Rapid Java Application Development Using JBuilder 4/5/6

Y. Daniel Liang

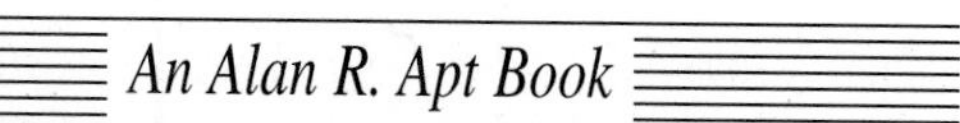

Prentica Hall
Upper Saddle River, New Jersey 07458
http://www.prenhall.com

Library of Congress Cataloging-in-Publication Data

Liang, Y. Daniel.
Rapid Java application development using JBuilder 4/5/6/ Y. Daniel Liang.
p. cm.
Includes bibliographical references and index.
ISBN 0-13-066550-9
1. Java (Computer program language) 2. JBuilder. I. Title
QA76.73.J38 L5343 2002
005.13'3—dc21 2001045948
CIP

Vice President and Editorial Director, ECS: *Marcia J. Horton*
Publisher: *Alan R. Apt*
Associate Editor: *Toni D. Holm*
Editorial Assistant: *Patrick Lindner*
Vice President and Director of Production and Manufacturing, ESM: *David W. Riccardi*
Executive Managing Editor: *Vince O'Brien*
Managing Editor: *David A. George*
Production Editor: *Patty Donovan*
Composition: *Pine Tree Composition*
Director of Creative Services: *Paul Belfanti*
Creative Director: *Carole Anson*
Art Director: *Heather Scott*
Assistant Art Director: *John Christiana*
Art Editor: *Greg Dulles*
Manufacturing Manager: *Trudy Pisciotti*
Manufacturing Buyer: *Lynda Castillo*
Senior Marketing Manager: *Jennie Burger*

Printed in the United States of America
10 9 8 7 6 5 4 3 2 1

ISBN 0-13-066550-9

Pearson Education Ltd., *London*
Pearson Education Australia Pty. Ltd., *Sydney*
Pearson Education Singapore, Pte. Ltd.
Pearson Education North Asia Ltd., *Hong Kong*
Pearson Education Canada, Inc., *Toronto*
Pearson Educacíon de Mexico, S.A. de C.V.
Pearson Education—Japan, *Tokyo*
Pearson Education Malaysia, Pte. Ltd.
Pearson Education, *Upper Saddle River, New Jersey*

To Samantha, Michael, and Michelle

PREFACE

When I began writing my first introductory Java text in the summer of 1996, only a few schools were teaching Java. Today, Java has become the programming language of choice for many schools. The incorporation of Java into the computer science curriculum has increased the need for an advanced Java text. This book covers the advanced Java features that are needed to support upper-level CS courses, such as software engineering, graphical user interface design, database programming, and distributed programming. It can be used as a text for advanced Java programming or as a supplement for upper-level CS courses. In addition, it is perfectly suitable for Java programmers who want to learn rapid application development techniques using JBuilder.

In this book I introduce the concepts of JavaBeans, bean event models, model-view control, developing customized components, Swing components, creating custom layout managers, bean persistence, bound properties and constraint properties, bean introspection and customization, Java database programming, and enterprise programming using remote method invocation and servlets. The promotion of rapid Java application development is the main thread of the book, however. Rapid application development, or RAD, is a software-development technology for developing programs efficiently and effectively. This technology has been successfully implemented in Visual Basic, Delphi, Power Builder, Oracle Developer 2000, and many other program-development tools. Using a RAD tool, projects can be developed quickly and efficiently with minimum coding. Projects developed using RAD are easy to modify and easy to maintain. The key elements in a RAD tool are the software components, such as buttons, labels, combo boxes, lists, check boxes, radio buttons, and menus. These components can be visually manipulated and tailored during design time in order to develop customized programs.

One of the central issues in software development is how to reuse programs effectively. Java is an object-oriented programming language that provides great flexibility, modularity, clarity, and reusability through method abstraction, class abstraction, and class inheritance. A Java program can be viewed as a collection of cooperating objects that are created during runtime. The JavaBeans technology is a significant extension and enhancement of the Java language that makes it possible for programmers to rapidly build applications by assembling objects and testing them during design time, thus making reuse of the software more productive.

To facilitate developing and managing Java programs, the book is aided by JBuilder, one of the best Java tools. JBuilder rapidly simplifies Java program development for maximum productivity. It provides a fully scalable, distributed, and cross-platform architecture for building reusable components. JBuilder provides a tightly integrated development environment that lets you visually design user interface and rapidly build applications using the UI designer and Menu designer. JBuilder BeansExpress makes it point-and-click easy to create JavaBeans components. JBuilder also contains many intelligent wizards that are convenient to use to generate source code automatically.

Throughout the book there are numerous examples with step-by-step instructions that will guide you in creating reusable components and using them to assemble large practical applications. It is assumed that you are familiar with the basics of Java programming, including creating graphical user interfaces using Swing, exception handling, internationalization, multithreads, IO streams, and Java Collections framework. These topics are covered in my introductory Java text, *Introduction to Java Programming with JBuilder 4/5/6* (Prentice-Hall, 2001).

One of the major considerations in choosing JBuilder to teach rapid Java application development is the clarity of the JBuilder-generated source code. The source code generated by JBuilder UI designer, Menu designer, and various wizards does not contain any proprietary code. Thus, the JBuilder-generated source code is easy to read and to maintain. With JBuilder, students can not only develop Java programs more productively, but can also learn advanced Java programming more effectively by following the source code.

You can use either JBuilder 4 or JBuilder 5 and 6 for this book, because JBuilder 4/5/6 have the same IDE except for a very few differences. For most of the book, JBuilder 4 Foundation or JBuilder 5 and 6 Personal is sufficient, but the BeansExpress wizard in Chapter 4, JBuilder data-aware components in Chapter 14, and servlets in Chapter 16 require JBuilder Professional. If you don't have it, you may type the code by hand instead of using the BeansExpress wizard.

All the examples in the text are developed and tested with JBuilder 4/5/6 Professional Edition. JBuilder 4/5/6 are the same except for a very few differences. The differences are highlighted in the "JBuilder 5 NOTE" box in the text and JBuilder 6 Notes at **www.cs.armstrong.edu/liang/radjb5.html**. You can use either JBuilder 4/5/6 for this book.

Most of the examples in this book are Java applets. A main method is provided for each applet to enable it to run standalone. However, for the sake of brevity, the main method is not listed in source code in the text.

Pedagogical Features of This Book

The philosophy of this book is "teaching by example and learning by doing." Basic features are explained by example so that you can learn by doing. The book uses the following elements to get the most out of the material:

- **Objectives** list what students learn from the chapter. This helps them to determine whether they have met the objectives after completing the chapter.
- **Introduction** opens the discussion with a brief overview of what to expect from the chapter.
- **Examples**, carefully chosen and presented in an easy-to-follow style, teach programming concepts. Each example is described, and includes the source code, a sample run, and an example review. The source code of the examples is contained in the companion CD-ROM. Almost all of the examples can run in two modes: standalone application or applets. Each program is com-

plete and ready to be compiled and executed. The sample run of the program is captured from the screen to give students a live presentation of the example. Reading these examples is much like entering and running them on a computer.

- **Chapter Summary** reviews the important subjects that students should understand and remember. It also helps students to reinforce the key concepts they have learned in the chapter.
- **Review Questions** help students to track their progress and evaluate their learning.
- **Programming Exercises** at the end of each chapter provide students opportunities to apply the skills on their own. The trick of learning programming is practice, practice, and practice. To that end, this book provides a large number of exercises.
- **Notes**, **Tips**, and **Cautions** are inserted throughout the text to offer students valuable advice and insight on important aspects of program development.

NOTE
Provides additional information on the subject and reinforces important concepts.

TIP
Teaches good programming style and practice.

CAUTION
Helps students steer away from the pitfalls of programming errors.

What's New in This Edition

This book expands and improves upon *Rapid Java Application Development Using JBuilder 3*. The major changes are as follows:

- The book is updated to JBuilder 4/5/6. The screen shots are taken from JBuilder 4. New features in JBuilder 5 are presented in the "JBuilder 5 NOTE" box in the text. New features in JBuilder 6 are presented in the JBuilder 6 Notes at **www.cs.armstrong.edu/lian/radjb5.html**.
- The book is completely revised and improved from start to finish with new chapters, new sections, new examples, and new illustrations.
- Chapter 16, "Servlets," is brand-new. The text of Chapter 16 in the previous edition, "Distributed Applications Using CORBA," has been moved to the companion Web site.
- UML graphical notations are used to describe classes and their relationships whenever appropriate.

- The book is reorganized to provide flexible ordering of chapters, as is explained in the Prerequisites and Chapter Dependency Chart.
- The comprehensive companion Web site includes supplements on Coding Style, Java Server Page, CORBA, and XML among many other useful materials.

The Organization of This Book

Java is a comprehensive and powerful language with many evolving features. There is plenty of room for an advanced Java text. This book is centered on rapid Java application development. It is divided into five parts that, taken together, form a comprehensive course on rapid Java application development.

The early chapters introduce JavaBeans, which are the basis of rapid Java application development. Subsequent chapters apply RAD techniques to build comprehensive, robust, and useful graphics applications, database and client/server applications, and distributed applications, with step-by-step instructions.

Part I: Introduction to JBuilder and JavaBeans

The first part of the book begins with an introduction to JBuilder, presents the concept of JavaBeans, discusses the bean event model, introduces the model-view architectures, and teaches developing and using beans in rapid Java application development.

Chapter 1, "Getting Started with JBuilder," gives an overview of JBuilder's integrated development environment. You will learn how to develop Java programs with a variety of JBuilder wizards for creating projects, applications, applets, and classes, and how to compile and run programs.

Chapter 2, "Introduction to JavaBeans," introduces the concept of JavaBeans. This chapter explains the relationship between JavaBeans and Java RAD builder tools, and shows you how to write simple JavaBeans and visually manipulate the beans in JBuilder.

Chapter 3, "Bean Events," covers the Java event delegation model, inner classes, and anonymous inner classes. You will learn how to develop source beans and listener beans and how to associate the listener beans with the source beans in JBuilder.

Chapter 4, "Developing and Using Components," discusses the differences between developing beans and using beans in rapid Java application development. This chapter introduces the model-view architecture. You will learn how to use the BeansExpress wizard to create properties and events and the Archive Builder to deploy applications and applets.

Part II: Rapid Application Development with Swing Components

The book's second section covers Swing components and their use in rapid Java application development. You will learn how to use a variety of Swing components to develop Java projects using JBuilder.

Chapter 5, "Swing Components," introduces the concept of Swing components and discusses the differences between lightweight components and heavyweight components. You will learn how to use various Swing components in rapid application development.

Chapter 6, "Containers and Layout Managers," introduces Swing containers and layout managers, examines the structure of Swing containers, and studies the layout managers provided in JBuilder. You will learn how to create custom layout managers and install them in JBuilder. The components `JTabbedPane`, and `JSplitPane` are also covered in this chapter.

Chapter 7, "Menus, Toolbars, and Dialogs," introduces menus, popup menus, toolbars, `JOptionPane` dialogs, custom dialogs, `JColorChooser`, and `JFileChooser`. This chapter also teaches how to use the Menu designer to visually design menus and popup menus.

Chapter 8, "Advanced Swing Components," shows how to use several advanced Swing components, such as `JList`, `JComboBox`, `JTable`, and `JTree`, in rapid application development. You will learn various data models, selection models, renderers, and editors for supporting these advanced components.

Part III: Bean Persistence, Introspection, and Customization

This part introduces the JavaBeans API. You will learn how to develop persistent beans, use bound and constraint properties, and create bean property editors.

Chapter 9, "Bean Persistence and Versioning," introduces object serialization, which is a built-in Java mechanism for persistently storing and restoring beans. You will learn how to use Sun's Beanbox, a tool for testing beans, which can be used to verify bean persistence. You will also learn to customize serialization and bean versioning.

Chapter 10, "Bound and Constraint Properties," introduces bound and constraint properties. A *bound property* of a component is one for which a property notification service is provided when the property changes. A *constraint property* allows the listener component to verify the property change to determine whether to accept or reject a change. These properties are useful for creating custom property editors. These properties can be used to simplify the model-view components.

Chapter 11, "Bean Introspection and Customization," takes an in-depth look at how builder tools learn bean information through introspection. You will learn how to create and deploy custom editors.

Part IV: Java Database Programming

This part of the book is devoted to developing database projects using Java. You will learn the Java database programming interface, handle database metadata, create and process SQL statements, and use JBuilder database beans for rapidly developing Java database applications.

Chapter 12, "Introduction to Java Database Programming," begins with an overview of the JDBC interface for accessing relational databases from Java. A thorough introduction to the four types of the JDBC drivers is presented through examples of the use of MS Access, Oracle, and JDataStore.

Chapter 13, "Advanced Java Database Programming," gives a comprehensive treatment of obtaining database metadata, and processing statements, prepared statements, and callable statements. You will also learn how to manipulate scrollable result sets.

Chapter 14, "JBuilder DataExpress and Data-Aware Components," teaches you how to use JBuilder's powerful data-access beans and data-aware Swing components for rapidly developing database applications.

Part V: Enterprise Java Programming

The book's final part introduces the development of distributed projects using Java remote method invocation (RMI) and servlets.

Chapter 15, "Remote Method Invocation," introduces remote method invocation, a technology that provides a framework for building distributed Java systems. You will learn how to use it to create useful distributed applications.

Chapter 16, "Servlets," introduces the technique of creating dynamic HTML contents using Java servlets. You will learn how to write server-side Java programs to access databases. You will also learn the techniques for session tracking.

Prerequisites and Chapter Dependency Chart

The book has been used as a text for advanced Java programming and rapid Java application development and as a supplement for software engineering, graphical user interface design, database and client/server programming, distributed systems and network programming, and Web application development. Instructors have used this book in many creative ways. Here is a recommended sequence.

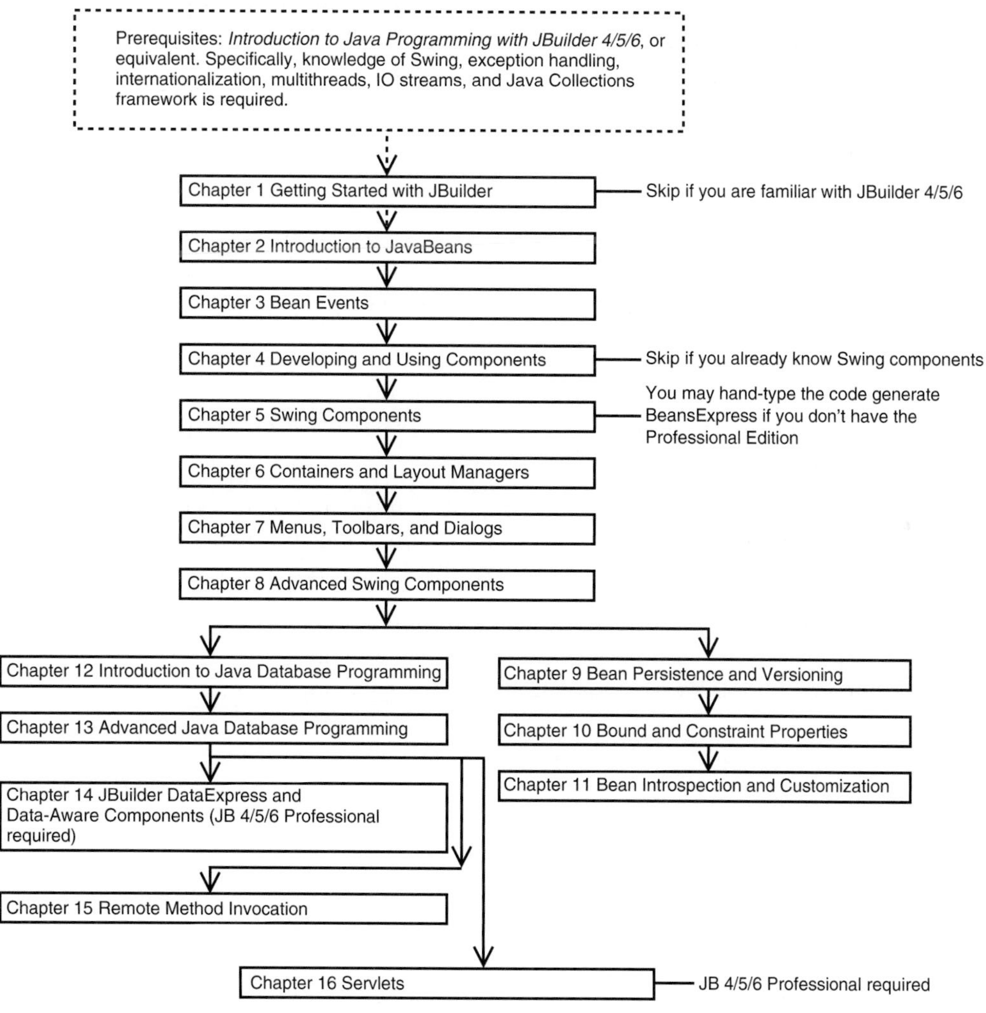

ABOUT THE AUTHOR

Y. Daniel Liang is the author of the Prentice-Hall Liang Java Series. He has taught more than 50 Java courses to university students and corporate employees.

Dr. Liang is currently a Yamacraw professor of software engineering in the Department of Computer Science at Armstrong Atlantic State University, Savannah, Georgia. He can be reached via the Internet at liangjava@yahoo.com or liang@armstrong.edu.

ACKNOWLEDGMENTS

I am grateful to the readers of my Java Series, both students and instructors, Iwho offered comments, suggestions, bug reports, and praise. Their enthusiastic support contributed to the success of these books.

This edition was greatly improved thanks to outstanding reviews by Professors David Scuse (University of Manitoba), Carolyn Schauble (Colorado State University), Kevin Parker (Idaho State), and Jun Ni (University of Iowa).

My students and colleagues at Armstrong Atlantic State University have been great supporters of this ongoing project. I would like to thank Ray Greenlaw for his support of incorporating Java into the CS curriculum, and for his tireless efforts to build a first-class undergraduate computer science program.

This edition has benefited from the previous editions of all my Java books. I would like to acknowledge the following people who contributed to the previous editions: Greg Geller, Ben Page, Michael Willig, Russell Minnich, Balaram Nair, Ben Stonebraker, Michael Sunderman and Russell R. Colegrove.

For this edition, I would like to thank Alan Apt, Toni Holm, Amy Todd, Jennie Burger, Cindy Szollose, Jake Warde, and their colleagues at Prentice-Hall for organizing and managing this project, and Patty Donovan, Robert Milch, Dana Smith and their colleagues at Pine Tree Composition for helping to produce the book.

As always, I am indebted to my wife, Samantha, for love, support, and encouragement.

Supplements to the Book

Student CD-ROM

The student CD-ROM comes with the book. Its contents are listed below:

- JBuilder 5 Enterprise Trial (It can be used as either the JBuilder 5 Enterprise Trial or JBuilder 5 Personal by requesting a set of keys at **www.borland.com/jbuilder/keys**)
- JBuilder 5 Enterprise Trial from Borland
- Solutions to even-numbered programming exercises
- Source code for the examples in the book
- Answers to review questions

Companion Web Site for the Book

The companion Web site for the book can be accessed from **www.cs.armstrong.edu/liang/radjb5.html** or **www.prenhall.com/liang**. The Web site contains the following resources:

- Java Programming Style and Documentation Guidelines
- JBuilder Supplements (Install Custom Layout Manager in JBuilder, and Resource Strings wizard in JBuilder)
- Java Supplements (Java Server Page, HTML Tutorial, Java Plug-in and HTML Converter, SQLJ, and Oracle Stored Procedures in Java)
- Microsoft PowerPoint slides for lectures
- Errata
- Useful Links
- FAQs

Instructor Resources

The Instructor's Resource CD-ROM is available for instructors using this book. It contains the following resources:

- Microsoft PowerPoint slides for lectures.
- Solutions to all exercises. Students will have access to the solutions to the even-numbered exercises in the book's companion CD-ROM.

To obtain the Instructor's Resource CD-ROM, contact your Prentice-Hall sales representative.

Contents at a Glance

TABLE OF CONTENTS

PART I

Introduction to JBuilder and JavaBeans

You have heard a lot about Java and its rapid application development capability. You are anxious to start rapid Java development. The first part of the book is a stepping stone that will prepare you to embark on the journey of rapid Java application development using JBuilder. You will begin to learn JBuilder, the concept of JavaBeans, and the bean event model, and to develop and use beans in rapid Java application development.

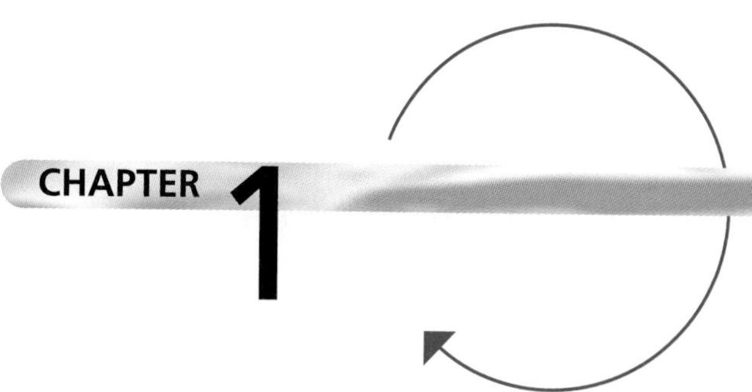

Getting Started with JBuilder

Objectives

- Get a quick start on JBuilder.
- Understand project properties and know how to set them.
- Become familiar with the wizards in the Object Gallery.
- Create projects using the Project wizard.
- Create applications using the Application wizard.
- Create applets using the Applet wizard.
- Learn how to use the UI designer to create user interfaces.
- Manage JBuilder projects.
- Customize JBuilder environments.
- Get online help from JBuilder.

Introduction

JBuilder is a premier Java development tool for developing Java programs. Borland products are known to be "best of breed" in the rapid application development tool market. Over the years, Borland has led the charge in creating visual development tools like Delphi and C++ Builder. And now Borland is leading the way in Java development tools with JBuilder. JBuilder delivers 100% pure Java code and is one of the most popular Java tools used by professional Java developers.

JBuilder provides a fully scalable, distributed, and cross-platform architecture for building reusable components. JBuilder provides a tightly integrated development environment that lets you visually design user interfaces and rapidly build applications with the UI designer and Menu designer. JBuilder BeansExpress makes it point-and-click easy to create standard Java bean components. JBuilder also comes with many intelligent wizards that are convenient for generating source code automatically. With JBuilder, you can create Java programs with minimum coding for maximum productivity.

JBuilder is written completely in Java. It uses the Swing component library, provided by JavaSoft (Sun Microsystems), as its foundation. This pure Java component library allows JBuilder to have a sophisticated user interface and remain 100% Java. The Swing library also gives the added benefit of a pluggable look-and-feel, which allows JBuilder to adjust its appearance to match the computer's native operating system UI without sacrificing the power and flexibility of the JBuilder UI. JBuilder runs on the Windows 98, NT, and 2000, Linux, Solaris, and Mac platforms.

JBuilder is available in three versions: JBuilder Foundation, JBuilder Professional, and JBuilder Enterprise.

- The JBuilder Foundation is ideal for beginners to learn the basics of Java programming. JBuilder Foundation was renamed JBuilder Personal Edition in JBuilder 5 and 6.
- JBuilder Professional contains the Borland data-aware components for developing Java database programs. It also contains the Borland BeansExpress wizard for creating JavaBeans components.
- JBuilder Enterprise contains all the components in JBuilder Professional, plus support for creating distributed applications using XML and CORBA.

NOTE

The book covers both JBuilder 4/5/6. Most of the features in these two versions are the same. The screen shots are taken from JBuilder 4. The new features of JBuilder 5 are presented in the JBuilder 5 NOTE box in the text and JBuilder 6 Notes at **www.cs.armstrong.edu/liang/radjb5.html**.

NOTE

For most of the book, JBuilder 4 Foundation or JBuilder 5 or 6 Personal is sufficient, but JBuilder Professional is required for the BeansExpress wizard in Chapter 4, JBuilder data-aware components in Chapter 14, "JBuilder DataExpress and Data-Aware Components," and the servlets in Chapter 16, "Servlets." The BeansExpress wizard helps generate the code for beans. If you don't have it, you may type the code by hand instead of using the BeansExpress wizard.

NOTE

Most of the examples in the book are Java applets with a main method, so you can run the programs either as applets or applications. You can view the applets from Netscape 6. To view applets from other browsers, such as IE 5.0 and Netscape 4.7, you have to use the Java Plug-In. Please see supplements for information on Java Plug-In, at **www.cs.armstrong.edu/liang/radjb5.html.**

Starting JBuilder

Assume you have successfully installed JBuilder on your machine. Start JBuilder from Windows, Linux, or Solaris. The main JBuilder user interface appears, as shown in Figure 1.1. If you don't see the Welcome project, choose Welcome Project (Sample) from the Help menu.

NOTE

To install JBuilder from the companion CD-ROM, please refer to www.cs.armstrong.edu/liang/radjb5.html.

NOTE

The screen shots in this book are from JBuilder Professional. *If you use JBuilder Foundation, or JBuilder Enterprise, your screen may look slightly different.*

Traditional IDE tools use many windows to accommodate various development tasks, such as editing, debugging, and browsing information. As a result, finding the window you need is often difficult. Because it is easy to get lost, beginners may be intimidated. For this reason, some new programmers prefer to use separate utilities, such as the JDK command line tools, for developing programs.

Borland is aware of the usability problem and has made significant efforts to simplify the JBuilder user interface. The JBuilder user interface presents a single window for managing Java projects, browsing files, compiling, running, and debugging programs. This user interface is called the *AppBrowser* in JBuilder 4/5/6.

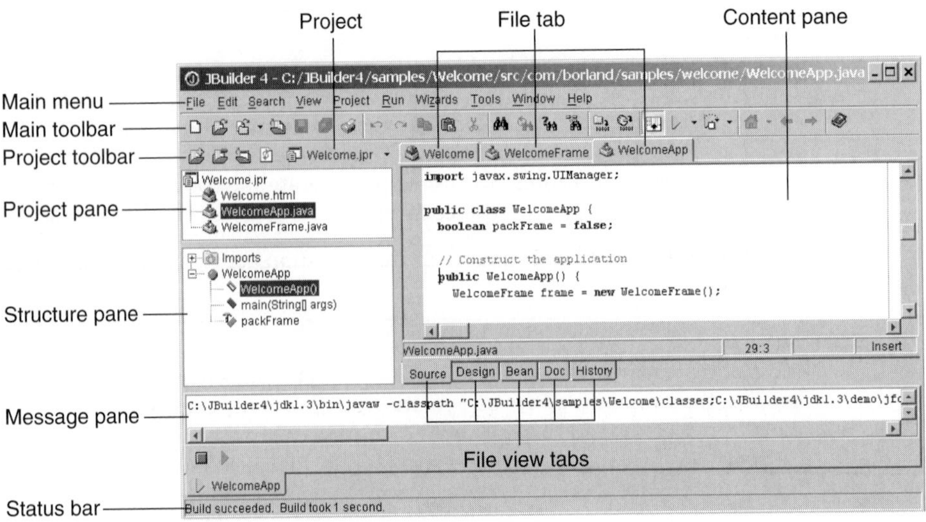

Figure 1.1 *The JBuilder user interface is a single window that performs functions for editing, compiling, debugging, and running programs.*

NOTE

The AppBrowser window and the main window are two separate windows in JBuilder 3, but are combined into one window in the versions after JBuilder 3.

The AppBrowser window primarily consists of the main menu, main toolbar, status bar, project pane, structure pane, and content pane.

The Main Menu

The main menu is similar to that of other Windows applications and provides most of the commands you need to use JBuilder, including those for creating, editing, compiling, running, and debugging programs. The menu items are enabled and disabled in response to the current context.

The Toolbar

The toolbar provides buttons for several frequently used commands on the menu bar. Clicking a toolbar is faster than using the menu bar. For some commands, you can also use function keys or keyboard shortcuts. For example, you can save a file in three ways:

- Select File, Save from the menu bar.
- Click the "save" toolbar button.
- Use the keyboard shortcut Ctrl+S.

TIP
You can display a label, known as the *ToolTip*, for a button by pointing the mouse to the button without clicking.

The Status Bar

The status bar displays a message to alert users to the operation status, such as file saved for the Save file command and compilation successful for the Compilation command.

The Project Pane

The *project pane* (known as the *navigation pane* in JBuilder 3) displays the contents of one or more projects opened in the AppBrowser. It consists of the following items, as shown in Figure 1.2.

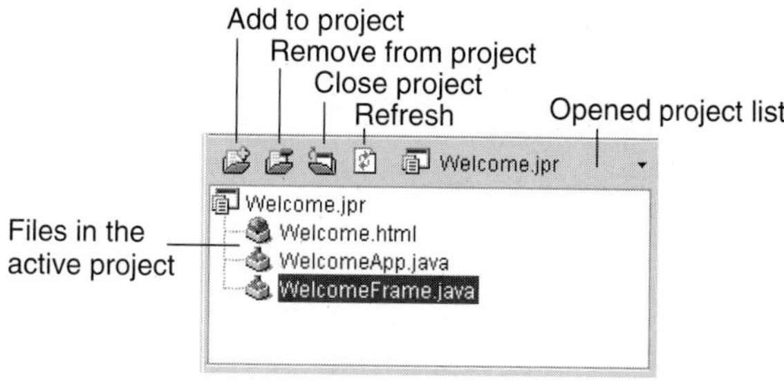

Figure 1.2 *The project pane manages JBuilder projects.*

- A small toolbar with four buttons (Add To Project, Remove From Project, Close Project, and Refresh).
- A drop-down list of all opened projects.
- A tree view of all the files that make up the active project.

The project pane shows a list of one or more files. In the case of the Project browser, you will see the project (.jpr or .jpx) file first. Attached to that is a list of the files in the project. The list can include .java, .html, text, or image files. You select a file in the project pane by clicking it. The content pane and the structure pane display information about the selected file. As you select different files in the project pane, each one will be represented in the content and structure panes.

The project pane shown in Figure 1.2 contains three files. The Add button is used to add new files to the project, and the Remove button to remove files from the project. For example, you can remove Welcome.html by selecting the file in the project pane and clicking the Remove button. You can then add the file back to the project, as follows:

1. Click the Add button to display the Add Files or Packages to Project dialog box shown in Figure 1.3.
2. Select Welcome.html. You will see Welcome.html displayed in the project pane.

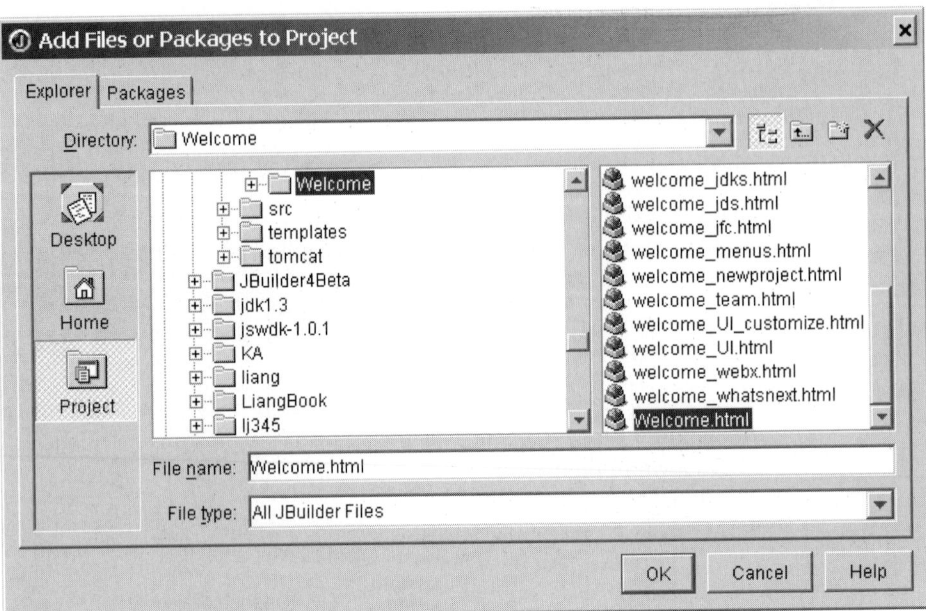

Figure 1.3 *The Add Files or Packages to Project dialog box enables you to add an existing file.*

TIP

You can select multiple files by clicking the files with the CTRL key pressed, or select multiple consecutive files with the SHIFT key pressed.

The Content Pane

The content pane displays all opened files as a set of tabs. To open a file in the content pane, double-click it in the project pane. The content pane displays the detailed content of the selected file. The editor or viewer used is determined by the file's extension. If you click the WelcomeApp.java file in the project pane, for example, you will see four tabs (Source, Design, Bean, Doc, and History) at the bottom of the content pane (see Figure 1.1). If you select the Source tab, you will see the JBuilder Java source code editor. This is a full-featured, syntax-highlighted programming editor.

If you select Welcome.html in the project pane, you will see the content pane become an HTML browser, as shown in Figure 1.4. If you choose the Source tab, you can view and edit the HTML code in the content pane, as shown in Figure 1.5.

The Structure Pane

The *structure pane* displays structural information about the files you selected in the project pane. All the items displayed in the structure pane are in the form of a hierarchical indexed list. The expand symbol (+) in front of an item indicates that it contains subitems. You can see the subitems by clicking on the expand symbol.

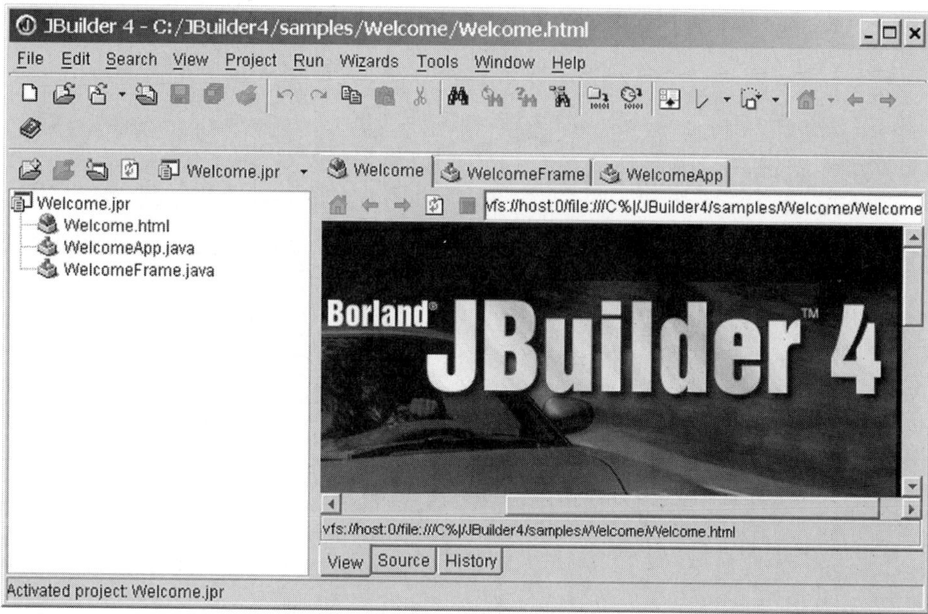

Figure 1.4 *You can view HTML files in the content pane.*

You can also use the structure pane as a quick navigational tool to the various structural elements in the file. If you select the WelcomeFrame.java file, for example, you see classes, variables, and methods in the structure pane. If you then click on any of those elements in the structure pane, the content pane will move to and highlight it in the source code.

If you click on the `jMenuFile` item in the structure pane, as shown in Figure 1.6, the content pane moves to and highlights the statement that defines the `jMenuFile`

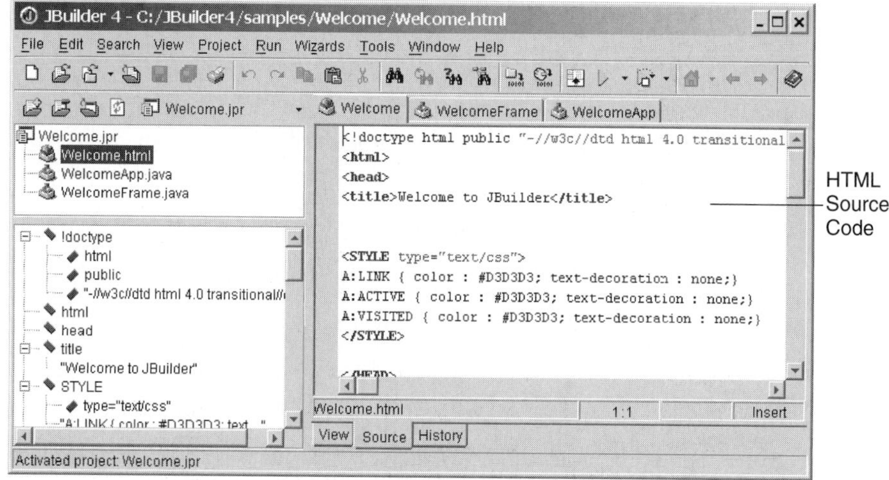

Figure 1.5 *You can edit HTML files in the content pane.*

data field. This provides a much faster way to browse and find the elements of a .java file than scrolling through it.

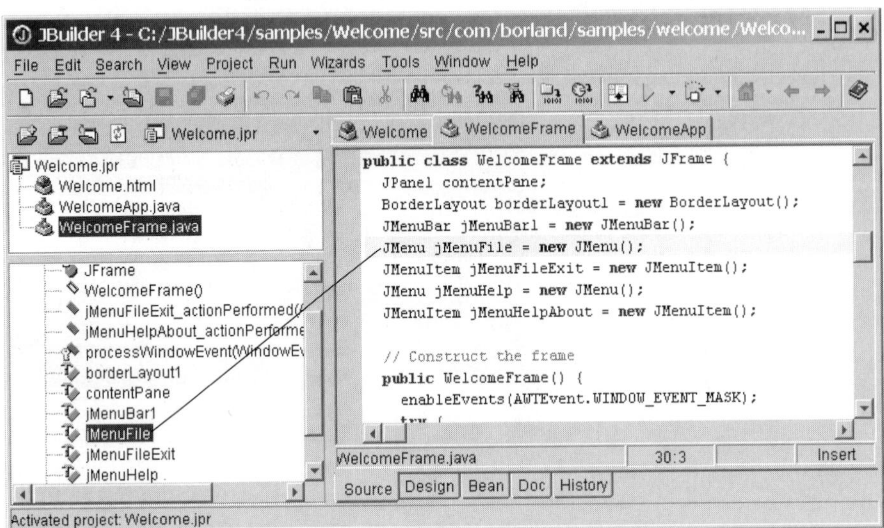

Figure 1.6 *You can cruise through the source code from the structure pane.*

Running the Examples in This Book

A good way to learn programming is through examples. There are abundant examples in this book. They are included in the file example.zip in the companion CD-ROM or can be downloaded at **www.cs.armstrong.edu/liang/radjb5.html**.

Assume that you have successfully uncompressed **example.zip** into **c:\radjb**. Here are the steps to run the clockdemo project in Example 4.2, "Creating a Clock Component," in Chapter 4, "Developing and Using Components."

1. Choose File, Open Project to bring up the Open Project dialog box, as shown in Figure 1.7.
2. Choose or type clockdemo.jpr in c:\radjb in the Open Project dialog box. The project should appear in the project pane of the AppBrowser window, as shown in Figure 1.8. Note that the icon for a Java project file in JBuilder is (icon).
3. Run SixClocks.java by right-clicking on SixCloks.java in the project pane and choosing Run from the context menu. Figure 1.9 is a sample run of the program.

NOTE

If you open a nonproject file, the file will be added to the current project in the AppBrowser.

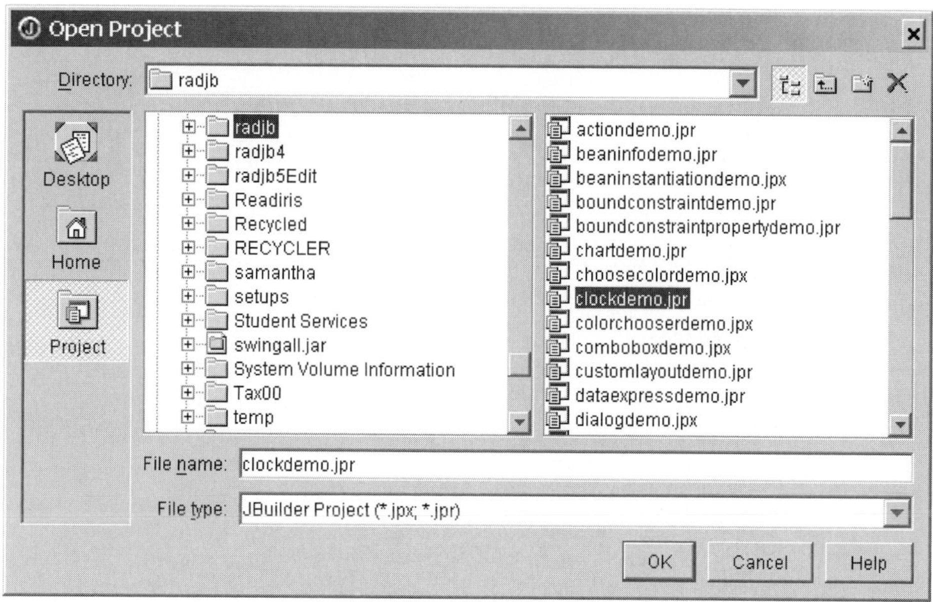

Figure 1.7 *The Open Project dialog box allows you to open an existing project using the project file.*

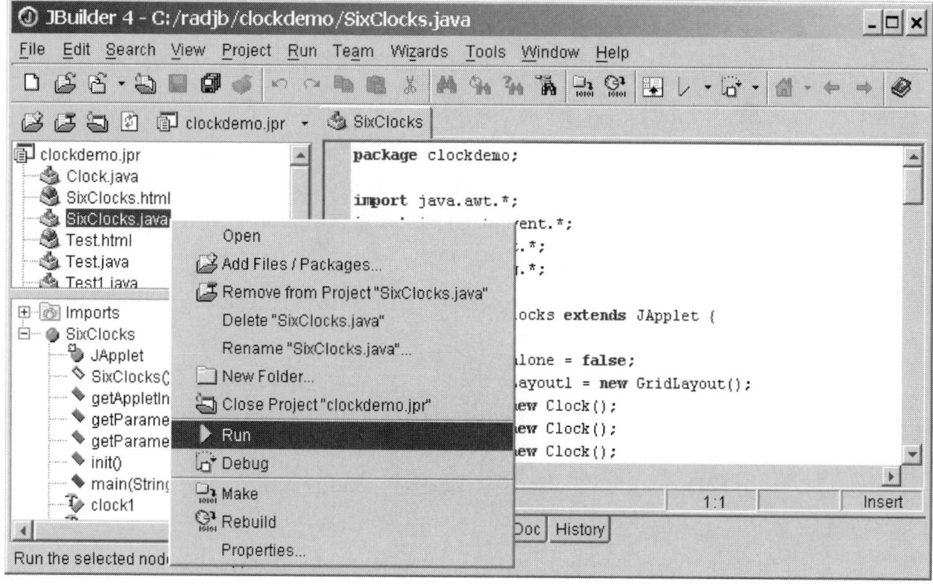

Figure 1.8 *The clockdemo project appears in the AppBrowser window.*

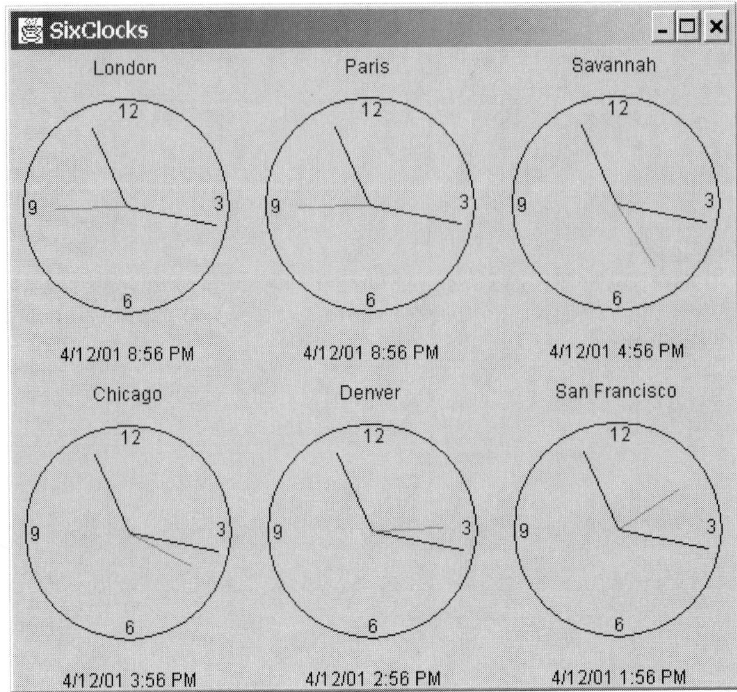

Figure 1.9 *The program displays six running clocks.*

Creating a Project

A project is like a holder that ties all the files together. The information about each JBuilder project is stored in a project file with a .jpr or .jpx file extension. The project file contains a list of all the files and project settings and properties. JBuilder uses this information to load and save all the files in the project and compile and run the programs. For simplicity, this book creates all projects under c:\radjb. Here are the steps to create a new project:

1. Choose File, New Project to bring up the Project wizard dialog box, as shown in Figure 1.10.
2. Type **introdemo** in the Project name field. You may choose either jpr or jpx for the project type. Type **c:/radjb** in the Root path field, and *empty* the Project directory name field, Source directory name field, and Output directory name field. Type **bak** in the Backup directory name. Click Next to display Step 2 of 3 of the Project wizard, as shown in Figure 1.11.
3. Click Next to display Step 3 of 3 of the Project wizard, as shown in Figure 1.12.

4. Fill in the title, author, company, and description fields. These optional fields provide a description for the project. 5. Click Finish. The new project is displayed in the project pane, as shown in Figure 1.13. The Project wizard created the project file (introdemo.jpr) and an HTML file (introdemo.html), and placed them in **c:\radjb**. The project file stores the information about the project, and the HTML file is used to describe the project.

NOTE

The forward slash / is the Java file path separator, whereas the backward slash \ is the Windows file path separator. You should use the forward slash / in JBuilder.

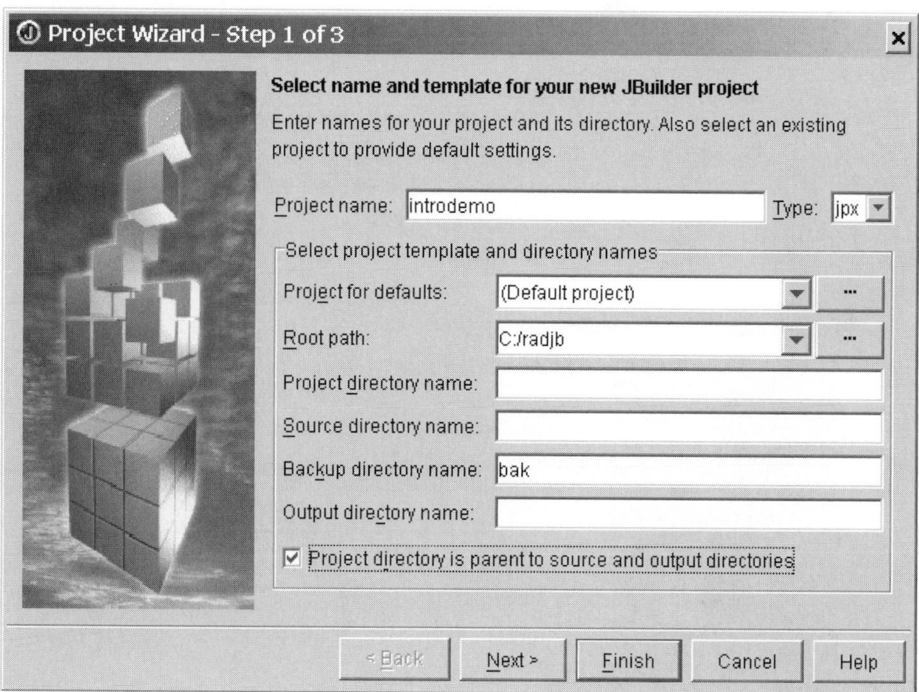

Figure 1.10 *The Project wizard dialog box enables you to specify the project file with other optional information.*

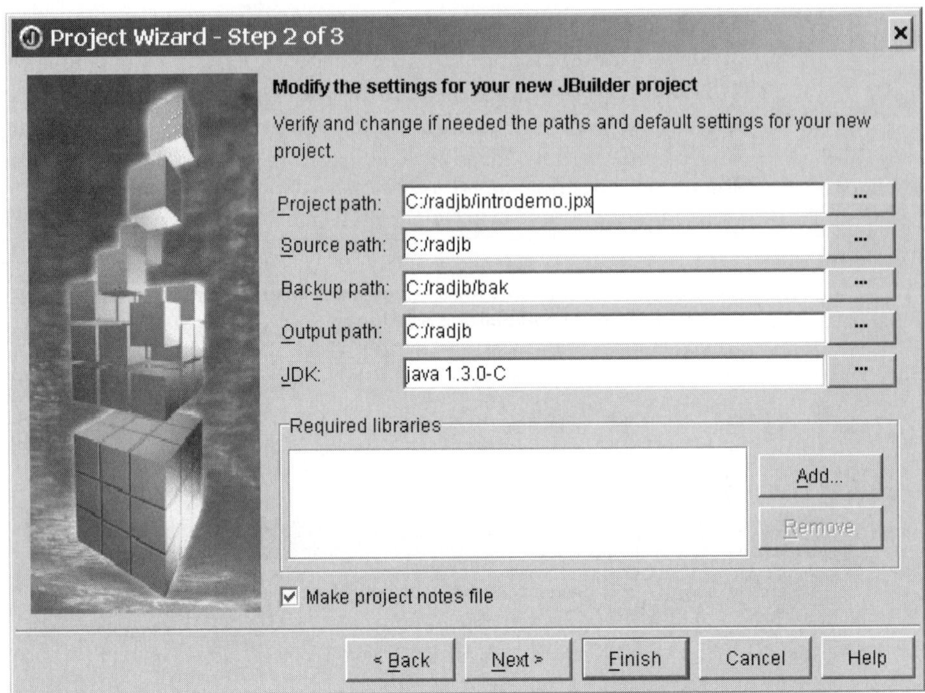

Figure 1.11 *The Project wizard Step 2 of 3 enables you to modify project settings.*

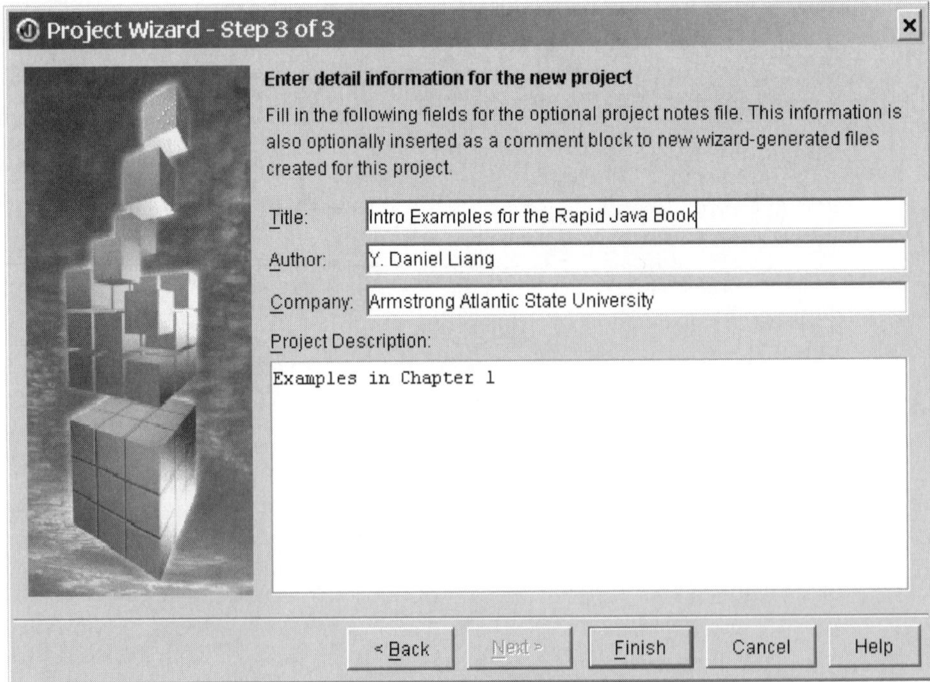

Figure 1.12 *Project wizard Step 3 of 3 collects optional information for the project.*

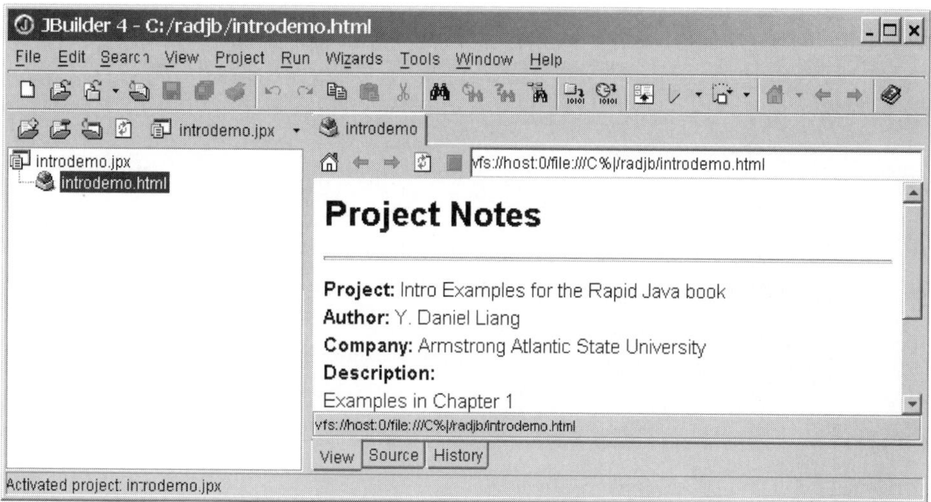

Figure 1.13 *A new project is created with the .jpx file and .html file.*

Note

JBuilder automatically generates many backup files. I use **bak** as the root directory for all these backup files so they can be easily located and removed.

Caution

Creating a project is a preliminary step before developing Java programs. Creating projects incorrectly is a common problem for new JBuilder users, and it can lead to frustrating mistakes. You may create your project exactly as shown in this section, or change the word *radjb* to your name like *liang*, so that your project source path and output path are c:\liang in Figure 1.10.

JBuilder 5 Note

The Project wizard in JBuilder 5 has an extra Documentation path, as shown in Figure 1.14. This is the root path for storing .html files generated from the javadoc utility.

Creating Java Applications

JBuilder provides numerous wizards for generating templates that you can use to speed up your development of applications, applets, beans, dialogs, and so forth. These wizards are contained in the Object Gallery (see Figure 1.15), which is accessible by choosing File, New from the main menu. You can use the Application wizard to generate the class templates for your application.

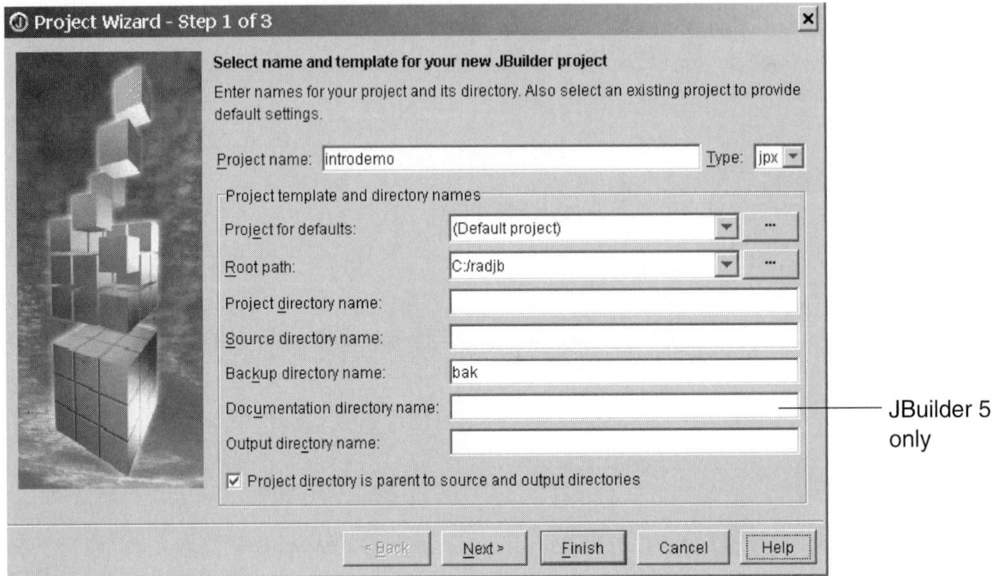

Figure 1.14 *The JBuilder 5 Project wizard dialog box has an extra documentation path.*

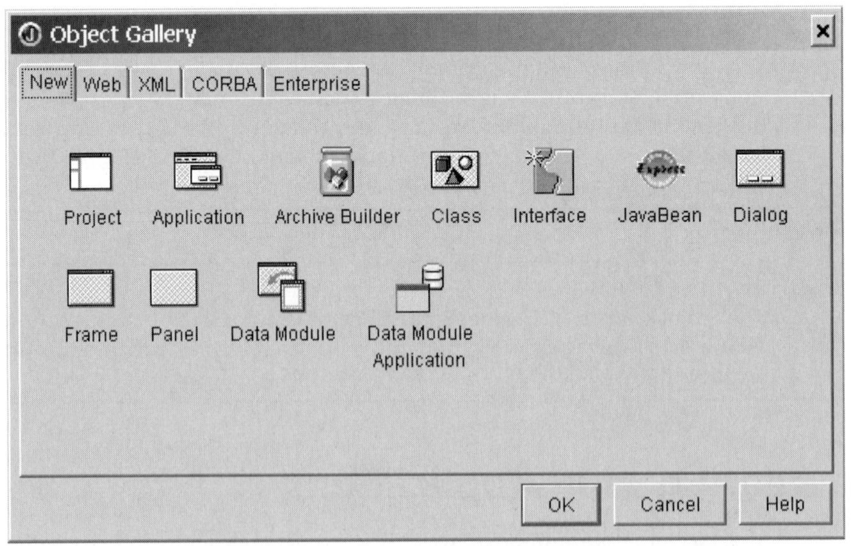

Figure 1.15 *The Object Gallery contains wizards for creating applications, applets, beans, dialogs, and so forth.*

JBUILDER 5 NOTE
JBuilder 5 regrouped wizards in the Object Gallery. For example, the Applet wizard is located under the Web tab in JBuilder 5.

This section shows you how to create Java applications using the Application wizard. You will write an application that adds two integers and displays the sum (see Figure 1.16).

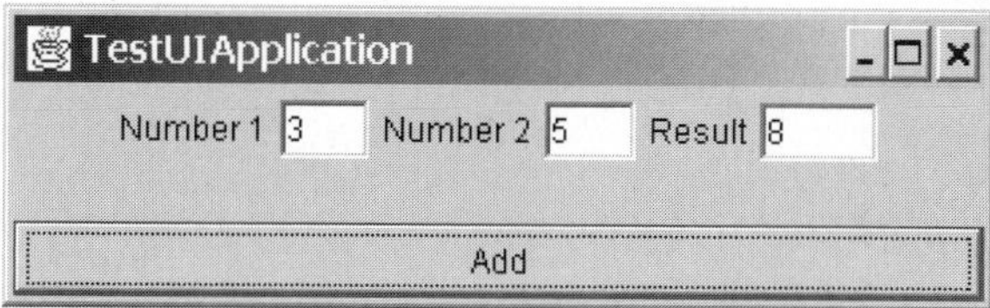

Figure 1.16 *The program adds the numbers from Number 1 and Number 2 and displays the result.*

Here are the steps to complete the project:

1. Make sure the introdemo project is displayed in the project pane. If not, open it by choosing File, Open Project.
2. Choose File, New to display the Object Gallery. Click the Application icon to bring up the Application wizard, as shown in Figure 1.17.
3. Type TestApplication in the Class field of the Application wizard's Step 1 of 2, and click Next to display the Application wizard's Step 2 of 2, as shown in Figure 1.18.
4. Type TestFrame in the Class field, check Center frame on screen. Click Finish.

The Application wizard creates the following two files:

- TestApplication.java, referred to as the *application class*.
- TestFrame.java, referred to as the *frame class*.

The Java interpreter executes the project, starting from the application class. The frame class creates the user interface and performs the actual operations.

The Application Class

The application class contains a constructor and a main method, as shown in Figure 1.19. The constructor creates an instance for the frame class and makes it visible. The `main` method is called by the Java interpreter to start the application class. You can navigate through the structure pane to show these two methods in the content pane. If you highlight TestApplication.java in the project pane, for example, and then highlight its constructor in the structure pane, you will see the source code for the constructor in the content pane.

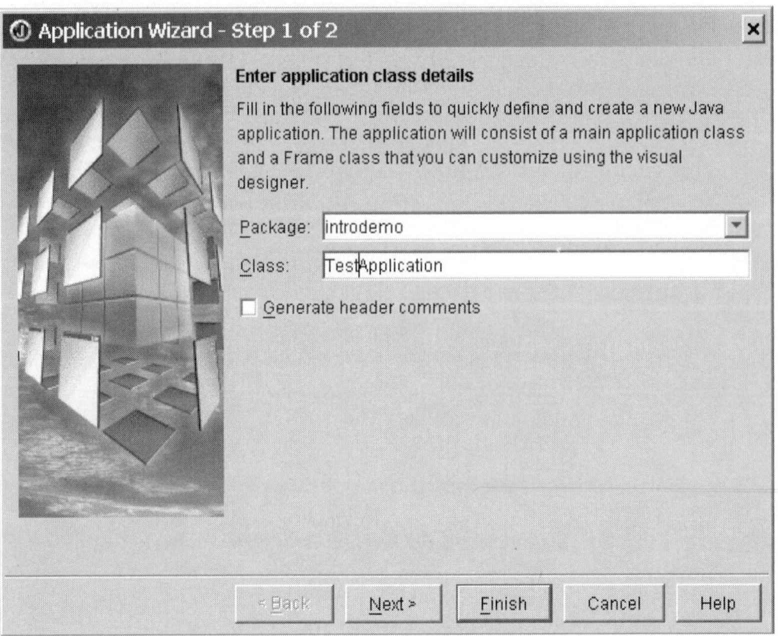

Figure 1.17 *The Application wizard's Step 1 of 2 dialog box prompts you to enter a package name and an application main class name.*

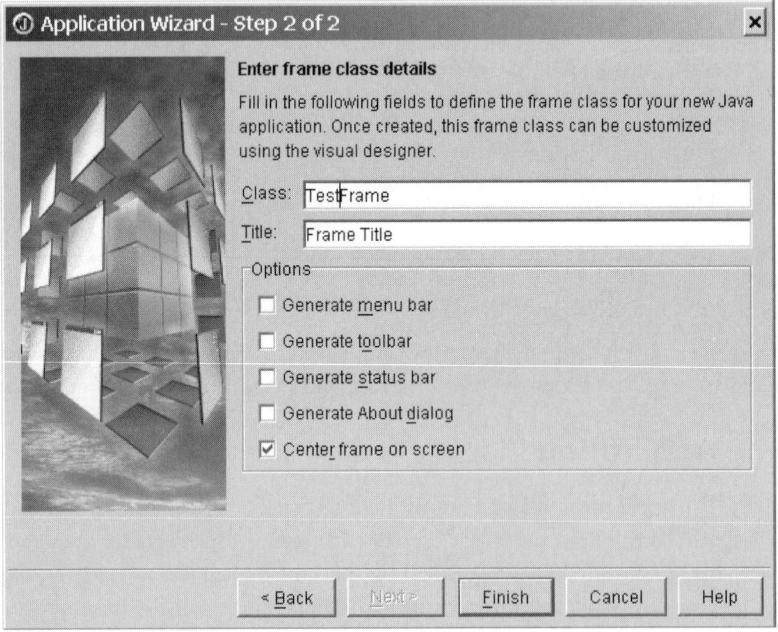

Figure 1.18 *The Application wizard's Step 2 of 2 dialog box prompts you to enter the frame class name and to specify frame style.*

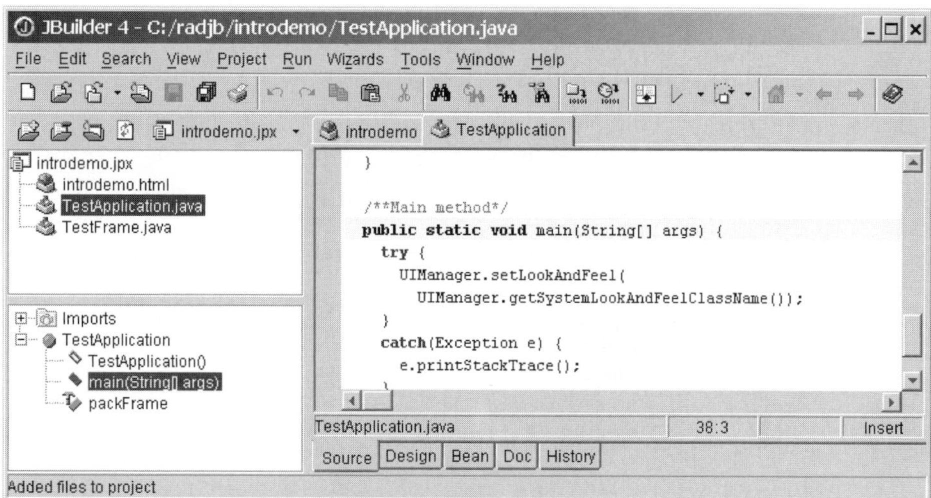

Figure 1.19 *The application class contains a main method and a constructor.*

The statement `package introdemo` in the first line tells JBuilder that the compiled bytecode of the application class will be saved in the introdemo subdirectory under the Output path. Since the Output path is set to **c:\radjb**, as shown in Figure 1.11 for Step 2 of the Project wizard, the .class files will be stored in **c:\radjb\introdemo** when the class is compiled. The source code for TestApplication is shown in Listing 1.1.

Note

The code that you manually typed is highlighted in the listing throughout the book. The coding style adopted in this book is summarized at **www.cs.armstrong.edu/liang/radjb5/codingstyle.html**.

Normally you should not add any code in the Application class except to set a different look-and-feel in the main method or to set the `packFrame` variable to false or true. The look and feel will be discussed in Chapter 5, "Swing Components." If `packFrame` is set to true, the frame's `pack()` method will be invoked to set the initial size for the frame. Often you need to modify the frame class to write the code for creating the user interface and carrying out operations for the project.

The Frame Class

Before modifying the frame class, let us take a look at the contents generated by the Application wizard. Highlighting TestFrame.java in the project pane displays the structure of the source code in the structure pane and the source code itself in the content pane (see Figure 1.20).

The `import` statements import Java packages used in this file. You can import additional packages if needed when you modify the code in the frame class. The gener-

```
package introdemo;

import javax.swing.UIManager;
import java.awt.*;

public class TestApplication {
  boolean packFrame = false;

  /** Construct the application */
  public TestApplication() {
    TestFrame frame = new TestFrame();
    //Validate frames that have preset sizes
    //Pack frames that have useful preferred size info, e.g.
   // from their layout
    if (packFrame) {
      frame.pack();
    }
    else {
      frame.validate();
    }

    // Center the window
    Dimension screenSize =
     Toolkit.getDefaultToolkit().getScreenSize();
    Dimension frameSize = frame.getSize();
    if (frameSize.height > screenSize.height) {
      frameSize.height = screenSize.height;
    }
    if (frameSize.width > screenSize.width) {
      frameSize.width = screenSize.width;
    }
    frame.setLocation((screenSize.width - frameSize.width) / 2,
     (screenSize.height - frameSize.height) / 2);
    frame.setVisible(true);
  }

  /** Main method */
  public static void main(String[] args) {
    try {
      UIManager.setLookAndFeel(
        UIManager.getSystemLookAndFeelClassName());
    }
    catch(Exception e) {
      e.printStackTrace();
    }
    new TestApplication();
  }
}
```

Listing 1.1 *TestApplication.java*

ated `TestFrame` class extends `JFrame`. You may click on `JFrame` in the structure pane to browse the source code for `JFrame`, as shown in Figure 1.21. You can see the documentation of `JFrame` by clicking the Doc tab in the content pane, as shown in Figure 1.22.

`TestFrame` has a method `jbInit` and a constructor. The `jbInit` method sets the frame's initial size, title, and the layout style. You also can modify or add new code in this method. The constructor uses the `enableEvents` method to enable window

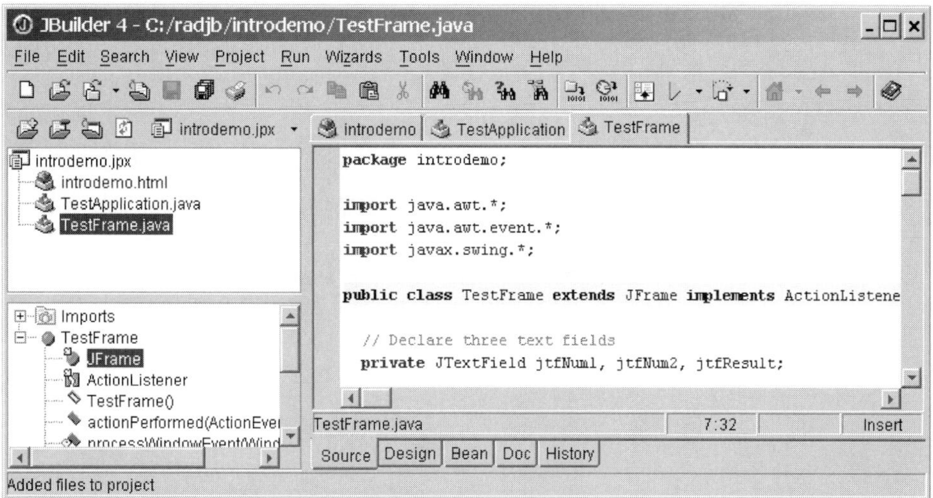

Figure 1.20 *The frame class contains the code that creates the user interface and carries out actual operations.*

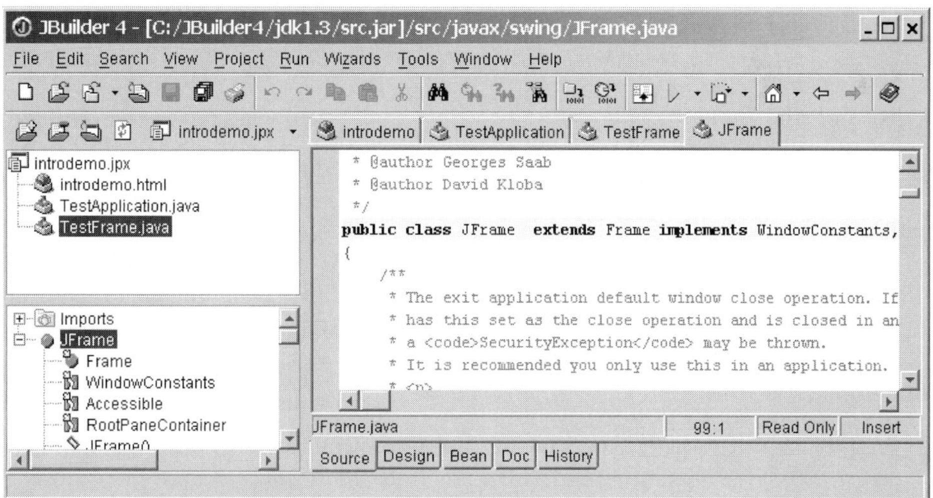

Figure 1.21 *You can browse the Java files you imported to your class in the content pane.*

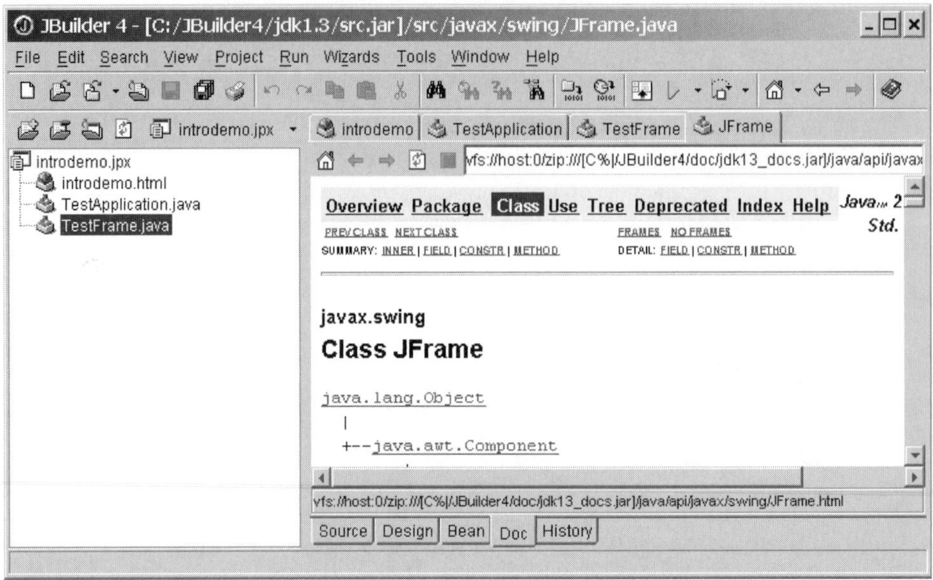

Figure 1.22 *You can browse the documentation of the Java class by clicking the Doc tab in the content pane.*

events and invokes the `jbInit` method. The `processWindowEvent` is overridden so that the program exits when the window is closed. In JDK 1.3, you could add `setDefaultCloseOperation(JFrame.EXIT_ON_CLOSE)` in the `jbInit` method to exit the program upon closing the window.

If you run the program now, you will see a blank frame.

Modifying the Code in the Frame Class

By now you know the files generated by the Application wizard as well as their contents. The Application wizard cannot generate everything you need in the project. To make the program work, you will have to modify the `TestFrame` class:

1. Add `implements ActionListener` in the class heading because `TestFrame` needs to listen to button actions and add `import java.awt.event.*`. (Alternatively, you can use the Implement Interface wizard to implement the `ActionListener` automatically from the Wizards menu.)

2. Add the code in the data declaration part of the program to declare instances of `JTextField` named `jtfNum1`, `jtfNum2`, and `jtfResult`, and an instance of `JButton` named `jbtAdd`, as shown in Listing 1.2.

3. Add the code in the `jbInit` method to create the user interface, and register the listener for `jbtAdd`, as shown in Listing 1.2.

4. Implement the `actionPerformed` method to add the numbers, and display the result, as shown in Listing 1.2.

5. Run the program. A sample run is shown in Figure 1.16.

```
package introdemo;

import java.awt.*;
import java.awt.event.*;
import javax.swing.*;

public class TestFrame extends JFrame implements ActionListener {
  // Declare three text fields
  private JTextField jtfNum1, jtfNum2, jtfResult;

  // Declare Add button
  private JButton jbtAdd;

  JPanel contentPane;
  BorderLayout borderLayout1 = new BorderLayout();

  /** Construct the frame */
  public TestFrame() {
    enableEvents(AWTEvent.WINDOW_EVENT_MASK);
    try {
      jbInit();
    }
    catch(Exception e) {
      e.printStackTrace();
    }
  }

  /** Component initialization */
  private void jbInit() throws Exception {
    //setIconImage(Toolkit.getDefaultToolkit().
    //  createImage(TestFrame.class.getResource("[Your Icon]")));
    contentPane = (JPanel)this.getContentPane();
    contentPane.setLayout(borderLayout1);
    this.setSize(new Dimension(400, 300));
    this.setTitle("TestUIApplication");

    // Place labels and text fields in a panel
    JPanel p1 = new JPanel();
    p1.setLayout(new FlowLayout());
    p1.add(new JLabel("Number 1"));
    p1.add(jtfNum1 = new JTextField(3));
    p1.add(new JLabel("Number 2"));
    p1.add(jtfNum2 = new JTextField(3));
    p1.add(new JLabel("Result"));
    p1.add(jtfResult = new JTextField(4));
    jtfResult.setEditable(false);  // Set it noneditable

    // Add the panel and the Add button in the frame
    contentPane.add(p1, BorderLayout.CENTER);
    contentPane.add(jbtAdd = new JButton("Add"), BorderLayout.SOUTH);

    // Register listener
    jbtAdd.addActionListener(this);
  }
```

Listing 1.2 *TestFrame.java*

```
    /** Handle add button action */
    public void actionPerformed(ActionEvent e) {
      int num1 =
        (Integer.valueOf(jtfNum1.getText().trim())).intValue();
      int num2 =
        (Integer.valueOf(jtfNum2.getText().trim())).intValue();
      int result = num1 + num2;

      // Display result
      jtfResult.setText(String.valueOf(result));
    }

    /** Overridden so we can exit when window is closed */
    protected void processWindowEvent(WindowEvent e) {
      super.processWindowEvent(e);
      if (e.getID() == WindowEvent.WINDOW_CLOSING) {
        System.exit(0);
      }
    }
  }
```

Listing 1.2 *Continued*

TIP

You can use JBuilder's Code Insight to display a context-sensitive popup window within the Editor, as shown in Figure 1.23. Code Insight helps you to complete the code. To adjust the option settings for Code Insight, choose Tools, Environment Options and click the Code Insight tab.

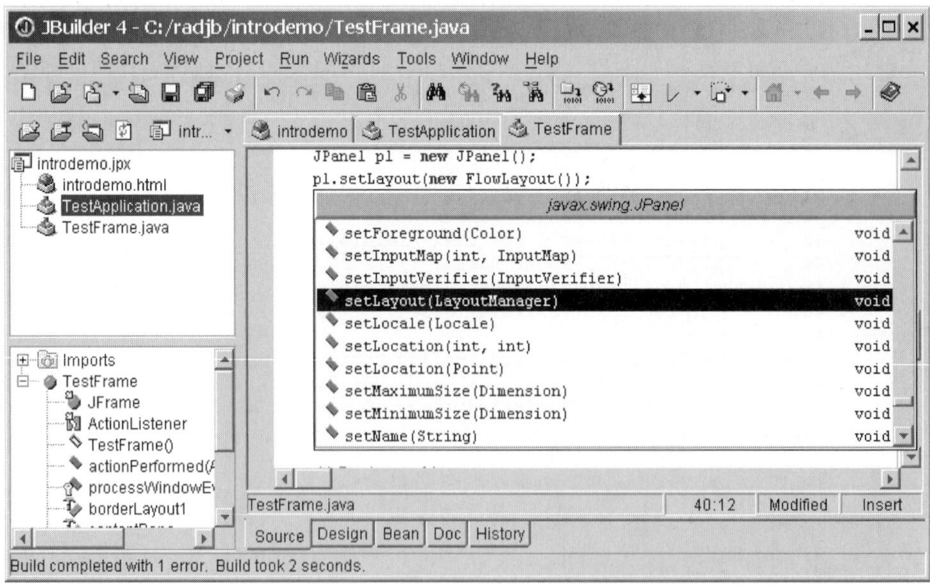

Figure 1.23 *Code Insight provides code completion and parameter lists for the methods.*

NOTE

All the applications will be created in the same way as TestApplication and TestFrame in this book, with the same options checked in the Application wizard unless explicitly noted otherwise.

NOTE

The bytecode is stored in Output path\Package Name. Therefore, TestFrame.class is stored in **c:\radjb\introdemo**, since the Output path is set to **c:\radjb** (see Figure 1.11) and the package name is **introdemo**. The file structures for the examples in this book are shown in Figure 1.24.

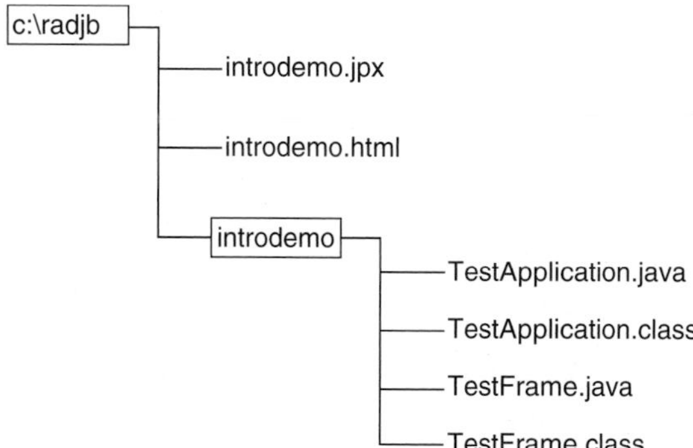

Figure 1.24 *TestApplication.java, TestApplication.class, TestFrame.java, and TestFrame.class are placed in c:\radjb\introdemo.*

Creating Java Applets

This section shows you how to create Java applets using the Applet wizard. You will write an applet to display a message on the applet at a specified location. The message and the location are passed as parameters using the `<param>` tag in HTML.

The Applet wizard uses three dialog boxes to collect applet information from the user, and it generates two files: an HTML file and an applet file. You can modify these two files if necessary to make them work for your project.

This section creates an applet to perform the same operation as in `TestFrame` in the previous section.

Here are the steps to create this applet:

1. In the introdemo project, choose File, New to display the Object Gallery. Double-click the Applet icon to display the Applet wizard, as shown in Figure 1.25.

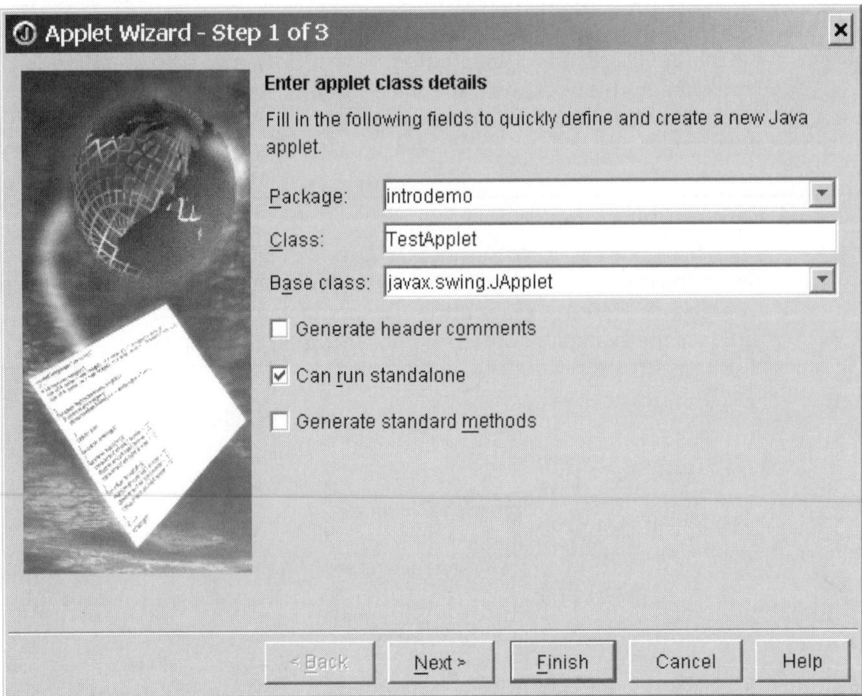

Figure 1.25 *Applet wizard Step 1 of 3 prompts you to enter the package name, the applet class name, and other optional information.*

2. In the Class field, type TestApplet, as shown in Figure 1.25. Check the option "Can run standalone" and choose `javax.swing.JApplet` in Base class. Click Finish to generate TestApplet.html and TestApplet.java.

JBUILDER 5 NOTE

The default Base class in JBuilder 5's Applet wizard is java.applet.Applet, but it is `java.applet.JApplet` in JBuilder 4.

The source code for TestApplet.html is shown in the content pane in the AppBrowser in Figure 1.26, and the source code of TestApplet.java is shown in Figure 1.27.

Modifying the Generated Applet Class

The Applet wizard creates the following two files:

- TestApplet.html contains an applet tag referencing your applet class. This is the file you should select to run or debug your applet. This file is stored in the output root directory.

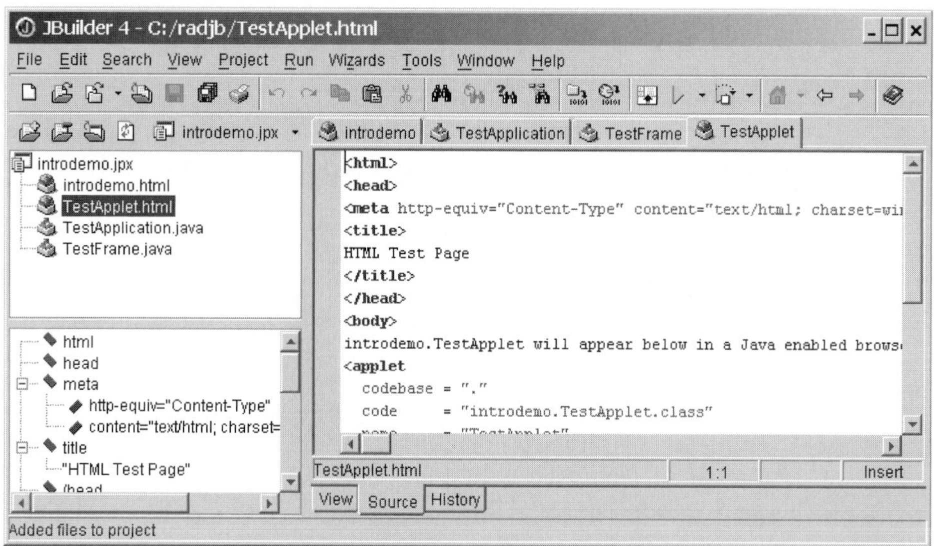

Figure 1.26 *The source code of TestApplet.html is shown in the AppBrowser.*

- TestApplet.java is your applet, which extends the `JApplet` class. This file is stored in the introdemo directory under the output root directory.

Although the Application wizard generates two .java files, the Applet wizard generates just one. In this example, the file is TestApplet.java. The `TestApplet` class contains a constructor, a main method, and five methods: `getAppletInfo`, `getParameter`, `getParameterInfo`, `init`, and `jbInit`. Since you checked the "Can

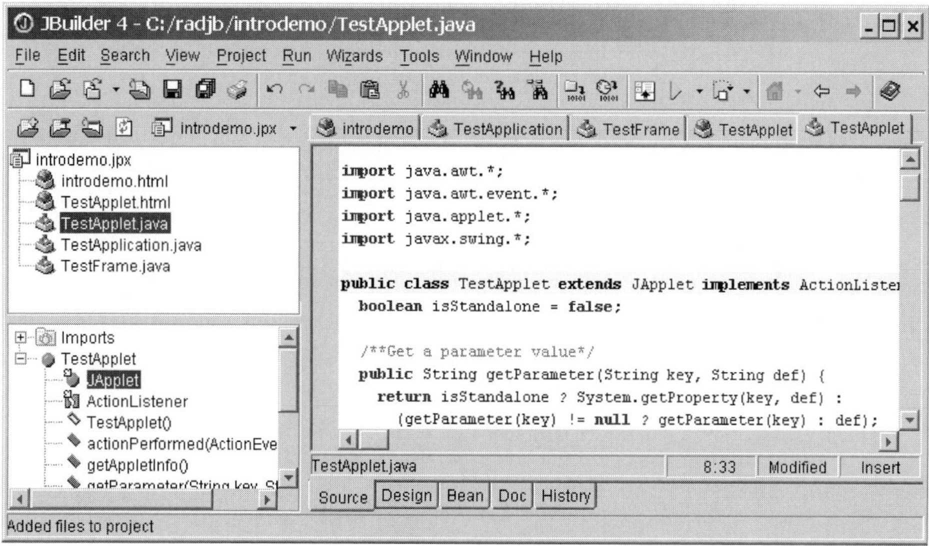

Figure 1.27 *The source code of* `TestApplet.java` *is shown in the AppBrowser.*

run standalone" option in Step 1 of 3 of the Applet wizard, JBuilder generates a `main` method for running the applet as a standalone application.

The methods `getAppletInfo`, `getParameterInfo`, and `init` are defined in the `java.applet.Applet` class and are overridden in the `TestApplet` class with concrete contents. The `jbInit` method initializes the applet user interface; this method is called by `init`.

NOTE

You can use the Applet wizard's Step 2 of 3 to specify HTML parameters, and the Applet wizard's Step 3 of 3 to specify the attributes in the applet tag in the HTML file. See **www.cs.armstrong.edu/liang/radjb5.html** for supplements on using the Applet wizard.

To make the applet perform the same function as `TestFrame` in the preceding example, you will have to modify the `TestApplet` class.

1. Add `implements ActionListener` in the class heading because `TestApplet` needs to listen to button actions and add `import java.awt.event.*`; (Alternatively, you can use the Implement Interface wizard to implement the `ActionListener` automatically from the Wizards menu.)
2. Add the code in the data declaration part of the program to declare instances of `JTextField` named `jtfNum1`, `jtfNum2`, and `jtfResult`, and an instance of `JButton` named `jbtAdd`, as shown in Listing 1.3.
3. Add the code in the `jbInit` method to create the user interface, and register the listener for `jbtAdd`, as shown in Listing 1.3.
4. Implement the `actionPerformed` method to add the numbers, and display the result, as shown in Listing 1.3.

```
package introdemo;

import java.awt.*;
import java.awt.event.*;
import java.applet.*;
import javax.swing.*;

public class TestApplet extends JApplet implements ActionListener {
  // Declare three text fields
  private JTextField jtfNum1, jtfNum2, jtfResult;

  // Declare Add button
  private JButton jbtAdd;

  boolean isStandalone = false;

  /** Get a parameter value */
  public String getParameter(String key, String def) {
    return isStandalone ? System.getProperty(key, def) :
      (getParameter(key) != null ? getParameter(key) : def);
  }
```

Listing 1.3 *TestApplet.java*

```

  /** Construct the applet */
  public TestApplet() {
  }

  /** Initialize the applet */
  public void init() {
    try {
      jbInit();
    }
    catch(Exception e) {
      e.printStackTrace();
    }
  }

  /** Component initialization */
  private void jbInit() throws Exception {
    this.setSize(new Dimension(400,300));

    // Place labels and text fields in a panel
    JPanel p1 = new JPanel();
    p1.setLayout(new FlowLayout());
    p1.add(new JLabel("Number 1"));
    p1.add(jtfNum1 = new JTextField(3));
    p1.add(new JLabel("Number 2"));
    p1.add(jtfNum2 = new JTextField(3));
    p1.add(new JLabel("Result"));
    p1.add(jtfResult = new JTextField(4));
    jtfResult.setEditable(false);  // Set it noneditable

    // Add the panel and the Add button in the frame
    this.getContentPane().add(p1, BorderLayout.CENTER);
    this.getContentPane().add(jbtAdd = new JButton("Add"),
      BorderLayout.SOUTH);

    // Register listener
    jbtAdd.addActionListener(this);
  }

  /** Get Applet information */
  public String getAppletInfo() {
    return "Applet Information";
  }

  /** Get parameter info */
  public String[][] getParameterInfo() {
    return null;
  }

  /** Main method */
  public static void main(String[] args) {
    TestApplet applet = new TestApplet();
    applet.isStandalone = true;
    JFrame frame = new JFrame();
    //EXIT_ON_CLOSE == 3
    frame.setDefaultCloseOperation(3);
    frame.setTitle("TestApplet");
    frame.getContentPane().add(applet, BorderLayout.CENTER);
    applet.init();
    applet.start();
    frame.setSize(400,320);
    Dimension d = Toolkit.getDefaultToolkit().getScreenSize();
```

Listing 1.3 *Continued*

```
    frame.setLocation((d.width - frame.getSize().width) / 2,
    (d.height - frame.getSize().height) / 2);
    frame.setVisible(true);
  }

  /** Handle add button action */
  public void actionPerformed(ActionEvent e) {
    int num1 =
      (Integer.valueOf(jtfNum1.getText().trim())).intValue();
    int num2 =
      (Integer.valueOf(jtfNum2.getText().trim())).intValue();
    int result = num1 + num2;

    // Display result
    jtfResult.setText(String.valueOf(result));
  }

  // static initializer for setting look & feel
  static {
    try {
      //UIManager.setLookAndFeel(UIManager.
      //   getSystemLookAndFeelClassName());
      //UIManager.setLookAndFeel(UIManager.
      //   getCrossPlatformLookAndFeelClassName());
    }
    catch(Exception e) {
    }
  }
}
```

Listing 1.3 *Continued*

You can run TestApplet.java as an applet or as an application. To run it as an applet, choose TestApplet.html in the project pane, and right-click the mouse button to display the context menu. Click Run from the menu. Figure 1.28 shows the output as an applet.

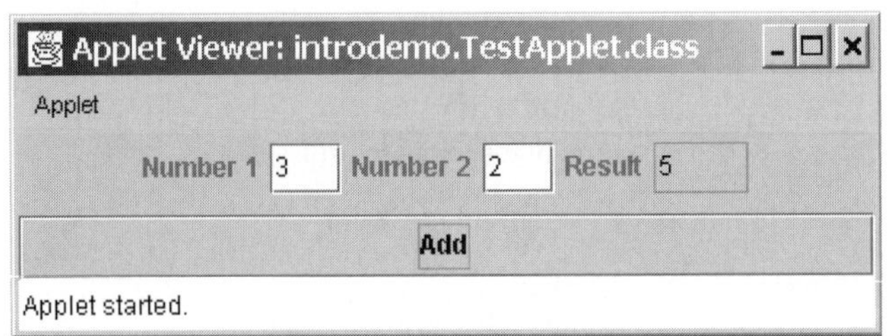

Figure 1.28 *The TestApplet runs from the applet viewer.*

You can also test the applet in the content pane from the AppBrowser. To do so, display TestApplet.html in the content pane and select the View button, as shown in Figure 1.29.

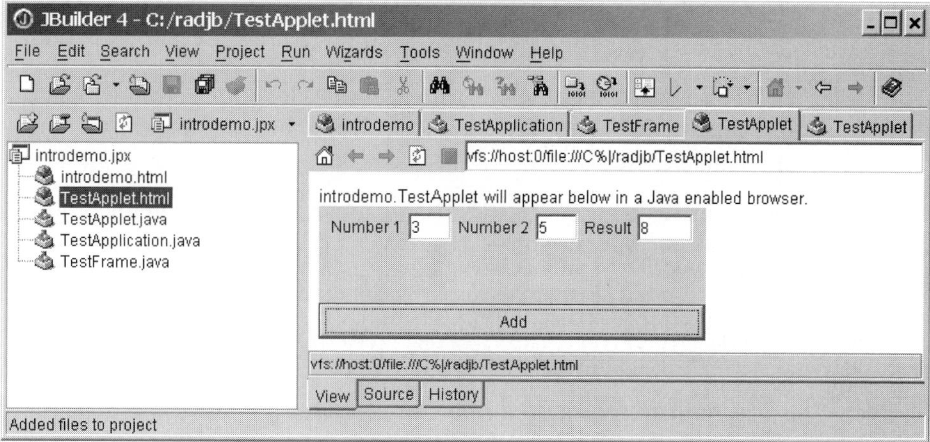

Figure 1.29 *You can view the applet within JBuilder.*

NOTE

Most of the examples in this book will be created using the Applet wizard. When using the Applet wizard, the base class selected is always javax.swing.JApplet, and the option "Can run standalone" is always checked. For brevity, the methods `main`, `getAppletInfo`, `getParameter`, and `getParameterInfo` will not be listed in future examples. The static block in the applet that specifies the look-and-feel of Motif, Metal, or Windows will not be listed either, for the same reason. Sometimes, the empty default constructor is also omitted.

Designing User Interfaces Using the UI Designer

JBuilder provides tools for visually designing and programming Java classes. This enables you to quickly and easily assemble the elements of a user interface (UI) for a Java application or applet. You can construct the UI with various building blocks chosen from the component palette that contains such components as buttons, text areas, lists, dialogs, and menus. Then you set the values of the component properties and attach event-handler code to the component events, telling the program how to respond to UI events.

JBuilder's visual tools make programming in Java easier and more productive. No tools, however, can accomplish everything you need. You have to modify the program produced by the tools. Thus, it is imperative to know the basic concept of Java graphics programming before starting to use the visual tools. This book assumes that you have a basic knowledge of Java, including creating graphical user interfaces using Swing, exception handling, internationalization, multithreads, IO streams, and the Java collections framework. Now you can use the UI designer to make programming more productive.

This section demonstrates using visual design tools to create the same program that you manually coded in the preceding section.

JBuilder's visual tools are designed to work well with the class templates created from the wizards. To use the UI designer, you should use the wizards in the Object Gallery to create classes.

Follow the steps below to create a new applet to demonstrate the UI designer in the introdemo project.

1. Choose File, Reopen to display a popup menu that includes a list of recently opened projects. Double-click introdemo.jpx on the list to open it. If it is not on the list, choose File, Open Project to open it.

2. Create a new applet class named `TestUIApplet` using the Applet wizard. In the Applet wizard, check the option "Can run standalone."

You wrote the code to create the UI in TestApplet.java. Now you will learn how to use the UI designer to create the user interface in TestUIApplet.java. The following are the steps to complete the example:

1. With TestUIApplet.java selected in the project pane, choose the Design tab in the content pane to switch to the UI designer, as shown in Figure 1.30.

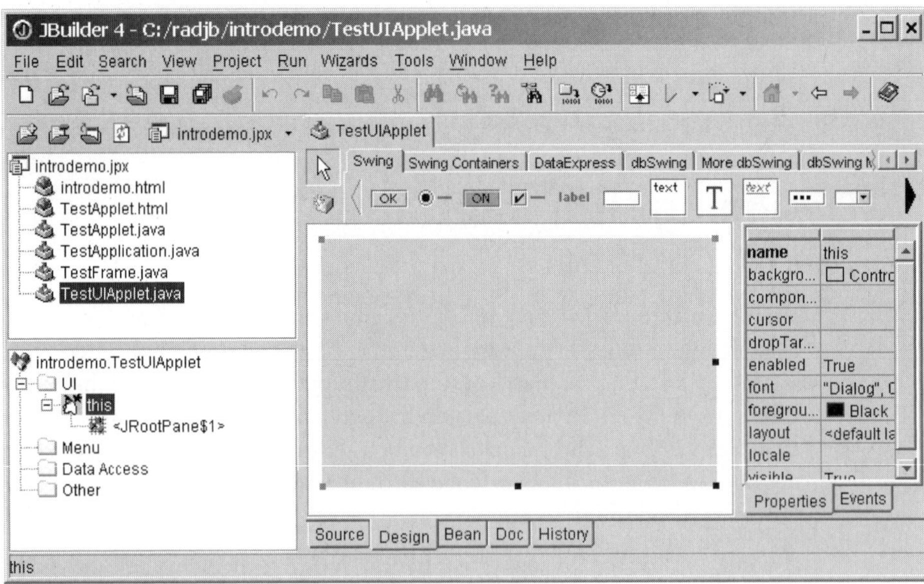

Figure 1.30 *The UI designer is shown in the content pane, and the component tree is shown in the structure pane.*

JBuilder 5 Note

Sometimes the layout property of the Applet wizard in JBuilder 5 does not show up because of a bug. In this case, you have to write the code in the `jbInit` method to change the layout of the content pane if you want to use a layout other than the default `BorderLayout`.

---

2. Click `JPanel` in the Swing Containers page of the component palette and drop it to the center of the UI designer or to the component tree. A new object named `jPanel1` is created. You can see it in the component tree under the `this` node (see Figure 1.31).

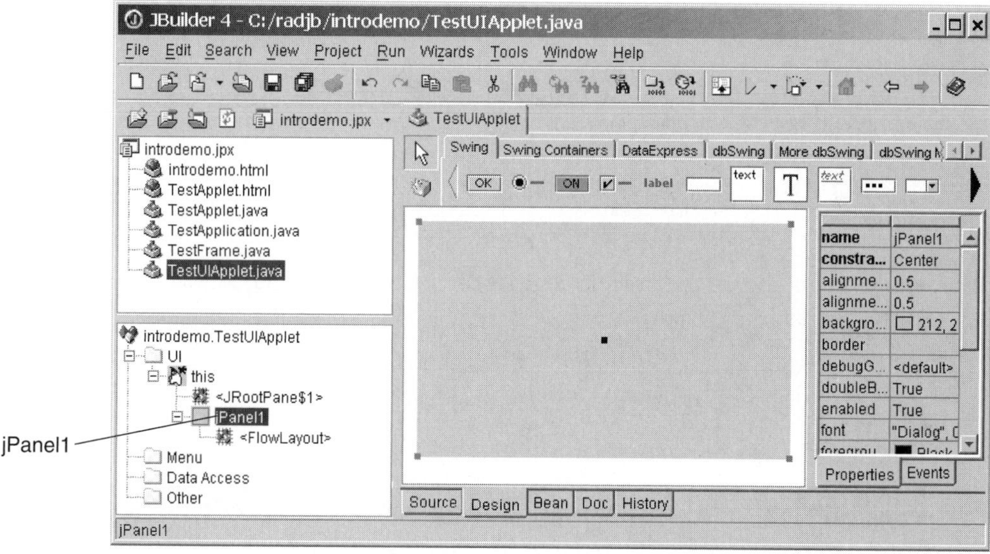

Figure 1.31 `jPanel1` *was added to the UI designer.*

3. Select `jPanel1` in the component tree. In the component inspector for `jPanel1`, set its `constraint` property to Center if it is not Center, and set its `layout` property to `FlowLayout`. (By default, the layout of a `JPanel` is `FlowLayout`.)

4. With the `this` node selected in the component tree, click `JButton` from the Swing page of the component palette and drop it to the south of the applet. An object named `jButton1` is created. You can see the object under the `this` Node in the component tree (see Figure 1.32).

5. Select `jButton1` in the component tree. In the inspector of `jButton1`, change its `name` property to `jbtAdd`, set its constraint to South, and change its `text` to Add. Whenever you make changes in the inspector, you will see their effects

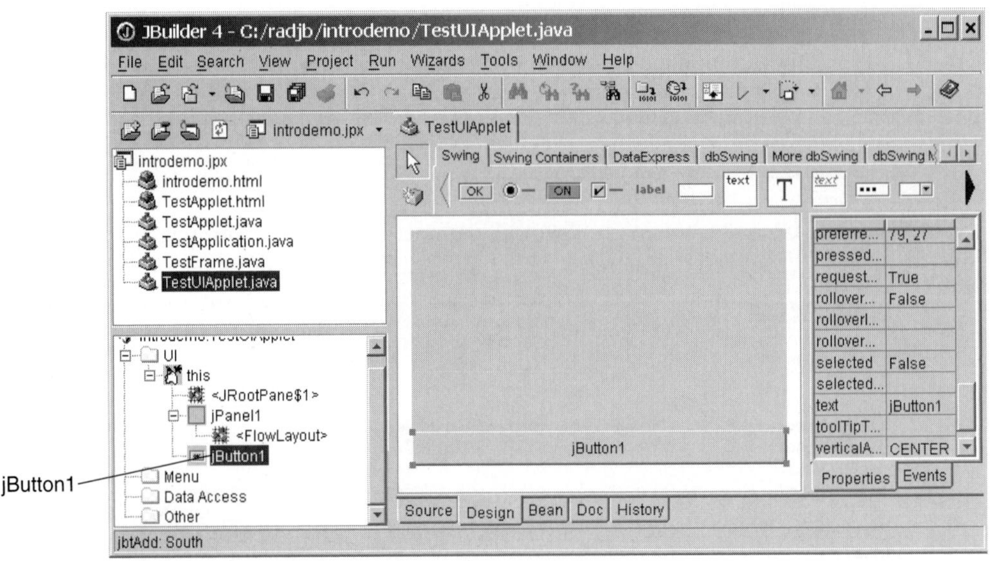

Figure 1.32 `jButton1` *was added to the applet.*

in the UI and in the component tree (see Figure 1.33) as well as in the source code (see Figure 1.34).

6. With `jPanel1` selected in the component tree, drop a `JLabel`, a `JTextField`, a `JLabel`, a `JTextField`, a `JLabel`, and a `JTextField` from the Swing page of the

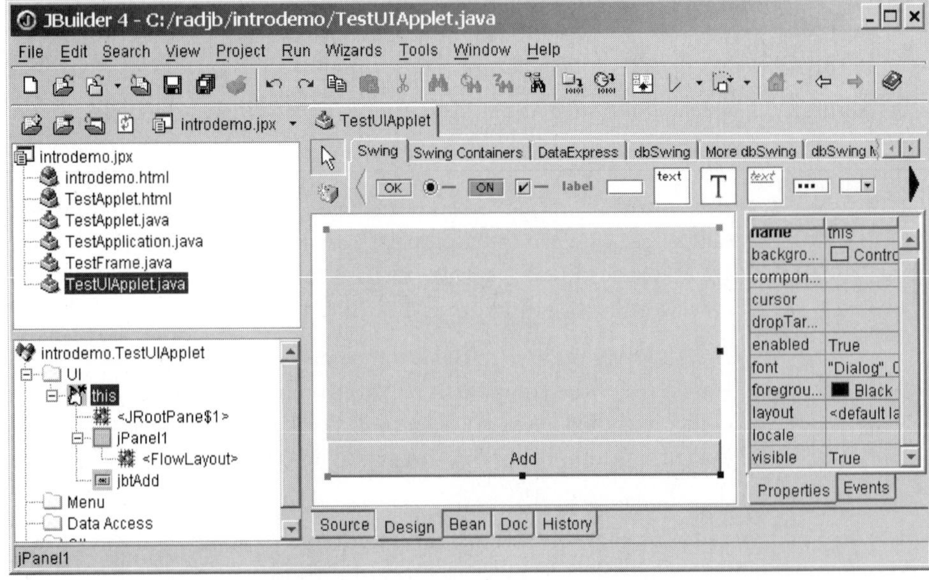

Figure 1.33 *The view of the AppBrowser is shown here after modifications of* `jbtAdd`*'s properties.*

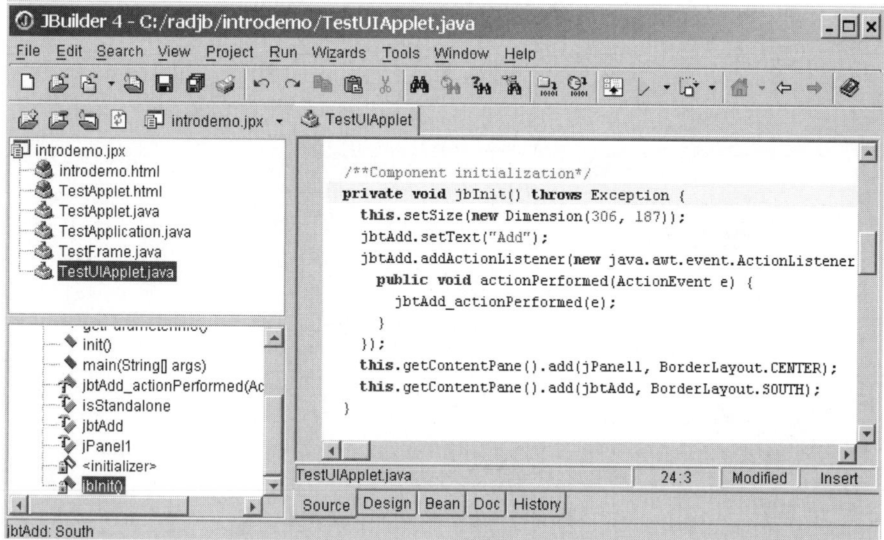

Figure 1.34 *The source code is synchronized with the UI designer.*

component palette into `jPanel1` to create objects named `jLabel1`, `jTextField1`, `jLabel2`, `jTextField2`, `jLabel3`, and `jTextField3`, as shown in Figure 1.35.

7. In the inspector of `jLabel1`, change its name to `jlblNum1` and its `text` property to Number 1. Similarly, change `jLabel2`'s name to `jlblNum2` and its `text` to Number 2, and `jLabel3`'s name to `jlblResult` and `text` to Result.

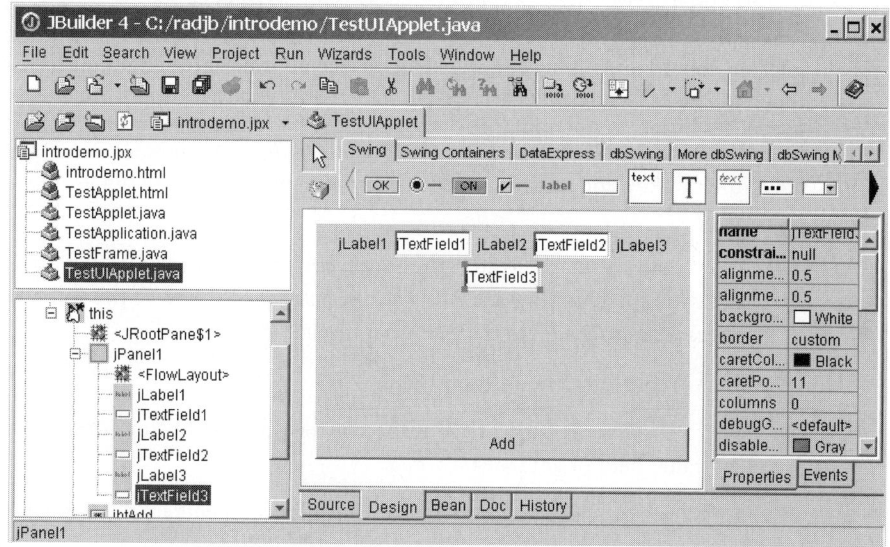

Figure 1.35 *The labels and text fields were created in the applet.*

8. In the inspector of `jTextField1`, change its `name` property to `jtfNum1`, set its `text` property to empty, and its `columns` to 3. Similarly, set `jTextField2`'s name to `jtfNum2`, `text` to empty, and `columns` to 3, and `jTextField3`'s name to `jtfResult`, `text` to empty, and `columns` to 4, as shown in Figure 1.36.

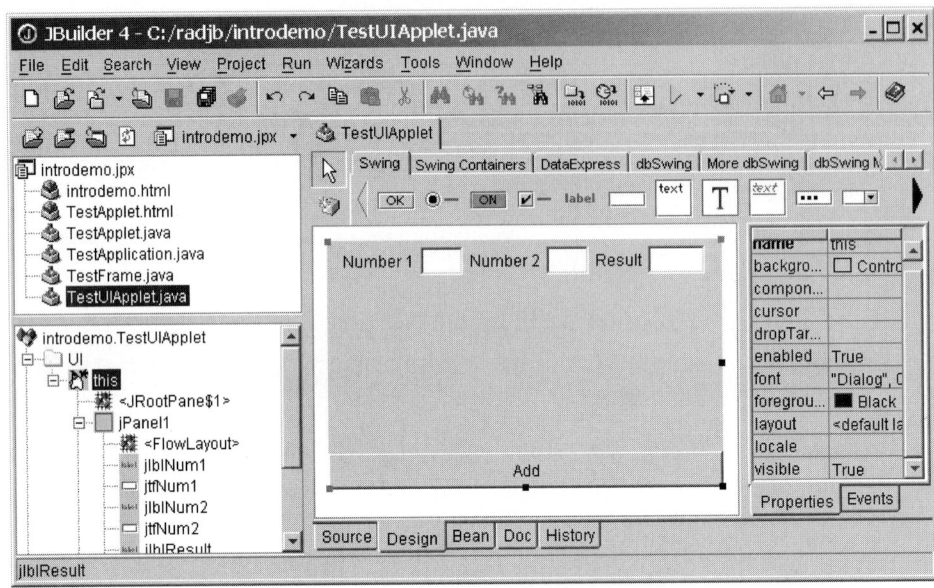

Figure 1.36 *The properties of labels and text fields were modified.*

TIP

You can set properties for multiple components. When more than one component is selected, the component inspector displays only the properties they have in common. When the values for the shared property differ among the selected components, the property value displayed is either the default or the value of the first component selected. When you change any of the shared properties in the component inspector, the property value changes to the new value in all the selected components. To select multiple components, hold down the Ctrl key and select each of the components in the UI designer.

---

9. Now that you have created the user interface, you are ready to implement the code for handling the Add button action. Use one of the following two approaches to generate the event handling code:

   - Double-click the Add button.
   - In the Events page of the inspector for the Add button, double-click the value field of `actionPerformed`.

   Either of the above actions will cause JBuilder to generate the following code:

- The line `import java.awt.event.*;` was inserted.
- A listener was created and registered with `jbtAdd` using the anonymous adapter as follows.

```
jbtAdd.addActionListener(new java.awt.event.ActionListener() {
   public void actionPerformed(ActionEvent e) {
     jbtAdd_actionPerformed(e);
   }
 });
```

- The method `jbtAdd_actionPerformed` for handling the action event is created. You need to fill in the code to carry out the actual action.

10. Implement `jbtAdd_actionPerformed` using the same code as in the `actionPerformed` method in TestApplet.java in the preceding section. The complete code for TestUIApplet.java is shown in Listing 1.4.

```
package introdemo;

import java.awt.*;
import java.awt.event.*;
import java.applet.*;
import javax.swing.*;

public class TestUIApplet extends JApplet {
  boolean isStandalone = false;
  JPanel jPanel1 = new JPanel();
  JButton jbtAdd = new JButton();
  JLabel jlblNum1 = new JLabel();
  JTextField jtfNum1 = new JTextField();
  JLabel jlblNum2 = new JLabel();
  JTextField jtfNum2 = new JTextField();
  JLabel jlblResult = new JLabel();
  JTextField jtfResult = new JTextField();

  /** Initialize the applet */
  public void init() {
    try {
      jbInit();
    }
    catch(Exception e) {
      e.printStackTrace();
    }
  }

  /** Component initialization */
  private void jbInit() throws Exception {
    this.setSize(new Dimension(306, 187));
    jbtAdd.setText("Add");
    jbtAdd.addActionListener(new java.awt.event.ActionListener() {
      public void actionPerformed(ActionEvent e) {
        jbtAdd_actionPerformed(e);
      }
    });
    jlblNum1.setText("Number 1");
    jtfNum1.setColumns(3);
```

Listing 1.4 *TestUIApplet.java*

```
      jlblNum2.setText("Number 2");
      jlblResult.setText("Result");
      jtfResult.setColumns(4);
      jtfNum2.setColumns(3);
      this.getContentPane().add(jPanel1, BorderLayout.CENTER);
      jPanel1.add(jlblNum1, null);
      jPanel1.add(jtfNum1, null);
      jPanel1.add(jlblNum2, null);
      jPanel1.add(jtfNum2, null);
      jPanel1.add(jlblResult, null);
      jPanel1.add(jtfResult, null);
      this.getContentPane().add(jbtAdd, BorderLayout.SOUTH);
    }

    void jbtAdd_actionPerformed(ActionEvent e) {
      int num1 =
        (Integer.valueOf(jtfNum1.getText().trim())).intValue();
      int num2 =
        (Integer.valueOf(jtfNum2.getText().trim())).intValue();
      int result = num1 + num2;

      // Display result
      jtfResult.setText(String.valueOf(result));
    }
  }
```

Listing 1.4 *Continued*

All the code in TestUIApplet.java was automatically generated except the body of the `jbtAdd_actionPerformed` method. The UI designer enables you to rapidly develop Java programs with minimum coding. All the components in the component palette are JavaBeans components. JavaBeans provides the foundations for rapid application development in Java. The rest of the book is centered on creating JavaBeans components and using the beans in rapid application development.

Managing Projects in JBuilder

JBuilder uses a project file to store project information. You cannot edit the project file manually; it is modified automatically, however, whenever you add or remove files from the project or set project options. You can see the project file as a node at the top of the project tree in the project pane (see Figure 1.8). JBuilder uses a Project Properties dialog box for setting project properties and provides a Project wizard to facilitate creating projects.

Setting Project Properties

JBuilder uses the Default Project Properties dialog box to set default environment properties for all the projects. An individual project has its own Project Properties dialog box, which can be used to set project-specific properties.

To display the default Project Properties dialog box, select Project, Default Properties, as shown in Figure 1.37. To display the Project Properties dialog box, select Project, Properties, as shown in Figure 1.38. You can also right-click the project file in the project pane and choose the Properties command to display the Project Properties dialog box.

The Default Project Properties dialog box (Figure 1.37) and the Project Properties dialog box (Figure 1.38) look the same but have different titles. Both dialog boxes contain Paths, General, Run, Debug, and Code Style. The Team tab is only available in JBuilder Enterprise. You can set options in these pages for the current project or the default project, depending on whether the dialog box is for the current project or for the default project. JBuilder Enterprise Edition has more options in the Project Properties dialog box.

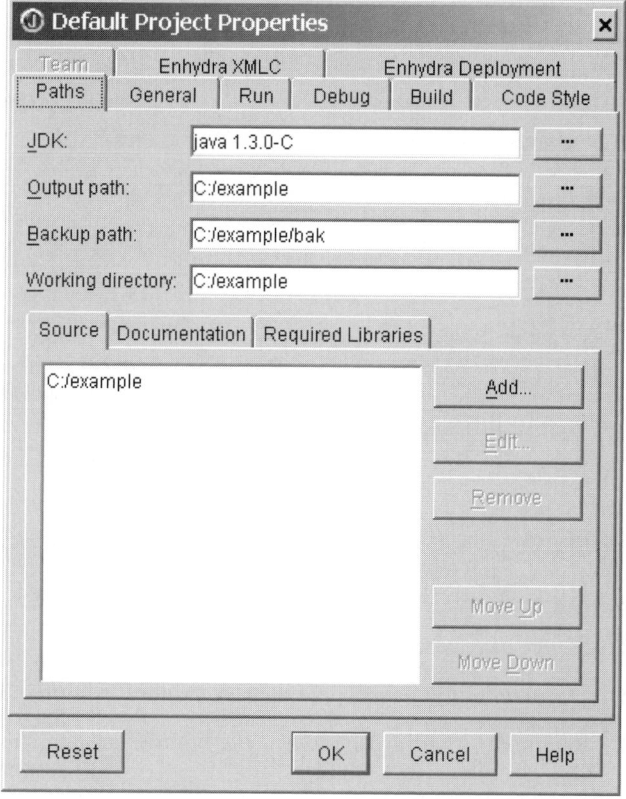

Figure 1.37 *The Default Project Properties dialog box enables you to set default properties to cover all the projects.*

The Paths Page

The Paths page of the Project Properties dialog box sets the following options:

- JDK version.
- Output path where the compilation output is stored.

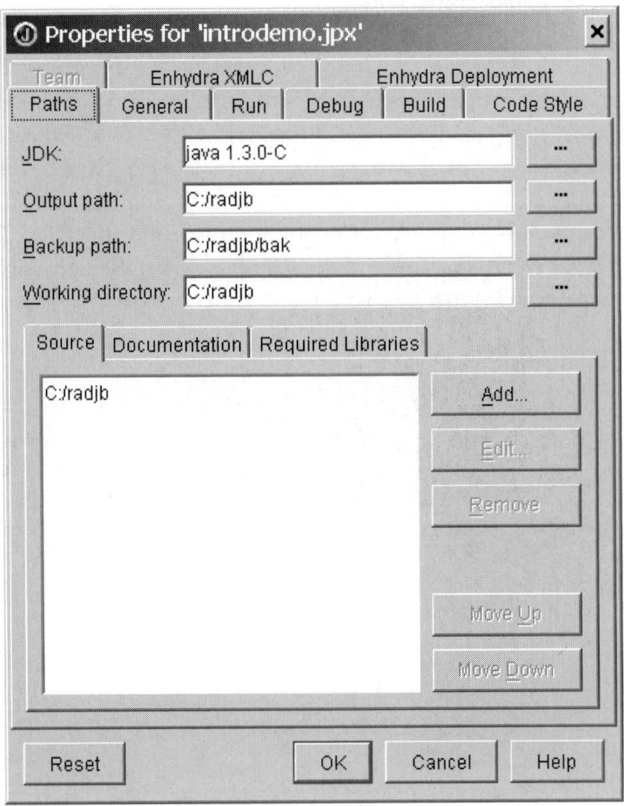

Figure 1.38 *Each project keeps its own project properties.*

- Backup path where the backup files are stored.
- Working directory where the temporary files are stored.
- Source page where the source files are stored.
- Documentation page where the javadoc files are stored.
- Required Libraries page where the libraries are searched for compiling and running.

JBuilder can compile and run against JDK 1.1, JDK 1.2, or JDK 1.3. To set up the list of available JDKs, click the ellipsis button to display the Available JDK Versions dialog box for adding new JDK compilers. This feature is available only in JBuilder Professional and Enterprise.

Setting proper paths is necessary for JBuilder to locate the associated files in the right directory for compiling and running the programs in the project. The Source page specifies one or more paths for the source file. The Output path specifies the path where the compiler places the .class files. Files are placed in a directory tree that is based on the Output path and the package name. For example, if the Output path is **c:\radjb** and the package name is introdemo in the source code, the

.class file is placed in **c:\radjb\introdemo**. The Backup path specifies a directory where the backup source files are stored. JBuilder automatically backs up the files before committing any change to the current file. Note that the .java files are backed up in the backup directory, but the other files, like .html and .jpx, are backed up in their original directory.

All the libraries you need for this book have already been taken care of. If you need to add the custom libraries to the project, click the Add button to display a list of available libraries. To remove a library, click the Remove button. To switch the order of libraries, use the Move Up and Move Down buttons.

The General Page

The General page (Figure 1.39) allows you to specify an encoding scheme used in JBuilder, enable or disable automatic source package discovery, and modify javadoc fields.

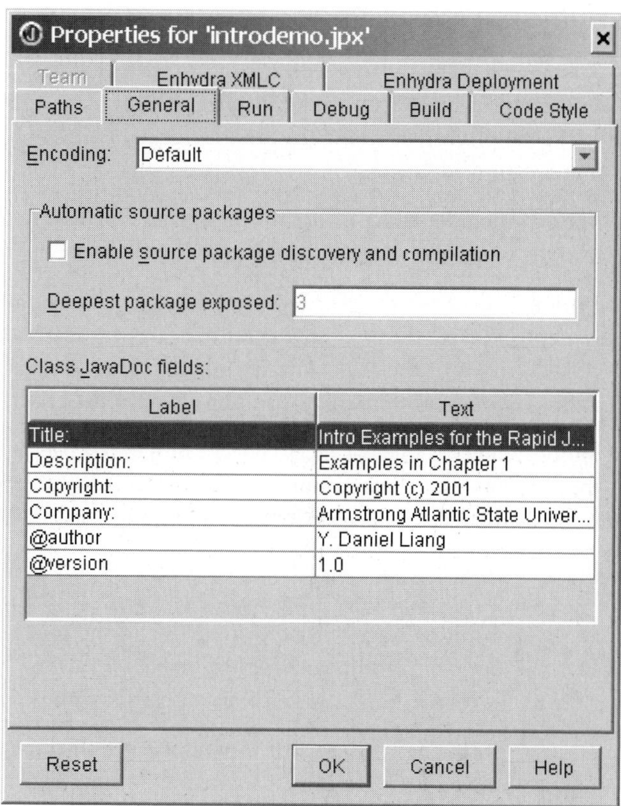

Figure 1.39 *The General page has options for selecting encoding type, enabling/disabling automatic source package discovery, and modifying javadoc fields.*

NOTE

The option "Enable source package discovery and compilation" is unchecked for all the projects in this book. If this option is checked, all the packages under **c:\radjb** would be displayed in the project pane. This option is not available in JBuilder Foundation.

The "Encoding" choice menu specifies the encoding that controls how the compiler interprets characters beyond the ASCII character set. If no setting is specified, the default native-encoding converter for the platform is used.

You can enable or disable automatic source package. This is a useful feature available only in JBuilder Professional and Enterprise. With automatic source package enabled, all packages in the project's source path automatically appear in the project pane, so you can navigate through the files without switching projects.

The Class Javadoc fields section specifies the javadoc tags generated in the class files when Generate Header Comments is enabled in a wizard.

The Run Page, Debug Page, and Build Page

The Run page sets the runtime configuration. The Debug page sets debug options. The Build page (Figure 1.40) sets compiler options. The options are applied to all the files in the project, as well as to files referenced by these files, stopping at packages that are marked "stable."

The option "Include debug information" includes symbolic debug information in the .class file when you compile, make, or rebuild a node.

The option "Show warnings" displays compiler warning messages. The option "Show deprecations" displays all deprecated classes, methods, properties, events, and variables used in the API. The option "Synchronize output dir" deletes class files on the output path for which you don't have source files before compiling.

The option "Check stable packages" checks files in the packages marked "stable" to see whether they and their imported classes need to be recompiled. This option shortens the edit/recompile cycle by not rechecking stable packages.

The option "Make package stable" checks all the classes of a package on the first build and marks the package "stable." If this option is unchecked, only the referenced classes of this package will be compiled, and the package will not be marked "stable." This option should be unchecked when working with partial projects. It is especially useful for working with a library of classes with no source code.

The option "Obfuscate" makes your programs less vulnerable to decompiling. Decompiling means to translate the Java bytecode to Java source code. After decompiling your obfuscated code, the generated source code contains altered symbol names for private symbols. This feature is available only in JBuilder Professional and Enterprise.

The "Exclude Class" choice lets you specify that a .class file is excluded from being compiled.

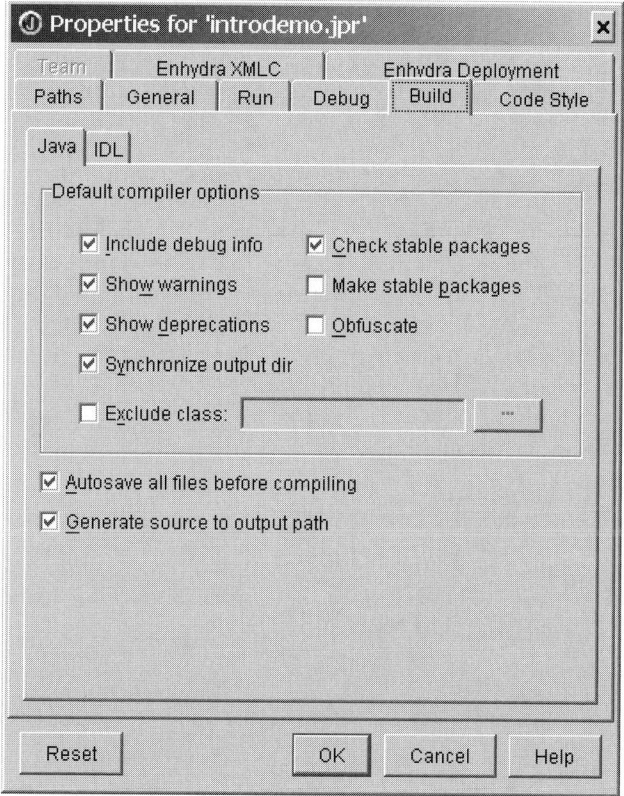

Figure 1.40 *The Build page sets compiler options.*

The option "Autosave all files before compiling" automatically saves all files in the project before each compile.

The option "Generate source to output path" is applicable only to RMI (Remote Method Invocation) and IDL (Interface Definition Language) files.

The Code Style Page

The Code Style page (Figure 1.41) enables you to specify the code style of the program generated by JBuilder.

With the option "End of line" selected, JBuilder will generate the code with opening braces inserted at the end of the line; otherwise, the opening braces are inserted at the beginning of the new line.

In the Event Handling section, you can choose one of the options to tell JBuilder to generate event-handling code using an anonymous adapter, standard adapter, or matching the existing style of the event-handling code. The adapters are used in the UI designer in JBuilder.

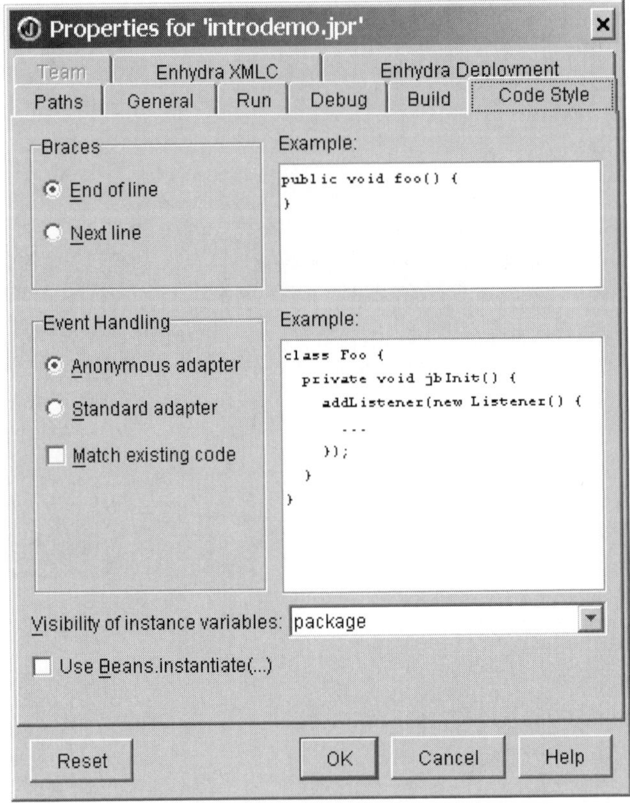

Figure 1.41 *The Code Style page of the Project Properties dialog box sets the options for the code style of the program generated by JBuilder.*

NOTE

The standard adapter would be generated if you selected the standard adapter option in the Code Style page of the Project Properties dialog box. Various adapters will be introduced in Chapter 3.

The option "Use Beans.instantiate" tells JBuilder to instantiate objects using `Beans.instantiate()` instead of the `new` operator. This feature is discussed Chapter 9, "Bean Persistence and Versioning."

Customizing JBuilder Environment

JBuilder allows you to customize your development environment by changing the IDE options or the Editor options. Certain options, such as syntax highlighting, can make your programs easy to read and help you to spot errors.

To set the IDE options, choose Tools, IDE Options to display the IDE Options dialog box, as shown in Figure 1.42. The dialog box contains three tabs: Browser, File Types, and Run/Debu.

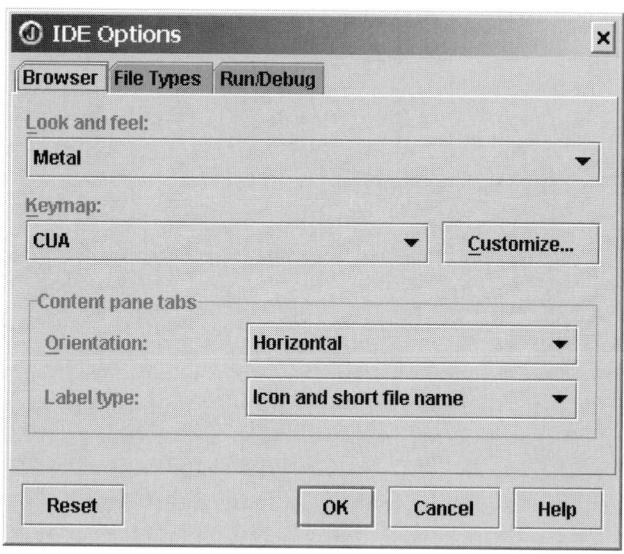

Figure 1.42 *The IDE Options dialog box enables you to set the options for the Browser, File Types, and Run/Debug.*

JBUILDER 5 NOTE

JBuilder 5's IDE Options dialog box enables you to set options for XML, Web, and Audio.

In the Browser tab, you can set the look-and-feel of the browser. Three types of look-and-feel (Metal, Motif, and Windows) are available in the Windows version of JBuilder. For example, if you choose Windows in the look-and-feel combo box, the IDE Options dialog would be displayed as shown in Figure 1.43.

In the IDE Options dialog box, you can also set the orientation of the tabs in the content pane and the label type for the tabs in the content pane. Figure 1.44 shows the new IDE after setting the orientation to vertical.

You can set the options for file extensions for the types of files in the File Types tab. You can also set runtime update intervals and debugger update intervals in the Run/Debug tab.

To set Editor options, choose Tools, Editor Options to display the Editor Options dialog box, as shown in Figure 1.45. The dialog box contains six tabs: Editor, Display, Color, CodeInsight, Templates, and Java Structure.

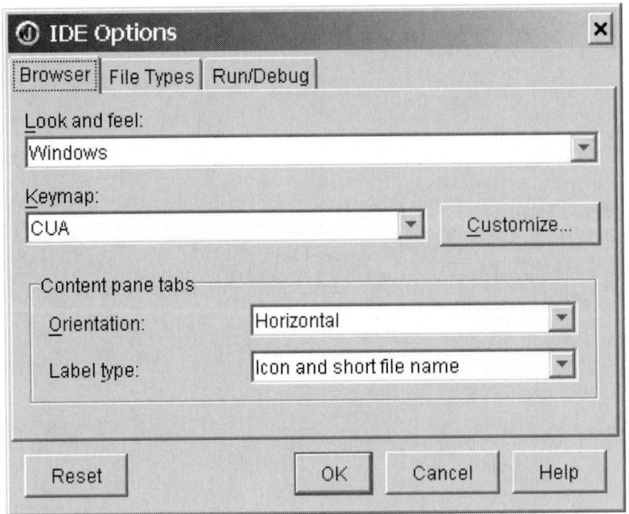

Figure 1.43 *The IDE Options dialog box appears in Windows look and feel.*

The Editor tab enables you to customize editing behavior in the content pane. You can set the smart key options, indent options, display options, save options, and search options.

The Display tab (see Figure 1.46) enables you to set the right margin and fonts for the content pane.

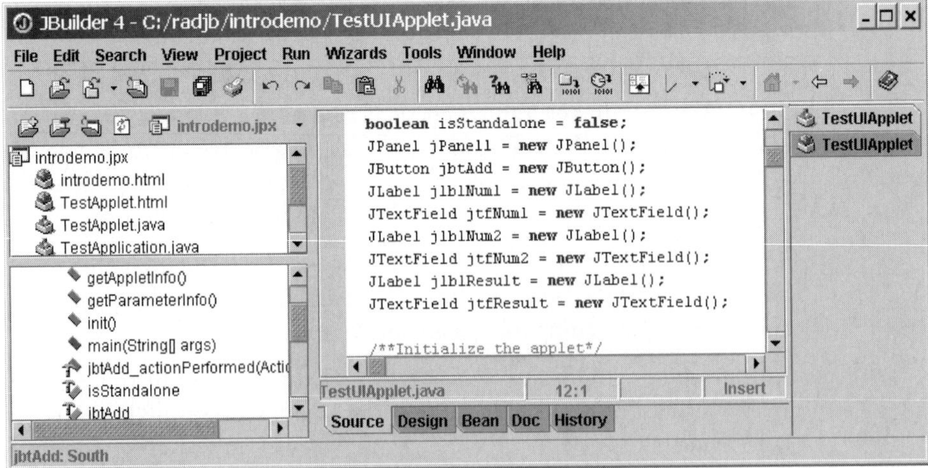

Figure 1.44 *The file tabs in the content pane are displayed vertically due to a change in the IDE option dialog box.*

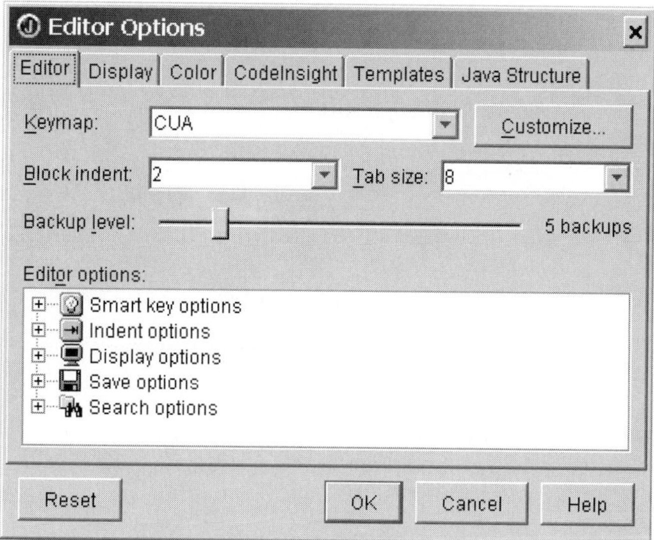

Figure 1.45 *The Editor Options dialog box enables you to set the options for editing in the content pane.*

The Colors tab (see Figure 1.47) specifies the colors of the different elements of your code in the source pane. You can specify foreground and background colors for the elements, such as Comment, Reserved word, String, Symbol, and Error line, in the Element list. The sample code at the bottom of the dialog box shows how your settings will appear in the source pane.

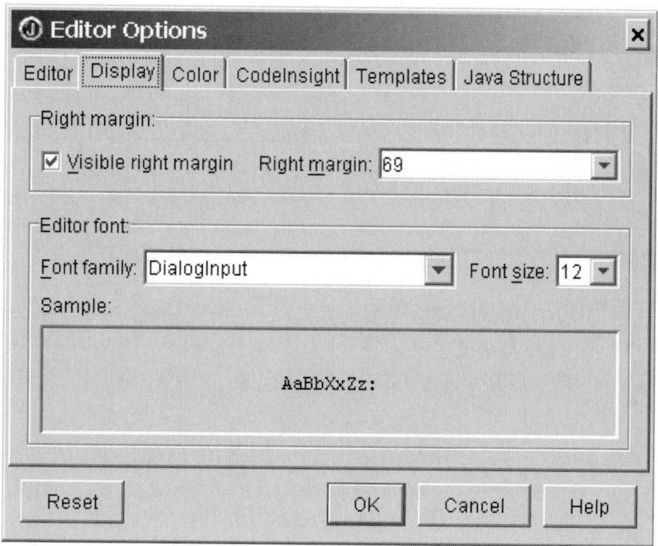

Figure 1.46 *You can customize display and font options for the content pane in the Display tab of the Editor Options dialog box.*

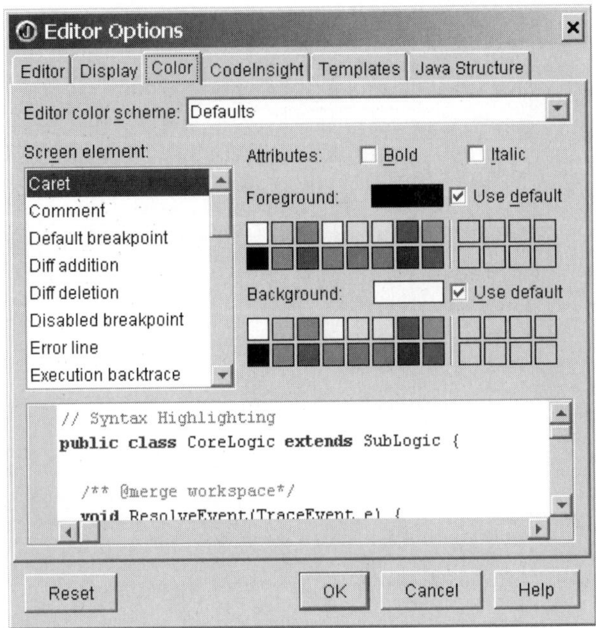

Figure 1.47 *You can customize colors for different elements of the source code.*

The CodeInsight tab (see Figure 1.48) enables you to configure Code Insight (Code completion assistant). JBuilder's Code Insight enhancements display a context-sensitive popup window within the Editor. Code Insight provides code completion, parameter lists, and tool tip expression evaluation. Code Insight highlights illegal class references not on the Class Path and invalid statements not found in the classes.

TIP

If the cursor is between the parentheses for a method call, pressing Ctrl+Shift+H or Ctrl+Shift+Space brings up a list of valid parameters.

The Templates tab (see Figure 1.49) displays JBuilder's predefined code templates. Code templates are snippets of frequently used code elements that you can insert into your code to avoid repetitive typing. To use code templates, choose one of the following two methods:

- Type the code template name, such as *forb*, in your code where you want the code to appear and press CTRL+J to generate the template for the `for` loop.
- Position the cursor where you want the code to appear and press CTRL+J to display a list of template names. Select a template from the list. The template is automatically created.

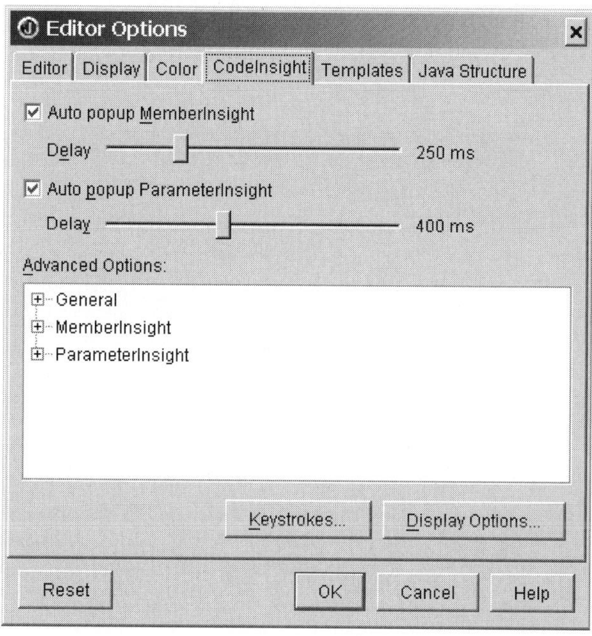

Figure 1.48 *You can specify whether and how Code Insight is used on the CodeInsight tab of the Editor Options dialog box.*

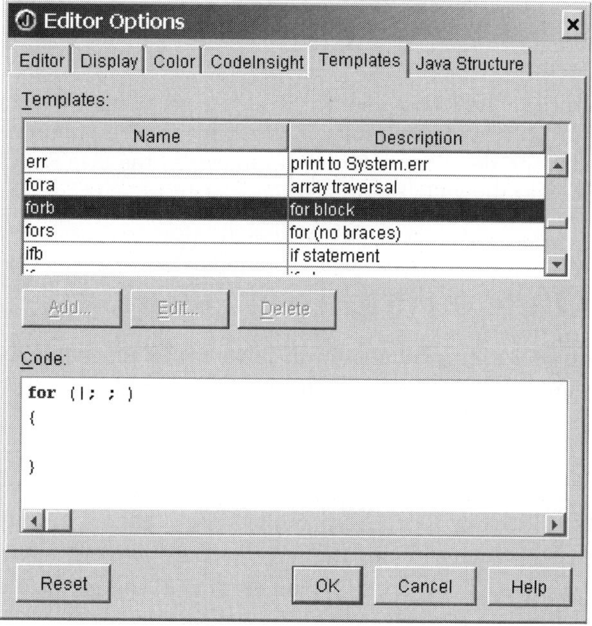

Figure 1.49 *You can add, edit, or delete code templates in the Templates tab.*

The Java Structure tab (see Figure 1.50) contains the options for specifying the appearance of the code elements in the structure pane.

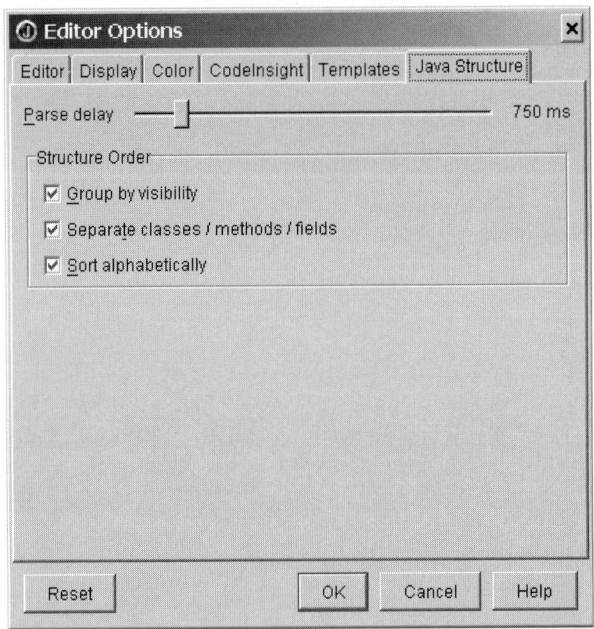

Figure 1.50 *The Java Structure tab enables you to specify the appearance of the code elements in the structure pane.*

TIP

The Java Structure dialog box can also be displayed by right-clicking the mouse button in the structure pane to display a popup menu. The popup menu contains the item named Properties. Choose Properties to display the Java Structure View Properties dialog box, as shown in Figure 1.51.

Getting Online Help from JBuilder

JBuilder provides a large number of documents online, giving you a great deal of information on a variety of topics pertaining to the use of JBuilder and Java.

To access online help, choose Help, Help Topics to display JBuilder Help, as shown in Figure 1.52.

JBuilder Help behaves like a Web browser and contains the main menus, navigation pane, and content pane. From the main menus, you can open a URL from the File menu, add bookmarks from the Bookmarks menu, and get help on using JBuilder Help from the Help menu.

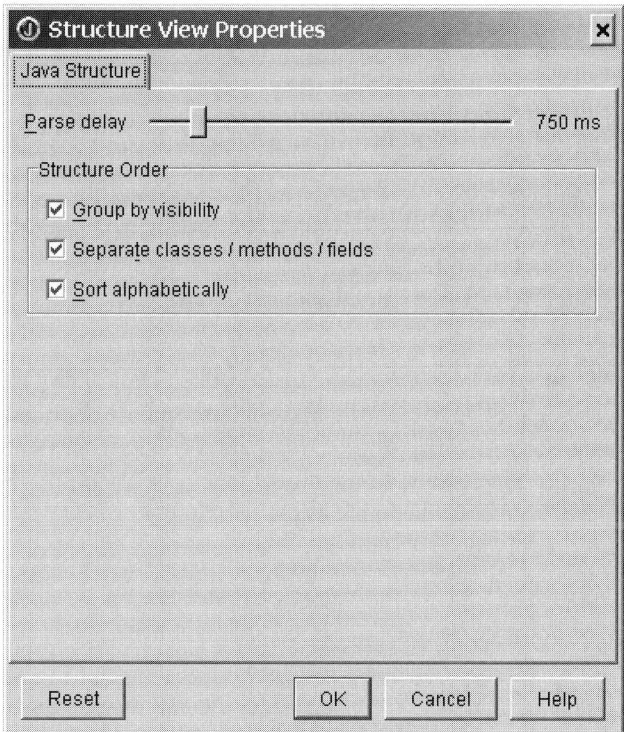

Figure 1.51 *The Structure View Properties dialog box can be displayed from the context menu in the structure pane.*

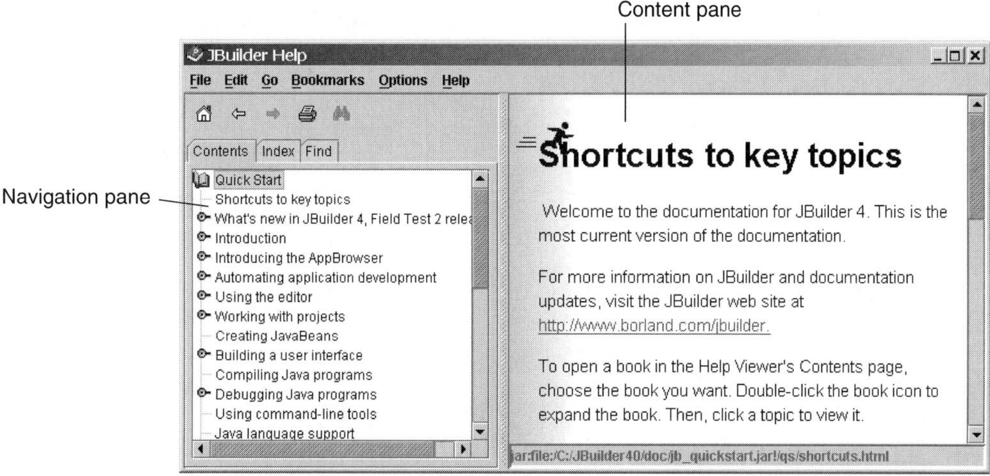

Figure 1.52 *All help documents are displayed in JBuilder Help.*

The navigation pane contains five action buttons on top of the three tabs. The buttons are **Home**, **Previous**, **Next**, **Print**, and **Find in Page**. The Home, Previous, and Next buttons go to the first, previous, and next topics in the history list. The Print button prints the document in the content pane. The Find in Page button enables you to search the current topic.

The three tabs are **Contents**, **Index,** and **Find**. The Contents tab displays available documents. The table of contents of the document is displayed in a tree-like list in the navigation pane. To view a given topic, select the node in the tree associated with the topic. JBuilder Help displays the document for the topic in the content pane.

The Index tab shows the index entries for the current document. The Find page shows the combined index entries for all the available documents in JBuilder. To display the index, simply type the first few letters in the entry. As you start typing, the index scrolls, doing an incremental search on the index entries to find the closest match. Select and double-click the index in the entry to display the document for the entry in the content pane.

TIP

The Help menu is not the only way to get help. There are many ways to get help on a topic when you are using JBuilder. For example, if you want to find out what a particular menu item does, highlight a menu item on a pull-down menu without activating the item and press F1. You can also get help on a Java keyword or on a class name in the Java library such as `Math`, by highlighting the keyword or class name in the content pane and pressing F1.

Chapter Summary

This chapter gave you a quick start on using JBuilder to develop Java programs. JBuilder contains numerous wizards in the Object Gallery that can be used to create program templates. You learned how to use the Project wizard, the Application wizard, and the Applet wizard to create projects, applications, and applets. You also learned how to customize project properties, including how to modify Source root directories and the Output root directory, how to set compiler options, how to specify the code style, how to customize environments, and how to get online help in JBuilder. Finally, you learned how to use the UI designer for creating user interfaces and generating event-handling code with minimum coding.

Review Questions

1.1. How do you create a Java project in JBuilder?

1.2. How do you compile a Java program in JBuilder?

1.3. How do you run a Java application in JBuilder?

1.4. How do you create a Java applet in JBuilder?

1.5. Where is the .class file stored after successful compilation in JBuilder?

1.6. What would happen if a Java source file was not in one of the Source root directories?

1.7. How do you add a file or a package to an existing project or remove one from a project? How do you add a package to a project or to remove one from a project? Does removing a file from a project cause the file to be deleted from the disk? Find out how to delete a file permanently.

1.8. How do you control the order of fields, methods, and separate classes displayed in the structure pane?

1.9. How do you set the option to enable JBuilder to save the files before compiling?

1.10. How do you set the option to enable JBuilder to generate the code with the new-line brace style?

1.11. Can you set the environment option not to save backup files?

1.12. How do you set the option so that the Java keywords are displayed in red in the content pane?

1.13. How do you turn off the Code Insight?

1.14. How do you open the UI designer? How do you set properties for a component? How do you set properties for multiple components at the same time?

1.15. If the message pane is not displayed, how do you show it?

1.16. How do you browse the source code of a Java file in the Java library?

1.17. Show at least two ways to display online documentation for JBuilder build options.

1.18. Suppose the output path is c:\smith, and the package statement in the source code is package homework.csci1301. Where is the .class file stored after successful compilation in JBuilder?

a. c:\jbuilder4\projects\classes
b. c:\smith
c. c:\smith\homework
d. c:\smith\homework\csci1301

1.19. Suppose the source path is c:\smith, and you specified exercise1 in the Package field in the Applet wizard, and Test in the Class name field. Where is the generated Test.java stored?

a. c:\jbuilder4\projects\src
b. c:\smith
c. c:\smith\exercise1
d. c:\smith\exercise1\test

Programming Exercises

1.1. Use the Application wizard and UI designer to create a project that converts a Celsius temperature to a Fahrenheit temperature with the following requirements:

a. Create a project file named exercise1_1.jpr using the Project wizard.
b. Create an application class named `ConvApplication` and a frame class named `ConvFrame` using the Application wizard.
c. Use the UI designer to create the user interface, as shown in Figure 1.53. Implement the code that converts the temperature when the Convert button is clicked and displays the resulting Fahrenheit temperature.

The formula for converting Celsius to Fahrenheit is as follows:

```
fahrenheit = (9.0/5.0)*celsius + 32.0
```

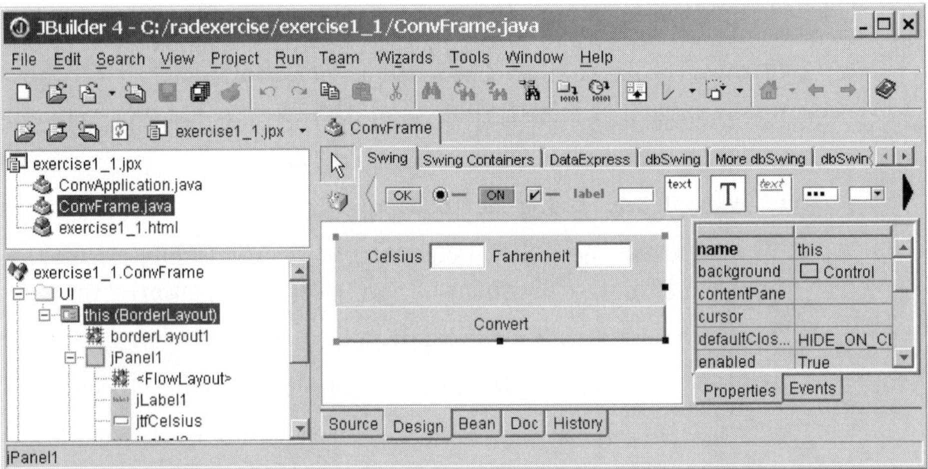

Figure 1.53 *The user enters a temperature in Celsius and clicks the Convert button to display the corresponding temperature in Fahrenheit.*

1.2. Use the Applet wizard and UI designer to create an applet that converts a Celsius temperature to a Fahrenheit temperature with the following requirements:

a. Create a project file named exercise1_2.jpr using the Project wizard.
b. Create an applet named `Exercise1_2` using the Applet wizard.
c. Use the UI designer to create the user interface, as shown in Figure 1.53.
d. Implement the code that converts the temperature when the Convert button is clicked and displays the resulting Fahrenheit temperature.

CHAPTER 2

INTRODUCTION TO JAVABEANS

Objectives

- Know what a JavaBeans component is.
- Discover the similarities and differences between beans and regular objects.
- Learn how to create JavaBeans components in JBuilder and install them in the component palette.
- Understand JavaBeans properties and naming patterns.
- Become familiar with JavaBeans property types.
- Know how to use the component inspector in JBuilder.

Introduction

JavaBeans technology is a significant extension and enhancement of the Java language. This technology enables programmers to rapidly build applications by assembling objects and testing them during design time. It is the foundation for the Java builder tools that support rapid Java application development.

JavaBeans are 100% pure Java programs. They are simple to develop and easy to use. JavaBeans are a special kind of Java class. If you know Java, you may have already developed JavaBeans. In fact, all the AWT and Swing user interface classes are JavaBeans components. With JavaBeans, you can create new applications by connecting various off-the-shelf software components using a builder tool, such as JBuilder, with minimum coding. The JavaBeans technology ushers in a new era of component computing. An application can be viewed as a framework consisting of various software components that can be added, removed, or customized, as needed.

This chapter introduces the concept of JavaBeans and the relationship between JavaBeans and Java RAD builder tools. You will begin to write simple JavaBeans and use them in JBuilder.

Beans and Objects

JavaBeans is a software component architecture that extends the power of the Java language to enable well-formed objects to be manipulated visually in a builder tool like JBuilder during design time. Such well-formed objects are referred to as *Java beans* or simply *beans*. The classes that define the beans, referred to as *JavaBeans components* or *bean components*, or simply *components*, must conform to the JavaBeans component model with the following requirements:

- A bean component must be a public class.
- A bean component must have a public default constructor (one that takes no arguments), although it can have other constructors, if needed. For example, a bean named `MyBean` must either have a constructor with the signature

  ```
  public MyBean();
  ```

  or have no constructor if its superclass has a default constructor.
- A bean component must implement the `Serializable` interface to ensure a persistent state. JavaBeans can be used in a wide variety of tools, such as Lotus, Delphi, MS Visual Basic, and MS Word. Bean persistence may be required when JavaBeans are used in other tools. Some tools need to save the beans and restore them later. Bean persistence ensures that the tools can reconstruct the properties and consistent behaviors of the bean to the state in which it was saved. Persistence and serialization will be further discussed in Chapter 9, "Bean Persistence and Versioning."
- A bean component usually has properties with public accessor methods that enable them to be seen and updated visually by a builder tool. To enable the properties to be manipulated, the accessor methods must conform to the naming patterns or be specified explicitly, using the `BeanInfo` interface. According to the accessor method naming pattern, the method must be named

`get<PropertyName>()` for getting the property value and `set<PropertyName>()` for setting the property value. The naming patterns of properties and their accessor methods will be discussed in detail in the section "Bean Properties." The `BeanInfo` interface will be introduced in Chapter 11, "Bean Introspection and Customization."

- A bean component may have events with public registration methods that enable it to add and remove listeners. If the bean plays a role as the source of events, it must provide registration methods. This will be discussed in depth in Chapter 3, "Bean Events."

The first three requirements must be observed by all beans, and therefore are referred to as *minimum JavaBeans component requirements*. The last two requirements are dependent on implementations. It is possible to write a bean without accessor methods and event registration methods.

A JavaBeans component is a special kind of Java class. The relationship of a JavaBean component and a Java class is illustrated in Figure 2.1.

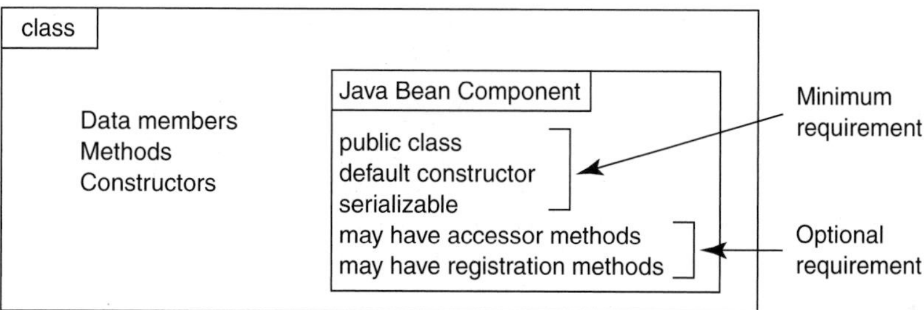

Figure 2.1 *A JavaBeans component is a serializable public class with a default constructor.*

Example 2.1 Writing a Simple JavaBeans Component

In this example, you will learn how to write a simple Java bean component named `MessagePanel` that displays a message on the panel. The UML diagram of this class is shown in Figure 2.2. The UML Graphical Notations are summarized in the book's companion Web site.

To see the development in action, follow these steps:

1. Create a new project named messagepaneldemo.jpx.
2. Choose File, New Class to bring up the Class wizard, as shown in Figure 2.3.
3. Type MessagePanel as Class name and type javax.swing.JPanel in the Base class field. Choose Public and "Generate default constructor" in the Options section.
4. Click OK to generate a template for MessagePanel.java, as shown in Figure 2.4.
5. Complete the code for `MessagePanel`, as shown in Listing 2.1.

continued

Example 2.1 continued

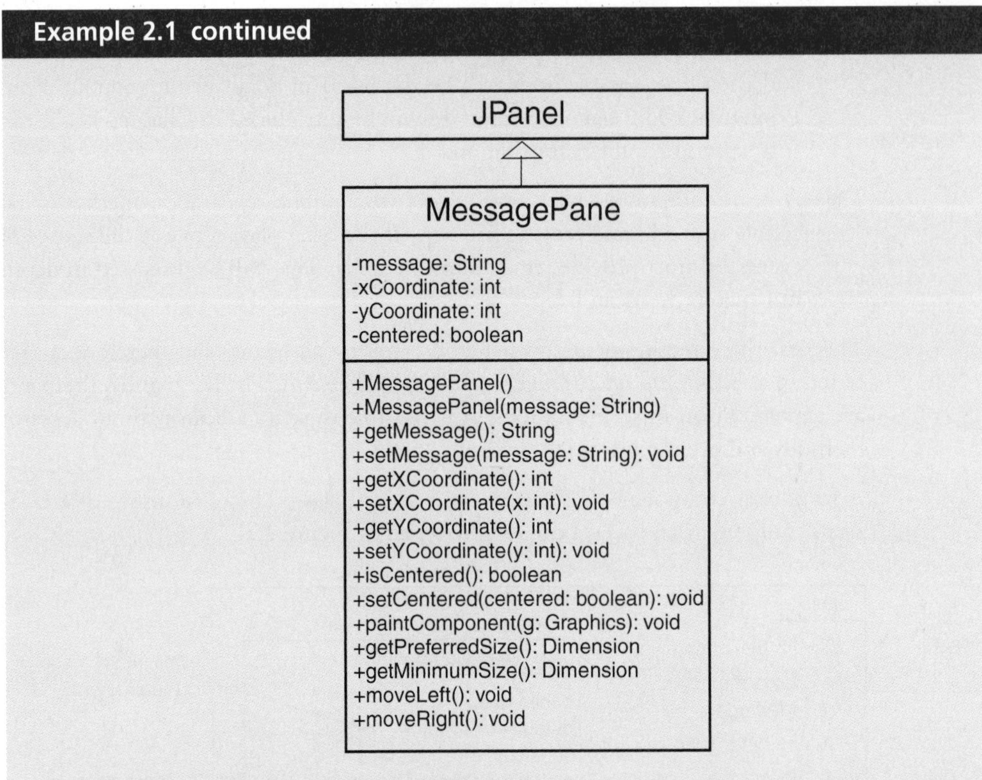

Figure 2.2 *The* `MessagePanel` *class extends* `JPanel` *to display a message.*

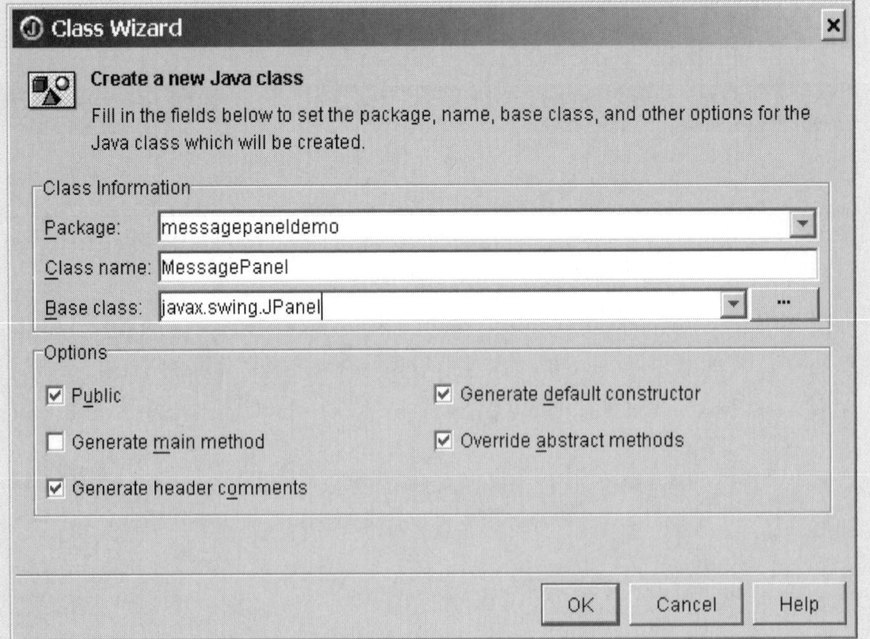

Figure 2.3 *You can create a new Java class using the Class wizard.*

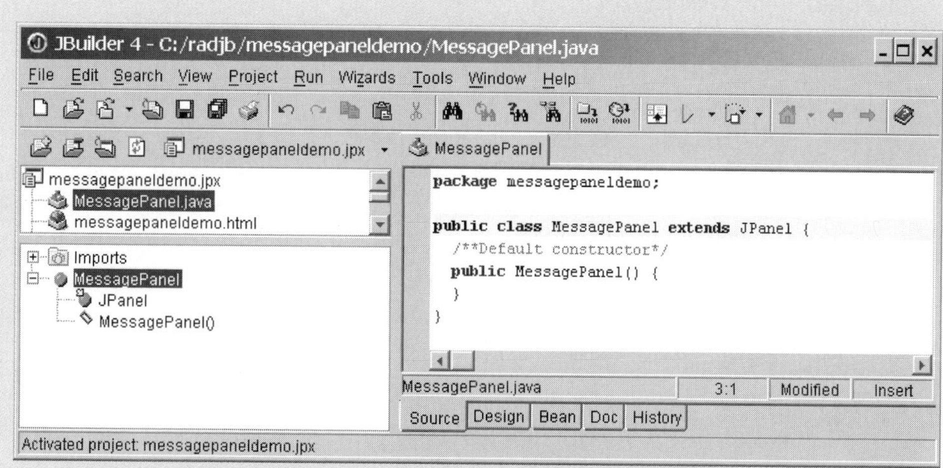

Figure 2.4 *The Class wizard generates a Java class template.*

```
package messagepaneldemo;

import java.awt.Font;
import java.awt.FontMetrics;
import java.awt.Dimension;
import java.awt.Graphics;
import javax.swing.JPanel;

public class MessagePanel extends JPanel {
  /** The message to be displayed */
  private String message = "Welcome to Java";

  /** The x coordinate where the message is displayed */
  private int xCoordinate = 20;

  /** The y coordinate where the message is displayed */
  private int yCoordinate = 20;

  /** Indicate whether the message is displayed in the center */
  private boolean centered;

  /** Default constructor */
  public MessagePanel() {
  }

  /** Constructor with a message parameter */
  public MessagePanel(String message) {
    this.message = message;
  }

  /** Return message */
  public String getMessage() {
    return message;
  }

  /** Set a new message */
  public void setMessage(String message) {
```

Listing 2.1 *MessagePanel.java*

continued

Example 2.1 continued

```
      this.message = message;
      repaint();
    }

    /** Return xCoordinator */
    public int getXCoordinate() {
      return xCoordinate;
    }

    /** Set a new xCoordinator */
    public void setXCoordinate(int x) {
      this.xCoordinate = x;
    }

    /** Return yCoordinator */
    public int getYCoordinate() {
      return yCoordinate;
    }

    /** Set a new yCoordinator */
    public void setYCoordinate(int y) {
      this.yCoordinate = y;
    }

    /** Return centered */
    public boolean isCentered() {
      return centered;
    }

    /** Set a new centered */
    public void setCentered(boolean centered) {
      this.centered = centered;
    }

    /** Paint the message */
    public void paintComponent(Graphics g) {
      super.paintComponent(g);

      if (centered) {
        // Get font metrics for the current font
        FontMetrics fm = g.getFontMetrics();

        // Find the center location to display
        int w = fm.stringWidth(message);  // Get the string width
        // Get the string height, from top to the baseline
        int h = fm.getAscent();
        xCoordinate = getWidth()/2-w/2;
        yCoordinate = getHeight()/2+h/2;
      }

      g.drawString(message, xCoordinate, yCoordinate);
    }

    /** Override get method for preferredSize */
    public Dimension getPreferredSize() {
      return new Dimension(200, 100);
    }

    /** Override get method for minimumSize */
    public Dimension getMinimumSize() {
```

Listing 2.1 *Continued*

```
97          return new Dimension(200, 100);
98        }
99
100       /** Move the message in the panel to the left */
101       public void moveLeft() {
102         if (getXCoordinate() > 10) {
103           // Shift the message to the left
104           setXCoordinate(getXCoordinate()-10);
105           repaint();
106         }
107       }
108
109       /** Move the message in the panel to the right */
110       public void moveRight() {
111         if (getXCoordinate() < getSize().width - 20) {
112           // Shift the message to the right
113           setXCoordinate(getXCoordinate()+10);
114           repaint();
115         }
116       }
117     }
```

Listing 2.1 *Continued*

Example Review

Since `javax.awt.Component` implements `Serializable`, and `MessagePanel` is a subclass of `JPanel`, which is a subclass of `Component`, `MessagePanel` is serializable.

The `MessagePanel` class is a public class with a default constructor, `MessagePanel()`. Since `MessagePanel` is a serializable public class with a default constructor, it is a JavaBeans component.

The `MessagePanel` class has the properties `message`, `xCoordinate`, `yCoordinate`, and `centered`. The `getMessage()`, `getXCoordinate()`, `getYCoordinate()`, and `isCentered()` methods read the `message`, `xCoordinate`, `yCoordinate`, and `centered` properties, respectively; and the `setMessage`, `setXCoordinate`, `setYCoordinate`, and `setCentered` methods update these properties. The message is painted on the panel starting at the position specified by coordinates `xCoordinate` and `yCoordinate`.

The `getPreferredSize()` (Lines 90–93) and `getMinimumSize()` (Lines 95–98) methods are overridden to specify the `preferredSize` and `minimumSize` properties for instances of `MessagePanel`. The `MessagePanel` class also contains two methods, `moveLeft()` (Lines 100–107) and `moveRight()` (Lines 109–116), for moving the message to the left and to the right on the panel.

CAUTION

The *MessagePanel* class uses the properties *xCoordinate* and *yCoordinate* to specify the position of the message displayed on the panel. Do not use property names *x*, and *y*, because they are already defined in the *Component* class to specify the position of the component in the parent's coordinate system.

continued

Example 2.1 continued

NOTE

You wrote the code for declaring the properties and their accessor methods in this example. In Chapter 4, "Developing and Using Components," you will learn to use JBuilder's BeansExpress to automatically generate the code.

JavaBeans and Java Builder Tools

Since a JavaBeans component is a Java class, it can be used wherever a class is applicable. You can create a JavaBeans component, access its properties, and invoke its methods in a scripting environment, just as you use regular classes. Nevertheless, JavaBeans components are specially designed for use in a builder tool that enables the bean user to visually manipulate the beans during design time. The builder tool may be a Java IDE like JBuilder or Visual Café, a non-Java IDE like Microsoft Visual Basic or Borland Delphi, a Web page builder like Microsoft FrontPage, or even a word processor like Microsoft Word.

A builder tool can discover the contents (properties, methods, and events) and expose them to the bean user for visual manipulation during design time. The contents are presented on a user interface, referred to as a *component inspector*, or simply *inspector*, in JBuilder, on which the user can update property values and register events of the bean. The JavaBeans architecture provides a core API to support builder tools that find out what is inside the beans. The process of discovering and analyzing a bean, referred to as *bean introspection*, will be covered in Chapter 11, "Bean Introspection and Customization."

A builder tool usually has an internal component, referred to as a *reflector,* which is responsible for communication between the bean and the component inspector during design time. The reflector analyzes the bean and presents its properties and events on the component inspector. When the bean user modifies the properties, the reflector applies the changes to the bean by invoking the set method of the properties. The relationship of component inspector, reflector, and bean is illustrated in Figure 2.5.

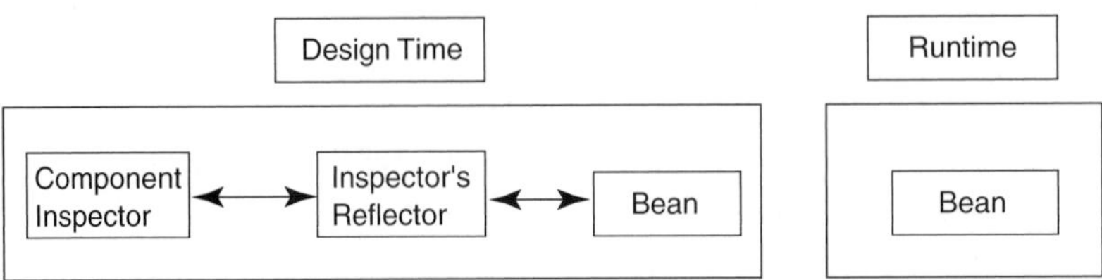

Figure 2.5 *During design time, the user interacts with the inspector, and the reflector controls the execution of the bean. During runtime, the bean runs just like a regular object.*

NOTE

The component inspector and the reflector are used during design time and play no role at runtime.

If the bean follows the naming patterns for properties and events, the reflector will automatically recognize and present it on the component inspector. If not, you have to provide a bean information class that implements the `BeanInfo` interface to describe the properties and events of the bean to the reflector in order for the inspector to reveal the properties and events to the user. How to write such a description class will be introduced in Chapter 11, "Bean Introspection and Customization."

Using JavaBeans in JBuilder

One of the major applications of JavaBeans is for rapid application development, or RAD, a powerful feature used in software development tools for visual programming. RAD allows you to select a component and drop it to a desired location. The click-and-drop capability enables you to write programs with little or no coding, thereby greatly improving software reusability and productivity.

RAD in JBuilder is completely based on JavaBeans, and each RAD component in JBuilder is a bean accessible from the component palette in the UI designer. In this section, you will learn how to add a bean to the component palette and utilize it in the applications, using the example of the `MessagePanel` bean presented in Example 2.1.

Adding a Bean to the Component Palette

All the classes in AWT and Swing are already beans. Some of them, such as `JButton`, `JCheckBox`, `JComboBox`, `JLabel`, `JList`, `JRadioButton`, `JTextArea`, `JTextField`, `JMenuBar`, `JPopupMenu`, `JScrollbar`, `JPanel`, and `JScrollPanel`, are already added into the Swing page and Swing Containers group in the component palette. This book uses Swing components to create graphics user interfaces. The necessary basic knowledge of Swing components is covered in my *Introduction to Java Programming with JBuilder 4*. Advanced features of Swing components will be covered in Part II, "Rapid Application Development with Swing Components."

Suppose you want to use the `MessagePanel` bean in the JBuilder visual environment. First you must add it to the component palette following the steps below.

1. Choose Tools, Configure Palette or right-click anywhere in the component palette and choose Properties. The Palette Properties dialog box appears, as shown in Figure 2.6.

2. Select the Pages tab and choose the page on the component palette on which you want the component to appear. Optionally, you may create a new page by clicking the Add button and entering the page name in the Add Page dialog box.

3. Suppose you want to add the `MessagePanel` bean to the `Other` group. Select `Other` in the pages column and click the Add components tab to display the dialog box for adding components, as shown in Figure 2.7.

4. Click the Install button to display the Browse for Class dialog box, as shown in Figure 2.8. Locate `MessagePanel` in the messagepaneldemo package. Click OK in the Browse for Class dialog box to display a dialog box, as shown in

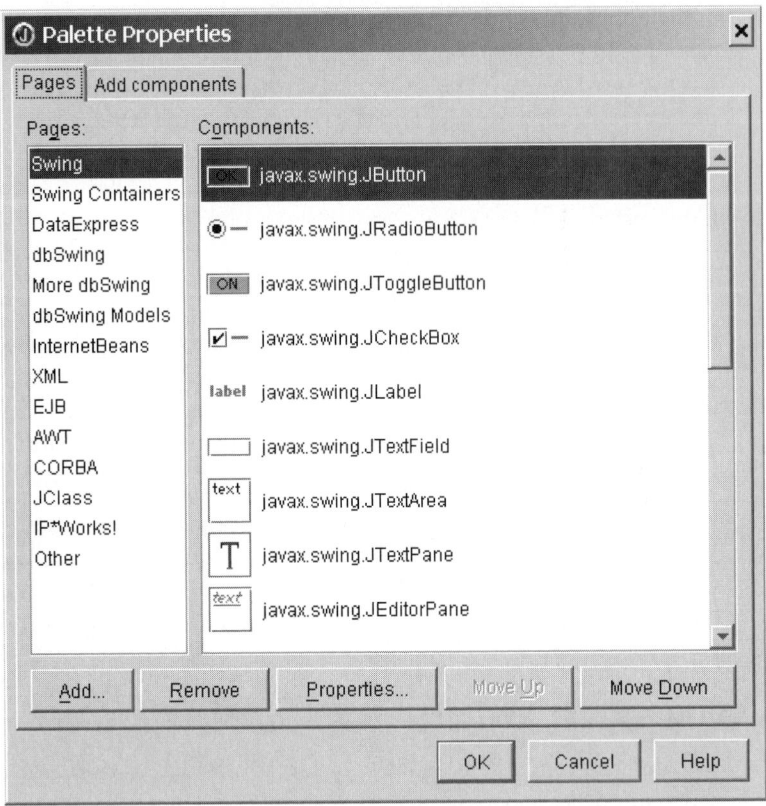

Figure 2.6 *The Palette Properties dialog box lets you add beans to the component palette.*

Figure 2.9. Click OK in this dialog box to confirm it. Click OK in the Palette Properties dialog box in Figure 2.7 to close this dialog box.

JBUILDER 5 NOTE

To add components from the current project in JBuilder 5, you have to create a library for the current project, then select this library from the Palette Properties dialog box, as shown in Figure 2.10. This dialog box also enables you to filter the JavaBeans in the library. To create a library, click Select Library to display the Select a Different Library dialog box, as shown in Figure 2.11. Click New in the Select a Different Library dialog box to display the New Library wizard, as shown in Figure 2.12. Enter the new library name (i.e. radjb) in the Name field and add the library path in the Library paths section. Click OK to add the library. The library appears under the User Home node in the Select a Different Library dialog box. Select radjb in the Select a Different Library dialog box and click OK to return to the Palette Properties dialog box in Figure 2.10. Click the Add from Selected Library button in the Palette Properties dialog box to display the Browse for Class dialog box, as shown in Figure 2.8. Now you can add a JavaBeans component from this library just as in JBuilder 4.

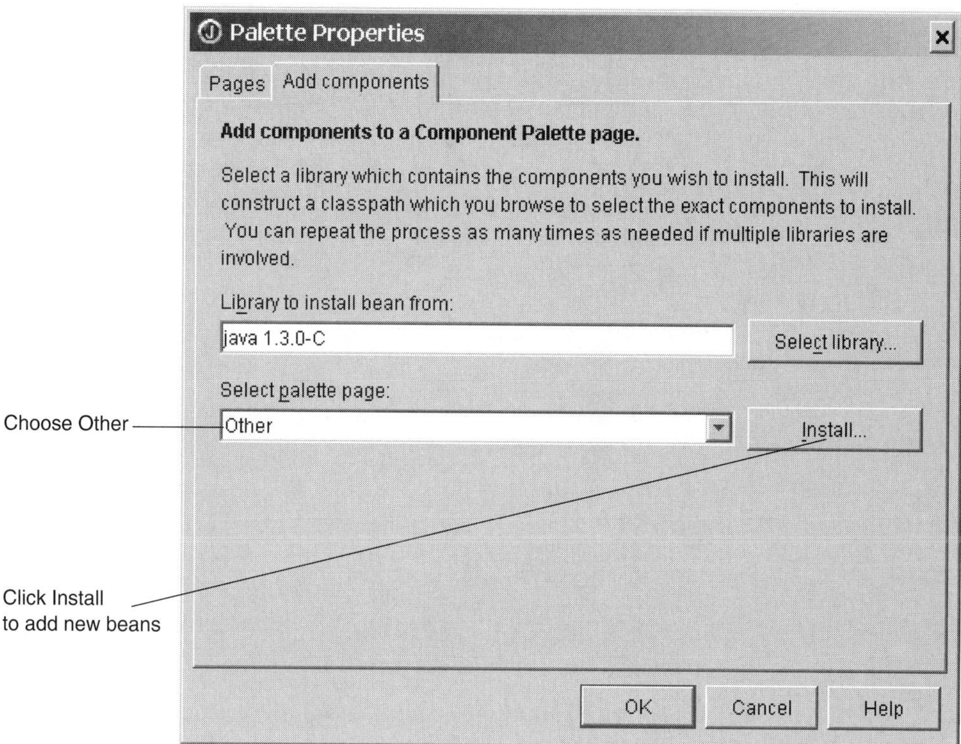

Figure 2.7 *You can install components to a selected page in the component palette.*

Using Beans in JBuilder

You are now ready to test the `MessagePanel` bean you just added to the component palette. Open project MessagePanel.jpx that was created in Example 2.1 and create a new applet named `TestMessagePanel` using the Applet wizard. In Step 1 of 3 of the Applet wizard, check "Can run standalone" so to generate the applet that can also run as application, and click Finish. TestMessagePanel.java is created and added in the messagepaneldemo project, as shown in Figure 2.13.

You can now add the `MessagePanel` bean to `TestMessagePanel`. Highlight TestMessagePanel.java in the project pane and choose the Design tab in the content pane to switch to the UI designer, as shown in Figure 2.14.

`TestMessagePanel` itself is a bean component. You can visually inspect and update its properties through the component inspector.

To add a `MessagePanel` bean, first choose `TestMessagePanel` in the component tree, then click the `MessagePanel` component from the Other tab in the component palette and drop it to the center of the applet, as shown in Figure 2.15.

JBuilder generates a bean named `messagePanel1`. You can change the bean's properties, including its name, from the component inspector. The inspector window is embedded inside the content pane shown in Figure 2.15. Whenever you start the UI designer, the inspector window is automatically displayed. When you select a component from the UI designer or from the component tree, the inspector window displays its properties and events.

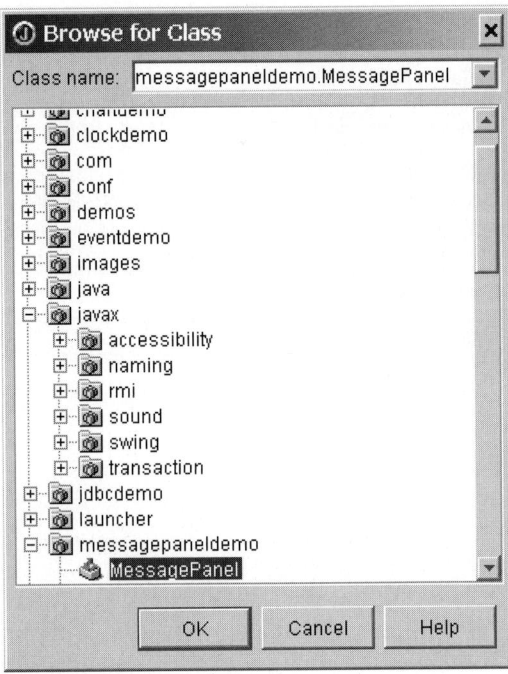

Figure 2.8 *Select the component from the Browse for Class dialog box to install in the component palette.*

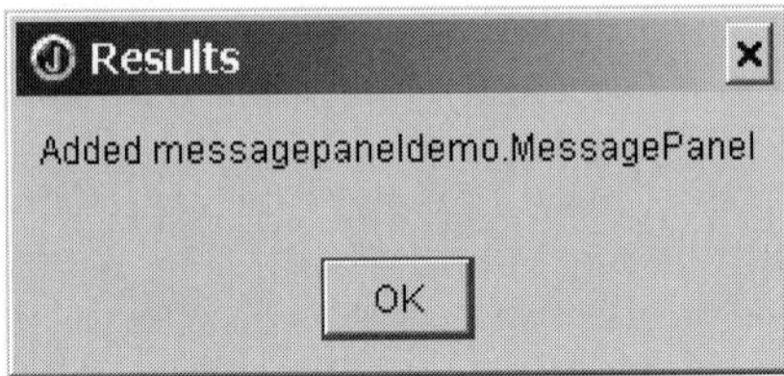

Figure 2.9 *Confirm the component to be installed.*

NOTE

JBuilder generates the source code to carry out all the changes made in the UI designer. For example, if you drop a bean into the UI designer, JBuilder generates the code to declare and create an instance of the bean; if you change a property value, JBuilder generates the code that invokes the property's set method to update the value.

NOTE

The name and constraints properties are highlighted in the component inspector. These two properties do not belong to a bean. JBuilder uses them to support the UI designer. The name property is for identifying the bean, and the constraints property is for locating the bean in its parent container.

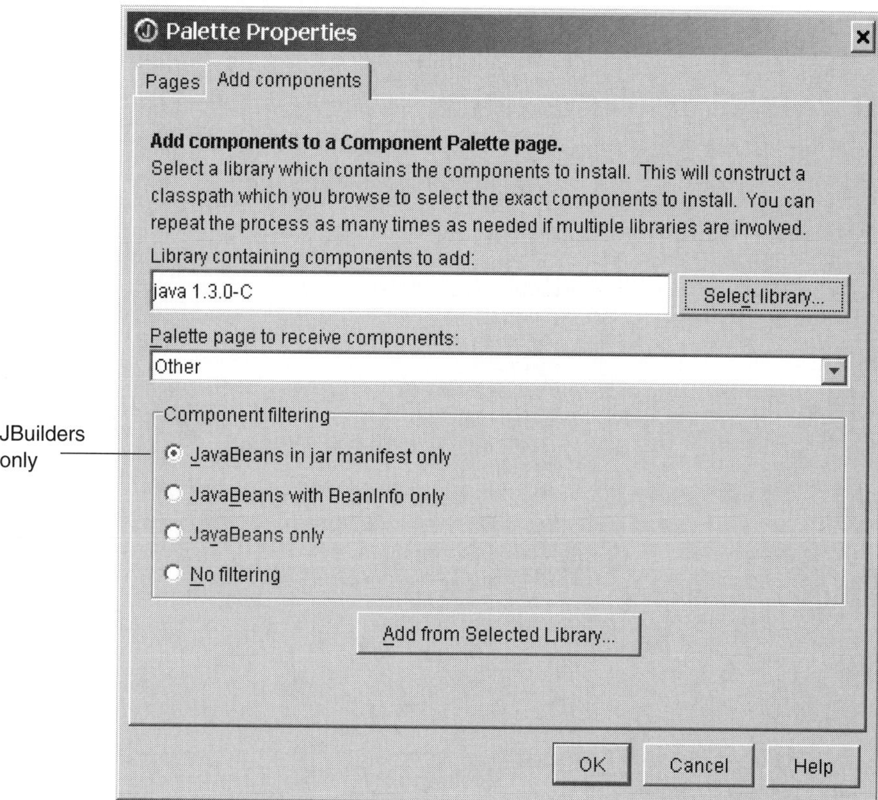

Figure 2.10 *The JBuilder 5 Palette Properties dialog box allows you to filter JavaBeans with various options.*

The inspector contains a property sheet and an event sheet that can be selected by choosing the Properties tab or the Events tab on the bottom of the component inspector.

The `name` property is for naming the bean; you may change it to a name of your choice. The properties `message`, `xCoordinate`, `yCoordinate`, and `centered` are defined in `MessagePanel`, and all the other properties are defined in the superclasses of `MessagePanel`. Type "Welcome to JavaBeans" in the `message` property and press the Enter key to let the change take effect. You will see "Welcome to JavaBeans" displayed on the panel. You don't need to run the program to see the changes. The changes can be verified instantaneously, since the bean is live during design time.

NOTE

If you change the *`centered`* property to True, the message is supposed to appear centered in the applet, but this does not happen, because the panel is not repainted by this property change. To repaint the panel, add the *`repaint()`* method in the *`setCentered`* method body or double-click *`messagePanel1`* to redisplay *`messagePanel1`*, which would cause the panel to be repainted.

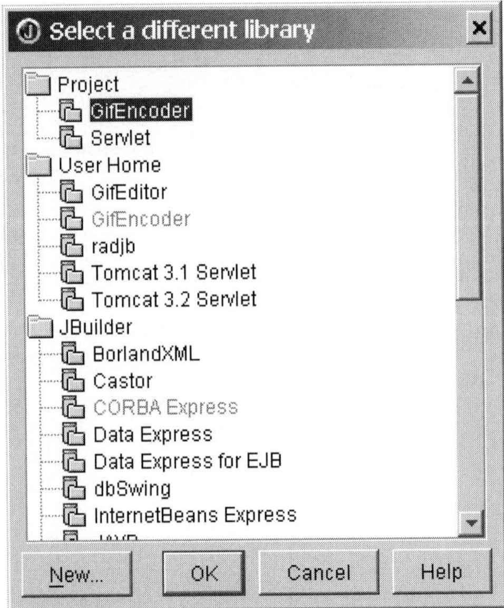

Figure 2.11 *You can select or create a new library from the Select a Different Library dialog box.*

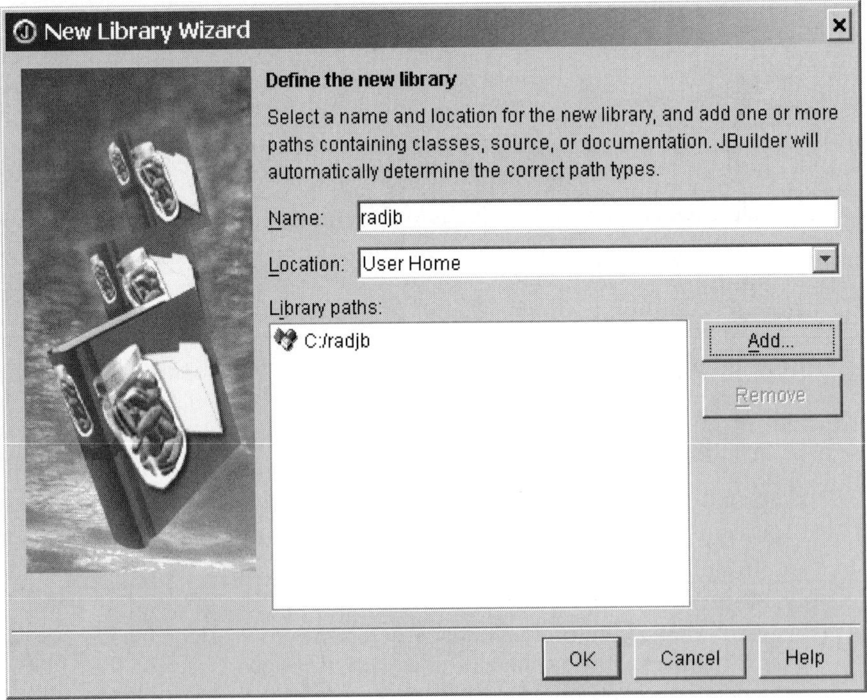

Figure 2.12 *You can define a new library in the New Library wizard.*

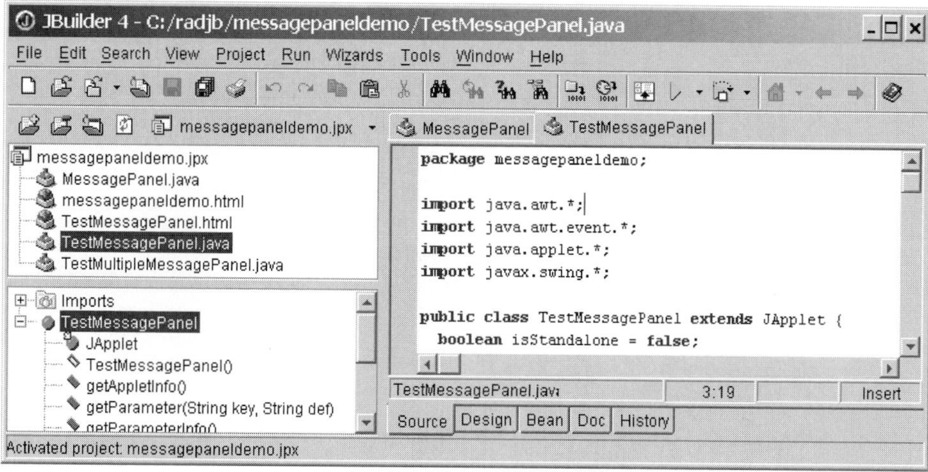

Figure 2.13 *TestMessagePanel.java is created to test the* `MessagePanel` *bean.*

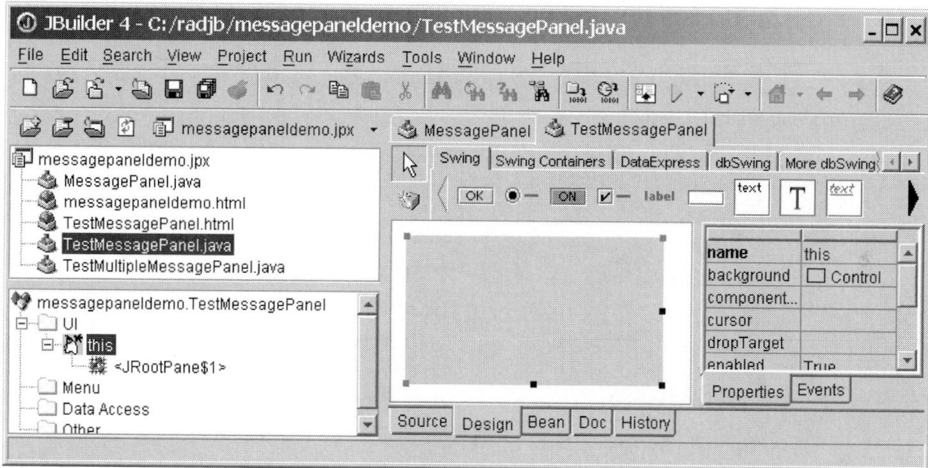

Figure 2.14 `TestMessagePanel` *is visually displayed in the content pane during design.*

Note

When a nondefault value is assigned to the property from the inspector, the set method is created in the source code to synchronize the change. When a default value is assigned to the property, the set method is deleted from the source code, so that the default value can take effect.

You have learned how to create a simple bean component, install it in the component palette, and manipulate it in the UI designer. Below, you will see an example that uses the `MessagePanel` in a project with other beans.

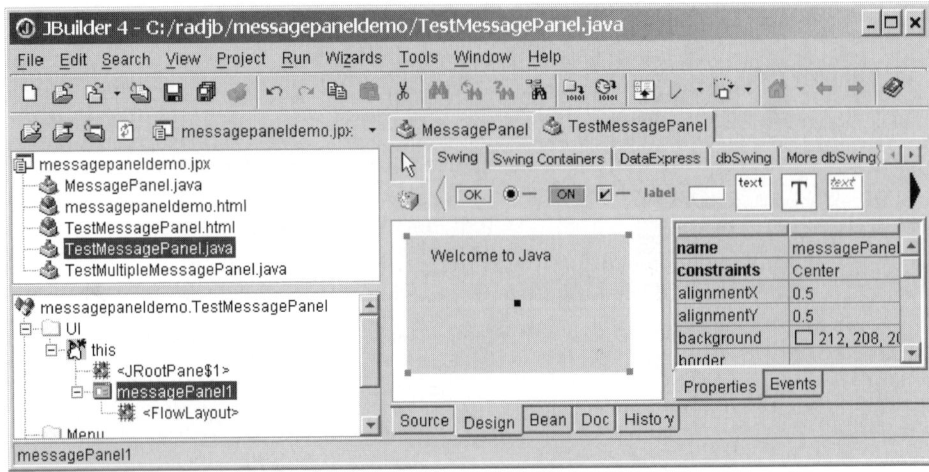

Figure 2.15 *A MessagePanel bean is placed inside TestMessagePanel.*

Example 2.2 Moving a Message on a Panel

This example involves a `MessagePanel` bean and two `JButton` beans. The `MessagePanel` bean displays a message and two `JButton` beans for moving the message to the left and right, respectively. A sample run of the program is shown in Figure 2.16.

Figure 2.16 *You can use the buttons to move the message to the left and the right.*

Here are the steps to complete the example.

1. Reopen project messagepaneldemo.jpx created in Example 2.1 and use the Applet wizard to create a new Java applet named `MoveMessage`.

2. With MoveMessage.java selected in the project pane, choose the Design tab in the content pane to start the UI designer. Drop a `MessagePanel` from the component palette to the center of the applet to create an instance of `MessagePanel`, named `messagePanel1`. Verify `messagePanel1`'s `constraints` property and set it to `Center` if it is not Center.

3. Drop `JPanel` from the Swing Containers page in the component palette to the south of the applet to create an instance of `JPanel`, named `jPanel1`.

Verify `jPanel1`'s constraint property and set it to South if it is not South. `jPanel1` may appear very small now, but its size will change after buttons are added to the panel.

4. Drop a `JButton` from the Swing page of the component palette to `jPanel1` twice to create `jButton1` and `jButton2`. In the component inspector, change their names to `jbtLeft` and `jbtRight`, and change their `text` properties to <= and =>, respectively. If the text is not displayed, double-click `jPanel1`. Usually, if the components are not displayed correctly, you can double-click the container of the components in the component tree to redisplay them.

5. Double-click the <= button in the UI designer to generate the handler for the `jbtLeft` button. Implement the handler `jbtLeft_actionPerformed (ActionEvent e)` to move the message to the left, as shown in Listing 2.2 (Line 47).

6. Double-click the => button in the UI designer to generate the handler for the `jbtRight` button. Implement the handler `jbtRight_actionPerformed (ActionEvent e)` to move the message to the right, as shown in Listing 2.2 (Line 51).

```
1  package messagepaneldemo;
2
3  import java.awt.*;
4  import java.awt.event.*;
5  import java.applet.*;
6  import javax.swing.*;
7
8  public class MoveMessage extends JApplet {
9    boolean isStandalone = false;
10   MessagePanel messagePanel1 = new MessagePanel();
11   JPanel jPanel1 = new JPanel();
12   JButton jbtLeft = new JButton();
13   JButton jbtRight = new JButton();
14
15   /** Initialize the applet */
16   public void init() {
17     try {
18       jbInit();
19     }
20     catch(Exception e) {
21       e.printStackTrace();
22     }
23   }
24
25   /** Component initialization */
26   private void jbInit() throws Exception {
27     this.setSize(new Dimension(400,300));
28     jbtLeft.setText("<=");
29     jbtLeft.addActionListener(new java.awt.event.ActionListener() {
30       public void actionPerformed(ActionEvent e) {
31         jbtLeft_actionPerformed(e);
32       }
33     });
34     jbtRight.setText("=>");
35     jbtRight.addActionListener(new java.awt.event.ActionListener() {
36       public void actionPerformed(ActionEvent e) {
```

Listing 2.2 *MoveMessage.java*

continued

Example 2.2 continued

```
          jbtRight_actionPerformed(e);
        }
      });
      this.getContentPane().add(messagePanel1, BorderLayout.CENTER);
      this.getContentPane().add(jPanel1, BorderLayout.SOUTH);
      jPanel1.add(jbtLeft, null);
      jPanel1.add(jbtRight, null);
    }

    void jbtLeft_actionPerformed(ActionEvent e) {
      messagePanel1.moveLeft();
    }

    void jbtRight_actionPerformed(ActionEvent e) {
      messagePanel1.moveRight();
    }
  }
```

Listing 2.2 *Continued*

Example Review

When the <= button is clicked, the `messagePanel1`'s `moveLeft()` method is invoked to move the message to the left if there is room for the move. When the => button is clicked, the `messagePanel1`'s `moveRight()` method is invoked to move the message to the right if there is room for the move.

At design time, you can set properties for each bean and generate handlers for bean events. You cannot test how beans interact with one another, however. For example, you cannot see the effect of clicking a button at design time. You will only see it at runtime.

Bean Properties

Properties are discrete, named attributes of a Java bean that can affect its appearance or behavior. They are often data fields of a bean. For example, the `MessagePanel` component has a property named `message` that represents the message to be displayed on the panel. Private data fields are often used to hide specific implementations from the user and prevent the user from accidentally corrupting the properties. Accessor methods are provided instead to let the user read and write the properties. To enable properties to be accessed from a builder tool, either the signatures of the accessor methods must conform to the accessor method naming pattern or the properties and their accessor methods have to be explicitly specified using a custom `BeanInfo` class.

Property-Naming Patterns

The bean property-naming pattern is a mechanism of the JavaBean component model that simplifies the bean developer's task of presenting properties for inspection in a builder tool. A property can be a primitive data type or an object type.

The property type dictates the signature of the accessor methods and determines how the user edits the property in the component inspector.

In general, the get method is named `get<PropertyName>()`, which takes no parameters and returns an object of the type identical to the property type. For example,

```
public String getMessage() { }

public int getXCoordinate() { }

public int getYCoordinate() { }
```

For a property of `boolean` type, the get method should be named `is<PropertyName>()`, which returns a `boolean` value. For example,

```
public boolean isCentered() { }
```

The set method should be named `set<PropertyName>()`, which takes a single parameter identical to the property type and returns `void`. For example,

```
public void setMessage(String s) { }

public void setXCoordinate(int x) { }

public void setYCoordinate(int y) { }

public void setCentered(boolean centered) { }
```

NOTE
A property may be read-only with a get method but no set method, or write-only with a set method but no get method. However, JBuilder cannot expose the property in the component inspector unless its get and set methods are both provided in the component.

Properties and Data Fields

Properties describe the state of the bean. Naturally, data fields are used to store properties. However, a bean property is not necessarily a data field. For example, you may create a new property named `messageLength` that represents the number of the characters in `message`. The get method for the property may be defined as follows.

```
public int getMessageLength() {
  return message.length();
}
```

To enable the property to be seen in the JBuilder's component inspector window, both the get and set methods must be provided. Since the `messageLength` property has no set method, you would not see it in the component inspector. To be able to see it, you must provide a set method with a dummy parameter that does nothing, as shown below:

```
public void setMessageLength(int dummy) { }
```

NOTE
You may have multiple get and set methods, but there must be one get or set method with a signature conforming to the accessor method patterns. Any other methods are for programmatic use, and are not available to the visual designer.

Property Types

Properties can have any legitimate data type, including primitive data types, arrays, and objects. Properties can be classified into four types: *simple*, *indexed*, *bound*, and *constraint*.

A *simple property* represents a single value of primitive data types or object types. A pair of get and set methods defines the simple property. The get method is constructed as get<Property> or is<Property> for boolean values. The set method is constructed as set<Property>.

An *indexed property*, or array property, represents an array of elements. The property supports getting and setting the entire array at once. Some builder tools may also support getting and setting individual elements. JBuilder provides a built-in editor for arrays of strings. The signatures of the accessor methods are:

```
public PropertyType[] get<Property>() { }

public void set<Property>(PropertyType[] a) { }
```

JavaBeans provides support for bound and constraint properties. A *bound property* of a component is one for which a notification service is provided when the property changes. The components interested in the property receive the notification and perform operations in response to the property change. These components are related through the bound property. Sometimes, when a property change occurs, the listener component for the bound property may wish to validate the change and reject it if it is inappropriate. Such a property is referred to as *constraint property*. These properties will be introduced in Chapter 10, "Bound and Constraint Properties."

Property Editors

The inspector uses property editors to update property values. JBuilder provides standard editors for the properties of primitive data types, array of strings, and several commonly used object types, such as Color and Font. The standard editors can be classified into *simple editor*, *array editor*, *choice-menu editor*, and *object editor* according to their appearance in the inspector.

- A simple editor edits a single value, such as a number, a character, or a string. The user edits the value of the property directly in the component inspector. For example, the property editors for message, xCoordinate, and yCoordinate in the MessagePanel component are examples of simple editors.
- An array editor edits an array of elements. The elements may be of any data type. The inspector has no built-in support for editing array properties except for arrays of strings. The component developer may provide a property editor for manipulating the array property.

- A choice-menu editor edits the value as numbers, characters, or strings, with all possible values enumerated in a choice menu. A `boolean` property is of the enumerated type with the values True and False, which is built into JBuilder. The component developer has to provide a property editor for any other choice-menu editor.
- An object editor edits an instance of the object. Properties of the object type must have their own property editors, except for several standard Java classes, such as `Color` and `Font`, whose editors are predefined in JBuilder.

The editors of array properties and object properties appear in the inspector with an ellipsis (. . .) at the right of the value when the property is selected. The user clicks the ellipsis to bring up the property editor.

The following example demonstrates the use of JBuilder's built-in property editors to manipulate array properties, enumerated type properties, and object properties. In Chapter 11, "Bean Introspection and Customization," you will learn how to write your own property editors.

Example 2.3 Using Editors for Array, Enumerated, and Object Properties

This example creates a bean to display a single message or a composite message. The composite message is constructed from an array of strings. The bean uses a `boolean` property, `displayed`, to turn the display on or off and another `boolean` property, `showingSingleMessage`, to determine whether a single message or a composite message is shown on the panel when `displayed` is true. The new component is shown in Figure 2.17.

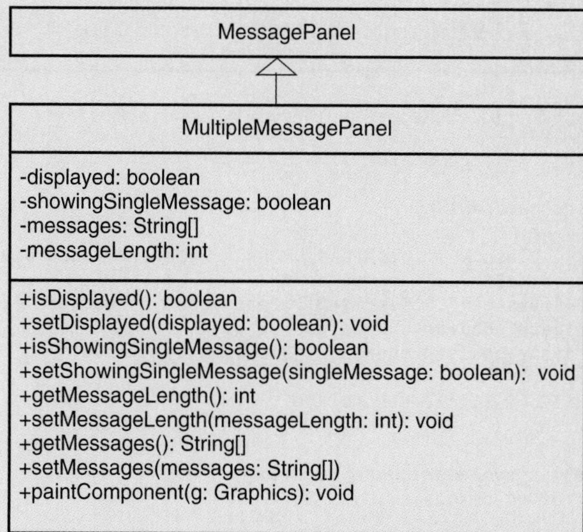

Figure 2.17 *The* `MultipleMessagePanel` *extends* `MessagePanel` *to display multiple messages.*

continued

Example 2.3 continued

Follow the steps below to complete the example.

1. Reopen the project messagepaneldemo.jpx and create a new class for the `MultipleMessagePanel` component using the Class wizard that extends `messagepaneldemo.MessagePanel`. Complete `MultipleMessagePanel` as shown in Listing 2.3. Compile it and install it in the component palette.
2. Create an applet named TestMultipleMessagePanel.java using the Applet wizard. With TestMultipleMessagePanel.java selected in the project pane, click the Design tab to display the UI designer.
3. Select `MultipleMessagePanel` from the component palette and drop it into TestMultipleMessagePanel to the applet to create `multipleMessagePanel1`. The AppBrowser for the project is shown in Figure 2.18.

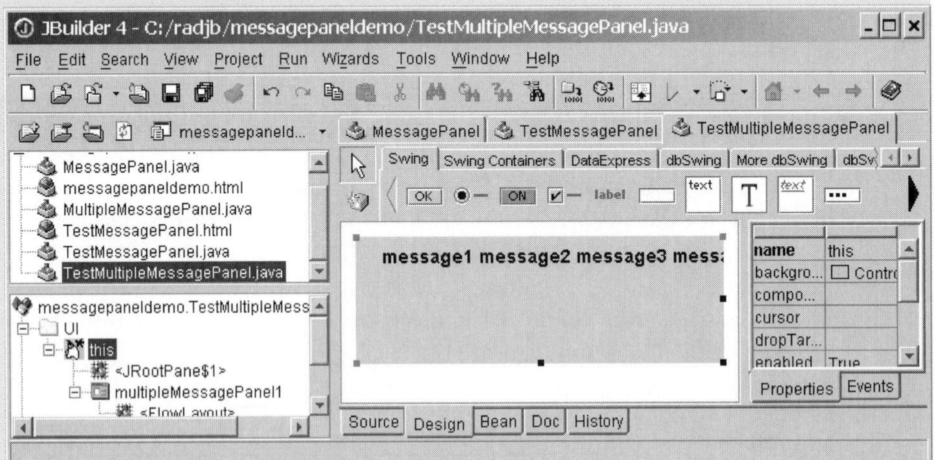

Figure 2.18 *A* `MultipleMessagePanel` *bean is placed into the applet.*

```
package messagepaneldemo;

import java.awt.*;

public class MultipleMessagePanel extends MessagePanel {
  private String[] messages =
    {"message1", "message2", "message3", "message4"};
  private boolean displayed = true;
  private boolean showingSingleMessage = false;

  public MultipleMessagePanel() {
  }

  public boolean isDisplayed() {
    return displayed;
  }

  public void setDisplayed(boolean displayed) {
    this.displayed = displayed;
  }

```

Listing 2.3 *MultipleMessagePanel.java*

```
  public int getMessageLength() {
    return getMessage().length();
  }

  public void setMessageLength(int dummy) {
  }

  public boolean isShowingSingleMessage() {
    return showingSingleMessage;
  }

  public void setShowingSingleMessage(boolean b) {
    this.showingSingleMessage = b;
  }

  public String[] getMessages() {
    return messages;
  }

  public void setMessages(String[] messages) {
    System.arraycopy(messages, 0, this.messages, 0, messages.length);
    repaint();
  }

  public void paintComponent(Graphics g) {
    // Clear the panel
    g.clearRect(0, 0, getSize().width, getSize().height);

    // Things to display
    String thingsToDisplay = new String();

    if (displayed) {
      if (showingSingleMessage)
        thingsToDisplay = getMessage();
      else {
        for (int i=0; i<messages.length; i++)
          thingsToDisplay += messages[i] + " ";
      }
    }

    if (isCentered()) {
      // Get font metrics for the font
      FontMetrics fm = g.getFontMetrics(getFont());

      // Find the center location to display
      int w = fm.stringWidth(thingsToDisplay); // Get the width
      int h = fm.getAscent(); // Get the string height
      setXCoordinate((getSize().width-w)/2);
      setYCoordinate((getSize().height+h)/2);
    }

    g.drawString(thingsToDisplay,
      getXCoordinate(), getYCoordinate());
  }
}
```

Listing 2.3 *Continued*

Example Review

The `MultipleMessagePanel` class extends the `MessagePanel` class created in Example 2.1.

continued

Example 2.3 continued

The `showingSingleMessage` is a `boolean` property that determines whether a single message or a composite message is displayed. By default, it is false, indicating that a composite message is displayed. If you change the property to True in the component inspector and double-click `multipleMessagePanel1`, you would see a single message, "Welcome to Java," displayed. The `boolean` property is an enumerated type with two values, True and False, for selection in a choice menu. Double-clicking `multipleMessagePanel1` in the component tree causes the `paintComponent` method to be executed. When you set the `showingSingleMessage` property, the `paintComponent` method is not invoked.

The `messageLength` property represents the number of characters in `message`. It is worth noting that it is not a data field in the `MultipleMessagePanel` component. The set method of the property does nothing, and its presence in the component is for the property to be read during design, since JBuilder requires both get and set methods to be present for the property to be shown in the inspector.

The `messages` property is an array property, consisting of four strings with initial values, "message1," "message2," "message3," and "message4." The strings in the array are separated by <NL>, the new-line symbol, as shown in the component inspector in Figure 2.19. Click the ellipsis to bring up the property editor shown in Figure 2.20. Change the strings to "Welcome," "to," Java," "!!!"; and click OK to finish editing. You will see "Welcome to Java!!!" displayed on the panel, if the `showingSingleMessage` property is false.

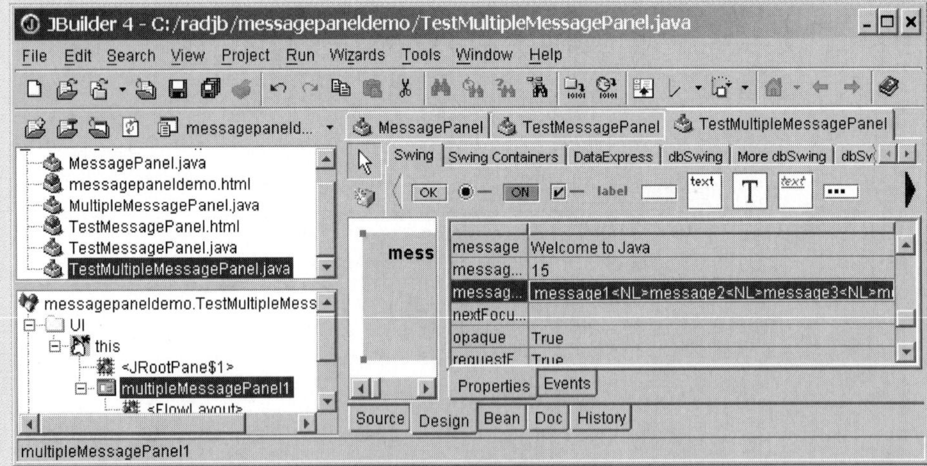

Figure 2.19 *You may edit an array of strings from the component inspector using a standard editor built into JBuilder.*

The `background`, `foreground`, and `font` are the object properties. They are defined in `java.awt.Component` and inherited by `MultipleMessagePanel`. JBuilder

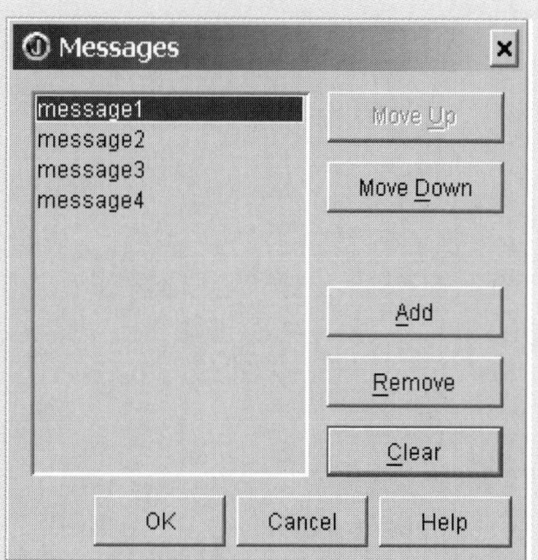

Figure 2.20 *JBuilder has a built-in property editor for manipulating an array of strings.*

provides built-in editors for the `Color` class and the `Font` class. For example, you can click the ellipsis on the `font` property to bring up the font property editor, as shown in Figure 2.21.

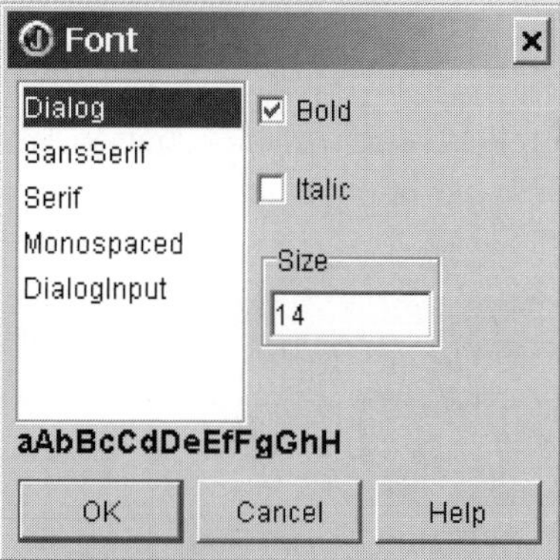

Figure 2.21 *The* `Font` *class property editor lets you choose desired type, style, and size for the font.*

This class can be improved to display the multiple messages on different lines. See Exercise 2.5.

Chapter Summary

In this chapter, you learned that a JavaBeans component is simply a Java class that is public and serializable and has a public default constructor. Beans are especially useful in builder tools that enable programmers to visually manipulate them through the component inspector during design time. You learned how to write simple beans, install beans in the component palette in JBuilder, and update bean properties during runtime.

Review Questions

2.1 What are the minimum requirements for a bean component? Is a bean component a Java class? Is a Java class a bean component?

2.2 How do you install a bean component into the component palette in JBuilder?

2.3 How do you display the component inspector?

2.4 How do you name a get method for a non-boolean property? How do you name a get method for a boolean property? How do you name a set method for a property?

2.5 List the types of properties.

2.6 Is a property always a data field of the class?

2.7 Some Java builder tools can work with read-only properties. Can JBuilder display read-only properties in the inspector?

2.8 If a superclass is not a bean component, can a subclass be a bean component?

2.9 Is a bean component always a GUI component?

Programming Exercises

2.1 Add a button labeled Up and a button labeled Down in Example 2.2 to move the message upward and downward, as shown in Figure 2.22.

Figure 2.22 *You can move the message up and down as well as left and right.*

2.2 Create a bean component named `Circle` that displays a circle in the center of the panel. The `Circle` component has a property named `radius` that determines the size of the circle, and it also contains a method for computing the area of the circle. Install the component in the component palette and use it to create an applet that enables the user to set the radius and displays the area of the circle. A sample run of the applet is shown in Figure 2.23.

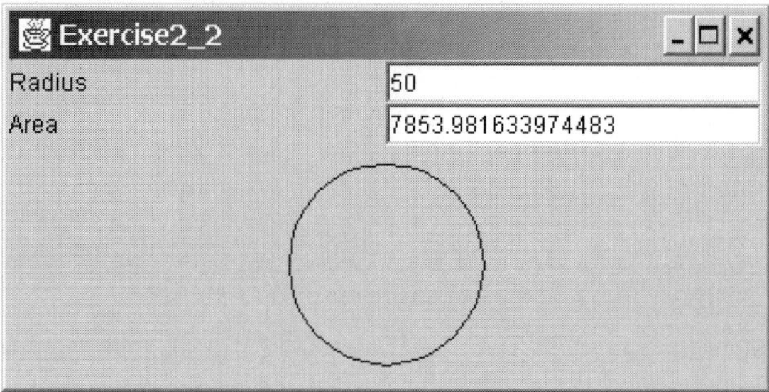

Figure 2.23 *You can set the radius of the circle and display its area.*

2.3 Create a bean component named `MessageControl`, which controls how a message is displayed. The message can blink or move from right to left circularly, or both at the same time. The properties of `MessageControl` are as follows:

- `message`: A string for the message to be displayed.
- `blinking`: A boolean value indicating whether the message should blink.
- `moving`: A boolean value indicating whether the message moves.

2.4 Create a bean component named `ImageControl` that displays an image for a specified image file. The properties of `ImageControl` are as follows:

- `filename`: The name of the file containing the image.
- `stretched`: A boolean value indicating whether the image is stretched to fill the entire view area.

Use the UI designer to create an applet with two objects of `ImageControl` placed in its content pane of the `GridLayout`, as shown in Figure 2.24.

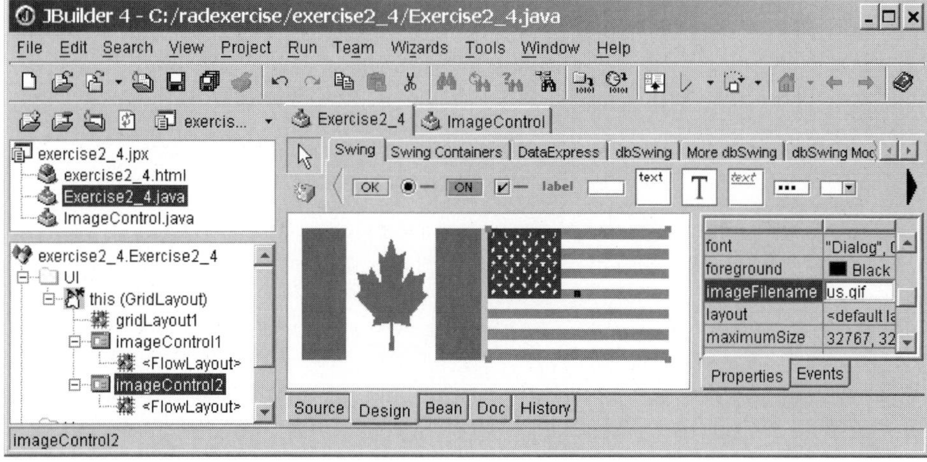

Figure 2.24 *The* `ImageControl` *component is used to display an image.*

2.5 Modify the `MultipleMessagePanel` class in Example 2.3 to display each message on a separate line. Add the property `vgap` to indicate the vertical gap between the lines. The messages are centered if the `centered` property is true, as shown in Figure 2.25.

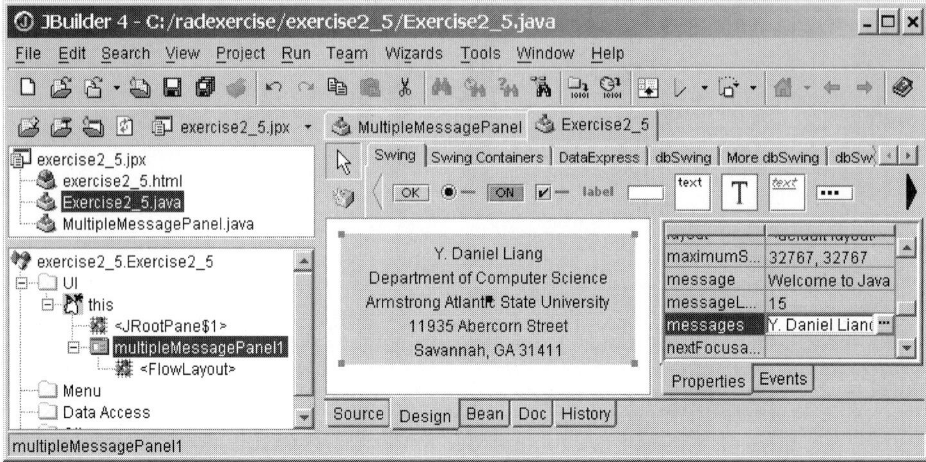

Figure 2.25 *Multiple messages are displayed on different lines.*

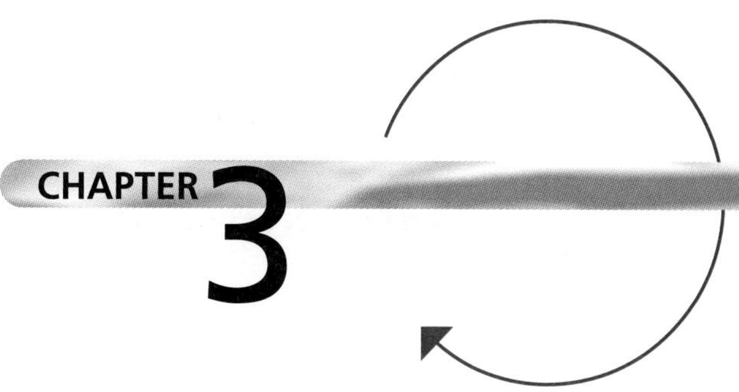

Bean Events

Objectives

- Review the Java event delegation model.
- Create a new event class and listener interface.
- Develop source components using new event sets or existing event sets.
- Make source components from scratch or from existing components.
- Implement listener components.
- Become familiar with adapters, inner classes, and anonymous classes.
- Learn how to hook up source components with listener components in JBuilder.

Introduction

A bean may communicate with other beans. The Java event delegation model provides the foundation for beans to send, receive, and handle events. When something happens to a bean, such as a mouse click on a `javax.swing.JButton` bean, an event object is created that encapsulates information pertaining to the event. The bean passes the event object to the interested beans for the event to be processed.

Events are typically generated by Java GUI components, such as `javax.swing.JButton`, but are not limited to GUI components. This chapter introduces the development of beans that can generate events and beans that listen for events. You will learn how to create custom events and link the beans via events in JBuilder.

Java Event Model

The Java event model consists of the following four types of classes. Their interrelationship is illustrated in Figure 3.1.

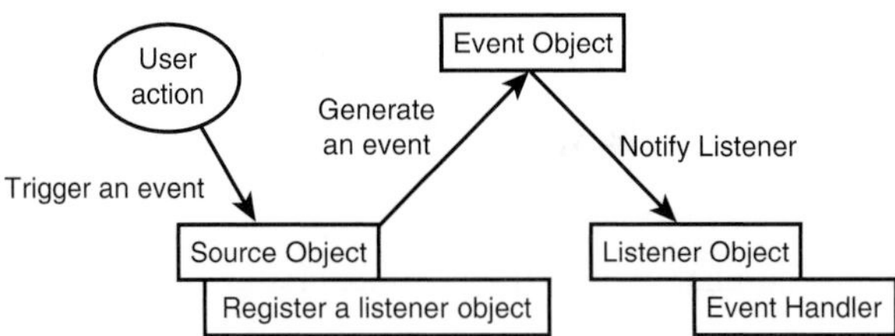

Figure 3.1 *An event is triggered by user or system actions on a source object, and the source object "fires" the event and invokes the handler of the listener object to process the event.*

- The event object
- The event source
- The event listener interface
- The event listener

An *event* is a signal to the program that something has happened. It can be generated by external user actions, such as mouse movements, mouse button clicks, and keystrokes, or by the operating system, such as a timer. An *event object* contains the information that describes the event. A *source object* is where the event originates. When an event occurs on the source object, an event object is created. An object interested in the event receives the event. Such an object is called a *listener*. Not all objects can receive events. To become a listener, the object must be registered as a listener by the source object. The source object maintains a list of listeners and notifies all the registered listeners by invoking the event-handling method implemented on the listener object. The handlers are defined in the class known as the *event listener interface*. Each class of an event object has a corresponding event listener interface.

> **NOTE**
> The Java event model is referred to as a *delegation-based model* because the source object delegates the event to the listeners for processing.

Event Objects

The Java event model is essential to Java graphics programming. Each GUI component is associated with one or more events, as shown in Figure 3.2.

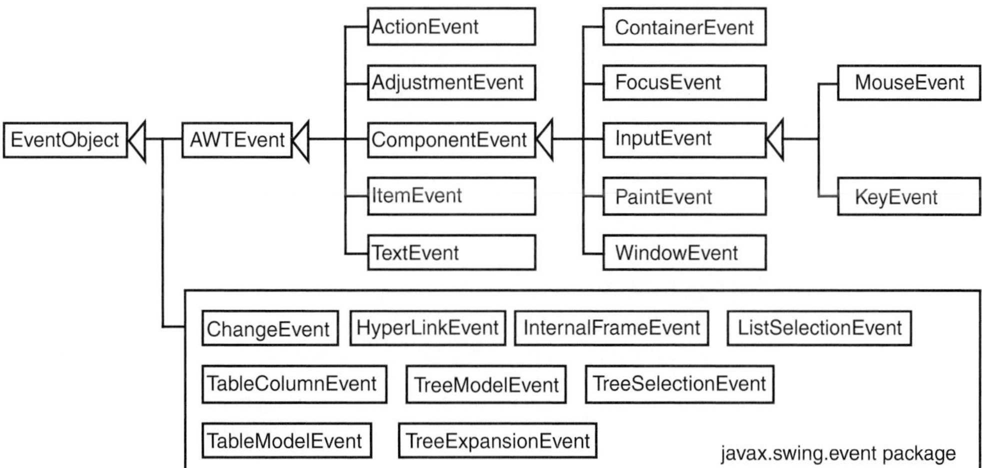

Figure 3.2 *The* `java.util.EventObject` *class is the root of all Java event classes.*

The event classes introduced in JDK 1.1 are grouped in the `java.awt.event` package. These classes were originally designed for AWT components, but many Swing components generate these events. The events in the `javax.swing.event` package are only applicable to Swing components.

The event class contains whatever data values and methods are pertinent to the particular event type. For example, the `KeyEvent` class describes the data values related to a key event and contains the methods, such as `getKeyChar()`, for retrieving the key associated with the event.

All the event classes extend `EventObject`. Below, in the section "Creating Custom Events," you will learn how to create custom event classes by extending `EventObject`.

Source Components

The component on which an event is generated is referred to as an *event source*. Every Java AWT and Swing user interface component is an *event source*. For example, `JButton` is an event source because it generates a `java.awt.event.ActionEvent` when a button object is clicked.

The source component contains the code that detects an external or internal action that triggers the event. Upon detecting the action, the source should fire an event to the listeners by invoking the event handler defined by listeners. The source component must also contain methods for registering and deregistering listeners.

Event Listener Interface

Every event class is associated with an event listener interface that defines one or more methods, referred to as *handlers*. The handlers are implemented by the listener components. The source component invokes the listeners' handlers when an event is detected.

Since an event class and its listener interface are coexistent, they are often referred to as an *event set* or *event pair*. The event listener interface must be named as *X*Listener for the *X*Event. For example, the listener interface for `ActionEvent` is `ActionListener`.

Listener Components

A listener component for an event must implement the event listener interface. The object of the listener component cannot receive event notifications from a source component unless the object is registered as a listener of the source.

A listener component may implement any number of listener interfaces to listen to several types of events. A source component may register many listeners. A source component may register itself as a listener.

Review of the *JButton* Component

To learn how to create custom event sets and your own source components, let us take a look at the `JButton` component and its associated event set and listener component.

TIP

You can find the source code of a class by choosing Search, Browse Classes to bring up a dialog box in which you can type a fully qualified class name to review its source code.

A `JButton` instance can fire an `ActionEvent`. `java.awt.event.ActionEvent` extends `java.awt.AWTEvent`, which extends `java.util.EventObject`. `ActionEvent` contains two constructors:

```
public ActionEvent(Object source, int id, String command)
public ActionEvent(Object source, int id, String command,
  int modifiers)
```

These constructors can be used by source components to create event objects.

A listener of `ActionEvent` must implement the `ActionListener` interface. `java.awt.event.ActionListener` extends `java.util.EventListener`. `ActionListener` simply contains the `actionPerformed` method, which must be implemented by the listener component that responds to `ActionEvent`.

The `JButton` is a subclass of `AbstractButton`. The `fireActionPerformed` method defined in `AbstractButton` is invoked when a `JButton` object is clicked. This method invokes the registered listener's `actionPerformed` handler.

The `AbstractButton` class also provides registration methods `addActionListener` and `removeActionListener` for listeners. These methods are defined as follows:

```
public synchronized void addActionListener(ActionListener l)
public synchronized void removeActionListener(ActionListener l)
```

As shown in Figure 3.3, a listener component implements the `ActionListener` interface and provides the actual code for handling the event in the `actionPerformed` method. The application class creates an instance of `JButton` and an instance of the listener component, and registers the listener with the source. When an `ActionEvent` occurs on a button, the button object invokes the listener's `actionPerformed` method to deal with the event.

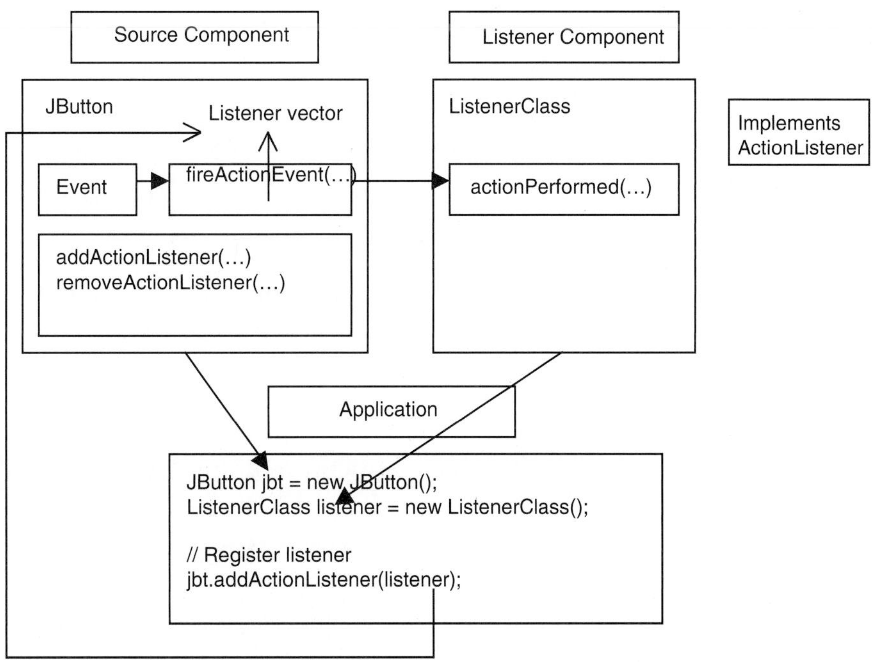

Figure 3.3 *The source component invokes the listener's handler to process the events.*

Creating Custom Event Sets and Source Components

You have already used event sets and event source components in Java graphics programming, since certain event sets and source components are provided as part of the Java API. In this section, you will learn how to create custom event sets and develop your own source components. By developing your own event sets and source components, you will gain a better understanding of the Java event model.

A custom event class must extend `java.util.EventObject` or a subclass of `java.util.EventObject`. Additionally, you need to provide data members and methods to describe and process the event.

A custom event listener interface must always extend `java.util.EventListener`. You need to define the signature of the handlers for the event. The listener interface should be named <*Event*>Listener for a builder tool to recognize it at design time.

A source component must have the appropriate registration methods for adding and removing listeners. To enable a builder tool to recognize events, the registration methods must conform to the registration method naming patterns. Events can be unicasted (only one object is notified of the event) or multicasted (each object in a list of listeners is notified of the event). The naming pattern for adding a unicast listener is

```
public void add<Event>Listener(<Event>Listener l) throws
   TooManyListenersException;
```

The naming pattern for adding a multicast listener is the same, except that it does not throw the `TooManyListenersException`.

```
public void add<Event>Listener(<Event>Listener l)
```

The naming pattern for removing a listener (either unicast or multicast) is:

```
public void remove<Event>Listener(<Event>Listener l)
```

A source component contains the code that creates an event object and passes it to the listening components by calling a method in the listener's event listener interface. You may use a standard Java event class like `ActionEvent` to create event objects or may define your own event classes if necessary.

Example 3.1 Creating a Custom Event Set and a Source Component

This example creates a custom event set named `TickEvent` and `TickListener` for describing tick events, and develops a source component that generates a tick event at every specified time interval in milliseconds. The event class shown in Listing 3.1 contains the information on tick count and tick interval.

```
package eventdemo;

public class TickEvent extends java.util.EventObject {
  /** tickCount counts the number of ticks for the event */
  private long tickCount;

  /** tickInterval is the interval between ticks in milliseconds */
  private long tickInterval;

  /** Construct a TickEvent */
  public TickEvent(Object o) {
    super(o);
  }

```

Listing 3.1 *TickEvent.java*

```
    /** Return tickCount */
    public long getTickCount() {
      return tickCount;
    }

    /** Set a new tickCount */
    public void setTickCount(long tickCount) {
      this.tickCount = tickCount;
    }

    /** Return tickInterval */
    public long getTickInterval() {
      return tickInterval;
    }

    /** Set a new tickInterval */
    public void setTickInterval(long milliseconds) {
      tickInterval = milliseconds;
    }
  }
```

Listing 3.1 *Continued*

An event listener interface must be defined for each new event class. The listener interface for `TickEvent` presented in Listing 3.2 contains a method, `handleTick`, that will be implemented by the listeners of `TickEvent`.

```
package eventdemo;

import eventdemo.TickEvent;

public interface TickListener extends java.util.EventListener {
  /** Handle a TickEvent, to be implemented by a listener */
  public void handleTick(TickEvent e);
}
```

Listing 3.2 *TickListener.java*

The source component is responsible for registering listeners, generating events, and notifying listeners by invoking the methods defined in the listeners' interfaces. The `Tick` component presented in Listing 3.3 is capable of registering multiple listeners, generating a `TickEvent` object at every specified time interval, and notifying the listeners by invoking the listeners' `handleTick` method.

Note

The TickListener interface can be created using the Interface wizard from the Wizards menu.

```
package eventdemo;

import eventdemo.*;
import java.util.Vector;

public class Tick implements Runnable {
  /** A thread to control tick */
  protected Thread thread = null;

```

Listing 3.3 *Tick.java*

continued

Example 3.1 continued

```
/** Whether the thread is suspended */
private boolean suspended;

/** Store Tick listeners in a vector */
private Vector tickListenerList;

/** Tick event e */
private TickEvent e;

/**  Tick count and Tick interval */
private long tickCount = 0;
private long tickInterval = 1000;

/** Default constructor */
public Tick() {
  // Create a TickEvent
  e = new TickEvent(this);

  // Create and start the thread
  thread = new Thread(this);
  thread.start();
}

/** Return tickInterval */
public long getTickInterval() {
  return tickInterval;
}

/** Set a tickInterval */
public void setTickInterval(long interval) {
  tickInterval = interval;
}

/** Run the thread */
public void run() {
  while (true) {
    try {
      Thread.sleep(tickInterval);
      synchronized (this) {
        while (suspended)
          wait();
      }
    }
    catch (InterruptedException e) {  }

    // Adjust Tick count and interval
    e.setTickCount(tickCount++);
    e.setTickInterval(tickInterval);

    // Fire TickEvent
    processEvent(e);
  }
}

/** Resume the thread */
public synchronized void resume() {
  if (suspended) {
    suspended = false;
```

Listing 3.3 *Tick.java*

```
      notify();
    }
  }

  /** Suspend the thread */
  public synchronized void suspend() {
    suspended = true;
  }

  /** Register a tick event listener */
  public synchronized void addTickListener(TickListener l) {
    Vector v = tickListenerList == null ?
      new Vector(2) : (Vector)tickListenerList.clone();
    if (!v.contains(l)) {
      v.addElement(l);
      tickListenerList = v;
    }
  }

  /** Remove a tick event listener */
  public synchronized void removeTickListener(TickListener l) {
    if (tickListenerList != null && tickListenerList.contains(l)) {
      tickListenerList.removeElement(l);
    }
  }

  /** Fire TickEvent */
  public void processEvent(TickEvent e) {
    Vector v;

    synchronized (this) {
      v = (Vector)tickListenerList.clone();
    }

    for (int i=0; i < v.size(); i++) {
      TickListener listener = (TickListener)v.elementAt(i);
      listener.handleTick(e);
    }
  }
}
```

Listing 3.3 *Continued*

Follow the steps below to complete the project:

1. Create a new project named eventdemo.jpr, and create an applet named `TestTick` using the Applet wizard. Create classes for `TickEvent`, `TickListener`, and `Tick` in the project, compile the classes, and install the `Tick` component into the component palette. See the section "Using JavaBeans in JBuilder" for installing a JavaBeans component to the component palette in JBuilder.

2. Click `Tick` from the component palette and drop it in the UI designer, as shown in Figure 3.4. Since `Tick` is not a UI component, it is not seen in the UI designer, but in the component tree you can see a bean named `tick1` whose properties and event handler can be visually manipulated in the component inspector. The inspector window in Figure 3.4 shows the bean property. To reveal the bean event handlers, choose the Event tab at

continued

Example 3.1 continued

the bottom of the component inspector, as shown in Figure 3.5. You will learn how to link the source component with listeners by implementing the handlers using JBuilder's visual designer in the section "Linking Components via Events in JBuilder."

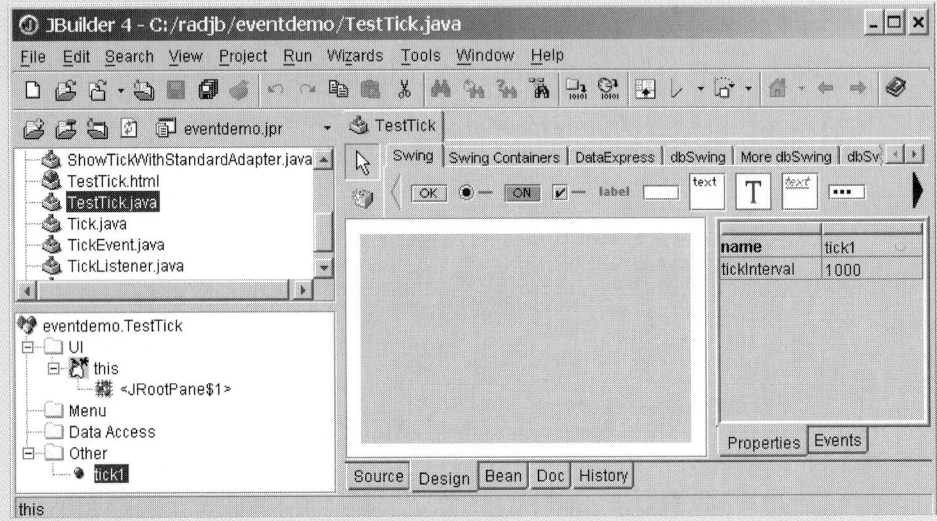

Figure 3.4 *You can add a non-UI JavaBeans component into the designer and manipulate its properties and event handlers from the component inspector.*

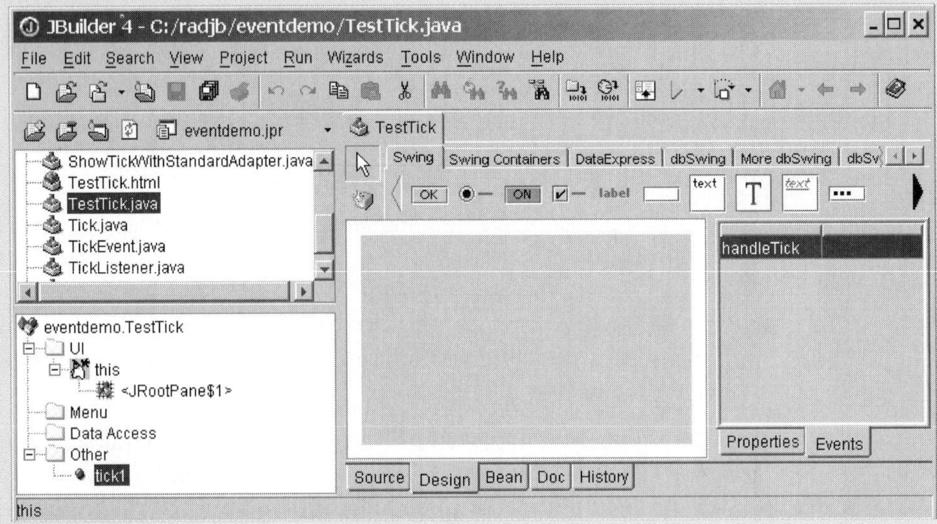

Figure 3.5 *The* `handleTick` *handler is shown in the component inspector, where you can link the source component to a listener in JBuilder.*

Example Review

The `Tick` class is a JavaBeans component; however, `TickEvent` and `TickListener` are not JavaBeans components. Therefore, `Tick` can be installed in the component palette, but not `TickEvent` and `TickListener`.

The `suspend()` (Lines 72–75) and `resume()` (Lines 64–70) methods defined in the `Tick` class are for suspending and resuming ticking. Their implementation is compatible with Java 2. The `suspend()` and `resume()` methods defined in the `Thread` class in Java 1 are deprecated because they are known to be deadlock-prone. Therefore, they are replaced by the new implementation in the `Tick` class. In the implementation for the `run()` method (Lines 43–62), the `wait()` method is used, along with a `boolean` variable, to indicate whether a thread is suspended.

`TickEvent` is a new event class. Most of the time you don't need to create your own event classes unless you want to encapsulate information not available in the existing event classes, as in the case of the `TickEvent` class that contains tick count and tick interval. In this case, you need to write an event set that includes the event class and its listener interface.

Since the source component `Tick` is designed for multiple listeners, a `java.util.Vector` instance `tickListenerList` is used to hold all the listeners for the source component. The data type of the elements in the vector is `Object`. To add a listener `listener` to the `tickListenerList` vector, use

```
tickListenerList.addElement(listener);
```

To remove a listener, `listener`, from `tickListenerList`, use

```
tickListenerList.removeElement(Listener);
```

The `addTickListener` method does not add the listener twice if it is already in the list. The `removeTickListener` method removes a listener if it is in list. `tickListenerList` is an instance of `Vector`, which is like a flexible array that can grow or shrink dynamically. Initially, `tickListenerList` is new `Vector(2)`, which implies that the capacity of the vector is 2, but the capacity can be changed dynamically. If more than two listeners are added to `tickListenerList`, the vector size will be automatically increased.

The `addTickListener` and `removeTickListener` methods are synchronized to prevent data corruption on `tickListenerList` when attempting to register multiple listeners concurrently.

The `processEvent` method is invoked at every `tickInterval` in milliseconds. This notifies the listeners in the `tickListenerList` vector by calling each listener's `handleTick` method to process the event. It is possible that a new listener may be added or an existing listener may be removed when `processEvent` is running. To avoid corruption on `tickListenerList`, a clone `v` of `tickListenerList` is created for use to notify listeners. To avoid corruption when creating the clone, all the methods of the object are synchronized as follows:

continued

Example 3.1 continued

```
    synchronized (this) {
      v = (Vector)tickListenerList.clone();
    }
```

The `Tick` component is created from scratch. If you build a new component that extends a component capable of generating events, the new component inherits the ability to generate the same type of events. For example, the `MessagePanel` component is derived from `javax.swing.JPanel`, which is a subclass of `java.awt.Component`. The `MessagePanel` component can detect and generate a number of events, such as key and mouse events. You don't need to write the code to generate these events and register listeners for them, since the code is already given in the superclass. However, you still need to write the code to make your component capable of firing events not supported in the superclass.

NOTE
You wrote the code for registering and deregistering events and for processing events in this example. In Chapter 4, "Developing and Using Components," you will learn to use JBuilder's BeansExpress to automatically generate the code.

Creating Listener Components

If a component is to be a listener for an event, it must implement the event listener interface and be registered with a source object. For example, to listen for `TickEvent`, the listener component must implement `TickListener`, and must be registered with an instance of a source component, such as `Tick`.

A builder tool can help to automate the process of creating a listener and registering it with a source. For example, in JBuilder, the code can be generated by selecting and pressing the event handler in the component inspector. To understand how JBuilder generates listeners, let us first look at the following example, which creates a listener manually.

Example 3.2 Writing a Listener Component Manually

In this example, a hand-coded class, named `ShowTick`, is given to display the tick count and tick interval when a tick event occurs. `ShowTick` is a subclass of `JFrame`. The display is shown in a `MessagePanel` bean placed in `ShowTick`. The `MessagePanel` component was presented in Example 2.1. A `Tick` bean is used to generate tick events. The `ShowTick` class is the listener for tick events. Figure 3.6 shows the relationship among these classes.

Follow the steps below to complete the example:

1. Reopen project eventdemo.jpr and create a class named `ShowTick` that extends `JFrame` using the Class wizard. In the Class wizard, check all the options, as shown in Figure 3.7.

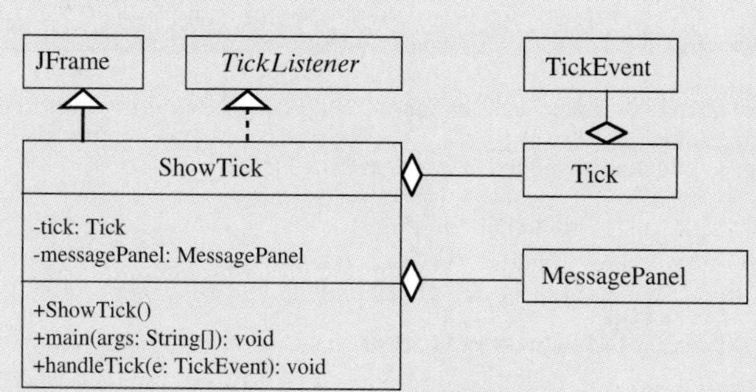

Figure 3.6 *The* `ShowTick` *class uses* `Tick` *and* `MessagePanel` *to control and display a message.*

Class Wizard

Create a new Java class

Fill in the fields below to set the package, name, base class, and other options for the Java class which will be created.

Class Information

Package: eventdemo

Class name: ShowTick

Base class: javax.swing.JFrame

Options

- [x] Public
- [x] Generate default constructor
- [x] Generate main method
- [x] Override abstract methods
- [x] Generate header comments

OK Cancel Help

Figure 3.7 *You can use the Class wizard to create a template for the* `ShowTick` *class.*

2. Choose Wizards, Implement Interface to bring up the Implement Interface wizard, as shown in Figure 3.8. Expand `eventdemo` to select the `eventdemo.TickListener` interface. Click OK to let JBuilder generate the code for implementing the interface in ShowTick.java.

3. Complete the code as shown in Listing 3.4. A sample run of the program is shown in Figure 3.9.

```
package eventdemo;

import javax.swing.*;
import messagepaneldemo.MessagePanel;
import java.awt.*;

```

Listing 3.4 *ShowTick.java*

continued

Example 3.2 continued

```
public class ShowTick extends JFrame implements TickListener {
  private Tick tick;
  private MessagePanel messagePanel;

  /** Default constructor */
  public ShowTick() {
    // Create a Tick event instance and set tick interval to 1000
    Tick tick = new Tick();
    tick.setTickInterval(1000);

    // Create a message panel instance
    messagePanel = new MessagePanel();

    // Place the message canvas to the frame
    this.getContentPane().setLayout(new BorderLayout());
    this.getContentPane().add(messagePanel);
    setTitle("ShowTick");

    // Register listener
    tick.addTickListener(this);
  }

  /** Main method */
  public static void main(String[] args) {
    ShowTick showTick = new ShowTick();
    showTick.setSize(100, 100);
    showTick.setVisible(true);
  }

  public void handleTick(TickEvent e) {
    //TODO: implement this eventdemo.TickListener method;
    messagePanel.setMessage("Tick count is " + e.getTickCount() +
      " and tick interval is " + e.getTickInterval());
  }
}
```

Listing 3.4 *Continued*

Example Review

The program starts from the main method, which creates an instance of `ShowTick` and displays the frame on the screen.

To make `ShowTick` a listener for `Tick`, `ShowTick` implements `TickListener` and provides the code for handling tick events in the `handleTick` method. You should also register the listener by invoking `TickListener`'s add listener method, as follows:

```
tick.addTickListener(this);
```

When an event occurs in `tick`, the `processEvent` method is invoked to notify the listener `ShowTick` by invoking its `handleTick` method. The flow of the event processing from the source to the listener is shown in Figure 3.10.

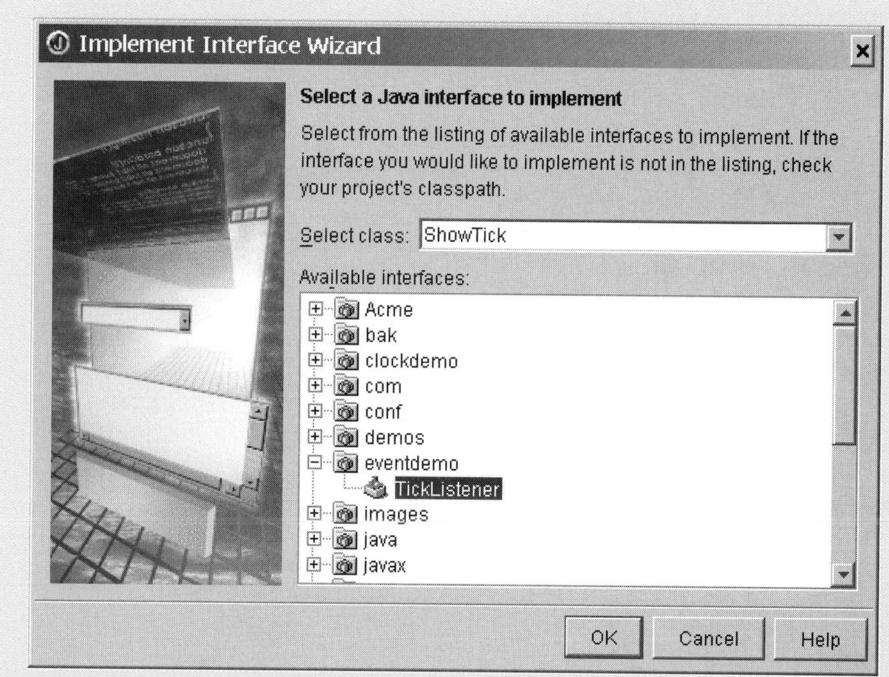

Figure 3.8 *The Implement Interface Wizard can help you to implement all the handlers in an interface.*

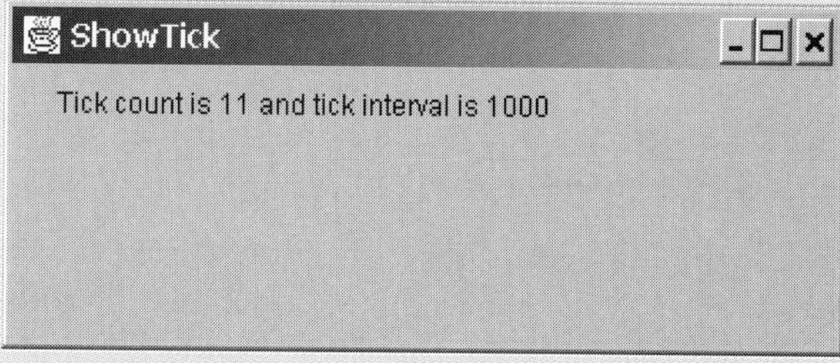

Figure 3.9 *The tick count is updated every 1 second.*

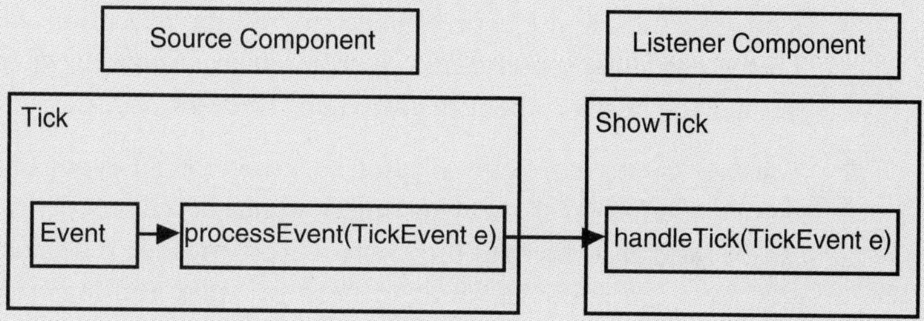

Figure 3.10 *When a Tick event occurs, the* `processEvent` *method is invoked, which invokes the* `handleTick` *method defined in the listener's interface and implemented in the listener.*

Event Adapters

The Java event model shown in Figure 3.1 is flexible, allowing modifications and variations. One useful variation of the model is the addition of adapters, as shown in Figure 3.11. When an event occurs, the source object notifies the adapter. The adapter then delegates the handling of the event to the real listener object, which is referred to as a *target*.

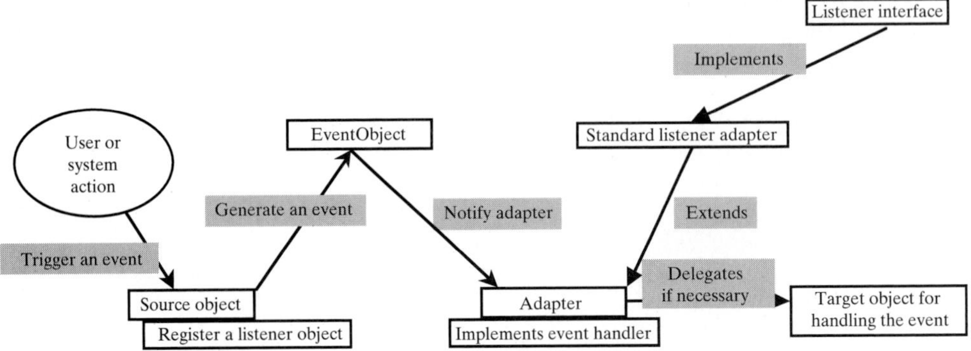

Figure 3.11 *The adapter listens for events and delegates handling to the actual listener (target).*

The adapter is a service object that provides a level of indirection between the source and the target. It is registered as a listener for the source event. Instead of passing the event object to the target, the source passes the event object to the adapter and lets it delegate to the target handler.

At first glance, the advantages of using adapters are not apparent. Adapters seem to make things more complex, but they are valuable in many situations. Here are some examples:

- If you need to hook a source to an existing bean that cannot be modified or extended, you can use an adapter as a listener to the source and register it with the source. When an event occurs, the source notifies the adapter, which then invokes the methods in the target.
- You can use an adapter to place all the event notifications from the source in a queue to allow the source object to resume execution without blocking. This is particularly useful in a distributed environment where the target object may be busy or not available when the event occurs.
- You can create a generic adapter to listen for all types of events from all sources, then deliver them to one or multiple targets. This generic adapter can be used as a filter for the events before they are delegated out to the targets. You can apply all kinds of business rules and logic to the delivery of events and sort the events by priority.

An adapter usually extends a convenience listener adapter. A *convenience listener adapter* is a support class that provides default implementations for all the methods in the listener interface. The default implementation is usually an empty body.

Java provides convenience listener adapters for all the AWT listener interfaces except the `ActionListener`. A convenience listener adapter is named *X*Adapter for *X*Listener. For example, `MouseAdapter` is a convenience listener adapter for `MouseListener`.

A listener interface may contain many methods for handling various types of actions of an event. For example, `MouseListener` contains `mouseClicked`, `mousePressed`, `mouseReleased`, `mouseEntered`, and `mouseExited`. The convenience listener adapter is convenient because a listener class may simply extend the adapter and implement only the method for the intended type of action instead of all the methods of the listener interface.

Adapters are an important addition to the Java event model. You will see more examples and different ways of using adapters. In the next section, you will see how adapters can make builder tools more efficient.

Using Adapters in JBuilder

A builder tool such as JBuilder uses adapters to delegate handling events to the target objects. For example, suppose a target object is a listener for two buttons named Ok and Cancel, respectively. JBuilder generates an adapter for the Ok button and an adapter for the Cancel button, as shown in Figure 3.12. The target object contains a method (say `ok_actionPerformed(...)`) for handling the Ok button and a separate method (say `cancel_actionPerformed(...)`) for handling the Cancel button. When you click the Ok button, it fires the `ActionEvent` to the Ok adapter, which then delegates the event to `ok_actionPerformed(...)`.

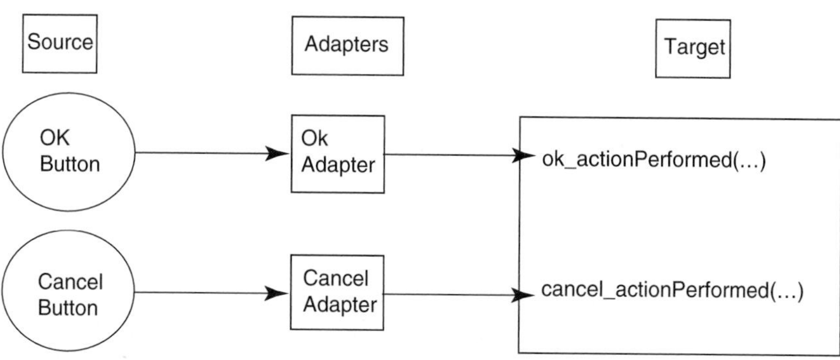

Figure 3.12 *JBuilder uses adapters to hook up source components with listeners.*

JBuilder greatly simplifies the task of creating listeners. It automatically registers listeners and provides an empty method for the user to fill in the code for handling the event. JBuilder can generate anonymous adapters or standard adapters. In the following example, you will learn how to use JBuilder's UI designer to link source components and listeners via standard adapters. Anonymous adapters will be introduced in the section "Anonymous Classes."

Example 3.3 Creating a Listener Component Using JBuilder

This example uses JBuilder's visual designer to develop the same program as in Example 3.2. Additionally, the program stops the tick when the mouse is pressed, and the tick resumes when the mouse is released. Suppose that the `MessagePanel` and `Tick` components are already placed in the component palette. To see the development in action, follow these steps:

1. Reopen the project eventdemo.jpr and create an applet named `ShowTickWithStandardAdapter` using the Applet wizard.
2. In the Project Properties for eventdemo.jpr, make sure you select Standard adapter for the event handling in the Code Style page of the dialog box, as shown in Figure 3.13. With this selection, JBuilder will generate standard adapters.

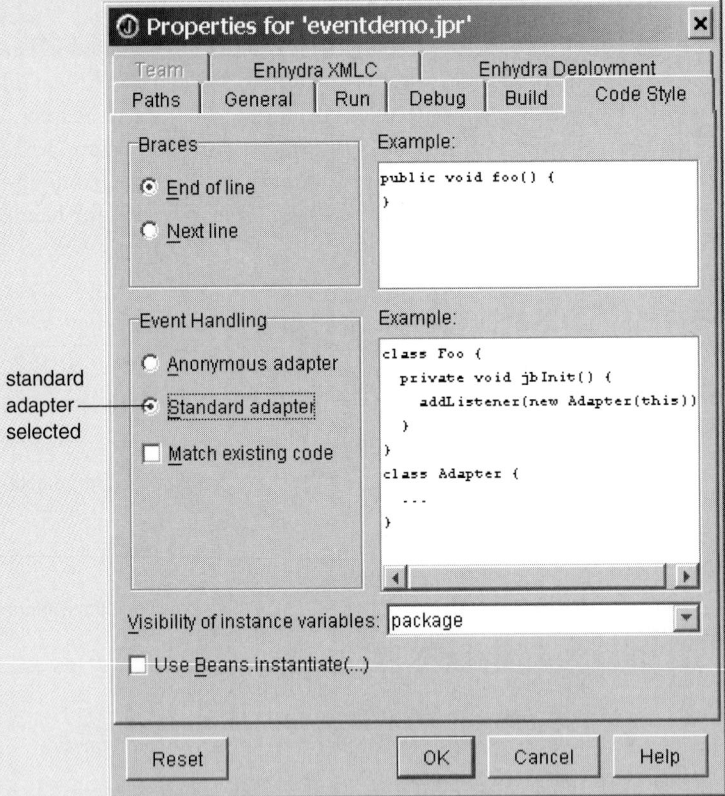

Figure 3.13 *You may choose an event-handling style from the Project Properties dialog.*

3. With ShowTickWithStandardAdapter.java selected in the project pane, choose the Design tab to display the UI designer. Drop a `MessagePanel` component to the center of the applet to create `messagePanel1`. Set its `background` to Cyan and `yCoordinate` to 30 in the component inspector.

4. Drop a `Tick` component to the frame. You will see `tick1` in the component tree under the node Other.

5. With `tick1` selected in the component tree, switch to the Events page of the component inspector. Select the `handleTick` event and double-click its value field in the component inspector. The following code is automatically generated.

➡ The following line was added into the `jbInit()` method to register the listener for `TickEvent`.

```
tick1.addTickListener(new
  ShowTickWithStandardAdapter_tick1_tickAdapter(this));
```

➡ An empty handler method is created for you to fill in the code for handling the `TickEvent`.

```
void tick1_handleTick(TickEvent e) {
}
```

➡ A new event listener adapter class was created, as shown below.

```
class ShowTickWithStandardAdapter_tick1_tickAdapter
  implements eventdemo.TickListener {
  ShowTickWithStandardAdapter adaptee;

  ShowTickWithStandardAdapter_tick1_tickAdapter(
    ShowTickWithStandardAdapter adaptee) {
    this.adaptee = adaptee;
  }

  public void handleTick(TickEvent e) {
    adaptee.tick1_handleTick(e);
  }
}
```

6. Fill in the following code in the method `tick1_handleTick` to handle the tick event.

```
void tick1_handleTick(TickEvent e) {
  messagePanel1.setMessage("Tick count is " + e.getTickCount() +
    " and tick interval is " + e.getTickInterval());
}
```

7. We now turn our attention to creating the code for handling the mouse events. In the Events page of the component inspector for `messagePanel1`, double-click the value field of the `mousePressed` event. The code shown below is automatically generated.

➡ The following line is added into the `jbInit` method to register the listener for `MouseEvent`.

```
messagePanel1.addMouseListener(new
  ShowTickWithStandardAdapter_messagePanel1_mouseAdapter(this));
```

continued

Example 3.3 continued

➡ An empty handler method was created for you to fill in the code for handling the `mousePressed` event.

```
void messagePanel1_mousePressed(MouseEvent e) {
}
```

➡ A new event listener adapter class was created, as follows.

```
class ShowTickWithStandardAdapter_messagePanel1_mouseAdapter
  extends java.awt.event.MouseAdapter {
  ShowTickWithStandardAdapter adaptee;

  ShowTickWithStandardAdapter_messagePanel1_mouseAdapter(
    ShowTickWithStandardAdapter adaptee) {
    this.adaptee = adaptee;
  }

  public void mousePressed(MouseEvent e) {
    adaptee.messagePanel1_mousePressed(e);
  }
}
```

8. Fill in the following code in the method `messagePanel1_mousePressed` to suspend the tick when the mouse is pressed.

```
void messagePanel1_mousePressed(MouseEvent e) {
  tick1.suspend();
}
```

9. To generate the code for handling the `mouseReleased` event, click the value field of `mouseReleased` in the Events page for `messagePanel1`. Since the adapter for the `MouseEvent` has already been created and is registered with the source as a `MouseEvent` listener, this code will not be regenerated. Instead the following code was generated.

➡ An empty handler method was created for you to fill in the code for handling the `mouseReleased` event.

```
void messagePanel1_mouseReleased(MouseEvent e) {
}
```

➡ A handler for the `mouseReleased` event was added to the adapter.

```
public void mouseReleased(MouseEvent e) {
  adaptee.messagePanel1_mouseReleased(e);
}
```

10. Fill in the following code in the method `messagePanel1_mouseReleased` to resume the tick when the mouse is pressed.

```
void messagePanel1_mouseReleased(MouseEvent e) {
  tick1.resume();
}
```

11. The ShowTickWithStandardAdapter.java code generated by JBuilder is shown in Listing 3.5. Run ShowTickWithStandardAdapter.java in the

project to test the program. The output of a sample run is shown in Figure 3.9, which is the same as in Example 3.1.

```
package eventdemo;

import java.awt.*;
import java.awt.event.*;
import java.applet.*;
import javax.swing.*;
import messagepaneldemo.*;

public class ShowTickWithStandardAdapter extends JApplet {
  boolean isStandalone = false;
  MessagePanel messagePanel1 = new MessagePanel();
  Tick tick1 = new Tick();


  /** Initialize the applet */
  public void init() {
    try {
      jbInit();
    }
    catch(Exception e) {
      e.printStackTrace();
    }
  }

  /** Component initialization */
  private void jbInit() throws Exception {
    this.setSize(new Dimension(400,300));
    messagePanel1.setBackground(Color.cyan);
    messagePanel1.setYCoordinate(30);
    messagePanel1.addMouseListener(new
      ShowTickWithStandardAdapter_messagePanel1_mouseAdapter(this));
    tick1.addTickListener(new
      ShowTickWithStandardAdapter_tick1_tickAdapter(this));
    this.getContentPane().add(messagePanel1, BorderLayout.CENTER);
  }

  void tick1_handleTick(TickEvent e) {
    messagePanel1.setMessage("Tick count is " + e.getTickCount() +
      " and tick interval is " + e.getTickInterval());
  }

  void messagePanel1_mousePressed(MouseEvent e) {
    tick1.suspend();
  }

  void messagePanel1_mouseReleased(MouseEvent e) {
    tick1.resume();
  }
}

class ShowTickWithStandardAdapter_tick1_tickAdapter
  implements eventdemo.TickListener {
  ShowTickWithStandardAdapter adaptee;

  ShowTickWithStandardAdapter_tick1_tickAdapter(
    ShowTickWithStandardAdapter adaptee) {
    this.adaptee = adaptee;
  }
```

Listing 3.5 *ShowTickWithStandardAdapter.java*

continued

Example 3.3 continued

```
    public void handleTick(TickEvent e) {
      adaptee.tick1_handleTick(e);
    }
  }

  class ShowTickWithStandardAdapter_messagePanel1_mouseAdapter
    extends java.awt.event.MouseAdapter {
    ShowTickWithStandardAdapter adaptee;

    ShowTickWithStandardAdapter_messagePanel1_mouseAdapter(
      ShowTickWithStandardAdapter adaptee) {
      this.adaptee = adaptee;
    }
    public void mousePressed(MouseEvent e) {
      adaptee.messagePanel1_mousePressed(e);
    }
    public void mouseReleased(MouseEvent e) {
      adaptee.messagePanel1_mouseReleased(e);
    }
  }
```

Listing 3.5 *Continued*

Example Review

The `Tick` component can generate `TickEvent`. `MessagePanel` can generate `MouseEvent`, since `MessagePanel` is a subclass of `java.awt.Component` and the `Component` class can generate `MouseEvent`.

JBuilder uses a listener adapter as an intermediary class interposed between an event source and the real listener, as shown in Figure 3.14 for the `TickEvent`, and in Figure 3.15 for the `MouseEvent`. The adapter plays the role of pairing a source event with a listener. When a `TickEvent` occurs, the `processEvent` method in the event source invokes the `handleTick` method in the adapter, which then invokes the real handler `tick1_handleTick` in the target component.

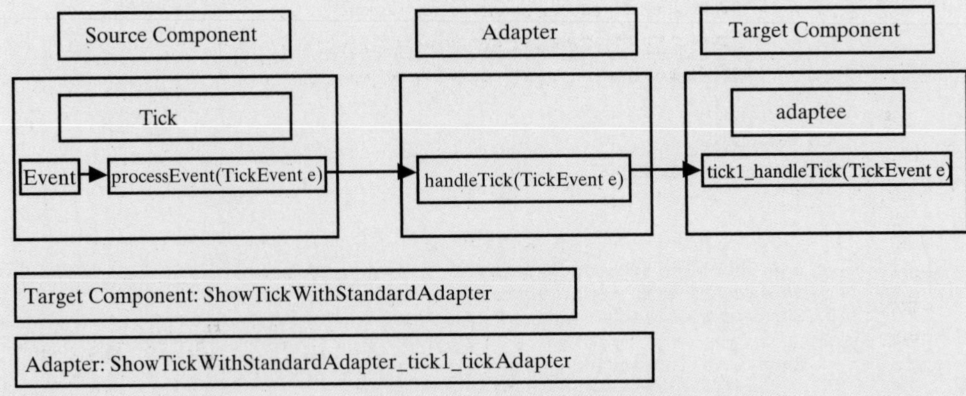

Figure 3.14 *When a* `TickEvent` *occurs, the* `processEvent` *method is invoked, which invokes the* `handleTick` *method in the adapter, which in turn invokes the real handler,* `handleTick`.

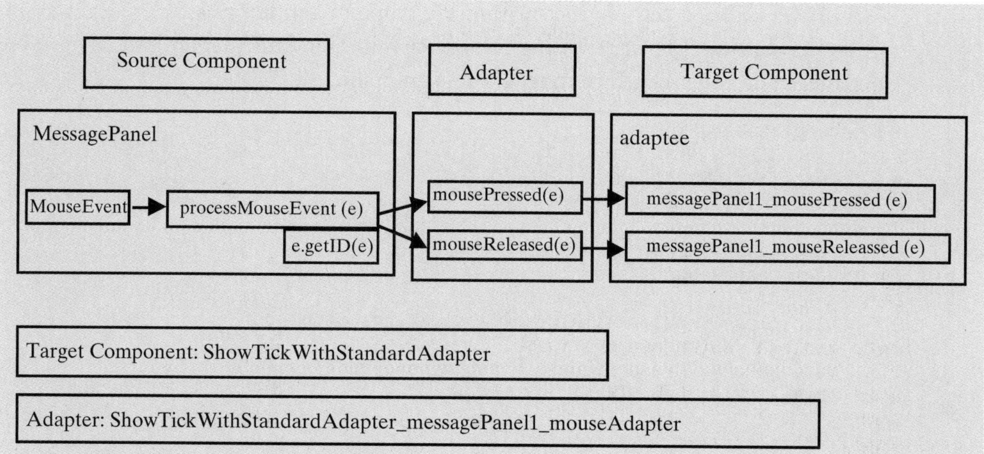

Figure 3.15 *When a* `MouseEvent` *occurs, the* `processMouseEvent` *method is invoked, which invokes the* `mousePressed` *method or* `mouseReleased` *method in the adapter, and then the real handler,* `messagePanel1_mousePressed` *or* `messagePanel1_mouseReleased`.

When a `MouseEvent` occurs, the `processMouseEvent` method in the event source invokes one of the five mouse events (`mousePressed`, `mouseReleased`, `mouseClicked`, `mouseEntered`, and `mouseExited`). Which of the five events is processed depends on the event ID. For the detailed code of the `processMouseEvent` method, please refer to `java.awt.Component`. Since you are only interested in the `mousePressed` and `mouseReleased` events, these two handlers are provided in the adapter. When one of these two handlers is invoked in the adapter, the corresponding real handler in the target component is invoked.

The adapter for the `TickEvent` implements the `TickListener` interface and the adapter for the `MouseEvent` extends the `MouseAdapter` convenience listener adapter class. JBuilder creates adapters by extending the listener interface's convenience adapter class, if the convenience adapter exists.

TIP

To delete an existing event handler, highlight the entire value field of the event handler in the Events page, press the Delete key, and then press the Enter key. JBuilder automatically deletes the adapter class and the registration method from the source code. The associated event-handling method is also deleted if it is empty.

Inner Classes and Anonymous Inner Classes

As you have just learned, JBuilder generates an event adapter for every type of event from the source in which the target is interested. Consequently, there are usually many classes in the project. You can use inner classes to reduce the proliferation of adapter classes and to shorten the program.

An *inner class* is a class defined within the scope of another class. Here is an example (see Listing 3.6) of rewriting ShowTickWithStandardAdapter.java using inner classes. The code related to inner classes is in italic.

```
package eventdemo;

import java.awt.*;
import java.awt.event.*;
import java.applet.*;
import javax.swing.*;
import messagepaneldemo.*;

public class ShowTickWithInnerClass extends JApplet {
  boolean isStandalone = false;
  MessagePanel messagePanel1 = new MessagePanel();
  Tick tick1 = new Tick();

  /** Initialize the applet */
  public void init() {
    try {
      jbInit();
    }
    catch(Exception e) {
      e.printStackTrace();
    }
  }

  /** Component initialization */
  private void jbInit() throws Exception {
    this.setSize(new Dimension(400,300));
    messagePanel1.setBackground(Color.cyan);
    messagePanel1.setYCoordinate(30);
    messagePanel1.addMouseListener(new
      ShowTickWithStandardAdapter_messagePanel1_mouseAdapter());
    tick1.addTickListener(new
      ShowTickWithStandardAdapter_tick1_tickAdapter());
    this.getContentPane().add(messagePanel1, BorderLayout.CENTER);
  }

  void tick1_handleTick(TickEvent e) {
    messagePanel1.setMessage("Tick count is " + e.getTickCount() +
      " and tick interval is " + e.getTickInterval());
  }

  void messagePanel1_mousePressed(MouseEvent e) {
    tick1.suspend();
  }

  void messagePanel1_mouseReleased(MouseEvent e) {
    tick1.resume();
  }

  /** Inner class */
  class ShowTickWithStandardAdapter_tick1_tickAdapter
    implements eventdemo.TickListener {
    public void handleTick(TickEvent e) {
      tick1_handleTick(e);
    }
  }

  /** Inner class */
  class ShowTickWithStandardAdapter_messagePanel1_mouseAdapter
```

Listing 3.6 *ShowTickWithInnerClass.java.*

```
      extends java.awt.event.MouseAdapter {
      public void mousePressed(MouseEvent e) {
        messagePanel1_mousePressed(e);
      }
      public void mouseReleased(MouseEvent e) {
        messagePanel1_mouseReleased(e);
      }
    }
  }
```

Listing 3.6 *Continued*

The adapters are simplified inside `ShowTickWithInnerClass` using inner classes. Inner classes are just like any regular classes with the following features:

- An inner class can reference the data and methods defined in its parent class so that you do not need to pass the reference of the parent class to the constructor of the inner class. Therefore, the constructors of the adapters are eliminated and the `handleTick` method invokes `tick1_handleTick`, which is defined in `ShowTickWithInnerClass`.
- Inner classes make programs simple and concise. As you can see, the new class is shorter and leaner.
- An inner class is only for supporting the work of its containing outer class, and it is compiled into a class named *`OutClassName$InnerClassName`*`.class`. For example, the inner class `ShowTickWithStandardAdapter_tick1_tickAdapter` in `ShowTickWithInnerClass` is compiled into

  ```
  ShowTickWithInnerClass$
    ShowTickWithStandardAdapter_tick1_tickAdapter.class.
  ```

- An inner class can be declared `public`, `protected`, or `private` subject to the same visibility rules applied to a member of the class.
- An inner class can be declared `static`. A `static` inner class can be accessed using the outer class name. A static inner class cannot access non-static members of the outer class.
- Objects of an inner class are often created in the outer class. But you can also create an object of an inner class from another class. If the inner class is non-static, you must first create an instance of the outer class, then use the following syntax to create an object for the inner class:

  ```
  OuterClass.InnerClass innerObject = outerObject.new InnerClass();
  ```

  If the inner class is static, use the following syntax to create an object for the inner class:

  ```
  OuterClass.InnerClass innerObject = new OuterClass.InnerClass();
  ```

The inner class can be further shortened by using an anonymous inner class. An *anonymous inner class* is an inner class without a name. An anonymous inner class combines declaring an inner class and creating an instance of the class in one step. An anonymous inner class is declared as shown here:

```
new SuperClassName() [or InterfaceName()] {
  // Implement or override methods in superclass or interface

  // Other methods if necessary
}
```

Since an anonymous inner class is a special kind of inner class, it is treated like an inner class in many ways. Additionally, an anonymous inner class has the following features:

- An anonymous inner class must always extend a superclass, or implement an interface, but it cannot have an explicit extends or implements clause.
- An anonymous inner class must implement all abstract methods in the superclass and in the interface.
- An anonymous inner class always uses the default constructor from its superclass to create an instance. If an anonymous inner class implements an interface, the default constructor is `Object()`.

Here is an example (see Listing 3.7) of rewriting ShowTickWithInnerClass.java using anonymous inner classes. The code related to anonymous inner classes is in italic.

```
package eventdemo;

import java.awt.*;
import java.awt.event.*;
import java.applet.*;
import javax.swing.*;
import messagepaneldemo.*;

public class ShowTickWithAnonymousAdapter extends JApplet {
  boolean isStandalone = false;
  MessagePanel messagePanel1 = new MessagePanel();
  Tick tick1 = new Tick();

  /** Initialize the applet */
  public void init() {
    try {
      jbInit();
    }
    catch(Exception e) {
      e.printStackTrace();
    }
  }

  /** Component initialization */
  private void jbInit() throws Exception {
    this.setSize(new Dimension(400,300));
    messagePanel1.setBackground(Color.cyan);
    messagePanel1.setYCoordinate(30);
    // Anonymous inner class adapter
    messagePanel1.addMouseListener(
      new java.awt.event.MouseAdapter() {
      public void mousePressed(MouseEvent e) {
```

Listing 3.7 *ShowTickWithAnonymousAdapter.java*

```
33          messagePanel1_mousePressed(e);
34        }
35        public void mouseReleased(MouseEvent e) {
36          messagePanel1_mouseReleased(e);
37        }
38      });
39      tick1.addTickListener(new eventdemo.TickListener() {
40        public void handleTick(TickEvent e) {
41          tick1_handleTick(e);
42        }
43      });
44      this.getContentPane().add(messagePanel1, BorderLayout.CENTER);
45    }
46
47    void tick1_handleTick(TickEvent e) {
48      messagePanel1.setMessage("Tick count is " + e.getTickCount() +
49        " and tick interval is " + e.getTickInterval());
50    }
51
52    void messagePanel1_mousePressed(MouseEvent e) {
53      tick1.suspend();
54    }
55
56    void messagePanel1_mouseReleased(MouseEvent e) {
57      tick1.resume();
58    }
59  }
```

Listing 3.7 *Continued*

In Lines 31–38 of Listing 3.7, the anonymous class extends `MouseAdapter` convenience adapter class and implemented the `mousePressed` and `mouseReleased` handlers. In Lines 39–43, the anonymous class implements the `TickListener` interface and the `handleTick handler`.

JBuilder lets you choose either anonymous adapters or standard adapters. If you checked the option "Anonymous adapter" for event handling in the Project Property dialog box in Figure 3.13, and repeat the same steps in Example 3.3 using new file named ShowTickWithAnonymousAdapter.java, JBuilder generates the code shown exactly in Listing 3.7.

NOTE

Since anonymous inner classes make the code condensed, from now on all the projects will use anonymous adapters for event handling.

Working with Existing Event Sets

You created `TickEvent` and `TickListener` in the section "Creating Custom Event Sets and Source Components." Most of the time you will not need to create event sets from scratch, since you will be able to use existing event sets. For example, suppose you don't need the tick count and tick interval contained in a tick event. There is no need to create a `TickEvent` class; instead you can use `java.awt.ActionEvent` and let the `Tick` class generate an `ActionEvent` instance when a tick event occurs.

Example 3.4 Developing a Source Component Using Existing Event Sets

This example presents a new component that generates an `ActionEvent` when a tick event occurs. The new source component named `TickUsingActionEvent` is created as shown in Listing 3.8. The code related to generating and handling the action event is in italic. The class `ShowTickUsingActionEvent` is created to test `TickUsingActionEvent`. Their relationship is shown in Figure 3.16.

```
package eventdemo;

import java.util.*;
import java.awt.event.*;

public class TickUsingActionEvent implements Runnable {
  /** A thread to control tick */
  protected Thread thread = null;

  /** Whether the thread is suspended */
  private boolean suspended;

  /** Store Tick listeners in a vector */
  private Vector tickListenerList;

  /** tickCount */
  private long tickCount = 0;

  /** tickInterval */
  private long tickInterval = 1000;

  /** Default constructor */
  public TickUsingActionEvent() {
    // Create and start the thread
    thread = new Thread(this);
    thread.start();
  }

  /** Return tickInterval */
  public long getTickInterval() {
    return tickInterval;
  }

  /** Return tickCount */
  public long getTickCount() {
    return tickCount;
  }

  /** Set a tickInterval */
  public void setTickInterval(long interval) {
    tickInterval = interval;
  }

  /** Run the thread */
  public void run() {
    while (true) {
      try {
        Thread.sleep(tickInterval);
        synchronized (this) {
          while (suspended)
            wait();
        }
```

Listing 3.8 *TickUsingActionEvent.java*

```
        }
        catch (InterruptedException e) {  }

        // Increase the tick count
        tickCount++;

        // Fire ActionEvent
        processEvent(new ActionEvent(this,
          ActionEvent.ACTION_PERFORMED, null));
      }
    }

    /** Resume the thread */
    public synchronized void resume() {
      if (suspended) {
        suspended = false;
        notify();
      }
    }

    /** Suspend the thread */
    public synchronized void suspend() {
      suspended = true;
    }

    /** Register an action event listener */
    public synchronized void addActionListener(ActionListener l) {
      Vector v = tickListenerList == null ?
        new Vector(2) : (Vector)tickListenerList.clone();
      if (!v.contains(l)) {
        v.addElement(l);
        tickListenerList = v;
      }
    }

    /** Remove an action event listener */
    public synchronized void removeActionListener(ActionListener l) {
      if (tickListenerList != null && tickListenerList.contains(l)) {
        tickListenerList.removeElement(l);
      }
    }

    /** Fire TickEvent */
    public void processEvent(ActionEvent e) {
      Vector v;

      synchronized (this) {
        v = (Vector)tickListenerList.clone();
      }

      for (int i=0; i < v.size(); i++) {
        ActionListener listener = (ActionListener)v.elementAt(i);
        listener.actionPerformed(e);
      }
    }
  }
```

Listing 3.8 *continued*

continued

Example 3.4 continued

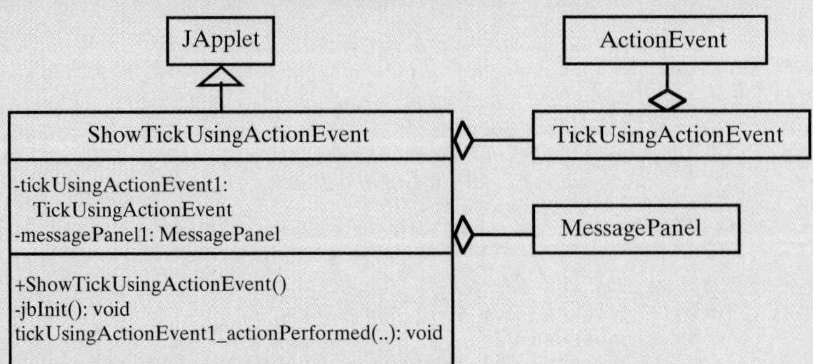

Figure 3.16 *The* `ShowTick` *class uses* `Tick` *and* `MessagePanel` *to control and display a message.*

Follow the steps below to complete the example.

1. Reopen the project eventdemo.jpr and create `ShowTickUsingActionEvent` using the Applet wizard.

2. Create `TickUsingActionEvent` as shown in Listing 3.8, compile, and place it in the component palette.

3. With ShowTickUsingActionEvent.java selected in the project pane, choose the Design tab to display the UI designer. Drop a `MessagePanel` component into the center of the applet to create `messagePanel1`. Change `messagePanel1`'s background to Cyan and `yCoordinate` to 30 in the inspector.

4. Drop the `TickUsingActionEvent` component on the frame. You will see `tickUsingActionEvent1` created in the component tree under the node Other.

5. With `tickUsingActionEvent1` selected in the component tree, switch to the Events page of the component inspector. Select the `actionPerformed` event and double-click its value field in the component inspector. JBuilder generates the adapter and an empty event-handling method, `tickUsingActionEvent1_actionPerformed()`. Fill in the following code in this method:

```
  void tickUsingActionEvent1_actionPerformed(ActionEvent e) {
    messagePanel1.setMessage("Tick count is " +
      tickUsingActionEvent1.getTickCount() + " and tick interval
is "
      +tickUsingActionEvent1.getTickInterval());
  }
```

TIP

The adapter for `ActionEvent` of a source object can be generated by double-clicking the object in the UI designer. This is quicker than generating the adapter from the inspector.

6. ShowTickUsingActionEvent.java is shown in Listing 3.9. Run ShowTickUsingActionEvent.java in the project to test the program. This program should run in the same way as Example 3.1.

```
package eventdemo;

import java.awt.*;
import java.awt.event.*;
import java.applet.*;
import javax.swing.*;
import messagepaneldemo.*;

public class ShowTickUsingActionEvent extends JApplet {
  boolean isStandalone = false;
  MessagePanel messagePanel1 = new MessagePanel();
  TickUsingActionEvent tickUsingActionEvent1 =
    new TickUsingActionEvent();

  /** Initialize the applet */
  public void init() {
    try {
      jbInit();
    }
    catch(Exception e) {
      e.printStackTrace();
    }
  }

  /** Component initialization */
  private void jbInit() throws Exception {
    this.setSize(new Dimension(400,300));
    messagePanel1.setBackground(Color.cyan);
    messagePanel1.setYCoordinate(30);
    tickUsingActionEvent1.addActionListener(
      new java.awt.event.ActionListener() {
      public void actionPerformed(ActionEvent e) {
        tickUsingActionEvent1_actionPerformed(e);
      }
    });
    this.getContentPane().add(messagePanel1, BorderLayout.CENTER);
  }

  void tickUsingActionEvent1_actionPerformed(ActionEvent e) {
    messagePanel1.setMessage("Tick count is " +
      tickUsingActionEvent1.getTickCount() + " and tick interval is "
      +tickUsingActionEvent1.getTickInterval());
  }
}
```

Listing 3.9 *ShowTickUsingActionEvent.java*

Example Review

`TickUsingActionEvent` is very similar to the `Tick` component presented in Example 3.1 except that it utilizes `ActionEvent` to generate events and register listeners. Invoking the following constructor generates an `ActionEvent`.

```
new ActionEvent(this, ActionEvent.ACTION_PERFORMED, null);
```

continued

Example 3.4 continued

The listener interface for `ActionEvent` is an `ActionListener` that contains a handler `actionPerformed` for the listener to implement. The registration methods `addActionListener` and `removeActionListener` are defined in the component for adding and removing listeners.

The `TickEvent` class contains methods `getTickCount()` and `getTickInterval()`, but the `ActionEvent` class does not contain these methods. Therefore, when processing the event using `actionPerformed(ActionEvent e)` handler, you cannot get tick count or tick interval from `e`. To enable the listener to obtain tick count and tick interval, `getTickCount()` and `getTickInterval()` are defined in the `TickUsingActionEvent` class. Since `tickUsingActionEvent1` is an instance of `TickUsingActionEvent`, you can get tick count and tick interval from `tickUsingActionEvent1`.

Chapter Summary

This chapter took you inside the Java delegation model and showed you the basics on event sets, source components, and listener components. The event delegation model separates the tasks of generating events from handling events, thus making it possible to develop source components and listener components independently. Adapters are used to listen for events and delegate them to the right components for handling them. You learned how to hook a listener with a source using standard adapters and anonymous inner class adapters.

You learned how to create a custom event like `TickEvent` by extending `java.util.EventObject` and an event listener interface like `TickListner` by extending `java.util.EventListener`. You can use custom event sets to create a source component like `Tick` and Java-provided event sets to create a source component like `TickUsingActionEvent`.

Review Questions

3.1 If an event class is named *X*Event, what should you name its associated listener interface? If an event listener interface is named *X*Listener, what should you name the registration methods in the source component?

3.2 Is an event class a subclass of `java.util.EventObject`? Is an event listener interface a subinterface of `java.util.EventListener`?

3.3 Show the code that generates and fires the event in the `Tick` component in Listing 3.3.

3.4 How do you register events for multicasting or for unicasting?

3.5 How are the listeners notified of the events?

3.6 How do you use the Implement Interface wizard to generate the code for implementing interfaces?

3.7 What is a convenience adapter? What are the benefits of convenience adapters?

3.8 How do you set the Project Properties to generate anonymous adapters or standard adapters?

3.9 What does JBuilder generate for handling a button click action using standard adapters? What does JBuilder generate for handling a button click action using anonymous adapters?

3.10 The `new` operator cannot be used to create an instance of an interface. Why does JBuilder generate the anonymous adapter using `new TickListener()` in Listing 3.7?

3.11 How do you construct an `ActionEvent`?

Programming Exercises

3.1 The `MessagePanel` class in Example 2.1 is a subclass of `JPanel`; it can fire a `MouseEvent`, `KeyEvent`, and `ComponentEvent`, but not an `ActionEvent`. Modify the `MessagePanel` class so that it can fire an `ActionEvent` when an instance of the `MessagePanel` class is clicked. Name the new class `MessagePanelWithActionEvent`. Test it with a Java applet that displays the current time in a message panel whenever the message panel is clicked, as shown in Figure 3.17.

Figure 3.17 *The current time is displayed whenever you click on the message panel.*

3.2 Develop a project that meets the following requirements:

Create a source component named `MemoryWatch` for monitoring memory. The component generates a `MemoryEvent` when the free memory space exceeds a specified `highLimit` or is below a specified `lowLimit`. The `highLimit` and `lowLimit` are customizable properties in `MemoryWatch`.

Create an event set named `MemoryEvent` and `MemoryListener`. The `MemoryEvent` simply extends `java.util.EventObject` and contains two methods, `freeMemory` and `totalMemory`, which return the free memory and total memory of the system. The `MemoryListener` interface contains two handlers: `sufficientMemory` and `insufficientMemory`. The `sufficientMemory` method is invoked when the free memory space exceeds the specified high limit, and `insufficientMemory` is invoked when the free memory space is lower than the specified low limit.

Develop a listener component that displays free memory, total memory, and whether the memory is sufficient or insufficient when a `MemoryEvent` occurs. Make the listener an applet with a main method to run standalone.

3.3 Create a class named `Hurricane` with properties `name` and `category` and its accessor methods. The `Hurricane` component generates an `ActionEvent` whenever its `category` property is changed. Write a listener that displays the hurricane category. If the category is 2 or greater, a message "Hurricane Warning!!!" is displayed.

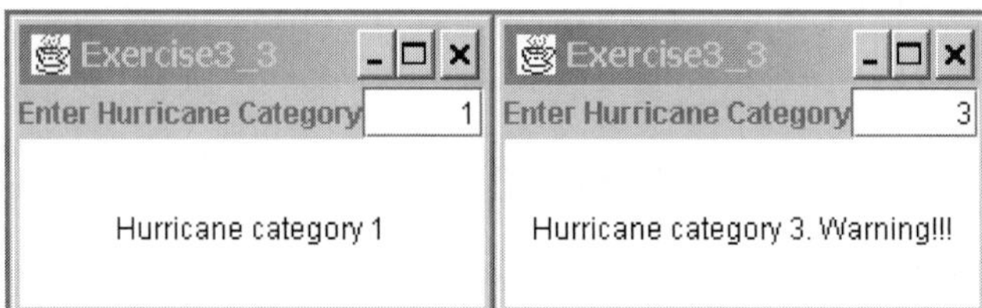

Figure 3.18 *Whenever the hurricane category is changed, an appropriate message is displayed in the message panel.*

CHAPTER 4

Developing and Using Components

Objectives

- Understand the differences between writing components and using components.
- Become familiar with the component-development process.
- Develop JavaBeans components using JBuilder's BeansExpress.
- Use the model-view approach to separate data and logic from the presentation of data.
- Understand the application-development process.
- Use JBuilder Archive Builder to deploy applications and applets.

Introduction

You developed the components `MessagePanel` and `MultipleMessagePanel` in Chapter 2, "Introduction to JavaBeans," and the components `Tick` and `TickUsingActionEvent` in Chapter 3, "Bean Events." From these examples, you learned the techniques of writing components. These techniques are not new. Developing JavaBeans components is nothing more than writing Java classes that follow some fairly strict naming conventions for accessor methods and event registration methods. There are, however, differences between developing components and using components. This chapter explores these differences, and, through comprehensive examples, introduces the process of developing components and using them in rapid Java application development. You will learn how to use JBuilder's BeansExpress to rapidly develop components and create components using the model-view approach.

Developing Components versus Using Components

Throughout the book, you will develop JavaBeans components and use them to build projects. Sometimes, you will play the role of both component writer and component user. It is important to note the differences between developing components and using components.

From a user's perspective, a component consists of properties, methods, and events. The user may use a component to create beans in a builder tool or in scripting programming. The user creates a bean and customizes its behavior by changing properties and writing code to carry out responses to events.

From a writer's perspective, a component is designed for use in a visual environment, where the component properties and events are exposed during design time. In order to expose the properties and events of the component in a builder tool, the component writer must follow property and event design patterns.

There are three major differences between developing components and using components.

- A component is a black box to the component user. The user manipulates the component through public accessor methods and events without knowing the implementation of the component. However, the component writer knows all the details of the component if the component is created from scratch. If the component is derived from a superclass, the writer has access to all the protected data fields and methods of the superclass.
- Components are usually designed for use by many different customers. To make your components useful in a wide range of applications, they should provide a variety of ways for customization through properties, methods, and events.

- Components are designed for reuse. Users can incorporate components in many different combinations, orders, and environments. Therefore, you should design a component that imposes no restrictions on what or when the user can do with it, design the properties to ensure that the user can set properties in any order and with any combination of values, and design events and methods to function independently of their order of occurrence at runtime.

Component-Development Process

As in the development of any software, developing JavaBeans components requires an engineering approach that involves the following steps:

1. Understand the requirements of the component and determine what functions it requires.

2. Design the properties, methods, and events to support the functions required by the component.

3. Based on the requirements, decide whether to create a UI component or a non-UI component. A UI component must extend `java.awt.Component` or its subclass. A non-UI component can extend any appropriate class. A UI component can have drawings on it and can become part of the user interface of the application. A non-UI component is invisible on the UI designer, but generally provides encapsulated functionality to interact with the UI components. The `MessagePanel` component in Example 2.1, "Writing a Simple JavaBeans Component," is a UI component, but the `Tick` component in Example 3.1, "Creating a Custom Event Set and a Source Component," is a non-UI component.

4. Create properties. Choose the names for properties to follow the JavaBeans property naming convention. Decide whether to use the default property editor or a customized property editor. Creating a customized property editor will be introduced in Chapter 11, "Bean Introspection and Customization."

5. Create the customized events your component needs by writing their event classes and event listener interfaces.

6. Implement the code that generates and fires events. Implement event registration methods and choose the names according to the naming conventions.

7. Implement public methods. Component methods encapsulate the behavior of the component. They are standard Java methods that can be called from other components. Unlike accessor methods, component methods cannot change the behavior of the bean during design time. The component methods are used only at runtime.

8. Create a `BeanInfo` class for the component to customize the exposure of the bean's properties and events, if necessary. Creating a component's `BeanInfo` class will be introduced in Chapter 11, "Bean Introspection and Customization."

9. Compile, install the component in the component palette, and test the component.

NOTE

The development process is cyclic. If the requirements are changed, you will have to redevelop or modify the component following the development process.

Components can be efficiently created using JBuilder's BeansExpress. In the following section, you will apply the development process and use BeansExpress to create a component for an image viewer and an analog clock.

NOTE

BeansExpress is a feature of JBuilder Professional and Enterprise. You may hand-code the program without using BeansExpress, if you are using JBuilder Foundation.

Using BeansExpress to Create Properties

BeansExpress is a visual bean designer that helps to create the JavaBeans component without writing extensive code. To activate BeansExpress, select the Bean tab in the content pane from the AppBrowser, as shown in Figure 4.1. BeansExpress contains the following tabs:

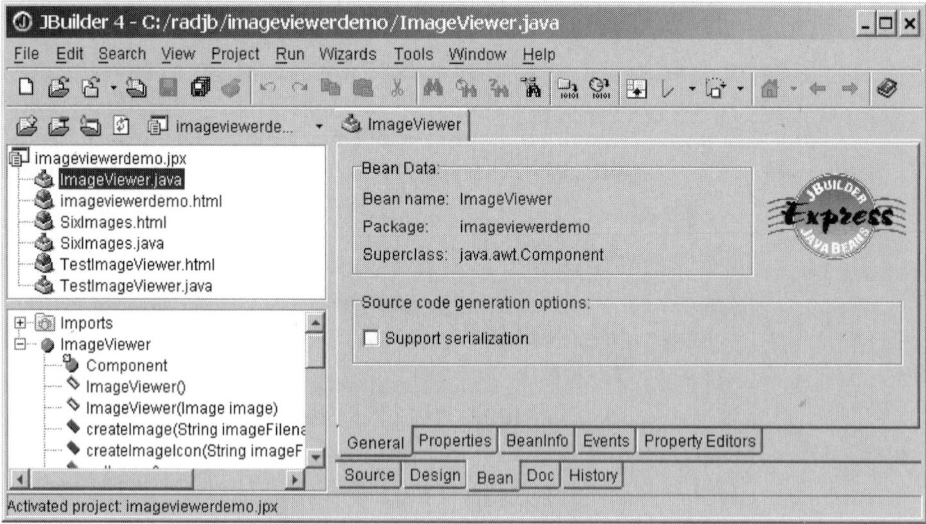

Figure 4.1 *You can use JBuilder's BeansExpress to assist in creating the bean component.*

- General: Displays general information about the bean. You can set the options for specifying "Support serialization."

- Properties: You can use the property designer to add or remove properties.
- BeanInfo: You can use the BeanInfo designer to customize the exposure of properties and events to the component users.
- Events: You can use the event designer to add or remove events that your component may generate.
- Property Editors: You can create customized property editors.

You will learn how to use the property designer to create properties in Examples 4.1 and 4.2, and how to use the event designer in Example 4.3. In Chapter 11, "Bean Introspection and Customization," you will learn how to use the BeanInfo designer and the property editor designer to generate `BeanInfo` classes and custom property editors.

Example 4.1 Creating an Image Viewer

This example creates an image viewer that displays an image in a component. This bean allows the user to customize an image viewer through the following properties:

- `image`: The image in the image viewer.
- `imageFilename`: The file name of the image.
- `stretched`: A `boolean` value indicating whether the image is stretched.
- `xCoordinate`: The x-Coordinate of the upper-left corner of the image in the component.
- `yCoordinate`: The y-Coordinate of the upper-left corner of the image in the component.

Figure 4.2 shows the properties of an `ImageViewer` bean in the component inspector.

This example demonstrates how BeansExpress can be used to create the properties. Here are the steps in creating the component:

1. Create a new project named imageviewerdemo.jpx and create a Java class named `ImageViewer` that extends `java.awt.Component` using the Class wizard.
2. With ImageViewer.java selected in the project pane, choose the Bean tab in the content pane to switch to BeansExpress, as shown in Figure 4.1.
3. Choose the Properties tab at the bottom of BeansExpress to switch to the Properties page, as shown in Figure 4.3.

continued

Example 4.1 continued

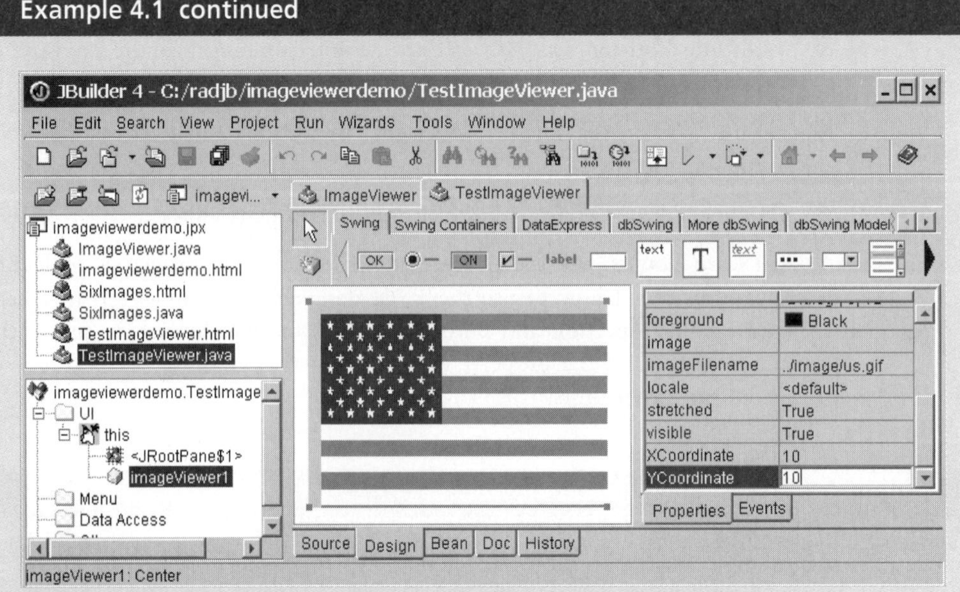

Figure 4.2 *When using the* `ImageViewer` *bean, you can customize it to suit your needs with a variety of properties provided by the component.*

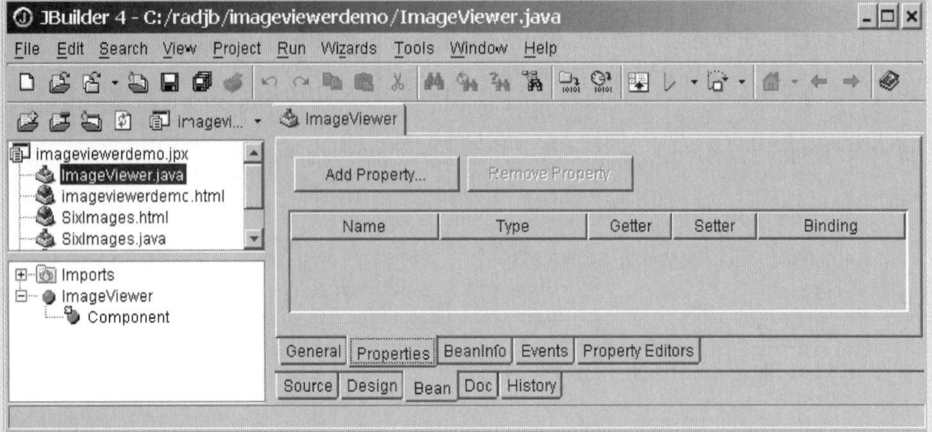

Figure 4.3 *You can add or remove properties from the Properties page in BeansExpress.*

4. Click the Add Property button to bring up the New Property dialog box, as shown in Figure 4.4. Enter `image` in the Property Name field and `Image` in the Type field. Press Apply to let JBuilder generate the source code for the property. You can view the generated source code for the data member and the accessor methods by choosing the Source tab in the content pane.

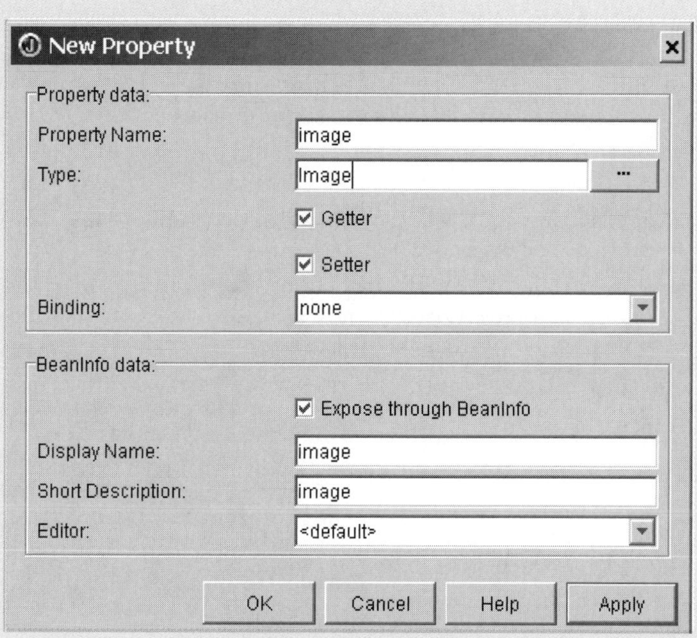

Figure 4.4 *The New Property dialog box lets you specify the property information, such as name, type, and editor.*

5. Repeatedly apply Step 4 to add the additional properties `imageFilename` (`String` type), `stretched` (`boolean` type), `xCoordinate` (`int` type), and `yCoordinate` (`int` type). The Properties page of BeansExpress is shown in Figure 4.5.

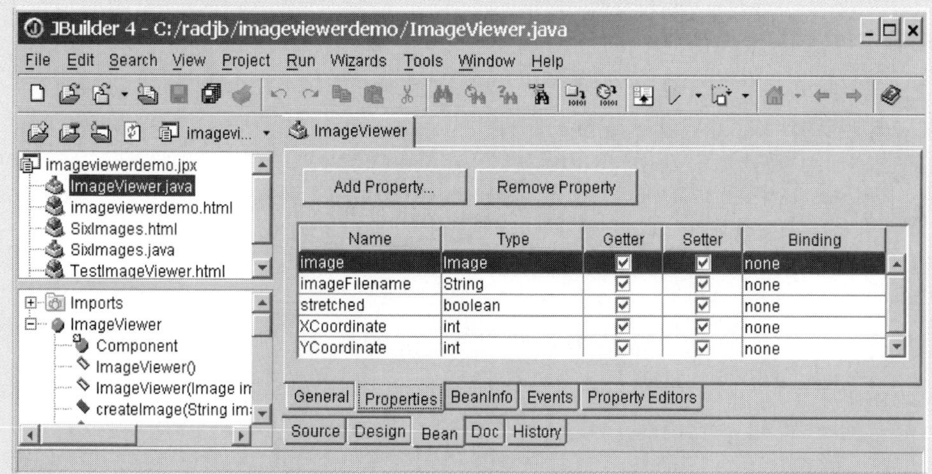

Figure 4.5 *The properties are displayed in the Properties page of BeansExpress.*

continued

Example 4.1 continued

TIP

I recommend providing default values for properties for the following three reasons:

- A default value gives the user an example of the property value.
- Some builder tools will not display a property unless a default value is provided for it.
- Using default values helps avoid runtime errors. For example, when using a property of object type, a null pointer exception would occur if the property were not initialized.

6. Override the `paint` method to draw the image in the component as shown in Listing 4.1.

7. Modify the set methods for the properties to repaint the component, as shown in Listing 4.1.

```
package imageviewerdemo;

import java.awt.*;
import javax.swing.*;
import java.net.URL;
import java.awt.image.ImageProducer;

public class ImageViewer extends Component {
  private Image image = null;
  private String imageFilename = "";
  private boolean stretched = true;
  private int xCoordinate;
  private int yCoordinate;

  public ImageViewer() {
  }

  public ImageViewer(Image image) {
    this.image = image;
    repaint();
  }

  public void setImageFilename(String imageFilename) {
    this.imageFilename = imageFilename;
    image = createImage(imageFilename, this);
    repaint();
  }

  /** Create an image icon from an image file through the resource
   * of the object.
   */
  public static ImageIcon createImageIcon(String imageFilename,
    Object object) {
    try {
      URL url = object.getClass().getResource(imageFilename);
      return new ImageIcon(url);
    }
```

Listing 4.1 *ImageViewer.java*

```
    catch (Exception ex) {
    }

    return null;
  }

  /** Create an image from an image file through the resource
   * of the object.
   */
  public static Image createImage(String imageFilename,
    Object object) {
    ImageIcon imageIcon = createImageIcon(imageFilename, object);
    if (imageIcon != null)
      return imageIcon.getImage();
    else
      return null;
  }

  public String getImageFilename() {
    return imageFilename;
  }

  public void paint(Graphics g) {
    if (image != null)
      if (isStretched())
        g.drawImage(image, xCoordinate, yCoordinate,
          getSize().width, getSize().height, this);
      else
        g.drawImage(image, xCoordinate, yCoordinate, this);
  }

  public void setStretched(boolean newStretched) {
    stretched = newStretched;
    repaint();
  }

  public void setImage(Image image) {
    this.image = image;
    repaint();
  }

  public Image getImage() {
    return image;
  }

  public boolean isStretched() {
    return stretched;
  }

  public void setXCoordinate(int newXCoordinate) {
    xCoordinate = newXCoordinate;
    repaint();
  }

  public int getXCoordinate() {
    return xCoordinate;
  }

```

Listing 4.1 *Continued*

continued

Example 4.1 continued

```
    public void setYCoordinate(int newYCoordinate) {
      yCoordinate = newYCoordinate;
      repaint();
    }

    public int getYCoordinate() {
      return yCoordinate;
    }
  }
```

To test the component, compile ImageViewer.java and install it in the component palette. You may simply drop the bean on the UI designer, change its properties from the component inspector, and see how the bean responds to the changes. Below you will use it to display six images in an applet. Here are the steps to complete the project.

1. Create a new applet named `SixImages` in the imageviewerdemo project using the Applet wizard. With SixImages.java selected in the project pane, switch to the UI designer. Set `layout` of the applet to `GridLayout`. In the component inspector of `gridLayout1`, set `rows` to 2, `hgap` to 10, and `vgap` to 10, so as to have three images in one row and three in the other row, with a 10-pixel gap horizontally and vertically.

2. Drop `ImageViewer` six times to the applet. Set the imageFilename properties to /image/us.gif, /image/ca.gif, /image/india.gif, /image/china.gif, /image/uk.gif, and /image/norway.gif. The generated source code for SixImages.java is shown in Listing 4.2. Figure 4.6 contains a sample run of the program.

Figure 4.6 *The* `ImageViewer` *bean is used to display six images.*

```
package imageviewerdemo;

import java.awt.*;
import java.awt.event.*;
import java.applet.*;
import javax.swing.*;

public class SixImages extends JApplet {
  boolean isStandalone = false;
  GridLayout gridLayout1 = new GridLayout();
  ImageViewer imageViewer1 = new ImageViewer();
  ImageViewer imageViewer2 = new ImageViewer();
  ImageViewer imageViewer3 = new ImageViewer();
  ImageViewer imageViewer4 = new ImageViewer();
  ImageViewer imageViewer5 = new ImageViewer();
  ImageViewer imageViewer6 = new ImageViewer();

  /** Construct the applet */
  public SixImages() {
  }

  /** Initialize the applet */
  public void init() {
    try {
      jbInit();
    }
    catch(Exception e) {
      e.printStackTrace();
    }
  }

  /** Component initialization */
  private void jbInit() throws Exception {
    gridLayout1.setRows(2);
    gridLayout1.setColumns(3);
    gridLayout1.setHgap(10);
    gridLayout1.setVgap(10);
    this.setSize(new Dimension(400,300));
    this.getContentPane().setLayout(gridLayout1);
    imageViewer1.setImageFilename("/image/us.gif");
    imageViewer2.setImageFilename("/image/ca.gif");
    imageViewer3.setImageFilename("/image/india.gif");
    imageViewer4.setImageFilename("/image/uk.gif");
    imageViewer5.setImageFilename("/image/china.gif");
    imageViewer6.setImageFilename("/image/norway.gif");
    this.getContentPane().add(imageViewer1, null);
    this.getContentPane().add(imageViewer2, null);
    this.getContentPane().add(imageViewer3, null);
    this.getContentPane().add(imageViewer4, null);
    this.getContentPane().add(imageViewer5, null);
    this.getContentPane().add(imageViewer6, null);
  }
}
```

Listing 4.2 *SixImages.java*

Example Review

The `Component` class is the root of all Java graphical user interface components. Since `ImageViewer` extends `java.awt.Component`, it can be used with both AWT components and Swing components.

continued

Example 4.1 continued

The `ImageViewer` class in Listing 4.1 provides two static methods, `createImageIcon` (Lines 29–42) and `createImage` (Lines 44–54). The `createImageIcon(imageFilename, object)` method returns an `ImageIcon` from the image file name through the resource of the object. The `createImage(imageFilename, object)` method returns an `Image` instance from the image file through the resource of the object.

The image icon is created using `new ImageIcon(url)` in the `createImageIcon` method, where `url` is obtained using the `getResource` method in a `Class` instance of the object. You may create an image icon directly from the absolute path of the image file, as follows:

```
new ImageIcon("c:\\radjb\\imageviewerdemo\\someimage.gif");
```

This approach is simple, but it works only with standalone applications. To load images in Java applets, you have to obtain the URL of the image and load the image through it. This approach works for both Java applications and applets.

The `createImage` method invokes the `createImageIcon` method to create an image icon and then returns the image from the image icon using the `getImage` method.

The `imageFilename` property enables you to set a filename for the image. The `setImageFilename` method sets the `imageFilename` and creates the image for the file.

The `ImageViewer` component also provides the `image` property. You can set the image directly using the `setImage` method. This is convenient if your program knows the image but not the filename for the image. This is a good example of a JavaBeans component that provides many ways to use the bean. You can use the `imageFilename` property or the image property to set the image for `ImageViewer`, whichever is convenient.

NOTE

The `createImageIcon` method and `createImage` method could have been eliminated and combined with the `setImageFilename` method. The purpose of creating these two static methods is for use by other programs. These two methods will be used throughout the book to create image icons and images.

NOTE

To paint a non-Swing component, you need to override the `paint` method in the `Component` class. To paint a Swing component, you need to override the `paintComponent` method in the `JComponent` class.

NOTE

You can use images in the Swing components, such as `JLabel` and `JButton`, but the images are not stretchable and image filenames cannot be used directly with these components. The `ImageViewer` component provides better support for displaying images.

TIP

If `ImageViewer` instances are not placed in the right order inside the content pane of the applet, you can either drag and move them in the UI designer or modify the source code.

Example 4.2 Creating a Clock Component

This example creates a useful bean for displaying an analog clock. This bean allows the user to customize a clock through the following properties:

- `secondHandColor`: The color of the second hand.
- `minuteHandColor`: The color of the minute hand.
- `hourHandColor`: The color of the hour hand.
- `headerColor`: The color of header. Header is an optional title for the clock, displayed above the analog clock.
- `header`: The contents of the header (a string).
- `showingHeader`: A `boolean` value indicating whether the header is displayed.
- `digitalDateTimeColor`: The color of the optional digital time, displayed below the analog clock.
- `showingDigitalDateTime`: A `boolean` value indicating whether the digital time is displayed.
- `dateStyle`: An `int` value representing four formats for displaying date. The values are `DateFormat.FULL` (0), `DateFormat.LONG` (1), `DateFormat.MEDIUM` (2), and `DateFormat.SHORT` (3).
- `timeStyle`: An `int` value representing four formats for displaying time. The values are `DateFormat.FULL` (0), `DateFormat.LONG` (1), `DateFormat.MEDIUM` (2), and `DateFormat.SHORT` (3).
- `usingTimeZoneID`: A `boolean` value indicating whether the `timeZoneID` property is used to set the `timeZoneOffset` property.

continued

Example 4.2 continued

- `timeZoneID`: A string representing a valid time zone. All the time zone IDs can be obtained in `TimeZone.getAvailableIDs()`.
- `timeZoneOffset`: An `int` value representing a time zone offset from GMT. The valid values are between -12 and 12.
- `running`: A boolean value indicating whether the clock is running.

Figure 4.7 shows the properties of a `Clock` bean in the component inspector.

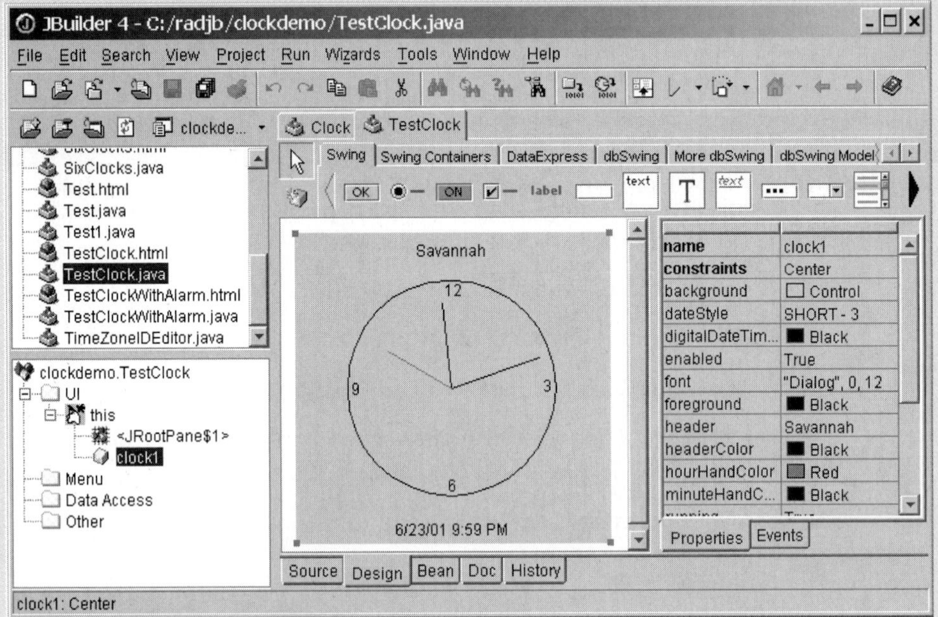

Figure 4.7 *When using the Clock bean, you can customize it to suit your needs with a variety of properties provided by the component.*

The `Clock` component also provides two public methods, `start()` and `stop()`, to let the component user start and stop the clock.

Here are the steps in creating the component:

1. Create a new project named clockdemo.jpr, and create a Java class named `Clock` that extends `java.awt.Component` using the Class wizard.
2. With Clock.java selected in the project pane, choose the Bean tab in the content pane to switch to BeansExpress, as shown in Figure 4.1.
3. Choose the Properties tab at the bottom of BeansExpress to switch to the Properties page, as shown in Figure 4.8.

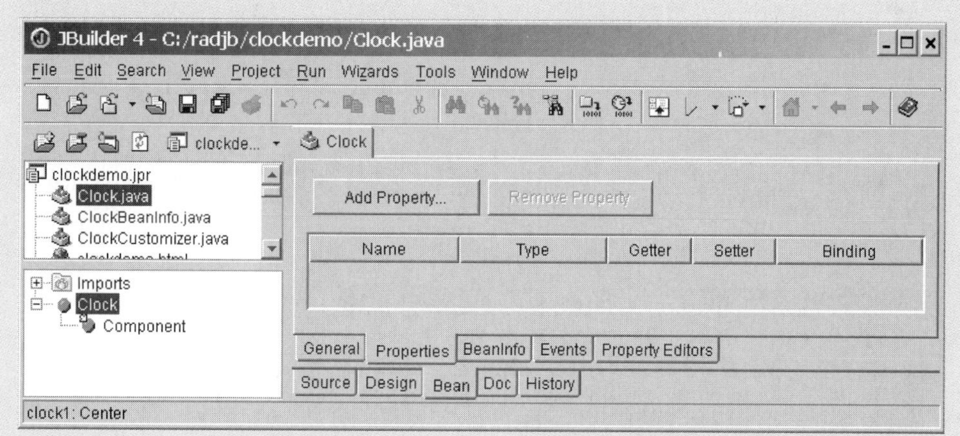

Figure 4.8 *You can add or remove properties from the Properties page in BeansExpress.*

4. Click the Add Property button to bring up the New Property dialog box, as shown in Figure 4.9. Enter `secondHandColor` in the Property Name field and `java.awt.Color` in the Type field. Press Apply to let JBuilder generate the source code for the property. If you choose the Source tab in the content pane, you will see that the data member and the accessor methods were automatically generated.

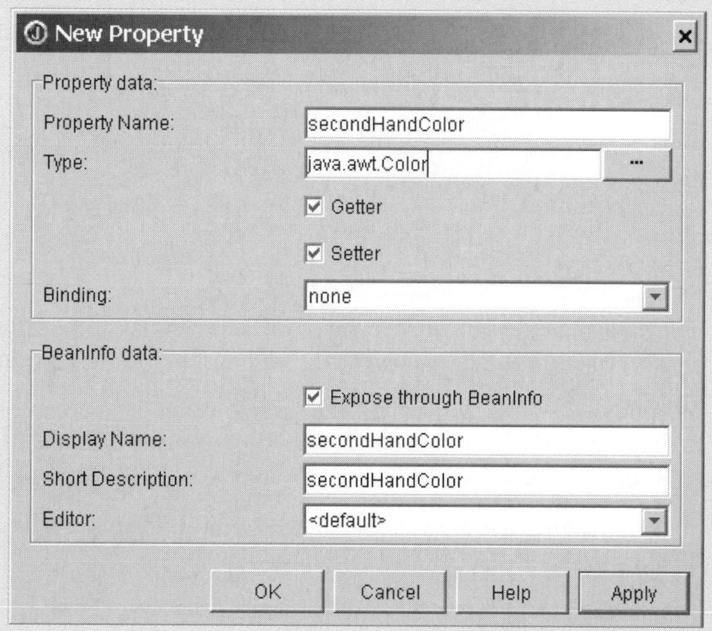

Figure 4.9 *The New Property dialog box lets you specify the property information, such as name, type, and editor.*

continued

Example 4.2 continued

5. Repeatedly apply Step 4 to add the additional properties `minuteHandColor`, `hourHandColor`, `digitalTimeColor`, `headerColor`, `running`, `showing-DigitalTime`, `showingHeader`, `header`, `timeZoneID`, `timeZoneOffset`, and `usingTimeZoneID`. The Properties page of the BeansExpress is shown in Figure 4.10.

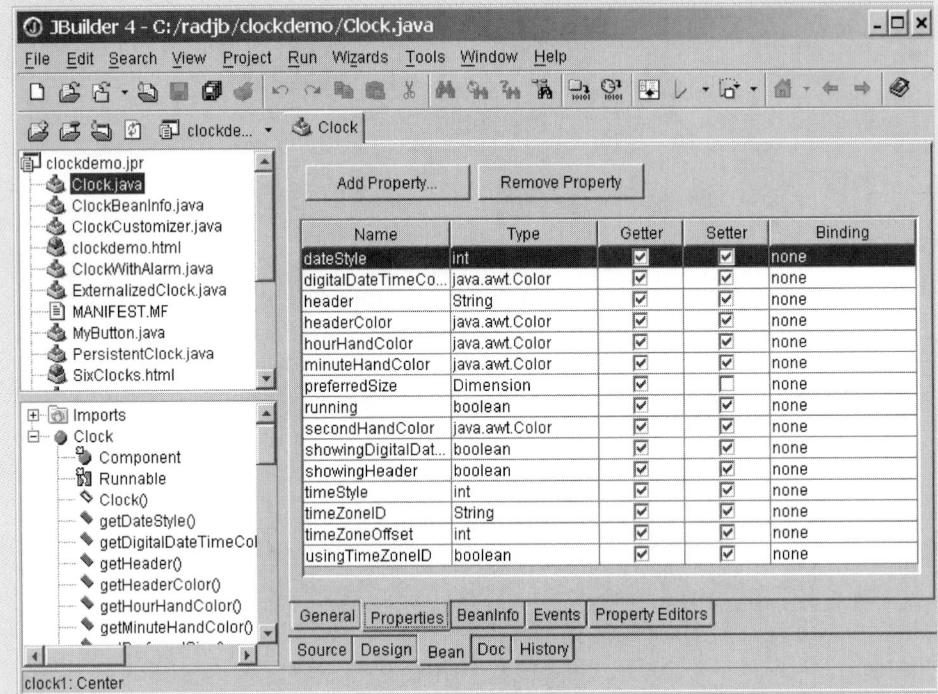

Figure 4.10 *The properties are displayed in the Properties page of BeansExpress.*

6. Modify the default implementation for the `setRunning` method and set the default values of the properties, as shown in Listing 4.3 (Lines 79–86).

7. Choose Wizards, Implement Interface to bring up the Implement Interface wizard. Choose and click `java.lang.Runnable` from the dialog box to generate code for implementing this interface.

8. Declare an instance of `Thread`, named `thread`, for running the clock and drawing it.

9. Override the `paint` method to paint the clock every second, as shown in Listing 4.3 (Lines 157–231).

10. Create public methods `start()` (Lines 247–253) and `stop()` (Lines 255–260) for starting and stopping the clock, as shown in Listing 4.3.

```
package clockdemo;

import java.awt.*;
import javax.swing.*;
import java.lang.Runnable;
import java.util.*;
import java.text.*;
import java.io.*;

public class Clock extends Component implements Runnable {
  // Create a thread to control clock running
  protected transient Thread thread;
  private java.awt.Color secondHandColor = Color.black;
  private java.awt.Color minuteHandColor = Color.black;
  private java.awt.Color hourHandColor = Color.red;
  private java.awt.Color digitalDateTimeColor = Color.black;
  private java.awt.Color headerColor = Color.black;
  private boolean running;
  private boolean showingDigitalDateTime = true;
  // TimeStyle 0-FULL, 1-LONG, 2-MEDIUM, 3-SHORT
  private int timeStyle = 3;
  // DateStyle 0-FULL, 1-LONG, 2-MEDIUM, 3-SHORT
  private int dateStyle = 3;
  private boolean showingHeader = true;
  private java.lang.String header = "Savannah";
  private java.lang.String timeZoneID = "EST";
  private int timeZoneOffset;
  private boolean usingTimeZoneID = true;

  /** Create TimeZone */
  protected TimeZone tz = TimeZone.getDefault();

  public Clock() {
    // Start clock
    setRunning(true);
  }

  public java.awt.Color getSecondHandColor() {
    return secondHandColor;
  }

  public void setSecondHandColor(java.awt.Color newSecondHandColor) {
    secondHandColor = newSecondHandColor;
  }

  public void setMinuteHandColor(java.awt.Color newMinuteHandColor) {
    minuteHandColor = newMinuteHandColor;
  }

  public java.awt.Color getMinuteHandColor() {
    return minuteHandColor;
  }

  public void setHourHandColor(java.awt.Color newHourHandColor) {
    hourHandColor = newHourHandColor;
  }

  public java.awt.Color getHourHandColor() {
    return hourHandColor;
  }

```

Listing 4.3 *Clock.java*

continued

Example 4.2 continued

```
  public void setDigitalDateTimeColor(
    java.awt.Color newDigitalDateTimeColor) {
    digitalDateTimeColor = newDigitalDateTimeColor;
  }

  public java.awt.Color getDigitalDateTimeColor() {
    return digitalDateTimeColor;
  }

  public void setHeaderColor(java.awt.Color newHeaderColor) {
    headerColor = newHeaderColor;
  }

  public java.awt.Color getHeaderColor() {
    return headerColor;
  }

  /** Start the clock */
  public void setRunning(boolean newRunning) {
    running = newRunning;
    if (running)
      start();
    else
      stop();
  }

  public boolean isRunning() {
    return running;
  }

  public void setShowingDigitalDateTime(boolean
    newShowingDigitalDateTime) {
    showingDigitalDateTime = newShowingDigitalDateTime;
  }

  public boolean isShowingDigitalDateTime() {
    return showingDigitalDateTime;
  }

  public void setTimeStyle(int newtimeStyle) {
    timeStyle = newtimeStyle;
  }

  public int getTimeStyle() {
    return timeStyle;
  }

  public void setDateStyle(int newDateStyle) {
    dateStyle = newDateStyle;
  }

  public int getDateStyle() {
    return dateStyle;
  }

  public void setShowingHeader(boolean newShowingHeader) {
    showingHeader = newShowingHeader;
  }

```

Listing 4.3 *Continued*

```
  public boolean isShowingHeader() {
    return showingHeader;
  }

  public void setHeader(java.lang.String newHeader) {
    header = newHeader;
  }

  public java.lang.String getHeader() {
    return header;
  }

  public void setTimeZoneID(java.lang.String newTimeZoneID) {
    timeZoneID = newTimeZoneID;
  }

  public java.lang.String getTimeZoneID() {
    return timeZoneID;
  }

  public void setTimeZoneOffset(int newTimeZoneOffset) {
    timeZoneOffset = newTimeZoneOffset;
  }

  public int getTimeZoneOffset() {
    return tz.getRawOffset()/(1000*3600);
  }

  public void setUsingTimeZoneID(boolean newUsingTimeZoneID) {
    usingTimeZoneID = newUsingTimeZoneID;
  }

  public boolean isUsingTimeZoneID() {
    return usingTimeZoneID;
  }

  /** Display the clock*/
  public void paint(Graphics g) {
    int clockRadius = (int)Math.min(getWidth(), getHeight()*0.7*0.5);
    int xCenter = (getWidth())/2;
    int yCenter = (getHeight())/2;

    // Draw circle
    g.setColor(Color.black);
    g.drawOval(xCenter - clockRadius, yCenter - clockRadius,
      2*clockRadius, 2*clockRadius);
    g.drawString("12", xCenter-5, yCenter-clockRadius+12);
    g.drawString("9", xCenter-clockRadius+3, yCenter+5);
    g.drawString("3", xCenter+clockRadius-10, yCenter+3);
    g.drawString("6", xCenter-3, yCenter+clockRadius-3);

    if (usingTimeZoneID)
      tz = TimeZone.getTimeZone(timeZoneID);
    else
      tz.setRawOffset(timeZoneOffset*1000*3600);

    // Get current time using GregorianCalendar
    GregorianCalendar cal = new GregorianCalendar(tz);

    // Draw second hand
    int s = (int)cal.get(GregorianCalendar.SECOND);
    int sLength = (int)(clockRadius*0.9);
```

Listing 4.3 *Continued*

continued

Example 4.2 continued

```
      int secondx =
        (int)(xCenter + sLength*Math.sin(s*(2*Math.PI/60)));
      int secondy =
        (int)(yCenter - sLength*Math.cos(s*(2*Math.PI/60)));
      g.setColor(secondHandColor);
      g.drawLine(xCenter, yCenter, secondx, secondy);

      // Draw minute hand
      int m = (int)cal.get(GregorianCalendar.MINUTE);
      int mLength = (int)(clockRadius*0.8);
      int minutex =
        (int)(xCenter + mLength*Math.sin(m*(2*Math.PI/60)));
      int minutey =
        (int)(yCenter - mLength*Math.cos(m*(2*Math.PI/60)));
      g.setColor(minuteHandColor);
      g.drawLine(xCenter, yCenter, minutex, minutey);

      // Draw hour hand
      int h = (int)cal.get(GregorianCalendar.HOUR_OF_DAY);
      int hLength = (int)(clockRadius*0.7);
      int hourx =
        (int)(xCenter + hLength*Math.sin((h+m/60.0)*(2*Math.PI/12)));
      int houry =
        (int)(yCenter - hLength*Math.cos((h+m/60.0)*(2*Math.PI/12)));
      g.setColor(hourHandColor);
      g.drawLine(xCenter, yCenter, hourx, houry);

      if (showingHeader) {
        // Display header
        FontMetrics fm = g.getFontMetrics();
        g.setColor(headerColor);
        g.drawString(header, (getWidth() -
          fm.stringWidth(header))/2, (yCenter-clockRadius)/2);
      }

      if (showingDigitalDateTime) {
        // Set display format in specified style, locale and timezone
        DateFormat myFormat = DateFormat.getDateTimeInstance
          (dateStyle, timeStyle, getLocale());
        myFormat.setTimeZone(tz);

        // Display time
        String today = myFormat.format(cal.getTime());
        FontMetrics fm = g.getFontMetrics();
        g.setColor(digitalDateTimeColor);
        g.drawString(today, (getWidth() -
          fm.stringWidth(today))/2, yCenter+clockRadius+30);
      }
    }

    /** Run the clock */
    public void run() {
      //TODO: implement this java.lang.Runnable method;
      while (true) {
        if (thread == null) return;

        try {
          thread.sleep(1000);
        }
```

Listing 4.3 *Continued*

```
        catch (InterruptedException e) {}
        repaint();
      }
    }

    /** Start the clock */
    public void start() {
      if (thread == null) {
        thread = new Thread(this);
        thread.start();
      }
    }

    /** Stop the clock */
    public void stop() {
      if (thread != null) {
        thread = null;
      }
    }

    /** Set the preferred size for the clock */
    public Dimension getPreferredSize() {
      return new Dimension(200, 200);
    }
  }
```

Listing 4.3 *Continued*

To test the component, compile Clock.java and install it in the component palette. You may simply drop the bean on the UI designer, change its properties from the component inspector, and see how the bean responds to the changes. Below you will use it to develop a program that shows a set of clocks for displaying the time in London, Paris, Savannah, Chicago, Denver, and San Francisco.

Here are the steps to complete the project.

1. Create a new applet named `SixClocks` in the clockdemo project using the Applet wizard. With SixClocks.java selected in the project pane, switch to the UI designer. Set `layout` of the applet to `GridLayout`. In the component inspector of `gridLayout1`, set `rows` to 2, `hgap` to 10, and `vgap` to 10, so as to have three clocks in one row and three in the other row, with a 10-pixel gap horizontally and vertically.

2. Add six clocks to the applet. Set the appropriate header and time zone ID for each clock. The generated source code for SixClocks.java is shown in Listing 4.4. Figure 4.11 contains a sample run of the program.

```
package clockdemo;

import java.awt.*;
import java.awt.event.*;
import java.applet.*;
import javax.swing.*;

```

Listing 4.4 *SixClocks.java*

continued

Example 4.2 continued

```
public class SixClocks extends JApplet {
  boolean isStandalone = false;
  GridLayout gridLayout1 = new GridLayout();
  Clock clock1 = new Clock();
  Clock clock2 = new Clock();
  Clock clock3 = new Clock();
  Clock clock4 = new Clock();
  Clock clock5 = new Clock();
  Clock clock6 = new Clock();

  /** Initialize the applet */
  public void init() {
    try {
      jbInit();
    }
    catch(Exception e) {
      e.printStackTrace();
    }
  }

  /** Component initialization */
  private void jbInit() throws Exception {
    gridLayout1.setRows(2);
    gridLayout1.setColumns(3);
    gridLayout1.setHgap(10);
    gridLayout1.setVgap(10);
    this.setSize(new Dimension(511, 368));
    this.getContentPane().setLayout(gridLayout1);
    clock1.setHeader("London");
    clock1.setTimeZoneID("GMT");
    clock6.setHeader("Paris");
    clock6.setTimeZoneID("PMT");
    clock5.setHeader("Savannah");
    clock5.setTimeZoneID("EST");
    clock4.setHeader("Chicago");
    clock4.setTimeZoneID("CST");
    clock3.setHeader("Denver");
    clock3.setTimeZoneID("MST");
    clock2.setHeader("San Francisco");
    clock2.setTimeZoneID("PST");
    this.getContentPane().add(clock1, null);
    this.getContentPane().add(clock6, null);
    this.getContentPane().add(clock5, null);
    this.getContentPane().add(clock4, null);
    this.getContentPane().add(clock3, null);
    this.getContentPane().add(clock2, null);
  }
}
```

Listing 4.4 *Continued*

Example Review

In the `Clock` component, `thread` is an instance of `Thread`. Since it cannot be serialized, the `transient` modifier was used to mark it so that `thread` is not stored when a `Clock` object is stored. If `transient` were not used, this example would work fine, because no objects are stored during design time in JBuilder. However, it might be erroneous if it is used in another development tool. To ensure

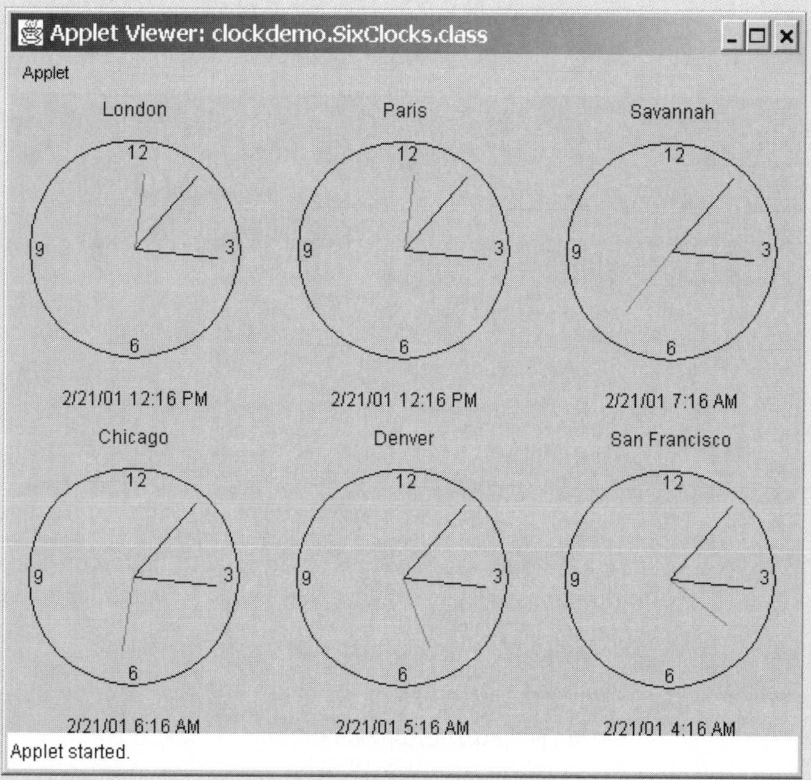

Figure 4.11 *The Clock bean is used to develop a set of six clocks.*

portability, make your beans serializable by marking `transient` on all nonserializable data fields. More discussions on the `transient` keyword and bean serialization will be presented in Chapter 9, "Bean Persistence and Versioning."

Since the `Thread thread` is `protected` rather than `private`, `thread` can be referenced in a subclass of `Clock` in Example 9.4, "Making the Clock Component Persistent," and Example 9.5, "Using the `Externalizable` Interface."

To make the bean versatile and useful, a variety of properties are provided in `Clock`. For instance, you can set the clock using the time zone ID or using the offset to the GMT time, whichever is convenient.

NOTE

The `timeZoneOffset` value is automatically adjusted when `timeZoneID` is changed. However, the reversal is not true. A time zone may have several IDs. For instance, IET (Indiana Eastern Time) and CST (Central Standard Time) are the same during the summer, and IET and EST (Eastern Standard Time) are the same during the winter. Therefore, when you set the `timeZoneOffset` property, the `timezoneID` property cannot be automatically adjusted.

Using BeansExpress to Create Events

In the preceding example you created a `Clock` component. Now your customers want to have an alarm clock. In this section, you will learn how to use Beans-Express to help develop a new clock component that fires an `ActionEvent` for the alarm.

Example 4.3 Creating an Alarm Clock

This example creates an alarm clock, named `ClockWithAlarm`, which extends the `Clock` component built in Example 4.2. This component contains two new properties:

- `alarmDate`: A string consisting of year, month, and day, separated by commas. For example, 1998,5,13 represents the year 1998, month 5, and day 13.
- `alarmTime`: A string consisting of hour, minute, and second, separated by commas. For example, 10,45,2 represents 10 hours, 45 minutes, and 2 seconds.

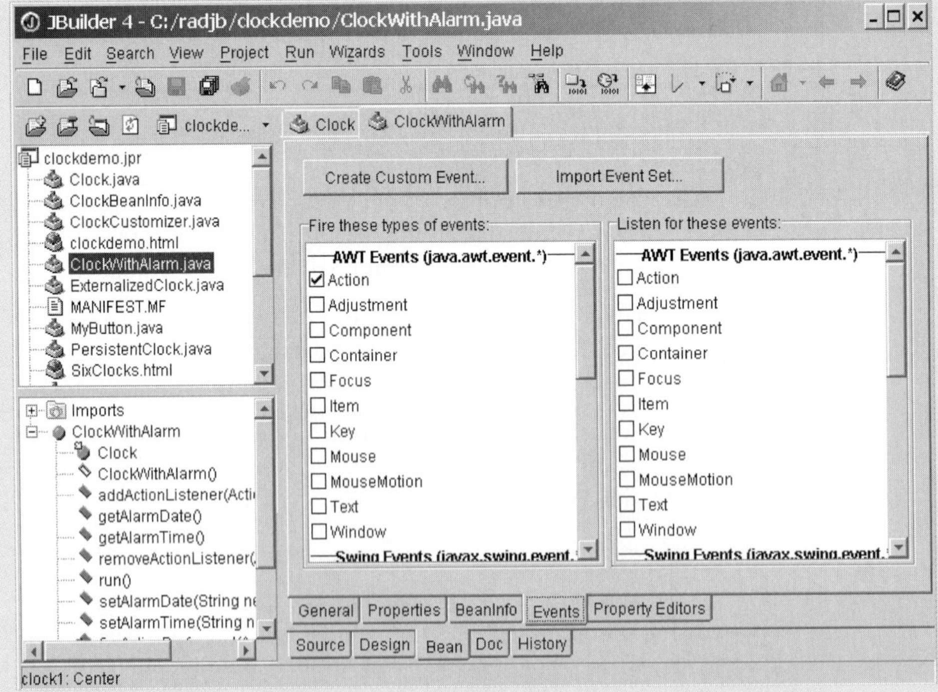

Figure 4.12 *You can use BeansExpress to generate event registration methods and the code for firing events.*

When the clock time matches the alarm time, `ClockWithAlarm` fires an `ActionEvent`.

Follow the steps below to create the `ClockWithAlarm` component.

1. Reopen the clockdemo project created in Example 4.2. Create a new class `ClockWithAlarm` that extends `Clock` using the Class wizard.
2. With ClockWithAlarm.java selected in the project pane, choose the Bean tab in the content pane to switch to BeansExpress. Add properties `alarmDate` and `alarmTime` using the Properties page in BeansExpress.
3. Choose the Events tab in BeansExpress to switch to the Events page, as shown in Figure 4.12. Check the box for Action in the "Fires these types of events" column. Checking it triggers JBuilder to automatically generate the event registration methods and the code for firing the `ActionEvent`. Unchecking the box would remove the code.
4. Initialize `alarmTime` and `alarmDate` in the `ClockWithAlarm` constructor, and override the `run()` method to run the clock and fire an `ActionEvent` when the clock matches the alarm time so to notify the listeners of the event, as shown in Listing 4.5.

```
package clockdemo;

import java.awt.*;
import java.util.*;
import java.awt.event.*;

public class ClockWithAlarm extends Clock {
  private java.lang.String alarmDate;
  private java.lang.String alarmTime;
  private transient Vector actionListeners;

  public ClockWithAlarm() {
    super();

    // Get initial date and time
    GregorianCalendar cal = new GregorianCalendar(tz);

    // Initialize alarm date, which consists of current
    // year, month, and date, separated by commas.
    alarmDate = cal.get(cal.YEAR) + "," + cal.get(cal.MONTH)
      + "," + cal.get(cal.DATE);

    // Initialize alarm time, which consists of current
    // hour, minute, and second, separated by commas.
    alarmTime = cal.get(cal.HOUR) + "," + cal.get(cal.MINUTE)
      + "," + cal.get(cal.SECOND);
  }

  public void run() {
    while (true) {
      try {
        thread.sleep(1000);
      }
```

Listing 4.5 *ClockWithAlarm.java*

continued

Example 4.3 continued

```
      catch (InterruptedException e) {}
      repaint();

      // Fire tick event if the current time matches alarm time
      GregorianCalendar rightNow = new GregorianCalendar(tz);
      String rightNowDate = rightNow.get(rightNow.YEAR)
        + "," +  rightNow.get(rightNow.MONTH) + "," +
        rightNow.get(rightNow.DATE);
      String rightNowTime = rightNow.get(rightNow.HOUR)
        + "," +  rightNow.get(rightNow.MINUTE) + "," +
        rightNow.get(rightNow.SECOND);
      if (rightNowDate.equals(alarmDate)
        && rightNowTime.equals(alarmTime))
        fireActionPerformed(new ActionEvent
          (this, ActionEvent.ACTION_PERFORMED, null));
    }
  }

  public void setAlarmDate(java.lang.String newAlarmDate) {
    alarmDate = newAlarmDate;
  }

  public java.lang.String getAlarmDate() {
    return alarmDate;
  }

  public void setAlarmTime(java.lang.String newAlarmTime) {
    alarmTime = newAlarmTime;
  }

  public java.lang.String getAlarmTime() {
    return alarmTime;
  }

  /** Generated by JBuilder */
  public synchronized void removeActionListener(ActionListener l) {
    if (actionListeners != null && actionListeners.contains(l)) {
      Vector v = (Vector) actionListeners.clone();
      v.removeElement(l);
      actionListeners = v;
    }
  }

  /** Generated by JBuilder */
  public synchronized void addActionListener(ActionListener l) {
    Vector v = actionListeners ==
      null ? new Vector(2) : (Vector) actionListeners.clone();
    if (!v.contains(l)) {
      v.addElement(l);
      actionListeners = v;
    }
  }

  /** Generated by JBuilder */
  protected void fireActionPerformed(ActionEvent e) {
    if (actionListeners != null) {
      Vector listeners = actionListeners;
      int count = listeners.size();
```

Listing 4.5 *Continued*

```
          for (int i = 0; i < count; i++)
            ((ActionListener) listeners.elementAt(i)).actionPerformed(e);
        }
      }
    }
```

Listing 4.5 *Continued*

To test the `ClockWithAlarm` component, follow the steps below to create an applet that makes a sound when the clock alarms.

1. Compile `ClockWithAlarm` and install it in the component palette. Create an applet named `TestClockWithAlarm` using the Applet wizard.

2. With TestClockWithAlarm.java selected in the project pane, switch to the UI designer in the content pane. Set the `layout` to `BorderLayout` for the applet. Drop a `ClockWithAlarm` to the applet to create `clockWithAlarm1`, and set its `alarmDate` and `alarmTime` to a later time, as shown in Figure 4.13.

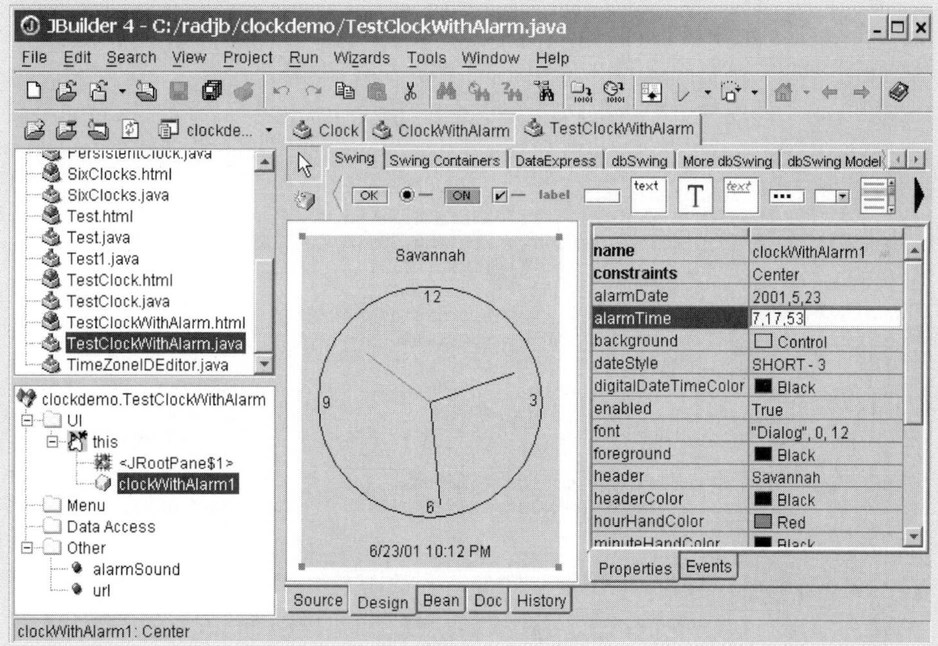

Figure 4.13 `alarmDate` *and* `alarmTime` *are the two new properties in the* `ClockWithAlarm` *component.*

3. Double-click `clockWithAlarm1` in the UI designer to generate the handler for handling the alarm event.

4. Declare an `AudioClip` instance named `alarmSound` for playing sound file alarmSound.au, create the audio clip in the `jbInit()` method, and

continued

Example 4.3 continued

complete the `clockWithAlarm1_actionPerformed` handler to play the audio clip, as shown in Listing 4.6.

```
package clockdemo;

import java.awt.*;
import java.awt.event.*;
import java.applet.*;
import javax.swing.*;
import java.net.*;

public class TestClockWithAlarm extends JApplet {
  boolean isStandalone = false;
  ClockWithAlarm clockWithAlarm1 = new ClockWithAlarm();

  /** Declare alarmSound */
  AudioClip alarmSound;

  /** Initialize the applet */
  public void init() {
    try {
      jbInit();
    }
    catch(Exception e) {
      e.printStackTrace();
    }
  }

  /** Component initialization */
  private void jbInit() throws Exception {
    this.setSize(new Dimension(400,300));
    clockWithAlarm1.setAlarmTime("7,17,53");
    clockWithAlarm1.addActionListener(
      new java.awt.event.ActionListener() {
      public void actionPerformed(ActionEvent e) {
        clockWithAlarm1_actionPerformed(e);
      }
    });
    this.getContentPane().add(clockWithAlarm1, BorderLayout.CENTER);

    // Get the URL for the file name
    URL url = this.getClass().getResource("alarmSound.au");

    // Get the audio clip
    alarmSound = Applet.newAudioClip(url);
  }

  void clockWithAlarm1_actionPerformed(ActionEvent e) {
    alarmSound.play();
  }
}
```

Listing 4.6 *TestClockWithAlarm.java*

Example Review

When designing a component, you may have two conflicting objectives. On the one hand, you want the bean to be simple, so that it will not intimidate an inexperienced user; on the other hand, you want the bean to be comprehensive, so that it will meet the needs of a variety of customers in various applications. The only way to resolve the conflict is to make several versions of the component available, and let each user choose the one that suits his needs. As in the case of the clock, if you don't need the alarm function, you could simply choose `Clock` rather than `ClockWithAlarm`.

`ClockWithAlarm` extends `Clock` with the capability of firing an `ActionEvent` when the clock time matches the alarm time. The `run()` method (Lines 29–50) is overridden to repaint the clock every second and check to see whether the current time matches the alarm time. When they match, an `ActionEvent` is fired.

BeansExpress generates the event registration methods and the code for firing `ActionEvent`. In Example 3.1, "Creating Custom Event Sets and a Source Component," and Example 3.4, "Developing Source Component Using Existing Event Sets," you hand-coded the registration methods and the events firing methods for the `Tick` component and the `TickUsingActionEvent` component. BeansExpress makes creating beans easy.

The test program makes a sound for the alarm. If you wish to embed the task of playing the audio in the `ClockWithAlarm` component, declare and create an `AudioClip` instance, say `alarmSound`, for alarmSound.au, in the `ClockWithAlarm` class. Play the `alarmSound` when the current time matches the specified alarm time.

The test program can run as an applet as well as an application. The `newAudioClip(url)` method is a new static method in the `Applet` class in Java 2 for creating an `AudioClip` in an applet or in an application.

There is an annoying problem in this example. When the alarm starts, the clock pauses. The clock resumes only after the audio clip finishes playing. To fix this problem, play the audio clip on a separate thread, as suggested in Exercise 4.3.

NOTE

When entering `alarmDate` and `alarmTime`, you must follow the pattern. Do not pad zeros before the number. For example, use 4 rather than 04 for number 4.

Developing Components Using the Model-View Approach

The model-view approach is a way of developing components by separating data storage and handling from the visual representation of the data. The component for storing and handling data, known as a *model*, contains the actual contents of the component. The component for presenting the data, known as a *view*, handles all essential component behaviors. It is the view that comes to mind when you think of the component. It does all the displaying of the components.

Separating a component into a model and a view has two major benefits:

- It makes multiple views possible so that data can be shared through the same model. For example, a model storing student names can simultaneously be displayed in a combo box or in a list box.
- It simplifies the task of writing complex applications and makes system maintenance easier. Changes can be made to the view without affecting the model, and vice versa.

A model contains data, whereas a view makes the data visible. Once a view is associated with a model, it immediately displays updates to the model. This ensures that all the views of the model display the same data consistently. To achieve consistency and synchronize the model with its dependent views, the model should notify the views when there is a change in a property in the model that is used in the view. In response to a change notification, the view is responsible for redisplaying the viewing area affected by the property change.

A view is responsible for presenting data. It can also be used as an interface to interact with the user and accept user input, as shown in Figure 4.14. Sometimes it is helpful to further separate user interaction from display using a component known as a *controller*. A controller is the means by which the user interacts with the application. A controller accepts input from the user and instructs the model and view to perform actions based on that input, as shown in Figure 4.15. In effect, the controller is responsible for mapping end-user action to application response. For example, if the user clicks the mouse button or chooses a menu item, the controller is responsible for determining how the application should respond. For this reason, the model-view approach is also known as the *model-view-controller architecture*. Whether to separate the controller from the view depends on whether the view and the controller are tightly intertwined or loosely connected. If there is a good deal of communication between the two, it makes sense to combine them. If they don't have to be used together, separating them makes these components more scalable and maintainable.

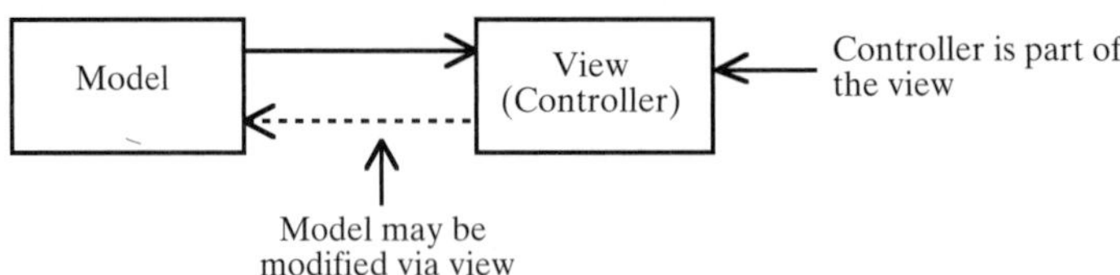

Figure 4.14 *The view can display data as well as interact with the user.*

Prior to JDK 1.1, you had to create a model by extending the `java.util.Observable` class and create a view by implementing the `java.util.Observer` interface. `Observable` and `Observer` were introduced in JDK 1.0, and their use is not consistent with the JDK 1.1 event model. With the arrival of the new Java event delegation model, using `Observable` and `Observer` is obsolete. The JDK event delegation

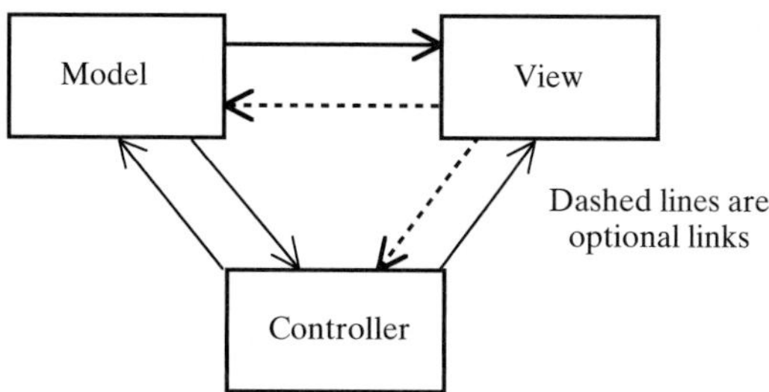

Figure 4.15 *The controller is separated from the view to facilitate interaction with the user.*

model provides a superior architecture for supporting model-view component development. The model can be implemented as a source with appropriate event and event listener registration methods. The view can be implemented as a listener. So, if data are changed in the model, the view will be notified. To enable the selection of the model during design time in a builder tool, simply add the model as a property in the view. You can easily create a property for each kind of model in the view with the event delegation model, but this task would be difficult with the Observable/Observer architecture.

Example 4.4 Developing Model-View Components

This example demonstrates the development of components using the model-view approach with the event delegation model. The example creates a model named `CircleModel`, and its two dependent views, named `CircleView` and `CircleEditor`. `CircleView` draws a circle according to the properties of the circle and enables changes that increase or decrease the circle's radius by a left mouse click or a right mouse click. `CircleEditor` displays all the circle properties and enables editing of the `radius` property in a text field. An applet is created to host the instances of `CircleModel`, `CircleView`, and `CircleEditor` and test the interaction among these instances. The relationship of these classes is shown in Figure 4.16. A sample run of the applet is shown in Figure 4.17.

The `CircleModel` contains the following properties:

- `radius`: The radius of the circle.
- `filled`: A boolean value indicating whether the circle is filled with a color.
- `color`: The color used to fill in the circle.

When a property value is changed, the `CircleModel` generates an `ActionEvent` and notifies its views of the associated change. Here are the steps in creating `CircleModel`:

1. Create a project named modelviewdemo.jpr. Use the Class wizard to create a template for CircleModel.java.

continued

Example 4.4 continued

CircleModel
-radius: double
-filled: boolean
-color: Color
// accessor methods for radius, filled,
// and color
+addActionListener(l: ActionListener): void
+removeActionListener(l: ActionListener): void

TestCircleModel
-circleModel1: CircleModel
-circleViewl: CircleView
-circleEditor1: CircleEditor
+ShowTick()
+main(args: String[]): void
+handleTick(e: TickEvent): void

CircleView

CircleEditor

Figure 4.16 *The* `CircleModel` *class contains data. The* `CircleView` *and* `CircleEditor` *classes display and control data.* `TestCircleModel` *is a test class for these components.*

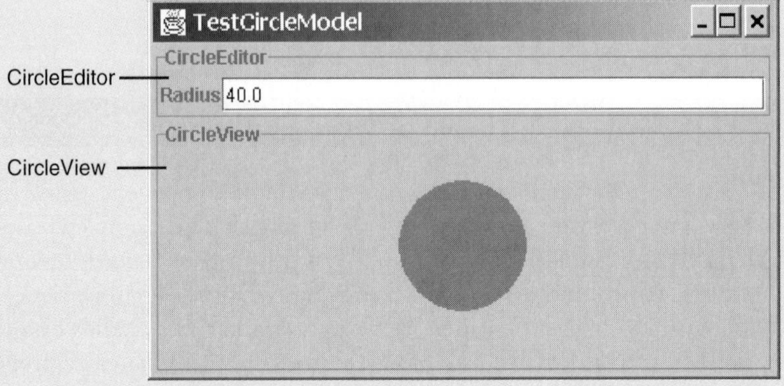

Figure 4.17 *A* `CircleEditor` *is shown in the north, and a* `CircleView` *is shown in the center of the applet. A* `CircleModel` *is shared by both* `CircleEditor` *and* `CircleView`.

2. With CircleModel.java selected in the project pane, choose the Bean tab in the content pane to start BeansExpress. In the Properties page of BeansExpress, click the Add Property button to add properties `radius`, `filled`, and `color`.

3. In the Events page of BeansExpress, check Action in the section "Fire these types of events" to generate the code for firing and registering `ActionEvent`.

4. Modify `setRadius`, `setFilled`, and `setColor` methods to invoke the `fireActionPerformed` method upon a property change, as shown in Listing 4.7.

```
package modelviewdemo;

import java.awt.event.*;
import java.util.*;

public class CircleModel {
  private double radius = 20;
  private boolean filled;
  private java.awt.Color color;

  private transient Vector actionListeners;

  public CircleModel() {
  }

  public double getRadius() {
    return radius;
  }

  public void setRadius(double newRadius) {
    radius = newRadius;

    // Notify the listener for the change on radius
    fireActionPerformed(
      new ActionEvent(this, ActionEvent.ACTION_PERFORMED, "radius"));
  }

  public void setFilled(boolean newFilled) {
    filled = newFilled;

    // Notify the listener for the change on filled
    fireActionPerformed(
      new ActionEvent(this, ActionEvent.ACTION_PERFORMED, "filled"));
  }

  public boolean isFilled() {
    return filled;
  }

  public void setColor(java.awt.Color newColor) {
    color = newColor;

    // Notify the listener for the change on color
    fireActionPerformed(
      new ActionEvent(this, ActionEvent.ACTION_PERFORMED, "color"));
  }

  public java.awt.Color getColor() {
    return color;
  }

  public synchronized void removeActionListener(ActionListener l) {
    if (actionListeners != null && actionListeners.contains(l))
    {
      Vector v = (Vector) actionListeners.clone();
      v.removeElement(l);
      actionListeners = v;
    }
  }

```

Listing 4.7 *CircleModel.java*

continued

Example 4.4 continued

```
    public synchronized void addActionListener(ActionListener l) {
      Vector v = actionListeners ==
        null ? new Vector(2) : (Vector) actionListeners.clone();
      if (!v.contains(l)) {
        v.addElement(l);
        actionListeners = v;
      }
    }

    protected void fireActionPerformed(ActionEvent e) {
      if (actionListeners != null) {
        Vector listeners = actionListeners;
        int count = listeners.size();
        for (int i = 0; i < count; i++)
          ((ActionListener) listeners.elementAt(i)).actionPerformed(e);
      }
    }
  }
```

Listing 4.7 *Continued*

Follow the steps below to create the `CircleView` component.

1. Choose File, New to display the Object Gallery. Click the JavaBean icon in the Object Gallery to display the JavaBean wizard. Create `CircleView` that extends `javax.swing.JPanel` using this wizard. The generated JavaBean uses the `BorderLayout` in the panel.

2. With CircleView.java selected in the project pane, choose the Bean tab in the content pane to start BeansExpress. In the Properties page of BeansExpress, add a property named `model` with type `CircleModel`.

3. In the Event page, check the Action box in the section "Listen for these events" to implement the `ActionListener` for `CircleView`, as shown in Figure 4.18. You could equally well use the Implement Interface wizard to generate the code for implementing the `ActionListener` interface, but using BeansExpress is more convenient.

NOTE

The Listen for These Events wizard in BeansExpress only generates listeners for an event listener interface, while the Implement Interface wizard can generate the code for implementing all kinds of interfaces.

---

4. Implement the `actionPerformed` method to add the `repaint()` method to repaint the circle upon receiving a property-change notification from the model. Implement the `paintComponent` method to paint the circle in the center of the panel.

5. Implement the `setModel` method to set the new model and register the view with the model, as shown in Listing 4.8 (Lines 29–39).

6. Choose the Design tab to switch to the UI designer. In the Events page of `CircleView`, double-click the value field of the `mouseClicked` handler to

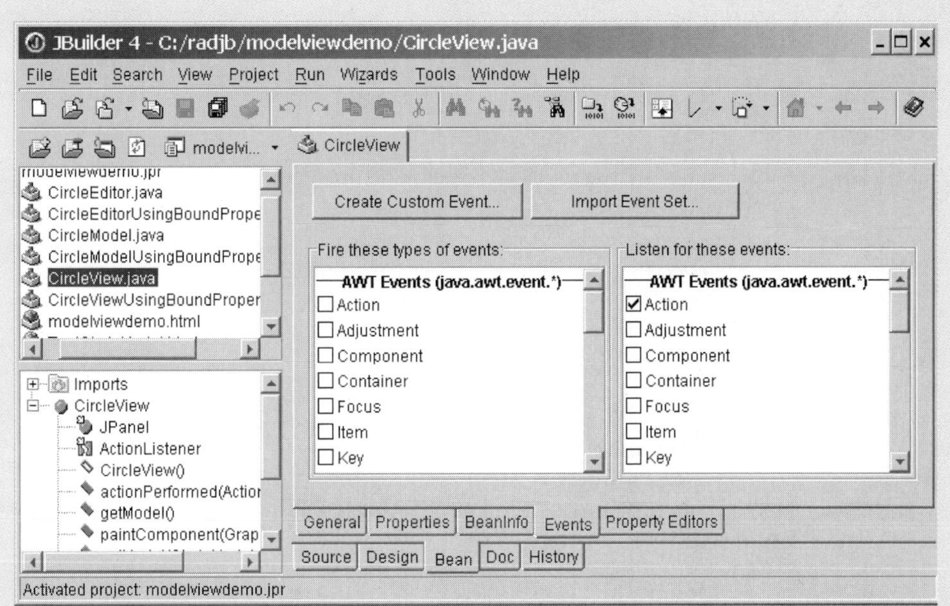

Figure 4.18 *You can generate the code for implementing an event listener interface from BeansExpress.*

generate the code for handling mouse-clicked events. Implement the `mouseClicked` method to handle the right-button click for increasing radius and the left-button click for decreasing radius, as shown in Listing 4.8 (Lines 73–80).

```
1     package modelviewdemo;
2
3     import java.awt.*;
4     import javax.swing.JPanel;
5     import java.awt.event.*;
6
7     public class CircleView extends JPanel implements ActionListener {
8       BorderLayout borderLayout1 = new BorderLayout();
9       private modelviewdemo.CircleModel model;
10
11      public CircleView() {
12        try {
13          jbInit();
14        }
15        catch(Exception ex) {
16          ex.printStackTrace();
17        }
18      }
19
20      private void jbInit() throws Exception {
21        this.addMouseListener(new java.awt.event.MouseAdapter() {
22          public void mouseClicked(MouseEvent e) {
23            this_mouseClicked(e);
24          }
25        });
```

Listing 4.8 *CircleView.java*

continued

Example 4.4 continued

```
    this.setLayout(borderLayout1);
  }

  /** Set a model */
  public void setModel(modelviewdemo.CircleModel newModel) {
    model = newModel;

    if (model != null) {
      // Register the view as listener for the model
      model.addActionListener(this);
    }
    else {
      model.removeActionListener(this);
    }

    repaint();
  }

  public modelviewdemo.CircleModel getModel() {
    return model;
  }

  public void actionPerformed(ActionEvent e) {
    repaint();
  }

  public void paintComponent(Graphics g) {
    super.paintComponent(g);

    if (model == null) return;

    g.setColor(model.getColor());

    int xCenter = getWidth()/2;
    int yCenter = getHeight()/2;
    int radius = (int)model.getRadius();

    if (model.isFilled()) {
      g.fillOval(xCenter - radius, yCenter - radius,
        2*radius, 2*radius);
    }
    else {
      g.drawOval(xCenter - radius, yCenter - radius,
        2*radius, 2*radius);
    }
  }

  void this_mouseClicked(MouseEvent e) {
    if (model == null) return;

    if (e.isMetaDown())
      model.setRadius(model.getRadius()-5);
    else
      model.setRadius(model.getRadius()+5);
  }
}
```

Listing 4.8 *Continued*

Follow the steps below to create the `CircleEditor` component.

1. Use the JavaBean wizard to create a `CircleEditor` that extends `javax.swing.JPanel`.

2. With CircleEditor.java selected in the project pane, choose the Design tab to switch to the UI designer. Drop a `JLabel` to the west of `CircleEditor`, and change the text of the label to Radius. Drop a `JTextField` to the center of `CircleEditor` and rename it `jtfRadius`.

3. Choose the Bean tab to switch to the BeansExpress. Add a property named `model` with type `CircleModel`. In the Events page of BeansExpress, check Action in the section "Listen for these events" to generate code for implementing `ActionListener`.

4. Modify the `setModel` method to register the view with the model, as shown in Listing 4.9 (Lines 34–44), and implement the `actionPerformed` method to set the radius from the model (Lines 57–60).

5. To enable `CircleEditor` to edit the radius in the `jtfRadius` text field, switch to the UI designer and double-click `jtfRadius` to generate `jtfRadius_actionPerformed` method and its associated event adapter. Implement `jtfRadius_actionPerformed` to set a new radius in the model, as shown in Listing 4.9.

```
1   package modelviewdemo;
2
3   import java.awt.*;
4   import javax.swing.*;
5   import java.awt.event.*;
6
7   public class CircleEditor extends JPanel implements ActionListener {
8     BorderLayout borderLayout1 = new BorderLayout();
9     JLabel jLabel1 = new JLabel();
10    JTextField jtfRadius = new JTextField();
11    private modelviewdemo.CircleModel model;
12
13    public CircleEditor() {
14      try {
15        jbInit();
16      }
17      catch(Exception ex) {
18        ex.printStackTrace();
19      }
20    }
21
22    private void jbInit() throws Exception {
23      jLabel1.setText("Radius");
24      this.setLayout(borderLayout1);
25      jtfRadius.addActionListener(new java.awt.event.ActionListener() {
26        public void actionPerformed(ActionEvent e) {
27          jtfRadius_actionPerformed(e);
28        }
29      });
```

Listing 4.9 *CircleEditor.java*

continued

Example 4.4 continued

```
      this.add(jLabel1, BorderLayout.WEST);
      this.add(jtfRadius, BorderLayout.CENTER);
    }

    public void setModel(modelviewdemo.CircleModel newModel) {
      model = newModel;

      if (model != null) {
        // Register the view as listener for the model
        model.addActionListener(this);
      }
      else {
        model.removeActionListener(this);
      }
    }

    public modelviewdemo.CircleModel getModel() {
      return model;
    }

    public void actionPerformed(ActionEvent e) {
      if (model != null)
        if (e.getActionCommand().equals("radius"))
          jtfRadius.setText(
            new Double(model.getRadius()).toString());
    }

    void jtfRadius_actionPerformed(ActionEvent e) {
      model.setRadius(
        new Double(jtfRadius.getText()).doubleValue());
    }
  }
```

Listing 4.9 *Continued*

After creating a model and two views, you are ready to put them together in an applet. Here are the steps in creating this applet:

1. Create an applet named `TestCircleModel` using the Applet wizard.
2. Install `CircleModel`, `CircleView`, and `CircleEditor` to the component palette. In the UI designer for TestCircleModel.java, drop a `CircleView` to the center of the applet to create `circleView1`, and drop a `CircleEditor` to the north of the applet to create `circleEditor1`.
3. Set the `border` property for `circleEditor` to `Titled` to create `titleBorder1`. You will see `titledBoder1` in the component tree. Set the title of `titledBorder1` to CircleEditor. Similarly, create a title named `CircleView` for `circleView1`.
4. Set the `model` property of `circleView1` and `circleEditor1` to `circleModel1`, as shown in Figure 4.19.
5. In the inspector for `circleModel1`, change `radius` to 40, `color` to Blue, and `filled` to True. You will see a circle to be drawn accordingly in `circleView1`, as shown in Figure 4.20. The code for `TestCircleModel` is shown in Listing 4.10.

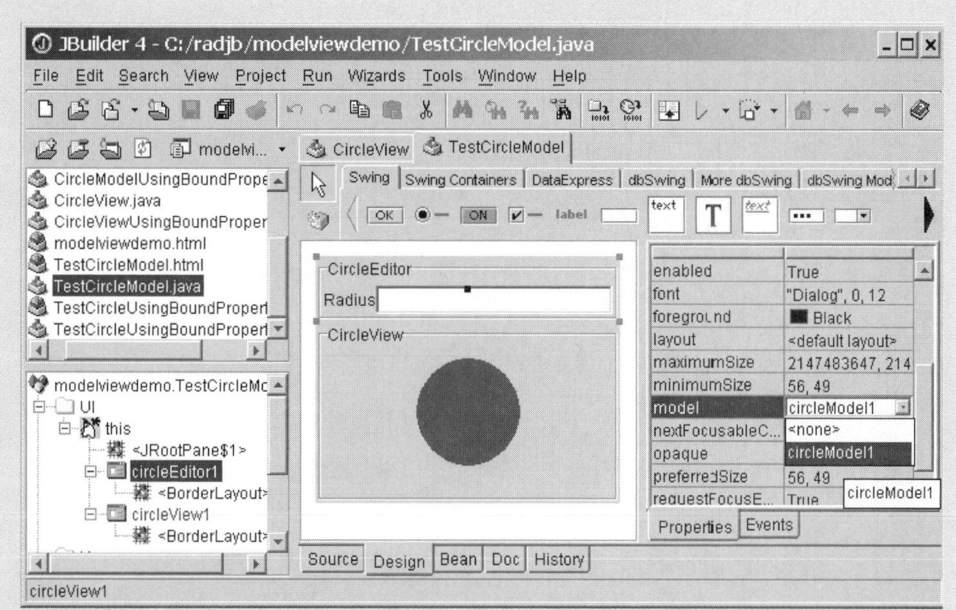

Figure 4.19 `circleModel1` *appears in the combo box of the* `model` *property in the inspector for* `circleEditor1`.

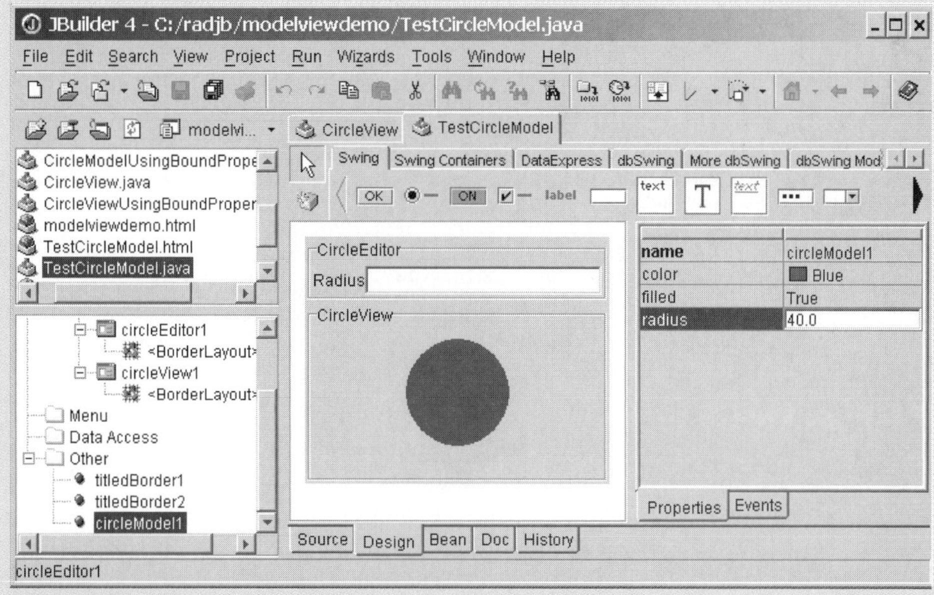

Figure 4.20 *Updates of* `circleModel1` *are immediately shown in* `circleView1` *in the App-Browser.*

continued

Example 4.4 continued

```
package modelviewdemo;

import java.awt.*;
import java.awt.event.*;
import java.applet.*;
import javax.swing.*;
import javax.swing.border.*;

public class TestCircleModel extends JApplet {
  boolean isStandalone = false;
  CircleEditor circleEditor1 = new CircleEditor();
  TitledBorder titledBorder1;
  CircleView circleView1 = new CircleView();
  TitledBorder titledBorder2;
  CircleModel circleModel1 = new CircleModel();

  /** Initialize the applet */
  public void init() {
    try {
      jbInit();
    }
    catch(Exception e) {
      e.printStackTrace();
    }
  }

  /** Component initialization */
  private void jbInit() throws Exception {
    titledBorder1 = new TitledBorder("");
    titledBorder2 = new TitledBorder("");
    this.setSize(new Dimension(234, 184));
    circleEditor1.setBorder(titledBorder1);
    circleEditor1.setModel(circleModel1);
    titledBorder1.setTitle("CircleEditor");
    circleView1.setBorder(titledBorder2);
    circleView1.setModel(circleModel1);
    titledBorder2.setTitle("CircleView");
    circleModel1.setRadius(40.0);
    circleModel1.setFilled(true);
    circleModel1.setColor(Color.blue);
    this.getContentPane().add(circleEditor1, BorderLayout.NORTH);
    this.getContentPane().add(circleView1, BorderLayout.CENTER);
  }
}
```

Listing 4.10 *TestCircleModel.java*

Example Review

The model stores and handles data, and the view is responsible for presenting data. The fundamental issue in the model-view approach is to ensure consistency between the views and the model. Any change in the model should be notified to the dependent views, and all the views should display the same data consistently. You can change the radius either by entering a value in the radius text field in `circleEditor1` or by clicking the left or right mouse button to increase or decrease it in `circleView1`. Both views will display the same radius at the same time.

All the code in CircleModel.java was automatically generated by JBuilder except that you added the code in `setRadius`, `setFilled`, and `setColor` to invoke the `fireActionPerformed` method. All the code in `CircleView` and `CircleEditor` was automatically generated except that you modified the `setModel` method and the methods for handling mouse-click events in `CircleView` and action events in `CircleEditor`. Finally, all the code in TestCircle.java was automatically generated.

The `setModel` method in `CircleView` and `CircleEditor` sets a new model and registered the view with the model by invoking the model's `addActionListener` method. This is the preferred approach to implement the view. It simplifies the use of the model-view components. If registration were not done in the `setModel` method, you would have to attach the view to the model in `TestCircle`.

There is no definitive definition for a controller. You may well consider `CircleEditor` as a controller, which accepts user input for the `CircleModel` and `CircleView`.

Rapid Application Development Process

Rapid Application Development, or RAD, is a software development technology introduced in the 1980s by researchers at the Xerox Palo Alto Research Lab. This technology for developing programs efficiently and effectively has been successfully implemented in program development tools like Visual Basic, Delphi, Power Builder, and Oracle Developer 2000, among many others. Using a RAD tool, projects can be developed quickly and efficiently with minimum coding. Projects developed using RAD are easy to modify and easy to maintain. The key elements in a Java RAD tool are the JavaBeans components. These components can be visually manipulated and tailored during design time in order to develop customized programs.

The application development process is similar to the component development process in many ways. Developing a software project is an engineering process. Software products, no matter how large or how small, have the same developmental phases: requirement specification, analysis, design, implementation, testing, deployment, and maintenance, as shown in Figure 4.21.

Requirements specification is a formal process that seeks to understand the problem and document in detail what it needs to do. This phase involves close interaction between users and designers. Most of the examples in this book are simple, and their requirements are clearly stated. In the real world, however, problems are not well defined. You need to study a problem carefully to identify its requirements.

System analysis seeks to analyze the business process in terms of data flow, and to identify the system's input and output.

System design is the process of designing the system's components. This phase involves the use of many levels of abstraction to decompose the problem into manageable components and design algorithms for each of them.

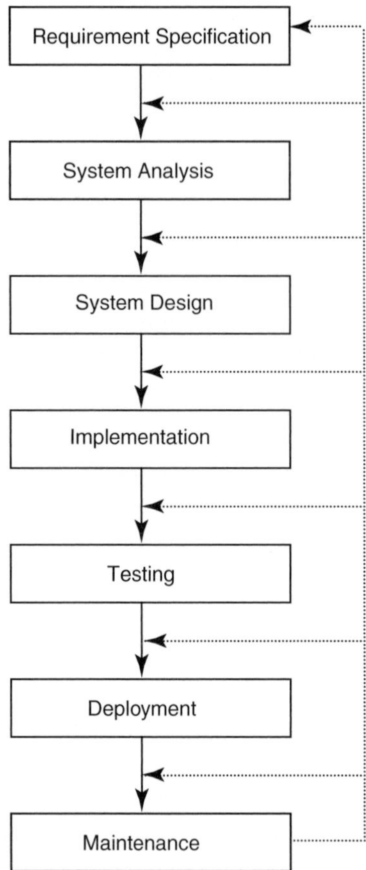

Figure 4.21 *Developing a project involves requirement specification, system analysis, system design, implementation, testing, deployment, and maintenance.*

Implementation is the process of translating the system design into programs. A program is written for each component, and they are put to work together. This phase requires the use of a specific programming language.

Testing ensures that the code meets the requirements specification and weeds out bugs. An independent team of software engineers not involved in design and implementation of the project usually conducts such testing.

Deployment makes the project available for use. For a Java applet, this means installing it on a Web server. For a Java application, install it on the client's computer. For a Java servlet or a server page, install it with a Web server that has a servlet engine. The project usually consists of many classes. An effective approach for deployment is to package all the classes into a Java archive file, which is introduced in the section "Packaging and Deploying Java Projects in JBuilder."

Maintenance is concerned with changing and improving the product. A software product must continue to perform and improve in a changing environment. This requires periodic upgrades of the product to fix newly discovered bugs and to incorporate changes.

The development phases are cyclic. You can use a CASE (Computer Aided Software Engineering) tool to aid software development. Requirements specification, analysis, and design are usually taught in a software engineering course. This chapter focuses on creating a project using rapid application development.

When writing a project using a RAD tool, you should first carefully plan the project before implementing it. The major part of the planning involves designing the user interface. You may draw a sketch of the screens that shows all the visible beans you plan to use. Indicate the layout for the containers, and identify all the objects with appropriate names.

The implementation is a two-step process that involves creating user interfaces and writing code. To create a user interface, click-and-drop the bean components, such as buttons, labels, combo boxes, lists, and text fields, from the component palette to the UI designer, and set the beans properties in the inspector.

After the user interface is created, you will add event handlers and write the code to carry out the actions for the associated events.

The following example illustrates the process for rapid Java application development.

Example 4.5 Developing a Mortgage Calculator

This example creates a mortgage calculator for computing mortgage payments, as shown in Figure 4.22. The mortgage calculator lets the user enter loan amount, interest rate, and years; when the user clicks the Compute button, monthly payment and total payment are displayed.

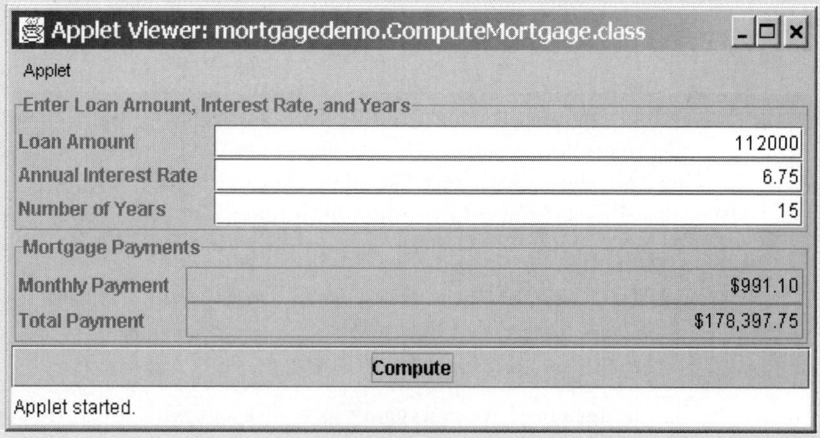

Figure 4.22 *The mortgage calculator gets input on loan amount, annual interest rate, and loan period in number of years, and computes monthly payment and total payment.*

continued

Example 4.5 continued

Here are the steps to complete the project:

1. It is often helpful to draw a sketch of a complex user interface, as shown in Figure 4.23.

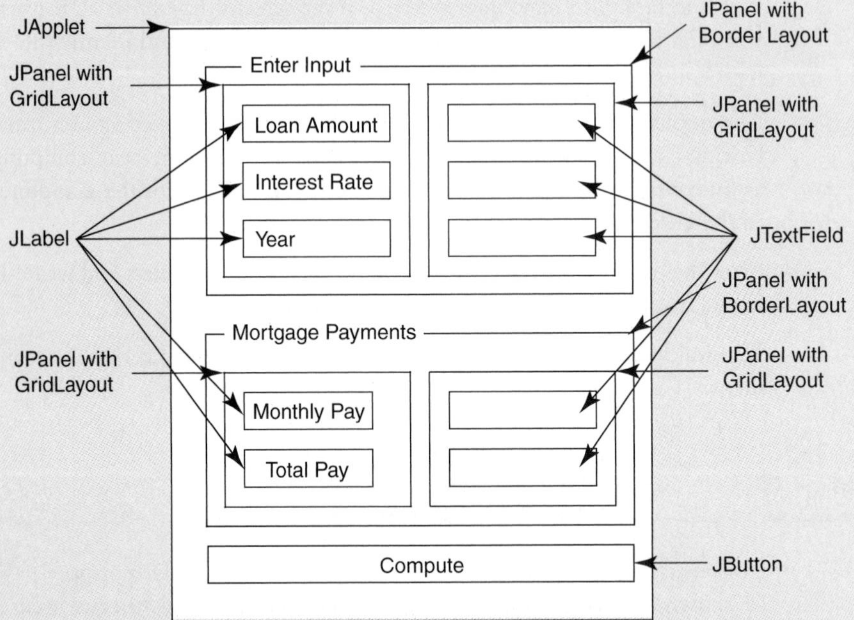

Figure 4.23 *The labels, text fields, borders, and a button are placed in the applet.*

2. Create a new project named mortgagedemo.jpr and create an applet named `ComputeMortgage` using the Applet wizard.

3. In the UI designer of ComputeMortgage.java, drop a `JPanel` to the north of the applet to create `jpInput`, and drop a `JPanel` to the center of the applet to create `jpResults`. Drop a `JButton` to the south of the applet to create `jbtCompute` with text Compute. Set the border title of `jpInput` and `jpResults` to "Enter Loan Amount, Interest Rate, and Years," and "Mortgage Payments," respectively.

4. Set the `layout` of `jpInput` to `BorderLayout`. Drop a `JPanel` to the west of `jpInput` to create `jpInputLabels`, and drop a `JPanel` to the center of `jpInput` to create `jpInputTextFields`.

5. Set the `layout` of `jpInputLabels` to `GridLayout` with three rows, and drop three labels with text "Loan Amount," "Interest Rate," and "Years." Set the `layout` of `jpInputTextFields` to `GridLayout` with three rows, and drop three text fields to create `jtfLoanAmount`, `jtfInterestRate`, and `jtfYears`.

6. Set the `layout` of `jpResults` to `BorderLayout`. Drop a `JPanel` to the west of `jpResults` to create `jpResultLabels`, and drop a `JPanel` to the center of `jpResults` to create `jpResultTextFields`.

7. Set the `layout` of `jpResultLabels` to `GridLayout` with two rows, and drop two labels with text "Monthly Payment" and "Total Payment." Set the `layout` of `jpResultTextFields` to `GridLayout` with two rows, and drop two text fields to create `jtfMonthlyPay` and `jtfTotalPay`. Set horizontal alignment for all text fields to `RIGHT`.

8. Double-click `jbtCompute` to generate the handler `jbtCompute_actionPerformed` for handling the button-click event. Fill in the code in this handler to read the input, compute, and display monthly payment and total payment. The code can be found in Listing 4.11 (Lines 110–127).

```
1   package mortgagedemo;
2
3   import java.awt.*;
4   import java.awt.event.*;
5   import java.applet.*;
6   import javax.swing.*;
7   import javax.swing.border.*;
8   import java.text.*;
9
10  public class ComputeMortgage extends JApplet {
11    boolean isStandalone = false;
12    JPanel jpInput = new JPanel();
13    JPanel jpResults = new JPanel();
14    JButton jbtCompute = new JButton();
15    JPanel jpInputLabels = new JPanel();
16    JLabel jlblLoanAmount = new JLabel();
17    BorderLayout borderLayout1 = new BorderLayout();
18    JLabel jlblInterestRate = new JLabel();
19    JLabel jlblYears = new JLabel();
20    GridLayout gridLayout1 = new GridLayout();
21    JPanel jpInputTextFields = new JPanel();
22    JTextField jtfLoanAmount = new JTextField();
23    JTextField jtfInterestRate = new JTextField();
24    JTextField jtfYears = new JTextField();
25    GridLayout gridLayout2 = new GridLayout();
26    TitledBorder titledBorder1;
27    JPanel jpResultLabels = new JPanel();
28    BorderLayout borderLayout2 = new BorderLayout();
29    JLabel jlbMonthlyPay = new JLabel();
30    JLabel jlblTotalPay = new JLabel();
31    GridLayout gridLayout3 = new GridLayout();
32    JPanel jpResultTextFields = new JPanel();
33    JTextField jtfMonthlyPay = new JTextField();
34    JTextField jtfTotalPay = new JTextField();
35    GridLayout gridLayout4 = new GridLayout();
36    TitledBorder titledBorder2;
37
38    /** Initialize the applet */
39    public void init() {
40      try {
41        jbInit();
42      }
43      catch(Exception e) {
44        e.printStackTrace();
45      }
46    }
47
48    /** Component initialization */
```

Listing 4.11 *MortgageApplet.java.*

continued

Example 4.5 continued

```
  private void jbInit() throws Exception {
    titledBorder1 = new TitledBorder("");
    titledBorder2 = new TitledBorder("");
    this.setSize(new Dimension(400,300));
    jbtCompute.setText("Compute");
    jbtCompute.addActionListener(
      new java.awt.event.ActionListener() {
      public void actionPerformed(ActionEvent e) {
        jbtCompute_actionPerformed(e);
      }
    });
    jlblLoanAmount.setText("Loan Amount");
    jpInput.setLayout(borderLayout1);
    jlblInterestRate.setText("Interest Rate");
    jlblYears.setText("Years");
    jpInputLabels.setLayout(gridLayout1);
    gridLayout1.setRows(3);
    jpInputTextFields.setLayout(gridLayout2);
    gridLayout2.setRows(3);
    borderLayout1.setHgap(10);
    borderLayout1.setVgap(10);
    jpInput.setBorder(titledBorder1);
    titledBorder1.setTitle("Enter Loan Amount, " +
      "Interest Rate, and Years");
    jpResults.setLayout(borderLayout2);
    jlbMonthlyPay.setText("Monthly Pay");
    jlblTotalPay.setText("Total Pay");
    jpResultLabels.setLayout(gridLayout3);
    gridLayout3.setRows(2);
    jpResultTextFields.setLayout(gridLayout4);
    gridLayout4.setRows(2);
    borderLayout2.setHgap(10);
    borderLayout2.setVgap(10);
    jpResults.setBorder(titledBorder2);
    titledBorder2.setTitle("Mortgage Payments");
    jtfLoanAmount.setHorizontalAlignment(SwingConstants.RIGHT);
    jtfInterestRate.setHorizontalAlignment(SwingConstants.RIGHT);
    jtfYears.setHorizontalAlignment(SwingConstants.RIGHT);
    jtfMonthlyPay.setEditable(false);
    jtfMonthlyPay.setHorizontalAlignment(SwingConstants.RIGHT);
    jtfTotalPay.setEditable(false);
    jtfTotalPay.setHorizontalAlignment(SwingConstants.RIGHT);
    this.getContentPane().add(jpInput, BorderLayout.NORTH);
    jpInput.add(jpInputLabels, BorderLayout.WEST);
    jpInputLabels.add(jlblLoanAmount, null);
    jpInputLabels.add(jlblInterestRate, null);
    jpInputLabels.add(jlblYears, null);
    jpInput.add(jpInputTextFields, BorderLayout.CENTER);
    jpInputTextFields.add(jtfLoanAmount, null);
    jpInputTextFields.add(jtfInterestRate, null);
    jpInputTextFields.add(jtfYears, null);
    this.getContentPane().add(jpResults, BorderLayout.CENTER);
    jpResults.add(jpResultLabels, BorderLayout.WEST);
    jpResultLabels.add(jlbMonthlyPay, null);
    jpResultLabels.add(jlblTotalPay, null);
    jpResults.add(jpResultTextFields, BorderLayout.CENTER);
    jpResultTextFields.add(jtfMonthlyPay, null);
    jpResultTextFields.add(jtfTotalPay, null);
    this.getContentPane().add(jbtCompute, BorderLayout.SOUTH);
  }

```

Listing 4.11 *Continued*

```
    /** Compute mortgage payments */
    void jbtCompute_actionPerformed(ActionEvent e) {
      // Retrieve input from user
      double loan = new Double(jtfLoanAmount.getText()).doubleValue();
      double interestRate =
        new Double(jtfInterestRate.getText()).doubleValue()/1200;
      int year = new Integer(jtfYears.getText()).intValue();

      // Calculate payment
      double monthlyPay =
        loan*interestRate/(1-(Math.pow(1/(1+interestRate),year*12)));
      double totalPay = monthlyPay*year*12;

      // Display results in currency format
      NumberFormat nf = NumberFormat.getCurrencyInstance(getLocale());
      jtfMonthlyPay.setText(nf.format(monthlyPay));
      jtfTotalPay.setText(nf.format(totalPay));
    }
  }
```

Listing 4.11 *Continued*

Example Review

This example uses many panels to group components in order to achieve the desired layout. Creating UI interfaces using Java is more complex than using Visual Basic or Delphi, mainly because Java has a variety of layout styles. However, VB and Delphi use the fixed-position layout. Chapter 6, "Containers and Layout Managers," presents a thorough discussion of Java layout managers.

The program displays monthly payment and total payment in locale-sensitive format. An instance, named `nf`, of `NumberFormat` is created to format the number in the applet's locale. The `format` method in `nf` is used to format the number into a locale-sensitive string. For more information on number formatting, please refer to Chapter 14, "Internationalization," in my *Introduction to Java Programming with JBuilder 4*.

You created the user interface with labels, text fields, and a button. The default name for an object is *xi*, where *x* stands for the name of the bean, and *i* is an integer indicating that it is the *i*th object created for the same type of bean. There are five labels named `jLabel1`, `jLabel2`, `jLabel3`, `jLabel4`, and `jLabel5`. For better identification, these names were changed to `lblLoanAmount`, `lblInterestRate`, `lblYears`, `lblMonthlyPay`, and `lblTotalPay`. For the same reason, five text fields were renamed `txtLoanAmount`, `txtInterestRate`, `txtYears`, `txtMonthlyPay`, and `txtTotalPay`.

TIP

I recommend replacing the default names of multiple objects of the same type with more descriptive names to help identify them. It is not necessary to rename the objects, however, if they are not used in handwritten code. For example, the five text fields are used in the handwritten code; thus renaming them makes referencing easier. But since the five labels are not referenced in the code, it is not necessary to rename them.

Packaging and Deploying Java Projects in JBuilder

Your project may consist of many classes and supporting files, such as image files and audio files. All of these files have to be provided to the end-users if your programs are to run on their side. For convenience, Java supports an archive file that can group all the project files in a compressed file.

The Java archive file format (JAR) is based on the popular ZIP file format. JAR can be used as a general archiving tool, but transporting Java applications, applets, and their requisite components (.class files, images, and sounds) in a single file was the primary motivation for its development.

This single file can be deployed on an end-user's machine as an application. It also can be downloaded to a browser in a single HTTP transaction, rather than opening a new connection for each piece. This greatly simplifies application deployment and improves the speed with which an applet can be loaded onto a Web page and begin functioning. The JAR format also supports compression, which reduces the size of the file and improves download time still further. Additionally, individual entries in a JAR file can be digitally signed by the applet author to authenticate their origin.

You can create an archive file using either the JDK **jar** command or the JBuilder Archive Builder wizard. The following command creates an archive file named ComputeMortgage.jar for classes ComputeMortgage.class and its inner class ComputeMortgage$1.class:

```
jar -cf ComputeMortgage.jar mortgagedemo/ComputerMortgage.class
mortgagedemo/ComputeMortgage$1.class
```

The **-c** option is for creating a new archive file, and the **-f** option specifies the archive file's name.

Using the Archive Builder to Package Projects

With the **jar** command, you have to manually identify the dependent files. JBuilder Professional provides the Archive Builder that gathers all the classes on which your program depends into one JAR archive that includes image and audio files.

Let us use the `ComputeMortgage` class from the preceding example to demonstrate packaging projects. Here are the steps to follow in generating the archive file:

1. Open the mortgagedemo.jpr project. Choose Wizards, Archive Builder to start Archive Builder, as shown in Figure 4.24.

JBUILDER 5 NOTE

JBuilder 5 has more options in the Archive type to enable you to create packages for various types of applications.

---

2. Since ComputeMortgage can run as an application, choose Application as Archive type. Click Next to display Archive Builder – Step 2 of 6, as shown

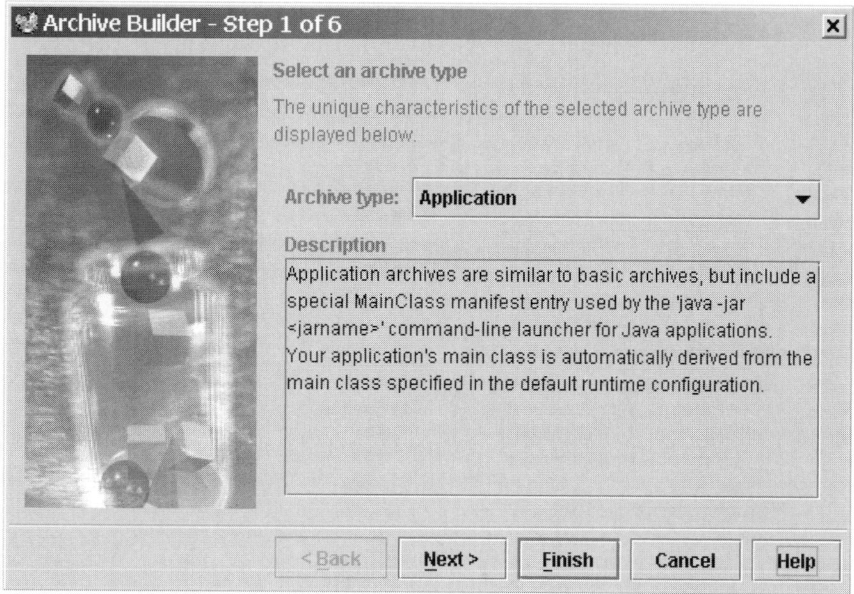

Figure 4.24 *You can use the Archive Builder wizard to create an archive file for the project.*

in Figure 4.25. Check Compress the contents of the archive. Enter ComputeMortgage.jar in the File field.

3. Click Next to display Step 3 of 6 of Archive Builder, as shown in Figure 4.26. Check "Include required classes and known resources." Click Add

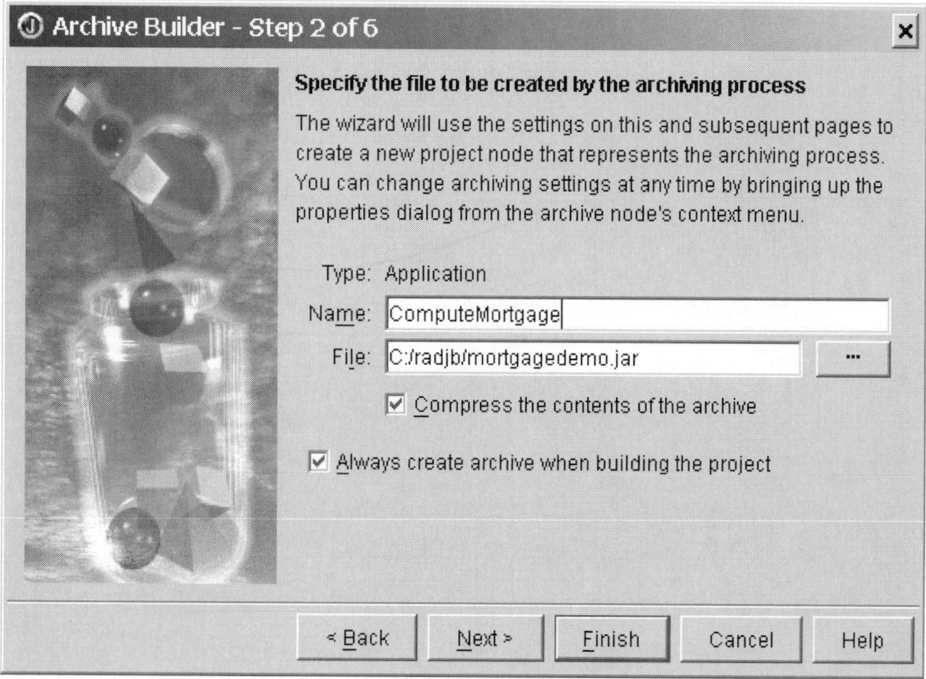

Figure 4.25 *You specify an archive file in Step 2 of Archive Builder.*

Class to display the Select a Class dialog box to select mortgagedemo.ComputeMortgage. Click Next continually to skip Steps 4 and 5. In Step 6 of 6 of Archive Builder, as shown in Figure 4.27, check Use the class specified below. Click the ellipses to display the Select Main Class for Archive dialog box to select mortgagedemo.ComputeMortgage.

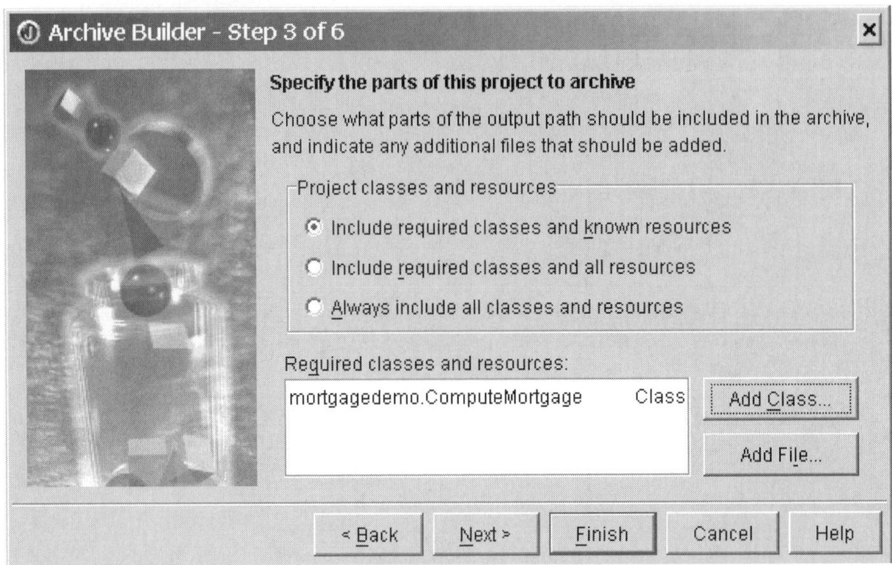

Figure 4.26 *You specify the parts of the project to archive in Step 3 of Archive Builder.*

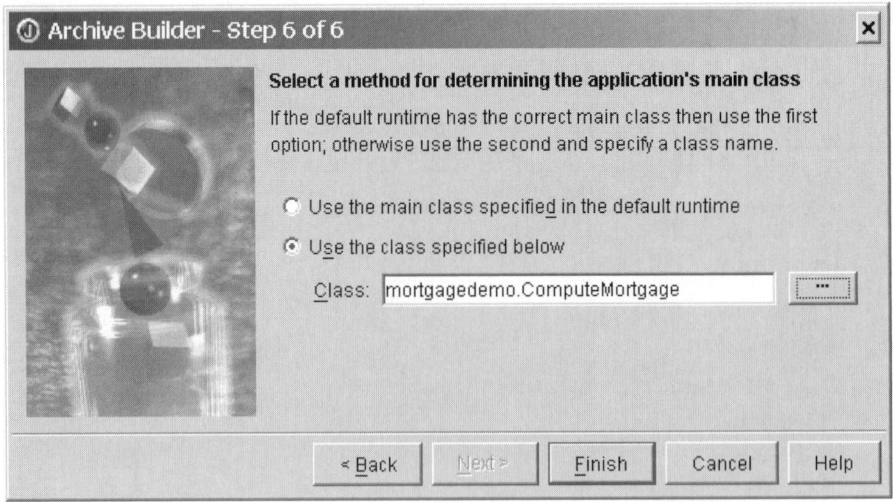

Figure 4.27 *You specify the main method for the archive file in Step 6 of Archive Builder.*

4. Click Finish to close the Archive Builder. Rebuild the project to create the archive file.

Note

You can view the contents of a .JAR file using WinZip, a popular compression utility for Windows, as shown in Figure 4.28.

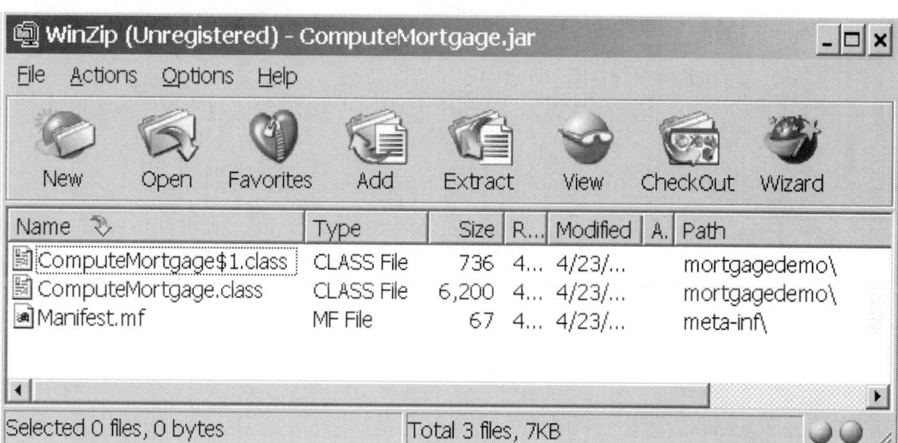

Figure 4.28 *You can view the files contained in the archive file using the WinZip utility.*

The Manifest File

As shown in Figure 4.28, a manifest file was created with the path name `meta-inf\`. The manifest is a special file that contains information about the files packaged in a JAR file. For instance, the manifest file in Figure 4.28 contains the following information:

```
Manifest-Version: 1.0
Main-Class: mortgagedemo.ComputeMortgage
```

The Main-Class line specifies that the jar file contains a Java application whose main class is mortgagedemo.ComputeMortgage.

Running Archived Projects

The Archive Builder packages all the class files and dependent resource files into an archive file that can be distributed to the end-user. If the project is a Java application, the user should have a Java Runtime Environment already installed. If it is not installed, the user can download Java Runtime Environment (JRE) from JavaSoft at www.javasoft.com/ and install it.

Note

The Java Runtime Environment is the minimum standard Java platform for running Java programs. It contains the Java interpreter, Java core classes, and supporting files. The JRE does not contain any of the development tools (such as Applet Viewer or javac) or classes that pertain only to a development environment. The JRE is a subset of JDK.

Running Archived Files from Java Applications

To run `ComputeMortgage` as an application from an archived file, simply type the following command:

```
java -jar ComputeMortgage.jar
```

NOTE

You can create an icon on the Windows Desktop to enable the end-user to run the program by double-clicking on it. To learn how to do it, see www.cs.armstrong.edu/liang/radjb5.html.

Running Archived Files from Java Applets

To run `ComputeMortgage` as an applet from an archived file, you need to modify the <APPLET> tag in the HTML file to include an ARCHIVE attribute. The ARCHIVE attribute specifies the archive file that contains the applet. For example, the HTML file for running the `ComputeMortgage` can be modified as follows:

```
<APPLET
  CODE     = "mortgagedemo.ComputeMortgage.class"
  ARCHIVE  = "ComputeMortgage.jar"
  WIDTH    = 400
  HEIGHT   = 300
  HSPACE   = 0
  VSPACE   = 0
  ALIGN    = Middle
>
</APPLET>
```

NOTE

If your Java source code is changed, you need to update the .jar file. To update the .jar file, right-click the project file in the project pane to display the context menu, and choose Rebuild.

Chapter Summary

This chapter introduced the process of developing bean components and developing applications using beans, the model-view approach, and JBuilder's powerful BeansExpress for creating bean properties and events with minimum coding. You learned the difference between a bean developer and a bean user, and learned how to apply the bean development process to create bean components. You used BeansExpress to create bean properties in the `Clock` component, and to create bean events in the `ClockWithAlarm` component. Finally, you learned how to package and deploy Java projects in JBuilder.

Review Questions

4.1 Describe the differences between developing beans and using beans.

4.2 Describe the component development process.

4.3 How do you start BeansExpress? How do you add or remove a property? How do you add or delete the code for generating and firing events? How do you add or delete the code for listening to events?

4.4 What are the differences between the Implement Interface wizard and the "Listen for These Events" wizard in BeansExpress?

4.5 What is the model-view approach? What are advantages of developing components using the model-view approach? How do you implement the model and the view so that they are synchronized when a property is changed?

4.6 Describe the project development process.

4.7 Describe the steps in developing projects using RAD.

4.8 Describe the preinstalled components in JBuilder's component palette.

4.9 How do you use the Archive Builder to package a Java project? How do you execute an application from an archive, and how do you specify an applet in an archive file?

Programming Exercises

4.1 Use the `Clock` component to develop an applet, as shown in Figure 4.29, that can display the time in London, New York, Savannah, Chicago, Denver, and San Francisco.

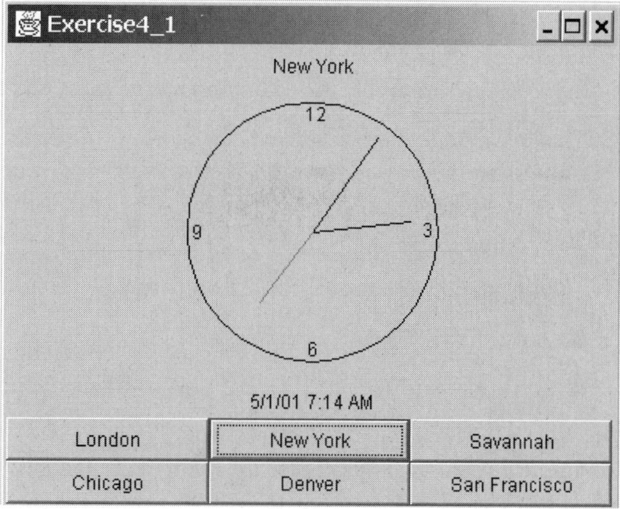

Figure 4.29 *The applet displays the clock for one of the six cities.*

4.2 Create a program that displays three clocks in a group. Each clock has individual Resume and Suspend control buttons. You can also resume or suspend all the clocks by using group control Resume All and Suspend All buttons, as shown in Figure 4.30.

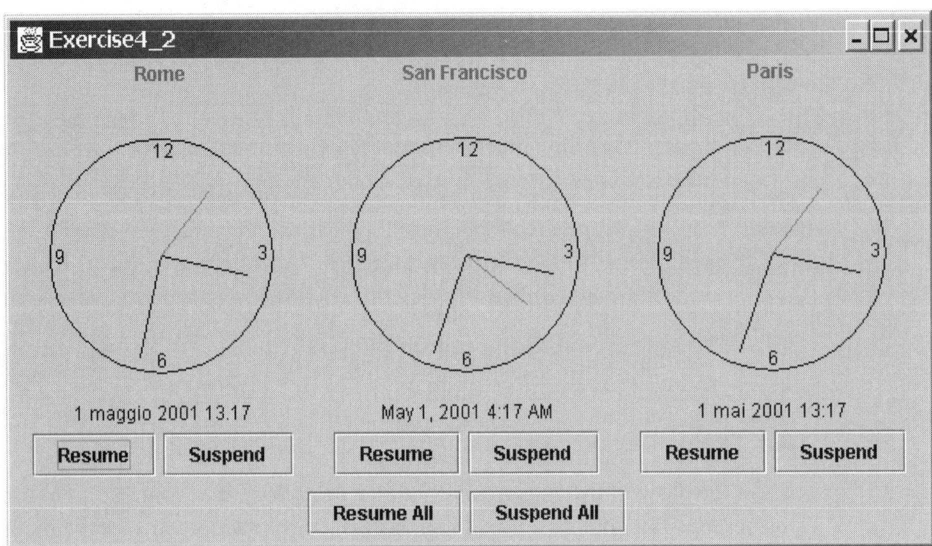

Figure 4.30 *Three clocks run independently with individual control and group control.*

4.3 Modify TestClockWithAlarm in Example 4.3 to play the alarm audio clip on a separate thread, so as to avoid interfering with repainting the clock.

4.4 Develop a model, named `Rectangle`, for describing rectangles. `Rectangle` contains the properties `width`, `height`, `color`, and `filled` and the methods `findArea` and `findPerimeter` for computing the area and the perimeter of the rectangle. Develop a view that displays the rectangle as a figure, and develop another view like a component inspector that displays all the properties of the rectangle. Assemble these components in a test program.

4.5 Create a model, named `Student`, for storing student information, including ssn, lastName, firstName, mi, streetAddress, city, state, phone, and imageFileName (for photo). Develop the following three views for `Student`:

- A panel that is similar to a component inspector to display the student's information and enable editing properties.
- A panel that displays a mailing label.
- A component (like an ID card) that contains the photo and other essential information on the card.

4.6 Create a project that meets the following requirements:

- Develop a `CalendarPanel` component with the properties `month` and `year`, as shown in Figure 4.31.
- Use the bean to create a program that displays the calendar based on the specified locale, as shown in Figure 4.32. The user can specify a locale from a combo box that consists of a list of all the available locales supported by the system.

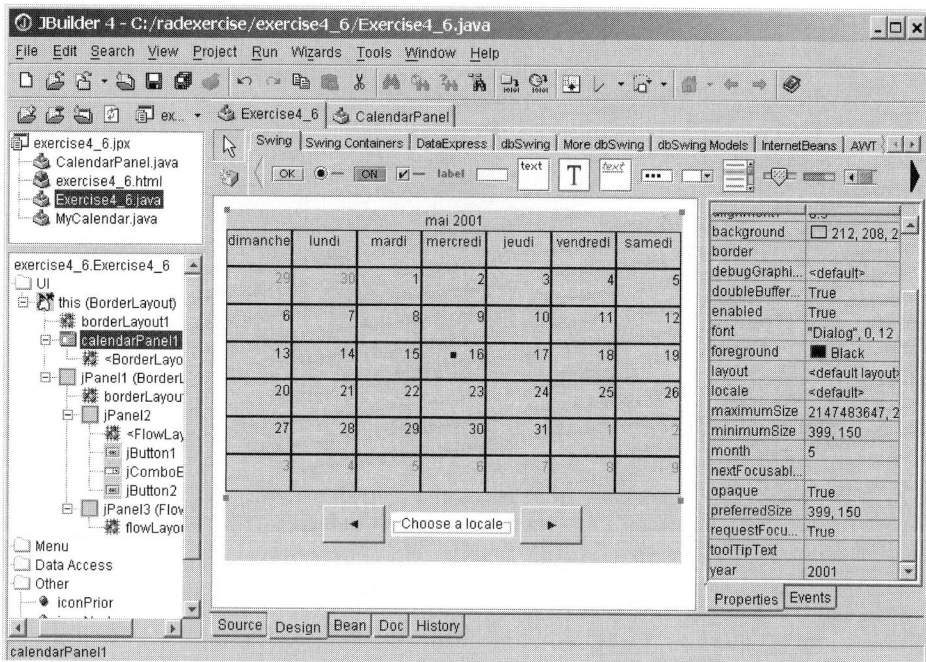

Figure 4.31 *An instance of* `CalendarPanel` *is shown in the UI designer.*

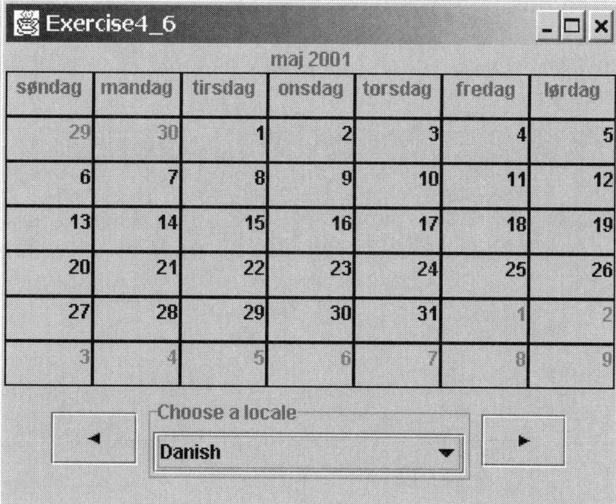

Figure 4.32 *The calendar applet displays the calendar with the Danish locale.*

4.7 Create a project that meets the following requirements:

- Develop a `Fan` bean that displays a fan with the properties `running`, `speed`, and `reversed`.
- Use the bean to create a program that displays and controls the fan, as shown in Figure 4.33.

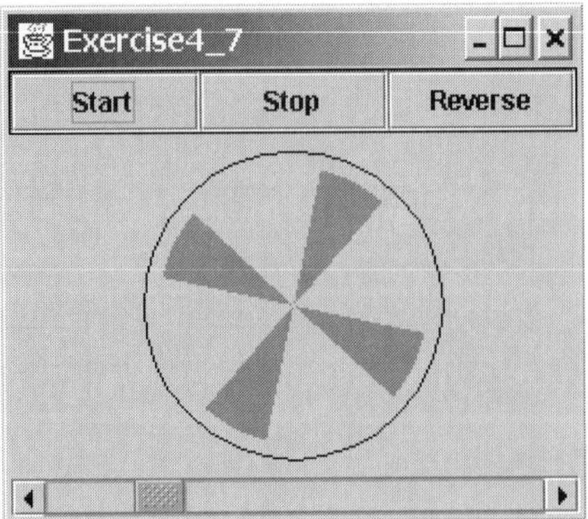

Figure 4.33 *The program simulates a running fan.*

4.8 Create a model that holds the data in an array of double elements, named `data`, and the names for the data in an array of strings, named `dataName`. For example, the enrollment data {200, 40, 50, 100, 40} stored in the array `data` are for {"CS", "Math", "Chem", "Biol", "Phys"} in the array `dataName`. These two properties have their respective get methods, but not individual set methods. Both properties are set together in the `setChartData(String[] newDataName, double[] newData)` method so that they can be displayed properly. Create a view named `PieChart` to present the data in a pie chart, and create a view named `BarChart` to present the data in a bar chart, as shown in Figure 4.34. In Exercise 8.10, you will create a controller that enables the user to insert, delete, and update data interactively using a table.

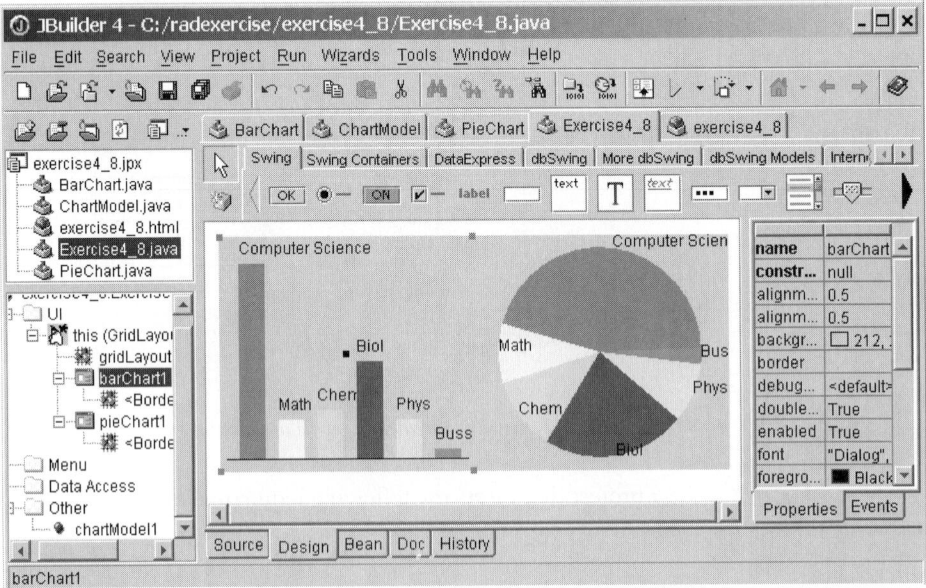

Figure 4.34 *The two views,* `PieChart` *and* `BarChart`*, receive data from the* `ChartModel`.

Hint: Each pie represents a percentage of the total data. Color the pie using the colors from an array named `colors`, which is {`Color.red`, `Color.yellow`, `Color.green`, `Color.blue`, `Color.cyan`, `Color.magenta`, `Color.orange`, `Color.pink`, `Color.darkGray`}. Use `colors[i%colors.length]` for the ith pie. Use black color to display the data names.

PART II

Rapid Application Development with Swing Components

Swing components are the essential elements in creating a graphical user interface. This part of the book covers Swing components and uses them in rapid Java application development. You will learn how to use a variety of Swing components to develop Java projects with JBuilder.

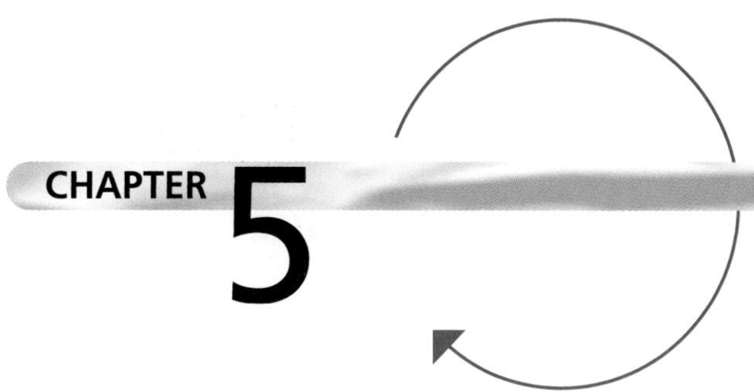

Swing Components

Objectives

- Know the differences between Swing components and AWT components.
- Understand Swing model-view architecture.
- Use the pluggable look-and-feel features of Swing components in JBuilder.
- Become familiar with the basic features of `JComponent`.
- Create projects using the Swing components `JButton`, `JRadioButton`, `JToggleButton`, `JCheckBox`, `JLabel`, `JTextField`, `JTextArea`, `JEditorPane`, `JScrollPane`, `JScrollBar`, `JSlider`, and `JProgressBar`.

Introduction

When Java was introduced, the graphics components were bundled in a library known as *Abstract Window Toolkit,* or *AWT.* For each platform on which Java runs, the AWT components are automatically mapped to the platform-specific components through their respective agents, known as *peers.* AWT is fine for developing simple GUI applications, but it is inadequate for developing comprehensive GUI applications. Besides, AWT is prone to platform-specific bugs, because its peer-based approach relies heavily on the underlying platform. With the release of JDK 1.2, the AWT user interface components were replaced by a more robust and versatile set of classes known as the *Swing components.* Swing components are painted directly on canvases using Java code, except for components that are subclasses of `java.awt.Window` or `java.awt.Panel`, which must be drawn using native GUI on a specific platform. Swing components are less dependent on the target platform and use fewer native GUI resources. For this reason, Swing components are referred to as *lightweight components,* and AWT components are referred to as *heavyweight components.* Although AWT components are still supported in Java 2, I recommend that you learn to program with the Swing components, because the AWT user interface components will eventually fade away. That is why this book uses Swing components exclusively.

Java provides a rich set of classes to help you build graphical user interfaces. You can use various GUI-building classes, such as frames, panels, labels, buttons, text fields, text areas, combo boxes, check boxes, radio buttons, menus, scroll bars, scroll panes, and tabbed panes, to construct user interfaces. This chapter introduces the basic Swing components. You will learn how to use them in rapid application development.

Lightweight Component Framework

Swing components are lightweight. To understand what a lightweight component is, it is necessary to review the design of the AWT components.

AWT provides a platform-independent interface to develop visual programs and graphical user interfaces. For each platform on which Java runs, the AWT components are automatically mapped to the platform-specific components. These platform-specific mappings, called *peers,* are defined in `java.awt.peer` package. The user interface components (`java.awt.Button`, `java.awt.Canvas`, `java.awt.Label`, etc.), `java.awt.Window`, and `java.awt.Panel` all have their supporting peers, named *X*Peer for component *X*. For example, the button peer is named `ButtonPeer`. Since the peers enable the user applications to be consistent with other applications running on the same platform, a Java user interface on Windows has the same look-and-feel as other Windows applications.

Peer architecture has the obvious advantage of simultaneously preserving the look-and-feel of each platform on which Java runs and maintaining a platform-independent API that can be used on all platforms. This architecture has two drawbacks, however.

- The peer architecture consumes a lot of resources. To create a new GUI class, you must subclass `java.awt.Canvas` or `java.awt.Panel`. Components that extend these classes have their own native windows. These native windows, the peers, exist along with the components you are creating. In essence, creating one component using this peer model consumes the resources of two. For this reason, the component with an underlying peer is referred to as *heavyweight*.
- The native windows are also opaque (nontransparent). This means that a window onscreen covers any other windows behind it; you can't "see through" such windows.

To alleviate these problems, Swing components with no native peer were introduced. These components are completely implemented in Java without an underlying native peer. Because they don't require native data structures or peer classes, they are indeed "lighter" in their consumption of resources. For this reason, they are referred to as *lightweight*.

Lightweight components extend `java.awt.Component` and `java.awt.Container` classes instead. As a result, these components no longer have native windows associated with them. Also, lightweight components need not be opaque. They can have transparent parts if their paint methods do not render the components.

CAUTION
Do not mix AWT peer components with Swing components. Mixing them may cause problems. This book only uses Swing components.

The Swing Model-View Architecture

In Chapter 4, "Developing and Using Components," you learned how to use the model-view approach in developing models and views that separate data storage and handling from the visual representation of the data. The model-view approach is the backbone of the Swing architecture. Most Swing user interface components are implemented using a variation of the classic model-view approach known as *Swing Model-View Architecture.*

A Swing user interface component usually consists of the following objects:

- A component, such as `JButton`, which extends `JComponent`.
- A UI delegate, such as `BasicButtonUI`, which is responsible for displaying the component.
- A model, such as `ButtonModel`, which maintains a component's data.

Swing components delegate visual presentation to their respective UI delegates. A UI delegate plays the role of the view in the classic model-view architecture. Programmers use Swing components to create user interfaces. Components indirectly create their UI delegates. The UI delegates work behind the scenes to paint the components whenever the models change. The UI delegates can be plugged into a component when the components are constructed. The major benefit of delegating painting to the UI delegates is for implementing pluggable look-and-feel, which is introduced in the next section.

Each UI delegate listens for the model change. The change listeners are implemented as inner classes for most of the UI delegates. A few listeners, such as `ButtonUIListener`, are implemented as separate classes, because `ButtonUIListener` is shared by `JButton`, `JToggleButton`, `JCheckBox`, and `JRadioButton`.

The models for most components are implemented by interfaces whose names end with Model. For example, the model for button component is `ButtonModel`; its default implementation is `DefaultButtonModel`. For convenience, most Swing components contain some properties of their models, and these properties can be modified directly from the component without knowing the existence of the model. For example, the properties `actionCommand` and `mnemonic` are defined in both `DefaultButtonModel` and `JButton`. Some Swing models even contain properties that are not stored in the model, but are used by the UI delegate for painting the component. In any case, all the data are synchronized behind the scenes. For instance, when one of its properties changes, the component notifies the model, and the model sends the change to the UI delegate. The UI delegate then repaints the component.

Most Swing user interface components have a property named `model` that enables programmers to access and manipulate the model through the component. When you create a Swing user interface component, a default model is assigned to the `model` property. For simple components like `JButton`, `JToggleButton`, `JCheckBox`, `JRadioButton`, `JTextField`, and `JTextArea`, you need not be concerned about the models. For advanced components like `JList`, `JComboBox`, `JTable`, and `JTree`, you have to work with their models directly and access the components through the models.

Pluggable Look-and-Feel

Lightweight components consume fewer resources and can be transparent, but they lack the AWT's platform-specific look-and-feel advantage. To address this problem, a new pluggable look-and-feel feature was introduced in Java.

The pluggable look-and-feel feature lets you design a single set of GUI components that automatically has the look-and-feel of any OS platform. The implementation of this feature is independent of the underlying native GUI, yet it can imitate the native behavior of the native GUI.

Currently, Java supports the following three look-and-feel styles:

- Metal
- Motif
- Windows

JavaSoft provides an example to demonstrate these three styles. To run this example, change the directory to c:\JBuilder4\jdk1.3\demo\jfc\SimpleExample and type the following command at the DOS prompt:

```
java -jar SimpleExample.jar
```

Figure 5.1 shows three sample runs of the example.

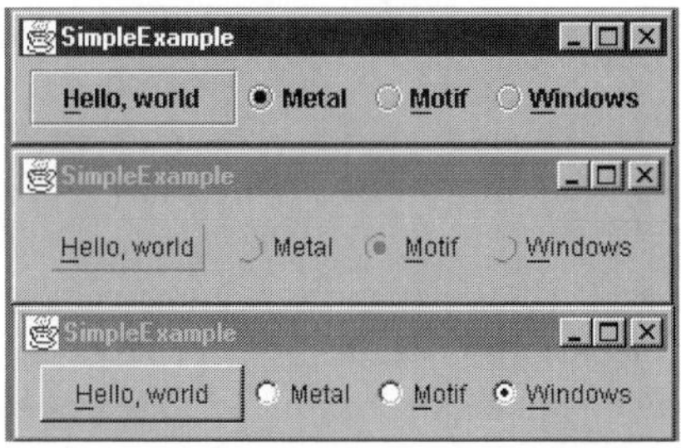

Figure 5.1 *The SimpleExample demonstrates three look-and-feel styles.*

The Metal style, also known as the *Java style*, gives you a consistent look regardless of operating systems. The Windows style is currently only available on Windows due to Windows copyright restrictions. The Motif style is used on Unix operating systems. Recall that JBuilder allows the user to set the look-and-feel as shown in Figure 1.43.

The `javax.swing.UIManager` class manages the look-and-feel of the user interface. You can use one of the following three methods to set the look-and-feel for Metal, Motif, and Windows:

```
UIManager.setLookAndFeel
  (UIManager.getCrossPlatformLookAndFeelClassName());

UIManager.setLookAndFeel
  (new javax.swing.plaf.motif.MotifLookAndFeel());

UIManager.setLookAndFeel
  (new javax.swing.plaf.windows.WindowsLookAndFeel());
```

The `setLookAndFeel` method throws `UnsupportedLookAndFeelException`, so you have to put the method inside a `try/catch` block for it to compile.

The look-and-feel can be plugged during design time or at runtime, but most often you set a look-and-feel during design time. To ensure that the setting takes effect, the `setLookAndFeel` method should be executed before any of the components are instantiated. Thus, you need to place the code in the beginning of the `main` method for applications and in the beginning of the `init` method for applets. Alternatively, you can put the code in an anonymous static block. The anonymous static block is always executed when the class is instantiated.

When you create an application with JBuilder's Application wizard, the following `main` method is automatically generated in the application class. The `getSystemLookAndFeelClassName` method returns the name of the `LookAndFeel` class that implements the native system's look-and-feel if there is one; otherwise the name of the default cross-platform LookAndFeel class is returned.

```
/** Main method */
public static void main(String[] args) {
  try {
    UIManager.setLookAndFeel
      (UIManager.getSystemLookAndFeelClassName());
  }
  catch(Exception e) {
    e.printStackTrace();
  }
  new Application1();
}
```

When you create an applet with JBuilder's Applet wizard, the following static initialization block is automatically generated in the applet class, in which two setLookAndFeel methods are commented. Static initialization blocks are executed when the class is loaded. For more information on static initialization blocks, please refer to Chapter 8, "Class Inheritance and Interfaces," in *Introduction to Java Programming with JBuilder 4*. You may uncomment one setLookAndFeel method in the following code to specify a look-and-feel.

```
static {
  try {
    //UIManager.setLookAndFeel(
    //  UIManager.getSystemLookAndFeelClassName());
    //UIManager.setLookAndFeel
    //  (UIManager.getCrossPlatformLookAndFeelClassName());
  }
  catch (Exception e) {}
}
```

NOTE

For simplicity, I deliberately deleted the static block in the code generated by the Applet wizard. Thus this block is not shown in the source code listing in the text.

TIP

You can preview a particular look-and-feel in your UI design from the UI designer in JBuilder, as follows:

1. Right-click in the UI designer and choose Look-and-Feel.
2. Select the look you want from the menu list, as shown in Figure 5.2.

The UI designer repaints the components to display the selected look-and-feel. Note that the preview does not set the look-and-feel for the runtime.

NOTE

By default, the Windows look-and-feel is used in the UI designer for the Windows version of JBuilder during design time. If a look-and-feel is not explicitly specified in the program, the Metal look-and-feel is used.

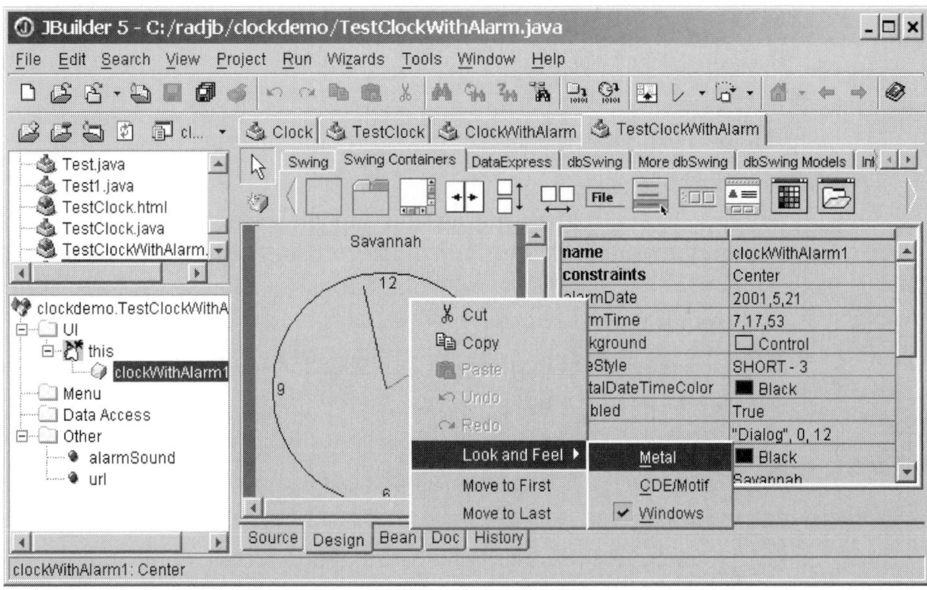

Figure 5.2 *You can review look-and-feel in the UI designer.*

Overview of the Swing Classes

The Swing classes are extensions of and enhancements to the Java API. There are more than 250 Swing classes grouped in the following packages:

- `javax.swing` contains the lightweight user interface components, including pure Java implementation of the standard AWT components, such as `JButton` for `java.awt.Button`, `JLabel` for `java.awt.Label`, and `JPanel` for `java.awt.Panel`, plus a rich set of advanced components, such as `JProgressBar`, `JTree`, and `JTable`.

- `javax.swing.border` contains classes that describe the borders of the Swing components. You can use the border styles, such as `BevelBorder`, `SoftBevelBorder`, `EtchedBorder`, `LineBorder`, `TitledBorder`, and `MatteBorder`, to create a (decorated or plain) area around the edge of a component with optional titles.

- `javax.swing.event` contains the event sets (the event classes and their listeners) for Swing components. Swing components use the event sets in the `java.awt.event` package as well as in the `javax.swing.event` package.

- `javax.swing.text` contains the classes for viewing and editing text.

- `javax.swing.text.html` contains the `HTMLEditorKit` class, which provides a default implementation of HTML editing functionality. The primary goal here is to be small but flexible. It is not intended to be a full-fledged HTML implementation, but it meets modest needs, with the idea that more substantial needs can be met with alternative implementations.

- `javax.swing.text.html.parser` contains the parser classes for HTML files.
- `javax.swing.text.rtf` contains the `RTFEditorKit` class, which provides a default implementation of RTF editing functionality.
- `javax.swing.undo` contains the classes for supporting the cut, copy, and paste operations.
- `javax.accessibility` provides the support for developers to make products that are compatible with Assistive Technologies (for alternative interfaces like Braille). All of the Swing components implement interface `Accessible`, which is the main interface for the accessibility package.
- `javax.swing.table` contains the classes for supporting `JTable`. `JTable` is a user interface component that presents data in a two-dimensional table format.
- `javax.swing.tree` contains the classes for supporting `JTree`. `JTree` is a user interface component that presents a set of hierarchical data as an outline.
- `javax.swing.colorchooser` contains support classes and interfaces for the `javax.swing.JColorChooser` component.
- `javax.swing.filechooser` contains support classes and interfaces for the `javax.swing.JFileChooser` component.
- `javax.swing.plaf` contains one interface and many abstract classes that Swing uses to provide its pluggable look-and-feel capabilities.
- `javax.swing.plaf.basic` provides user interface objects built according to the basic look-and-feel.
- `javax.swing.plaf.metal` provides user interface objects built according to the Metal look-and-feel.

Figures 5.3 and 5.4 illustrate the hierarchical relationship of Swing classes using the UML graphical notations. An open triangle pointing to the superclass is used to denote the inheritance relationship between the two classes involved. A filled diamond is attached to the composed class to denote the composition relationship, and a hollow diamond is attached to the aggregated class to denote the aggregation relationship. Abstract class names, interface names, and abstract methods are italicized. Dashed lines and open triangles are used to point to the interface. For more information, see UML Graphical Notations at the book's companion Web site.

The *JComponent* Class

All Swing components preinstalled in the Swing page and the Swing Containers page in the component palette extend `javax.swing.JComponent` or a subclass of `JComponent`. `JComponent` is derived from `java.awt.Container`. `JComponent` provides the following basic features of Swing components:

- A pluggable look-and-feel feature that can be specified by the programmer or (optionally) selected by the user at runtime.
- Comprehensive keystroke handling that works with nested components.

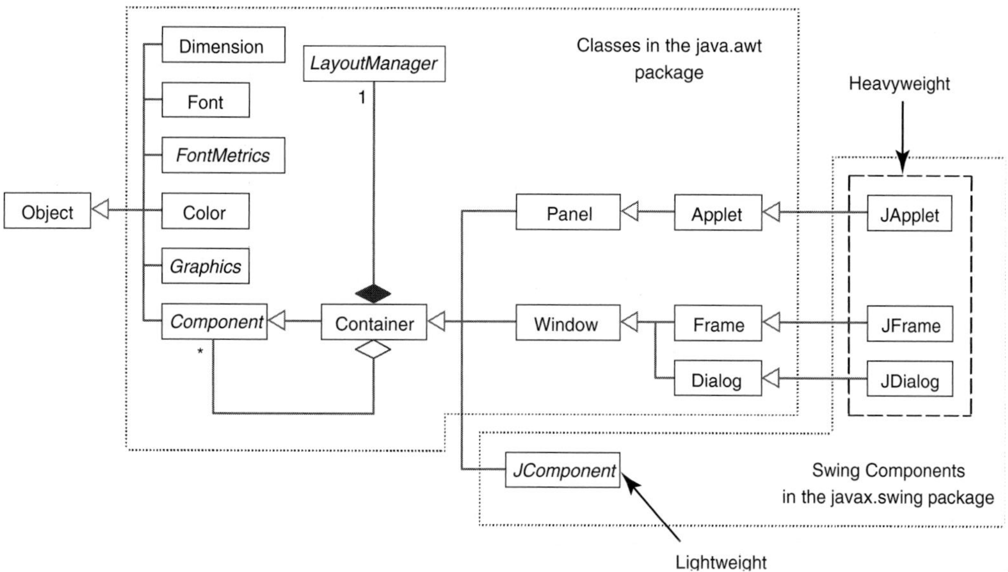

Figure 5.3 *Java graphics programming utilizes the classes shown in this hierarchical diagram.*

- Action objects for single-point control of program actions initiated by multiple components.
- Support for accessibility. Accessibility involves magnifying fonts for sight-impaired users or displaying captions associated with sounds for hearing-impaired users.

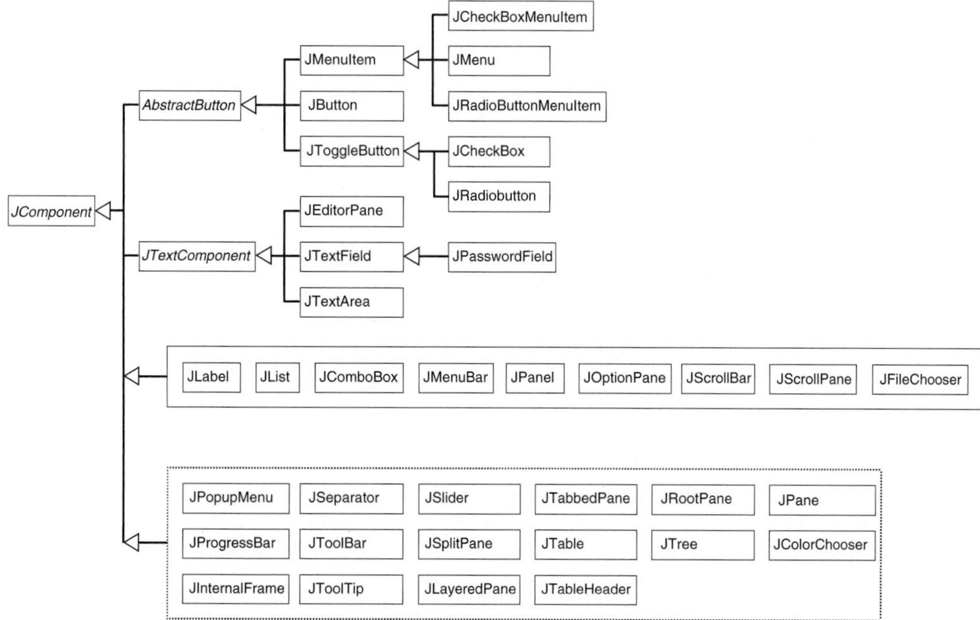

Figure 5.4 *The* `JComponent` *and its subclasses are the basic elements for building graphical user interfaces.*

- Support for international localization. Each swing component has a `locale` property that encapsulates information about a specific locale. A locale determines how locale-sensitive information like date, time, and number is displayed, and how locale-sensitive operations like sorting strings are performed. Swing components can also display Unicode characters.

Keystroke Handling

The `JComponent` architecture makes it easy to handle keyboard events in nested components. You can register interest in a particular combination of keystrokes by creating a `KeyStroke` object and registering it with the component. When you register the keystroke combination and its associated action, you also specify one of the following conditions to determine when the action is initiated:

- The component has the focus.
- A child or grandchild of the component has the focus.

You can use this capability to define global actions for a composite component. For example, a tree control could act on the Plus key to expand all elements in the tree, as long as any component in the tree has the focus.

The window in which the component is located has the focus. In other words, if the component is a child or grandchild of a window, and any component in the window has the focus, then the component receives the event. You can use this capability to direct the keystroke combination Alt+C to the Cancel button in a dialog, for example, as long any component in the dialog has the focus.

An example of keystroke handling is given in Example 7.1, "Using Menu Designer."

Action Objects

Action-interface objects provide a single point of control for program actions. For example, a toolbar icon and a menu item can reference the same action object. When the action object is disabled, the GUI items that reference it are automatically disabled. The `Action` interface extends `java.awt.event.ActionListener`, specifying an `enabled` property as well as properties for text descriptions and graphic icons.

An example of using action objects is given in Example 7.4, "Using Actions."

JComponent Properties

Since `JComponent` is the root for all Swing GUI components, all the properties of `JComponent` are inherited by other Swing GUI components, and thus it is important to understand the properties. Figure 5.5 shows the `JComponent` properties in the component inspector.

- `alignmentX`: This is the preferred horizontal alignment of the component, which specifies how the component would like to be aligned relative to other

name	jComponent1
actionMap	
alignmentX	0.5
alignmentY	0.5
autoscrolls	False
background	☐ 212, 208, 200
border	
debugGraphicsOptions	
doubleBuffered	True
enabled	True
font	"Dialog", 0, 12
foreground	■ Black
inputVerifier	
layout	<default layout>
maximumSize	32767, 32767
minimumSize	10, 10
nextFocusableComponent	
opaque	True
preferredSize	10, 10
requestFocusEnabled	True
toolTipText	
verifyInputWhenFocusTarget	True

Properties | Events

Figure 5.5 *The properties of* `JComponent` *are shown in the component inspector.*

components along the x-axis. The value should be a number between 0 and 1, where 0 represents alignment along the origin, 1 is aligned the farthest away from the origin, 0.5 is centered, etc. This property is used with the `BoxLayout`, which is introduced in Chapter 6, "Containers and Layout Managers."

- `alignmentY`: This is the preferred vertical alignment of the component, which specifies how the component would like to be aligned relative to other components along the y-axis. The value should be a number between 0 and 1, where 0 represents alignment along the origin, 1 is aligned the farthest away from the origin, 0.5 is centered, etc. This property is used with the `BoxLayout`.
- `autoscrolls`: This is a `boolean` property to enable automatic scrolling in a list, table, or tree that occurs when the user is dragging the mouse. By default, it is `false`.
- `border`: This specifies a border of the component with an optional title. Many types of border styles are available, and they can be combined to create compound borders.
- `debugGraphicsOption`: This allows you to set slow-motion graphics rendering, so that you can see what is being displayed on screen and whether or not it is being overwritten. This feature is useful in debugging.

- `doubleBuffered`: This specifies whether the component is painted using double-buffering. This is a technique for reducing flickering. In AWT programming, you have to manually implement this technique in the program. With Swing, this capability is automatically supported if the `doubleBuffered` property is set to `true`. By default, it is `true`.
- `enabled`: This determines whether the component is enabled. An enabled component can respond to user input and generate events. By default, `enabled` is true.
- `font`: The font used to display text on the component.
- `foreground`: The foreground color of the component.
- `background`: The background color of the component.
- `layout`: This specifies a layout manager in the component. Although this property is available to all subclasses of `JComponent`, it is used when the component is a container, such as `JPanel`. You could use a `JButton` to contain other components, if you wish, but `JPanel` should be used instead.
- `maximumSize`: This specifies the maximum size the component needs so that the layout manager won't waste space giving it to a component that does not need it. For instance, `BorderLayout` could limit the center component's size to its maximum size, and then either give the space to edge components or limit the size of the outer window when resized.
- `minimumSize`: This specifies the minimum size for the component to be useful. For most Swing components, `minimumSize` is the same as `preferredSize`. Layout managers generally respect `minimumSize` rather than `preferredSize`.
- `preferredSize`: This indicates the ideal size for the component to look best. This property may or may not be considered by some layout managers, depending on their rules. For example, a component uses its preferred size in a container with a `FlowLayout` manager, but its preferred size may be ignored if it is placed in a container with a `GridLayout` manager.
- `nextFocusableComponent`: This specifies the next focusable component or null if the focus manager should choose the next focusable component automatically.
- `requestFocusEnabled`: This determines whether the receiving component can obtain the focus by calling the `requestFocus()` method. The default value is true.
- `opaque`: This specifies whether the component is opaque. By default it is true.
- `toolTipText`: This is the text displayed when the mouse points on the component without clicking. This text is generally used to give the user a tip about the function of the component.
- `visible`: This is a `boolean` value indicating whether the component is visible.
- `size`: This is the size of the component displayed. This property's type is `java.awt.Dimension`.

Note
The `background`, `enabled`, `font`, `foreground`, `maximumSize`, `minimumSize`, and `preferredSize` properties are defined in `java.awt.Component`; the `alignmentX`, `alignmentY`, and `layout` properties are defined in `java.awt.Container`.

Note
The subclasses of `JComponent` may change the default values of the properties initialized in `JComponent`. For example, the default value for `doubleBuffered` property in `JButton` is false.

The SwingSet Demo

Swing comes with a variety of samples that demonstrate various aspects of the Swing components. By far the most interesting of all the samples is the SwingSet example, which is an excellent demonstration of many important and useful features of Swing components. To run the example, change the directory to c:\JBuilder4\jdk1.3\demo\jfc\SwingSet2 and type the following command at the DOS prompt:

```
java -jar SwingSet2.jar
```

A sample run of the example is shown in Figure 5.6.

JButton

`JButton` is the Swing version of a button component. You can have a text on the button, an image icon on the button, or both a text and an image icon at the same time. You can have a pressed icon, which appears when the button is pressed. You can have a rollover icon, which appears when the mouse points to the button without clicking. Figure 5.7 shows buttons in the SwingSet demo.

`JButton` is a subclass of `AbstractButton`, which defines the common behaviors for `JButton`, `JToggleButton`, `JCheckBox`, and `JRadioButton`. All the properties of `JButton` are defined in its superclass, such as `JComponent` and `AbstractButton`.

The following properties are defined in the `AbstractButton` class.

- `text`: This is the label on the button. You can set a label using the `setText` method.
- `horizontalAlignment`: This is one of the three values (`SwingConstants.LEFT`, `SwingConstants.CENTER`, `SwingConstants.RIGHT`) that specify how the text is placed horizontally on a button. The default horizontal alignment is `SwingConstants.CENTER`.
- `horizontalTextPosition`: This is one of the five values (`SwingConstants.LEFT`, `SwingConstants.CENTER`, `SwingConstants.RIGHT`, `SwingConstants.LEADING`, `SwingConstants.TRAILLING`) that specify the horizontal position of the text relative to the icon. The default horizontal text position is `SwingConstants.RIGHT`.

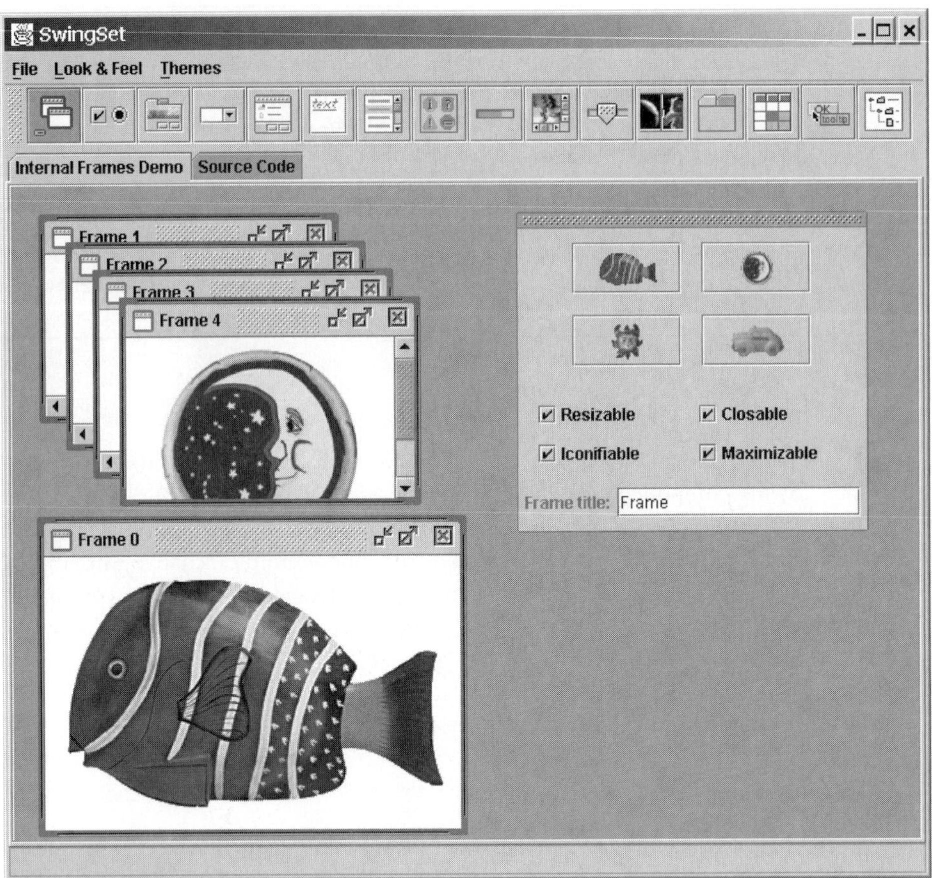

Figure 5.6 *The SwingSet applet is a comprehensive example that demonstrates many interesting features of the Swing components.*

- `verticalAlignment`: This is one of the three values (`SwingConstants.TOP`, `SwingConstants.CENTER`, `SwingConstants.BOTTOM`) that specify how the label is placed vertically on a button. The default vertical alignment is `SwingConstants.CENTER`.
- `verticalTextPosition`: This is one of the three values (`SwingConstants.TOP`, `SwingConstants.CENTER`, `SwingConstants.BOTTOM`) that specify the vertical position of the text relative to the icon. The default vertical text position is `SwingConstants.CENTER`.
- `actionCommand`: This specifies an action command string associated with the button. By default, the action command is the same as the button text. The action command string is passed to the `ActionEvent` when an `ActionEvent` is generated on the button.
- `mnemonic`: This specifies a shortcut key. You can select the button by pressing the ALT key and the mnemonic key at the same time. The mnemonic is underlined. As shown in Figure 5.7, B is the mnemonic for the Pain Border check box. You can check or uncheck the option by pressing Alt + B.

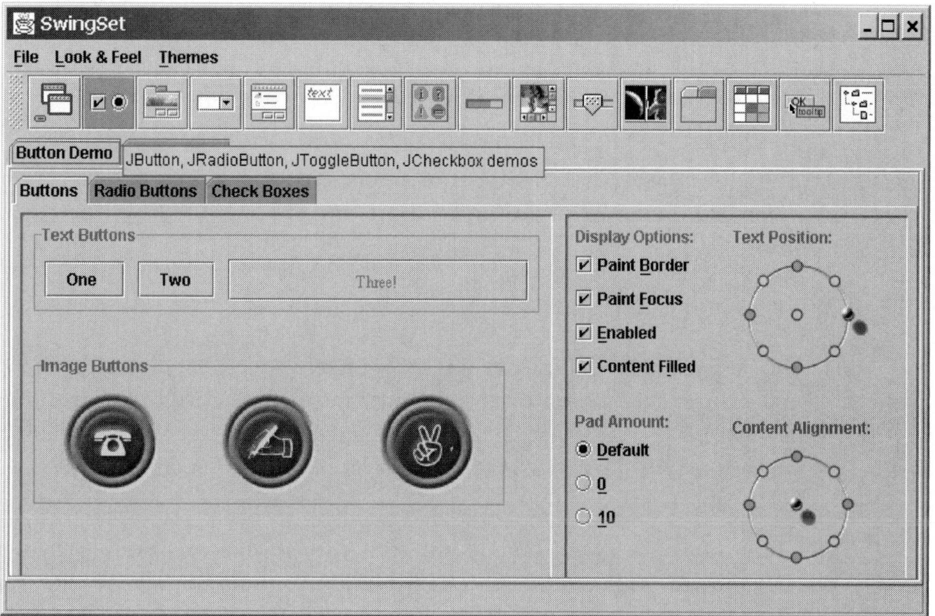

Figure 5.7 *The SwingSet demo demonstrates the features of* `JButton`.

- `disabledIcon`: This is the icon displayed when the button is disabled. You can set a disabled icon using the `setDisableIcon` method.
- `icon`: This is the image icon on the button. You can set an icon using the `setIcon` method.
- `pressedIcon`: An icon that is displayed when a button is pressed.
- `rolloverIcon`: An icon that is displayed when the mouse points to the button without clicking. To see a rollover icon, the `rolloverEnabled` property must be `true`.
- `rolloverEnabled`: This determines whether rollover is enabled. By default, it is `true`. When you set a rollover icon in the component inspector, the `rolloverEnabled` property is automatically set to `true`.
- `borderPainted`: This determines whether the button border is painted. By default, it is true.
- `contentAreaFilled`: This determines whether the button should paint the content area or leave it transparent. By default, the content area is painted.
- `focusPainted`: This determines whether a focus indicator is painted when a button has the focus. By default, it is true.
- `margin`: This is the space between the button's border and its content. The margin property type is `java.awt.Insets`.
- `model`: This is the model that a button represents. Rarely used with buttons.

- `selected`: This property has no meaning in `JButton` but is used in `JRadioButton`, `JCheckBox`, and `JToggleButton`.
- `selectedIcon`: This property has no meaning in `JButton` but is used in `JRadioButton`, `JCheckBox`, and `JToggleButton`.

Buttons can generate many types of events, but often you use the `ActionEvent` to respond to button-click action. Most of the events are inherited from `JButton`'s superclass.

JToggleButton

Toggle buttons are buttons that have two states: selected and deselected. `JToggleButton` is a subclass of `AbstractButton` and a superclass of `JRadioButton` and `JCheckBox`. `JToggleButton` provides an implementation of a two-state button, which is the basis for `JRadioButton` and `JCheckBox`.

All the properties of the `JToggleButton` class are inherited from its superclass. These properties are the same as the properties of `JButton`. `JToggleButton` can fire all the events that can be generated by a `JButton` object. Whenever a button is clicked, an `ActionEvent` and an `ItemEvent` are generated.

`JRadioButton` and `JCheckBox` are subclasses of `JToggleButton`. These two classes are often used instead of the `JToggleButton` class.

JCheckBox

A check box is a component that enables the user to toggle a choice on or off, like a light switch. Check boxes are usually displayed in a group and allow multiple selections. Figure 5.8 shows the use of `JCheckBox` in the SwingSet demo.

`JCheckBox` is a subclass of `JToggleButton`. All the properties of `JCheckBox` are inherited from its superclasses. These properties are the same as the properties in `JToggleButton`, but the default values may be different. By default, `borderPainted` is `false` for a `JCheckBox` object. If an image icon is used, the image icon replaces the check box indicator.

`JCheckBox` can fire all the events that can be generated by its superclass. Whenever a check box is checked or unchecked, an `ActionEvent` and an `ItemEvent` are generated.

JRadioButton

Radio buttons, also known as *option buttons*, are often used to choose one item exclusively from a list of choices. In appearance they are similar to check boxes. A check box displays a square that is either checked or blank, and a radio button displays a circle that is either filled (if selected) or blank (if not selected). Figure 5.9 demonstrates the use of `JRadioButton` in the SwingSet demo.

`JRadioButton` is a subclass of `JToggleButton`. All the properties of `JRadioButton` are inherited from its superclasses. These properties are the same as the properties in

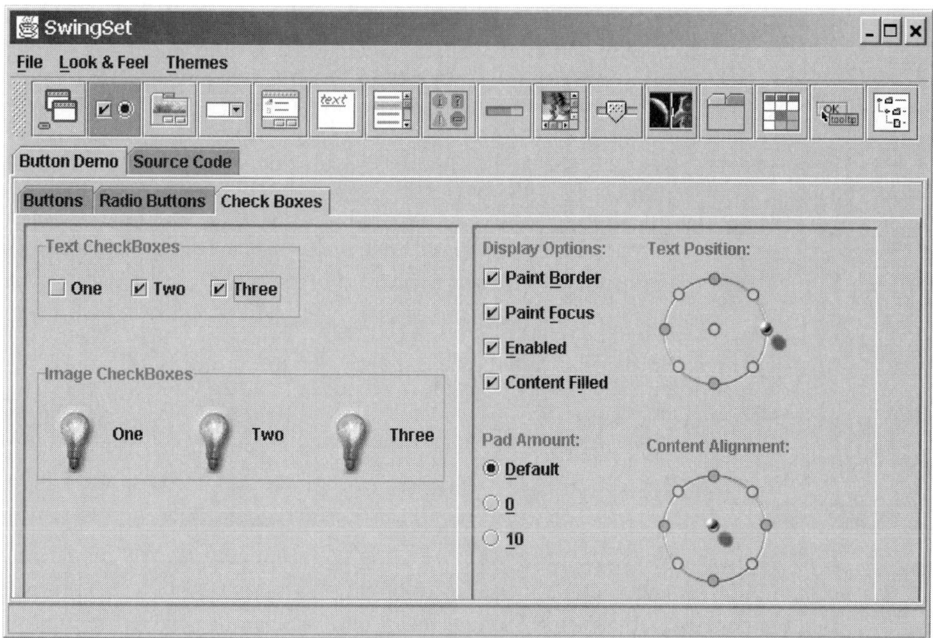

Figure 5.8 *The SwingSet demo demonstrates the features of* `JCheckBox`.

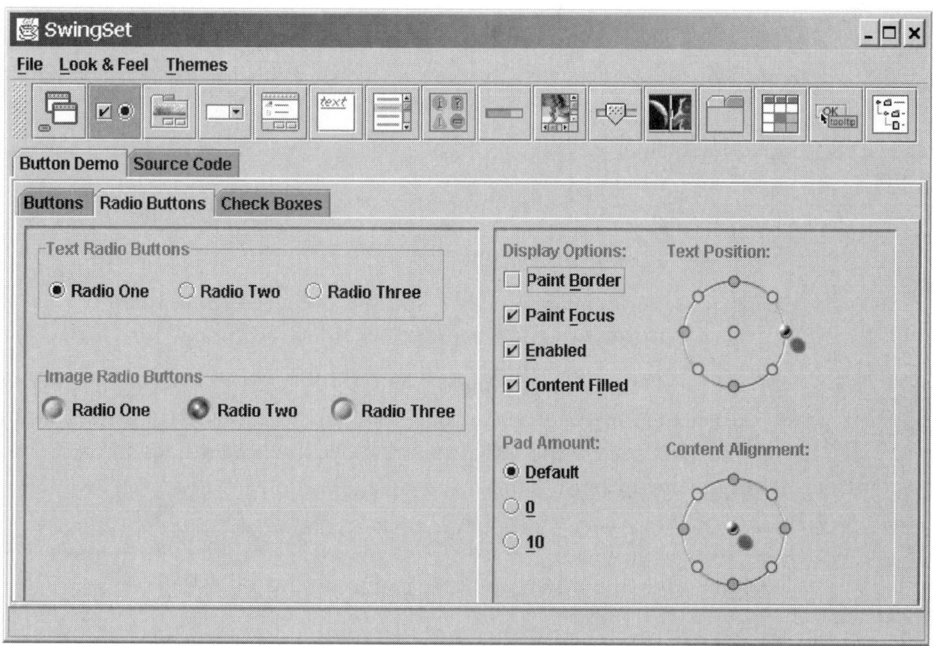

Figure 5.9 *The SwingSet demo demonstrates the features of* `JRadioButton`.

JToggleButton, but the default values may be different. By default, borderPainted is false for a JRadioButton object. If an image icon is used, the image icon replaces the radio button indicator.

JRadioButton can fire all the events that can be generated by its superclass. Whenever a radio button is checked or unchecked, an ActionEvent and an ItemEvent are generated.

To group radio buttons, create an instance of ButtonGroup and place the radio buttons into the group using the add method. For example, the following statements group radio buttons jrb1, jrb2, and jrb3:

```
ButtonGroup btg = new ButtonGroup();
btg.add(jrb1);
btg.add(jrb2);
btg.add(jrb3);
```

Border

Border, one of the interesting new Swing components features, renders a border around the edges of a Swing component. The BevelBorder, SoftBevelBorder, EtchedBorder, LineBorder, TitledBorder, and MatteBorder classes are used to create specific border styles. You can use EmptyBorder to create a plain border, and CompoundBorder to nest multiple border objects, creating a single, combined border.

To create a titled border, use the following statement:

```
Border titledBorder = new TitledBorder("A Title");
```

Border is the interface for all types of borders. TitledBorder is an implementation of Border with a title. You can create a desired border using the following properties:

- title: The title of the border.
- titleColor: The color of the title.
- titleFont: The font of the title.
- titleJustification: This specifies Border.LEFT, Border.CENTER, or Border.RIGHT for left, center, or right title justification.
- titlePosition: This is one of the six values (Border.ABOVE_TOP, Border.TOP, Border.BELOW_TOP, Border.ABOVE_BOTTOM, Border.BOTTOM, Border.BELOW_BOTTOM) that specify the title position above the border line, on the border line, or below the border line.
- border: This is the property in TitledBorder for building composite borders.

The other types of borders can be created using the following classes:

- BevelBorder: This creates a border with a 3-D look that can be lowered or raised. To construct a BevelBorder, use the following constructor, which creates a `BevelBorder` with the specified `bevelType` (`BevelBorder.LOWERED` or `BevelBorder.BevelBorder`).

```
public BevelBorder(int bevelType)
```

- `EtchedBorder`: This creates an etched border which can either be etched-in or etched-out. You can use its default constructor to construct an `EtchedBorder` with lowered border. `EtchedBorder` has a property `etchType` with values `LOWERED` or `RAISED`.
- `LineBorder`: This creates a line border of arbitrary thickness in a single color. To create a `LineBorder`, use the following constructor:

  ```
  public LineBorder(Color c, int thickness)
  ```

- `MatteBorder`: This creates a matte-like border padded with icon images. To create a `MatteBorder`, use the following constructor:

  ```
  public MatteBorder(Icon tileIcon)
  ```

- `EmptyBorder`: This creates a border with border space but no drawings. To create an `EmptyBorder`, use the following constructor:

  ```
  public EmptyBorder(int top, int left, int bottom, int right)
  ```

NOTE

All the border classes and interfaces are grouped in the `javax.swing.border` package.

Swing also provides the `javax.swing.BorderFactory` class, which contains static methods for creating borders. Some of the static methods are:

- `public static TitledBorder createTitledBorder(String title)`
- `public static Border createLoweredBevelBorder()`
- `public static Border createRaisedBevelBorder()`
- `public static Border createLineBorder(Color color)`
- `public static Border createLineBorder(Color color, int thickness)`
- `public static Border createEtchedBorder()`
- `public static Border createEtchedBorder(Color highlight, Color shadow)`
- `public static Border createEmptyBorder()`
- `public static MatteBorder createEmptyBorder(int top, int left, int bottom, int right)`
- `public static MatteBorder createMatteBorder(int top, int left, int bottom, int right, Color color)`

- `public static MatteBorder createMatteBorder(int top, int left, int bottom, int right, Icon tileIcon)`
- `public static Border createCompoundBorder(Border outsideBorder, Border insideBorder)`

For example, to create an etched border, simply use the following statement:

```
Border border = BorderFactory.createEtchedBorder();
```

`Border` instances can be shared. Rather than create a new border object using one of the border classes, you can create a shared instance of the common border types. You can also create a custom border class, which inherits `AbstractBorder`.

NOTE

The `border` property in the component inspector has a combo box and an ellipsis, as shown in Figure 5.10. You can choose simple border styles from the combo box and create composite borders from the Border dialog box, as shown in Figure 5.11. The Border dialog box is displayed when you click the ellipsis.

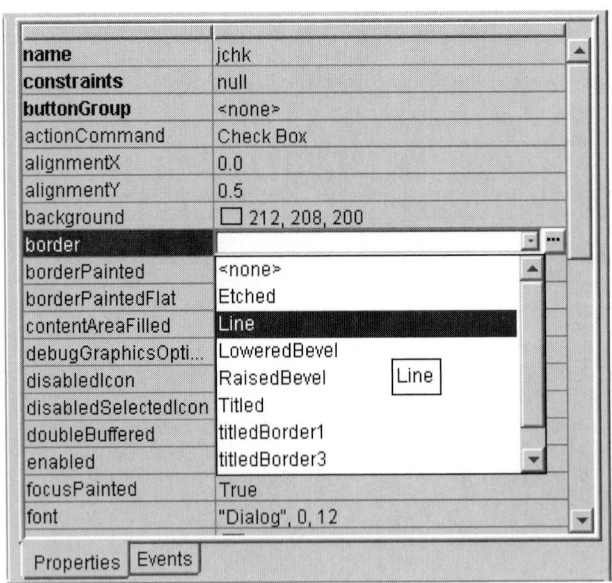

Figure 5.10 *You can choose a fixed border from the combo box or create a composite border by clicking the ellipsis.*

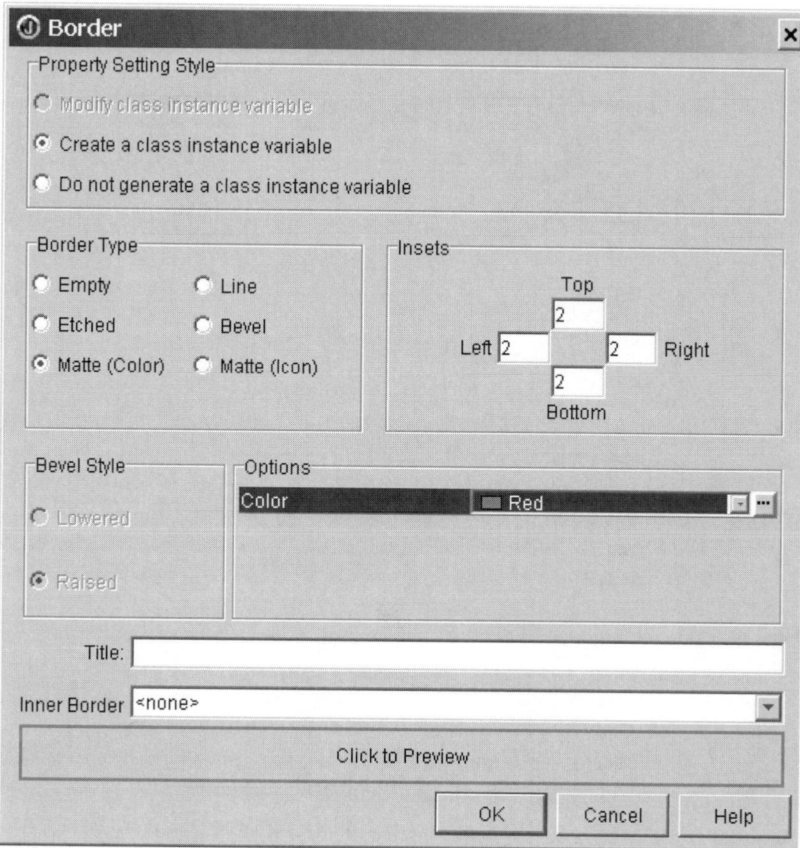

Figure 5.11 *You can create a composite border from the Border dialog box.*

Example 5.1 Using `JButton`, `JToggleButton`, `JCheckBox`, `JRadioButton`, and Borders

This example demonstrates the use of `JButton`, `JToggleButton`, `JCheckBox`, `JRadioButton`, and borders. A sample run of the example is shown in Figure 5.12. The program enables you to dynamically set the properties of `JButton`, `JToggleButton`, `JCheckBox`, and `JRadioButton` at runtime.

Here are the steps to complete the project:

1. Create a new project named dynamicsettingsdemo.jpr and an applet named DynamicSetting.java using the Applet wizard.
2. Select DynamicSetting.java in the project pane, and choose the Design tab in the content pane to switch to the UI designer. Drop a `JPanel` into the center of the applet and rename it `jpButtons`. Drop a `JPanel` into the south of the applet and rename it `jpSettings`.

continued

Example 5.1 continued

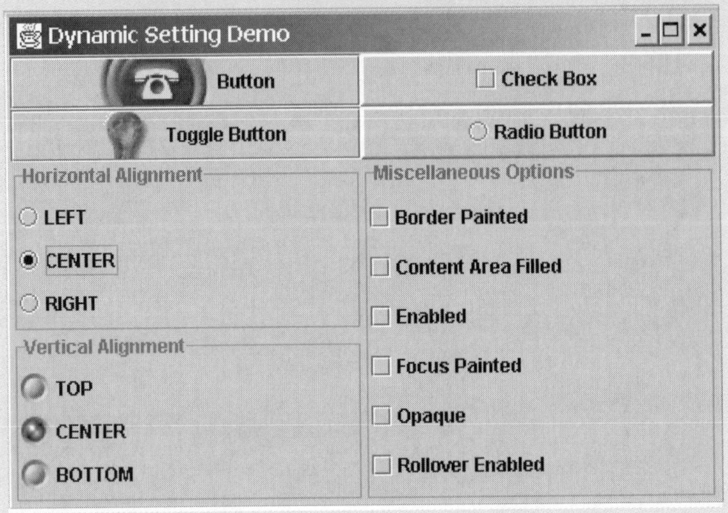

Figure 5.12 *You can set the properties of the button, toggle button, check box, and radio button dynamically.*

3. Drop a `JButton`, a `JToggleButton`, a `JCheckBox`, and a `JRadioButton` into `jpButtons`, and rename them `jbt`, `jtb`, `jchk`, and `jrb`. Set their texts to Button, Toggle Button, Check Box, and Radio Button, and `tooltip` to appropriate strings. Set the `layout` property of `jpButtons` to `GridLayout`, and set the `row` and `column` of the `GridLayout` to 2.

4. Set the layout of `jpSettings` to `GridLayout`. Drop a `JPanel` twice into `jpSettings` to create two panels, and rename them `jpAlignment`, and `jpMiscSettings`.

5. Set the layout of `jpAlignment` to `GridLayout`, and set the row of the `GridLayout` to 2. Drop a `JPanel` twice into `jpAlignment` to create two panels named `jpHorizontalAlignment` and `jpVerticalAlignment`.

6. Drop a `JRadioButton` three times into `jpHorizontalAlignment` to create three radio buttons named `jrbLeft`, `jrbCenter`, and `jrbRight` with text set to LEFT, CENTER, and RIGHT. Set the `layout` of `jpHorizontalAlignment` to `GridLayout` with the `row` property set to 3.

7. Drop a `JRadioButton` three times into `jpVerticalAlignment` to create three radio buttons named `jrbTop`, `jrbVCenter`, and `jrbBottom` with text set to TOP, CENTER, and BOTTOM. Set the `layout` of `jpVerticalAlignment` to `GridLayout` with the `row` property set to 3.

8. Drop a `JCheckBox` six times into `jpMiscSettings` to create six check boxes named `jchkBorderPainted`, `jchkContentAreaFilled`, `jchkEnabled`, `jchkFocusPainted`, `jchkOpaqued`, and `jchkRolloverEnabled` with text set to

Border Painted, Content Area Filled, Enabled, Focus Painted, Opaque, and Rollover Enabled. Set the `layout` of `jpMiscSettings` to `GridLayout` with the `row` property set to 6.

9. To set the borders, choose `titled` in the border property of `jpHorizontalAlignment` to create `titledBorder1`. Select `titledBorder1` in the Other node in the component tree, and set the `title` property to "Horizontal Alignment." Similarly, you can create a titled border for `jpVerticalAlignment`, and `jpMiscSettings`.

10. Declare image icons for use in `jbt`, `jtb`, `jrbTop`, `jrbVCenter`, and `jrbBottom` as regular icon, pressed icon, rollover icon, selected icon, and rollover selected icon. These icons are declared as fields in the class. Create the image icons in the `jbInit` method, as shown in Listing 5.1 (Lines 80–92).

11. In the designer, set properties `icon`, `pressedIcon`, `rolloverIcon`, `rolloverSelectedIcon`, and `selectedIcon` for `jbt`, `jtb`, `jrbTop`, `jrbVCenter`, and `jrbBottom`. Note that the `rolloverSelectedIcon` property and the `selectedIcon` property are not applicable for `jbt`. So don't set them.

12. Declare two `ButtonGroup` instances named `btg1` and `btg2`, and write the code to add the radio buttons for horizontal alignment to `btg1`, and the radio buttons for vertical alignment to `btg2` in the `jbInit` method (Lines 259–267).

13. Generate action events for the radio buttons in the `jpHorizontalAlignment` panel, in the `jpVerticalAlignment` panel, and in the `jpMiscSettings` panel, and implement these handlers for setting the properties of the buttons in the `jpButtons` panel, as shown in Listing 5.1.

```
1    package dynamicsettingdemo;
2
3    import java.awt.*;
4    import java.awt.event.*;
5    import java.applet.*;
6    import javax.swing.*;
7    import javax.swing.border.*;
8    import imageviewerdemo.ImageViewer;
9
10   public class DynamicSetting extends JApplet {
11     // Create button group
12     ButtonGroup btg1 = new ButtonGroup();
13     ButtonGroup btg2 = new ButtonGroup();
14
15     // Create image icons for buttons
16     ImageIcon btIcon; // Regular icon
17     ImageIcon btpIcon; // Pressed icon
18     ImageIcon btrIcon; // Rollover icon
19
20     // Create image icons for the toggle button
21     ImageIcon tbIcon; // Regular icon
22     ImageIcon tbrIcon;  // Rollover icon
23     ImageIcon tbrsIcon; // Rollover selected icon
24     ImageIcon tbsIcon;  // Selected icon, same as pressed
25
```

Listing 5.1 *DynamicSetting.java*

continued

Example 5.1 continued

```
  // Create image icons for radio buttons
  ImageIcon rbIcon;  // Regular icon
  ImageIcon rbpIcon; // Pressed icon
  ImageIcon rbrIcon; // Rollover icon
  ImageIcon rbsIcon; // Selected icon
  ImageIcon rbrsIcon; // Rollover selected icon

  // Generated by JBuilder
  boolean isStandalone = false;
  JPanel jpButtons = new JPanel();
  JPanel jpSettings = new JPanel();
  JPanel jpAlignment = new JPanel();
  GridLayout gridLayout1 = new GridLayout();
  JButton jbt = new JButton();
  JToggleButton jtb = new JToggleButton();
  JCheckBox jchk = new JCheckBox();
  JRadioButton jrb = new JRadioButton();
  TitledBorder titledBorder1;
  TitledBorder titledBorder3;
  JPanel jpMiscSettings = new JPanel();
  JCheckBox jchkBorderPainted = new JCheckBox();
  JCheckBox jchkContentAreaFilled = new JCheckBox();
  JCheckBox jchkEnabled = new JCheckBox();
  JCheckBox jchkFocusPainted = new JCheckBox();
  JCheckBox jchkOpaque = new JCheckBox();
  JCheckBox jchkRolloverEnabled = new JCheckBox();
  GridLayout gridLayout4 = new GridLayout();
  JRadioButton jrbLeft = new JRadioButton();
  JRadioButton jrbRight = new JRadioButton();
  JRadioButton jrbCenter = new JRadioButton();
  GridLayout gridLayout3 = new GridLayout();
  GridLayout gridLayout2 = new GridLayout();
  JPanel jpHorizontalAlignment = new JPanel();
  JPanel jpVerticalAlignment = new JPanel();
  GridLayout gridLayout5 = new GridLayout();
  BorderLayout borderLayout1 = new BorderLayout();
  JRadioButton jrbTop = new JRadioButton();
  JRadioButton jrbVCenter = new JRadioButton();
  JRadioButton jrbBottom = new JRadioButton();
  TitledBorder titledBorder2;
  GridLayout gridLayout6 = new GridLayout();

  /** Initialize the applet */
  public void init() {
    try {
      jbInit();
    }
    catch(Exception e) {
      e.printStackTrace();
    }
  }

  /** Component initialization */
  private void jbInit() throws Exception {
    // Load icon images
    btIcon = ImageViewer.createImageIcon("/image/b.gif", this);
    btpIcon = ImageViewer.createImageIcon("/image/bp.gif", this);
    btrIcon = ImageViewer.createImageIcon("/image/br.gif", this);
    tbIcon = ImageViewer.createImageIcon("/image/tb.gif", this);
    tbrIcon = ImageViewer.createImageIcon("/image/tbr.gif", this);
```

Listing 5.1 *Continued*

```
      tbsIcon = ImageViewer.createImageIcon("/image/tbs.gif", this);
      tbrsIcon = ImageViewer.createImageIcon("/image/tbrs.gif", this);
      rbIcon = ImageViewer.createImageIcon("/image/rb.gif", this);
      rbpIcon = ImageViewer.createImageIcon("/image/rbp.gif", this);
      rbrIcon = ImageViewer.createImageIcon("/image/rbr.gif", this);
      rbsIcon = ImageViewer.createImageIcon("/image/rbs.gif", this);
      rbrsIcon = ImageViewer.createImageIcon("/image/rbrs.gif", this);

      //  Generated by JBuilder
      titledBorder1 = new TitledBorder("");
      titledBorder3 = new TitledBorder("");
      titledBorder2 = new TitledBorder("");
      this.setSize(new Dimension(400,300));
      this.getContentPane().setLayout(borderLayout1);
      jpButtons.setLayout(gridLayout1);
      jbt.setToolTipText("This is a JButton");
      jbt.setIcon(btIcon);
      jbt.setPressedIcon(btpIcon);
      jbt.setRolloverIcon(btrIcon);
      jbt.setText("Button");
      jtb.setIcon(tbIcon);
      jtb.setToolTipText("This is a JToggleButton");
      jtb.setRolloverIcon(tbrIcon);
      jtb.setRolloverSelectedIcon(tbrsIcon);
      jtb.setSelectedIcon(tbsIcon);
      jtb.setPressedIcon(tbsIcon);
      jtb.setText("Toggle Button");
      jchk.setToolTipText("This is a JCheckBox");
      jchk.setRolloverIcon(btrIcon);
      jchk.setBorderPainted(true);
      jchk.setPressedIcon(btpIcon);
      jchk.setText("Check Box");
      jrb.setToolTipText("This is a radio button");
      jrb.setRolloverIcon(btrIcon);
      jrb.setBorderPainted(true);
      jrb.setPressedIcon(btpIcon);
      jrb.setText("Radio Button");
      gridLayout1.setRows(2);
      titledBorder1.setTitle("Horizontal Alignment");
      jpAlignment.setLayout(gridLayout3);
      jpMiscSettings.setBorder(titledBorder3);
      jpMiscSettings.setLayout(gridLayout4);
      titledBorder3.setTitle("Miscellaneous Options");
      jchkBorderPainted.setText("Border Painted");
      jchkBorderPainted.addActionListener(
        new java.awt.event.ActionListener() {
        public void actionPerformed(ActionEvent e) {
          jchkBorderPainted_actionPerformed(e);
        }
      });
      jchkContentAreaFilled.setText("Content Area Filled");
      jchkContentAreaFilled.addActionListener(
        new java.awt.event.ActionListener() {
        public void actionPerformed(ActionEvent e) {
          jchkContentAreaFilled_actionPerformed(e);
        }
      });
      jchkEnabled.setText("Enabled");
      jchkEnabled.addActionListener(
        new java.awt.event.ActionListener() {
        public void actionPerformed(ActionEvent e) {
```

Listing 5.1 *Continued*

continued

Example 5.1 continued

```
          jchkEnabled_actionPerformed(e);
        }
      });
      jchkFocusPainted.setText("Focus Painted");
      jchkFocusPainted.addActionListener(
        new java.awt.event.ActionListener() {
        public void actionPerformed(ActionEvent e) {
          jchkFocusPainted_actionPerformed(e);
        }
      });
      jchkOpaque.setText("Opaque");
      jchkOpaque.addActionListener(
        new java.awt.event.ActionListener() {
        public void actionPerformed(ActionEvent e) {
          jchkOpaque_actionPerformed(e);
        }
      });
      jchkRolloverEnabled.setText("Rollover Enabled");
      jchkRolloverEnabled.addActionListener(
        new java.awt.event.ActionListener() {
        public void actionPerformed(ActionEvent e) {
          jchkRolloverEnabled_actionPerformed(e);
        }
      });
      gridLayout4.setRows(6);
      jrbLeft.setText("LEFT");
      jrbLeft.addActionListener(new java.awt.event.ActionListener() {
        public void actionPerformed(ActionEvent e) {
          jrbLeft_actionPerformed(e);
        }
      });
      jrbRight.setText("RIGHT");
      jrbRight.addActionListener(new java.awt.event.ActionListener() {
        public void actionPerformed(ActionEvent e) {
          jrbRight_actionPerformed(e);
        }
      });
      jrbCenter.setText("CENTER");
      jrbCenter.addActionListener(
        new java.awt.event.ActionListener() {
        public void actionPerformed(ActionEvent e) {
          jrbCenter_actionPerformed(e);
        }
      });
      gridLayout3.setRows(2);
      jpHorizontalAlignment.setLayout(gridLayout5);
      gridLayout5.setRows(3);
      jpHorizontalAlignment.setBorder(titledBorder1);
      jrbTop.setIcon(rbIcon);
      jrbTop.setRolloverIcon(rbrIcon);
      jrbTop.setRolloverSelectedIcon(rbrsIcon);
      jrbTop.setSelectedIcon(rbsIcon);
      jrbTop.setText("TOP");
      jrbTop.setPressedIcon(rbpIcon);
      jrbTop.addActionListener(new java.awt.event.ActionListener() {
        public void actionPerformed(ActionEvent e) {
          jrbTop_actionPerformed(e);
        }
      });
      jrbVCenter.setIcon(rbIcon);
```

Listing 5.1 *Continued*

```
        jrbVCenter.setRolloverIcon(rbrIcon);
        jrbVCenter.setRolloverSelectedIcon(rbrsIcon);
        jrbVCenter.setSelectedIcon(rbsIcon);
        jrbVCenter.setSelected(true);
        jrbVCenter.setText("CENTER");
        jrbVCenter.setPressedIcon(rbpIcon);
        jrbVCenter.addActionListener(
          new java.awt.event.ActionListener() {
          public void actionPerformed(ActionEvent e) {
            jrbVCenter_actionPerformed(e);
          }
        });
        jrbBottom.setIcon(rbIcon);
        jrbBottom.setRolloverIcon(rbrIcon);
        jrbBottom.setRolloverSelectedIcon(rbsIcon);
        jrbBottom.setSelectedIcon(rbsIcon);
        jrbBottom.setText("BOTTOM");
        jrbBottom.setPressedIcon(rbpIcon);
        jrbBottom.addActionListener(
          new java.awt.event.ActionListener() {
          public void actionPerformed(ActionEvent e) {
            jrbBottom_actionPerformed(e);
          }
        });
        jpVerticalAlignment.setBorder(titledBorder2);
        jpVerticalAlignment.setLayout(gridLayout6);
        gridLayout6.setRows(3);
        titledBorder2.setTitle("Vertical Alignment");
        this.getContentPane().add(jpButtons, BorderLayout.CENTER);
        jpButtons.add(jbt, null);
        jpButtons.add(jchk, null);
        jpButtons.add(jtb, null);
        jpButtons.add(jrb, null);
        this.getContentPane().add(jpSettings, BorderLayout.SOUTH);
        jpSettings.setLayout(gridLayout2);
        jpSettings.add(jpAlignment, null);
        jpAlignment.add(jpHorizontalAlignment, null);
        jpHorizontalAlignment.add(jrbLeft, null);
        jpHorizontalAlignment.add(jrbCenter, null);
        jpHorizontalAlignment.add(jrbRight, null);
        jpAlignment.add(jpVerticalAlignment, null);
        jpVerticalAlignment.add(jrbTop, null);
        jpVerticalAlignment.add(jrbVCenter, null);
        jpVerticalAlignment.add(jrbBottom, null);
        jpSettings.add(jpMiscSettings, null);
        jpMiscSettings.add(jchkBorderPainted, null);
        jpMiscSettings.add(jchkContentAreaFilled, null);
        jpMiscSettings.add(jchkEnabled, null);
        jpMiscSettings.add(jchkFocusPainted, null);
        jpMiscSettings.add(jchkOpaque, null);
        jpMiscSettings.add(jchkRolloverEnabled, null);

        // Group radio buttons for setting horizontal alignment
        btg1.add(jrbLeft);
        btg1.add(jrbCenter);
        btg1.add(jrbRight);

        // Group radio buttons for setting horizontal alignment
        btg2.add(jrbTop);
        btg2.add(jrbVCenter);
```

Listing 5.1 *Continued*

continued

Example 5.1 continued

```
      btg2.add(jrbBottom);
    }

    /** Handle check box borderPainted */
    void jchkBorderPainted_actionPerformed(ActionEvent e) {
      jbt.setBorderPainted(jchkBorderPainted.isSelected());
      jtb.setBorderPainted(jchkBorderPainted.isSelected());
      jchk.setBorderPainted(jchkBorderPainted.isSelected());
      jrb.setBorderPainted(jchkBorderPainted.isSelected());
    }

    /** Handle check box contentAreaFilled */
    void jchkContentAreaFilled_actionPerformed(ActionEvent e) {
      jbt.setContentAreaFilled(jchkContentAreaFilled.isSelected());
      jtb.setContentAreaFilled(jchkContentAreaFilled.isSelected());
      jchk.setContentAreaFilled(jchkContentAreaFilled.isSelected());
      jrb.setContentAreaFilled(jchkContentAreaFilled.isSelected());
    }

    /** Handle check box enabled */
    void jchkEnabled_actionPerformed(ActionEvent e) {
      jbt.setEnabled(jchkEnabled.isSelected());
      jtb.setEnabled(jchkEnabled.isSelected());
      jchk.setEnabled(jchkEnabled.isSelected());
      jrb.setEnabled(jchkEnabled.isSelected());
    }

    /** Handle check box focusPainted */
    void jchkFocusPainted_actionPerformed(ActionEvent e) {
      jbt.setFocusPainted(jchkFocusPainted.isSelected());
      jtb.setFocusPainted(jchkFocusPainted.isSelected());
      jchk.setFocusPainted(jchkFocusPainted.isSelected());
      jrb.setFocusPainted(jchkFocusPainted.isSelected());
    }

    /** Handle check box opaque */
    void jchkOpaque_actionPerformed(ActionEvent e) {
      jbt.setOpaque(jchkOpaque.isSelected());
      jtb.setOpaque(jchkOpaque.isSelected());
      jchk.setOpaque(jchkOpaque.isSelected());
      jrb.setOpaque(jchkOpaque.isSelected());
    }

    /** Handle check box rolloverEnabled */
    void jchkRolloverEnabled_actionPerformed(ActionEvent e) {
      jbt.setRolloverEnabled(jchkRolloverEnabled.isSelected());
      jtb.setRolloverEnabled(jchkRolloverEnabled.isSelected());
      jchk.setRolloverEnabled(jchkRolloverEnabled.isSelected());
      jrb.setRolloverEnabled(jchkRolloverEnabled.isSelected());
    }

    /** Handle the radio button to set left horizontal alignment */
    void jrbLeft_actionPerformed(ActionEvent e) {
      if (jrbLeft.isSelected())
        setHorizontalAlignment(SwingConstants.LEFT);
    }

    /** Handle the radio button to set center horizontal alignment */
    void jrbCenter_actionPerformed(ActionEvent e) {
```

Listing 5.1 *Continued*

```
      if (jrbCenter.isSelected())
        setHorizontalAlignment(SwingConstants.CENTER);
    }

    /** Handle the radio button to set right horizontal alignment */
    void jrbRight_actionPerformed(ActionEvent e) {
      if (jrbRight.isSelected())
        setHorizontalAlignment(SwingConstants.RIGHT);
    }

    /** Handle the radio button to set top vertical alignment */
    void jrbTop_actionPerformed(ActionEvent e) {
      if (jrbTop.isSelected())
        setVerticalAlignment(SwingConstants.TOP);
    }

    /** Handle the radio button to set center vertical alignment */
    void jrbVCenter_actionPerformed(ActionEvent e) {
      if (jrbVCenter.isSelected())
        setVerticalAlignment(SwingConstants.CENTER);
    }

    /** Handle the radio button to set bottom vertical alignment */
    void jrbBottom_actionPerformed(ActionEvent e) {
      if (jrbBottom.isSelected())
        setVerticalAlignment(SwingConstants.BOTTOM);
    }

    /** Set horizontal alignment */
    private void setHorizontalAlignment(int alignment) {
      jbt.setHorizontalAlignment(alignment);
      jtb.setHorizontalAlignment(alignment);
      jchk.setHorizontalAlignment(alignment);
      jrb.setHorizontalAlignment(alignment);
    }

    /** Set vertical alignment */
    private void setVerticalAlignment(int alignment) {
      jbt.setVerticalAlignment(alignment);
      jtb.setVerticalAlignment(alignment);
      jchk.setVerticalAlignment(alignment);
      jrb.setVerticalAlignment(alignment);
    }
  }
```

Listing 5.1 *Continued*

Example Review

Each button has an icon, a pressed icon, a rollover icon, a rollover selected icon, and a selected icon. When you point the mouse to the button, the rollover icon is displayed if the Rollover Enabled option box is checked. When you press the button, the pressed icon is displayed. When you roll over a selected toggle button, radio button, and check box button, the rollover-selected icon is displayed.

Using the radio buttons in the Horizontal Alignment and Vertical Alignment panels, you can set the horizontal alignment and vertical alignment of the icon and the button.

continued

Example 5.1 continued

By default, the border of `JButton` and `JToggleButton` is painted and the border of `JCheckBox` and `JRadioButton` is not painted. You can use the `borderPainted` property to specify a border. When an icon is associated with `JCheckBox` or `JRadioButton`, the check box or the radio button is replaced by the icon.

The program contains 369 lines of code, but JBuilder generates most of the code automatically. The code is easy to read and easy to maintain. This example and many other examples in this book demonstrate the power of rapid Java application development.

As mentioned in Example 4.1, you may create an image icon using the absolute filename, as follows:

```
ImageIcon btIcon = new ImageIcon("c:\\radjb4\\image\\b.gif");
```

This approach works fine with Java applications, but it would fail to load images in Java applets, because applets cannot directly access the local file system. So you should use the static `createImageIcon` method in the `ImageViewer` class to create the image icon through the URL of the filename. The URL of the filename is obtained through the resource of this class.

JBUILDER 5 NOTE

Due to a bug in JBuilder 5, the image icons are not displayed in the UI designer using the `ImageViewer.createImageIcon` method. To fix it, replace

```
btIcon = ImageViewer.createImageIcon("/image/b.gif", this);
```

by

```
Toolkit toolkit = Toolkit.getDefaultToolkit();
java.net.URL url = this.getClass().getResource("/image/b.gif");
btIcon = new ImageIcon(toolkit.getImage(url));
```

TIP

The icons and borders can be shared. You can modify this program to share icons and borders among different components. See Exercise 5.5.

JLabel

`JLabel` is a Swing implementation of a `java.awt.Label`. A `JLabel` object can display text, an image, or both.

`JLabel` inherits all the properties from `JComponent` and has many properties used in `JButton`, such as `text`, `icon`, `horizontalAlignment`, and `verticalAlignment`. Setting the vertical and horizontal alignments specifies the label's location. By default, labels are vertically centered in their display area, text-only labels are left-aligned, and image-only labels are horizontally centered. You can also specify the position of the text relative to the image. By default, the text is to the right of the image, with the text and image vertically aligned.

JScrollPane

`JScrollPane` is a component that supports *automatically* scrolling without coding. You can add a Swing component to a scroll pane. The scroll pane takes care of scrolling.

A scroll pane can be viewed as a specialized container with a view port for displaying the contained component. In addition to horizontal and vertical scroll bars, a `JScrollPane` can have a column header, a row header, and corners, as shown in Figure 5.13.

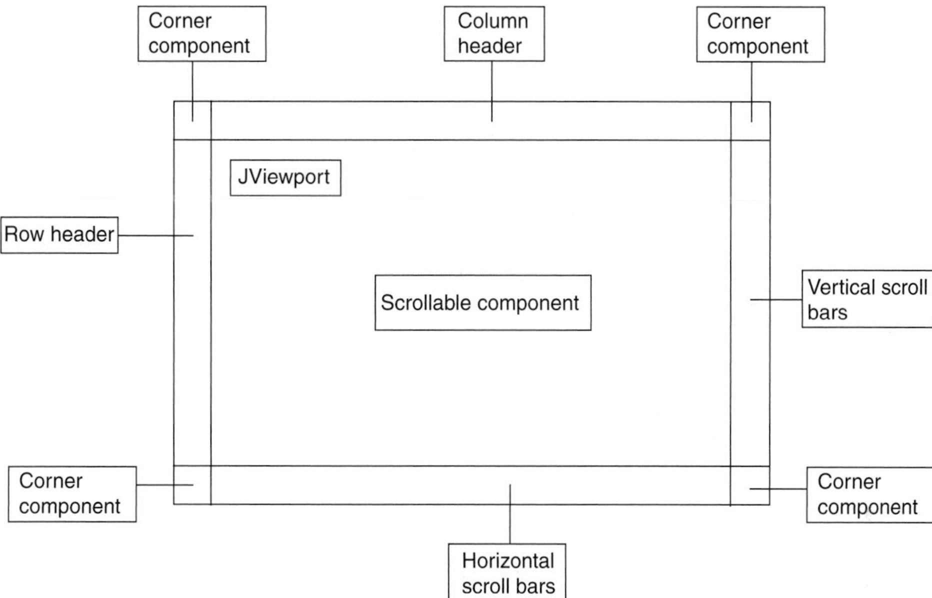

Figure 5.13 *A* `JScrollPane` *has a view port, optional horizontal and vertical bars, optional column and row headers, and optional corners.*

The view port is an instance of `JViewport` through which a scrollable component is displayed. Adding a component to the scroll pane actually places it in the scroll pane's view port.

The following properties of `JScrollPane` are often useful:

- `horizontalScrollBarPolicy`: This determines when the horizontal scrollbar appears in the scroll pane.
- `verticalScrollBarPolicy`: This determines when the vertical scrollbar appears in the scroll pane.
- `viewportView`: This specifies the component to be viewed in the view port.
- `viewportBorder`: This specifies a border around the view port in the scroll pane.
- `rowHeaderView`: This specifies the row-header view component to be used in the scroll pane.

- `columnHeaderView`: This specifies the column-header view component to be used in the scroll pane.

To set a corner component, use the following method:

```
public void setCorner(String key, Component corner)
```

Legal values for the `key` parameter are the following:

- `JScrollPane.LOWER_LEFT_CORNER`
- `JScrollPane.LOWER_RIGHT_CORNER`
- `JScrollPane.UPPER_LEFT_CORNER`
- `JScrollPane.UPPER_RIGHT_CORNER`

Example 5.2 Using Labels and Scroll Panes

This example uses a scroll pane to browse large maps. The program lets the user choose a map from a radio button and displays the map in the scroll pane, as shown in Figure 5.14.

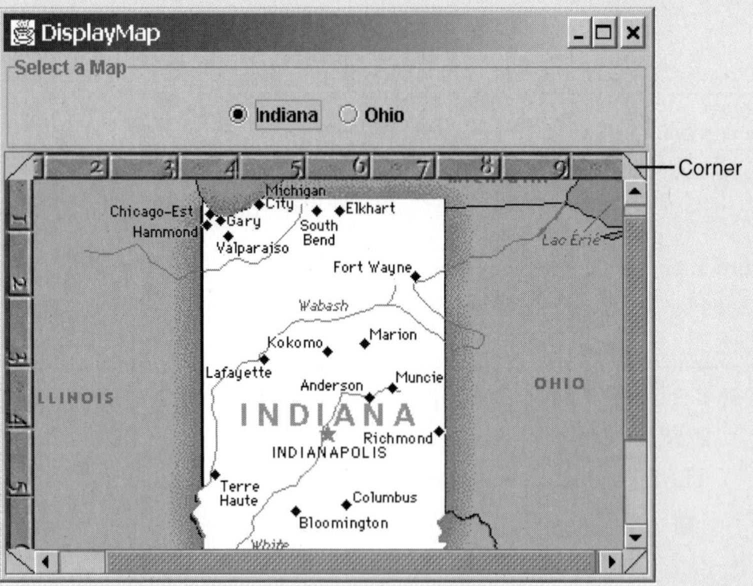

Figure 5.14 *You can choose a map from a radio button and display it in a scroll pane.*

Here are the steps to complete the example:

1. Create a new project named displaymapdemo.jpr and an applet named DisplayMap.java using the Applet wizard.

2. Create a class named `CornerPanel` for displaying scroll pane corners, as shown in Listing 5.3. This class extends `JPanel` and draws simple lines on a panel for decorating the scroll pane corners.

3. With DisplayMap.java selected in the project pane, choose the Design tab in the content pane to display the UI designer. Drop a `JScrollPane` to the center of the applet and rename it `jspMap`. Drop a `JPanel` to the north of the applet and rename it `jpSelection`.

4. Drop a `JRadioButton` twice into `jpSelection` to create `jrbMap1` and `jrbMap2`. Set the `text` property of these two radio buttons "Indiana" and "Ohio."

5. Drop a `JLabel` to `jspMap` and rename it `jlblMap`.

6. Declare and create two image icons named `map1` and `map2` for two image maps using the static `createImageIcon` method in the `ImageViewer` class. Set row header, column header, and corner header in the `jbInit()` method, as shown in Listing 5.2 (Lines 73–83).

7. Generate action-event handlers for the two radio buttons, and implement the handlers for map selections, as shown in Listing 5.2 (Lines 90–96).

```
1   // DisplayMap.java: Display maps in a label placed in a scroll pane
2   package displaymapdemo;
3
4   import java.awt.*;
5   import java.awt.event.*;
6   import java.applet.*;
7   import javax.swing.*;
8   import javax.swing.border.*;
9   import imageviewerdemo.ImageViewer;
10
11  public class DisplayMap extends JApplet {
12    // Create image icons for maps
13    ImageIcon map1;
14    ImageIcon map2;
15
16    // Create a button group
17    ButtonGroup btg = new ButtonGroup();
18
19    // Generated by JBuilder
20    boolean isStandalone = false;
21    JScrollPane jspMap = new JScrollPane();
22    JLabel jlblMap = new JLabel();
23    JPanel jpSelection = new JPanel();
24    JRadioButton jrbMap2 = new JRadioButton();
25    JRadioButton jrbMap1 = new JRadioButton();
26    FlowLayout flowLayout1 = new FlowLayout();
27    TitledBorder titledBorder1;
28
29    /** Initialize the applet */
30    public void init() {
31      try {
```

Listing 5.2 *DisplayMap.java*

continued

Example 5.2 Using Labels and Scroll Panes

```
      jbInit();
    }
    catch(Exception e) {
      e.printStackTrace();
    }
  }

  /** Component initialization */
  private void jbInit() throws Exception {
    // Load images
    map1 = ImageViewer.createImageIcon(
      "/image/indianaMap.gif", this);
    map2 =  ImageViewer.createImageIcon("/image/ohioMap.gif", this);
    ImageIcon hRuler = ImageViewer.createImageIcon(
      "/image/horizontalRuler.gif", this);
    ImageIcon vRuler = ImageViewer.createImageIcon(
      "/image/verticalRuler.gif", this);

    titledBorder1 = new TitledBorder("");
    this.setSize(new Dimension(400,300));
    jpSelection.setLayout(flowLayout1);
    jrbMap1.setText("Indiana");
    jrbMap1.addActionListener(new java.awt.event.ActionListener() {
      public void actionPerformed(ActionEvent e) {
        jrbMap1_actionPerformed(e);
      }
    });
    jrbMap2.setText("Ohio");
    jrbMap2.addActionListener(new java.awt.event.ActionListener() {
      public void actionPerformed(ActionEvent e) {
        jrbMap2_actionPerformed(e);
      }
    });
    jpSelection.setBorder(titledBorder1);
    titledBorder1.setTitle("Select a Map");
    this.getContentPane().add(jspMap, BorderLayout.CENTER);
    this.getContentPane().add(jpSelection, BorderLayout.NORTH);
    jpSelection.add(jrbMap1, null);
    jpSelection.add(jrbMap2, null);
    jspMap.getViewport().add(jlblMap, null);

    // Set row header, column header and corner header
    jspMap.setColumnHeaderView(new JLabel(hRuler));
      jspMap.setRowHeaderView(new JLabel(vRuler));
    jspMap.setCorner(JScrollPane.UPPER_LEFT_CORNER,
      new CornerPanel(JScrollPane.UPPER_LEFT_CORNER));
    jspMap.setCorner(ScrollPaneConstants.UPPER_RIGHT_CORNER,
      new CornerPanel(JScrollPane.UPPER_RIGHT_CORNER));
    jspMap.setCorner(JScrollPane.LOWER_RIGHT_CORNER,
      new CornerPanel(JScrollPane.LOWER_RIGHT_CORNER));
    jspMap.setCorner(JScrollPane.LOWER_LEFT_CORNER,
      new CornerPanel(JScrollPane.LOWER_LEFT_CORNER));

    // Group buttons
    btg.add(jrbMap1);
    btg.add(jrbMap2);
  }

```

Listing 5.2 *Continued*

```
    void jrbMap1_actionPerformed(ActionEvent e) {
      if (jrbMap1.isSelected()) jlblMap.setIcon(map1);
    }

    void jrbMap2_actionPerformed(ActionEvent e) {
      if (jrbMap2.isSelected()) jlblMap.setIcon(map2);
    }
  }
```

Listing 5.2 *Continued*

```
// CornerPanel.java: A panel displaying a line used for scroll
// pane corner
package displaymapdemo;

import javax.swing.*;
import java.awt.*;

public class CornerPanel extends JPanel
  implements ScrollPaneConstants {
  /** Line location */
  private String location;

  /** Construct a corner panel */
  public CornerPanel(String location) {
    this.location = location;
  }

  /** Draw a line depending on the location */
  public void paintComponent(Graphics g) {
    super.paintComponents(g);

    if (location == "UPPER_LEFT_CORNER")
      g.drawLine(0, getSize().height, getSize().width, 0);
    else if (location == "UPPER_RIGHT_CORNER")
      g.drawLine(0, 0, getSize().width, getSize().height);
    else if (location == "LOWER_RIGHT_CORNER")
      g.drawLine(0, getSize().height, getSize().width, 0);
    else if (location == "LOWER_LEFT_CORNER")
      g.drawLine(0, 0, getSize().width, getSize().height);
  }
}
```

Listing 5.3 *CornerPanel.java*

Example Review

`JLabel` can be used to display images as well as text. The program displays an image map in a label, and places the label in the scroll pane. You cannot directly place an image into a scroll pane, because an image is not a component.

The scroll pane holds a label in its view port. Choosing a radio button causes an image icon to be set in the label and displayed in the view port. The scroll pane has a row header, column header, and corners. The row header, column header, and corners can be any components. The program places a label with a horizontal-ruler image as the row header, and another label with a vertical ruler as the column header. The corners are instances of `CornerPanel`. The `CornerPanel` class is a subclass of `JPanel`, which draws simple lines on the panel.

JTextField

JTextField is a Swing implementation of java.awt.TextField that allows the editing of a single line of text. The setEchoChar and getEchoChar methods in TextField are not provided in JTextField in order to avoid a new implementation of a pluggable look-and-feel inadvertently exposing password characters. To provide password-like services, a separate class, JPasswordField, extends JTextField to provide this service with an independently pluggable look-and-feel.

JTextField has capabilities not found in TextField. For example, the horizontal alignment of JTextField can be set to be left-justified, centered, or right-justified if the required size of the field text is smaller than the size allocated to it. This is determined by the horizontalAlignment property. The default is to be left-justified.

In addition to properties like text and horizontalAlignment, JTextField has the following useful properties:

- actionCommand: This specifies an action command string associated with the text. By default, the action command is the same as the text. The action command string is passed to the ActionEvent when an ActionEvent is generated on the button.
- editable: This is a boolean property indicating whether the text field can be edited by the user.
- columns: This specifies the width of the text field.

JTextField can fire ActionEvent and ItemEvent, among many other events. Pressing Enter in a text field triggers the ActionEvent. Changing contents in a text field triggers the TextEvent.

JTextArea

JTextArea is a Swing implementation of java.awt.TextArea, a multi-line area that displays plain text. JTextArea and JTextField are subclasses of JTextComponent. In addition to properties like text, editable, and columns shared with JTextField, JTextArea has the following properties:

- lineWrap: This is a boolean property indicating whether the line in the text area is automatically wrapped.
- wrapStyleWord: This is a boolean property indicating whether the line is wrapped on word or character. The default value is false, which indicates that the line is wrapped on character boundaries.
- rows: This specifies the number of lines in the text area.
- lineCount: This specifies the number of lines in the text.
- tabSize: This specifies the number of characters inserted when the Tab key is pressed.

You can use the following methods to insert, append, and replace text:

- public void insert(String s, int pos)

This inserts string s in the specified position in the text area.

- `public void append(String s)`

  This appends string s to the end of the text.

- `public void replaceRange(String s, int start, int end)`

  This replaces partial texts in the range from position `start` to position `end` with string `s`.

`JTextArea` does not handle scrolling, but you can create a `JScrollPane` object to hold an instance of `JTextArea` and let the scroll pane handle scrolling for `JTextArea`.

JEditorPane

Swing provides a new component named `javax.swing.JEditorPane`, which can be used to display HTML files. `JEditorPane` is a subclass of `JTextArea`. Thus it inherits all the behavior and properties from `JTextArea`. Additionally, it is capable of rendering an HTML file with a given URL, as shown in Figure 5.15.

Figure 5.15 *The* `JEditorPane` *is demonstrated in the SwingSet example.*

The `JEditorPane` class has a `page` property that can be used to specify a URL for the HTML file. The signature of the setPage method is as follows:

```
public void setPage(URL url) IOException
```

`JEditorPane` generates `javax.swing.event.HyperlinkEvent` when a hyperlink in the editor pane is clicked. Through this event, you can get the URL of the hyperlink and display the content again, using the `setPage(url)` method.

Example 5.3 Using JEditorPane

This example creates a simple Web browser to render HTML files. The program lets the user enter an HTML file in a text field and press the Enter key to display the HTML file in an editor pane, as shown in Figure 5.16.

Figure 5.16 *You can specify a URL in the text field and display the HTML file in an editor pane.*

Here are the steps to complete the project:

1. Create a new project named viewhtmldemo.jpr and an applet named ViewHTML.java using the Applet wizard.
2. With ViewHTML.java selected in the project pane, choose the Design tab to display the UI designer. Drop a `JScrollPane` to the center of the applet, and drop a `JEditorPane` to the scroll pane and rename it `jep`. Drop a `JPanel` to the north of the applet and rename it `jpURL`.
3. Set the `layout` of `jpURL` to `BorderLayout`. Drop a `JLabel` to the west of `jpURL` and a `JTextField` to the center of `jpURL` and rename it `jtfURL`.
4. Generate an action-event handler for the text field, and implement the handler for displaying the URL in the editor pane, as shown in Listing 5.4.
5. Generate a hyperlink event handler for the editor pane, and implement it to display the content of the hyperlink in the editor pane, as shown in Listing 5.4.

```
// ViewHTML.java: Display HTML file in JEditorPane
package viewhtmldemo;

import java.awt.*;
import java.awt.event.*;
import java.applet.*;
import javax.swing.*;
import java.net.URL;
import javax.swing.event.*;
import java.io.*;

public class ViewHTML extends JApplet {
  boolean isStandalone = false;

  JScrollPane jScrollPane1 = new JScrollPane();
  JEditorPane jep = new JEditorPane();
  JPanel jpURL = new JPanel();
  JLabel jLabel1 = new JLabel();
  BorderLayout borderLayout1 = new BorderLayout();
  JTextField jtfURL = new JTextField();

  /** Initialize the applet */
  public void init() {
    try {
      jbInit();
    }
    catch(Exception e) {
      e.printStackTrace();
    }
  }

  /** Component initialization */
  private void jbInit() throws Exception {
    this.setSize(new Dimension(400,300));
    jep.setEditable(false);
    jep.addHyperlinkListener(
      new javax.swing.event.HyperlinkListener() {
      public void hyperlinkUpdate(HyperlinkEvent e) {
        jep_hyperlinkUpdate(e);
      }
    });
    jLabel1.setText("URL");
    jpURL.setLayout(borderLayout1);
    jtfURL.addActionListener(new java.awt.event.ActionListener() {
      public void actionPerformed(ActionEvent e) {
        jtfURL_actionPerformed(e);
      }
    });
    this.getContentPane().add(jScrollPane1, BorderLayout.CENTER);
    this.getContentPane().add(jpURL, BorderLayout.NORTH);
    jpURL.add(jLabel1, BorderLayout.WEST);
    jpURL.add(jtfURL, BorderLayout.CENTER);
    jScrollPane1.getViewport().add(jep, null);
  }

  void jep_hyperlinkUpdate(HyperlinkEvent e) {
    try {
      jep.setPage(e.getURL());
    }
    catch (IOException ex) {
```

Listing 5.4 *ViewHTML.java*

continued

Example 5.3 continued

```
        ex.printStackTrace();
      }
    }

    void jtfURL_actionPerformed(ActionEvent e) {
      try {
        // Get the URL of the HTML file
        URL url = new URL(jtfURL.getText().trim());

        // Display the HTML file
        jep.setPage(url);
      }
      catch (IOException ex) {
        ex.printStackTrace();
      }
    }
  }
```

Listing 5.4 *Continued*

Example Review

In this example, a simple Web browser is created using the `JEditorPane` class. `JEditorPane` is capable of displaying files in the HTML format or in the RTF format. To enable scrolling, the editor pane is placed inside a scroll pane.

The user enters a URL of the HTML file in the text field and presses the Enter key to fire an action event to display the URL in the editor pane. To display the URL in the editor pane, simply set the URL in the `page` property of the editor pane.

The editor pane does not have all the functions of a commercial Web browser, but it is convenient for displaying HTML files, including embedded images.

This program cannot view a local HTML file. To view a remote HTML file, you have to enter a URL beginning with http://. In Exercise 5.6, you will modify the program so that it can also view an HTML file from the local host and accept URLs beginning with either http:// or www.

JScrollBar

You used scroll panes to view large contents with automatically scrolling. In many cases, a scroll pane is simple, convenient, and sufficient to provide scrolling functions, but occasionally you need to use scroll bars to manually control scrolling. A *scroll bar* is a control that enables the user to select from a range of values. A scroll bar appears in two styles, *horizontal* and *vertical*, as shown in Figure 5.17.

`JScrollBar` has the following properties.

- `orientation`: This specifies horizontal or vertical style, with 0 for horizontal and 1 for vertical.

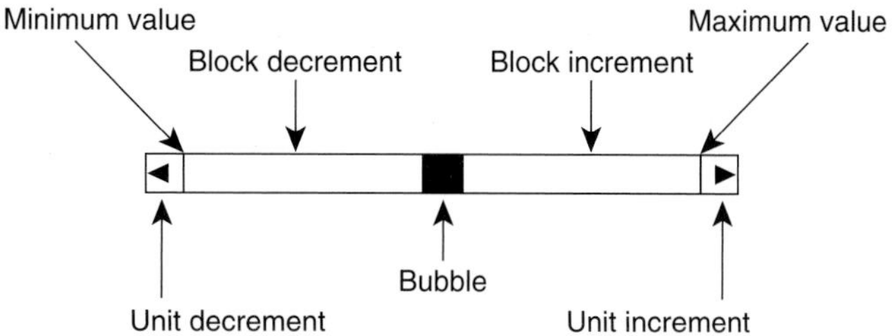

Figure 5.17 *A scroll bar represents a range of values graphically.*

- `maximum`: This specifies the maximum value the scroll bar represents when the bubble reaches to the right end of the scroll bar for horizontal style or to the bottom of the scroll bar for vertical style.
- `minimum`: This specifies the minimum value the scroll bar represents when the bubble reaches to the left end of the scroll bar for horizontal style or to the top of the scroll bar for vertical style.
- `visibleAmount`: This specifies the relative width of the scroll bar's bubble. The actual width appearing on the screen is determined by the maximum value and the value of `visibleAmount`.
- `value`: This is the current value of the scroll bar. Normally, a program should change a scroll bar's value by calling the `setValue` method. The `setValue` method simultaneously and synchronously sets the minimum, maximum, visible amount, and value properties of a scroll bar, so that they are mutually consistent.
- `blockIncrement`: This is the value that is added (subtracted) when the user activates the block increment (decrement) area of the scroll bar, as shown in Figure 5.17. The `blockIncrement` property, which is new in JDK 1.1, supersedes the `pageIncrement` property used in JDK 1.02.
- `unitIncrement`: This is the value that is added (subtracted) when the user activates the unit increment (decrement) area of the scroll bar, as shown in Figure 5.17. The `unitIncrement` property, which is new in JDK 1.1, supersedes the `lineIncrement` property used in JDK 1.02.

Note

The actual width of the scroll bar's track is `maximum+visibleAmount`. When the scroll bar is set to its maximum value, the left side of the bubble is at `maximum`, and the right side is at `maximum+visibleAmount`.

Normally, the user changes the value of the scroll bar by making a gesture with the mouse. For example, the user can drag the scroll bar's bubble up and down or click in the scroll bar's unit increment or block increment area. Keyboard gestures can also be mapped to the scroll bar. By convention, the Page Up and Page Down keys are equivalent to clicking in the scroll bar's block increment and block decrement areas.

When the user changes the value of the scroll bar, the scroll bar generates an instance of `AdjustmentEvent` that is passed to any registered listeners. Any object that wishes to be notified of changes to the scroll bar's value should implement the `adjustmentValueChanged` method in the `AdjustmentListener` interface defined in the package `java.awt.event`.

Example 5.4 Using Scroll Bars

This example uses three scroll bars to specify the red, green, and blue components of a color and set the color as the background color for a panel, as shown in Figure 5.18.

Figure 5.18 *The background color of the panel changes as you adjust the scroll bars.*

Here are the steps to complete the project:

1. Create a new project named displaycolordemo.jpr and a new applet named DisplayColor.java using the Applet wizard.
2. In the UI designer for DisplayColor.java, drop a `JPanel` to the center of the applet and rename it `jpColor`, and drop a `JPanel` to the south of the applet and rename it `jpSelections`.
3. Set the `layout` of `jpSelections` to `BorderLayout`. Drop a `JPanel` to the west of `jpSelections` and rename it `jpLabels`, and drop a `JPanel` to the Center of `jpSelections` and rename it `jpScrollBars`.
4. Set the `layout` of `jpLabels` to `GridLayout` and set the `row` property of the `GridLayout` to 3. Drop a `JLabel` three times into `jpLabels`, and set the `text` of the labels to Red, Green and Blue.
5. Set the `layout` of `jpScrollBars` to `GridLayout`, and set the `row` property of the `GridLayout` to 3. Drop a `JScrollBar` three times and rename them `jscbRed`, `jscbGreen`, and `jscbBlue`. Set `orientation` and `maximum` of each scroll bar to `VERTICAL` and 128.
6. Declare variables `redValue`, `greenValue`, and `blueValue` for representing the red, green, and blue components of the color. Generate adjustment-event handlers for the scroll bars, and implement them to adjust these

variables and update the background color in the panel `jpColor`, as shown in Listing 5.5 (Lines 109–112).

```
1  // DisplayColor.java: Use scroll bars to select colors and
2  // display colors in a panel
3  package displaycolordemo;
4
5  import java.awt.*;
6  import java.awt.event.*;
7  import java.applet.*;
8  import javax.swing.*;
9
10 public class DisplayColor extends JApplet {
11   // Declare color component values
12   int redValue, greenValue, blueValue;
13   Color color;
14
15   boolean isStandalone = false;
16   JPanel jpColor = new JPanel();
17   JPanel jpSelections = new JPanel();
18   JPanel jpLabels = new JPanel();
19   JPanel jpScrollBars = new JPanel();
20   JLabel jLabel1 = new JLabel();
21   BorderLayout borderLayout1 = new BorderLayout();
22   JLabel jLabel2 = new JLabel();
23   JLabel jLabel3 = new JLabel();
24   GridLayout gridLayout1 = new GridLayout();
25   JScrollBar jscbRed = new JScrollBar();
26   JScrollBar jscbGreen = new JScrollBar();
27   JScrollBar jscbBlue = new JScrollBar();
28   GridLayout gridLayout2 = new GridLayout();
29
30   /** Initialize the applet */
31   public void init() {
32     try {
33       jbInit();
34     }
35     catch(Exception e) {
36       e.printStackTrace();
37     }
38   }
39
40   /** Component initialization */
41   private void jbInit() throws Exception {
42     this.setSize(new Dimension(400,300));
43     jLabel1.setText("Red");
44     jpSelections.setLayout(borderLayout1);
45     jLabel2.setText("Green");
46     jLabel3.setText("Blue");
47     jpLabels.setLayout(gridLayout1);
48     gridLayout1.setRows(3);
49     jscbRed.setOrientation(JScrollBar.HORIZONTAL);
50     jscbRed.setMaximum(128);
51     jscbRed.setBorder(BorderFactory.createEtchedBorder());
52     jscbRed.addAdjustmentListener(
53       new java.awt.event.AdjustmentListener() {
54       public void adjustmentValueChanged(AdjustmentEvent e) {
55         jscbRed_adjustmentValueChanged(e);
56       }
57     });
```

Listing 5.5 *DisplayColor.java*

continued

Example 5.4 continued

```
      jscbBlue.setOrientation(JScrollBar.HORIZONTAL);
      jscbBlue.setMaximum(128);
      jscbBlue.setBorder(BorderFactory.createEtchedBorder());
      jscbBlue.addAdjustmentListener(
        new java.awt.event.AdjustmentListener() {
        public void adjustmentValueChanged(AdjustmentEvent e) {
          jscbBlue_adjustmentValueChanged(e);
        }
      });
      jscbGreen.setOrientation(JScrollBar.HORIZONTAL);
      jscbGreen.setMaximum(128);
      jscbGreen.setBorder(BorderFactory.createEtchedBorder());
      jscbGreen.addAdjustmentListener(
        new java.awt.event.AdjustmentListener() {
        public void adjustmentValueChanged(AdjustmentEvent e) {
          jscbGreen_adjustmentValueChanged(e);
        }
      });
      jpScrollBars.setLayout(gridLayout2);
      gridLayout2.setRows(3);
      jpSelections.setBorder(BorderFactory.createEtchedBorder());
      this.getContentPane().add(jpColor, BorderLayout.CENTER);
      this.getContentPane().add(jpSelections, BorderLayout.SOUTH);
      jpSelections.add(jpLabels, BorderLayout.WEST);
      jpLabels.add(jLabel1, null);
      jpLabels.add(jLabel2, null);
      jpLabels.add(jLabel3, null);
      jpSelections.add(jpScrollBars, BorderLayout.CENTER);
      jpScrollBars.add(jscbRed, null);
      jpScrollBars.add(jscbGreen, null);
      jpScrollBars.add(jscbBlue, null);
    }

    /** Handle jscbRed */
    void jscbRed_adjustmentValueChanged(AdjustmentEvent e) {
      redValue = jscbRed.getValue();
      updateColor();
    }

    /** Handle jscbGreen */
    void jscbGreen_adjustmentValueChanged(AdjustmentEvent e) {
      greenValue = jscbGreen.getValue();
      updateColor();
    }

    /** Handle jscbBlue */
    void jscbBlue_adjustmentValueChanged(AdjustmentEvent e) {
      blueValue = jscbBlue.getValue();
      updateColor();
    }

    void updateColor() {
      color = new Color(redValue, greenValue, blueValue);
      jpColor.setBackground(color);
    }
  }
```

Listing 5.5 *Continued*

Example Review

The color of the panel above the scroll bars changes as you adjust the scroll bars. The colors are determined by the values represented in the scroll bars. Since the red, green, and blue component values range from 0 to 128, the maximum values of the scroll bars are set at 128.

Whenever the user adjusts a scroll bar, an `AdjustmentEvent` is fired. The event handler obtains the current value of the color and updates the background color of the panel.

JSlider

`JSlider` is similar to `JScrollBar` in the sense that both can be used to represent a range of values, but `JSlider` has more properties than `JScrollBar` and can appear in many forms and styles, as shown in Figure 5.19.

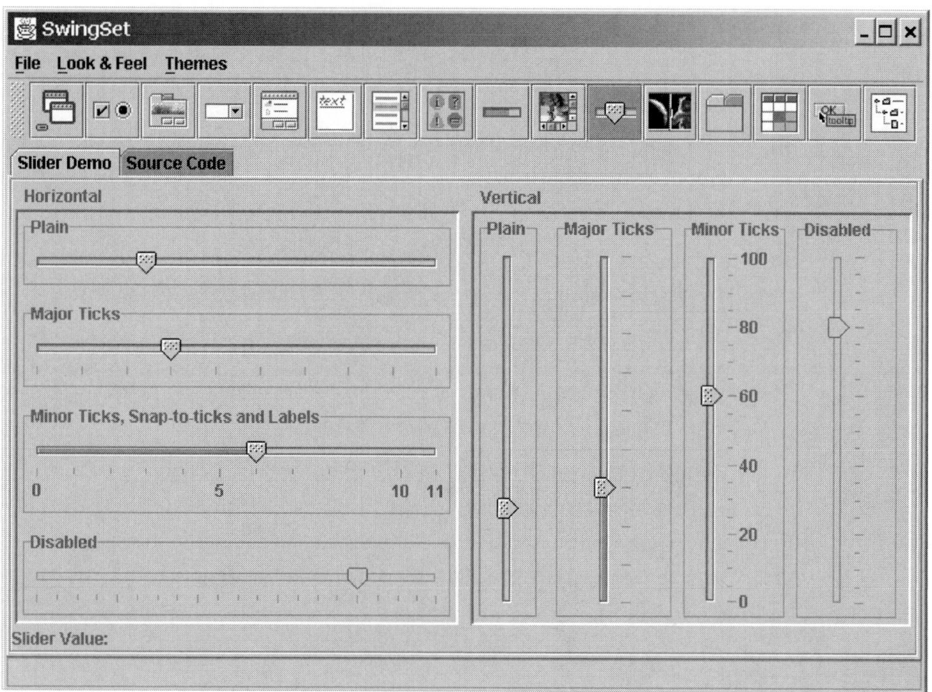

Figure 5.19 *The SwingSet demo demonstrates the features of* `JSlider`.

`JSlider` lets the user graphically select a value by sliding a knob within a bounded interval. The slider can show both major tick marks and minor tick marks between them. The number of pixels between the tick marks is controlled with `setMajorTickSpacing` and `setMinorTickSpacing`. Sliders can be displayed horizontally or vertically, with or without ticks, and with or without labels.

The following properties are defined in the `JSlider` class.

- `extend`: This is the size of the range covered by the knob. Default value is 0.
- `inverted`: This is a `boolean` value. If `true`, indicating values increase from right to left or from top to bottom. If `false`, indicating values increase from left to right or from bottom to top. The default value is `false`.
- `maximum`: This is the maximum value the slider represents. The default value is 100.
- `minimum`: This is the minimum value the slider represents. The default value is 0.
- `majorTickSpacing`: This is the number of units between major ticks. The default value is 0.
- `minorTickSpacing`: This is the number of units between minor ticks. The default value is 0.
- `orientation`: This is the orientation of the slider, either `HORIZONTAL` or `VERTICAL`. The default value is `HORIZONTAL`.
- `paintLabels`: This is a `boolean` value indicating whether the labels are painted at tick marks. The default value is false, which indicates that the labels are not painted.
- `paintTicks`: This is a `boolean` value indicating whether the tick marks are painted. The default value is `false`, which indicates that the tick marks are not painted.
- `paintTrack`: This is a `boolean` value indicating whether the track is painted. The default value is true, which indicates that the track is painted.
- `value`: This is the current value of the slider. The default value is 50.
- `valueIsAdjusting`: This is a `boolean` value indicating whether the knob is being dragged. The default value is `false`.

When the user changes the value of the slider, the slider generates an instance of `javax.swing.event.ChangeEvent`, which is passed to any registered listeners. Any object that wishes to be notified of changes to the slider's value should implement `stateChanged` method in the `ChangeListener` interface defined in the package `javax.swing.event`.

JProgressBar

`JProgressBar` is a component that displays a value graphically within a bounded interval. A progress bar is typically used to show the percentage of completion of a lengthy operation; it comprises a rectangular bar that is "filled in" from left to right horizontally or from bottom to top vertically as the operation is performed. It provides the user with feedback on the progress of the operation. For example, when a file is being read, it alerts the user to the progress of the operation, thereby keeping the user attentive.

You can choose the ProgressBar toolbar to see the demo for using `JProgressBar` in the SwingDemo project, as shown in Figure 5.20.

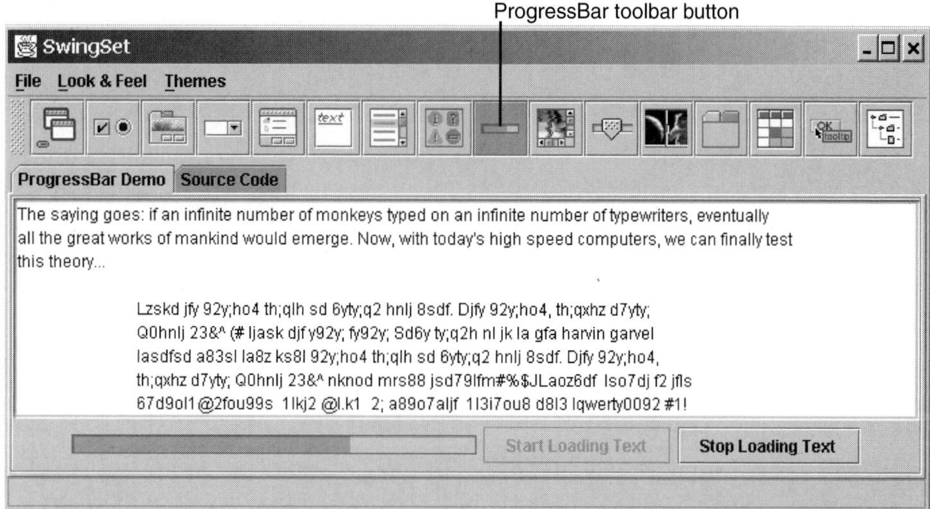

Figure 5.20 *The ProgressBar Demo demonstrates the features of* `JProgressBar`.

When the SwingSet demo starts, a progress bar displays the loading status of all the panels. The progress bar can be displayed horizontally or vertically, as determined by its `orientation` property. The `minimum`, `value`, and `maximum` properties determine the minimum, current, and maximum length on the progress bar.

Example 5.5 Using the Progress Bar

This example creates a program that lets you copy files. A progress bar is used to show the progress of the copying operation, as shown in Figure 5.21.

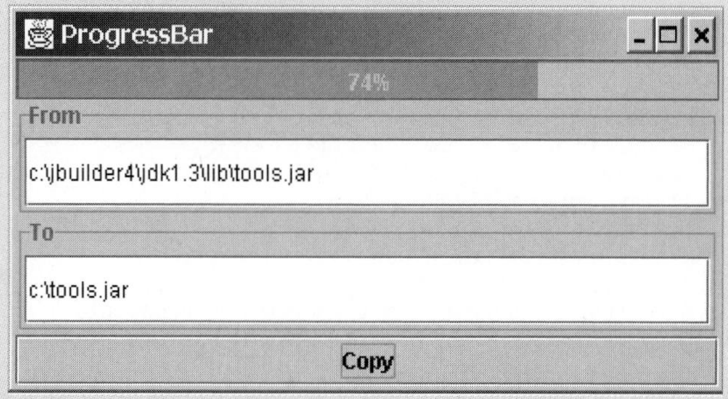

Figure 5.21 *The user enters the files in the text fields and clicks the Copy button to start copying files.*

continued

Example 5.5 continued

Here are the steps to complete the project.

1. Create a new project named progressbardemo.jpr and use the Applet wizard to create an applet named `ProgressBar`.
2. In the UI designer of ProgressBar.java, drop a `JProgressBar` from the Swing page to the north of the frame, a `JButton` to the south of the frame, and a `JPanel` to the center of the frame. Rename the generated objects `jpb`, `jbtCopy`, and `jpFiles`.
3. Set the `stringPainted` property of `jpb` to True, so that the percentage of completion will be displayed in the progress bar.
4. Set the `layout` of `jpFiles` to `GridLayout` with two rows. Drop a `JPanel` twice into `jpFiles` to create `jpFromFile` and `jpToFile`. Set the border with title "From" for `jpFromFile` and the border with title "To" for `jpToFile`.
5. Set the layout of `jpFromFile` and `jpToFile` to `BorderLayout`. Drop a `JTextField` to the center of `jpFromFile` and the center of `jpToFile` to create `jtfFrom` and `jtfTo`.
6. Generate and implement the code for handling the Copy button, as shown in Listing 5.6 (Lines 66–70).
7. Create a thread class for copying files and updating the progress bar.

```
1   package progressbardemo;
2
3   import java.awt.*;
4   import java.awt.event.*;
5   import java.applet.*;
6   import javax.swing.*;
7   import javax.swing.border.*;
8   import java.io.*;
9
10  public class ProgressBar extends JApplet {
11    boolean isStandalone = false;
12    BorderLayout borderLayout1 = new BorderLayout();
13    JProgressBar jpb = new JProgressBar();
14    JPanel jPanel1 = new JPanel();
15    JButton jbtCopy = new JButton();
16    JPanel jPanel2 = new JPanel();
17    JPanel jPanel3 = new JPanel();
18    GridLayout gridLayout1 = new GridLayout();
19    TitledBorder titledBorder1;
20    TitledBorder titledBorder2;
21    JTextField jtfFrom = new JTextField();
22    JTextField jtfTo = new JTextField();
23    BorderLayout borderLayout2 = new BorderLayout();
24    BorderLayout borderLayout3 = new BorderLayout();
25
26    /** Initialize the applet */
27    public void init() {
28      try {
```

Listing 5.6 *ProgressBar.java*

```
      jbInit();
    }
    catch(Exception e) {
      e.printStackTrace();
    }
  }

  /** Component initialization */
  private void jbInit() throws Exception {
    titledBorder1 = new TitledBorder("");
    titledBorder2 = new TitledBorder("");
    this.getContentPane().setLayout(borderLayout1);
    this.setSize(new Dimension(348, 193));
    jbtCopy.setText("Copy");
    jbtCopy.addActionListener(new java.awt.event.ActionListener() {
      public void actionPerformed(ActionEvent e) {
        jbtCopy_actionPerformed(e);
      }
    });
    jPanel1.setLayout(gridLayout1);
    gridLayout1.setRows(2);
    jPanel2.setBorder(titledBorder1);
    jPanel2.setLayout(borderLayout2);
    jPanel3.setBorder(titledBorder2);
    jPanel3.setLayout(borderLayout3);
    titledBorder1.setTitle("From");
    titledBorder2.setTitle("To");
    jpb.setStringPainted(true);
    this.getContentPane().add(jpb, BorderLayout.NORTH);
    this.getContentPane().add(jPanel1, BorderLayout.CENTER);
    jPanel1.add(jPanel2, null);
    jPanel2.add(jtfFrom, BorderLayout.CENTER);
    jPanel1.add(jPanel3, null);
    jPanel3.add(jtfTo, BorderLayout.CENTER);
    this.getContentPane().add(jbtCopy, BorderLayout.SOUTH);
  }

  void jbtCopy_actionPerformed(ActionEvent e) {
    // Create a thread for copying files
    CopyFileThread thread = new CopyFileThread(this);
    thread.start();
  }
}

// Copy file and update progress bar in a separate thread
class CopyFileThread extends Thread {
  int currentValue;
  Runnable updateProgressBar;
  ProgressBar applet;

  public CopyFileThread(final ProgressBar applet) {
    this.applet = applet;

    updateProgressBar = new Runnable() {
      public void run() {
        JProgressBar jpb = applet.jpb;
        jpb.setValue(currentValue);
      }
    };
  }

```

Listing 5.6 *Continued*

continued

Example 5.5 continued

```
    public void run() {
      BufferedInputStream in = null;
      BufferedOutputStream out = null;
      try  {
        // Create file input stream
        File inFile = new File(applet.jtfFrom.getText().trim());
        in = new BufferedInputStream(new FileInputStream(inFile));

        // Create file output stream
        File outFile = new File(applet.jtfTo.getText());
        out =  new BufferedOutputStream(new FileOutputStream(outFile));

        // Get total bytes in the file
        long totalBytes = in.available();

        // Start progress meter bar
        applet.jpb.setValue(0);
        applet.jpb.setMaximum(100);

        int r;
        long bytesRead = 0;
        byte[] b = new byte[512];
        while ((r = in.read(b, 0, b.length)) != -1) {
          out.write(b, 0, r);
          bytesRead += r;
          currentValue = (int)(bytesRead*100/totalBytes);

          // Update the progress bar
          SwingUtilities.invokeLater(updateProgressBar);
        }
      }
      catch (FileNotFoundException ex) {
        ex.printStackTrace();
      }
      catch (IOException ex) {
        ex.printStackTrace();
      }
      finally {
        try {
          if (in != null) in.close();
          if (out != null) out.close();
        }
        catch (Exception ex) {}
      }
    }
  }
```

Listing 5.6 *Continued*

Example Review

The class `CopyFileThread` is a subclass of `Thread`. This class is for copying a file on a separate thread. Swing components are not *thread-safe*, meaning that they can only be accessed from the event dispatch thread once they are displayed. The event dispatch thread is the thread that invokes callback methods like `update` and `paint` as well as the event handlers in the event listener interface. Occasionally, you need to update GUI components from a nonstandard event, as in this case, where the progress bar is repainted in the thread that copies files. To ensure that the progress bar is updated in the event dispatch thread, you need to use the `SwingUtilities`'s `invokeLater` method to invoke the thread for updating the progress bar (Lines 117–118).

The object `updateProgessBar` is an instance of `Runnable`, which is created using an anonymous inner class. This object is responsible for updating the progress bar, which must run from the event dispatch thread.

Chapter Summary

Swing lightweight components are written in Java, without platform-specific code. This facilitates a customizable look-and-feel without relying on the native windowing system, and simplifies the deployment of applications. Swing also supports a pluggable look-and-feel architecture. Thanks to this feature, users can switch the look-and-feel of an application or an applet without restarting it and without the developer having to subclass the entire component set.

This chapter introduced the basic features of Swing components. You learned how to create projects using the components `JButton`, `JRadioButton`, `JToggleButton`, `JCheckBox`, `Border`, `JLabel`, `JScrollPane`, `JTextField`, `JTextArea`, `JEditorPane`, `JScrollBar`, `JSlider`, and `JProgressBar` in JBuilder.

Review Questions

5.1 Why are the AWT user interface components considered heavyweight? Why are the Swing user interface components considered lightweight?

5.2 Describe the Swing model-view architecture.

5.3 How do you specify a particular look-and-feel in Java programs?

5.4 How do you preview a particular look-and-feel in JBuilder?

5.5 Describe the properties of `JComponent`.

5.6 Describe the properties of `AbstractButton`.

5.7 How do you create a scrollable text area?

5.8 How do you display an HTML page in a `JEditorPane`?

5.9 Describe the similarities and differences between `JScrollPane` and `JScrollBar`.

5.10 Describe the similarities and differences between `JScrollBar` and `JSlider`.

5.11 Why is it necessary to use the `invokeLater` method in Example 5.5?

5.12 What is the property that displays the percentage of work completed in `JProgressBar`?

5.13 Suppose you want to display four identical buttons in a panel of grid layout. You create one button and add this button four times into the panel. Can you see four buttons displayed in the panel?

Programming Exercises

5.1 Develop a program to set the horizontal alignment and column size properties of a text field dynamically, as shown in Figure 5.22.

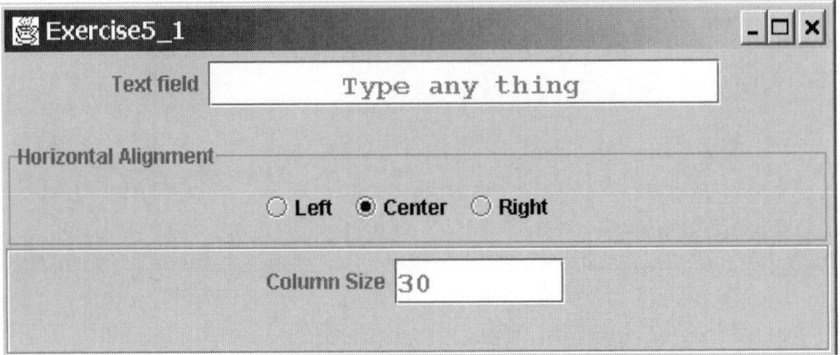

Figure 5.22 *You can set the horizontal alignment and column size properties of a text field dynamically.*

5.2 Create a program that demonstrates the wrapping styles of the text area. The program uses a check box to indicate whether the text area is wrapped. In the case where the text area is wrapped, you need to specify whether it is wrapped by characters or by words, as shown in Figure 5.23.

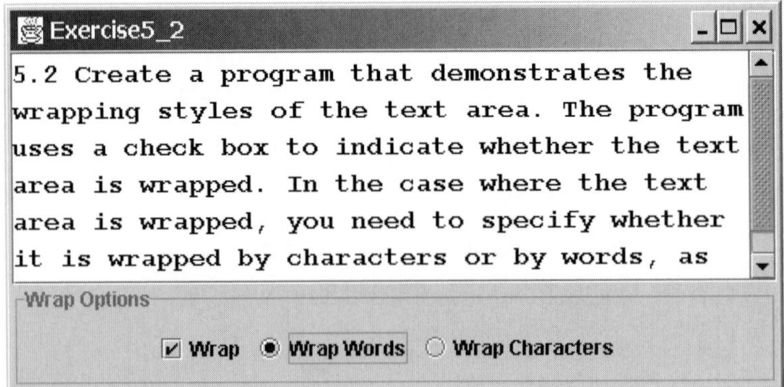

Figure 5.23 *You can set the options to wrap a text area by characters or by words dynamically.*

5.3 Modify Example 5.4 and use the `JSlider` to select colors instead of using `JScrollBar`.

5.4 Create a program that displays an instance of `JProgressBar` and sets its `value` property randomly every 500 milliseconds infinitely.

5.5 Modify Example 5.1 to set the icons for the radio buttons in Horizontal Alignment section, as shown in Figure 5.24. The icons are the same as used by the radio buttons in the Vertical Alignment section. Create a composite matte border of red color with 2 pixels thick. Share this border among four buttons in the top panel. The top panel shares the same border.

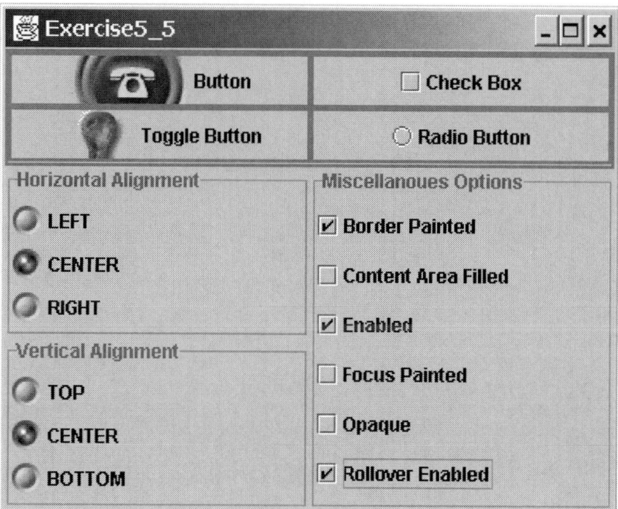

Figure 5.24 *The icons and borders can be shared.*

5.6 Modify Example 5.3, "Using `JEditorPane`," as follows:

- It accepts an HTML file from a local host. Assume that a local HTML filename begins neither with http:// nor with www.
- It accepts a remote HTML file. A remote HTML filename begins with either http:// or www.

CHAPTER 6

Containers and Layout Managers

Objectives

- Know the structures of the Swing container.
- Understand how a layout manager works in Java.
- Examine the layout managers provided in JBuilder.
- Create custom layout managers and install custom layout managers in JBuilder.
- Use `JTabbedPane` to create tabbed panes.
- Use `JSplitPane` to create split panes.

Introduction

If you have used a Windows-based RAD tool like Visual Basic, you know that it is easier to create user interfaces with Visual Basic than with a Java RAD tool like JBuilder. This is mainly because the components are placed in absolute positions and sizes in Visual Basic, whereas they are placed in containers using a variety of layout managers in Java. Absolute positions and sizes are fine if the application is developed and deployed on the same platform, but what looks fine on a development system may not look right on a deployment system on a different platform. To solve this problem, Java provides a set of layout managers that place components in containers in a way that is independent of fonts, screen resolutions, and platform differences.

A *container* is an object that holds and groups components. A *layout manager* is a special object used to place components in a container. Containers and layout managers play a crucial role in creating user interfaces. This chapter presents a conceptual overview of containers, reviews the layout managers in Java, and introduces the new layout managers provided by JBuilder. You will also learn how to create your own layout manager and install it in JBuilder.

About Containers

User interface components like `JButton` cannot be displayed without being placed in a container. A container is a component that is capable of containing other components. You do not display a user interface component; you place it in a container, and the container displays the components it contains.

The base class for all containers is `java.awt.Container`, which is a subclass of `java.awt.Component`. The `Container` class has the following essential functions:

- It adds and removes components using various `add` and `remove` methods.
- It maintains a `layout` property for specifying a layout manager that is used to lay out components in the container. Every container has a default layout manager.
- It provides registration methods for the `java.awt.event.ContainerEvent`.

In AWT programming, the `java.awt.Frame` class is used as a top-level container for Java applications, `java.awt.Applet` class is used for all Java applets, and `java.awt.Dialog` is used for dialog windows. These classes do not work properly with Swing lightweight components. Special versions of `Frame`, `Applet`, and `Dialog` named `JFrame`, `JApplet`, and `JDialog` have been developed to accommodate Swing components. `JFrame` is a subclass of `Frame`, `JApplet` is a subclass of `Applet`, and `JDialog` is a subclass of `Dialog`. `JFrame` and `JApplet` inherit all the functions of their heavyweight counterparts, but they have a more complex internal structure with several layered panes, as shown in Figure 6.1.

`javax.swing.JRootPane` is a lightweight container used behind the scenes by Swing's top-level containers, such as `JFrame`, `JApplet`, and `JDialog`.

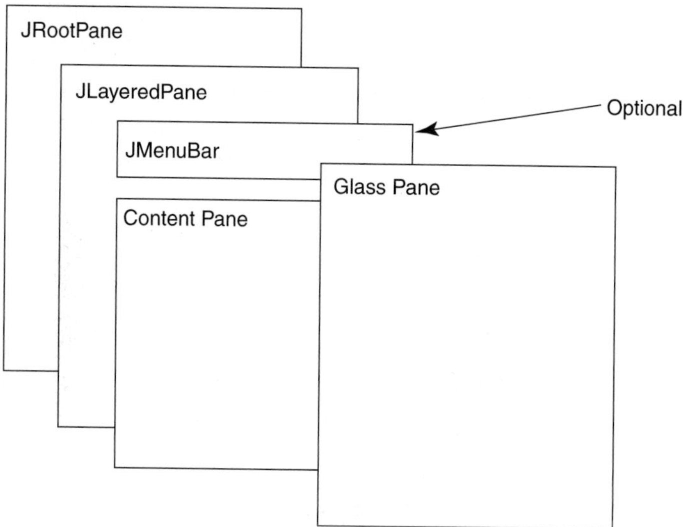

Figure 6.1 *Swing top-level containers use layers of panes to group lightweight components and make them work properly.*

`javax.swing.JLayeredPane` is a container that manages the optional menu bar and the content pane. The content pane is an instance of `Container` with default `BorderLayout`. This is the container where the user interface components are added. To obtain the content pane in a `JFrame` or in a `JApplet`, use the `getContentPane()` method. The glass pane floats on top of everything. `java.swing.JGlassPane` is a hidden pane by default. If you make the glass pane visible, then it's like a sheet of glass over all the other parts of the root pane. It's completely transparent unless you implement the glass pane's paint method so that it does something, and it intercepts input events for the root pane. In general, `JRootPane`, `JLayeredPane`, and `JGlassPane` are not used directly.

Now let us review the three most frequently used Swing containers: `JFrame`, `JApplet`, and `JPanel`.

JFrame

`JFrame`, a Swing version of `Frame`, is a top-level container for Java graphics applications. Like `Frame`, `JFrame` is displayed as a standalone window with a title bar and a border. The following properties are often useful in `JFrame`.

- `contentPane`: This is the content pane of the frame.
- `iconImage`: This is the image that represents the frame. This image replaces the default Java image on the frame's title bar and is also displayed when the frame is minimized. This property type is `Image`. You can get an image using the `ImageIcon` class, as follows:

```
Image image = (new ImageIcon(filename)).getImage();
```

- jMenuBar: This is the optional menu bar for the frame.
- layout: This is inherited from Frame, but is not used in JFrame because the components are not directly placed in the frame; instead they are placed in the content pane. In JBuilder, this property is associated with the content pane of the frame. When you set a new layout, JBuilder sets the layout in the content pane of JFrame.
- resizable: This is a boolean value indicating whether the frame is resizable. The default value is true.
- title: This specifies the title of the frame.

All the above properties are inherited from Frame except contentPane and jMenuBar.

NOTE

JFrame is a top-level container. You can also create internal frames using the JInternalFrame class. Creating internal frames is presented in the companion Web site.

JApplet

JApplet is a Swing version of Applet. Since it is a subclass of Applet, it has all the functions required by the Web browser. Here are the four essential methods defined in Applet:

```
// Called by the browser when the Web page containing
// this applet is initially loaded
public void init()

// Called by the browser after the init() method and
// every time the Web page is visited.
public void start()

// Called by the browser when the page containing this
// applet becomes inactive.
public void stop()

// Called by the browser when the Web browser exits.
public void destroy()
```

Additionally, JApplet has the contentPane and jMenuBar properties, among others. As with JFrame, you do not place components directly into JApplet; instead you place them into the content pane of the applet. The Applet class cannot have the menu bar, but the JApplet class allows you to set the menu bar using the setJMenuBar method.

TIP

contentPane and jMenuBar are hidden properties in JApplet. By default, these properties do not appear in the inspector. To display hidden properties, right-click the inspector, choose Property Exposure Level, hidden.

NOTE

To use the Swing components in an applet, the applet must extend `JApplet` or a subclass of `JApplet` instead of `Applet`. To use the Swing components in an application, the application must extend `JFrame` or a subclass of `JFrame`.

JPanel

Panels act as smaller containers for grouping user interface components. `javax.swing.JPanel` is different from `JFrame` and `JApplet`. First, `JPanel` is not a top-level container; it must be placed inside another container, and it can be placed inside another `JPanel`. Second, since `JPanel` is a subclass of `JComponent`, `JPanel` is a lightweight component, but `JFrame` and `JApplet` are heavyweight components.

`JPanel` is a Swing version of `Panel`, but it is not a subclass of `Panel`. Nevertheless, you can use `JPanel` the same way you use `Panel`. As a subclass of `JComponent`, `JPanel` can take advantage of `JComponent`, such as double buffering and borders. You should draw figures on `JPanel` rather than `JFrame` or `JApplet`, because `JPanel` supports double buffering, which is the technique for eliminating flickers.

Layout Managers

Every container has a layout manager that is responsible for arranging its components. The container's `setLayout` method can be used to set a layout manager. Certain types of containers have default layout managers. For instance, the content pane of `JFrame` or `JApplet` uses `BorderLayout`, and `JPanel` uses `FlowLayout`.

A container's `layout` property appears in the inspector for the container, as shown in Figure 6.2. You can specify a layout manager for a container by selecting one from a list of available layout managers. JBuilder automatically updates the container's call to `setLayout`.

The layout manager places the components in accordance with its own rules and property settings, and with the constraints associated with each component.

Every layout manager has its own specific set of rules. For example, the `FlowLayout` manager places components in rows from left to right and starts a new row when the previous row is filled. The `BorderLayout` manager places components in the north, south, east, west, or center of the container. The `GridLayout` manager places components in a grid of cells in rows and columns from left to right in order.

Some layout managers have properties that can affect the sizing and location of the components in the container. For example, `BorderLayout` has properties called `hgap` (horizontal gap) and `vgap` (vertical gap) that determine the distance between components horizontally and vertically. `FlowLayout` has properties that can be used to specify the alignment (left, center, right) of the components and properties for specifying the horizontal or vertical gap between the components. `GridLayout` has properties that can be used to specify the horizontal or vertical gap between columns and rows and the properties for specifying the number of rows and

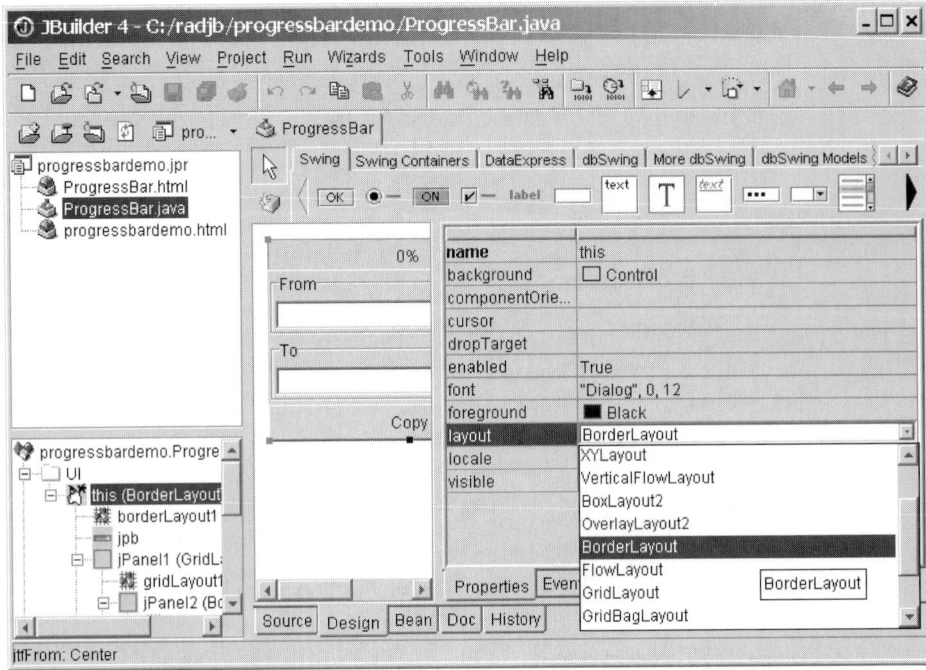

Figure 6.2 *Every container has a* `layout` *property. You can choose a layout from a drop-down list of layout managers in JBuilder.*

columns. These properties can be viewed and edited in the inspector when the layout manager is selected in the component tree. As shown in Figure 6.3, the layout manager is displayed as an item in the component tree just below the container to which it is attached.

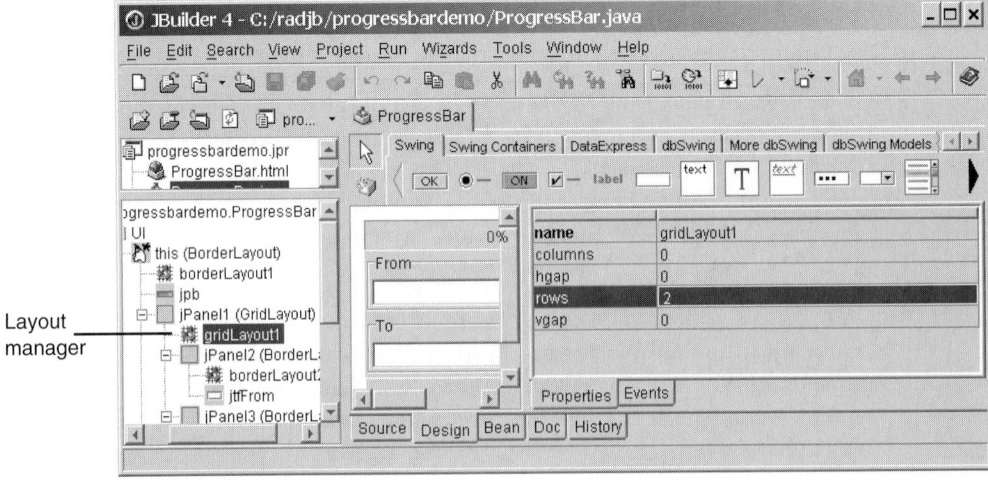

Figure 6.3 *You can view and edit the properties of a layout manager in the UI Designer.*

For each component you drop into a container, JBuilder uses the *constraints* property to provide additional information about how the layout manager should locate and size this specific object. For example, a component added to a container with BorderLayout has the constraints property with selectable values North, South, East, West, and Center. When a component is created, an initial value is assigned to constraints depending on where this component is placed in the container. The constraints value of a component added to a container with FlowLayout or GridLayout is always null. The constraints property is associated with a component, but it is not specified until the component is added to a container.

NOTE

The constraints property is JBuilder-specific, and is created for every object that is added to a container. This property can be viewed and edited in the inspector. The type of object or value created depends on the type of layout manager being used. Modifications of the constraints property are synchronized with the updates of the container's add method in the source code.

The size of a component in a container is determined by many factors, such as:

- The type of layout manager used by the container.
- The layout constraints associated with each component.
- The size of the container.
- Certain properties common to all components (such as preferredSize, minimumSize, maximumSize, alignmentX, and alignmentY).

The preferredSize property indicates the ideal size for the component to look best. Depending on the rules of the particular layout manager, this property may or may not be considered. For example, the preferred size of a component is used in a container with a FlowLayout manager, but ignored if it is placed in a container with a BorderLayout manager.

The minimumSize property specifies the minimum size for the component to be useful. For most GUI components, minimumSize is the same as preferredSize. Layout managers generally respect minimumSize more than preferredSize.

The maximumSize property specifies the maximum size needed by a component, so that the layout manager won't wastefully give space to a component that does not need it. For instance, BorderLayout could limit the center component's size to its maximum size, and then either give the space to edge components or limit the size of the outer window when resized.

The alignmentX property specifies how the component would like to be aligned relative to other components along the x-axis. This value should be a number between 0 and 1, where 0 represents alignment along the origin, 1 is aligned the farthest away from the origin, 0.5 is centered, etc.

The alignmentY property specifies how the component would like to be aligned relative to other components along the y-axis. The value should be a number between 0 and 1, where 0 represents alignment along the origin, 1 is aligned the farthest away from the origin, 0.5 is centered, etc.

Working with Layout Managers

Java provides a variety of layout managers. In addition, you can create custom layout managers. BorderLayout, FlowLayout, GridLayout, CardLayout, GridBagLayout, and Null were introduced with Java AWT. BoxLayout and OverlayLayout were introduced in Swing. BoxLayout2, OverlayLayout2, XYLayout, PaneLayout, and VerticalLayout are custom layout managers provided by JBuilder.

BorderLayout

BorderLayout arranges and resizes its components to fit in five regions: North, South, East, West, and Center. The components are laid out according to their preferred sizes and constraints. The North and South components may be stretched horizontally; the East and West components may be stretched vertically; the Center component may stretch both horizontally and vertically to fill any space left over.

By default, a BorderLayout puts no gap between the components in the container. However, you can specify the horizontal gap (hgap) and the vertical gap (hgap) in the inspector.

BorderLayout is ideal for docking components to one or more edges of a container, and for filling up the center of the container with a component. Use BorderLayout if you want a single component to occupy the entire container.

FlowLayout

FlowLayout arranges components according to their preferredSize in a left-to-right flow, much like lines of text in a paragraph.

You can choose how to place components in the rows by specifying an alignment justification of left, right, or center on the alignment property in the inspector for the layout manager. You can also specify the size of the horizontal or vertical gap between the components, using the hgap and vgap properties. By default, the gap is 5 pixels.

GridLayout

GridLayout arranges components in a rectangular grid of cells. The container is divided into equal-sized rectangles, and one component is placed in each rectangle. GridLayout expands each component to fill the entire cell.

You can specify the number of columns and rows in the grid; one of these can be zero, but at least one must be nonzero. For example, if you specify four columns and zero rows, GridLayout creates a grid with four columns and a variant number of rows depending on the number of components that are added to the container. You can also specify the gap between rows and columns. By default, the gap is 0.

GridLayout is ideal when you want the components in a container to be the same size. In Example 4.2, "Creating a Clock Component," you put six clocks in the applet using GridLayout to ensure that all the clocks were the same size.

CardLayout

CardLayout places components in the container as cards. Only one card is visible at a time, and the container acts as a stack of cards. The ordering of cards is determined by the container's own internal ordering of its component objects. CardLayout defines a set of methods that allow an application to flip through the cards sequentially or to show a specified card directly.

You can specify the size of the horizontal and vertical gap surrounding a stack of components in a CardLayout manager.

CardLayout is ideal when you need to manage two or more panels that have to share the same display area. In many situations, CardLayout can be replaced by JTabbedPane, which is introduced later in this chapter.

GridBagLayout

GridBagLayout is the most flexible and the most complex. It is similar to GridLayout in the sense that both layout managers arrange components in a grid. However, in GridBagLayout the components can vary in size and can be added in any order.

GridBagLayout uses a dynamic rectangular grid of cells, with each component occupying one or more cells called its *display area*. Each component managed by a GridBagLayout manager is associated with a GridBagConstraints instance that specifies how the component is laid out within its display area. How a GridBagLayout places a set of components depends on each component's GridBagConstraints and minimum size, as well as the preferred size of the components' container.

To use GridBagLayout effectively, you must customize one or more of its components' GridBagConstraints. You customize a GridBagConstraints object by setting one or more of its instance variables:

- gridx and gridy: These variables specify the cell at the upper left of the component's display area, where the upper-left-most cell has address gridx=0, gridy=0. Note that gridx specifies the column in which the component will be placed, and gridy specifies the row in which the component will be placed.
- gridwidth and gridheight: These variables specify the number of cells in a row (for gridwidth) or column (for gridheight) in the component's display area. The default value is 1.

- weightx and weighty: These variables specify the extra space to allocate the component horizontally and vertically when the window is resized. Unless you specify a weight for at least one component in a row (weightx) and column (weighty), all the components clump together in the center of their container. This is because when the weight is zero (the default), the GridBagLayout puts any extra space between its grid of cells and the edges of the container.
- fill: This specifies how the component should be resized if its viewing area is larger than its current size. Valid values are GridBagConstraints.NONE (the default), GridBagConstraints.HORIZONTAL (make the component wide enough to fill its display area horizontally, but don't change its height), GridBagConstraints.VERTICAL (make the component tall enough to fill its display area vertically, but don't change its width), and GridBagConstraints.BOTH (make the component fill its display area entirely).
- anchor: This specifies where the component is placed in the area when it does not fill in the entire area. Valid values are GridBagConstraints.CENTER (the default), GridBagConstraints.NORTH, GridBagConstraints.NORTHEAST, GridBagConstraints.EAST, GridBagConstraints.SOUTHEAST, GridBagConstraints.SOUTH, GridBagConstraints.SOUTHWEST, GridBagConstraints.WEST, and GridBagConstraints.NORTHWEST.
- insets: This specifies the minimum amount of external space (padding) in pixels between the component and the edges of its display area.

The fill and anchor parameters deal with how to fill and place the component when the viewing area is larger than the requested area. The fill and anchor parameters are class variables, while gridx, gridy, width, height, weightx, and weighty are instance variables.

GridBagLayout is a complex layout manager that many people find difficult to use. JBuilder greatly simplifies the use of GridBagLayout with a Constraint property editor. The Constraint property editor enables you to edit all the GridBagConstraints values, as shown in Figure 6.4. To open the editor, either right-click the component in the UI designer and choose Constraints or select the constraints property in the inspector and click the ellipsis button.

By right-clicking on a component and choosing Show Grid, you can display a grid on the UI designer that lets you see exactly where and how components are placed in the container. The grid is only visible when a component inside a GridBagLayout is selected. When you right-click on a component, you also see other choices on the popup menu, and these let you quickly set or remove certain constraints without using the Constraint property editor, as shown in Figure 6.5.

TIP

While GridBagLayout can accommodate a complex grid, it behaves more predictably if you organize your components into smaller panels, nested inside the GridBagLayout container. These nested panels can use other layouts and can contain additional panels if necessary.

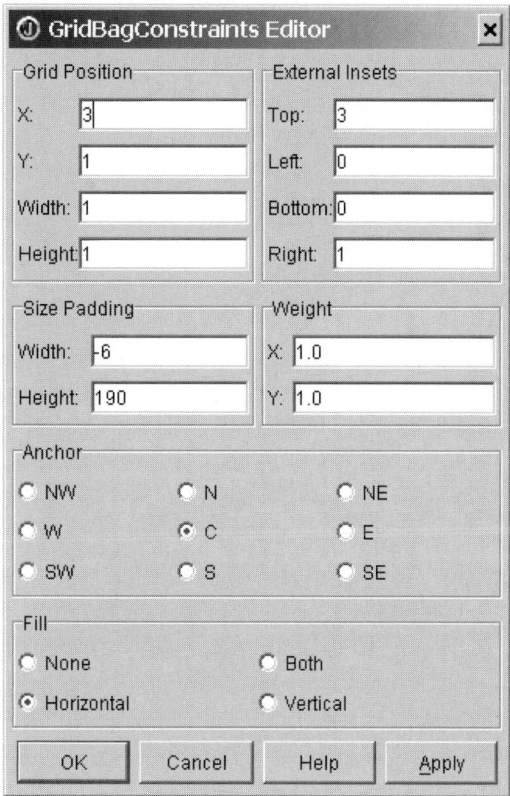

Figure 6.4 *The* `GridBagConstraints` *property editor lets you edit all the properties of a component's constraints.*

Null

Null means that no layout manager is assigned to the container. The components in the container are arranged in absolute positions and sizes. It is easy to use, but lacks portability, because when you resize a container, the components do not reposition or resize. You should avoid using `NULL` for cross-platform projects.

BoxLayout and *Box* Class

`BoxLayout` is a Swing layout manager that arranges components in a row or a column. The `JToolBar` component introduced in Chapter 7, "Menus, Toolbars, and Dialogs," uses `BoxLayout`. You can use `BoxLayout` in any container, but it is simpler to use the `Box` class, which is a container of `BoxLayout`. To create a `Box` container, use one of the following two static methods:

```
Box box1 = Box.createHorizontalBox();
Box box2 = Box.createVerticalBox();
```

The former creates a box that contains components horizontally, and the latter creates a box that contains components vertically. These two types of boxes are prein-

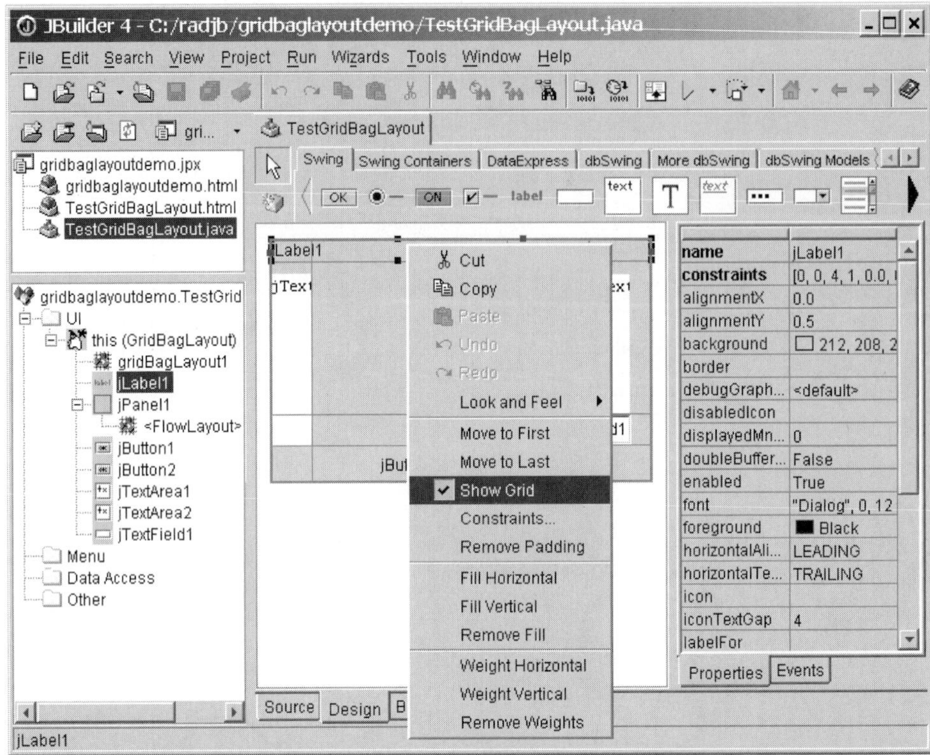

Figure 6.5 *You can set the constraints of a component with* `GridBagLayout` *in a popup menu in the UI designer.*

stalled in the Swing Containers page of the component palette in JBuilder. As a result, you can create horizontal or vertical boxes using JBuilder's UI designer.

You can add components to a box programmatically in the same way that you add them to the containers of `FlowLayout` or `GridLayout` using the `add` method, as follows:

```
box1.add(new JButton("A Button"));
```

You can drop components to a box in the same way that you drop components to a container. The components are laid left to right in a horizontal box, and top to bottom in a vertical box.

`BoxLayout` is similar to `GridLayout`, but `BoxLayout` has many unique features.

First, `BoxLayout` respects a component's preferred size, maximum size, and minimum size. If the total preferred size of all the components in the box is less than the box size, then the components are expanded up to their maximum size. If the total preferred size of all the components in the box is greater than the box size, then the components are shrunk down to their minimum size. If the components do not fit at their minimum width, some of them will not be shown. In the `GridLayout`, the container is divided into cells of equal size, and the components are fit in regardless of their preferred maximum or minimum size.

Second, unlike other layout managers, `BoxLayout` considers the component's `alignmentX` or `alignmentY` property. The `alignmentX` property is used to place the component in a vertical box layout, and the `alignmentY` property is used to place it in a horizontal box layout.

Third, `BoxLayout` does not have gaps between the components, but you can use fillers to separate components. A filler is an invisible component. There are three kinds of fillers: struts, rigid areas, and glues.

A *strut* simply adds some space between components. You can use the static method `createHorizontalStrut()` in the `Box` class to create a horizontal strut, and the static method `createVerticalStrut()` to create a vertical strut. For example, the following code adds a vertical strut of 8 pixels between two buttons in a vertical box.

```
box2.add(new JButton("Button 1"));
box2.add(Box.createVerticalStrut(8));
box2.add(new JButton("Button 2"));
```

A *rigid area* is a two-dimensional space that can be created using the static method `createRigidArea(dimension)` in the `Box` class. For example, the following code adds a rigid area 10 pixels wide and 20 pixels high into a box.

```
box2.add(Box.createRigidArea(new Dimension(10, 20));
```

A *glue* separates components as much as possible. For example, by adding a glue between two components in a horizontal box, you place one component at the left end and the other at the right end. A glue can be created using the `Box.createGlue()` method.

JBuilder installs three fillers in the Swing page of the component palette:

- ( ) `Box.createGlue()`
- ( ) `Box.createHorizontalStrut(8)`
- ( ) `Box.createVerticalStrut(8)`

BoxLayout2

`BoxLayout2`, a JBuilder custom layout manager, is a Swing `BoxLayout` wrapped as a bean so that it can be selected as a layout in the inspector. `BoxLayout2` places components in a row or a column and expands them to fill the available space in the container.

You can choose whether the components are placed in a row or in a column by specifying the axis of `x-axis` or `y-axis` in the inspector of the layout manager.

XYLayout

Like the Null layout manager, `XYLayout` arranges components in absolute positions and sizes. `XYLayout` is a JBuilder layout manager that has more functions than the Java's standard `Null` layout manager.

The `constraints` property can be modified to set the location and size for the component. This can also be done by using the mouse. You can align the components and give them the same width and height. To perform the alignment operations, select the components you want to align, right-click in the UI designer, and select the desired operations from the popup menu, as shown in Figure 6.6.

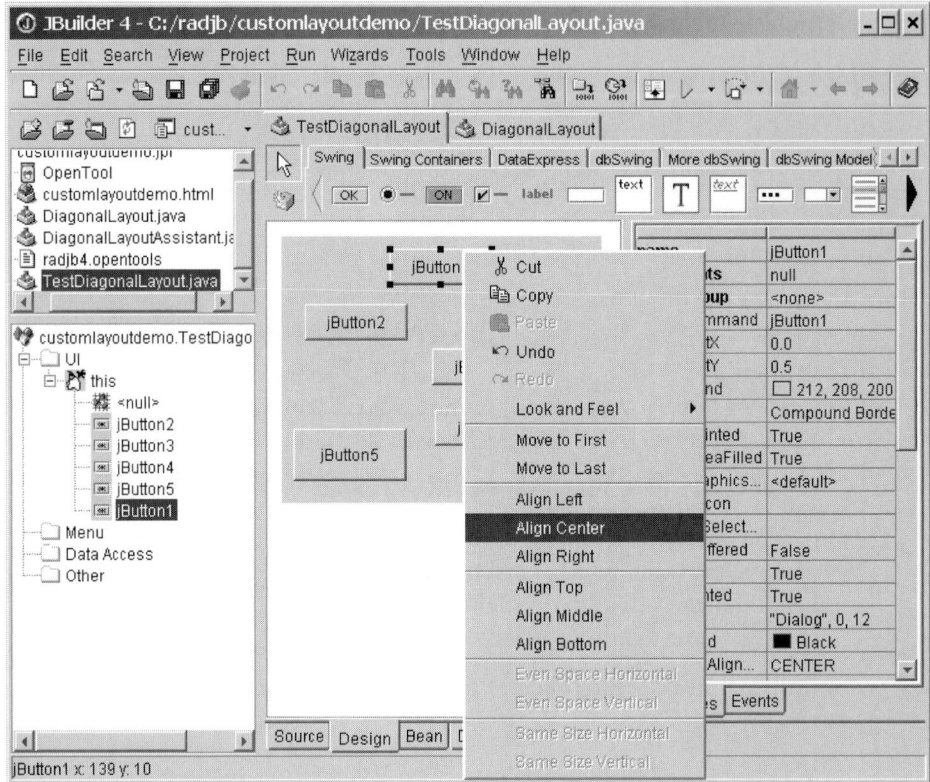

Figure 6.6 *The alignment operations make it easy to organize components in a clean look.*

`XYLayout` is very useful for prototyping UI design. You can use `XYLayout` to design complex UI with multiple, nested panels, then convert the design using portable layout managers. It is particularly convenient to use `XYLayout` for prototyping designs involving `GridBagLayout`. This can speed up your design work. JBuilder intelligently converts the layout to `GridBagLayout`.

CAUTION

Save the source code before converting from one layout to the other, because sometimes the conversion distorts the UI design and makes it unusable.

TIP

When prototyping with `XYLayout`, use `XYLayout` for all the nested containers. When converting the design, start from the inner containers.

OverlayLayout2

OverlayLayout2, a JBuilder custom layout manager, is Swing's OverlayLayout wrapped as a bean so that it can be selected as a layout in the inspector. It is similar to CardLayout in that it places the components on top of one other. Unlike CardLayout, where only one component is visible at a time, the components can be visible at the same time if you make each component in the container transparent. For example, to make a composite graphics, you could overlay multiple transparent images on top of one other in the container.

PaneLayout

PaneLayout is a JBuilder custom layout manager that lets you specify the size of a component in relation to its sibling components. PaneLayout was introduced before the Swing components were proposed. The usefulness of PaneLayout has diminished with the introduction of JSplitPane. JSplitPane is more versatile and flexible than PaneLayout. I recommend the use of JSplitPane to create split panes. JSplitPane is covered later in this chapter.

VerticalFlowLayout

VerticalFlowLayout is a JBuilder custom layout manager. While FlowLayout arranges components in a left-to-right flow, VerticalFlowLayout arranges components in columns from top to bottom, then left to right, based on the components' preferredSize.

Like FlowLayout, you can specify alignment and horizontal and vertical gaps in VerticalFlowLayout. You can also specify whether all the components are placed in one column using the horizontalFill property and whether the last component fills the remaining height of the container using the verticalFill property. By default, horizontalFill is true, and verticalFill is false.

TIP

The standard Java layout managers are sufficient in most situations. I recommend that you avoid using the layout managers provided in JBuilder. Although the JBuilder layout managers are 100% pure Java, you need to import them to your project and package them for deployment.

NOTE

The layout managers provided by Borland are contained in the *JBuilder Component Library* (JBCL). It contains many Swing-like components in the com.borland.control package, layout managers in the com.borland.layout package, and utilities in the com.borland.util package. JBCL was developed before Java Swing components. The JBCL UI interface components have been replaced by Swing components; for example, ButtonControl has been replaced by JButton. However, some of the layout managers and utilities are still useful. The JBCL library is automatically added to the project if you select a JBCL layout from the UI designer. If the JBCL library is not in the project, you may add it to the Required Libraries of the project, as shown in Figure 6.7.

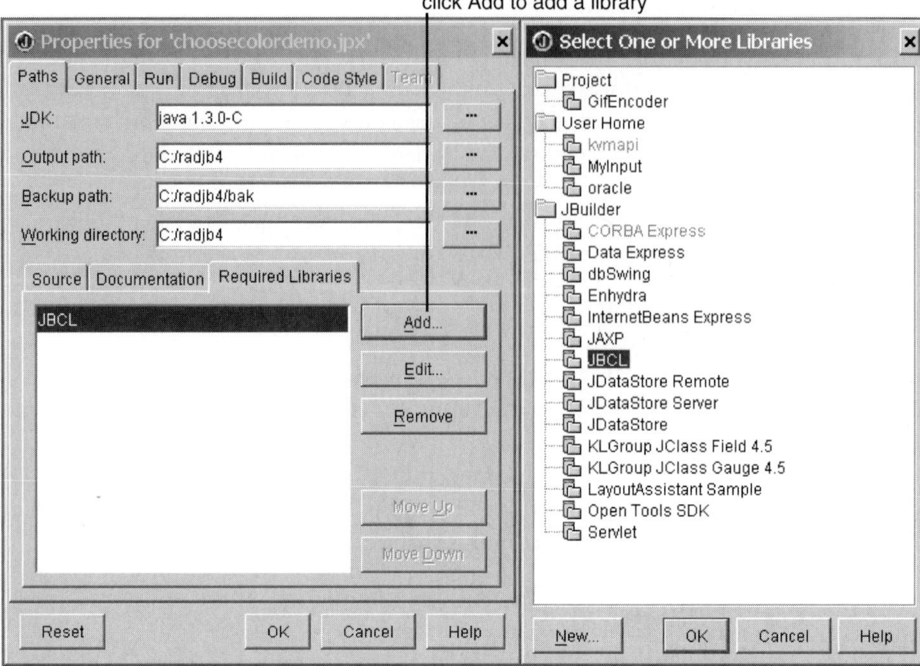

Figure 6.7 *You can add the JBCL library from the Project Properties dialog box.*

The following example demonstrates the use of a variety of Swing containers and layout managers to create projects in JBuilder.

Example 6.1 Choosing Colors

This example creates a project that selects a standard color from a combo box or selects any color by specifying an RGB value or an HSB value. A sample run of the project is shown in Figure 6.8.

The three color-selection panels titled Red, Green, and Blue in the Choose Color panel have similar functions. This makes it ideal to create a bean component for modeling these panels. Let the bean component be named `ColorPanel`. This component generates an `ActionEvent` to notify listeners whenever the color value changes in the panel.

Here are the steps in creating `ColorPanel`.

1. Create a new project named choosecolordemo.jpr, choose File, and create a bean named `ColorPanel` using the JavaBeans wizard that extends `JPanel`.
2. Click the Bean tab in the content pane to switch to BeansExpress. Choose Properties to add three properties: `colorType` (a string value either RGB or HSB), `colorValue` (an `int` value), and `title` (a string for the title on the border of the panel).

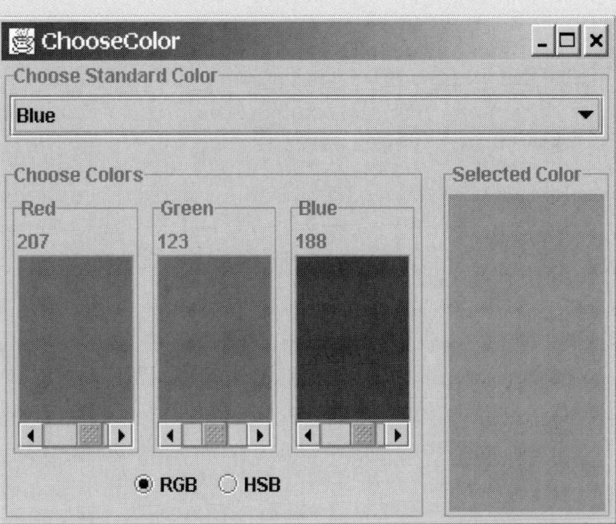

Figure 6.8 *You can choose a standard color from the combo box or choose any color by specifying either RGB or HSB values.*

3. Choose the Events tab in BeansExpress and check Action to enable the bean to fire Action events. The Action event is needed to notify the listeners that a new color has been selected.

4. Click the Design tab to switch to the UI Designer. Set the `layout` of the panel to `BorderLayout`. Set the `border` to titled to create `titledBorder1`. Drop a `JLabel` to the North, a `JTextField` to the Center and a `JScrollBar` to the South of the panel. Rename these components `jlblColor`, `jtfColor`, and `jscbColor`. The UI layout of `ColorPanel` is shown in Figure 6.9.

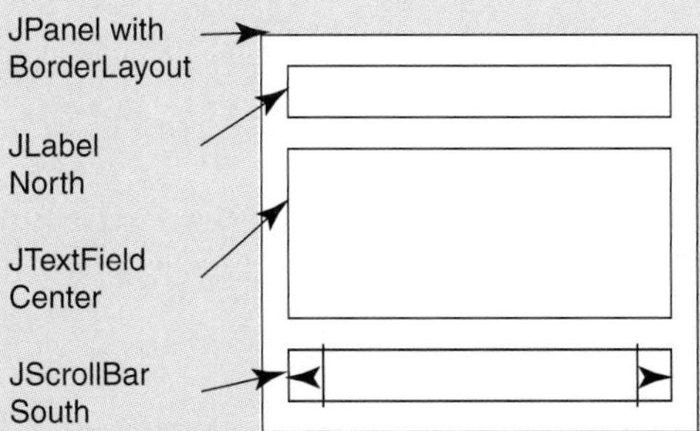

Figure 6.9 *The* `ColorPanel` *consists of a* `JScrollBar` *for selecting values, a* `JTextField` *for showing the color, and a* `JLabel` *for displaying the value.*

continued

Example 6.1 continued

5. In the Events page of `jscbColor`, click the value field of `adjustmentValueChanged` to generate the code for handling the adjustment value change of the scroll bar. Fill in the code as shown in Listing 6.1 (Lines 78–95).

6. Modify the `getTitle` and `setTitle` methods to get the title from `titledBorder1` and set it to `titledBorder1`. Delete the declaration for the `title` variable, since it is not used to maintain the `title` property.

7. Create a variable named `buttonType` to indicate whether RGB radio button or HSB radio button is selected. Code the `switchButton` method to switch to either the RGB mode or the HSB mode, as shown in Listing 6.1 (Lines 97–110).

8. Install `ColorPanel` in the component palette for use in the `ChooseColor` class.

```
1    package choosecolordemo;
2
3    import java.awt.*;
4    import javax.swing.*;
5    import javax.swing.border.*;
6    import java.awt.event.*;
7    import java.util.*;
8
9    public class ColorPanel extends JPanel {
10     BorderLayout borderLayout1 = new BorderLayout();
11     JScrollBar jscbColor = new JScrollBar();
12     JTextField jtfColor = new JTextField();
13     JLabel jlblColorValue = new JLabel();
14
15     private String colorType = "Red";
16     private String buttonType = "RGB";
17     private int colorValue = 0;
18
19     private transient Vector actionListeners;
20     TitledBorder titledBorder1;
21
22     /** Constructor */
23     public ColorPanel() {
24       try {
25         jbInit();
26       }
27       catch (Exception ex) {
28         ex.printStackTrace();
29       }
30     }
31
32     /** Component initialization */
33     private void jbInit() throws Exception {
34       titledBorder1 = new TitledBorder("");
35       jscbColor.addAdjustmentListener(
36         new java.awt.event.AdjustmentListener() {
```

Listing 6.1 *ColorPanel.java*

```
      public void adjustmentValueChanged(AdjustmentEvent e) {
        jscbColor_adjustmentValueChanged(e);
      }
    });
    jscbColor.setOrientation(JScrollBar.HORIZONTAL);
    jtfColor.setEditable(false);
    jlblColorValue.setText("jLabel1");
    this.setLayout(borderLayout1);
    this.setBorder(titledBorder1);
    this.add(jscbColor, BorderLayout.SOUTH);
    this.add(jtfColor, BorderLayout.CENTER);
    this.add(jlblColorValue, BorderLayout.NORTH);

    setTitle("Color type");
  }

  /** Set colorType */
  public void setColorType(String newColorType) {
    colorType = newColorType;
  }

  /** Return colorType */
  public String getColorType() {
    return colorType;
  }

  /** Return colorValue */
  public int getColorValue() {
    return colorValue;
  }

  /** Set title */
  public void setTitle(String newTitle) {
    titledBorder1.setTitle(newTitle);
  }

  /** Get title */
  public String getTitle() {
    return titledBorder1.getTitle();
  }

  void jscbColor_adjustmentValueChanged(AdjustmentEvent e) {
    colorValue = jscbColor.getValue();
    jlblColorValue.setText(colorValue+"");

    if (buttonType.equals("RGB")) {
      if (colorType.equals("Red"))
        jtfColor.setBackground(new Color(colorValue, 0, 0));
      else if (colorType.equals("Green"))
        jtfColor.setBackground(new Color(0, colorValue, 0));
      else if (colorType.equals("Blue"))
        jtfColor.setBackground(new Color(0, 0, colorValue));

      jtfColor.repaint();
    }

```

Listing 6.1 *Continued*

continued

Example 6.1 continued

```
      fireActionPerformed(
        new ActionEvent(this, ActionEvent.ACTION_PERFORMED, null));
    }

    public void switchButton(String s) {
      if (s.equals("RGB"))
        jscbColor.setMaximum(255);
      else if (s.equals("HSB"))
        jscbColor.setMaximum(100);

      jtfColor.setBackground(Color.white);
      jtfColor.repaint();
      jscbColor.setValue(0);

      this.repaint();

      buttonType = s;
    }

    /** Remove listener. Generated by JBuilder */
    public synchronized void removeActionListener(ActionListener l) {
      if (actionListeners != null && actionListeners.contains(l)) {
        Vector v = (Vector) actionListeners.clone();
        v.removeElement(l);
        actionListeners = v;
      }
    }

    /** Add listener. Generated by JBuilder */
    public synchronized void addActionListener(ActionListener l) {
      Vector v = actionListeners ==
        null ? new Vector(2) : (Vector) actionListeners.clone();
      if (!v.contains(l)) {
        v.addElement(l);
        actionListeners = v;
      }
    }

    /** Fire ActionEvent. Generated by JBuilder */
    protected void fireActionPerformed(ActionEvent e) {
      if (actionListeners != null) {
        Vector listeners = actionListeners;
        int count = listeners.size();
        for (int i = 0; i < count; i++)
          ((ActionListener) listeners.elementAt(i)).actionPerformed(e);
      }
    }
  }
```

Listing 6.1 *Continued*

Note

You will not see the variable `title` in the structure pane of `ColorPanel` because `title` is not declared as a data field in the class. But `title` is a JavaBeans property. Recall that a bean property is not necessarily a data field (see the section "Properties and Data Members" in Chapter 2, "Introduction to JavaBeans.")

Let us turn our attention to the main part of this example for creating the `ChooseColor` class.

1. Use the Applet wizard to create the `ChooseColor` class. With ChooseColor.java selected in the navigation pane, switch to the UI designer and create the UI, as shown in Figure 6.10.

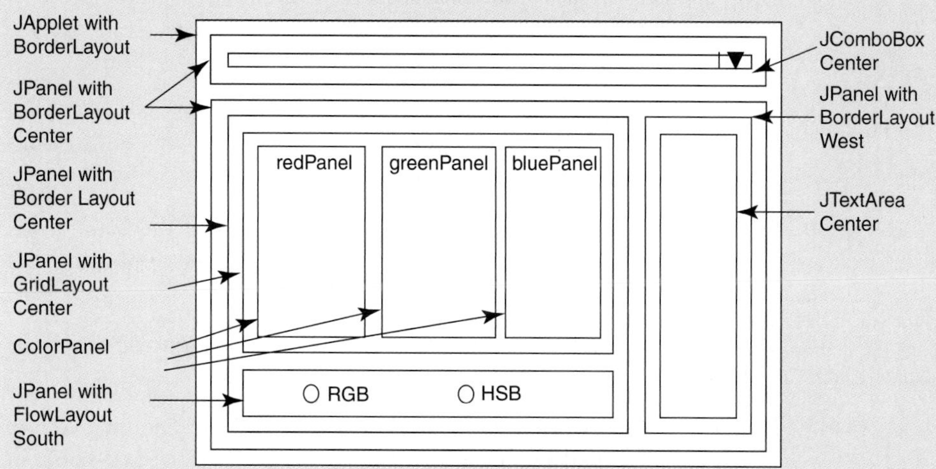

Figure 6.10 *The user interface employs nested panels to group the components in order to achieve the desired layout.*

2. Drop a `JPanel` to the north of the applet and rename it `jpStandardColor`. Set the `layout` of `jpStandardColor` to `BorderLayout`; drop a `JComboBox` to the center of `jpStandardColor` and rename it `jcboStandardColor`. Drop a `JPanel` to the center of the applet and rename it `jpSelection`.

3. Set the `layout` of `jpSelection` to `BorderLayout`. Drop a `JPanel` to the center and a `JPanel` to the east of `jpSelection`, and rename them `jpSelectColor` and `jpSelectedColor`.

4. Set the `layout` of `jpSelectedColor` to `BorderLayout`, and the width (the first argument) of the `preferredSize` property to 80. Drop a `JTextArea` to the center of `jpSelectedColor` and rename it `jtaSelectedColor`.

5. Set the `layout` of `jpSelectColor` to `BorderLayout`. Drop a `JPanel` to the center and drop a `JPanel` to the south of `jpSelectColor`. Rename them `jpColors` and `jpRadioButtons`.

continued

Example 6.1 continued

6. Set the `layout` of `jpColors` to `GridLayout` and drop a `ColorPanel` to `jpColors` three times to create `redPanel`, `greenPanel`, and `bluePanel`. Set the title properties of these three panels to "Red," "Green," and "Blue," respectively.

7. Drop a `JRadioButtons` into `jpRadioButtons` to create `jrbRGB`, and set its `text` to `RGB`. Drop a `JRadioButton` into `jpRadioButtons` to create `jrbHSB`, and set its text to `HSB`.

8. Set a border with the title "Choose Standard Color" in `jpStandardColor`, a border with the title "Choose Colors" in `jpSelection`, and a border with the title "Selected Color" in `jpSelectedColor`.

9. Add items "Red," "Green," "Blue," and "Yellow" into the combo box `jcboStandardColor` in the `jbInit()` method, as shown in Listing 6.2 (Lines 129–133).

10. Declare an instance of `ButtonGroup`, named `btg`, for grouping the RGB and HSB radio buttons (Lines 135–137).

11. Double-click `jcboStandardColor` to generate the code for handling combo item selection. Implement the handler to display the selected color in `jtaSelectedColor` (Lines 210–221).

12. In the Events page of `redPanel`, click the value field of `actionPerformed` to generate the code for handling the color value change action. This action is generated when the color value changes. Implement the handler to display the selected color in `jtaSelectedColor`, as shown in Listing 6.2. Similarly, create the code for handling actions from `greenPanel` and `bluePanel` (Lines 179–192).

13. Double-click on `jrbRGB` to generate the code for handling the radio button switch. Implement the handler to switch the RGB mode for selecting colors (Lines 143–146). Similarly, generate and implement the code for handling the HSB radio button (Lines 148–151).

```
1    package choosecolordemo;
2
3    import java.awt.*;
4    import java.awt.event.*;
5    import java.applet.*;
6    import javax.swing.*;
7    import javax.swing.border.*;
8
9    public class ChooseColor extends JApplet {
10     boolean isStandalone = false;
11     BorderLayout borderLayout1 = new BorderLayout();
12     JPanel jpSelection = new JPanel();
```

Listing 6.2 *ChooseColor.java*

```
  BorderLayout borderLayout2 = new BorderLayout();
  JPanel jpSelectColor = new JPanel();
  BorderLayout borderLayout4 = new BorderLayout();
  JPanel jpColors = new JPanel();
  JPanel jpRadioButtons = new JPanel();
  GridLayout gridLayout2 = new GridLayout();
  JRadioButton jrbRGB = new JRadioButton();
  JRadioButton jrbHSB = new JRadioButton();
  ColorPanel redPanel = new ColorPanel();
  ColorPanel greenPanel = new ColorPanel();
  ColorPanel bluePanel = new ColorPanel();
  JPanel jpStandardColor = new JPanel();
  BorderLayout borderLayout5 = new BorderLayout();
  JComboBox jcboStandardColor = new JComboBox();
  JPanel jpSelectedColor = new JPanel();
  BorderLayout borderLayout3 = new BorderLayout();

  JTextArea jtaSelectedColor = new JTextArea();
  TitledBorder titledBorder1;
  TitledBorder titledBorder2;
  TitledBorder titledBorder3;

  // Declare a ButtonGroup for grouping RGB and HSB radio buttons
  ButtonGroup btg = new ButtonGroup();

  /** Initialize the applet */
  public void init() {
    try {
      jbInit();
    }
    catch (Exception e) {
      e.printStackTrace();
    }
  }

  /** Component initialization */
  private void jbInit() throws Exception {
    titledBorder1 = new TitledBorder("");
    titledBorder2 = new TitledBorder("");
    titledBorder3 = new TitledBorder("");
    this.getContentPane().setLayout(borderLayout1);
    this.setSize(400,300);
    jpSelection.setLayout(borderLayout2);
    borderLayout1.setVgap(10);
    borderLayout1.setHgap(10);
    borderLayout2.setVgap(10);
    borderLayout2.setHgap(10);
    gridLayout2.setHgap(5);
    gridLayout2.setColumns(3);
    jrbRGB.setText("RGB");
    jrbRGB.setSelected(true);
    jrbRGB.addActionListener(new java.awt.event.ActionListener() {
      public void actionPerformed(ActionEvent e) {
        jrbRGB_actionPerformed(e);
      }
    });
    jrbHSB.setText("HSB");
```

Listing 6.2 *Continued*

continued

Example 6.1 continued

```
    jrbHSB.addActionListener(new java.awt.event.ActionListener() {
      public void actionPerformed(ActionEvent e) {
        jrbHSB_actionPerformed(e);
      }
    });
    redPanel.setTitle("Red");
    redPanel.addActionListener(new java.awt.event.ActionListener() {
      public void actionPerformed(ActionEvent e) {
        redPanel_actionPerformed(e);
      }
    });
    greenPanel.setColorType("Green");
    greenPanel.setTitle("Green");
    greenPanel.addActionListener(
      new java.awt.event.ActionListener() {
      public void actionPerformed(ActionEvent e) {
        greenPanel_actionPerformed(e);
      }
    });
    bluePanel.setColorType("Blue");
    bluePanel.setTitle("Blue");
    jcboStandardColor.setToolTipText(
      "You may choose a standard color from here");
    jcboStandardColor.addActionListener(
      new java.awt.event.ActionListener() {
      public void actionPerformed(ActionEvent e) {
        jcboStandardColor_actionPerformed(e);
      }
    });
    bluePanel.addActionListener(new java.awt.event.ActionListener() {
      public void actionPerformed(ActionEvent e) {
        bluePanel_actionPerformed(e);
      }
    });
    jpSelectedColor.setLayout(borderLayout3);
    jpStandardColor.setLayout(borderLayout5);
    jpColors.setLayout(gridLayout2);
    jpSelectColor.setLayout(borderLayout4);
    jtaSelectedColor.setPreferredSize(new Dimension(100, 18));
    jpStandardColor.setBorder(titledBorder1);
    titledBorder1.setTitle("Choose Standard Color");
    jpSelectColor.setBorder(titledBorder2);
    titledBorder2.setTitle("Choose Colors");
    jpSelectedColor.setBorder(titledBorder3);
    titledBorder3.setTitle("Selected Color");
    this.getContentPane().add(jpSelection, BorderLayout.CENTER);
    jpSelection.add(jpSelectColor, BorderLayout.CENTER);
    jpSelectColor.add(jpColors, BorderLayout.CENTER);
    jpColors.add(redPanel, null);
    jpColors.add(greenPanel, null);
    jpColors.add(bluePanel, null);
    jpSelectColor.add(jpRadioButtons, BorderLayout.SOUTH);
    jpRadioButtons.add(jrbRGB, null);
    jpRadioButtons.add(jrbHSB, null);
    jpSelection.add(jpSelectedColor, BorderLayout.EAST);
    jpSelectedColor.add(jtaSelectedColor, BorderLayout.CENTER);
    this.getContentPane().add(jpStandardColor, BorderLayout.NORTH);
    jpStandardColor.add(jcboStandardColor, BorderLayout.CENTER);
```

Listing 6.2 *Continued*

```
      // Intialize combo box
      jcboStandardColor.addItem("Red");
      jcboStandardColor.addItem("Green");
      jcboStandardColor.addItem("Blue");
      jcboStandardColor.addItem("Yellow");

      // Group radio buttons
      btg.add(jrbRGB);
      btg.add(jrbHSB);

      // Set RGB radio button by default
      switchButton("RGB");
    }

    /** Handle jrbRGB */
    void jrbRGB_actionPerformed(ActionEvent e) {
      switchButton("RGB");
    }

    /** Handle jrbHSB */
    void jrbHSB_actionPerformed(ActionEvent e) {
      switchButton("HSB");
    }

    /** Switch to RGB or HSB for selecting colors */
    private void switchButton(String radioButtonName) {
      if (radioButtonName.equals("RGB")) {
        redPanel.setTitle("Red");
        redPanel.setToolTipText("Specify red component of the color");
        greenPanel.setTitle("Green");
        greenPanel.setToolTipText(
          "Specify green component of the color");
        bluePanel.setTitle("Blue");
        bluePanel.setToolTipText(
          "Specify blue component of the color");
      }
      else {
        redPanel.setTitle("Hue");
        redPanel.setToolTipText("Specify hue of the color");
        greenPanel.setTitle("Saturation");
        greenPanel.setToolTipText("Specify saturation of the color");
        bluePanel.setTitle("Brightness");
        bluePanel.setToolTipText("Specify brightness of the color");
      }

      redPanel.switchButton(radioButtonName);
      greenPanel.switchButton(radioButtonName);
      bluePanel.switchButton(radioButtonName);
    }

    /** Handle red color change in redPanel */
    void redPanel_actionPerformed(ActionEvent e) {
      showSelectedColor();
    }

    /** Handle green color change in greenPanel */
    void greenPanel_actionPerformed(ActionEvent e) {
      showSelectedColor();
    }

```

Listing 6.2 *Continued*

continued

Example 6.1 continued

```
    /** Handle blue color change in bluePanel */
    void bluePanel_actionPerformed(ActionEvent e) {
      showSelectedColor();
    }

    /** Get selected colors and display it in the text area */
    private void showSelectedColor() {
      if (jrbRGB.isSelected()) {
        Color c = new Color(redPanel.getColorValue(),
          greenPanel.getColorValue(),
        bluePanel.getColorValue());
        jtaSelectedColor.setBackground(c);
      }
      else {
        Color c = Color.getHSBColor(redPanel.getColorValue(),
          greenPanel.getColorValue(),
        bluePanel.getColorValue());
        jtaSelectedColor.setBackground(c);
      }
    }

    /** Handle selecting a standard color in the combo box */
    void jcboStandardColor_actionPerformed(ActionEvent e) {
      String s = (String)jcboStandardColor.getSelectedItem();
      if (s.equals("Red"))
        jtaSelectedColor.setBackground(Color.red);
      else if (s.equals("Green"))
        jtaSelectedColor.setBackground(Color.green);
      else if (s.equals("Blue"))
        jtaSelectedColor.setBackground(Color.blue);
      else if (s.equals("Yellow"))
        jtaSelectedColor.setBackground(Color.yellow);
    }
  }
```

Listing 6.2 *Continued*

Example Review

You can choose a color either by using the scroll bar to specify the red, green, and blue components of the color or by selecting a standard color from the combo box. The selected color is displayed as the background of the text area. This program does not synchronize the color selected in the combo box with the color displayed in the `jpColors` panel. You can fix the problem by adding a set method for the `colorValue` property in the `ColorPanel` class and set the red, green, and blue components in the `redPanel`, `greenPanel`, and `bluePanel` to match the selected color in the combo box. See Exercise 6.4 for more details.

This is a quite sophisticated project with pages of source code, but the amount of the code you hand-wrote is very small. Most of the code was generated automatically by JBuilder. Once again, this demonstrates that you can develop powerful programs in Java using JBuilder with minimal coding.

> **Tip**
> You can nest panels within other panels to gain more control over the placement of components. Each panel may use a different layout manager to achieve the desired look.

> **Tip**
> Sometimes it is very difficult to put a component into a small or obscured container in the UI designer. In these situations, drop the component on the container displayed in the component tree. To do so, select the component in the component palette, then click the container in the component tree.

How Does a Layout Manager Lay Out Components?

A container's `setLayout` method specifies a layout manager for the container. The layout manager is responsible for laying out the components and displaying them in a desired location with an appropriate size. Many introductory Java texts state that once a layout manager is selected for a container, it works dutifully behind the scenes to place the components in the right place and automatically display them in the right size. This statement is true, but it does not explain how a layout manager works and interacts with the components. This section will help you understand the nuts and bolts of layout managers so that you can create your own custom layout managers in the next section, "Creating Custom Layout Managers."

Every layout manager must directly or indirectly implement the `LayoutManager` interface. For instance, `FlowLayout` directly implements `LayoutManager`, and `BorderLayout` implements `LayoutManager2`, which implements `LayoutManager`. The `LayoutManager` interface provides the following methods for laying out components in a container:

- `public void addLayoutComponent(String name, Component comp)`

  Adds the specified component with the specified name to the container.

- `public void layoutContainer(Container parent)`

  Lays out the components in the specified container. In this method, you should provide concrete instructions that specify where the components are to be placed.

- `public Dimension minimumLayoutSize(Container parent)`

  Calculates the minimum size dimensions for the specified panel, given the components in the specified parent container.

- `public Dimension preferredLayoutSize(Container parent)`

  Calculates the preferred size dimensions for the specified panel, given the components in the specified parent container.

- `public void removeLayoutComponent(Component comp)`

  Removes the specified component from the layout.

These methods in `LayoutManager` are invoked by the methods in the `java.awt.Container` class through the layout manager in the container. `Container` contains a property named `layout` (an instance of `LayoutManager`) and the methods for adding and removing components from the container. There are five overloading `add` methods defined in `Container` for adding components with various options. The `remove` method removes a component from the container. The `add` method invokes `addImpl`, which then invokes the `addLayoutComponent` method defined in the `LayoutManager` interface. The `layoutContainer` method in the `LayoutManager` interface is indirectly invoked by `validate` through several calls. The `remove` method invokes `removeLayoutComponent` in `LayoutManager`. The `validate` method is invoked to refresh the container after the components it contains have been added to or modified. The relationship of `Container` and `LayoutManager` is shown in Figure 6.11.

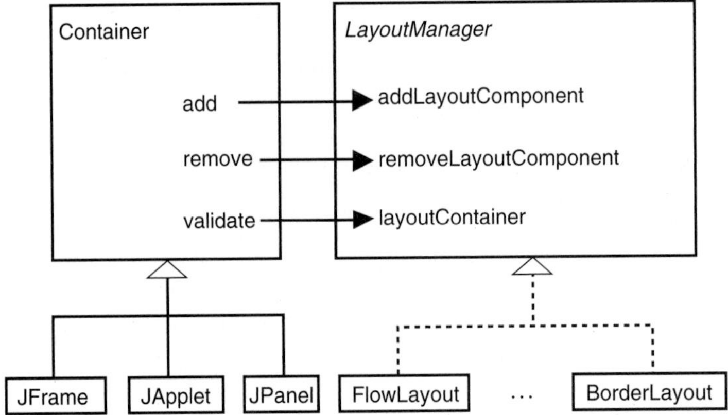

Figure 6.11 *The* `add`, `remove`, *and* `validate` *methods in* `Container` *invoke the methods defined in the* `LayoutManager` *interface.*

Creating Custom Layout Managers

In addition to the layout managers provided in JBuilder, you can create your own layout managers and install them in JBuilder.

A custom layout manager can be created by simply implementing the `LayoutManager` interface. In the following example, you will learn how to create a custom layout manager and install it in JBuilder.

Example 6.2 Creating a Custom Layout Manager

This example creates a layout manager named `DiagonalLayout` that places the components in a diagonal, as shown in Figure 6.12.

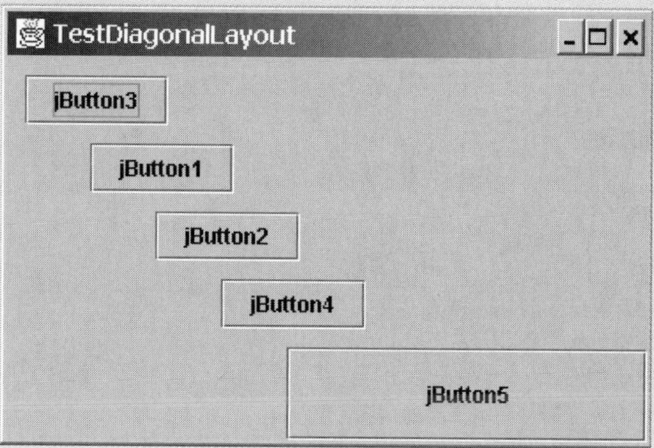

Figure 6.12 *The* `DiagonalLayout` *manager places the components in a diagonal in the container.*

The `DiagonalLayout` class is similar to `FlowLayout` and `VerticalFlowLayout`. `DiagonalLayout` arranges components along a diagonal using each component's natural `preferredSize`. It contains three constraints: `gap`, `lastFill`, and `majorDiagonal`.

- `gap`: This specifies the gap between the components.
- `lastFill`: This specifies whether the last component in the container is stretched to fill the rest of the space.
- `majorDiagonal`: This specifies whether components are placed along the major diagonal or the subdiagonal.

Here are the steps to complete the project.

1. Create a new project named customlayoutdemo.jpr and a JavaBeans Component named `DiagonalLayout` using the JavaBean wizard.
2. With DiagonalLayout.java selected in the navigation pane, choose Wizards, Implement Interface to bring up the Implement Interface wizard. Select `LayoutManager` under `java.awt`, and click OK to generate code for implementing the methods in the `LayoutManager` interface.
3. Choose the Bean tab to start BeansExpress for creating the properties `gap`, `lastFill`, and `majorDiagonal`, as shown in Figure 6.13.
4. Implement `layoutContainer`, as shown in Listing 6.3 (Lines 38–79). Compile DiagonalLayout.java.

continued

Example 6.2 continued

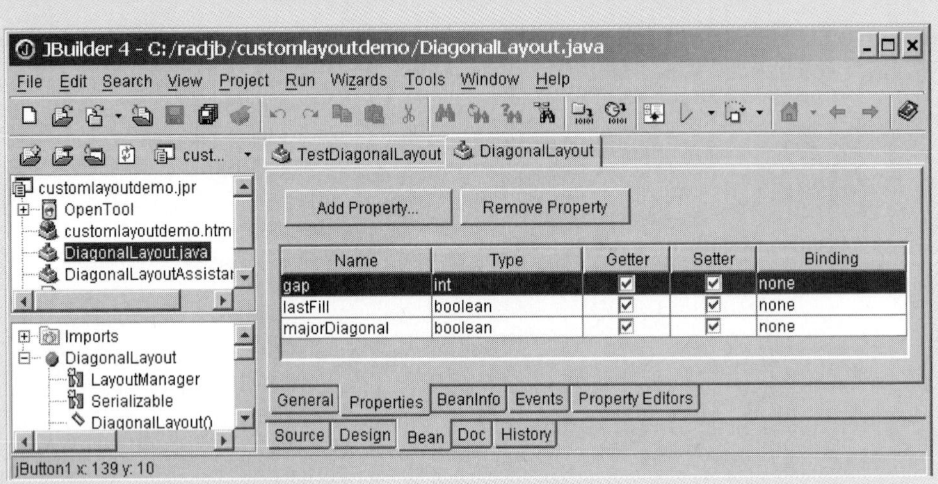

Figure 6.13 *You use BeansExpress to create three properties:* `gap`, `lastFill`, *and* `majorDiagonal`.

5. To install `DiagonalLayout` in JBuilder 4 and 5, please refer to "Installing Custom Layout Managers in JBuilder" at **www.cs.armstrong.edu/liang/radjb5.html**.

6. Now use the `DiagonalLayout` layout manager in JBuilder. Restart JBuilder. Reopen customlayoutdemo.jpr. Use the Applet wizard to create an applet named `TestDiagonalLayout`.

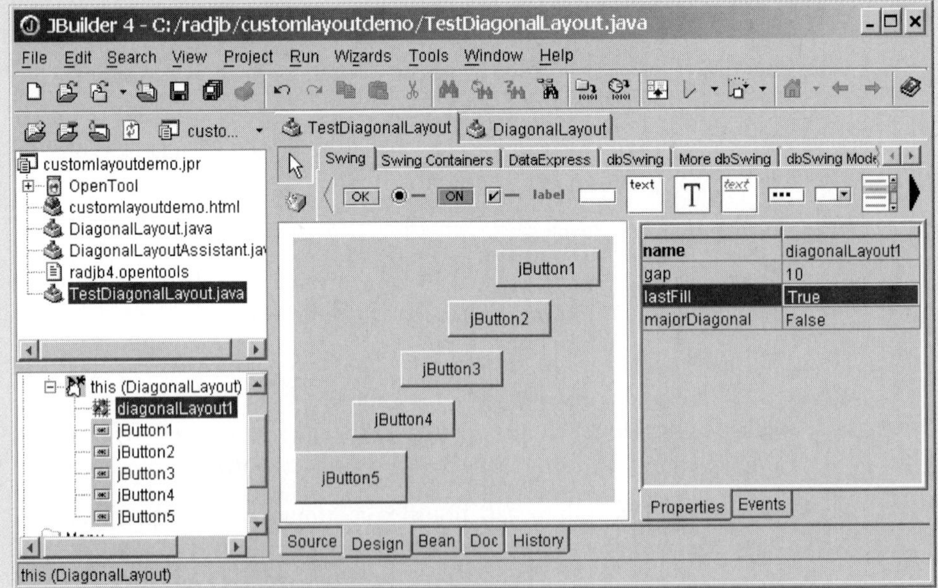

Figure 6.14 *You can modify the parameters* `gap`, `lastFill`, *and* `majorDiagonal` *in the inspector for an object of* `DiagonalLayout`.

7. With TestDiagonalLayout.java selected, click the Design tab to switch to the UI designer in the content pane. Change the layout to `DiagonalLayout`. Drop a `JButton` from the Swing page five times to the applet. You will see the buttons placed in a diagonal in the applet, as shown in Figure 6.14.

```
package customlayoutdemo;

import java.awt.*;

public class DiagonalLayout implements LayoutManager,
  java.io.Serializable {
  /** Vertical gap between the components */
  private int gap = 10;

  /** True if components are placed along the major diagonal */
  private boolean majorDiagonal = true;

  /*True if the last component is stretched to fill the space */
  private boolean lastFill = false;

  /** Constructor */
  public DiagonalLayout() {
  }

  public void addLayoutComponent(String name, Component comp) {
    //TODO: implement this java.awt.LayoutManager method;
  }

  public void removeLayoutComponent(Component comp) {
    //TODO: implement this java.awt.LayoutManager method;
  }

  public Dimension preferredLayoutSize(Container parent) {
    //TODO: implement this java.awt.LayoutManager method;
    return minimumLayoutSize(parent);
  }

  public Dimension minimumLayoutSize(Container parent) {
    //TODO: implement this java.awt.LayoutManager method;
    return new Dimension(0, 0);
  }

  public void layoutContainer(Container parent) {
    //TODO: implement this java.awt.LayoutManager method;
    int numberOfComponents = parent.getComponentCount();

    Insets insets = parent.getInsets();
    int w = parent.getSize().width - insets.left - insets.right;
    int h = parent.getSize().height - insets.bottom - insets.top;

    if (majorDiagonal) {
      int x = 10, y = 10;

      for (int j=0; j<numberOfComponents; j++) {
        Component c = parent.getComponent(j);
        Dimension d = c.getPreferredSize();

```

Listing 6.3 *DiagonalLayout.java*

continued

Example 6.2 continued

```
        if (c.isVisible())
          if (lastFill && (j == numberOfComponents -1))
            c.setBounds(x, y, w-x, h-y);
          else
            c.setBounds(x, y, d.width, d.height);
        x += d.height+gap;
        y += d.height+gap;
      }
    }
    else { // It is subdiagonal
      int x = w-10, y = 10;

      for (int j=0; j<numberOfComponents; j++) {
        Component c = parent.getComponent(j);
        Dimension d = c.getPreferredSize();

        if (c.isVisible())
          if (lastFill & (j == numberOfComponents -1))
            c.setBounds(0, y, x, h-y);
          else
            c.setBounds(x-d.width, y, d.width, d.height);

        x -= (d.height+gap);
        y += d.height+gap;
      }
    }
  }

  public int getGap() {
    return gap;
  }

  public void setGap(int gap) {
    this.gap = gap;
  }

  public void setMajorDiagonal(boolean newMajorDiagonal) {
    majorDiagonal = newMajorDiagonal;
  }

  public boolean isMajorDiagonal() {
    return majorDiagonal;
  }

  public void setLastFill(boolean newLastFill) {
    lastFill = newLastFill;
  }

  public boolean isLastFill() {
    return lastFill;
  }
}
```

Listing 6.3 *Continued*

Example Review

When you change the layout of a container to `DiagonalLayout`, an object named `diagonalLayout1` is created, and it appears under the container's name in the component tree. You can modify three parameters, `gap`, `lastFill`, and `major-`

`Diagonal`, in the property editor of the inspector for `diagonalLayout1`, as shown in Figure 6.14.

The modification of the parameters is reflected in the source code. If no immediate changes are taken in the UI designer, double-click `diagonalLayout1` in the component tree. This would force the `validate` method to be invoked. The `validate` method invokes the `layoutContainer` method in the `DiagonalLayout` class to display the components.

The `Insets` class describes the size of the borders of a container. It contains the variables `left`, `right`, `bottom`, and `top`, which correspond to the measurements for the *left border*, *right border*, *top border*, and *bottom border*.

The `Dimension` class encapsulates the width and height of a component in a single object. The class is associated with certain properties of components. Several methods defined by the `Component` class and the `LayoutManager` interface return a `Dimension` object.

JTabbedPane

`JTabbedPane` is a useful Swing container that provides a set of mutually exclusive tabs for accessing multiple components. Usually you place the panels inside a `JTabbedPane` and associate a tab with each panel. `JTabbedPane` is easy to use, since the selection of the panel is handled automatically by clicking the corresponding tab. You can switch between a group of panels by clicking on a tab with a given title and/or icon.

`JTabbedPane` has the following useful properties:

- `selectedComponent`: This is the component that is currently selected.
- `selectedIndex`: This is the index of the currently selected tab.
- `tabPlacement` is the location of the tabs. Valid values are `JTabbedPane.TOP`, `JTabbedPane.LEFT`, `JTabbedPane.BOTTOM`, and `JTabbedPane.RIGHT`.

The following methods in the `JTabbedPane` class are often useful:

- `public void setIconAt(int index, Icon icon)`

  Sets icon at the tab with the specified index.

- `public int getTabCount()`

  Returns the number of tabs in the tabbed pane.

- `public void setTitleAt(int index, Icon icon)`

  Sets title at the tab with the specified index.

Example 6.3 Using JTabbedPane

This example uses a tabbed pane with four tabs to display four types of figures: Square, Rectangle, Circle, and Oval. You can select a figure to display by clicking the corresponding tab, as shown in Figure 6.15.

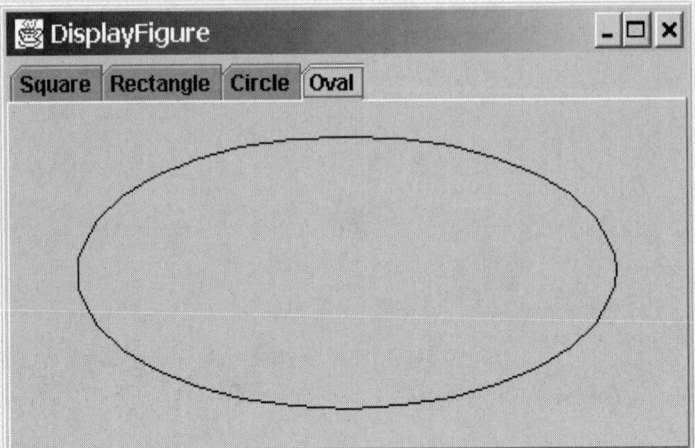

Figure 6.15 *The tabbed pane lets you automatically select figure panels with tabs.*

The figures are displayed in a panel, which is created as follows:

1. Create a new project named displayfiguredemo.jpr, and create a JavaBean component named `FigurePanel` that extends `JPanel` using the JavaBean Wizard.

2. Select FigurePanel.java in the navigation pane, and choose the Bean tab in the content pane to start BeansExpress. Click the Properties tab in BeansExpress to add a new `int` property named `figureType` to represent figure types: 1 for Square, 2 for Rectangle, 3 for Circle, 4 for Oval.

3. Override the `paintComponent` method, as shown in Listing 6.4 (Lines 31–56).

4. Compile and install `FigurePanel` in the component palette.

```
1   package displayfiguredemo;
2
3   import java.awt.*;
4   import javax.swing.JPanel;
5
6   public class FigurePanel extends JPanel {
7     BorderLayout borderLayout1 = new BorderLayout();
8     private int figureType = 1;
9
10    // Define constants
11    public static final int SQUARE = 1;
12    public static final int RECTANGLE = 2;
13    public static final int CIRCLE = 3;
14    public static final int OVAL = 4;
15
```

Listing 6.4 *FigurePanel.java*

```
    /** Constructor */
    public FigurePanel() {
      try {
        jbInit();
      }
      catch(Exception ex) {
        ex.printStackTrace();
      }
    }

    /** Initialize component */
    private void jbInit() throws Exception {
      this.setLayout(borderLayout1);
    }

    /** Draw a figure on the panel */
    public void paintComponent(Graphics g) {
      super.paintComponent(g);

      // Get the appropriate size for the figure
      int width = getSize().width;
      int height = getSize().height;
      int side = (int)(0.80*Math.min(width, height));

      switch (figureType) {
        case SQUARE: // Display a square
          g.drawRect((width-side)/2, (height-side)/2, side, side);
          break;
        case RECTANGLE: // Display a rectangle
          g.drawRect((int)(0.1*width), (int)(0.1*height),
            (int)(0.8*width), (int)(0.8*height));
          break;
        case CIRCLE: // Display a circle
          g.drawOval((width-side)/2, (height-side)/2, side, side);
          break;
        case OVAL: // Display an oval
          g.drawOval((int)(0.1*width), (int)(0.1*height),
            (int)(0.8*width), (int)(0.8*height));
          break;
      }
    }

    /** Setter figureType */
    public void setFigureType(int newFigureType) {
      figureType = newFigureType;
    }

    /** Return figureType */
    public int getFigureType() {
      return figureType;
    }

    /** Specify preferred size */
    public Dimension getPreferredSize() {
      return new Dimension(80, 80);
    }
  }
```

Listing 6.4 *Continued*

continued

Example 6.3 continued

Now turn your attention to the main program that creates a tabbed pane and places the figure panels in the tabbed pane.

1. Create a new Java applet named DisplayFigure.java using the Applet wizard.
2. In the UI designer for `DisplayFigure`, drop a `JTabbedPane` from the Swing Containers page and rename it `jtpFigures`.
3. Drop a `FigurePanel` four times to `jtpFigures` and rename them `squarePanel`, `rectanglePanel`, `circlePanel`, and `ovalPanel`. Set the `figureType` property to 1 for `squarePanel`, 2 for `rectanglePanel`, 3 for `circlePanel`, and 4 for `ovalPanel`.
4. The tabs are created with default name, which is the same as the component's name. To change the name, you need to modify the `constraints` property for the panel in the inspector. For example, to set the tab name for `ovalPanel`, change the `constraints` property to Oval in the inspector for `ovalPanel`. The source code for DisplayFigure.java is shown in Listing 6.5.

```
package displayfiguredemo;

import java.awt.*;
import java.awt.event.*;
import java.applet.*;
import javax.swing.*;

public class DisplayFigure extends JApplet {
  boolean isStandalone = false;
  JTabbedPane jtpFigures = new JTabbedPane();
  FigurePanel squarePanel = new FigurePanel();
  FigurePanel rectanglePanel = new FigurePanel();
  FigurePanel circlePanel = new FigurePanel();
  FigurePanel ovalPanel = new FigurePanel();

  /** Initialize the applet */
  public void init() {
    try {
      jbInit();
    }
    catch(Exception e) {
      e.printStackTrace();
    }
  }

  /** Component initialization */
  private void jbInit() throws Exception {
    this.setSize(new Dimension(400,300));
    squarePanel.setFigureType(FigurePanel.SQUARE);
    rectanglePanel.setFigureType(FigurePanel.RECTANGLE);
    circlePanel.setFigureType(FigurePanel.CIRCLE);
    ovalPanel.setFigureType(FigurePanel.OVAL);
    this.getContentPane().add(jtpFigures, BorderLayout.CENTER);
```

Listing 6.5 *DisplayFigure.java*

```
        jtpFigures.add(squarePanel, "Square");
        jtpFigures.add(rectanglePanel, "Rectangle");
        jtpFigures.add(circlePanel, "Circle");
        jtpFigures.add(ovalPanel, "Oval");
    }
  }
```

Listing 6.5 *Continued*

Example Review

The program creates a tabbed pane to hold four panels, each of which displays a figure. A panel is associated with a tab. Tabs are titled Square, Rectangle, Circle, and Oval, which can be set using the `constraints` property.

By default, the tabs are placed at the top of the tabbed pane. You can select a different placement using the `tabPlacement` property.

JSplitPane

`JSplitPane` is a convenient Swing container that contains two components with a separate bar known as a *divider*. The bar can divide the container horizontally or vertically, and can be dragged to change the amount of space occupied by each component.

`JSplitPane` has the following useful properties:

- `bottomComponent`: This is the component to the left or below the divider.
- `continousLayout`: This is a boolean value indicating whether the components in the split pane are continuously resized and repainted as the bar moves. By default, it is `false`.
- `dividerLocation`: This is an `int` value that specifies the location of the divider from the top or left edge of the split pane in pixels.
- `dividerSize`: This is the size of the divider in pixels.
- `lastDividerLocation`: This is the previous location of the divider.
- `leftComponent`: This is the component to the left of or above the divider.
- `oneTouchExpandable`: This is a `boolean` property with a default value `false`. If the property is true, the divider has an expanding and contracting look, so that the divider can expand and contract with one touch.
- `orientation`: This property specifies whether the container is divided horizontally or vertically. The possible values are `JSplitPane.HORIZONTAL_SPILT` and `JSplitPane.VERTICAL_SPLIT`. The default value is `JSplitPane.HORIZONTAL_SPILT`, which divides the container into a left part and a right part.
- `rightComponent`: This is the same as `bottomComponent`.
- `topComponent`: This is the same as `leftComponent`.

You can also set the divider location as a percentage of `JSplitPane`'s size using the following method:

```
public void setDividerLocation(double proportionalLocation)
```

where `proportionalLocation` is a value between 0.0 and 1.0.

Example 6.4 Using JSplitPane

This example demonstrates the use of split panes. It lets the user select a layout manager dynamically and use the layout manager to show buttons in a panel. The usage of the layout manager is displayed in an instance of `JEditorPane` at the same time. A sample run of the program is shown in Figure 6.16.

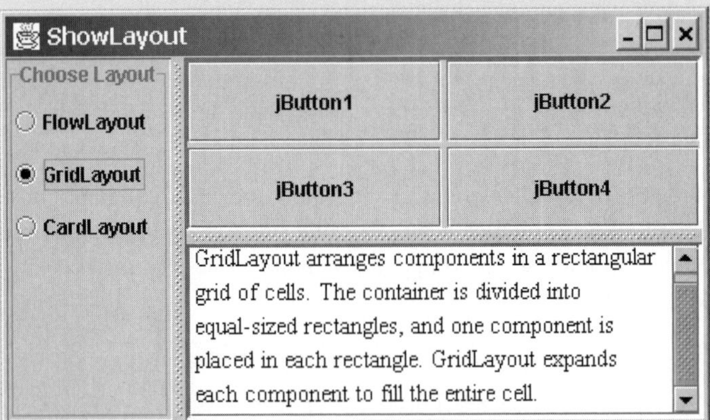

Figure 6.16 *The split pane lets you adjust the component size in the split panes.*

Here are the steps to complete the project:

1. Create a new project named splitpanedemo.jpr and a Java applet named ShowLayout.java using the Applet wizard.
2. In the UI designer for ShowLayout.java, drop a `JSplitPane` from the Swing Containers page to create `jSplitPane1`. Drop a `JPanel` to the left part of `jSplitPane1` to create `jpChooseLayout`, and drop a `JSplitPane` to the right part of `jSplitPane1` to create `jSplitPane2`.
3. Set the `orientation` of `jSplitPane2` to `VERTICAL_SPLIT`. Drop a `JPanel` to the top part of `jSplitPane2` to create `jpComponents`, and drop a `JScroll-Pane` to the bottom part of `jSplitPane2` to create `jScrollPane1`.
4. Drop a `JButton` four times to `jpComponents` to create `jButton1`, `jButton2`, `jButton3`, and `jButton4`.
5. Set the layout of `jpChooseLayout` to `GridLayout` with three rows. Drop a `JRadionButton` three times to `jpChooseLayout` to create `jrbFlowLayout`, `jr-`

bGridLayout, and jrbCardLayout, and set the text of radio buttons to FlowLayout, GridLayout, and CardLayout.

6. Drop a JEditorPane to jScrollPane1 to create jEditorPane1. Set the editable property of jEditorPane1 to false.

7. Create an instance of ButtonGroup to group the radio buttons. Generate handlers for three radio buttons, and implement the handlers, as shown in Listing 6.6 (Lines 111–130).

```
1  package splitpanedemo;
2
3  import java.awt.*;
4  import java.awt.event.*;
5  import java.applet.*;
6  import javax.swing.*;
7  import javax.swing.border.*;
8  import java.net.URL;
9  import java.io.*;
10
11 public class ShowLayout extends JApplet {
12   boolean isStandalone = false;
13   JSplitPane jSplitPane1 = new JSplitPane();
14   JSplitPane jSplitPane2 = new JSplitPane();
15   JPanel jpChooseLayout = new JPanel();
16   JRadioButton jrbFlowLayout = new JRadioButton();
17   JRadioButton jrbGridLayout = new JRadioButton();
18   JRadioButton jrbCardLayout = new JRadioButton();
19   TitledBorder titledBorder1;
20   GridLayout gridLayout1 = new GridLayout();
21   JPanel jpComponents = new JPanel();
22   JButton jButton1 = new JButton();
23   JButton jButton2 = new JButton();
24   JButton jButton3 = new JButton();
25   JButton jButton4 = new JButton();
26   JScrollPane jScrollPane1 = new JScrollPane();
27   JEditorPane jEditorPane1 = new JEditorPane();
28
29   // Create a button group
30   ButtonGroup btg = new ButtonGroup();
31
32   // Create layout managers
33   FlowLayout flowLayout = new FlowLayout();
34   GridLayout gridLayout = new GridLayout(2, 2, 3, 3);
35   CardLayout cardLayout = new CardLayout();
36
37   // get the url for HTML files
38   URL urlFlowLayoutHTML =
39     this.getClass().getResource("FlowLayout.html");
40   URL urlGridLayoutHTML =
41     this.getClass().getResource("GridLayout.html");
42   URL urlCardLayoutHTML =
43     this.getClass().getResource("CardLayout.html");
44
45   /** Initialize the applet */
46   public void init() {
47     try {
48       jbInit();
49     }
```

Listing 6.6 *ShowLayout.java*

continued

Example 6.4 continued

```
    catch(Exception e) {
      e.printStackTrace();
    }
  }

  /** Component initialization */
  private void jbInit() throws Exception {
    titledBorder1 = new TitledBorder("");
    this.setSize(new Dimension(400,300));
    jSplitPane2.setOrientation(JSplitPane.VERTICAL_SPLIT);
    jrbFlowLayout.setText("FlowLayout");
    jrbFlowLayout.addActionListener(
      new java.awt.event.ActionListener() {
      public void actionPerformed(ActionEvent e) {
        jrbFlowLayout_actionPerformed(e);
      }
    });
    jrbGridLayout.setText("GridLayout");
    jrbGridLayout.addActionListener(
      new java.awt.event.ActionListener() {
      public void actionPerformed(ActionEvent e) {
        jrbGridLayout_actionPerformed(e);
      }
    });
    jrbCardLayout.setText("CardLayout");
    jrbCardLayout.addActionListener(
      new java.awt.event.ActionListener() {
      public void actionPerformed(ActionEvent e) {
        jrbCardLayout_actionPerformed(e);
      }
    });
    jpChooseLayout.setBorder(titledBorder1);
    jpChooseLayout.setLayout(gridLayout1);
    titledBorder1.setTitle("Choose Layout");
    gridLayout1.setRows(6);
    jButton1.setText("jButton1");
    jButton2.setText("jButton2");
    jButton3.setText("jButton3");
    jButton4.setText("jButton4");
    jEditorPane1.setText("jEditorPane1");
    jEditorPane1.setEditable(false);
    this.getContentPane().add(jSplitPane1, BorderLayout.CENTER);
    jSplitPane1.add(jSplitPane2, JSplitPane.RIGHT);
    jSplitPane2.add(jpComponents, JSplitPane.TOP);
    jpComponents.add(jButton1, null);
    jpComponents.add(jButton2, null);
    jpComponents.add(jButton3, null);
    jpComponents.add(jButton4, null);
    jSplitPane2.add(jScrollPane1, JSplitPane.BOTTOM);
    jScrollPane1.getViewport().add(jEditorPane1, null);
    jSplitPane1.add(jpChooseLayout, JSplitPane.LEFT);
    jpChooseLayout.add(jrbFlowLayout, null);
    jpChooseLayout.add(jrbGridLayout, null);
    jpChooseLayout.add(jrbCardLayout, null);

    // Group radio buttons
    btg.add(jrbFlowLayout);
    btg.add(jrbGridLayout);
```

Listing 6.6 *Continued*

```
    btg.add(jrbCardLayout);
  }

  /** Handle jrbFlowLayout */
  void jrbFlowLayout_actionPerformed(ActionEvent e) {
    jpComponents.setLayout(flowLayout);
    jpComponents.doLayout();
    displayHTML(urlFlowLayoutHTML);
  }

  /** Handle jrbGridLayout */
  void jrbGridLayout_actionPerformed(ActionEvent e) {
    jpComponents.setLayout(gridLayout);
    jpComponents.doLayout();
    displayHTML(urlGridLayoutHTML);
  }

  /** Handle jrbCardLayout */
  void jrbCardLayout_actionPerformed(ActionEvent e) {
    jpComponents.setLayout(cardLayout);
    jpComponents.doLayout();
    displayHTML(urlCardLayoutHTML);
  }

  /** Display an HTML file in EditorPane */
  void displayHTML(URL url) {
    try {
      // Render the HTML file
      jEditorPane1.setPage(url);
    }
    catch (IOException ex) {
      System.out.println(ex);
    }
  }
}
```

Listing 6.6 *Continued*

Example Review

Split panes can be embedded. Adding a split pane to an existing split results in three split panes. The program creates two split panes to hold a panel for radio buttons, a panel for buttons, and a scroll pane.

The radio buttons are used to select layout managers. A selected layout manager is used in the panel for laying out the buttons. The scroll pane contains a `JEditorPane` for displaying the HTML file that describes the selected layout manager.

The HTML files are preloaded using the `getResource` method in the `Class` class. The `displayHTML` method is invoked by the radio button handler for displaying a specified HTML file in the `JEditorPane`.

Chapter Summary

A Java container is an object that holds and groups user interface components. A *layout manager* is a special object used to manage how the components in the container are displayed. Java provides a set of layout managers that you can use to intelligently place components that are independent of fonts, screen resolutions, and platform. This chapter discussed Swing containers and reviewed the layout managers provided in JBuilder. You learned how to use two useful Swing containers, `JTabbedPane` and `JSplitPane`. You also learned how to create custom layout managers and install them in JBuilder.

Review Questions

6.1 How does the layout in Java differ from the ones in Visual Basic and Delphi?

6.2 Are the following statements correct?

- Each layout has a set of properties applied to all the components in the container.
- The constraints property is associated with a component.

6.3 Describe the various preinstalled layout managers in JBuilder.

6.4 When should `OverlayLayout` be used?

6.5 How do you use `JTabbedPane` and `JSplitPane`? Can you specify a layout manager in these two containers?

6.6 How do you create a custom layout manager and install it in JBuilder?

Programming Exercises

6.1 Create a program that enables the user to set the properties of a `FlowLayout` manager dynamically, as shown in Figure 6.17. The `FlowLayout` manager is used to place 15 components in a panel. You can set the `alignment`, `hgap`, and `vgap` properties of the `FlowLayout` dynamically.

6.2 Create a program that enables the user to set the properties of a `GridLayout` manager dynamically, as shown in Figure 6.18. The `GridLayout` manager is used to place 15 components in a panel. You can set the `rows`, `columns`, `hgap`, and `vgap` properties of the `GridLayout` dynamically.

6.3 Create a program that uses `OverlayLayout` to display two overlaid labels with images and texts in a panel, as shown in Figure 6.19.

6.4 Modify Example 6.1 to set the red, green, and blue components in the `redPanel`, `greenPanel`, and `bluePanel` to match the selected color in the combo box.

6.5 Create a program that displays four figures in split panes, as shown in Figure 6.20. The figures are defined in the `FigurePanel` class defined in Example 6.3.

6.6 Modify Example 6.3 to add a panel of radio buttons for specifying the tab placement of the tabbed pane, as shown in Figure 6.21.

6.7 Create a program that enables the user to set the properties of a split pane dynamically, as shown in Figure 6.22.

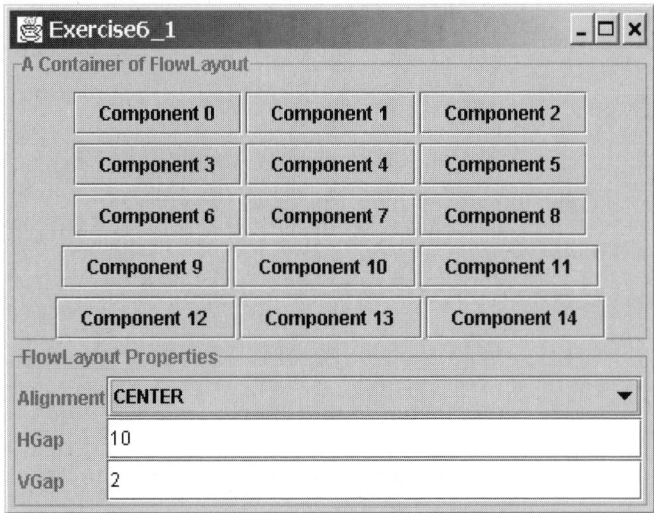

Figure 6.17 *The program enables you to set the properties of a* `FlowLayout` *manager dynamically.*

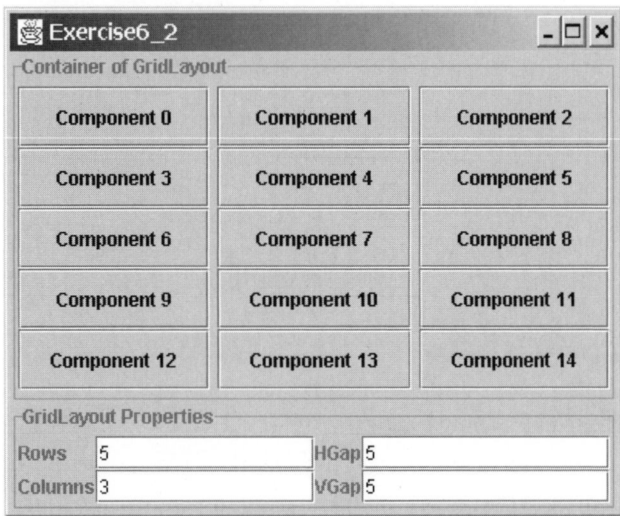

Figure 6.18 *The program enables you to set the properties of a* `GridLayout` *manager dynamically.*

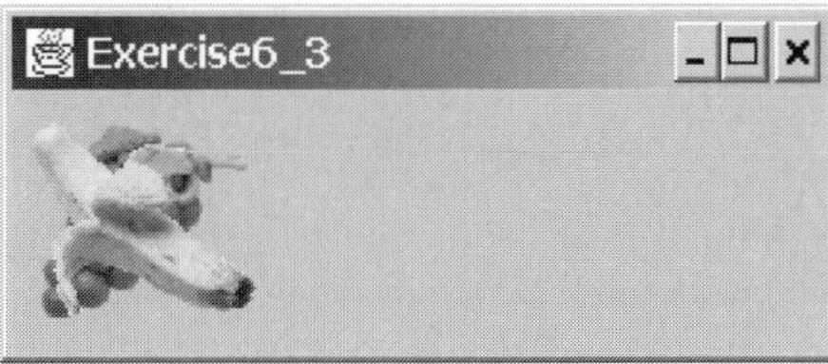

Figure 6.19 *You can display components transparently at the same time using* `OverlayLayout`.

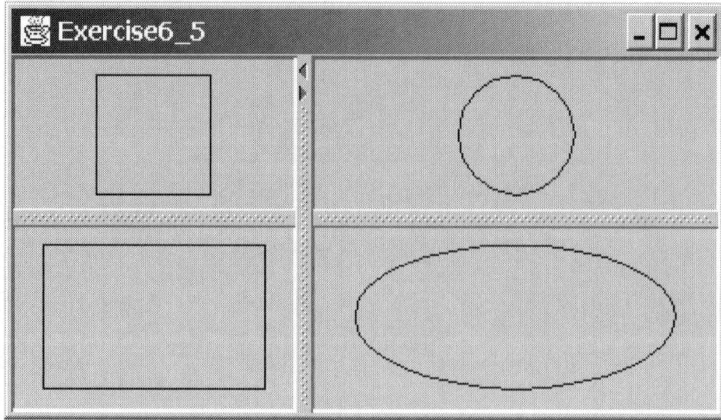

Figure 6.20 *Four figures are displayed in split panes.*

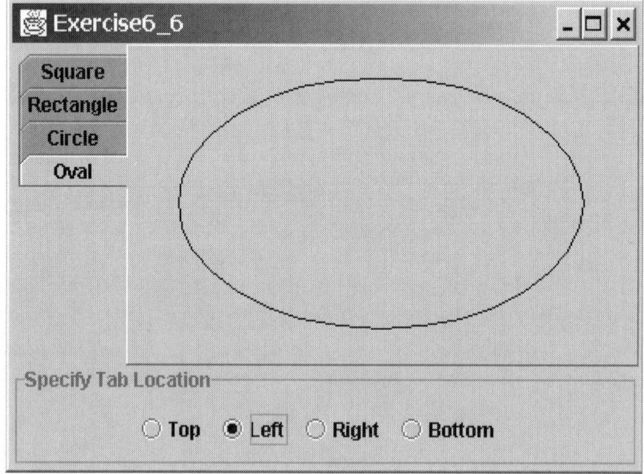

Figure 6.21 *The radio buttons let you choose the tab placement of the tabbed pane.*

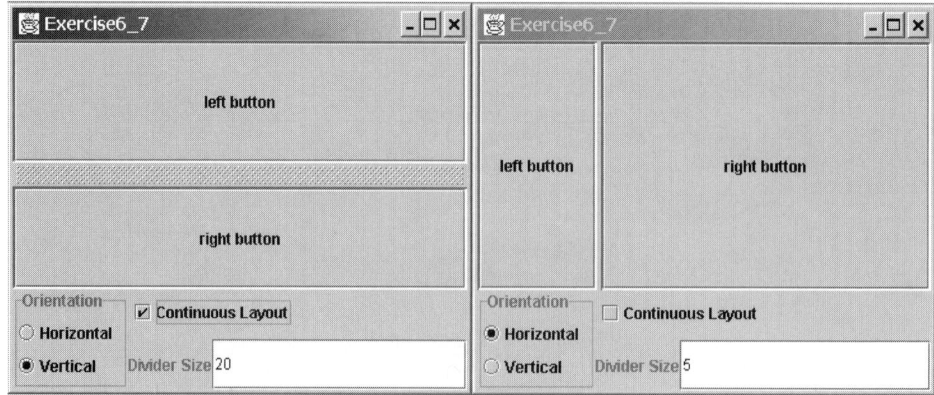

Figure 6.22 *The program enables you to set the properties of a split pane dynamically.*

6.8 Rewrite Example 6.1, "Choosing Colors" using the `GridBagLayout`.

CHAPTER 7

Menus, Toolbars, and Dialogs

Objectives

- Learn the menu components `JMenuBar`, `JMenu`, `JPopupMenu`, `JMenuItem`, `JCheckBoxMenuItem`, and `JRadioButtonMenuItem`.
- Create menus and popup menus using the Menu designer.
- Use `JToolBar` to create tool bars.
- Use the `Action` objects to centralize the code for processing action.
- Create standard dialogs using the `JOptionPane` class.
- Extend the `JDialog` class to create custom dialogs.
- Select colors using `JColorChooser`.
- Use `JFileChooser` to display Open and Save File dialogs.

Introduction

In the preceding two chapters, you learned how to use Swing components, containers, and layout managers. This chapter introduces menus, popup menus, tool bars, and dialogs. Using these components effectively can greatly boost your programming productivity.

Menus

Menus make selection easier and are widely used in Windows applications. Java provides five classes, `JMenuBar`, `JMenu`, `JMenuItem`, `JCheckBoxMenuItem`, and `JRadioButtonMenuItem`, to implement menus.

`JMenuBar`, the top-level menu component, is used to hold the menus. Menus consist of *menu items* that the user can select (or toggle on or off). Menu items can be an instance of `JMenuItem`, `JCheckBoxMenuItem`, or `JRadioButtonMenuItem`.

The sequence of implementing menus in Java is as follows:

1. Create a menu bar and associate it with a frame.

   ```
   JFrame frame = new JFrame();
   frame.setSize(300, 200);
   frame.setVisible(true);
   JMenuBar jmb = new JMenuBar();
   frame.setJMenuBar(jmb);  // Attach a menu bar to a frame
   ```

   This code creates a frame and a menu bar, and sets the menu bar in the frame.

2. Create menus.

   You can use the following constructor to create a menu:

   ```
   public JMenu(String label)
   ```

   The following is an example of creating menus:

   ```
   JMenu fileMenu = new JMenu("File");
   JMenu helpMenu = new JMenu("Help");
   jmb.add(fileMenu);
   jmb.add(helpMenu);
   ```

   This creates two menus labeled `File` and `Help`, as shown in Figure 7.1. The menus will not be seen until they are added to `JMenuBar`.

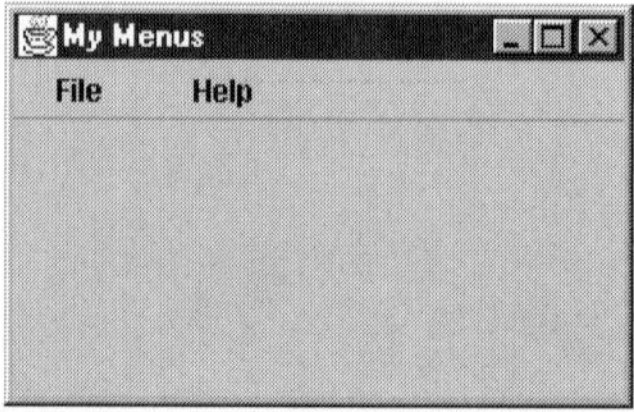

Figure 7.1 *The menu bar appears below the title bar on the frame.*

3. Create menu items and add them to menus.

```
fileMenu.add(new JMenuItem("New"));
fileMenu.add(new JMenuItem("Open"));
fileMenu.addSeparator();
fileMenu.add(new JMenuItem("Print"));
fileMenu.addSeparator();
fileMenu.add(new JMenuItem("Exit"));
```

This code adds the menu items New, Open, a separator bar, Print, another separator bar, and Exit in this order into the File menu, as shown in Figure 7.2.

The `addSeparator()` method adds a separate bar in the menu.

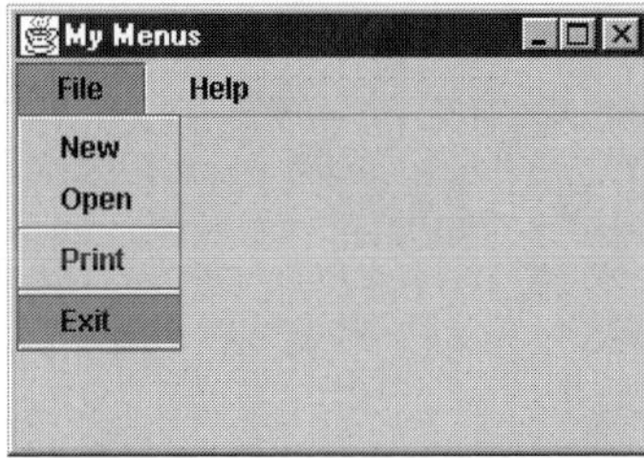

Figure 7.2 *Clicking a menu on the menu bar reveals the items under the menu.*

You can also embed menus inside menus so that the embedded menus become submenus. Here is an example:

```
JMenu softwareHelpSubMenu = new JMenu("Software");
JMenu hardwareHelpSubMenu = new JMenu("Hardware");
helpMenu.add(softwareHelpSubMenu);
helpMenu.add(hardwareHelpSubMenu);
softwareHelpSubMenu.add(new JMenuItem("Unix"));
softwareHelpSubMenu.add(new JMenuItem("NT"));
softwareHelpSubMenu.add(new JMenuItem("Win95"));
```

This code adds two submenus, `softwareHelpMenu` and `hardwareHelpMenu`, in `helpMenu`. The menu items `Unix`, `NT`, and `Win95` are added into `softwareHelpMenu` (see Figure 7.3).

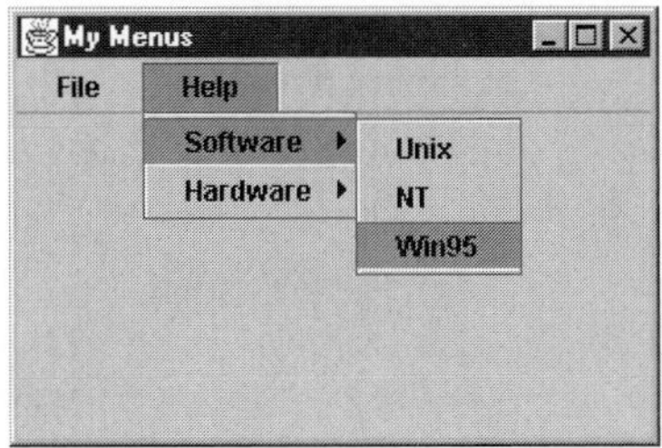

Figure 7.3 *Clicking a menu item reveals the secondary items under the menu item.*

You can also add a `JCheckBoxMenuItem` to a `JMenu`. `JCheckBoxMenuItem` is a subclass of `JMenuItem` that adds a `boolean` state to the `JMenuItem`, and displays a check when its state is true. You can click the menu item to turn it on and off. For example, the following statement adds the check box menu item `Check it` (see Figure 7.4).

```
helpMenu.add(new JCheckBoxMenuItem("Check it"));
```

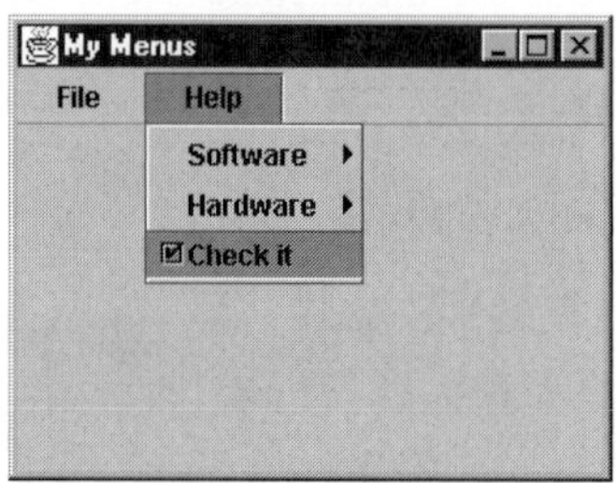

Figure 7.4 *A check box menu item, just like a check box, lets you check or uncheck a menu item.*

You can also add radio buttons in a menu using the `JRadioButtonMenuItem` class. This is often useful when you have a group of mutually exclusive choices in the menu. For example, the following statements add a submenu named Color and a set of radio buttons for choosing a color (see Figure 7.5).

```
JMenu colorHelpSubMenu = new JMenu("Color");
helpMenu.add(colorHelpSubMenu);

JRadioButtonMenuItem jrbmiBlue, jrbmiYellow, jrbmiRed;
colorHelpSubMenu.add(jrbmiBlue =
  new JRadioButtonMenuItem("Blue"));
colorHelpSubMenu.add(jrbmiYellow =
  new JRadioButtonMenuItem("Yellow"));
colorHelpSubMenu.add(jrbmiRed = new JRadioButtonMenuItem("Red"));

ButtonGroup btg = new ButtonGroup();
btg.add(jrbmiBlue);
btg.add(jrbmiYellow);
btg.add(jrbmiRed);
```

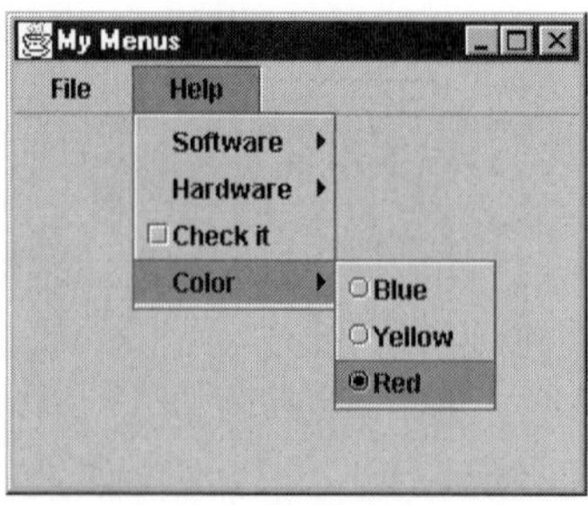

Figure 7.5 *You can use* `JRadioButtonMenuItem` *to choose a mutually exclusive menu choice.*

4. The menu items generate `ActionEvent`. Your program must implement the `actionPerformed` handler to respond to the menu selection. The following is an example:

```
public void actionPerformed(ActionEvent e) {
  String actionCommand = e.getActionCommand();

  // Make sure the source is JMenuItem
  if (e.getSource() instanceof JMenuItem)
    if ("New".equals(actionCommand))
      respondToNew();
}
```

This code executes the method `respondToNew()` when the menu item labeled New is selected.

Image Icons, Keyboard Mnemonics, and Keyboard Accelerators

The menu components `JMenu`, `JMenuItem`, `JCheckBoxMenuItem`, and `JRadioButtonMenuItem` have `icon` and `mnemonic` properties. For example, you can set icons for the New and Open menu items and set keyboard mnemonic for File, Help, New, and Open using the code shown below:

```
JMenuItem jmiNew, jmiOpen;
fileMenu.add(jmiNew = new JMenuItem("New"));
fileMenu.add(jmiOpen = new JMenuItem("Open"));
jmiNew.setIcon(new ImageIcon("/image/new.gif"));
jmiOpen.setIcon(new ImageIcon("/image/open.gif"));
helpMenu.setMnemonic('H');
fileMenu.setMnemonic('F');
jmiNew.setMnemonic('N');
jmiOpen.setMnemonic('O');
```

The new icons and mnemonics are shown in Figure 7.6. You can also use `JMenuItem` constructors like the following to construct and set an icon or a mnemonic in one statement.

```
public JMenuItem(String label, Icon icon);

public JMenuItem(String label, int mnemonic);
```

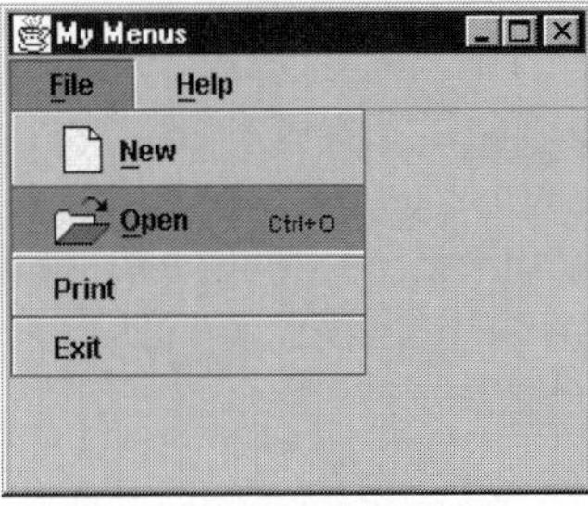

Figure 7.6 *You can set image icons, keyboard mnemonics, and keyboard accelerators in menus.*

To select a menu, press the ALT key and the mnemonic key. For example, press ALT+F to select the File menu. You can then press ALT+O to select the Open menu item. Keyboard mnemonics are useful, but they only let you select menu items from the currently open menu. Key accelerators, however, let you select a menu item directly by pressing the CTRL key and the accelerator key. For example, you can attach the accelerator key CTRL+O to the Open menu item using the following code:

```
jmiOpen.setAccelerator(KeyStroke.getKeyStroke
  (KeyEvent.VK_O, ActionEvent.CTRL_MASK));
```

The `setAccelerator()` method takes an object of the `KeyStroke` class. The static method `getKeyStoke()` in the `KeyStroke` class creates an instance of the keystroke. `VK_O` is a constant representing the O key, and `CTRL_MASK` is a constant indicating that the CTRL key is associated with the keystroke.

Using the JBuilder Menu Designer

JBuilder has a Menu designer that can be used to simplify the task of designing menus. This section demonstrates the use of the Menu designer with simple examples.

Example 7.1 Using Menu Designer

This example demonstrates how to create menus using JBuilder Menu designer, as shown in Figure 7.7. You will learn how to add and remove menus, menu items, separator bars, submenus, check box menus, and radio button menus.

Here are the steps to complete the project.

1. Create a new project named menudemo.jpr and create an applet named `TestMenuDesigner` using the Applet wizard.
2. With TestMenuDesigner.java selected in the navigation pane, switch to the UI designer. Drop a `JMenuBar` in the Swing Containers page to the UI designer to create `jMenuBar1`.
3. To activate the Menu designer, double-click `jMenuBar1` under the Menu node in the component tree, as shown in Figure 7.7.
4. You are going to create a new menu named File and add four menu items named New, Open, Print, and Exit into the File menu. Add a separator bar between Open and Print, and another separator between Print and Exit, as follows:

   4.1. Click the empty menu, type **File**, then press the Enter key.

   4.2. The first menu item under File is automatically highlighted. Type **New** and press Enter.

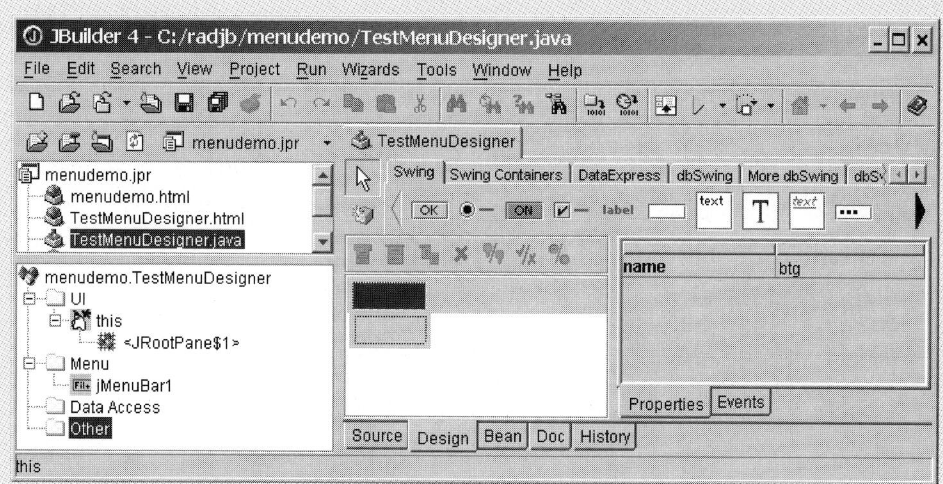

Figure 7.7 *You can visually add and remove menus, menu items, separator bars, submenus, check box menus, and radio button menus.*

4.3. The next menu item after New is automatically highlighted. Type **Open** and press Enter.

4.4. The next menu item after Open is now highlighted. Click the Insert Separator button (the second button on the top of the menu) to create a separator bar.

4.5. The next menu item after the separator is highlighted. Type **Print** and press Enter.

4.6. The next menu item after Print is now highlighted. Click the Insert Separator button to create a separator bar.

4.7. The next menu item after the separator is highlighted. Type **Exit** and press Enter.

5. You are going to create a new menu named Help after the File menu and create submenus, check box menu items, and radio button menu items under Help, as follows:

5.1. Click the empty menu on the right of the File menu, type **Help**, then press the Enter key.

5.2. The first menu item under Help is automatically highlighted. Type **Software** and press Enter to create a menu item for Software. Select Software and right-click the mouse to display a popup menu, as shown in Figure 7.8. Choose Insert Nested Menu to create three submenu items named Unix, Windows, and Linux, as shown in Figure 7.9. Note that the Software menu item is automatically converted to a Software menu.

continued

Example 7.1 continued

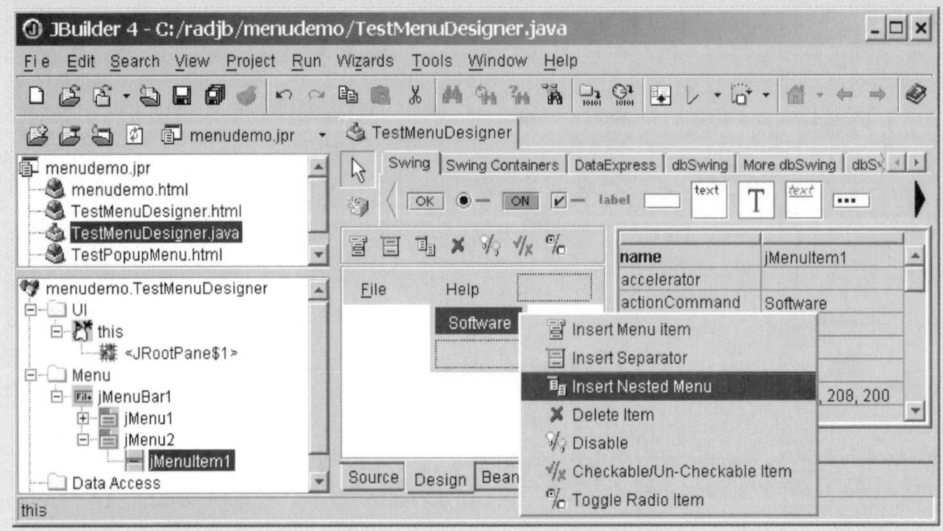

Figure 7.8 *The popup menu gives you the options for inserting menu items, deleting menu items, inserting submenus, disabling menu items, creating check box menu items, or creating radio button menu items.*

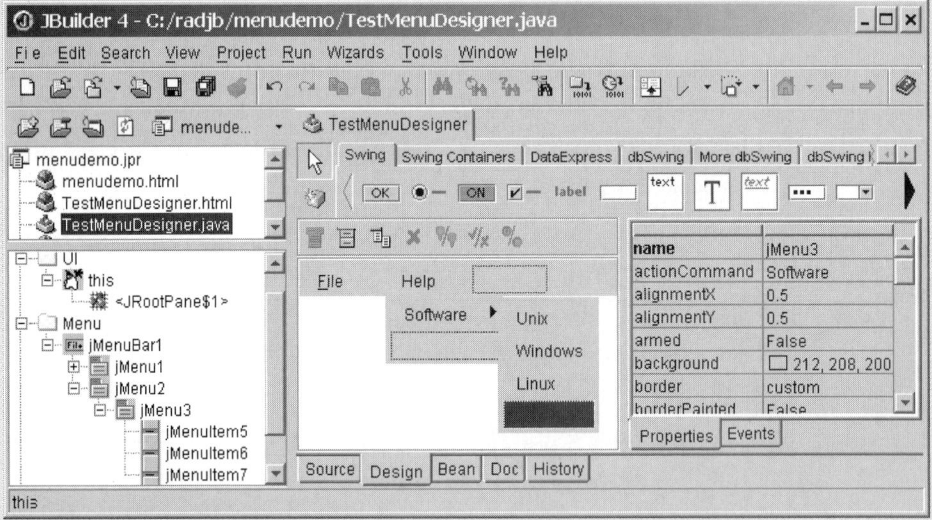

Figure 7.9 *Three submenu items are created in the Software menu.*

5.3. Highlight the next menu item below Software, type **Hardware**, and press Enter.

5.4. The next menu item after Hardware is now highlighted. Type **Check It** and press Enter to create a menu item for Check It. Select Check

It and choose Checkable/Uncheckable Item in the popup menu. The menu item for Check It is converted to a check box menu item.

5.5. Highlight the next menu item after Check It. Type **Color** and press Enter to create a menu item for Color. Select Color and choose Toggle Radio Item in the popup menu. The menu item for Color is converted to a radio button menu. Add three radio buttons named Red, Green, and Blue in the Color menu, as shown in Figure 7.10.

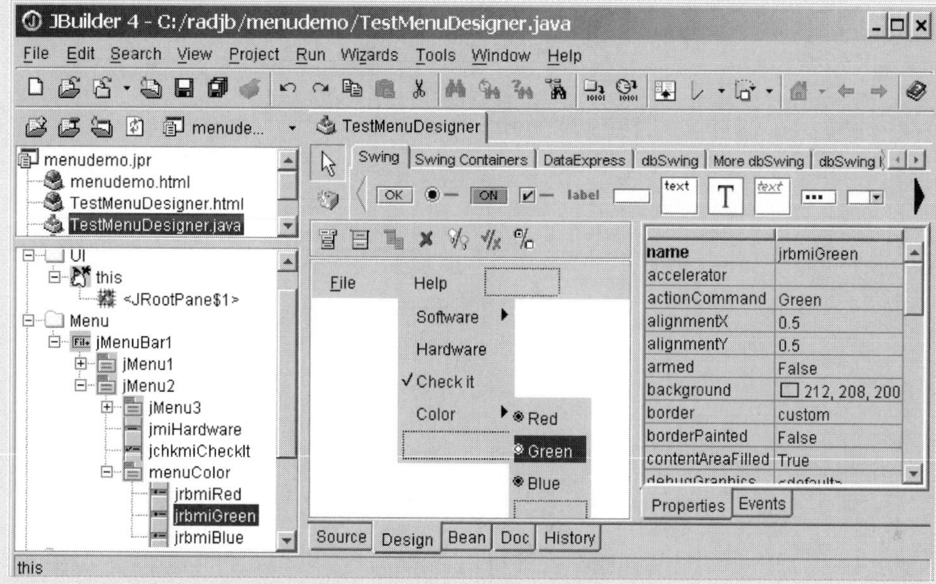

Figure 7.10 *Three radio button menu items are created in the Color menu.*

6. Rename the menus and menu items to `menuFile`, `jmiNew`, `jmiOpen`, `jmiPrint`, `jmiExit`, `menuHelp`, `menuSoftware`, `jmiHardware`, `jchkmiCheckIt`, `menuColor`, `jrbmiRed`, `jrbmiGreen`, and `jrbmiBlue`.

7. Create an instance of `ButtonGroup` to group the radio buttons, as shown in Listing 7.1 (Lines 112–115).

8. Declare three image icons named `newImageIcon`, `openImageIcon`, and `printImageIcon`, and load the image icons, as shown in Listing 7.1 (Lines 52–58). In the Menu designer, set the icon properties of `jmiNew`, `jmiOpen`, and `jmiPrint` to `newImageIcon`, `openImageIcon`, and `printImageIcon`, respectively.

9. Set the `mnemonic` properties of `menuFile`, `jmiNew`, `jmiOpen`, `jmiPrint`, and `jmiExit` to F, N, O, P, and E, respectively.

10. To create an accelerator for the Open menu, click the ellipse button in the accelerator field to display the Accelerator dialog box shown in Figure 7.11. Choose Key Pressed for the event type and press Ctrl+O. You will see Ctrl+O in the keystroke combination field.

continued

Example 7.1 continued

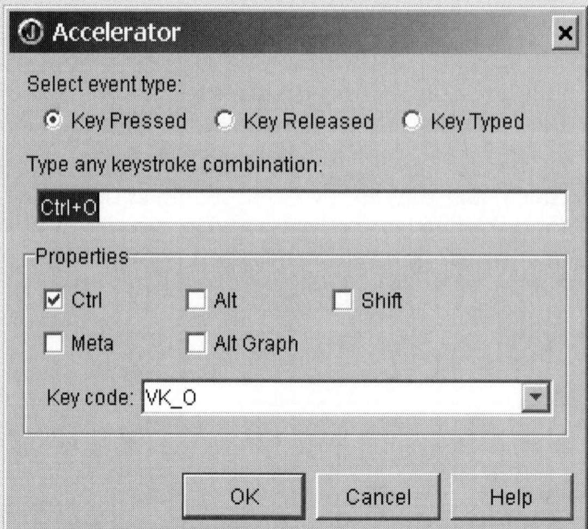

Figure 7.11 *You can use the Accelerator dialog box to create accelerators for menu items.*

11. Switch the UI designer by clicking the `this` under the UI node. Right-click the inspector for the applet to display hidden properties. Set the `JMenuBar` property to `jMenuBar1` to attach the menu bar to the applet.

12. In the Events page of the inspector for `jmiExit`, double-click the value field of `actionPerformed` to generate the code for handling the Exit menu item. Add the code to terminate the program in the handler, as shown in Listing 7.1 (Line 119).

```
1    package menudemo;
2
3    import java.awt.*;
4    import java.awt.event.*;
5    import java.applet.*;
6    import javax.swing.*;
7    import imageviewerdemo.ImageViewer;
8
9    public class TestMenuDesigner extends JApplet {
10     boolean isStandalone = false;
11     JMenuBar jMenuBar1 = new JMenuBar();
12     JMenu menuFile = new JMenu();
13     JMenuItem jmiNew = new JMenuItem();
14     JMenuItem jmiOpen = new JMenuItem();
15     JMenuItem jmiPrint = new JMenuItem();
16     JMenuItem jmiExit = new JMenuItem();
17     JMenu menuHelp = new JMenu();
18     JMenu menuSoftware = new JMenu();
19     JMenuItem jMenuItem5 = new JMenuItem();
20     JMenuItem jMenuItem6 = new JMenuItem();
21     JMenuItem jMenuItem7 = new JMenuItem();
22     JMenuItem jmiHardware = new JMenuItem();
23     JCheckBoxMenuItem jchkmiCheckIt = new JCheckBoxMenuItem();
24     JMenu menuColor = new JMenu();
```

Listing 7.1 *TestMenuDesigner.java*

```
  JRadioButtonMenuItem jrbmiRed = new JRadioButtonMenuItem();
  JRadioButtonMenuItem jrbmiGreen = new JRadioButtonMenuItem();
  JRadioButtonMenuItem jrbmiBlue = new JRadioButtonMenuItem();

  // Group radio buttons
  ButtonGroup btg = new ButtonGroup();

  // Declare image icons
  ImageIcon newImageIcon;
  ImageIcon openImageIcon;
  ImageIcon printImageIcon;

  /** Construct the applet */
  public TestMenuDesigner() {
  }
  /** Initialize the applet */
  public void init() {
    try {
      jbInit();
    }
    catch(Exception e) {
      e.printStackTrace();
    }
  }

  /** Component initialization */
  private void jbInit() throws Exception {
    // Create image icons
    newImageIcon = ImageViewer.createImageIcon(
      "/image/new.gif", this);
    openImageIcon = ImageViewer.createImageIcon(
      "/image/open.gif", this);
    printImageIcon = ImageViewer.createImageIcon(
      "/image/print.gif", this);

    this.setJMenuBar(jMenuBar1);
    this.setSize(new Dimension(245, 158));
    menuFile.setMnemonic('F');
    menuFile.setText("File");
    jmiNew.setIcon(newImageIcon);
    jmiNew.setMnemonic('N');
    jmiNew.setText("New");
    jmiOpen.setIcon(openImageIcon);
    jmiOpen.setMnemonic('O');
    jmiOpen.setText("Open");
    jmiOpen.setAccelerator(javax.swing.KeyStroke.getKeyStroke(79,
      java.awt.event.KeyEvent.CTRL_MASK, false));
    jmiPrint.setIcon(printImageIcon);
    jmiPrint.setMnemonic('P');
    jmiPrint.setText("Print");
    jmiExit.setMnemonic('E');
    jmiExit.setText("Exit");
    jmiExit.addActionListener(new java.awt.event.ActionListener() {
      public void actionPerformed(ActionEvent e) {
        jmiExit_actionPerformed(e);
      }
    });
    menuHelp.setText("Help");
    menuSoftware.setText("Software");
    jMenuItem5.setText("Unix");
```

Listing 7.1 *Continued*

continued

Example 7.1 continued

```
        jMenuItem6.setText("Windows");
        jMenuItem7.setText("Linux");
        jmiHardware.setText("Hardware");
        jchkmiCheckIt.setText("Check it");
        menuColor.setText("Color");
        jrbmiRed.setText("Red");
        jrbmiGreen.setText("Green");
        jrbmiBlue.setText("Blue");
        jMenuBar1.add(menuFile);
        jMenuBar1.add(menuHelp);
        menuFile.add(jmiNew);
        menuFile.add(jmiOpen);
        menuFile.addSeparator();
        menuFile.add(jmiPrint);
        menuFile.addSeparator();
        menuFile.add(jmiExit);
        menuHelp.add(menuSoftware);
        menuHelp.add(jmiHardware);
        menuHelp.add(jchkmiCheckIt);
        menuHelp.add(menuColor);
        menuSoftware.add(jMenuItem5);
        menuSoftware.add(jMenuItem6);
        menuSoftware.add(jMenuItem7);
        menuColor.add(jrbmiRed);
        menuColor.add(jrbmiGreen);
        menuColor.add(jrbmiBlue);

        // Group radio buttons
        btg.add(jrbmiRed);
        btg.add(jrbmiGreen);
        btg.add(jrbmiBlue);
      }

      void jmiExit_actionPerformed(ActionEvent e) {
        System.exit(0);
      }
    }
```

Listing 7.1 *Continued*

Example Review

Before starting the Menu designer, you need to create an instance of `JMenuBar` by dropping it to the UI designer from the Swing Containers page in the component palette.

The Menu designer appears in the content pane of the AppBrowser when a menu item in the component tree is double-clicked. It has its own toolbar and recognizes keystrokes, such as the navigation cursors and the *INS* and *DEL* keys.

JBuilder IDE maintains everything in sync as you work. As you edit menu items in the Menu designer, all changes are reflected immediately to the AppBrowser and the inspector. When you make changes to the menus in the source code or the inspector, they are reflected in the Menu designer, and vice versa.

The program exits when you click the Exit menu item. The Exit command is ignored if the applet runs from a Web browser.

NOTE

The menu bar is usually attached to the window using the `setJMenuBar` method. However, like any other component, it can be placed in a container. For instance, you can place a menu bar in the south of the container with `BorderLayout`.

TIP

To switch to the Menu designer, click any item under the node Menu. To switch back to the UI designer, click any item under the node labeled `"this"`.

Popup Menus

A popup menu, also known as *a context menu,* is like a regular menu, but does not have a menu bar and can float anywhere on the screen. You create a popup menu the same way you create a regular menu using JBuilder's Menu designer.

A regular menu is always attached to a menu bar using the `setJMenuBar` method, but a popup menu is associated with a parent component and is displayed using the `show` method in the `JPopupMenu` class. You specify the parent component and the location of the popup menu, using the coordinate system of the parent like this:

```
popupMenu.show(component, x, y);
```

The popup menu usually contains the commands for an object. Customarily, you display a popup menu by pointing to the object and clicking a certain mouse button, the so-called *popup trigger.* Popup triggers are system-dependent. In Windows, the popup menu is displayed when the right mouse button is released. In Motif, the popup menu is displayed when the third mouse button is pressed and held down.

Example 7.2 Using Popup Menus

This example demonstrates creating popup menus using JBuilder Menu designer. The program creates a text area in a scroll pane. The popup menu is displayed when the mouse pointed to the text area triggers the popup menu, as shown in Figure 7.12.

continued

Example 7.2 continued

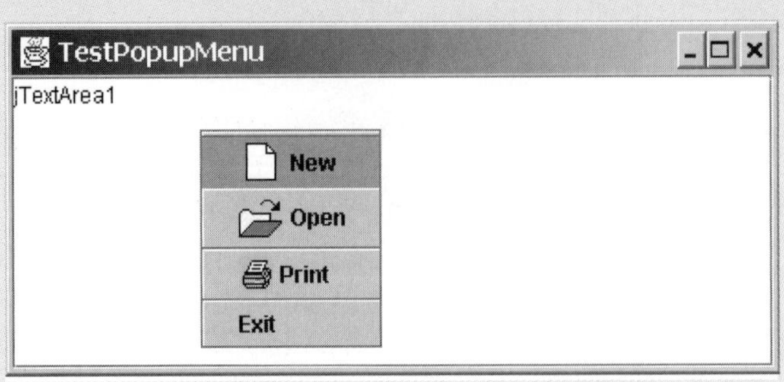

Figure 7.12 *A popup menu is displayed when the popup trigger is issued on the text area.*

Here are the steps to complete the project.

1. Reopen project menudemo.jpr and create an applet named `TestPopupMenu` using the Applet wizard.

2. In the UI designer of TestPopupMenu.java, drop a `JScrollPane` to the center of the applet, and drop a `JTextArea` into the scroll pane to create `jTextArea1`.

3. Drop a `JPopupMenu` from the Swing Containers page to the applet to create `jPopupMenu1`. Double-click `jPopupMenu1` in the component tree to switch to the Menu designer, as shown in Figure 7.13.

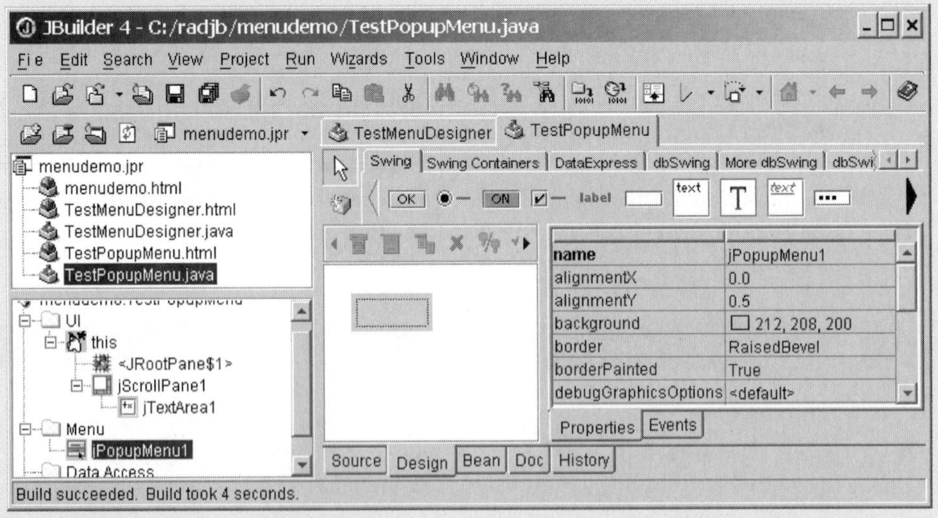

Figure 7.13 *You can design popup menus the same way you design regular menus in the Menu designer.*

4. Create menu items New, Open, a separator, a menu item Print, a separator, and a menu item Exit in the popup menu. Rename the menu items `jmiNew`, `jmiOpen`, `jmiPrint`, and `jmiExit`.

5. Generate and implement the handler for the Exit menu to exit the program.

6. Declare and create image icons and set the image icons for `jmiNew`, `jmiOpen`, and `jmiPrint`, the same as in the previous example.

7. Switch to the UI designer by double-clicking `jTextArea1`. In the Events page of `jTextArea1`, double-click the value field of `mousePressed` and `mouseReleased` to generate the code for displaying the popup menu, as shown in Listing 7.2 (Lines 81–89).

```
1   package menudemo;
2
3   import java.awt.*;
4   import java.awt.event.*;
5   import java.applet.*;
6   import javax.swing.*;
7   import java.beans.*;
8   import imageviewerdemo.ImageViewer;
9
10  public class TestPopupMenu extends JApplet {
11    boolean isStandalone = false;
12    JScrollPane jScrollPane1 = new JScrollPane();
13    JTextArea jTextArea1 = new JTextArea();
14    JPopupMenu jPopupMenu1 = new JPopupMenu();
15    JMenuItem jmiNew = new JMenuItem();
16    JMenuItem jmiOpen = new JMenuItem();
17    JMenuItem jmiPrint = new JMenuItem();
18    JMenuItem jmiExit = new JMenuItem();
19
20    // Declare image icons
21    ImageIcon newImageIcon;
22    ImageIcon openImageIcon;
23    ImageIcon printImageIcon;
24
25    /** Initialize the applet */
26    public void init() {
27      try {
28        jbInit();
29      }
30      catch(Exception e) {
31        e.printStackTrace();
32      }
33    }
34
35    /** Component initialization */
36    private void jbInit() throws Exception {
37      // Create image icons
38      newImageIcon = ImageViewer.createImageIcon(
39        "/image/new.gif", this);
40      openImageIcon = ImageViewer.createImageIcon(
41        "/image/open.gif", this);
```

Listing 7.2 *TestPopupMenu.java*

continued

Example 7.2 continued

```
      printImageIcon = ImageViewer.createImageIcon(
        "/image/print.gif", this);

      this.setSize(new Dimension(251, 161));
      jTextArea1.setText("jTextArea1");
      jTextArea1.addMouseListener(new java.awt.event.MouseAdapter() {
        public void mousePressed(MouseEvent e) {
          jTextArea1_mousePressed(e);
        }
        public void mouseReleased(MouseEvent e) {
          jTextArea1_mouseReleased(e);
        }
      });
      jmiNew.setText("New");
      jmiOpen.setText("Open");
      jmiPrint.setText("Print");
      jmiExit.setText("Exit");
      jmiNew.setIcon(newImageIcon);
      jmiOpen.setIcon(openImageIcon);
      jmiPrint.setIcon(printImageIcon);
      jmiExit.addActionListener(new java.awt.event.ActionListener() {
        public void actionPerformed(ActionEvent e) {
          jmiExit_actionPerformed(e);
        }
      });
      this.getContentPane().add(jScrollPane1, BorderLayout.CENTER);
      jScrollPane1.getViewport().add(jTextArea1, null);
      jPopupMenu1.add(jmiNew);
      jPopupMenu1.add(jmiOpen);
      jPopupMenu1.addSeparator();
      jPopupMenu1.add(jmiPrint);
      jPopupMenu1.addSeparator();
      jPopupMenu1.add(jmiExit);
    }

    void jmiExit_actionPerformed(ActionEvent e) {
      System.exit(0);
    }

    /** Display popup menu for Motif */
    void jTextArea1_mousePressed(MouseEvent e) {
      showPopup(e);
    }

    /** Display popup menu for Windows */
    void jTextArea1_mouseReleased(MouseEvent e) {
      showPopup(e);
    }

    /** Display popup menu when triggered */
    private void showPopup(MouseEvent e) {
      if (e.isPopupTrigger())
        jPopupMenu1.show(e.getComponent(), e.getX(), e.getY());
    }
  }
```

Listing 7.2 *Continued*

Example Review

The process of creating popup menus is the same as the process for creating regular menus. To create a popup menu, drop a `JPopupMenu` from the component palette to the UI designer to create an instance of `JPopupMenu`. You can start the Menu designer by double-clicking the instance under the Menu node in the component tree.

To show a popup menu, the applet uses the `show` method by specifying the parent component and the location for the popup menu. The `show` method is invoked when the popup menu is triggered by a particular mouse click on the text area. Popup triggers are system-dependent. This program implements the `mouseReleased` handler for displaying the popup menu in the Windows and the `mousePressed` handler for displaying the popup menu in the Motif.

JToolBar

In user interfaces, a *toolbar* is often used to hold commands that also appear in the menus. Frequently used commands are placed in a toolbar for quick access. Clicking a command in the toolbar is faster than choosing it from the menu.

Swing provides the `JToolBar` class as the container to hold tool bar components. `JToolBar` uses `BoxLayout` to manage components. The components usually appear as icons. Since icons are not components, they cannot be placed into a tool bar directly. Instead you may place buttons into the tool bar and set the icons on the buttons. An instance of `JToolBar` is like a regular container. Often it is placed in the north, west, or east of a container of `BorderLayout`.

The following properties in the `JToolBar` class are often useful:

- `orientation`: This specifies whether the items in the tool bar appear horizontally or vertically. The possible values are `JToolBar.HORIZONTAL` and `JToolBar.VERTICAL`. The default value is `JToolBar.HORIZONTAL`.
- `floatable`: This is a `boolean` value that specifies whether the tool bar can be floated. By default, the tool bar is floatable.

Example 7.3 Creating Tool Bars

This example demonstrates creating a tool bar for the commands New, Open, and Print, as shown in Figure 7.14.

Here are the steps to complete the example:

1. Create a new project named toolbardemo.jpr and an applet named `TestToolBar` using the Applet wizard.

continued

Example 7.3 continued

Figure 7.14 *The tool bar contains the icons representing the commands New, Open, and Print.*

2. In the UI designer of TestToolBar.java, drop a `JToolBar` from the Swing Containers page into the north of the applet to create `jToolBar1`.
3. Drop a `JButton` three times into `jToolBar1` and name the buttons `jbtNew`, `jbtOpen`, and `jbtPrint`.
4. Switch to the source code. Declare and create image icons named `newImageIcon`, `openImageIcon`, and `printImageIcon` for New, Open, and Print, as shown in Listing 7.3 (Lines 33–39).
5. Switch to the UI designer. Set the `icon` property of `jbtNew`, `jbtOpen`, and `jbtPrint` to `newImageIcon`, `openImageIcon`, and `printImageIcon`, as shown in Figure 7.15. You may adjust the `margin` property of the button to resize the button.

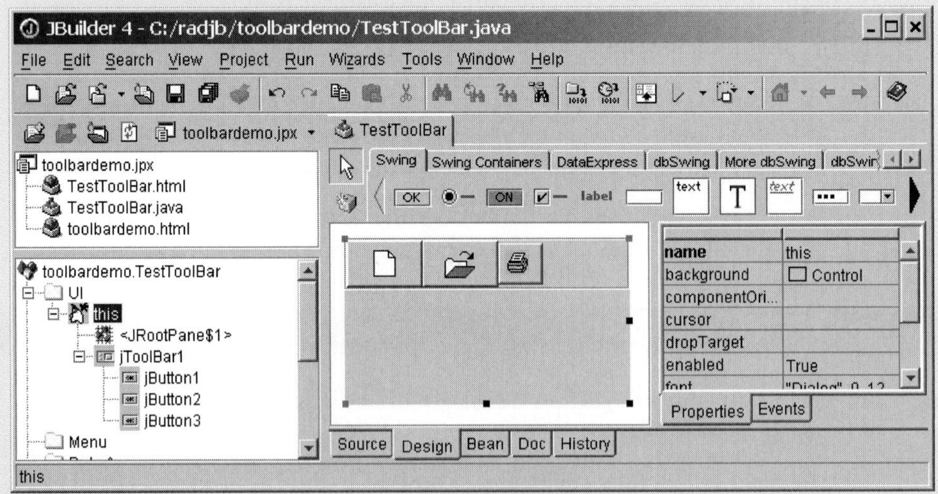

Figure 7.15 *The buttons are added to the tool bar, and the icons are set on the buttons.*

JBUILDER 5 NOTE

As addressed in Example 5.1, there is a bug in JBuilder 5 that prevents the image icons from being displayed in the UI designer using the `ImageViewer.createImageIcon` method. To show the image icon in the JBuilder 5 UI designer, replace

```
btIcon = ImageViewer.createImageIcon("/image/new.gif", this);
```

with

```
Toolkit toolkit = Toolkit.getDefaultToolkit();
java.net.URL url = this.getClass().getResource("/image/new.gif");
newImageIcon = new ImageIcon(toolkit.getImage(url));
```

```
package toolbardemo;

import java.awt.*;
import java.awt.event.*;
import java.applet.*;
import javax.swing.*;
import imageviewerdemo.ImageViewer;

public class TestToolBar extends JApplet {
  boolean isStandalone = false;
  JToolBar jToolBar1 = new JToolBar();
  JButton jButton1 = new JButton();
  JButton jButton2 = new JButton();
  JButton jButton3 = new JButton();

  // Declare image icons
  ImageIcon newImageIcon;
  ImageIcon openImageIcon;
  ImageIcon printImageIcon;

  /** Initialize the applet */
  public void init() {
    try {
      jbInit();
    }
    catch(Exception e) {
      e.printStackTrace();
    }
  }

  /** Component initialization */
  private void jbInit() throws Exception {
    // Create image icons
    newImageIcon = ImageViewer.createImageIcon(
      "/image/new.gif", this);
    openImageIcon = ImageViewer.createImageIcon(
      "/image/open.gif", this);
    printImageIcon = ImageViewer.createImageIcon(
      "/image/print.gif", this);

    this.setSize(new Dimension(270, 159));
    jButton1.setIcon(newImageIcon);
    jButton2.setIcon(openImageIcon);
    jButton3.setIcon(printImageIcon);
```

Listing 7.3 *TestToolBar.java*

continued

Example 7.3 continued

```
        jButton3.setMargin(new Insets(2, 2, 4, 8));
        this.getContentPane().add(jToolBar1, BorderLayout.NORTH);
        jToolBar1.add(jButton1, null);
        jToolBar1.add(jButton2, null);
        jToolBar1.add(jButton3, null);
    }
}
```

Listing 7.3 *Continued*

Example Review

The tool bar is a container with `BoxLayout`. The layout is fixed and cannot be changed. Using the `orientation` property, you can specify whether components in the tool bar are organized horizontally or vertically.

By default, the tool bar is floatable, and a floatable controller is displayed in front of its components. You can drag the floatable controller to move the tool bar to different locations of the window or can show the tool bar in a separate window, as shown in Figure 7.16.

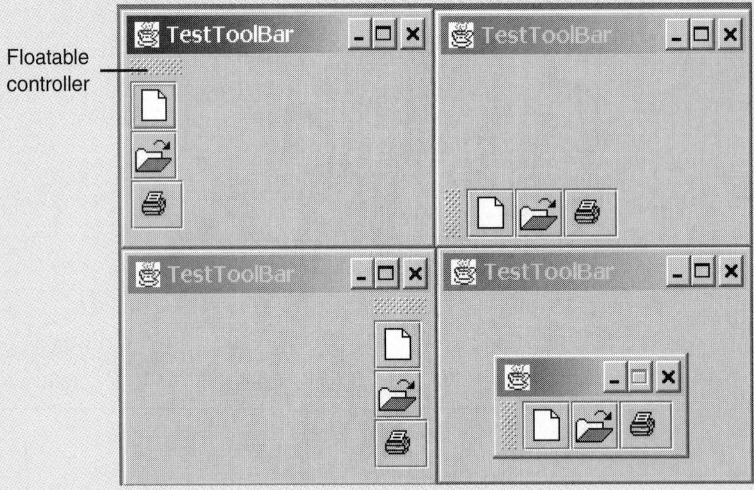

Figure 7.16 *The toolbar buttons are floatable.*

Processing Actions Using the *Action* Interface

Often menus and tool bars contain some common actions. For example, you can display the Object Gallery by choosing File, New, or by clicking the new button in the tool bar. Swing provides the `Action` interface, which can be used to create action objects for processing actions. Using `Action` objects, common action processing can be centralized and separated from the other application code.

The `Action` interface is a subinterface of `ActionListener`. Additionally, it defines several methods for retrieving and setting the associated action value, for checking whether the action is enabled, and for enabling and disabling the action. These methods are:

- `public boolean isEnabled()`

  Returns true if action is enabled.

- `public void setEnabled(boolean newValue)`

  Enables or disables the action.

- `public void putValue(String key, Object value)`

  Associates a key/value pair with the action. Key can be any string, but four names have predefined meanings:

Name	*Value*
`Action.NAME`	A name for the action
`Action.SMALL_ICON`	A small icon for the action
`Action.SHORT_DESCRIPTION`	A tool tip for the action
`Action.LONG_DESCRIPTION`	A description for online help

- `public Object getValue(String key)`

  Returns the object of the key/value pair.

`AbstractAction` is a default implementation of the `Action` interface. It implements all the methods in the `Action` interface except the `actionPerformed` method. The constructors of `AbstractionAction` are as follows:

- `public AbstractAction()`

  Defines an `Action` object with a default description string and default icon.

- `public AbstractAction(String name)`

  Defines an `Action` object with the specified description string and a default icon.

- `public AbstractAction(String name, Icon icon)`

  Defines an `Action` object with the specified description string and the specified icon.

Since `AbstractAction` is an abstract class, you cannot create an instance using its constructor. However, you can create a concrete subclass of `AbstractAction` and implement the `actionPerformed` method. This subclass can be defined as an anonymous inner class. For example, the following code creates an `Action` object for terminating the program.

```
Action exitAction = new AbstractAction("Exit") {
  public void actionPerformed(ActionEvent e) {
    System.exit(0);
  }
};
```

Certain containers, such as `JMenu` and `JToolBar`, know how to add an `Action` object. When an `Action` object is added to such a container, the container automatically creates an appropriate component for the `Action` object, and registers a listener with the `Action` object. Here is an example of adding an `Action` object to a menu and a tool bar:

```
jMenu.add(exitAction);
jToolBar.add(exitAction);
```

`Action` objects can also be used to respond to keystrokes. To associate actions with keystrokes, you need to create an instance of the `KeyStroke` class using the static `getKeyStroke` method, as follows:

```
KeyStroke exitKey =
  KeyStroke.getKeyStroke(KeyEvent.VK_E, KeyEvent.CTRL_MASK);
```

You can now associate an action with the keystroke by registering with an instance of `JComponent`. For example, the following code associates `exitAction` with `exitKey`, and registers this action with `jPanel1`.

```
jPanel1.registerKeyboardAction
   (exitAction, exitKey, JComponent.WHEN_IN_FOCUSED_WINDOW);
```

The `registerKeyboardAction(ActionListener anAction, KeyStroke aKeyStroke, int aCondition)` method is defined in the `JComponent` class. The argument `aCondition` indicates under what condition the action should be invoked. Three possible values for the condition are `WHEN_FOCUSED`, `WHEN_IN_FOCUSED_WINDOW`, and `WHEN_ANCESTOR_OF_FOCUSED_COMPONENT`. Keystrokes are delivered to the component that has focus. Actions are invoked when keystrokes are detected in the focused component, in the focus window, and in the focused ancestor component under these conditions.

Example 7.4 Using Actions

This example demonstrates processing actions using the `Action` interface. The program creates three menu items Left, Center, Right, three tool bar buttons Left, Center, Right, and three regular buttons Left, Center, Right, as shown in Figure 7.17. The actions of these components are processed through common action handlers.

Here are the steps to complete the example:

1. Create a new project named actiondemo.jpr and an applet named `TestActionInterface` using the Applet wizard.
2. In the UI designer of TestActionInterface.java, drop a `JToolBar` from the Swing Containers page into the north of the applet to create `jToolBar1`.

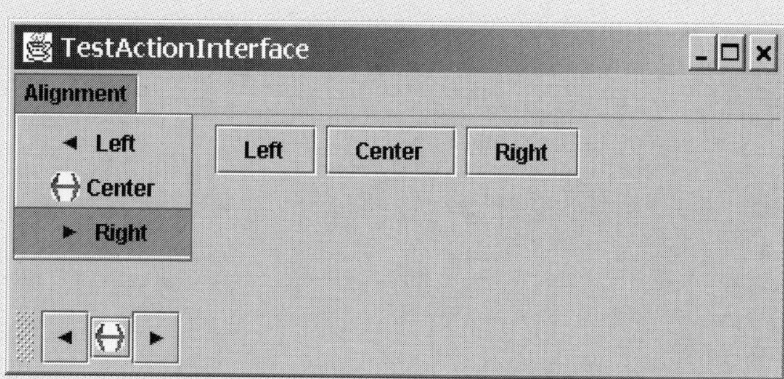

Figure 7.17 *Left, Center, and Right appear in the menu, in the toolbar, and in regular buttons.*

3. Drop a `JPanel` to the center of the applet. Drop `JButton` three times into the panel and name the buttons `jbtLeft`, `jbtCenter`, and `jbtRight`.

4. Drop a `JMenuBar` to the applet to create `jMenuBar1`. Create a menu named `jmiAlignment`.

5. Write the code for an inner class `MyAction` that extends `AbstractAction` as shown in Listing 7.4 (Lines 88–100).

6. Write the code to create image icons (Lines 32–38). Write the code to create `leftAction`, `centerAction`, and `rightAction` (Lines 40–43). Write the code to create keystrokes and register for the actions (Lines 71–85).

```
1   package actiondemo;
2
3   import java.awt.*;
4   import java.awt.event.*;
5   import java.applet.*;
6   import javax.swing.*;
7   import imageviewerdemo.ImageViewer;
8
9   public class TestActionInterface extends JApplet {
10    boolean isStandalone = false;
11    JMenuBar jMenuBar1 = new JMenuBar();
12    JMenu jMenu1 = new JMenu();
13    JMenuItem jmiExit = new JMenuItem();
14    JPanel jPanel1 = new JPanel();
15    JButton jbtLeft = new JButton();
16    JButton jbtCenter = new JButton();
17    JButton jbtRight = new JButton();
18    JToolBar jToolBar1 = new JToolBar();
19
20    /** Initialize the applet */
21    public void init() {
22      try {
23        jbInit();
24      }
25      catch(Exception e) {
26        e.printStackTrace();
27      }
28    }
29
```

Listing 7.4 *TestActionInterface.java*

continued

Example 7.4 Using Actions

```
    /** Component initialization */
    private void jbInit() throws Exception {
      // Create image icons
      ImageIcon leftImageIcon = ImageViewer.createImageIcon(
        "/image/prior.gif", this);
      ImageIcon centerImageIcon = ImageViewer.createImageIcon(
        "/image/center16.gif", this);
      ImageIcon rightImageIcon = ImageViewer.createImageIcon(
        "/image/next.gif", this);

      // Create actions
      Action leftAction = new MyAction("Left", leftImageIcon);
      Action centerAction = new MyAction("Center", centerImageIcon);
      Action rightAction = new MyAction("Right", rightImageIcon);

      this.setSize(new Dimension(400,300));
      jMenu1.setText("Alignment");
      jbtLeft.setText("Left");
      jbtCenter.setText("Center");
      jbtRight.setText("Right");
      jMenuBar1.add(jMenu1);
      jMenu1.add(leftAction);
      jMenu1.add(centerAction);
      jMenu1.add(rightAction);
      this.getContentPane().add(jPanel1, BorderLayout.CENTER);
      jPanel1.add(jbtLeft, null);
      jPanel1.add(jbtCenter, null);
      jPanel1.add(jbtRight, null);
      this.getContentPane().add(jToolBar1, BorderLayout.NORTH);
      this.setJMenuBar(jMenuBar1);

      // Add actions to the toolbar
      jToolBar1.add(leftAction);
      jToolBar1.add(centerAction);
      jToolBar1.add(rightAction);

      // Add actions to the buttons
      jbtLeft.addActionListener(leftAction);
      jbtCenter.addActionListener(centerAction);
      jbtRight.addActionListener(rightAction);

      // Create KeyStroke instances
      KeyStroke leftKey =
        KeyStroke.getKeyStroke(KeyEvent.VK_L, KeyEvent.CTRL_MASK);
      KeyStroke centerKey =
        KeyStroke.getKeyStroke(KeyEvent.VK_C, KeyEvent.CTRL_MASK);
      KeyStroke rightKey =
        KeyStroke.getKeyStroke(KeyEvent.VK_R, KeyEvent.CTRL_MASK);

      // Register keystrokes
      jPanel1.registerKeyboardAction
        (leftAction, leftKey, JComponent.WHEN_IN_FOCUSED_WINDOW);
      jPanel1.registerKeyboardAction
        (centerAction, centerKey, JComponent.WHEN_IN_FOCUSED_WINDOW);
      jPanel1.registerKeyboardAction
        (rightAction, rightKey, JComponent.WHEN_IN_FOCUSED_WINDOW);
    }

```

Listing 7.4 *Continued*

```
    private class MyAction extends AbstractAction {
      String name;

      MyAction(String name, Icon icon) {
        super(name, icon);
        putValue(Action.SHORT_DESCRIPTION, name);
        this.name = name;
      }

      public void actionPerformed(ActionEvent e) {
        System.out.println("It is " + name);
      }
    }
  }
```

Listing 7.4 *Continued*

Example Review

The inner class `MyAction` extends `AbstractAction` with a constructor to construct an action with a name and an icon. It implements the `actionPerformed` method to display the action to the console.

Three actions, `leftAction`, `centerAction`, and `rightAction`, were created from the `MyAction` class. Each action has a name and an associated icon. The actions are for the menu items and the toolbar button. The menu and toolbar know how to add these objects. The tool tip is effective in the toolbar, but is ignored (not displayed) in the menu.

Since `Action` is a subinterface of `ActionListener`, `leftAction` is an instance of `ActionListener`. Therefore, to associate actions with the regular buttons, you can use the `addActionListener` method, such as `jbtLeft.addActionListener(leftAction)`.

JOptionPane Dialogs

A *dialog box* is normally used as a temporary window to receive additional information from the user or to provide notification that some event has occurred. Java provides the `JOptionPane` class, which can be used to create standard dialogs. You can also build custom dialogs by extending the `JDialog` class.

The `JOptionPane` class can be used to create four kinds of standard dialogs:

- Message dialog: This shows a message and waits for the user to click OK.
- Confirmation dialog: This shows a question and asks for confirmation, such as OK and Cancel.
- Input dialog: This shows a question and gets the user's input from a text field, combo box, or list.
- Option dialog: This shows a question and gets the user's answer from a set of options.

These dialogs are created using the static methods `showXxxDialog` and generally appear as shown in Figure 7.18.

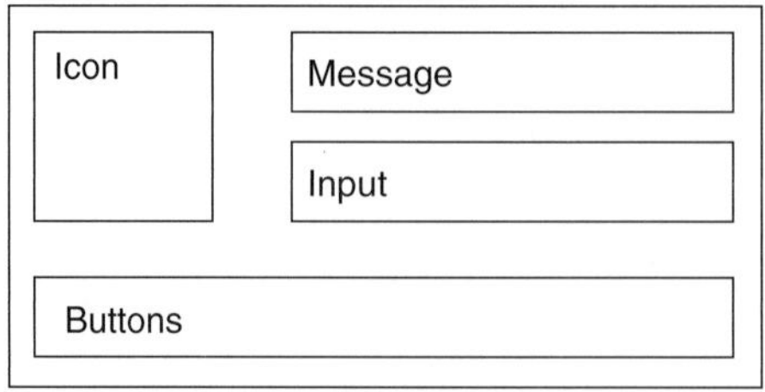

Figure 7.18 *A standard dialog can display an icon, a message, an input, and option buttons.*

For example, you can use the following method to create a message dialog box, as shown in Figure 7.19.

```
JOptionPane.showMessageDialog(this, "SSN not found",
  "For Your Information", JOptionPane.INFORMATION_MESSAGE);
```

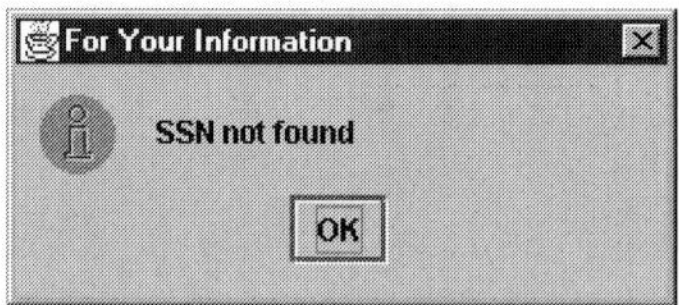

Figure 7.19 *The Message dialog displays a message and waits for the user to click OK.*

Message Dialogs

A *message dialog* box simply displays a message to alert the user and waits for the user to click the OK button to close the dialog. The methods for creating message dialogs are shown below:

```
public static void showMessageDialog(Component parentComponent,
                                     Object message)

public static void showMessageDialog(Component parentComponent,
                                     Object message,
                                     String title,
                                     int messageType)

public static void showMessageDialog(Component parentComponent,
                                     Object message,
                                     String title,
                                     int messageType,
                                     Icon icon)
```

The `parentComponent` can be any component. The `message` is an object, but often a string is used. These two parameters must always be specified. The `title` is a string displayed in the title bar of the dialog with default value “Message.”

The `messageType` is one of the following constants:

- `JOptionPane.ERROR_MESSAGE`
- `JOptionPane.INFORMATION_MESSAGE`
- `JOptionPane.PLAIN_MESSAGE`
- `JOptionPane.WARNING_MESSAGE`
- `JOptionPane.QUESTION_MESSAGE`

By default, `messageType` is `JOptionPane.INFORMATION_MESSAGE`. Each type has an associated icon except the `PLAIN_MESSAGE` type, as shown in Figure 7.20. You can also supply your own `icon` in the `icon` parameter.

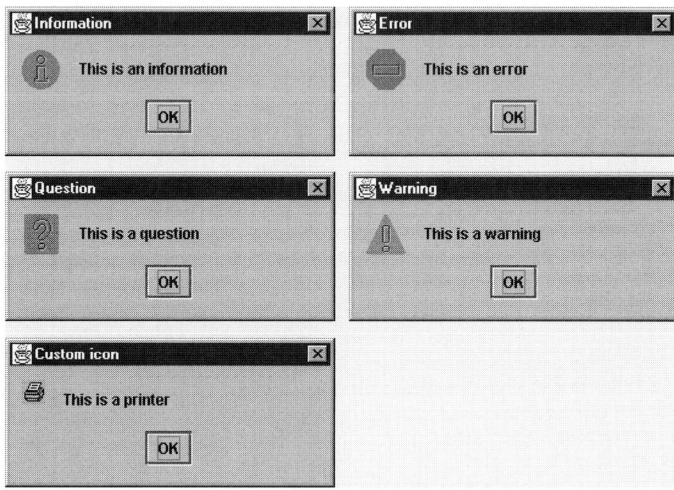

Figure 7.20 *There are five types of message dialog boxes.*

The `message` parameter is an object. If it is a GUI component, the component is displayed. If it is a non-GUI component, the string representation of the object is displayed. For example, the following statement displays a clock in a message dialog, as shown in Figure 7.21.

```
JOptionPane.showMessageDialog(this, new Clock(),
  "Current Time", JOptionPane.PLAIN_MESSAGE);
```

Confirmation Dialogs

A message dialog box displays a message and waits for the user to click the OK button to dismiss the dialog. The message dialog does not return any value. A *confirmation dialog* asks a question and requires the user to respond with an appropriate button. The confirmation dialog returns a value that corresponds to a selected button.

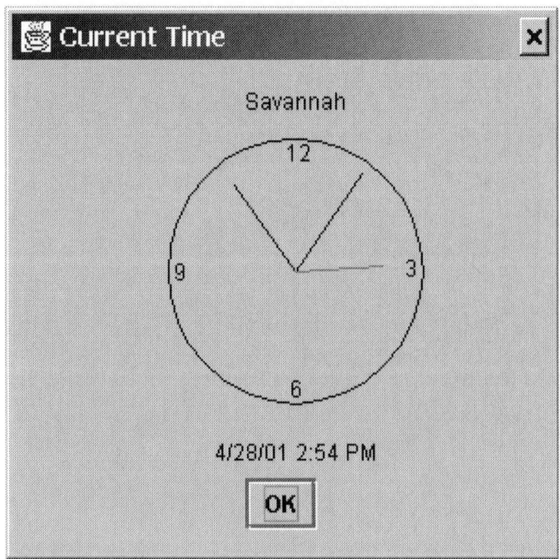

Figure 7.21 *A clock is displayed in a message dialog.*

The methods for creating confirmation dialogs are as follows:

```
public static int showConfirmDialog(Component parentComponent,
                                    Object message)

public static int showConfirmDialog(Component parentComponent,
                                    Object message,
                                    String title,
                                    int optionType)

public static int showConfirmDialog(Component parentComponent,
                                    Object message,
                                    String title,
                                    int optionType,
                                    int messageType)

public static int showConfirmDialog(Component parentComponent,
                                    Object message,
                                    String title,
                                    int optionType,
                                    int messageType,
                                    Icon icon)
```

The parameters `parentComponent`, `message`, `title`, `icon`, and `messageType` are the same as in the `showMessageDialog` method. The default value for `title` is "Select an Option" and for `messageType` is `QUESTION_MESSAGE`. The `optionType` determines which buttons are displayed in the dialog. The possible values are as follows:

- `JOptionPane.YES_NO_OPTION`
- `JOptionPane.YES_NO_CANCEL_OPTION`
- `JOptionPane.OK_CANCEL_OPTION`

Figure 7.22 shows the confirmation dialogs with these options.

The `showConfirmDialog` method returns one of the following `int` values corresponding to the selected option.

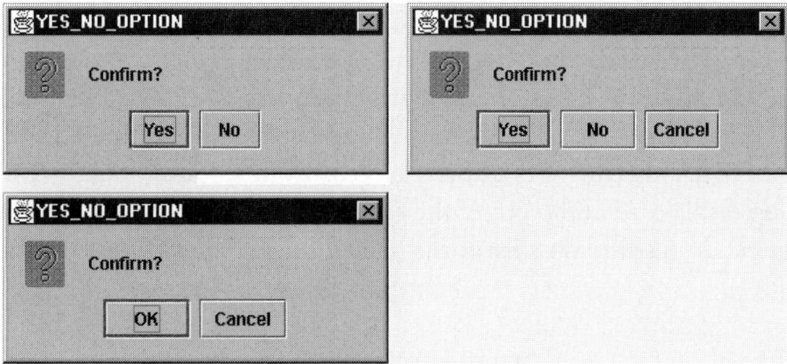

Figure 7.22 *The confirmation dialog displays a question and three types of option buttons, and requires responses from the user.*

- `JOptionPane.YES_OPTION`
- `JOptionPane.NO_OPTION`
- `JOptionPane.CANCEL_OPTION`
- `JOptionPane.OK_OPTION`
- `JOptionPane.CLOSED_OPTION`

These options correspond to the button that was activated, except for the `CLOSED_OPTION`, which implies that the dialog box is closed with buttons activated.

Input Dialogs

An *input dialog* box is used to receive input from the user. The input can be entered from a text field or selected from a combo box or a list. Selectable values can be specified in an array, and a particular value can be designated as the initial selected value. If no selectable value is specified when an input dialog is created, a text field is used for entering input. If fewer than 20 selection values are specified, a combo box is displayed in the input dialog. If 20 or more selection values are specified, a list is used in the input dialog.

The methods for creating input dialogs are shown below:

```
public static String showInputDialog(Object message)

public static String showInputDialog(Component parentComponent,
                                     Object message)

public static String showInputDialog(Component parentComponent,
                                     Object message,
                                     String title,
                                     int messageType)

public static Object showInputDialog(Component parentComponent,
                                     Object message,
                                     int messageType,
                                     Icon icon,
                                     Object[] selectionValues,
                                     Object initialSelectionValue)
```

The first three methods listed above use text field for input, as shown in Figure 7.23. The last method listed above specifies an array of `Object` type as selection values in addition to an object that is specified as an initial selection. The first three methods return a `String` that is entered from the text field in the input dialog. The last method returns an `Object` selected from a combo box or a list. The input dialog displays a combo box if the selection values are fewer than 20, as shown in Figure 7.24; it displays a list if the selection values are 20 or more, as shown in Figure 7.25.

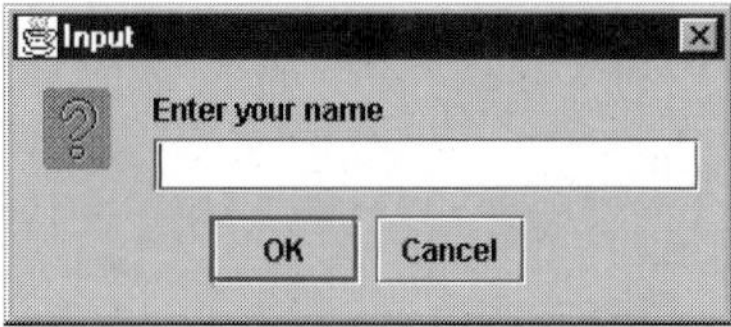

Figure 7.23 *When creating an input dialog without specifying selection values, the input dialog displays a text field for data entry.*

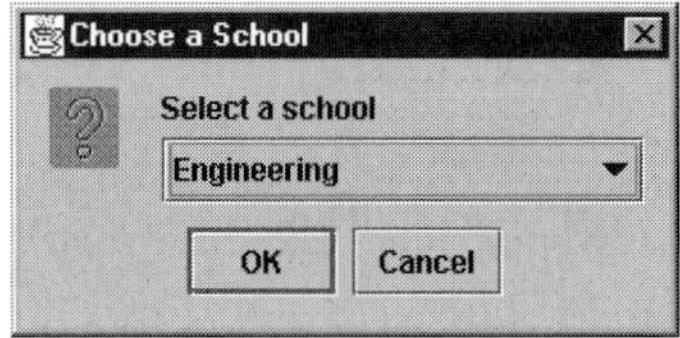

Figure 7.24 *When creating an input dialog with selection values, the input dialog displays a combo box if the selection values are fewer than 20.*

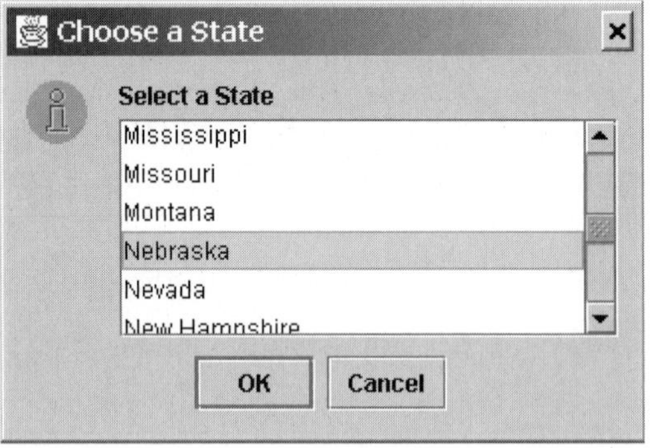

Figure 7.25 *When creating an input dialog with selection values, the input dialog displays a list if the selection values are 20 or more.*

NOTE

The `showInputDialog` method does not have the `optionType` parameter. The buttons for input dialog are not configurable. The OK and Cancel buttons are always used.

Option Dialogs

An *option dialog* allows you to create custom buttons. You can create an option dialog using the following method:

```
public static int showOptionDialog(Component parentComponent,
                                   Object message,
                                   String title,
                                   int optionType,
                                   int messageType,
                                   Icon icon,
                                   Object[] options,
                                   Object intialValue)
```

The buttons are specified using the `options` parameter. The `intialValue` parameter allows you to specify a button to receive initial focus. The `showOptionDialog` method returns an `int` value indicating the button that was activated. For example, here is the code that creates an option dialog, as shown in Figure 7.26.

```
int value =
  JOptionPane.showOptionDialog(this, "Select a button",
    "Option Dialog", JOptionPane.DEFAULT_OPTION,
    JOptionPane.PLAIN_MESSAGE, null,
     new Object[]{"Button 0", "Button 1", "Button 2"}, "Button 1");
```

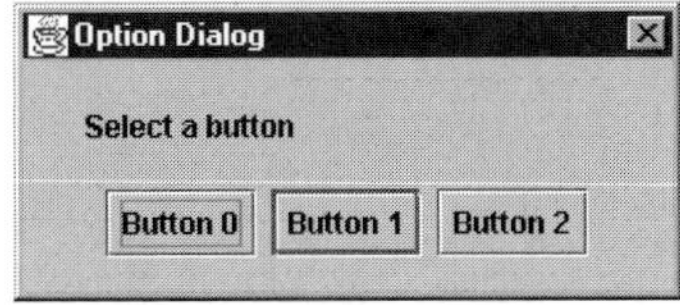

Figure 7.26 *The option dialog displays the custom buttons.*

Example 7.5 Creating Standard Dialogs

This example demonstrates creating message dialogs, confirmation dialogs, input dialogs, and option dialogs. The example uses menus to display the dialogs, as shown in Figure 7.27.

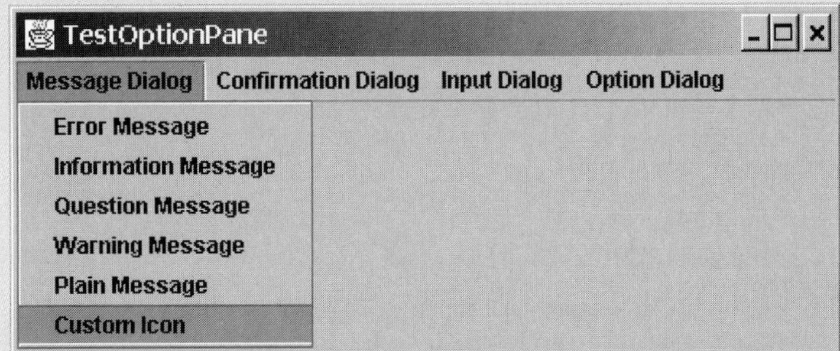

Figure 7.27 *You can display a dialog box by clicking a menu item.*

continued

Example 7.5 continued

Here are the steps to complete the project:

1. Create a new project named dialogdemo.jpr and an applet named `TestOptionPane` using the Applet wizard.
2. In the UI designer of TestOptionPane.java, drop a `JLabel` to the south of the applet to create `jlblStatus`.
3. Drop a `JMenuBar` to the applet to create `jMenuBar1`. Double-click `jMenuBar1` to switch to the Menu designer. Add menus Message Dialog, Confirmation Dialog, Input Dialog, and Option Dialog, and their appropriate menu items.
4. In the component inspector for the applet, set its `JMenuBar` property to `jMenuBar1`.
5. Generate and implement the handlers for the menu items to display dialog boxes, as shown in Listing 7.5.

```
package dialogdemo;

import java.awt.*;
import java.awt.event.*;
import java.applet.*;
import javax.swing.*;
import clockdemo.Clock;
import imageviewerdemo.ImageViewer;

public class TestOptionPane extends JApplet {
  boolean isStandalone = false;
  JMenuBar jMenuBar1 = new JMenuBar();
  JMenu jMenu1 = new JMenu();
  JMenuItem jmiErrorMessage = new JMenuItem();
  JMenuItem jmiInformationMessage = new JMenuItem();
  JMenuItem jmiQuestionMessage = new JMenuItem();
  JMenuItem jmiWarningMessage = new JMenuItem();
  JMenuItem jmiPlainMessage = new JMenuItem();
  JMenuItem jmiCustomIcon = new JMenuItem();
  JMenu jMenu2 = new JMenu();
  JMenuItem jmiYesNo = new JMenuItem();
  JMenuItem jmiYesNoCancel = new JMenuItem();
  JMenuItem jmiOkCancel = new JMenuItem();
  JLabel jlblStatus = new JLabel();
  JMenu jMenu3 = new JMenu();
  JMenuItem jmiTfInput = new JMenuItem();
  JMenuItem jmiCboInput = new JMenuItem();
  JMenuItem jmiLstInput = new JMenuItem();
  JMenu jMenu4 = new JMenu();
  JMenuItem jmiCustomOption = new JMenuItem();

  ImageIcon printImageIcon;

  /** Initialize the applet */
  public void init() {
    try {
      jbInit();
    }
```

Listing 7.5 *TestOptionPane.java*

```
    catch(Exception e) {
      e.printStackTrace();
    }
  }

  /** Component initialization */
  private void jbInit() throws Exception {
    this.setSize(new Dimension(400, 298));
    jMenu1.setText("Message Dialog");
    jmiErrorMessage.setText("Error Message");
    jmiErrorMessage.addActionListener(
      new java.awt.event.ActionListener() {
      public void actionPerformed(ActionEvent e) {
        jmiErrorMessage_actionPerformed(e);
      }
    });
    jmiInformationMessage.setText("Information Message");
    jmiInformationMessage.addActionListener(
      new java.awt.event.ActionListener() {
      public void actionPerformed(ActionEvent e) {
        jmiInformationMessage_actionPerformed(e);
      }
    });
    jmiQuestionMessage.setText("Question Message");
    jmiQuestionMessage.addActionListener(
      new java.awt.event.ActionListener() {
      public void actionPerformed(ActionEvent e) {
        jmiQuestionMessage_actionPerformed(e);
      }
    });
    jmiWarningMessage.setText("Warning Message");
    jmiWarningMessage.addActionListener(
      new java.awt.event.ActionListener() {
      public void actionPerformed(ActionEvent e) {
        jmiWarningMessage_actionPerformed(e);
      }
    });
    jmiPlainMessage.setText("Plain Message");
    jmiPlainMessage.addActionListener(
      new java.awt.event.ActionListener() {
      public void actionPerformed(ActionEvent e) {
        jmiPlainMessage_actionPerformed(e);
      }
    });
    jmiCustomIcon.setText("Custom Icon");
    jmiCustomIcon.addActionListener(
      new java.awt.event.ActionListener() {
      public void actionPerformed(ActionEvent e) {
        jmiCustomIcon_actionPerformed(e);
      }
    });
    jMenu2.setText("Confirmation Dialog");
    jmiYesNo.setText("YES_NO_OPTION");
    jmiYesNo.addActionListener(new java.awt.event.ActionListener() {
      public void actionPerformed(ActionEvent e) {
        jmiYesNo_actionPerformed(e);
      }
    });
    jmiYesNoCancel.setText("YES_NO_CANCEL_OPTION");
```

Listing 7.5 *Continued*

continued

Example 7.5 continued

```
      jmiYesNoCancel.addActionListener(
        new java.awt.event.ActionListener() {
        public void actionPerformed(ActionEvent e) {
          jmiYesNoCancel_actionPerformed(e);
        }
      });
      jmiOkCancel.setText("OK_CANCEL_OPTION");
      jmiOkCancel.addActionListener(
        new java.awt.event.ActionListener() {
        public void actionPerformed(ActionEvent e) {
          jmiOkCancel_actionPerformed(e);
        }
      });
      jMenu3.setText("Input Dialog");
      jmiTfInput.setText("TextField Input");
      jmiTfInput.addActionListener(
        new java.awt.event.ActionListener() {
        public void actionPerformed(ActionEvent e) {
          jmiTfInput_actionPerformed(e);
        }
      });
      jmiCboInput.setText("ComboBox Input");
      jmiCboInput.addActionListener(
        new java.awt.event.ActionListener() {
        public void actionPerformed(ActionEvent e) {
          jmiCboInput_actionPerformed(e);
        }
      });
      jmiLstInput.setText("List Input");
      jmiLstInput.addActionListener(
        new java.awt.event.ActionListener() {
        public void actionPerformed(ActionEvent e) {
          jmiLstInput_actionPerformed(e);
        }
      });
      jMenu4.setText("Option Dialog");
      jmiCustomOption.setText("Custom Option");
      jmiCustomOption.addActionListener(
        new java.awt.event.ActionListener() {
        public void actionPerformed(ActionEvent e) {
          jmiCustomOption_actionPerformed(e);
        }
      });
      jMenuBar1.add(jMenu1);
      jMenuBar1.add(jMenu2);
      jMenuBar1.add(jMenu3);
      jMenuBar1.add(jMenu4);
      jMenu1.add(jmiErrorMessage);
      jMenu1.add(jmiInformationMessage);
      jMenu1.add(jmiQuestionMessage);
      jMenu1.add(jmiWarningMessage);
      jMenu1.add(jmiPlainMessage);
      jMenu1.add(jmiCustomIcon);
      jMenu2.add(jmiYesNo);
      jMenu2.add(jmiYesNoCancel);
      jMenu2.add(jmiOkCancel);
      this.getContentPane().add(jlblStatus, BorderLayout.SOUTH);
      jMenu3.add(jmiTfInput);
      jMenu3.add(jmiCboInput);
      jMenu3.add(jmiLstInput);
```

Listing 7.5 *Continued*

Creating Custom Dialogs

Standard dialogs are sufficient in most cases. Occasionally, you need to create custom dialogs. In Swing, the `JDialog` class can be extended to create custom dialogs. In JBuilder, the Dialog wizard can be used to generate a dialog class.

`JDialog` is a subclass of `java.awt.Dialog` fitted with an instance of `JRootPane`. As with `JFrame`, components are added to the `contentPane` of `JDialog`. Creating a custom dialog usually involves laying out user interface components in the dialog, adding buttons for dismissing the dialog, and installing listeners that respond to button actions.

The standard dialog is *modal*, which means that no other window can be accessed before the dialog is dismissed. However, the custom dialogs derived from `JDialog` are not modal by default. To make the dialog modal, set its `modal` property to `true`. To display an instance of `JDialog`, set its `visible` property to `true`.

Example 7.6 Creating Custom Dialogs

This example demonstrates creating custom dialogs using the Dialog wizard in JBuilder. The example creates a button. When you click the button, a dialog for selecting colors is displayed, as shown in Figure 7.28.

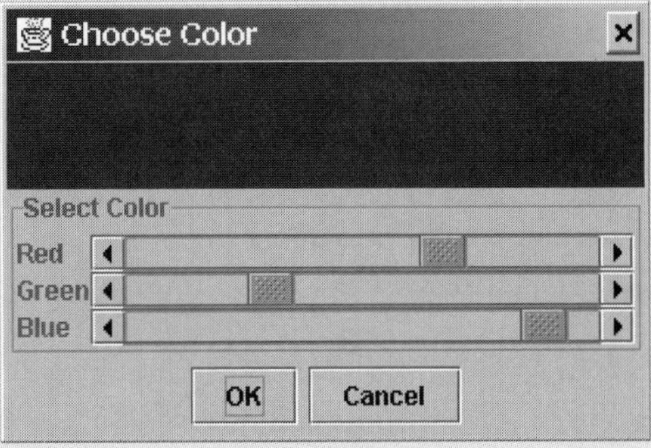

Figure 7.28 *The custom dialog allows you to choose the color from the button's foreground.*

The color dialog can be created as follows:

1. Reopen the project dialogdemo.jpr and double-click the Dialog icon in the Object Gallery to display the Dialog wizard, as shown in Figure 7.29. Enter ColorDialog in the Name field, and click OK to generate ColorDialog.java.

2. Select ColorDialog.java in the navigation pane, click the Design tab to switch to the UI designer. You will see `panel1` in the UI in component tree. `panel1` was created and added to the dialog by the Dialog wizard.

continued

Example 7.6 continued

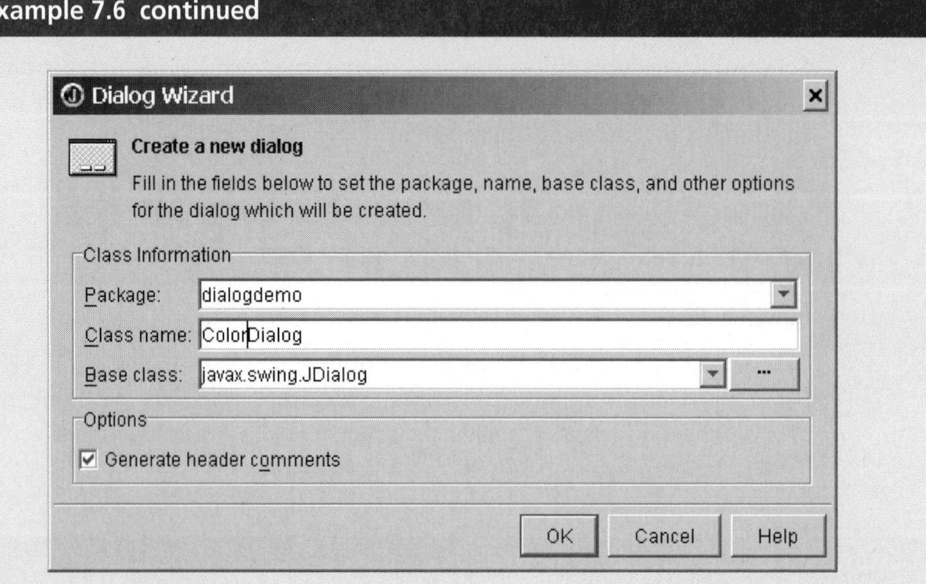

Figure 7.29 *The Dialog wizard can be used to generate custom dialogs.*

3. Drop a `JPanel` to the center of `panel1` to create `jpColor`, and set its `layout` to `BorderLayout`. Drop a `JPanel` to the south of panel to create `jpButtons`, and set its `layout` to `FlowLayout` with left alignment.

4. Drop a `JPanel` to the center of `jpColor` to create `jpSelectedColor`, and drop a `JPanel` to the south of `jpColor` to create `jpSelectColor`. Set the `layout` of `jpSelectColor` to `BorderLayout`. Set the `border` property of `jpSelectColor` to `titledBorder` to create `titledBorder1`, and set the `title` of `titledBorder1` to "Select Color."

5. Drop a `JPanel` to the west of `jpSelectColor` to create `jpLabels`. Drop a `JPanel` to the center of `jpSelectColor` to create `jpScrollBars`.

6. Set the `layout` of `jpLabels` and `jpScrollBar` to `GridLayout` with three rows. Drop three labels to `jpLabels` and three scroll bars to `jpScrollBar`. Rename the scroll bars `jscbRed`, `jscbGreen`, and `jscbBlue`.

7. Declare a variable named `color` of the `Color` type for the currently selected color. Declare variables named `redValue`, `greenValue`, and `blueValue` for the currently selected red, green, and blue colors.

8. Generate and implement the handlers for handling the `adjustmentValueChanged` event in the scroll bars as shown in Listing 7.6 (Lines 116–132). Generate and implement the handlers for handling the action event in the buttons (Lines 134–141).

```
package dialogdemo;

import java.awt.*;
import javax.swing.*;
import javax.swing.border.*;
import java.awt.event.*;

public class ColorDialog extends JDialog {
  JPanel panel1 = new JPanel();
  BorderLayout borderLayout1 = new BorderLayout();
  JPanel jpSelectedColor = new JPanel();
  JPanel jpSelectColor = new JPanel();
  TitledBorder titledBorder1;
  BorderLayout borderLayout2 = new BorderLayout();
  JPanel jpLabels = new JPanel();
  JLabel jLabel1 = new JLabel();
  JLabel jLabel2 = new JLabel();
  JLabel jLabel3 = new JLabel();
  GridLayout gridLayout1 = new GridLayout();
  JPanel jpScrollBars = new JPanel();
  JScrollBar jscbRed = new JScrollBar();
  JScrollBar jscbGreen = new JScrollBar();
  JScrollBar jscbBlue = new JScrollBar();
  GridLayout gridLayout2 = new GridLayout();
  JPanel jpColor = new JPanel();
  BorderLayout borderLayout3 = new BorderLayout();
  JPanel jpButtons = new JPanel();
  JButton jbOK = new JButton();
  JButton jbCancel = new JButton();
  FlowLayout flowLayout1 = new FlowLayout();

  // Declare color component values and selected color
  int redValue, greenValue, blueValue;
  Color color = null;

  public ColorDialog(Frame frame, String title, boolean modal) {
    super(frame, title, modal);
    try {
      jbInit();
      pack();
    }
    catch(Exception ex) {
      ex.printStackTrace();
    }
  }

  public ColorDialog() {
    this(null, "", false);
  }

  void jbInit() throws Exception {
    titledBorder1 = new TitledBorder("");
    panel1.setLayout(borderLayout1);
    jpSelectColor.setBorder(titledBorder1);
    jpSelectColor.setLayout(borderLayout2);
    titledBorder1.setTitle("Select Color");
    jLabel1.setText("Red");
    jLabel2.setText("Green");
    jLabel3.setText("Blue");
```

Listing 7.6 *ColorDialog.java*

continued

Example 7.6 continued

```
    jpLabels.setLayout(gridLayout1);
    gridLayout1.setRows(3);
    jscbRed.setOrientation(JScrollBar.HORIZONTAL);
    jscbRed.addAdjustmentListener(
      new java.awt.event.AdjustmentListener() {
      public void adjustmentValueChanged(AdjustmentEvent e) {
        jscbRed_adjustmentValueChanged(e);
      }
    });
    jscbGreen.setOrientation(JScrollBar.HORIZONTAL);
    jscbGreen.addAdjustmentListener(
      new java.awt.event.AdjustmentListener() {
      public void adjustmentValueChanged(AdjustmentEvent e) {
        jscbGreen_adjustmentValueChanged(e);
      }
    });
    jscbBlue.setOrientation(JScrollBar.HORIZONTAL);
    jscbBlue.addAdjustmentListener(
      new java.awt.event.AdjustmentListener() {
      public void adjustmentValueChanged(AdjustmentEvent e) {
        jscbBlue_adjustmentValueChanged(e);
      }
    });
    jpScrollBars.setLayout(gridLayout2);
    gridLayout2.setRows(3);
    jpColor.setLayout(borderLayout3);
    jbOK.setText("OK");
    jbOK.addActionListener(new java.awt.event.ActionListener() {
      public void actionPerformed(ActionEvent e) {
        jbOK_actionPerformed(e);
      }
    });
    jbCancel.setText("Cancel");
    jbCancel.addActionListener(new java.awt.event.ActionListener() {
      public void actionPerformed(ActionEvent e) {
        jbCancel_actionPerformed(e);
      }
    });
    jpButtons.setLayout(flowLayout1);
    getContentPane().add(panel1);
    panel1.add(jpColor, BorderLayout.CENTER);
    jpColor.add(jpSelectedColor, BorderLayout.CENTER);
    jpColor.add(jpSelectColor, BorderLayout.SOUTH);
    jpSelectColor.add(jpLabels, BorderLayout.WEST);
    jpLabels.add(jLabel1, null);
    jpLabels.add(jLabel2, null);
    jpLabels.add(jLabel3, null);
    jpSelectColor.add(jpScrollBars, BorderLayout.CENTER);
    jpScrollBars.add(jscbRed, null);
    jpScrollBars.add(jscbGreen, null);
    jpScrollBars.add(jscbBlue, null);
    panel1.add(jpButtons, BorderLayout.SOUTH);
    jpButtons.add(jbOK, null);
    jpButtons.add(jbCancel, null);
  }

  void jscbRed_adjustmentValueChanged(AdjustmentEvent e) {
    redValue = jscbRed.getValue();
    color = new Color(redValue, greenValue, blueValue);
```

Listing 7.6 *Continued*

```
      jpSelectedColor.setBackground(color);
    }

    void jscbGreen_adjustmentValueChanged(AdjustmentEvent e) {
      greenValue = jscbGreen.getValue();
      color = new Color(redValue, greenValue, blueValue);
      jpSelectedColor.setBackground(color);
    }

    void jscbBlue_adjustmentValueChanged(AdjustmentEvent e) {
      blueValue = jscbBlue.getValue();
      color = new Color(redValue, greenValue, blueValue);
      jpSelectedColor.setBackground(color);
    }

    void jbOK_actionPerformed(ActionEvent e) {
      setVisible(false);
    }

    void jbCancel_actionPerformed(ActionEvent e) {
      color = null;
      setVisible(false);
    }

    public Dimension getPreferredSize() {
      return new Dimension(200, 200);
    }
  }
```

Listing 7.6 *Continued*

Now you create a test class to use the color dialog, as follows:

1. Reopen the project dialogdemo.jpr and create an applet named `TestCustomDialog` using the Applet wizard.
2. In the UI designer of `TestCustomDialog`, set the `layout` of the applet to `FlowLayout`. Drop a `JButton` in the applet to create `jbtChangeColor`. Set the `text` of the button to "Change Button Text Color."
3. Install `ColorDialog` to the component palette and drop a `ColorDialog` to the applet to create `colorDialog1`. Set the `modal` property of the dialog to `True`.
4. Generate and implement the handler for the button to show the dialog, as shown in Listing 7.7 (Lines 39–44).

```
1     package dialogdemo;
2
3     import java.awt.*;
4     import java.awt.event.*;
5     import java.applet.*;
6     import javax.swing.*;
7
8     public class TestCustomDialog extends JApplet {
9       boolean isStandalone = false;
10      FlowLayout flowLayout1 = new FlowLayout();
```

Listing 7.7 *TestCustomDialog.java*

continued

Example 7.6 continued

```
  JButton jbtChangeColor = new JButton();
  ColorDialog colorDialog1 = new ColorDialog();

  /** Initialize the applet */
  public void init() {
    try {
      jbInit();
    }
    catch(Exception e) {
      e.printStackTrace();
    }
  }

  /** Component initialization */
  private void jbInit() throws Exception {
    jbtChangeColor.setText("Change Button Text Color");
    jbtChangeColor.addActionListener(
      new java.awt.event.ActionListener() {
      public void actionPerformed(ActionEvent e) {
        jbtChangeColor_actionPerformed(e);
      }
    });
    this.setSize(new Dimension(400,300));
    this.getContentPane().setLayout(flowLayout1);
    colorDialog1.setModal(true);
    this.getContentPane().add(jbtChangeColor, null);
  }

  void jbtChangeColor_actionPerformed(ActionEvent e) {
    colorDialog1.setVisible(true);

    if (colorDialog1.color != null)
      jbtChangeColor.setForeground(colorDialog1.color);
  }
}
```

Listing 7.7 *Continued*

Example Review

The custom dialog box allows the user to use the scroll bars to select colors. The selected color is stored in the `color` variable. When the user clicks the Cancel button, color becomes `null`, which implies that no selection has been made.

The dialog box is displayed when the user clicks the "Change Button Text Color" button and is closed when the OK button or the Cancel button is clicked.

TIP

Not setting the dialog modal when needed is a common mistake. In this example, if the dialog is not modal, all the statements in the "Change Button Text Color" button handler are executed before the color is selected from the dialog box.

JColorChooser

You created a color dialog in the previous example. This dialog is a subclass of `JDialog`, which is a subclass of `java.awt.Dialog`. Therefore, it cannot be added to a container as a component. Color dialogs are commonly used in graphics programming. Swing provides a convenient and versatile color dialog named `javax.swing.JColorChooser`. Like `JOptionPane`, `JColorChooser` is a lightweight component inherited from `JComponent`. It can be added to any container. Figure 7.30 shows a `JColorChooser` in an applet.

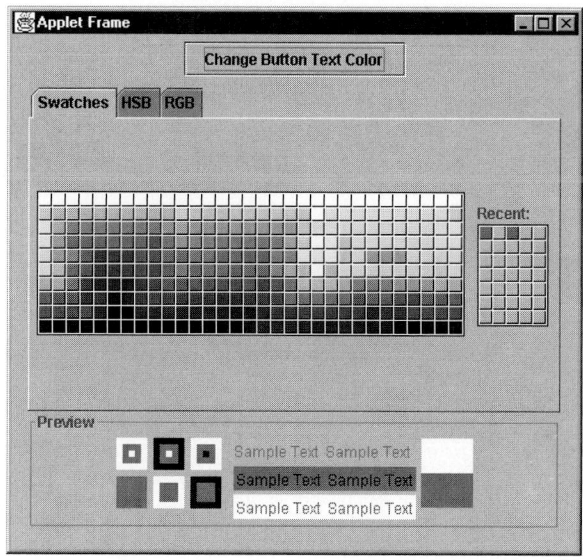

Figure 7.30 *An instance of* `JColorChooser` *is displayed in an applet.*

Often an instance of `JColorChooser` is added to a dialog window to display a color dialog. To display color chooser in a dialog box, use `JColorChooser`'s static `showDialog` method:

```
public static Color showDialog(Component parentComponent,
                               String title,
                               Color initialColor)
```

This method creates an instance of `JDialog` with three buttons, OK, Cancel, and Reset, to hold a `JColorChooser` object, as shown in Figure 7.31. The method displays a modal dialog. If the user clicks the OK button, the method dismisses the dialog and returns the selected color. If the user clicks the Cancel button or closes the dialog, the method dismisses the dialog and returns null.

`JColorChooser` consists of a tabbed pane and a color preview panel. The tabbed pane has three tabs for choosing colors using Swatches, HSB, and RGB, as shown in Figure 7.32. The preview panel shows the effect of the selected color.

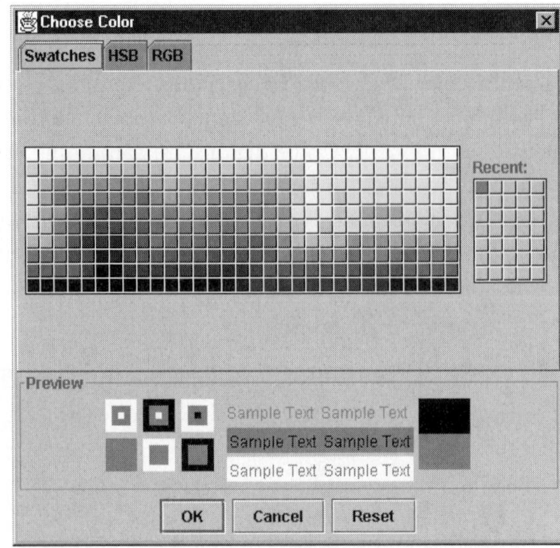

Figure 7.31 *An instance of* `JColorChooser` *is displayed in a dialog box with the OK, Cancel, and Reset buttons.*

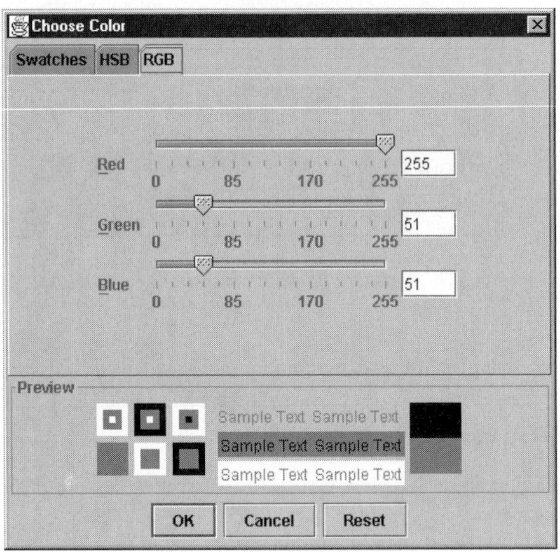

Figure 7.32 *The* `JColorChooser` *class contains a tabbed pane with three tabs for selecting colors using Swatches, HSB, and RGB.*

NOTE

`JColorChooser` is very flexible. It allows you to replace the tabbed pane or the color preview panel with custom components. The default tabbed pane and the color preview panel are sufficient. You rarely need to use custom components.

JFileChooser

Swing provides the `javax.swing.JFileChooser` class that displays a dialog box from which the user can navigate through the file system and select files for loading or saving, as shown in Figure 7.33.

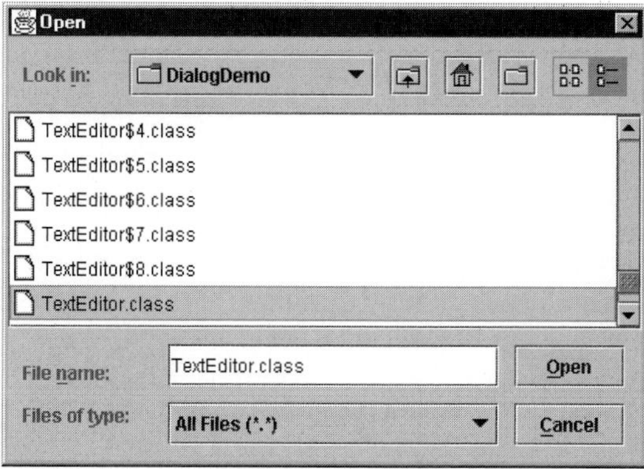

Figure 7.33 *The Swing* `JFileChooser` *shows files and directories, and enables the user to navigate through the file system visually.*

Like `JColorChooser`, `JFileChooser` is a lightweight component inherited from `JComponent`. It can be added to any container if desired, but often you create an instance of `JFileChooser` and display it standalone.

`JFileChooser` is a subclass of `JComponent`. There are several ways to construct a file dialog box. The simplest is to use `JFileChooser`'s default constructor.

The file dialog box can appear in two types: *open* and *save*. The *open type* is for opening a file, and the *save type* is for storing a file. To create an open file dialog, use the following method:

```
public int showOpenDialog(Component parent)
```

This method creates a dialog box that contains an instance of `JFileChooser` for opening a file. The method returns an `int` value, either `APPROVE_OPTION` or `CANCEL_OPTION`, which indicates whether the OK button or the Cancel button was clicked.

Similarly, you can use the following method to create a dialog for saving files.

```
public int showSaveDialog(Component parent)
```

The file dialog box created with the `showOpenDialog` or `showSaveDialog()` is modal. The `JFileChooser` class has the properties inherited from `JComponent`. Additionally, it has the following useful properties:

- `dialogType`: This specifies the type of this dialog. Use `OPEN_DIALOG` when you want to bring up a file chooser that the user can use to open a file. Likewise, use `SAVE_DIALOG` to let the user choose a file for saving.

- `dialogTitle`: The string that is displayed in the title bar of the dialog box.
- `currentDirectory`: This is the current directory of the file. The type of this property is `java.io.File`. If you want the current directory to be used, use `setCurrentDirectory(new File("."))`.
- `SelectedFile`: This is the file you have selected. You can use `getSelectedFile()` to return the selected file from the dialog box. The type of this property is `java.io.File`. If you have a default file name that you expect to use, use `setSelectedFile(new File(filename))`.
- `selectedFiles`: This is a list of the files selected if the file chooser is set to allow multi-selection. The type of this property is `File[]`.
- `multiSelectionEnabled`: This is a `boolean` value indicating whether multiple files can be selected. By default, it is `false`.

Example 7.7 Creating a Text Editor

This example uses Swing menus, tool bar, file chooser, and color chooser to create a simple text editor, as shown in Figure 7.34, which allows the user to open and save text files, clear text, and change the color and font of the text.

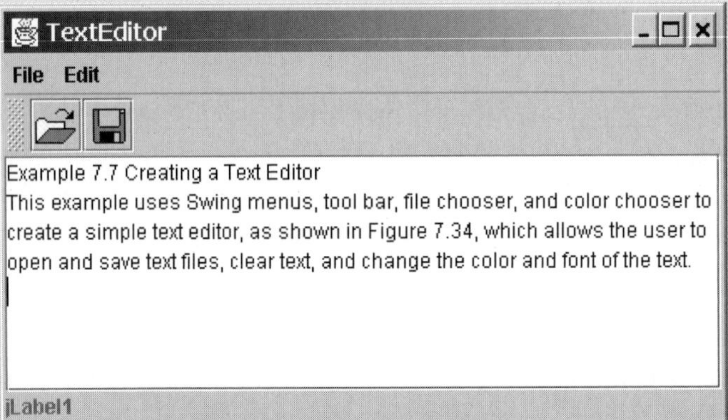

Figure 7.34 *The editor enables you to open and save text files from the File menu or from the tool bar, and to change the color and font of the text from the Edit menu.*

Follow the steps below to complete the project.

1. Reopen the project dialogdemo.jpr and create an applet named `TextEditor` using the Applet wizard.
2. With TextEditor.java selected in the navigation pane, switch to the UI designer in the content pane. Drop a `JScrollPane` to the center of the applet, and drop a `JTextArea` to the scroll pane and name it `jta`.

3. Drop a `JToolBar` to the north of the applet to create `jToolBar1`. Drop a `JButton` twice to `jToolBar1` to create `jbtOpen` and `jbtSave`. Drop a `JLabel` to the south of the applet to create `jlblStatus`.

4. Select the UI node and drop a `JFileChooser` from the Swing Containers page to the UI node to create an instance of `jFileChooser1`.

5. Drop a `JMenuBar` to the applet to create `jMenuBar1`. Right-click the inspector for the applet to display hidden properties. Set the `JMenuBar` property to `jMenuBar1`.

6. Double-click `jMenuBar1` to switch to the Menu designer. Add the menus File and Edit. In the File menu, add the menu items Open, Save, and Clear. In the Edit menu, add the menu items Foreground Color and Background Color. Rename the menu items `jmiOpen`, `jmiSave`, `jmiClear`, `jmiExit`, `jmiForeground`, and `jmiBackground`.

7. Switch to the source code editor, declare and create image icons named `openImageIcon` and `saveImageIcon`. Set the `icon` property of `jtbOpen` and `jmiOpen` to `openImageIcon`, and the `icon` property of `jtbSave` and `jmiSave` to `saveImageIcon`.

8. Generate the action event handlers for buttons and menu items. Implement the handlers, as shown in Listing 7.8.

```
package dialogdemo;

import java.awt.*;
import java.awt.event.*;
import java.applet.*;
import javax.swing.*;
import java.io.*;
import imageviewerdemo.ImageViewer;

public class TextEditor extends JApplet {
  boolean isStandalone = false;
  JToolBar jToolBar1 = new JToolBar();
  JButton jbtOpen = new JButton();
  JButton jbtSave = new JButton();
  JScrollPane jScrollPane1 = new JScrollPane();
  JTextArea jta = new JTextArea();
  JMenuBar jMenuBar1 = new JMenuBar();
  JMenu jMenu1 = new JMenu();
  JMenuItem jmiOpen = new JMenuItem();
  JMenuItem jmiSave = new JMenuItem();
  JMenuItem jmiClear = new JMenuItem();
  JMenuItem jmiExit = new JMenuItem();
  JMenu jMenu2 = new JMenu();
  JMenuItem jmiForeground = new JMenuItem();
  JMenuItem jmiBackground = new JMenuItem();
  JFileChooser jFileChooser1 = new JFileChooser();
  JLabel jlblStatus = new JLabel();

```

Listing 7.8 *TextEditor.java*

continued

Example 7.7 continued

```
  // Declare image icons
  ImageIcon openImageIcon;
  ImageIcon saveImageIcon;

  /** Initialize the applet */
  public void init() {
    try {
      jbInit();
    }
    catch(Exception e) {
      e.printStackTrace();
    }
  }

  /** Component initialization */
  private void jbInit() throws Exception {
    // Create image icons
    openImageIcon = ImageViewer.createImageIcon(
      "/image/open.gif", this);
    saveImageIcon = ImageViewer.createImageIcon(
      "/image/save.gif", this);

    this.setJMenuBar(jMenuBar1);
    this.setSize(new Dimension(400,300));
    jta.setWrapStyleWord(true);
    jta.setLineWrap(true);
    jta.setText("jTextArea1");
    jbtOpen.setIcon(openImageIcon);
    jbtOpen.addActionListener(new java.awt.event.ActionListener() {
      public void actionPerformed(ActionEvent e) {
        jbtOpen_actionPerformed(e);
      }
    });
    jbtSave.setIcon(saveImageIcon);
    jbtSave.addActionListener(new java.awt.event.ActionListener() {
      public void actionPerformed(ActionEvent e) {
        jbtSave_actionPerformed(e);
      }
    });
    jMenu1.setText("File");
    jmiOpen.setIcon(openImageIcon);
    jmiOpen.setText("Open");
    jmiOpen.addActionListener(new java.awt.event.ActionListener() {
      public void actionPerformed(ActionEvent e) {
        jmiOpen_actionPerformed(e);
      }
    });
    jmiSave.setIcon(saveImageIcon);
    jmiSave.setText("Save");
    jmiSave.addActionListener(new java.awt.event.ActionListener() {
      public void actionPerformed(ActionEvent e) {
        jmiSave_actionPerformed(e);
      }
    });
    jmiClear.setText("Clear");
    jmiClear.addActionListener(new java.awt.event.ActionListener() {
      public void actionPerformed(ActionEvent e) {
```

Listing 7.8 *Continued*

```
        jmiClear_actionPerformed(e);
      }
    });
    jmiExit.setText("Exit");
    jmiExit.addActionListener(new java.awt.event.ActionListener() {
      public void actionPerformed(ActionEvent e) {
        jmiExit_actionPerformed(e);
      }
    });
    jMenu2.setText("Edit");
    jmiForeground.setText("Foreground Color");
    jmiForeground.addActionListener(
      new java.awt.event.ActionListener() {
      public void actionPerformed(ActionEvent e) {
        jmiForeground_actionPerformed(e);
      }
    });
    jmiBackground.setText("Background Color");
    jmiBackground.addActionListener(
      new java.awt.event.ActionListener() {
      public void actionPerformed(ActionEvent e) {
        jmiBackground_actionPerformed(e);
      }
    });
    jlblStatus.setText("jLabel1");
    this.getContentPane().add(jToolBar1, BorderLayout.NORTH);
    jToolBar1.add(jbtOpen, null);
    jToolBar1.add(jbtSave, null);
    this.getContentPane().add(jScrollPane1, BorderLayout.CENTER);
    this.getContentPane().add(jlblStatus, BorderLayout.SOUTH);
    jScrollPane1.getViewport().add(jta, null);
    jMenuBar1.add(jMenu1);
    jMenuBar1.add(jMenu2);
    jMenu1.add(jmiOpen);
    jMenu1.add(jmiSave);
    jMenu1.add(jmiClear);
    jMenu1.addSeparator();
    jMenu1.add(jmiExit);
    jMenu2.add(jmiForeground);
    jMenu2.add(jmiBackground);

    // Set current directory
    jFileChooser1.setCurrentDirectory(new File("."));
  }

  void jmiOpen_actionPerformed(ActionEvent e) {
    open();
  }

  void jbtOpen_actionPerformed(ActionEvent e) {
    open();
  }

  void jmiSave_actionPerformed(ActionEvent e) {
    save();
  }

  void jmiClear_actionPerformed(ActionEvent e) {
    jta.setText(null);
  }

```

Listing 7.8 *TextEditor.java*

continued

Example 7.7 continued

```
  void jmiExit_actionPerformed(ActionEvent e) {
    System.exit(0);
  }

  void jbtSave_actionPerformed(ActionEvent e) {
    save();
  }

  void jmiForeground_actionPerformed(ActionEvent e) {
    Color selectedColor =
      JColorChooser.showDialog(this, "Choose Foreground Color",
        jta.getForeground());

    if (selectedColor != null)
      jta.setForeground(selectedColor);
  }

  void jmiBackground_actionPerformed(ActionEvent e) {
    Color selectedColor =
      JColorChooser.showDialog(this, "Choose Background Color",
        jta.getForeground());

    if (selectedColor != null)
      jta.setBackground(selectedColor);
  }

  /** Open file */
  private void open() {
    if (jFileChooser1.showOpenDialog(this) ==
      JFileChooser.APPROVE_OPTION) {
      open(jFileChooser1.getSelectedFile());
    }
  }

  /** Open file with the specified File instance */
  private void open(File file) {
    try {
      // Read from the specified file and store it in jta
      BufferedInputStream in = new BufferedInputStream(
        new FileInputStream(file));
      byte[] b = new byte[in.available()];
      in.read(b, 0, b.length);
      jta.append(new String(b, 0, b.length));
      in.close();

      // Display the status of the Open file operation in jlblStatus
      jlblStatus.setText(file.getName() + " Opened");
    }
    catch (IOException ex) {
      jlblStatus.setText("Error opening " + file.getName());
    }
  }

  /** Save file */
  private void save() {
```

Listing 7.8 *Continued*

```
    if (jFileChooser1.showSaveDialog(this) ==
      JFileChooser.APPROVE_OPTION) {
      save(jFileChooser1.getSelectedFile());
    }
  }

  /** Save file with specified File instance */
  private void save(File file) {
    try {
      // Write the text in jta to the specified file
      BufferedOutputStream out = new BufferedOutputStream(
        new FileOutputStream(file));
      byte[] b = (jta.getText()).getBytes();
      out.write(b, 0, b.length);
      out.close();

      // Display the status of the save file operation in jlblStatus
      jlblStatus.setText(file.getName()  + " Saved ");
    }
    catch (IOException ex) {
      jlblStatus.setText("Error saving " + file.getName());
    }
  }
}
```

Listing 7.8 *Continued*

Example Review

The program creates the File and Edit menus. The File menu contains the menu commands Open for loading a file, Save for saving a file, Clear for clearing the text editor, and Exit for terminating the program. The Edit menu contains the menu commands Foreground Color and Background Color for setting foreground color and background color in the text. The Open and Save menu commands can also be accessed by the tool bar. The status of executing Open and Save is displayed in the status label.

An instance `jFileChooser1` of `JFileChooser` is created for displaying the file dialog box to open and save files. The `setCurrentDirectory(new File("."))` method is used to set the current directory to the directory where the class is stored.

The `open` method is invoked when the user clicks the Open menu command. The `showOpenDialog` method displays an Open dialog box, as shown in Figure 7.33. Upon receiving the selected file, the method `open(file)` is invoked to load the file to the text area using a `BufferedInputStream` wrapped on a `FileInputStream`.

The `save` method is invoked when the user clicks the Save menu command. The `showSaveDialog` method displays a Save dialog box. Upon receiving the selected file, the method `save(file)` is invoked to save the contents from the text area to the file using a `BufferedOutputStream` wrapped on a `FileOutputStream`.

Example 7.7 continued

The color dialog is displayed using the static method `showDialog` of `JColorChooser`. Thus you don't need to create an instance of `JFileChooser`. The `showDialog` method returns the selected color if the OK button is clicked after a color is selected.

Chapter Summary

You learned how to create menus visually using JBuilder's Menu designer and how to create tool bars using `JToolBar`. You learned how to display standard dialogs using `JOptionPane`, how to create custom dialog by directly extending the `JDialog` class, and how to use `JColorChooser` and `JFileChooser` for selecting colors and files.

Review Questions

7.1 How do you display the Menu designer? How do you switch to the UI designer from the Menu designer?

7.2 How do you create a submenu? How do you create a check box menu item? How do you create a radio button menu item?

7.3 How do you display the `JMenuBar` property of `JFrame`, `JApplet`, or `JDialog` in the component inspector?

7.4 How do you create a popup menu in JBuilder? How do you show a popup menu? Describe popup trigger.

7.5 Describe the standard dialog boxes created using the `JOptionPane` class.

7.6 How do you create a message dialog? What are the message types? What is the button in the message dialog?

7.7 How do you create a confirmation dialog? What are button option types?

7.8 How do you create an input dialog with a text field for entering input? How do you create a combo box dialog for selecting values as input? How do you create a list dialog for selecting values as input?

7.9 How do you show an instance of `JDialog`? Is a standard dialog box created using the static methods in `JOptionPane` modal? Is an instance of `JDialog` modal?

7.10 How do you display an instance of `JColorChooser`? Is an instance of `JColorChooser` modal? How do you obtain the selected color?

7.11 How do you display an instance of `JFileChooser`? Is an instance of `JFileChooser` modal? How do you obtain the selected file?

Programming Exercises

7.1 Write a program to calculate the future value of an investment at a given interest rate for a specified number of years. The formula for the calculation is as follows:

```
futureValue = investmentAmount * (1 + monthlyInterestRate)^(years x 12)
```

Use text fields for interest rate, investment amount, and years. Display the future amount in a text field when the user clicks the Calculate button or chooses Calculate from the Operation menu (see Figure 7.35). Show a message dialog box when the user clicks the About menu item from the Help menu.

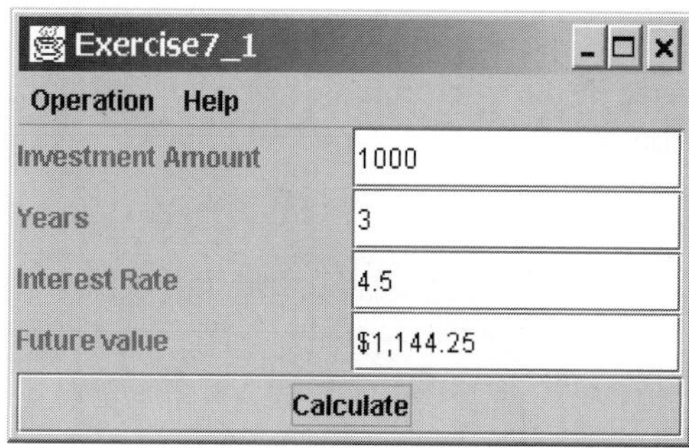

Figure 7.35 *The user enters the investment amount, years, and interest rate to compute future value.*

7.2 Write a program to emulate a paint utility. Your program should enable the user to choose options and draw shapes or get characters from the keyboard based on the selected options (see Figure 7.36). The options are displayed in a tool bar. To draw a line, the user first clicks the line icon in the tool bar and then uses the mouse to draw a line in the same way you would draw using Microsoft Paint.

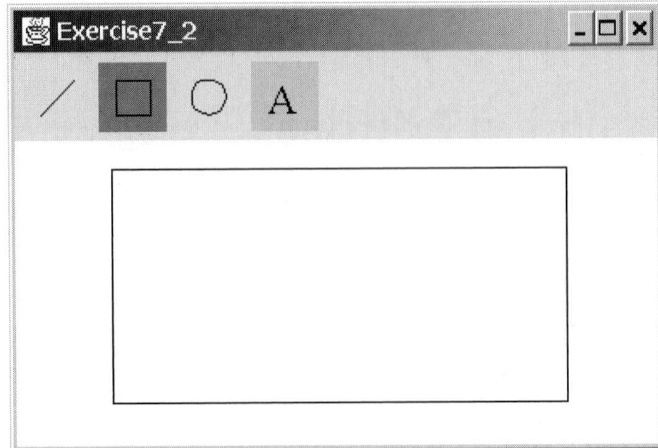

Figure 7.36 *This exercise produces a prototype drawing utility that enables you to draw lines, rectangles, ovals, and characters.*

7.3 JBuilder displays a dialog for choosing fonts when you click the `font` property in the inspector, as shown in Figure 7.37. Create this dialog as an exercise.

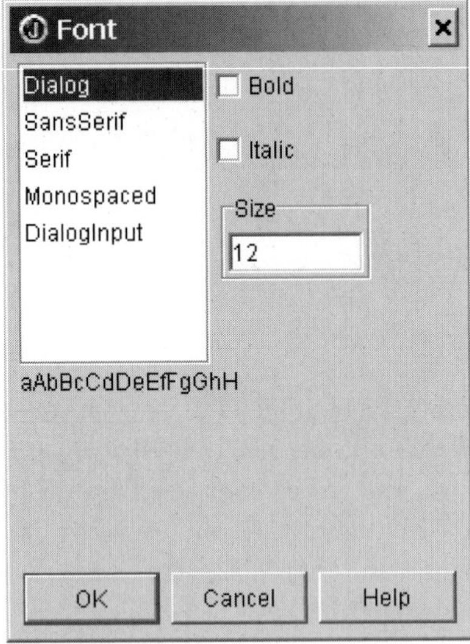

Figure 7.37 *The font dialog box allows you to choose a font by specifying font name, font style, and font size.*

CHAPTER 8

ADVANCED SWING COMPONENTS

Objectives

- Use `JList` to select single or multiple items in a list.
- Use `JComboBox` to select a single item from a combo box.
- Use `JTable` to display and process tables.
- Use `JTree` to display data in a tree hierarchy.
- Learn how to create custom renderers for `JList`, `JComboBox`, `JTable`, and `JTree`.
- Learn how to create custom editors for `JComboBox`, `JTable`, and `JTree`.

Introduction

In the preceding three chapters, you learned how to use Swing components, containers, layout managers, menus, tool bars, and dialog boxes. This chapter will show you how to work with some of the complex Swing components. You will learn how to use `JList`, `JComboBox`, `JTable`, and `JTree` to create advanced graphical user interfaces.

JList

A *list* is a component that enables you to choose one or more items. It is useful in limiting a range of choices and avoids the cumbersome validation of data input. `JList` is the Swing version of a list. Functionally it is similar to a set of check boxes or radio buttons, but the selectable items are placed in a list and are chosen by clicking on the items themselves. Figure 8.1 shows an example of `JList`.

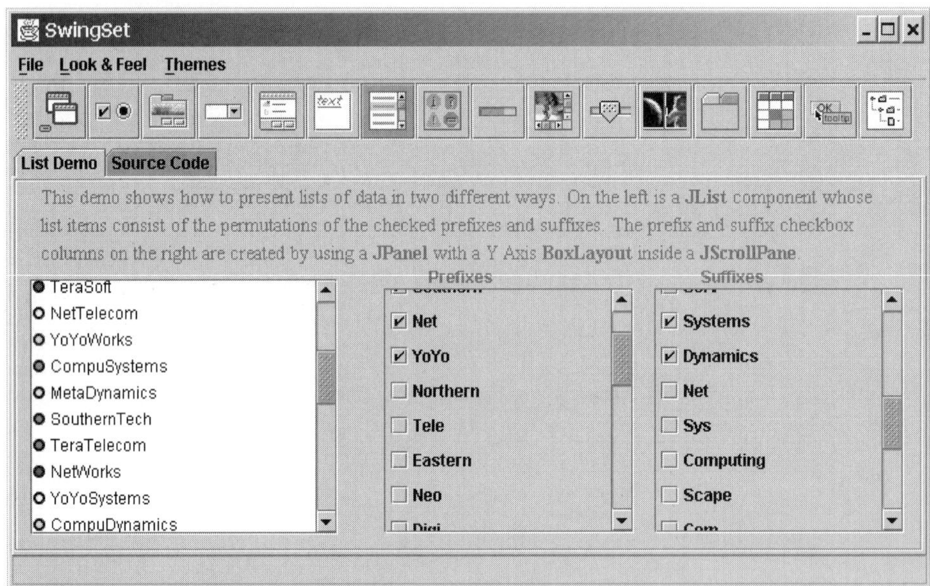

Figure 8.1 *SwingSet2 demonstrates the features of* `JList`.

`JList` doesn't support scrolling directly. To create a scrollable list, you need to create a `JScrollPane` and add an instance of `JList` to it. An instance of `JList` can be created using its default constructor or one of these three constructors:

- `public JList(ListModel dataModel)`
- `public JList(Object[] listData)`
- `public JList(Vector listData)`

If you have a list of a fixed number of string items, an instance of `JList` can easily be created as follows:

```
String[] listData = {"Item 1", "Item 2", "Item 3"};
JList jlst = new JList(listData);
```

`JList` supports three selection modes: single selection, single-interval selection, and multiple-interval selection. *Single selection* allows only one item to be selected. *Single-interval selection* allows multiple selections, but the selected items must be contiguous. *Multiple-interval selection* is the most flexible, because it allows selections of any items.

`JList` has the following useful properties:

- `cellRenderer`: This is an object used to render the cells in a list. By default, an instance of `DefaultListCellRenderer` is used to display items in a list that can display strings or icons. Using custom cell renderer is introduced in the section "List Cell Renderers."
- `listData`: This is a write-only property used to set an array or a vector of objects for the list.
- `fixedCellHeight`: This specifies the height of a list cell. All the cells in a list have the same height. If this property is not specified, the tallest item in the list dictates the cell height for all the cells.
- `fixedCellWidth`: This specifies the width of a list cell. All the cells in a list have the same width. If this property is not specified, the widest item in the list dictates the cell width for all the cells.
- `model`: This is an object that maintains the data for the list. List models must be used explicitly when adding or deleting items in a list. List models are introduced in the section "List Models."
- `prototypeCellValue`: This is an object whose cell size dictates the cell size of the list.
- `selectedIndex`: This is an `int` value indicating the index of the selected item in the list.
- `selectedIndices`: This is an array of `int` values representing the indices of the selected items in the list.
- `selectedValue`: This is the first selected value in the list.
- `selectedValues`: This is an array of objects representing selected values in the list. This property is read-only.
- `selectionBackground`: This is the background color for selected cells.
- `selectionForeground`: This is the foreground color for selected cells.
- `selectionMode`: This is one of the three values (`SINGLE_SELECTION`, `SINGLE_INTERVAL_SELECTION`, `MULTIPLE_INTERVAL_SELECTION`) that indicate whether single items, single-interval items, or multiple-interval items can be selected.

- `selectionModel`: This is an object that tracks list selection. List-selection models are rarely used explicitly. They are discussed in the section "List-Selection Models."
- `visibleRowCount`: This is the preferred number of rows in the list that can be displayed without a scroll bar. The default value is 8.

`JList` generates `javax.swing.event.ListSelectionEvent` to notify the listeners of the selections. The listener must implement the `valueChanged` handler to process the event.

Example 8.1 Simple List Demo

This example creates a list of a fixed number of items displayed as strings. The example allows you to set a selection mode dynamically from a combo box, as shown in Figure 8.2. When you select one or more items, their values are displayed in a status label below the list.

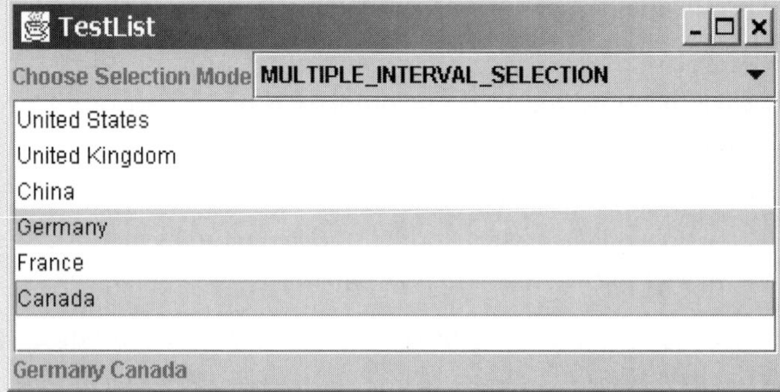

Figure 8.2 *You can choose single selection, single-interval selection, or multiple-interval selection in a list.*

Here are the steps to complete the project:

1. Create a new project named listdemo.jpr and a new applet named TestList.java using the Applet wizard.
2. In the UI designer of TestList.java, drop a `JPanel` to the north of the applet to create `jpSelectionMode`. Drop a `JScrollPane` to the center of the applet, and drop a `JList` to the scroll pane to create `jList1`. Drop a `JLabel` to the south of the applet to create `jlblStatus`.
3. Set `layout` of `jpSelectionMode` to `BorderLayout`. Drop a `JLabel` and a `JComboBox` to `jpSelectionMode`, and rename the combo box `jcboSelectionMode`.
4. Create an array of strings named `countries` for the names of several countries. Add countries to the list using the following method:

```
jList1.setListData(countries);
```

5. Add three items "SINGLE_SELECTION," "SINGLE_INTERVAL_SELECTION," and "MULTIPLE_INTERVAL_SELECTION" to the combo box using the `addItem` method (Lines 61–64).

6. Generate the `ActionEvent` handler for the combo box, and implement it to set a selection mode for the list, as shown in Listing 8.1 (Lines 67–80).

7. Generate the `ListSelectionEvent` handler for the list, and implement it to display the selected items in the label, as shown in Listing 8.1 (Lines 82–93).

```
1  package listdemo;
2
3  import java.awt.*;
4  import java.awt.event.*;
5  import javax.swing.*;
6  import javax.swing.event.*;
7
8  public class TestList extends JApplet {
9    boolean isStandalone = false;
10   JScrollPane jScrollPane1 = new JScrollPane();
11   JList jList1 = new JList();
12
13   JPanel jpSelectionMode = new JPanel();
14   JComboBox jcboSelectionMode = new JComboBox();
15   JLabel jlblStatus = new JLabel();
16
17   JLabel jLabel1 = new JLabel();
18   BorderLayout borderLayout1 = new BorderLayout();
19
20   // Create an array of strings for country names
21   String[] countries = {"United States", "United Kingdom", "China",
22     "Germany", "France", "Canada"};
23
24   /** Initialize the applet */
25   public void init() {
26     try {
27       jbInit();
28     }
29     catch(Exception e) {
30       e.printStackTrace();
31     }
32   }
33
34   /** Component initialization */
35   private void jbInit() throws Exception {
36     this.setSize(new Dimension(400, 300));
37
38     jList1.setListData(countries);
39     jList1.addListSelectionListener(
40       new javax.swing.event.ListSelectionListener() {
41       public void valueChanged(ListSelectionEvent e) {
42         jList1_valueChanged(e);
43       }
44     });
45     jpSelectionMode.setLayout(borderLayout1);
46     jcboSelectionMode.addActionListener(
47       new java.awt.event.ActionListener() {
```

Listing 8.1 *TestList.java*

continued

Example 8.1 continued

```
        public void actionPerformed(ActionEvent e) {
          jcboSelectionMode_actionPerformed(e);
        }
      });
      jlblStatus.setText("Status");
      jLabel1.setText("Choose Selection Mode");
      this.getContentPane().add(jScrollPane1, BorderLayout.CENTER);
      jScrollPane1.getViewport().add(jList1, null);
      this.getContentPane().add(jpSelectionMode, BorderLayout.NORTH);
      jpSelectionMode.add(jLabel1, BorderLayout.WEST);
      jpSelectionMode.add(jcboSelectionMode, BorderLayout.CENTER);
      this.getContentPane().add(jlblStatus, BorderLayout.SOUTH);

      // Add selection modes to the combo box
      jcboSelectionMode.addItem("SINGLE_SELECTION");
      jcboSelectionMode.addItem("SINGLE_INTERVAL_SELECTION");
      jcboSelectionMode.addItem("MULTIPLE_INTERVAL_SELECTION");
    }

    /** Handle item selection from a combo box */
    void jcboSelectionMode_actionPerformed(ActionEvent e) {
      String selectedMode =
        (String)jcboSelectionMode.getSelectedItem();

      if (selectedMode.equals("SINGLE_SELECTION"))
        jList1.setSelectionMode(ListSelectionModel.SINGLE_SELECTION);
      else if (selectedMode.equals("SINGLE_INTERVAL_SELECTION"))
        jList1.setSelectionMode(
          ListSelectionModel.SINGLE_INTERVAL_SELECTION);
      if (selectedMode.equals("MULTIPLE_INTERVAL_SELECTION"))
        jList1.setSelectionMode(
          ListSelectionModel.MULTIPLE_INTERVAL_SELECTION);
    }

    /** Handle item selection in the list */
    void jList1_valueChanged(ListSelectionEvent e) {
      int[] indices = jList1.getSelectedIndices();
      Object[] selectedItems = jList1.getSelectedValues();
      String display = "";

      for (int i=0; i<indices.length; i++) {
        display += (String)selectedItems[i] + " ";
      }

      jlblStatus.setText(display);
    }
  }
```

Listing 8.1 *Continued*

Example Review

The program creates an array of strings and sets the array as `listData` in the list. The list is placed in a scroll pane so that you can scroll it when the number of items in the list exceeds the viewing area.

When the user selects an item in the list, the `valueChanged` handler is executed, which gets the selected items and displays all the items in the label.

The example enables you to specify selection mode from a combo box. When you choose SINGLE_SELECTION, only one item can be selected at a given time. When you choose SINGLE_INTERVAL_SELECTION, multiple consecutive items can be selected all together by holding down the SHIFT key. When you choose MULTIPLE_INTERVAL_SELECTION, you can choose any number of items anywhere in the list by holding down the CTRL key.

List Models

The preceding example constructs a list with a fixed set of strings. If you want to add new items to the list or delete existing items, you have to use a list model. This section introduces list models.

The `JList` class delegates the responsibilities of storing and maintaining data to its data model. The `JList` class itself does not have methods for adding or removing items from the list. These methods are supported in the list model.

All list models implement the `ListModel` interface, which defines the registration methods for `ListDataEvent`. The instances of `ListDataListener` are notified when the items in the list are modified. `ListModel` also defines the methods `getSize` and `getElementAt`. The `getSize` method returns the length of the list, and the `getElementAt` method returns the element at the specified index.

`AbstractListModel` implements the `ListModel` and `Serializable` interfaces. `AbstractListModel` implements the registration methods in the `ListModel`, but does not implement the `getSize` and `getElementAt` methods.

`DefaultListModel` extends `AbstractListModel` and implements the two methods `getSize` and `getElementAt`, which are not implemented by `AbstractListModel`. The relationship among `ListModel`, `AbstractListModel`, and `DefaultListModel` is shown in Figure 8.3.

The methods in `DefaultListModel` are similar to those in the `java.util.Vector` class. You use the `add` method to insert an element to the list, the `remove` method to remove an element from the list, the `clear` method to clear the list, the `getSize` method to return the number of elements in the list, and the `getElementAt` method to retrieve an element. In fact, the `DefaultListModel` stores data in an instance of `Vector`, which is essentially a resizable array. Swing components were developed before the Java Collections Framework. In the future implementation, `Vector` may be replaced by `java.util.ArrayList`.

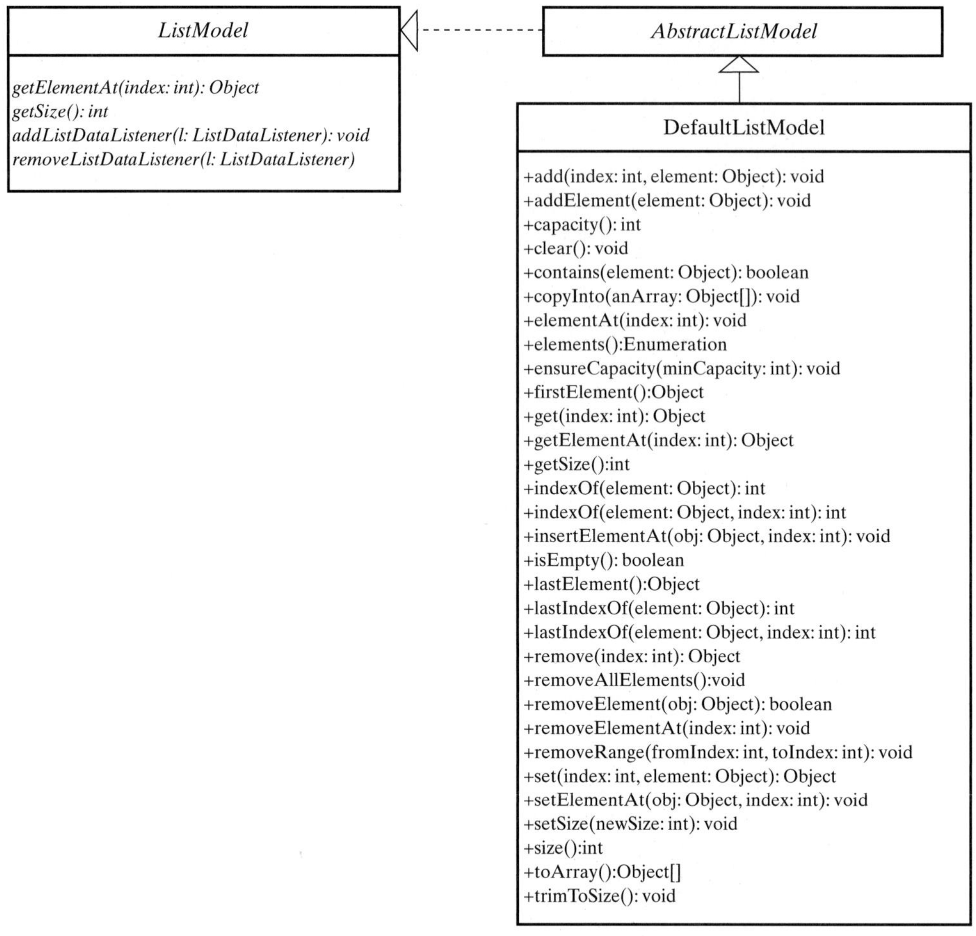

Figure 8.3 `DefaultListModel` *is a concrete implementation of* `ListModel`.

Example 8.2 List Model Demo

This example creates a list using a list model and allows the user to add and delete items in the list. A sample run of the program is shown in Figure 8.4.

Here are the steps to complete the project:

1. Reopen project listdemo.jpr and create a new applet named TestListModel.java using the Applet wizard.

2. In the UI designer of TestListModel.java, drop a `JPanel` to the north of the applet to create `jpSettings`. Drop a `JScrollPane` to the center of the applet, and drop a `JList` to the scroll pane to create `jList1`. Drop a `JLabel` to the south of the applet to create `jlblStatus`.

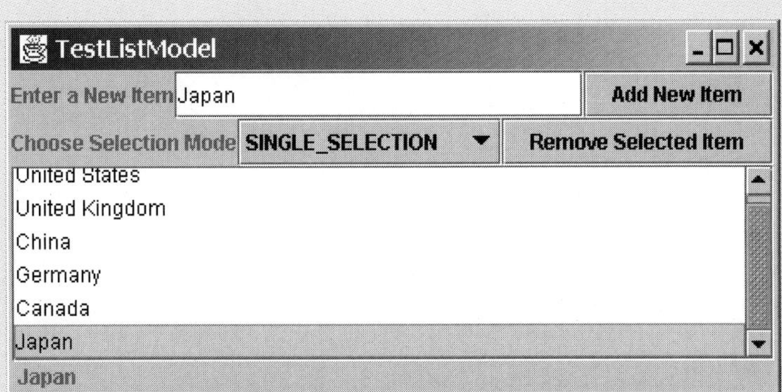

Figure 8.4 *You can add elements and remove elements in a list using list models.*

3. Set `layout` of `jpSettings` to `BorderLayout`, and drop a `JPanel` to the north and a `JPanel` to the south of `jpSettings` to create `jpAdd` and `jpRemove`. Set `layout` of `jpAdd` and `jpRemove` to `BorderLayout`. Drop a `JLabel`, a `JTextField`, and a `JButton` to the east, center, and west of `jpAdd`, and rename the text field and button `jtfNewItem` and `jbtAdd`. Drop a `JLabel`, a `JComboBox`, and a `JButton` to the east, center, and west of `jpRemove`, and rename the combo box and button `jcboSelectionMode` and `jbtRemove`.

4. Switch to the source pane to create an instance of `DefaultListModel` named `listModel`, and add items to the model using `listModel.addElement()`, as shown in Listing 8.2 (Lines 88–94). Add three items "SINGLE_SELECTION," SINGLE_INTERVAL_SELECTION," and "MULTIPLE_INTERVAL_SELECTION" to the combo box `jcboSelectionMode` (Lines 96–99).

5. Switch to the UI designer and set the `model` property of `jList1` to `listModel`.

6. Generate the `ActionEvent` handlers for the combo box, the Add New Item button, and the Remove Selected Item button, and implement these handlers for setting a selection mode, adding a new element, and deleting elements in the list, as shown in Listing 8.2.

7. Generate the `ListSelectionEvent` handler for the list and implement it to display the selected items in the label, as shown in Listing 8.2 (Lines 131–142).

```
1    package listdemo;
2
3    import java.awt.*;
4    import java.awt.event.*;
5    import javax.swing.*;
6    import javax.swing.event.*;
7
8    public class TestListModel extends JApplet {
9      boolean isStandalone = false;
10     JScrollPane jScrollPane1 = new JScrollPane();
11     JList jList1 = new JList();
```

Listing 8.2 *TestListModel.java*

continued

Example 8.2 continued

```
  JPanel jpSettings = new JPanel();
  JLabel jLabel1 = new JLabel();
  JTextField jtfNewItem = new JTextField();
  JButton jbtAdd = new JButton();
  JButton jbtRemove = new JButton();
  JPanel jpAdd = new JPanel();
  JPanel jpRemove = new JPanel();
  JComboBox jcboSelectionMode = new JComboBox();
  BorderLayout borderLayout1 = new BorderLayout();
  BorderLayout borderLayout2 = new BorderLayout();
  BorderLayout borderLayout3 = new BorderLayout();
  JLabel jlblStatus = new JLabel();
  JLabel jLabel2 = new JLabel();

  // Create a list model
  DefaultListModel listModel = new DefaultListModel();

  /** Initialize the applet */
  public void init() {
    try {
      jbInit();
    }
    catch(Exception e) {
      e.printStackTrace();
    }
  }

  /** Component initialization */
  private void jbInit() throws Exception {
    this.setSize(new Dimension(400, 300));
    jLabel1.setText("Enter a New Item");
    jbtAdd.setText("Add New Item");
    jbtAdd.addActionListener(new java.awt.event.ActionListener() {
      public void actionPerformed(ActionEvent e) {
        jbtAdd_actionPerformed(e);
      }
    });
    jbtRemove.setText("Remove Selected Item");
    jbtRemove.addActionListener(
      new java.awt.event.ActionListener() {
      public void actionPerformed(ActionEvent e) {
        jbtRemove_actionPerformed(e);
      }
    });

    jList1.setModel(listModel);
    jList1.addListSelectionListener(
      new javax.swing.event.ListSelectionListener() {
      public void valueChanged(ListSelectionEvent e) {
        jList1_valueChanged(e);
      }
    });
    jpAdd.setLayout(borderLayout1);
    jpSettings.setLayout(borderLayout2);
    jpRemove.setLayout(borderLayout3);
    jcboSelectionMode.addActionListener(
      new java.awt.event.ActionListener() {
      public void actionPerformed(ActionEvent e) {
        jcboSelectionMode_actionPerformed(e);
      }
```

Listing 8.2 *Continued*

```
    });
    jlblStatus.setText("Status");
    jLabel2.setText("Choose Selection Mode");
    this.getContentPane().add(jScrollPane1, BorderLayout.CENTER);
    jScrollPane1.getViewport().add(jList1, null);
    this.getContentPane().add(jpSettings, BorderLayout.NORTH);
    jpSettings.add(jpRemove, BorderLayout.SOUTH);
    jpRemove.add(jcboSelectionMode, BorderLayout.CENTER);
    jpRemove.add(jbtRemove, BorderLayout.EAST);
    jpRemove.add(jLabel2, BorderLayout.WEST);
    jpSettings.add(jpAdd, BorderLayout.NORTH);
    jpAdd.add(jLabel1, BorderLayout.WEST);
    jpAdd.add(jtfNewItem, BorderLayout.CENTER);
    jpAdd.add(jbtAdd, BorderLayout.EAST);
    this.getContentPane().add(jlblStatus, BorderLayout.SOUTH);

    // Add items to the list model
    listModel.addElement("United States");
    listModel.addElement("United Kingdom");
    listModel.addElement("China");
    listModel.addElement("Germany");
    listModel.addElement("France");
    listModel.addElement("Canada");

    // Add selection modes to the combo box
    jcboSelectionMode.addItem("SINGLE_SELECTION");
    jcboSelectionMode.addItem("SINGLE_INTERVAL_SELECTION");
    jcboSelectionMode.addItem("MULTIPLE_INTERVAL_SELECTION");
  }

  /** Add an element to the list */
  void jbtAdd_actionPerformed(ActionEvent e) {
    listModel.addElement(jtfNewItem.getText());
  }

  /** Removing elements from the list */
  void jbtRemove_actionPerformed(ActionEvent e) {
    int selectedIndices[] = jList1.getSelectedIndices();

    for (int i=0; i<selectedIndices.length; i++) {
      listModel.removeElementAt(selectedIndices[i] - i);
    }
  }

  /** Choose a selection mode */
  void jcboSelectionMode_actionPerformed(ActionEvent e) {
    String selectedMode =
      (String)jcboSelectionMode.getSelectedItem();

    if (selectedMode.equals("SINGLE_SELECTION"))
      jList1.setSelectionMode(ListSelectionModel.SINGLE_SELECTION);
    else if (selectedMode.equals("SINGLE_INTERVAL_SELECTION"))
      jList1.setSelectionMode(
        ListSelectionModel.SINGLE_INTERVAL_SELECTION);
    if (selectedMode.equals("MULTIPLE_INTERVAL_SELECTION"))
      jList1.setSelectionMode(
        ListSelectionModel.MULTIPLE_INTERVAL_SELECTION);
  }

  /** Select items in the list */
  void jList1_valueChanged(ListSelectionEvent e) {
    int[] indices = jList1.getSelectedIndices();
```

Listing 8.2 *Continued*

continued

Example 8.2 continued

```
134         Object[] selectedItems = jList1.getSelectedValues();
135         String display = "";
136
137         for (int i=0; i<indices.length; i++) {
138           display += " " + (String)selectedItems[i];
139         }
140
141         jlblStatus.setText(display);
142       }
143     }
```

Listing 8.2 *Continued*

Example Review

The program creates `listModel`, which is an instance of `DefaultListModel`, and uses it to manipulate data in the list. The model enables you to add and remove items in the list,

To add an element, the user enters the new element in the text field, and clicks the Add New Item button to add the element to the model. The model notifies the list's UI delegate to display the new element in the list.

To remove elements, the user specifies a selection mode, selects the elements, and clicks the Remove Selected Item to remove the item(s) from the model. The `getSelectedIndices()` method returns the indices of all selected items in strict order. Whenever an item is removed from the list, the indices of the items are immediately rearranged. Thus, the current index of the *i*th item to remove is `selectedIndices[i] - i`, as shown in Listing 8.2 (Line 112).

List-selection models

Unlike most Swing components, `JList` has two models: a list model and a list-selection model. List models handle data management, and list-selection models deal with data selection. A list-selection model must implement the `ListModelSelection` interface, which defines constants for three selection modes (`SINGLE_SELECTION`, `SINGLE_INTERVAL_SELECTION`, and `MULTIPLE_INTERVAL_SELECTION`), and registration methods for `ListSectionListener`. It also defines the methods for adding and removing selection intervals, and the access methods for the properties, such as `selectionMode`, `anchorSelectionIndex`, `leadSelectionIndex`, and `valueIsAdjusting`.

By default, an instance of `JList` uses `DefaultListSelectionModel`, which is a concrete implementation of `ListSelectionModel`. Usually, you do not need to provide a custom list-selection model, because the `DefaultListSelectionModel` class is sufficient in most cases. Unlike the list data model, you do not need to access the list-selection model directly, because most of the methods you need from the list-selection model are also defined in `Jlist`.

List Cell Renderers

The preceding example displays items as strings in a list. `JList` is very flexible and versatile, and it can be used to display images and drawings in addition to simple text. This section introduces list cell renderers for displaying graphics.

In addition to delegating data storage and processing to list models, `JList` delegates the rendering of the list cells to list cell renderers. All list cell renderers implement the `ListCellRenderer` interface, which defines a single method, `getListCellRendererComponent`, as follows:

```
public Component getListCellRendererComponent
  (JList list, Object value, int index, boolean isSelected,
   boolean cellHasFocus)
```

This method is passed with a list, the value associated with the cell, the index of the value, and information regarding whether the value is selected and whether the cell has the focus. The component returned from the method is painted on the cell in the list.

By default, `JList` uses `DefaultListCellRenderer` to render its cells. The `DefaultListCellRenderer` class implements `ListCellRenderer`, extends `JLabel`, and can display either a string or an icon, but not both in the same cell. You can create a custom renderer by implementing `ListCellRenderer`.

Example 8.3 List Cell Renderer Demo

This example creates a list of countries and displays the country flag and the country name in the list, as shown in Figure 8.5. When a country is selected in the list, its flag is displayed in a panel next to the list.

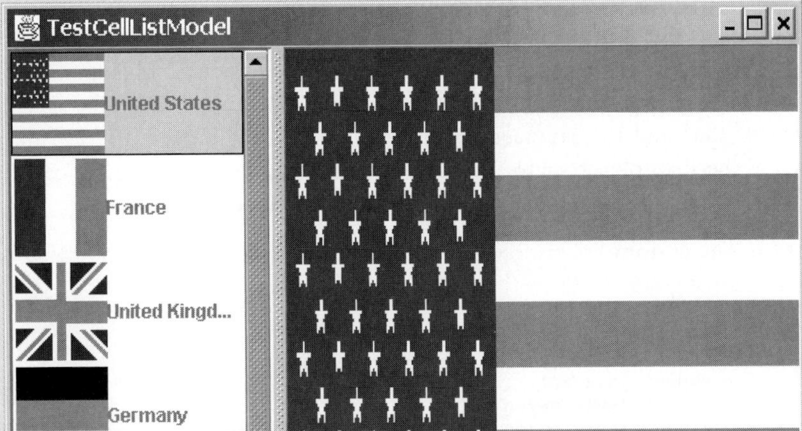

Figure 8.5 *The image and the text are displayed in the list cell.*

continued

Example 8.3 continued

The program requires a custom list cell renderer to display an image and a text in the same cell. Often you need to create a new list model that provides additional information for rendering the cell. In this example, each item has an image and a label, which should be stored in the list model for use by the list cell renderer as well as by the users of the list. The new list model named `MyListModel` is given in Listing 8.3.

```
package listdemo;

import javax.swing.*;
import java.awt.*;

public class MyListModel extends DefaultListModel {
  public MyListModel(String[] name, Image[] image) {
    for (int i=0; i<name.length; i++) {
      addElement(new Object[] {name[i], image[i]});
    }
  }

  /** Override the getName method in DefaultListModel */
  public String getName(Object value) {
    Object[] array = (Object[])value;
    return (String)array[0];
  }

  /** Override the getImage method in DefaultListModel */
  public Image getImage(Object value) {
    Object[] array = (Object[])value;
    return (Image)array[1];
  }
}
```

Listing 8.3 *MyListModel.java*

The `MyListModel` class extends `DefaultListModel` and is constructed with an array of country names and country flag images. Each pair consisting of a country name and a country flag image is stored as an array object in the list model. The `getName(value)` method returns the country name for the specified object value, and the `getImage(value)` method returns the country flag image for the specified object value. These two methods are used by the list cell renderer to obtain the name and image of the value of the cell.

The custom list cell renderer that displays the image and the name is given in Listing 8.4.

```
package listdemo;

import java.awt.*;
import javax.swing.*;
import javax.swing.border.*;
import imageviewerdemo.ImageViewer;

public class MyListCellRenderer implements ListCellRenderer {
  JPanel listCellPanel = new JPanel();
```

Listing 8.4 *MyListCellRenderer.java*

```
  ImageViewer imageViewer = new ImageViewer();
  JLabel jlbl = new JLabel(" ", JLabel.LEFT);
  Border lineBorder =
    BorderFactory.createLineBorder(Color.black, 1);
  Border emptyBorder =
    BorderFactory.createEmptyBorder(2, 2, 2, 2);

  public MyListCellRenderer() {
    listCellPanel.setOpaque(true);
    jlbl.setPreferredSize(new Dimension(100, 60));
    listCellPanel.setLayout(new BorderLayout());
    listCellPanel.add(imageViewer, BorderLayout.CENTER);
    listCellPanel.add(jlbl, BorderLayout.EAST);
  }

  /** Implement this method in ListCellRenderer */
  public Component getListCellRendererComponent
    (JList list, Object value, int index, boolean isSelected,
      boolean cellHasFocus) {
    MyListModel listModel =
      (MyListModel)list.getModel();
    String country = listModel.getName(value);
    Image image = listModel.getImage(value);
    jlbl.setText(country);
    imageViewer.setImage(image);

    if (isSelected) {
      listCellPanel.setForeground(list.getSelectionForeground());
      listCellPanel.setBackground(list.getSelectionBackground());
    }
    else {
      listCellPanel.setForeground(list.getForeground());
      listCellPanel.setBackground(list.getBackground());
    }

    if (cellHasFocus)
      listCellPanel.setBorder(lineBorder);
    else
      listCellPanel.setBorder(emptyBorder);

    return listCellPanel;
  }
}
```

Listing 8.4 *Continued*

The `MyListCellRenderer` class implements the `getListCellRendererComponent` method in the `ListCellRenderer` interface. The `getListCellRendererComponent` method obtains the list model of list, and obtains the name and image of the cell value through the list model. It then displays the image in an image panel and the name in a label. The image panel and the label are placed in a panel (`listCellPanel`) that is the returned component of the `getListCellRendererComponent` method.

The `ImageViewer` class for displaying an image was presented in Example 4.1, "Creating an Image Viewer."

continued

Example 8.3 continued

Finally, let us construct the main program that utilizes the custom list model and custom list cell renderer in a list. Here are the steps to complete the project:

1. Reopen project listdemo.jpr and create a new applet named TestListCellRenderer.java using the Applet wizard.

2. In the UI designer of TestListCellRenderer.java, drop a `JSplitPanel` to the center of the applet. Drop a `JScrollPane` to the left part of the split pane and a `JList` to the scroll pane to create `jList1`. Drop an `ImageViewer` to the right part of the split pane to create `imageViewer1`.

3. Switch to the source pane to create images for the flags of several countries, as shown in Listing 8.5 (Lines 49–67). Create an instance of `MyListModel` named `listModel` (Lines 69–76), and set the `model` property of `jList1` to this instance (Lines 78–79). Create an instance of `MyListCellRenderer`(Lines 19–20), and set the `cellRenderer` property of `jList1` to this instance (Lines 81–82).

4. Generate the `ListSelectionEvent` handler (`valueChanged` for the list, and implement it to display the selected flag in `imageViewer1` (Lines 85–89).

```
1   package listdemo;
2
3   import java.awt.*;
4   import java.awt.event.*;
5   import java.applet.*;
6   import javax.swing.*;
7   import javax.swing.event.*;
8   import imageviewerdemo.ImageViewer;
9
10  public class TestListCellRenderer extends JApplet {
11    boolean isStandalone = false;
12    JSplitPane jSplitPane1 = new JSplitPane();
13    JScrollPane jScrollPane1 = new JScrollPane();
14    JList jList1 = new JList();
15    ImageViewer imageViewer1 = new ImageViewer();
16
17    MyListModel listModel;
18
19    // Create a list cell renderer
20    ListCellRenderer myListCellRenderer = new MyListCellRenderer();
21
22    /** Initialize the applet */
23    public void init() {
24      try {
25        jbInit();
26      }
27      catch(Exception e) {
28        e.printStackTrace();
29      }
30    }
31
32    /** Component initialization */
33    private void jbInit() throws Exception {
34      this.setSize(new Dimension(400, 300));
35      jList1.setFixedCellHeight(65);
```

Listing 8.5 *TestListCellRenderer.java*

```
      jList1.setFixedCellWidth(150);
      jList1.addListSelectionListener(
        new javax.swing.event.ListSelectionListener() {
        public void valueChanged(ListSelectionEvent e) {
          jList1_valueChanged(e);
        }
      });
      jSplitPane1.setContinuousLayout(true);
      this.getContentPane().add(jSplitPane1, BorderLayout.NORTH);
      jSplitPane1.add(jScrollPane1, JSplitPane.TOP);
      jSplitPane1.add(imageViewer1, JSplitPane.BOTTOM);
      jScrollPane1.getViewport().add(jList1, null);

      // Create images
      Image imageUS = ImageViewer.createImage(
        "/image/us.gif", this);
      Image imageFrance = ImageViewer.createImage(
        "/image/fr.gif", this);
      Image imageUK = ImageViewer.createImage(
        "/image/uk.gif", this);
      Image imageGermany = ImageViewer.createImage(
        "/image/germany.gif", this);
      Image imageIndia = ImageViewer.createImage(
        "/image/india.gif", this);
      Image imageNorway = ImageViewer.createImage(
        "/image/norway.gif", this);
      Image imageChina = ImageViewer.createImage(
        "/image/china.gif", this);
      Image imageCanada = ImageViewer.createImage(
        "/image/ca.gif", this);
      Image imageDenmark = ImageViewer.createImage(
        "/image/denmark.gif", this);

      // Create a list model
      listModel = new MyListModel(
        new String[]
        {"United States", "France", "United Kingdom", "Germany",
         "India", "Norway", "China", "Canada", "Denmark"},
         new Image[]
         {imageUS, imageFrance, imageUK, imageGermany, imageIndia,
          imageNorway, imageChina, imageCanada, imageDenmark});

      // Set list model
      jList1.setModel(listModel);

      // Set list cell renderer
      jList1.setCellRenderer(myListCellRenderer);
    }

    /** Handle list selection event */
    void jList1_valueChanged(ListSelectionEvent e) {
      Image image = listModel.getImage(jList1.getSelectedValue());
      imageViewer1.setImage(image);
    }
  }
```

Example Review

The example consists of four classes: `MyListModel`, `MyListCellRenderer`, `ImageViewer`, and `TestListCellRenderer`. The `MyListModel` class is responsible for storing data that include image and text for the list. The `MyListCellRenderer`

continued

Example 8.3 continued

class is responsible for rendering the cell with image and text. The `ImageViewer` class displays an image in the panel. The `TestListCellRenderer` class tests the list with the custom list cell renderer.

When you choose a country in the list, the list selection event handler is invoked. This handler obtains the list model for the list, uses the list model to retrieve the country's flag image, and displays the image in the image panel on the right side of the split pane.

The `getListCellRendererComponent` method in `MyListCellRenderer` is passed with the parameters `list`, `value`, `index`, `isSelected`, and `isFocused`. The `list` is used to obtain the list model. The `value` determines the image and name of the country displayed in the cell. If the cell is selected, the background and foreground of the cell are set to the list's selection background and foreground. If the cell is focused, the cell's border is set to the line border; otherwise, it is set to the empty border. The empty border serves as divider between the cells.

NOTE
The images may not be displayed immediately, because it takes time to load them. You can use image tracker techniques to ensure that the images are loaded before they are displayed. Tracking loading images is introduced in Chapter 16, "Multimedia," in my *Introduction to Java Programming with JBuilder 4*.

TIP
The label's preferred size is set to 100 by 60 in the `MyListCellRenderer` class (Line 19), so it will be limited to 100 by 60 and the rest of the space in the cell renderer is allocated to the image.

JComboBox

A *combo box* is a component similar to a list. Both combo box and list are used for selecting items from a list. A combo box allows the user to select one item at a time, while a list permits multiple selections. A combo box displays a drop-down list contained in a popup menu when the combo box is clicked. The selected item can be edited in the cell as if it were a text field.

The constructors of `JComboBox` are similar to those of `JList`. An instance of `JComboBox` can be created using its default constructor or one of the following three constructors:

- `public JComboBox(ComboBoxModel model)`
- `public JComboBox(Object[] objectArray)`
- `public JComboBox(Vector vector)`

The following properties of JComboBox are often useful:

- actionCommand: An action command string associated with the JComboBox.
- editable: This is a boolean value indicating whether the combo box can be edited. The default value is false.
- itemCount: This counts the number of items in the combo box. This property is read-only.
- maximumRowCount: This specifies the maximum number of rows that can be seen without scrolling. The default value is 8.
- model: This is an object that maintains the data for the list. Combo box models must be used explicitly to add or delete items in a combo box.
- popupVisible: This is a boolean value indicating whether the popup menu that contains the list is displayed. The default value is false, which means that the user has to click the combo box to display the popup menu.
- renderer: This is an instance of the class that implements the ListCellRenderer interface. The renderer is responsible for rendering the cell in the combo box.
- selectedIndex: This is the index of the selected item in the combo box.
- selectedItem: This is the current selected object in the combo box.

Like JList, the JComboBox class delegates the responsibilities of storing and maintaining data to its data model. All combo box models implement the ComboBoxModel interface, which extends the ListModel interface and defines the getSelectedItem and setSelectedItem methods for retrieving and setting a selected item. The methods for adding and removing items are defined in the MutableComboBoxModel interface, which extends ComboBoxModel.

When an instance of JComboBox is created without explicitly specifying a model, an instance of DefaultComboBoxModel is used. The DefaultComboBoxModel class extends AbstractListModel and implements MutableComboBoxModel. Recall that the DefaultListModel class also extends AbstractListModel. So DefaultComboBoxModel and DefaultListModel share many common methods.

Unlike JList, the JComboBox class has the methods for adding or removing items from the list. The following methods are useful in operating a JComboBox object:

- public void addItem(Object item)

  Adds the item of any object into the combo box.

- public Object getItemAt(int index)

  Returns an item from the combo box at the specified index.

- public void removeItem(Object anObject)

  Removes an item from the item list.

- `public void removeAllItems()`

  Removes all items from the item list.

Combo boxes render cells exactly like lists, because the combo box items are displayed in a list contained in a popup menu.

`JComboBox` can generate `ActionEvent` and `ItemEvent`, among many other events. Whenever a new item is selected, `JComboBox` generates `ItemEvent` twice, once for deselecting the previously selected item, and the other for selecting the currently selected item. `JComboBox` generates an `ActionEvent` after generating `ItemEvent`.

Example 8.4 Combo Box Demo

This example creates a combo box that contains a list of countries and displays the country flag and the country name in the list cell, as shown in Figure 8.6. When a country is selected in the list, its flag is displayed in a panel below the combo box.

Figure 8.6 *The image and the text are displayed in the list cell of a combo box.*

This example is similar to Example 8.3. A custom data model named `MyComboBoxModel` is created to store data (flag image and country name), as shown in Listing 8.6. A custom cell renderer, named `MyComboBoxRenderer`, is created to render the cells, as shown in Listing 8.7. These two classes are almost identical to the data model and list renderer in Example 8.3, except for the following differences:

- `MyComboBoxModel` extends `DefaultComboBoxModel`, but `MyListModel` extends `DefaultListModel`.
- The data model obtained from the `list` parameter in the `getListCellRendererComponent` method is casted to `MyComboBoxModel`, while the data model in `MyListCellRenderer` is casted to `MyListModel`.

```
package comboboxdemo;

import javax.swing.*;
import java.awt.*;

public class MyComboBoxModel extends DefaultComboBoxModel {
  public MyComboBoxModel(String[] name, Image[] image) {
    for (int i=0; i<name.length; i++) {
      addElement(new Object[] {name[i], image[i]});
    }
  }

  /** Override this method in DefaultComoboBoxModel */
  public String getName(Object value) {
    Object[] array = (Object[])value;
    return (String)array[0];
  }

  /** Override this method in DefaultComoboBoxModel */
  public Image getImage(Object value) {
    Object[] array = (Object[])value;
    return (Image)array[1];
  }
}
```

Listing 8.6 *MyComboBoxModel.java*

```
package comboboxdemo;

import java.awt.*;
import javax.swing.*;
import javax.swing.border.*;
import imageviewerdemo.ImageViewer;

public class MyComboBoxRenderer implements ListCellRenderer {
  JPanel listCellPanel = new JPanel();
  ImageViewer imageViewer = new ImageViewer();
  JLabel jlbl = new JLabel(" ", JLabel.LEFT);
  Border lineBorder =
    BorderFactory.createLineBorder(Color.black, 1);
  Border emptyBorder =
    BorderFactory.createEmptyBorder(2, 2, 2, 2);

  public MyComboBoxRenderer() {
    jlbl.setPreferredSize(new Dimension(100, 60));
    listCellPanel.setLayout(new BorderLayout());
    listCellPanel.add(imageViewer, BorderLayout.CENTER);
    listCellPanel.add(jlbl, BorderLayout.EAST);
  }

  /** Override this method in ListCellRenderer */
  public Component getListCellRendererComponent
    (JList list, Object value, int index, boolean isSelected,
     boolean cellHasFocus) {
    MyComboBoxModel listModel =
      (MyComboBoxModel)list.getModel();
    String country = listModel.getName(value);
    Image image = listModel.getImage(value);
    jlbl.setText(country);
    imageViewer.setImage(image);

```

Listing 8.7 *MyComboBoxRenderer.java*

continued

Example 8.4 continued

```
      if (isSelected) {
        listCellPanel.setForeground(list.getSelectionForeground());
        listCellPanel.setBackground(list.getSelectionBackground());
      }
      else {
        listCellPanel.setForeground(list.getForeground());
        listCellPanel.setBackground(list.getBackground());
      }

      if (cellHasFocus)
        listCellPanel.setBorder(lineBorder);
      else
        listCellPanel.setBorder(emptyBorder);

      return listCellPanel;
    }
  }
```

Listing 8.7 *Continued*

Let us construct the main program that utilizes the custom combo box model and custom combo box cell renderer in a combo box. Here are the steps to complete the project:

1. Create a new project comboboxdemo.jpr, and create a new applet named TestComboBox.java using the Applet wizard.
2. In the UI designer of TestComboBox.java, drop an `ImageViewer` to the center of the applet to create `imageViewer1`, and drop a `JComboBox` to create `jcboCountries`.
3. Switch to the content pane to create images for the flags of several countries, as shown in Listing 8.8 (Lines 42–60). Create an instance of `MyComboBoxModel` named `comboBoxModel`, and set the `model` property of `jcboCountries` to this instance. Create an instance of `MyComboBoxRenderer`, and set the `renderer` property of `jcboCountries` to this instance.
4. Generate the `ActionEvent` handler for the combo box, and implement it to display the selected flag in `imageViewer1` (Lines 79–84).

```
1   package comboboxdemo;
2
3   import java.awt.*;
4   import java.awt.event.*;
5   import java.applet.*;
6   import javax.swing.*;
7   import imageviewerdemo.ImageViewer;
8
9   public class TestComboBox extends JApplet {
10    boolean isStandalone = false;
11    ImageViewer imageViewer1 = new ImageViewer();
12    JComboBox jcboCountries = new JComboBox();
13
14    MyComboBoxModel comboBoxModel;
15
```

Listing 8.8 *TestComboBox.java*

```
  // Create a list cell renderer
  MyComboBoxRenderer myComboBoxRenderer = new MyComboBoxRenderer();

  /** Initialize the applet */
  public void init() {
    try {
      jbInit();
    }
    catch(Exception e) {
      e.printStackTrace();
    }
  }

  /** Component initialization */
  private void jbInit() throws Exception {
    this.setSize(new Dimension(400,300));
    jcboCountries.addActionListener(
      new java.awt.event.ActionListener() {

      public void actionPerformed(ActionEvent e) {
        jcboCountries_actionPerformed(e);
      }
    });
    this.getContentPane().add(imageViewer1, BorderLayout.CENTER);
    this.getContentPane().add(jcboCountries, BorderLayout.NORTH);

    // Create images
    Image imageUS = ImageViewer.createImage(
      "/image/us.gif", this);
    Image imageFrance = ImageViewer.createImage(
      "/image/fr.gif", this);
    Image imageUK = ImageViewer.createImage(
      "/image/uk.gif", this);
    Image imageGermany = ImageViewer.createImage(
      "/image/germany.gif", this);
    Image imageIndia = ImageViewer.createImage(
      "/image/india.gif", this);
    Image imageNorway = ImageViewer.createImage(
      "/image/norway.gif", this);
    Image imageChina = ImageViewer.createImage(
      "/image/china.gif", this);
    Image imageCanada = ImageViewer.createImage(
      "/image/ca.gif", this);
    Image imageDenmark = ImageViewer.createImage(
      "/image/denmark.gif", this);

    // Create a list model
    comboBoxModel = new MyComboBoxModel(
      new String[]
      {"United States", "France",
       "United Kingdom", "Germany",
       "India", "Norway", "China", "Canada", "Denmark"},
      new Image[]
      {imageUS, imageFrance, imageUK, imageGermany, imageIndia,
       imageNorway, imageChina, imageCanada, imageDenmark});

    // Set list model
    jcboCountries.setModel(comboBoxModel);

```

Listing 8.8 *Continued*

continued

Example 8.4 continued

```
      // Set list cell renderer
      jcboCountries.setRenderer(myComboBoxRenderer);
    }

    /** Handle the combo box selection */
    void jcboCountries_actionPerformed(ActionEvent e) {
      Image image = comboBoxModel.getImage(
        jcboCountries.getSelectedItem());
      imageViewer1.setImage(image);
    }
  }
```

Listing 8.8 *Continued*

Example Review

If you don't need to provide custom methods in the data model, you can simply use the `DefaultComboBoxModel`, which is used by all the combo boxes if no data model is explicitly specified. In fact, you don't need the combo box data model as much as you need the list data model for `JList`, because `JComboBox` directly supports the methods for adding and removing items in the combo box, but `JList` does not contain those methods.

Each combo box has a default cell renderer that displays a string or an icon, but not both at the same time. To display a combination of images, drawings, and text, you need to create a custom renderer.

This example creates a custom data model to hold country names and flag images, and to provide the methods for getting names and images. The methods are used in the custom renderer for displaying images and names in cells in the combo box. The combo box renderer is the same as the list box renderer. They all implement the `ListCellRenderer` interface. In fact, a combo box cell is displayed in a list contained in a popup menu. You can modify Examples 8.3 and 8.4 so that they can share the same renderer.

Editing Combo Boxes

Unlike lists, combo boxes can be edited. By default, a combo box is not editable. To make a combo box editable, set its `editable` property to `true`. Editing only affects the current item and does not change the contents of the list. Editing changes are lost after another item in the combo box is selected. To make changes permanent, you have to implement the `ActionEvent` handler to replace the current item with the modified item.

Example 8.5 Editing in a Combo Box

This example creates a simple Web browser to render HTML files. The program lets the user enter a URL in a combo box and save it. When the user presses the Enter key after entering the URL or selects an existing URL from the combo box, the HTML file is displayed in an editor pane, as shown in Figure 8.7.

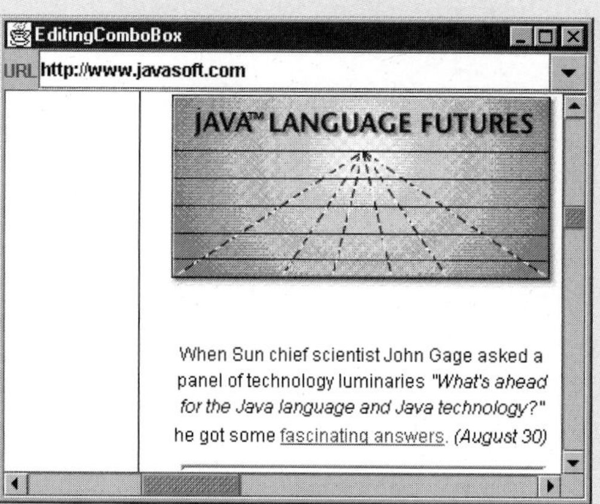

Figure 8.7 *You can enter a URL in the combo box and display the HTML file in an editor pane.*

Here are the steps to complete the project:

1. Reopen the project comboboxdemo.jpr, and create a new applet named EditingComboBox.java.

2. In the UI designer of EditingComboBox.java, drop a `JScrollPane` to the center of the applet, and drop a `JEditorPane` to the scroll pane and rename it `jep`. Drop a `JPanel` to the north of the applet to create `jpURL`.

3. Set `layout` of `jpURL` to `BorderLayout`. Drop a `JLabel` to the west of `jpURL`, and drop a `JComboBox` to the center of `jpURL` to create `jcboURL`. Set `editable` of `jcboURL` to True.

4. Generate an `ActionEvent` handler for `jcboURL`, and implement the handler to display the contents at URL in the editor pane, and add the URL to the combo box, as shown in Listing 8.9 (Lines 55–66).

5. Generate a hyperlink event handler for the editor pane, and implement it to display the content of the hyperlink in the editor pane, as shown in Listing 8.9 (Lines 68–76).

```
1   package comboboxdemo;
2
3   import java.awt.*;
4   import java.awt.event.*;
5   import java.applet.*;
6   import javax.swing.*;
7   import javax.swing.event.*;
8   import java.io.IOException;
9   import java.net.URL;
10
11  public class EditingComboBox extends JApplet {
12    boolean isStandalone = false;
13    JScrollPane jScrollPane1 = new JScrollPane();
```

Listing 8.9 *EditingComboBox.java*

continued

Example 8.5 continued

```
    JEditorPane jep = new JEditorPane();
    JPanel jPanel1 = new JPanel();
    JLabel jLabel1 = new JLabel();
    JComboBox jcboURL = new JComboBox();
    BorderLayout borderLayout1 = new BorderLayout();

    /** Initialize the applet */
    public void init() {
      try {
        jbInit();
      }
      catch(Exception e) {
        e.printStackTrace();
      }
    }

    /** Component initialization */
    private void jbInit() throws Exception {
      this.setSize(new Dimension(400,300));
      jep.setText("jEditorPane1");
      jep.addHyperlinkListener(
        new javax.swing.event.HyperlinkListener() {
        public void hyperlinkUpdate(HyperlinkEvent e) {
          jep_hyperlinkUpdate(e);
        }
      });
      jLabel1.setText("URL");
      jPanel1.setLayout(borderLayout1);
      jcboURL.setEditable(true);
      jcboURL.addActionListener(new java.awt.event.ActionListener() {
        public void actionPerformed(ActionEvent e) {
          jcboURL_actionPerformed(e);
        }
      });
      this.getContentPane().add(jScrollPane1, BorderLayout.CENTER);
      this.getContentPane().add(jPanel1, BorderLayout.NORTH);
      jPanel1.add(jLabel1, BorderLayout.WEST);
      jPanel1.add(jcboURL, BorderLayout.CENTER);
      jScrollPane1.getViewport().add(jep, null);
    }

    /** Handle combo box action */
    void jcboURL_actionPerformed(ActionEvent e) {
      jcboURL.addItem(jcboURL.getSelectedItem());

      try {
        // Display the HTML file
        jep.setPage(new URL((String)(jcboURL.getSelectedItem())));
      }
      catch (IOException ex) {
        System.out.println(ex);
      }
    }

    /** Process hyperlinks in the HTML file */
    void jep_hyperlinkUpdate(HyperlinkEvent e) {
      try {
        jep.setPage(e.getURL());
      }
```

Listing 8.9 *Continued*

```
        catch (IOException ex) {
          System.out.println(ex);
        }
      }
    }
```

Listing 8.9 *Continued*

Example Review

To enable editing, the `editable` property of the combo box must be `true`. By default, `editable` is `false`.

The user enters a URL of the HTML file in the combo box and presses the Enter key to fire an `ActionEvent`. The `ActionEvent` handler stores the URL and displays the URL in the editor pane. You can also select a URL from the combo box.

JTable

`JTable` is a Swing component that displays data in rows and columns in a two-dimensional grid. Figure 8.8 shows the Swing table in the SwingSet demo.

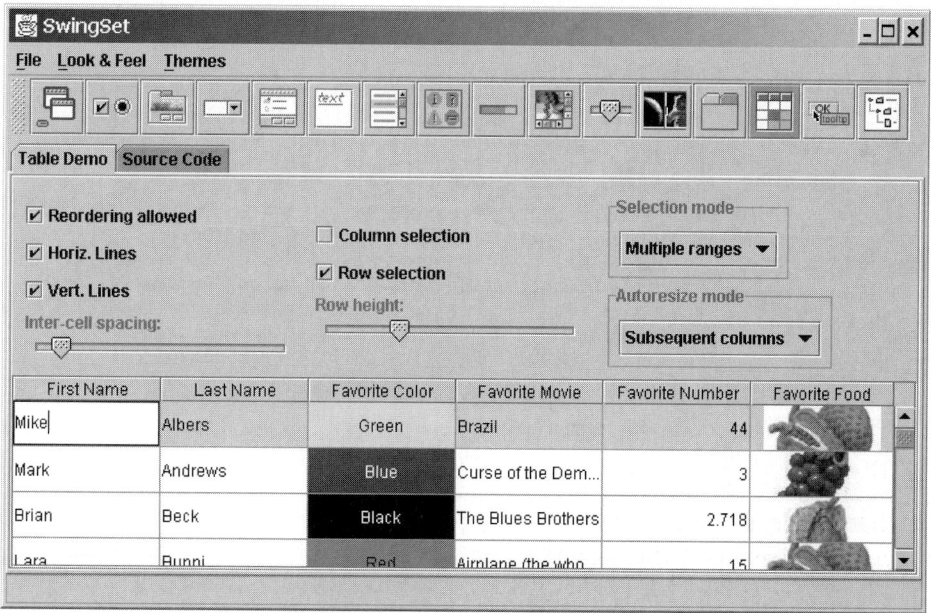

Figure 8.8 *The SwingSet demo demonstrates the features of* `JTable`.

`JTable` doesn't directly support scrolling. To create a scrollable table, you need to create a `JScrollPane` and add an instance of `JTable` to the scroll pane. If a table is not placed in a scroll pane, its column header will not be visible, because the column header is placed in the header of the view port of a scroll pane.

`JTable` has three different models: a table model, a column model, and a list-selection model. The *table model* is for storing and processing data. The *column model* deals with column management. The *list-selection model* is the same used by `JList` for selecting rows, columns, and cells in a table.

Like `JList` and `JComboBox`, `JTable` has renderers and editors. `JTable` has many features that make it possible to customize its rendering and editing. `JTable` also provides many convenient, easy-to-use renderers and editors.

There are seven constructors in the `JTable` class. The builder tool always uses the default constructor to create an instance of `JTable`. The constructor shown below constructs a table from a two-dimensional array representing data and an array representing column names:

```
public JTable(Object[][] rowData, Object[] columnNames)
```

For instance, the following statements construct a table, as shown in Figure 8.9.

```
// Create table column names
String[] columnNames =
  {"Title", "Author", "Publisher", "In-stock"};

// Create table data
Object[][] data = {
  {"Introduction to Java Programming", "Y. Daniel Liang",
   "Que Education & Training", new Boolean(false)},
  {"Introduction to Java Programming, Second Edition",
   "Y. Daniel Liang", "Que Education & Training",
   new Boolean(true)},
  {"Introduction to Java Programming, Third Edition",
   "Y. Daniel Liang", "Prentice Hall", new Boolean(true)},
  {"Introduction to Java Programming With Visual J++ 6",
   "Y. Daniel Liang", "Prentice Hall", new Boolean(true)},
  {"Introduction to Java Programming with JBuilder 3",
   "Y. Daniel Liang", "Prentice Hall", new Boolean(true)},
  {"Rapid Java Application Development Using JBuilder 3",
   "Y. Daniel Liang", "Prentice Hall", new Boolean(true)},
  {"Rapid Java Application Development Using JBuilder 4 and 5",
   "Y. Daniel Liang", "Prentice Hall", new Boolean(true)},
  {" Introduction to Java Programming with JBuilder 4",
   "Y. Daniel Liang", "Prentice Hall", new Boolean(true)},
};

// Create a table
JTable jTable1 = new JTable(data, columnNames);
```

NOTE

`JTable` has many supporting classes. For convenience, all the table classes except `JTable` are grouped in the `javax.swing.table` package.

JTable Properties

`JTable` is a powerful control with a variety of properties and methods that provide many ways to customize tables. The following properties are often used:

- `autoCreateColumnsFromModel`: This is a `boolean` value indicating whether the columns are created in the table. The default value is `true`.

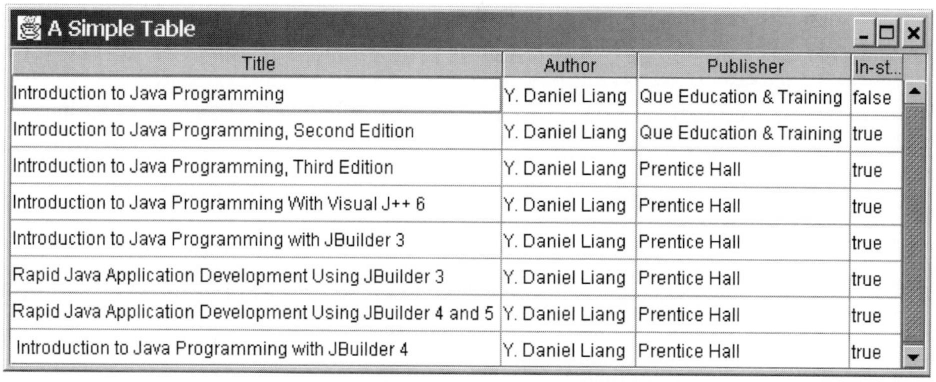

A Simple Table

Title	Author	Publisher	In-st...
Introduction to Java Programming	Y. Daniel Liang	Que Education & Training	false
Introduction to Java Programming, Second Edition	Y. Daniel Liang	Que Education & Training	true
Introduction to Java Programming, Third Edition	Y. Daniel Liang	Prentice Hall	true
Introduction to Java Programming With Visual J++ 6	Y. Daniel Liang	Prentice Hall	true
Introduction to Java Programming with JBuilder 3	Y. Daniel Liang	Prentice Hall	true
Rapid Java Application Development Using JBuilder 3	Y. Daniel Liang	Prentice Hall	true
Rapid Java Application Development Using JBuilder 4 and 5	Y. Daniel Liang	Prentice Hall	true
Introduction to Java Programming with JBuilder 4	Y. Daniel Liang	Prentice Hall	true

Figure 8.9 *You can construct a simple table using the* `JTable` *constructor.*

- `autoResizingMode`: This specifies how columns are resized (you can resize table columns but not rows). Possible values are:

```
JTable.AUTO_RESIZE_OFF
JTable.AUTO_RESIZE_LAST_COLUMN
JTable.AUTO_RESIZE_SUBSEQUENT_COLUMNS
JTable.AUTO_RESIZE_NEXT_COLUMN
JTable.AUTO_RESIZE_ALL_COLUMNS
```

- `cellSelectionEnabled`: This is a `boolean` value specifying whether individual cells can be selected.
- `columnModel`: This is an object that maintains the table column data. Table column models are introduced in the section "Table Column Models."
- `columnSelectionAllowed`: This is a `boolean` value specifying whether column selection is allowed.
- `defaultEditor`: This is the default editor for table cells. `JTable` provides a set of default editors that can be overridden, if desired. The editors are introduced in the section "Table Renderers and Editors."
- `defaultRenderer`: This is the default renderer for table cells. `JTable` provides a set of default renderers that can be overridden, if desired. The renderers are introduced in the section "Table Renderers and Editors."
- `editingColumn`: The column of the cell that is currently being edited.
- `editingRow`: The row of the cell that is currently being edited.
- `gridColor`: The color used to draw grid lines.
- `intercellSpacing`: This is a dimension that represents the horizontal and vertical margins between cells.
- `model`: This is an object that maintains the table data. Table models are introduced in the section "Table Models."
- `rowHeight`: This specifies the row height of the table. The default value is 16 pixels.

- `rowMargin`: This specifies the vertical margin between rows.
- `rowCount`: This counts the number of rows in a table.
- `rowSelectionAllowed`: This is a `boolean` value specifying whether the rows can be selected.
- `selectionBackground`: The background color of selected cells.
- `SelectionForeground`: The foreground color of selected cells.
- `selectionMode`: This specifies how table cells can be selected. This property is write-only. The possible values are:

  ```
  ListSelectionModel.SINGLE_SELECTION
  ListSelectionModel.SINGLE_INTERVAL_SELECTION
  ListSelectionModel.MULTIPLE_INTERVAL_SELECTION
  ```

- `selectionModel`: This is an object that tracks the selection of table cells. The table-selection model is the same as the list-selection model.
- `showGrid`: This is a `boolean` value indicating whether the grid lines are displayed. The default value is `true`.
- `showHorizontalGrid`: This is a `boolean` value indicating whether the horizontal grid lines are displayed. The default value is `true`.
- `showVerticalGrid`: This is a `boolean` value indicating whether the vertical grid lines are displayed. The default value is `true`.
- `tableHeader`: This is an instance of `JTableHeader` that is displayed in the header of the view port in a scroll pane. Table header is usually specified as an array of strings in the table model.

Example 8.6 Testing Table Properties

This example demonstrates the use of several `JTable` properties. The example creates a table and allows the user to choose an Auto Resize Mode, specify the row height and margin, and indicate whether the grid is shown. A sample run of the program is shown in Figure 8.10.

Here are the steps to complete the project:

1. Create a new project named tabledemo.jpr, and create a new applet named TestTable.java.
2. In the UI designer of TestTable.java, drop a `JScrollPane` to the center of the applet, and drop a `JTable` to the scroll pane to create `jTable1`. Drop a `JPanel` to north of the applet to create `jpProperties`.
3. Set `layout` of `jpProperties` to `BorderLayout`. Drop a `JPanel` to the north of `jpProperties` to create `jpAutoResizeMode`. Drop a `JPanel` to the south of `jpProperties` to create `jpRowGrid`.

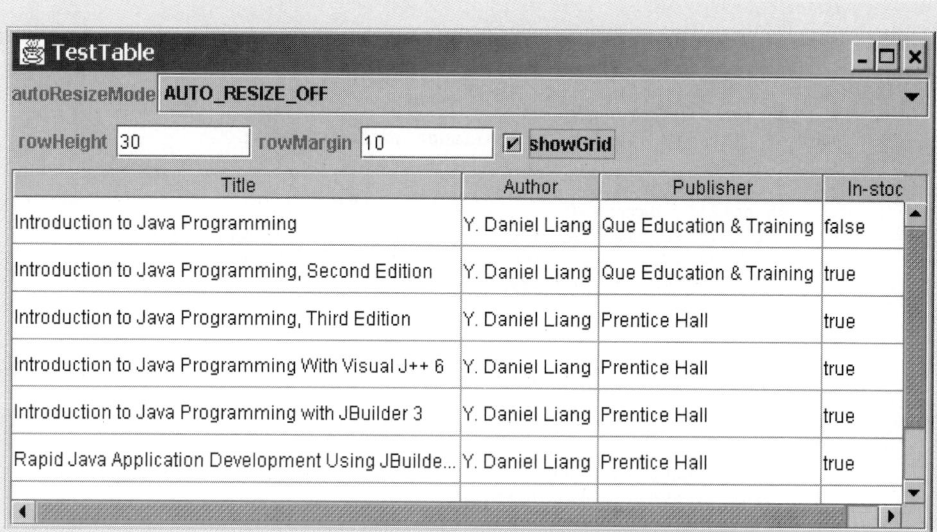

Figure 8.10 *You can specify an auto-resizing mode, the table's row height and row margin, and whether to show the grid in the table.*

4. Set layout of `jpAutoResizingMode` to `BorderLayout`. Drop a `JLabel` to the west of `jpAutoResizingMode`, and drop a `JComboBox` to the center of `jpAutoResizingMode` to create `jcboAutoResizingMode`.

5. Set layout of `jpRowGrid` to `FlowLayout` with left alignment. Drop a `JLabel`, a `JTextField`, a `JLabel`, a `JTextField`, and a `JCheckBox` to `jpRowGrid`. Set text of the labels to rowHeight and rowMargin. Rename the text fields to `jtfRowHeight` and `jtfRowMargin`. Rename the check box `jchkShowGrid`.

6. Initialize the table with table data and column header (Lines 13–25). Add five autoresizing modes to the combo box (Lines 103–108).

7. Generate and implement the code for handling combo box selection, for obtaining and using values in the text fields, and for checking and unchecking the showGrid check box, as shown in Listing 8.10 (Lines 129–146).

```
1   package tabledemo;
2
3   import java.awt.*;
4   import java.awt.event.*;
5   import java.applet.*;
6   import javax.swing.*;
7   import java.util.*;
8
9   public class TestTable extends JApplet {
10    boolean isStandalone = false;
11    JScrollPane jScrollPane1 = new JScrollPane();
12
```

Listing 8.10 *TestTable.java*

continued

Example 8.6 continued

```
  // Create table column names
  String[] columnNames =
    {"Title", "Author", "Publisher", "In-stock"};

  // Create table data
  Object[][] data = {
    {"Introduction to Java Programming", "Y. Daniel Liang",
      "Que Education & Training", new Boolean(false)},
    // Omitted for brevity
  };

  // Create a table
  JTable jTable1 = new JTable(data, columnNames);

  JPanel jpProperties = new JPanel();
  JPanel jpRowGrid = new JPanel();
  JPanel jpAutoResizeMode = new JPanel();
  JLabel jLabel1 = new JLabel();
  JComboBox jcboAutoResizeMode = new JComboBox();
  BorderLayout borderLayout1 = new BorderLayout();
  BorderLayout borderLayout3 = new BorderLayout();
  FlowLayout flowLayout1 = new FlowLayout();
  JLabel jLabel2 = new JLabel();
  JTextField jtfRowHeight = new JTextField();
  JLabel jLabel3 = new JLabel();
  JTextField jtfRowMargin = new JTextField();
  JCheckBox jchkShowGrid = new JCheckBox();

  /** Initialize the applet */
  public void init() {
    try {
      jbInit();
    }
    catch(Exception e) {
      e.printStackTrace();
    }
  }

  /** Component initialization */
  private void jbInit() throws Exception {
    this.setSize(new Dimension(400,300));
    jTable1.setRowHeight(40);
    jLabel1.setText("autoResizeMode");
    jpAutoResizeMode.setLayout(borderLayout3);
    jpRowGrid.setLayout(flowLayout1);
    jpProperties.setLayout(borderLayout1);
    jcboAutoResizeMode.addActionListener(
      new java.awt.event.ActionListener() {
      public void actionPerformed(ActionEvent e) {
        jcboAutoResizeMode_actionPerformed(e);
      }
    });
    jLabel2.setText("rowHeight");
    jtfRowHeight.setColumns(8);
    jtfRowHeight.addActionListener(
      new java.awt.event.ActionListener() {
      public void actionPerformed(ActionEvent e) {
        jtfRowHeight_actionPerformed(e);
      }
    });
```

Listing 8.10 *Continued*

```
    jLabel3.setText("rowMargin");
    jtfRowMargin.setCaretPosition(0);
    jtfRowMargin.setColumns(8);
    jtfRowMargin.addActionListener(
      new java.awt.event.ActionListener() {
      public void actionPerformed(ActionEvent e) {
        jtfRowMargin_actionPerformed(e);
      }
    });
    jchkShowGrid.setText("showGrid");
    jchkShowGrid.addActionListener(
      new java.awt.event.ActionListener() {
      public void actionPerformed(ActionEvent e) {
        jchkShowGrid_actionPerformed(e);
      }
    });
    flowLayout1.setAlignment(FlowLayout.LEFT);
    this.getContentPane().add(jScrollPane1, BorderLayout.CENTER);
    this.getContentPane().add(jpProperties, BorderLayout.NORTH);
    jpProperties.add(jpAutoResizeMode, BorderLayout.NORTH);
    jpAutoResizeMode.add(jLabel1, BorderLayout.WEST);
    jpAutoResizeMode.add(jcboAutoResizeMode, BorderLayout.CENTER);
    jpProperties.add(jpRowGrid, BorderLayout.SOUTH);
    jpRowGrid.add(jLabel2, null);
    jpRowGrid.add(jtfRowHeight, null);
    jpRowGrid.add(jLabel3, null);
    jpRowGrid.add(jtfRowMargin, null);
    jpRowGrid.add(jchkShowGrid, null);
    jScrollPane1.getViewport().add(jTable1, null);

    // Add auto resize modes to jcboAutoResizeMode
    jcboAutoResizeMode.addItem("AUTO_RESIZE_OFF");
    jcboAutoResizeMode.addItem("AUTO_RESIZE_LAST_COLUMN");
    jcboAutoResizeMode.addItem("AUTO_RESIZE_SUBSEQUENT_COLUMNS");
    jcboAutoResizeMode.addItem("AUTO_RESIZE_NEXT_COLUMN");
    jcboAutoResizeMode.addItem("AUTO_RESIZE_ALL_COLUMNS");
  }

  /** Choose auto resize mode */
  void jcboAutoResizeMode_actionPerformed(ActionEvent e) {
    String selectedItem =
      (String)jcboAutoResizeMode.getSelectedItem();

    if (selectedItem.equals("AUTO_RESIZE_OFF"))
      jTable1.setAutoResizeMode(JTable.AUTO_RESIZE_OFF);
    else if (selectedItem.equals("AUTO_RESIZE_LAST_COLUMN"))
      jTable1.setAutoResizeMode(JTable.AUTO_RESIZE_LAST_COLUMN);
    else if (selectedItem.equals("AUTO_RESIZE_SUBSEQUENT_COLUMNS"))
      jTable1.setAutoResizeMode(
        JTable.AUTO_RESIZE_SUBSEQUENT_COLUMNS);
    else if (selectedItem.equals("AUTO_RESIZE_NEXT_COLUMN"))
      jTable1.setAutoResizeMode(JTable.AUTO_RESIZE_NEXT_COLUMN);
    else if (selectedItem.equals("AUTO_RESIZE_ALL_COLUMNS"))
      jTable1.setAutoResizeMode(JTable.AUTO_RESIZE_ALL_COLUMNS);
  }

  /** Set row height */
  void jtfRowHeight_actionPerformed(ActionEvent e) {
    int rowHeight = new Integer(
      jtfRowHeight.getText().trim()).intValue();
```

Listing 8.10 *Continued*

continued

Example 8.6 continued

```
      jTable1.setRowHeight(rowHeight);
    }

    /** Set row margin */
    void jtfRowMargin_actionPerformed(ActionEvent e) {
      int rowMargin = new Integer(
        jtfRowMargin.getText().trim()).intValue();
      jTable1.setRowMargin(rowMargin);
    }

    /** Set showGrid property */
    void jchkShowGrid_actionPerformed(ActionEvent e) {
      jTable1.setShowGrid(jchkShowGrid.isSelected());
    }
  }
```

Listing 8.10 *Continued*

Example Review

Initially, each column in the table occupies the same width (75 pixels). You can resize the columns but not the rows. There are five options for resizing columns: `AUTO_RESIZE_OFF`, `AUTO_RESIZE_LAST_COLUMN`, `AUTO_RESIZE_SUBSEQUENT_COLUMNS`, `AUTO_RESIZE_NEXT_COLUMN`, and `AUTO_RESIZE_ALL_COLUMNS`. With `AUTO_RESIZE_OFF`, resizing a column does not affect the widths of the other columns. With `AUTO_RESIZE_LAST_COLUMN`, resizing a column affects the width of the last column. With `AUTO_RESIZE_SUBSEQUENT_COLUMNS`, resizing a column affects the widths of all the subsequent columns. With `AUTO_RESIZE_NEXT_COLUMN`, resizing a column affects the widths of the next columns. With `AUTO_RESIZE_ALL_COLUMNS`, resizing a column affects the widths of all the columns.

`rowHeight` and `rowMargin` are properties in the `JTable` class. To set the width and margin for columns, you need to use the `TableColumn` class and the table's column model, which are introduced in the sections "Table Column Models" and "The `TableColumn` Class."

`JTable` does not provide methods for manipulating data, such as adding or removing rows and columns. Those methods are defined in the table models and table column models.

Table Models

Like `JList` and `JComboBox`, `JTable` delegates data storing and processing to its table data model. A table data model must implement the `TableModel` interface, which defines the methods for registering table model listeners, manipulating cells, and obtaining row count, column count, column class, and column name.

The `AbstractTableModel` class provides default implementations for most of the methods in `TableModel`. It takes care of the management of listeners and provides some conveniences for generating `TableModelEvents` and dispatching them to the listeners. To create a concrete `TableModel`, you can simply extend `AbstractTableModel` and implement at least the following three methods:

- `public int getRowCount();`
- `public int getColumnCount();`
- `public Object getValueAt(int row, int column);`

The `DefaultTableModel` class extends `AbstractTableModel` and implements these three methods. Additionally, `DefaultTableModel` provides concrete storage for data. The data are stored in a vector. The elements in the vector are arrays of objects, each of which represents an individual cell value.

The following methods in `DefaultTableModel` for accessing and modifying data are often useful:

```
// For processing cells
public Object getValueAt(int row, int column)
public void setValueAt(Object value, int row, int column)
public boolean isCellEditable(int row, int column)

// For processing columns
public void addColumn(Object columnName)
public void addColumn(Object columnName, Object[] columnData)
public void addColumn(Object columnName, Vector columnData)
public int getColumnCount()
public Class getColumnClass(int column)
public String getColumnName()

// For processing rows
public void addRow(Object[] rowData)
public void addRow(Vector rowData)
public int getRowCount()
public void insertRow(int index, Object[] rowData)
public void insertRow(int index, Vector rowData)
public void moveRow(int startIndex, int endIndex, int toIndex)
```

An instance of `DefaultTableModel` can be constructed using these constructors:

```
public DefaultTableModel()
public DefaultTableModel(int numRows, int numColumns)
public DefaultTableModel(Object[] columnNames, int numRows)
public DefaultTableModel(Object[][] data, object[] columnNames)
public DefaultTableModel(Vector columnNames, int numRows)
public DefaultTableModel(Vector data, Vector columnNames)
```

Table Column Models

Table column models manage columns in a table. They can be used to select, add, move, and remove table columns. A table column model must implement the `TableColumnModel` interface, which defines the methods for registering table column model listeners, and for accessing and manipulating columns.

The `DefaultTableColumnModel` class is a concrete implementation of `TableColumnModel`. The `DefaultTableColumnModel` class stores its columns in a vector and contains an instance of `ListSelectionModel` for selecting columns.

The following methods in `DefaultColumnModel` for manipulating and selecting columns are often useful:

```
// For manipulating columns
public void addColumn(TableColumn tableColumn)
public void removeTableColumn(TableColumn tableColumn)
public void moveColumn(int fromIndex, int toIndex)
public int getColumnMargin()
public void setColumnMargin(int newMargin)
public TableColumn getColumn(int columnIndex)
public int getColumnCount()
public int getColumnIndex(Object columnIdentifier)
public Enumeration getColumns()
public int getTotalColumnWidth()

// For selecting columns
public boolean getColumnSelectionAllowed()
public void setColumnSelectionAllowed(boolean flag)
public int getSelectedColumnCount()
public int getSelectedColumns()
public ListSelectionModel getSelectionModel()
public void setSelectionModel(ListSelectionModel newModel)
```

The *TableColumn* Class

The column model deals with all the columns in a table. The `TableColumn` class is used to represent an individual column in the table. An instance of `TableColumn` for a specified column can be obtained using the `getColumn(index)` method in `TableColumnModel`, or the `getColumn(columnIdentifier)` method in `JTable`.

The following methods in `TableColumn` are used for manipulating column width and specifying cell renderer, cell editor, and header renderer.

```
// Column width, max width, min width, and preferred width
public int getWidth()
public void setWidth(int width)
public int getMaxWidth()
public void setMaxWidth(int maxWidth)
public int getMinWidth()
public void setMinWidth(int minWidth)
public int getPreferredWidth()
public void setPreferredWidth(int minWidth)

// Resizes the column to fit the width of its header cell
public void sizeWidthToFit()

// Renderers and editors for the cells in the column
public TableCellEditor getCellEditor()
public void setCellEditor(TableCellEditor anEditor)
public TableCellRenderer getCellRenderer()
public void setCellRenderer(TableCellRenderer aRenderer)
public TableCellRenderer getHeaderRenderer()
public void setHeaderRenderer(TableCellRenderer aRenderer)
```

Example 8.7 Using Table Models

This example demonstrates the use of table models, table column models, list-selection models, and the `TableColumn` class. The program allows the user to choose selection mode and selection type, and to add or remove rows and columns, as shown in Figure 8.11.

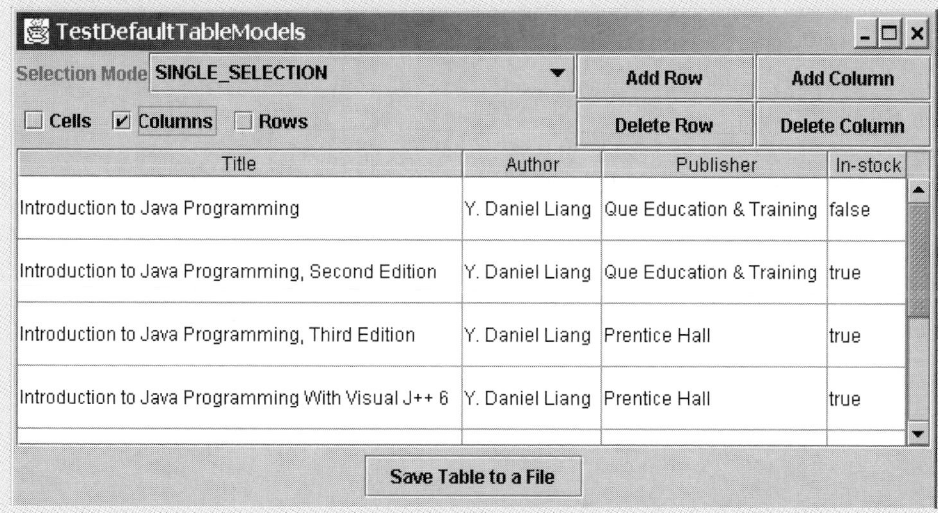

Figure 8.11 *You can add or remove rows and columns in a table.*

Here are the steps to complete the project:

1. Reopen project tabledemo.jpr, and create a new applet named TestDefaultTableModels.java.
2. In the UI designer of TestDefaultTableModels.java, drop a `JScrollPane` to the center of the applet, and drop a `JTable` to the scroll pane to create `jTable1`. Drop a `JPanel` to north of the applet to create `jpOperations`.
3. Set `layout` of `jpOperations` to `BorderLayout`. Drop a `JPanel` to the center of `jpOperations` to create `jpSelections`. Drop a `JPanel` to the east of `jpOperations` to create `jpAddRemove`.
4. Set `layout` of `jpSelections` to `BorderLayout`. Drop a `JPanel` to the north of `jpSelections` to create `jpSelectionMode`, and drop a `JPanel` to the south of `jpSelections` to create `jpSelectionType`.
5. Set `layout` of `jpSelectionMode` to `BorderLayout`. Drop a `JLabel` to the west of `jpSelectionMode`, and drop a `JComboBox` to the center of `jpSelectionMode`.
6. Set `layout` of `jpSelectionType` to `FlowLayout` with left alignment. Drop a `JCheckBox` three times into `jpSelectionType` to create `jchkCells`, `jchkColumns`, and `jchkRows`.

continued

Example 8.7 continued

7. Set `layout` of `jpAddRemove` to `GridLayout` with two rows and two columns. Drop a `JButton` four times to create `jbtAddRow`, `jbtAddColumn`, `jbtDeleteRow`, and `jbtDeleteColumn`.

8. Drop a `JPanel` to the south of the applet. Drop a `JButton` to the panel. Set the button's text to "Save Table to a File." Drop a `JFileChooser` to the UI node in the component tree to create `jFileChooser1`.

9. Create an instance, named `tableModel`, of `DefaultTableModel` with table data and column, as shown in Listing 8.11 (Lines 40–42), and set the `model` property of `jTable1` to `tableModel`.

10. Generate the `ActionEvent` handlers for combo box, check boxes, and buttons, and implement the handlers for choosing a selection mode, choosing selection types, adding or removing rows and columns, and saving the current contents of the table to a file, as shown in Listing 8.11.

```
1  package tabledemo;
2
3  import java.awt.*;
4  import java.awt.event.*;
5  import java.applet.*;
6  import javax.swing.*;
7  import javax.swing.table.*;
8  import java.util.*;
9  import java.io.*;
10
11 public class TestDefaultTableModels extends JApplet {
12   boolean isStandalone = false;
13   JScrollPane jScrollPane1 = new JScrollPane();
14   JTable jTable1 = new JTable();
15   JPanel jpOperations = new JPanel();
16   JPanel jpSelections = new JPanel();
17   JPanel jpSelectionType = new JPanel();
18   JPanel jpSelectionMode = new JPanel();
19   JLabel jLabel1 = new JLabel();
20   JComboBox jcboSelectionMode = new JComboBox();
21   BorderLayout borderLayout1 = new BorderLayout();
22   BorderLayout borderLayout2 = new BorderLayout();
23   BorderLayout borderLayout3 = new BorderLayout();
24   JCheckBox jchkCells = new JCheckBox();
25   JCheckBox jchkColumns = new JCheckBox();
26   JCheckBox jchkRows = new JCheckBox();
27   FlowLayout flowLayout1 = new FlowLayout();
28
29   // Create table column names
30   String[] columnNames =
31     {"Title", "Author", "Publisher", "In-stock"};
32
33   // Create table data
34   Object[][] data = {
35     {"Introduction to Java Programming", "Y. Daniel Liang",
36      "Que Education & Training", new Boolean(false)},
37     // Omitted for brevity
38   };
39
```

Listing 8.11 *TestDefaultTableModels.java*

```
    // Create table model
    DefaultTableModel tableModel =
      new DefaultTableModel(data, columnNames);

    JPanel jpAddRemove = new JPanel();
    JButton jbtDeleteColumn = new JButton();
    JButton jbtDeleteRow = new JButton();
    JButton jbtAddColumn = new JButton();
    JButton jbtAddRow = new JButton();
    GridLayout gridLayout1 = new GridLayout();
    JPanel jPanel1 = new JPanel();
    JButton jbtSave = new JButton();
    JFileChooser jFileChooser1 = new JFileChooser();

    /** Initialize the applet */
    public void init() {
      try {
        jbInit();
      }
      catch(Exception e) {
        e.printStackTrace();
      }
    }

    /** Component initialization */
    private void jbInit() throws Exception {
      this.setSize(new Dimension(452, 294));
      jTable1.setModel(tableModel);
      jTable1.setRowHeight(40);
      jLabel1.setText("Selection Mode");
      jpSelectionMode.setLayout(borderLayout3);
      jpSelectionType.setLayout(flowLayout1);
      jpSelections.setLayout(borderLayout1);
      jpOperations.setLayout(borderLayout2);
      jcboSelectionMode.addActionListener(
        new java.awt.event.ActionListener() {
        public void actionPerformed(ActionEvent e) {
          jcboSelectionMode_actionPerformed(e);
        }
      });
      jchkCells.setText("Cells");
      jchkCells.addActionListener(
        new java.awt.event.ActionListener() {
        public void actionPerformed(ActionEvent e) {
          jchkCells_actionPerformed(e);
        }
      });
      jchkColumns.setText("Columns");
      jchkColumns.addActionListener(
        new java.awt.event.ActionListener() {
        public void actionPerformed(ActionEvent e) {
          jchkColumns_actionPerformed(e);
        }
      });
      jchkRows.setText("Rows");
      jchkRows.addActionListener(
        new java.awt.event.ActionListener() {
        public void actionPerformed(ActionEvent e) {
          jchkRows_actionPerformed(e);
```

Listing 8.11 *Continued*

continued

Example 8.7 continued

```
      }
    });
    flowLayout1.setAlignment(FlowLayout.LEFT);
    jbtDeleteColumn.setText("Delete Column");
    jbtDeleteColumn.addActionListener(
      new java.awt.event.ActionListener() {
      public void actionPerformed(ActionEvent e) {
        jbtDeleteColumn_actionPerformed(e);
      }
    });
    jbtDeleteRow.setText("Delete Row");
    jbtDeleteRow.addActionListener(
      new java.awt.event.ActionListener() {
      public void actionPerformed(ActionEvent e) {
        jbtDeleteRow_actionPerformed(e);
      }
    });
    jbtAddColumn.setText("Add Column");
    jbtAddColumn.addActionListener(
      new java.awt.event.ActionListener() {
      public void actionPerformed(ActionEvent e) {
        jbtAddColumn_actionPerformed(e);
      }
    });
    jbtAddRow.setText("Add Row");
    jbtAddRow.addActionListener(
      new java.awt.event.ActionListener() {
      public void actionPerformed(ActionEvent e) {
        jbtAddRow_actionPerformed(e);
      }
    });
    jpAddRemove.setLayout(gridLayout1);
    gridLayout1.setColumns(2);
    gridLayout1.setRows(2);
    jbtSave.setText("Save Table to a File");
    jbtSave.addActionListener(new java.awt.event.ActionListener() {
      public void actionPerformed(ActionEvent e) {
        jbtSave_actionPerformed(e);
      }
    });
    this.getContentPane().add(jScrollPane1, BorderLayout.CENTER);
    jScrollPane1.getViewport().add(jTable1, null);
    this.getContentPane().add(jpOperations, BorderLayout.NORTH);
    jpOperations.add(jpSelections, BorderLayout.CENTER);
    jpSelections.add(jpSelectionMode, BorderLayout.NORTH);
    jpSelectionMode.add(jLabel1, BorderLayout.WEST);
    jpSelectionMode.add(jcboSelectionMode, BorderLayout.CENTER);
    jpSelections.add(jpSelectionType, BorderLayout.CENTER);
    jpSelectionType.add(jchkCells, null);
    jpSelectionType.add(jchkColumns, null);
    jpSelectionType.add(jchkRows, null);
    jpOperations.add(jpAddRemove, BorderLayout.EAST);
    jpAddRemove.add(jbtAddRow, null);
    jpAddRemove.add(jbtAddColumn, null);
    jpAddRemove.add(jbtDeleteRow, null);
    jpAddRemove.add(jbtDeleteColumn, null);
    this.getContentPane().add(jPanel1, BorderLayout.SOUTH);
    jPanel1.add(jbtSave, null);

```

Listing 8.11 *Continued*

```
      // Add selection modes to jcboSelectionMode
      jcboSelectionMode.addItem("SINGLE_SELECTION");
      jcboSelectionMode.addItem("SINGLE_INTERVAL_SELECTION");
      jcboSelectionMode.addItem("MULTIPLE_INTERVAL_SELECTION");
    }

    /** Choose a selection mode */
    void jcboSelectionMode_actionPerformed(ActionEvent e) {
      String selectedItem =
        (String)jcboSelectionMode.getSelectedItem();

      if (selectedItem.equals("SINGLE_SELECTION"))
        jTable1.setSelectionMode(ListSelectionModel.SINGLE_SELECTION);
      else if (selectedItem.equals("SINGLE_INTERVAL_SELECTION"))
        jTable1.setSelectionMode(
          ListSelectionModel.SINGLE_INTERVAL_SELECTION);
      else if (selectedItem.equals("MULTIPLE_INTERVAL_SELECTION"))
        jTable1.setSelectionMode(
          ListSelectionModel.MULTIPLE_INTERVAL_SELECTION);
    }

    /** Cell selection enabled */
    void jchkCells_actionPerformed(ActionEvent e) {
      jTable1.setCellSelectionEnabled(
        jchkCells.isSelected());
    }

    /** Column selection enabled */
    void jchkColumns_actionPerformed(ActionEvent e) {
      jTable1.setColumnSelectionAllowed(
        jchkColumns.isSelected());
    }

    /** Row selection enabled */
    void jchkRows_actionPerformed(ActionEvent e) {
      jTable1.setRowSelectionAllowed(
        jchkRows.isSelected());
    }

    /** Add a new row */
    void jbtAddRow_actionPerformed(ActionEvent e) {
      tableModel.addRow(new Object[]{
        " ", " ", " ", new Boolean(false)});
    }

    /** Add a new column */
    void jbtAddColumn_actionPerformed(ActionEvent e) {
      tableModel.addColumn(new String("New Column"),
        new Object[] {"1", "2", "3", "4", "5", "6", "7"});
    }

    /** Remove the selected row */
    void jbtDeleteRow_actionPerformed(ActionEvent e) {
      tableModel.removeRow(jTable1.getSelectedRow());
    }

    /** Remove the selected column */
    void jbtDeleteColumn_actionPerformed(ActionEvent e) {
      DefaultTableColumnModel tableColumnModel =
        (DefaultTableColumnModel)jTable1.getColumnModel();
```

Listing 8.11 *Continued*

continued

Example 8.7 continued

```
      int selectedColumn = jTable1.getSelectedColumn();
      tableColumnModel.removeColumn(
        tableColumnModel.getColumn(selectedColumn));
    }

    void jbtSave_actionPerformed(ActionEvent e) {
      if (jFileChooser1.showSaveDialog(this) ==
        JFileChooser.APPROVE_OPTION) {
        save(jFileChooser1.getSelectedFile());
      }
    }

    /** Save file with specified File instance */
    private void save(File file) {
      try {
        // Write table to the specified file
        BufferedWriter out = new BufferedWriter(new FileWriter(file));
        String header = "";

        // Write header to the file
        for (int i=0; i<jTable1.getColumnCount(); i++)
          header += jTable1.getColumnName(i) + '\t';
        out.write(header);
        out.newLine();

        // Write rows to the file
        for (int i=0; i<jTable1.getRowCount(); i++) {
          for (int j=0; j<jTable1.getColumnCount(); j++) {
            out.write(jTable1.getValueAt(i, j).toString() + '\t');
          }
          out.newLine();
        }

        out.close();
      }
      catch (IOException ex) {
        ex.printStackTrace();
      }
    }
  }
```

Listing 8.11 *Continued*

Example Review

The table selection model is the same as the list selection mode. You can choose to select a single object, objects in a single interval, or objects in multiple intervals. The objects can be cells, columns, or rows. The selectable object types can be specified using the following `JTable` `boolean` properties:

- `cellSelectionAllowed`
- `columnSelectionAllowed`
- `rowSelectionAllowed`

When you click the Add Row button, a new row is appended to the table. When you click the Add Column button, a new column entitled "New Column" is appended to the table. To delete a row, first select a row, then click the

Delete Row button. To delete a column, first select a column, then click the Delete Column button. The program only deletes one row or one column at a time, but you can modify the handlers to enable the deletion of multiple rows and columns.

When you click the Save Table to a File button, a file save dialog box is displayed. You can choose or specify a filename, then click OK to save the current contents of the table to a file.

Some of the methods defined in the table model and the table column model are also defined in the table model or in the `JTable` class for convenience. For instance, the `getColumnCount()` method is defined in `JTable`, `TableModel`, and `TableColumnModel`, the `addColumn` method defined in the column model is also defined in the table model, and the `getColumn()` method defined in the column model is also defined in the `JTable` class.

NOTE

Due to a bug, `TableModel` and `TableColumnModel` are not synchronized. If you add or delete a column from `TableColumnModel`, the change is not effected in `TableModel`. However, the change does take place in `JTable`. Always use the methods from `JTable` as much as possible. For example, to get the column count, use the `getColumnCount` method from the `JTable` class instead of from the `TableColumnModel` class. Therefore, in the `save` method in this example, `jTable1.getColumnCount()` was used instead of `tableModel.getColumnCount()`.

Table Renderers and Editors

Table cells are painted by cell renderers. By default, a cell object's string representation is displayed and the string can be edited as it was in a text field. `JTable` maintains a set of predefined renderers and editors, listed in Table 8.1, which can be specified to replace default string renderers and editors.

The predefined renderers and editors are automatically located and loaded to match the class return from the `getColumnClass()` method in the table model. To

TABLE 8.1 Predefined renderers and editors for tables

Class	*Renderer*	*Editor*
`Object`	`JLabel` (left aligned)	`JTextField`
`Date`	`JLabel` (right aligned)	`JTextField`
`Number`	`JLabel` (right aligned)	`JTextField`
`ImageIcom`	`JLabel` (center aligned)	
`Boolean`	`JCheckBox` (center aligned)	`JCheckBox` (center aligned)

use a predefined renderer or editor for a class other than `String`, you need to create your own table model by extending a subclass of `TableModel`. In your table model class, you need to override the `getColumnClass()` method to return the class of the column, as follows:

```
public Class getColumnClass(int column) {
  return getValueAt(0, column).getClass();
}
```

Example 8.8 Using Predefined Table Renderers and Editors

This example demonstrates using predefined table renderers and editors for `boolean` values, dates, and image icons, as shown in Figure 8.12.

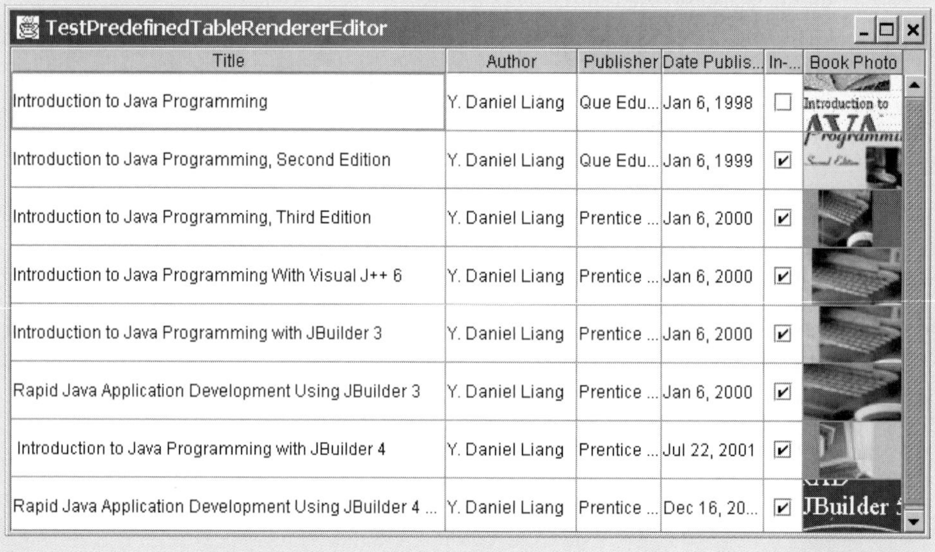

TestPredefinedTableRendererEditor

Title	Author	Publisher	Date Publis...	In-...	Book Photo
Introduction to Java Programming	Y. Daniel Liang	Que Edu...	Jan 6, 1998	☐	
Introduction to Java Programming, Second Edition	Y. Daniel Liang	Que Edu...	Jan 6, 1999	☑	
Introduction to Java Programming, Third Edition	Y. Daniel Liang	Prentice ...	Jan 6, 2000	☑	
Introduction to Java Programming With Visual J++ 6	Y. Daniel Liang	Prentice ...	Jan 6, 2000	☑	
Introduction to Java Programming with JBuilder 3	Y. Daniel Liang	Prentice ...	Jan 6, 2000	☑	
Rapid Java Application Development Using JBuilder 3	Y. Daniel Liang	Prentice ...	Jan 6, 2000	☑	
Introduction to Java Programming with JBuilder 4	Y. Daniel Liang	Prentice ...	Jul 22, 2001	☑	
Rapid Java Application Development Using JBuilder 4 ...	Y. Daniel Liang	Prentice ...	Dec 16, 20...	☑	

Figure 8.12 `JTable` *uses predefined renderers and editors for* `boolean` *values, dates, and image icons.*

Here are the steps to complete the project:

1. Reopen project tabledemo.jpr. Create a new class named `MyTableModel` that extends `DefaultTableModel`, as shown in Listing 8.12. Create a new applet named TestPredefinedTableRendererEditor.java using the Applet wizard.

2. In the UI designer of TestPredefinedTableRendererEditor.java, drop a `JScrollPane` to the center of the applet, and drop a `JTable` to the scroll pane to create `jTable1`.

3. Create an instance, named `tableModel`, of `MyTableModel` with table data and column, as shown in Listing 8.13 and set the `model` property of `jTable1` to `tableModel`.

```
package tabledemo;

import javax.swing.*;
import javax.swing.table.*;
import java.util.*;

public class MyTableModel extends DefaultTableModel {
  public MyTableModel(Object[][] data, Object[] columnNames) {
    super(data, columnNames);
  }

  /** Override this method to return a class for the column */
  public Class getColumnClass(int column) {
    return getValueAt(0, column).getClass();
  }

  /** Override this method to return true if cell is editable */
  public boolean isCellEditable(int row, int column) {
    Class columnClass = getColumnClass(column);
    return columnClass != ImageIcon.class &&
      columnClass != Date.class;
  }
}
```

Listing 8.12 *MyTableModel.java*

```
package tabledemo;

import java.awt.*;
import java.awt.event.*;
import java.applet.*;
import javax.swing.*;
import java.util.*;
import imageviewerdemo.ImageViewer;

public class TestPredefinedTableRendererEditor extends JApplet {
  boolean isStandalone = false;
  JScrollPane jScrollPane1 = new JScrollPane();
  JTable jTable1 = new JTable();

  // Create table column names
  String[] columnNames =
    {"Title", "Author", "Publisher", "Date Published", "In-stock",
      "Book Photo"};

  /** Initialize the applet */
  public void init() {
    try {
      jbInit();
    }
    catch(Exception e) {
      e.printStackTrace();
    }
  }

  /** Component initialization */
  private void jbInit() throws Exception {
    // Create images
    ImageIcon intro1eImageIcon = ImageViewer.createImageIcon(
      "/image/intro1e.gif", this);

```

Listing 8.13 *TestPredefinedTableRendererEditor.java*

continued

Example 8.8 continued

```
      // Create image icons, omitted for brevity

      // Create table data
      Object[][] data = {
        {"Introduction to Java Programming", "Y. Daniel Liang",
         "Que Education & Training",
          new GregorianCalendar(1998, 1-1, 6).getTime(),
          new Boolean(false), intro1eImageIcon},
        // Omitted for brevity
      };

      // Create table model
      MyTableModel tableModel = new MyTableModel(data, columnNames);

      this.setSize(new Dimension(400,300));
      jTable1.setModel(tableModel);
      jTable1.setRowHeight(40);
      this.getContentPane().add(jScrollPane1, BorderLayout.CENTER);
      jScrollPane1.getViewport().add(jTable1, null);
    }
  }
```

Listing 8.13 *Continued*

Example Review

The example creates two classes: `MyTableModel` and `TestPredefinedTableRendererEditor`. `MyTableModel` is an extension of `DefaultTableModel`. The purpose of `MyTableModel` is to override the default implementation of the `getColumnClass()` method to return the class of the column, so that an appropriate predefined `JTable` can be used for the column. By default, `getColumnClass()` returns `Object.class`.

`MyTableModel` also overrides the `isCellEditable()` method. By default, `isCellEditable()` returns `true`. You can override it to prohibit editing of a cell. This example does not allow the user to edit image icons and dates. For a cell to be editable, both `isCellEditable()` in the table model and `isEditing` in `JTable` class must be `true`.

The `TestPredefinedTableRendererEditor` class creates a table model using `MyTableModel`. `JTable` assigns a predefined cell renderer and a predefined editor to the cell, whose class is specified in the `getColumnClass()` method in `MyTableModel`.

Custom Table Renderers and Editors

Predefined renderers and editors are convenient and easy to use, but their functions are limited. The predefined image icon renderer displays the image icon in a label. The image icon cannot be scaled. If you want the whole image to fit in a cell, you need to create a custom renderer.

A custom renderer can be created by extending the `DefaultTableCellRenderer`, which is a default implementation for the `TableCellRender` interface. The custom renderer must override the `getTableCellRendererComponent()` to return a component for rendering the table cell.

The `getTableCellRendererComponent` is defined as follows:

```
public Component getTableCellRendererComponent
  (JTable table, Object value, boolean isSelected,
   boolean isFocused, int row, int column)
```

This method signature is very similar to the `getListCellRendererComponent` method used to create custom list cell renderers. Their implementations are similar too. The following class, `MyImageCellRenderer`, shown in Listing 8.14, creates a renderer for displaying image icons in a panel.

```
package tabledemo;

import javax.swing.*;
import javax.swing.table.*;
import imageviewerdemo.ImageViewer;
import java.awt.*;

public class MyImageCellRenderer extends DefaultTableCellRenderer {
  /** Override this method in DefaultTableCellRenderer */
  public Component getTableCellRendererComponent
    (JTable table, Object value, boolean isSelected,
     boolean isFocused, int row, int column) {
    Image image = ((ImageIcon)value).getImage();
    ImageViewer imageViewer = new ImageViewer(image);
    return imageViewer;
  }
}
```

Listing 8.14 *MyImageCellRenderer.java*

You can also create a custom editor. `JTable` provides the `DefaultCellEditor` class, which can be used to edit a cell in a text field, a check box, or a combo box. To use it, simply create a text field, a check box, or a combo box, and pass it to `DefaultCellEditor`'s constructor to create an editor.

Example 8.9 Using Custom Table Renderers and Editors

This example demonstrates using custom table renderers to display image icons and using a custom combo editor to edit items. A sample run of the program is shown in Figure 8.13.

Here are the steps to complete the project:

1. Reopen project tabledemo.jpr. Create a new class named `MyImageCellRenderer` that extends `DefaultTableCellRenderer`, as shown in Listing 8.14. Create a new applet named TestCustomTableRendererEditor.java using the Applet wizard.

2. In the UI designer of TestCustomTableRendererEditor.java, drop a `JScrollPane` to the center of the applet, and drop a `JTable` to the scroll pane to create `jTable1`.

3. Switch to the content pane to create an instance, named `tableModel`, of `MyTableModel` with table data and column names, and set the `model` property of `jTable1` to `tableModel`.

continued

Example 8.9 continued

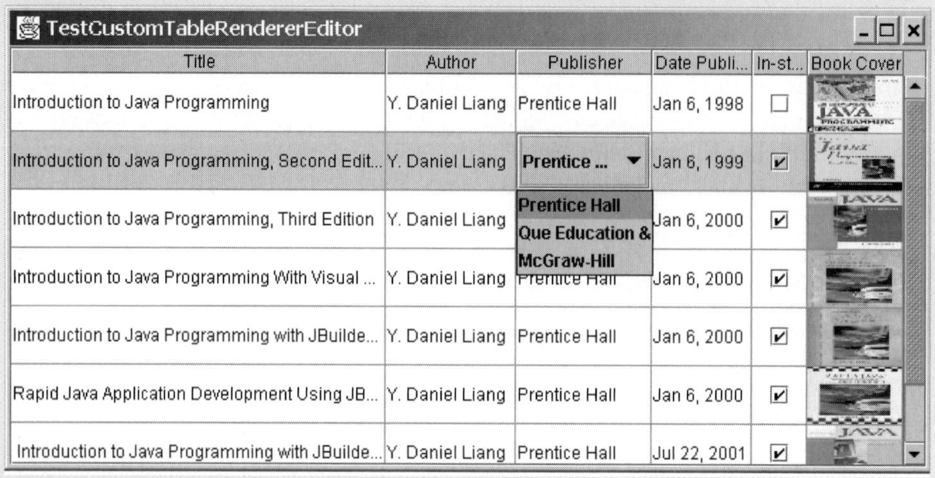

TestCustomTableRendererEditor

Title	Author	Publisher	Date Publi...	In-st...	Book Cover
Introduction to Java Programming	Y. Daniel Liang	Prentice Hall	Jan 6, 1998	☐	
Introduction to Java Programming, Second Edit...	Y. Daniel Liang	Prentice ...	Jan 6, 1999	☑	
Introduction to Java Programming, Third Edition	Y. Daniel Liang	Prentice Hall / Que Education & / McGraw-Hill	Jan 6, 2000	☑	
Introduction to Java Programming With Visual ...	Y. Daniel Liang	Prentice Hall	Jan 6, 2000	☑	
Introduction to Java Programming with JBuilde...	Y. Daniel Liang	Prentice Hall	Jan 6, 2000	☑	
Rapid Java Application Development Using JB...	Y. Daniel Liang	Prentice Hall	Jan 6, 2000	☑	
Introduction to Java Programming with JBuilde...	Y. Daniel Liang	Prentice Hall	Jul 22, 2001	☑	

Figure 8.13 *A custom renderer displays a scaled image, and a custom editor edits the Publisher column using a combo box.*

4. Create an instance of `MyImageCellRenderer` and set it as the cell renderer for the Book Cover column (Lines 52–54).

5. Create an instance of `JComboBox` and add three publisher names, as shown in Listing 8.15 (Lines 56–60). Pass the combo box to the constructor of `DefaultCellEditor` to create a custom editor and set it as the cell editor for the Publisher column.

```
1   package tabledemo;
2
3   import java.awt.*;
4   import java.awt.event.*;
5   import java.applet.*;
6   import javax.swing.*;
7   import javax.swing.table.*;
8   import java.util.*;
9   import imageviewerdemo.ImageViewer;
10
11  public class TestCustomTableRendererEditor extends JApplet {
12    boolean isStandalone = false;
13    JScrollPane jScrollPane1 = new JScrollPane();
14    JTable jTable1 = new JTable();
15
16    /** Initialize the applet */
17    public void init() {
18      try {
19        jbInit();
20      }
21      catch(Exception e) {
22        e.printStackTrace();
23      }
24    }
25
26    /** Component initialization */
```

Listing 8.15 *TestCustomTableRendererEditor.java*

```
27        private void jbInit() throws Exception {
28          // Create images
29          ImageIcon intro1eImageIcon = ImageViewer.createImageIcon(
30            "/image/intro1e.gif", this);
31
32          // Create other images omitted for brevity
33
34          // Create table data
35          Object[][] data = {
36            {"Introduction to Java Programming", "Y. Daniel Liang",
37             "Que Education & Training",
38              new GregorianCalendar(1998, 1-1, 6).getTime(),
39              new Boolean(false), intro1eImageIcon},
40            // Omitted for brevity
41          };
42
43          // Create table model
44          MyTableModel tableModel = new MyTableModel(data, columnNames);
45
46          this.setSize(new Dimension(400,300));
47          jTable1.setModel(tableModel);
48          jTable1.setRowHeight(40);
49          this.getContentPane().add(jScrollPane1, BorderLayout.CENTER);
50          jScrollPane1.getViewport().add(jTable1, null);
51
52          // Set custom renderer for displaying images
53          TableColumn bookCover = jTable1.getColumn("Book Cover");
54          bookCover.setCellRenderer(new MyImageCellRenderer());
55
56          // Create a combo box for publishers
57          JComboBox jcboPublishers = new JComboBox();
58          jcboPublishers.addItem("Prentice Hall");
59          jcboPublishers.addItem("Que Education & Training");
60          jcboPublishers.addItem("McGraw-Hill");
61
62          // Set combo box as the editor for the publisher column
63          TableColumn publisherColumn = jTable1.getColumn("Publisher");
64          publisherColumn.setCellEditor(
65            new DefaultCellEditor(jcboPublishers));
66        }
67      }
```

Listing 8.15 *Continued*

Example Review

This example uses the same table model (`MyTableModel`) that was created in the previous example. By default, image icons are displayed using the predefined image icon renderer. To use `MyImageCellRenderer` to display the image, you have to explicitly specify the `MyImageCellRenderer` renderer for the Book Cover column (Line 54). Likewise, you have to explicitly specify the combo box editor for the Publisher column (Line 64); otherwise the default editor would be used.

When you edit a cell in the Publisher column, a combo box of three items is displayed. When you select an item from the box, it is displayed in the cell. You did not write the code for handling selections. The selections are handled by the `DefaultCellEditor` class.

When you resize the Book Cover column, the image is resized to fit into the whole cell. With the predefined image renderer, you can only see part of the image if the cell is smaller than the image.

Table Events

Table events are fired by table models, table column models, and table selection models whenever changes are made to these models. The `JTable` class does not fire table events. Table models fire `TableModelEvent` when table data are changed. Table column models fire `TableColumnModelEvent` when columns are added, removed, or moved, or when the column selection changes. Table selection models fire `ListSelectionEvent` when the selection changes.

To listen for these events, a listener must be registered with an appropriate model and implement the correct listener interface. The following example demonstrates using these events.

Example 8.10 Using Table Events

This example demonstrates handling table events. The program displays messages on a label when a row or a column is selected, when a cell is edited, or when a column is removed. Figure 8.14 is a sample run of the example.

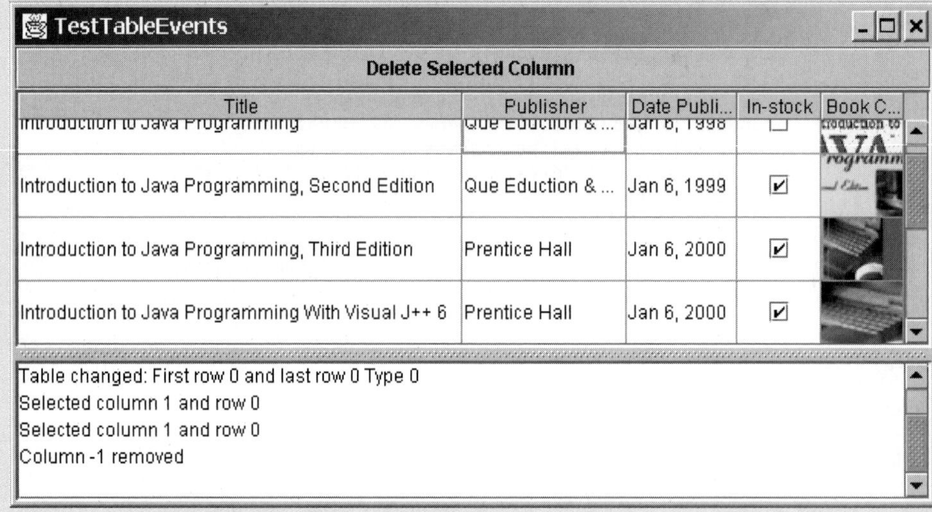

Figure 8.14 *Table event handlers display table events on a text area.*

Here are the steps to complete the project:

1. Reopen project tabledemo.jpr. Create a new applet named TestTableEvents.java using the Applet wizard.

2. In the UI designer of TestTableEvents.java, drop a `JSplitPane` to the center of the applet and set its `orientation` to `VERTICAL`. Drop a `JScrollPane` to the top of the split pane, and drop a `JTable` to the scroll pane to create `jTable1`. Drop a `JScrollPane` to the bottom of the split pane, and drop a `JTextArea` to the scroll pane to create `jtaMessage`. Drop a `JButton` to the north of the applet to create `jbtDeleteColumn`.

3. Switch to the content pane to create an instance named `tableModel` of `MyTableModel` with table data and column names (Line 63), and set the `model` property of `jTable1` to `tableModel`. Create an instance named `tableColumnModel` obtained from `jTable1.getColumnModel()` (Line 66). Create an instance named `selectionModel` obtained from `jTable1.getSelectionModel()` (Line 69).

4. Switch to the UI designer. In the component tree, select `tableModel` in the Other node. In the Events page of the component inspector for `tableModel`, double-click the value field of `tableChanged` item to generate the handler for table model changed event. Implement the handler to display the changes in the text area, as shown in Listing 8.16 (Lines 121–126).

5. Select `tableModel` in the Other node in the component tree. In the Events page of the component inspector for `tableColumnModel`, double-click the value field of `columnRemoved` item to generate the handler for column removed event. Implement the handler to display the remove column index in the text area, as shown in Listing 8.16 (Lines 128–132).

6. Select `selectionModel` in the Other node in the component tree. In the Events page of the component inspector for `selectionModel`, double-click the value field of `valueChanged` item to generate the handler for selection event. Implement the handler to display the selected row and column in the text area, as shown in Listing 8.16 (Lines 134–139).

7. Double-click the Delete Selected Column button to generate a handler for button action. Implement the handler to delete the currently selected column, as shown in Listing 8.16 (Lines 141–146).

```
1   package tabledemo;
2
3   import java.awt.*;
4   import java.awt.event.*;
5   import java.applet.*;
6   import javax.swing.*;
7   import javax.swing.table.*;
8   import javax.swing.event.*;
8   import java.util.*;
19  import imageviewerdemo.ImageViewer;
11
12  public class TestTableEvents extends JApplet {
13    boolean isStandalone = false;
14    JSplitPane jSplitPane1 = new JSplitPane();
15    JScrollPane jScrollPane1 = new JScrollPane();
16    JButton jbtDeleteColumn = new JButton();
17    JScrollPane jScrollPane2 = new JScrollPane();
18    JTextArea jtaMessage = new JTextArea();
19    JTable jTable1 = new JTable();
20
21    // Table model
22    MyTableModel tableModel;
23
24    // Table column model
25    TableColumnModel tableColumnModel;
26
```

Listing 8.16 *TestTableEvents.java*

continued

Example 8.10 continued

```
  // Table selection model
  ListSelectionModel selectionModel;

  /** Initialize the applet */
  public void init() {
    try {
      jbInit();
    }
    catch(Exception e) {
      e.printStackTrace();
    }
  }

  /** Component initialization */
  private void jbInit() throws Exception {
    // Create table column names
    String[] columnNames =
      {"Title", "Author", "Publisher", "Date Published", "In-stock",
        "Book Cover"};

    // Create images
    ImageIcon intro1eImageIcon = ImageViewer.createImageIcon(
      "/image/intro1e.gif", this);

    // Create other images, omitted for brevity

    // Create table data
    Object[][] data = {
      {"Introduction to Java Programming", "Y. Daniel Liang",
       "Que Education & Training",
       new GregorianCalendar(1998, 1-1, 6).getTime(),
       new Boolean(false), intro1eImageIcon},
        // Omitted for brevity
    };

    // Create table model
    tableModel = new MyTableModel(data, columnNames);

    // Create table column model
    tableColumnModel = jTable1.getColumnModel();

    // Create table selection model
    selectionModel = jTable1.getSelectionModel();

    this.setSize(new Dimension(400,300));
    jTable1.setColumnSelectionAllowed(true);
    jTable1.setModel(tableModel);
    jTable1.setRowHeight(40);
    selectionModel.addListSelectionListener(
      new javax.swing.event.ListSelectionListener() {
      public void valueChanged(ListSelectionEvent e) {
        selectionModel_valueChanged(e);
      }
    });
    tableModel.addTableModelListener(
      new javax.swing.event.TableModelListener() {
      public void tableChanged(TableModelEvent e) {
        tableModel_tableChanged(e);
      }
    });
```

Listing 8.16 *Continued*

```
      jbtDeleteColumn.setText("Delete Selected Column");
      jbtDeleteColumn.addActionListener(
        new java.awt.event.ActionListener() {
        public void actionPerformed(ActionEvent e) {
          jbtDeleteColumn_actionPerformed(e);
        }
      });
      tableColumnModel.addColumnModelListener(
        new javax.swing.event.TableColumnModelListener() {
        public void columnAdded(TableColumnModelEvent e) {
        }

        public void columnMarginChanged(ChangeEvent e) {
        }

        public void columnMoved(TableColumnModelEvent e) {
        }

        public void columnRemoved(TableColumnModelEvent e) {
          tableColumnModel_columnRemoved(e);
        }

        public void columnSelectionChanged(ListSelectionEvent e) {
        }
      });
      this.getContentPane().add(jbtDeleteColumn, BorderLayout.NORTH);
      this.getContentPane().add(jSplitPane1, BorderLayout.CENTER);
      jSplitPane1.setOrientation(JSplitPane.VERTICAL_SPLIT);
      jSplitPane1.add(jScrollPane1, JSplitPane.TOP);
      jScrollPane1.getViewport().add(jTable1);
      jSplitPane1.add(jScrollPane2, JSplitPane.BOTTOM);
      jScrollPane2.getViewport().add(jtaMessage);
    }

    /** Handle table change events */
    void tableModel_tableChanged(TableModelEvent e) {
      jtaMessage.append("Table changed: First row " + e.getFirstRow()
        + " and last row " + e.getLastRow() + " Type " +
        e.getType() + '\n');
    }

    /** Handle column removed event */
    void tableColumnModel_columnRemoved(TableColumnModelEvent e) {
      jtaMessage.append("Column " + jTable1.getSelectedColumn() +
        " removed " + '\n');
    }

    /** Handle selection events */
    void selectionModel_valueChanged(ListSelectionEvent e) {
      jtaMessage.append("Selected column " +
        jTable1.getSelectedColumn() + " and row " +
        jTable1.getSelectedRow() + '\n');
    }

    /** Handle deleting a selected column */
    void jbtDeleteColumn_actionPerformed(ActionEvent e) {
      int selectedColumn = jTable1.getSelectedColumn();
      tableColumnModel.removeColumn(
        tableColumnModel.getColumn(selectedColumn));
    }
  }
```

Listing 8.16 *Continued*

continued

Example 8.10 continued

Example Review

This example creates a table model for the table, and gets the default table column model and selection model from the table. To make those model instances visible in the component tree, they are declared as data members of the class. The event handlers for the models are created from the Events page in the component inspector.

When a row or a column is selected, a `ListSelectionEvent` is fired by `selectionModel`, which invokes the handler to display the selected row and column in the text area. When the content or structure of the table is changed, a `TableModelEvent` is fired by `tableModel`, which invokes the handler to display the last row, last column, and event type in the text area. When a column is deleted by clicking the Delete Selected Column button, a `ColumnModelEvent` is fired by `tableColumnModel`, which invokes the handler to display the index of the deleted column.

JTree

`JTree` is a Swing component that displays data in a treelike hierarchy. Figure 8.15 shows the Swing tree in the SwingSet demo.

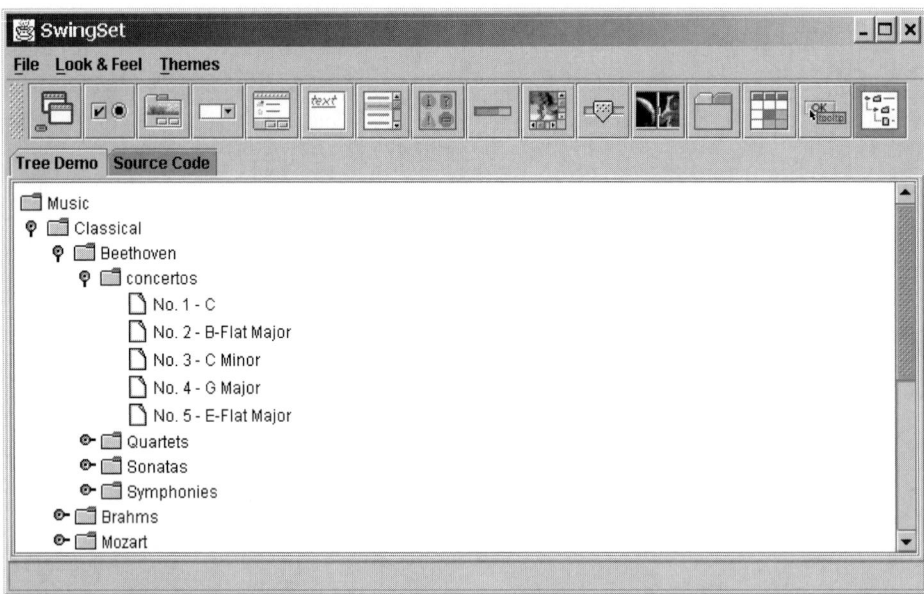

Figure 8.15 *The SwingSet demo demonstrates the features of* `JTree`.

All the nodes displayed in the tree are in the form of a hierarchical indexed list. The tree can be used to navigate structured data with hierarchical relationships. The JBuilder project pane, structure pane, and component tree are examples of displaying items as nodes in a treelike structure. A node can have child nodes. A node is called a *leaf* if it has no children; a node with no parent is called the *root* of its tree. A tree may consist of many subtrees, each node acting as the root for its own subtree.

A nonleaf node can be expanded or collapsed by double-clicking on the node or on the node's handle in front of the node. The handle usually has a visible sign to indicate whether the node is expanded or collapsed. For example, on Windows, the + symbol indicates that the node is collapsed, and the – symbol, that it is expanded.

Like `JTable`, `JTree` is a very complex component with many supporting interfaces and classes. `JTree` is in the `javax.swing` package, but its supporting classes are all included in the `javax.swing.tree` package. These supporting classes are `DefaultMutableTreeNode`, `DefaultTreeModel`, `TreeSelectionModel`, `DefaultTreeCellEditor`, `DefaultTreeCellRenderer`, and `TreePath`.

While `JTree` displays the tree, the data representation of the tree is handled by the `DefaultMutableTreeNode` class, which provides operations for creating nodes, for examining and modifying a node's parent and children, and also for examining the tree to which the node belongs. While the `DefaultMutableTreeNode` represents a node, the `DefaultTreeModel` represents the entire tree. Unlike the `ListModel` or `TableModel`, the tree model does not directly store or manage tree data. Tree data are stored and managed by the `DefaultMutableTreeNode` class. To create a tree model, you first create an instance of `DefaultMutableTreeNode` to represent the root of the tree, and then create an instance of `DefaultTreeModel` fitted with the root.

The `TreeSelectionModel` class handles tree node selection. The `DefaultTreeCellRenderer` class provides a default tree node renderer that can display a label and/or an icon in a node. The `DefaultTreeCellEditor` can be used to edit the cells in a text field. The `TreePath` class is a support class that represents a set of nodes in a path.

`JTree` has the following useful properties:

- `cellEditor`: This is an object used to edit the cell in a tree node. By default, an instance of `DefaultCellEditor` is used to edit the cells in a text field. Using custom tree cell renderer is introduced in the section "Tree Node Rendering and Editing."
- `cellRenderer`: This is an object used to render the cells in a tree node. By default, an instance of `DefaultTreeCellRenderer` is used to display nodes in a tree that can display strings or icons. Using custom tree cell renderer is introduced in the section "Tree Node Rendering and Editing."
- `editable`: This is a `boolean` value indicating whether the cell is editable. The default value is `false`.
- `model`: This is an instance of `TreeModel`.
- `rootVisible`: This is a `boolean` value indicating whether the root is displayed in the tree. The default value is `true`.
- `rowHeight`: This specifies the height of the row for the node displayed in the tree. The default height is 16 pixels.
- `selectionModel`: This is an instance of `TreeSelectionModel`.

Creating Trees

`JTree` doesn't directly support scrolling. To create a scrollable tree, you need to create a `JScrollPane` and add an instance of `JTree` to the scroll pane.

There are several constructors that can be used to create a `JTree`. You can create a `JTree` with an array of objects, a vector, or a hash table. The builder tool always uses the default constructor to create an instance of `JTree` with a default tree model. The default tree is shown in Figure 8.16, because the default tree model is defined in the `getDefaultTreeModel` method of the `JTree` class as follows:

```
// Excerpted from JTree.java
protected static TreeModel getDefaultTreeModel() {
  DefaultMutableTreeNode root = new DefaultMutableTreeNode("JTree");
  DefaultMutableTreeNode parent;

  parent = new DefaultMutableTreeNode("colors");
  root.add(parent);
  parent.add(new DefaultMutableTreeNode("blue"));
  parent.add(new DefaultMutableTreeNode("violet"));
  parent.add(new DefaultMutableTreeNode("red"));
  parent.add(new DefaultMutableTreeNode("yellow"));

  parent = new DefaultMutableTreeNode("sports");
  root.add(parent);
  parent.add(new DefaultMutableTreeNode("basketball"));
  parent.add(new DefaultMutableTreeNode("soccer"));

  // Omitted for brevity

  return new DefaultTreeModel(root);
}
```

Figure 8.16 *The default tree constructed with the default constructor of* `JTree` *displays sample data.*

As demonstrated in the following example, a custom tree model can be created in the same way as the default model.

Example 8.11 Creating Custom Trees

This example creates a tree to display the table of contents of this book, as shown in Figure 8.17.

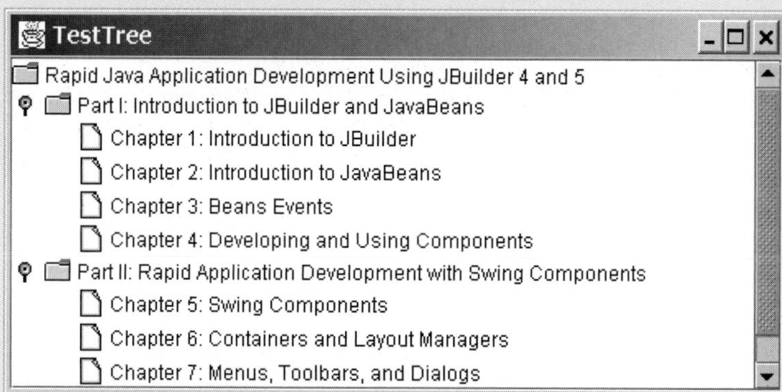

Figure 8.17 *The table of contents of this book is displayed in a tree.*

Here are the steps to complete the example:

1. Create a new project named treedemo.jpr and an applet named TestTree.java.
2. In the UI designer of TestTree.java, drop a `JScrollPane` to the center of the applet, and drop a `JTree` to the scroll pane to create `jTree1`.
3. Create a method named `createTreeModel()` to create a tree model, as shown in Listing 8.17 (Lines 36–69). Declare and create an instance of `TreeModel` named `treeModel`. Set the `model` property of `jTree1` to `treeModel` (Line 29).

```
1   package treedemo;
2
3   import java.awt.*;
4   import java.awt.event.*;
5   import java.applet.*;
6   import javax.swing.*;
7   import javax.swing.tree.*;
8
9   public class TestTree extends JApplet {
10    boolean isStandalone = false;
11    JScrollPane jScrollPane1 = new JScrollPane();
12    JTree jTree1 = new JTree();
13    DefaultTreeModel treeModel;
14
```

Listing 8.17 *TestTree.java*

continued

Example 8.11 continued

```
  /** Initialize the applet */
  public void init() {
    try {
      jbInit();
    }
    catch(Exception e) {
      e.printStackTrace();
    }
  }

  /** Component initialization */
  private void jbInit() throws Exception {
    // Create a tree model and set the tree model in jTree1
    treeModel = createTreeModel();
    jTree1.setModel(treeModel); // Set this value manually

    this.setSize(new Dimension(400,300));
    this.getContentPane().add(jScrollPane1, BorderLayout.CENTER);
    jScrollPane1.getViewport().add(jTree1, null);
  }

  /** Create a tree model */
  private DefaultTreeModel createTreeModel() {
    DefaultMutableTreeNode root = new DefaultMutableTreeNode
      ("Rapid Java Application Development Using JBuilder 4 and 5");

    DefaultMutableTreeNode parent = new DefaultMutableTreeNode
      ("Part I: Introduction to JBuilder and JavaBeans");
    root.add(parent);

    parent.add(new DefaultMutableTreeNode
      ("Chapter 1: Introduction to JBuilder"));
    parent.add(new DefaultMutableTreeNode
      ("Chapter 2: Introduction to JavaBeans"));
    parent.add(new DefaultMutableTreeNode
      ("Chapter 3: Beans Events"));
    parent.add(new DefaultMutableTreeNode
      ("Chapter 4: Developing and Using Components"));

    parent = new DefaultMutableTreeNode("Part II: Rapid Application "
      + "Development Using Swing Components");
    root.add(parent);

    parent.add(new DefaultMutableTreeNode
      ("Chapter 5: Swing Components"));
    parent.add(new DefaultMutableTreeNode
      ("Chapter 6: Containers and Layout Managers"));
    parent.add(new DefaultMutableTreeNode
      ("Chapter 7: Menus, Toolbars, and Dialogs"));
    parent.add(new DefaultMutableTreeNode
      ("Chapter 8: Advanced Swing Components"));

    // Omitted for brevity
    return new DefaultTreeModel(root);
  }
}
```

Listing 8.17 *Continued*

Example Review

The example creates a tree for the table of contents of this book. Each node is created using the `DefaultMutableTreeNode` class. The `createTreeModel()` method returns a `TreeModel` fitted with the root of the tree.

When you drop a `JTree` to the UI designer, the default tree model is used. Thus you see the sample data created in the default model. Once you set the `model` property with the new model, the new data replace the sample data.

NOTE

There is a bug to set the `model` property of an instance of `JTree` from the inspector. Write the code to set this property value programmatically.

Processing Tree Nodes

Swing uses the `TreeNode` interface to model a single node. The `MutableTreeNode` interface extends `TreeNode`. The `DefaultMutableTreeNode` class is an implementation of `MutableTreeNode`. The `DefaultMutableTreeNode` class stores data for a node and provides methods for tree traversal in various orders or for following the path between two nodes. Breadth-first traversal, depth-first traversal, postorder traversal, and preorder traversal are supported. These traversals are often used in algorithm design and are popular topics in courses on data structures.

The following methods in `DefaultMutableTreeNode` are often useful:

```
// The useful methods in DefaultMutableTreeNode
public TreeNode getParent() // Return the parent node
public Enumeration children() // Get all children
public boolean isLeaf() // Is the node a leaf
public Enumeration breadthFirstEnumeration()
public Enumeration depthFirstEnumeration()
public Enumeration preorderEnumeration()
public Enumeration postOrderEnumeration()
```

The last four methods create and return an enumeration that traverses the subtree rooted at this node in breadth-first order, depth-first order, preorder, or postorder, respectively. The code shown below displays the nodes in breadth-first traversal order:

```
Enumeration bf = root.breadthFirstEnumeration();
while (bf.hasMoreElements()) {
  System.out.print(bf.nextElement().toString());
}
```

Swing uses the `TreePath` class to represent a path between an ancestor and a descendant in the tree. Instances of `TreePath` are often instantiated by Swing classes. For instance, the `getLeadSelectionPath()` method in the `TreeSelectionModel` returns the path from the root to the selected node. There are many ways to extract the nodes from a tree path. Often you use the `getLastPathComponent()` method to obtain the last node in the path, and then the `getParent()` method to get all the nodes in the path upward through the link.

The selection of tree nodes is defined in the `TreeSelectionModel` interface. The `DefaultTreeSelectionModel` class is an implementation of the `TreeSelectionModel`, which maintains an array of `TreePath` objects representing the current selection. The last `TreePath` selected, called the *lead path*, can be obtained using the `getLeadSelectionPath()` method. To obtain all the selection paths, use the `getSelectionPaths()` method, which returns an array of tree paths.

`TreeSelectionModel` supports three selection modes: contiguous selection, discontiguous selection, and single selection. *Single selection* allows only one item to be selected. *Contiguous selection* allows multiple selections, but the selected items must be contiguous. *Discontigous selection* is the most flexible; it allows any item to be selected at a given time. The default tree selection mode is discontiguous. To set a selection mode, use the `setSelectionMode` method in `TreeSelectionModel`. The constants for the three modes are the following:

- `CONTIGUOUS_TREE_SELECTION`
- `DISCONTIGUOUS_TREE_SELECTION`
- `SINGLE_TREE_SELECTION`

The `TreeModel` interface defines operations for inserting or removing tree nodes. The `DefaultTreeModel` class is a concrete implementation of `TreeModel`. To insert or remove a node, use the following methods:

```
public void insertNodeInto(MutableTreeNode newNode,
                           MutablTreeNode parent,
                           int index)

public void removeNodeFromParent(MutableTreeNode theNode)
```

Example 8.12 Adding and Removing Nodes

This example uses the classes `DefaultMutableTreeNode`, `TreePath`, `DefaultTreeSelectionModel`, and `DefaultTreeModel`. The example enables the user to add or remove nodes from a tree, as shown in Figure 8.18.

Here are the steps to complete the example:

1. Reopen the project treedemo.jpr and create an applet named ProcessTree.java using the Applet wizard.
2. In the UI designer of ProcessTree.java, drop a `JScrollPane` to the center of the applet, and drop a `JTree` to the scroll pane to create `jTree1`. Drop a `JPanel` to create `jpButtons`, and add two buttons named `jbtAdd` and `jbtRemove` into `jpButtons`.
3. Declare and obtain the tree model and the selection model from `jTree1` using the `getModel()` and `getSelectionModel()` methods. Set the selection mode to single selection.
4. Generate and implement the code for handling `jbtAdd` and `jtbRemove`, as shown in Listing 8.18.

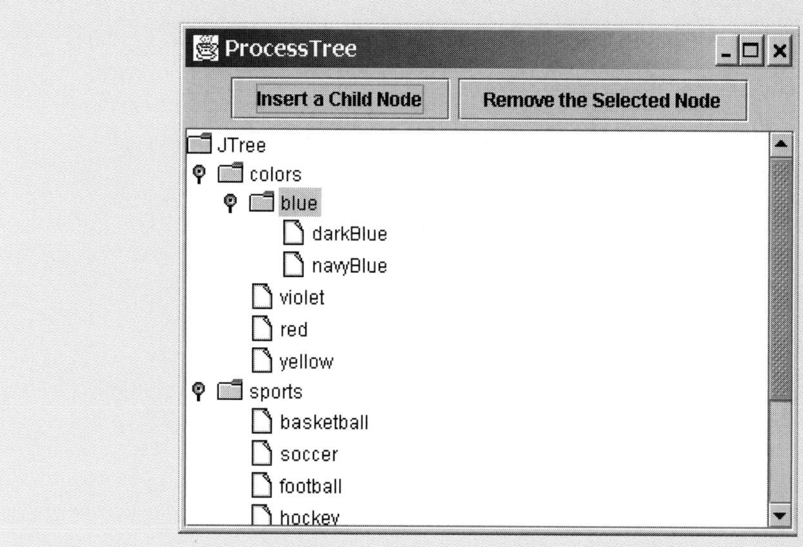

Figure 8.18 *You can add or remove nodes dynamically in a tree.*

```
package treedemo;

import java.awt.*;
import java.awt.event.*;
import java.applet.*;
import javax.swing.*;
import javax.swing.tree.*;

public class ProcessTree extends JApplet {
  boolean isStandalone = false;
  JScrollPane jScrollPane1 = new JScrollPane();
  JTree jTree1 = new JTree();
  JPanel jpButtons = new JPanel();
  JButton jbtAdd = new JButton();
  JButton jbtRemove = new JButton();

  // Get selection model
  TreeSelectionModel selectionModel = jTree1.getSelectionModel();

  // Get tree model
  DefaultTreeModel treeModel = (DefaultTreeModel)jTree1.getModel();

  /** Initialize the applet */
  public void init() {
    try {
      jbInit();
    }
    catch(Exception e) {
      e.printStackTrace();
    }
  }

  /** Component initialization */
  private void jbInit() throws Exception {
    this.setSize(new Dimension(400,300));
```

Listing 8.18 *ProcessTree.java*

continued

Example 8.12 continued

```
      jbtAdd.setText("Insert a Child Node");
      jbtAdd.addActionListener(new java.awt.event.ActionListener() {
        public void actionPerformed(ActionEvent e) {
          jbtAdd_actionPerformed(e);
        }
      });
      jbtRemove.setText("Remove the Selected Node");
      jbtRemove.addActionListener(
        new java.awt.event.ActionListener() {
        public void actionPerformed(ActionEvent e) {
          jbtRemove_actionPerformed(e);
        }
      });
      this.getContentPane().add(jScrollPane1, BorderLayout.CENTER);
      this.getContentPane().add(jpButtons, BorderLayout.NORTH);
      jpButtons.add(jbtAdd, null);
      jpButtons.add(jbtRemove, null);
      jScrollPane1.getViewport().add(jTree1, null);

      // Set single selection
      selectionModel.setSelectionMode(
        TreeSelectionModel.SINGLE_TREE_SELECTION);
    }

    void jbtAdd_actionPerformed(ActionEvent e) {
      // Get the selection path
      TreePath path = selectionModel.getLeadSelectionPath();

      // Get the last node in the path
      DefaultMutableTreeNode treeNode =
        (DefaultMutableTreeNode)path.getLastPathComponent();

      // Enter a new node
      String nodeName = JOptionPane.showInputDialog(
        this, "Enter a name for this new node", "Add a Child",
        JOptionPane.QUESTION_MESSAGE);

      // Insert the new node as a child of treeNode
      treeModel.insertNodeInto(new DefaultMutableTreeNode(nodeName),
        treeNode, treeNode.getChildCount());
    }

    void jbtRemove_actionPerformed(ActionEvent e) {
      // Get the selection path
      TreePath path = selectionModel.getLeadSelectionPath();

      // Get the last node in the path
      DefaultMutableTreeNode treeNode =
        (DefaultMutableTreeNode)path.getLastPathComponent();

      if (treeNode == treeModel.getRoot()) {
        JOptionPane.showMessageDialog(this, "Cannot remove the root");
      }
      else
        // Remove the selected node
        treeModel.removeNodeFromParent(treeNode);
    }
  }
```

Listing 8.18 *Continued*

Example Review

The example creates a tree using the default constructor. The `getModel()` method returns the tree model, and the `getSelectionModel()` method obtains the tree selection model. The methods for inserting and removing nodes are provided in the tree model, and the tree selection model can be used to find the selected path using the `getLeadSelectionPath()` method. The selected node is the last node in the lead path, which can be found using the `getLastPathComponent()` method.

To insert a node, first select a parent in the tree, then click the Insert a Child Node button, which displays an input dialog box to receive the new node name. The new node is added as a child of the selected node.

To remove a node, first select the node in the tree, then click the Remove the Selected Node button. If you attempt to remove the root, a message dialog is displayed to alert you that the root cannot be removed.

Tree Node Rendering and Editing

Like all the advanced Swing components, `JTree` delegates node rendering to a renderer. The `DefaultTreeCellRenderer` interface defines how cells are rendered, which is implemented by the `DefaultTreeCellRenderer` class. The `DefaultTreeCellRenderer` class maintains three icon properties named `leafIcon`, `openIcon`, and `closedIcon` for leaf nodes, expanded nodes, and collapsed nodes. It also provides colors for text and background. The following code sets new leaf, open and closed icons, and new background selection color in the tree.

```
DefaultTreeCellRenderer renderer =
  (DefaultTreeCellRenderer)jTree1.getCellRenderer();
renderer.setLeafIcon(leafImageIcon);
renderer.setOpenIcon(openImageIcon);
renderer.setClosedIcon(closedImageIcon);
renderer.setBackgroundSelectionColor(Color.red);
```

NOTE

The default leaf icon, open icon, and closed icon are dependent on the look-and-feel. For instance, on Windows look-and-feel, the open icon is -, and the closed icon is +.

`JTree` comes with a default cell editor. If `JTree`'s `editable` property is `true`, the default editor activates a text field for editing when the node is clicked three times. By default, this property is set to `false`. To create a custom editor, you need to extend the `DefaultCellEditor` class, which is the same class you used in table cell editing. You can use a text field, a check box, or a combo box, and pass it to `DefaultCellEditor`'s constructor to create an editor. The following code uses a combo box for editing colors. The combo box editor is shown in Figure 8.19.

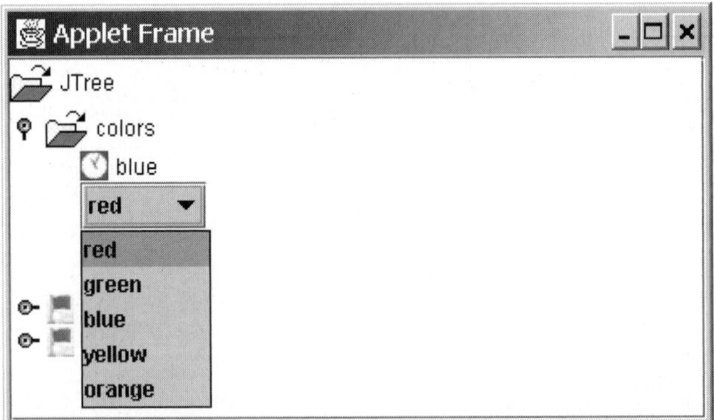

Figure 8.19 *You can supply a custom editor for editing tree nodes.*

```
// Customize editor
JComboBox jcboColor = new JComboBox();
jcboColor.addItem("red");
jcboColor.addItem("green");
jcboColor.addItem("blue");
jcboColor.addItem("yellow");
jcboColor.addItem("orange");

jTree1.setCellEditor(new DefaultCellEditor(jcboColor));
jTree1.setEditable(true);
```

There are two annoying problems with the editor created in the preceding code. First, it is activated with just one mouse click. Second, it overlaps the node's icon, as shown in Figure 8.19. The first problem can be fixed by creating a subclass of `DefaultCellEditor` that overrides the `isCellEditable()` method, which returns true if the mouse click count is 3. The second problem can be fixed by using the `DefaultTreeCellEditor`, as shown below. The new editor is shown in Figure 8.20.

```
jTree1.setCellEditor
  (new DefaultTreeCellEditor(jTree1,
    new DefaultTreeCellRenderer(),
    new DefaultCellEditor(jcboColor)));
```

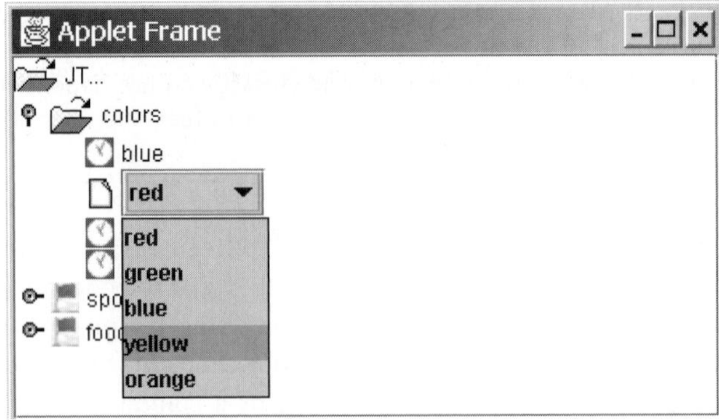

Figure 8.20 *The* `DefaultTreeCellEditor` *displays an editor that does not overlap a node's icon.*

Tree Events

`JTree` can fire `TreeSelectionEvent` and `TreeExpansionEvent`, among many other events. Whenever a new node is selected, `JTree` fires a `TreeSelectionEvent`. Whenever a node is expanded or collapsed, `JTree` fires a `TreeExpansionEvent`. To handle the tree selection event, a listener must implement the `TreeSelectionListener` interface, which contains a single handler named `valueChanged`. `TreeExpansionListener` contains two handlers named `treeCollapsed` and `treeExpanded` for handling node expansion or node closing.

The following code displays a selected node:

```
void jTree1_valueChanged(TreeSelectionEvent e) {
  TreePath path = e.getNewLeadSelectionPath();
  TreeNode treeNode = (TreeNode)path.getLastPathComponent();
  System.out.println("The selected node is " + treeNode.toString());
}
```

Chapter Summary

This chapter introduced four advanced Swing components: `JList`, `ComboBox`, `JTable`, and `JTree`. You learned how to use their data models to store and process data, and how to use selection models to handle data selection, renderer classes to display views, and the editor class to edit cells in these components.

Review Questions

8.1 Does `JList` have a method, such as `addItem()`, for adding an item to a list? How do you add items to a list? Can `JList` display icons and custom GUI objects in a list? Can a list item be edited? How do you initialize data in a list? How do you specify the maximum number of visible rows in a list without scrolling? How do you specify the height of a list cell? How do you specify the horizontal margin of list cells?

8.2 How do you create a list model? How do you add items to a list model? How do you remove items from a list model?

8.3 What are the three list-selection modes? Can you set the selection modes directly in an instance of `JList`? How do you obtain the selected item(s)?

8.4 How do you create a custom list cell renderer?

8.5 What is the handler for handling the `ListSelectionEvent`?

8.6 Can multiple items be selected from a combo box? Can a combo box item be edited? How do you specify the maximum number of visible rows in a combo box without scrolling? Can you specify the height of a combo box cell using a method in `JComboBox`? How do you obtain the selected item in a combo box?

8.7 How do you add or remove items from a combo box?

8.8 Why is the cell renderer for a combo box the same as the renderer for a list?

8.9 How do you initialize a table? Can you specify the maximum number of visible rows in a table without scrolling? How do you specify the height of a table cell? How do you specify the horizontal margin of table cells?

8.10 How do you modify table contents? How do you add or remove a row? How do you add or remove a column?

8.11 What is auto-resizing of a table column? How many types of auto resizing are available?

8.12 What are the properties that show grids, horizontal grids, and vertical grids? What are the properties that specify the table row height, vertical margin, and horizontal margin?

8.13 What are the default table renderers and editors? How do you create a custom table cell renderer and editor?

8.14 How do you create a tree? How do you specify the row height of a tree node? How do you obtain the default tree model and tree selection model from an instance of `JTree`?

8.15 How do you initialize data in a tree using `TreeModel`? How do you add a child to an instance of `DefaultMutableTreeNode`?

8.16 How do you add or remove a node from a tree?

8.17 How do you obtain a selected tree node?

Programming Exercises

8.1 Create a program that shows a list of geometrical shapes along with a label in an instance of `JList`, as shown in Figure 8.21. Display the selected figure in a panel when selecting a figure from the list. The figures are represented in the `FigurePanel` class in Example 6.3, "Using `JTabbedPane`."

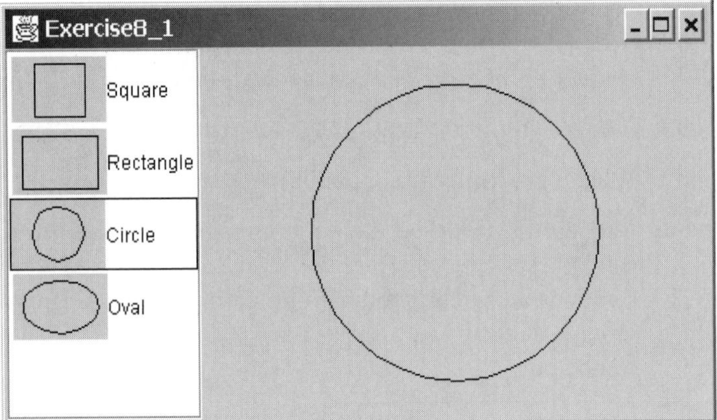

Figure 8.21 *The list displays geometrical shapes and their names.*

8.2 Create a program that shows a list of geometrical shapes along with a label in a combo box, as shown in Figure 8.22. This exercise may share the list cell renderer with the preceding exercise.

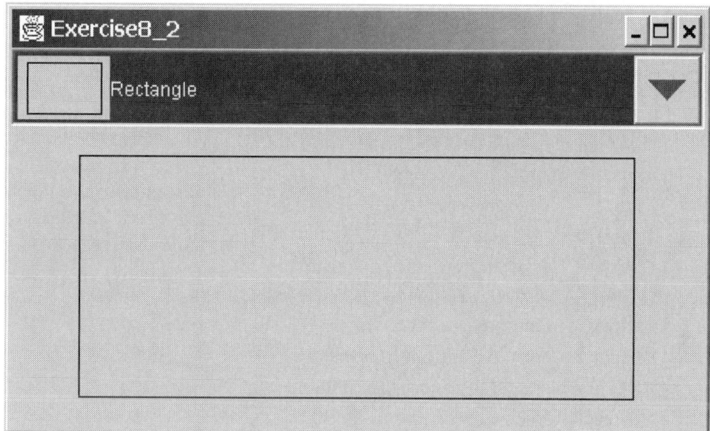

Figure 8.22 *The combo box contains a list of geometrical shapes and the shape names.*

8.3 Create a table for student records. Each record consists of name, birthday, class status, in-state, and a photo, as shown in Figure 8.23. The name is of the `String` type; birthday is of the `Date` type; class status is one of the following five values: Freshman, Sophomore, Junior, Senior, and Graduate; in-state is a `boolean` value indicating whether the student is a resident of the state; and photo is an image icon. The program enables the user to add, remove, or edit a record. Use the default editors for name, birthday, and in-state. Supply a combo box as custom editor for class status. (Note: The photos in Figure 8.23 are not real images of the students.)

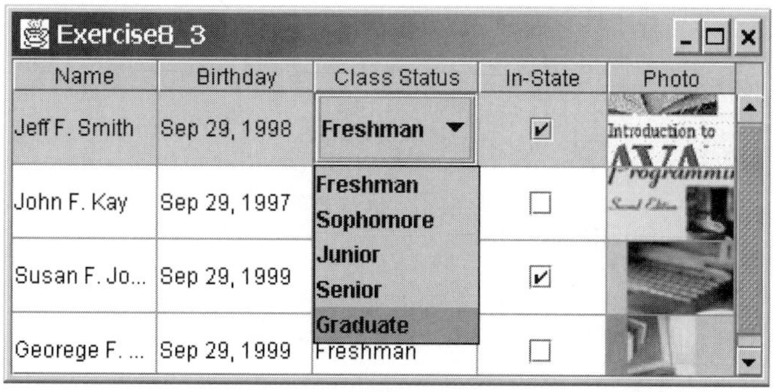

Figure 8.23 *The table displays student records and supports add, remove, and edit operations.*

8.4 Modify Example 8.11 as follows:

- Run it in the look-and-feel of Motif, Metal, or Windows.
- Display the nodes in breadth-first order, depth-first order, preorder, and postorder.

- Set custom icons for leaf, open, and closed nodes, and create custom editors for choosing colors in a combo box.
- Display a paragraph in a text area for each node in the tree, as shown in Figure 8.24.

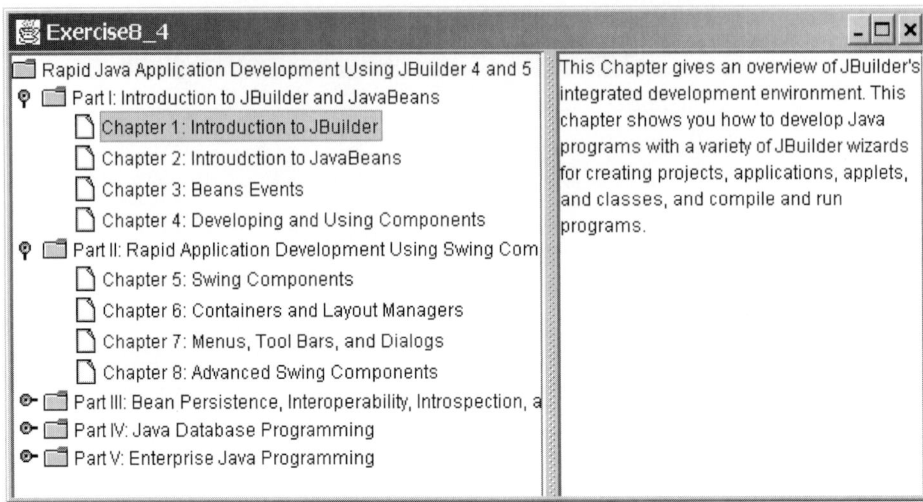

Figure 8.24 *The content of the node is displayed in a text area when a node is clicked.*

8.5 Suppose a table is stored in a text file. The first line in the file is the header, and the remaining lines correspond to rows in the table. The elements are separated by the Tab characters. Write a program to display the table using the `JTable` component.

8.6 Modify Example 8.10, "Using Table Events," to delete a row or a column by pressing the DELETE key.

8.7 Modify Example 8.12, "Adding and Removing Nodes," to add a new child node by pressing the INSERT key, and delete a node by pressing the DELETE key.

8.8 Create a custom tree node renderer that uses a combo box to choose colors, as shown in Figure 8.20. Display the combo box upon three consecutive mouse clicks on the node.

8.9 Modify Example 8.3, "List Cell Renderer Demo," and Example 8.4, "Combo Box Demo," to share the same renderer class:

- Create an interface named `ImageModel`, as follows:

```
public interface ImageModel {
  public String getName(Object value);
  public Image getImage(Object value);
}
```

- Modify `MyListModel` to implement the `ImageModel` interface.
- Modify `MyComboBoxModel` to implement the `ImageModel` interface.
- Modify `MyListCellRenderer.java` to replace `MyListModel` by `ImageModel`.
- You should be able to run `TestListCellRenderer` with no changes.
- In the `TestComboBox` class, change any reference to `MyComboBoxRenderer` to `MyListCellRenderer`. Now `TestComboBox` and `TestListCellRenderer` share the same renderer.

8.10 In Exercise 4.8, you created a chart model (`ChartModel`) and two views (`PieChart` and `BarChart`). Create a controller to enable the user to modify the data, as shown in Figure 8.25. You will see the changes take effect in the pie chart view and bar chart view. Your exercise consists of the following classes:

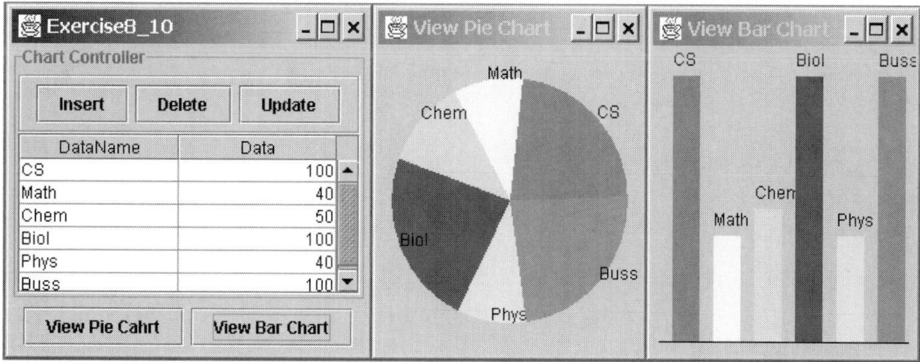

Figure 8.25 *You can modify the data in the controller. The views are synchronized with the controller.*

- The controller named `ChartController`. This class uses a table to display data. You can modify the data in the table. Click the Insert button to insert a new row above the selected row in the table, click the Delete button to delete the selected row in the table, and click the Update button to update the changes you made in the table.
- The class `MyTableModel`. This class extends `DefaultTableModel` to override the `getColumnClass` method so that you can use the `JTable`'s default editor for numerical values.
- The classes `ChartModel`, `PieChart`, and `BarChart` from Exercise 4.8.
- The main class `Exercise8_10`. This class creates a user interface with a controller, and two buttons, View Pie Chart and View Bar Chart. Click the View Pie Chart button to pop up a frame to display a pie chart, and click the View Bar Chart button to pop up a frame to display a bar chart.

PART III

Bean Persistence, Introspection, and Customization

This part of the book introduces JavaBeans API. You will learn how to develop persistent beans, use beans in other tools, implement bound and constraint properties, and create bean property editors.

CHAPTER 9

Bean Persistence and Versioning

Objectives

- Understand the concept of bean persistence.
- Know object serialization and use it to store and restore beans persistently.
- Use the `Beans.instantiate` method to load serialized beans.
- Become familiar with Sun's BeanBox and use it to test bean persistence.
- Customize Object Serialization.
- Use bean versioning to make beans of different versions compatible.

Introduction

JBuilder does not store beans during design time. Changes in properties from the inspector are stored in the source code. The UI designer reconstructs the user interface by parsing source code. However, other tools, such as Sun's Beanbox, IBM Visual Age for Java, and MS Visual Basic, need to store the beans and then restore them later during design time. Bean persistence ensures that these tools can correctly reconstruct the properties of the bean to the state when it was saved.

This chapter introduces object serialization, which is a built-in Java mechanism that stores and restores beans persistently. You will learn Sun's Beanbox, a tool for testing beans, which can be used to verify bean persistence. You will also learn how to customize serialization and use bean versioning to handle different versions of beans.

Object Serialization and Deserialization

In order to be persistent, a bean has to implement the `java.io.Serializable` interface. The `Serializable` interface is a marker interface. It has no methods, so you don't need to add additional code in your class that implements `Serializable`. Implementing this interface enables the Java serialization mechanism to automate the process of storing the object.

To appreciate this automation feature and understand how an object is stored, consider what you need to do in order to store an object without using this feature. Suppose you want to store an object of the `MessagePanel` class in Example 2.1 "Writing a Simple Java Bean." To do this you need to store all the current values of the properties in a `MessagePanel` object. The properties defined in `MessagePanel` are `message (String)`, `centered (boolean)`, `xCoordinate (int)`, and `yCoordinate (int)`. Since `MessagePanel` is a subclass of `JPanel`, the property values of `JPanel` have to be stored as well as the properties of all the `superclasses` of `JPanel`. If a property is of an object type, storing it requires storing all the property values inside this object. As you can see, this is a very tedious process. Fortunately you don't have to go through this process with Java. Since JDK 1.1, Java has provided a built-in mechanism that automates the process of writing objects. This process is referred to as *object serialization*. In contrast, the process of reading objects is referred to as *object deserialization*.

To store and restore an object, you need to use the `ObjectOutputStream` class for storing objects and the `ObjectInputStream` class for restoring objects. These two classes are built upon several other classes. Figure 9.1 shows the hierarchic relationship of these related classes.

`ObjectOutputStream` implements `ObjectOutput`, which inherits `DataOutput`. `DataOutput` provides methods for writing Java primitive-type values. `ObjectOutput` extends `DataOutput` to include output of objects, arrays, and strings. An `ObjectOutputStream` writes Java primitive-type values and objects to an `OutputStream`. Persistent storage can be accomplished using a file for the stream. The format of the

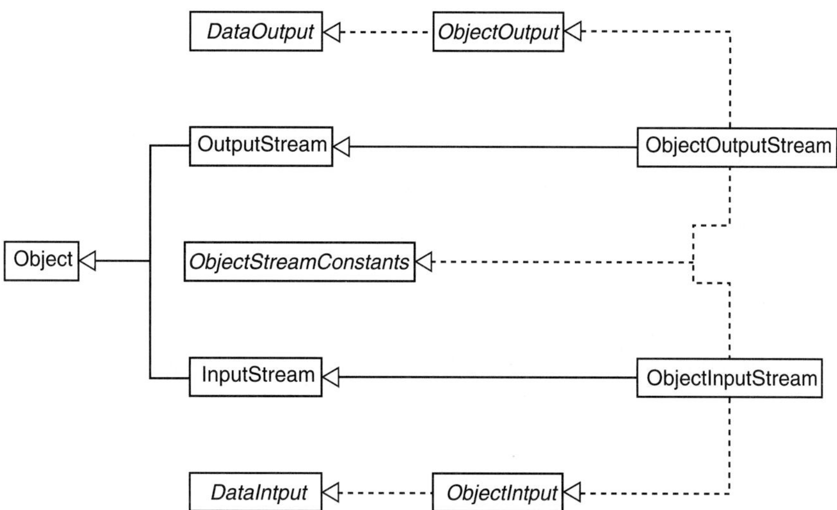

Figure 9.1 `ObjectOutputStream` *extends* `OutputStream` *and implements* `ObjectOutput` *and* `ObjectStreamConstants`. `ObjectInputStream` *extends* `InputStream` *and implements* `ObjectInput` *and* `ObjectStreamConstants`.

output is platform-independent. The `OutputStream` can also be a network socket stream.

`ObjectInputStream` is the inverse of `ObjectOutputStream`. `ObjectInputStream` implements `ObjectInput`, which inherits `DataInput`. `DataInput` provides methods for reading primitive-type values. `ObjectInput` extends `DataInput` to include input of objects, arrays, and strings. An `ObjectInputStream` reads the data previously written using an `ObjectOutputStream` with a file stream and a network socket stream.

Only objects whose class implements the `java.io.Serializable` interface can use `ObjectOutputStream` and `ObjectInputStream`. The method `writeObject` is used to write an object to the `ObjectOutputStream`, and `readObject` is used to read an object from the `ObjectInputStream`. Attempting to store an object that does not support the `Serializable` interface would cause `java.io.NotSerializableException`.

When a serializable object is stored, the class of the object is encoded; this includes the class name and the signature of the class, the values of the object's fields and arrays, and any other objects referenced from the initial object. When a primitive-type value is stored, appropriate methods, such as `writeInt`, `writeBoolean` in the `DataOutput` interface, are used. Multiple objects or primitives can be written to the stream. The objects must be read back from the corresponding `ObjectInputstream` with the same types and in the same order as they were written. Java's safe casting should be used to get the desired type. For instance, when reading an object of the `MessagePanel` class, the object should be cast to `MessagePanel`.

Here is an example of creating an `ObjectOutputStream` and storing an object `messagePanel1` of `MessagePanel` and an `int` value to the file named beans.dat.

```
ObjectOutputStream out = new ObjectOutputStream(
  new FileOutputStream("beans.dat"));
out.writeObject(messagePanel1);
out.writeInt(5);
```

The corresponding code to restore the object and the `int` value is as follows.

```
ObjectInputStream in = new ObjectInputStream(
  new FileInputStream("beans.dat"));
MessagePanel c = (MessagePanel)in.readObject();
int x = in.readInt();
```

Example 9.1 Testing Object Serialization

This example creates a program to manipulate `MessagePanel`, as shown in Figure 9.2. You will use radio buttons to set the background color, and two buttons, <= and =>, to move the message to left and right. The Store button is provided to save a `MessagePanel` object, and the Restore button is used to reload the saved `MessagePanel` object.

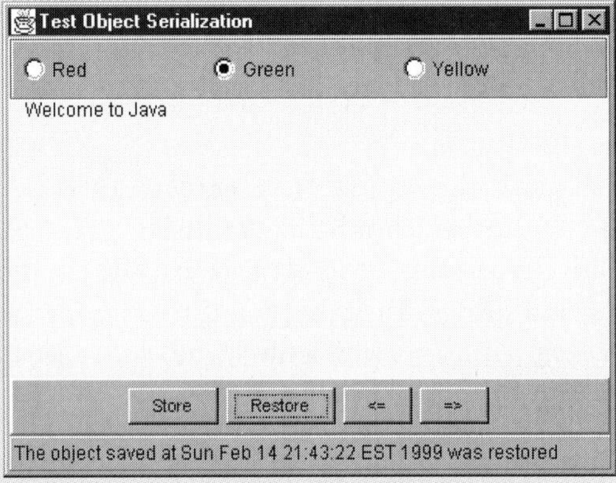

Figure 9.2 *You can use the Store button to save the* `MessagePanel` *object shown in the middle of the window, and the Restore button to reload the saved object later.*

Follow the steps below to complete the project.

1. Create a new project named serializationdemo.jpr and create SerializationApplication.java and SerializationFrame.java using the Application wizard. In Step 2 of 2 of the Application wizard, check the options "Generate status bar" and "Center frame on screen," and type "Test Object Serialization" in the Title field.

2. In the UI designer of SerializationFrame.java, drop a `JPanel` to the center of the frame to create `jpSerialization`. Set the layout of `jpSerialization` to `BorderLayout`. Drop a `JPanel` to the north of `jpSerialization` to create `jpRadioButtons`, drop a `MessagePanel` in the center of `jpSerialization` to

create messagePanel1, and drop a JPanel to the south of jpSerialization to create jpButtons.

3. Set the border property of jpRadioButtons and jpButtons to Etched, and messagePanel1 to RaisedBevel.

4. Drop a JRadioButton three times to jpRadioButtons to create jrbRed, jrbGreen, and jrbYellow with text property set to Red, Green, and Yellow. Drop a JButton four times to jpButtons to create jbtStore, jbtRestore, jbtLeft, and jbtRight with text property set to Store, Restore, <=, and =>.

5. Create an instance of ButtonGroup to group the buttons in the jbInit() method (Lines 104–108).

6. Generate and implement the code for handling the radio buttons and buttons, as shown in Listing 9.1.

```
1   package serializationdemo;
2
3   import java.awt.*;
4   import java.awt.event.*;
5   import javax.swing.*;
6   import messagepaneldemo.*;
7   import java.io.*;
8   import java.util.*;
9
10  public class SerializationFrame extends JFrame {
11    JLabel statusBar = new JLabel();
12    BorderLayout borderLayout1 = new BorderLayout();
13    JPanel jpSerialization = new JPanel();
14    BorderLayout borderLayout2 = new BorderLayout();
15    JPanel jpRadioButtons = new JPanel();
16    MessagePanel messagePanel1 = new MessagePanel();
17    JPanel jpButtons = new JPanel();
18    JRadioButton jrbRed = new JRadioButton();
19    JRadioButton jrbGreen = new JRadioButton();
20    JRadioButton jrbYellow = new JRadioButton();
21    JButton jbtStore = new JButton();
22    JButton jbtRestore = new JButton();
23    JButton jbtLeft = new JButton();
24    JButton jbtRight = new JButton();
25
26    /** Construct the frame */
27    public SerializationFrame() {
28      enableEvents(AWTEvent.WINDOW_EVENT_MASK);
29      try {
30        jbInit();
31      }
32      catch(Exception e) {
33        e.printStackTrace();
34      }
35    }
36
37    /** Component initialization */
38    private void jbInit() throws Exception {
```

Listing 9.1 *SerializationFrame.java*

continued

Example 9.1 continued

```
        this.getContentPane().setLayout(borderLayout1);
        this.setSize(new Dimension(400, 300));
        this.setTitle("Test Object Serialization");
        statusBar.setText(" ");
        jpSerialization.setLayout(borderLayout2);
        jrbRed.setText("Red");
        jrbRed.addActionListener(new java.awt.event.ActionListener() {
          public void actionPerformed(ActionEvent e) {
            jrbRed_actionPerformed(e);
          }
        });
        jrbGreen.setText("Green");
        jrbGreen.addActionListener(new java.awt.event.ActionListener() {
          public void actionPerformed(ActionEvent e) {
            jrbGreen_actionPerformed(e);
          }
        });
        jrbYellow.setText("Yellow");
        jrbYellow.addActionListener(
          new java.awt.event.ActionListener() {
          public void actionPerformed(ActionEvent e) {
            jrbYellow_actionPerformed(e);
          }
        });
        jbtStore.setText("Store");
        jbtStore.addActionListener(new java.awt.event.ActionListener() {
          public void actionPerformed(ActionEvent e) {
            jbtStore_actionPerformed(e);
          }
        });
        jbtRestore.setText("Restore");
        jbtRestore.addActionListener(
          new java.awt.event.ActionListener() {
          public void actionPerformed(ActionEvent e) {
            jbtRestore_actionPerformed(e);
          }
        });
        jbtLeft.setText("<=");
        jbtLeft.addActionListener(new java.awt.event.ActionListener() {
          public void actionPerformed(ActionEvent e) {
            jbtLeft_actionPerformed(e);
          }
        });
        jbtRight.setText("=>");
        jbtRight.addActionListener(new java.awt.event.ActionListener() {
          public void actionPerformed(ActionEvent e) {
            jbtRight_actionPerformed(e);
          }
        });
        jpRadioButtons.setBorder(BorderFactory.createEtchedBorder());
        jpButtons.setBorder(BorderFactory.createEtchedBorder());
        messagePanel1.setBorder(BorderFactory.createRaisedBevelBorder());
        this.getContentPane().add(statusBar, BorderLayout.SOUTH);
        this.getContentPane().add(jpSerialization, BorderLayout.CENTER);
        jpSerialization.add(jpRadioButtons, BorderLayout.NORTH);
        jpRadioButtons.add(jrbRed, null);
        jpRadioButtons.add(jrbGreen, null);
        jpRadioButtons.add(jrbYellow, null);
```

Listing 9.1 *Continued*

```
    jpSerialization.add(messagePanel1, BorderLayout.CENTER);
    jpSerialization.add(jpButtons, BorderLayout.SOUTH);
    jpButtons.add(jbtStore, null);
    jpButtons.add(jbtRestore, null);
    jpButtons.add(jbtLeft, null);
    jpButtons.add(jbtRight, null);

    // Group radio buttons
    ButtonGroup btg = new ButtonGroup();
    btg.add(jrbRed);
    btg.add(jrbGreen);
    btg.add(jrbYellow);
  }

  /** Overridden so we can exit on System Close */
  protected void processWindowEvent(WindowEvent e) {
    super.processWindowEvent(e);
    if(e.getID() == WindowEvent.WINDOW_CLOSING) {
      System.exit(0);
    }
  }

  /** Handle selecting red background in messagePanel1 */
  void jrbRed_actionPerformed(ActionEvent e) {
    messagePanel1.setBackground(Color.red);
  }

  /** Handle selecting green background in messagePanel1 */
  void jrbGreen_actionPerformed(ActionEvent e) {
    messagePanel1.setBackground(Color.green);
  }

  /** Handle selecting yellow background in messagePanel1 */
  void jrbYellow_actionPerformed(ActionEvent e) {
    messagePanel1.setBackground(Color.yellow);
  }

  /** Handle storing the objects */
  void jbtStore_actionPerformed(ActionEvent e) {
    try {
      ObjectOutputStream out =
        new ObjectOutputStream(new FileOutputStream("beans.dat"));
      out.writeObject(messagePanel1);
      out.writeObject(new Date());
      out.close();
      statusBar.setText("The object is stored in beans.dat");
    }
    catch (IOException ex) {
      System.out.println(ex);
    }
  }

  /** Handle restoring the objects */
  void jbtRestore_actionPerformed(ActionEvent e) {
    try {
      ObjectInputStream in =
        new ObjectInputStream(new FileInputStream("beans.dat"));
      MessagePanel c = (MessagePanel)in.readObject();
      Date d = (Date)in.readObject();
      jpSerialization.remove(messagePanel1);
```

Listing 9.1 *Continued*

continued

Example 9.1 continued

```
      messagePanel1 = c;
      jpSerialization.add(messagePanel1, BorderLayout.CENTER);
      jpSerialization.repaint();
      in.close();
      statusBar.setText("The object saved at " + d.toString()
        + " is restored");
    }
    catch (IOException ex1) {
      System.out.println(ex1);
    }
    catch (ClassNotFoundException ex2) {
      System.out.println(ex2);
    }
  }

  /** Handle moving the message left */
  void jbtLeft_actionPerformed(ActionEvent e) {
    messagePanel1.moveLeft();
  }

  /** Handle moving the message right */
  void jbtRight_actionPerformed(ActionEvent e) {
    messagePanel1.moveRight();
  }
}
```

Listing 9.1 *Continued*

Example Review

When you click the Store button, the current state of the `messagePanel1` and the current time (`new Date()`) are saved to file beans.dat using `ObjectOutputStream`. When you click the Restore button, these objects are read back from the same file. They must be read back in the same order as they were stored. Explicit type casting must be used to ensure that the objects read are of the right type.

In the handler for the Restore button, `messagePanel1` was removed from `jpSerialization`, and then a new `messagePanel1` was created and added to `jpSerialization`. This is necessary to ensure that the newly restored `messagePanel1` is used in the windows, not the old copy.

Like many Java classes, `java.awt.Component` and `java.util.Date` implement `java.io.Serializable`, so the objects of these classes or their subclasses can be stored using object streams.

The *transient* Keyword

By default, all the nonstatic properties of a serialized object are written to the object stream. However, not all the nonstatic properties can be serialized. For example, since the `java.awt.Thread` class does not implement `Serializable`, a `Thread` object cannot be serialized. The `transient` keyword should be used to mark a nonserializable property, as shown in Example 4.2, "Creating a `Clock` Component," so that it is not stored during serialization of the object that contains the property.

The `transient` keyword can also be used to mark a property not to be stored for security reasons. Since the state of the object is stored into a stream of bytes using a file stream or a network socket stream, the stream could be modified to result in a change in the actual value of the property. To see how easy it would be to tamper with the data, just modify beans.dat using a Hex editor like Hex Workshop, which is a shareware product available from Break Point Software at **www.bpsoft.com**. Suppose you change the word Java to C++ in beans.dat, as shown in Figure 9.3. `Welcome to C++` is displayed on the panel when the Restore button is clicked, as shown in Figure 9.4.

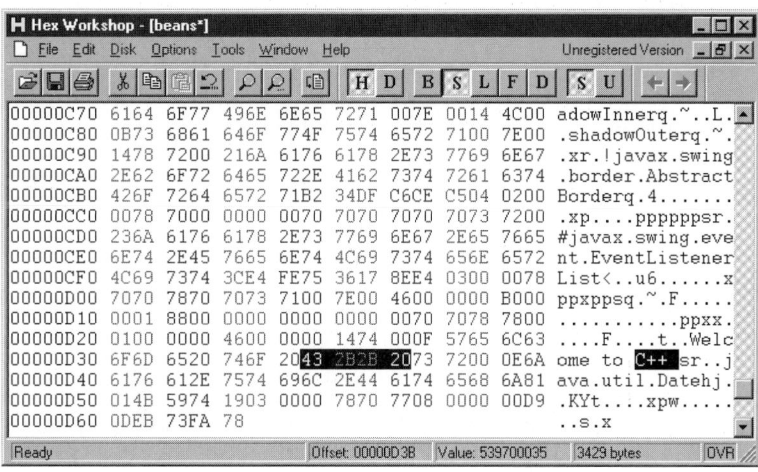

Figure 9.3 *You can use Hex Workshop to modify the beans.dat file.*

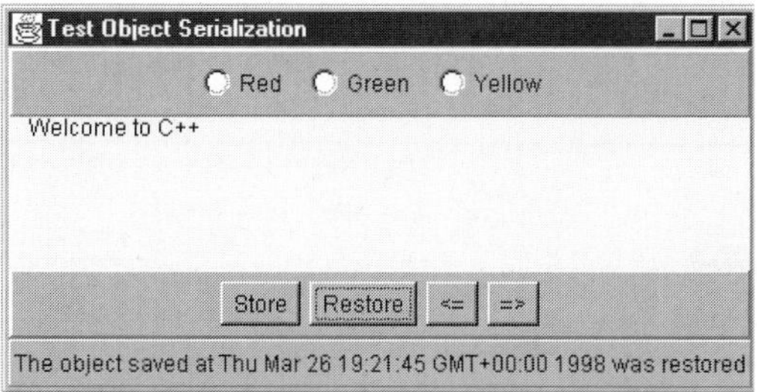

Figure 9.4 *The contents of beans.dat are restored. The modified message* `Welcome to C++` *is displayed.*

Instantiating Serialized Beans

A serialized bean can be directly loaded to the program without using the `new` operator. This important advance in component-based software deployment makes it possible to provide different versions of the bean without changing the application. Suppose your application requires a `Clock` bean; you can ship it to London with a serialized Clock bean tailored for British users, and to Paris with different serialized `Clock` bean tailored for French users.

The static method `instantiate` in the `java.beans.Beans` class is designed to dynamically load the serialized bean.

```
public static Object instantiate(ClassLoader cls, String beanName)
  throws IOException, ClassNotFoundException
```

The first argument is a class loader. If it is `null`, the system class loader is used. The second argument is the name of the bean. This method searches for the bean with the specified name and a .ser file extension. If not found, an attempt is made to find a class file with the specified name. If this attempt fails, a `ClassNotFoundException` is thrown. The `instantiate` method may also throw `IOException` if the serialized bean file is corrupted.

You can customize JBuilder so that the code it generates uses `Beans.instantiate(…)` instead of the `new` operator by checking the "Use Beans.instantiate" option in the Code Style page of the Project Properties dialog box.

It is not difficult to write a program to store a bean, but the simplest way to serialize a bean is to use the UI designer. Here are the steps for serializing a `MessagePanel` bean in Example 9.1.

1. Select `messagePanel1` in the UI designer in Example 9.1.
2. Customize `messagePanel1` to set the `message` property to Welcome to HTML, `xCoordinate` to 40, and `yCoordinate` to 40.
3. Right-click `messagePanel1` in the component tree to display a popup menu, as shown in Figure 9.5.

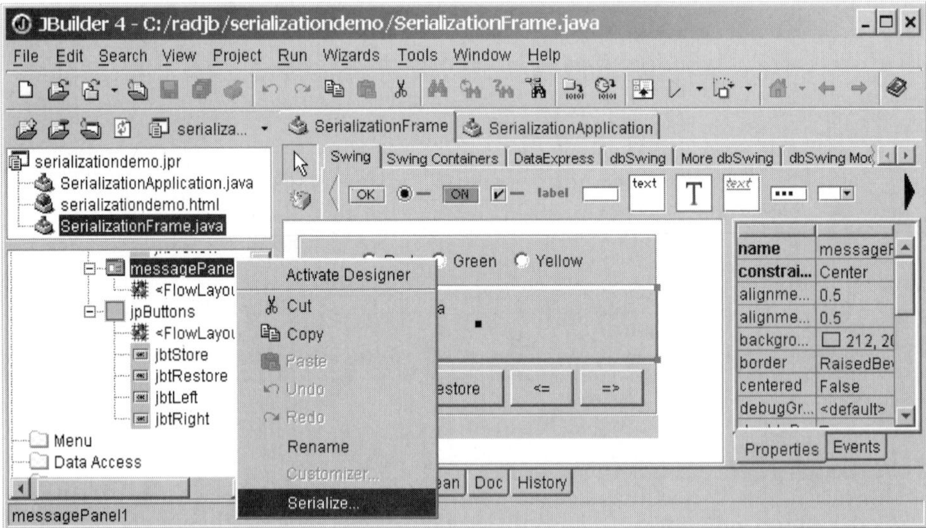

Figure 9.5 *You can customize a bean and save it in a file by choosing Serialize in the UI designer.*

4. Choose Serialize on the menu to bring up a dialog box, as shown in Figure 9.6. Click OK to save the bean in a file named after the class with a .ser extension.

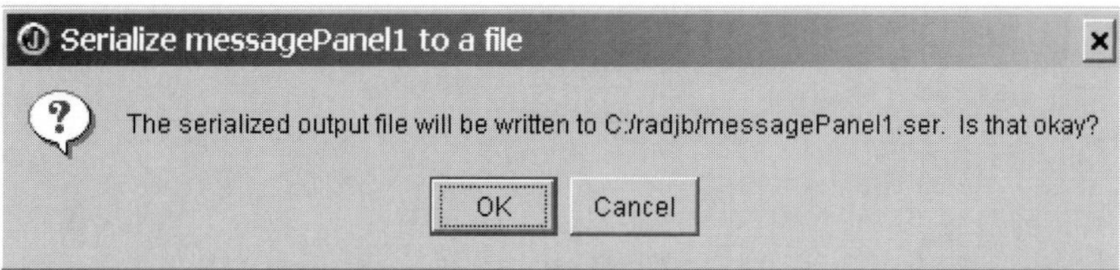

Figure 9.6 *The bean is saved to a file named after the class of the bean with a .ser extension.*

Example 9.2 Instantiating Beans

This example demonstrates generating code using the `Beans.instantiate` method in JBuilder. You will create a program similar to Example 2.2, "Moving Message on a Panel." A sample run of the program is shown in Figure 9.7.

Figure 9.7 *You can move the message to left and right using the buttons.*

Follow the steps below to complete the project.

1. Create a new project named beaninstantiationdemo.jpr, and check the option "Use Beans.instantiate" in the Code Style page of the Project Properties dialog box. Create TestBeanInstantiation.java using the Applet wizard.

2. In the UI designer of TestBeanInstantiation.java, drop a `MessagePanel` to the center of the applet to create `messagePanel1`, and drop a `JPanel` to the south to create `jPanel1`.

3. Drop a `JButton` twice to `jPanel1` to create `jButton1` and `jButton2`. Rename them `jbtLeft` and `jbtRight`.

4. Double-click `jbtLeft` in the UI designer to generate the code for moving the message to the left. Implement `jbtLeft_actionPerformed`, as shown in Listing 9.2 (Lines 56–58). You can generate and implement `jbtRight_actionPerformed` the same way (Lines 60–62).

continued

Example 9.2 continued

```
package beaninstantiationdemo;

import java.awt.*;
import java.awt.event.*;
import java.applet.*;
import javax.swing.*;
import messagepaneldemo.*;
import java.beans.*;

public class TestBeanInstantiation extends JApplet {
  boolean isStandalone = false;
  MessagePanel messagePanel1;
  JPanel jPanel1;
  JButton jbtLeft;
  JButton jbtRight;

  /** Initialize the applet */
  public void init() {
    try {
      jbInit();
    }
    catch(Exception e) {
      e.printStackTrace();
    }
  }

  /** Component initialization */
  private void jbInit() throws Exception {
    messagePanel1 = (MessagePanel)Beans.instantiate(getClass().
      getClassLoader(), MessagePanel.class.getName());
    jPanel1 = (JPanel) Beans.instantiate(getClass().
      getClassLoader(), JPanel.class.getName());
    jbtLeft = (JButton) Beans.instantiate(getClass().
      getClassLoader(), JButton.class.getName());
    jbtRight = (JButton) Beans.instantiate(getClass().
      getClassLoader(), JButton.class.getName());
    this.setSize(new Dimension(400,300));
    jbtLeft.setText("<=");
    jbtLeft.addActionListener(new java.awt.event.ActionListener() {
      public void actionPerformed(ActionEvent e) {
        jbtLeft_actionPerformed(e);
      }
    });
    jbtRight.setText("=>");
    jbtRight.addActionListener(new java.awt.event.ActionListener() {
      public void actionPerformed(ActionEvent e) {
        jbtRight_actionPerformed(e);
      }
    });
    this.getContentPane().add(messagePanel1, BorderLayout.CENTER);
    this.getContentPane().add(jPanel1, BorderLayout.SOUTH);
    jPanel1.add(jbtLeft, null);
    jPanel1.add(jbtRight, null);
  }

  void jbtLeft_actionPerformed(ActionEvent e) {
    messagePanel1.moveLeft();
  }

```

Listing 9.2 *TestBeanInstantiation.java*

```
    void jbtRight_actionPerformed(ActionEvent e) {
      messagePanel1.moveRight();
    }
  }
```

Listing 9.2 *TestBeanInstantiation.java*

Example Review

Since you have set the option "Use Beans.instantiate" for the project, JBuilder uses the `Beans.instantiate` method to instantiate a bean whenever the bean is dropped on the UI designer. The `getClass()` method defined in the `Object` class returns the runtime class of the object. The `getClassLoader()` method determines the class loader for the class.

`messagepaneldemo.MessagePanel.class` is an instance of the `Class` class, which is generated when the Java Virtual Machine loads the `MessagePanel` class. `MessagePanel.class`, referred to as a companion class for `MessagePanel`, provides useful information about the `MessagePanel`, such as its name and the names of variables and methods in the `MessagePanel`. `messagepaneldemo.MessagePanel.class.getName()` returns the name of the class, which is `MessagePanel`.

You may wonder why JBuilder does not generate "`messagepaneldemo.MessagePanel`" to replace `messagepaneldemo.MessagePanel.class.getName()`. If it did, it would work fine locally on the machine that you use to develop this program, but it would fail on a network, because the applets are prohibited from accessing local files.

The BeanBox

You want to know whether the components can be used in a variety of tools after they are developed. JavaSoft provides a BeanBox for testing bean properties, events, and persistence, and for demonstrating the use of beans. The BeanBox utility is compressed in a file named bdk1_1-win.exe, which can be obtained from **`http://www.javasoft.com/beans/software/bdk_download.html`**.

TIP

Double-click bdk1_1-win.exe in the windows to install the BeanBox. In the Choose Install Folder dialog of the BDK installation, choose c:\BDK1.1 instead of c:\Programs Files\BDK1.1, as shown in Figure 9.8. Installing into a directory path that contains spaces may cause problems for environment variables used by the various tools that come with JDK.

After a successful installation, you can start to run BeanBox from the DOS prompt by the **run** command at the beanbox directory. The beanbox directory is under the BDK1.1 directory. When the BeanBox starts, you first see a message box indicating that the BeanBox is analyzing the packages and loading the beans. The beans are packaged in the .jar archive files stored in the **jars** directory. Several .jar files are

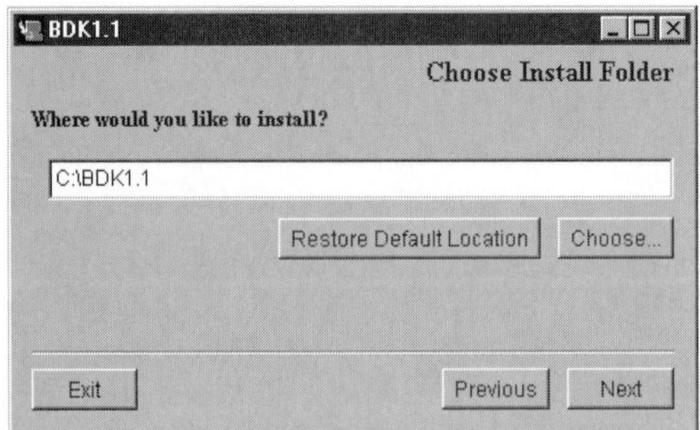

Figure 9.8 *You should install BDK in a directory path without spaces.*

installed by default in this directory, and the beans in these .jar files are analyzed and loaded during startup. If you want your beans to be loaded when the BeanBox starts, place their .jar files in this directory.

NOTE

Running the BeanBox requires that the JDK bin directory be in the DOS environment path. To set the path, type the following command:

```
set path=%path%;c:\jbuilder4\jdk1.3\bin
```

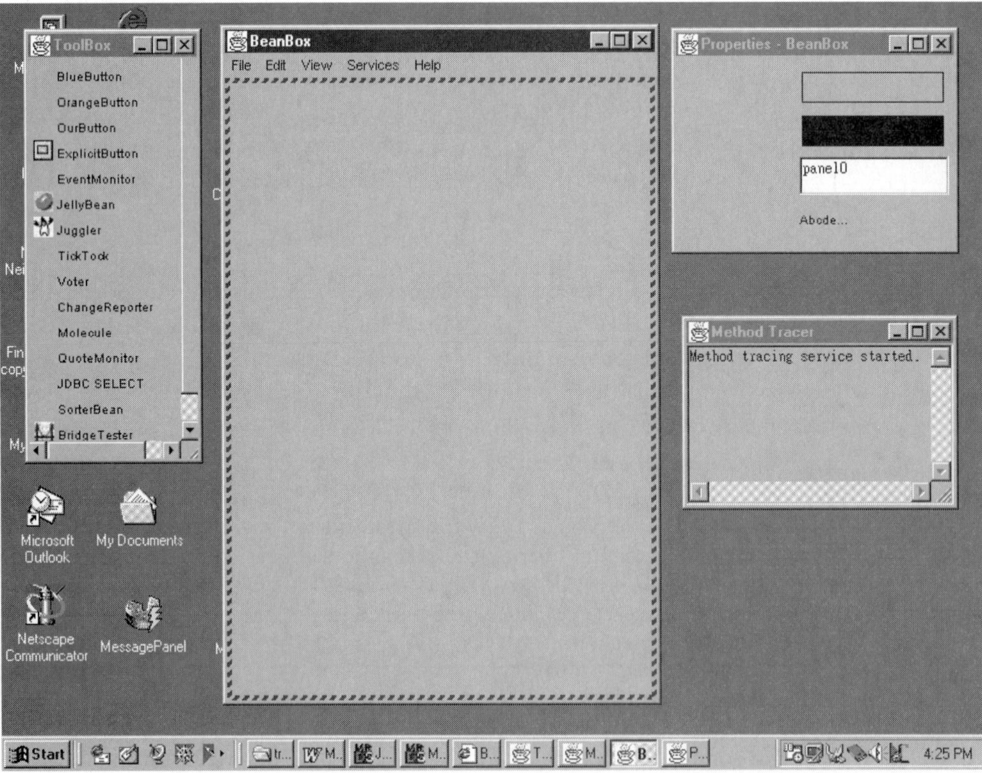

Figure 9.9 *The BeanBox consists of four independent windows entitled ToolBox, BeanBox, Properties, and Method Tracer.*

After the BeanBox is started, you will see four separate windows entitled ToolBox, BeanBox, Properties, and Method Tracer, as shown in Figure 9.9. The ToolBox consists of all the beans available for use by the BeanBox. The BeanBox window is where you test and manipulate beans installed in the ToolBox window. The Property window enables you to set or modify bean properties. The Method Tracer traces the methods in the bean.

By default, the ToolBox contains 16 beans. Some beans have associated icons appearing on the left of the bean name. You will learn how to specify bean icons in Chapter 11, "Bean Introspection and Customization." A new bean can be added to the ToolBox by placing its .jar file in the jars directory or by choosing File, LoadJar from the menu. The BeanBox can be used to test bean properties, events, and persistence, and it can also be used to create applets from the beans. Here is an example of using the BeanBox to create an applet for controlling clocks.

Example 9.3 Using BeanBox

This example installs a `Clock` component to ToolBox and uses the BeanBox to assemble an applet with a Start button and a Stop button to control the clock in the BeanBox. Recall that the `Clock` bean was created in Example 4.2. Here are the steps to complete the project.

1. The BeanBox requires the beans to be packaged in a JAR file with an appropriate manifest file that describes beans. The JBuilder Archive Builder does not generate this required file. Therefore, you have to create the manifest file and the JAR file manually from the command line using the `jar` command. Here are the steps to create a JAR file for the `Clock` component:

   a. Create a text file named temp.mf, as follows:

   ```
   Manifest-Version: 1.0

   Name: ClockDemo/Clock.class
   Java-Bean: True
   ```

NOTE

You need to leave a blank line after java-Bean: True.

   b. Change directory to c:\radjb and type the following command to generate the archive file Clock.jar.

   ```
   jar -cfm Clock.jar temp.mf clockdemo\Clock.class
   ```

2. Start BeanBox. Choose File, LoadJar to load the `Clock` bean into the ToolBox from C:\radjb\Clock.jar.

continued

Example 9.3 continued

3. Select the `Clock` bean in the ToolBox. The cursor becomes a crosshair upon selected. Drop it in the BeanBox, as shown in Figure 9.10. With the bean selected in the BeanBox (a hatched border indicates that the bean has been selected), you can move it to the desired location or resize it to the preferred size. With the `Clock` bean selected in the BeanBox, set `showingHeader` to True and `hourHandColor` to red in the Properties window.

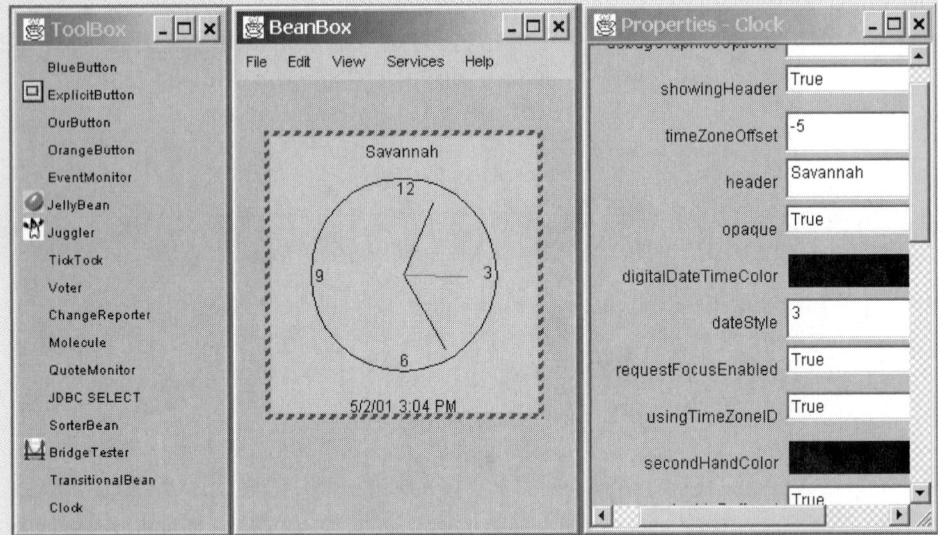

Figure 9.10 *A* `Clock` *bean is created in the BeanBox with its* `hourHandColor` *set to red, and* `showingHeader` *set to True.*

TIP

If you accidentally select a bean other than the `Clock` bean in the ToolBox, you have to remove it from the BeanBox by choosing Edit, Cut to delete it.

NOTE

A property will not be shown in the Property window if it has no default value explicitly specified in the bean component. For example, if the default header "Savannah" were not given in the `Clock` class, the property `header` would not be shown in the Properties window.

---

4. Select `OurButton` from the ToolBox, drop it to the BeanBox, and set its label to Start in the Properties window. Repeat the same operation to create another button labeled Stop.

5. Now you are ready to hook up the Start button to the `start()` method, and the Stop button to the `stop()` method, in the `Clock` bean. With the Start button selected, choose Edit, Events, mouse, mouseClicked, as shown in Figure 9.11. You will see a red line originating from the Start button, as shown in Figure 9.12. Click on the `Clock` bean to hook up the button with the bean. You will see a list of methods in Figure 9.13. Select start and press OK to let BeanBox generate adapters and other needed code to carry out the button-click action. Similarly you can hook the Stop button to the `stop()` method in the `Clock` bean.

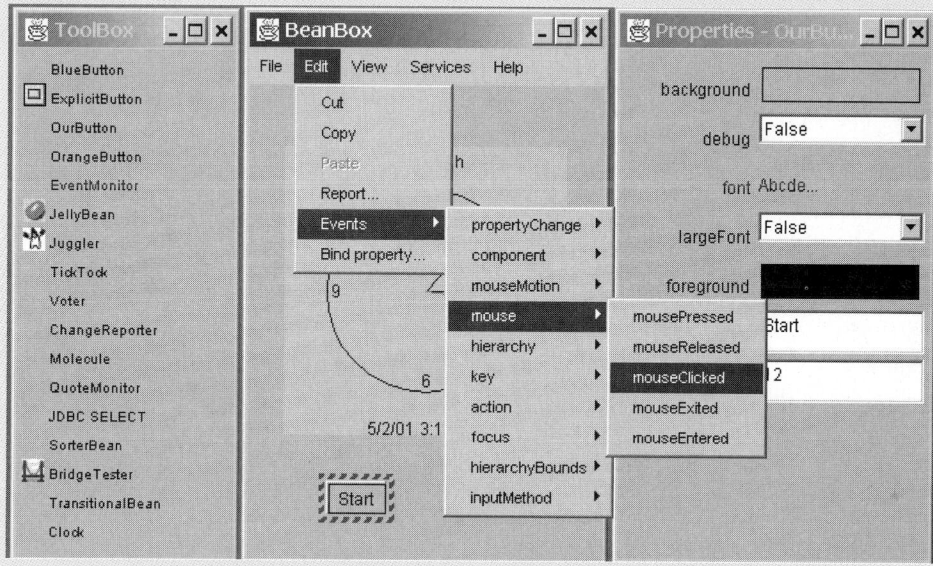

Figure 9.11 *With the Start button selected, you can implement mouse-click events on the button.*

6. By now you have created two buttons and associated the button-press action to the `start()` and `stop()` methods in the `Clock` bean. To put all the beans in the BeanBox in a new applet, choose File, Make Applet. A dialog box pops up to let you specify a JAR file name and an applet class name, as shown in Figure 9.14. Accept the default names and press OK to let the BeanBox generate the JAR file and the myApplet.html for running the applet.

The BeanBox generates an applet corresponding to a BeanBox layout. The data and classes needed for this applet are packaged into a JAR file. Run myApplet.html from appletviewer or from a Java Plug-in in a Web browser to test the applet. Figure 9.15 shows a sample run of the applet in appletviewer.

continued

Example 9.3 continued

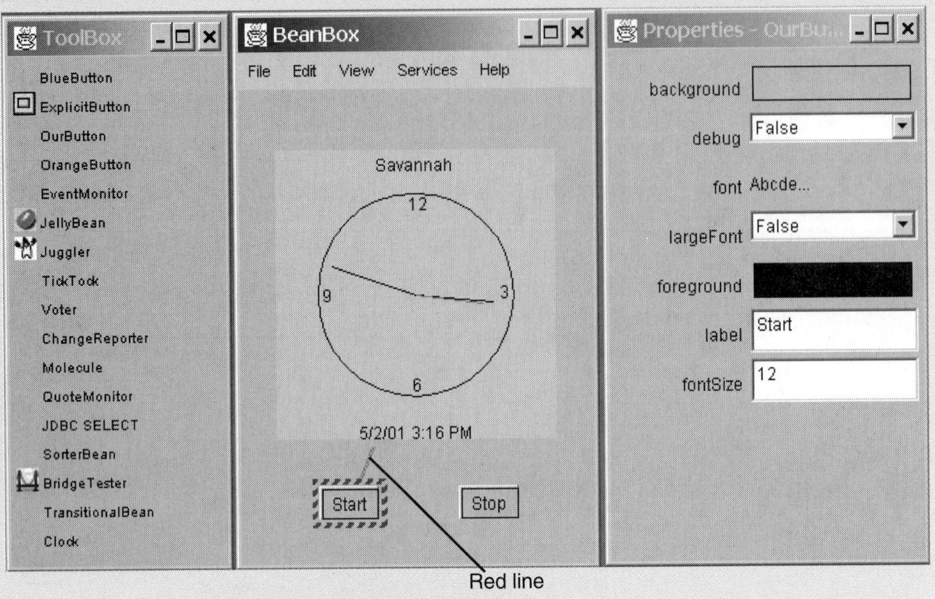

Figure 9.12 *The red line originating from the Start button indicates that the Start button is the source of the event.*

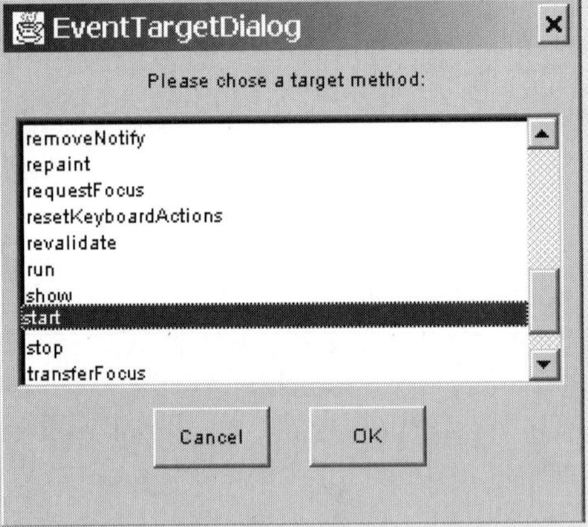

Figure 9.13 *The EventTargetDialog allows you to choose a method on the target for handling the source object event.*

Example Review

Although BeanBox is not a full-fledged Java builder tool, it demonstrates an interesting way to create applications. Unlike JBuilder, BeanBox does not generate source code for the project. The applet was generated in the form of stored objects using serialization. Figure 9.16 shows the contents of the generated JAR

Figure 9.14 *The BeanBox generates files for running the applet when you click OK in the Make an Applet dialog box.*

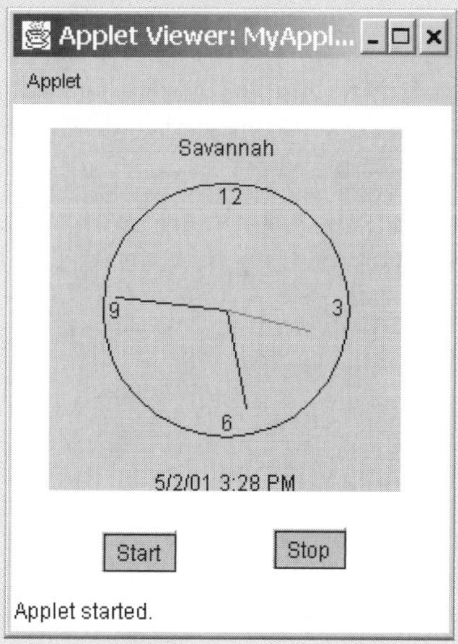

Figure 9.15 *The clock starts when the Start button is pressed, and stops when the Stop button is pressed.*

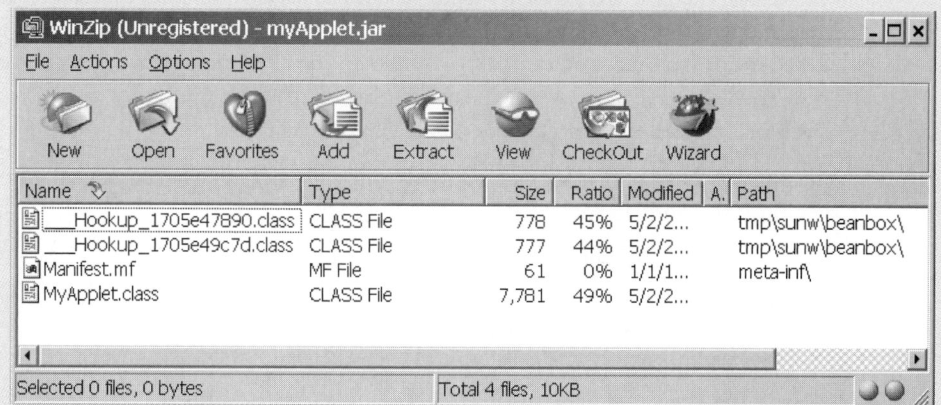

Figure 9.16 *The generated JAR file contains MyApplet.class, two adapter classes and a serialized data file for the* `Clock` *bean, and two button beans.*

continued

Example 9.3 continued

file in WinZip. The data file contains the beans in the applet. These beans are loaded when the applet starts.

Creating applets is not the only thing you do with the BeanBox. You can use it to test bean persistence. JBuilder does not have a utility for testing persistence. In fact, the beans you have developed with JBuilder may not be persistent. A bean that can be saved in BeanBox with the Save command from the File menu is serializable. If the bean restores all the previous behaviors after it is loaded back from its saved file using the Load command from the File menu, then the bean is persistent.

You can test the bean in the BeanBox by selecting `Disable Design Mode`. The ToolBox and Properties windows disappear when the BeanBox is in runtime mode. To switch back to design mode, select `Enable Design Mode` from the View menu.

It is interesting to see how a button is hooked with the clock in the BeanBox by originating a line from a button (Source) to the clock (target). This approach, referred to as *visual event design,* is also used in IBM Visual Age for Java and Visual Café.

Customizing Serialization

A serialized bean is not guaranteed to be persistent. If you save a clock bean in the BeanBox and then reload it, you will notice that the clock is not ticking. Obviously the clock is not restored to the correct running state. This is because the thread that controls the clock is not restarted after being restored. To make the `Clock` bean persistent, you need to recreate the thread and start it after the bean is loaded. The bean is saved using the `writeObject` method and loaded to the BeanBox using the `readObject` method by Java's built-in serialization system. You can implement these methods to add customized operations to preserve bean persistence. In the case of the `Clock` bean, you can add code to stop the clock before saving bean properties and add code to create and start the thread after the properties are restored, as will be demonstrated in Example 9.4.

The `writeObject` and `readObject` methods you will implement must have the exact signatures shown below.

```
private void writeObject(java.io.ObjectOutputStream out)
  throws IOException

private void readObject(java.io.ObjectInputStream in)
  throws IOException, ClassNotFoundException
```

The `writeObject` method is responsible for saving the state of the object. The default mechanism for saving the Object's fields can be invoked by calling `out.defaultWriteObject(…)`. The `readObject()` method is responsible for restoring the state of the object by reading the data stored by the `writeObject` method. The default mechanism for restoring the object can be invoked by calling `in.defaultReadObject()`, which restores the fields that were written using the `out.defaultWriteObject(...)` method.

Example 9.4 Making the `Clock` Component Persistent

This example implements the `writeObject` and `readObject` methods to add additional operations to make the `Clock` bean persistent. The new Clock component named `PersistentClock` is presented in Listing 9.3.

```
package clockdemo;

import java.io.*;

public class PersistentClock extends Clock {
  /** Restore clock to the persistent state */
  private void readObject(ObjectInputStream in)
    throws IOException, ClassNotFoundException {
    in.defaultReadObject();
    thread = new Thread(this);
    thread.start();
  }

  /** Store clock */
  private void writeObject(ObjectOutputStream out)
    throws IOException {
    thread = null;
    out.defaultWriteObject();
  }
}
```

Listing 9.3 *PersistentClock.java*

Example Review

You have to use the exact signatures for the `readObject` and `writeObject` methods. It is often thought, erroneously, that these two methods are defined in the `Serializable` interface. In fact, however, they are unique methods in the Java serialization mechanism, which are invoked when an object of the class is serialized or deserialized.

The default `readObject` and `writeObject` methods are usually sufficient to maintain bean persistence. Customizing serialization is needed when the bean contains nonserializable data, such as a thread, that needs to be restored, as in the case of the `Clock` bean.

The `Serializable` interface provides a valuable mechanism to automate the process of storing and restoring the state of a bean. You can define your own mechanism to store and restore object data by implementing the `Externalizable` interface. This interface is a subinterface of `Serializable` and has two public methods, `writeExternal` and `readExternal`, with the following signatures:

```
public void writeExternal(ObjectOutput out) throws IOException

public void readExternal(ObjectInput in)
  throws IOException, ClassNotFoundException
```

Example 9.5 Using the `Externalizable` Interface

This example uses the `Externalizable` interface to store and restore a `Clock` bean. The new `Clock` component, named `ExternalizedClock`, is presented in Listing 9.4.

```
package clockdemo;

import java.awt.*;
import java.io.*;

public class ExternalizedClock extends PersistentClock
  implements Externalizable {
  /** Restore clock */
  public void readExternal(ObjectInput in)
    throws IOException, ClassNotFoundException {
    setShowingDigitalDateTime(in.readBoolean());
    setTimeZoneID(in.readUTF());
    setSecondHandColor((Color)in.readObject());
    setMinuteHandColor((Color)in.readObject());
    setHourHandColor((Color)in.readObject());
    setDigitalDateTimeColor((Color)in.readObject());
    setRunning(in.readBoolean());
    thread = new Thread(this);
    thread.start();
  }

  /** Store clock */
  public void writeExternal(ObjectOutput out) throws IOException {
    thread = null;
    out.writeBoolean(isShowingDigitalDateTime());
    out.writeUTF(getTimeZoneID());
    out.writeObject(getSecondHandColor());
    out.writeObject(getMinuteHandColor());
    out.writeObject(getHourHandColor());
    out.writeObject(getDigitalDateTimeColor());
    out.writeBoolean(isRunning());
  }
}
```

Listing 9.4 *ExternalizedClock.java*

Example Review

When a bean of the component that implements `Externalizable` is stored in a builder tool like BeanBox, the builder tool invokes the bean's `writeExternal()` method. The builder tool invokes the `readExternal()` method to restore the bean. These methods are fully responsible for storing and restoring object data. You have total control over what data are stored (including the data defined in the superclass).

NOTE

The `readObject` and `writeObject` methods are private and use `InputObjectStream` and `OutputObjectStream`, but the `readExternal` and `writeExternal` methods are public, and read and write data using `InputObject` and `OutputObject`.

Bean Versioning

The bean components you have developed are subject to upgrade and modification. For example, you may add a new property named `showing` in `messagepaneldemo.MessagePanel` to control whether the message is shown. If you have stored a `MessagePanel` bean in the beans.dat file using `serializationdemo.SerializationApplication` with the old version of `MessagePanel`, you cannot restore the bean from the file using the new `MessagePanel`, as shown in Figure 9.17. The error message shown in Figure 9.18 would appear in the DOS window when you attempt to read the old file using `serializationdemo.SerializationApplication` with the new bean.

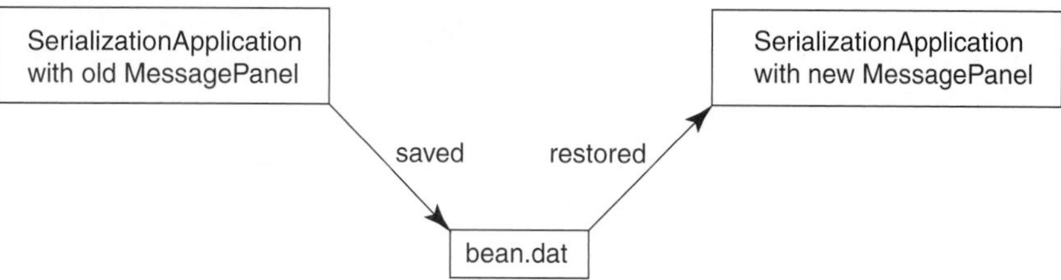

Figure 9.17 *The beans saved in beans.dat cannot be restored with the new* `MessagePanel` *unless you use bean versioning.*

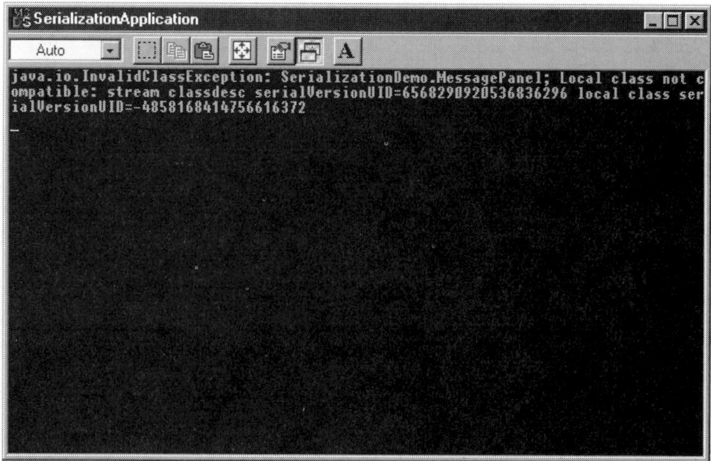

Figure 9.18 *The* `InvalidClassException` *indicates that a different version of class is used.*

The bean was stored in the old version, but the program that reads the bean uses a new version. This difference is detected by the Java runtime system. Java assigns every class a unique ID, known as the *serialVersionUID*, which is determined by the structure of the class, including package name, class name, interface name, data fields, and methods defined in the class. When a bean is saved, its ID is saved. When the bean is restored, its ID is compared with the current bean ID. The Java runtime system refuses to restore the saved bean if its ID differs from the current bean ID. However, a class can indicate that it is compatible with an old version of itself by specifying the ID of the old version in the new class, which forces the Java runtime system to assign the new bean the specified ID. For this to occur, you must first find the ID of the old class. JDK contains a command-line utility `serialver` to let you find the ID of a class. For example, the command

```
serialver messagepaneldemo.MessagePanel
```

gets the ID of the class, as shown in Figure 9.19. If you type the command **serialver -show**, a graphic dialog box is displayed, as shown in Figure 9.20.

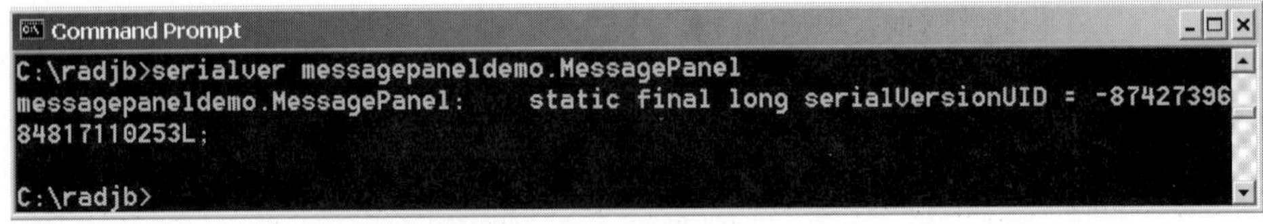

Figure 9.19 *The serialver command finds the ID of the class.*

Serial Version Inspector
Full Class Name: messagepaneldemo.MessagePanel Show
Serial Version: static final long serialVersionUID = -8742739684817110253L;

Figure 9.20 *The graphic version of the serialver command finds the ID of the class.*

To specify that the new class is compatible with its old version, add the old class's ID as a static final long constant named `serialVersionUID` in the new class, so that the new class uses the same ID as its old version. For example, to make the new `MessagePanel` compatible with its old version, add the following statement in the new `MessagePanel`:

```
static final long serialVersionUID = -8742739684817110253L;
```

With this declaration, the new program can read beans saved with the old version, and the old program can read beans saved with the new version, because the beans of both versions have the same ID. If two beans differ only in the methods, then reading the objects poses no problem. However, if the beans differ in data fields, special handling is needed to convert the stream object to the current version. Consider the following cases.

- If two fields have the same name but different types, the `InvalidClassException` is thrown with the message, indicating that the two data types are incompatible.
- If the object in the stream has a data field that is not present in the current version, these data are ignored.

- If the current version has data that are not in the object in the stream, they are set to their default values when restored. For example, the data are null for objects, `false` for `boolean` type, and zero for numbers.

Example 9.6 Testing Bean Versioning

This example uses bean versioning to restore old files using new classes. You will add a new field `showing` to `MessagePanel` to control whether the message is shown. Here are the steps to complete the project:

1. Run `serializationdemo.SerializationApplication`, select yellow color, and press the Store button to store the current `MessagePanel` in beans.dat file.

2. Record the ID of the `MessagePanel` class using the serialver utility, and create a new `MessagePanel` class in the serializationdemo project, as shown in Listing 9.5 with the same ID as the old version's. This new class replaces the old `MessagePanel` in the same directory.

3. Compile the new class and restart `serializationdemo.SerializationApplication`. Press the Restore button in the frame. You will see a yellow background message panel with no message shown. This is because the `showing` property is not defined in the old version and becomes `false` when the object is loaded from the stream.

```
package serializationdemo;

import javax.swing.*;
import java.awt.*;

public class MessagePanel extends JPanel {
  // Specify the bean ID using the ID of the previous version
  static final long serialVersionUID = -8742739684817110253L;

  // Add a new property
  private boolean showing = true;

  private String message = "Welcome to Java"; // Message to display

  // (x, y) coordinates where the message is displayed
  private int xCoordinate = 20;
  private int yCoordinate = 20;

  // Indicating whether the message is displayed in the center
  private boolean centered;

  /** Default constructor */
  public MessagePanel() {
    repaint();
  }

```

Listing 9.5 *The new MessagePanel.java*

continued

Example 9.6 continued

```
  /** Construct with a message parameter */
  public MessagePanel(String message) {
    this.message = message;
    repaint();
  }

  public String getMessage() {
    return message;
  }

  public void setMessage(String message) {
    this.message = message;
  }

  public int getXCoordinate() {
    return xCoordinate;
  }

  public void setXCoordinate(int x) {
    this.xCoordinate = x;
  }

  public int getYCoordinate() {
    return yCoordinate;
  }

  public void setYCoordinate(int y) {
    this.yCoordinate = y;
  }

  public boolean isCentered() {
    return centered;
  }

  public void setCentered(boolean centered) {
    this.centered = centered;
  }

  /** Display the message at specified location */
  public void paintComponent(Graphics g) {
    super.paintComponent(g);

    if (centered) {
      // Get font metrics for the font
      FontMetrics fm = g.getFontMetrics(getFont());

      // Find the center location to display
      int w = fm.stringWidth(message);  // Get the string width
      int h = fm.getAscent(); // Get the string height
      xCoordinate = (getSize().width-w)/2;
      yCoordinate = (getSize().height+h)/2;
    }

    g.drawString(message, xCoordinate, yCoordinate);
  }

```

Listing 9.5 *Continued*

```
    public Dimension getPreferredSize() {
      return new Dimension(200, 100);
    }

    public Dimension getMinimumSize() {
      return new Dimension(200, 100);
    }

    /** Move the message in the pane to the left */
    public void moveLeft() {
      if (getXCoordinate() > 10) {
        // Shift the message to the left
        setXCoordinate(getXCoordinate()-10);
        repaint();
      }
    }

    /** Move the message in the panel to the right */
    public void moveRight() {
      if (getXCoordinate() < getSize().width - 20) {
        // Shift the message to the right
        setXCoordinate(getXCoordinate()+10);
        repaint();
      }
    }

    /** The getter method for the showing property */
    public boolean isShowing() {
      return showing;
    }

    /** The setter method for the showing property */
    public void setShowing(boolean showing) {
      this.showing = showing;
      repaint();
    }
  }
```

Listing 9.5 *Continued*

Example Review

There are two MessagePanel.java files. One is in the project messagepaneldemo, which was created in Example 2.1. The other is the new one created in this example, which is stored in the project serializationdemo. After this new file is created, the new `MessagePanel` class is used when running `serializationdemo.SerializationApplication`. The new `MessagePanel` is assigned the same ID as its previous version, so you can restore the `MessagePanel` beans that were saved with the previous version of `MessagePanel`.

Assigning the new class the same ID as its old version does not guarantee compatibility. To ensure that the new class is backward-compatible with the old version, do not delete a data field, change its declaration to `transient` or `static`, or change it to a different type.

Chapter Summary

This chapter addressed the issues of bean interoperability and compatibility. Bean persistence ensures that a bean can be restored to the same state as when it was saved. This feature makes beans useful in the Java and non-Java builder tools that require beans to be stored during design time. Bean versioning makes different versions of the beans compatible.

Review Questions

9.1 How do you declare a class so that its objects will be serializable?

9.2 How do you serialize an object, and how do you deserialize an object?

9.3 How do you serialize a component in the UI designer?

9.4 What is the `transient` modifier for?

9.5 How do you load a bean directly without using the `new` operator?

9.6 How do you set the JBuilder project to generate code using the `Beans.instantiate(...)` method to instantiate beans?

9.7 How do you install a bean into the ToolBox window in the BeanBox? How do you associate a source bean with a target bean in the BeanBox?

9.8 How do you customize serialization by implementing the `readObject()` and `writeObject()` methods? How do you customize serialization using the `Externalizable` interface? Is `Externalizable` a subinterface of `Serializable`?

9.9 How do you enable the new class to deserialize a bean that was serialized with the old version of the class? How do you create the *serialVersionUID*?

Programming Exercises

9.1 Create an application to register students, as shown in Figure 9.21. Student information is defined in a serializable class, as follows:

```
// Student.java: Student class encapsulates student information
import java.io.*;

public class Student implements Serializable {
  private String name;
  private String street;
  private String city;
  private String state;
  private String zip;

  /** Default constructor */
  public Student() {
  }

  /** Construct a Student with specified name, street, city, state,
    and zip */
```

```
    public Student(String name, String street, String city,
      String state, String zip) {
      this.name = name;
      this.street = street;
      this.city = city;
      this.state = state;
      this.zip = zip;
    }

    public String getName() {
      return name;
    }

    public String getStreet() {
      return street;
    }

    public String getCity() {
      return city;
    }

    public String getState() {
      return state;
    }

    public String getZip() {
      return zip;
    }
  }
```

Your program stores student objects in a data file.

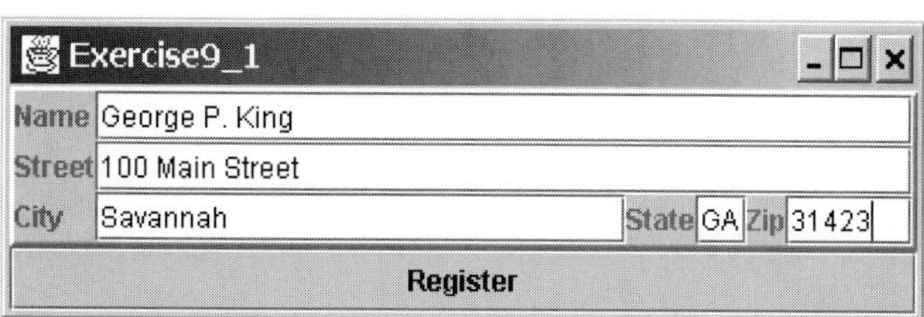

Figure 9.21 *The program gathers the name and address, and stores it in a file.*

9.2 In the UI designer of JBuilder, create an instance of Clock, customize it for London, and serialize it as London.ser. Customize it for New York, and serialize it as NewYork.ser. Create an applet that contains these two clocks using the `Beans.instantiate` method.

9.3 Modify Example 8.7, "Using Table Models," to save the table in a vector to a data file.

CHAPTER 10

Bound and Constraint Properties

Objectives

- Understand the concept of bound and constraint properties.
- Know the role of bound properties in implementing property editors in the builder tools.
- Learn to implement bound and constraint properties.
- Create bound and constraint properties using BeansExpress.
- Use bound properties to simplify the implementation of model-view components.

Introduction

A *bound property* of a component is one for which a property notification service is provided when the property changes. Bound properties are very useful in the implementation of property editors for beans, and they notify the beans of changes of property values in the editor. *Constraint properties* allow the listener component to verify the property change to determine whether to accept or reject it.

Implementing Bound Properties

The implementation of bound properties is based on the JavaBeans event model. The event set `java.beans.PropertyChangeEvent` and `java.beans.PropertyChangeListener` is provided to facilitate bean communications through bound properties. When a change is detected, the source bean creates a `PropertyChangeEvent` and invokes the listener's `propertyChange` method defined in `PropertyChangeListener`.

The `PropertyChangeListener` interface is used to provide notification of changes in bound properties. In order to support bound properties, the source component must declare a variable of `PropertyChangeListener` and implement a pair of `PropertyChangeListener` registration methods. When a change in the bound property occurs in the source bean, a `PropertyChangeEvent` is constructed and passed to the `propertyChange` method implemented in the listener bean.

To construct a `PropertyChangeEvent`, use the constructor

```
PropertyChangeEvent(source, propertyName, oldValue, newValue)
```

In the listener handler, you can get the property name using the `getPropertyName()` method, and the old and new values of the bound property using the `getOldValue()` and `getNewValue()` methods from an instance of `PropertyChangeEvent`.

Example 10.1 Beans Communications Through Bound Properties

This example creates a property editor for the `Clock` component in Example 4.2, "Creating a `Clock` Component." This property editor can be used during runtime to change the properties of `Clock`. The property editor window is popped up, as shown in Figure 10.1, when the user presses on the clock using the right mouse button. A change in a property in the editor is passed to the `Clock` bean through its bound property.

For simplicity, the property editor will contain only five representative properties from the `Clock` component: `hourHandColor`, `showingDigitalTime`, `timeZone`, `timeZoneOffset`, and `usingTimeZoneID`. Here are the steps to create the editor:

1. Create a new project named boundconstraintpropertydemo.jpr. Create ClockEditor.java using the Frame wizard in the Object Gallery. Switch to the UI designer of ClockEditor.java.

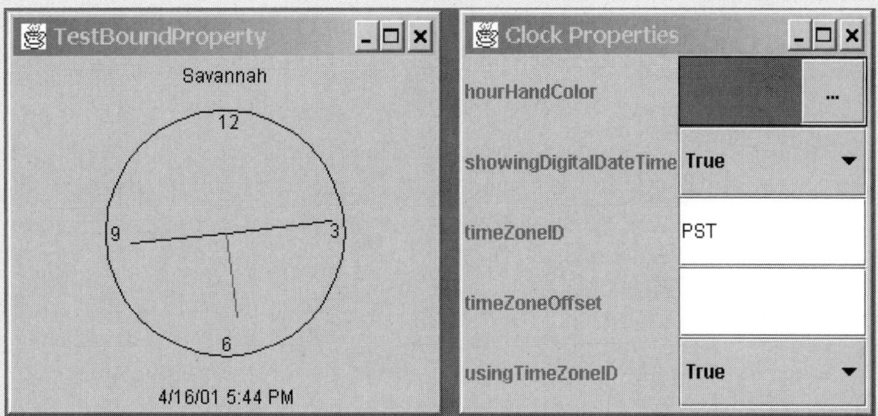

Figure 10.1 *You can set the property values in* `Clock` *from the property editor.*

2. Drop a `JPanel` to the west of the frame to create `jpLabels`, and drop a `JPanel` to the center of the frame to create `jpProperties`.

3. Set the `layout` property of `jpLabels` to `GridLayout` with five rows. Drop a `JLabel` to `jpLabels` five times, and set the `text` property of the labels to `hourHandColor`, `showingDigitalDateTime`, `timeZoneID`, `timeZoneOffset`, and `usingTimeZoneID`.

4. Set the `layout` property of `jpProperties` to `GridLayout` with five rows. Drop a `JPanel` to `jpProperties` to create `jpColor`. Set its layout to `BorderLayout` and its `border` to Line. Drop a `JLabel` to the center of `jpColor` to create `jlblColor`, and drop a `JButton` to `jpColor` to create `jbtColor`. Set the `opaque` property of `jlblColor` to True. Set the `text` property of `jbtColor` to an ellipsis symbol (...).

5. Drop a `JComboBox` to `jpProperties` to create `jcboShowingDigitalDateTime`. Drop a `JTextField` twice into `jpProperties` to create `jtfTimeZoneID` and `jtfTimeZoneOffset`. Drop a `JComboBox` to `jpProperties` to create `jcboUsingTimeZoneID`.

6. Select the UI designer in the component tree, and drop a `JColorChooser` from the Swing Containers page to the UI to create `jColorChooser1`.

7. Now that you have created the UI for the property editor, you are ready to write the code to send the bound properties to the listener. Import `java.beans.*`, declare a listener to be `PropertyChangeListener` (Line 29), and implement the registration methods `addPropertyChangeListener` and `removePropertyChangeListener`, as shown in Listing 10.1 (Lines 114–123).

8. Double-click on `jbtColor` to generate the adapter and handler `jbtColor_actionPerformed(ActionEvent e)` for the button. Implement the handler and the `fire()` method, as shown in Listing 10 (Lines 125–150).

continued

Example 10.1 continued

9. Add the items "True" and "False" into `jcboShowingDigitalDateTime` and `jcboUsingTimeZoneID` in the `jbInit()` method, as follows:

```
jcboShowingDigitalDateTime.addItem("True");
jcboShowingDigitalDateTime.addItem("False");
jcboUsingTimeZoneID.addItem("True");
jcboUsingTimeZoneID.addItem("False");
```

10. Double-click `jcboShowingDigitalDateTime` to generate the adapter and handler for handling the selection of True and False from the combo box. Implement the handler as shown in Listing 10.1. Similarly, generate the code for handling the selection of the item in `jcboUsingTimeZone`.

11. Double-click `jtfTimeZoneID` to generate the adapter and handler for changing the time zone value, and implement as shown in Listing 10.1 (Lines 167–173). You can generate and implement the handler for `jtfTimeZoneOffset` the same way (Lines 175–183).

```
1  package boundconstraintpropertydemo;
2
3  import java.awt.*;
4  import javax.swing.*;
5  import java.beans.*;
6  import java.awt.event.*;
7
8  public class ClockEditor extends JFrame {
9    JPanel jpLabels = new JPanel();
10   JLabel jLabel1 = new JLabel();
11   JLabel jLabel2 = new JLabel();
12   GridLayout gridLayout1 = new GridLayout();
13   JLabel jLabel3 = new JLabel();
14   JLabel jLabel4 = new JLabel();
15   JLabel jLabel5 = new JLabel();
16   JPanel jpProperties = new JPanel();
17   GridLayout gridLayout2 = new GridLayout();
18   JPanel jpColor = new JPanel();
19   JComboBox jcboShowingDigitalDateTime = new JComboBox();
20   JTextField jtfTimeZoneID = new JTextField();
21   JTextField jtfTimeZoneOffset = new JTextField();
22   JComboBox jcboUsingTimeZoneID = new JComboBox();
23   BorderLayout borderLayout1 = new BorderLayout();
24   JLabel jlblColor = new JLabel();
25   JButton jbtColor = new JButton();
26   JColorChooser jColorChooser1 = new JColorChooser();
27
28   // The ClockEditor component is the source of PropertyChangeEvent
29   private PropertyChangeListener listener;
30
31   // Track the previous property values
32   private String oldShowingDigitalDateTime = new String();
33   private String oldUsingTimeZoneID = new String();
34   private String oldTimeZoneID = new String();
35   private int oldTimeZoneOffset = 0;
36
```

Listing 10.1 *ClockEditor.java*

```
  /** Default constructor */
  public ClockEditor() {
    try {
      jbInit();
    }
    catch(Exception e) {
      e.printStackTrace();
    }
  }

  private void jbInit() throws Exception {
    jLabel1.setText("hourHandColor");
    jLabel2.setText("showingDigitalDateTime");
    jpLabels.setLayout(gridLayout1);
    gridLayout1.setRows(5);
    jLabel3.setText("timeZoneID");
    jLabel4.setText("timeZoneOffset");
    jLabel5.setText("usingTimeZoneID");
    jpProperties.setLayout(gridLayout2);
    gridLayout2.setRows(5);
    jpColor.setLayout(borderLayout1);
    jbtColor.setText("...");
    jbtColor.addActionListener(new java.awt.event.ActionListener() {
      public void actionPerformed(ActionEvent e) {
        jbtColor_actionPerformed(e);
      }
    });
    this.setTitle("Clock Properties");
    jColorChooser1.setName("");
    jpColor.setBorder(BorderFactory.createLineBorder(Color.black));
    jcboShowingDigitalDateTime.addActionListener(
      new java.awt.event.ActionListener() {
      public void actionPerformed(ActionEvent e) {
        jcboShowingDigitalDateTime_actionPerformed(e);
      }
    });
    jtfTimeZoneID.addActionListener(
      new java.awt.event.ActionListener() {
      public void actionPerformed(ActionEvent e) {
        jtfTimeZoneID_actionPerformed(e);
      }
    });
    jtfTimeZoneOffset.addActionListener(
      new java.awt.event.ActionListener() {
      public void actionPerformed(ActionEvent e) {
        jtfTimeZoneOffset_actionPerformed(e);
      }
    });
    jcboUsingTimeZoneID.addActionListener(
      new java.awt.event.ActionListener() {
      public void actionPerformed(ActionEvent e) {
        jcboUsingTimeZoneID_actionPerformed(e);
      }
    });
    jlblColor.setOpaque(true);
    this.getContentPane().add(jpLabels, BorderLayout.WEST);
    jpLabels.add(jLabel1, null);
    jpLabels.add(jLabel2, null);
    jpLabels.add(jLabel3, null);
    jpLabels.add(jLabel4, null);
```

Listing 10.1 *Continued*

continued

Example 10.1 continued

```
      jpLabels.add(jLabel5, null);
      this.getContentPane().add(jpProperties, BorderLayout.CENTER);
      jpProperties.add(jpColor, null);
      jpColor.add(jlblColor, BorderLayout.CENTER);
      jpColor.add(jbtColor, BorderLayout.EAST);
      jpProperties.add(jcboShowingDigitalDateTime, null);
      jpProperties.add(jtfTimeZoneID, null);
      jpProperties.add(jtfTimeZoneOffset, null);
      jpProperties.add(jcboUsingTimeZoneID, null);

      // Initialize combo boxes
      jcboShowingDigitalDateTime.addItem("True");
      jcboShowingDigitalDateTime.addItem("False");
      jcboUsingTimeZoneID.addItem("True");
      jcboUsingTimeZoneID.addItem("False");
    }

    /** Add property change listener */
    public void addPropertyChangeListener(PropertyChangeListener l) {
      listener = l;
    }

    /** Remove property change listener */
    public void removePropertyChangeListener(
      PropertyChangeListener l) {
      listener = null;
    }

    /** Choose hour hand color */
    void jbtColor_actionPerformed(ActionEvent e) {
      Color oldColor = jlblColor.getBackground();
      jColorChooser1.setColor(oldColor);

      Color selectedColor =
        JColorChooser.showDialog(this, "Choose Color",
          jlblColor.getBackground());

      if ((selectedColor != null) &&
        !(oldColor.equals(selectedColor))) {
        jlblColor.setBackground(selectedColor);
        fire("hourHandColor", selectedColor);
        oldColor = jlblColor.getBackground();
      }

      if (selectedColor != null)
        jlblColor.setBackground(selectedColor);
    }

    /** Fire property change event */
    private void fire(String propertyName, Object newValue) {
      if (listener != null)
        listener.propertyChange(
          new PropertyChangeEvent(this, propertyName, null, newValue));
    }

    /** Change showingDigitalDateTime property */
    void jcboShowingDigitalDateTime_actionPerformed(ActionEvent e) {
      if (!(oldShowingDigitalDateTime.equals
```

Listing 10.1 *Continued*

```
      (jcboShowingDigitalDateTime.getSelectedItem()))) {
      if (jcboShowingDigitalDateTime.getSelectedItem().equals(
          "True"))
        fire("showingDigitalDateTime", new Boolean(true));
      else
        fire("showingDigitalDateTime", new Boolean(false));

      oldShowingDigitalDateTime =
        (String)jcboShowingDigitalDateTime.getSelectedItem();
    }
  }

  /** Change timeZoneID property */
  void jtfTimeZoneID_actionPerformed(ActionEvent e) {
    if (!(oldTimeZoneID.equals(jtfTimeZoneID.getText().trim()))) {
      fire("timeZoneID", jtfTimeZoneID.getText().trim());
      oldTimeZoneID = jtfTimeZoneID.getText().trim();
    }
  }

  /** Change timeZoneOffset property */
  void jtfTimeZoneOffset_actionPerformed(ActionEvent e) {
    int newTimeZoneOffset =
      new Integer(jtfTimeZoneOffset.getText().trim()).intValue();
    if (!(oldTimeZoneOffset == newTimeZoneOffset)) {
      fire("timeZoneOffset", new Integer(newTimeZoneOffset));
      oldTimeZoneOffset = newTimeZoneOffset;
    }
  }

  /** Change usingTimeZoneID property */
  void jcboUsingTimeZoneID_actionPerformed(ActionEvent e) {
    if (!(oldUsingTimeZoneID.equals
      (jcboUsingTimeZoneID.getSelectedItem()))) {
      if (jcboUsingTimeZoneID.getSelectedItem().equals("True"))
        fire("usingTimeZoneID", new Boolean(true));
      else
        fire("usingTimeZoneID", new Boolean(false));
      oldUsingTimeZoneID =
        (String)jcboUsingTimeZoneID.getSelectedItem();
    }
  }
}
```

Listing 10.1 *Continued*

Any beans that implement the `PropertyChangeListener` can be the listeners for the `ClockEditor` component. As shown in Listing 10.2, the component `ClockBoundPropertyListener`, derived from `Clock`, listens for changes in the bound properties `handHourColor`, `showingDigitalDateTime`, `TimeZoneID`, and `TimeZoneOffset`.

```
package boundconstraintpropertydemo;

import clockdemo.Clock;
import java.awt.*;
import java.beans.*;

```

Listing 10.2 *ClockBoundPropertyListener.java*

continued

Example 10.1 continued

```
public class ClockBoundPropertyListener
  extends Clock implements PropertyChangeListener {
  public ClockBoundPropertyListener() {
  }

  public void propertyChange(PropertyChangeEvent e) {
    if (e.getPropertyName().equals("hourHandColor"))
      setHourHandColor((Color)e.getNewValue());

    if (e.getPropertyName().equals("showingDigitalDateTime"))
      setShowingDigitalDateTime(
        ((Boolean)e.getNewValue()).booleanValue());

    if (e.getPropertyName().equals("timeZoneID"))
      setTimeZoneID((String)e.getNewValue());

    if (e.getPropertyName().equals("timeZoneOffset"))
      setTimeZoneOffset(
        ((Integer)e.getNewValue()).intValue());

    if (e.getPropertyName().equals("usingTimeZoneID"))
      setUsingTimeZoneID(((Boolean)e.getNewValue()).booleanValue());
  }
}
```

Listing 10.2 *Continued*

Follow the steps below to create a test program to hook the listener bean with the source bean and see how they interact.

1. Create an applet named TestBoundProperty.java using the Applet wizard. In the UI designer of TestBoundProperty.java, drop a `ClockBoundPropertyListener` from the component palette to the center of the applet to create an instance renamed `clock`. Select UI from the component tree and drop a `ClockEditor` from the component palette to the applet to create an instance renamed `editor`.

2. In the inspector of `editor`, double-click the value field of `propertyChange` in the Events page to generate the adapter and handler for bound property change. Implement the `editor_propertyChange` method, as shown in Listing 10.3 (Lines 42–45), to notify bound property changes to `clock`. The `clock` object becomes a listener for `editor`.

3. In the Events page of `clock`, double-click the value field of `mousePressed` to generate the adapter and handler. Implement the `clock_mousePressed` method, as shown in Listing 10.3 (Lines 47–53), to handle mouse-press actions.

4. Run `TestBoundProperty` to test the project. Point the mouse to the clock and click the right mouse button to bring up the property editor, as shown in Figure 10.1. Click the ellipsis button to bring up the dialog box for choosing color. Choose True in the value field of `showingDigitalDateTime` to display date and time. Type a time zone ID (i.e., CST) and press

return to set the time zone for the clock. Type a numeric value (i.e., -6) for setting a new time with the specified offset to GMT with `usingTimeZoneID` set to False.

```
package boundconstraintpropertydemo;

import java.awt.*;
import java.awt.event.*;
import java.applet.*;
import javax.swing.*;
import java.beans.*;

public class TestBoundProperty extends JApplet {
  boolean isStandalone = false;
  ClockBoundPropertyListener clock =
    new ClockBoundPropertyListener();
  ClockEditor editor = new ClockEditor();

  /** Initialize the applet */
  public void init() {
    try {
      jbInit();
    }
    catch(Exception e) {
      e.printStackTrace();
    }
  }

  /** Component initialization */
  private void jbInit() throws Exception {
    this.setSize(new Dimension(400,300));
    editor.addPropertyChangeListener(
      new java.beans.PropertyChangeListener() {
      public void propertyChange(PropertyChangeEvent e) {
        editor_propertyChange(e);
      }
    });
    clock.addMouseListener(new java.awt.event.MouseAdapter() {
      public void mousePressed(MouseEvent e) {
        clock_mousePressed(e);
      }
    });
    this.getContentPane().add(clock, BorderLayout.CENTER);
  }

  /** Change property values in clock */
  void editor_propertyChange(PropertyChangeEvent e) {
    clock.propertyChange(e);
  }

  /** Activate the property editor */
  void clock_mousePressed(MouseEvent e) {
    if (e.isMetaDown()) { // Detect right button pressed
      editor.pack();
      editor.setVisible(true);
    }
  }
}
```

Listing 10.3 *TestBoundProperty.java*

continued

Example 10.1 continued

Example Review

The implementation of this project and the relationship of the classes in the project are shown in Figure 10.2.

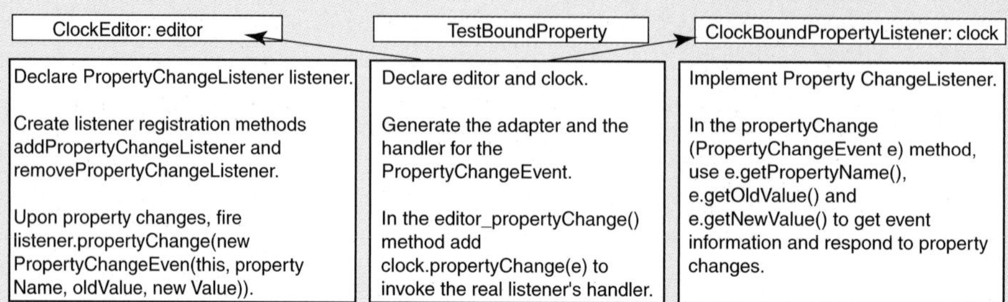

Figure 10.2 *Changes in bound properties in* `editor` *are notified to* `clock` *through the adapter created in* `TestBoundProperty`.

The use of `PropertyChangeEvent` is usually associated with a bound property of the bean. Theoretically, however, it could be used with no relation to any property of the bean.

A `PropertyChangeEvent` is fired in `editor` when changes occur in the bound property. The bean fires the `PropertyChangeEvent` only when the new value of the property is different from its old value.

The `ClockEditor` class uses unicasting for simplicity. It can be modified to enable multicasting. When adapters are used in tools like JBuilder, the effect of multicasting can be easily achieved for unicasting source components. For example, if you have two clocks (say `clock1` and `clock2`) in the applet, you could simply write the code in the `editor_propertyChange` method like this to invoke the handlers from `clock1` and `clock2`:

```
void editor_propertyChange(PropertyChangeEvent e) {
  clock1.propertyChange(e);
  clock2.propertyChange(e);
}
```

However, this approach is not equivalent to multicasting. For instance, if an exception is raised in the course of executing `clock1.propertyChange(e)`, `clock2` will not have a chance to respond to the `PropertyChangeEvent`.

NOTE

The constructor of `PropertyChangeEvent` is

```
PropertyChangeEvent(Object source, string propertyName,
  Object oldValue, Object newValue);
```

If the property is of the primitive data type, its value has to be wrapped using the wrapper class in order to pass it the `PropertyChangeEvent`.

The *PropertyChangeSupport* Class

Java also provides a utility class called `java.beans.PropertyChangeSupport` that can be used to simplify creating source components with bound properties. You can either inherit from this class or use an instance of the class as a member field of your bean and delegate various kinds of work to it. To use it for supporting bound properties in the `ClockEditor` class, follow the steps below.

1. Declare an instance of `PropertyChangeSupport`, or its subclass. For example,

   ```
   private PropertyChangeSupport changes =
     new PropertyChangeSupport(this);
   ```

2. To report a bound property update to any registered listener, invoke the `firePropertyChange` method:

   ```
   changes.firePropertyChange(
     "color", null, jColorChooser1.getColor());
   ```

3. The `firePropertyChange` method automatically checks whether the new value is the same as the old value and fires the event only when they are different.

4. Implement the registration methods:

   ```
   public void addPropertyChangeListener(PropertyChangeListener l) {
     changes.addPropertyChangeListener(l);
   }

   public void removePropertyChangeListener
     (PropertyChangeListener l) {
     changes.removePropertyChangeListener(l);
   }
   ```

NOTE

Contrary to many support classes in Java, `PropertyChangeSupport` does not implement `PropertyChangeListener`. You create an instance of `PropertyChangeSupport` for the source bean using its constructor, `PropertyChangeSupport(sourceBean)`, and this instance handles property changes in the source bean.

You will see examples of using `PropertyChangeSupport` in the next section.

Using BeansExpress to Create Bound Properties

You can use BeansExpress to create a bound property and generate the necessary code for handling it. BeansExpress uses the `PropertyChangeSupport` class to support bound properties. The following example demonstrates the use of BeansExpress to create bound properties.

Example 10.2 Using BeansExpress to Create Bound Properties

This example rewrites ClockEditor.java, as presented in Example 10.1, using BeansExpress.

Here are the steps to complete the project.

1. Reopen project boundconstraintpropertydemo.jpr. Create a new frame named ClockEditorUsingSupportClass.java using the Frame wizard.

2. Repeat Steps 2, 3, 4, 5, and 6 in the example for creating `ClockEditor` to create the same UI for `ClockEditorUsingSupportClass`, or copy and paste the UI from ClockEditor.java. You may have to adjust the layout after copying it.

3. With ClockEditorUsingSupportClass.java selected in the project pane, choose the Bean tab in the content pane to start BeansExpress. In the Properties page of BeansExpress, click "Add Properties" to bring up the New Property dialog box, as shown in Figure 10.3.

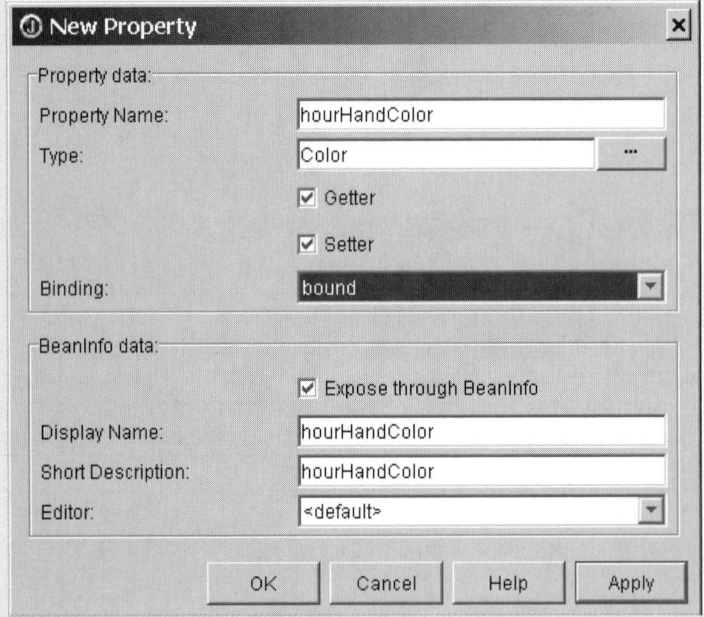

Figure 10.3 *Choose bound in the Binding field of the New Property dialog box to create a bound property.*

4. Type hourHandColor in the Name field, type Color in the Type field, and choose bound in Binding, as shown in Figure 10.3. Click Apply to create the bound property `hourHandColor`. JBuilder automatically generates the code for this bound property and the property change listener.

5. Similarly, create the bound properties `showingDigitalDateTime (boolean)`, `timeZoneID (String)`, `timeZoneOffset (int)`, and `usingTimeZoneID (boolean)`, as shown in Figure 10.4.

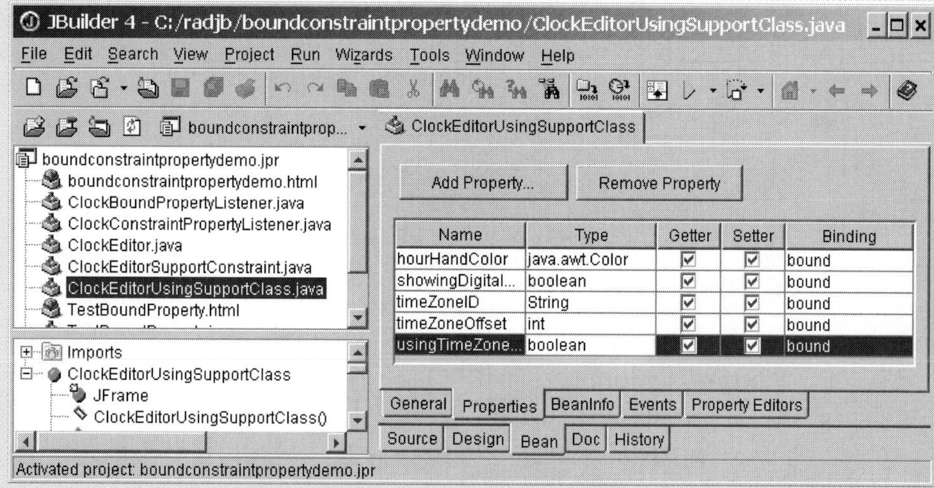

Figure 10.4 `ClockEditorUsingSupportClass` *contains five bound properties.*

6. With ClockEditorUsingSupportClass.java selected in the project pane, click the Design tab to switch to the UI designer. Generate the event handlers for `jbtColor`, `jcboShowingDigitalDateTime`, `jtfTimeZoneID`, `jtfTimeZoneOffset`, and `jcboUsingTimeZoneID`. Implement these handlers as shown in Listing 10.4.

7. Change the following statement

```
ClockEditor editor = new ClockEditor();
```

in TestBoundProperty.java to

```
ClockEditorUsingSupportClass editor =
  new ClockEditorUsingSupportClass();
```

8. Run the program. It should work the same as Example 10.1.

```
package boundconstraintpropertydemo;

import java.awt.*;
import javax.swing.*;
import java.beans.*;
import java.awt.event.*;

public class ClockEditorUsingSupportClass extends JFrame {
  private java.awt.Color hourHandColor;
  private transient PropertyChangeSupport propertyChangeListeners
```

Listing 10.4 *ClockEditorUsingSupportClass.java*

continued

Example 10.2 continued

```
      = new PropertyChangeSupport(this);
  private boolean showingDigitalDateTime;
  private String timeZoneID;
  private boolean usingTimeZoneID;

  JPanel jpLabels = new JPanel();
  JLabel jLabel1 = new JLabel();
  JLabel jLabel2 = new JLabel();
  GridLayout gridLayout1 = new GridLayout();
  JLabel jLabel3 = new JLabel();
  JLabel jLabel4 = new JLabel();
  JLabel jLabel5 = new JLabel();
  JPanel jpProperties = new JPanel();
  GridLayout gridLayout2 = new GridLayout();
  JPanel jpColor = new JPanel();
  JComboBox jcboShowingDigitalDateTime = new JComboBox();
  JTextField jtfTimeZoneID = new JTextField();
  JTextField jtfTimeZoneOffset = new JTextField();
  JComboBox jcboUsingTimeZoneID = new JComboBox();
  BorderLayout borderLayout1 = new BorderLayout();
  JLabel jlblColor = new JLabel();
  JButton jbtColor = new JButton();
  JColorChooser jColorChooser1 = new JColorChooser();
  private int timeZoneOffset;

  public ClockEditorUsingSupportClass() {
    try {
      jbInit();
    }
    catch(Exception e) {
      e.printStackTrace();
    }
  }

  public java.awt.Color getHourHandColor() {
    return hourHandColor;
  }

  public void setHourHandColor(java.awt.Color newHourHandColor) {
    java.awt.Color oldHourHandColor = hourHandColor;
    hourHandColor = newHourHandColor;
    propertyChangeListeners.firePropertyChange
      ("hourHandColor", oldHourHandColor, newHourHandColor);
  }

  public synchronized void removePropertyChangeListener
    (PropertyChangeListener l) {
    super.removePropertyChangeListener(l);
    propertyChangeListeners.removePropertyChangeListener(l);
  }

  public synchronized void addPropertyChangeListener
    (PropertyChangeListener l) {
    super.addPropertyChangeListener(l);
    propertyChangeListeners.addPropertyChangeListener(l);
  }

  public void setShowingDigitalDateTime
    (boolean newShowingDigitalDateTime) {
```

Listing 10.4 *Continued*

```
      boolean oldShowingDigitalDateTime = showingDigitalDateTime;
      showingDigitalDateTime = newShowingDigitalDateTime;
      propertyChangeListeners.firePropertyChange(
        "showingDigitalDateTime", new Boolean(oldShowingDigitalDateTime),
        new Boolean(newShowingDigitalDateTime));
    }

    public boolean isShowingDigitalDateTime() {
      return showingDigitalDateTime;
    }

    public void setTimeZoneID(String newTimeZoneID) {
      String oldTimeZoneID = timeZoneID;
      timeZoneID = newTimeZoneID;
      propertyChangeListeners.firePropertyChange("timeZoneID",
        oldTimeZoneID, newTimeZoneID);
    }

    public String getTimeZoneID() {
      return timeZoneID;
    }

    public void setTimeZoneOffset(int newTimeZoneOffset) {
      int oldTimeZoneOffset = timeZoneOffset;
      timeZoneOffset = newTimeZoneOffset;
      propertyChangeListeners.firePropertyChange("timeZoneOffset",
        new Integer(oldTimeZoneOffset),
        new Integer(newTimeZoneOffset));
    }

    public int getTimeZoneOffset() {
      return timeZoneOffset;
    }

    public void setUsingTimeZoneID(boolean newUsingTimeZoneID) {
      boolean oldUsingTimeZoneID = usingTimeZoneID;
      usingTimeZoneID = newUsingTimeZoneID;
      propertyChangeListeners.firePropertyChange("usingTimeZoneID",
        new Boolean(oldUsingTimeZoneID),
        new Boolean(newUsingTimeZoneID));
    }

    public boolean isUsingTimeZoneID() {
      return usingTimeZoneID;
    }

    private void jbInit() throws Exception {
      jLabel1.setText("hourHandColor");
      jLabel2.setText("showingDigitalDateTime");
      jpLabels.setLayout(gridLayout1);
      gridLayout1.setRows(5);
      jLabel3.setText("timeZoneID");
      jLabel4.setText("timeZoneOffset");
      jLabel5.setText("usingTimeZoneID");
      jpProperties.setLayout(gridLayout2);
      gridLayout2.setRows(5);
      jpColor.setLayout(borderLayout1);
      jbtColor.setText("...");
```

Listing 10.4 *Continued*

continued

Example 10.2 continued

```
    jbtColor.addActionListener(new java.awt.event.ActionListener() {
      public void actionPerformed(ActionEvent e) {
        jbtColor_actionPerformed(e);
      }
    });
    this.setTitle("Clock Properties");
    jColorChooser1.setName("");
    jpColor.setBorder(BorderFactory.createLineBorder(Color.black));
    jcboShowingDigitalDateTime.addActionListener(
      new java.awt.event.ActionListener() {
      public void actionPerformed(ActionEvent e) {
        jcboShowingDigitalDateTime_actionPerformed(e);
      }
    });
    jtfTimeZoneID.addActionListener(
      new java.awt.event.ActionListener() {
      public void actionPerformed(ActionEvent e) {
        jtfTimeZoneID_actionPerformed(e);
      }
    });
    jtfTimeZoneOffset.addActionListener(
      new java.awt.event.ActionListener() {
      public void actionPerformed(ActionEvent e) {
        jtfTimeZoneOffset_actionPerformed(e);
      }
    });
    jcboUsingTimeZoneID.addActionListener(
      new java.awt.event.ActionListener() {
      public void actionPerformed(ActionEvent e) {
        jcboUsingTimeZoneID_actionPerformed(e);
      }
    });
    jlblColor.setOpaque(true);
    this.getContentPane().add(jpLabels, BorderLayout.WEST);
    jpLabels.add(jLabel1, null);
    jpLabels.add(jLabel2, null);
    jpLabels.add(jLabel3, null);
    jpLabels.add(jLabel4, null);
    jpLabels.add(jLabel5, null);
    this.getContentPane().add(jpProperties, BorderLayout.CENTER);
    jpProperties.add(jpColor, null);
    jpColor.add(jlblColor, BorderLayout.CENTER);
    jpColor.add(jbtColor, BorderLayout.EAST);
    jpProperties.add(jcboShowingDigitalDateTime, null);
    jpProperties.add(jtfTimeZoneID, null);
    jpProperties.add(jtfTimeZoneOffset, null);
    jpProperties.add(jcboUsingTimeZoneID, null);

    // Initialize combo boxes
    jcboShowingDigitalDateTime.addItem("True");
    jcboShowingDigitalDateTime.addItem("False");
    jcboUsingTimeZoneID.addItem("True");
    jcboUsingTimeZoneID.addItem("False");
  }

  /** Choose hour hand color */
  void jbtColor_actionPerformed(ActionEvent e) {
    jColorChooser1.setColor(jlblColor.getBackground());

```

Listing 10.4 *Continued*

```
        Color selectedColor =
          JColorChooser.showDialog(this, "Choose Color",
            jlblColor.getBackground());

        if (selectedColor != null) {
          setHourHandColor(selectedColor);
          jlblColor.setBackground(selectedColor);
        }
      }

      /** Change showingDigitalDateTime property */
      void jcboShowingDigitalDateTime_actionPerformed(ActionEvent e) {
        if (jcboShowingDigitalDateTime.getSelectedItem().equals("True"))
          setShowingDigitalDateTime(true);
        else
          setShowingDigitalDateTime(false);
      }

      /** Change timeZoneID property */
      void jtfTimeZoneID_actionPerformed(ActionEvent e) {
        setTimeZoneID(jtfTimeZoneID.getText().trim());
      }

      /** Change timeZoneOffset property */
      void jtfTimeZoneOffset_actionPerformed(ActionEvent e) {
        setTimeZoneOffset(
          new Integer(jtfTimeZoneOffset.getText().trim()).intValue());
      }

      /** Change usingTimeZoneID property */
      void jcboUsingTimeZoneID_actionPerformed(ActionEvent e) {
        if (jcboUsingTimeZoneID.getSelectedItem().equals("True"))
          setUsingTimeZoneID(true);
        else
          setUsingTimeZoneID(false);
      }
    }
```

Listing 10.4 *Continued*

Implementing Constraint Properties

When a constraint property changes, the source bean creates an instance of `PropertyChangeEvent` and invokes the `vetoableChange` method. If the listener rejects the change, it throws a `PropertyVetoException`. The source bean then catches this exception and reverts to the old value.

Often the bound property and the constraint property are used together to verify and update the property in a so-called *two-phase approach*. The constraint property is used first to check whether the change is valid. If it is, the bound property is used to actually commit the change; if it is invalid, no change is made.

As in the case of the `PropertyChangeSupport` class, JavaBeans provides `java.beans.VetoableChangeSupport` to simplify the implementation of the constraint properties. The use of `VetoableChangeSupport` is similar to the use of the `PropertyChangeSupport` class.

Example 10.3 Using Constraint Properties

This example modifies Example 10.2 to allow the listener (clock) to reject any values of `timeZoneOffset` not in the range between -12 and 12. The example creates a new editor bean component, `ClockEditorSupportConstraint`, that generates constraint property changes, and a new clock component, `ClockConstraintPropertyListener`, to listen for constraint property changes. Since `ClockEditorSupportConstraint` extends `ClockEditor`, and `ClockConstraintPropertyListener` extends `ClockBoundPropertyListener`, these two new classes need to reference superclass data members and override some handlers. For convenience, this example will be created in the project boundconstraintproperty-demo.

Follow the steps below to complete the project.

1. Reopen project boundconstraintpropertydemo.jpr and create `ClockEditorSupportConstraint`, which extends `EditorClass` with the capability of firing constraint properties on `timeZoneOffset`, as shown in Listing 10.5 (Lines 28–40). Compile and install it in the component palette.
2. Create `ClockConstraintPropertyListener`, which extends `ClockBoundPropertyListener` and implements `VetoableChangeListener` with the capability of handling constraint property changes, as shown in Listing 10.6 (Lines 12–19). Compile and install it in the component palette.
3. Create a new applet named TestConstraintProperty.java using the Applet wizard. In the UI designer of TestConstraintProperty.java, drop a `ClockConstraintPropertyListener` to the center of the applet, and a `ClockEditorSupportConstraint` to the applet, and change their names to `clock` and `editor`, respectively.
4. In the Events page of `editor`, double-click on the value field of `propertyChange` to generate the adapter and handler for bound property change. Double-click on the value field of `vetoableChange` to generate the adapter and handler for constraint property change. Implement these two handlers as shown in Listing 10.7 (Lines 54–57 and 67–71).
5. In the Events page of `clock`, double-click on the value field of `mousePressed` to generate the adapter and handler for mouse-pressed action on `clock`. Implement the handler, as shown in Listing 10.7 (Lines 59–65), to display the editor upon a right-click of the mouse.
6. Run TestConstraintProperty to test the project. Point the mouse at the clock and click the right mouse button to display the property editor. Select False in `usingTimeZoneID` field, type 10 in the `timeZoneOffset` field, and press the ENTER key. You will see that the hour hand moves. Enter 13 in the `timeZoneOffset` field and press the ENTER key. You will see that nothing happens, because this value is rejected by the listener.

```
package boundconstraintpropertydemo;

import java.awt.*;
import java.beans.*;
import java.awt.event.*;

public class ClockEditorSupportConstraint
  extends ClockEditorUsingSupportClass {
  // Declare an instance of VetoableChangeSupport for verifying
  // property change
  private VetoableChangeSupport vetoes =
    new VetoableChangeSupport(this);

  public ClockEditorSupportConstraint() {
  }

  /** Add listener for vetoable change */
  public void addVetoableChangeListener(VetoableChangeListener l) {
    vetoes.addVetoableChangeListener(l);
  }

  /** Remove listener for vetoable change */
  public void removeVetoableChangeListener
    (VetoableChangeListener l) {
    vetoes.removeVetoableChangeListener(l);
  }

  /** Override this method defined in the super class */
  void jtfTimeZoneOffset_actionPerformed(ActionEvent e) {
    try {
      vetoes.fireVetoableChange("timeZoneOffset",
        new Integer(getTimeZoneOffset()),
        new Integer(jtfTimeZoneOffset.getText().trim()));
      super.jtfTimeZoneOffset_actionPerformed(e);
    }
    catch (PropertyVetoException ex) {
      jtfTimeZoneOffset.setText(
        new Integer(getTimeZoneOffset()).toString());
    }
  }
}
```

Listing 10.5 *ClockEditorSupportConstraint.java*

```
package boundconstraintpropertydemo;

import java.awt.*;
import java.beans.*;

public class ClockConstraintPropertyListener
  extends ClockBoundPropertyListener
  implements VetoableChangeListener {
  public ClockConstraintPropertyListener() {
  }

  public void vetoableChange(PropertyChangeEvent e)
    throws PropertyVetoException {
    if (e.getPropertyName() == "timeZoneOffset") {
      int timeZoneOffset = ((Integer)e.getNewValue()).intValue();
```

Listing 10.6 *ClockConstraintPropertyListener.java*

continued

Example 10.3 continued

```
        if (timeZoneOffset > 12 || timeZoneOffset < -12)
          throw new PropertyVetoException("Invalid timeZoneOffset", e);
      }
    }
  }
```

Listing 10.6 *Continued*

```
package boundconstraintpropertydemo;

import java.awt.*;
import java.awt.event.*;
import java.applet.*;
import javax.swing.*;
import java.beans.*;

public class TestConstraintProperty extends JApplet {
  boolean isStandalone = false;
  ClockConstraintPropertyListener clock =
    new ClockConstraintPropertyListener();
  ClockEditorSupportConstraint editor =
    new ClockEditorSupportConstraint();

  /** Construct the applet */
  public TestConstraintProperty() {
  }

  /** Initialize the applet */
  public void init() {
    try {
      jbInit();
    }
    catch(Exception e) {
      e.printStackTrace();
    }
  }

  /** Component initialization */
  private void jbInit() throws Exception {
    this.setSize(new Dimension(400,300));
    editor.addPropertyChangeListener(
      new java.beans.PropertyChangeListener() {
      public void propertyChange(PropertyChangeEvent e) {
        editor_propertyChange(e);
      }
    });
    clock.addMouseListener(new java.awt.event.MouseAdapter() {
      public void mousePressed(MouseEvent e) {
        clock_mousePressed(e);
      }
    });
    editor.addVetoableChangeListener(
      new java.beans.VetoableChangeListener() {
      public void vetoableChange(PropertyChangeEvent e)
        throws PropertyVetoException {
        editor_vetoableChange(e);
      }
    });
```

Listing 10.7 *TestConstraintProperty.java*

```
      this.getContentPane().add(clock, BorderLayout.CENTER);
    }

    /** Change property values in clock */
    void editor_propertyChange(PropertyChangeEvent e) {
      clock.propertyChange(e);
    }

    /** Activate the property editor */
    void clock_mousePressed(MouseEvent e) {
      if (e.isMetaDown()) { // Detect right button pressed
        editor.pack();
        editor.setVisible(true);
      }
    }

    /** Veto property values in clock if necessary */
    void editor_vetoableChange(PropertyChangeEvent e)
      throws PropertyVetoException {
      clock.vetoableChange(e);
    }
  }
```

Listing 10.7 *Continued*

Example Review

The implementation of the project and the relationship of the classes in the project are shown in Figure 10.5.

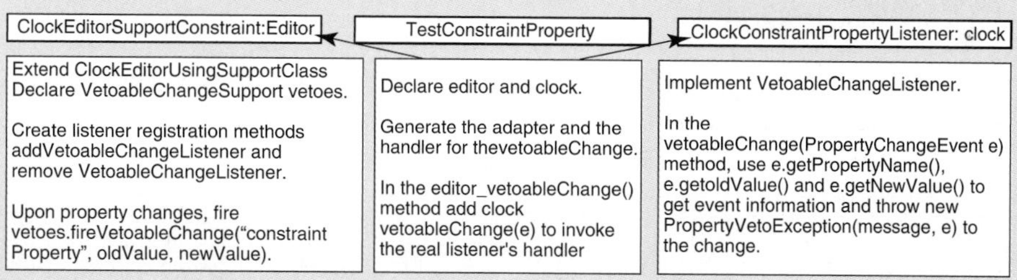

Figure 10.5 *Changes of constraint properties in* `editor` *are notified to* `clock` *through the adapter created in* `TestConstraintProperty`.

Note that Java does not have a class named `VetoableChangeEvent`. Both `VetoChangeListener` and `PropertyChangeListener` listen for `PropertyChangeEvent`.

When invoking `firePropertyChange` in `ClockEditorSupportConstraint`, all three parameters (`propertyName`, `oldValue`, and `newValue`) must be given, and they must be non-null. Like the `firePropertyChange` method, the `fireVetoableChange` method does not fire `PropertyChangeEvent` if the new value is the same as the old value, which reduces the danger of infinite loops when methods are cross-connected in classes.

continued

Example 10.3 continued

When `fireVetoableChange`, invoked from the `jtfTimeZoneOffset_actionPerformed` method in the `ClockEditorSupportConstraint` class, throws a `PropertyVetoException`, the other statements in this method are skipped. In consequence, the property is not changed in the clock. Furthermore, `timeZoneOffset` is reset to the previous value in the catch clause.

Just as you created bound properties using BeansExpress, you can use it to create constraint properties and generate the code needed to carry out the task of handling constraint properties.

Implementing Model-View Components Using Bound and Constraint Properties

Bound properties are ideal for implementing the model-view components. In Example 4.4, "Developing Model-View Components," you created a model, named `CircleModel`, which notifies the listeners of its property changes through an `ActionEvent`. The notification is implemented in the property's set method using the `fireActionPerformed` method. Instead of firing an `ActionEvent` with every property change, you can simply make it either a bound or a constraint property. Using bound and constraint properties simplifies the task of creating the model and the views.

The following example demonstrates creating model-view components using bound properties.

Example 10.4 Implementing Model-View Components Using Bound Properties

This example rewrites Example 4.4 to create a new circle model, circle editor, and circle view, named `CircleModelUsingBoundProperties`, `CircleEditorUsingBoundProperties`, and `CircleViewUsingBoundProperties`, respectively. The `CircleEditorUsingBoundProperties` class is like a property editor that enables you to change the properties of the circle. The `CircleViewBoundProperties` class displays the circle visually and enables you to increase or decrease the radius with a mouse click on the left or right button. Both `CircleEditorUsingBoundProperties` and `CircleViewUsingBoundProperties` are views that use the data stored in `CircleModelUsingBoundProperties`. A sample run of the test program that uses these three components is shown in Figure 10.6.

The following are the steps to create `CircleModelUsingBoundProperties`.

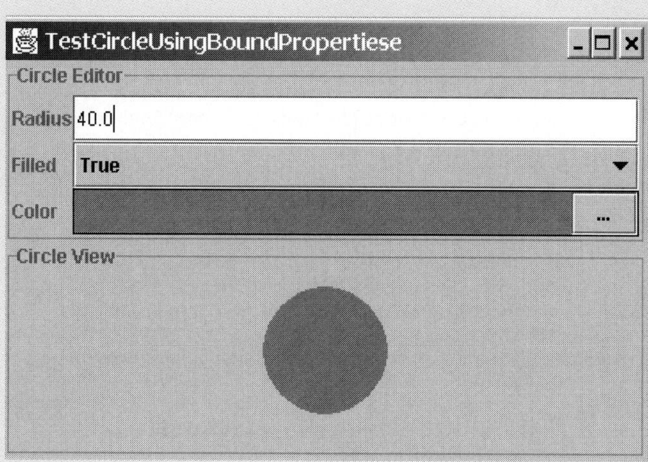

Figure 10.6 *You can change the circle property from the circle editor and increase or decrease the circle radius by clicking the left or right button.*

1. Reopen the modelviewdemo project created in Chapter 4, "Developing and Using Components." Create `CircleModelUsingBoundProperties` using the JavaBean wizard.

2. With CircleModelUsingBoundProperties.java selected in the project pane, choose the Bean tab in the content pane to start BeansExpress. Choose the Properties tab, and click the Add Properties button to bring up the New Property dialog box. Add three bound properties, `color`, `filled`, and `radius`, with type `java.awt.Color`, `boolean`, and `double`, respectively. For each property, choose bound in the binding field. `CircleModelUsingBoundProperties` is generated, as shown in Listing 10.8.

```
package modelviewdemo;

import java.beans.*;

public class CircleModelUsingBoundProperties {
  private double radius;
  private transient PropertyChangeSupport propertyChangeListeners
    = new PropertyChangeSupport(this);
  private boolean filled = true;
  private java.awt.Color color;

  public CircleModelUsingBoundProperties() {
  }

  public double getRadius() {
    return radius;
  }

  public void setRadius(double newRadius) {
    double oldRadius = radius;
```

Listing 10.8 *CircleModelUsingBoundProperties.java*

continued

Example 10.4 continued

```
      radius = newRadius;
      propertyChangeListeners.firePropertyChange(
        "radius", new Double(oldRadius), new Double(newRadius));
    }

    public synchronized void removePropertyChangeListener
      (PropertyChangeListener l) {
      propertyChangeListeners.removePropertyChangeListener(l);
    }

    public synchronized void addPropertyChangeListener
      (PropertyChangeListener l) {
      propertyChangeListeners.addPropertyChangeListener(l);
    }

    public void setFilled(boolean newFilled) {
      boolean oldFilled = filled;
      filled = newFilled;
      propertyChangeListeners.firePropertyChange(
        "filled", new Boolean(oldFilled), new Boolean(newFilled));
    }

    public boolean isFilled() {
      return filled;
    }

    public void setColor(java.awt.Color newColor) {
      java.awt.Color oldColor = color;
      color = newColor;
      propertyChangeListeners.firePropertyChange
        ("color", oldColor, newColor);
    }

    public java.awt.Color getColor() {
      return color;
    }
  }
```

Listing 10.8 *Continued*

The following are the steps to create `CircleEditorUsingBoundProperties`.

1. Create `CircleEditorUsingBoundProperties`, which extends `JPanel` using the JavaBean wizard.

2. In the UI designer of CircleEditorUsingBoundProperties.java, drop a `JPanel` to the west of the panel to create `jpLabels`, and drop a `JPanel` to the center of the applet to create `jpProperties`.

3. Set the `layout` of `jpLabels` to `GridLayout` with three rows. Drop a `JLabel` three times to jpLabels to create labels "Radius," "Filled," and "Color." Set the `layout` of `jpProperties` to `GridLayout` with three rows. Drop a `JTextField`, a `JComboBox`, and a `JPanel` into `jpProperties` to create `jtfRadius`, `jcbFilled`, and `jpColor`. Set the layout of `jpColor` to `BorderLayout`. Drop a `JLabel` and `JButton` into the center and east of `jpColor` to create `jlblColor` and `jbtColor`.

4. Select UI in the component tree, and drop a `JColorChooser` to create `jColorChooser1`.

5. Choose the Bean tab in the content pane to switch to BeansExpress. Add a property named `model` with type `CircleModelUsingBoundProperties`. Modify the `setModel` method to register `model` and initialize value in the editor.

6. Choose the Design tab to switch back to the UI designer. Double-click `jtfRadius` to generate the code for handling text input. Double-click `jcboFilled` to generate the code for handling the selection of combo box values. Double-click `jbtColor` to generate the code for handling the button action. Implement these event handlers as shown in Listing 10.9.

7. Add items True and False in the `jcbFilled` combo box (Lines 80–82).

8. Use the Implement Interface wizard to implement the `PropertyChangeListener`, and implement the handler `propertyChange` to update the values in the editor.

```
1  package modelviewdemo;
2
3  import java.awt.*;
4  import javax.swing.*;
5  import java.awt.event.*;
6  import java.beans.PropertyChangeEvent;
7  import java.beans.PropertyChangeListener;
8
9  public class CircleEditorUsingBoundProperties
10   extends JPanel implements PropertyChangeListener {
11   JPanel jpLabels = new JPanel();
12   JPanel jpProperties = new JPanel();
13   JLabel jLabel1 = new JLabel();
14   JLabel jLabel2 = new JLabel();
15   JLabel jLabel3 = new JLabel();
16   JTextField jtfRadius = new JTextField();
17   JComboBox jcboFilled = new JComboBox();
18   JPanel jpColor = new JPanel();
19   JLabel jlblColor = new JLabel();
20   JButton jbtColor = new JButton();
21   BorderLayout borderLayout2 = new BorderLayout();
22   BorderLayout borderLayout1 = new BorderLayout();
23   GridLayout gridLayout1 = new GridLayout();
24   GridLayout gridLayout2 = new GridLayout();
25
26   private CircleModelUsingBoundProperties model;
27
28   public CircleEditorUsingBoundProperties() {
29     try {
30       jbInit();
31     }
32     catch (Exception ex) {
33       ex.printStackTrace();
34     }
35   }
36
```

Listing 10.9 *CircleEditorUsingBoundProperties.java*

continued

Example 10.4 continued

```
  private void jbInit() throws Exception {
    jLabel1.setText("Radius");
    jLabel2.setText("Filled");
    jLabel3.setText("Color");
    jlblColor.setBackground(Color.black);
    jlblColor.setOpaque(true);
    jpColor.setLayout(borderLayout2);
    jbtColor.setText("jButton1");
    jbtColor.setText("...");
    jbtColor.addActionListener(new java.awt.event.ActionListener() {
      public void actionPerformed(ActionEvent e) {
        jbtColor_actionPerformed(e);
      }
    });
    jtfRadius.addActionListener(
      new java.awt.event.ActionListener() {
      public void actionPerformed(ActionEvent e) {
        jtfRadius_actionPerformed(e);
      }
    });
    this.setLayout(borderLayout1);
    jpLabels.setLayout(gridLayout1);
    gridLayout1.setRows(3);
    jpProperties.setLayout(gridLayout2);
    gridLayout2.setRows(3);
    jcboFilled.addActionListener(
      new java.awt.event.ActionListener() {
      public void actionPerformed(ActionEvent e) {
        jcboFilled_actionPerformed(e);
      }
    });
    jpColor.setBorder(BorderFactory.createLineBorder(Color.black));
    this.add(jpLabels, BorderLayout.WEST);
    jpLabels.add(jLabel1, null);
    jpLabels.add(jLabel2, null);
    jpLabels.add(jLabel3, null);
    this.add(jpProperties, BorderLayout.CENTER);
    jpProperties.add(jtfRadius, null);
    jpProperties.add(jcboFilled, null);
    jpProperties.add(jpColor, null);
    jpColor.add(jlblColor, BorderLayout.CENTER);
    jpColor.add(jbtColor, BorderLayout.EAST);

    // Add items True and False in the combo box
    jcboFilled.addItem("True");
    jcboFilled.addItem("False");
  }

  void jtfRadius_actionPerformed(ActionEvent e) {
    model.setRadius(
      new Double(jtfRadius.getText()).doubleValue());
  }

  public void setModel(
    CircleModelUsingBoundProperties newModel) {
    model = newModel;

```

Listing 10.9 *Continued*

```
      // Register listener
      if (model != null) {
        model.addPropertyChangeListener(this);
        updateEditor();
      }
      else {
        model.removePropertyChangeListener(this);
      }
    }

    public CircleModelUsingBoundProperties getModel() {
      return model;
    }

    public void propertyChange(PropertyChangeEvent e) {
      // TODO: implement this java.beans.PropertyChangeListener method;
      updateEditor();
    }

    /** Update property values in the editor */
    private void updateEditor() {
      // Update radius
      jtfRadius.setText(new Double(model.getRadius()).toString());

      // Update filled
      if (model.isFilled()) {
        jcboFilled.setSelectedIndex(0);
      }
      else {
        jcboFilled.setSelectedIndex(1);
      }

      // Update color
      jlblColor.setBackground(model.getColor());
    }

    void jcboFilled_actionPerformed(ActionEvent e) {
      if (((String)jcboFilled.getSelectedItem()).equals("True")) {
        if (model != null) model.setFilled(true);
      }
      else {
        if (model != null) model.setFilled(false);
      }
    }

    void jbtColor_actionPerformed(ActionEvent e) {
      Color selectedColor =
        JColorChooser.showDialog(this, "Choose Color",
          jlblColor.getBackground());

      if (selectedColor != null) {
        model.setColor(selectedColor);
        jlblColor.setBackground(selectedColor);
      }
    }
  }
```

Listing 10.9 *Continued*

continued

Example 10.4 continued

The following are the steps to create `CircleViewUsingBoundProperties`.

1. Create `CircleViewUsingBoundProperties` to extend `JPanel` using the JavaBean wizard.

2. Choose the Bean tab in the content pane to switch to BeansExpress. Add a property named `model` with type `CircleModelUsingBoundProperties`. Modify the `setModel` method to register `model` and initialize value in the view.

3. Use the Implement Interface wizard to implement the `PropertyChangeListener`, and implement the handler `propertyChange` to repaint the circle in the view.

4. Override the `paintComponent` method to draw the circle on the panel, as shown in Listing 10.10.

```
package modelviewdemo;

import java.awt.*;
import javax.swing.*;
import java.beans.PropertyChangeEvent;
import java.beans.PropertyChangeListener;
import java.awt.event.*;

public class CircleViewUsingBoundProperties
  extends JPanel implements PropertyChangeListener {
  BorderLayout borderLayout1 = new BorderLayout();
  private CircleModelUsingBoundProperties model;

  public CircleViewUsingBoundProperties() {
    try {
      jbInit();
    }
    catch (Exception ex) {
      ex.printStackTrace();
    }
  }

  private void jbInit() throws Exception {
    this.setOpaque(false);
    this.addMouseListener(new java.awt.event.MouseAdapter() {
      public void mouseClicked(MouseEvent e) {
        this_mouseClicked(e);
      }
    });
    this.setLayout(borderLayout1);
  }

  public void propertyChange(PropertyChangeEvent evt) {
    // TODO: implement this java.beans.PropertyChangeListener method;
    repaint();
  }

```

Listing 10.10 *CircleViewUsingBoundProperties.java*

```
    public void setModel(CircleModelUsingBoundProperties newModel) {
      model = newModel;

      // Register listener
      if (model != null) {
        model.addPropertyChangeListener(this);
      }
      else {
        model.removePropertyChangeListener(this);
      }
    }

    public CircleModelUsingBoundProperties getModel() {
      return model;
    }

    /** Paint the circle */
    public void paintComponent(Graphics g) {
      super.paintComponent(g);

      if (model == null) return;

      g.setColor(model.getColor());

      int xCenter = getSize().width/2;
      int yCenter = getSize().height/2;
      int radius = (int)model.getRadius();

      if (model.isFilled()) {
        g.fillOval(xCenter - radius, yCenter - radius,
          2*radius, 2*radius);
      }
      else {
        g.drawOval(xCenter - radius, yCenter - radius,
          2*radius, 2*radius);
      }
    }

    void this_mouseClicked(MouseEvent e) {
      if (model == null) return;

      if (e.isMetaDown())
        model.setRadius(model.getRadius()-5);
      else
        model.setRadius(model.getRadius()+5);
    }
  }
```

Listing 10.10 *Continued*

Finally, let us put the model and views together to create a test program, as follows:

1. Create an applet named `TestCircleUsingBoundProperties` using the Applet wizard.

2. Drop a `CircleEditorUsingBoundProperties` to the north of the applet to create `editor`. Drop a `CircleViewUsingBoundProperties` to the center of the applet to create `view`. Set the `border` title of `editor` to Circle Editor, and the `border` title of `view` to Circle View.

continued

Example 10.4 continued

3. Drop a `CircleModelUsingBoundProperties` to the UI designer to create `circleModel`. Set the model property of `editor` and `view` to `circleModel`.

The generated code for `TestCircleUsingBoundProperties` is shown in Listing 10.11.

```
package modelviewdemo;

import java.awt.*;
import java.awt.event.*;
import java.applet.*;
import javax.swing.*;
import javax.swing.border.*;

public class TestCircleUsingBoundProperties extends JApplet {
  boolean isStandalone = false;
  CircleEditorUsingBoundProperties editor
    = new CircleEditorUsingBoundProperties();
  CircleViewUsingBoundProperties view
    = new CircleViewUsingBoundProperties();
  CircleModelUsingBoundProperties circleModel
    = new CircleModelUsingBoundProperties();
  BorderLayout borderLayout1 = new BorderLayout();
  TitledBorder titledBorder1;
  TitledBorder titledBorder2;

  /** Initialize the applet */
  public void init() {
    try {
      jbInit();
    }
    catch(Exception e) {
      e.printStackTrace();
    }
  }

  /** Component initialization */
  private void jbInit() throws Exception {
    this.setSize(new Dimension(400,300));
    titledBorder1 = new TitledBorder("");
    titledBorder2 = new TitledBorder("");
    this.setSize(400,300);
    this.getContentPane().setLayout(borderLayout1);
    editor.setBorder(titledBorder1);
    editor.setModel(circleModel);
    view.setBorder(titledBorder2);
    view.setModel(circleModel);
    circleModel.setRadius(20.0);
    titledBorder1.setTitle("Circle Editor");
    titledBorder2.setTitle("Circle View");
    this.getContentPane().add(editor, BorderLayout.NORTH);
    this.getContentPane().add(view, BorderLayout.CENTER);
  }
}
```

Listing 10.11 *TestCircleUsingBoundProperties.java*

Example Review

Through the `Model` property, the objects `editor`, `view`, and `circleModel` are glued together. The property values of these objects are synchronized. A change in a property value in one object is immediately changed in the other objects.

The properties `radius`, `filled`, and `color` are defined as bound properties in the `CircleModelUsingBoundProperties` model. The editor and view are the listeners of these properties. Whenever there is a change in one of these properties, the listeners of the model are notified to update the property values through `circleModel`.

`CircleEditorUsingBoundProperties` and `CircleViewUsingBoundProperties` are both views for the data model `CircleModelUsingBoundProperties`.

`CircleEditorUsingBoundProperties` allows you to edit circle properties `radius`, `filled`, and `color`. `CircleViewUsingBoundProperties` allows you to increase the radius with a right mouse click and decrease the radius with a left mouse click.

Chapter Summary

Bound and constraint properties provide a mechanism that notifies the listener beans of changes to the properties of one bean. Constraint properties allow the listener beans to veto the change. Bound and constraint properties are useful in developing beans that are related through mutual properties.

Review Questions

10.1 Does a bound property or a constraint property use a special data type for declaration? How do you declare a bound property? How do you declare a constraint property?

10.2 Is `PropertyChangeSupport` a subclass of `PropertyChangeListener`? What are the differences between using `PropertyChangeSupport` and `PropertyChangeListener`?

Programming Exercises

10.1 Rewrite Exercise 4.4 using bound properties.

10.2 Rewrite Exercise 4.5 using bound properties.

CHAPTER 11

Bean Introspection and Customization

Objectives

- Use a bean information class to control the properties and events of the component to be exposed in builder tools.
- Analyze beans using the `java.beans.Introspector` class.
- Become familiar with the BeanInsight wizard.
- Develop and deploy custom property editors.
- Create custom property editors and generate `BeanInfo` classes using BeansExpress.
- Create GUI custom property editors.
- Create customizers for editing a group of related properties.

Introduction

If your component follows the standard design patterns, the builder tool can automatically recognize the properties and events it supports through introspection of a bean during design time. You can then use the property editors from the component inspector to view and modify the bean's properties. You can also inspect the events and let the builder tool generate event listener adapters for them. The design patterns provide a simple framework that allows you to develop components that support introspection. You are not limited to using the standard patterns, however. You can choose to provide your own bean information class to describe the properties and events to be exposed, and it would supersede the standard design patterns for the properties and events.

In this chapter, you will learn how to use `BeanInfo` classes to describe beans to a builder tool, create customer editors for editing individual properties, and use customizers for editing a group of related properties.

Creating *BeanInfo* Classes

To specify component information, you need to create a class that describes your component, thereby allowing you to hide or expose properties and events, give them aliases for design purposes, and give them brief descriptions that will be visible in design tools. This class is referred to as the *bean information* class (or `BeanInfo`) for the component. The bean information class causes specified properties and events of a component to appear in the component inspector.

The bean information class can be outlined as follows:

```
public class MyClassBeanInfo implements BeanInfo {
  public BeanDescriptor getBeanDescriptor() {
    // TODO: implement this java.beans.BeanInfo method;
  }

  public EventSetDescriptor[] getEventSetDescriptors() {
    // TODO: implement this java.beans.BeanInfo method;
  }

  public int getDefaultEventIndex() {
    // TODO: implement this java.beans.BeanInfo method;
  }

  public PropertyDescriptor[] getPropertyDescriptors() {
    // TODO: implement this java.beans.BeanInfo method;
  }

  public int getDefaultPropertyIndex() {
    // TODO: implement this java.beans.BeanInfo method;
  }

  public MethodDescriptor[] getMethodDescriptors() {
    // TODO: implement this java.beans.BeanInfo method;
  }
```

```
    public BeanInfo[] getAdditionalBeanInfo() {
      // TODO: implement this java.beans.BeanInfo method;
    }

    public Image getIcon(int iconKind) {
      // TODO: implement this java.beans.BeanInfo method;
    }
  }
```

Place the bean information class in the same package with the component. By default, the bean information class should be named <Component>BeanInfo, which directly implements the `java.beans.BeanInfo` interface or extends the `java.beans.SimpleBeanInfo` class. The `BeanInfo` interface provides methods for learning about properties and events, and for specifying bean image icons. You can create a customer bean information class by directly implementing the `BeanInfo` interface, but it is easier to extend the `SimpleBeanInfo` class. `SimpleBeanInfo` is a support class that itself implements the `BeanInfo` interface. All the methods in `SimpleBeanInfo` return `null`. You can override these methods to provide explicit information on the properties, events, and methods of the beans.

You need to provide your own `BeanInfo` classes if

- You have existing classes that don't follow the naming patterns for properties or events. These classes were developed before JavaBeans API was introduced.
- You don't want to give the user of your bean access to every public property at design time.
- You wish to use a particular custom editor with some property that might otherwise be assigned a default editor.

A `BeanInfo` class contains the following methods to describe bean properties, events, and other useful information to the builder tool.

- The `getPropertyDescriptors` method describes properties and returns an array of objects of the `PropertyDescriptor` class.
- The `getEventSetDescriptors` method describes event sets and returns an array of objects of the `EventSetDescriptor` class.
- The `getIcon` method describes an icon that can be used to represent the bean in the builder tool.
- The `getBeanDescriptor` method describes the customizer for the bean. The customizer is introduced in the section "Creating Component Customizers."

To provide property information, you need to override `getPropertyDescriptors` with the code to instantiate an array of `PropertyDescriptor` objects containing information on each property of the component you want the builder tool to access.

To provide event information, you need to override `getEventSetDescriptors` with the code to instantiate an array of `EventSetDescriptor` objects containing information on each event set your bean may generate.

The *PropertyDescriptor* Class

A `PropertyDescriptor` object describes a property, its accessor methods, and the custom editor for the property to the builder tool. Suppose you developed the `Circle` class before the JavaBeans standards were introduced. The property `radius` of `Circle` is read and written using the methods `readRadius` and `writeRadius`, rather than the standard names `getRadius` and `setRadius`. To describe `radius` as a bean property to the builder tool, construct a `PropertyDescriptor` object, as follows:

```
new PropertyDescriptor("radius", Circle.class, "readRadius",
  "writeRadius");
```

This object describes the `radius` property in the `Circle` class with the get and set methods `readRadius` and `writeRadius`. If the accessor methods conform to the design patterns, you could simply construct a property descriptor using this constructor:

```
new PropertyDescriptor("radius", Circle.class);
```

The following instance methods of the `PropertyDescriptor` objects are useful to get property information and set custom property editors.

- `public Class getPropertyType()`

  Returns the data type of the property. The `java.lang.Class` class encapsulates the class information, including the class name, data members, methods, and superclass.

- `public Method getReadMethod()`

  Returns the method that is used to read the property if the method is defined in the component; otherwise, it returns `null`. The `java.lang.reflect.Method` class encapsulates the method information, including the method name, return type, and parameter profile.

- `public Class getPropertyEditorClass()`

  Returns a custom editor class that has been registered for this property. The custom editor class is registered using the `setPropertyEditorClass()` method, as follows:

- `public void setPropertyEditorClass(Class propertyEditorClass)`

  Usually a default property editor is used. However, if for some reason you want to associate a certain property editor with a given property, you can do it with this method. You will learn how to customize editors in the section "Customizing Property Editors."

The *EventSetDescriptor* Class

An `EventSetDescriptor` describes a group of events fired by a given Java bean. The events in a given group are all delivered as method calls on a single event listener interface, and an event listener object can be registered via a call on a registration method supplied by the event source.

Suppose your `Circle` component fires `SmallRadiusEvent` when radius is less than 10. The listener interface of the event is `SRListener`, and two methods, `radiusChanging` and `radiusChanged`, are defined in the interface. You may create an `EventSetDescriptor` object to describe the event set to the builder tool:

```
new EventSetDesriptor(Circle.class, "SmallRadiusEvent", "SRListener",
  {"radiusChanging", "radiusChanged"},
  "addRadiusListener", "removeRadiusListener");
```

The `EventSetDescriptor` provides instance methods to get the event set information, such as the listener type (`getListenerType`) and listener registration methods (`getListenerMethods`).

The *MethodDescriptor* Class

A `MethodDescriptor` describes a specific method of external access from other components that is supported by a Java bean. The `MethodDescriptor` class provides the `getMethod` method for getting the method that this `MethodDescriptor` encapsulates, and the `getParameterDescriptor` method for getting the `ParameterDescriptor` for each of this `MethodDescriptor`'s method's parameters.

Specifying Image Icons

By overriding the `getIcon()` method, whose signature is shown below, you can specify an image icon to graphically represent a bean in the component palette of the builder tool.

```
public Image getIcon(int iconKind)
```

Four types of icons are represented in the following constants:

- `ICON_COLOR_16x16`: A 16 × 16-pixel color icon
- `ICON_MONO_16x16`: A 16 × 16-pixel monochrome icon
- `ICON_COLOR_32x32`: A 32 × 32-pixel color icon
- `ICON_MONO_32x32`: A 32 × 32-pixel monochrome icon

The `iconKind` parameter is determined by the builder tool that displays the bean icon. You override the `getIcon` method with the code that loads the image based on `iconKind`. To load, use the `loadImage` method provided in the `SimpleBeanInfo` class. This method returns `null` if loading fails.

NOTE

Some builder tools (not JBuilder) allow you to inspect all the public methods; you can provide custom information on the methods by overriding the `getMethodDescriptors()` method with the code to instantiate an array of `MethodDescriptor` objects containing information on the public methods in the component.

Example 11.1 Using the `BeanInfo` Class

This example demonstrates how to develop and use the `BeanInfo` class for a bean component. First, a new component named `Circle` will be created with a property field `radius`, whose accessor methods are deliberately named `readRadius` and `writeRadius`, which do not follow the standard design patterns. Another property named `filled`, with standard accessor methods, `isFilled` and `setFilled`. Second, you will create the `CircleBeanInfo` class to describe the properties and events.

Follow the steps below to complete the project.

1. Create a new project named beaninfodemo.jpr, and create a new class named `Circle` using the Class wizard, as shown in Listing 11.1.

```
package beaninfodemo;

import javax.swing.*;
import java.awt.*;

public class Circle extends JPanel {
  private int radius = 30;
  private boolean filled;

  public Circle() {
  }

  public int readRadius() {
    return radius;
  }

  public void writeRadius(int radius) {
    this.radius = radius;
  }

  public boolean isFilled() {
    return filled;
  }

  public void setFilled(boolean filled) {
    this.filled = filled;
  }

  public void paintComponent(Graphics g) {
    super.paintComponent(g);

    int xCenter = getSize().width/2;
    int yCenter = getSize().height/2;

    if (filled)
      g.fillOval(xCenter - radius, yCenter - radius,
        2*radius, 2*radius);
    else
      g.drawOval(xCenter - radius, yCenter - radius,
        2*radius, 2*radius);
  }
}
```

Listing 11.1 *Circle.java*

2. Suppose you want the properties `radius` and `filled`, and the mouse event to be exposed to the builder tool, and you also want to provide two color icons (circle16.gif and circle32.gif) for the builder tool to use. Create `CircleBeanInfo`, as shown in Listing 11.2.

```
package beaninfodemo;

import java.beans.*;
import java.awt.event.MouseListener;
import java.awt.Image;

public class CircleBeanInfo extends SimpleBeanInfo {
  public PropertyDescriptor[] getPropertyDescriptors() {
    try {
      PropertyDescriptor pdsRadius = new PropertyDescriptor
        ("radius", Circle.class, "readRadius", "writeRadius");
      PropertyDescriptor pdsFilled = new PropertyDescriptor
        ("filled", Circle.class);
      PropertyDescriptor[] pds = {pdsRadius, pdsFilled};
      return pds;
    }
    catch (IntrospectionException e) {
      return null;
    }
  }

  public EventSetDescriptor[] getEventSetDescriptors() {
    try {
      String[] methodNames = {"mouseClicked", "mouseEntered",
        "mouseExited", "mousePressed", "mouseReleased"};
      EventSetDescriptor esMouseEvent = new EventSetDescriptor
        (Circle.class, "MouseEvent", MouseListener.class,
         methodNames, "addMouseListener", "removeMouseListener");
      EventSetDescriptor[] es = {esMouseEvent};
      return es;
    }
    catch (IntrospectionException e) {
      return null;
    }
  }

  public Image getIcon(int iconKind) {
    if (iconKind == BeanInfo.ICON_COLOR_16x16)
      return loadImage("circle16.gif");
    else if (iconKind == BeanInfo.ICON_COLOR_32x32)
      return loadImage("circle32.gif");
    return null;
  }
}
```

Listing 11.2 *CircleBeanInfo.java*

3. Install `Circle` in the component palette. Create TestCircle.java using the Applet wizard.

4. In the UI designer of TestCircle.java, drop a `Circle` bean to the frame. You will see the properties `radius` and `filled` in the inspector shown in Figure 11.1, and the `MouseEvent` handlers on the Event page of the inspector shown in Figure 11.2.

continued

Example 11.1 continued

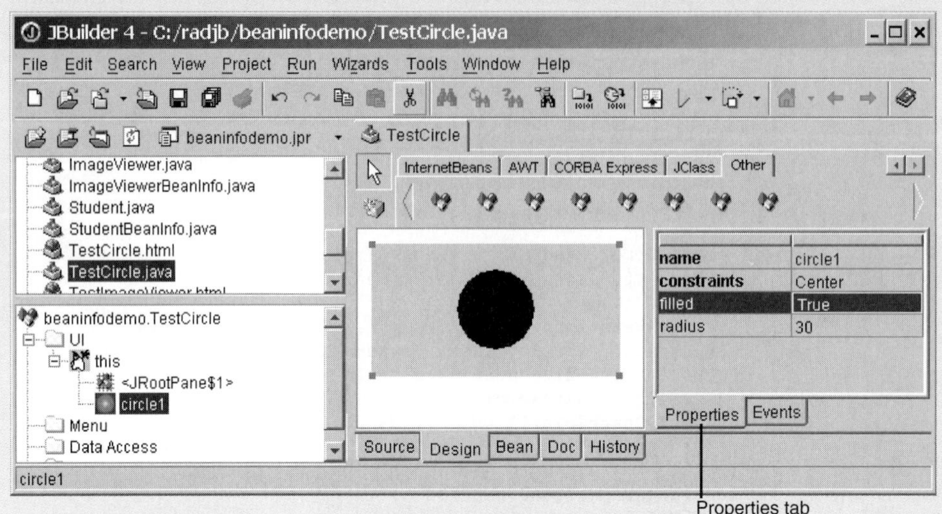

Figure 11.1 *The properties described in the* `CircleBeanInfo` *class are shown on the Properties page of the inspector.*

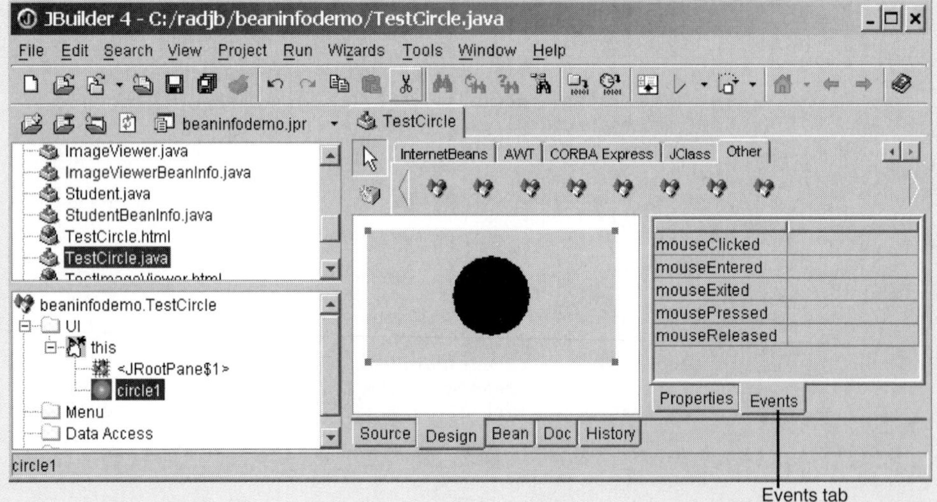

Figure 11.2 *The event listener methods described in the* `CircleBeanInfo` *classes are shown on the Events page of the inspector.*

Example Review

The `PropertyDescriptor` object `pdsRadius`, shown below, describes property `radius` and its accessor methods, `readRadius` and `writeRadius`.

```
PropertyDescriptor pdsRadius = new PropertyDescriptor
  ("radius", Circle.class, "readRadius", "writeRadius");
```

The PropertyDescriptor object pdsFilled, shown below, indicates that the property filled uses its default accessor methods.

```
PropertyDescriptor pdsFilled =
  new PropertyDescriptor("filled", Circle.class);
```

The EventSetDescriptor object esMouseEvent, shown below, describes the mouse event source, mouse event name, mouse event listener, mouse event handlers, and mouse event registration methods, where methodNames is an array of strings containing all the handlers.

```
EventSetDescriptor esMouseEvent = new EventSetDescriptor
  (Circle.class, "MouseEvent", MouseListener.class,
   methodNames, "addMouseListener", "removeMouseListener");
```

Since the constructors for PropertyDescriptor and EventSetDescriptor may throw IntrospectionException, the try/catch block is necessary to wrap the code that invokes the constructors.

If you don't override getPropertyDescriptors(), the builder tool will obtain the bean properties through automatic analysis based on the design patterns. If getPropertyDescriptors() is overridden, only the properties described in the method are accessible in the inspector. The same principle applies to the getEventSetDescriptors() method.

The CircleBeanInfo provides two color icons for the bean. If the builder tool does not support color icons, a builder tool default icon will be used.

Inspecting Bean Components

To programmatically discover which properties and events are exposed during *runtime* in a bean, you can use the java.beans.Introspector class to analyze the bean. This class uses the Java Reflection API to expose the properties, events, and methods that the bean supports. The Reflection API comprises the Class class in the java.lang package and the Constructor, Field, Member, Method, and Modifier classes in the java.lang.reflect package.

All the builder tools use the java.beans.Introspector class to analyze beans and present the analysis to the user in the inspector. The Introspector class provides a standard way for tools to learn about the properties, events, and methods supported by a target Java bean.

For each of these three kinds of information, the Introspector will separately analyze the bean's class and superclasses, looking for explicit or implicit information, and will use this information to build a BeanInfo object that comprehensively describes the target bean.

If the component's BeanInfo class exists, the non-null return values of the getPropertyDescriptors, getEventSetDescriptors, and getMethodDescriptors provide the information on the properties, event sets, and methods. If the return value is null or the component's BeanInfo class does not exist, the Introspector uses standard design patterns to analyze the bean.

To use the `Introspector` class programmatically, simply use the static method `getBeanInfo(beanClass)` in the `Introspector` class to create an object of the `BeanInfo` interface. You can then use the `BeanInfo` object's `getPropertyDescriptors()`, `getEventSetDescriptors()`, and `getMethodDescriptors()` methods to get properties, event sets, and methods.

Example 11.2 Analyzing Components

This example uses the `Introspector` class to create a program to discover the properties, event sets, and methods of the components. The program enables you to enter a fully qualified class name and select the type of information (properties, events, and methods). The information is displayed in a text area, as shown in Figure 11.3.

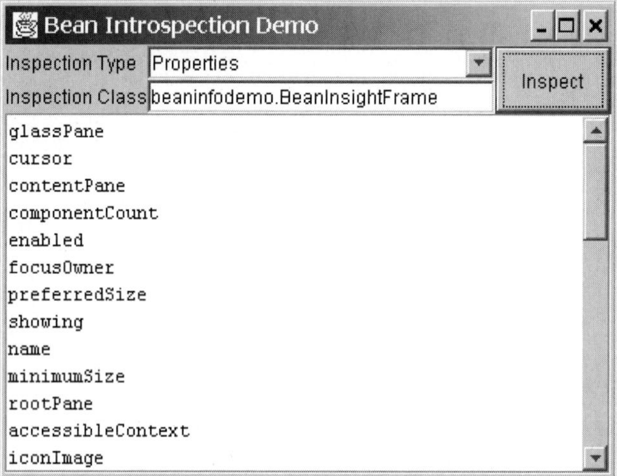

Figure 11.3 *The program lets you specify a class and choose the type of information for introspection.*

Follow the steps below to build the project.

1. In the beaninfodemo project, create BeanInsightApplication.java and BeanInsightFrame.java using the Application wizard.

2. With BeanInsightFrame.java selected in the project pane, switch to the UI designer. Drop a `JPanel` into the north of the frame to create `jpInspect`. Drop a `JScrollPane` to the center of the frame, and drop a `JTextArea` into the scroll pane to create `jta`.

3. Set the `layout` of `jpInspect` to `BorderLayout`. Drop a `JPanel` to the west of `jpInspect` to create `jpLabels`, drop a `JPanel` to the center of the `jpInspect` to create `jpSelections`, and drop a `JButton` to the east of `jpInspect` to create `jbtInspect`.

4. Set the layout of `jpLabels` to `GridLayout` with two rows, and drop a `JLabel` twice into `jpLabels` to create the labels with `text` "Inspection Type" and "Inspection Class."

5. Set the layout of `jpSelections` to `GridLayout` with two rows. Drop a `JComboBox` into it to create `jcboTypes`, and drop a `JTextField` into it to create `jtfClass`.

6. Insert the code in the `jbInit()` method to add the items into the combo box, as follows:

```
jcboTypes.addItem("Properties");
jcboTypes.addItem("Events");
jcboTypes.addItem("Methods");
```

7. Double-click `jcboTypes` to generate the code for handling selection of inspection types. Implement the handler as shown in Listing 11.3 (Lines 89–91).

8. Double-click `jbtInspect` to generate the code for inspecting the bean. Implement the handler as shown in Listing 11.3 (Lines 93–101).

9. Hand-code the `introspectBean()` method to introspect the selected information from the component (Lines 103–129). The complete code for BeanInsightFrame.java is listed below. Run BeanInsightApplication.java to test the program.

```
1   package beaninfodemo;
2
3   import java.awt.*;
4   import java.awt.event.*;
5   import javax.swing.*;
6   import java.beans.*;
7
8   public class BeanInsightFrame extends JFrame {
9     BorderLayout borderLayout1 = new BorderLayout();
10    JPanel jpInspect = new JPanel();
11    JScrollPane jScrollPane1 = new JScrollPane();
12    JTextArea jta = new JTextArea();
13    JPanel jpLabels = new JPanel();
14    JLabel jLabel1 = new JLabel();
15    JLabel jLabel2 = new JLabel();
16    BorderLayout borderLayout2 = new BorderLayout();
17    GridLayout gridLayout1 = new GridLayout();
18    JPanel jpSelections = new JPanel();
19    GridLayout gridLayout2 = new GridLayout();
20    JComboBox jcboTypes = new JComboBox();
21    JTextField jtfClass = new JTextField();
22    JButton jbtInspect = new JButton();
23
24    // Declare introspection type
25    private String introspectionType = "Properties";
26
27    /** Construct the frame */
28    public BeanInsightFrame() {
29      enableEvents(AWTEvent.WINDOW_EVENT_MASK);
```

Listing 11.3 *BeanInsightFrame.java*

continued

Example 11.2 continued

```
    try {
      jbInit();
    }
    catch(Exception e) {
      e.printStackTrace();
    }
  }

  /** Component initialization */
  private void jbInit() throws Exception {
    this.getContentPane().setLayout(borderLayout1);
    this.setSize(new Dimension(400, 300));
    this.setTitle("Bean Introspection Demo");
    jLabel1.setText("Inspection Type");
    jLabel2.setText("Inspection Class");
    jpInspect.setLayout(borderLayout2);
    jpLabels.setLayout(gridLayout1);
    gridLayout1.setRows(2);
    jpSelections.setLayout(gridLayout2);
    gridLayout2.setRows(2);
    jbtInspect.setText("Inspect");
    jbtInspect.addActionListener(
      new java.awt.event.ActionListener() {
      public void actionPerformed(ActionEvent e) {
        jbtInspect_actionPerformed(e);
      }
    });
    jcboTypes.addActionListener(
      new java.awt.event.ActionListener() {
      public void actionPerformed(ActionEvent e) {
        jcboTypes_actionPerformed(e);
      }
    });
    this.getContentPane().add(jpInspect, BorderLayout.NORTH);
    jpInspect.add(jpLabels, BorderLayout.WEST);
    jpLabels.add(jLabel1, null);
    jpLabels.add(jLabel2, null);
    jpInspect.add(jpSelections, BorderLayout.CENTER);
    jpSelections.add(jcboTypes, null);
    jpSelections.add(jtfClass, null);
    jpInspect.add(jbtInspect, BorderLayout.EAST);
    this.getContentPane().add(jScrollPane1, BorderLayout.CENTER);
    jScrollPane1.getViewport().add(jta, null);

    // Initialize combo box
    jcboTypes.addItem("Properties");
    jcboTypes.addItem("Events");
    jcboTypes.addItem("Methods");
  }

  /** Overridden so we can exit on System Close */
  protected void processWindowEvent(WindowEvent e) {
    super.processWindowEvent(e);
    if(e.getID() == WindowEvent.WINDOW_CLOSING) {
      System.exit(0);
    }
  }

  /** Handle selecting inspection types */
```

Listing 11.3 *Continued*

```
    void jcboTypes_actionPerformed(ActionEvent e) {
      introspectionType = (String)jcboTypes.getSelectedItem();
    }

    /** Handle the Inspect button */
    void jbtInspect_actionPerformed(ActionEvent e) {
      try {
        introspectBean(Class.forName(jtfClass.getText()));
      }
      catch (ClassNotFoundException ex) {
        System.out.println("class not found");
      }
    }

    /** Invoked from the button action to introspect a bean */
    public void introspectBean(Class beanClass) {
      try {
        BeanInfo bi = Introspector.getBeanInfo(beanClass);
        if (introspectionType.equals("Properties")) {
          PropertyDescriptor[] pd = bi.getPropertyDescriptors();
          jta.setText(null);
          for (int i=0; i<pd.length; i++)
            jta.append(pd[i].getName() + "\n");
        }
        else if (introspectionType.equals("Events")) {
          EventSetDescriptor[] ed = bi.getEventSetDescriptors();
          jta.setText(null);
          for (int i=0; i<ed.length; i++)
            jta.append(ed[i].getName() + "\n");
        }
        else if (introspectionType.equals("Methods")) {
          MethodDescriptor[] md = bi.getMethodDescriptors();
          jta.setText(null);
          for (int i=0; i<md.length; i++)
            jta.append(md[i].getName() + "\n");
        }
      }
      catch (IntrospectionException ex) {
        System.out.println("Error during introspection");
      }
    }
  }
```

Listing 11.3 *Continued*

Example Review

The `getBeanInfo(beanClass)` method is static and may throw `IntrospectionException`. The `Introspector` class also provides another overloaded method, `getBeanInfo(beanClass, stopClass)`, to let you introspect a Java bean and learn all about its properties, events, and methods in the class/superclass chain up to the `stopClass`.

You need to provide a fully qualified class name in the text field for introspection. For example, enter `BeanInsightDemo.BeanInsightFrame` for introspection of `BeanInsightFrame.class`.

Using the BeanInsight Wizard

JBuilder provides a convenient wizard called *BeanInsight* to let you inspect the bean and view its detailed information on BeanInfo, properties, event set, property editors, and so forth. You can start BeanInsight from the Tools menu to display the BeanInsight dialog box, as shown in Figure 11.4. To examine a bean, click the Select Bean button to select a bean, or type a bean in the text field to examine it, then click the Examine button to see the results. To view details, click View Details to display the View Details dialog box, as shown in Figure 11.5.

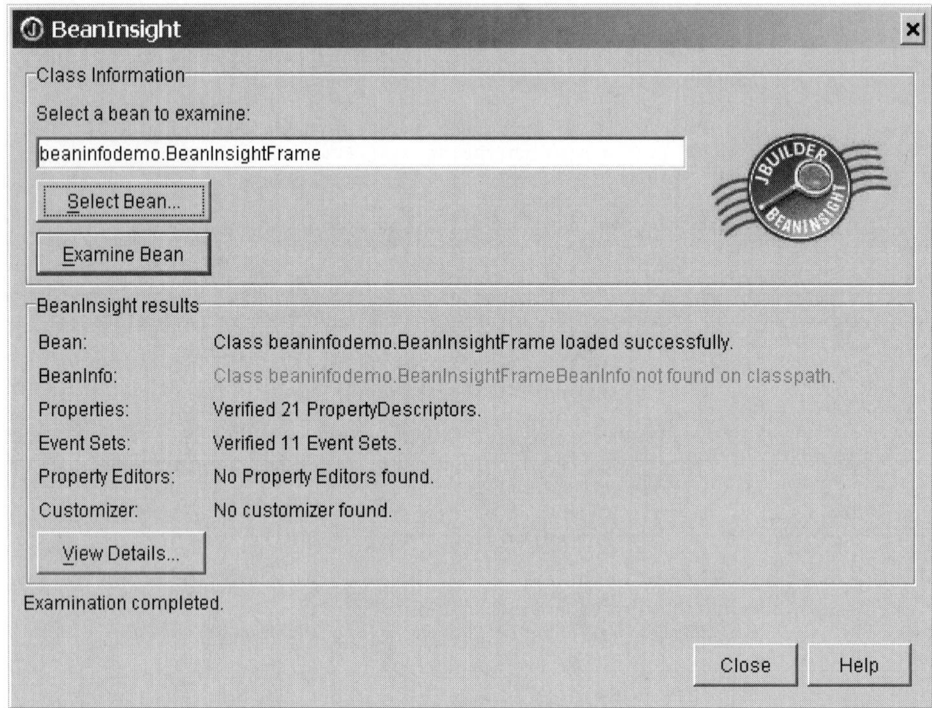

Figure 11.4 *The BeanInsight wizard lets you inspect a bean and reveal its details.*

Customizing Property Editors

JBuilder provides standard editors for the properties of primitive data types, arrays of strings, and several commonly used object types, such as `Color` and `Font`. You can, however, create your own property editors to complement or customize property editing.

To create your own property editor and enable the inspector to use it to edit the property, you must

- Create a property editor class that directly implements the `java.beans.PropertyEditor` interface, or extends the `java.beans.PropertyEditorSupport` class.
- Specify that the custom editor for the property in the `BeanInfo` class is to supersede the standard editor for the property.

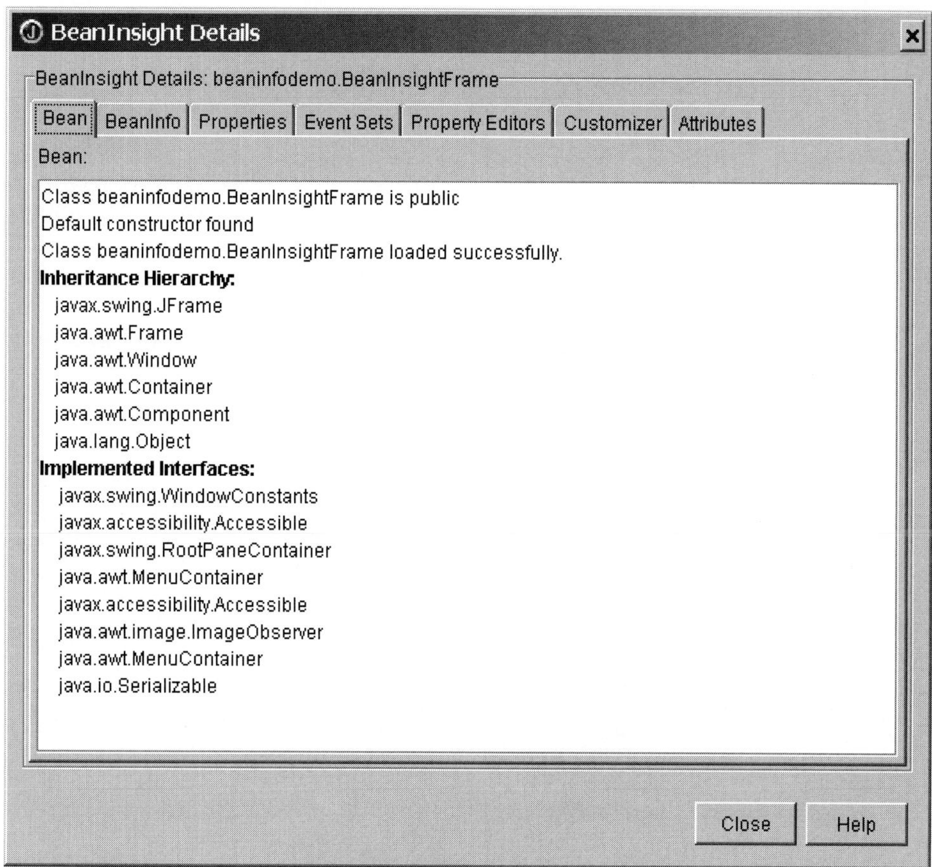

Figure 11.5 *The BeanInsight Details dialog box lets you inspect the details of a bean.*

The `PropertyEditor` interface, shown in Figure 11.6, provides several ways to update and display property values. How property values are displayed and edited depends on which methods of the `PropertyEditor` interface you implement.

PropertyEditor
getAsText(): String *getCustomEditor(): Component* *getJavaInitializationString(): String* *getTags(): String[]* *getValue(): Object* *isPaintable(): boolean* *paintValue(gfx: Graphics, box: java.awt.Rectangle): void* *setAsText(text: String): void* *setValue(Object value): void* *supportsCustomEditor(): boolean* *addPropertyChangeListener(listener: PropertyChangeListener): void* *removePropertyChangeListener(listener: PropertyChangeListener): void*

Figure 11.6 *The* `PropertyEditor` *interface provides support for the component inspector to allow users to edit a property value of a given type.*

Displaying Property Values

The builder tool invokes one of the following three methods in the `PropertyEditor` to display a property value:

- `public String getAsText()`

  Returns the property value as a string to be displayed in the component inspector.

- `public String[] getTags()`

  Returns a list of allowed property values to be displayed as a drop-down menu in the component inspector.

- `public void paintValue()`

  Paints a representation of the value into the value field of the property in the component inspector. You need to return `true` in the `isPaintable()` method to enable the `paintValue()` method. An example of using the `paintValue()` method is the `Color` property value, in which a small rectangle for color is displayed along with a description of the color.

Editing Property Values

The builder tool invokes one of the following two methods in the `PropertyEditor` to edit a property value:

- `public void setAsText(String text) throws IllegalArgumentException`

  This method can be used to retrieve the value as text from the component inspector, parse the text to an appropriate value, and then invoke the `setValue` method to set the value in `PropertyEditor`. This method may throw `java.lang.IllegalArgumentException` if the `text` is badly formatted or if this kind of property cannot be expressed as text.

- `public Component getCustomEditor()`

  Returns a GUI component that serves as a custom editor for the property. Examples of such editors are the color editor and font editor in JBuilder.

Creating Property Editors

Each property editor must implement the `getJavaInitializationString()` method, which returns a string representation of the property value for use by the builder tool to generate the code for the property change. For example, if you change the `message` property for a `MessagePanel` bean in the component inspector to "Welcome to HTML," JBuilder generates the code `setMessage("Welcome to HTML")` in the `jbInit()` method. The "Welcome to HTML" is returned from invoking the `getJavaInitializationString()` method.

Each property editor must maintain a list of event listeners that are interested in changes to the property value. When the user changes the value in the component inspector through the `setAsText` method or through a GUI editor, it must send a

PropertyChangeEvent to all registered listeners. The PropertyEditor class defines the standard event registration and removal methods addPropertyChangeListener and removePropertyChangeListener.

The PropertyEditorSupport class is often used to create custom editors. This support class implements all of the methods in the PropertyEditor interface. As an example, this is how the getAsText and setAsText methods are implemented:

```
public String getAsText() {
  return ("" + value); // Return a string
}

public void setAsText(String text)
  throws java.lang.IllegalArgumentException {
  if (value instanceof String) {
    setValue(text);
    return;
  }
  throw new java.lang.IllegalArgumentException(text);
}
```

The PropertyEditorSupport also notifies the property changes in the setValue method. This is how the setValue method is implemented:

```
public void setValue(Object value) {
  this.value = value;
  firePropertyChange();
}
```

The variable value is defined in the PropertyEditorSupport class to hold the property. The setValue method fires the PropertyChangeEvent to the builder tool so that it can respond to the property change and display the new property in the component inspector by invoking the getAsText method.

Example 11.3 Providing Custom Property Editors

This example creates a class named Student that describes student information, containing student full name, age, and gender. The full name, consisting of the first name, the middle name, and the last name, is edited using JBuilder's standard string editor. The example creates an editor for the age property to restrict the age to the range between 0 and 150, inclusively. For the gender property, the example provides an editor that lets the user choose Male and Female from a combo box.

The Student class with properties fullName, age, and gender is created using the JavaBean wizard, and its source code is given in Listing 11.4. The properties are displayed in the text fields in a panel.

```
package beaninfodemo;

import java.awt.*;
import javax.swing.*;
```

Listing 11.4 *Student.java*

continued

Example 11.3 continued

```
import java.util.*;

public class Student extends JPanel {
  BorderLayout borderLayout1 = new BorderLayout();
  JPanel jPanel1 = new JPanel();
  JLabel jLabel1 = new JLabel();
  JLabel jLabel2 = new JLabel();
  JLabel jLabel3 = new JLabel();
  GridLayout gridLayout1 = new GridLayout();
  JPanel jPanel2 = new JPanel();
  JTextField jtfName = new JTextField();
  JTextField jtfAge = new JTextField();
  JTextField jtfGender = new JTextField();
  GridLayout gridLayout2 = new GridLayout();

  // Student properties
  private String firstName = "Jim";
  private String middleName = "A";
  private String lastName = "Richards";
  private int age = 19;
  private String gender = "male";

  public Student() {
    try {
      jbInit();
    }
    catch(Exception ex) {
      ex.printStackTrace();
    }
  }

  private void jbInit() throws Exception {
    this.setLayout(borderLayout1);
    jLabel1.setText("Name");
    jLabel2.setText("Age");
    jLabel3.setText("Gender");
    jPanel1.setLayout(gridLayout1);
    gridLayout1.setRows(3);
    jPanel2.setLayout(gridLayout2);
    gridLayout2.setRows(3);
    this.add(jPanel1, BorderLayout.WEST);
    jPanel1.add(jLabel1, null);
    jPanel1.add(jLabel2, null);
    jPanel1.add(jLabel3, null);
    this.add(jPanel2, BorderLayout.CENTER);
    jPanel2.add(jtfName, null);
    jPanel2.add(jtfAge, null);
    jPanel2.add(jtfGender, null);
  }

  public String getFullName() {
    return firstName + "," + middleName + "," + lastName;
  }

  public void setFullName(String fullname) {
    StringTokenizer st = new StringTokenizer(fullname, ",");
    try {
      firstName = st.nextToken();
```

Listing 11.4 *Continued*

```
          middleName = st.nextToken();
          lastName = st.nextToken();
        }
        catch (Exception e) {
          System.out.println("Names are not formed right");
        }

        jtfName.setText(firstName + " " + middleName + " " + lastName);
      }

      public int getAge() {
        return age;
      }

      public void setAge(int age) {
        this.age = age;
        jtfAge.setText(new Integer(age).toString());
      }

      public String getGender() {
        return gender;
      }

      public void setGender(String gender) {
        this.gender = gender;
        jtfGender.setText(gender);
      }
    }
```

Listing 11.4 *Continued*

The editor `AgeEditor` for editing the `age` property shown in Listing 11.5 restricts the user to enter an integer between 0 and 150 for `age`.

```
    package beaninfodemo;
    import java.beans.PropertyEditorSupport;

    public class AgeEditor extends PropertyEditorSupport {
      /** Override this method from PropertyEditorSupport */
      public String getAsText() {
        return getValue().toString();
      }

      /** Override this method from PropertyEditorSupport */
      public void setAsText(String text)
        throws IllegalArgumentException {
        Integer val = new Integer(text);
        if (val.intValue()<= 0)
          throw new IllegalArgumentException(
            "Age may not be negative or zero");
        else if (val.intValue() >= 150)
          throw
            new IllegalArgumentException(
              "Age may not be greater than or equal to 150");
        setValue(val);
      }

      /** Override this method from PropertyEditorSupport */
      public String getJavaInitializationString() {
```

Listing 11.5 *AgeEditor.java*

continued

Example 11.3 continued

```
        return getAsText();
      }
    }
```

Listing 11.5 *Continued*

The editor `GenderEditor` for editing the `gender` property (see Listing 11.6) lets the user choose the value "Male" or "Female" from a combo box.

```
package beaninfodemo;

import java.beans.PropertyEditorSupport;

public class GenderEditor extends PropertyEditorSupport {
  /** Override this method from PropertyEditorSupport */
  public String[] getTags() {
    String[] choices = {"Male", "Female"};
    return choices;
  }

  /** Override this method from PropertyEditorSupport */
  public String getJavaInitializationString() {
    return "\"" + getValue().toString() + "\"";
  }
}
```

Listing 11.6 *GenderEditor.java*

As can be seen in Listing 11.7, you need to provide a `BeanInfo` class `StudentBeanInfo` to describe the custom editor to the builder tool.

```
package beaninfodemo;

import java.beans.*;

public class StudentBeanInfo extends SimpleBeanInfo {
  /** Override this method from PropertyEditorSupport */
  public PropertyDescriptor[] getPropertyDescriptors() {
    try {
      PropertyDescriptor pdsFullName = new 1PropertyDescriptor
        ("fullName", Student.class);
      PropertyDescriptor pdsAge = new PropertyDescriptor
        ("age", Student.class);
      pdsAge.setPropertyEditorClass(AgeEditor.class);
      PropertyDescriptor pdsGender = new PropertyDescriptor
        ("gender", Student.class);
      pdsGender.setPropertyEditorClass(GenderEditor.class);
      PropertyDescriptor[] pds = {pdsFullName, pdsAge, pdsGender};
      return pds;
    }
    catch (IntrospectionException e) {
      return null;
    }
  }
}
```

Listing 11.7 *StudentBeanInfo.java*

Follow the steps below to complete the example.

1. In the beaninfodemo project, create an applet TestSimplePropertyEditor.java using the Applet wizard.
2. Create and compile `Student`, `AgeEditor`, `GenderEditor`, and `StudentBeanInfo`, and install `Student` in the component palette.
3. With TestSimplePropertyEditor.java selected in the project pane, switch to the UI designer and drop a `Student` bean to the center of the applet to create `student1`.
4. With `student1` selected, test edit the `age` property by entering integers in and out of the permissible age range, and test edit the property by choosing Male or Female from a combo box, as shown in Figure 11.7.

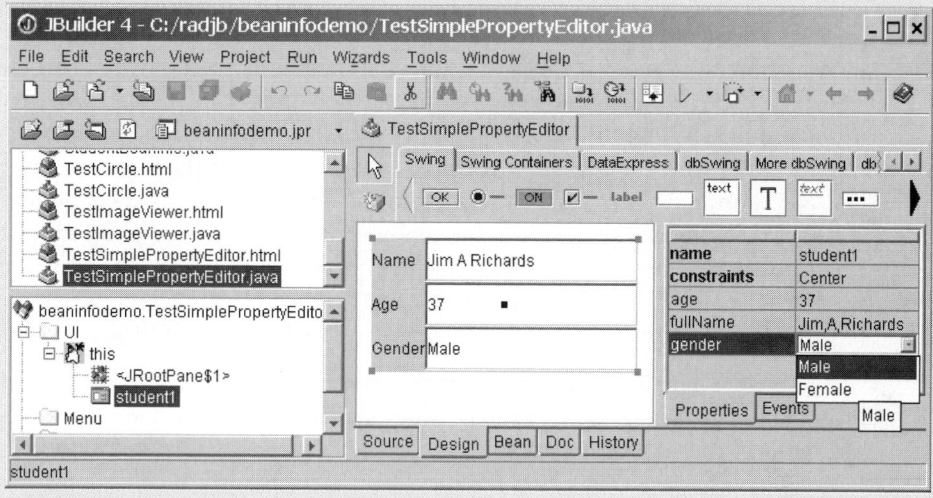

Figure 11.7 *The built-in property is used for editing* `fullName`*, and the custom property editors* `AgeEditor` *and* `GenderEditor` *are used for editing* `age` *and* `gender`.

Example Review

The `fullName` property is a string consisting of `firstName`, `middleName`, and `lastName` separated by commas, such as "Jim,A,Richards." Adhere to this pattern when modifying the property. The property editor does not validate the change. For example, if you change the value of `fullName` to "Jim A Richards," JBuilder would generate the following incorrect code in the `jbInit()` method:

```
student1.setFullName("Jim A Richards");
```

The `AgeEditor` can validate changes in the value of the `age` property. If you enter a value that is not within the permissible range, the property editor rejects it and generates no code. To understand how this editor works, let us examine it at the component inspector. When the user presses the RETURN key with the mouse pointed at the value column of the `age` property, the builder tool invokes

continued

Example 11.3 continued

the property editor's `setAsText` method, which reads the value as text from the component inspector and validates the value. If the value is valid, the `setValue` method sets the value as an `Integer` object; otherwise, an `IllegalArgumentException` is raised and the change is aborted. In the case of a valid change, the builder tool invokes the `getAsText` method to get the `Integer` object and converts it into text for display on the component inspector. Finally, a builder tool generates the following code to reflect the change by invoking the `getJavaInitializationString` method:

```
student1.setAge(ageEditor.getJavaInitializationString());
```

Here, `ageEditor` is an instance of `AgeEditor`.

The `GenderEditor` is an enumeration-type editor that allows the user to choose a value from a drop-down choice list, thus eliminating the necessity of data validation. When the user double-clicks the value column of the `gender` property, the component inspector displays a list of values by invoking the property editor's `getTags` method, which predefines a list of values for the user to choose. Upon choosing a value from the choice menu, a builder tool invokes `getAsText` to get the value and present it to the component inspector. Finally, the builder tool generates the code for setting `gender` property programmatically in the source code by invoking the `getJavaInitializationString` method, which returns the text of the selected value enclosed by double-quote symbols.

The builder tool does not recognize the custom editors unless they are described in the `BeanInfo` class. The customer editor should be stored in the same directory with the `BeanInfo` class. The `setPropertyEditor(editorClassName)` of a `PropertyDescriptor` object sets the editor for the property. The following statements set the property editors for the properties `age` and `gender`:

```
pdsAge.setPropertyEditorClass(AgeEditor.class);
pdsGender.setPropertyEditorClass(GenderEditor.class);
```

The *FeatureDescriptor* Class

The `FeatureDescriptor` class is the common base class for the bean descriptor classes, such as `PropertyDescriptor`, `EventSetDescriptor`, and `MethodDescriptor`. The following methods of the `FeatureDescriptor` class are often used to set and retrieve common information for any of the introspection descriptors in the `BeanInfo` class.

- `public void setHidden(boolean hidden)`

  Specifies whether the property is hidden. By default it is not hidden. A hidden property is not displayed in the builder tool. In JBuilder, you can right-click the inspector and set Property Exposure Level hidden to reveal hidden properties of the component. Recall that the `jMenuBar` property in the `JApplet` class is a hidden property.

- `public void setDisplayName(String displayName)`

  Sets a display name for this feature. For example, you can use it to set a display name for a property descriptor. This name is displayed as a tool tip in the inspector.

- `public void setValue(String attributeName, Object value)`

  Associates a named attribute with this feature. You can use it to associate string values to an enumeration property.

Using BeansExpress to Create Property Editors and Generate *BeanInfo* Classes

You can use BeansExpress to create property editor templates and generate the `BeanInfo` class automatically, as demonstrated in the following example. You can then modify the `BeanInfo` class if necessary to insert additional features.

Example 11.4 Creating the `TimeZoneIDEditor` and the `BeanInfo` Class for the `Clock` Component

The `Clock` component in Example 4.2, "Creating a Clock Component," contains a `timeZoneID` property. In this example, you will create a drop-down menu for the `timeZoneID` property so that the user can select a `timeZoneID` from a list of available IDs.

Here are the steps in creating a property editor named `TimeZoneIDEditor`.

1. Open project clockdemo.jpr. With Clock.java selected in the project pane, choose the Bean tab in the content pane to switch to BeansExpress.
2. In BeansExpress, choose the Property Editor tab to create or import property editors. Click "Create Custom Property Editor" to bring up the New Property Editor dialog box, as shown in Figure 11.8.
3. Type TimeZoneIDEditor in the Editor Name field, and choose String List in the Editor Type. Click OK to generate TimeZoneIDEditor.java, as shown in Figure 11.9.
4. Select TimeZoneIDEditor.java in the project pane, and modify the `getTags()` method to return a list of available time zone IDs, as shown in Listing 11.8.
5. With Clock.java selected in the project pane, choose the BeanInfo tab in BeansExpress to generate the BeanInfo class. Check the option "Expose superclass BeanInfo" to expose all the properties and events in the superclass of `Clock`, as shown in Figure 11.10. In the Editor column, choose

continued

Example 11.4 continued

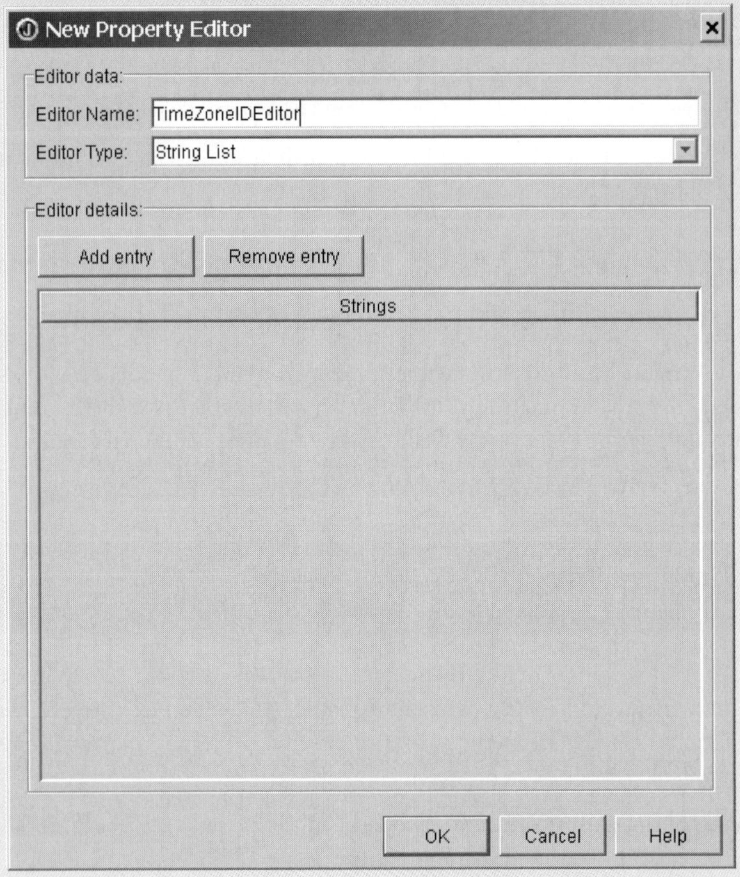

New Property Editor

Editor data:

Editor Name: TimeZoneIDEditor

Editor Type: String List

Editor details:

Add entry Remove entry

Strings

OK Cancel Help

Figure 11.8 *You can use the New Property Editor dialog box to create templates for property editors.*

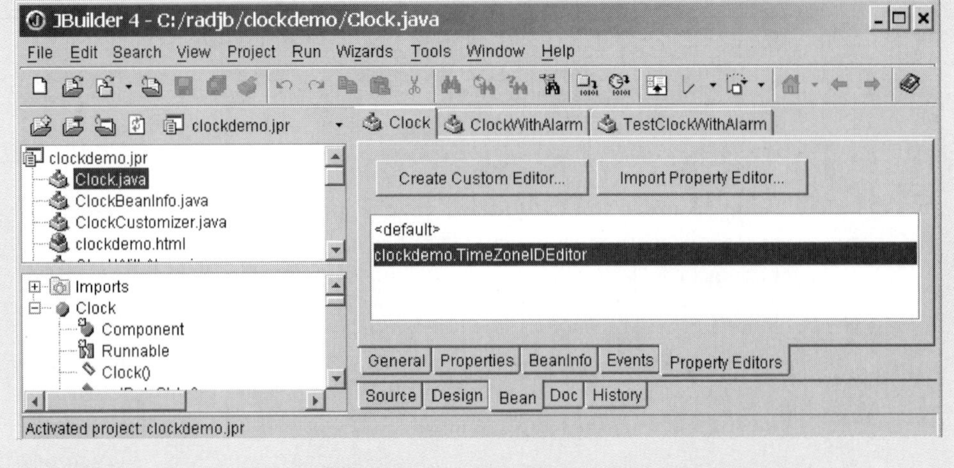

Figure 11.9 *The* `TimeZoneIDEditor` *was created by BeansExpress.*

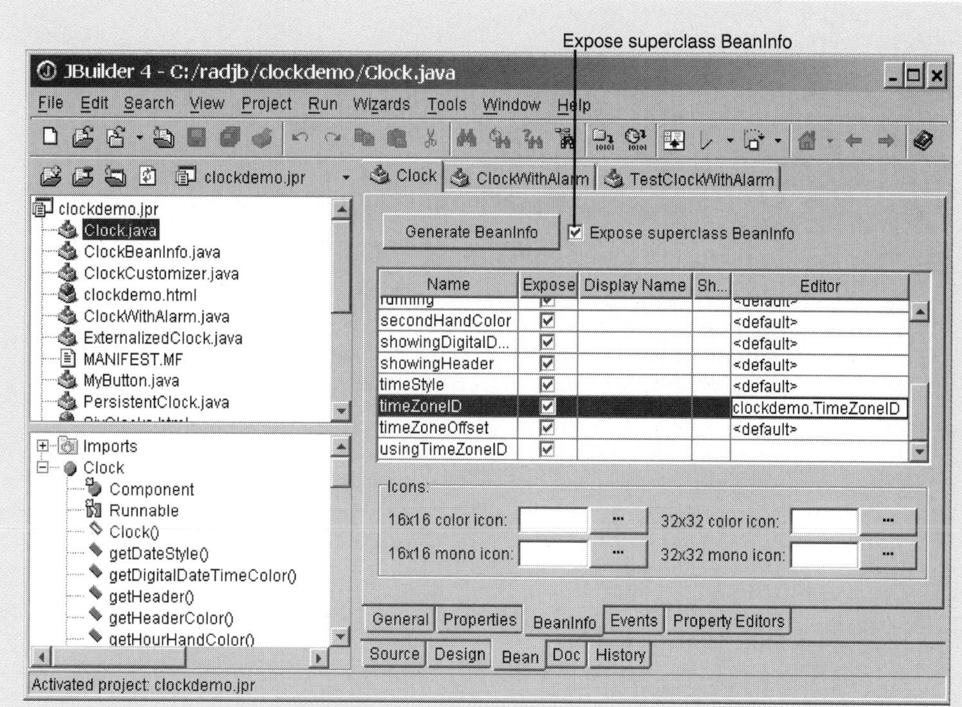

Figure 11.10 *BeansExpress can automatically generate the* `BeanInfo` *class.*

`TimeZoneIDEditor` for the `timeZoneID` property. In the Display Name column for the property `running`, type "Enable the clock to run." The Display Name is a ToolTip for the property in the component inspector. In the Icons section, choose clock16.gif and clock32.gif for the respective color icons.

6. Click the button "Generate Bean Info" to generate ClockBeanInfo.

7. Modify the generated `ClockBeanInfo` class to add the feature for displaying enumeration values for the properties `dateStyle` and `timeStyle` using the `setValue()` method in the `FeatureDescriptor` class, as shown in Listing 11.9.

```
package clockdemo;

import java.beans.*;
import java.util.TimeZone;

public class TimeZoneIDEditor extends PropertyEditorSupport {
  public TimeZoneIDEditor() {
  }

```

Listing 11.8 *TimeZoneIDEditor.java*

continued

Example 11.4 continued

```
  /** Override this method from PropertyEditorSupport */
  public String[] getTags() {
    return TimeZone.getAvailableIDs();
  }

  /** Override this method from PropertyEditorSupport */
  public String getJavaInitializationString() {
    return "\"" + getAsText() + "\"";
  }

  public void setAsText(String text)
    throws IllegalArgumentException {
    setValue(text);
  }
}
```

Listing 11.8 *Continued*

```
package clockdemo;

import java.beans.*;

public class ClockBeanInfo extends SimpleBeanInfo {
  Class beanClass = Clock.class;

  public ClockBeanInfo() {
  }

  /** Specify the customizer (to be introduced in Example 11.6 */
  public BeanDescriptor getBeanDescriptor() {
    return new BeanDescriptor(Clock.class, ClockCustomizer.class);
  }

  public PropertyDescriptor[] getPropertyDescriptors() {
    try {
      PropertyDescriptor _dateStyle = new PropertyDescriptor
        ("dateStyle", beanClass, "getDateStyle", "setDateStyle");
      PropertyDescriptor _digitalDateTimeColor =
        new PropertyDescriptor("digitalDateTimeColor", beanClass,
          "getDigitalDateTimeColor", "setDigitalDateTimeColor");
      PropertyDescriptor _header = new PropertyDescriptor
        ("header", beanClass, "getHeader", "setHeader");
      PropertyDescriptor _headerColor = new PropertyDescriptor
        ("headerColor", beanClass, "getHeaderColor",
        "setHeaderColor");
      PropertyDescriptor _hourHandColor = new PropertyDescriptor
        ("hourHandColor", beanClass,
         "getHourHandColor", "setHourHandColor");
      PropertyDescriptor _minuteHandColor = new PropertyDescriptor
        ("minuteHandColor", beanClass,
         "getMinuteHandColor", "setMinuteHandColor");
      PropertyDescriptor _preferredSize = new PropertyDescriptor
        ("preferredSize", beanClass, "getPreferredSize", null);
      PropertyDescriptor _running = new PropertyDescriptor
        ("running", beanClass, "isRunning", "setRunning");
      _running.setDisplayName("Enable the clock to run");
      PropertyDescriptor _secondHandColor = new PropertyDescriptor
        ("secondHandColor", beanClass,
```

Listing 11.9 *ClockBeanInfo.java*

```
            "getSecondHandColor", "setSecondHandColor");
        PropertyDescriptor _showingDigitalDateTime =
          new PropertyDescriptor("showingDigitalDateTime", beanClass,
           "isShowingDigitalDateTime", "setShowingDigitalDateTime");
        PropertyDescriptor _showingHeader = new PropertyDescriptor
          ("showingHeader", beanClass,
           "isShowingHeader", "setShowingHeader");
        PropertyDescriptor _timeStyle =
          new PropertyDescriptor("timeStyle",
            beanClass, "getTimeStyle", "setTimeStyle");
        PropertyDescriptor _timeZoneID = new PropertyDescriptor
          ("timeZoneID", beanClass, "getTimeZoneID", "setTimeZoneID");
        _timeZoneID.setPropertyEditorClass(
          clockdemo.TimeZoneIDEditor.class);
        PropertyDescriptor _timeZoneOffset = new PropertyDescriptor
          ("timeZoneOffset", beanClass,
           "getTimeZoneOffset", "setTimeZoneOffset");
        PropertyDescriptor _usingTimeZoneID = new PropertyDescriptor
          ("usingTimeZoneID", beanClass, "isUsingTimeZoneID",
          "setUsingTimeZoneID");

        // Set the enumeration values in the timeStyle property
        _timeStyle.setValue("enumerationValues", new Object[] {
          "FULL - 0", new Integer(0), "0",
          "LONG - 1", new Integer(1), "1",
          "MEDIUM - 2", new Integer(2), "2",
          "SHORT - 3", new Integer(3), "3",
        });

        // Set the enumeration values in the dateStyle property
        _dateStyle.setValue("enumerationValues", new Object[] {
          "FULL - 0", new Integer(0), "0",
          "LONG - 1", new Integer(1), "1",
          "MEDIUM - 2", new Integer(2), "2",
          "SHORT - 3", new Integer(3), "3",
        });

        PropertyDescriptor[] pds = new PropertyDescriptor[] {
          _dateStyle,
          _digitalDateTimeColor,
          _header,
          _headerColor,
          _hourHandColor,
          _minuteHandColor,
          _preferredSize,
          _running,
          _secondHandColor,
          _showingDigitalDateTime,
          _showingHeader,
          _timeStyle,
          _timeZoneID,
          _timeZoneOffset,
          _usingTimeZoneID,};
        return pds;
      }
      catch(IntrospectionException ex) {
        ex.printStackTrace();
        return null;
      }
    }

```

Listing 11.9 *Continued*

continued

Example 11.4 continued

```
  /** Expose PME( Properties, Methods, and Events in the superclass */
  public BeanInfo[] getAdditionalBeanInfo() {
    Class superclass = beanClass.getSuperclass();
    try {
      BeanInfo superBeanInfo = Introspector.getBeanInfo(superclass);
      return new BeanInfo[] { superBeanInfo };
    }
    catch(IntrospectionException ex) {
      ex.printStackTrace();
      return null;
    }
  }

  /** Specify an image icon */
  public java.awt.Image getIcon(int iconKind) {
    if (iconKind == BeanInfo.ICON_COLOR_16x16)
      return loadImage("clock16.gif");
    else if (iconKind == BeanInfo.ICON_COLOR_32x32)
      return loadImage("clock32.gif");
    return null;
  }
}
```

Listing 11.9 *Continued*

Example Review

Since you chose the String List as the Editor Type for the property editor in the New Property Editor dialog box in Figure 11.8, BeansExpress generates the TimeZoneIDEditor.java with a default `getTags()` method for displaying the `timeZoneID` property in a drop-down choice menu. The `getTags()` method returns a list of available time zone IDs, which can be obtained using the `TimeZone.getAvailableIDs()` method.

The `ClockBeanInfo` class was generated with no coding. The `getAdditionalBeanInfo()` method in the `BeanInfo` interface allows a `BeanInfo` object to return an arbitrary collection of other `BeanInfo` objects that provide additional information on the current bean. In this example, it returns the `BeanInfo` object of its superclass. If there are conflicts or overlaps between the information provided by different `BeanInfo` objects, then the current `BeanInfo` takes precedence over the `getAdditionalBeanInfo` objects, and later elements in the array take precedence over earlier ones.

The `setDisplayName` method of a `PropertyDescriptor` object sets a ToolTip for property. You can see the ToolTip in the component inspector, as shown in Figure 11.11.

The `setDisplayName` is actually defined in the `FeatureDescriptor` class, which is a base class for `PropertyDescriptor`, `EventSetDescriptor`, and `MethodDescriptor`. It supports some common information that can be set and retrieved for any of the introspection descriptors. In addition to setting a ToolTip using the `setDisplayName` method, you can use the `setValue` method in the `FeatureDescriptor` class to associate a property value with a string representing the

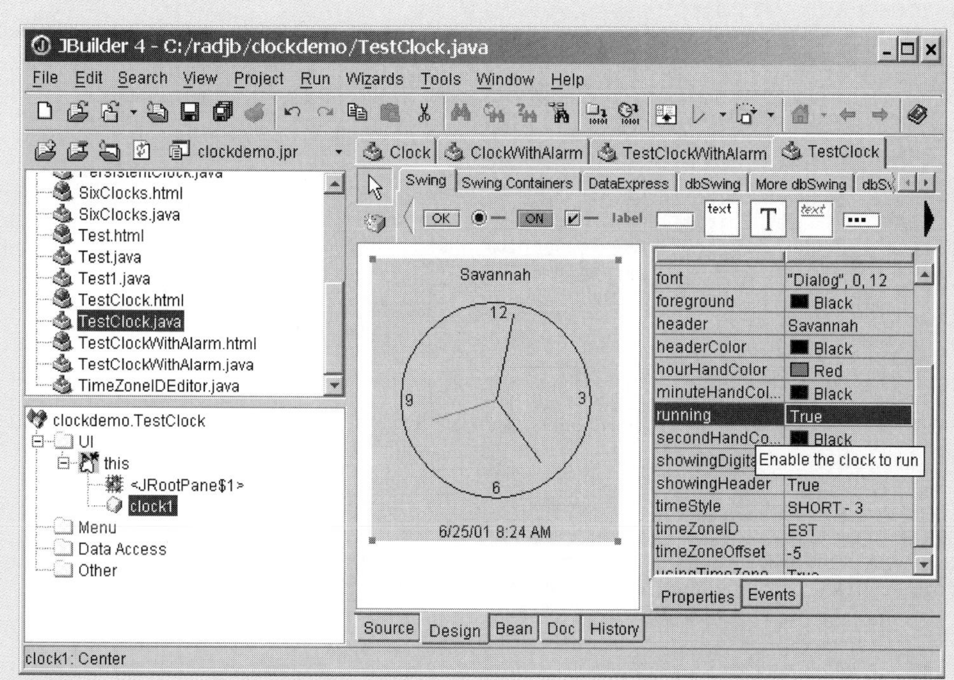

Figure 11.11 *The Display Name "Enable the clock to run" for the* `running` *property is shown as a ToolTip in the component inspector.*

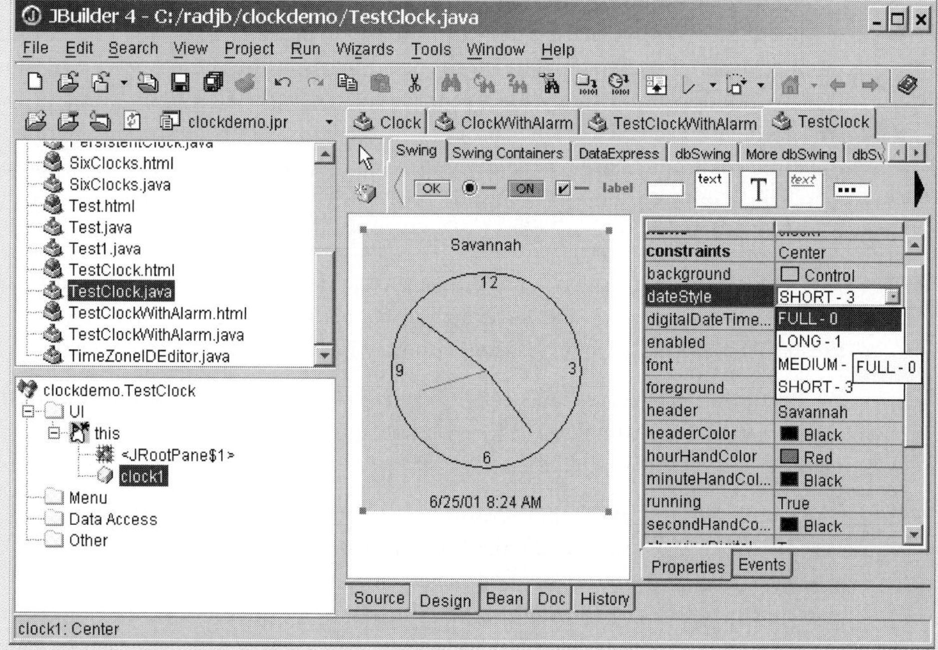

Figure 11.12 *The* `dateStyle` *property values (0, 1, 2, 3) are represented by strings in a drop-down choice menu.*

Example 11.4 continued

value in the component inspector. For example, you can associate the `dateStyle` property values with strings using the following statement:

```
_dateStyle.setValue("enumerationValues",
  new Object[] {
   "FULL - 0", new Integer(0), "0",
   "LONG - 1", new Integer(1), "1",
   "MEDIUM - 2", new Integer(2), "2",
   "SHORT - 3", new Integer(3), "3",
  });
```

You will see strings "FULL - 0," "LONG - 1," "MEDIUM - 2," and "SHORT - 3" in the value field of `dateStyle` as a drop-down choice menu, as shown in Figure 11.12.

NOTE

JBuilder's BeansExpress does not work with properties and events that violate the standard naming conventions. You cannot use BeansExpress to generate a `BeanInfo` class that contains nonstandard properties or events.

Creating GUI Custom Editors

While standard editors, customized simple editors, or enumeration-type editors will meet most of your needs, there are situations in which you might want to use more specialized and sophisticated editors. For example, the `Color` editor allows you to choose colors visually for a property of the `Color` type. The property with advanced editors appears in the component inspector with an ellipsis at the right of the value column when the property is selected. The editor pops up a GUI component when the user clicks the ellipsis. Therefore, the advanced editor is also referred to as a *popup property editor*, or GUI property editor.

To create a GUI property editor like the `Color` editor, override the methods `supportsCustomEditor()` and `getCustomEditor()` in addition to other methods in the `PropertyEditorSupport` class that you may need to use.

By default, `supportsCustomEditor()` returns `false`. To use a GUI editor, this method must return `true` to enable a builder tool to invoke the `getCustomEditor()` method to start the GUI editor.

By default, `getCustomEditor()` returns `null`. You need to implement `getCustomEditor()` to return a `Component` as the GUI editor. You need to create a class that extends `Component` or a subclass of `Component` so that you can create an object of this class and have it returned from the `getCustomEditor()` method. JBuilder automatically creates a standard dialog box to hold the object, as in the Color editor shown in Figure 11.13.

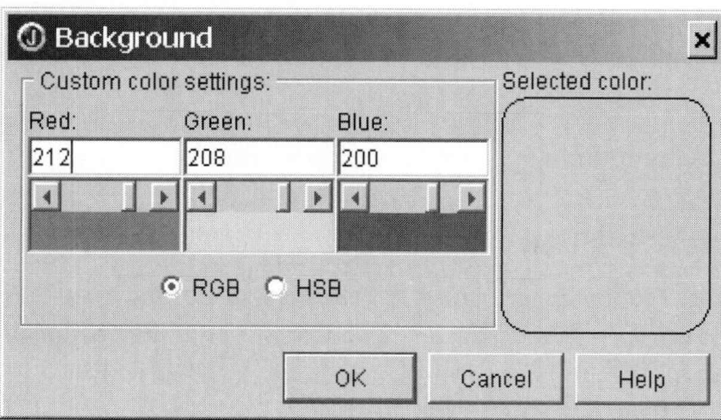

Figure 11.13 *The editor is placed in the dialog box created by JBuilder.*

The dialog window has three buttons: "OK," "Cancel," and "Help." "OK" signifies acceptance of the selected value, "Cancel" voids the selected value, and "Help" brings up the JBuilder Help Viewer.

Example 11.5 Creating GUI Property Editors

This example creates an editor for selecting an image file. The editor enables the user to browse a set of eight images and select one of them. A sample run of the property editor is shown in Figure 11.14.

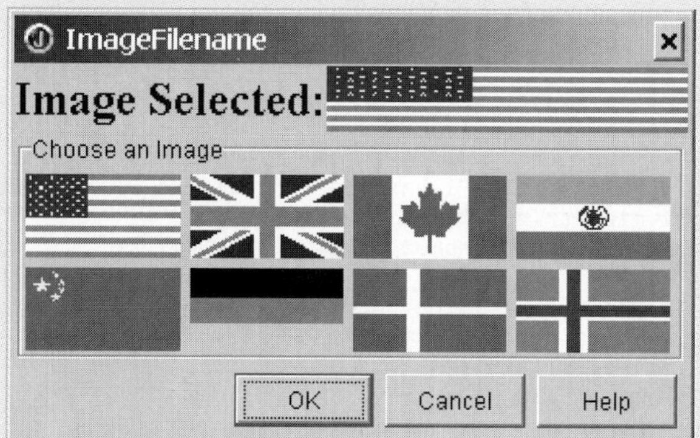

Figure 11.14 *The user selects an image by pointing the mouse, double-clicking on the image, and pressing OK.*

The example involves the following classes:

`ImageViewer`: This is the component for displaying an image. This component was developed in Example 4.1, "Creating an Image Viewer." The component contains five properties: `image`, `imageFilename`, `stretched`, `xCoordinate`, and `yCoordinate`. The `image` property specifies the image to be displayed. The `imageFilename` property specifies the filename for the image to be displayed.

continued

Example 11.5 continued

You can set images using either the `image` property or the `imageFilename` property. The `stretched` property indicates whether the image is stretched to fill in the entire viewing area. The `xCoordinate` and `yCoordinate` properties specify the upper-left corner of the image.

`ImageFilenameEditor`: This is the property editor for `imageFilename`. This class extends `PropertyEditorSupport` and contains an object of `ImageFilenameGUIEditor` as the GUI editor. The complete code of this class is shown in Listing 11.10.

`ImageFilenameGUIEditor`: This is the GUI component for choosing `imageFilename`. This class extends `JPanel` and implements `MouseListener`. It displays eight images for selection using the mouse. An instance of this class is returned from the `getCustomEditor()` method. A builder tool invokes `getCustomEditor()` to get the GUI editor and display it from the component inspector. The complete code of this class is shown in Listing 11.11.

`ImageViewerBeanInfo`: This is the `BeanInfo` class for `ImageViewer`. This class describes all the properties of the `ImageViewer` class and the GUI property editor for `imageFilename` to the builder tool. This class can be generated using BeansExpress. The complete code of this class is shown in Listing 11.12.

`TestImageViewer`: This is for testing the `ImageViewer` class and its supporting classes: `ImageFilenameEditor`, `ImageFilenameGUIEditor`, and `ImageViewerBeanInfo`.

```
package guipropertyeditordemo;

import java.awt.*;
import java.beans.*;

public class ImageFilenameEditor extends PropertyEditorSupport {
  private String imageFilename = "";
  private ImageFilenameGUIEditor guiEditor;

  /** Override this method from PropertyEditorSupport */
  public void setAsText(String text) {
    setValue(text);
  }

  /** Override this method from PropertyEditorSupport */
  public void setValue(Object o) {
    imageFilename = (String)o;
    if (guiEditor != null)
            guiEditor.imageFilename = imageFilename;

    firePropertyChange();
  }

  /** Override this method from PropertyEditorSupport */
  public Object getValue() {
    if (guiEditor != null)
      this.imageFilename = guiEditor.imageFilename;

```

Listing 11.10 *ImageFilenameEditor.java*

```
      return imageFilename;
    }

    /** Override this method from PropertyEditorSupport */
    public String getAsText() {
      return imageFilename;
    }

    /** Override this method from PropertyEditorSupport */
    public boolean supportsCustomEditor() {
      return true;
    }

    /** Override this method from PropertyEditorSupport */
    public Component getCustomEditor() {
      if (guiEditor == null)
        guiEditor =  new ImageFilenameGUIEditor(imageFilename);
      return guiEditor;
    }

    /** Override this method from PropertyEditorSupport */
    public String getJavaInitializationString() {
      return "\"" + getAsText() + "\"";
    }
  }
```

Listing 11.10 *Continued*

```
package guipropertyeditordemo;

import java.awt.*;
import java.awt.event.*;
import javax.swing.*;
import javax.swing.border.*;

public class ImageFilenameGUIEditor extends JPanel
  implements MouseListener {
  private ImageViewer selectedImageViewer = new
    ImageViewer();
  String imageFilename = "";

  public ImageFilenameGUIEditor(String imageFilename) {
    // Create panel p for holding images for selection
    JPanel p = new JPanel();
    p.setLayout(new GridLayout(2, 4, 5, 5));
    p.setBorder(new TitledBorder("Choose an Image"));

    // Place images in the panel p
    ImageViewer[] imageViewers = new ImageViewer[8];
    for (int i=0; i<8; i++) {
      imageViewers[i] = new ImageViewer();
      imageViewers[i].addMouseListener(this);
      p.add(imageViewers[i]);
    }

    imageViewers[0].setImageFilename("/image/us.gif");
    imageViewers[1].setImageFilename("/image/uk.gif");
    imageViewers[2].setImageFilename("/image/ca.gif");
    imageViewers[3].setImageFilename("/image/india.gif");
    imageViewers[4].setImageFilename("/image/china.gif");
```

Listing 11.11 *ImageFilenameGUIEditor.java*

continued

Example 11.5 continued

```
      imageViewers[5].setImageFilename("/image/germany.gif");
      imageViewers[6].setImageFilename("/image/denmark.gif");
      imageViewers[7].setImageFilename("/image/norway.gif");

      // Panel p1 for organizing the selected image
      JPanel p1 = new JPanel();
      p1.setLayout(new BorderLayout());

      // Create a label
      JLabel jlbl;
      p1.add(jlbl = new JLabel("Image Selected:"), BorderLayout.WEST);
      jlbl.setFont(new Font("TimesRoman", Font.BOLD, 24));

      // Create selectedImageViewer
      selectedImageViewer.setBackground(Color.yellow);
      selectedImageViewer.setImageFilename(imageFilename);
      p1.add(selectedImageViewer, BorderLayout.CENTER);

      // Place p and p1 in the main panel
      this.setLayout(new BorderLayout());
      this.add(p1, BorderLayout.NORTH);
      this.add(p, BorderLayout.CENTER);
    }

    /** Override this method from JPanel */
    public Dimension getPreferredSize() {
      return new Dimension(350, 150);
    }

    public void mouseClicked(MouseEvent e) {
      ImageViewer imageViewer = (ImageViewer)e.getComponent();
      imageFilename = imageViewer.getImageFilename();
      selectedImageViewer.setImageFilename(imageFilename);
    }

    public void mousePressed(MouseEvent e) {
    }

    public void mouseReleased(MouseEvent e) {
    }

    public void mouseEntered(MouseEvent e) {
    }

    public void mouseExited(MouseEvent e) {
    }
  }
```

Listing 11.11 *Continued*

```
package guipropertyeditordemo;

import java.beans.*;

public class ImageViewerBeanInfo extends SimpleBeanInfo {
  Class beanClass = ImageViewer.class;

  public ImageViewerBeanInfo() {
  }

```

Listing 11.12 *ImageViewerBeanInfo.java*

```
    public PropertyDescriptor[] getPropertyDescriptors() {
      try {
        PropertyDescriptor _image = new PropertyDescriptor("image",
          beanClass, "getImage", "setImage");
        PropertyDescriptor _imageFilename = new PropertyDescriptor(
          "imageFilename", beanClass, "getImageFilename",
          "setImageFilename");
        _imageFilename.setPropertyEditorClass(
          ImageFilenameEditor.class);
        PropertyDescriptor _stretched = new PropertyDescriptor(
          "stretched", beanClass, "isStretched", "setStretched");
        PropertyDescriptor _XCoordinate = new PropertyDescriptor(
          "XCoordinate", beanClass, "getXCoordinate",
          "setXCoordinate");
        PropertyDescriptor _YCoordinate = new PropertyDescriptor(
          "YCoordinate", beanClass, "getYCoordinate",
            "setYCoordinate");
        PropertyDescriptor[] pds = new PropertyDescriptor[] {
          _image,
          _imageFilename,
          _stretched,
          _XCoordinate,
          _YCoordinate};
        return pds;
      }
      catch(IntrospectionException ex) {
        ex.printStackTrace();
        return null;
      }
    }

    public BeanInfo[] getAdditionalBeanInfo() {
      Class superclass = beanClass.getSuperclass();
      try {
        BeanInfo superBeanInfo = Introspector.getBeanInfo(superclass);
        return new BeanInfo[] { superBeanInfo };
      }
      catch(IntrospectionException ex) {
        ex.printStackTrace();
        return null;
      }
    }
  }
```

Listing 11.12 *Continued*

Follow the steps below to complete the example.

1. Create a new project named guipropertyeditordemo.jpr.
2. Create and compile `ImageViewer`, `ImageFilenameEditor`, `ImageFilenameGUIEditor`, and `ImageViewerBeanInfo`, and install `ImageViewer` in the component palette.
3. Create TestImageViewer.java using the Applet wizard. With TestImageViewer.java selected in the project pane, switch to the UI designer. Drop a `JTabbedPane` from the Swing Containers page to the applet to create `jTabbedPane1`.

continued

Example 11.5 continued

4. With `jTabbedPane1` selected, drop an *ImageViewer* from the component palette four times to create `imageViewer1`, `imageViewer2`, `imageViewer3`, and `imageViewer4`.

5. In the inspector of `imageViewer1`, double-click the ellipsis button in the value field of the *imageFilename* property to display the editor for *imageFilename*, as shown in Figure 11.14. Double-click the first image icon and then press OK; you will see the new image displayed in `imageViewer1` and `imageViewer1.setImageFilename("/image/us.gif")` inserted in the `jbInit` method. The filename /image/us.gif now appears in the imageFilename, as shown in Figure 11.15.

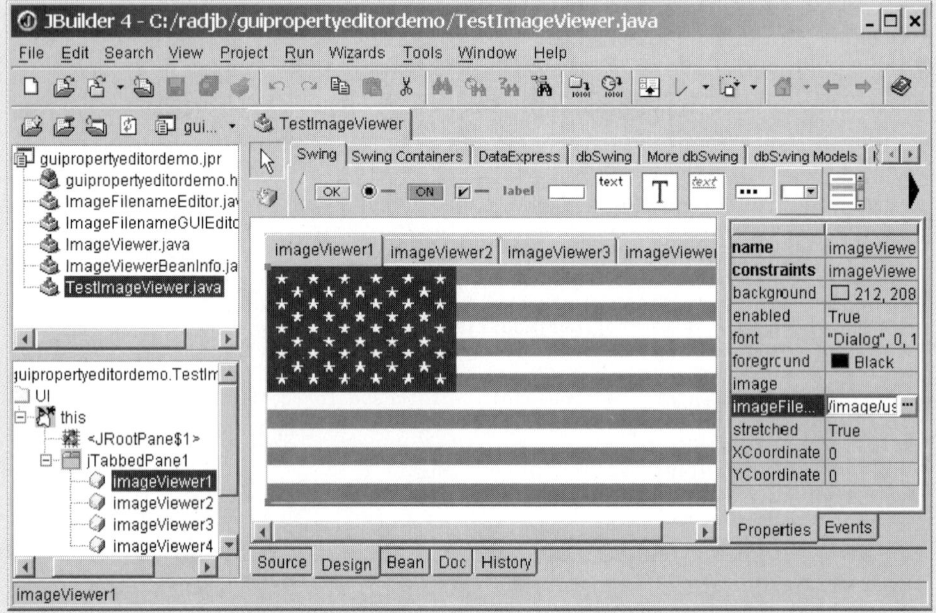

Figure 11.15 *The* `imageFilename` *is selected from a GUI property editor, which is shown in Figure 11.14.*

6. Repeat Step 5 for `imageViewer2`, `imageViewer3`, and `imageViewer4`, choose an image from the editor.

7. Run the program. Select four tabs in the tab set panel to see the images. The complete code for TestImageViewer.java is shown in Listing 11.13.

```
package guipropertyeditordemo;

import java.awt.*;
import java.awt.event.*;
import java.applet.*;
import javax.swing.*;

```

Listing 11.13 *TestImageViewer.java*

```
public class TestImageViewer extends JApplet {
  boolean isStandalone = false;
  JTabbedPane jTabbedPane1 = new JTabbedPane();
  ImageViewer imageViewer1 = new ImageViewer();
  ImageViewer imageViewer2 = new ImageViewer();
  ImageViewer imageViewer3 = new ImageViewer();
  ImageViewer imageViewer4 = new ImageViewer();

  /** Initialize the applet */
  public void init() {
    try {
      jbInit();
    }
    catch(Exception e) {
      e.printStackTrace();
    }
  }

  /** Component initialization */
  private void jbInit() throws Exception {
    this.setSize(new Dimension(367, 204));
    imageViewer2.setStretched(true);
    imageViewer3.setStretched(true);
    imageViewer4.setStretched(true);
    imageViewer4.setImageFilename("/image/norway.gif");
    imageViewer3.setImageFilename("/image/india.gif");
    imageViewer2.setImageFilename("/image/ca.gif");
    imageViewer1.setImageFilename("/image/us.gif");
    this.getContentPane().add(jTabbedPane1, BorderLayout.CENTER);
    jTabbedPane1.addTab("imageViewer1", imageViewer1);
    jTabbedPane1.addTab("imageViewer2", imageViewer2);
    jTabbedPane1.addTab("imageViewer3", imageViewer3);
    jTabbedPane1.addTab("imageViewer4", imageViewer4);
  }
}
```

Listing 11.13 *Continued*

Example Review

The `ImageFilenameEditor` class, extending `PropertyEditorSupport`, facilitates intercommunication between the GUI property editor and the builder tool, as shown in Figure 11.16.

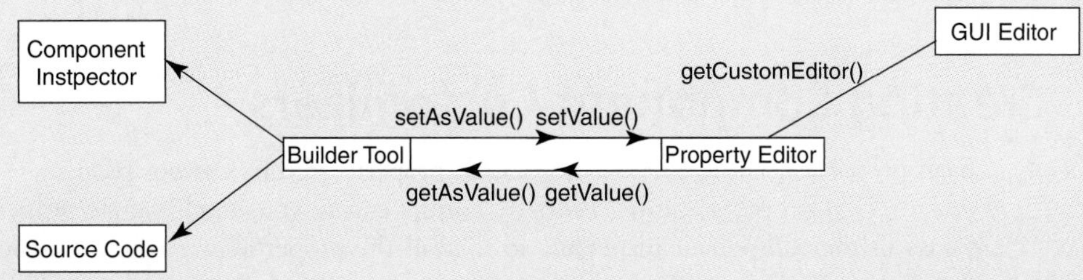

Figure 11.16 *The user selects an image from the GUI editor; the builder tool displays the image file name on the component inspector and updates the source code for setting the image in* `jbInit`.

continued

Example 11.5 continued

Since `supportsCustomEditor()` returns `true`, the GUI property editor `guiEditor` (an instance of `ImageFilenameGUIEditor`) is used for editing `guiEditor.imageFilename`, which lets the user choose an image graphically and sets the corresponding file name for the image in `guiEditor.imageFilename`.

The `getValue()` method returns the `imageFilename` value chosen from the `guiEditor` instance, and `getAsText()` returns `imageFilename` as a string. The `setAsText()` method invokes `setValue()` to set `imageFilename` from the component inspector to `guiEditor.imageFilename`.

The `ImageViewerBeanInfo` class describes the `imageFilename` property of the `ImageViewer` class and specifies its custom editor `ImageFilenameEditor`.

`TestImageViewer` uses a `JTabbedPane` to hold four instances of `ImageViewer`. The `ImageFilenameEditor`, `ImageFilenameGUIEditor`, and `ImageViewerBeanInfo` classes are used only during design time and are not needed at runtime.

NOTE
The GUI property is cached in JBuilder. If you change the code in ImageFilenameGUIEditor.java, you have to restart JBuilder.

NOTE
JBuilder requires that a property be a noncontainer in order for a GUI customer editor to work correctly. Since `ImageViewer` extends `Component`, it is not a subclass of `Container`. If `ImageViewer` were a subclass of `Container`, the GUI editor would not be displayed.

NOTE
Since `ImageViewer` and its bean info class, `ImageViewerBeanInfo`, must be in the same folder, the `ImageViewer` that was used in Example 4.1 was copied into the guipropertyeditordemo package.

Creating Component Customizers

Bean properties can be edited with default property editors, custom property editors, or GUI property editors. Property editors enable you to edit single property values in the component inspector, so that all the properties are edited independently. Some properties, however, are related. The value of one property may affect the selection of the values of other properties. For example, the `Clock` component contains the properties `showingDigitalDateTime`, `dateStyle`, and `timeStyle`. These three properties are related. You do not have to set `dateStyle` and `timeStyle` if `showingDigitalDateTime` is false. It would be nice to disable the selection of `dateStyle` and `timeStyle` when `showingDigitalDateTime` is false. This feature cannot be implemented by property editors, but it can be done with customizers.

A *customizer* is a GUI component that makes it possible to edit a group of properties at once. You can implement the rules of editing in a customizer to edit the properties interactively. A customizer is usually a panel displayed in a dialog box created by the builder tool. The dialog box in JBuilder is similar to the one used by the GUI property editor. A customizer is not limited to just one window. You can create many wizard-like dialog boxes to collect information from the user and edit the properties based on the user's responses.

A customizer must implement the `Customizer` interface. The `Customizer` interface contains the following three methods:

- `public abstract void setObject(Object bean)`
  Passes the bean to be customized to the customizer, so that it can find the state of the bean, update the bean, and interact with the bean. The builder tool starts a customizer by invoking this method.

- `public abstract void addPropertyChangeListener(PropertyChangeListener listener)`
  Registers a listener for the `PropertyChange` event. When a build tool starts a customizer, it creates an instance of the customizer and registers a listener to listen for property changes by invoking this method. Whenever a property is changed, the customizer should fire a `PropertyChange` event to notify the builder tool so that it can update the bean accordingly.

- `public abstract void removePropertyChangeListener(PropertyChangeListener listener)`
  Removes a listener for the `PropertyChange` event.

By convention, the name of a customizer should be the same as the name of the component it customizes, with "Customizer" appended to it. For example, if your component is named `Clock`, the customizer should be named `ClockCustomizer`. Following this naming convention, a customizer can be automatically recognized by builder tools without the need to create a `BeanInfo` class. If a `BeanInfo` class is used to describe a component, you have to specify the name of the customizer in the `getBeanDescriptor()` method. For example, since you created `ClockBeanInfo` for the `Clock` class, you must implement the `getBeanDescriptor()` method in the `ClockBeanInfo` class, as follows:

```
public BeanDescriptor getBeanDescriptor() {
  return new BeanDescriptor(Clock.class, ClockCustomizer.class);
}
```

Finally, how does a user start a customizer? It depends on the builder tool. In JBuilder, you start the customizer as follows:

1. Select the bean in the component tree.
2. Right-click the mouse button to display a popup menu.
3. Choose the Customizer item from the popup menu. (If the bean does not have a customizer, this item will not be shown in the menu.)

Example 11.6 Creating a Customizer for the `Clock` Component

In this example, a customizer is created to set values for properties `showingDigitalDateTime`, `dateStyle`, and `timeStyle` in the `Clock` component, as shown in Figure 11.17.

Figure 11.17 *This customizer enables you to set values for properties that specify whether and how to display a digital date and time in a clock.*

Follow the steps below to complete the example.

1. Reopen the clockdemo project, and create `ClockCustomizer` to extend `JPanel`, using the JavaBean wizard from the Object Gallery.
2. In the UI designer for `ClockCustomizer`, set the `layout` of the panel (this) to `BorderLayout`. Drop a `JCheckBox` to the south of the panel to create `jCheckBox1`.
3. Drop a `JPanel` to the center of the panel to create `jPanel1` with `GridLayout`. Drop a `JPanel` twice into `jPanel1` to create `jPanel2` and `jPanel3`. Rename `jPanel2` to `jpDateStyle`, `jPanel3` to `jpTimeStyle`. In the inspector for `jpDateStyle`, select `titled` from the drop-down choice menu for the `border` property to create `titleBorder1`. `titleBorder1` is an instance of `TitleBorder` and appears under the Other node in the component tree. In the inspector for `titleBorder1`, change the `title` to "Date Style." Similarly, create a border titled "Time Style" for `jpTimeStyle`.
4. With `jpDateStyle` selected in the component tree, set its `layout` to `GridLayout` with four rows. Drop a `JRadioButton` four times to `jpDateStyle` to create `jRadioButton1`, `jRadioButton2`, `jRadioButton3`, and `jRadioButton4`. Set the `text` property of the buttons to `FULL`, `LONG`, `MEDIUM`, and `SHORT`, respectively. Similarly, add four instances of `JRadioButton` named `jRadioButton5`, `jRadioButton6`, `jRadioButton7`, and `jRadioButton8` with text FULL, LONG, MEDIUM, and SHORT into the `jpTimeStyle` panel.

5. Declare and create two instances of `ButtonGroup`, named `buttonGroup1` and `buttonGroup2` (Lines 15–18). Group the date style radio buttons in `buttonGroup1` and group the time style radio buttons in `groupButton2` using the `add` method, as shown in Listing 11.14 (Lines 84–94).

6. Implement the `java.beans.Customizer` interface using the Implement Interface wizard to generate the methods `setObject`, `addPropertyChangeListener`, and `removePropertyChangeListener`. Declare and create an instance of `PropertyChangeSupport`, and complete these methods as shown in Listing 11.14 (Lines 107–148).

7. Implement the `ItemListener` interface using the Implement Interface wizard. Register the customizer (`this`) as the listener for all the radio buttons and the check box. Implement the `itemStateChanged` handler to process the change in the state of the check box and eight radio buttons, as shown in Listing 11.14 (Lines 150–217).

```
1   package clockdemo;
2
3   import java.awt.*;
4   import javax.swing.*;
5   import javax.swing.border.*;
6   import java.awt.event.*;
7   import java.text.DateFormat;
8   import java.beans.*;
9
10  public class ClockCustomizer extends JPanel
11    implements Customizer, ItemListener {
12    // **variables declared manually
13    // Declare a variable for notifying property change
14    PropertyChangeSupport pcs = null;
15    // Declare buttonGroup1 to group date style radio buttons
16    ButtonGroup buttonGroup1 = new ButtonGroup();
17    // Declare buttonGroup2 to group time style radio buttons
18    ButtonGroup buttonGroup2= new ButtonGroup();
19    // Declare a variable for Clock
20    Clock clock = null;
21
22    // —Variables created automatically
23    BorderLayout borderLayout1 = new BorderLayout();
24    JCheckBox jCheckBox1 = new JCheckBox();
25    JPanel jPanel1 = new JPanel();
26    GridLayout gridLayout1 = new GridLayout();
27    JPanel jpDateStyle = new JPanel();
28    JPanel jpTimeStyle = new JPanel();
29    TitledBorder titledBorder1;
30    TitledBorder titledBorder2;
31    JRadioButton jRadioButton1 = new JRadioButton();
32    JRadioButton jRadioButton2 = new JRadioButton();
33    JRadioButton jRadioButton3 = new JRadioButton();
34    JRadioButton jRadioButton4 = new JRadioButton();
35    JRadioButton jRadioButton5 = new JRadioButton();
36    JRadioButton jRadioButton6 = new JRadioButton();
37    JRadioButton jRadioButton7 = new JRadioButton();
```

Listing 11.14 *ClockCustomizer.java*

continued

Example 11.6 continued

```
    JRadioButton jRadioButton8 = new JRadioButton();
    GridLayout gridLayout2 = new GridLayout();
    GridLayout gridLayout3 = new GridLayout();

    public ClockCustomizer() {
      // Delete the code for invoking jbInit() here.
      // jbInit() should be invoked from setObject(),
      // because setObject() must be called before jbInit().
    }

    private void jbInit() throws Exception {
      titledBorder1 = new TitledBorder("Date Style");
      titledBorder2 = new TitledBorder("Time Style");
      jpTimeStyle.setLayout(gridLayout3);
      jpTimeStyle.setBorder(titledBorder2);
      jRadioButton1.setText("FULL");
      jRadioButton2.setText("LONG");
      jRadioButton3.setText("MEDIUM");
      jRadioButton3.setName("");
      jRadioButton4.setText("SHORT");
      jRadioButton5.setText("FULL");
      jRadioButton6.setText("LONG");
      jRadioButton7.setText("MEDIUM");
      jRadioButton8.setText("SHORT");
      jpDateStyle.setBorder(titledBorder1);
      jpDateStyle.setLayout(gridLayout2);
      jCheckBox1.setText("Show Digital Time");
      jCheckBox1.setHorizontalAlignment(0);
      gridLayout1.setHgap(5);
      jPanel1.setLayout(gridLayout1);
      this.setLayout(borderLayout1);
      gridLayout2.setRows(4);
      gridLayout3.setRows(4);
      this.add(jCheckBox1, BorderLayout.SOUTH);
      this.add(jPanel1, BorderLayout.CENTER);
      jPanel1.add(jpDateStyle, null);
      jpDateStyle.add(jRadioButton1, null);
      jpDateStyle.add(jRadioButton2, null);
      jpDateStyle.add(jRadioButton3, null);
      jpDateStyle.add(jRadioButton4, null);
      jPanel1.add(jpTimeStyle, null);
      jpTimeStyle.add(jRadioButton5, null);
      jpTimeStyle.add(jRadioButton6, null);
      jpTimeStyle.add(jRadioButton7, null);
      jpTimeStyle.add(jRadioButton8, null);

      // Group date style radio buttons
      buttonGroup1.add(jRadioButton1);
      buttonGroup1.add(jRadioButton2);
      buttonGroup1.add(jRadioButton3);
      buttonGroup1.add(jRadioButton4);

      // Group date style radio buttons
      buttonGroup2.add(jRadioButton5);
      buttonGroup2.add(jRadioButton6);
      buttonGroup2.add(jRadioButton7);
      buttonGroup2.add(jRadioButton8);
```

Listing 11.14 *Continued*

```
    // Register listeners
    jRadioButton1.addItemListener(this);
    jRadioButton2.addItemListener(this);
    jRadioButton3.addItemListener(this);
    jRadioButton4.addItemListener(this);
    jRadioButton5.addItemListener(this);
    jRadioButton6.addItemListener(this);
    jRadioButton7.addItemListener(this);
    jRadioButton8.addItemListener(this);
    jCheckBox1.addItemListener(this);
  }

  public void setObject(Object bean) {
    // TODO: implement this java.beans.Customizer method;
    // jbInit() is fired from here instead of the constructor because
    // it is assumed in the Beans Spec that setObject() is called
    //first.
    try { jbInit(); } catch (Exception e) { e.printStackTrace(); }

    if(bean instanceof Clock) {
      clock = (Clock)bean;

      jCheckBox1.setSelected(clock.isShowingDigitalDateTime());

      switch (clock.getDateStyle()) {
        case 0: jRadioButton1.setSelected(true); break;
        case 1: jRadioButton2.setSelected(true); break;
        case 2: jRadioButton3.setSelected(true); break;
        case 3: jRadioButton4.setSelected(true); break;
      }

      switch (clock.getTimeStyle()) {
        case 0: jRadioButton5.setSelected(true); break;
        case 1: jRadioButton6.setSelected(true); break;
        case 2: jRadioButton7.setSelected(true); break;
        case 3: jRadioButton8.setSelected(true); break;
      }
    }
  }

  /** Required by implementation of Customizer Interface */
  public void addPropertyChangeListener(
    PropertyChangeListener parm1) {
    if (pcs == null)
      pcs = new PropertyChangeSupport(this);
    pcs.addPropertyChangeListener(parm1);
  }

  /** Required by implementation of Customizer Interface */
  public void removePropertyChangeListener
    (PropertyChangeListener parm1) {
    if (pcs != null)
      pcs.removePropertyChangeListener(parm1);
  }

  public void itemStateChanged(ItemEvent e) {
    if (e.getSource() instanceof JCheckBox) {
      if (clock != null)
        clock.setShowingDigitalDateTime(jCheckBox1.isSelected());
```

Listing 11.14 *Continued*

continued

Example 11.6 continued

```
        if (pcs != null)
          pcs.firePropertyChange("showingDigitalDateTime",
            new Boolean(!jCheckBox1.isSelected()),
            new Boolean(jCheckBox1.isSelected()));

        // Enable radio buttons for date style and time style
        // if showingDigitalDateTime is checked
        if (jCheckBox1.isSelected()) {
          jRadioButton1.setEnabled(true);
          jRadioButton2.setEnabled(true);
          jRadioButton3.setEnabled(true);
          jRadioButton4.setEnabled(true);
          jRadioButton5.setEnabled(true);
          jRadioButton6.setEnabled(true);
          jRadioButton7.setEnabled(true);
          jRadioButton8.setEnabled(true);
        }
        else {
          jRadioButton1.setEnabled(false);
          jRadioButton2.setEnabled(false);
          jRadioButton3.setEnabled(false);
          jRadioButton4.setEnabled(false);
          jRadioButton5.setEnabled(false);
          jRadioButton6.setEnabled(false);
          jRadioButton7.setEnabled(false);
          jRadioButton8.setEnabled(false);
        }
      }
      else { // A radio button is changed
        int currentDateStyle = clock.getDateStyle();
        int newDateStyle = currentDateStyle;

        if (jRadioButton1.isSelected())
          newDateStyle = 0;
        else if (jRadioButton2.isSelected())
          newDateStyle = 1;
        else if (jRadioButton3.isSelected())
          newDateStyle = 2;
        else if (jRadioButton4.isSelected())
          newDateStyle = 3;

        clock.setDateStyle(newDateStyle);
        if (pcs != null)
          pcs.firePropertyChange("dateStyle",
            new Integer(currentDateStyle), new Integer(newDateStyle));

        int currentTimeStyle = clock.getTimeStyle();
        int newTimeStyle = currentTimeStyle;

        if (jRadioButton5.isSelected())
          newTimeStyle = 0;
        else if (jRadioButton6.isSelected())
          newTimeStyle = 1;
        else if (jRadioButton7.isSelected())
          newTimeStyle = 2;
        else if (jRadioButton8.isSelected())
          newTimeStyle = 3;

```

Listing 11.14 *Continued*

```
          clock.setTimeStyle(newTimeStyle);
          if (pcs != null)
            pcs.firePropertyChange("timeStyle",
              new Integer(currentTimeStyle), new Integer(newTimeStyle));
        }
      }
    }
```

Listing 11.14 *Continued*

Example Review

ClockCustomizer implements the Customizer interface. The setObject method is invoked first by the builder tool when the customizer starts. For this reason, the statement for invoking the jbInit() statement is moved from the constructor to the setObject method, so that you can initialize the customizer to display the current state of the clock passed from the builder tool. The implementation of addPropertyChangeListener and removePropertyChangeListener involves registering and unregistering the listener with an instance of PropertyChangeSupport named pcs.

You could use the UI designer to generate nine ItemEvent adapters for the check box and eight radio buttons. However, a more efficient way in this example is to use a single centralized adapter to handle all the item events from the check box and the radio buttons.

When a check box is unchecked, all the radio buttons are disabled, since there is no need to set date style or time style when the date and time are not displayed. Whenever a property is changed, the builder tool is notified by invoking pcs.firePropertyChange("propertyName", oldValue, newValue). The builder tool updates the bean property by generating a statement in the jbInit method code using the property's set method. To ensure that a change takes effect during design, you need to invoke the property's set method in the customizer. For instance, the following code

```
clock.setShowingDigitalDateTime(jCheckBox1.isSelected());
```

updates clock's showingDigitalDateTime property in the UI designer.

The customizer is contained in a dialog box created by JBuilder. The dialog box contains an OK button and a Cancel button. You can close the customizer by clicking either of them. The functions of these two buttons are identical in the customizers, since the builder tool has already been notified of the property changes through the property change listener pcs. Recall that the OK and Cancel buttons in the dialog box for a GUI property editor are different. Clicking OK saves the editing change, whereas clicking Cancel does not.

Chapter Summary

This chapter introduced the JavaBeans API that a builder tool can use to discover the properties, methods, and events of a bean so that it can be manipulated visually during design time. You learned how to create custom property editors, GUI property editors, and customizers for editing bean properties. You also learned how to use the BeanInsight wizard to inspect beans and BeansExpress to create `BeanInfo` classes.

Review Questions

11.1 Are the `BeanInfo` class, the property editor class, and the customizer class necessary at runtime?

11.2 How do you expose properties whose get and set methods do not follow standard naming patterns?

11.3 How do you expose events whose registration and removal methods do not follow standard naming patterns?

11.4 How do you programmatically inspect bean properties and events at runtime?

11.5 Describe the methods `getAsText`, `setAsText`, `getValue`, `setValue`, and `getTags` in the `PropertyEditor` interface.

11.6 Describe the implementation of the `PropertyEditorSupport` class. How are the methods `getAsText`, `setAsText`, `getValue`, `setValue`, and `getTags` implemented in the `PropertyEditorSupport` class?

11.7 How do you create a custom property editor to display property values in a choice menu in the component inspector?

11.8 How do you specify a custom property editor in the `BeanInfo` class?

11.9 Describe the role of the methods `setDisplayName` and `setValue` in the `FeatureDescriptor` class.

11.10 How do you create a property editor using BeansExpress? How do you generate a `BeanInfo` class using BeansExpress?

11.11 How should the methods `getCustomEditor` and `supportsCustomEditor` be implemented to create a GUI property editor? How do you start a GUI property editor in the component inspector? How is a GUI property displayed?

11.12 Describe the methods `setObject`, `addPropertyChangeListener`, and `removePropertyChangeListener` in the `Customizer` interface. How do you start a customizer? How is a customizer displayed? How do you specify a customizer in the `BeanInfo` class?

Programming Exercises

11.1 The `CalendarPanel` class in Exercise 4.6 contains a `month` property and a `year` property. Both properties are `int` values. Create a property editor for the `month` property to display locale-sensitive month names in a choice menu, as shown in Figure 11.18, and create a property editor for the `year` property to display and validate `year` to ensure that `year` is non-negative.

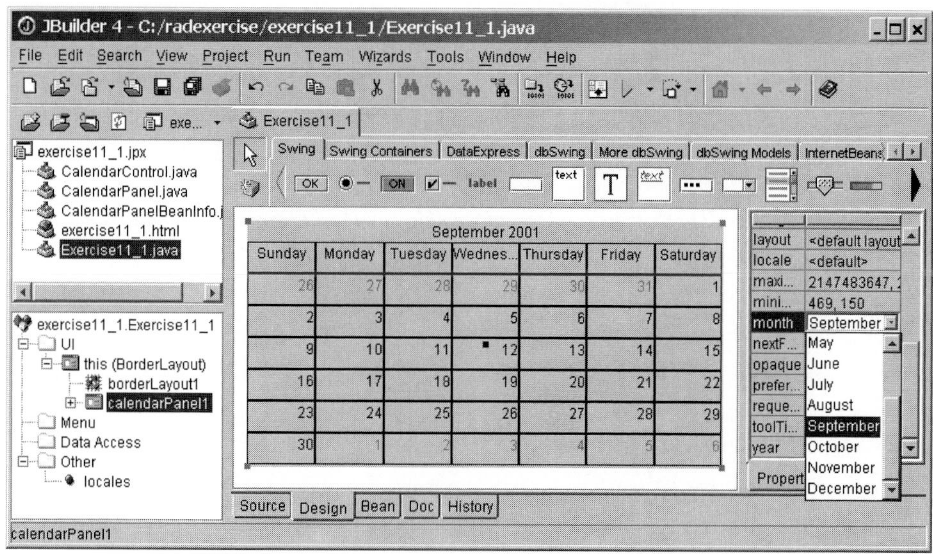

Figure 11.18 *The* `month` *property is displayed in a choice menu of month names.*

11.2 Create a GUI property editor for selecting colors just like the one used in JBuilder.

11.3 The Student class in Example 11.3 contains a property named `fullName`, which consists of first name, middle name, and last name. The entire full name must be edited once in the component inspector. Create a customizer for the Student class to enable the user to edit first name, middle name, and last name separately. The customizer is shown in Figure 11.19. The name labels are placed in a `JPanel` named `labelPanel` of `GridLayout`, and the text fields are placed in a `JPanel` named `textPanel` of `GridLayout`. `labelPanel` and `textPanel` are placed in a `JPanel` of `BorderLayout`, with `labelPanel` on the east and `textPanel` in the center. The Apply button applies the change to the bean, and the Revert button restores the original names in the bean.

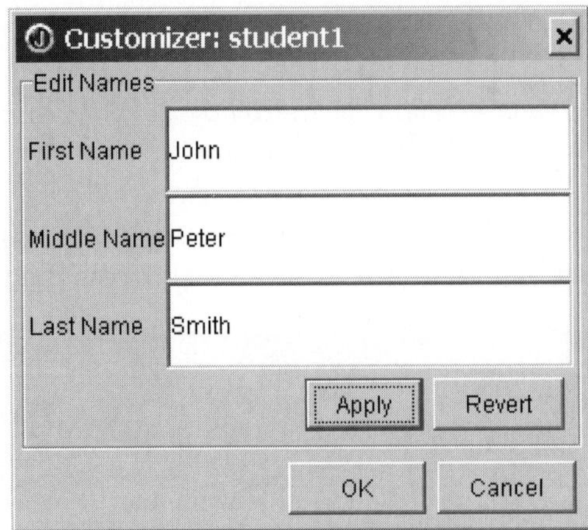

Figure 11.19 *The* `StudentCustomizer` *enables you to edit first name, middle name, and last name separately.*

PART IV

JAVA DATABASE PROGRAMMING

This part of the book discusses how to use Java to develop database projects. You will learn JDBC interfaces and classes, create and process SQL statements, obtain database metadata, and use JBuilder database beans to rapidly develop Java database applications.

CHAPTER 12

Introduction to Java Database Programming

Objectives

- Understand the architecture of JDBC.
- Know the four types of JDBC drivers.
- Use JDBC drivers.
- Be able to write simple JDBC programs.

Introduction

JDBC is a Java API that provides Java programmers with a uniform interface for accessing and manipulating a wide range of relational databases. Before JDBC, database clients were typically developed using Microsoft Visual Basic, Borland Delphi, and other development tools provided by database vendors, such as PowerBuilder by Sybase and Oracle Developer 2000 by Oracle. These are excellent rapid application development tools, but the programs developed with them can only run on certain platforms. With JDBC, you can write database programs that run on any platform that has a Java Virtual Machine with an appropriate JDBC driver.

The relationships between Java programs, JDBC API, JDBC drivers, and relational databases are shown in Figure 12.1. The JDBC API is a set of Java interfaces and classes used to write Java programs for accessing and manipulating relational databases. Since a JDBC driver serves as the interface to facilitate communications between JDBC and a proprietary database, JDBC drivers are database-specific. You need Oracle JDBC drivers to access Oracle database, and Sybase JDBC drivers to access Sybase database. Even for the same vendor, the drivers may be different for different versions of a database. For instance, the JDBC driver for Oracle 8 is different from the one for Oracle 7. A JDBC-ODBC bridge driver is included in JDK to support Java programs that access databases through ODBC drivers. The ODBC driver, introduced before Java, defines a protocol and API for accessing relational databases.

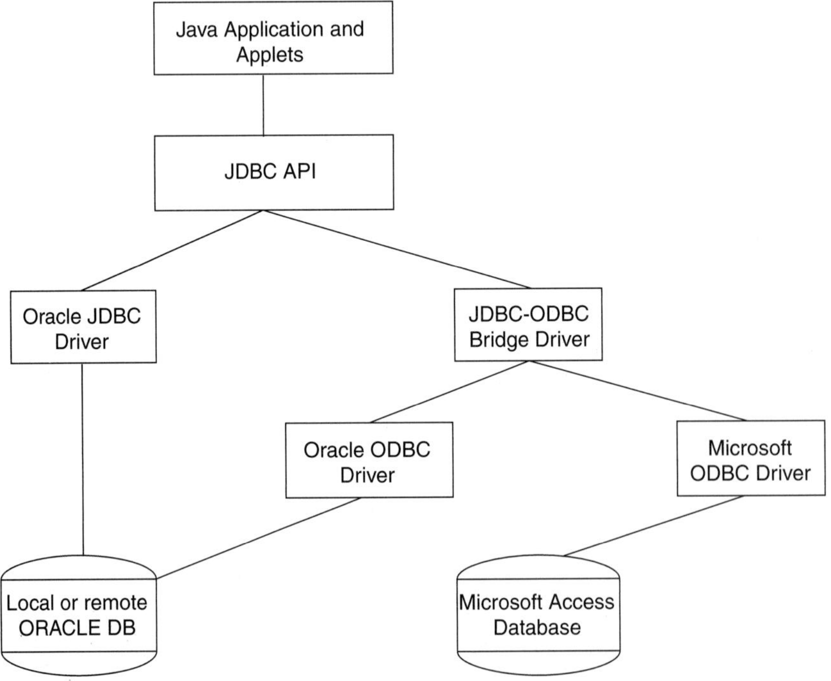

Figure 12.1 *Java programs access and manipulate databases through JDBC drivers.*

Note

JDBC is the trademarked name of a Java API that supports Java programs to access relational databases. JDBC is not an acronym, but it is often thought to stand for Java Database Connectivity.

Overview of the JDBC API

The JDBC API is a Java application programming interface to generic SQL databases that enables Java developers to develop DBMS-independent Java applications using a uniform interface.

The JDBC API consists of classes and interfaces for establishing connections with databases, sending SQL statements to databases, processing the results of the SQL statements, and obtaining database metadata. The JDBC interfaces and classes can be classified by type as drivers, connections, statements, result sets, metadata, processing supports, and exceptions, as shown in Table 12.1.

Note

The initial design of JDBC API was based on JDK 1.02, known as *JDBC 1*. When JDBC 1 was released, many important Java technologies, such as JavaBeans and Java Internationalization, had not yet been developed. With the release of JDK 1.2 of Java 2, JavaSoft added new features and enhancements to JDBC 1. The new JDBC product is known as *JDBC 2*. JDBC 1 is compatible with Java 2. Any application developed with JDBC 1 will continue to work under JDK 1.2. However, you will need JDBC 2 drivers to use the new features in JDBC 2. The JDBC-ODBC driver, which is bundled with JDK 1.3, does not support all features of JDBC 2. If you run a program that uses the unsupported new features, an exception indicating that the operations are not supported would occur.

The interfaces define a framework for generic SQL database access. The JDBC driver vendors provide implementation for these interfaces. The relationship of these interfaces and classes is shown in Figure 12.2. A JDBC application loads an appropriate driver using the `Driver` interface, connects to the database using the `Connection` interface, creates and executes SQL statements using the `Statement` interface, and processes the result using the `ResultSet` interface if the statements return results. Note that some statements, such as SQL data definition statements and SQL data modification statements, do not return results.

The *Driver* Interface

The `Driver` interface is database-specific. The JDBC vendor should implement this interface and provide proprietary database information to enable Java programs to communicate with the database.

An appropriate driver must be loaded before your application can connect to a database. The driver can be loaded using the following statement:

```
Class.forName("TheDriverName")
```

TABLE 12.1 JDBC Classes

Type	*Class/Interface*
Driver management	`java.sql.Driver (Interface)`
	`java.sql.DriverPropertyInfo`
	`java.sql.DriverManager`
Establishing connections	`java.sql.Connection (Interface)`
Processing statements	`java.sql.Statement (Interface)`
	`java.sql.PreparedStatement (Interface)`
	`java.sql.CallableStatement (Interface)`
Handling result sets	`java.sql.ResultSet (Interface)`
Metadata	`java.sql.DatabaseMetaData (Interface)`
	`java.sql.ResultSetMetaData (Interface)`
Exceptions	`java.sql.SQLException`
	`java.sql.SQLWarning`
	`java.sql.DataTruncation`
	`java.sql.BatchUpdateException (JDBC 2)`
Support classes	`java.sql.Date`
	`java.sql.Time`
	`java.sql.TimeStamp`
	`java.sql.Types`
	`java.sql.Blob (JDBC 2)`
	`java.sql.Clob (JDBC 2)`
	`java.sql.Array (JDBC 2)`
	`java.sql.SQLInput (JDBC 2)`
	`java.sql.SQLOutput (JDBC 2)`
	`java.sql.Ref (JDBC 2)`
	`java.sql.Struct (JDBC 2)`

This statement attempts to locate, load, and link the driver class. If it succeeds, it returns an anonymous `Class` object representing the driver class. You don't need to return an explicit driver reference, because each newly loaded driver is capable of registering itself with the `DriverManager`.

The driver is anonymous; you don't need to reference it explicitly to make a database connection. After the driver is registered, the `DriverManager` can use it to make database connections. If the driver is not found, the method throws a `ClassNotFoundException`.

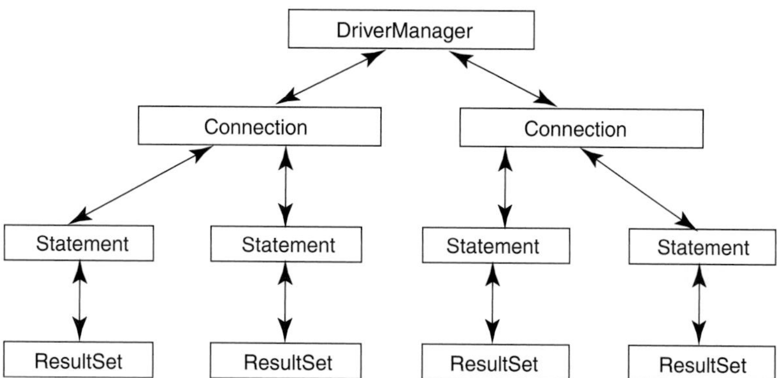

Figure 12.2 *JDBC classes enable Java programs to connect to the database, send SQL statements, and process results.*

The *DriverManager* Class

The `DriverManager` class, a layer of JDBC working between the driver and the user, is responsible for registering and managing the drivers. It serves as a ringmaster to keep track of all the registered drivers, establishing a connection between the database and an appropriate driver.

All the methods in `DriverManager` are static. A programmer can use its `getConnection()` method to get a connection to the database, which returns an object of `Connection`. For example, the following statement connects the database at specified `url` with `username` and `password`:

```
Connection connection =
  DriverManager.getConnection(url, username, password);
```

The *DriverPropertyInfo* Class

The `DriverPropertyInfo` class is used by advanced programmers to manage specific properties of a `Driver` instance. It should be used only by developers who need to interact with a driver to discover and supply properties for connections.

The *Connection* Interface

A `Connection` instance represents a session with a specific database. In the context of a `Connection` instance, SQL statements are sent to the database for execution, and the results of the execution, if any, are returned. Think of a connection as a pipeline through which database transactions travel back and forth between your program and the database.

A `Connection` instance can be used to create various `Statement` objects for executing SQL statements and stored procedures using the `createStatement` method. You can also use it to set transaction properties for the connection. By default the `Connection` instance automatically commits changes after executing each statement. If auto-commit has been disabled, an explicit commit must be done or database changes will not be saved.

You can use the `getMetaData()` method to get an object of `DataBaseMetaData` that describes the connected database information on the tables, views, supported SQL grammar, stored procedures, and capabilities of this connection. Chapter 13, "Advanced Java Database Programming," gives an in-depth look at retrieving metadata.

The *Statement*, *PreparedStatement*, and *CallableStatement* Interfaces

The `Statement`, `PreparedStatement`, and `CallableStatement` interfaces are related in a hierarchical relationship. `CallableStatement` inherits `PreparedStatement`, which inherits `Statement`. These interfaces are used for sending SQL statements to the database for execution on a given connection. A `Statement` object is used to execute a static SQL statement; a `PreparedStatement` object is used to execute a precompiled SQL statement with or without IN parameters; and a `CallableStatement` object is used to execute a call to a stored procedure in the database.

The `executeQuery` method of the object is used if the statement is a SQL SELECT query, and the `executeUpdate` method is used if the statement is a SQL INSERT, UPDATE, or DELETE and also a SQL DDL (Data Definition Language) statement like `CREATE TABLE`, `CREATE VIEW`, `DROP TABLE`, or `DROP VIEW`.

The `executeQuery` method returns the query result in a `ResultSet` object. Only one `ResultSet` per `Statement` can be open at any single point in time. Therefore, if the reading of one `ResultSet` is interleaved with the reading of another, each must have been generated by a different statement. All statement-execute methods implicitly close a statement's current `ResultSet` if an open one exists.

When executing a stored procedure, the execution may return multiple result sets. The `execute` method should be used to execute the SQL statement in this case. You can then use `getResultSet` or `getUpdateCount` to retrieve the result, and `getMoreResults` to move to the next result set.

The *ResultSet* Interface

A `ResultSet` provides access to a table of data generated by executing a statement.

A `ResultSet` maintains a cursor pointing to its current row of data. The current row can be set using the cursor movement methods, such as `absolute`, `first`, `last`, `next`, and `previous`. Initially the cursor is positioned before the first row. The `next` method moves the cursor to the next row. The first call to `next` makes the first row the current row, the second call makes the second row the current row, and so on.

Various get methods are provided to retrieve column values for the current row. You can retrieve values by using either the index number of the column or the name of the column. For example, to retrieve a column of the `String` type, you may use `rs.getString("ColumnName")`, where `rs` is an object of `ResultSet`.

The column values within a row can be accessed in any order.

The *SQL Exception* Classes

The JDBC methods may raise the `SQLException`, `SQLWarning`, `DataTruncation`, and `BatchUpdateException` exceptions. `SQLException` is the root of all the exceptions in the JDBC.

The `SQLException` class provides information on a database access error. The `SQLWarning` exception, a subclass of `SQLException`, provides information on a database access warning. A warning is silently chained to the object whose method caused it to be reported. A `SQLWarning` exception may be ignored in order to allow the normal course of the execution to proceed. A `DataTruncation` exception, a subclass of `SQLWarning`, is raised when JDBC unexpectedly truncates a data value. A `BatchUpdateException` exception, a subclass of `SQLException`, is raised if exceptions occur during a batch operation.

The *DatabaseMetaData* Interface

The `DatabaseMetaData` interface enables you to obtain information about the database, such as tables, views, columns, primary keys, and foreign keys.

Many of these methods return the information in `ResultSet`. You can use the normal `ResultSet` methods, such as `getString` and `getInt`, to retrieve the data from these result sets. If a given form of metadata is not available, these methods should throw a `SQLException`. For example, to find all the catalogs in the database, you can use the `getCatalogs` method to return a list of catalogs in an object of `ResultSet`, then retrieve all the catalogs from the result set.

The *ResultSetMetaData* Interface

The `ResultSetMetaData` interface provides various methods for getting information about a `ResultSet` object. You can use a `ResultSetMetaData` object to get the number of columns and find out about the types and properties of the columns in a `ResultSet`.

The JDBC Support Classes

JDBC provides many support classes. The `Date`, `Time`, and `TimeStamp` classes are for accepting and processing SQL DATE, TIME, and TIMESTAMP values. All these classes extend the `java.util.Date` class.

The `Types` class contains a list of predefined constants for identifying SQL types that can be used in JDBC, such as `INTEGER`, `FLOAT`, `DOUBLE`, `VARCHAR`, `BLOB`, `CLOB`, and so on. No methods are defined in this class.

The `Blob`, `Clob`, `Array`, `Ref`, `Struct`, `SQLInput`, and `SQLOutput` are new support classes introduced in JDBC 2. The `Blob` class represents a SQL BLOB type for storing a binary large object, such as an image. The `Clob` class represents a SQL CLOB type for storing character large object such as a text dcoument. The `Array` class represents a SQL ARRAY type for storing a sequence of values. The `Ref` class is a reference to a SQL structured type value in the database. The `Struct` class maps to a SQL structured type. The `SQLInput` and `SQLOutput` classes provide a mechanism for mapping structured SQL types to Java objects.

Developing JDBC Applications

The JDBC interfaces and classes are the building blocks in the development of Java database programs. A typical Java program takes the following steps to access the database, as shown in Figure 12.2.

1. Load drivers.

   JDBC allows multiple drivers to be loaded in one program. A program can load a JDBC driver at any time. For example, `MyDriver` is loaded with the following statement:

   ```
   Class.forName("MyDriver");
   ```

   The statement loads the driver. The driver is automatically registered with the driver manager. You may use the static method `registerDriver` in the `DriverManager` class to explicitly register a driver with the driver manager. For example, this statement registers `MyDriver`:

   ```
   DriverManager.registerDriver(new MyDriver());
   ```

2. Establish connections.

   Once the driver is loaded and registered with the driver manager, the `DriverManager` is capable of choosing an appropriate one from a list of registered drivers to fulfill the connection to the database. You simply invoke `DriverManager.getConnection()` to establish a session with the database. In the unusual situation where more than one driver is suitable to connect to a database and you want a particular driver to be chosen, the `connect` method in a `Driver` object can be invoked directly to use that driver to connect to a given database.

3. Create statements.

   You can create statements for executing SQL in three types: `Statement`, `PreparedStatement`, or `CallableStatement`. The `Statement` class is used to execute static SQL. The `PreparedStatement` and `CallableStatement` classes are used to construct dynamic SQL.

4. Execute statements.

   Statements can be executed using the `executeQuery`, `executeUpdate`, or `execute` method. The result of the query is returned in `ResultSet`.

5. Process `ResultSet`.

   The `ResultSet` maintains a table whose current row can be retrieved. The initial row position is `null`. The methods, such as `absolute`, `first`, `last`, `next`, and `previous`, can be used to set the row position. The various get methods are used to retrieve values from a current row.

Here is a simple example (see Listing 12.1) of connecting to a database, executing a simple query, and processing the query result.

```
package jdbcdemo;

import java.sql.*;

public class SimpleJdbc {
  public static void main(String[] args)
    throws SQLException, ClassNotFoundException {
    // Load the JDBC driver
    Class.forName("sun.jdbc.odbc.JdbcOdbcDriver");
    System.out.println("Driver loaded");

    // Establish a connection
    Connection connection = DriverManager.getConnection
      ("jdbc:odbc:LiangBookDB_MDB", "", "" );
    System.out.println("Database connected");

    // Create a statement
    Statement stmt = connection.createStatement();

    // Select the columns from the Student table
    ResultSet rset = stmt.executeQuery
      ("select firstName, mi, lastName from Student");

    // Iterate through the result and print the student names
    while (rset.next())
      System.out.println(rset.getString(1) + " " + rset.getString(2)
        + ". " + rset.getString(3));
  }
}
```

Listing 12.1 *SimpleJDBC.java*

The statement

```
Class.forName("sun.jdbc.odbc.JdbcOdbcDriver")
```

loads the `JdbcOdbcDriver` for connecting to an ODBC data source, such as Microsoft Access Database. In Example 12.1, you will learn how to set up the ODBC data source to test this program.

The statement

```
Connection connection = DriverManager.getConnection
  ("jdbc:odbc:LiangBookDB_MDB", "", "");
```

creates a `Connection` object `connection`, which represents a logical session for sending SQL statements and getting query results back from the database. You can create an instance of `Statement` for executing static queries as used in the example, create `PreparedStatement` for precompiled SQL statements, or create `CallableStatement` for executing stored procedures. Their applications are discussed in Chapter 13, "Advanced Java Database Programming."

The statement

```
ResultSet rset = stmt.executeQuery
  ("select firstName, mi, lastName from Student");
```

executes the query and returns the result in a `ResultSet` object, which can be perceived as a table of three columns consisting of firstName, mi, and lastName. The `getString(1)`, `getString(2)`, and `getString(3)` methods retrieve the column values for firstName, mi, and lastName, respectively. Alternatively, you can use `getString("firstName")`, `getString("mi")`, and `getString("lastName")` to retrieve the same three column values.

The first execution of the `next()` method sets the current row to the first row in the result set, and subsequent invocation of the `next()` method sets the current row to the second, third, and so on, to the last row.

NOTE
The MS Access database (LiangBookDB_MDB.mdb) in the book is created using Microsoft Access 2000. This database cannot be used with MS Access 97. If you use MS Access 97 or 95, please create your own database.

JDBC Drivers

A JDBC driver is a software component that works between JDBC and the database. The driver is responsible for accepting SQL statements, sending them to the database system, and returning the execution results to JDBC. The driver is specific to each database. For instance, to enable JDBC to connect to the Oracle database, you need a JDBC driver that works specifically for Oracle. Even among Oracle databases, the drivers are different for various versions of Oracle DBMS.

There are many JDBC drivers now available on the market. They can be classified into the four types listed in Table 12.2.

Table 12.2 JDBC Driver Types

Types of drivers	Description
Type 1: JDBC-ODBC Bridge	Provides access through ODBC drivers
Type 2: Native-API	Provides access through native database API
Type 3: Middle-tier	Provides access through a middle-tier server
Type 4: Native-protocol	Provides access through a network protocol used by DBMS

Type 1: JDBC-ODBC Bridge Driver

ODBC (Open DataBase Connectivity) is an API for accessing relational databases. It was originally designed to enable database clients on PCs to access databases on a server by Microsoft. It became a popular industry standard API for connecting to the relational databases for the client on all types of platforms. Since ODBC is widely available, it makes sense to provide a driver that accesses the database through ODBC drivers. Such a driver is referred to as a *JDBC-ODBC bridge driver.*

A JDBC-ODBC driver is bundled with JDK 1.3. This driver bridges JDBC with ODBC by mapping the JDBC calls into ODBC calls; the ODBC calls interact with the database, as shown in Figure 12.3.

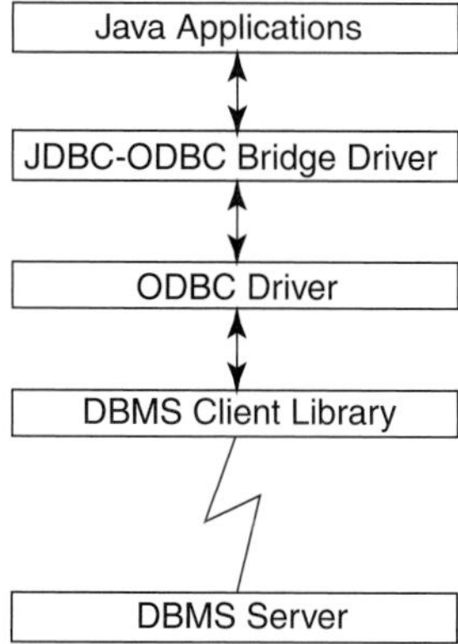

Figure 12.3 *The JDBC-ODBC bridge driver maps JDBC calls to ODBC calls.*

The JDBC-ODBC bridge driver provides convenient access to all the existing systems, since most of the database systems already have ODBC drivers. However, the driver is slow and is not suitable for applets. The ODBC drivers are specific to the database. For example, you need an Oracle ODBC driver to access Oracle databases. The JDBC application using the JDBC-ODBC bridge driver requires that the ODBC driver and the client database library must be loaded on the client machine. This approach is obviously not efficient, because it requires the JDBC driver to talk to the database via an ODBC driver. Since the ODBC driver is written in C, it cannot be downloaded and used by applets.

Type 2: Native-API Driver

The native-API driver converts JDBC calls into native database calls and communicates directly with the database server, as shown in Figure 12.4.

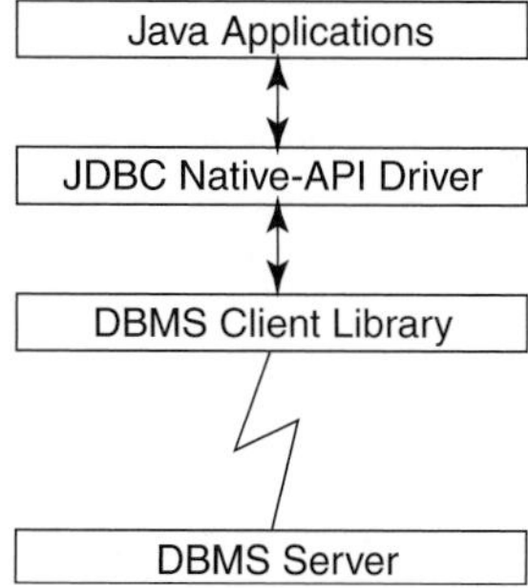

Figure 12.4 *The JDBC native-API driver maps JDBC calls to native API calls.*

Native-API drivers are usually provided by database vendors. For example, Oracle provides a native-API driver that maps JDBC with the Oracle Call Interface. Like the bridge driver, this driver requires some binary code for the native database API to be loaded on the client machine. But it is more efficient than the JDBC-ODBC bridge approach, since it allows you to talk to the database directly.

Type 3: Middle-Tier Driver

The middle-tier driver converts JDBC calls into a DBMS-independent network protocol and sends them to a middle-tier server. The server then translates the calls to a DBMS-specific protocol for Oracle, Sybase, DB2, InterBase, or other DBMS, as shown in Figure 12.5.

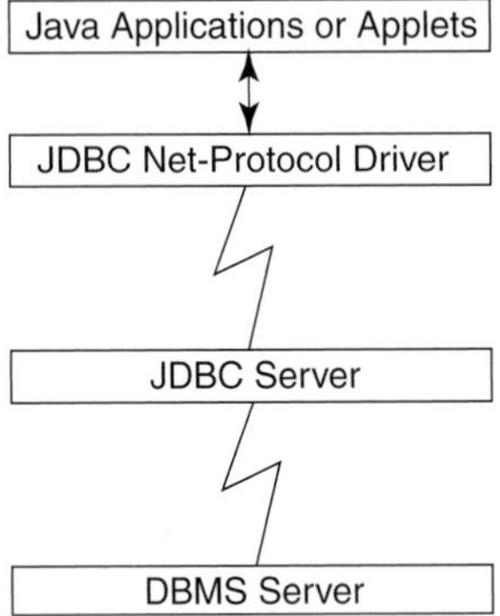

Figure 12.5 *The middle-tier driver maps JDBC calls to a DBMS-independent middle-tier server that communicates with proprietary DBMS.*

The middle-tier JDBC server connects to Java applications or applets with a database server. Borland's InterClient and Symantec's dbAnyWhere are middle-tier servers based on this kind of architecture. The middle-tier server can reside on a machine different from the client and the DBMS server.

The middle-tier driver is a pure Java JDBC driver that enables platform-independent, client/server development for the Internet. The advantage of a pure Java driver, as opposed to a native-code driver, is that you can deploy applets without having to manually load platform-specific JDBC drivers on each client system. Since the Web servers automatically download the driver's classes along with the applets, there is no need to manage local native database libraries, and this simplifies administration and maintenance of customer applications. As part of a Java applet, the driver can be dynamically updated, further reducing the cost of application deployment and maintenance.

An example of using a middle-tier driver with Borland's InterClient and InterBase database can be obtained from `www.cs.armstrong.edu/liang/radjb5.html`.

Type 4: Native-Protocol Driver

The native-protocol driver converts JDBC calls into network protocol used by a DBMS and communicates with the DBMS directly, as shown in Figure 12.6.

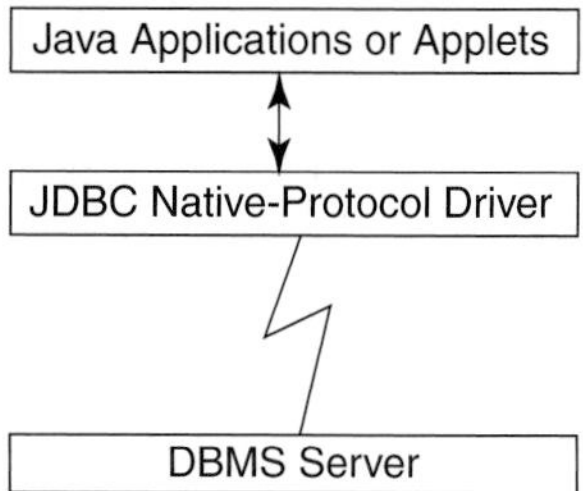

Figure 12.6 *The native-protocol driver facilitates communications between Java applications and applets with a DBMS server.*

Like the middle-tier driver, the native-protocol driver does not require any database-specific binary code to be loaded on the client. The native-protocol driver, however, is more flexible than the middle-tier driver, because it eliminates the middle-tier JDBC server.

NOTE
The JDBC-ODBC driver and the native-API driver use native methods, which makes them platform-specific. They are not suitable for Java applets intended to be downloaded into browsers running on universal platforms. Middle-tier drivers are preferred for use with multi-tier architecture where connectors are used to link clients with database servers. Native-protocol drivers are ideal for direct access to the database. Both middle-tier and native-protocol drivers are written in 100% pure Java; thus they are suitable for Java applets.

Connecting to Databases Using JDBC Drivers

A number of JDBC drivers have already been developed. Many of them can be downloaded from vendors for 30 or more days of evaluation. Information for locating the drivers can be obtained from the following URL:

```
http://industry.java.sun.com/products/jdbc/drivers
```

This section provides examples of using JDBC drivers. Specifically, you will use the Sun JDBC-ODBC driver, the Oracle JDBC OCI driver (native-API), and the Oracle thin-client driver (native-protocol).

NOTE
A driver is not just of a single class. In fact a JDBC driver is a set of classes that provide mappings between JDBC and a specific database. The driver must include classes that implement the eight interfaces in the `java.sql` package: `Driver`, `Connection`, `Statement`, `PreparedStatement`, `CallableStatement`, `ResultSet`, `DatabaseMetaData`, and `ResultSetMetaData`. For example, the `oracle.jdbc.drive.OracleStatement` class implements `java.sql.Statement`. Figure 12.7 lists all the classes in the Oracle 8i JDBC Thin driver bundled in the classes12.zip file using the WinZip utility. These classes are used by JDBC, not directly by JDBC programmers.

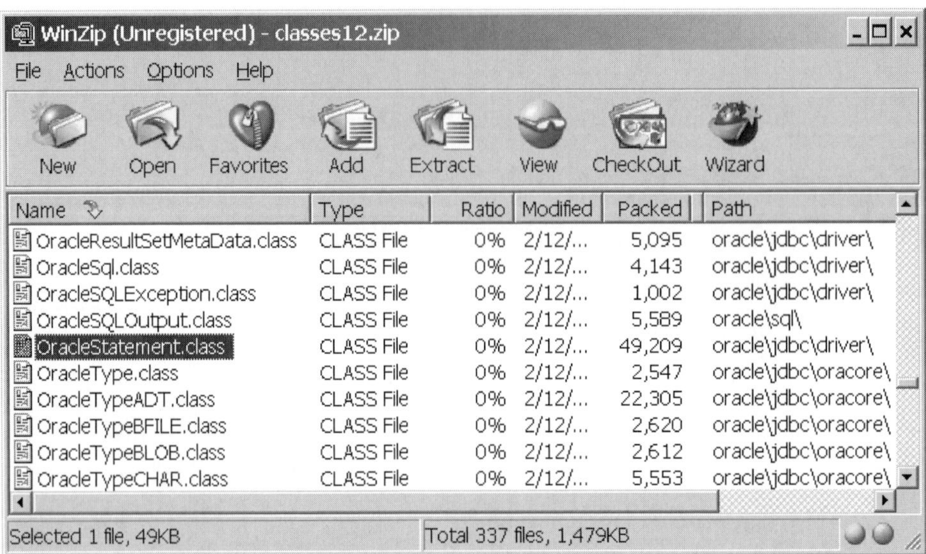

Figure 12.7 *A JDBC driver contains classes that enable JDBC to interact with a specific database.*

JDBC URL Naming Conventions

How does a Java program find its database? It finds the database by using its JDBC URL. A JDBC URL provides a way for the appropriate driver to identify the database. The standard syntax of a URL is:

```
jdbc:<subprotocol>:<datasource>
```

The first part of the syntax is always `jdbc`. The second part is the `subprotocol` specified by the driver vendor. For example, the `subprotocol` for Sun drivers is always sun, and the `subprotocol` for Oracle drivers is always oracle. The `datasource` consists of the database name and the host machine where the database resides. Information needed to access the data source, such as the user's login name and password, may be included in `datasource`, or may be supplied separately.

The `subprotocol` is used by the `DriverManager` class to associate an appropriate driver with the database. When the `DriverManager` class presents the `subprotocol` of the URL to its list of registered drivers, the driver that matches the protocol is used to establish a connection to the database specified in the data source. The `subprotocol` name is defined by the vendor, but it must be registered with JavaSoft to avoid naming conflicts. JavaSoft acts as an informal registry for JDBC `subprotocol` names.

The `subprotocol` `odbc` is reserved for JDBC-ODBC bridge drivers. For example, the URL to access an ODBC data source "MyDataSource" through a JDBC-ODBC driver is

```
jdbc:odbc:MyDataSource
```

In this example, the `subprotocol` is `odbc`, and the data source is the ODBC data source "MyDataSource."

The subprotocol may consist of several words. For example, the subprotocol `oracle:oci8` is reserved for accessing Oracle 8 database through native Oracle OCI (Oracle Call Interface), and `oracle:thin` is reserved for accessing oracle 8 using the Type 4 native-protocol driver.

The JDBC URL provides an indirection in the data source. You may use a logical host or database name that is dynamically translated to an actual name by a network naming system. For example, the URL to access a remote Oracle 8 database using the Oracle JDBC Thin driver may look like:

```
jdbc:oracle:thin:scott/tiger@liang.armstrong.edu:1521:test
```

This URL implies that the Oracle database with the ID oracle runs at port 1521 on `liang.armstrong.edu`. The user name is scott and the password is tiger.

Using the JDBC-ODBC Driver

To use the JDBC-ODBC driver to access databases in Java, two drivers must be installed on the client machine: a universal JDBC-ODBC bridge driver and a vendor-specific ODBC driver. The JDBC-ODBC driver comes with Java 2 SDK 1.3 or higher, or any Java development tool that supports JDK 1.2, or higher. The ODBC driver is not included in JDK and is usually provided by database vendors. The example chosen to demonstrate the JDBC-ODBC approach in this section is the Microsoft ODBC driver for the MS-Access database on Windows, since it is bundled with Microsoft Office Suite and widely available to many readers. This section uses the ODBC driver on Windows 2000.

NOTE
Using the JDBC-ODBC approach, the database is not necessarily on the same machine with the client. For example, you may use an Oracle ODBC driver to access a remote Oracle database.

Example 12.1 Using the JDBC-ODBC Bridge Driver

This example develops a Java program that creates a table named Student in an MS Access database. Each record consists of student firstName, mi, and lastName. Your program inserts two records into Student and then displays all the records on the console.

Follow the steps below to complete the project.

1. Install an MS ODBC driver for MS Access if necessary.

   By default the ODBC driver is installed on Windows 2000. If not, install MS Access to get the proper ODBC driver on your system. Upon successful installation, you should see the icon Data Sources (ODBC) in the Administrative Tools subwindow under the control panel for Windows

continued

Example 12.1 continued

2000. For Windows 98 and NT, you should see a "32-bit ODBC" icon appearing on the control panel.

2. Set up a Data Source as the database for storing the Student table.

2.1. From the Windows Start button, choose Setting, Control Panel to bring up the Control Panel dialog box.

2.2. Double-click Administrative Tools, and then double-click Data Sources (ODBC) to display the "ODBC Data Source Administrator," as shown in Figure 12.8.

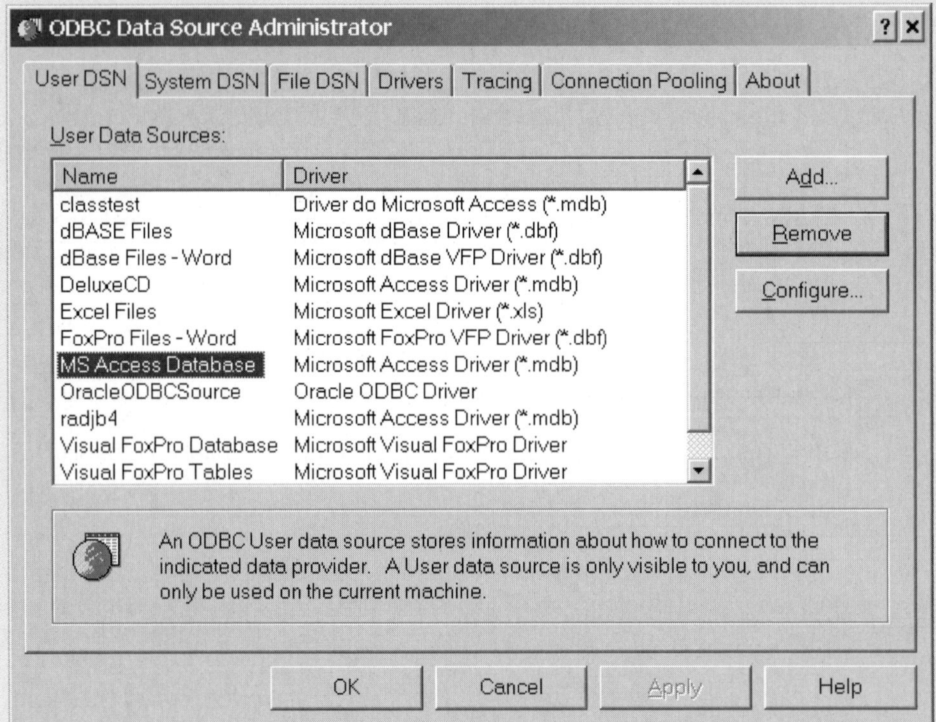

Figure 12.8 *The ODBC Data Source Administrator is the main dialog box to manage the data source and the drivers.*

2.3. Click Add to bring up the "Create New Data Source" dialog box, as shown in Figure 12.9.

2.4. Select Microsoft Access Driver and Press "Finish" to bring the "ODBC Microsoft Access Setup" dialog window, as shown in Figure 12.10. Type "LiangBookDB_MDB" in the Data Source Name field, and type "Liang Book MS Access database" in the Description filed. Press

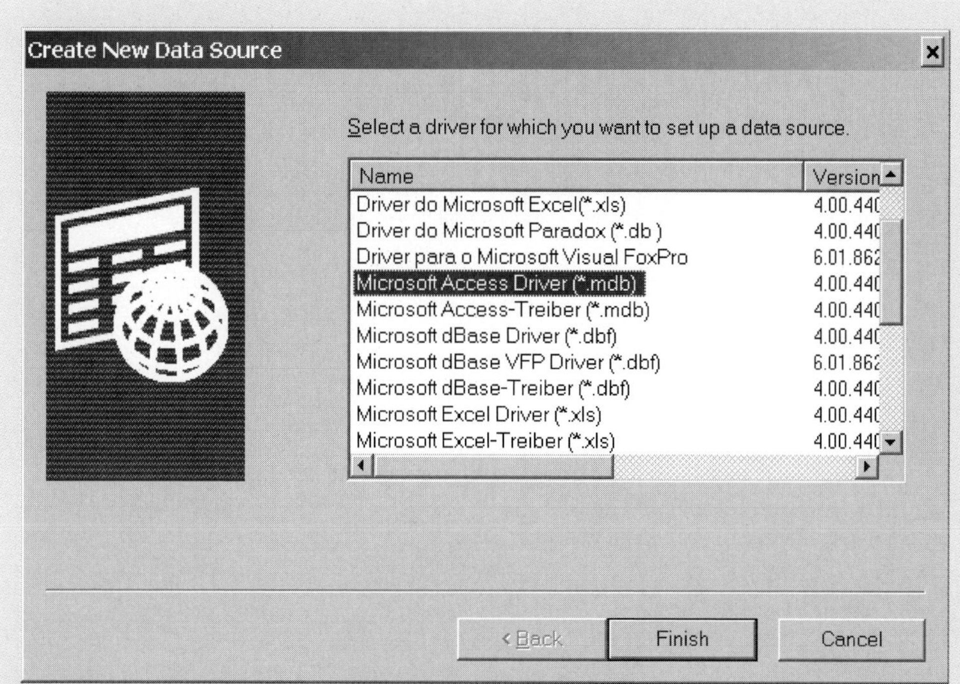

Figure 12.9 *Select a proper driver for the data source in the "Create New Data Source" window.*

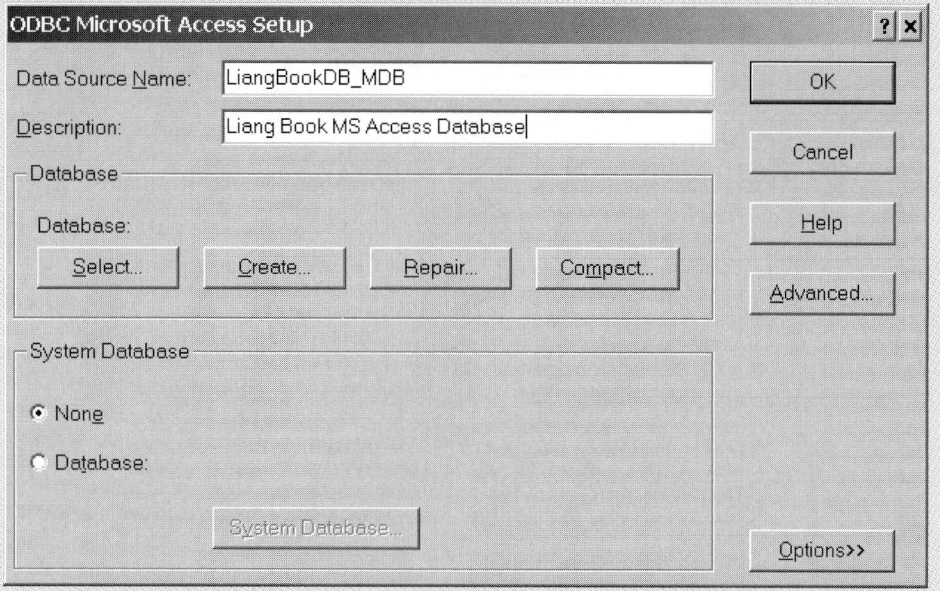

Figure 12.10 *Specify the Data Source Name to associate it with a database in the "ODBC Microsoft Access Setup" window.*

continued

Example 12.1 continued

Select to bring up the "Select Database" dialog window, as shown in Figure 12.11.

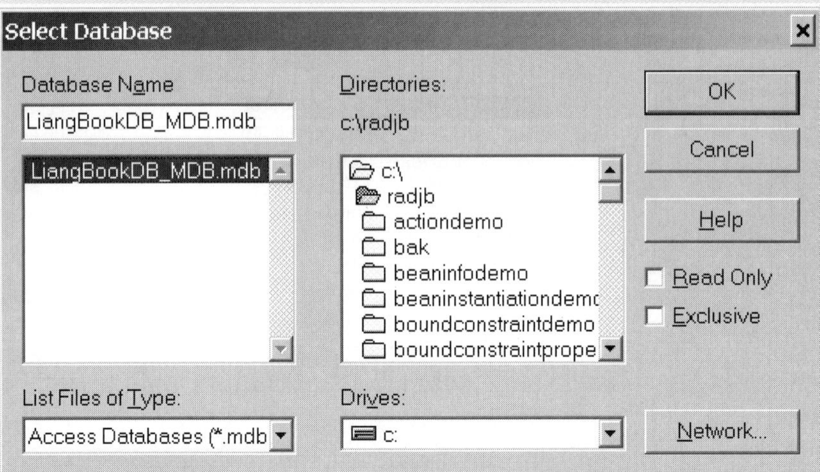

Figure 12.11 *Specify the physical database file name that corresponds to the data source name in the "Select Database" window.*

2.5. Since LiangBookDB_MDB.mdb has already been created, select LiangBookDB_MDB.mdb from the directory **c:\radjb**. Press OK to close the Select Database dialog window, click OK to close the ODBC Microsoft Access Setup window, and click OK to close the ODBC Data Source Administrator window.

3. Create a new project named jdbcdemo.jpr and create a class named `TestJdbcOdbc` (see Listing 12.2) to create a Student table, insert two records, and retrieve the records from the database.

```
package jdbcdemo;

import java.sql.*;

public class TestJdbcOdbc {
  public static void main(String[] args)
    throws SQLException, ClassNotFoundException {
    // Load the JDBC-ODBC bridge driver
    Class.forName("sun.jdbc.odbc.JdbcOdbcDriver");
    System.out.println("Driver sun.jdbc.odbc.JdbcOdbcDriverloaded");

    // Establish connection
    Connection connection = DriverManager.getConnection
      ("jdbc:odbc:LiangBookDB_MDB", "", "");
    System.out.println("Database LiangBookDB_MDB connected");

```

Listing 12.2 *TestJdbcOdbc.java*

```
      // Create a statement
      Statement stmt = connection.createStatement();

      try {
        // Create the Student TABLE
        stmt.executeUpdate(
          "create table Student(firstName varchar(20), "
          + "mi varchar(1), lastName varchar(20))");

        // Insert two records into the Student TABLE
        stmt.executeUpdate(
          "insert into Student values ('John', 'F', 'Smith')");
        stmt.executeUpdate(
          "insert into Student values ('Wade', 'E', 'Bush')");
      }
      catch (SQLException ex) {
        System.out.println("Table Student already exists");
      }

      // Select the column student from the Student table
      ResultSet rset = stmt.executeQuery
        ("select firstName, mi, lastName from Student");

      // Iterate through the result and print the student names
      while (rset.next())
        System.out.println(rset.getString(1) + " " +
          rset.getString(2) + ". " + rset.getString(3));

      // Close the connection
      connection.close();
    }
  }
```

4. Compile and test the program. A sample run of the program is shown in Figure 12.12.

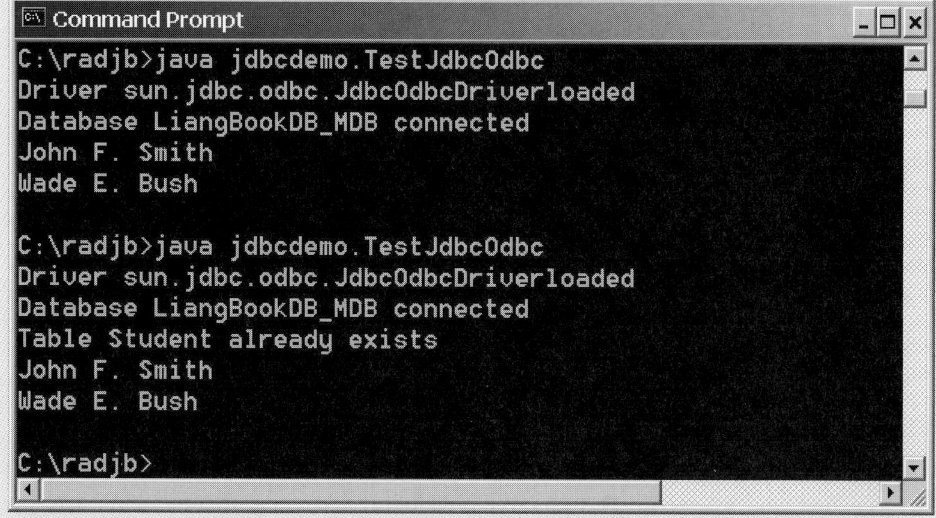

Figure 12.12 *The Java program accesses an MS Access data source through the JDBC-ODBC bridge driver.*

continued

Example 12.1 continued

Example Review

Java does not run on 16-bit platforms. You must use a 32-bit ODBC driver, not a 16-bit ODBC driver. The program was tested using MS Access 2000. It should also work with MS Access 97.

The URL of a data source for a JDBC-ODBC connection is `jdbc:odbc:ODBC-Source-Name`. So `jdbc:odbc:LiangBookDB_MDB` is the URL used in the statement

```
Connection connection = DriverManager.getConnection
  ("jdbc:odbc:LiangBookDB_MDB", "", "" );
```

to establish a connection to the data source LiangBookDB_MDB.

The program creates the Student table, inserts two records, and displays the records in the table. The SQL statements are passed as string arguments.

TIP

The statement `connection.close()` closes the connection, but it is not necessary in this example because the connection is automatically closed upon exiting the program. However, I recommend that you use this statement whenever a connection is no longer needed. Closing it would release the resource associated with the connection.

NOTE

When executing this example using MS Access 97, close MS Access, because only one active session is allowed on MS Access 97. Access Windows 2000 running on Windows 2000 does not have this restriction.

Using the Native-Protocol Driver

A native-protocol driver translates JDBC calls into network protocol used by a DBMS and communicates with the DBMS directly. Since some part of the network protocol for facilitating database communications is vendor-specific, a driver of this kind is usually provided by the vendor. The driver is written in 100% pure Java to implement high-level network communication to the server. Since the native-protocol driver, unlike the native-API driver, does not require that any database-specific binary code be loaded on the client, it is suitable for deploying Java applets.

Oracle, the most popular database, is used by many large corporations. In this section, you will learn how to use the Oracle JDBC thin driver to develop Java applets for accessing remote Oracle databases. Oracle's JDBC thin driver is a native-protocol driver that provides an implementation of the Oracle high-level communications protocol known as TNS (Transparent Network Substrate). This driver can access local or remote servers of Oracle 8i or higher from a client on any platform.

NOTE

You have to use a correct version of Oracle driver for the database. The Oracle JDBC OCI drivers for Oracle 7 and Oracle 8 are different.

Example 12.2 Using the Oracle JDBC Thin Driver

This example develops a Java applet that connects to a remote Oracle 8i server using an Oracle JDBC Thin driver. After the connection is established, the program obtains the system time from the server and displays it on the applet.

Follow the steps below to complete the project.

1. If you have already installed Oracle 8i, it is likely you have the JDBC driver installed in \jdbc\lib of your Oracle installation directory. If not, join Oracle Tech Network to download it. It is bundled with Personal Oracle 8i.

2. In the jdbcdemo project, create an applet named `TestOraJdbcThin` that connects to the test database on liang.armstrong.edu, obtains current system time from the server, and displays it on the applet. The program is given in Listing 12.3.

3. Add $ORACLE_HOME\jdbc\lib\classes12.zip in the libraries in the Project Properties in JBuilder if you are using JBuilder. Add $ORACLE_HOME\jdbc\lib\classes12.zip in the classpath if you are running the program from the DOS prompt. Compile TestOraJdbcThin.java and run the program. A sample run of the program is shown in Figure 12.13.

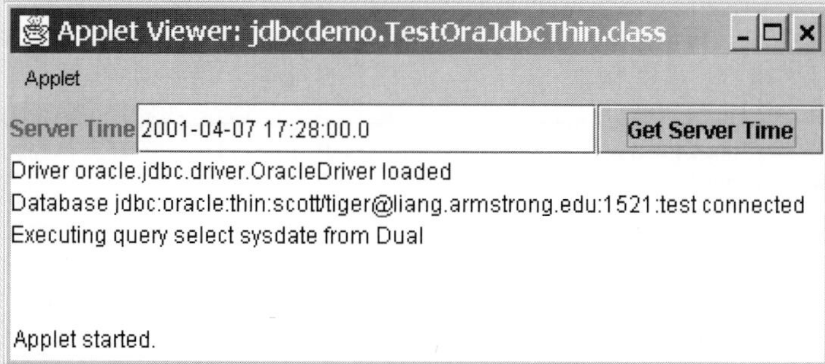

Figure 12.13 *Using the Oracle JDBC Thin driver, the Java applet accesses a remote database and obtains the time from the server.*

```
package jdbcdemo;

import java.awt.*;
import java.awt.event.*;
import java.applet.*;
```

Listing 12.3 *TestOraJdbcThin.java*

continued

Example 12.2 continued

```
import javax.swing.*;
import java.sql.*;

public class TestOraJdbcThin extends JApplet {
  // SQL Statement
  Statement stmt;

  boolean isStandalone = false;
  JPanel jPanel1 = new JPanel();
  JTextArea jtaOutput = new JTextArea();
  BorderLayout borderLayout1 = new BorderLayout();
  JLabel jLabel1 = new JLabel();
  JTextField jtfTime = new JTextField();
  JButton jbtGetTime = new JButton();

  /** Initialize the applet */
  public void init() {
    try {
      jbInit();
    }
    catch(Exception e) {
      e.printStackTrace();
    }
  }

  /** Component initialization */
  private void jbInit() throws Exception {
    this.setSize(new Dimension(399, 166));
    jPanel1.setLayout(borderLayout1);
    jLabel1.setText("Server Time");
    jbtGetTime.setText("Get Server Time");
    jbtGetTime.addActionListener(
      new java.awt.event.ActionListener() {
      public void actionPerformed(ActionEvent e) {
        jbtGetTime_actionPerformed(e);
      }
    });
    this.getContentPane().add(jPanel1, BorderLayout.NORTH);
    jPanel1.add(jLabel1, BorderLayout.WEST);
    jPanel1.add(jtfTime, BorderLayout.CENTER);
    jPanel1.add(jbtGetTime, BorderLayout.EAST);
    this.getContentPane().add(jtaOutput, BorderLayout.CENTER);

    // Initialized JDBC
    initializeJDBC();
  }

  private void initializeJDBC() {
    try {
      // Load the Oracle JDBC Thin driver
      Class.forName("oracle.jdbc.driver.OracleDriver");
      jtaOutput.append("Driver oracle.jdbc.driver.OracleDriver" +
        " loaded"+'\n');

      // Connect to the sample database
      Connection connection = DriverManager.getConnection
        ("jdbc:oracle:thin:@liang.armstrong.edu:1521:test",
         "scott", "tiger");
```

Listing 12.3 *Continued*

```
        jtaOutput.append("Database jdbc:oracle:thin:scott/tiger" +
          "@liang.armstrong.edu:1521:test connected"+'\n');

        // Create a Statement
        stmt = connection.createStatement();
      }
      catch (Exception ex) {
        jtaOutput.append(ex.getMessage() + '\n');
      }
    }

    void jbtGetTime_actionPerformed(ActionEvent e) {
      String query = "select sysdate from Dual";

      if (e.getSource() instanceof JButton) {
        try {
          // Execute the query
          jtaOutput.append("Executing query " + query + "\n");
          ResultSet rset = stmt.executeQuery(query);

          // Display the time
          while (rset.next())
            jtfTime.setText(rset.getString(1));
        }
        catch (Exception ex) {
          jtaOutput.append(ex.getMessage() + '\n');
        }
      }
    }
  }
```

Listing 12.3 *Continued*

Example Review

The Oracle JDBC Thin connection URL is `jdbc:oracle:thin:@hostname:port:sid`. So the following statement

```
Connection conn = DriverManager.getConnection
  ("jdbc:oracle:thin:@liang.armstrong.edu:1521:test",
   "scott", "tiger");
```

establishes a connection to the remote database on liang.armstrong.edu using username **scott** and password **tiger** to the database with a system id test whose listener is at port 1521.

You can test the applet using the appletviewer utility, as shown in Figure 12.14. If this applet is deployed on the server where the database is located, any client on the Internet can run it from a Web browser. Since the client may not have the Oracle Thin driver, you should make the driver available along with the applet in one archive file. This archive file can be created as follows:

1. Copy $ORACLE_HOME\jdbc\lib\classes12.zip to TestOraJdbcThin.zip.
2. Add TestOraJdbcThin.class into TestOraJdbcThin.zip using the WinZip utility.

continued

Example 12.2 continued

3. Add TestOraJdbcThin$1.class into TestOraJdbcThin.zip using the WinZip utility. TestOraJdbcThin$1.class is for the anonymous inner event adapter class for listening to the button action.

You need to deploy TestOraJdbcThin.zip and TestOraJdbcThin.html on the server. TestOraJdbcThin.html should use the applet tag with a reference to the Zip file, as follows:

```
<applet
  code="jdbcdemo.TestOraJdbcThin"
  archive="TestOraJdbcThin.zip"
  width=500
  height=200
>
</applet>
```

NOTE

You can also create the archive file using the Archive Builder. Be careful, however, because the Archive Builder wizard is not very intelligent. It does not package the Oracle driver classes to the JAR file unless you check the option "Include all classes and resources" in Step 3 of 5 of the Archive Builder. With this option checked, the Archive Builder packages all the classes and files in the project, though many of the files are not needed for this applet. To circumvent the problem, create a new project that only contains classes for the applet and its dependent files, then package all the classes in the project into one archive file.

NOTE

To access the database from an applet, it is necessary, because of security restrictions, for the applet to be downloaded from the server where the Oracle database is located. Hence, you have to deploy the applet on the server.

NOTE

Do not use a semicolon (;) to end the Oracle SQL command. The semicolon does not work with the Oracle JDBC drivers, but it does work with the other drivers used in the book.

Using the Native-API Driver

A native-API driver translates JDBC calls directly into calls on the DBMS-specific client API. Thus, you must install the JDBC driver as well as the DBMS client-side library. Major enterprise database vendors like Oracle, Sybase, and IBM already provide native support of database connectivity for development tools, such as Visual Basic and Borland Delphi, among many others, through their proprietary client API. The support extended by these companies enables JDBC to talk directly to the client API through the native-API driver.

This section demonstrates developing a Java application that accesses a remote Oracle database via the Oracle JDBC OCI driver. Oracle's JDBC OCI driver is a native-API driver that provides an implementation of the JDBC interfaces on top of the OCI (Oracle Call Interface) to interact with an Oracle database. This driver can access a local or remote Oracle database from a client on Windows.

Example 12.3 Using the Oracle JDBC OCI Driver

This example develops a Java program that gets the system time from a remote database. The server is accessible on the Internet with the host name liang.armstrong.edu (IP address 130.254.204.33). An Oracle 8i database is running on the server. You can access the database using username **scott** and password **tiger**.

Follow the steps below to set up the client on Windows.

1. Install Oracle 8i client if necessary. Oracle 8i client includes SQL*Net and all other dependent files required to support JDBC OCI driver to connect to the Oracle server. SQL*NET is an Oracle proprietary product that supports network service to the server from the client.

2. Install the Oracle 8i JDBC driver if necessary. Oracle 8 JDBC OCI driver and JDBC thin driver are bundled in the same file classes/2.zip.

3. Add the Oracle TNS alias name for the sample database in the \network\admin\tnsname.ora file as follows, so that this program can access the Oracle test database for this book.

```
liang =
  (description =
    (address_list =
      (address =
        (protocol = TCP)
        (host = liang.Armstrong.edu)
        (port = 1521)
      )
    )
    (connect_data =
      (sid = test)
    )
  )
```

4. In the jdbcdemo project, create a class name TestOraJdbcOci8, as shown in Listing 12.4.

continued

Example 12.3 Using the Oracle JDBC OCI Driver

5. To run the program from the DOS prompt, add $ORACLE_HOME\jdbc\lib in the path, and add $ORACLE_HOME\jdbc\lib\classes12.zip in the classpath. To run the program from JBuilder, add $ORACLE_HOME\jdbc\lib\ classes12.zip in the Java libraries in the Project Properties.

```
package jdbcdemo;

import java.sql.*;

public class TestOraJdbcOci8 {
  public static void main(String[] args)
    throws SQLException, ClassNotFoundException {
    // Load the Oracle JDBC driver
    Class.forName ("oracle.jdbc.driver.OracleDriver");
    System.out.println("Driver loaded");

    // Connect to the sample database
    Connection connection = DriverManager.getConnection
      ("jdbc:oracle:oci8:@liang", "scott", "tiger");
    System.out.println("Database connected");

    // Create a Statement
    Statement stmt = connection.createStatement();

    // Select the date and time from the server
    ResultSet rset = stmt.executeQuery("select sysdate from Dual");

    // Show the system date and time
    while (rset.next())
      System.out.println(rset.getString(1));
  }
}
```

Listing 12.4 *TestOraJdbcOCI8.java*

6. Compile and run the program. A sample run of the program is shown in Figure 12.14.

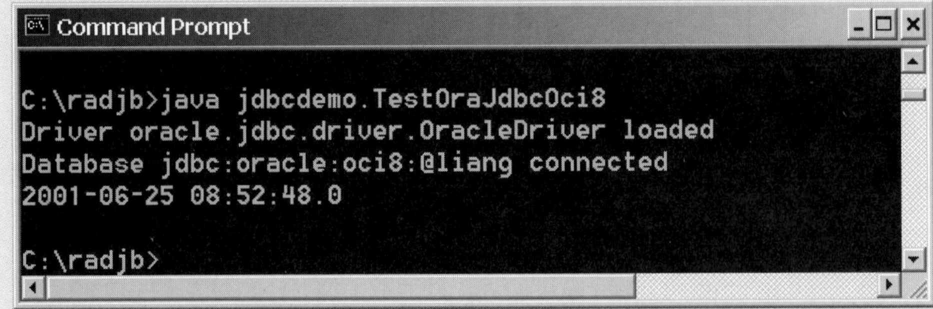

Figure 12.14 *Using an Oracle 8 JDBC OCI driver, the Java program accesses a remote database and obtains the time from the server.*

Example Review

The Oracle 8 JDBC OCI connection url is jdbc:oracle:oci8@tnsname. So the following statement

```
Connection connection = DriverManager.getConnection
  ("jdbc:oracle:oci8:@liang", "scott", "tiger");
```

establishes a connection to the remote database on the host liang.armstrong.edu through the TNS alias name liang using username **scott** and password **tiger**.

The SQL statement "select sysdate from Dual" is specific to Oracle, which returns the current system date and time on the database server.

The success of this example depends on a sequence of steps, each of which must be done exactly right to avoid frustrating errors. Here is a list of things to check:

- Check whether you can log on to the database using **sqlplus scott/tiger@liang**. If this fails, check whether you have created the right alias in the tnsname.ora file for the database server.
- If you get a `ClassNotFoundException`, it is likely that you did not set $ORACLE_HOME\jdbc\lib\classes12.zip in the classpath.
- If you get an error indicating that ocijdbc8.dll file was not found when you ran this program from the DOS prompt, it is because you did not add $ORACLE_HOME\jdbc\bin in the path.

A Universal SQL Client

You have learned how to use various drivers to connect to the database, create statements for executing SQL statements, and process the results from SQL queries. This section presents a bean component for connecting to databases, and a useful utility for processing interactive SQL commands.

Example 12.4 Creating a Connection Dialog Component

This example develops a dialog bean component to connect to a database, as shown in Figure 12.15. The user enters or selects a JDBC driver, a database URL, a username, and a password, and clicks the Connect button to connect to the database. Once connected, an instance of the `Connection` interface can be obtained from the `getConnection` method in the dialog bean.

Here are the steps to create this component.

1. In the jdbcdemo.jpr project, create a dialog class named `DBConnectDialog` using the Dialog wizard from the Object Gallery. The Dialog wizard creates a panel named `panel1` of `BorderLayout` in the dialog container.

continued

Example 12.4 continued

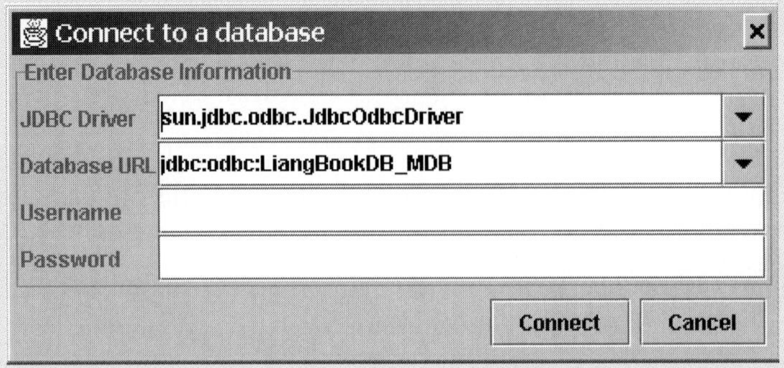

Figure 12.15 *The Connect to Database dialog box enables you to connect to any JDBC data source.*

2. In the UI designer for DBConnectDialog.java, set the `modal` property of the dialog to `true`, and the `title` to "Connect to a database." Drop a `JPanel` to the center of `panel1` to create `jPanel1`, and drop a `JPanel` to the south of `panel1` to create `jPanel2`.

3. In `jPanel1`, set the `layout` to `BorderLayout`, and choose `titled` in the `border` property to create `titledBorder1`. Set the `title` property of `titledBorder1` to "Enter database information" in the property editor for `titleBorder1`.

4. Drop a `JPanel` to the west of `jPanel1` to create `jPanel3`, and drop a `JPanel` to the center of `jPanel1` to create `jPanel4`. Set the `layout` of both `jPanel3` and `jPanel4` to `GridLayout`, with the `row` property set to 4 and the `column` property set to 1.

5. Drop a `JLabel` four times to `jPanel3`, and set the `text` of the labels to "JDBC Driver," "Database URL," "Username," and "Password." Drop a `JComboBox` twice to `jPanel4`, and rename the combo boxes `jcboDriver`, and `jcboURL`. Set the `editable` property of the combo boxes to `true` so as to allow the user to type in a driver name and URL in addition to selecting them from the combo boxes. Drop a `JTextField` to `jPanel4` and rename the object `jtfUsername`. Drop a `JPasswordField` to `jPanel4` and rename the object `jpfPassword`.

6. Set the `layout` of `jPanel2` to `FlowLayout` with right alignment. Drop a `JButton` twice to create buttons Connect and Cancel, and rename the buttons `jbtConnect` and `jbtCancel`.

7. Click the Bean tab in the content pane to switch to BeansExpress. Choose the Properties tab and click the Add Properties button to add a property named `connection` of the `java.sql.Connection` type with a get method. This field stores the connection to the database once a connected session is established.

8. Use the `addItem` method to add JDBC driver classes, and database URLs to `jcboDriver` and `jcboURL`. Generate and implement the handlers for the Connect and Cancel buttons, as shown in Example 12.5 (Lines 126–152).

```
1   package jdbcdemo;
2
3   import java.awt.*;
4   import javax.swing.*;
5   import javax.swing.border.*;
6   import java.awt.event.*;
7   import java.sql.*;
8
9   public class DBConnectDialog extends JDialog {
10    // Generated from BeansExpress
11    private java.sql.Connection connection;
12
13    JPanel panel1 = new JPanel();
14    BorderLayout borderLayout1 = new BorderLayout();
15    JPanel jPanel1 = new JPanel();
16    JPanel jPanel2 = new JPanel();
17    FlowLayout flowLayout1 = new FlowLayout();
18    JButton jbtConnect = new JButton();
19    JButton jbtCancel = new JButton();
20    TitledBorder titledBorder1;
21    BorderLayout borderLayout2 = new BorderLayout();
22    JPanel jPanel3 = new JPanel();
23    JPanel jPanel4 = new JPanel();
24    GridLayout gridLayout1 = new GridLayout();
25    JLabel jLabel1 = new JLabel();
26    JLabel jLabel2 = new JLabel();
27    JLabel jLabel3 = new JLabel();
28    JLabel jLabel4 = new JLabel();
29    GridLayout gridLayout2 = new GridLayout();
30    JComboBox jcboDriver = new JComboBox();
31    JComboBox jcboURL = new JComboBox();
32    JTextField jtfUsername = new JTextField();
33    JPasswordField jpfPassword = new JPasswordField();
34
35    /** Construct a dialog with specified frame, title, and modal */
36    public DBConnectDialog(Frame frame, String title, boolean modal) {
37      super(frame, title, modal);
38      try {
39        jbInit();
40        pack();
41      }
42      catch (Exception ex) {
43        ex.printStackTrace();
44      }
45    }
46
47    /** Default constructor */
48    public DBConnectDialog() {
49      this(null, "", false);
50    }
51
```

Listing 12.5 *DBConnectDialog.java*

continued

Example 12.4 continued

```
  void jbInit() throws Exception {
    titledBorder1 = new TitledBorder("");
    panel1.setLayout(borderLayout1);
    jPanel2.setLayout(flowLayout1);
    flowLayout1.setAlignment(2);
    jbtConnect.setText("Connect");
    jbtConnect.addActionListener(
      new java.awt.event.ActionListener() {
      public void actionPerformed(ActionEvent e) {
        jbtConnect_actionPerformed(e);
      }
    });
    jbtCancel.setText("Cancel");
    jbtCancel.addActionListener(
      new java.awt.event.ActionListener() {
      public void actionPerformed(ActionEvent e) {
        jbtCancel_actionPerformed(e);
      }
    });
    jPanel1.setBorder(titledBorder1);
    jPanel1.setLayout(borderLayout2);
    titledBorder1.setTitle("Enter Database Information");
    jPanel3.setLayout(gridLayout1);
    jLabel1.setText("JDBC Driver");
    jLabel2.setText("Database URL");
    jLabel3.setText("Username");
    jLabel4.setText("Password");
    gridLayout1.setColumns(1);
    gridLayout1.setRows(4);
    jPanel4.setLayout(gridLayout2);
    gridLayout2.setColumns(1);
    gridLayout2.setHgap(10);
    gridLayout2.setRows(4);
    this.setTitle("Connect to a database");
    this.setModal(true);
    jcboDriver.setEditable(true);
    jcboURL.setEditable(true);
    getContentPane().add(panel1);
    panel1.add(jPanel1, BorderLayout.CENTER);
    jPanel1.add(jPanel3, BorderLayout.WEST);
    jPanel3.add(jLabel1, null);
    jPanel3.add(jLabel2, null);
    jPanel3.add(jLabel3, null);
    jPanel3.add(jLabel4, null);
    jPanel1.add(jPanel4, BorderLayout.CENTER);
    jPanel4.add(jcboDriver, null);
    jPanel4.add(jcboURL, null);
    jPanel4.add(jtfUsername, null);
    jPanel4.add(jpfPassword, null);
    panel1.add(jPanel2, BorderLayout.SOUTH);
    jPanel2.add(jbtConnect, null);
    jPanel2.add(jbtCancel, null);

    // Add items to the combo boxes
    jcboDriver.addItem("sun.jdbc.odbc.JdbcOdbcDriver");
    jcboURL.addItem("jdbc:odbc:LiangBookDB_MDB");
    jcboDriver.addItem("oracle.jdbc.driver.OracleDriver");
    jcboURL.addItem
      ("jdbc:oracle:thin:@liang.armstrong.edu:1521:test");
    // Oracle Type 2 JDBC Connection
```

Listing 12.5 *Continued*

```
    jcboURL.addItem("jdbc:oracle:oci8:@liang");
    jcboDriver.addItem(
      "com.borland.datastore.jdbc.DataStoreDriver");
    jcboURL.addItem
      ("jdbc:borland:dslocal:C:\\radjb\\LiangBookDB.jds");
    jcboDriver.addItem("interbase.interclient.Driver");
    jcboURL.addItem
      ("jdbc:interbase://localhost/C:/LiangBook/LiangBookDB.gdb");

    // Username and password for Interbase SYSDBA/masterkey
    // Username and password for Oracle scott/tiger
    // Username and password for JDataStore system/manager
  }

  /** Handle the Connect button */
  void jbtConnect_actionPerformed(ActionEvent e) {
    // Get database information from the user input
    String driver = (String)jcboDriver.getSelectedItem();
    String url = (String)jcboURL.getSelectedItem();
    String username = jtfUsername.getText().trim();
    String password = new String(jpfPassword.getPassword());

    // Connection to the database
    try {
      Class.forName(driver);
      System.out.println("Driver " + driver + "loaded\n");
      connection = DriverManager.getConnection(
        url, username, password);
      System.out.println("Connected to " + url + '\n');
      setVisible(false);
    }
    catch (java.lang.Exception ex) {
      ex.printStackTrace();
    }
  }

  /** Handle the Cancel button */
  void jbtCancel_actionPerformed(ActionEvent e) {
    // Close the dialog box
    setVisible(false);
  }

  /** Return connection */
  public java.sql.Connection getConnection() {
    return connection;
  }
}
```

Listing 12.5 *Continued*

Example Review

An example of using this dialog component will be given in the next example.

The `modal` property of the dialog box is set to `true` to ensure that the Connect to Database dialog is dealt with before performing other tasks.

You can choose a JDBC driver (or a database URL) from the combo box or enter a driver class (or a database URL) in the combo box.

Once a connection is established, the `getConnection` method returns the `Connection` object. If the return value is null, there is no active connection.

Example 12.5 Creating an Interactive SQL Client

This example creates a Java applet for submitting and executing SQL commands interactively, as shown in Figure 12.16. The client can connect to any JDBC data source, and submit SQL SELECT commands and non-SELECT commands for execution. The execution result is displayed for the SELECT queries, and the execution status is displayed for the non-SELECT commands.

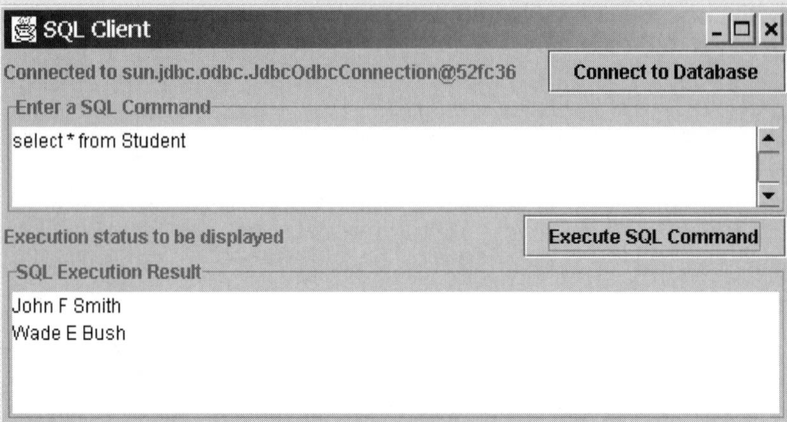

Figure 12.16 *You can connect to any JDBC data source and execute SQL commands interactively.*

Here are the steps to create this applet.

1. In the jdbcdemo project, create a new applet named SQLClient.java using the Applet wizard from the Object Gallery.

2. In the UI designer for SQLClient.java, drop a `JPanel` to the north of the applet to create `jPanel1`, and drop a `JScrollPane` to the center of the applet to create `jScrollPane1`.

3. In `jPanel1`, set the `layout` to `BorderLayout`. Drop a `JPanel` to the north of `jPanel1` to create `jPanel2`. Drop a `JScrollPane` to the center of `jPanel1` to create `jScrollPane2`. Drop a `JPanel` to the south of `jPanel1` to create `jPanel3`.

4. In `jPanel2`, set the `layout` to `BorderLayout`. Drop a `JLabel` to the west of `jPanel2` and rename the label `jlblConnectionStatus`. Drop a `JButton` to the east of `jPanel2` and rename the button `jbtConnect`. Set the `text` of the button to Connect.

5. In `jScrollPane2`, choose `titled` in the `border` property to create `titledBorder1`. Set the `title` property of `titledBorder1` to "Enter a SQL Command." Drop a `JTextArea` into `jScrollPane2` to create `jtaSQLCommand`.

6. In `jPanel3`, set the `layout` to `BorderLayout`. Drop a `JLabel` to the west of `jPanel3` and rename the label `jlblExecutionStatus`. Drop a `JButton` to the east of `jPanel3` and rename the button `jbtExecuteSQL`. Set the `text` of the button to "Execute SQL Command."

7. In `jScrollPane1`, choose `titled` in the `border` property to create `titledBorder2`. Set the `title` property of `titledBorder2` to "SQL Execution Result." Drop a `JTextArea` into `jScrollPane1` to create `jtaSQLResult`.

8. Install the `DBConnectDialog` component into the Component palette. `DBConnectDialog` was created in Example 12.4. Drop a `DBConnectDialog` from the component palette to the UI designer to create `dBConnectDialog1`.

8. Generate and implement the handlers for the Connect button and the Execute SQL Command button, as shown in Listing 12.6.

```
package jdbcdemo;

import java.awt.*;
import java.awt.event.*;
import java.applet.*;
import javax.swing.*;
import javax.swing.border.*;
import java.sql.*;

public class SQLClient extends JApplet {
  // Connection to the database
  Connection connection;

  // Statement to execute SQL commands
  Statement statement;

  boolean isStandalone = false;
  JPanel jPanel1 = new JPanel();
  JPanel jPanel2 = new JPanel();
  BorderLayout borderLayout1 = new BorderLayout();
  JScrollPane jScrollPane1 = new JScrollPane();
  JTextArea jtasqlCommand = new JTextArea();
  JLabel jlblStatus = new JLabel();
  JButton jbtConnectDB = new JButton();
  BorderLayout borderLayout2 = new BorderLayout();
  TitledBorder titledBorder1;
  JScrollPane jScrollPane2 = new JScrollPane();
  JTextArea jtaSQLResult = new JTextArea();
  DBConnectDialog dBConnectDialog1 = new DBConnectDialog();
  JPanel jPanel3 = new JPanel();
  JButton jbtExecuteSQL = new JButton();
  TitledBorder titledBorder2;
  JLabel jlblExecutionStatus = new JLabel();
  BorderLayout borderLayout3 = new BorderLayout();

  /** Initialize the applet */
  public void init() {
    try {
      jbInit();
    }
    catch(Exception e) {
      e.printStackTrace();
    }
  }

```

Listing 12.6 *SQLClient.java*

continued

Example 12.5 continued

```
  /** Component initialization */
  private void jbInit() throws Exception {
    titledBorder1 = new TitledBorder("");
    titledBorder2 = new TitledBorder("");
    this.setSize(new Dimension(400,300));
    jPanel1.setLayout(borderLayout1);
    jtasqlCommand.setPreferredSize(new Dimension(57, 50));
    jlblStatus.setText("No connection now");
    jbtConnectDB.setText("Connect to Database");
    jbtConnectDB.addActionListener(
      new java.awt.event.ActionListener() {
      public void actionPerformed(ActionEvent e) {
        jbtConnectDB_actionPerformed(e);
      }
    });
    jPanel2.setLayout(borderLayout2);
    jScrollPane1.setVerticalScrollBarPolicy(
      JScrollPane.VERTICAL_SCROLLBAR_ALWAYS);
    jScrollPane1.setBorder(titledBorder1);
    titledBorder1.setTitle("Enter a SQL Command");
    jbtExecuteSQL.setText("Execute SQL Command");
    jbtExecuteSQL.addActionListener(
      new java.awt.event.ActionListener() {
      public void actionPerformed(ActionEvent e) {
        jbtExecuteSQL_actionPerformed(e);
      }
    });
    jPanel3.setLayout(borderLayout3);
    jScrollPane2.setBorder(titledBorder2);
    titledBorder2.setTitle("SQL Execution Result");
    jlblExecutionStatus.setText("Execution status to be displayed");
    this.getContentPane().add(jPanel1, BorderLayout.NORTH);
    jPanel1.add(jPanel2, BorderLayout.NORTH);
    jPanel2.add(jlblStatus, BorderLayout.CENTER);
    jPanel2.add(jbtConnectDB, BorderLayout.EAST);
    jPanel1.add(jScrollPane1, BorderLayout.CENTER);
    jPanel1.add(jPanel3, BorderLayout.SOUTH);
    jPanel3.add(jlblExecutionStatus, BorderLayout.CENTER);
    jPanel3.add(jbtExecuteSQL, BorderLayout.EAST);
    this.getContentPane().add(jScrollPane2, BorderLayout.CENTER);
    jScrollPane2.getViewport().add(jtaSQLResult, null);
    jScrollPane1.getViewport().add(jtasqlCommand, null);
  }

  /** Connect to DB */
  void jbtConnectDB_actionPerformed(ActionEvent e) {
    dBConnectDialog1.setVisible(true);
    connection = dBConnectDialog1.getConnection();
    if (connection != null) {
      jlblStatus.setText("Connected to " + connection);
    }
  }

  /** Execute SQL commands */
  void jbtExecuteSQL_actionPerformed(ActionEvent e) {
    if (connection == null) {
      jtaSQLResult.setText("Please connect to a database first");
      return;
    }
```

Listing 12.6 *Continued*

```
    else {
      String sqlCommand = jtasqlCommand.getText().trim();
      if (sqlCommand.toUpperCase().startsWith("SELECT")) {
        processSQLSelect(sqlCommand);
      }
      else {
        processSQLNonSelect(sqlCommand);
      }
    }
  }

  /** Execute SQL SELECT commands */
  private void processSQLSelect(String sqlCommand) {
    try {
      // Get a new statement for the current connection
      statement = connection.createStatement();

      // Execute a SELECT SQL command
      ResultSet resultSet = statement.executeQuery(sqlCommand);

      // Find the number of columns in the result set
      int columnCount = resultSet.getMetaData().getColumnCount();
      String row = "";

      while (resultSet.next()) {
        for (int i=1; i<=columnCount; i++) {
          row += resultSet.getString(i) + " ";
        }

        jtaSQLResult.append(row + '\n');

        // Reset row to empty
        row = "";
      }
    }
    catch (SQLException ex) {
      jlblExecutionStatus.setText(ex.toString());
    }
  }

  /** Execute SQL DDL, and modification commands */
  private void processSQLNonSelect(String sqlCommand) {
    try {
      // Get a new statement for the current connection
      statement = connection.createStatement();

      // Execute a non-SELECT SQL command
      statement.executeUpdate(sqlCommand);

      jlblExecutionStatus.setText("SQL command executed");
    }
    catch (SQLException ex) {
      jlblExecutionStatus.setText(ex.toString());
    }
  }
}
```

Listing 12.6 *Continued*

continued

Example 12.5 continued

Example Review

The Connect button displays the dialog box for connecting to a database. You can retrieve the connection from the `getConnection` method in `dBConnectDialog1`.

The Execute SQL Command button gets the SQL command from the text area (`jtaSQLCommand`), and determines whether the command is a SELECT query or a DDL or data modification statement. If the command is a SELECT query, the `executeQuery` method is invoked to obtain the query result. The result is displayed in the text area (`jtaSQLResult`). If the command is a non-SELECT query, the `executeUpdate` method is invoked to execute the SQL command. The result of execution is displayed in the label (`jlblExecutionStatus`).

The `getMetaData` method in the `ResultSet` interface is used to obtain an instance of `ResultSetMetaData`. `ResultSetMetaData` can be used to find the metadata information on the result set, including the number of columns in the result set. `ResultSetMetaData` will be further discussed in Chapter 13, "Advanced Java Database Programming." In Exercise 13.3, you will modify this program to display the query result in a table.

If you connect to an Oracle database, do not use a semicolon at the end of the SQL command.

JDataStore Database

JDataStore is an embedded relational database system developed by Borland using Java. It is bundled in JBuilder 4 and 5 Professional and Enterprise Editions. Since it is small and developed in 100% pure Java, it can be used in various types of embedded systems. It is SQL92 compliant and requires no administration. The entire database is stored in one file, so it is easy to transport. You can use JDataStore databases through the JDataStore drivers locally or remotely.

JDataStore Explorer

JDataStore Explorer is a utility for managing and manipulating JDataStore databases. You can use it to browse and edit the contents of a JDataStore database.

To create a JDataStore database, choose Tools, JDataStore Explorer to display the JDataStore Explorer, as shown in Figure 12.17.

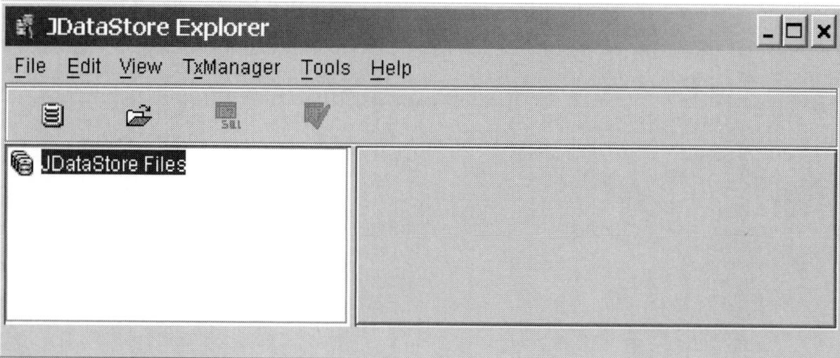

Figure 12.17 *JDataStore Explorer can be used to manage JDataStore databases.*

To create a new database, choose File, New to display the New JDataStore dialog box, as shown in Figure 12.18. Type C:\radjb\LiangBookDB.jds in the File name field, and choose all the default options. Click OK to create the database.

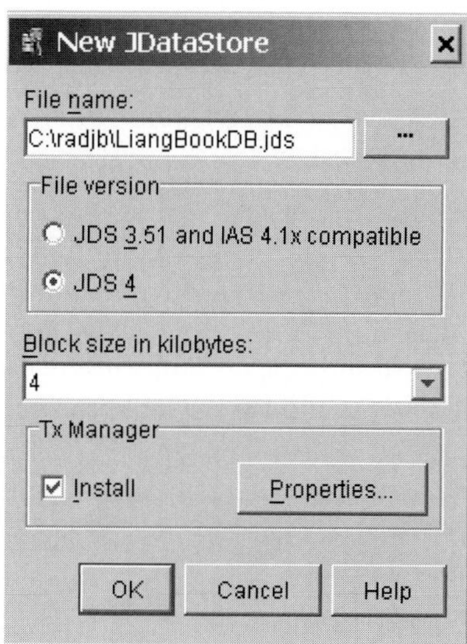

Figure 12.18 *You can create a JDataStore database in the New JDataStore dialog box.*

You can create tables and indexes, use SQL statements, and create user accounts from the Tools menu. If you don't create a user, you can open the database with any username without a password.

You can manipulate tables in a JDataStore database using the SQL commands from the SQL window, as shown in Figure 12.19. The SQL window can be displayed by choosing Tools, SQL.

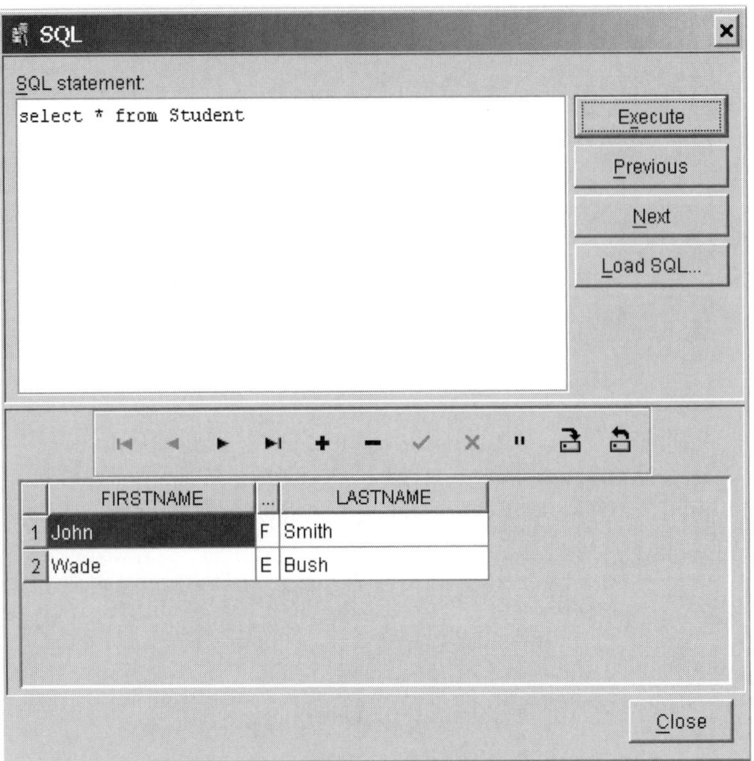

Figure 12.19 *The SQL window enables you to type and execute SQL commands.*

You can also browse and edit the tables by choosing the table in the left pane and choose the View tab to display the table contents in the right pane, as shown in Figure 12.20.

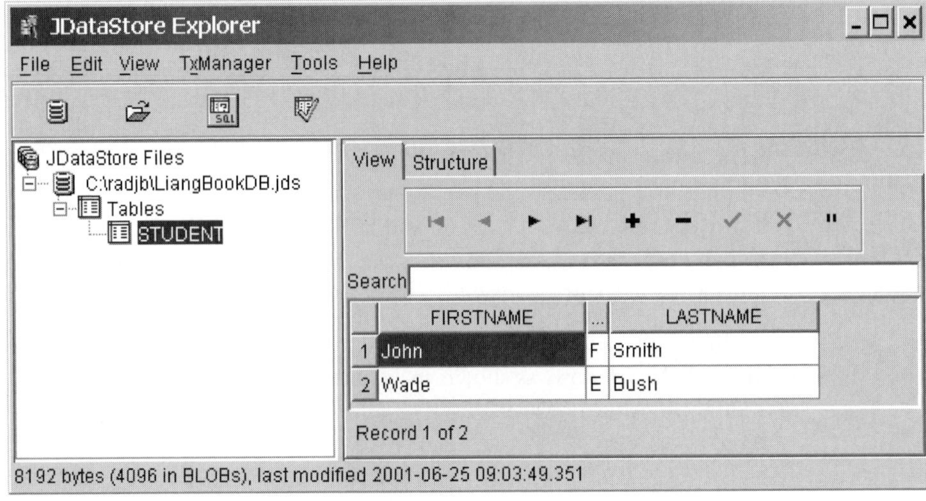

Figure 12.20 *You can browse and edit the contents of a table in the View page in the JDataStore Explorer.*

JDataStore JDBC Driver and URL

You can develop Java clients to access the JDataStore databases through the JDBC drivers. The JDataStore JDBC driver is `com.borland.datastore.jdbc.DataStoreDriver`. To access a local JDataStore database, use the URL

jdbc:borland:dslocal:complete-datastore-filename.

For example, the URL is jdbc:borland:dslocal:c:\radjb\LiangBookDB.jds to use the local JDataStore c:\radjb\LiangBookDB.jds.

To access a remote JDataStore database, use the URL

jdbc:borland:dsremote://<hostname>/<filename>

For example, the URL is jdbc:borland:dsremote://liang.armstrong.edu/c:/radjb/LiangBookDB.jds to use the remote JDataStore on host liang.armstrong.edu.

JDBC Explorer

JBuilder Professional and Enterprise has the JDBC Explorer. This is a pure-Java utility that enables you to browse a set of databases, its associated tables, views, indexes, primary keys, and stored procedures in addition to database metadata. You can also use it to edit data. To display the JDBC Explorer, choose Tools, JDBC Explorer from the JBuilder menu, as shown in Figure 12.21.

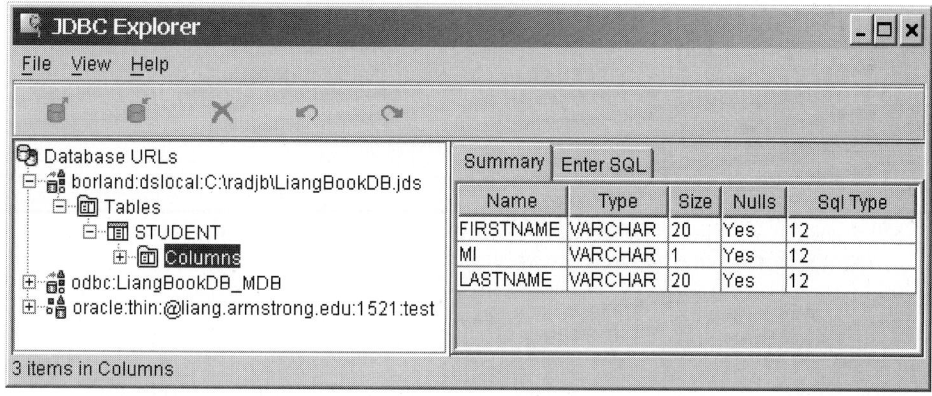

Figure 12.21 *The JDBC Explorer enables you to browse databases and execute SQL statements.*

The JDBC Explorer has two panes. The left pane, referred to as the *structure pane*, displays the database URLs and a hierarchical view of the tables, views, indexes, primary keys, and stored procedures. The right pane, referred to as the *content pane*, displays the contents of the tables, views, indexes, and primary keys.

To add a new database in the JDBC Explorer, highlight the node Database URLs in the structure pane, and choose File, New to display the New URL dialog box for entering a driver and a URL. When a database URL is opened, you can expand the tree to display child objects. Columns are child objects of a particular database table. As shown in Figure 12.21, when the Column object is selected for a table, the Summary page in the right pane lists the columns, their data type, size, and other information.

To display the contents of a table, enter a SQL select statement in the Enter SQL tab of the content pane. The contents of the query will be displayed in the content pane after you click the Execute button, as shown in Figure 12.22.

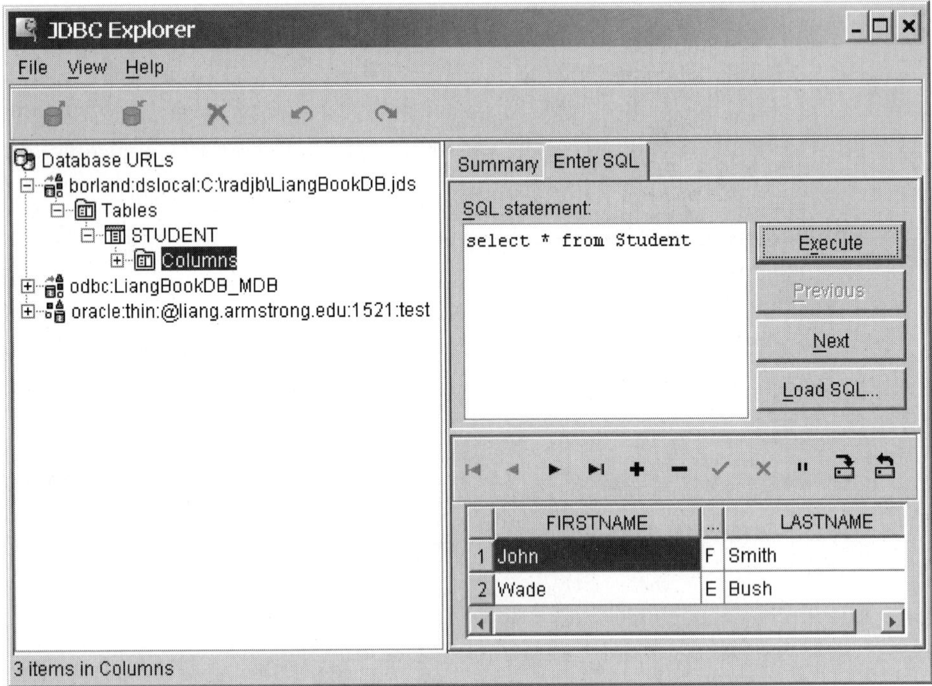

Figure 12.22 *You can view the contents of the tables from the JDBC Explorer.*

Editing Data

You can edit data in the JDataStore databases through the JDBC Explorer. For a demonstration, create a JDataStore database, and create a table in the database. Select the table in the navigation pane and click the Data tab in the content pane, as shown in Figure 12.23. You can now edit the data in the content pane. For more information, please refer to "JDBC Explorer User Guide" in JBuilder Help.

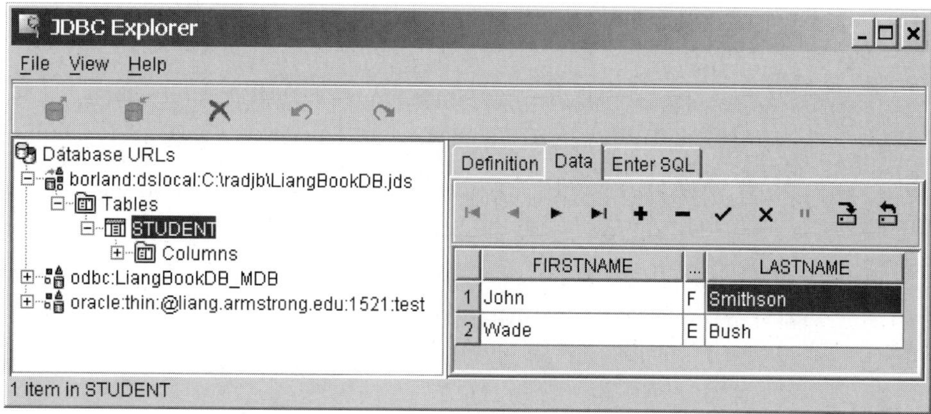

Figure 12.23 *You can edit the contents of the tables from the JDBC Explorer.*

Chapter Summary

This chapter introduced JDBC, which is the Java API for accessing relational databases. You learned how to write a simple JDBC program by loading the driver, connecting to the database, creating statements, executing the statements, and processing statements. The chapter gave step-by-step instructions for working with several representative JDBC drivers. It also provided a database connection dialog bean component and a universal interactive SQL client.

Review Questions

12.1 Describe the following JDBC interfaces: `Driver`, `Connection`, `Statement`, `ResultSet`.

12.2 How do you load a JDBC driver?

12.3 How do you create a JDBC connection? What is the syntax for a JDBC URL?

12.4 How do you create an instance of `Statement`? How do you execute a statement? Does every execution of the statement return a `ResultSet`?

12.5 How do you retrieve values in a `ResultSet`?

12.6 What are the four types of JDBC drivers? Which types of drivers require the DBMS client library? Which types of drivers can be downloaded and maintained on the server side?

Programming Exercises

12.1 Write an applet that shows the number of visits made to a Web page. The count should be stored on the server side in a database table. Every time the page is visited or reloaded, the applet should send a request to the server, and the server should increase the count and send it to the applet. The applet should then display the count in a message, such as You are visitor number: 1000.

12.2 Write an applet that gets stock quotes. The stock information is stored in a table consisting of six fields: stock symbol, stock share value, the high of the day, the low of the day, the highest value in the last 52 weeks, and the lowest value in the last 52 weeks. To get a stock quote, the user enters the stock symbol and presses ENTER in the text field for the stock symbol to display the stock information.

12.3 Write a Java applet that views, inserts, and updates staff information stored in a database, as shown in Figure 12.24. The Staff table is created as follows:

```
create table Staff
(
  id char(9) not null,
  lastName varchar(15),
  firstName varchar(15),
  mi char(1),
  address varchar(20),
  city varchar(20),
  state char(2),
  telephone char(10),
  email varchar(40),
  primary key (id)
);
```

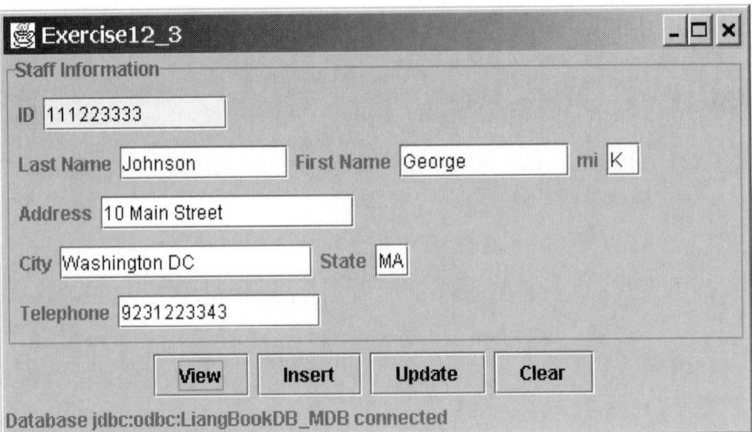

Figure 12.24 *The applet lets you view, insert, and update staff information.*

12.4 Modify Example 12.5 to add a File menu with a menu item named Connect to connect a database using the `DBConnectDialog` component, as shown in Figure 12.25.

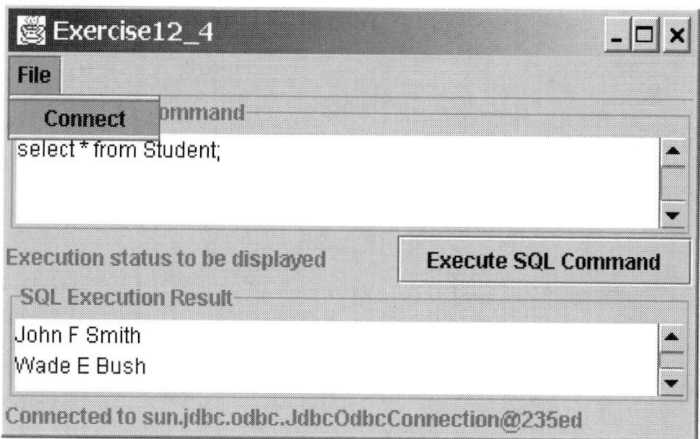

Figure 12.25 *The Connect menu item connects to a database using the* `DBConnectDialog` *component.*

12.5 Rewrite Exercise 4.8 to display the number of employees in each department in a pie chart and a bar chart, as shown in Figure 12.26. The number of employees for each department can be obtained dynamically from the database tables Department and Employee. The Department table has three columns: deptno, deptname, and deptchair. The Employee table has four columns: empno, name, office, and deptno. The number of employees in each department can be obtained using the following SQL statement:

```
select deptname, count(*)
from Department, Employee
where department.deptno = employee.deptno
group by deptname;
```

The `PieChart` component and the `BarChart` component were created in Exercise 4.8.

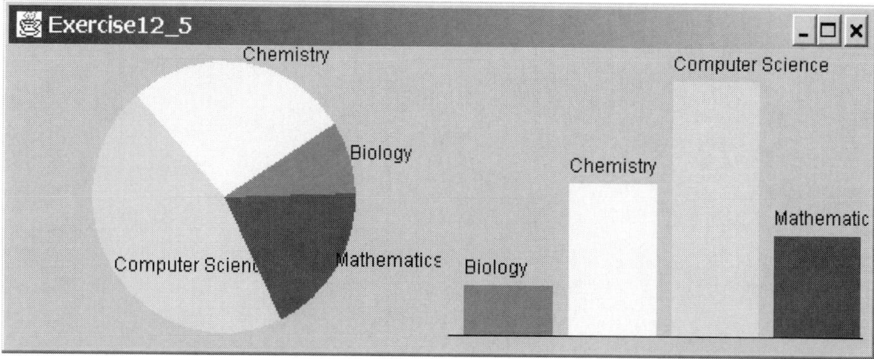

Figure 12.26 *The PieChart and BarChart display the query data obtained from the data module.*

CHAPTER 13

Advanced Java Database Programming

Objectives

- Handle transactions in the `Connection` interface.
- Explore database metadata using the `DatabaseMetaData` and `ResultSetMetaData` interfaces.
- Create and execute statements using the `Statement`, `PreparedStatement`, and `CallableStatement` interfaces.
- Process updateable and scrollable result sets.
- Store and retrieve images in JDBC.

Introduction

Chapter 12, "Introduction to Java Database Programming," presented an overview of the JDBC concept and examples of using various drivers to connect to databases. JDBC is a comprehensive approach to the development of platform-independent Java database applications. This chapter gives an in-depth look at transaction processing in the `Connection` interface, retrieving metadata in the `DatabaseMetaData` interface and result set metadata in the `ResultSetMetaData` interface, creating and executing static statements, dynamic statements and callable statements, processing scrollable and updateable result sets, and storing and retrieving images from the database.

Handling Transactions in the *Connection* Interface

The `Connection` interface establishes a connection to a database. Within the context of a connection, SQL statements are executed and results are returned. A connection also provides access to database metadata information that describes database tables, supported SQL grammar, stored procedures, the capabilities of the database, and so on. This information is obtained by invoking the `getMetaData` method from a `Connection` object. Database metadata will be introduced in the section "Getting Database Metadata."

TABLE 13.1 Some Methods Defined in the `Connection` Interface

Method	*Description*
`void clearWarnings()`	Clears all warnings reported for this connection.
`void close()`	Closes this connection and releases its associated resource.
`void commit()`	Saves all changes made since the previous commit/rollback.
`Statement createStatement()`	Creates a statement to execute static SQL commands.
`Statement createStatement(int resultSetType, int resultSetConcurrency)`	Creates a statement that executes static SQL commands with a specified result set type and currency mode.
`boolean getAutoCommit()`	Gets current auto-commit mode.
`String getCatalog()`	Gets the catalog for the connection.
`DatabaseMetaData getMetaData()`	Gets the database metadata catalog.
`int getTransactionIsolation()`	Gets the connection's current transaction isolation level.
`Map getTypeMap()`	Gets the type map object associated with this connection. (JDBC 2)

continued

TABLE 13.1 continued

Method	*Description*
`SQLWarning getWarnings()`	Gets the first warning on this connection.
`boolean isClosed()`	Returns `true` if the connection is closed.
`boolean isReadOnly()`	Returns `true` if the connection is in read-only mode.
`String nativeSQL(String sql)`	Converts the given SQL statement into the system's native SQL grammar.
`CallableStatement prepareCall(String sql)`	Creates a statement to execute stored procedures.
`CallableStatement prepareCall(String sql, int resultSetType, int resultSet-Concurrency)`	Creates a statement to execute stored procedures with specified result set type, and concurrency mode. (JDBC 2)
`PreparedStatement prepareStatement (String sql)`	Creates a statement to execute dynamic SQL statements.
`PreparedStatement prepareStatement (String sql, int resultSetType, int resultSetConcurrency)`	Creates a statement to execute dynamic SQL statements with specified result set and concurrency mode. (JDBC 2)
`void rollback()`	Rollbacks all changes made since the previous commit/rollback.
`void setAutoCommit(boolean autoCommit)`	Specifies an auto-commit mode.
`void setCatalog(String catalog)`	Sets a catalog name for this connection.
`void setReadOnly(boolean readOnly)`	Sets read-only `true` or `false` for this connection.
`void setTransactionIsolation(int level)`	Sets a new transaction level.
`void setTypeMap(java.util.Map map)`	Installs the given type map as the type map for this connection. The type map will be used for the custom mapping of SQL-structured types and distinct types. (JDBC 2)

The `Connection` interface handles transactions and specifies how they are processed. By default, a new connection is in auto-commit mode, and all its SQL statements are executed and committed as individual transactions. The commit occurs when the statement completes or the next execute occurs, whichever comes first. In the case of statements returning a result set, the statement completes when the last row of the result set has been retrieved or the result set has been closed. If a single statement returns multiple results, the commit occurs when all results have been retrieved.

You can use the `setAutoCommit(false)` method to disable auto-commit, so that all SQL statements are grouped into one transaction that is terminated by a call to either the `commit` or the `rollback` Method. By default, new connections are in auto-commit mode. Table 13.1 lists all the methods in the `Connection` interface.

Getting Database Metadata

Database *metadata* is information that describes the database itself. JDBC provides the `DatabaseMetaData` interface for obtaining database-wide information and the `ResultSetMetaData` interface for obtaining information on the specific `ResultSet`.

The `DatabaseMetaData` interface provides more than 100 methods for getting database metadata concerning the database as a whole. These methods can be divided into three groups: for retrieving general information, for finding database capabilities, and for getting object descriptions. The general information includes the URL, username, product name, product version, driver name, driver version, available functions, available data types, and so on. Information on database capabilities includes such matters as whether the database supports the GROUP BY operator, the ALTER TABLE command with add column option, and entry-level or full ANSI92 SQL grammar. Examples of database objects are tables, views, and procedures.

Obtaining General Database Information

The methods for general information usually return a string, an integer, except that the method for retrieving available data types returns a `ResultSet`. Most methods of this type don't have parameters. Table 13.2 lists some of the methods for retrieving database information.

Finding Database Capabilities

The methods for finding database capabilities return a `boolean` value indicating whether the database possesses a certain capability. Most methods of this type don't have parameters and are named with prefix *supports*. Table 13.3 lists some of these methods for finding database capabilities.

Getting Database Objects

The methods that get database objects shown in Table 13.4 return lists of information in `ResultSets`. You can use the normal `ResultSet` methods, such as `getString` and `getInt`, to retrieve data from these `ResultSets`. If a given form of metadata is not available, these methods should throw a `SQLException`.

Many of these methods take arguments that are string patterns. Within a pattern string, "%" means a match with any substring of 0 or more characters, and "_" means a match with any one character. Only metadata entries matching the search pattern are returned. If a search pattern argument is set to a `null` reference, it means that the argument's criteria should be dropped from the search.

TABLE 13.2 Some Methods for Retrieving General Information in the `DatabaseMetaData` Interface

Method Name	*Description*
`getURL`	Gets the URL of the database.
`getUserName`	Gets the username of the currently connected user.
`getDataBaseProductName`	Gets the name of the database product.
`getDataBaseProductVersion`	Gets the version of the database product.
`getDriverName`	Gets the JDBC driver name for connecting to the database.
`getDriverVersion`	Gets the JDBC driver version.
`getNumericFunctions`	Gets a list of comma-separated numeric functions.
`getStringFunctions`	Gets a list of comma-separated string functions.
`getSystemFunctions`	Gets a list of comma-separated system functions.
`getTimeDateFunctions`	Gets a list of comma-separated time and date functions.
`getMaxConnections`	Gets the maximum number of active connections to the database.
`getMaxCursorNameLength`	Gets the maximum cursor name length.
`getMaxSchemaNameLength`	Gets the maximum schema name length.
`getMaxRowLength`	Gets the maximum length of a single row.
`getMaxStatementLength`	Gets the maximum length of a SQL statement.
`getMaxTableNameLength`	Gets the maximum length of a table name.
`getTypeInfo`	Returns a `ResultSet` of all the SQL types supported by this database.

Retrieving Tables

The `getTables` method is used to find tables in a database. For example, you can use the following method to obtain all user-defined tables in the database:

```
DatabaseMetaData dbMetaData = connection.getMetaData();
ResultSet rsTables = dbMetaData.getTables(null, null, null,
  new String[] {"TABLE"});
```

The parameters of the `getTables` are `catalog` (`String`), `schemaPattern` (`String`), `tableNamePattern` (`String`), and `tableTypes` (`String[]`). The parameter `tableTypes` is an array of `String`. Each string specifies a table type. Typical types are "TABLE," "VIEW," "SYSTEM TABLE," "GLOBAL TEMPORARY," "LOCAL TEMPORARY," "ALIAS," and "SYNONYM." The arguments for `catalog`, `schemaPattern`, and `tableNamePattern` are null in the statement, so all the tables are returned with or without a catalog or a schema. The returned table information is in the `ResultSet`, which has the following five columns:

TABLE 13.3 Some Methods for Finding Database Capabilities in the `DatabaseMetaData` Interface

Method Name	*Description*
`allProceduresAreCallable`	Returns `true` if all the procedures returned by `getProcedures` (in Table 13.4) can be called by the current user.
`allTablesAreSelectable`	Returns `true` if all the tables returned by `getTables` (in Table 13.4) can be selected by the current user.
`isReadOnly`	Returns `true` if the database is in read-only mode.
`supportsAlterTableWithAddColumn`	Returns `true` if "ALTER TABLE" with add column is supported.
`supportsAlterTableWithDropColumn`	Returns `true` if "ALTER TABLE" with drop column is supported.
`supportsANSI92EntryLevelSQL`	Returns `true` if the ANSI92 entry-level SQL grammar is supported. All DBC-Compliant drivers must return `true`.
`supportsANSI92FullSQL`	Returns `true` if the ANSI full-SQL grammar is supported.
`supportsANSI92IntermediateSQL`	Returns `true` if the ANSI92 intermediate-SQL grammar is supported.
`supportsBatchUpdates`	Returns `true` if batch update is supported. (JDBC 2)
`supportsFullOuterJoins`	Returns `true` if full-nested outer join is supported.
`supportsGroupBy`	Returns `true` if some form of "GROUP BY" clause is supported.
`supportsGroupByBeyondSelect`	Returns `true` if a "GROUP BY" clause can add columns not in the select provided it specifies all the columns in the select.
`supportsIntegrityEnhancement-Facility`	Returns `true` if the SQL Integrity Enhancement Facility is supported.
`storesLowerCaseIdentifiers`	Returns `true` if the database treats mixed-case unquoted SQL identifiers as case insensitive and stores them in lower case.
`storesLowerCaseQuotedIdentifiers`	Returns `true` if the database treats mixed-case quoted SQL identifiers as case insensitive and stores them in lower case.

continued

TABLE 13.3 continued

Method Name	*Description*
`storesMixedCaseIdentifiers`	Returns `true` if the database treats mixed-case unquoted SQL identifiers as case insensitive and stores them in mixed case.
`supportsMultipleTransactions`	Returns `true` if multiple transactions are allowed.
`supportsOrderUnrelated`	Returns `true` if an "ORDER BY" clause can use columns not in the select.
`supportsOuterJoin`	Returns `true` if some form of outer join is supported.
`supportsPositionDelete`	Returns `true` if positioned DELETE supported.
`supportsPositionUpdate`	Returns `true` if positioned UPDATE is supported.
`supportsResultSetType(int type)`	Returns `true` if the given type is supported in the result set. (JDBC 2)
`supportsResultSetConcurrency(int type, int concurrency)`	Returns `true` if the database supports the concurrency type in combination with the given result set type. (JDBC 2)
`supportsUnion`	Returns `true` if SQL UNION is supported.
`supportsUnionALL`	Returns `true` if SQL UNION ALL is supported.
`useLocalFiles`	Returns `true` if the database stores tables in a local file.
`useLocalFilesPerTable`	Returns `true` if the database uses a file for each table.

Column Name	*Value*
`TABLE_CAT`	A `String` object for the table catalog.
`TABLE_SCHEM`	A `String` object for the table schema.
`TABLE_NAME`	A `String` object for the table name.
`TABLE_TYPE`	A `String` object for the table type.
`REMARKS`	A `String` object describing the table.

You can now print the table name using the following loop:

```
while (rsTables.next())
  System.out.println(rsTables.getString("TABLE_NAME"));
```

TABLE 13.4 Some Methods for Getting Database Objects in the `DatabaseMetaData` Interface

Method Name	*Parameter*	*Description*
`getCatalogs`	`()`	Gets catalog names in this database.

`getColumns`	`(String catalog,`
	`String schemaPattern,`
	`String tableNamePattern,`
	`String columnNamePattern)`
		Gets a description of columns.

`getColumnPrivileges`	`(String catalog,`
	`String schemaPattern,`
	`String tableNamePattern,`
	`String columnNamePattern)`
		Gets a description of the access rights of a table's columns.

`getExportedKeys`	`(String catalog,`
	`String schema,`
	`String table)`
		Gets a description of the primary key columns that are referenced by a table's foreign key columns.

`getImportedKeys`	`(String catalog,`
	`String schema,`
	`String table)`
		Gets a description of the primary key columns referenced by a table's foreign key columns.

`getIndexInfo`	`(String catalog,`
	`String schema,`
	`String table,`
	`boolean unique,`
	`boolean approximate)`
		Gets a description of a table's indices and statistics.

`getPrimaryKeys`	`(String catalog,`
	`String schema,`
	`String table)`
		Gets the primary key in a table.

`getProcedures`	`(String catalog,`
	`String schemaPattern,`
	`String procedureNamePattern)`
		Gets a description of stored procedures.

`getProcedureColumns`	`(String catalog,`
	`String schemaPattern,`
	`String procedureNamePattern,`
	`String columnNamePattern)`
		Gets a description of a catalog's stored procedure parameters and result columns.

continued

Retrieving Column Names

To find all the column names for a specified table, use the `getColumns` method. For example, you can use the following method to obtain all the columns in the table Address.

TABLE 13.4 continued

Method Name	*Parameter*	*Description*
`getSchemas`	`()`	Gets all the schemas in this database.
`getTables`	`(String catalog, String schemaPattern String tableNamePattern, String[] tableTypes)`	Gets a description of tables.
`getTableTypes`	`()`	Gets table types available in the database. Typical types are "TABLE," "VIEW," "SYSTEM TABLE," "GLOBAL TEMPORARY," "LOCAL TEMPORARY," "ALIAS," and "SYNONYM."
`getTablePrivileges`	`(String catalog, String schemaPattern, String tableNamePattern)`	Gets a description of the access rights for each table available in a catalog.

```
ResultSet rsColumns = dbMetaData.getTables(null, null,
  "Address", null);
```

The parameters of the `getColumns` are `catalog` (`String`), `schemaPattern` (`String`), `tableNamePattern` (`String`), and `tableTypes`. The arguments for `catalog`, `schemaPattern`, and `tableTypes` are null in the statement, so all the column names in the table Address are returned with or without a catalog or a schema. The returned column information is in the `ResultSet`, which contains 18 columns. The columns shown below are often used:

Column Name	*Value*
TABLE_CAT	A `String` object for the table catalog.
TABLE_SCHEM	A `String` object for the schema of the table that contains the column.
TABLE_NAME	A `String` object for the table name that contains the column.
COLUMN_NAME	A `String` object for the column name.
TYPE_NAME	A `String` object specifying the SQL type for the column.
COLUMN_SIZE	The maximum size of characters in the case of character or date types, or the precision of NUMERIC OR DECIMAL types.

TABLE 13.5 Methods in the `ResultSetMetaData` Interface

Method Name	*Description*
`getCatalogName(int column)`	Gets the catalog name of the table of the column.
`getColumnClassName(int column)` `(int column)`	Gets the class name (a string) of the column.
`getColumnCount()`	Gets the number of columns in the ResultSet.
`getColumnDisplaySize(int column)`	Gets the column's maximum width in characters.
`getColumnLabel(int column)`	Gets the column's title for use in printouts and displays.
`getColumnName(int column)`	Gets the column's name.
`getColumnType(int column)`	Gets the column's type in int, listed in `java.sql.Types.`
`getColumnTypeName(int column)`	Gets the column's type in `String`.
`getPrecision(int column)`	Gets the column's decimal precision.
`getScale(int column)`	Gets the column's number of digits to right of the decimal point.
`getSchemaName(int column)`	Gets the schema name of the table of the column.
`getTableName(int column)`	Gets the table name of the column.
`isAutoIncrement(int column)`	Is the column automatically numbered, thus read-only?
`isCaseSensitive(int column)`	Is the column case-sensitive?
`isCashValue(int column)`	Is the column a monetary value?
`isDefinitelyWritable(int column)`	Will a write on the column definitely succeed?
`isNullable(int column)`	Does the column accept null?
`isReadOnly(int column)`	Is the column read-only?
`isSearchable(int column)`	Can the column be used in a where clause?
`isSigned(int column)`	Is the column a signed number?
`isWritable(int column)`	Is it possible for a write on the column to succeed?

You can now print all the columns and their information:

```
// Get column count
int columnCount = rsColumns.getMetaData().getColumnCount();

// Store rows to rowData
while (rsColumns.next()) {
  for (int i=0; i<columnCount; i++) {
    System.out.print(rsColumns.getObject(i+1) + " ");
    System.out.println();
  }
```

The *ResultSetMetaData* Interface

The `ResultSetMetaData` interface describes information pertaining to the result set. A `ResultSetMetaData` object can be used to find out about the types and properties of the columns in a `ResultSet`. The methods in `ResultSetMetaData` have a single `int` parameter representing the column, except that the `getColumnCount` method has no parameters. All these methods return `int`, `boolean`, or `String`. The `ResultSetMetaData` interface has fewer methods than the `DatabaseMetaData` interface. Table 13.5 lists all the methods defined in `ResultSetMetaData`.

For more detailed information about the methods defined in the `DatabaseMetaData` and `ResultSetMetaDate` interfaces, please consult the JDBC API documentation.

NOTE

A `SQLException` will be thrown if a driver does not support a metadata method. In the case of methods that return a `ResultSet`, either a `ResultSet` (which may be empty) is returned or a `SQLException` is thrown.

Example 13.1 Exploring Databases

In this example, you will develop a useful utility to discover database information. A sample run of the utility is shown in Figure 13.1. The utility contains the Connection menu with the Connect to Database command. Clicking this command displays a dialog box, as shown in Figure 13.2, which lets you specify a database to connect. Once a database is connected, its structural information is displayed in a tree. You can navigate the database, the table types, tables, and columns from the tree. The metadata for the database, tables, and the columns are displayed in the content pane.

The utility consists of four classes: `DBExplorer` (see Listing 13.1), `DBConnectDialog` (created in Example 12.4, "Creating a Connection Dialog Component"), `DBInfoPanel` (see Listing 13.2), and `TableInfoPanel` (see Listing 13.3). `DBExplorer` displays the main interface with the menu, a split pane, and a status label. The split pane holds a tree on the left and a content pane on the right. The status label displays the database-connection information. `DBConnectDialog` is a subclass of `JDialog` for gathering the connection information of the database and establishing connections. Once a database is connected, its URL is displayed as the root of the tree. The table types are the children of root, the tables are the children of the table types, and the columns are the children of the tables.

When you select the root, an instance of `DBInfoPanel` with the connection for the database is placed in the right section of the split pane. The `DBInfoPanel` class contains five tabs: General, Capabilities, Functions, Data Types, and Table Types.

continued

Example 13.1 continued

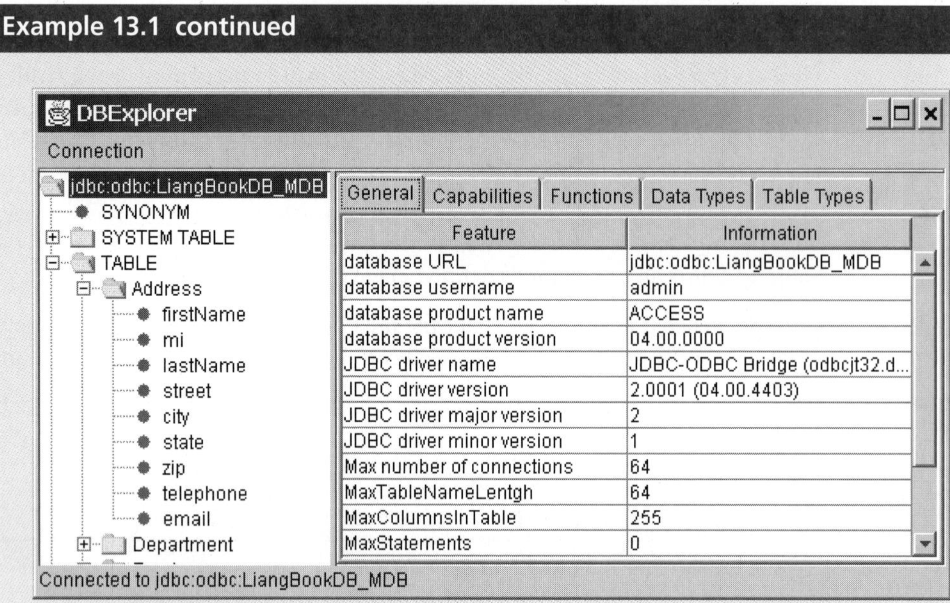

Figure 13.1 *The DBExplorer utility explores database information.*

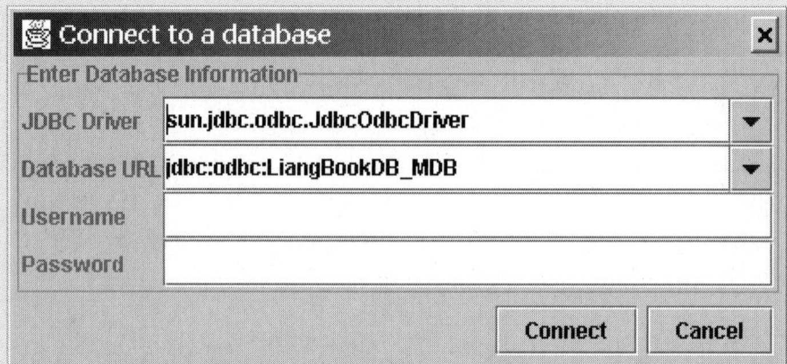

Figure 13.2 *You can specify a database to connect in the Database Connect dialog box.*

- The General tab uses the `showGeneralInfo()` method to show general information about the database, such as the database URL, current user name, and the JDBC driver name (see Figure 13.1).
- The Capabilities tab uses the `showCapability()` method to show the database capabilities, such as whether the database uses local files, uses local file per table, supports group by, and so on (see Figure 13.3).
- The Functions tab uses the `showFunctions()` method to show the standard functions supported by the database (see Figure 13.4).
- The Data Types tab uses the `showDataTypes()` method to show the data types supported by the database (see Figure 13.5).

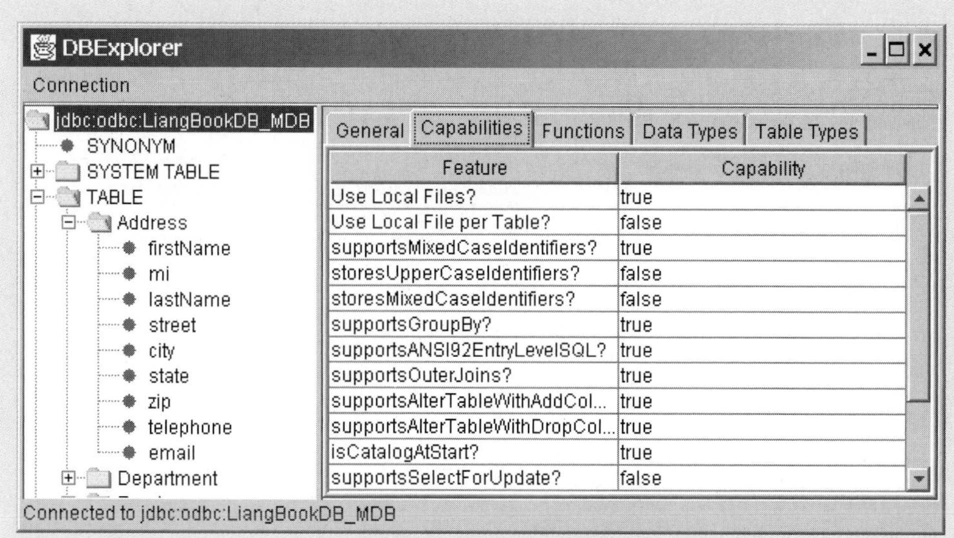

Figure 13.3 *You can choose a table name and show its primary key, its column definition, and its contents in the Extract Table Metadata dialog box.*

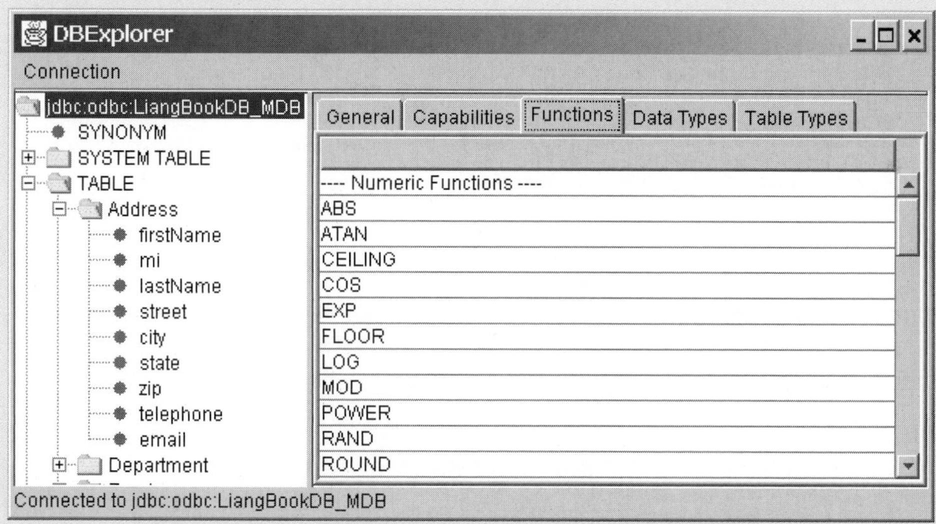

Figure 13.4 *The Functions tab displays the functions supported in the database.*

- The Table Types tab uses the `showTableTypes()` method to show the table types supported by the database (see Figure 13.6).

When you select a table, an instance of `TableInfoPanel` is placed in the right section of the split pane. You need to set connection and table name in this instance in order to display the table data and table definition. The `TableInfoPanel` class contains two tabs: Data and Definition.

continued

Example 13.1 continued

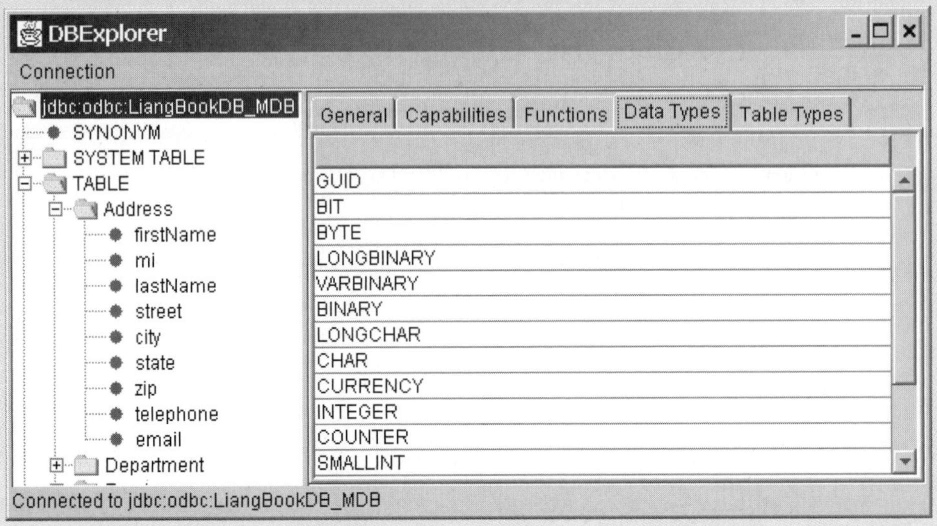

Figure 13.5 *The Data Types tab displays the data types supported in the database.*

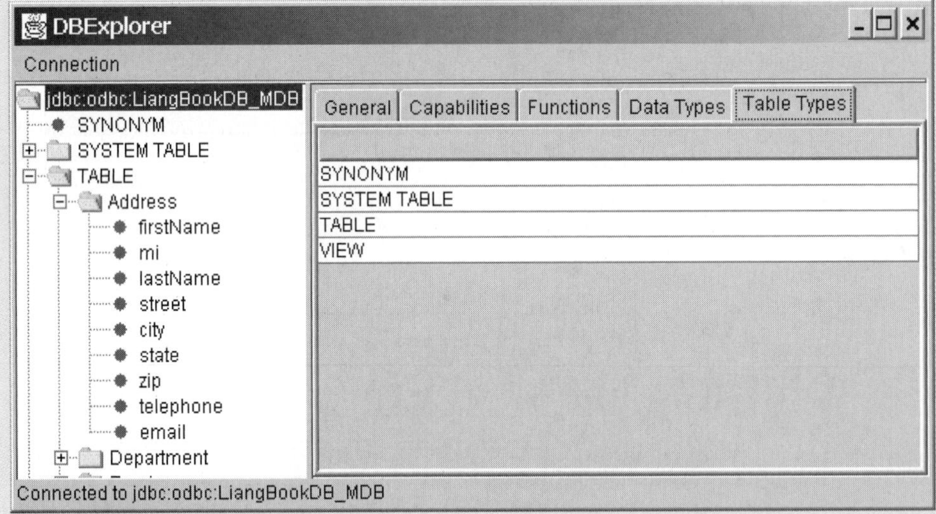

Figure 13.6 *The Table Types tab displays the table types available in the database.*

- The Data tab uses the `showData()` method to display the table data (see Figure 13.7).
- The Definition tab uses the `showTableDef()` method to display the column name, column name type, and column size (see Figure 13.8).

Here are the steps to complete the project.

1. In the jdbcdemo.jpr project, create an applet named `DBExplorer` using the Applet wizard, create a JavaBeans component named `DBInfoPanel` that ex-

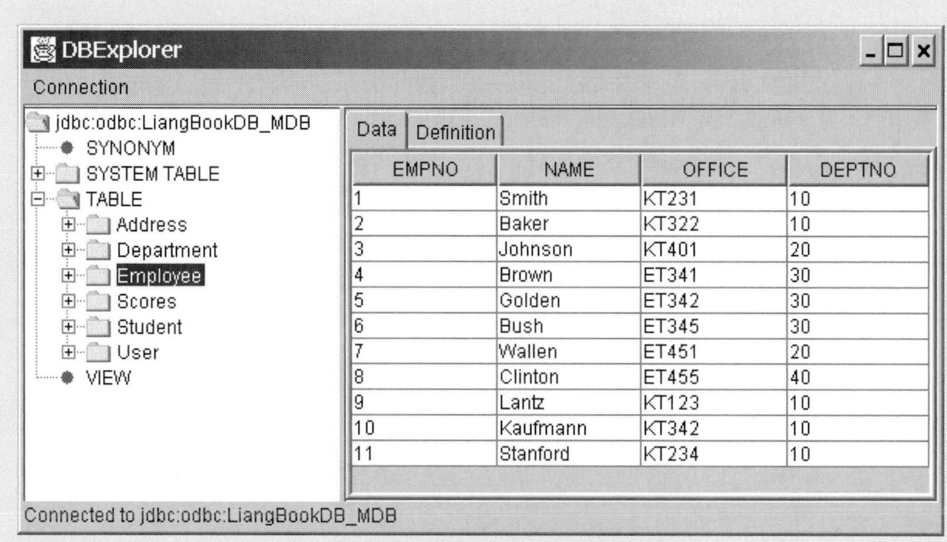

Figure 13.7 *The Data tab displays the contents for the specified table.*

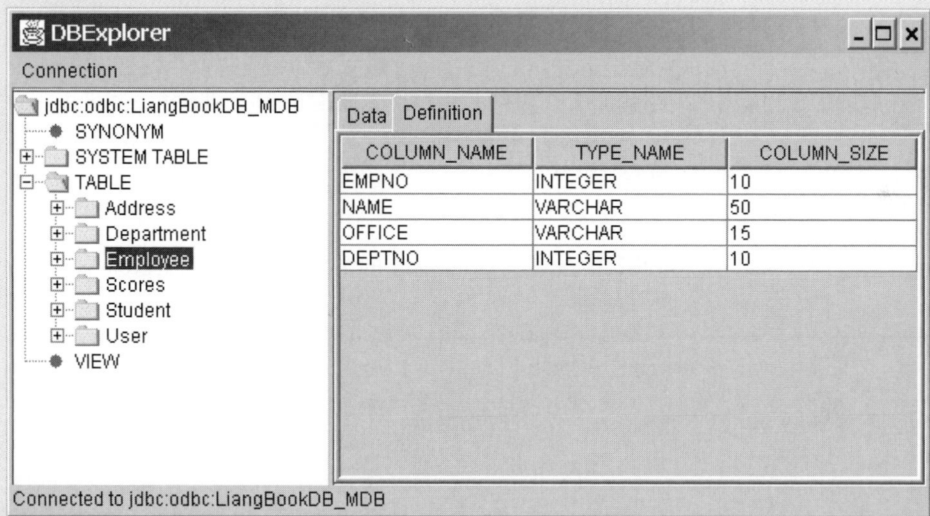

Figure 13.8 *The Definition tab displays column name, type, and size for the specified table.*

tends `JPanel`, and create a JavaBeans component named `TableInfoPanel` that extends `JPanel` using the JavaBeans wizard in the Object Gallery.

2. Build `DBExplorer` as follows:

   2.1. With DBExplorer.java selected in the project pane, switch to the UI designer. Drop a `JSplitPane` from the Swing Containers page to the center of the applet (this) to create `jSplitPane1`. Drop a `JTree` to the left of `jSplitPane1`. Drop a `JLabel` to the south of the applet to create `jlblStatus`.

continued

Example 13.1 continued

2.2. Drop a `JMenuBar` from the Swing Containers page to the UI to create `jMenuBar1`. Double-click `jMenuBar1` to switch to the Menu designer. Add a menu labeled Connection with two menu items "Connect to Database" and "Exit," and add a separator between them. Rename the menu item components to `jmiConnect` and `jmiExit`.

2.3. Set the `JMenuBar` property of the applet to `jMenuBar1`.

2.4. Install `DBConnectDialog` (created in Example 12.4) in the component palette, and drop a `DBConnectDialog` to the UI node in the applet to create `dBConnectDialog1`. Set its `modal` property to True.

2.5. Generate and implement the code for handling the action events for menu items (Connect to Database and Exit), as shown in Listing 13.1 (Lines 83–102).

2.6. Implement the `updateTree()` method to build the tree, as shown in Listing 13.1 (Lines 104–137).

2.7. Install DBInfoPanel and DBTablePanel into the component palette and drop them to the UI node of the structure pane of the applet to create `dBInfoPanel1` and `tableContentPanel1`. Generate the `valueChanged` handler in `jTree1`, and implement the `jTree1_valueChanged` method to handle the selection event for the root and the table nodes, as shown in Listing 13.1 (Lines 139–163).

3. Build `DBInfoPanel` as follows:

3.1. With DBInfoPanel.java selected in the project pane, switch to UI designer. Drop a `JTabbedPane` to the center of the panel, and drop a `JScrollPane` five times into the tabbed pane. Set the constraints property of the scroll panes to General, Capabilities, Functions, Data Types, and Table Types. Drop a `JTable` to each scroll pane to create `jTable1`, `jTable2`, `jTable3`, `jTable4`, and `jTable5`.

3.2. Declare five default table models named `model1`, `model2`, `model3`, `model4`, and `model5`, and set them in the `model` property for each table, as shown in Listing 13.2 (Lines 25–30).

3.3. Click the Bean tab in the content pane to switch to BeansExpress. In the Properties page, add property named `connection` with type `java.sql.Connection` with a set method. Implement the `setConnection` method to invoke the method `showMetaData`, which then invokes the methods `showGeneralInfo`, `showCapability`, `showFunctions`, `showDataTypes`, and `showTableTypes` to fill in database metadata information in the appropriate tables, as shown in Listing 13.2.

4. Build `TableInfoPanel` as follows:

   4.1. With TableInfoPanel.java selected in the project pane, switch to UI designer. Drop a `JTabbedPane` to the center of the panel, and drop a `JScrollPane` two times into the tabbed pane. Set the constraints property of the scroll panes to Data and Definition. Drop a `JTable` to each scroll pane to create `jTable1` and `jTable2`.

   4.2. Declare two default table models named `model1` and `model2`, and set them in the `model` property for each table, as shown in Listing 13.3 (Lines 17–19).

   4.3. Implement the `setConnectionAndTable` method to set a database connection and a table name in `TableInfoPanel` (Lines 44–50).

   4.4. Choose the Bean tab in the content pane to switch to BeansExpress. In the Properties page, add property named `connection` with type `java.sql.Connection` with a set method. Implement the `setConnection` method to invoke the methods `ShowData` and `showTableDef` to fill in database metadata information into appropriate tables, as shown in Listing 13.2 (Lines 52–125).

```
package jdbcdemo;

import java.awt.*;
import java.awt.event.*;
import javax.swing.*;
import javax.swing.tree.*;
import javax.swing.event.*;
import java.sql.*;

public class DBExplorer extends JApplet {
  // Create tree root
  DefaultMutableTreeNode root = new DefaultMutableTreeNode(
    "No database connected");

  // Create the tree model
  DefaultTreeModel treeModel = new DefaultTreeModel(root);

  // Database connection and meta data for the connection
  Connection connection;
  DatabaseMetaData dbMetaData;

  boolean isStandalone = false;
  JTree jTree1 = new JTree();
  JSplitPane jSplitPane1 = new JSplitPane();
  JLabel jlblStatus = new JLabel();
  JMenuBar jMenuBar1 = new JMenuBar();
  JMenu jMenu1 = new JMenu();
  JMenuItem jmiConnect = new JMenuItem();
  JMenuItem jmiExit = new JMenuItem();
  DBConnectDialog dBConnectDialog1 = new DBConnectDialog();
```

Listing 13.1 *DBExplorer.java*

continued

Example 13.1 continued

```
  DBInfoPanel dBInfoPanel1 = new DBInfoPanel();
  TableInfoPanel tableContentPanel1 = new TableInfoPanel();

  /** Initialize the applet */
  public void init() {
    try {
      jbInit();
    }
    catch (Exception e) {
      e.printStackTrace();
    }
  }

  /** Component initialization */
  private void jbInit() throws Exception {
    this.setJMenuBar(jMenuBar1);
    this.setSize(new Dimension(400,300));
    dBConnectDialog1.setModal(true);
    jlblStatus.setText("Choose Connection, Connect to a Database");

    jMenu1.setText("Connection");
    jmiConnect.setText("Connect to Database");
    jmiConnect.addActionListener(
      new java.awt.event.ActionListener() {
      public void actionPerformed(ActionEvent e) {
        jmiConnect_actionPerformed(e);
      }
    });

    jmiExit.setText("Exit");
    jmiExit.addActionListener(new java.awt.event.ActionListener() {
      public void actionPerformed(ActionEvent e) {
        jmiExit_actionPerformed(e);
      }
    });
    jTree1.setModel(treeModel);
    jTree1.addTreeSelectionListener(
      new javax.swing.event.TreeSelectionListener() {
      public void valueChanged(TreeSelectionEvent e) {
        jTree1_valueChanged(e);
      }
    });
    jSplitPane1.setRightComponent(null);
    this.getContentPane().add(jSplitPane1, BorderLayout.CENTER);
    jSplitPane1.add(jTree1, JSplitPane.LEFT);
    this.getContentPane().add(jlblStatus, BorderLayout.SOUTH);
    jMenuBar1.add(jMenu1);
    jMenu1.add(jmiConnect);
    jMenu1.addSeparator();
    jMenu1.add(jmiExit);
  }

  void jmiConnect_actionPerformed(ActionEvent e) {
    dBConnectDialog1.setVisible(true);

    try {
      connection = dBConnectDialog1.getConnection();
      if (connection != null) {
        dbMetaData = dBConnectDialog1.getConnection().getMetaData();
        jlblStatus.setText("Connected to " + dbMetaData.getURL());
```

Listing 13.1 *Continued*

```
            updateTree();
        jSplitPane1.add(jTree1, JSplitPane.LEFT);
      }
    }
    catch (SQLException ex) {
      jlblStatus.setText(ex.getMessage());
    }
  }

  void jmiExit_actionPerformed(ActionEvent e) {
    System.exit(0);
  }

  private void updateTree() throws SQLException {
    root.setUserObject(dbMetaData.getURL());

    ResultSet rsTableTypes = dbMetaData.getTableTypes();

    while (rsTableTypes.next()) {
      String tableType = rsTableTypes.getString("TABLE_TYPE");

      // Add table names to the tree node under database
      DefaultMutableTreeNode tableTypeNode =
        new DefaultMutableTreeNode(tableType);
      root.add(tableTypeNode);

      ResultSet rsTables = dbMetaData.getTables(null, null, null,
        new String[] {tableType});

      while (rsTables.next()) {
        String tableName = rsTables.getString("TABLE_NAME");
        // Add table names to the tree node under database
        DefaultMutableTreeNode tableNode =
          new DefaultMutableTreeNode(tableName);
        tableTypeNode.add(tableNode);

        ResultSet rsColumns = dbMetaData.getColumns(
          null, null, tableName, null);

        // Add column names to the table
        while (rsColumns.next()) {
          tableNode.add(new DefaultMutableTreeNode
            (rsColumns.getString("COLUMN_NAME")));
        }
      }
    }
  }

  void jTree1_valueChanged(TreeSelectionEvent e) {
    TreePath path = jTree1.getSelectionPath();
    if (path == null) return;

    String tableName = null;

    switch (path.getPathCount()) {
      case 1:
        dBInfoPanel1.setConnection(connection);
        jSplitPane1.setDividerLocation(0.2);
        jSplitPane1.add(dBInfoPanel1, JSplitPane.RIGHT);
        break;
```

Listing 13.1 *Continued*

continued

Example 13.1 continued

```
      case 3:
        tableName = (String)(((DefaultMutableTreeNode)
          (path.getPathComponent(2))).getUserObject());
        tableContentPanel1.setConnectionAndTable(
          connection, tableName);
        jSplitPane1.setDividerLocation(0.2);
        jSplitPane1.add(tableContentPanel1, JSplitPane.RIGHT);
        break;
      default:
        jSplitPane1.remove(dBInfoPanel1);
        jSplitPane1.remove(tableContentPanel1);
    }
  }
}
```

Listing 13.1 *Continued*

```
package jdbcdemo;

import java.awt.*;
import javax.swing.*;
import javax.swing.table.*;
import java.util.*;
import java.sql.*;

public class DBInfoPanel extends JPanel {
  BorderLayout borderLayout1 = new BorderLayout();
  JTabbedPane jTabbedPane1 = new JTabbedPane();
  JScrollPane jScrollPane1 = new JScrollPane();
  JScrollPane jScrollPane2 = new JScrollPane();
  JScrollPane jScrollPane3 = new JScrollPane();
  JScrollPane jScrollPane4 = new JScrollPane();
  JScrollPane jScrollPane5 = new JScrollPane();
  JTable jTable1 = new JTable();
  JTable jTable2 = new JTable();
  JTable jTable3 = new JTable();
  JTable jTable4 = new JTable();
  JTable jTable5 = new JTable();
  private java.sql.Connection connection;
  DatabaseMetaData dbMetaData;

  // Table models for the five tables
  DefaultTableModel model1 = new DefaultTableModel();
  DefaultTableModel model2 = new DefaultTableModel();
  DefaultTableModel model3 = new DefaultTableModel();
  DefaultTableModel model4 = new DefaultTableModel();
  DefaultTableModel model5 = new DefaultTableModel();

  public DBInfoPanel() {
    try {
      jbInit();
    }
    catch(Exception ex) {
      ex.printStackTrace();
    }
  }

```

Listing 13.2 *DBInfoPanel.java*

```
  private void jbInit() throws Exception {
    this.setLayout(borderLayout1);
    jTable1.setModel(model1);
    jTable2.setModel(model2);
    jTable3.setModel(model3);
    jTable4.setModel(model4);
    jTable5.setModel(model5);
    this.add(jTabbedPane1, BorderLayout.CENTER);
    jTabbedPane1.add(jScrollPane1, "General");
    jScrollPane1.getViewport().add(jTable1, null);
    jTabbedPane1.add(jScrollPane2, "Capabilities");
    jScrollPane2.getViewport().add(jTable2, null);
    jTabbedPane1.add(jScrollPane3, "Functions");
    jScrollPane3.getViewport().add(jTable3, null);
    jTabbedPane1.add(jScrollPane4, "Data Types");
    jScrollPane4.getViewport().add(jTable4, null);
    jTabbedPane1.add(jScrollPane5, "Table Types");
    jScrollPane5.getViewport().add(jTable5, null);
  }

  public void setConnection(java.sql.Connection newConnection) {
    connection = newConnection;

    try {
      showMetaData();
    }
    catch (SQLException ex) {
      ex.printStackTrace();
    }
  }

  /** Show database meta data */
  private void showMetaData() throws SQLException {
    dbMetaData = connection.getMetaData();
    showGeneralInfo();
    showCapability();
    showFunctions();
    showDataTypes();
    showTableTypes();
  }

  /** Find general database information */
  private void  showGeneralInfo() throws SQLException {
    Object[][] data = new Object[][] {
      {"database URL", dbMetaData.getURL()},
      {"database username", dbMetaData.getUserName()},
      {"database product name", dbMetaData.getDatabaseProductName()},
      {"database product version", dbMetaData.getDatabaseProductVersion()},
      {"JDBC driver name", dbMetaData.getDriverName()},
      {"JDBC driver version", dbMetaData.getDriverVersion()},
      {"JDBC driver major version",
          new Integer( dbMetaData.getDriverMajorVersion()) },
      {"JDBC driver minor version",
        new Integer(dbMetaData.getDriverMinorVersion())},
      {"Max number of connections",
        new Integer(dbMetaData.getMaxConnections())},
      {"MaxTableNameLength",
        new Integer(dbMetaData.getMaxTableNameLength())},
      {"MaxColumnsInTable",
        new Integer(dbMetaData.getMaxColumnsInTable())},
```

Listing 13.2 *Continued*

continued

Example 13.1 continued

```
      {"MaxStatements",
        new Integer(dbMetaData.getMaxStatements())},
      {"MaxColumnsInSelect",
        new Integer(dbMetaData.getMaxColumnsInSelect())},
      {"getSchemaTerm", dbMetaData.getSchemaTerm()},
      {"getProcedureTerm", dbMetaData.getProcedureTerm()},
      {"getCatalogTerm", dbMetaData.getCatalogTerm()}};

    Object[] columnNames = new Object[]{"Feature", "Information"};

    // Set new data to the table model
    model1.setDataVector(data, columnNames);
  }

  /** Find database capability */
  private void showCapability() throws SQLException {
    Object[][] data2 = new Object[][] {
      {"Use Local Files?",
        new Boolean(dbMetaData.usesLocalFiles())},
      {"Use Local File per Table?",
        new Boolean(dbMetaData.usesLocalFilePerTable())},
      {"supportsMixedCaseIdentifiers?",
        new Boolean(dbMetaData.supportsMixedCaseIdentifiers())},
      {"storesUpperCaseIdentifiers?",
        new Boolean(dbMetaData.storesUpperCaseIdentifiers())},
      {"storesMixedCaseIdentifiers?",
        new Boolean(dbMetaData.storesMixedCaseIdentifiers())},
      {"supportsGroupBy?",
        new Boolean(dbMetaData.supportsGroupBy())},
      {"supportsANSI92EntryLevelSQL?",
        new Boolean(dbMetaData.supportsANSI92EntryLevelSQL())},
      {"supportsOuterJoins?",
        new Boolean(dbMetaData.supportsOuterJoins())},
      {"supportsAlterTableWithAddColumn?",
        new Boolean(dbMetaData.supportsAlterTableWithAddColumn())},
      {"supportsAlterTableWithDropColumn?",
        new Boolean(dbMetaData.supportsAlterTableWithDropColumn())},
      {"isCatalogAtStart?",
        new Boolean(dbMetaData.isCatalogAtStart())},
      {"supportsSelectForUpdate?",
        new Boolean(dbMetaData.supportsSelectForUpdate())},
      {"supportsStoredProcedures?",
        new Boolean(dbMetaData.supportsStoredProcedures())},
      {"supportsUnion?",
        new Boolean(dbMetaData.supportsUnion())},
      {"supportsTransactions?",
        new Boolean(dbMetaData.supportsTransactions())},
      {"supportsDataDefinitionAndDataManipulationTransactions? ",
        new Boolean(dbMetaData.
          supportsDataDefinitionAndDataManipulationTransactions())}};

    Object[] columnNames2 = new Object[]{"Feature", "Capability"};
    model2.setDataVector(data2, columnNames2);
  }

  /** Find functions available in the database */
  private void showFunctions() throws SQLException {
    model3.setColumnCount(1); // Set column count
    jTable3.removeAll(); // Clear the table

```

Listing 13.2 *Continued*

```
    model3.setColumnIdentifiers(new Object[]{" "}); // No column name
    model3.addRow(new Object[]{"-- Numeric Functions --"});
    addFunctions(dbMetaData.getNumericFunctions());
    model3.addRow(new Object[]{" "});
    model3.addRow(new Object[]{"-- String Functions --"});
    addFunctions(dbMetaData.getStringFunctions());
    model3.addRow(new Object[]{" "});
    model3.addRow(new Object[]{"-- System Functions --"});
    addFunctions(dbMetaData.getSystemFunctions());
    model3.addRow(new Object[]{" "});
    model3.addRow(new Object[]{"-- Date and Time Functions --"});
    addFunctions(dbMetaData.getTimeDateFunctions());
  }

  private void addFunctions(String s) {
    StringTokenizer st = new StringTokenizer(s, ",");

    while (st.hasMoreTokens())
      model3.addRow(new Object[]{st.nextToken()});
  }

  /** Show available data types */
  private void showDataTypes() throws SQLException {
    model4.setColumnCount(1); // Set column count
    model4.setColumnIdentifiers(new Object[]{" "}); // No column name

    jTable4.removeAll(); // Clear the table

    ResultSet rs = dbMetaData.getTypeInfo();
    while (rs.next())
      model4.addRow(new Object[]{rs.getString("TYPE_NAME")});
  }

  /** Show available table types */
  private void showTableTypes() throws SQLException {
    model5.setColumnCount(1); // Set column count
    model5.setColumnIdentifiers(new Object[]{" "}); // No column name

    jTable5.removeAll(); // Clear the table

    ResultSet rs = dbMetaData.getTableTypes();
    while (rs.next())
      model5.addRow(new Object[]{rs.getString("TABLE_TYPE")});
  }
}
```

Listing 13.2 *Continued*

```
package jdbcdemo;

import java.awt.*;
import javax.swing.*;
import java.sql.*;
import java.util.*;
import javax.swing.table.*;

public class TableInfoPanel extends JPanel {
  BorderLayout borderLayout1 = new BorderLayout();
  JTabbedPane jTabbedPane1 = new JTabbedPane();
```

Listing 13.3 *TableInfoPanel.java*

continued

Example 13.1 continued

```
  JScrollPane jScrollPane1 = new JScrollPane();
  JScrollPane jScrollPane2 = new JScrollPane();
  JTable jTable1 = new JTable();
  JTable jTable2 = new JTable();

  // Create data model for jtbData and jtbDef
  DefaultTableModel model1 = new DefaultTableModel();
  DefaultTableModel model2 = new DefaultTableModel();

  private java.sql.Connection connection;
  private String tableName;

  public TableInfoPanel() {
    try {
      jbInit();
    }
    catch(Exception ex) {
      ex.printStackTrace();
    }
  }

  private void jbInit() throws Exception {
    this.setLayout(borderLayout1);
    jTable1.setModel(model1);
    jTable2.setModel(model2);
    this.add(jTabbedPane1, BorderLayout.CENTER);
    jTabbedPane1.add(jScrollPane1, "Data");
    jScrollPane1.getViewport().add(jTable1, null);
    jTabbedPane1.add(jScrollPane2, "Definition");
    jScrollPane2.getViewport().add(jTable2, null);
  }

  public void setConnectionAndTable(Connection newConnection,
    String newTableName) {
    connection = newConnection;
    tableName = newTableName;
    showData();
    showTableDef();
  }

  private void showData() {
    try {
      Statement statement = connection.createStatement();

      // Vector to store rows
      Vector rowData = new Vector();

      ResultSet rs = statement.executeQuery(
        "select * from " + tableName + ";");

      // Get column count
      int columnCount = rs.getMetaData().getColumnCount();

      // Store rows to rowData
      while (rs.next()) {
        Vector singleRow = new Vector();
        for (int i=0; i<columnCount; i++)
          // Store cells to a row
          singleRow.addElement(rs.getObject(i+1));
```

Listing 13.3 *Continued*

```
          rowData.addElement(singleRow);
        }

        // Vector to store column names
        Vector columnNames = new Vector();

        // Column name result set
        ResultSet rsColumns = connection.getMetaData().getColumns(
          null, null, tableName, null);

        // Add column names to the table
        while (rsColumns.next()) {
          columnNames.addElement(rsColumns.getString("COLUMN_NAME"));
        }

        // Set new data to the table model
        model1.setDataVector(rowData, columnNames);
      }
      catch (Exception ex) {
        ex.printStackTrace();
      }
    }

    private void showTableDef() {
      try {
        // Vector to store rows
        Vector rowData = new Vector();

        // Column name result set
        ResultSet rsColumns = connection.getMetaData().getColumns(
          null, null, tableName, null);

        // Store rows to rowData
        while (rsColumns.next()) {
          Vector singleRow = new Vector();
          // Store cells to a row
          singleRow.addElement(rsColumns.getObject("COLUMN_NAME"));
          singleRow.addElement(rsColumns.getObject("TYPE_NAME"));
          singleRow.addElement(rsColumns.getObject("COLUMN_SIZE"));
          rowData.addElement(singleRow);
        }

        // Vector to store column names
        Vector columnNames = new Vector();
        columnNames.addElement("COLUMN_NAME");
        columnNames.addElement("TYPE_NAME");
        columnNames.addElement("COLUMN_SIZE");

        // Set new data to the table model
        model2.setDataVector(rowData, columnNames);
      }
      catch (Exception ex) {
        ex.printStackTrace();
      }
    }
  }
```

Listing 13.3 *Continued*

continued

Example 13.1 continued

Example Review

The variable `connection` encapsulates all the work in the `DBConnectDialog` class. An instance of `DBConnectDialog` is created in `DBExplorer`, and the dialog box is displayed when the Connect to Database menu command is issued. The program attempts to establish a connection when the OK button is clicked in the dialog box. This variable is non-null if a connection to the database is established. The classes `DBConnectDialog`, `DBExplorer`, `DBInfoPanel`, and `TableInfoPanel` are related through the `connection` variable.

Once connected, the database structural information is displayed in the tree. The `updateTree()` method in `DBExplorer` builds the tree. The database URL is shown as the root. The second level of the tree contains the table types supported by the database. The third level of the tree displays the tables. The fourth level of the tree displays the columns of the tables.

Each node is an instance of `DefaultMutableTreeNode`. When you select a tree node, a `TreeSelectionEvent` occurs. The `jTree1_valueChanged` handler responds to the selection of a node. How do you know whether a root or a table node is selected? The solution is to get the selected path and use the `getPathCount` method of the path to determine the level of the selected node. If the root is selected, the `getPathCount()` method returns 1. If a table node is selected, the `getPathCount()` method returns 3.

When the root is selected, an instance of `DBInfoPanel` is placed into the right section of `jSplitPane1` after setting the database connection in the instance. When a table node is selected, the table name is retrieved through the `getPathComponent` method on the path. The table name and the database connection are set to the instance of `DBInfoPanel`, which is then placed into the right section of `jSplitPane1`. If a selected node is not the root or a table node, the content displayed in the split pane is removed.

The `setConnectionAndTable` method in the `TableInfoPanel` class sets a database connection and a table name. You could break this into two methods, one to set the connection, and the other to set the table name. However, the combined method is more appropriate because table data and definition cannot be obtained until both the connection property and the table name property are set.

Processing Statements

Once a connection to a particular database is established, it can be used to send SQL statements from your program to the database. JDBC provides the `Statement`, `PreparedStatement`, and `CallableStatement` interfaces to facilitate sending statements to a database for execution and receiving execution results from the database, as shown in Figure 13.9.

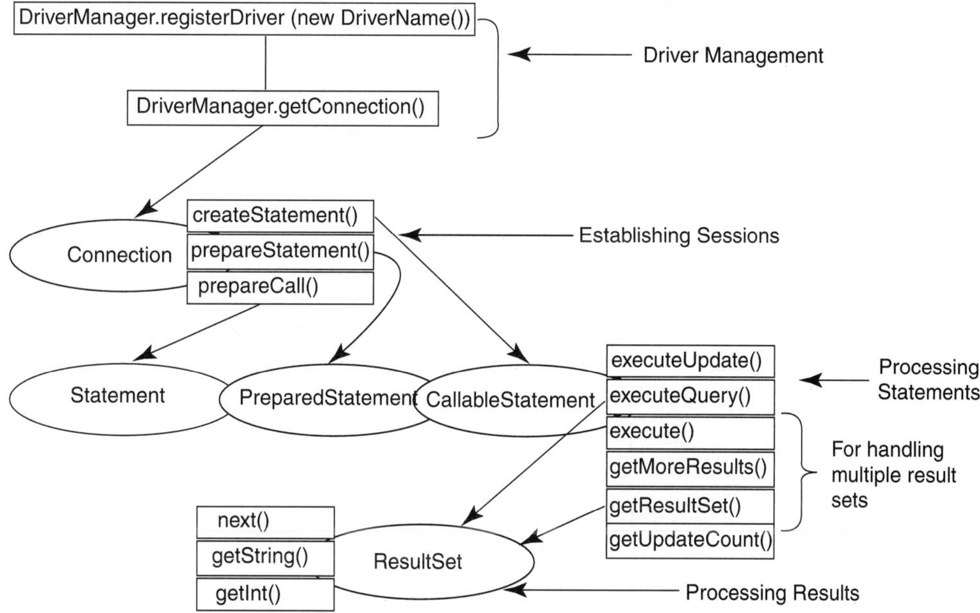

Figure 13.9 *JDBC classes enable Java programs to connect to the database, send SQL statements, and process results.*

The `Statement` interface is used to execute static SQL statements that contain no parameters. The `PreparedStatement`, extending `Statement`, is used to execute a precompiled SQL statement with or without IN parameters. The `CallableStatement`, extending `PreparedStatement`, is used to execute a call to a database-stored procedure.

If a `Connection` object can be envisioned as a cable linking your program to a database, an object of `Statement` or its subclass can be viewed as a cart that takes the SQL statements for execution by the database and brings the result back to the program. A `Statement` object is created using the `createStatement()` method in the `Connection` interface. For example, the following code creates a `Statement stmt` on a particular `Connection connection`.

```
Connection connection = DriverManager.getConnection
  ("jdbc:odbc:LiangBookDB_MDB", "", "" );
Statement stmt = connection.createStatement();
```

The `Statement` interface provides many methods listed in Table 13.6 to execute various types of SQL statements, getting execution results and information, and controlling the executions.

The *execute, executeQuery,* and *executeUpdate* Methods

The methods for executing SQL statements are `execute`, `executeQuery`, and `executeUpdate`, each of which accepts a string containing a SQL statement as an argument. This string is passed to the database for execution. The `execute` method

TABLE 13.6 `Statement` Methods

Method Name	*Description*
`void addBatch(String sql)`	Adds a SQL command to the current batch of commands for the statement. (JDBC 2)
`void cancel()`	Called by one thread to cancel a statement being executed by another thread.
`void clearBatch()`	Clears the current batch of commands for the statement. (JDBC 2)
`void clearWarnings()`	Clears the warnings for the current SQL statement.
`void close()`	Closes the statement for immediately releasing the associated resource.
`boolean execute(String sql)`	Executes a SQL statement that may return multiple result sets.
`int[] executeBatch()`	Executes all the SQL commands in the current batch for the statement. (JDBC 2)
`ResultSet executeQuery(String sql)`	Executes a SQL statement that returns a single result set.
`int executeUpdate(String sql)`	Executes a SQL INSERT, UPDATE, DELETE, or SQL DDL statement.
`Connection getConnection()`	Gets the connection object that produced this `Statement` object. (JDBC 2)
`int getFetchDirection()`	Gets the direction for fetching rows in a table. (JDBC 2)
`int getFetchSize()`	Gets the number of the rows to be fetched. (JDBC 2)
`int getMaxFieldSize()`	Gest a maximum size for all the columns a result set can have.
`int getMaxRows()`	Gets the maximum numbers of rows a result set can contain.

continued

should be used if the execution produces multiple result sets, multiple update counts, or a combination of result sets and update counts. The `executeQuery` method should be used if the execution produces a single result set, such as the SQL select statement. The `executeUpdate` method should be used if the statement results in a single update count or no update count, such as a SQL INSERT, DELETE, UPDATE, or DDL statement.

TABLE 13.6 continued

Method Name	*Description*
`boolean getMoreResults()`	Moves to the next result set. Used for SQL statements that return multiple results.
`int getQueryTimeout()`	Gets the number of seconds the driver will wait for a statement to execute.
`ResultSet getResultSet()`	Returns a `ResultSet` for the current result.
`int getResultSetConcurrency()`	Returns the result set concurrency. (JDBC 2)
`int getResultSetType()`	Returns the result set type. (JDBC 2)
`int getUpdateCount()`	Returns current result as an update count.
	Used for SQL INSERT, UPDATE, and DELETE statements.
`SQLWarning getWarnings()`	Returns a `SQLWarning` for the current statement.
`void setCursorName(String name)`	Sets the cursor name for subsequent use in SQL positioned update/delete statements.
`void setEscapeProcessing(boolean enable)`	Sets true or false on escape processing for the statement.
`void setFetchDirection(int direction)`	Sets the number of the rows to be fetched. (JDBC 2)
`void setFetchSize(int rows)`	Sets the number of the rows to be fetched. (JDBC 2)
`void setMaxFieldSize(int max)`	Sets the maximum size for a column in a result set.
`void setMaxRows(int max)`	Sets the maximum number of rows in a result set.
`void setQueryTimeout(int seconds)`	Sets the maximum time for a driver to wait for a statement to execute.

The `executeQuery` method returns a `ResultSet` object. The `executeUpdate` returns an update count, that is, an `int` value for the number of rows affected by the SQL statements. This value is the number of rows inserted, deleted, or updated for successful execution of a SQL INSERT, DELETE, or UPDATE statement. This value is 0 for a SQL DDL statement.

The `execute` method returns a `boolean` value. The value is `true` if the first result is a `ResultSet`, false if it returns an update count or there are no more results. The `getResultSet()` and `getUpdateCount()` are called to process the result produced by the `execute` method. The `getResultSet()` method is used to get the current result set. If the current result is an update count, or there are no more results, `getResultSet()` returns `null`. The `getUpdateCount()` method returns the current result as an update count; if the result is a `ResultSet` or there are no more results, -1 is returned. When `getUpdateCount()` returns -1, this means that the result is a `ResultSet` or that there are no more results. To determine what -1 really means, you can call `getResultSet()`. If `getResultSet()` returns `null` and `getUpdateCount()` returns -1, there are no more results.

After the current result, whether a `ResultSet` or an update count, you need to call `getMoreResults()` to move to a statement's next result. This method returns a `boolean` value, which returns `true` if the result is a `ResultSet`; `false` if it is an update count or there are no more results. If `getMoreResults()` returns `false` and `getUpdateCount()` returns -1, there are no more results.

Example 13.2 Using Statement to Execute Static SQL Statements

In this example, you will write a program to create an address book for viewing addresses and inserting new addresses. The addresses are stored in an Address table consisting of the following fields: firstName, mi, lastName, street, city, state, zip, telephone, and email, defined in the following statement:

```
create table Address
(
  firstname varchar(25),
  mi char(1),
  lastname varchar(25),
  street varchar(40),
  city varchar(20),
  state varchar(2),
  zip varchar(5),
  telephone varchar(10),
  email varchar(30)
)
```

The program contains two menus: File and Operation. The File menu contains menu items "Connect to Database" and "Exit," as shown in Figure 13.10. The Operation menu contains a single menu item, "Using Static SQL Statements." Choosing "Connect to Database" brings up a dialog box, as shown in Figure 13.2, to let you connect to a database. After your program is connected to the database, you may choose "Using Static SQL Statements" to view and insert an address, as shown in Figure 13.11. To view an address, enter the first name and the last name, then click the Search button. The Insert button inserts a new address in the database. The Clear button clears all the fields.

The project can be divided into two steps: creating the applet with menus, and creating the panel for processing the address. The panel is placed onto the applet when the "Using Static SQL Statements" menu is selected after connecting to a particular database.

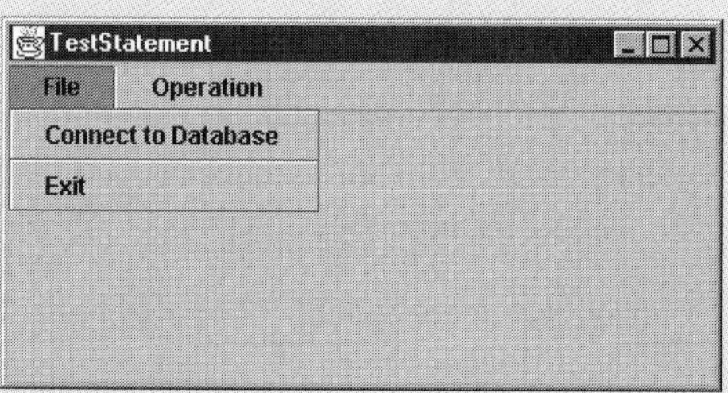

Figure 13.10 *You may connect to a JDBC-compliant database and test static SQL statements in this program.*

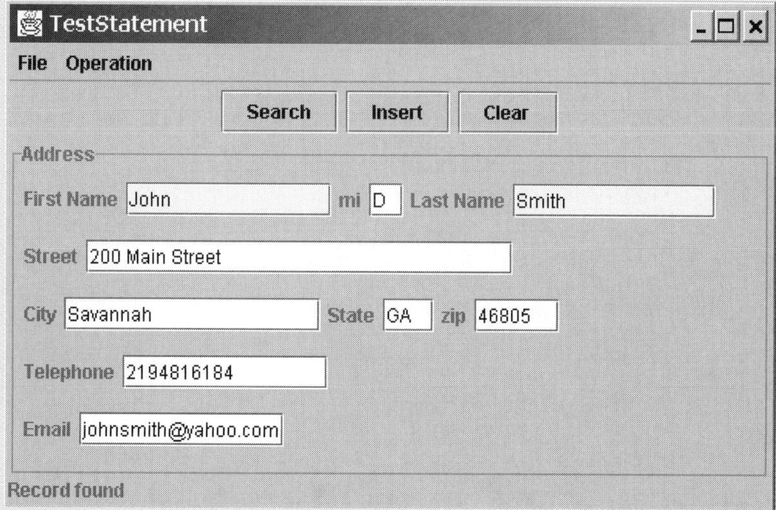

Figure 13.11 *Static SQL statements are used in this program to retrieve and modify database information.*

1. Creating the applet with menus
   1.1. In the jdbcdemo project, create an applet named TestStatement using the Applet wizard.
   1.2. With TestStatement.java selected in the project pane, switch to the UI designer in the content pane. Drop a `JMenuBar` to the content pane to create `jMenubar1`. Double-click `jMenuBar1` in the component tree to bring up the Menu designer.
   1.3. Create the File menu and add menu items "Connect to Database," a separator, and "Exit" in the File menu. Create the Operation menu and add the menu item "Using Static SQL Statements" to it. Change the menu item names to `jmiConnect`, `jmiExit`, and `jmiStaticSQL`.

continued

Example 13.2 continued

1.4. Drop a `DBConnectDialog` from the component palette to create `dBConnectDialog1`. Set its `modal` property to True. `DBConnectDialog` was created in Example 12.4.

1.5. Set the `JMenuBar` property of the applet to `jMenuBar1`.

1.6. Generate and implement the code for handling the menu commands "Connect to Database," "Exit," and "Using Static SQL Statements," as shown in Listing 13.4 (Lines 64–77).

```
1    package jdbcdemo;
2
3    import java.awt.*;
4    import java.awt.event.*;
5    import java.applet.*;
6    import javax.swing.*;
7    import jdbcdemo.*;
8
9    public class TestStatement extends JApplet {
10     boolean isStandalone = false;
11     JMenuBar jMenuBar1 = new JMenuBar();
12     JMenu jMenu1 = new JMenu();
13     JMenuItem jmiConnect = new JMenuItem();
14     JMenu jMenu2 = new JMenu();
15     JMenuItem jmiStaticSQL = new JMenuItem();
16     JMenuItem jmiExit = new JMenuItem();
17     DBConnectDialog dBConnectDialog1 = new DBConnectDialog();
18
19     /** Initialize the applet */
20     public void init() {
21       try {
22         jbInit();
23       }
24       catch(Exception e) {
25         e.printStackTrace();
26       }
27     }
28
29     /** Component initialization */
30     private void jbInit() throws Exception {
31       this.setJMenuBar(jMenuBar1);
32       this.setSize(new Dimension(400,300));
33       jMenu1.setText("File");
34       jmiConnect.setText("Connect to Database");
35       jmiConnect.addActionListener(
36         new java.awt.event.ActionListener() {
37         public void actionPerformed(ActionEvent e) {
38           jmiConnect_actionPerformed(e);
39         }
40       });
41       jMenu2.setText("Operation");
42       jmiStaticSQL.setText("Using Static SQL Statements");
43       jmiStaticSQL.addActionListener(
44         new java.awt.event.ActionListener() {
```

Listing 13.4 *TestStatement.java*

```
      public void actionPerformed(ActionEvent e) {
        jmiStaticSQL_actionPerformed(e);
      }
    });
    jmiExit.setText("Exit");
    jmiExit.addActionListener(new java.awt.event.ActionListener() {
      public void actionPerformed(ActionEvent e) {
        jmiExit_actionPerformed(e);
      }
    });
    dBConnectDialog1.setModal(true);
    jMenuBar1.add(jMenu1);
    jMenuBar1.add(jMenu2);
    jMenu1.add(jmiConnect);
    jMenu1.addSeparator();
    jMenu1.add(jmiExit);
    jMenu2.add(jmiStaticSQL);
  }

  /** Handle Connect menu command */
  void jmiConnect_actionPerformed(ActionEvent e) {
    dBConnectDialog1.setVisible(true);
  }

  /** Handle static SQL demo */
  void jmiStaticSQL_actionPerformed(ActionEvent e) {
    addAddressPanel(new AddressPanel(
      dBConnectDialog1.getConnection()));
  }

  void jmiExit_actionPerformed(ActionEvent e) {
    System.exit(0);
  }

  /** Add an address panel to the center of applet */
  void addAddressPanel(AddressPanel addressPanel) {
    if (dBConnectDialog1.getConnection() != null) {
      // Remove UI components from the applet
      this.getContentPane().removeAll();

      // Add AddressPanel panel to the applet
      this.getContentPane().add(addressPanel,
        BorderLayout.CENTER);

      this.validate();
    }
    else
      System.out.println("Database not connected");
  }
}
```

Listing 13.4 *Continued*

2. Creating the `AddressPanel` panel

   2.1. Create `AddressPanel`, which inherits `JPanel`, using the JavaBean wizard from the Object Gallery.

   2.2. Use the UI designer to lay out the UI components in the panel.

continued

Example 13.2 continued

2.3. Drop a `JPanel` to the center of `AddressPanel` to create `jpAddress`. Set its `layout` to `GridLayout`, with `row` set to 5 and `column` set to 1. Drop a `JPanel` five times to `jpAddress`, and drop appropriate labels and text fields for displaying address into these panels. Set the `text` property of the labels to "First Name," "MI," "Last Name," "Street," "City," "State," "Zip," "Telephone," and "Email." Rename the text fields `jtfFirstName`, `jtfMi`, `jtfLastName`, `jtfStreet`, `jtfCity`, `jtfState`, `jtfZip`, `jtfTelephone`, and `jtfEmail`. Set an appropriate value in the `column` property of each text field.

2.4. Drop a `JPanel` to the north of `AddressPanel` to create `jpButton`. Drop a `JButton` three times into `jpButton` to create the Search, Insert, and Clear buttons. Rename them `jbtSearch`, `jbtInsert`, and `jbtClear`.

2.5. Drop a `JLabel` to the south of `AddressPanel` to create `jlblStatus`.

2.6. Create a variable `connection` of the `java.sql.Connection` type in `AddressPanel`, and create a new constructor with a parameter of the `Connection` type, as shown in Listing 13.5 (Lines 61–66).

2.7. Generate and implement the code for handling the three buttons, as shown in Listing 13.5 (Lines 159–169).

```
1    package jdbcdemo;
2
3    import java.awt.*;
4    import javax.swing.*;
5    import javax.swing.border.*;
6    import java.awt.event.*;
7    import java.sql.*;
8
9    public class AddressPanel extends JPanel {
10     BorderLayout borderLayout1 = new BorderLayout();
11     JPanel jpAddress = new JPanel();
12     JPanel jpButtons = new JPanel();
13     GridLayout gridLayout1 = new GridLayout();
14     JPanel jPanel3 = new JPanel();
15     JPanel jPanel4 = new JPanel();
16     JPanel jPanel5 = new JPanel();
17     JPanel jPanel6 = new JPanel();
18     JPanel jPanel7 = new JPanel();
19     JLabel jLabel1 = new JLabel();
20     JTextField jtfFirstName = new JTextField();
21     JLabel jLabel2 = new JLabel();
22     JTextField jtfMi = new JTextField();
23     JLabel jLabel3 = new JLabel();
24     JTextField jtfLastName = new JTextField();
25     FlowLayout flowLayout1 = new FlowLayout();
26     TitledBorder titledBorder1;
27     JLabel jLabel4 = new JLabel();
28     JTextField jtfStreet = new JTextField();
29     FlowLayout flowLayout2 = new FlowLayout();
```

Listing 13.5 *AddressPanel.java*

```
    JLabel jLabel5 = new JLabel();
    JTextField jtfCity = new JTextField();
    JLabel jLabel6 = new JLabel();
    JTextField jtfState = new JTextField();
    JLabel jLabel7 = new JLabel();
    JTextField jtfZip = new JTextField();
    FlowLayout flowLayout3 = new FlowLayout();
    JLabel jLabel8 = new JLabel();
    JTextField jtfTelephone = new JTextField();
    FlowLayout flowLayout4 = new FlowLayout();
    FlowLayout flowLayout5 = new FlowLayout();
    JLabel jLabel9 = new JLabel();
    JTextField jtfEmail = new JTextField();
    JButton jbtSearch = new JButton();
    JButton jbtInset = new JButton();
    JButton jbtClear = new JButton();
    JLabel jlblStatus = new JLabel();

    // Database connection passed from DBConnectDialog
    Connection connection;

    /** Default constructor */
    public AddressPanel() {
      try {
        jbInit();
      }
      catch(Exception ex) {
        ex.printStackTrace();
      }
    }

    /** Construct an AddressPanel with a specified connection */
    public AddressPanel(Connection connection) {
      this();
      this.connection = connection;
      jlblStatus.setText("Using static SQL statements");
    }

    private void jbInit() throws Exception {
      titledBorder1 = new TitledBorder("");
      this.setLayout(borderLayout1);
      jpAddress.setLayout(gridLayout1);
      gridLayout1.setRows(5);
      jLabel1.setText("First Name");
      jtfFirstName.setBackground(Color.yellow);
      jtfFirstName.setColumns(12);
      jLabel2.setText("mi");
      jtfMi.setColumns(2);
      jLabel3.setText("Last Name");
      jtfLastName.setBackground(Color.yellow);
      jtfLastName.setColumns(12);
      jPanel3.setLayout(flowLayout1);
      flowLayout1.setAlignment(FlowLayout.LEFT);
      jLabel4.setText("Street");
      jtfStreet.setColumns(25);
      jPanel4.setLayout(flowLayout2);
      flowLayout2.setAlignment(FlowLayout.LEFT);
      jLabel5.setText("City");
      jtfCity.setColumns(15);
      jLabel6.setText("State");
```

Listing 13.5 *Continued*

continued

Example 13.2 continued

```
      jtfState.setColumns(3);
      jLabel7.setText("zip");
      jtfZip.setColumns(5);
      jPanel5.setLayout(flowLayout3);
      flowLayout3.setAlignment(FlowLayout.LEFT);
      jLabel8.setText("Telephone");
      jtfTelephone.setColumns(12);
      jPanel6.setLayout(flowLayout4);
      flowLayout4.setAlignment(FlowLayout.LEFT);
      jPanel7.setLayout(flowLayout5);
      flowLayout5.setAlignment(FlowLayout.LEFT);
      jLabel9.setText("Email");
      jtfEmail.setColumns(12);
      jbtSearch.setText("Search");
      jbtSearch.addActionListener(new java.awt.event.ActionListener() {
        public void actionPerformed(ActionEvent e) {
          jbtSearch_actionPerformed(e);
        }
      });
      jbtInset.setText("Insert");
      jbtInset.addActionListener(new java.awt.event.ActionListener() {
        public void actionPerformed(ActionEvent e) {
          jbtInset_actionPerformed(e);
        }
      });
      jbtClear.setText("Clear");
      jbtClear.addActionListener(new java.awt.event.ActionListener() {
        public void actionPerformed(ActionEvent e) {
          jbtClear_actionPerformed(e);
        }
      });
      titledBorder1.setTitle("Address");
      jpAddress.setBorder(titledBorder1);
      jlblStatus.setText("jLabel10");
      this.add(jpAddress, BorderLayout.CENTER);
      jpAddress.add(jPanel3, null);
      jPanel3.add(jLabel1, null);
      jPanel3.add(jtfFirstName, null);
      jPanel3.add(jLabel2, null);
      jPanel3.add(jtfMi, null);
      jPanel3.add(jLabel3, null);
      jPanel3.add(jtfLastName, null);
      jpAddress.add(jPanel4, null);
      jPanel4.add(jLabel4, null);
      jPanel4.add(jtfStreet, null);
      jpAddress.add(jPanel5, null);
      jPanel5.add(jLabel5, null);
      jPanel5.add(jtfCity, null);
      jPanel5.add(jLabel6, null);
      jPanel5.add(jtfState, null);
      jPanel5.add(jLabel7, null);
      jPanel5.add(jtfZip, null);
      jpAddress.add(jPanel6, null);
      jPanel6.add(jLabel8, null);
      jPanel6.add(jtfTelephone, null);
      jpAddress.add(jPanel7, null);
      jPanel7.add(jLabel9, null);
      jPanel7.add(jtfEmail, null);
      this.add(jpButtons, BorderLayout.NORTH);
      jpButtons.add(jbtSearch, null);
```

Listing 13.5 *Continued*

```
      jpButtons.add(jbtInset, null);
      jpButtons.add(jbtClear, null);
      this.add(jlblStatus, BorderLayout.SOUTH);
    }

    public void setConnection(java.sql.Connection newConnection) {
      connection = newConnection;
    }

    void jbtSearch_actionPerformed(ActionEvent e) {
      select();
    }

    void jbtInset_actionPerformed(ActionEvent e) {
      insert();
    }

    void jbtClear_actionPerformed(ActionEvent e) {
      clear();
    }

    protected void select() {
      String query = "select * from Address where " +
        "firstName = " +
        "'" + jtfFirstName.getText().trim() + "'" +
        " and lastName = " +
        "'" + jtfLastName.getText().trim() + "'";

      try {
        Statement stmt = connection.createStatement();
        ResultSet rs = stmt.executeQuery(query);

        if (rs.next()) {
          jtfMi.setText(rs.getString(2));
          jtfStreet.setText(rs.getString(4));
          jtfCity.setText(rs.getString(5));
          jtfState.setText(rs.getString(6));
          jtfZip.setText(rs.getString(7));
          jtfTelephone.setText(rs.getString(8));
          jtfEmail.setText(rs.getString(9));

          jlblStatus.setText("Record found");
        }
        else {
          jlblStatus.setText("Record not found");
        }
      }
      catch (SQLException ex) {
        jlblStatus.setText(ex.getMessage());
      }
    }

    protected void insert() {
      String sqlInsert = "insert into Address values (" +
        "'" + jtfFirstName.getText().trim() + "'" + "," +
        "'" + jtfMi.getText().trim() + "'" + "," +
        "'" + jtfLastName.getText().trim() + "'" + "," +
        "'" + jtfStreet.getText().trim() + "'" + "," +
        "'" + jtfCity.getText().trim() + "'" + "," +
        "'" + jtfState.getText().trim() + "'" + "," +
```

Listing 13.5 *Continued*

continued

Example 13.2 continued

```
        "'" + jtfZip.getText().trim() + "'" + "," +
        "'" + jtfTelephone.getText().trim() + "'" + "," +
        "'" + jtfEmail.getText().trim()+ "'" + ")";

      try {
        Statement stmt = connection.createStatement();
        int t = stmt.executeUpdate(sqlInsert);
        jlblStatus.setText("Insertion succeeded");
      }
      catch (SQLException ex) {
        jlblStatus.setText(ex.getMessage());
      }
    }

    protected void clear() {
      jtfFirstName.setText(null);
      jtfMi.setText(null);
      jtfLastName.setText(null);
      jtfStreet.setText(null);
      jtfCity.setText(null);
      jtfState.setText(null);
      jtfZip.setText(null);
      jtfTelephone.setText(null);
      jtfEmail.setText(null);
    }
  }
```

Listing 13.5 *Continued*

Example Review

You click the Connect to Database menu command to create an instance of `DBConnectDialog` and display the dialog box for establishing a database connection. After a connection to a particular database is established, you can click the Using Static SQL Statements menu command to display the `AddressPanel` panel. The constructor of `AddressPanel` has a parameter of the `Connection` type. The `dBconnectDialog1.getConnection()` is passed to the constructor of `AddressPanel` to create an instance of `AddressPanel`.

Static SQL statements are constructed to perform SQL select and SQL INSERT operations. A SQL `Statement` instance `stmt` is created to execute the static SQL statements. `stmt.executeQuery(sqlSelect)` executes a SQL select statement in the string `sqlSelect`, which returns a `ResultSet`; `stmt.executeUpdate(sqlInsert)` executes a SQL INSERT statement. In the example, only the first record in the `ResultSet` is displayed on the `AddressPanel` panel.

Batch Processing

In all the preceding examples, SQL commands are submitted to the database for execution one at a time. This is inefficient for processing a large number of updates. For example, suppose you want to insert a thousand rows into a table. Submitting one INSERT command at a time would take nearly a thousand times longer than submitting all the INSERT commands in a batch at once. To improve performance, JDBC 2 introduced the batch update for processing nonselect SQL commands. A batch update consists of a sequence of nonselect SQL commands. These commands are collected in a batch and submitted to the database all together.

To use the batch update, you add nonselect commands to a batch using the `addBatch` method in the `Statement` interface. After all the SQL commands are added to the batch, use the `executeBatch` method to submit the batch to the database for execution.

For example, the following code adds a create table command, two insert statements in a batch, and executes the batch.

```
Statement stmt = conn.createStatement();

// Add SQL commands to the batch
stmt.addBatch("CREATE TABLE T (C1 NUMBER, C2 VARCHAR(15))");
stmt.addBatch("insert into TABLE T values " +
  "(100, \'Smith\')");
stmt.addBatch("insert into TABLE T values " +
  "(200, \'Jones\')");

// Execute the batch
int count[] = stmt.executeBatch();
```

The `executeBatch` method returns an array of counts, each of which counts the number of the rows affected by the SQL command. The first count returns 0 because it is a DDL command. The rest of the commands return 1 because only one row is affected.

Example 13.3 Copying Text Files to Tables

In this example, you will write a program that gets data from a text file and copies the data to a table, as shown in Figure 13.12. The text file consists of the lines, each of which corresponds to a row in the table. The fields in a row are separated by commas. The string values in a row are enclosed in single quotes. You can view the text file by clicking the View button and copy the text to the table by clicking the Copy button. The table must already be defined in the database.

continued

Example 13.3 continued

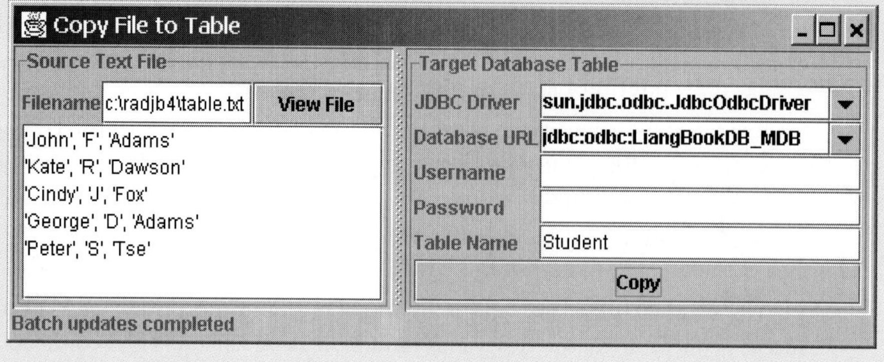

Figure 13.12 *The Copy File to Table utility copies text files to database tables.*

Here are the steps to create the project:

1. In the jdbcdemo project, create a new applet named CopyFileToTable.java.

2. In the UI designer for CopyFileToTable.java, drop a `JSplitPane` to the center of the applet to create `jSplitPane1`, and drop a `JLabel` to the south of the applet, and rename it `jlblStatus`.

3. Drop a `JPanel` to the left pane of `jSplitPane1` to create `jPanel1` and `jPanel2`. Set the border title of `jPanel1` and `jPanel2` to "Source Text File" and "Target Database Table," respectively. Set the `layout` of `jPanel1` and `jPanel2` to `BorderLayout`.

4. Drop a `JPanel` to the north of `jPanel1` to create `jPanel3`. Drop a `JScroll-Pane` to the center of the `jPanel1`. Drop a `JTextArea` into the scroll pane, and rename it `jtaFile`.

5. Set the `layout` of `jPanel3` to `BorderLayout`. Drop a `JLabel`, a `JTextField`, and a `JButton` to the west, center, and east of `jPanel3`. Rename the text filed `jtfFilename`, and the button `jbtViewFile`. Set the text of the label to Filename, and the button to View File.

6. Set the `layout` of `jPanel2` to `BorderLayout`. Drop a `JPanel` twice to the west and center of `jPanel2` to create `jPanel4` and `jPanel5`. Set their `layout` to GridLayout with five rows and two columns. Drop a `JButton` to the south of the `jPanel2`, rename it `jbtCopy`, and set its `text` to Copy.

7. Drop a `JLabel` five times to `jPanel4` and set their `text` to "JDBC Driver," "Database URL," "Username," "Password," and "Table Name." Drop a `JcomboBox` twice to `jPanel5` to create `jcboDriver` and `jcboURL`. Set their `editable` to True. Drop a `JTextField` three times to create `jtfUsername`, `jtfPassword`, and `jtfTableName`.

8. Use the addItem method to add JDBC driver classes, and database URLs to jcboDriver and jcboURL. Generate and implement the code for handling the buttons View File and Copy, as shown in Listing 13.6.

```
package jdbcdemo;

import java.awt.*;
import java.awt.event.*;
import java.applet.*;
import javax.swing.*;
import javax.swing.border.*;
import java.io.*;
import java.sql.*;

public class CopyFileToTable extends JApplet {
  boolean isStandalone = false;
  TitledBorder titledBorder1;
  JPanel jPanel2 = new JPanel();
  JPanel jPanel3 = new JPanel();
  JLabel jlblStatus = new JLabel();
  TitledBorder titledBorder2;
  JPanel jPanel4 = new JPanel();
  BorderLayout borderLayout1 = new BorderLayout();
  JLabel jLabel2 = new JLabel();
  JTextField jtfFilename = new JTextField();
  JButton jbtViewFile = new JButton();
  BorderLayout borderLayout2 = new BorderLayout();
  JScrollPane jScrollPane1 = new JScrollPane();
  JTextArea jtaFile = new JTextArea();
  GridLayout gridLayout2 = new GridLayout();
  JPanel jPanel5 = new JPanel();
  JPanel jPanel6 = new JPanel();
  JLabel jLabel3 = new JLabel();
  GridLayout gridLayout4 = new GridLayout();
  JLabel jLabel4 = new JLabel();
  JLabel jLabel5 = new JLabel();
  JLabel jLabel6 = new JLabel();
  JLabel jLabel7 = new JLabel();
  BorderLayout borderLayout3 = new BorderLayout();
  GridLayout gridLayout3 = new GridLayout();
  JComboBox jcboDriver = new JComboBox();
  JComboBox jcboURL = new JComboBox();
  JTextField jtfUsername = new JTextField();
  JTextField jtfPassword = new JPasswordField();
  JTextField jtfTableName = new JTextField();
  JButton jtbCopy = new JButton();
  JSplitPane jSplitPane1 = new JSplitPane();

  /** Initialize the applet */
  public void init() {
    try {
      jbInit();
    }
    catch(Exception e) {
      e.printStackTrace();
    }
  }

```

Listing 13.6 *CopyFileToTable.java*

continued

Example 13.3 continued

```
    /** Component initialization */
    private void jbInit() throws Exception {
      titledBorder1 = new TitledBorder("");
      titledBorder2 = new TitledBorder("");
      this.setSize(new Dimension(598, 170));
      titledBorder1.setTitle("Source Text File");
      jlblStatus.setText("Status label");
      jPanel2.setBorder(titledBorder1);
      jPanel2.setLayout(borderLayout1);
      jPanel3.setBorder(titledBorder2);
      jPanel3.setLayout(borderLayout3);
      titledBorder2.setTitle("Target Database Table");
      jLabel2.setText("Filename");
      jbtViewFile.setText("View File");
      jbtViewFile.addActionListener(
        new java.awt.event.ActionListener() {
        public void actionPerformed(ActionEvent e) {
          jbtViewFile_actionPerformed(e);
        }
      });
      jPanel4.setLayout(borderLayout2);
      gridLayout2.setColumns(1);
      gridLayout2.setRows(5);
      jLabel3.setText("JDBC Driver");
      jPanel5.setLayout(gridLayout4);
      gridLayout4.setRows(5);
      jLabel4.setText("Database URL");
      jLabel5.setText("Username");
      jLabel6.setText("Password");
      jLabel7.setText("Table Name");
      jPanel6.setLayout(gridLayout3);
      gridLayout3.setRows(5);
      jtbCopy.setText("Copy");
      jtbCopy.addActionListener(new java.awt.event.ActionListener() {
        public void actionPerformed(ActionEvent e) {
          jtbCopy_actionPerformed(e);
        }
      });
      jcboDriver.setEditable(true);
      jcboURL.setEditable(true);
      this.getContentPane().add(jlblStatus, BorderLayout.SOUTH);
      this.getContentPane().add(jSplitPane1, BorderLayout.CENTER);
      jSplitPane1.add(jPanel2, JSplitPane.LEFT);
      jPanel2.add(jPanel4, BorderLayout.NORTH);
      jPanel4.add(jLabel2, BorderLayout.WEST);
      jPanel4.add(jtfFilename, BorderLayout.CENTER);
      jPanel4.add(jbtViewFile, BorderLayout.EAST);
      jPanel2.add(jScrollPane1, BorderLayout.CENTER);
      jSplitPane1.add(jPanel3, JSplitPane.RIGHT);
      jPanel3.add(jPanel5, BorderLayout.WEST);
      jPanel5.add(jLabel3, null);
      jPanel5.add(jLabel4, null);
      jPanel5.add(jLabel5, null);
      jPanel5.add(jLabel6, null);
      jPanel5.add(jLabel7, null);
      jPanel3.add(jPanel6, BorderLayout.CENTER);
      jPanel6.add(jcboDriver, null);
      jPanel6.add(jcboURL, null);
      jPanel6.add(jtfUsername, null);
```

Listing 13.6 *Continued*

```
    jPanel6.add(jtfPassword, null);
    jPanel6.add(jtfTableName, null);
    jPanel3.add(jtbCopy, BorderLayout.SOUTH);
    jScrollPane1.getViewport().add(jtaFile, null);

    // Add items to the combo boxes
    jcboDriver.addItem("sun.jdbc.odbc.JdbcOdbcDriver");
    jcboDriver.addItem("interbase.interclient.Driver");
    jcboDriver.addItem("oracle.jdbc.driver.OracleDriver");
    jcboURL.addItem("jdbc:odbc:LiangBookDB_MDB");
    jcboURL.addItem(
      "jdbc:interbase://localhost/C:/LiangBook/LiangBookDB.gdb");
    jcboURL.addItem("jdbc:oracle:thin:@sesrv00.ipfw.edu:1521:test");

    // Interbase login SYSDBA/masterkey and Oracle login scott/tiger
  }

  void jbtViewFile_actionPerformed(ActionEvent e) {
    showFile();
  }

  /** Display the file in the text area */
  private void showFile() {
    // Use a BufferedReader to read text from the file
    BufferedReader infile = null;

    // Get file name from the text field
    String filename = jtfFilename.getText().trim();

    String inLine;

    try {
      // Create a buffered stream
      infile = new BufferedReader(new FileReader(filename));

      // Read a line and append the line to the text area
      while ((inLine = infile.readLine()) != null) {
        jtaFile.append(inLine + '\n');
      }
    }
    catch (FileNotFoundException ex) {
      System.out.println("File not found: " + filename);
    }
    catch (IOException ex) {
      System.out.println(ex.getMessage());
    }
    finally {
      try {
        if (infile != null) infile.close();
      }
      catch (IOException ex) {
        System.out.println(ex.getMessage());
      }
    }
  }

  void jtbCopy_actionPerformed(ActionEvent e) {
    try {
      copyFile();
    }
```

Listing 13.6 *Continued*

continued

Example 13.3 continued

```
      catch (Exception ex) {
        jlblStatus.setText(ex.toString());
      }
    }

    private void copyFile() throws Exception {
      // Load the JDBC driver
      System.out.println((String)jcboDriver.getSelectedItem());
      Class.forName(((String)jcboDriver.getSelectedItem()).trim());
      System.out.println("Driver loaded");

      // Establish a connection
      Connection conn = DriverManager.getConnection
        (((String)jcboURL.getSelectedItem()).trim(),
          jtfUsername.getText().trim(),
         jtfPassword.getText().trim());
      System.out.println("Database connected");

      // Read each line from the text file and insert it to the table
      insertRows(conn);
    }

    private void insertRows(Connection connection) {
      // Build the INSERT statement
      String sqlInsert = "insert into " + jtfTableName.getText()
        + " values (";

      // Use a BufferedReader to read text from the file
      BufferedReader infile = null;

      // Get file name from the text field
      String filename = jtfFilename.getText().trim();

      String inLine;

      try {
        // Create a buffered stream
        infile = new BufferedReader(new FileReader(filename));

        // Create a statement
        Statement statement = connection.createStatement();

        System.out.println("Driver major version? " +
          connection.getMetaData().getDriverMajorVersion());

        // Determine if the supportsBatchUpdates method supported in
        // DatabaseMetadata
        boolean batchUpdatesSupported = false;

        try {
          if (connection.getMetaData().supportsBatchUpdates()) {
            batchUpdatesSupported = true;
            System.out.println("batch updates supported");
          }
          else {
            System.out.println("The driver is of JDBC 2 type, but " +
              "does not support batch updates");
          }
        }
```

Listing 13.6 *Continued*

```
        catch (Exception ex) {
          System.out.println("The driver does not support JDBC 2");
        }

        // Determine if the driver is capable of batch updates
        if (batchUpdatesSupported) {
          // Read a line and add the insert table command to the batch
          while ((inLine = infile.readLine()) != null) {
            statement.addBatch(sqlInsert + inLine + ")");
          }

          statement.executeBatch();

          jlblStatus.setText("Batch updates completed");
        }
        else {
          // Read a line and execute insert table command
          while ((inLine = infile.readLine()) != null) {
            statement.executeUpdate(sqlInsert + inLine + ")");
          }

          jlblStatus.setText("Single row update completed");
        }
      }
      catch (SQLException ex) {
        System.out.println(ex);
      }
      catch (FileNotFoundException ex) {
        System.out.println("File not found: " + filename);
      }
      catch (IOException ex) {
        System.out.println(ex.getMessage());
      }
      finally {
        try {
          if (infile != null) infile.close();
        }
        catch (IOException ex) {
          System.out.println(ex.getMessage());
        }
      }
    }
  }
```

Listing 13.6 *Continued*

Example Review

The `insertRows` method uses the batch updates to submit SQL INSERT commands to the database for execution, if the driver supports batch updates. Not all JDBC drivers support JDBC 2. Even if a driver supports JDBC 2, it may not support every feature of JDBC 2. The `DatabaseMetaData` interface does not have a method to verify whether the driver supports JDBC 2. To find out whether the driver supports JDBC 2, invoke the `supportsBatchUpdates` method in the `DatabaseMetaData` interface. If the driver does not support JDBC 2, a `java.lang.UnsupportedOperationException` would occur. If the driver supports JDBC 2, but does not support batch updates, invoking `supportsBatchUpdates` would return false.

continued

Example 13.3 continued

The JDBC-ODBC driver in JDK 1.2 does not support JDBC 2, but the JDBC-ODBC driver in JDK 1.3 supports JDBC 2. The Oracle Thin driver for Oracle 8i supports JDBC 2.

The tables are already created in the database. The file format and contents must match the database table specification. Otherwise, the SQL INSERT command would fail.

In Exercise 13.4, you will write a program to insert 1000 records to a database and compare the performance with and without batch updates.

PreparedStatement

The `PreparedStatement` interface is designed to execute dynamic SQL statements and SQL-stored procedures with IN parameters. These SQL statements and stored procedures are precompiled for efficient use when repeatedly executed.

A `PreparedStatement` object is created using the `preparedStatement()` method in the `Connection` interface. For example, the following code creates a `PreparedStatement pstmt` on a particular `Connection connection` for a SQL INSERT statement.

```
Statement pstmt = connection.prepareStatement
  ("insert into Address (firstName, mi, lastName)
    values (?, ?, ?));
```

This INSERT statement has three question marks as placeholders for parameters representing values for firstName, mi, and lastName in a record of the Address table.

As a subclass of `Statement`, the `PreparedStatement` interface inherits all the methods defined in `Statement`. Additionally, it provides the methods for setting parameters in the object of `PreparedStatement`. These methods are used to set the values for the parameters before executing statements or procedures. In general, the set methods have the following name and signature:

```
setX(int parameterIndex, X value);
```

where *X* is the type of the parameter, and `parameterIndex` is the index of the parameter in the statement. For example, the method `setString(int parameterIndex, String value)` sets a `String` value to the specified parameter. Table 13.7 contains a complete list of the methods in `PreparedStatement`.

The following statements pass parameters "Jack," "A," "Ryan" to the placeholder (?) for firstName, mi, and lastName in the `PreparedStatement pstmt`.

```
pstmt.setString(1, "Jack");
pstmt.setString(2, "A");
pstmt.setString(3, "Ryan");
```

TABLE 13.7 `PreparedStatement` Methods

Method Name	*Description*
`clearParameters`	Clears all the parameters in the statement.
`execute`	Executes a prepared statement that may return multiple result sets.
`executeQuery`	Executes a prepared statement that returns a single result set.
`executeUpdate`	Executes a prepared INSERT, UPDATE, DELETE, or SQL DDL statement.
`setAsciiStream`	Sets a parameter to an ASCII stream.
`setBigDecimal`	Sets a parameter to a `java.lang.BigDecimal` value.
`setBinaryStream`	Sets a parameter to a binary stream.
`setBoolean`	Sets a parameter to a Java `boolean` value.
`setByte`	Sets a parameter to a Java `byte` value.
`setBytes`	Sets a parameter to a Java array of `byte` values.
`setDate`	Sets a parameter to a `java.sql.Date` value.
`setDouble`	Sets a parameter to a Java `double` value.
`setFloat`	Sets a parameter to a Java `float` value.
`setInt`	Sets a parameter to a Java `int` value.
`setLong`	Sets a parameter to a Java `long` value.
`setNull`	Sets a parameter to a SQL NULL value.
`setObject`	Sets a parameter to a Java object.
`setShort`	Sets a parameter to a Java `short` value.
`setString`	Sets a parameter to a Java `String` value.
`setTime`	Sets a parameter to a `java.sql.Time` value.
`setTimestamp`	Sets a parameter to a `java.sql.Timestamp` value.
`setUnicodeStream`	Sets a parameter to a Unicode stream.

After setting parameters, you can execute the prepared statement by invoking `execute()`, `executeQuery()`, or `executeUpdate()`, depending on the type of SQL statement. The `execute()`, `executeQuery()`, and `executeUpdate()` methods are similar to the ones defined in the `Statement` interface except that they have no parameters, since the SQL statements are already specified in the `preparedStatement` method when the object of `PreparedStatement` is created.

Example 13.4 Using PreparedStatement to Execute Dynamic SQL Statements

In this example, you will use dynamic SQL statements to select addresses and insert new addresses. A new menu, "Using Dynamic SQL Statements," will be added to the applet from the previous example. This new menu will bring up the same user interface as the menu "Using Static SQL Statements" with identical functions, but the dynamic SQL statements will be used to implement the SELECT and INSERT operations.

The example consists of two new classes: `TestPreparedStatement` and `AddressPanelUsingDynamicSQL`. `TestPreparedStatement` adds a new menu item, "Using Dynamic SQL," to the previous example, and `AddressPanelUsingDynamicSQL` extends `AddressPanel` and uses the dynamic statements to override the `select()` and `insert()` methods.

Follow the steps below to complete the project.

1. In the jdbcdemo.jpr, select TestStatement.java in the project pane. Choose File, Save As to save it into a new file named TestPreparedStatement.java.
2. Replace TestStatement with TestPreparedStatement.
3. In the Menu designer of `TestPreparedStatement`, add a menu item "Using Dynamic SQL Statements" in the Operation menu, and change the menu item's name to `jmiDynamicSQL`. Implement the menu item handler, as follows:

```
void jmiDynamicSQL_actionPerformed(ActionEvent e) {
  addAddressPanel(
    new AddressPanelUsingDynamicSQL(
          dBConnectDialog1.getConnection()));
}
```

4. Create a new class `AddressPanelUsingDynamicSQL` that extends `AddressPanel` and implements the `select()` and `insert()` methods using dynamic SQL statements, as shown in Listing 13.7 (Lines 26–72).
5. Run `TestPreparedStatement` to test the program. The main frame is shown in Figure 13.13. When selecting "Using Dynamic SQL State-

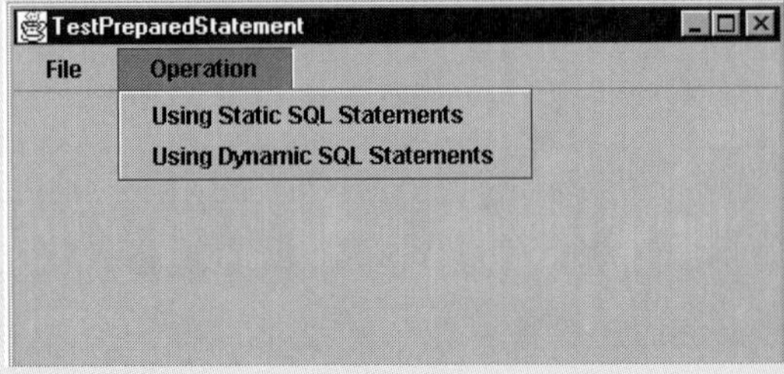

Figure 13.13 *The menu "Using Dynamic SQL Statements" was added to test* `PreparedStatement`.

ments," the same user interface as shown in Figure 13.11 appears in the frame for searching and inserting addresses.

```
package jdbcdemo;

import java.sql.*;

public class AddressPanelUsingDynamicSQL extends AddressPanel {
  PreparedStatement pstmt1;
  PreparedStatement pstmt2;

  public AddressPanelUsingDynamicSQL(Connection connection) {
    super(connection);

    // Create prepared SQL statements
    try {
      pstmt1 = connection.prepareStatement("select * from Address " +
        "where firstName = ? AND lastName = ?");
      pstmt2 = connection.prepareStatement("insert into Address " +
        "values (?, ?, ?, ?, ?, ?, ?, ?, ?)");
    }
    catch (SQLException ex) {
      jlblStatus.setText(ex.getMessage());
    }

    jlblStatus.setText("Using dynamic SQL statements");
  }

  /** Override this method from AddressPanel */
  protected void select() {
    try {
      pstmt1.setString(1, jtfFirstName.getText().trim());
      pstmt1.setString(2, jtfLastName.getText().trim());
      ResultSet rs = pstmt1.executeQuery();

      if (rs.next()) {
        jtfMi.setText(rs.getString(2));
        jtfStreet.setText(rs.getString(4));
        jtfCity.setText(rs.getString(5));
        jtfState.setText(rs.getString(6));
        jtfZip.setText(rs.getString(7));
        jtfTelephone.setText(rs.getString(8));
        jtfEmail.setText(rs.getString(9));
        jlblStatus.setText("Dynamic SQL selection succeeded");
      }
      else {
        jlblStatus.setText("no record found");
      }
    }
    catch (SQLException ex) {
      jlblStatus.setText(ex.getMessage());
    }
  }

  /** Override this method from AddressPanel */
  protected void insert() {
    try {
      pstmt2.setString(1, jtfFirstName.getText().trim());
      pstmt2.setString(2, jtfMi.getText().trim());
      pstmt2.setString(3, jtfLastName.getText().trim());
```

Listing 13.7 *AddressPanelUsingDynamicSQL.java*

continued

Example 13.4 continued

```
        pstmt2.setString(4, jtfStreet.getText().trim());
        pstmt2.setString(5, jtfCity.getText().trim());
        pstmt2.setString(6, jtfState.getText().trim());
        pstmt2.setString(7, jtfZip.getText().trim());
        pstmt2.setString(8, jtfTelephone.getText().trim());
        pstmt2.setString(9, jtfZip.getText().trim());

        pstmt2.executeUpdate();

        jlblStatus.setText("Dynamic SQL Insertion succeeded");
      }
      catch (SQLException ex) {
        jlblStatus.setText(ex.getMessage());
      }
    }
  }
```

Listing 13.7 *Continued*

Example Review

AddressPanelUsingDynamicSQL extends AddressPanel created in Example 13.2. The select() and insert() methods in AddressPanel were overridden to accommodate using the prepared statements pstmt1 and pstmt2, where pstmt1 can be used to select records from the Address table, and pstmt2 can be used to insert records into Address table in the database.

A new method addAddressPanel was created in TestPreparedStatement, which enables you to add an instance of AddressPanel to the center of the applet's content pane. First, all the components in the applet's content pane were removed, using the removeAll() method. Then the menu bar and the AddressPanel instance were added to the applet. You may use the remove() method to remove a specified component from a container, if you assign a name for an instance of AddressPanel rather than use an anonymous instance.

PreparedStatement is more efficient than Statement in the project for viewing and inserting new records because the SQL statements are precompiled and reused without recompiling. Please refer to Exercise 13.1 for performance evaluations of using static SQL statements and dynamic SQL statements.

CAUTION

To override a method in the superclass, the method has to be declared exactly as in its superclass. It would be a mistake, for example, if you missed the protected keyword for the select() or the insert() method, because this keyword is used for declaring these methods in its superclass.

CallableStatement

The CallableStatement interface is designed to execute SQL-stored procedures with OUT or IN OUT parameters. An OUT parameter returns a value after the procedure is completed, but it contains no value when the procedure is called. An

IN OUT parameter contains a value passed to the procedure when it is called and returns a value after it is completed. For example, the following procedure in Oracle PL/SQL has IN parameter p1, OUT parameter p2, and IN OUT parameter p3.

```
create or replace procedure sample
  (p1 in varchar, p2 out number, p3 in out integer) is
begin
  --doing something
  null;
end sample;
/
```

NOTE

The syntax of stored procedures is vendor-specific. Oracle PL/SQL is used for demonstrations of stored procedures in this book. PL/SQL is a procedural language extension of SQL. It is a fully functional programming language whose syntax is very similar to Ada. In Oracle 8i, you can write stored procedures using Java. For more information, see the companion Web site at `www.cs.armstrong.edu/liang/radjb5.html`.

A `CallableStatement` object can be created using the `prepareCall(String call)` method in the `Connection` interface. For example, the following code creates a `CallableStatement cstmt` on `Connection connection` for procedure `sample`.

```
CallableStatement cstmt = connection.prepareCall(
  "{call Sample(?, ?, ?)}");
```

`{call Sample(?, ?, ...)}` is referred to as the *SQL escape syntax*, which signals the driver that the code within it should be handled differently. The driver parses the escape syntax and translates it into code that the database understands. For this case, Sample is an Oracle PL/SQL procedure. The call is translated to a string `"begin sample(?, ?, ?); end"` and passed to an Oracle database for execution.

You can call procedures as well as functions. The syntax to create a SQL callable statement for a function is:

```
{? = call FunctionName(?, ?, ...)}
```

`CallableStatement` inherits `PreparedStatement`. Additionally, the `CallableStatement` interface provides methods for registering OUT parameters and for getting values from OUT parameters. These methods are listed in Table 13.8.

Before calling a SQL procedure, you need to use appropriate set methods to pass values to IN and IN OUT parameters, and use `registerOutParameter` to register OUT and IN OUT parameters. For example, before calling procedure Sample, the following statements pass values to parameters `p1` (IN) and `p3` (IN OUT) and register parameters `p2` (OUT) and `p3` (IN OUT):

```
cstmt.setString(1, "dummy");
cstmt.setLong(3, 1);
cstmt.registerOutParameter(2, java.sql.Types.DOUBLE);
cstmt.registerOutParameter(3, java.sql.Types.INTEGER);
```

You may use `execute()` or `executeUpdate()` to execute the procedure depending on the type of SQL statement, then use get methods to retrieve values from the OUT

TABLE 13.8 `CallableStatement` Methods

Method Name	*Description*
`getBigDecimal`	Gets an OUT parameter as a `java.math.BigDecimal` object.
`getBoolean`	Gets a `boolean` from an OUT parameter.
`getByte`	Gets a `byte` from an OUT parameter.
`getBytes`	Gets an OUT parameter as an array of `byte` values.
`getDate`	Gets an OUT parameter as a `java.sql.Date` object.
`getDouble`	Gets a `double` from an OUT parameter.
`getFloat`	Gets a `float` from an OUT parameter.
`getInt`	Gets an `int` from an OUT parameter.
`getLong`	Gets a `long` from an OUT parameter.
`getObject`	Gets an OUT parameter as a Java `Object`.
`getShort`	Gets a `short` from an OUT parameter.
`getString`	Gets a `string` from an OUT parameter.
`getTime`	Gets an OUT parameter as `java.sql.Time` object.
`getTimeStamp`	Gets an OUT parameter as `java.sql.TimeStamp` object.
`registerOutParameter`	Registers an OUT parameter's data type.
`wasNull`	Returns null if an OUT parameter is SQL NULL.

parameters. For example, the next statements retrieve the values from parameters `p2` and `p3`.

```
double d = cstmt.getDouble(2);
int i = cstmt.getInt(3);
```

Example 13.5 Using CallableStatement to Execute SQL Stored Procedures

In this example, you will use a SQL stored function to check whether an address is already in the database before inserting a new address. The example is a continuation of Example 13.4. You will add a new menu, "Using Callable Statements," to demonstrate using stored procedures.

The following Oracle PL/SQL function returns the number of the records in the table that match the specified firstName and lastName in the table Address.

```
create or replace function addressFound
  (first varchar2, last varchar2)
  -- Do not name firstName and lastName. 6/4/00 YDL
  return number is
  numberOfSelectedRows number := 0;
begin

  select count(*) into numberOfSelectedRows
  from Address
```

```
    where Address.firstName = first and
      Address.lastName = last;

    return numberOfSelectedRows;
  end addressFound;
  /
```

Suppose table Address and function `addressFound` are already created in the database. The example consists of two new classes: `TestCallableStatement` and `AddressPanelUsingStoredProc`. `TestCallableStatement` adds a new menu item, "Using Callable Statements," to the previous example; `AddressPanelUsingStoredProc` extends `AddressPanelUsingDynamicSQL` and overrides the `insert()` method to check whether an address for the given first name and last name is already in the database. If so, nothing is done; if not, the superclass's `insert()` method is invoked to insert a new record.

To see the development in action, follow the steps below:

1. In the jdbcdemo project, select TestPreparedStatement.java in the project pane, and choose File, Save As to save the file as TestCallableStatement.java.
2. Replace TestPreparedStatement with TestCallableStatement in TestCallableStatement.java.
3. In the Menu designer for `TestCallableStatement`, add a new menu item, "Using Callable Statements," in the Operation menu. Change the menu name to `jmiStoredProc`. Generate and implement the code for handling the menu command, as follows:

```
void jmiStoredProc_actionPerformed(ActionEvent e) {
  addAddressPanel(
    new AddressPanelUsingStoredProc(
      dBConnectDialog1.getConnection()));
}
```

4. Create the class `AddressPanelUsingStoredProc` that extends `AddressPanelUsingDynamicSQL` with additional features that check whether an address already exists before executing the insertion, as shown in Listing 13.8.
5. Run TestCallableStatement.java to test the program. The main frame is shown in Figure 13.14. When "Using Stored Procedures" is selected, the

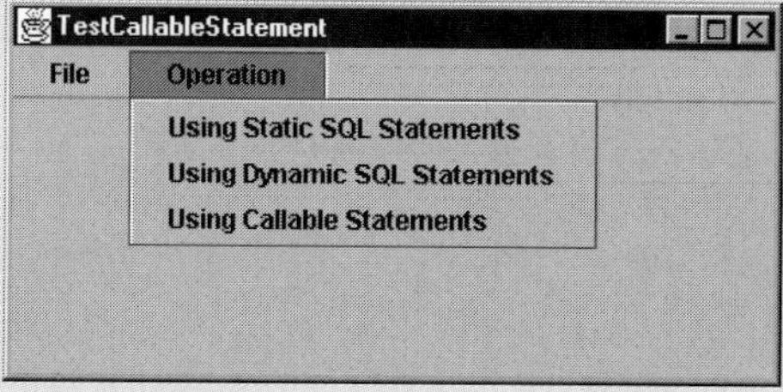

Figure 13.14 *The menu "Using Callable Statements" was added to test* `CallableStatement`.

continued

Example 13.5 continued

same user interface as shown in Figure 13.11 appears in the frame for searching and inserting addresses.

```
package jdbcdemo;

import java.sql.*;

public class AddressPanelUsingStoredProc
  extends AddressPanelUsingDynamicSQL {
  CallableStatement cstmt;

  public AddressPanelUsingStoredProc(Connection connection) {
    super(connection);

    try {
      // Create a callable statement
      cstmt = connection.prepareCall
        ("{ ? = call AddressFound(?, ?)}");
    }
    catch (SQLException ex) {
      jlblStatus.setText(ex.getMessage());
    }

    jlblStatus.setText("Using stored SQL procedures");
  }

  /** Override this method from AddressPanelUsingDynamicSQL */
  protected void insert() {
    try {
      if (addressFound() == 1)
        jlblStatus.setText("Address already exists");
      else
        super.insert();
    }
    catch (SQLException ex) {
      jlblStatus.setText(ex.getMessage());
    }
  }

  /** Return true if an address matching the given firstname and
    * lastname is already in the database  */
  int addressFound() throws SQLException {
    cstmt.setString(2, jtfFirstName.getText().trim());
    cstmt.setString(3, jtfLastName.getText().trim());
    cstmt.registerOutParameter(1, Types.INTEGER);
    cstmt.execute();
    return cstmt.getInt(1);
  }
}
```

Listing 13.8 *AddressPanelUsingStoredProc.java*

Example Review

Since the syntax and capabilities of stored procedures vary among vendors, JDBC's escape syntax for invoking procedures is translated into vendor-specific code for invoking procedures. To see whether the database supports stored procedures, call `supportsStoredProcedures()` in the `DatabaseMetaData` interface.

Use PreparedStatement or CallableStatement to process stored procedures with IN parameters. You must use CallableStatement to process stored procedures with OUT parameters. Before executing a stored procedure with the OUT parameter, you must use registerOutParameter() to register the OUT parameter with a data type specified in java.sql.Types.

CAUTION

Putting a semicolon (;) at the end of the escape syntax for invoking stored procedures is a common mistake. It causes a runtime error in Oracle drivers.

Scrollable and Updateable Result Set

The result sets used in the previous examples are read sequentially. A result set maintains a cursor pointing to its current row of data. Initially the cursor is positioned before the first row. The next method moves the cursor forward to the next row. This is known as *sequential forward reading*. It is only way supported in JDBC 1 for processing the rows in a result set.

With JDBC 2, you can scroll the rows both forward and backward and move the cursor to a desired location using the first, last, next, previous, absolute, or relative method. Additionally, you can insert, delete, or update a row in the result set and have the changes automatically reflected in the database.

To obtain a scrollable or updateable result set, you must first create a statement with an appropriate type and concurrency mode. For a static statement, use

```
Statement statement = connection.createStatement
  (int resultSetType, int resultSetConcurrency);
```

For a prepared statement, use

```
PreparedStatement statement = connection.prepareStatement
  (String sql, int resultSetType, int resultSetConcurrency);
```

For a callable statement, use

```
CallableStatement statement = connection.prepareCall
  (String sql, int resultSetType, int resultSetConcurrency);
```

The possible values of resultSetType are the constants defined in the ResultSet:

- TYPE_FORWARD_ONLY: The result set is accessed forward sequentially.
- TYPE_SCROLL_INSENSITIVE: The result set is scrollable, but not sensitive to changes in the database.
- TYPE_SCROLL_SENSITIVE: The result set is scrollable and sensitive to changes made by others. Use this type if you want the result set to be scrollable and updateable.

The possible values of `resultSetConcurrency` are the constants defined in the `ResultSet`:

- `CONCUR_READ_ONLY`: The result set cannot be used to update the database.
- `CONCUR_UPDATABLE`: The result set can be used to update the database.

NOTE
In English, updatable should be spelled updateable. But it is spelled `CONCUR_UPDATABLE` in Java.

For example, if you want the result set to be scrollable and updateable, you can create a static statement:

```
Statement statement = connection.createStatement
  (ResultSet.TYPE_SCROLL_INSENSITIVE, ResultSet.CONCUR_UPDATABLE)
```

You use the `executeQuery` method in a `Statement` object to execute a SQL query that returns a result set as follows:

```
ResultSet resultSet = statement.executeQuery(query);
```

The methods `first`, `next`, `previous`, and `last` are used to move the cursor to the first row, next row, previous row, and last row; and the `getXxx(int columnIndex)` or `getXxx(String columnName)` method is used to retrieve the value of a specified field at the current row. The methods `insertRow`, `deleteRow`, and `updateRow` can also be used to insert, delete, and update the current row. Before applying `insertRow` or `updateRow`, you need to use the method `update(int columnIndex, Xxx value)` or `update(String columnName, Xxx value)` to write a new value to the field at the current row.

The methods for manipulating a result set are shown in Table 13.9.

TABLE 13.9 `ResultSet` Methods

Method Name	*Description*
`boolean absolute(int row)`	Moves the cursor in the specified row.
`boolean afterLast()`	Moves the cursor to the end of the result set, just after the last row
`void beforeFirst()`	Moves the cursor to the front of the result set, just before the first row.
`void cancelRowUpdates()`	Cancels the updates made to a row.
`void clearWarnings()`	After this call, `getWarnings` returns null until a new warning is reported for this result set.
`void close()`	Closes result set and releases its resource.
`void deleteRow()`	Deletes the row from the result set and the underlying database.

continued

TABLE 13.9 continued

Method Name	*Description*
`int findColumn(String columnName)`	Finds the column index for the column name.
`boolean first()`	Moves the cursor to the first row.
`getXxx(String columnName)`	Various get methods to get the cell value for the column at the current row.
`getXxx(int columnIndex)`	Various get methods to get the cell value for the column at the current row.
`ResultSetMetaData getMetaData()`	Gets `ResultSetMetaData` for the result set.
`SQLWarning getWarnings()`	Gets SQL warning from the result set.
`void insertRow()`	Inserts the contents of the row to the result set and its underlying database.
`boolean isAfterLast()`	Returns true if the cursor is after the last row.
`boolean isBeforeFirst()`	Returns true if the cursor is before the first row.
`boolean isFirst()`	Returns true if the cursor is at the first row.
`boolean isLast()`	Returns true if the cursor is at the last row.
`boolean last()`	Moves the cursor to the last row.
`void moveToCurrentRow()`	Moves the cursor to the remembered cursor position after inserting or deleting a row.
`void moveToInsertRow()`	Moves the cursor to the insert row.
`boolean next()`	Moves the cursor to the next row.
`boolean previous()`	Moves the cursor to the previous row.
`void refreshRow()`	Refreshes the current row with its most recent value in the database.
`boolean relative(int rows)`	Moves the cursor a relative number of the rows.
`boolean rowDeleted()`	Indicates whether a row has been deleted.
`boolean rowInserted()`	Indicates whether a row has been inserted.
`boolean rowUpdated()`	Indicates whether a row has been updated.
`boolean updateRow()`	Updates the underlying database with the new contents of the current row.
`void updateXxx(String columnName, Xxx value)`	Updates the value for the column with the specified column name at the current row.
`void updateXxx(int columnIndex, Xxx value)`	Updates the value for the column with the specified index at the current row.
`boolean wasNull()`	Indicates whether the last column read had a value of SQL NULL.

Example 13.6 Scrolling and Updating Tables

In this example, you will develop a useful utility that displays all the rows of a database table in a `JTable` and uses a scrollable and updateable result set to navigate the table and modify its contents.

As shown in Figure 13.15, you enter or select a JDBC Driver and Database, enter a username and a password, and specify a table name to connect the database and display the table contents in the `JTable`. You can then use the buttons First, Next, Prior, and Last to move the cursor to the first row, next row, previous row, and last row in the table, and use the buttons Insert, Delete, and Update to modify the table contents. When clicking the Insert button, a dialog box is displayed to receive input, as shown in Figure 13.16.

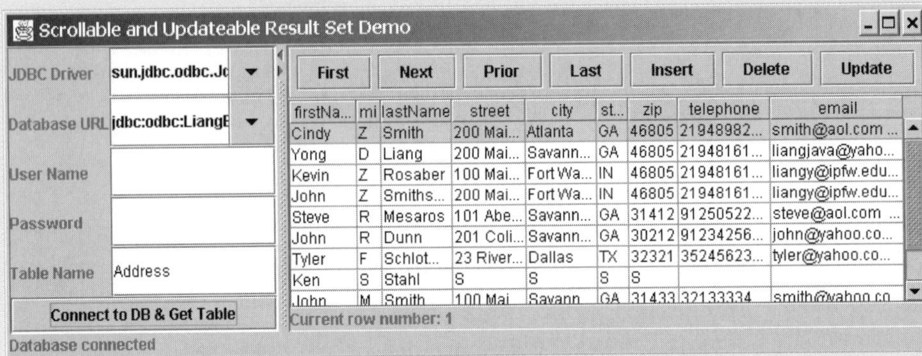

Figure 13.15 *The program enables you to navigate and modify the table.*

firstName	mi	lastName	street	city	state	zip	telephone	email
Tyler	C	Jones	110 Deer	Savannah	GA	32423	91234343...	tyler@hot...

Figure 13.16 *The Insert a New Record dialog box lets the user enter a new record.*

The status bar at the bottom of the window shows the current row in the result set and the `JTable`. The cursor in the result set and the row in the `JTable` are synchronized. You can move the cursor by using the navigation buttons or by selecting a row in the `JTable`.

The example consists of three classes: `TestTableEditor` (see Listing 13.9), `TableEditor` (see Listing 13.10), and `NewRecordDialog` (see Listing 13.11). `TestTableEditor` is the main class that enables the user to enter the database connection information and a table name. Once the database is connected, the table contents are displayed in an instance of `TableEditor`. The `TableEditor` class is a JavaBeans component that can be used to browse a table and modify a table. An instance of `NewRecordDialog` is displayed to let you enter a new record when you click the Insert button in `TableEditor`.

Follow the steps below to create this project.

1. In the jdbcdemo project, create a new applet named `TestTableEditor`, create a new JavaBeans component named `TableEditor` that extends `JPanel` using the JavaBean wizard, and create a new dialog component named `NewRecordDialog` using the Dialog wizard.
2. Build `TestTableEditor` as follows:

    2.1. With TestTableEditor.java selected in the project pane, switch the UI designer. Drop a `JSplitPane` from the Swing Containers page to the center of the applet to create `jSplitPane1`, and drop a `JLabel` to the south of the applet and rename it `jlblStatus`.

    2.2. Drop a `JPanel` to the left of `jSplitPane1` to create `jPanel1`, and set the layout of `jPanel1` to `BorderLayout`. Drop a `JPanel` to the west of `jPanel1` to create `jPanel2`, drop a `JPanel` to the center of `jPanel1` to create `jPanel3`, and drop a `JButton` to the south of `jPanel1` to create `jbtConnect` with the text "Connect to DB & Get Table." Panel `jPanel2` holds the labels for "JDBC Driver," "Database URL," "Username," "Password," and "Table Name." Panel `jPanel3` holds combo boxes and text fields for storing and entering information. These panels can be created in the same way as in Example 13.3, or you can simply copy them from Example 13.3 and paste them into this example.

    2.3. Compile TableEditor.java, install it in the component palette, and drop it to the right of `jSplitPane1` to create `tableEditor1`.

    2.4. Generate the handler for "Connect to DB & Get Table," and implement it to connect to the database. Set the connection and table name to `tableEditor1`, as shown in Listing 13.9 (Lines 107–118).

3. Build `TableEditor` as follows:

    3.1. With TableEditor.java selected in the project pane, switch the UI designer. Drop a `JPanel` to the north, a `JScrollPane` to the center, and a `JLable` to the south to create `jPanel1`, `jScrollPane1`, and `jlblStatus`.

    3.2. Drop a `JButton` seven times into `jPanel1` to create buttons with the text First, Next, Prior, Last, Insert, Delete, and Update. Rename the buttons `jbtFirst`, `jbtNext`, `jbtPrior`, `jbtLast`, `jbtInsert`, `jbtDelete`, and `jbtUpdate`.

    3.3. Drop a `JTable` into the `jScrollPane1` to create `jTable1`. Create a table model named `tableModel`, and set it to the `model` property of `jTable1`. Create a list selection model named `listSelectionModel`, and set it to the `selectionModel` of `jTable1`.

continued

Example 13.6 continued

3.4. Write the code to implement the buttons. Declare variables for JDBC `Connection`, `Statement`, and `ResultSet`. Declare the variable `rowVectors` to store the row data of `JTable`. Declare the variable `columnHeaderVector` to store the column names in `JTable`. Declare the variable `columnCount` to store the number of columns in `JTable`.

3.5. Create the method `setConnectionAndTable` to set a database connection and a table name for the component. Create the method `showTable()` to initialize the Swing table.

3.6. Generate the handler for the navigation buttons First, Next, Prior, and Last, implement these buttons to move the cursor in the result set, and set the corresponding row in `jTable1`.

3.7. In the component inspector for `listSelectModel`, choose the Events tab. Double-click the value field of the `valueChanged` event to generate a handler for processing a list selection change event. Implement the handler to set the cursor of the result set to the row selected in the table.

3.8. Generate the handler for the buttons Insert, Delete, and Update, and implement these buttons to modify the database. To insert a record to the database, you use a dialog box to obtain the new record.

4. Build `NewRecordDialog` as follows:

4.1. In the UI designer for NewRecordDialog.java, set the `title` property to "Insert a New Record," and the `modal` property to true. Set the hidden property `size` to 400, 100. Drop a `JScrollPane` to center of `panel1`, and drop a `JTable` to the scroll pane to create `jTable1`. Drop a `JPanel` to the south of `panel1` to create `jPanel1`. Drop a `JButton` twice to the panel to create `jbtOK` and `jbtCancel` with `text` properties OK and Cancel.

4.2. Click the Bean tab in the UI designer to switch to BeansExpress. Click the Properties tab, and click the Add Properties button to add a new property named `newRecord` of the `Vector` type with a getter method.

4.3. Declare the variable `tableModel` as the model for `jTable1`. Set the `model` property of `jTable1` to `tableModel`.

4.4. Generate and implement the handlers for the OK and Cancel buttons, as shown in Listing 13.11.

```
package jdbcdemo;

import java.awt.*;
import java.awt.event.*;
import java.applet.*;
import javax.swing.*;
import javax.swing.table.*;
```

Listing 13.9 *TestTableEditor.java*

```
import javax.swing.event.*;
import java.sql.*;
import java.util.*;

public class TestTableEditor extends JApplet {
  boolean isStandalone = false;
  JComboBox jcboURL = new JComboBox();
  JComboBox jcboDriver = new JComboBox();
  JTextField jtfTableName = new JTextField();
  JButton jtbConnect = new JButton();
  JPanel jPanel3 = new JPanel();
  JPanel jPanel2 = new JPanel();
  JPanel jPanel1 = new JPanel();
  JTextField jtfUserName = new JTextField();
  GridLayout gridLayout4 = new GridLayout();
  GridLayout gridLayout3 = new GridLayout();
  JTextField jtfPassword = new JPasswordField();
  BorderLayout borderLayout3 = new BorderLayout();
  JLabel jLabel5 = new JLabel();
  JLabel jLabel4 = new JLabel();
  JLabel jLabel3 = new JLabel();
  JLabel jLabel2 = new JLabel();
  JLabel jLabel1 = new JLabel();
  JSplitPane jSplitPane1 = new JSplitPane();
  JLabel jlblStatus = new JLabel();
  TableEditor tableEditor = new TableEditor();

  /** Initialize the applet */
  public void init() {
    try {
      jbInit();
    }
    catch(Exception e) {
      e.printStackTrace();
    }
  }

  /** Component initialization */
  private void jbInit() throws Exception {
    this.setSize(new Dimension(555, 224));
    jcboURL.setEditable(true);
    jcboDriver.setEditable(true);
    jtbConnect.setText("Connect to DB & Get Table");
    jtbConnect.addActionListener(
      new java.awt.event.ActionListener() {
      public void actionPerformed(ActionEvent e) {
        jtbConnect_actionPerformed(e);
      }
    });
    jPanel3.setLayout(gridLayout3);
    jPanel2.setLayout(gridLayout4);
    jPanel1.setLayout(borderLayout3);
    gridLayout4.setRows(5);
    gridLayout3.setRows(5);
    jLabel5.setText("Table Name");
    jLabel4.setText("Password");
    jLabel3.setText("User Name");
    jLabel2.setText("Database URL");
    jLabel1.setText("JDBC Driver");
    jlblStatus.setText("Status label");
    jSplitPane1.setContinuousLayout(true);
```

Listing 13.9 *Continued*

continued

Example 13.6 continued

```
    jSplitPane1.setOneTouchExpandable(true);
    jPanel3.setMinimumSize(new Dimension(50, 130));
    jPanel3.setPreferredSize(new Dimension(50, 130));
    this.getContentPane().add(jlblStatus, BorderLayout.SOUTH);
    this.getContentPane().add(jSplitPane1, BorderLayout.CENTER);
    jSplitPane1.add(jPanel1, JSplitPane.LEFT);
    jSplitPane1.add(tableEditor, JSplitPane.RIGHT);
    jPanel1.add(jPanel2, BorderLayout.WEST);
    jPanel2.add(jLabel1, null);
    jPanel2.add(jLabel2, null);
    jPanel2.add(jLabel3, null);
    jPanel2.add(jLabel4, null);
    jPanel2.add(jLabel5, null);
    jPanel1.add(jPanel3, BorderLayout.CENTER);
    jPanel3.add(jcboDriver, null);
    jPanel3.add(jcboURL, null);
    jPanel3.add(jtfUserName, null);
    jPanel3.add(jtfPassword, null);
    jPanel3.add(jtfTableName, null);
    jPanel1.add(jtbConnect, BorderLayout.SOUTH);

    // Add items to the combo boxes
    jcboURL.addItem("jdbc:odbc:LiangBookDB_MDB");
    jcboURL.addItem(
      "jdbc:oracle:thin:@liang.armstrong.edu:1521:test");
    jcboURL.addItem
      ("jdbc:borland:dslocal:C:\\radjb4\\LiangBookDB.jds");
    jcboURL.addItem
      ("jdbc:interbase://localhost/C:/radjb4/LiangBookDB.gdb");
    jcboDriver.addItem("sun.jdbc.odbc.JdbcOdbcDriver");
    jcboDriver.addItem("oracle.jdbc.driver.OracleDriver");
    jcboDriver.addItem(
      "com.borland.datastore.jdbc.DataStoreDriver");
    jcboDriver.addItem("interbase.interclient.Driver");

    // Pass this (applet) to the dialog box
  }

  /** Handle the "Connect to DB and Get Table" button */
  void jtbConnect_actionPerformed(ActionEvent e) {
    try {
      // Connect to the database
      Connection connection = getConnection();
      tableEditor.setConnectionAndTable(connection,
        jtfTableName.getText().trim());
    }
    catch (Exception ex) {
      jlblStatus.setText(ex.toString());
    }
  }

  /** Connect to a database */
  private Connection getConnection() throws Exception {
    // Load the JDBC driver
    System.out.println((String)jcboDriver.getSelectedItem());
    Class.forName(((String)jcboDriver.getSelectedItem()).trim());
    System.out.println("Driver loaded");

    // Establish a connection
    Connection connection = DriverManager.getConnection
```

Listing 13.9 *Continued*

```
        (((String)jcboURL.getSelectedItem()).trim(),
        jtfUserName.getText().trim(), jtfPassword.getText().trim());
      System.out.println("Database connected");
      jlblStatus.setText("Database connected");

      return connection;
    }
  }
```

Listing 13.9 *Continued*

```
package jdbcdemo;

import java.awt.*;
import javax.swing.*;
import java.awt.event.*;
import javax.swing.table.*;
import javax.swing.event.*;
import java.util.*;
import java.sql.*;

public class TableEditor extends JPanel {
  BorderLayout borderLayout1 = new BorderLayout();
  JButton jbtNext = new JButton();
  JButton jbtLast = new JButton();
  JPanel jPanel1 = new JPanel();
  JButton jbtInsert = new JButton();
  JButton jbtPrior = new JButton();
  JButton jbtDelete = new JButton();
  JButton jbtUpdate = new JButton();
  JButton jbtFirst = new JButton();
  JScrollPane jScrollPane1 = new JScrollPane();
  JTable jTable1 = new JTable();
  JLabel jlblStatus = new JLabel();

  // Dialog box for inserting a new record
  NewRecordDialog newRecordDialog1 = new NewRecordDialog();

  // JDBC Connection
  Connection connection;

  // Table name
  String tableName;

  // JDBC Statement
  Statement statement;

  // Result set for the table
  ResultSet resultSet;

  // Table model
  DefaultTableModel tableModel = new DefaultTableModel();

  // Table selection model
  DefaultListSelectionModel listSelectionModel =
    new DefaultListSelectionModel();

  // New row vector
  Vector rowVectors = new Vector();

```

Listing 13.10 *TableEditor.java*

continued

Example 13.6 continued

```
    // columnHeaderVector to hold column names
    Vector columnHeaderVector = new Vector();

    // Column count
    int columnCount;

    public TableEditor() {
      try {
        jbInit();
      }
      catch(Exception ex) {
        ex.printStackTrace();
      }
    }

    private void jbInit() throws Exception {
      jPanel1.setBorder(BorderFactory.createEtchedBorder());
      jbtLast.setText("Last");
      jbtLast.addActionListener(new java.awt.event.ActionListener() {
        public void actionPerformed(ActionEvent e) {
          jbtLast_actionPerformed(e);
        }
      });
      jbtNext.addActionListener(new java.awt.event.ActionListener() {
        public void actionPerformed(ActionEvent e) {
          jbtNext_actionPerformed(e);
        }
      });
      jbtNext.setText("Next");
      this.setLayout(borderLayout1);
      jbtInsert.setText("Insert");
      jbtInsert.addActionListener(new java.awt.event.ActionListener() {
        public void actionPerformed(ActionEvent e) {
          jbtInsert_actionPerformed(e);
        }
      });
      jbtPrior.addActionListener(new java.awt.event.ActionListener() {
        public void actionPerformed(ActionEvent e) {
          jbtPrior_actionPerformed(e);
        }
      });
      jbtPrior.setText("Prior");
      jbtDelete.setText("Delete");
      jbtDelete.addActionListener(new java.awt.event.ActionListener() {
        public void actionPerformed(ActionEvent e) {
          jbtDelete_actionPerformed(e);
        }
      });
      jbtUpdate.addActionListener(new java.awt.event.ActionListener() {
        public void actionPerformed(ActionEvent e) {
          jbtUpdate_actionPerformed(e);
        }
      });
      jbtUpdate.setText("Update");
      jbtFirst.addActionListener(new java.awt.event.ActionListener() {
        public void actionPerformed(ActionEvent e) {
          jbtFirst_actionPerformed(e);
        }
      });
```

Listing 13.10 *Continued*

```
      jbtFirst.setText("First");
      jlblStatus.setText("Status label");
      this.add(jPanel1, BorderLayout.NORTH);
      jPanel1.add(jbtFirst, null);
      jPanel1.add(jbtNext, null);
      jPanel1.add(jbtPrior, null);
      jPanel1.add(jbtLast, null);
      jPanel1.add(jbtInsert, null);
      jPanel1.add(jbtDelete, null);
      jPanel1.add(jbtUpdate, null);
      this.add(jScrollPane1, BorderLayout.CENTER);
      this.add(jlblStatus, BorderLayout.SOUTH);
      jScrollPane1.getViewport().add(jTable1, null);
      jTable1.setModel(tableModel);
      jTable1.setSelectionModel(listSelectionModel);
      listSelectionModel.addListSelectionListener(
        new javax.swing.event.ListSelectionListener() {
        public void valueChanged(ListSelectionEvent e) {
          listSelectionModel_valueChanged(e);
        }
      });
    }

    /** Handle the Update button */
    void jbtUpdate_actionPerformed(ActionEvent e) {
      try {
        // Get the current row
        int row = jTable1.getSelectedRow();

        // Gather data from the UI and update the database fields
        for (int i=1;
          i<=resultSet.getMetaData().getColumnCount(); i++) {
          resultSet.updateObject(i, tableModel.getValueAt(row, i-1));
        }

        // Invoke the update method in the result set
        resultSet.updateRow();
        refreshResultSet();
      }
      catch (Exception ex) {
        jlblStatus.setText(ex.toString());
      }
    }

    /** Handle the First button */
    void jbtFirst_actionPerformed(ActionEvent e) {
      moveCursor("first");
    }

    /** Set cursor in the table and set the row number in the status */
    private void setTableCursor() throws Exception {
      int row = resultSet.getRow();
      listSelectionModel.setSelectionInterval(row-1, row-1);
      jlblStatus.setText("Current row number: " + row);
    }

    /** Handle the Last button */
    void jbtLast_actionPerformed(ActionEvent e) {
      moveCursor("last");
    }

```

Listing 13.10 *Continued*

continued

Example 13.6 continued

```
      /** Handle the Prior button */
      void jbtPrior_actionPerformed(ActionEvent e) {
        moveCursor("previous");
      }

      /** Handle the Next button */
      void jbtNext_actionPerformed(ActionEvent e) {
        moveCursor("next");
      }

      /** Move cursor to the next record */
      private void moveCursor(String whereToMove) {
        try {
          if (whereToMove.equals("first"))
            resultSet.first();
          else if (whereToMove.equals("next"))
            resultSet.next();
          else if (whereToMove.equals("previous"))
            resultSet.previous();
          else if (whereToMove.equals("last"))
            resultSet.last();
          setTableCursor();
        }
        catch (Exception ex) {
          jlblStatus.setText(ex.toString());
        }
      }

      /** Handle the Insert button */
      void jbtInsert_actionPerformed(ActionEvent e) {
        // Display the dialog box
        newRecordDialog1.displayTable(columnHeaderVector);
        Vector newRecord = newRecordDialog1.getNewRecord();

        if (newRecord == null) return;

        // Insert the record to the Swing table
        tableModel.addRow(newRecord);

        // Insert the record to the database table
        try {
          for (int i=1; i<=columnCount; i++) {
            resultSet.updateObject(i, newRecord.elementAt(i-1));
          }

          resultSet.insertRow();
          refreshResultSet();
        }
        catch (Exception ex) {
          jlblStatus.setText(ex.toString());
        }
      }

      void jbtDelete_actionPerformed(ActionEvent e) {
        try {
          // Delete the record from the database
          resultSet.deleteRow();
          refreshResultSet();

```

Listing 13.10 *Continued*

```
      // Remove the row in the table
      tableModel.removeRow(
        listSelectionModel.getLeadSelectionIndex());
    }
    catch (Exception ex) {
      jlblStatus.setText(ex.toString());
    }
  }

  /** Refresh the result set */
  private void refreshResultSet() {
    try {
      resultSet = statement.executeQuery(
        "SELECT * FROM " + tableName);
      // Set the cursor to the first record in the table
      moveCursor("first");
    }
    catch (SQLException ex) {
      ex.printStackTrace();
    }
  }

  /** Set database connection and table name in the TableEditor */
  public void setConnectionAndTable(Connection newConnection,
    String newTableName) {
    connection = newConnection;
    tableName = newTableName;
    try {
      statement = connection.createStatement(ResultSet.
        TYPE_SCROLL_SENSITIVE, ResultSet.CONCUR_UPDATABLE);
      showTable();
      moveCursor("first");
    }
    catch (SQLException ex) {
      ex.printStackTrace();
    }
  }

  /** Display database table to a Swing table */
  private void showTable() throws SQLException {
    // Clear vectors to store data for a new table
    rowVectors.clear();
    columnHeaderVector.clear();

    // Obtain table contents
    resultSet = statement.executeQuery(
      "select * from " + tableName + ";");

    // Get column count
    columnCount = resultSet.getMetaData().getColumnCount();

    // Store rows to rowVectors
    while (resultSet.next()) {
      Vector singleRow = new Vector();
      for (int i=0; i<columnCount; i++)
        // Store cells to a row
        singleRow.addElement(resultSet.getObject(i+1));
      rowVectors.addElement(singleRow);
    }

```

Listing 13.10 *Continued*

continued

Example 13.6 continued

```
      // Get column name and add to columnHeaderVector
      ResultSet rsColumns = connection.getMetaData().getColumns(
        null, null, tableName, null);
      while (rsColumns.next()) {
        columnHeaderVector.addElement(
          rsColumns.getString("COLUMN_NAME"));
      }

      // Set new data to the table model
      tableModel.setDataVector(rowVectors, columnHeaderVector);
    }

    /** Handle the selection in the table */
    void listSelectionModel_valueChanged(ListSelectionEvent e) {
      int selectedRow = jTable1.getSelectedRow();

      try {
        resultSet.absolute(selectedRow+1);
        setTableCursor();
      }
      catch (Exception ex) {
        jlblStatus.setText(ex.toString());
      }
    }
  }
```

Listing 13.10 *Continued*

```
  package jdbcdemo;

  import java.awt.*;
  import javax.swing.*;
  import javax.swing.table.*;
  import java.util.*;
  import java.awt.event.*;

  public class NewRecordDialog extends JDialog {
    // Table model
    DefaultTableModel tableModel = new DefaultTableModel();

    JPanel panel1 = new JPanel();
    BorderLayout borderLayout1 = new BorderLayout();
    JScrollPane jScrollPane1 = new JScrollPane();
    JPanel jPanel1 = new JPanel();
    JButton jbtOK = new JButton();
    JButton jbtCancel = new JButton();
    JTable jTable1 = new JTable();
    private Vector newRecord;

    public NewRecordDialog(Frame frame, String title, boolean modal) {
      super(frame, title, modal);
      try {
        jbInit();
        pack();
      }
      catch(Exception ex) {
        ex.printStackTrace();
      }
    }

```

Listing 13.11 *NewRecordDialog.java*

```
    public NewRecordDialog() {
      this(null, "", false);
    }

    void jbInit() throws Exception {
      panel1.setLayout(borderLayout1);
      jbtOK.setText("OK");
      jbtOK.addActionListener(new java.awt.event.ActionListener() {
        public void actionPerformed(ActionEvent e) {
          jbtOK_actionPerformed(e);
        }
      });
      jbtCancel.setText("Cancel");
      jbtCancel.addActionListener(new java.awt.event.ActionListener() {
        public void actionPerformed(ActionEvent e) {
          jbtCancel_actionPerformed(e);
        }
      });
      this.setSize(new Dimension(400, 100));
      this.setTitle("Insert a New Record");
      this.setModal(true);
      jTable1.setModel(tableModel);
      getContentPane().add(panel1);
      panel1.add(jScrollPane1, BorderLayout.CENTER);
      jScrollPane1.getViewport().add(jTable1, null);
      panel1.add(jPanel1, BorderLayout.SOUTH);
      jPanel1.add(jbtOK, null);
      jPanel1.add(jbtCancel, null);
    }

    public java.util.Vector getNewRecord() {
      return newRecord;
    }

    /** Display the table */
    void displayTable(Vector columnHeaderVector) {
      this.setSize(new Dimension(400, 100));

      tableModel.setDataVector(new Vector(),
        columnHeaderVector);

      // Must create a new vector for a new record
      newRecord = new Vector();
      tableModel.addRow(newRecord);

      setVisible(true);
    }

    void jbtOK_actionPerformed(ActionEvent e) {
      setVisible(false);
    }

    void jbtCancel_actionPerformed(ActionEvent e) {
      newRecord = null;
      setVisible(false);
    }
  }
```

Listing 13.11 *Continued*

continued

Example 13.6 continued

Example Review

The key class in this example is `TableEditor`, which can be used to navigate and modify the table contents. To use it, simply create an instance of `TableEditor`, set the database connection and the table name in the instance, and place it in a graphical user interface. The `setConnectionAndTableName` method involves creating a statement, obtaining a result set, and displaying the result set in the Swing table. The statement is created with the arguments `TYPE_SCROLL_SENSITIVE` and `CONCUR_UPDATABLE` for obtaining scrollable and updateable result sets.

The `showTable()` method is responsible for transferring data from the database table to the Swing table. The column names and column count are obtained using the `ResultSetMetaData` interface. An instance of the `ResultSetMetaData` interface is obtained using the `getMetaData` method for the result set. Each record from the result set is copied to a row vector. The row vector is added to another vector that stores all the rows for the table model (`tableModel`) for the `JTable`.

The handling of the navigation buttons First, Next, Prior, and Last is simply to invoke the methods `first`, `next`, `previous`, and `last` to move the cursor in the result set and, at the same time, set the selected row in the Swing table.

The handling of the Insert button involves displaying the "Insert a New Record" dialog box (`newRecordDialog1`) for receiving the new record. Once the record is entered, clicking the OK button dismisses the dialog box. The new record is obtained by invoking the `newRecordDialog1.getNewRecord()` method. To insert the new record into the database, use the `updateXxx` method to update the fields and then use the `insertRow` method to insert the record to the database table. To insert the new record to the Swing table, use the `addRow` method to add the vector to the table model (`tableModel`). Finally, you need to refresh the result set by re-executing the query. Theoretically, you should not have to refresh the result set. The driver should automatically reflect the changes in the database to the result set. However, none of the drivers I have tested supports this.

To implement the Delete button, invoke the `deleteRow` method in the result set to remove the record from the database, and use the `removeElementAt` method in the `Vector` class to remove the record from `rowVectors`.

To implement the Update button, invoke the `updateXxx` method in the result set, and then invoke the `updateRow` method to update the result set.

To implement the handler for list selection event on `jTable1`, set the cursor in the result set to match the row selected in `jTable1`.

NOTE
To ensure the effect of editing a field in the table, you need to press the Enter key or move the cursor to other fields.

NOTE
I have tested the program using several drivers. The only driver that completely supports this program is the JDBC-ODBC driver in JDK 1.3. The Oracle driver bundled with Oracle Enterprise Server 8i supports the read-only scrollable result set but not the updateable scrollable result set. Thus you cannot modify the result set. You can use `supportsResultSetType(int type)` and `supportsResultSetConcurrency(int type, int concurrency)` in the `DatabaseMetaData` interface to find out which result type and currency modes are supported by the JDBC driver. But even if a driver supports the scrollable and updateable result set, a result set for a complex query might not be able to perform update. For example, the result set for a query that involves several tables is likely not to support update operations.

Storing and Retrieving Images in JDBC

One of the frequently asked questions is how to store and retrieve images from a database. Images are stored in binary in a table cell. The data type for the cell is BLOB (Binary Large OBject), which is a new SQL type in SQL3 for storing binary data. Another new SQL3 type is CLOB (Character Large OBject) for storing a large text in the character format. JDBC 2 introduced the interfaces `java.sql.Blob` and `java.sql.Clob` to support mapping for these new SQL types. JBDC 2 also added new methods, such as `getBlob`, `setBinaryStream`, `getClob`, `setBlob`, and `setClob` in the interfaces `ResultSet`, `PreparedStatement`, and `CallableStatement`, to access SQL BLOB and CLOB values.

To store an image into a cell in a table, the corresponding column for the cell must be of the BLOB type. For example, the following SQL statement creates a table whose type for the flag column is BLOB.

```
create table Country(name varchar(30), flag blob,
  description varchar(500));
```

In the preceding statement, the `description` column is limited to 500 characters. The upper limit for the VARCHAR type is 32,672 bytes. For a large character field, you can use the CLOB type, which can store up to 2 GB characters.

To insert a record with images to a table, define a prepared statement like this one:

```
PreparedStatement pstmt = connection.prepareStatement(
  "insert into Country values(?, ?, ?)");
```

Images are usually stored in files. You may first get an instance of `InputStream` for an image file and then use the `setBinaryStream` method to associate the input stream with cell in the table, as follows:

```
// Store image to the table cell
File file = new File(imageFilenames[i]);
InputStream inputImage = new FileInputStream(file);
pstmt.setBinaryStream(2, inputImage, (int)(file.length()));
```

To retrieve an image from a table, use the `getBlob` method, as shown below:

```
// Store image to the table cell
Blob blob = rs.getBlob(1);
ImageIcon imageIcon = new ImageIcon(
  blob.getBytes(1, (int)blob.length()));
```

Example 13.7 Storing and Retrieving Images in JDBC

In this example, you will create a table, populate it with data, including images, and retrieve and display images. The table is named Country. Each record in the table consists of three fields: name, flag, and description. Flag is an image field. The program first creates the table and stores data to it. Then the program retrieves the country names from the table and adds them to a combo box. When the user selects a name from the combo box, the country's flag and description are displayed, as shown in Figure 13.17.

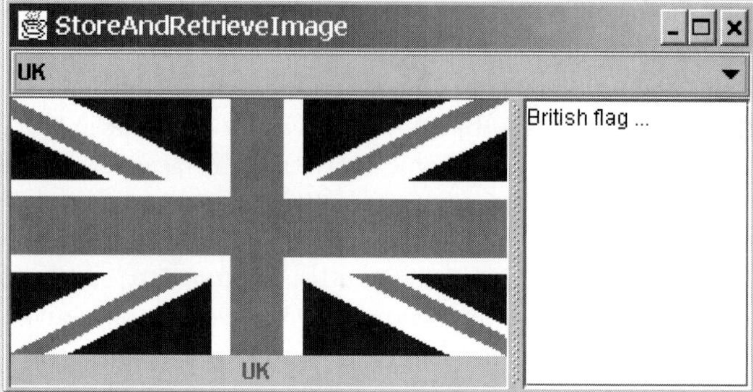

Figure 13.17 *The program enables you to retrieve data, including images, from a table and displays them.*

The example consists of two classes: `DescriptionPanel` (see Listing 13.12) and `StoreAndRetrieveImage` (see Listing 13.13). `DescriptionPanel` is a component for displaying a country (name, flag, and description). `StoreAndRetrieveImage` is the main class that initializes the table and creates the user interface using a `DescriptionPanel` and a combo box.

Follow the steps below to create this project.

1. In the jdbcdemo project, create a new applet named `StoreAndRetrieveImage`, and create a new JavaBeans component named `DescriptionPanel` that extends `JPanel` using the JavaBeans wizard.

2. Build `DescriptionPanel` as follows:

   2.1. With DescriptionPanel.java selected in the project pane, switch the UI designer. Drop a `JSplitPane` from the Swing Containers page to the center of the panel to create `jSplitPane1`, and drop a `JPanel` to the left of the split pane to create `jPanel1` and a `JScrollPane` to the right of the split pane.

   2.2. Set the layout of `jPanel1` to `BorderLayout`. Drop an `ImageViewer` (created in Example 4.1) to the center of `jPanel1` to create `imageViewer1`, and drop a `JLabel` to the south of `jPanel1` to create `jLabel1`. Drop a `JTextArea` to the scroll pane to create `jTextArea1`.

   2.3. Use BeansExpress to create properties `name`, `imageIcon`, and `description`. Modify the set method in these properties to display the properties in `imageViewer1`, `jLabel1`, and `jTextArea1`, as shown in Listing 13.11.

3. Build `StoreAndRetrieveImage` as follows:

   3.1. In the UI designer for StoreAndRetrieveImage.java, drop a `JComboBox` to the north of the applet to create `jComboBox1`, and drop a `DescriptionPanel` to the center of the applet to create `descriptionPanel1`.

   3.2. In the event tab of the inspector for `jComboBox1`, double-click the value field of `itemStateChanged` to generate a handler for the `ItemEvent`. Implement the handler to retrieve data from the database and display them in `descriptionPanel1`, as shown in Listing 13.12 (Lines 132–134).

   3.3. Implement the code for connecting the database, for creating the table, for populating data, including images, into the table, for retrieving data, and for displaying data, as shown in Listing 13.12.

```
1    package jdbcdemo;
2
3    import java.awt.*;
4    import javax.swing.*;
5    import imageviewerdemo.*;
6
7    public class DescriptionPanel extends JPanel {
8      BorderLayout borderLayout1 = new BorderLayout();
9      JPanel jPanel1 = new JPanel();
10     JScrollPane jScrollPane1 = new JScrollPane();
11     JTextArea jTextArea1 = new JTextArea();
12     BorderLayout borderLayout2 = new BorderLayout();
13     ImageViewer imageViewer1 = new ImageViewer();
14     JLabel jLabel1 = new JLabel();
15     private String name;
16     private String description;
17     private javax.swing.ImageIcon imageIcon;
18     JSplitPane jSplitPane1 = new JSplitPane();
19
```

Listing 13.12 *DescriptionPanel.java*

continued

Example 13.7 continued

```
    public DescriptionPanel() {
      try {
        jbInit();
      }
      catch(Exception ex) {
        ex.printStackTrace();
      }
    }

    private void jbInit() throws Exception {
      this.setLayout(borderLayout1);
      jTextArea1.setText("jTextArea1");
      jPanel1.setLayout(borderLayout2);
      jLabel1.setHorizontalAlignment(SwingConstants.CENTER);
      jLabel1.setText("jLabel1");
      this.add(jSplitPane1, BorderLayout.CENTER);
      jSplitPane1.add(jPanel1, JSplitPane.LEFT);
      jPanel1.add(imageViewer1, BorderLayout.CENTER);
      jPanel1.add(jLabel1, BorderLayout.SOUTH);
      jSplitPane1.add(jScrollPane1, JSplitPane.RIGHT);
      jScrollPane1.getViewport().add(jTextArea1, null);
    }

    public void setName(String newName) {
      name = newName;
      jLabel1.setText(name);
    }

    public String getName() {
      return name;
    }

    public void setDescription(String newDescription) {
      description = newDescription;
      jTextArea1.setText(description);
    }

    public String getDescription() {
      return description;
    }

    public void setImageIcon(javax.swing.ImageIcon newImageIcon) {
      imageIcon = newImageIcon;
      imageViewer1.setImage(imageIcon.getImage());
    }

    public javax.swing.ImageIcon getImageIcon() {
      return imageIcon;
    }
  }
```

Listing 13.12 *Continued*

```
package jdbcdemo;

import java.awt.*;
import java.awt.event.*;
import java.applet.*;
import javax.swing.*;
```

Listing 13.13 *StoreAndRetrieveImage.java*

```
import java.sql.*;
import java.io.*;

public class StoreAndRetrieveImage extends JApplet {
  boolean isStandalone = false;
  DescriptionPanel descriptionPanel1 = new DescriptionPanel();
  JComboBox jComboBox1 = new JComboBox();

  // Connection to the database
  Connection connection;

  // Statement for static SQL statements
  Statement stmt;

  // Prepared statement
  PreparedStatement pstmt = null;


  /** Initialize the applet */
  public void init() {
    try {
      jbInit();
    }
    catch(Exception e) {
      e.printStackTrace();
    }
  }

  /** Component initialization */
  private void jbInit() throws Exception {
    this.setSize(new Dimension(400,300));
    jComboBox1.addItemListener(new java.awt.event.ItemListener() {
      public void itemStateChanged(ItemEvent e) {
        jComboBox1_itemStateChanged(e);
      }
    });
    this.getContentPane().add(descriptionPanel1,
      BorderLayout.CENTER);
    this.getContentPane().add(jComboBox1, BorderLayout.NORTH);

    connectDB(); // Connect to DB
    storeDataToTable(); // Store data to the table (including image)
    fillDataInComboBox(); // Fill in combo box
    retrieveFlagInfo((String)(jComboBox1.getSelectedItem()));
  }

  private void connectDB() throws Exception {
    // Load the driver
    Class.forName("oracle.jdbc.driver.OracleDriver");
    System.out.println("Driver loaded");

    // Establish connection
    connection = DriverManager.getConnection
      ("jdbc:oracle:thin:@liang.armstrong.edu:1521:test",
       "scott", "tiger");
    System.out.println("Database connected");

    // Create a statement for static SQL
    stmt = connection.createStatement();

```

Listing 13.13 *Continued*

continued

Example 13.7 continued

```
    // Create a prepared statement to retrieve flag and description
    pstmt = connection.prepareStatement("select flag, description " +
      "from Country where name = ?");
  }

  private void storeDataToTable() {
    String[] countries = {"Canada", "UK", "USA", "Germany",
      "Indian", "China"};

    String[] imageFilenames = {"c:\\radjb\\image\\ca.gif",
      "c:\\radjb\\image\\uk.gif", "c:\\radjb\\image\\us.gif",
      "c:\\radjb\\image\\germany.gif", "c:\\radjb\\image\\india.gif",
      "c:\\radjb\\image\\china.gif"};

    String[] descriptions = {"A text to describe Canadian " +
      "flag is omitted", "British flag ...", "American flag ...",
      "German flag ...", "Indian flag ...", "Chinese flag ..."};

    try {
      stmt.executeUpdate("drop table Country" );
      System.out.println("Table Country removed.");
    }
    catch (Exception ex) {
      System.out.println(ex);
    }

    try {
      // Create the Country table
      stmt.executeUpdate("create table Country(" +
        "name varchar(30) not null, " +
        "flag blob, description varchar(1000), " +
        "primary key(name))");
      System.out.println("Table Country created");

      // Create a prepared statement to insert records
      PreparedStatement pstmt = connection.prepareStatement(
        "insert into Country values(?, ?, ?)");

      // Store all predefined records
      for (int i=0; i<countries.length; i++) {
        pstmt.setString(1, countries[i]);

        // Store image to the table cell
        File file = new File(imageFilenames[i]);
        InputStream inputImage = new FileInputStream(file);
        pstmt.setBinaryStream(2, inputImage, (int)(file.length()));

        pstmt.setString(3, descriptions[i]);
        pstmt.executeUpdate();
      }

      System.out.println("Table Country populated");
    }
    catch (Exception ex) {
      ex.printStackTrace();
    }
  }

```

Listing 13.13 *Continued*

```
    private void fillDataInComboBox() throws Exception {
      ResultSet rs = stmt.executeQuery("select name from Country");
      while (rs.next()) {
        jComboBox1.addItem(rs.getString(1));
      }
    }

    void jComboBox1_itemStateChanged(ItemEvent e) {
      retrieveFlagInfo((String)(e.getItem()));
    }

    private void retrieveFlagInfo(String name) {
      try {
        pstmt.setString(1, name);
        ResultSet rs = pstmt.executeQuery();
        if (rs.next()) {
          Blob blob = rs.getBlob(1);
          ImageIcon imageIcon = new ImageIcon(
            blob.getBytes(1, (int)blob.length()));
          descriptionPanel1.setImageIcon(imageIcon);
          descriptionPanel1.setName(name);
          String description = rs.getString(2);
          descriptionPanel1.setDescription(description);
        }
      }
      catch (Exception ex) {
        System.err.println(ex);
      }
    }
  }
```

Listing 13.13 *Continued*

Example Review

Not all databases and their drivers support the SQL BLOB type. This example was tested using the Oracle type-4 driver on Oracle 8i. The example does not work on Microsoft Access and Borland JDataStore, but you can modify the program to make it work with a JDataStore database. See Exercise 13.8 for details.

The `storeDataToTable` method first drops the Country table if it exists, creates the Country table, and populates the table with data. The `fillDataInComboBox` method retrieves the country names and adds them to the combo box. The `retrieveFlagInfo(name)` method retrieves the flag and description for the specified country name.

Chapter Summary

This chapter gave an in-depth look at metadata, statements, result sets, and connections. You learned how to use the `DatabaseMetaData` interface to obtain database-wide information and the `ResultSetMetaData` interface to obtain metadata information on a specific `ResultSet`. You learned how to create and process statements using static SQL statements, prepared SQL statements, and callable SQL statements. You learned how to process batch updates, and how to process scrollable and updateable result sets. You learned how to use the methods in the `Connection` interface for processing transactions. You also learned to store and retrieve images using JDBC.

Review Questions

13.1 How do you set auto-commit to true?

13.2 Describe the methods for retrieving general information in the `DatabaseMetaData` interface.

13.3 Describe the methods for finding database capabilities in the `DatabaseMetaData` interface.

13.4 Describe the methods for getting database objects in the `DatabaseMetaData` interface.

13.5 How do you create an instance of `DatabaseMetaData`?

13.6 What is `ResultSetMetaData` for? Describe the methods in `ResultSetMetaData`. How do you create an instance of `ResultSetMetaData`?

13.7 Describe static statements, prepared statements, and callable statements and their interrelationships. How do you create instances of `Statement`, `PreparedStatement`, and `CallableStatement`? How do you execute these statements?

Programming Exercises

13.1 Write a program to insert 100 records into a table using static SQL statements, and another inserting the same 100 records into a table using dynamic SQL statements. Compare the two.

13.2 Modify Example 13.5 to create three tabs, "Static SQL," "Dynamic SQL," and "Callable SQL," instead of using menus.

13.3 Modify Example 12.5 to use a table to display the result set, as shown in Figure 13.18. Use `ResultSetMetaData` to obtain the column names, and use `DatabaseMetaData` to display the database URL and the username, once the connection is established.

13.4 Write a program to insert 1000 records to a database and compare the performance with and without batch updates, as shown in Figure 13.19. Suppose the table is defined as follows:

```
CREATE TABLE TEMP(NUM1 NUMBER, NUM2 NUMBER, NUM3 NUMBER)
```

Use the `Math.random()` method to generate random numbers for each record. Test this program with a local database and a remote database.

13.5 Write a program to use the buttons First, Next, Prior, Last, Insert, Delete, and Update display and modify a single record in the Address table, as shown in Figure 13.20.

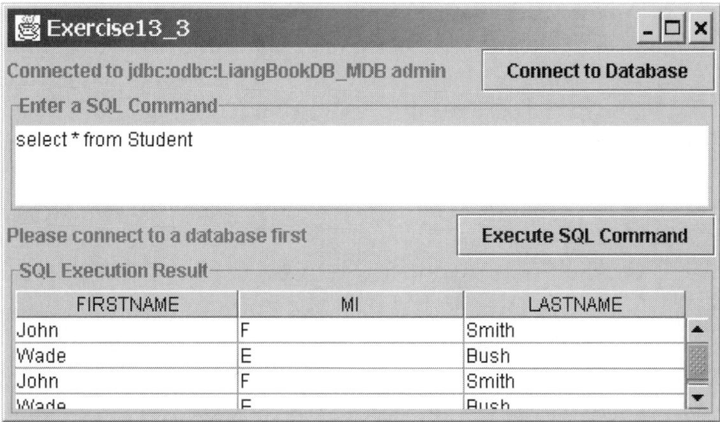

Figure 13.18 *The result set from the SQL select command is displayed in a table.*

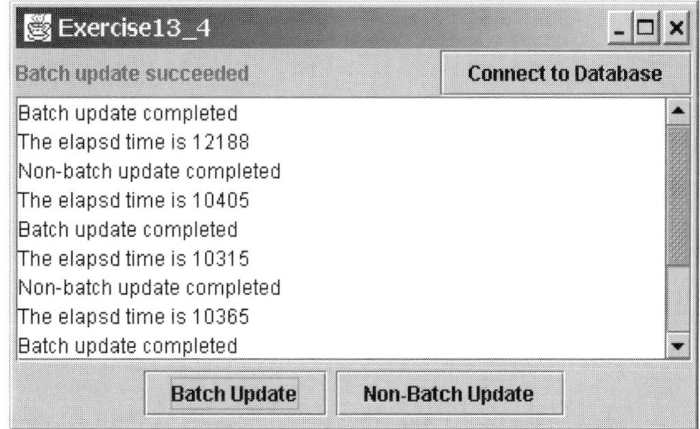

Figure 13.19 *The program demonstrates the performance improvements that result from using the batch updates.*

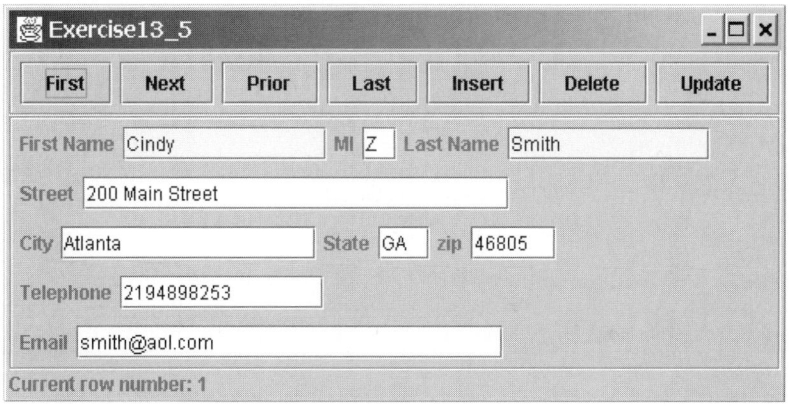

Figure 13.20 *You can use the buttons to display and modify a single record in the Address table.*

13.6 Modify Example 13.6 to display all the tables in the database for the specified user in a tree, as shown in Figure 13.21. You can choose a table from the tree instead of typing a table name in the text field, as in Example 13.6. Connect to the database using the `DBConnectDialog` class from a menu command in the Connection menu.

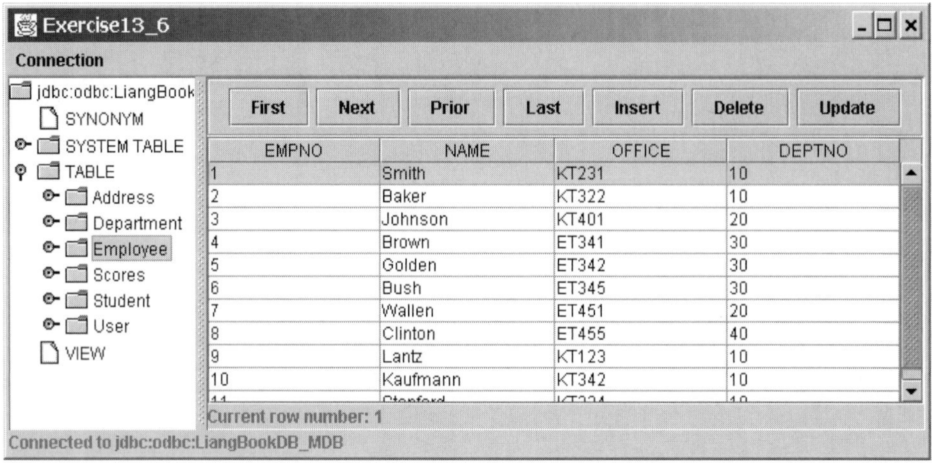

Figure 13.21 *You can choose a table from a tree.*

13.7 Improve Example 13.1 as follows:

1. Display the true/false value in the Capabilities tab in a check box, as shown in Figure 13.22.

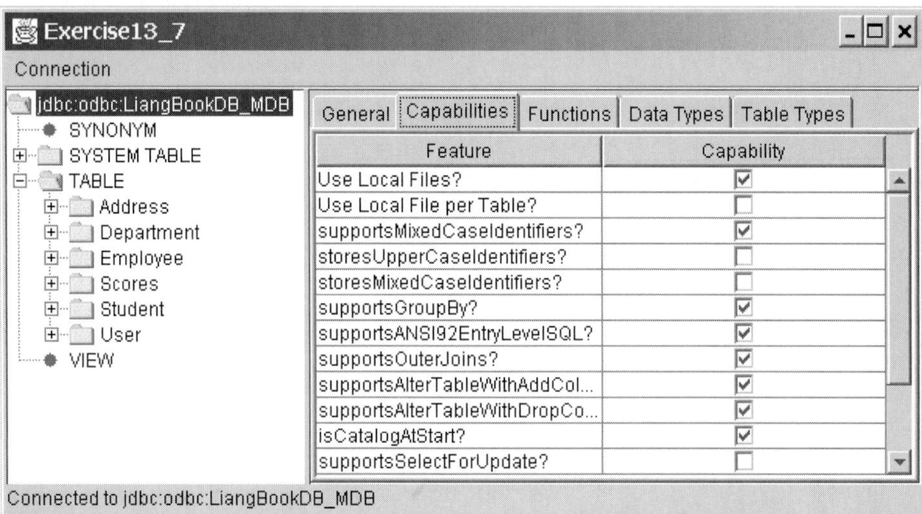

Figure 13.22 *The true/false value is displayed in a check box.*

2. Display functions in four tabs: Numeric, String, System, and Date and Time, as shown in Figure 13.23.

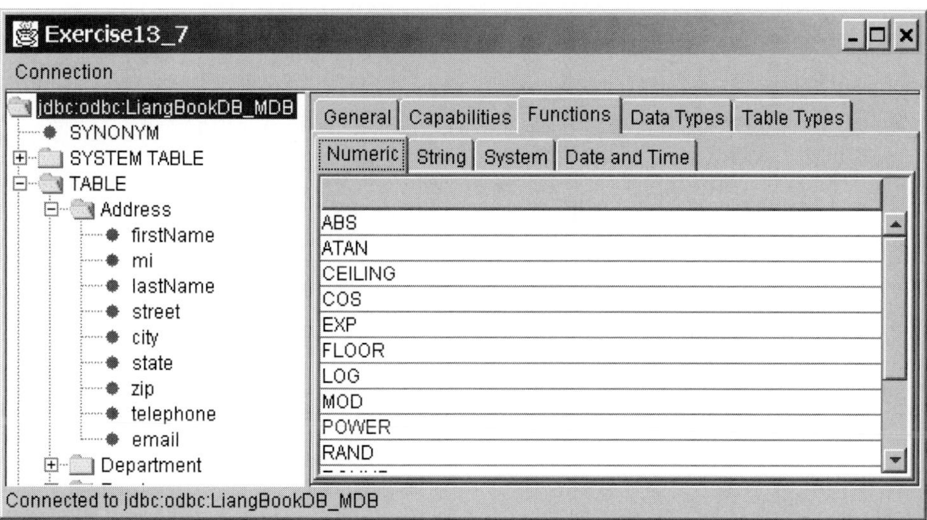

Figure 13.23 *The functions are displayed in groups using tabbed panes.*

3. Enable DBExplorer to display multiple connections, as shown in Figure 13.24.

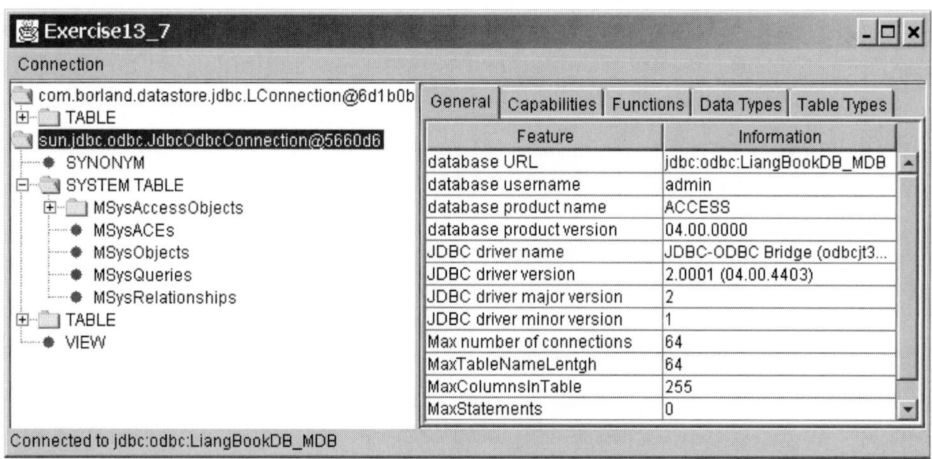

Figure 13.24 *Multiple connections are displayed in the explorer.*

4. Add a menu command Disconnect that removes a selected database connection from the tree, as shown in Figure 13.25.

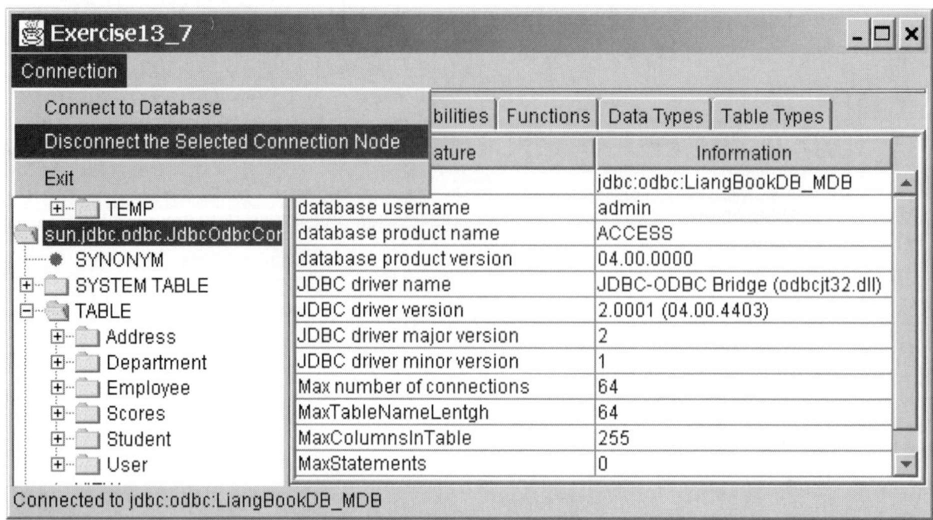

Figure 13.25 *You can remove a connection from DBExplorer.*

13.8 Example 13.7 does not work with a JDataStore database because JDataStore does not support the SQL BLOB type. However, it has the `InputStream` data type, which can be used to hold binary data. Rewrite Example 13.7 using a JDataStore database instead of Oracle, as follows:

- Create the table using the following statement:

```
create table Country(name varchar(30), flag inputstream,
  description varchar(500));
```

- Rewrite the `retrieveFlagInfo` method using the `setBinaryStream` method to set the image instead of using the `getBlob` method.

13.9 Write a program that uses `JTable` to display the Country table created in Example 13.7, as shown in Figure 13.26.

Figure 13.26 *The Country table is displayed in a* `JTable` *instance.*

CHAPTER 14

JBuilder DataExpress and Data-Aware Components

Objectives

- Understand the DataExpress API.
- Develop database applications using DataExpress and data-aware dbSwing components.
- Create master-detail forms using DataExpress and dbSwing components.
- Use a data module to separate data from GUI.

Introduction

JDBC provides a generic, low-level SQL database-access interface. It defines Java interfaces to represent database connections, SQL statements, result sets, database metadata, and so on. With the support of these interfaces, Java programmers issue SQL statements and process results. JDBC works well in this capacity and is easier to understand than ODBC, but it was designed to be a base upon which to build high-level interfaces and tools. JBuilder DataExpress API is a more user-friendly and convenient API built upon the JDBC API to provide powerful support for accessing and manipulating relational databases.

JBuilder also provides a data-aware version of Swing components, known as *dbSwing components*, that seamlessly bind to data sets defined in the DataExpress API. You can use these components to develop pure, powerful Java database applications with minimal coding.

NOTE
The DataExpress and dbSwing components are available in JBuilder 4 and 5 Professional and Enterprise.

DataExpress API

The DataExpress API consists of the following major classes contained in the `com.borland.dx.dataset`, `com.borland.dx.sql.dataset`, and `com.borland.datastore` packages. Some of these classes are installed in the Data Express page of the component palette.

- `Database`: This component installed in the component palette encapsulates a database connection through JDBC to a DBMS server and also provides lightweight transaction support. It combines the JDBC functions of loading the driver and connecting the database into one component.
- `DataSet`: This is an abstract class that provides basic editing, view, and cursor functionality for access to two-dimensional data. It supports the concept of a current row position, which allows for navigation of the data in the `DataSet`. The `DataSet` also manages a pseudo-record, an area in memory that temporarily stores a newly inserted row or changes to the current row.
- `StorageDataSet`: This is an abstract class that extends the `DataSet` class by providing basic cursor functionality to structural changes to the `DataSet`. It supports storage of data using `MemoryStore` or `DataStore`.
- `QueryDataSet`: This component installed in the component palette is a subclass of `StorageDataSet` for storing the results of a query string executed against a server database. It provides functionality to run a SQL query with or without parameters. This component works with the `Database` component to connect to a database server and executes queries. Once the resulting data

are stored in the `QueryDataSet`, you can manipulate them using the `DataSet` API.

- `ProcedureDataSet`: This component installed in the component palette is a subclass of `StorageDataSet` that provides functionality to run a stored procedure against data stored in a SQL database, passing in parameters if the procedure expects them.
- `TableDataSet`: This component installed in the component palette is a subclass of `StorageDataSet` for importing data from a text file.
- `DataSetView`: This component extends `DataSet` functionality by presenting an alternative view of the data in the `DataSet`. The `DataSetView` itself has no storage of data but sees all the unfiltered data contained in its `storageDataSet` property to which you can apply a different sort order and filter criterion from the original `StorageDataSet`. The navigation of `DataSetView` data is separate from that of its `StorageDataSet`.
- `DataStore`: This component provides high-performance data caching and compact persistence for `StorageDataSet`. By default, `StorageDataSet` uses a `MemoryStore` if the `store` property of `StorageDataSet` is not set. The `MemoryStore` class defines in-memory storage behavior for data that have been loaded into a JBuilder `DataSet` component. This class is used internally by other JBuilder classes. You should never use it directly.

When using the JDBC API to create a database application, you load the appropriate driver, establish a database connection, create and execute statements, and process the execution results. A typical procedure for developing database applications using the DataExpress API is as follows:

1. Use the `Database` class to specify a driver and connect to the database.
2. Use the `QueryDataSet`, `TableDataSet`, or `ProcedureDataSet` class to create and execute queries.
3. Use the methods in the `QueryDataSet`, `TableDataSet`, and `ProcedureDataSet` classes to process the query results.

Example 14.1 Creating an Address Book Using the DataExpress Components

This example creates a program to manage an online address book similar to the one in Example 13.2, "Using `Statement` to Execute Static SQL Statements." The address book was developed with the JDBC API in Example 13.2. This example uses DataExpress components to create a new address book component named `DataExpressAddressPanel` that extends the `jdbcdemo.AddressPanel` class and places the bean in an applet. Figure 14.1 shows a sample run of the applet.

continued

Example 14.1 continued

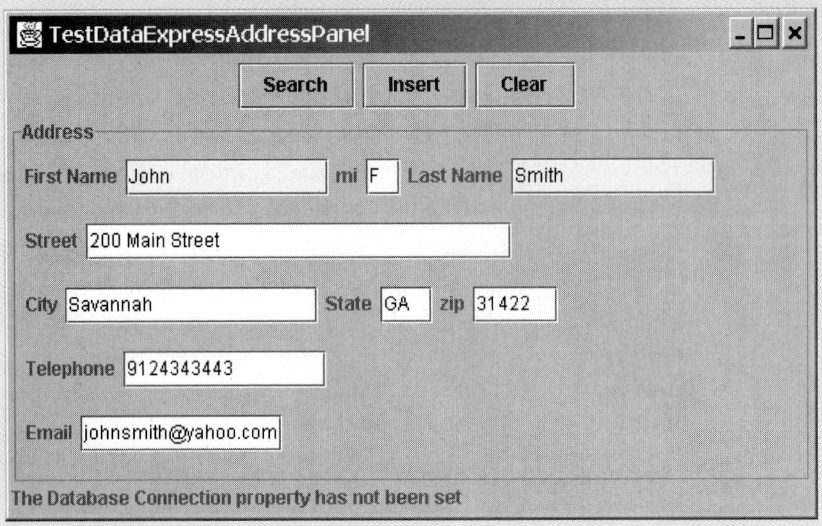

Figure 14.1 *You can search a record to match First Name and Last Name, insert a new record, or clear a record.*

Here are the steps to complete the project.

1. Create a new project named dataexpressdemo.jpr, and create a new class named `DataExpressAddressPanel` that extends `jdbcdemo.AddressPanel` using the Class wizard.

2. Follow the steps below to establish a database connection.

   2.1. In the UI designer of DataExpressAddressPanel.java, drop a `Database` from the Data Express page of the component palette to create `database1`, which will appear under the Data Access node in the component tree.

   2.2 In the inspector of `database1`, click the ellipsis button in the value field of property `connection` to display the Connection dialog box, as shown in Figure 14.2.

   2.3. Choose an appropriate driver and a URL. Enter Username and Password if necessary.

   2.4. Click Test connection in the Connection dialog box to test the selected connection. Check Prompt user password, and click OK to close the Connection dialog box.

3. The Search button searches the address to match the specified firstname and last name. These two names are parameters in the SQL SELECT statement. You need to use the `ParameterRow` class to define two parameters for first name and last name. Follow the steps below to create a `ParameterRow`.

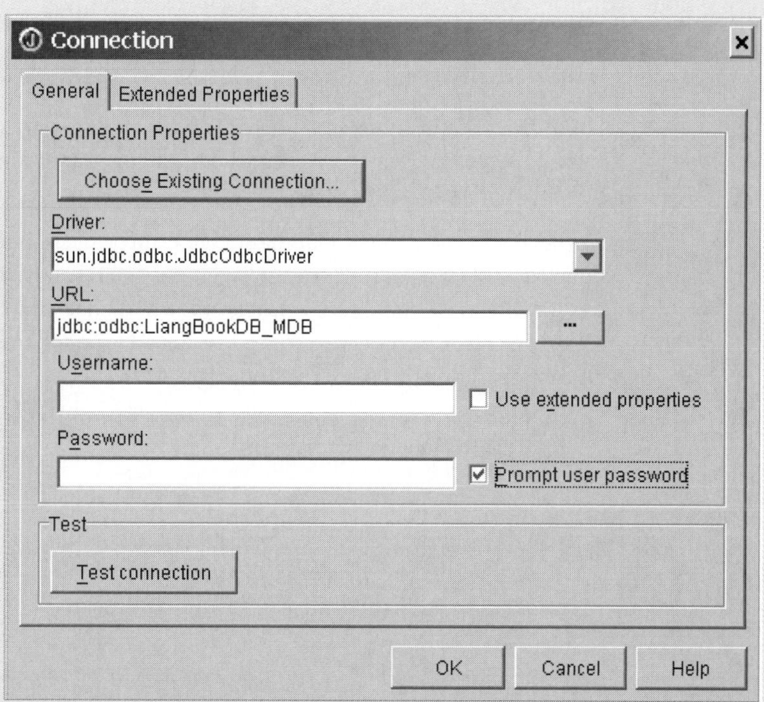

Figure 14.2 *The Connection dialog box gathers information about the database you want to connect.*

3.1. Drop a `ParameterRow` from the Data Express page of the component palette to create `parameterRow1, which will appear` under the Data Access node in the component tree.

3.2. Expand `parameterRow1` by clicking the + button in front of `parameterRow1` in the component tree. You will see <new column> under `parameterRow1`.

3.3. Choose <new column>. In the inspector of <new column>, set `caption` and `columnName` to firstName, and set `parameterType` to IN. You will see a new parameter named `firstName` appearing under `parameterRow1` in the component tree.

NOTE

If you don't see firstname in the component tree, close the project and re-open it.

3.4. Choose <new column> again. In the inspector of <new column>, set caption and columnName to lastName, and set parameterType to IN. You will see a new parameter named `lastName` appearing under `parameterRow1` in the component tree.

continued

Example 14.1 continued

4. Follow the steps below to create a `QueryDataSet`.

   4.1. Drop a `QueryDataSet` from the Data Express page of the component palette to create `queryDataSet1`, which will appear under the Data Access node in the component tree.

   4.2. In the inspector of `queryDataSet1`, click the ellipsis button in the value field of `metaDataUpdate` to display the MetaDataUpdate dialog box, as shown in Figure 14.3. Click None and click OK to close this dialog box. It is necessary to make this field None for the Insert and Update operations to work in this program.

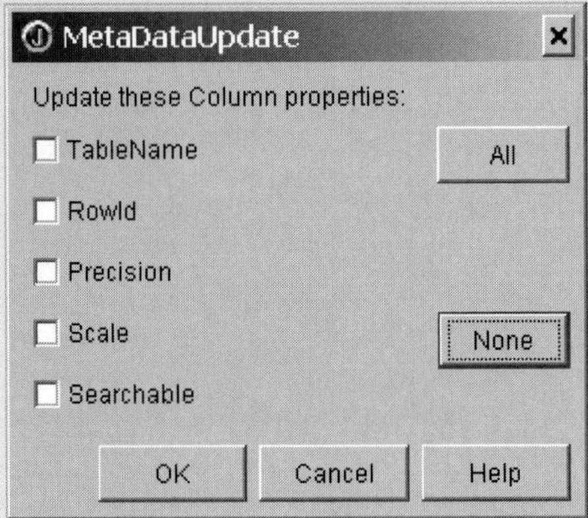

Figure 14.3 *The MetaDataUpdate property editor lets you set the meta data properties for the query.*

   4.3. In the inspector of `queryDataSet1`, click the ellipsis button in the value field `query` to bring up the Query dialog box, as shown in Figure 14.4.

   4.4. Choose `database1` in the Database choice menu to associate the query to the `database1` data source. Type the following SQL statement in the text area:

```
select * from Address where
  firstName = :firstName and lastName = :lastName
```

   4.5. Choose the Parameters tab in the Query dialog box (see Figure 14.5), select `parameterRow1`, and click OK.

   4.6. Switch to the Query page in the Query dialog box. You can also use SQL Builder to construct SQL statements instead of typing the statement manually, as shown in Figure 14.6. You can browse the tables by clicking the Browse Tables button and test the query by clicking the Test Query button.

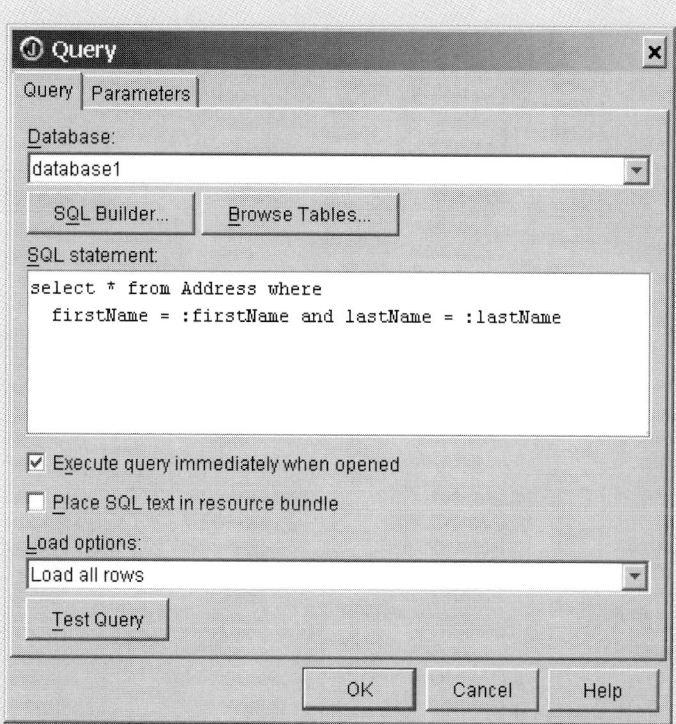

Figure 14.4 *The Query dialog box lets you construct and test a query with or without parameters.*

4.7. Expand `queryDataSet1` in the component tree to see the columns appearing under `queryDataSet1`. In the inspector of firstName and lastName, set the `rowid` property to true. Thus, firstName and lastName together form the primary key. This is necessary to ensure that insert operations work without the need to supply a row ID.

4.8. Set Address in the `tableName` property of `queryDataSet1`. This property is needed to ensure that the table can be updated.

5. Override the methods `select()`, `insert()`, and `update()` in the AddressPanel class using `queryDataSet1` and `parameterRow1`, as shown in Listing 14.1.

6. Create a Java applet named TestDataExpressAddressPanel.java. Install DataExpressAddressPanel in the component palette and drop it to the center of the applet. Run the applet. When the user presses the Search or Insert button for the first time, a dialog box is displayed to prompt the user to enter the password, as shown in Figure 14.7. Enter username and password to enter database. If your database does not require a password, close the dialog box. Test the Search and Insert buttons, as shown in Figure 14.1.

continued

Example 14.1 continued

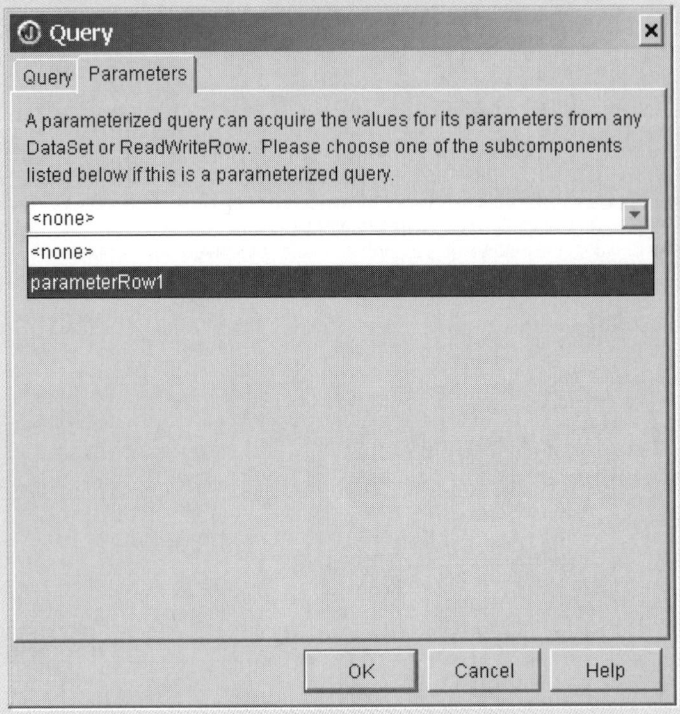

Query

Query | Parameters

A parameterized query can acquire the values for its parameters from any DataSet or ReadWriteRow. Please choose one of the subcomponents listed below if this is a parameterized query.

<none>

<none>

parameterRow1

OK | Cancel | Help

Figure 14.5 *You can associate parameters with the query from the Parameters page of the Query dialog box.*

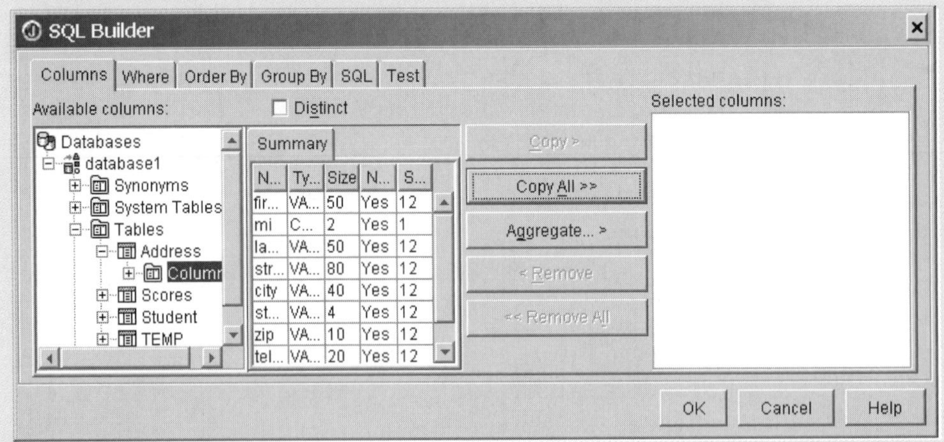

Figure 14.6 *The SQL Builder tool helps you build a SQL statement.*

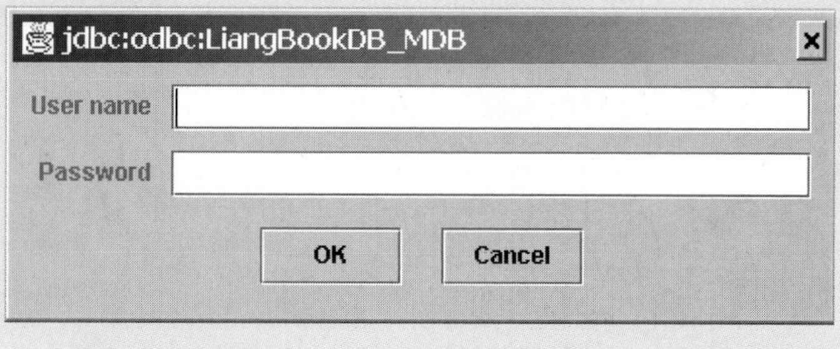

jdbc:odbc:LiangBookDB_MDB

User name

Password

OK Cancel

Figure 14.7 *The Password dialog box prompts the user to enter a password to establish a database connection.*

```
package dataexpressdemo;

import jdbcdemo.AddressPanel;
import com.borland.dx.sql.dataset.*;
import com.borland.dx.dataset.*;

public class DataExpressAddressPanel extends AddressPanel {
  Database database1 = new Database();
  ParameterRow parameterRow1 = new ParameterRow();
  Column column1 = new Column();
  Column column2 = new Column();
  QueryDataSet queryDataSet1 = new QueryDataSet();
  Column column3 = new Column();
  Column column4 = new Column();

  public DataExpressAddressPanel() {
    try {
      jbInit();
    }
    catch(Exception e) {
      e.printStackTrace();
    }
  }

  private void jbInit() throws Exception {
    column4.setColumnName("lastname");
    column4.setDataType(com.borland.dx.dataset.Variant.STRING);
    column4.setPrecision(25);
    column4.setRowId(true);
    column4.setServerColumnName("lastname");
    column4.setSqlType(12);
    column3.setColumnName("firstname");
    column3.setDataType(com.borland.dx.dataset.Variant.STRING);
    column3.setPrecision(25);
    column3.setRowId(true);
    column3.setServerColumnName("firstname");
    column3.setSqlType(12);
    queryDataSet1.setMetaDataUpdate(MetaDataUpdate.NONE);
    queryDataSet1.setTableName("Address");
    queryDataSet1.setQuery(new com.borland.dx.sql.dataset.
      QueryDescriptor(database1,
      "select * from Address where firstName = :firstName " +
      " and lastName = :lastName", parameterRow1, true, Load.ALL));
```

Listing 14.1 *DataExpressAddressPanel.java*

continued

Example 14.1 continued

```
    column2.setCaption("lastName");
    column2.setColumnName("lastName");
    column2.setDataType(com.borland.dx.dataset.Variant.STRING);
    column2.setParameterType(ParameterType.IN);
    column2.setServerColumnName("NewColumn2");
    column2.setSqlType(0);
    column1.setCaption("firstName");
    column1.setColumnName("firstName");
    column1.setDataType(com.borland.dx.dataset.Variant.STRING);
    column1.setParameterType(ParameterType.IN);
    column1.setServerColumnName("NewColumn1");
    column1.setSqlType(0);
    database1.setConnection(new com.borland.dx.sql.dataset.
      ConnectionDescriptor("jdbc:odbc:LiangBookDB_MDB", "",
      null, true, "sun.jdbc.odbc.JdbcOdbcDriver"));
    parameterRow1.setColumns(new Column[] {column1, column2});
    queryDataSet1.setColumns(new Column[] {column3, column4});
  }

  /**  Override this method from the AddressPanel class */
  protected void select() {
    try {
      parameterRow1.setString("firstname",
        jtfFirstName.getText().trim());
      parameterRow1.setString("lastname",
        jtfLastName.getText().trim());
      queryDataSet1.refresh();
      displayAddress();
    }
    catch (Exception ex) {
      jlblStatus.setText(ex.toString());
    }
  }

  /**  Display address in the UI */
  void displayAddress() {
    try {
      jtfMi.setText(queryDataSet1.getString(1));
      jtfStreet.setText(queryDataSet1.getString(3));
      jtfCity.setText(queryDataSet1.getString(4));
      jtfState.setText(queryDataSet1.getString(5));
      jtfZip.setText(queryDataSet1.getString(6));
      jtfTelephone.setText(queryDataSet1.getString(7));
      jtfEmail.setText(queryDataSet1.getString(8));
      jlblStatus.setText("Record found");
    }
    catch (Exception ex) {
      jlblStatus.setText(ex.getMessage());
    }
  }

  /** Override this method from the AddressPanel class */
  protected void insert() {
    try {
      if (!queryDataSet1.isOpen()) queryDataSet1.open();
      queryDataSet1.insertRow(false);
      update();
    }
```

Listing 14.1 *Continued*

```
      catch (Exception ex) {
        jlblStatus.setText(ex.getMessage());
      }
    }

    /** Update the current record */
    void update() {
      try {
        queryDataSet1.setString(0, jtfFirstName.getText());
        queryDataSet1.setString(1, jtfMi.getText());
        queryDataSet1.setString(2, jtfLastName.getText());
        queryDataSet1.setString(3, jtfStreet.getText());
        queryDataSet1.setString(4, jtfCity.getText());
        queryDataSet1.setString(5, jtfState.getText());
        queryDataSet1.setString(6, jtfZip.getText());
        queryDataSet1.setString(7, jtfTelephone.getText());
        queryDataSet1.setString(8, jtfEmail.getText());
        queryDataSet1.saveChanges();
        jlblStatus.setText("Record inserted");
      }
      catch (Exception ex) {
         jlblStatus.setText(ex.getMessage());
      }
    }
  }
```

Listing 14.1 *Continued*

Example Review

As you can see in the example, JBuilder provides easy-to-use and powerful property editors for many DataExpress components. You can create instances of these components and set their properties using the UI designer with no coding. The code generated by JBuilder can be modified and maintained.

The `connection` property editor of the `Database` component lets you choose a database URL, set user name and password, and test the connection during design time. JBuilder generates a `ConnectionDescriptor` object to store the connection properties. You can connect several `DataSet` components to a `Database` component.

The `query` property editor of the `QueryDataSet` dialog box allows you to choose a database and construct a SQL statement with or without parameters. It also allows testing the query. Once a Database object is created, it automatically appears in the choice list of the database field in the Query dialog box. A database must be chosen for a `QueryDataSet` object. JBuilder generates a `QueryDescriptor` object to store the query properties.

The `ResultSet` in JDBC is absorbed in `QueryDataSet`. The execution result of the query is stored in the `QueryDataSet`. This allows for much greater flexibility in navigation of the resulting data. The `QueryDataSet` inherits the `maxRows` property from `StorageDataSet`. This allows you to set the maximum number of rows that can be initially stored in the `QueryDataSet` from a query execution.

continued

Example 14.1 continued

When you created the database table Address in Example 13.2, you did not specify the primary key. For the insert operation to work properly, you set the `rowid` property on the columns firstName and lastName to true so that they would form the primary key. If the primary key were declared in the table, the property field of the column would automatically set to true.

To ensure that `QueryDataSet` can be updated, set the `tableName` property to Address and set the `metaDataUpdate` property to `MetaDataUpdate.NONE`, in addition to having a `rowid` in the table.

`QueryDataSet` contains a variety of methods. Among these are `open` for opening a query, `refresh` for refreshing a query, `addRow` for adding a new row, `insertRow` for inserting a new row, `delete` for deleting the current row, `getXXX` for retrieving a field of the appropriate type, `setXXX` for setting a new value in the field of the appropriate type, and `saveChanges()` for saving changes in the table. Like the `getXXX` method in the JDBC `ResultSet` class, the `getXXX` method has two versions: `getXXX(int)` and `getXXX(String)`. `getXXX(0)` in `QueryDataSet` refers to the field value for the first column, whereas `getXXX(1)` in `ResultSet` refers to the field value for the first column.

To assign parameter values in a parameterized query, you must first create a `ParameterRow` and add named columns that will be the placeholders for the values to be passed to the query. In this example, you created `parameterRow1`, an instance of `ParameterRow`, and added the columns `firstname` and `lastname`, which are the parameters used in the SQL query. `ParameterRow` is a subclass of `ReadWriteRow`, which contains one row of storage. You can get a parameter using a statement like the one shown below:

```
parameterRow1.getString("firstName");
```

You can set the value of a parameter using a statement like this one:

```
parameterRow1.setString("firstName", aString);
```

Data-Aware Components

JBuilder provides many data-aware components to simplify creating a data-aware user interface. These components, referred to as *dbSwing components*, are installed in the dbSwing, More dbSwing, and dbSwing Models pages of the component palette. Using these components greatly speeds up the Java database development process. The dbSwing components are data-aware versions of the Swing components. They are capable of accessing a database through DataExpress data sets. Most of the dbSwing components are subclasses of Swing components. For example, `JdbTextField` is a subclass of `JTextField`, `JdbComboBox` is a subclass of `JComboBox`, and `JdbTable` is a subclass of `JTable`. The dbSwing visual components are named with the prefix `Jdb`.

Most dbSwing data-aware components have a `dataSet` property and a `columnName` property. These properties bind the component to a specific `DataSet`, and a specific `Column` within that `DataSet`. (Some components work with all the columns of a `DataSet`, and therefore only have a `dataSet` property.) You should first choose a `DataSet` in the `dataset` property of the dbSwing component, then specify a column from the `dataset`.

The following dbSwing components are often useful:

- `JdbCheckBox`: A data-aware extension of the `JCheckBox` component. To make `JdbCheckBox` data-aware, set its `dataSet` and `columnName` properties so that it is linked to the desired column in the data set. Values in the column must denote a `boolean` value. If this is the case, a value that evaluates to `true` checks the check box, and a `false` value removes the checkmark. If the user checks the check box, a value that equates to `true` is entered in the column of the active record in the data set. Unchecking the check box puts a value that equates to `false` in the data set.
- `JdbLabel`: A data-aware extension of the `JLabel` component. To make `JdbLabel` data-aware, set its `dataSet` and `columnName` properties to link the text property to the data value for the column of the current row.
- `JdbComboBox`: A data-aware extension of the `JComboBox` component. To make `JdbComboBox` data-aware, set its `dataSet` and `columnName` properties to display the values in the specified column of the data set.
- `JbdList`: A data-aware extension of the `JList` component. To make `JdbList` data-aware, set its `dataSet` and `columnName` properties to display the values in the specified column of the data set.
- `JdbTextField`: A data-aware extension of the `JTextField` component. To make `JdbTextField` data-aware, set its `dataSet` and `columnName` properties to display the data value for the column of the current row.
- `JdbTextArea`: A data-aware extension of the `JTextArea` component. To make `JdbTextArea` data-aware, set its `dataSet` and `columnName` properties to display the value for the column of the current row in the text area.
- `JdbTable`: A data-aware extension of the `JTable` component. To make `JdbTable` data-aware, set its `dataSet`. The table cells can be edited. To make `JdbTable` scrollable, you must place it inside an instance of `TableScrollPane`, which is an extension of `JScrollPane` designed specifically for use with a `JdbTable`.
- `JdbNavToolBar`: A data-aware control that contains multiple preset buttons for performing operations on the data, such as searching, inserting, deleting, posting changes, and refreshing data source.
- `JdbStatusLabel`: This is a component that displays custom messages. If its `dataset` property is set, it displays status messages generated by its associated `DataSet`. These include row position, row count, validation errors, and data update notifications.

- `JdbNavField`: A `JTextField` with built-in row-locating functionality when its `dataSet` property is set. If its `columnName` property is set, it locates data in that column only. If the `columnName` property is not set, it locates data in the `DataSet` column that had focus last. If no column had focus, the first column in the `DataSet` that supports locate operations is chosen. Unlike `JdbTextField`, `JdbNavField` never writes to a `DataSet` column.

If the searched column is of the `String` type, the search occurs incrementally as characters are typed. If the search string is all lower-case, then the search is case-insensitive. If the search string is mixed-case, then the search is case-sensitive.

If the searched column is not of the `String` type, the search doesn't occur until the Enter key is pressed.

To search for prior and next matches, use the up and down arrow keys, respectively.

If a `JdbStatusLabel` is present, it displays usage information about the `JdbNavField` currently in use.

Example 14.2 Using dbSwing Data-Aware Components

In this example, you will develop a new address book (see Figure 14.8) using the JBCL data-aware components `JdbNavToolBar`, `JdbTable`, `JdbNavField`, `JdbTextField`, and `JdbStatusLabel`.

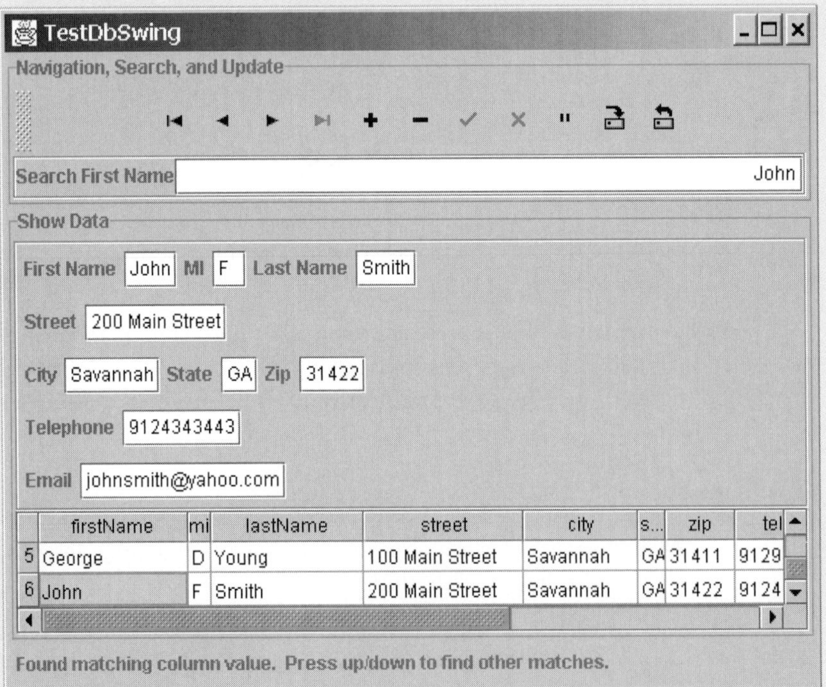

Figure 14.8 *You can display, search, and modify records using data-aware dbSwing components.*

You will use the same database as in Example 14.1. The query in the `QueryDataSet` is "select * from Address." You can use `JdbNavToolBar` to cruise through the `QueryDataSet` and to insert and delete records in it. `JdbTable` displays all the records in the `QueryDataSet`, and the Show Data panel displays the current row in the `QueryDataSet`. You can search the record according to firstName by entering a value in the Search Value field. `JdbStatusLabel` displays the message indicating the status of the operations.

Here are the steps to complete the project.

1. In the dataexpressdemo project, create a new applet named `TestDbSwing` using the Applet wizard.

2. With TestDbSwing.java selected in the project pane, switch to the UI designer.

3. Establish a database connection and create a query set as follows:

    3.1. Drop a `Database` from the Data Express page to create `database1`. In the inspector of `database1`, double-click the ellipsis button to bring up the Connection dialog box. Choose the same URL, username, and password as in Example 14.1. Close the Connection dialog box.

    3.2. Drop a `QueryDataSet` from the Data Express page to create `queryDataSet1`. In the inspector of `queryDataSet1`, set the `metaDataUpdate` property to None, set the `tableName` property to Address, and create "select * from Address" in the query property using the Query dialog box.

4. Create the user interface as follows (shown in Figure 14.8). The generated code is shown in Listing 14.2.

    4.1. Drop a `JPanel` to the north of the applet to create `jpControl`, drop a `JPanel` to the center of the applet to create `jpData`, and drop a `JdbStatusLabel` to the south of the applet to create `jdbStatusLabel1`. Set the border with title "Navigation, Search, and Update" on `jpControl` and the border with title "Show Data" on `jpData`. Set the `dataSet` property of `jdbStatusLabel1` to `queryDataSet1`.

    4.2. Set the `layout` of `jpControl` to `BorderLayout`. Drop a `JdbNavToolBar` to the north of `jpControl` to create `jdbNavToolBar1`. Set the `dataSet` property of `jdbNavToolBar1` to `queryDataSet1`.

    4.3. Drop a `JPanel` to the center of the `jpControl` to create `jpSearchField` with an `Etched` border and a `BorderLayout`. Drop a `JLabel` to the west of `jpSearchField` with text "Search First Name." Drop a `JdbNavField` from the More Swing page of the component palette to the center of `jpSearchField` to create `jdbNavField1`. Set the `dataSet` property of `jdbNavField1` to `queryDataSet1` and the `columnName` to firstName.

continued

Example 14.2 continued

4.4. Set the `layout` of `jpData` to `BorderLayout`. Drop a `TableScrollPane` from the dbSwing page to the center of `jpData`, and drop a `JdbTable` to the scroll pane to create `jdbTable1`. Set its `dataSet` property to `queryDataSet1`. Drop a `JPanel` to the north of `jpData` to create `jpRecord`. Set its layout to `GridLayout` with five rows.

4.5. Use `JLabel` and `JdbTextField` to create user interface for displaying a single record in `jpRecord`. For each instance of `JdbTextField`, set its `dataSet` property to `queryDataSet1` and its `columnName` to an appropriate column. For example, for the text field for firstName, set its `columnName` to firstName.

```
package dataexpressdemo;

import java.awt.*;
import java.awt.event.*;
import java.applet.*;
import javax.swing.*;
import com.borland.dx.sql.dataset.*;
import com.borland.dx.dataset.*;
import com.borland.dbswing.*;
import javax.swing.border.*;

public class TestDbSwing extends JApplet {
  boolean isStandalone = false;
  Database database1 = new Database();
  QueryDataSet queryDataSet1 = new QueryDataSet();
  TableScrollPane tableScrollPane1 = new TableScrollPane();
  JdbTable jdbTable1 = new JdbTable();
  JdbNavToolBar jdbNavToolBar1 = new JdbNavToolBar();
  JdbStatusLabel jdbStatusLabel1 = new JdbStatusLabel();
  Column column1 = new Column();
  Column column2 = new Column();
  JPanel jpControl = new JPanel();
  BorderLayout borderLayout1 = new BorderLayout();
  JdbNavField jdbNavField1 = new JdbNavField();
  JPanel jpData = new JPanel();
  BorderLayout borderLayout2 = new BorderLayout();
  JPanel jpRecord = new JPanel();
  JPanel jPanel1 = new JPanel();
  JdbTextField jdbTextField1 = new JdbTextField();
  GridLayout gridLayout1 = new GridLayout();
  JLabel jLabel1 = new JLabel();
  JLabel jLabel2 = new JLabel();
  JdbTextField jdbTextField2 = new JdbTextField();
  JLabel jLabel3 = new JLabel();
  JdbTextField jdbTextField3 = new JdbTextField();
  FlowLayout flowLayout1 = new FlowLayout();
  JPanel jPanel2 = new JPanel();
  JLabel jLabel4 = new JLabel();
  JdbTextField jdbTextField4 = new JdbTextField();
  FlowLayout flowLayout2 = new FlowLayout();
  JPanel jPanel3 = new JPanel();
  JLabel jLabel5 = new JLabel();
```

Listing 14.2 *TestdbSwing.java*

```
  JdbTextField jdbTextField5 = new JdbTextField();
  FlowLayout flowLayout3 = new FlowLayout();
  JLabel jLabel6 = new JLabel();
  JdbTextField jdbTextField6 = new JdbTextField();
  JLabel jLabel7 = new JLabel();
  JdbTextField jdbTextField7 = new JdbTextField();
  JPanel jPanel4 = new JPanel();
  JLabel jLabel8 = new JLabel();
  FlowLayout flowLayout4 = new FlowLayout();
  JdbTextField jdbTextField8 = new JdbTextField();
  JPanel jPanel5 = new JPanel();
  JLabel jLabel9 = new JLabel();
  JdbTextField jdbTextField9 = new JdbTextField();
  FlowLayout flowLayout5 = new FlowLayout();
  TitledBorder titledBorder1;
  TitledBorder titledBorder2;
  JLabel jLabel10 = new JLabel();
  JPanel jpSearchField = new JPanel();
  BorderLayout borderLayout3 = new BorderLayout();

  /** Initialize the applet */
  public void init() {
    try {
      jbInit();
    }
    catch(Exception e) {
      e.printStackTrace();
    }
  }

  /** Component initialization */
  private void jbInit() throws Exception {
    titledBorder1 = new TitledBorder("");
    titledBorder2 = new TitledBorder("");
    queryDataSet1.setMetaDataUpdate(MetaDataUpdate.NONE);
    queryDataSet1.setTableName("Address");
    queryDataSet1.setQuery(new com.borland.dx.sql.dataset.
      QueryDescriptor(database1, "select * from Address;\n",
      null, true, Load.ALL));
    database1.setConnection(new com.borland.dx.sql.dataset.
      ConnectionDescriptor("jdbc:odbc:LiangBookDB_MDB", "", "",
      false, "sun.jdbc.odbc.JdbcOdbcDriver"));
    this.setSize(new Dimension(437, 385));
    jdbTable1.setDataSet(queryDataSet1);
    jdbNavToolBar1.setDataSet(queryDataSet1);
    jdbStatusLabel1.setText("jdbStatusLabel1");
    jdbStatusLabel1.setDataSet(queryDataSet1);
    column1.setColumnName("firstName");
    column1.setDataType(com.borland.dx.dataset.Variant.STRING);
    column1.setPrecision(15);
    column1.setRowId(true);
    column1.setTableName("Address");
    column1.setServerColumnName("firstName");
    column1.setSqlType(12);
    column2.setColumnName("lastName");
    column2.setDataType(com.borland.dx.dataset.Variant.STRING);
    column2.setPrecision(15);
    column2.setRowId(true);
    column2.setTableName("Address");
    column2.setServerColumnName("lastName");
```

Listing 14.2 *Continued*

continued

Example 14.2 continued

```
        column2.setSqlType(12);
        queryDataSet1.setColumns(new Column[] {column1, column2});
        jpControl.setLayout(borderLayout1);
        jdbNavField1.setText("jdbNavField1");
        jdbNavField1.setHorizontalAlignment(SwingConstants.RIGHT);
        jdbNavField1.setColumnName("firstName");
        jdbNavField1.setDataSet(queryDataSet1);
        jpData.setLayout(borderLayout2);
        jdbTextField1.setColumnName("firstName");
        jdbTextField1.setDataSet(queryDataSet1);
        jpRecord.setLayout(gridLayout1);
        jLabel1.setText("First Name");
        jLabel2.setText("MI");
        jdbTextField2.setColumns(2);
        jdbTextField2.setColumnName("Mi");
        jdbTextField2.setDataSet(queryDataSet1);
        jLabel3.setText("Last Name");
        jdbTextField3.setColumnName("lastName");
        jdbTextField3.setDataSet(queryDataSet1);
        jPanel1.setLayout(flowLayout1);
        flowLayout1.setAlignment(FlowLayout.LEFT);
        gridLayout1.setRows(5);
        jLabel4.setText("Street");
        jdbTextField4.setColumnName("street");
        jdbTextField4.setDataSet(queryDataSet1);
        jPanel2.setLayout(flowLayout2);
        flowLayout2.setAlignment(FlowLayout.LEFT);
        jLabel5.setText("City");
        jdbTextField5.setColumnName("city");
        jdbTextField5.setDataSet(queryDataSet1);
        jPanel3.setLayout(flowLayout3);
        flowLayout3.setAlignment(FlowLayout.LEFT);
        jLabel6.setText("State");
        jdbTextField6.setColumnName("state");
        jdbTextField6.setDataSet(queryDataSet1);
        jLabel7.setText("Zip");
        jdbTextField7.setColumnName("zip");
        jdbTextField7.setDataSet(queryDataSet1);
        jLabel8.setText("Telephone");
        jPanel4.setLayout(flowLayout4);
        flowLayout4.setAlignment(FlowLayout.LEFT);
        jdbTextField8.setColumnName("telephone");
        jdbTextField8.setDataSet(queryDataSet1);
        jLabel9.setText("Email");
        jdbTextField9.setText("jdbTextField9");
        jdbTextField9.setColumnName("email");
        jdbTextField9.setDataSet(queryDataSet1);
        jPanel5.setLayout(flowLayout5);
        flowLayout5.setAlignment(FlowLayout.LEFT);
        jpControl.setBorder(titledBorder1);
        titledBorder1.setTitle("Navigation, Search, and Update");
        jpData.setBorder(titledBorder2);
        titledBorder2.setTitle("Show Data");
        jLabel10.setText("Search First Name");
        jpSearchField.setBorder(BorderFactory.createEtchedBorder());
        jpSearchField.setLayout(borderLayout3);
        jpRecord.setBorder(BorderFactory.createEtchedBorder());
        this.getContentPane().add(jdbStatusLabel1, BorderLayout.SOUTH);
        this.getContentPane().add(jpControl, BorderLayout.NORTH);
```

Listing 14.2 *Continued*

```
        jpControl.add(jdbNavToolBar1, BorderLayout.NORTH);
        jpControl.add(jpSearchField, BorderLayout.CENTER);
        jpSearchField.add(jLabel10, BorderLayout.WEST);
        jpSearchField.add(jdbNavField1, BorderLayout.CENTER);
        this.getContentPane().add(jpData, BorderLayout.CENTER);
        jpData.add(tableScrollPane1, BorderLayout.CENTER);
        jpData.add(jpRecord, BorderLayout.NORTH);
        jpRecord.add(jPanel1, null);
        jPanel1.add(jLabel1, null);
        jPanel1.add(jdbTextField1, null);
        jPanel1.add(jLabel2, null);
        jPanel1.add(jdbTextField2, null);
        jPanel1.add(jLabel3, null);
        jPanel1.add(jdbTextField3, null);
        jpRecord.add(jPanel2, null);
        jPanel2.add(jLabel4, null);
        jPanel2.add(jdbTextField4, null);
        jpRecord.add(jPanel3, null);
        jPanel3.add(jLabel5, null);
        jPanel3.add(jdbTextField5, null);
        jPanel3.add(jLabel6, null);
        jPanel3.add(jdbTextField6, null);
        jPanel3.add(jLabel7, null);
        jPanel3.add(jdbTextField7, null);
        jpRecord.add(jPanel4, null);
        jPanel4.add(jLabel8, null);
        jPanel4.add(jdbTextField8, null);
        jpRecord.add(jPanel5, null);
        jPanel5.add(jLabel9, null);
        jPanel5.add(jdbTextField9, null);
        tableScrollPane1.getViewport().add(jdbTable1, null);
    }
  }
```

Listing 14.2 *Continued*

Example Review

The dbSwing package contains components that extend the Swing components, such as `JdbTable` and `JdbTextField`, which are extensions of `javax.swing.JTable`, `javax.swing.JTextField` with built-in database support. The dbSwing package also contains components that complement the standard Swing components, such as `JdbNavToolBar` and `JdbNavField`. To make these components data-aware, set their `dataSet` property to bind the component to a `DataSet`, and set the `columnName` property to the desired column name.

All the data-aware components bound to a data set display or control data automatically. As in this example, a `JdbTextField` displays the value of the column of the current row. The buttons in the `JdbNavToolBar` are implemented to perform common database operations on the associated data set, and the `JdbTable` displays all the records in the query set. The `JdbNavField` automatically searches for the value on the specified column.

The buttons on the `JdbNavToolBar` can be customized. You can hide a button; for instance, you can hide the Next button by setting the `buttonStateNext` property to HIDDEN.

continued

Example 14.2 continued

`JdbNavField` performs an incremental search for string columns as each character is typed into the component. The search allows for a partial match. If the column is not a character column, such as a number or a time, no partial locate is performed as keys are typed. A nonstring search is performed only when the Enter key is typed.

`JdbTable` is a powerful and sophisticated component. It displays data in a two-dimensional tabular form. This component contains many properties for customization. You can specify whether to display column headers and customize them. By default, the headers are shown using the column name. You can specify where grid lines are visible or not, whether column width can be changed at runtime or not, and so on.

`JdbStatusLabel` is commonly used with a `DataSet`. It automatically displays status messages generated by the `DataSet` to provide valuable information on the status of the operations.

As this project demonstrates, the support of data-aware components enables you to rapidly develop complete and comprehensive database applications with almost no coding. The project is easy to maintain and scalable.

Master-Detail Relationship

The projects presented thus far involve single tables. A practical database may have many tables storing interrelated data that represent an enterprise. In a relational database, all data are related whether they are in the same table or in different tables. Data in different tables are linked together through foreign keys. Loosely speaking, foreign keys are common columns shared by two or more tables. A *master-detail relationship* is usually a one-to-many type relationship based on foreign keys between two tables. For example, a table called Department describing university academic departments consists of the columns deptNo, deptName, and deptChair, and a table called Employee representing employees consists of the columns empNo, empName, office, and deptNo. The column deptNo is shared in both tables. You can create a master-detail relationship that will enable you to cruise through the Department table and display the employees in the current department.

Master-detail forms are common in database applications. JBuilder makes it easy to develop master-detail forms using the powerful DataExpress and dbSwing components. To create a master-detail form, you simply create two query data sets and link them together through the `masterLink` property in the query data set for the detailed table. You can then use components like `JdbTable` to control and display records in the master table and the detail table.

Example 14.3 Creating Master-Detail Forms

This example creates two tables, Department and Employee, and develops a master-detail form to navigate through Department to display all the employees in the selected department, as shown in Figure 14.9.

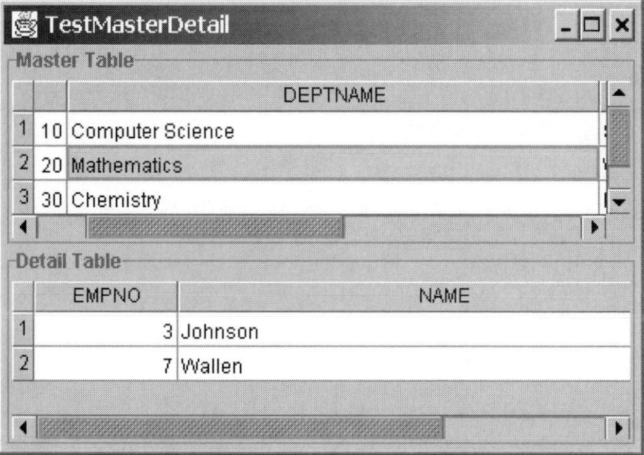

Figure 14.9 *You can select a department in the master table to display all the employees associated with the department in the detail table.*

Here are the steps to complete the project.

1. Create the tables Department and Employee in the database. The SQL statements for creating the tables are as follows:

```
create table Department
(
  deptNo number not null,
  deptName varchar(50),
  deptChair varchar(50),
  primary key (deptNo)
);

create table Employee
(
  empNo number not null,
  name varchar(50),
  office varchar(15),
  deptNo number,
  primary key (empNo)
);
```

2. In the dataexpressdemo project, create an applet named TestMasterDetail using the Applet wizard.

3. Establish a database connection and create a query data set, as follows:

   3.1. With TestMasterDetail.java selected in the project pane, switch to the UI designer.

continued

Example 14.3 continued

3.2. Drop a `Database` from the Data Express page to the UI to create `database1`. In the inspector of `database1`, click the ellipsis button to display the Connection dialog box to connect to the LiangBookDB_MDB.

3.3. Drop a `QueryDataSet` twice from the Data Express page to the UI to create `queryDataSet1` and `queryDataSet2`. `queryDataSet1` will serve as the master table, and `queryDataSet2` will serve as the detail table. In the `query` property editor of `queryDataSet1`, enter the following SQL statement in the SQL statement text box:

```
select * from Department
```

3.4. In the `query` property editor of `queryDataSet2`, enter the following SQL statement in the SQL statement text box:

```
select * from Employee
```

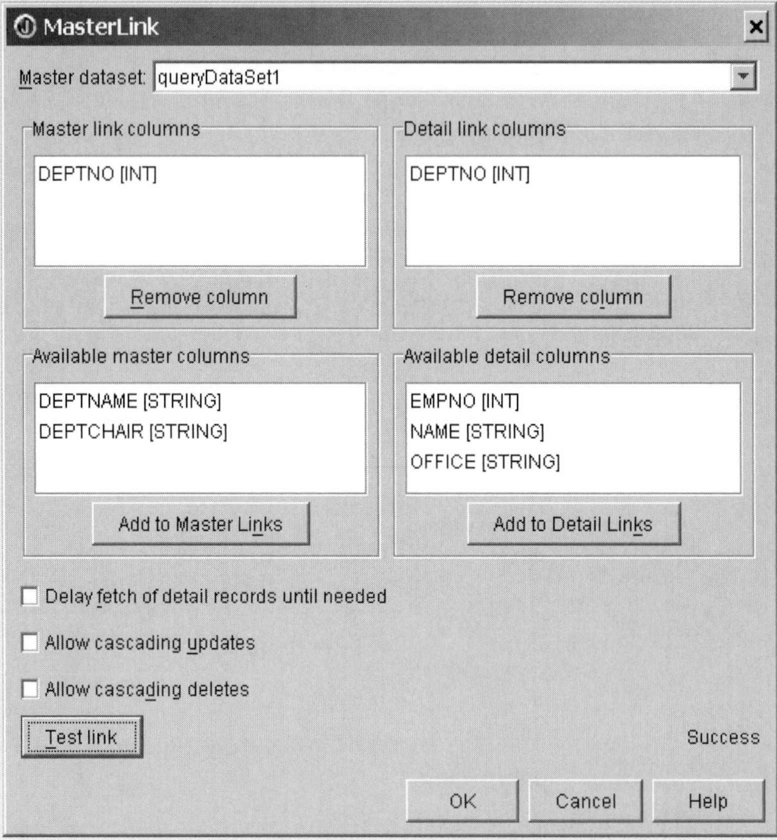

Figure 14.10 *The MasterLink dialog box allows you to set the links.*

3.5. In the inspector of `queryDataSet2`, double-click the value field of the `masterLink` property to bring up the `masterLink` dialog box, as shown in Figure 14.10. Choose `queryDataSet1` in the Master DataSet choice menu. Add `deptNo` to the Master link columns and the Detail link columns. Uncheck three check boxes in this dialog box. Press the Test link button to test the link before clicking OK to close the dialog box.

4. Create the UI. Drop a `JPanel` to the center of the applet. Change the panel's `layout` to `GridLayout` with two rows. Drop a `TableScrollPane` twice into the panel, and set their border titles, "Master Table" and "Detail Table," respectively. Drop a `JdbTable` to the first scroll pane and another `JdbTable` to the second scroll pane. Set the `dataSet` property of the tables to `queryDataSet1` and `queryDataSet2`, respectively. Listing 14.3 contains the code generated from the design.

5. Run the program. When selecting a department in the master table, you will see the corresponding employees in the department displayed in the detail table.

```
package dataexpressdemo;

import java.awt.*;
import java.awt.event.*;
import java.applet.*;
import javax.swing.*;
import com.borland.dx.sql.dataset.*;
import com.borland.dbswing.*;
import javax.swing.border.*;

public class TestMasterDetail extends JApplet {
  boolean isStandalone = false;
  Database database1 = new Database();
  QueryDataSet queryDataSet1 = new QueryDataSet();
  QueryDataSet queryDataSet2 = new QueryDataSet();
  JPanel jPanel1 = new JPanel();
  GridLayout gridLayout1 = new GridLayout();
  TableScrollPane tableScrollPane1 = new TableScrollPane();
  TableScrollPane tableScrollPane2 = new TableScrollPane();
  TitledBorder titledBorder1;
  TitledBorder titledBorder2;
  JdbTable jdbTable1 = new JdbTable();
  JdbTable jdbTable2 = new JdbTable();

  /** Initialize the applet */
  public void init() {
    try {
      jbInit();
    }
    catch(Exception e) {
      e.printStackTrace();
    }
  }

```

Listing 14.3 *TestMasterDetail.java*

continued

Example 14.3 continued

```
  /** Component initialization */
  private void jbInit() throws Exception {
    titledBorder1 = new TitledBorder("");
    titledBorder2 = new TitledBorder("");
    queryDataSet2.setQuery(new com.borland.dx.sql.dataset.
      QueryDescriptor(database1, "select * from Employee",
      null, true, Load.ALL));
    queryDataSet1.setQuery(new com.borland.dx.sql.dataset.
      QueryDescriptor(database1, "select * from Department",
      null, true, Load.ALL));
    database1.setConnection(new com.borland.dx.sql.dataset.
      ConnectionDescriptor("jdbc:odbc:LiangBookDB_MDB", "", "",
      false, "sun.jdbc.odbc.JdbcOdbcDriver"));
    this.setSize(new Dimension(400,300));
    queryDataSet2.setMasterLink(new com.borland.dx.dataset.
      MasterLinkDescriptor(queryDataSet1, new String[] {"DEPTNO"},
      new String[] {"DEPTNO"}, false, false, false));
    jPanel1.setLayout(gridLayout1);
    gridLayout1.setRows(2);
    gridLayout1.setColumns(1);
    tableScrollPane1.setBorder(titledBorder1);
    titledBorder1.setTitle("Master Table");
    tableScrollPane2.setBorder(titledBorder2);
    titledBorder2.setTitle("Detail Table");
    jdbTable1.setDataSet(queryDataSet1);
    jdbTable2.setDataSet(queryDataSet2);
    this.getContentPane().add(jPanel1, BorderLayout.CENTER);
    jPanel1.add(tableScrollPane1, null);
    tableScrollPane1.getViewport().add(jdbTable1, null);
    jPanel1.add(tableScrollPane2, null);
    tableScrollPane2.getViewport().add(jdbTable2, null);
  }
}
```

Listing 14.3 *Continued*

Example Review

This project was created without coding. JBuilder DataExpress components greatly simplify the development of database applications. A complex project like this one can be rapidly developed with little or no coding. Such a project is easy to maintain and highly scalable.

In a master-detail relationship, the values in the master fields determine which detail records will be displayed. The records for the detail data set can be fetched all at once or for a particular master when needed. By default, the option "Delay fetch of detail records until needed" in the masterLink dialog box is unchecked to allow all the detail records to be fetched.

By default, detail link columns are not displayed in a `JdbTable`, because they duplicate the values in the master link columns, which are displayed. You can insert, delete, and update records in the both master and the detail table. When a new record is inserted in the detail table, JBuilder uses the current value of the link columns. You can choose whether to allow cascading updates or cascading deletes in the masterLink dialog box.

Data Modules

Data modules, also known as *data models*, are specialized containers where data access components and their associated properties are collected into a reusable component. You define your data module once, then use it in various applications, or in various frames within a single application.

Data modules can be used to separate database access logic and business rules from the application user interface. This enables you to modularize your code and maintain control over the use of data modules. You can put data modules into a central location (a server, for example) so that the most recent version of the business logic is immediately available to the user without requiring changes of user applications.

To create a data module, you need to implement the `DataModule` interface, which declares the basic behavior of a data module. The `DataModule` interface is a marker interface, it does not contain any variables, properties, methods, or events. However, by implementing it you declare that your class is a data module.

Example 14.4 Using Data Modules

This example creates a project with three frames:

- A main frame, as shown in Figure 14.11, that contains two buttons that can be clicked to show or hide the other two frames.

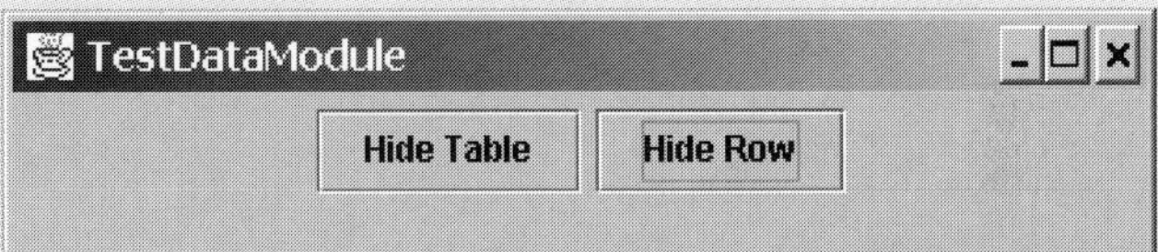

Figure 14.11 *The main frame contains two buttons for controlling two subframes.*

- A frame, as shown in Figure 14.12, that contains a `JdbTable` to show the whole table.
- A frame, as shown in Figure 14.13, that contains a `JdbNavToolBar`, and a panel for displaying a single row in the table.

The project can be divided into the following four tasks:

1. Create the main frame.
2. Create the data module to encapsulate the database information.
3. Create the frame for displaying the whole table.
4. Create the frame for displaying a row in the table.

continued

Example 14.4 continued

Show Table

	firstName	mi	lastName	street	city	state	zip	
1	CindyR	Z	Smith	200 Main Street	Atlanta	GA	46805	2
2	Yong	D	Liang	200 Main Street	Savannah	GA	46805	2
3	Kevin	Z	Rosaber	100 Main Street	Fort Wayne	IN	46805	2
4	John	Z	Smithson	200 Main Street	Fort Wayne	IN	46805	2
5	Steve	R	Mesaros	101 Abercorn	Savannah	GA	31412	9
6	John	R	Dunn	201 Coliseum	Savannah	GA	30212	9
7	Tyler	F	Schlotman	23 River Run	Dallas	TX	32321	3
8	Ken	S	Stahl	S	S	S	S	

Figure 14.12 *The whole table is displayed in a* `JdbTable`.

Figure 14.13 *The* `JdbNavToolBar` *navigates through the table to display the current row.*

1. Create the main frame.

   1.1. In the dataexpressdemo project, create TestDataModule.java using the Applet wizard.

   1.2. With TestDataModule.java selected in the project pane, switch to the UI designer. Drop a `JPanel` to the center of the frame. Drop a `JButton` twice to the frame to create `jbtShowTable` and `jbtShowRow`.

   1.3. Double-click `jbtShowTable` to generate the method `jbtShowTable_actionPerformed` for handling the Show Whole Table button. Implement the method as shown in Listing 14.4 (Lines 50–60).

   1.4. Double-click `jbtShowRow` to generate the method `jbtShowRow_actionPerformed` for handling the Show One Row button. Implement the method as shown in Listing 14.5 (Lines 62–72).

```
package dataexpressdemo;

import java.awt.*;
import java.awt.event.*;
import java.applet.*;
import javax.swing.*;

public class TestDataModule extends JApplet {
  boolean isStandalone = false;
  JPanel jPanel1 = new JPanel();
  JButton jbtShowTable = new JButton();
  JButton jbtShowRow = new JButton();

  // Create two frames
  TableFrame tableFrame = new TableFrame();
  RowFrame rowFrame = new RowFrame();

  /** Initialize the applet */
  public void init() {
    try {
      jbInit();
    }
    catch(Exception e) {
      e.printStackTrace();
    }
  }

  /** Component initialization */
  private void jbInit() throws Exception {
    this.setSize(new Dimension(400,300));
    jbtShowTable.setText("Show Table");
    jbtShowTable.addActionListener(
      new java.awt.event.ActionListener() {
      public void actionPerformed(ActionEvent e) {
        jbtShowTable_actionPerformed(e);
      }
    });
    jbtShowRow.setText("Show Row");
    jbtShowRow.addActionListener(
      new java.awt.event.ActionListener() {
      public void actionPerformed(ActionEvent e) {
        jbtShowRow_actionPerformed(e);
      }
    });
    this.getContentPane().add(jPanel1, BorderLayout.CENTER);
    jPanel1.add(jbtShowTable, null);
    jPanel1.add(jbtShowRow, null);
  }

  void jbtShowTable_actionPerformed(ActionEvent e) {
    if (jbtShowTable.getText().equals("Show Table")) {
      jbtShowTable.setText("Hide Table");
      tableFrame.pack();
      tableFrame.setVisible(true);
    }
    else if (jbtShowTable.getText().equals("Hide Table")) {
      jbtShowTable.setText("Show Table");
      tableFrame.setVisible(false);
    }
  }

```

Listing 14.4 *TestDataModule.java*

continued

Example 14.4 continued

```
    void jbtShowRow_actionPerformed(ActionEvent e) {
      if (jbtShowRow.getText().equals("Show Row")) {
        jbtShowRow.setText("Hide Row");
        rowFrame.pack();
        rowFrame.setVisible(true);
      }
      else if (jbtShowRow.getText().equals("Hide Row")) {
        jbtShowRow.setText("Show Row");
        rowFrame.setVisible(false);
      }
    }
  }
```

Listing 14.4 *Continued*

2. Create the data module.

   2.1. Double-click the Data Module icon in the Object Gallery to display the Data Module wizard, as shown in Figure 14.14. Check the option "Invoke Data Modeler." Type AddressDM in the Class name field, and click OK to generate the data module AddressDM.java to display a detailed data modeler, as shown in Figure 14.15.

TIP

If your database is not listed in the Current Query section, add it from the Database menu.

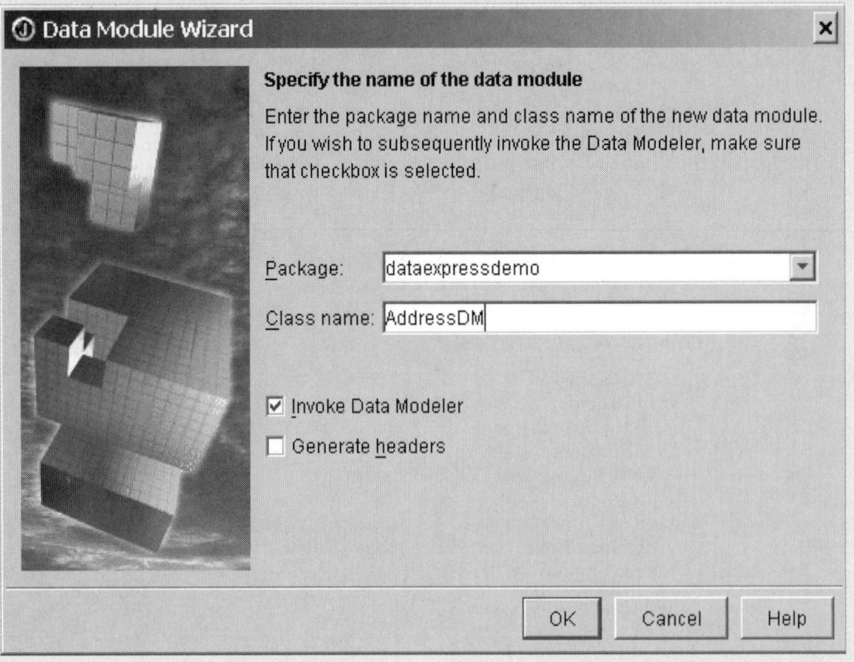

Figure 14.14 *The New DataModule dialog box creates a data module.*

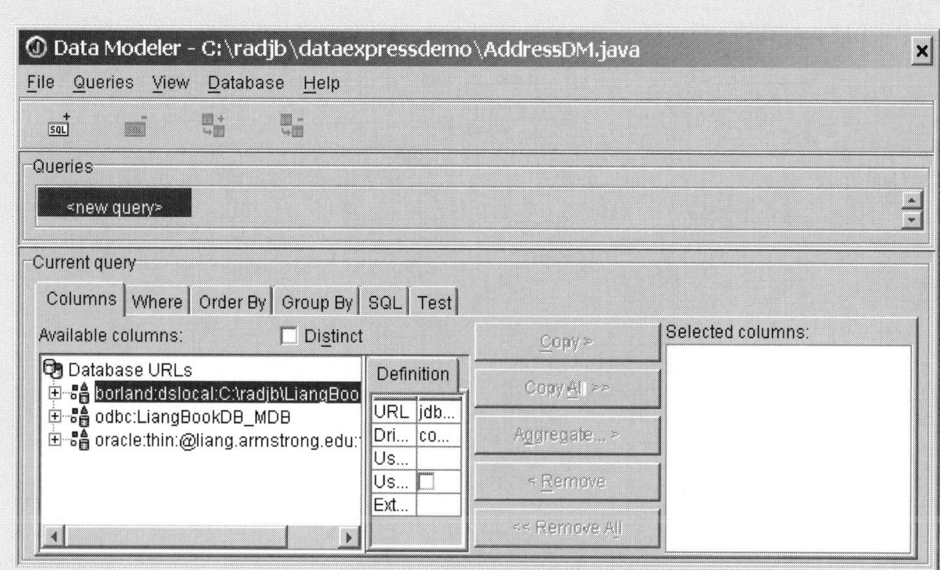

Figure 14.15 *You can select a database and create a query for the data model.*

2.2. Select the node odbc:LiangBookDB_MDB and login to this database. Choose the SQL tab. Type "select * from Address," as shown in Figure 14.16. Choose Test and click Execute Query to test it.

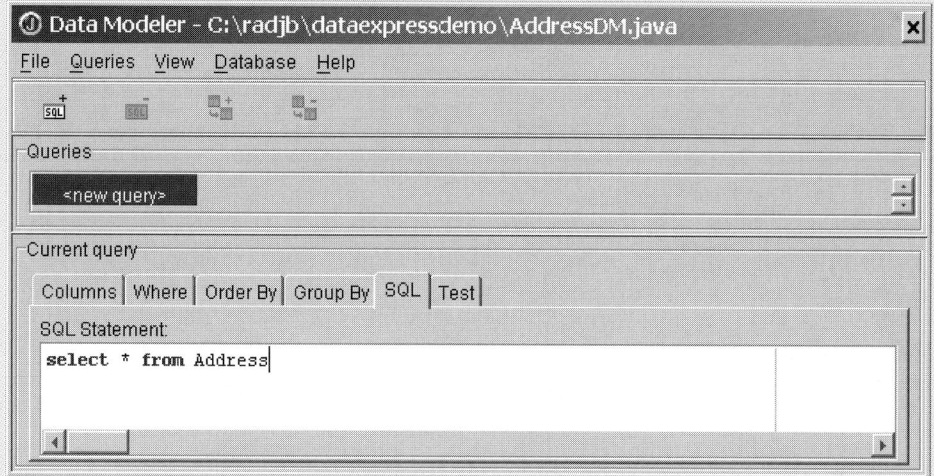

Figure 14.16 *You can create a query and test it in the data modeler.*

2.3. Choose File, Save to generate the source code for AddressDM.java. The generated code for the data module is shown in Listing 14.5. Choose File, Exit to exit Data Modeler.

continued

Example 14.4 continued

2.4. Select AddressDM.java in the project pane. Switch to the UI designer. Select address in the component tree. Set the `metaDataUpdate` property to None. Set the `rowId` property for both `firstName` and `lastName` to True. This is necessary to ensure that the records can be updated.

```
package dataexpressdemo;

import java.awt.*;
import java.awt.event.*;
import com.borland.dx.dataset.*;
import com.borland.dx.sql.dataset.*;

public class AddressDM implements DataModule {
  private static AddressDM myDM;
  Database database1 = new Database();
  QueryDataSet address = new QueryDataSet();
  Column column1 = new Column();
  Column column2 = new Column();

  public static AddressDM getDataModule() {
    if (myDM == null) {
      myDM = new AddressDM();
    }
    return myDM;
  }

  public AddressDM() {
    try {
      jbInit();
    }
    catch(Exception e) {
      e.printStackTrace();
    }
  }

  private void jbInit() throws Exception {
    column2.setColumnName("lastName");
    column2.setDataType(com.borland.dx.dataset.Variant.STRING);
    column2.setPrecision(15);
    column2.setRowId(true);
    column2.setTableName("Address");
    column2.setServerColumnName("lastName");
    column2.setSqlType(12);
    column1.setColumnName("firstName");
    column1.setDataType(com.borland.dx.dataset.Variant.STRING);
    column1.setPrecision(15);
    column1.setRowId(true);
    column1.setTableName("Address");
    column1.setServerColumnName("firstName");
    column1.setSqlType(12);
    address.setMetaDataUpdate(MetaDataUpdate.NONE);
    address.setQuery(new com.borland.dx.sql.dataset.QueryDescriptor
      (database1, "SELECT * FROM Address", null, true, Load.ALL));
    database1.setConnection(new com.borland.dx.sql.dataset.
      ConnectionDescriptor("jdbc:odbc:LiangBookDB_MDB", "", "",
      false, "sun.jdbc.odbc.JdbcOdbcDriver"));
```

Listing 14.5 *AddressDM.java*

```
      address.setColumns(new Column[] {column1, column2});
    }

    public Database getDatabase1() {
      return database1;
    }

    public QueryDataSet getAddress() {
      return address;
    }
  }
```

Listing 14.5 *Continued*

3. Create the frame for displaying the whole table.

   3.1. Create a new frame named TableFrame.java using the Frame wizard in the Object Gallery.

   3.2. With TableFrame.java selected in the project pane, choose Wizards, Use Data Module to bring up the Use DataModule wizard, as shown in Figure 14.17. Choose AddressDM in the DataModule class section, and check the radio button Share (static) instance of `DataModule`. Click OK to close the dialog box. You will see `addressDM1` created in the source code.

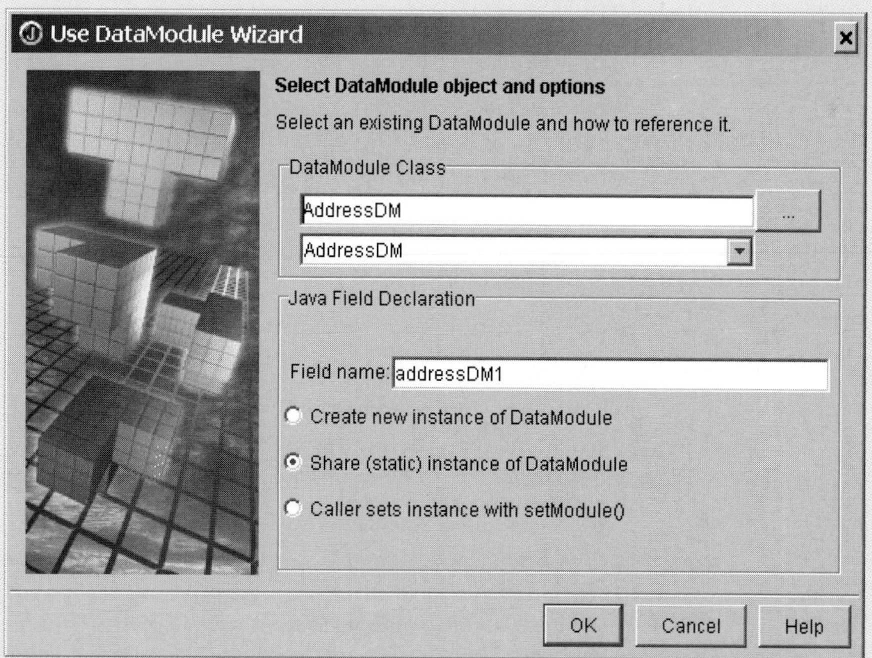

Figure 14.17 *The Choose a DataModule dialog box lets you choose a DataModule from the current project or from the library.*

continued

Example 14.4 continued

3.3. Drop a `TableScrollPane` from the dbSwing page to the center of the frame, and drop a `JdbTable` to the scroll pane to create `jdbTable1`. Set its `dataSet` property to `addressDM1`.

The generated code for TableFrame.java is shown in Listing 14.6.

```
package dataexpressdemo;

import java.awt.*;
import javax.swing.JFrame;
import com.borland.dbswing.*;

public class TableFrame extends JFrame {
  AddressDM addressDM1;
  TableScrollPane tableScrollPane1 = new TableScrollPane();
  JdbTable jdbTable1 = new JdbTable();

  public TableFrame() {
    try {
      jbInit();
    }
    catch(Exception e) {
      e.printStackTrace();
    }
  }

  private void jbInit() throws Exception {
    addressDM1 = dataexpressdemo.AddressDM.getDataModule();
    jdbTable1.setDataSet(addressDM1.getAddress());
    this.setTitle("Show Table");
    this.getContentPane().add(tableScrollPane1, BorderLayout.CENTER);
    tableScrollPane1.getViewport().add(jdbTable1, null);
  }
}
```

Listing 14.6 *TableFrame.java*

4. Create the frame for displaying a row in the table.

4.1. Create a new frame named RowFrame.java using the Frame wizard.

4.2. With RowFrame.java selected in the project pane, choose Wizards, Use Data Module to bring up the Use DataModule wizard. Choose AddressDM in the DataModule class section, and check the radio button Share (static) instance of DataModule. Click OK to close the wizard. You will see `addressDM1` created in the source code.

4.3. With RowFrame.java selected in the project pane, switch to the UI designer. Drop a `JdbNavToolBar` from the dbSwing page to the north of the frame to create `jdbNavToolBar1`. Set its `dataSet` property to `addressDM1`.

4.4. Drop a `JPanel` to the center of the frame to create `jpRow`. Set the `layout` property of `jpRow` to `GridLayout` with five rows. Drop a `JPanel` five times to `jpRow` to create five panels for containing the labels and text fields for records to display a row in the Address table.

4.5. Add appropriate labels and text fields to the panels using `JLabel` and `JdbTextField` in the same way as in Example 14.2. Be sure to bind the text field's `dataSet` to `addressDM1` and select the appropriate column names.

The generated code for RowFrame.java is shown in Listing 14.7.

```
package dataexpressdemo;

import java.awt.*;
import com.borland.dbswing.*;
import javax.swing.*;

public class RowFrame extends JFrame {
  AddressDM addressDM1;
  JdbNavToolBar jdbNavToolBar1 = new JdbNavToolBar();
  JPanel jpRow = new JPanel();
  GridLayout gridLayout1 = new GridLayout();

  JPanel jPanel1 = new JPanel();
  JdbTextField jdbTextField1 = new JdbTextField();
  JLabel jLabel1 = new JLabel();
  JLabel jLabel2 = new JLabel();
  JdbTextField jdbTextField2 = new JdbTextField();
  JLabel jLabel3 = new JLabel();
  JdbTextField jdbTextField3 = new JdbTextField();
  FlowLayout flowLayout1 = new FlowLayout();
  JPanel jPanel2 = new JPanel();
  JLabel jLabel4 = new JLabel();
  JdbTextField jdbTextField4 = new JdbTextField();
  FlowLayout flowLayout2 = new FlowLayout();
  JPanel jPanel3 = new JPanel();
  JLabel jLabel5 = new JLabel();
  JdbTextField jdbTextField5 = new JdbTextField();
  FlowLayout flowLayout3 = new FlowLayout();
  JLabel jLabel6 = new JLabel();
  JdbTextField jdbTextField6 = new JdbTextField();
  JLabel jLabel7 = new JLabel();
  JdbTextField jdbTextField7 = new JdbTextField();
  JPanel jPanel4 = new JPanel();
  JLabel jLabel8 = new JLabel();
  FlowLayout flowLayout4 = new FlowLayout();
  JdbTextField jdbTextField8 = new JdbTextField();
  JPanel jPanel5 = new JPanel();
  JLabel jLabel9 = new JLabel();
  JdbTextField jdbTextField9 = new JdbTextField();
  FlowLayout flowLayout5 = new FlowLayout();

  public RowFrame() {
    try {
      jbInit();
    }
    catch(Exception e) {
      e.printStackTrace();
    }
  }

```

Listing 14.7 *RowFrame.java*

continued

Example 14.4 continued

```
    private void jbInit() throws Exception {
      addressDM1 = AddressDM.getDataModule();
      jpRow.setLayout(gridLayout1);
      gridLayout1.setRows(5);
      jdbNavToolBar1.setDataSet(addressDM1.getAddress());
      jdbTextField1.setColumns(10);
      jdbTextField1.setColumnName("firstName");
      jdbTextField1.setDataSet(addressDM1.getAddress());
      this.setTitle("Show One Row");
      this.getContentPane().add(jdbNavToolBar1, BorderLayout.NORTH);
      this.getContentPane().add(jpRow, BorderLayout.CENTER);

      jLabel1.setText("FirstName");
      jLabel2.setText("MI");
      jdbTextField2.setColumns(2);
      jdbTextField2.setColumnName("MI");
      jdbTextField2.setDataSet(addressDM1.getAddress());
      jLabel3.setText("LastName");
      jdbTextField3.setColumnName("lastName");
      jdbTextField3.setDataSet(addressDM1.getAddress());
      jPanel1.setLayout(flowLayout1);
      flowLayout1.setAlignment(FlowLayout.LEFT);
      gridLayout1.setRows(5);
      jLabel4.setText("Address");
      jdbTextField4.setColumnName("street");
      jdbTextField4.setDataSet(addressDM1.getAddress());
      jPanel2.setLayout(flowLayout2);
      flowLayout2.setAlignment(FlowLayout.LEFT);
      jLabel5.setText("City");
      jdbTextField5.setColumnName("city");
      jdbTextField5.setDataSet(addressDM1.getAddress());
      jPanel3.setLayout(flowLayout3);
      flowLayout3.setAlignment(FlowLayout.LEFT);
      jLabel6.setText("State");
      jdbTextField6.setColumnName("state");
      jdbTextField6.setDataSet(addressDM1.getAddress());
      jLabel7.setText("Zip");
      jdbTextField7.setColumnName("zip");
      jdbTextField7.setDataSet(addressDM1.getAddress());
      jLabel8.setText("Telephone");
      jPanel4.setLayout(flowLayout4);
      flowLayout4.setAlignment(FlowLayout.LEFT);
      jdbTextField8.setColumnName("telephone");
      jdbTextField8.setDataSet(addressDM1.getAddress());
      jLabel9.setText("Email");
      jdbTextField9.setColumnName("email");
      jdbTextField9.setDataSet(addressDM1.getAddress());
      jPanel5.setLayout(flowLayout5);
      flowLayout5.setAlignment(FlowLayout.LEFT);
      jpRow.setBorder(BorderFactory.createEtchedBorder());
      jpRow.add(jPanel1, null);
      jPanel1.add(jLabel1, null);
      jPanel1.add(jdbTextField1, null);
      jPanel1.add(jLabel2, null);
      jPanel1.add(jdbTextField2, null);
      jPanel1.add(jLabel3, null);
      jPanel1.add(jdbTextField3, null);
      jpRow.add(jPanel2, null);
      jPanel2.add(jLabel4, null);
```

Listing 14.7 *Continued*

```
        jPanel2.add(jdbTextField4, null);
        jpRow.add(jPanel3, null);
        jPanel3.add(jLabel5, null);
        jPanel3.add(jdbTextField5, null);
        jPanel3.add(jLabel6, null);
        jPanel3.add(jdbTextField6, null);
        jPanel3.add(jLabel7, null);
        jPanel3.add(jdbTextField7, null);
        jpRow.add(jPanel4, null);
        jPanel4.add(jLabel8, null);
        jPanel4.add(jdbTextField8, null);
        jpRow.add(jPanel5, null);
        jPanel5.add(jLabel9, null);
        jPanel5.add(jdbTextField9, null);
    }
}
```

Listing 14.7 *Continued*

Example Review

As you can see from this example, data modules offer the significant advantage of separating database connection and query information from the user interface, which enables multiple frames or applets to share the same application logic and business rules.

For example, suppose you wish to log the transaction for the delete record operation on the Address table. All you need to do is to modify the AddressDM data module without requiring modifications of the other programs.

The data module does not need to be in the same directory with the application project. In fact, it can be stored on a server. Database applications based on data modules are easy to maintain, and clients can always get the latest version of the business logic from a centralized data module.

You can create a custom data module class manually, but the Data Module wizard greatly simplifies the process of creating a data module. The wizard automatically creates code that instantiates your data components at the level of the data module class. In addition, property settings made in the inspector are reflected in a `jbinit()` method. Individual get methods are also created that return each `Database`, `DataSet`, `DataStore` (and so on) in your data module. This allows `DataSet` components to be visible to the `dataSet` property of data-aware components in the component inspector when the data modules are used with data-aware components in the same application. As you can see in this example, `addressDM1` appears in the `dataSet` property of `jdbTable1` in TableFrame.java and also in `jdbNavToolBar1` of RowFrame.java.

The property settings and business rules code you created in the data module cannot be overridden in the application that uses the data module. If you have rules that do not apply across all the applications that use this data module, you should create a separate data module to isolate the differences.

continued

Example 14.4 continued

To reference your data module in your current application, select the Use Data-Module option from the Wizards menu to display the wizard. This dialog box displays all the data modules in your project, allows you to browse to find other data modules in the library, and lets you choose the kind of constructor you want. In this example, you chose the option "Share (static) instance of Data-Module." This option lets you access a single instance of your data module shared across your application instead of allocating memory for multiple instances. The static instance was automatically generated by the Data Module wizard. If you create a data module manually, make sure to write the code to declare the static instance. `addressDM1` in both `TableFrame` and `RowFrame` refers to the same object that is created using `AddressDM.getDataModule()`.

Chapter Summary

This chapter introduced the development of Java database applications using the JBuilder DataExpress API, dbSwing components, and data modules. You learned how to use the `DataBase` component to connect to a JDBC source and the `QueryDataSet` component to create queries. You also learned how to create applications using data-aware dbSwing components that link to `QueryDataSet`, how to create master-detail link forms, and how to create a data module to separate data from the GUI.

Review Questions

14.1 Describe the DataExpress API. How do you connect to a data source using the `Database` component? How do you associate a query in `QueryDataSet` with a database?

14.2 What properties do you have to set in the `QueryDataSet` to enable insertion and deletion of records in a table?

14.3 What properties do you need to bind a dbSwing component with a data source?

14.4 Describe the components `JdbNavToolBar` and `JdbNavField`.

14.5 Describe the process of creating a master-detail link between two instances of `QueryDataSet`.

14.6 What are the advantages of database data modules? How do you create a data module?

14.7 How do you create a data module object to be shared by several classes in a project?

Programming Exercises

14.1 Modify Example 14.1 to add a new button that enables the user to update a record and another button that enables the user to delete a record.

14.2 Modify Example 14.2 to add a `JComboBox` with the values firstName and lastName. When firstName is chosen, the search in the `JdbNavField` is based on the firstName column of the table. When lastName is chosen, the search is based on the lastName column of the table.

14.3 Modify Example 14.3 to add a `JdbNavToolBar` and a `JdbStatusLabel` for each table, so that the user can manipulate the tables using the `JdbNavToolBar` buttons and get the message from the `JdbStatusLabel`.

14.4 Rewrite Exercise 12.5 to display the number of employees in each department in a pie chart and a bar chart. Use a data module for this query and pass the data to the `PieChart` component and the `BarChart` component.

PART V

Enterprise Java Programming

The final part of the book introduces server-side Java programming. You will learn how to use remote method invocation to develop distributed applications, and Java servlets to generate dynamic contents.

CHAPTER 15

Remote Method Invocation

Objectives

- Understand how RMI works.
- Learn the process of developing RMI applications.
- Know the differences between RMI and socket-level programming.
- Develop three-tier applications using RMI.
- Use callbacks to develop interactive applications.

Introduction

The Java language is superior for developing reusable software components, and the JavaBeans technology enables you to create Java applications by using a builder tool to assemble JavaBeans components during design time. Remote Method Invocation (RMI) technology provides a framework for building distributed Java systems. Using RMI, a Java object on one system can invoke a method in an object on another system on the network. A *distributed Java system* can be defined as a collection of cooperative distributed objects on the network. This chapter introduces RMI basics. You will learn how to use RMI to create useful distributed applications.

RMI Basics

RMI is the Java Distributed Object Model for facilitating communications among distributed objects. RMI is a higher-level API built on top of sockets. Socket-level programming allows you to pass data through sockets among computers. RMI enables you not only to pass data among objects on different systems, but also to invoke methods in a remote object.

RMI is similar to Remote Procedure Calls (RPC) in the sense that both RMI and RPC enable you to invoke methods, but there are some important differences. With RPC, you call a standalone procedure. With RMI, you invoke a method within a specific object. RMI can be viewed as object-oriented RPC.

In many ways, RMI is an evolution of the client/server architecture. A *client* is a component that issues requests for services, and a *server* is a component that delivers the requested services. Like the client/server architecture, RMI maintains the notion of clients and servers, but the RMI approach is more flexible than the client/server paradigm.

- An RMI component can act as both a client and a server, depending on the scenario in question.
- An RMI system can pass functionality from a server to a client, and vice versa. A client/server system typically only passes data back and forth between server and client.

How Does RMI Work?

For an object to be invoked remotely, it must be defined in a Java interface accessible to both the server and the client. Furthermore, the interface must extend the `java.rmi.Remote` interface. Like the `java.io.Serializable` interface, `java.rmi.Remote` is a marker interface that contains no constants or methods. It is only used to identify remote objects. The implementation of the remote object interface, referred to as *server implementation*, resides on the server machine and is registered with the RMI registry, as shown in Figure 15.1. A client looks through the RMI registry for the remote object. Once it is located, it can be used in the same way as a local object.

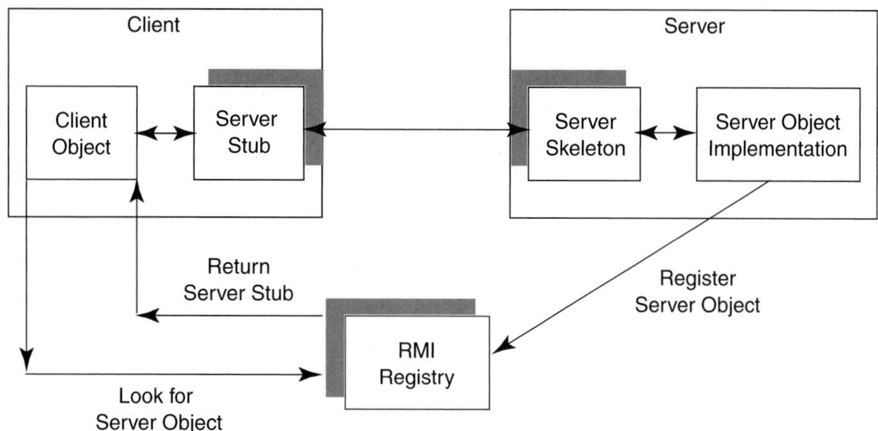

Figure 15.1 *Java RMI uses a registry to provide naming services for remote objects, and uses the stub and skeleton to facilitate communications between client and server.*

Obviously, invoking methods in a remote object on a server is very different from invoking methods in a local object on a client, since the remote object is in a different address space on a separate machine. The following steps are usually involved in invoking a remote method:

1. The client sends method parameters to the server.
2. The server receives the method parameter and executes the method.
3. The server sends the result back to the client.
4. The client receives the results.

Implementing this service is complicated, but the good news is that RMI provides a mechanism that liberates you from writing the tedious code for handling parameter passing and invoking remote methods. The basic idea is to use two helper classes known as *stub* and *skeleton* for handling communications between client and server, as shown in Figure 15.1.

The stub and the skeleton can be automatically generated from the server implementation using an RMI utility called `rmic`. The stub resides on the client machine. It contains all the reference information the client needs to know about the server object. When a client invokes a method on a server object, it actually invokes a method that is encapsulated in the stub. The stub is responsible for sending parameters to the server, and for receiving the result from the server and returning it to the client.

The skeleton communicates with the stub on the server side. The skeleton receives parameters from the client, passes them to the server for execution, and returns the result to the stub.

Passing Parameters

When a client invokes a remote method with parameters, passing the parameters is handled by the stub and the skeleton. Let us consider three types of parameters:

- Primitive data types. A parameter of primitive type, such as `char`, `int`, `double`, or `boolean`, is passed by value like a local call.
- Local object types. A parameter of local object type, such as `java.lang.String`, is also passed by value, but this is completely different from passing an object parameter in a local call. In a local call, an object parameter's reference is passed, which corresponds to the memory address of the object. In a remote call, there is no way to pass the object reference because the address on one machine is meaningless to a different Java VM. Any object can be used as a parameter in a remote call as long as it is serializable. The stub serializes the object parameter and sends it in a stream across the network. The skeleton deserializes the stream into an object.

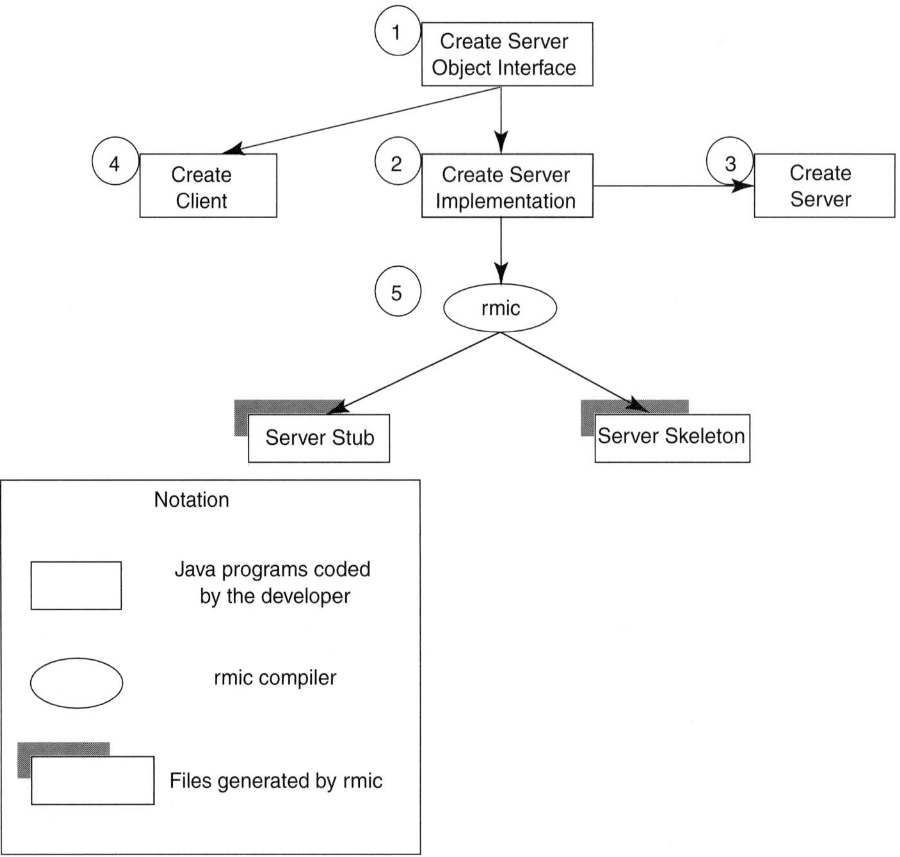

Figure 15.2 *The steps in developing RMI applications.*

- Remote object types. Remote objects are passed differently from local objects. When a client invokes a remote method with a parameter of a remote object type, the stub of the remote object is passed. The server receives the stub and manipulates the parameter through it. See Example 15.3, "The RMI TicTacToe Implementation," for details.

Developing RMI Applications

Now that you have a basic understanding of RMI, you are ready to write simple RMI applications. The steps in developing an RMI application are shown in Figure 15.2.

The following example demonstrates the development of an RMI application through these steps.

Example 15.1 Retrieving Student Scores from an RMI Server

This example creates a client to retrieve student scores from an RMI server. The client, shown in Figure 15.3, displays the score for the specified name.

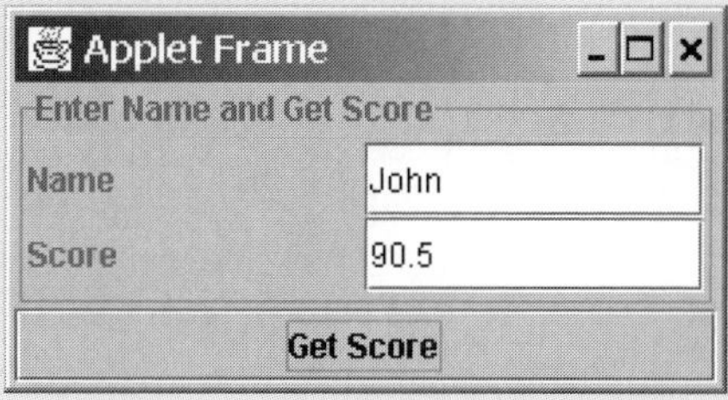

Figure 15.3 *You can get the score by entering a student name and clicking the Get Score button.*

Here are the steps to complete this example:

1. Create a new project named rmidemo.jpr. Uncheck "Synchronize output dir" in the Build page of the Project Properties dialog box, as shown in Figure 15.4. Later on in this project, we will generate two class files (skeleton and stub) that have no corresponding source files. With "Synchronized output dir" checked, these two files would be removed when you build the project. Without "Synchronized output dir" checked, you would receive a warning message, but the class files are not removed.

2. Create the server interface named Student.java, as shown in Listing 15.1. The interface tells the client how to invoke the server's `findScore` method to retrieve a student score.

continued

Example 15.1 continued

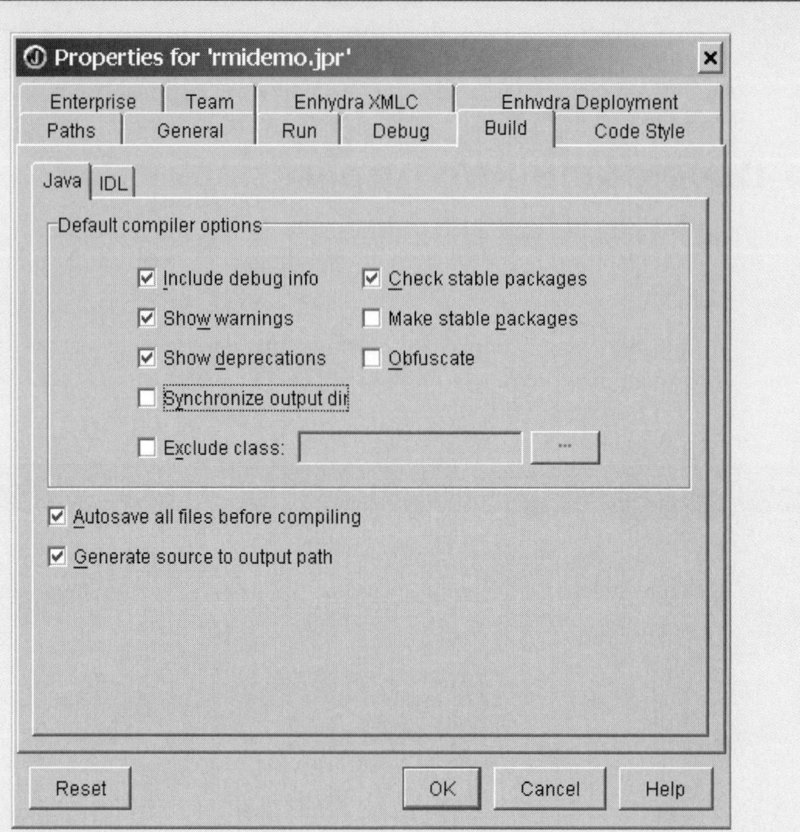

Figure 15.4 *With "Synchronized output dir" unchecked, the class files without corresponding source file are not removed in the project.*

3. Create StudentImpl.java (Listing 15.2) to implement the `Student` interface. The `findScore` method returns the score for a specified student. This method returns -1 if the score is not found.

4. Create a server program named `StudentServer` that creates an instance of server implementation, and register it with the RMI registry. StudentServer.java is shown in Listing 15.3.

5. Now turn your attention to developing the client.

   5.1. Create an applet named `StudentClient` using the Applet wizard.

   5.2. Create the user interface. In the UI designer for StudentClient.java, drop a `JPanel` to the center of the applet to create `jPanel1`, and drop a `JButton` to the south of the applet to create `jButton1`. Rename the button `jbtGetScore` and change the panel's `layout` to `GridLayout` to create `gridLayout1`. Select `gridLayout1` in the component tree, and set `columns` and `rows` to 2. Drop a `JLabel`, a `JTextField`, a `JLabel`, and a `JTextField` to the applet, and rename them to `jlblName`, `jtfName`, `jlblScore`, and `jtfScore`. Set the `text` property of `jlblName` to "Name," and the `text` property of `jlblScore` to "Score."

5.3. Create the method `initializeRMI` for locating the `Student` server, as shown in Listing 15.4 (Lines 82–107). Add the code to invoke this method from the `jbInit` method (Lines 61–62).

5.4. In the UI designer, double-click `jbtGetScore` to generate the supporting code for the handler `jbtGetScore_actionPerformed()`. Implement this handler for finding and displaying the student's score, as shown in Listing 15.4 (Lines 109–124).

6. Generate the stub and the skeleton as follows. Right-click on StudentImpl.java in the project pane and choose Properties to display the Properties dialog box for StudentImple.java, as shown in Figure 15.5. Choose the Build page and click the ellipse button to display the Additional RMI Options dialog box, as shown in Figure 15.6. Choose Java 2 only, because you are using JDK with JBuilder 4 and 5. The generated stub named StudentImpl Stub.class and the skeleton named StudentImpl_Skel.class are in the rmidemo folder.

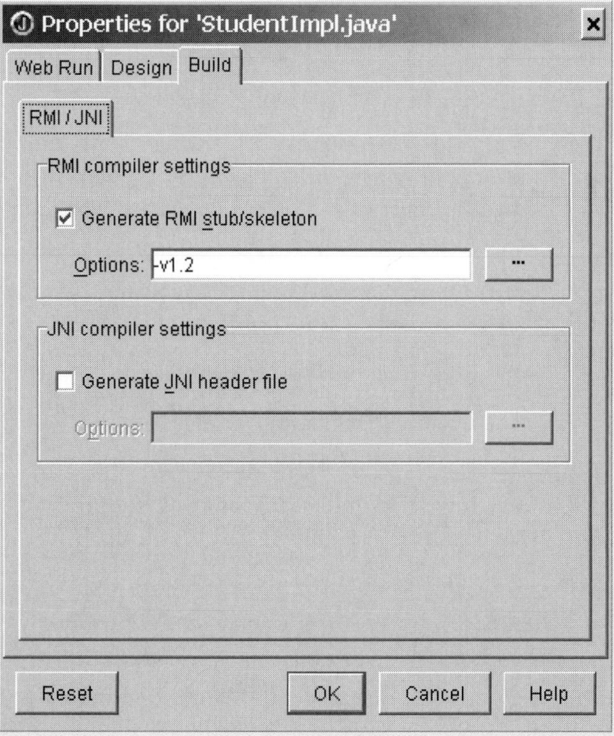

Figure 15.5 *You can set the option for JBuilder to generate stub and skeleton automatically.*

continued

Example 15.1 continued

Figure 15.6 *You can specify the skeleton type for Java 2, JDK 1.1 or 2 compatible, or JDK 1.1 only.*

NOTE
Alternatively, you can generate the stub and skeleton using the DOS command. To do so, at a DOS prompt, change the directory to c:\radjb, and type the following command to generate the stub and skeleton:

```
C:\radjb>rmic rmidemo.StudentImpl
```

---

7. Follow the steps below to run this example.

   7.1. Start the RMI registry by typing "**start rmiregistry**" at a DOS prompt from the radjb directory. By default, port number 1099 is used by rmiregistry. To use a different port number, type the command "**start rmiregistry *portnumber***" at a DOS prompt.

   7.2. Start `StudentServer` using the following command at C:\radjb directory:

   ```
   C:\radjb>java rmidemo.StudentServer
   ```

   7.3. Run `StudentClient` as an application. A sample run of the application is shown in Figure 15.3.

   7.4. Run rmidemo.StudentClient.html from the appletviewer. A sample run is shown in Figure 15.7.

NOTE
You must start rmiregistry from the directory where you will run the RMI server. Otherwise, you will receive the error `ClassNotFoundException` on `StudentImpl_Stub`. You can start the RMI registry from the Tools menu, but since there is a bug in JBuilder 4, you should start the it from the DOS prompt.

Figure 15.7 *You can run StudentClient as an applet.*

```java
// Student.java: Student server interface
package rmidemo;

import java.rmi.*;

public interface Student extends Remote {
  /**
   * Return the score for specified the name
   * @param   name   the student name
   * @return  an double score or -1 if the student
   *     is not found
   */
  public double findScore(String name) throws RemoteException;
}
```

Listing 15.1 *Student.java*

```java
// StudentImpl.java: implementation for Student.java
package rmidemo;

import java.rmi.*;
import java.rmi.server.*;
import java.util.*;

public class StudentImpl extends UnicastRemoteObject
  implements Student {
  // Stores scores in a map indexed by name
  private HashMap scores = new HashMap();

  /** Constructor */
  public StudentImpl() throws RemoteException {
    initializeStudent();
  }

  /** Initialize student information */
  protected void initializeStudent() {
    scores.put("John", new Double(90.5));
    scores.put("Michael", new Double(100));
    scores.put("Michelle", new Double(98.5));
  }

  /** Implement the findScore method from the Student interface */
  public double findScore(String name) throws RemoteException {
    Double d = (Double)scores.get(name);

```

Listing 15.2 *StudentImpl.java*

continued

Example 15.1 continued

```
    if (d == null) {
      System.out.println("Student " + name + " is not found ");
      return -1;
    }
    else {
      System.out.println("Student " + name + "\'s score is "
        + d.doubleValue());
      return d.doubleValue();
    }
  }
}
```

Listing 15.2 *Continued*

```
// StudentServer.java: register StudentImpl with the RMI registry
package rmidemo;

import java.rmi.*;
import java.rmi.server.*;

public class StudentServer {
  public static void main(String args[]) {
    // Set RMI security manager
    if (System.getSecurityManager() == null) {
      System.setSecurityManager(new RMISecurityManager());
    }

    // Create and register the server implementation
    try {
      StudentImpl studentImpl = new StudentImpl();
      // To register the object on remote host, use
      // Naming.bind("//hostname:port#/Student Server", studentImpl);
      Naming.bind("Student Server", studentImpl);
      System.out.println("Server " + studentImpl + " registered");
    }
    catch(Exception ex) {
      System.out.println(ex);
    }
  }
}
```

Listing 15.3 *StudentServer.java*

```
// StudentClient.java: Student RMI Client
package rmidemo;

import java.rmi.*;
import javax.swing.*;
import java.awt.*;
import java.awt.event.*;
import javax.swing.border.*;

public class StudentClient extends JApplet {
  // Declare a Student instance
  Student student;

  boolean isStandalone = false;
  JLabel jlblName = new JLabel();
  JTextField jtfName = new JTextField();
  JButton jbtGetScore = new JButton();
```

Listing 15.4 *StudentClient.java*

```
  JTextField jtfScore = new JTextField();
  JPanel jPanel1 = new JPanel();
  GridLayout gridLayout1 = new GridLayout();
  BorderLayout borderLayout1 = new BorderLayout();
  TitledBorder titledBorder1;
  JLabel jlblScore = new JLabel();

  /** Initialize the applet */
  public void init() {
    try {
      jbInit();
    }
    catch (Exception e) {
      e.printStackTrace();
    }
  }

  /** RMI initialization and Component initialization */
  private void jbInit() throws Exception {
    titledBorder1 = new TitledBorder("");
    this.getContentPane().setLayout(borderLayout1);
    jlblName.setText("Name");
    jbtGetScore.setText("Get Score");
    jbtGetScore.addActionListener(
      new java.awt.event.ActionListener() {
      public void actionPerformed(ActionEvent e) {
        jbtGetScore_actionPerformed(e);
      }
    });

    jPanel1.setLayout(gridLayout1);
    gridLayout1.setRows(2);
    gridLayout1.setColumns(2);
    jPanel1.setBorder(titledBorder1);
    titledBorder1.setTitle("Enter Name and Get Score");
    jlblScore.setText("Score");
    this.getContentPane().add(jPanel1, BorderLayout.CENTER);
    jPanel1.add(jlblName, null);
    jPanel1.add(jtfName, null);
    jPanel1.add(jlblScore, null);
    jPanel1.add(jtfScore, null);
    this.getContentPane().add(jbtGetScore, BorderLayout.SOUTH);

    // Initialize RMI
    initializeRMI();
  }

  /** Main method */
  public static void main(String[] args) {
    StudentClient applet = new StudentClient();
    applet.isStandalone = true;
    JFrame frame = new JFrame();
    frame.setTitle("StudentClient");
    frame.getContentPane().add(applet, BorderLayout.CENTER);
    applet.init();
    applet.start();
    frame.setSize(250, 150);
    Dimension d = Toolkit.getDefaultToolkit().getScreenSize();
    frame.setLocation((d.width - frame.getSize().width) / 2,
      (d.height - frame.getSize().height) / 2);
```

Listing 15.4 *Continued*

continued

Example 15.1 continued

```
      frame.setVisible(true);
      frame.setDefaultCloseOperation(3);
    }

    /** Initialize RMI */
    protected void initializeRMI() {
      String url;

      if (isStandalone) {
        // System.setSecurityManager(new RMISecurityManager());

        url = "rmi:///";
        // Use rmi://hostname/ if the server is located on hostname,
        // i.e. rmi://liangy.ipfw.edu/
      }
      else {
        // Initialize RMI for an applet
        url = getCodeBase().getHost();
        if (url.equals("default")) url = "";
        url = "rmi://" + url + "/";
      }

      try {
        student = (Student)Naming.lookup(url + "Student Server");
        System.out.println("Server object " + student + " found");
      }
      catch(Exception ex) {
        System.out.println(ex);
      }
    }

    /** Handle the Get Score button */
    void jbtGetScore_actionPerformed(ActionEvent e) {
      try {
        // Get student score
        double score = student.findScore(jtfName.getText().trim());

        // Display the result
        if (score < 0)
          jtfScore.setText("Not found");
        else
          jtfScore.setText(new Double(score).toString());
      }
      catch(Exception ex) {
        System.out.println(ex);
      }
    }
  }
```

Listing 15.4 *Continued*

Example Review

Any object that can be used remotely must be defined in an interface that extends the `java.rmi.Remote` interface. The `Student` interface, extending `Remote`, defines the `findScore` method that can be remotely invoked by a client to find a student's score. Each method in this interface must declare that it may throw a `java.rmi.RemoteException`. So your client code that invokes this method must be prepared to catch this exception in a try-catch block.

On the server side, the `StudentImpl` class implements the `Student` interface. This class must also extend the `java.rmi.server.RemoteServer` class or its subclass. `RemoteServer` is an abstract class that defines the methods needed to create and export remote objects. Often its subclass `java.rmi.server.UnicastRemoteObject` is used. This subclass implements all the abstract methods defined in `RemoteServer`.

`StudentImpl` implements the `findScore` method defined in the `Student` interface. For simplicity, three students, John, Michael, and Michelle, and their corresponding scores are stored in an instance of `java.util.HashMap` named `scores`. `HashMap` is a concrete class of the Map interface in the Java Collections Framework, which makes it possible to search and retrieve a value using a key. Both values and keys are of the `Object` type. The `findScore` method returns the score if the name is in the hash map, and returns -1 if the name is not found.

`StudentServer` is responsible for starting the server. It performs the following tasks:

1. Installing an RMI security manager to control the classes that are dynamically loaded with the following code:

   ```
   System.setSecurityManager(new RMISecurityManager());
   ```

2. Creating an instance of the server implementation and registering it in the RMI registry with the following code:

   ```
   Naming.rebind("Student Server", studentImpl);
   ```

`java.rmi.Naming` provides the bootstrap mechanism for locating remote objects. The server registers with the service, and the client retrieves the stub of the remote object through the service. The static `bind` method binds the name to a specified remote object. You can also use the `rebind` method to rebind the name to a new object and replace any existing binding associated with the name.

`StudentClient` invokes the `findScore` method on the server to find the score for a specified student. The key method in `StudentClient` is the `initializeRMI` method, which is responsible for locating the server stub. The stub is specified in an RMI URL using the usual host name, port, and server name:

rmi://hostname:port/servername

where *hostname* is the host name of the RMI registry (defaults to local host), *port* is the port number of the RMI registry (defaults to the registry port number), and *servername* is the name for a remote object, such as "Student Server" in this example.

The `initializeRMI()` method treats standalone applications differently from applets. The hostname should be the name where the applet is downloaded. It can be obtained using the `Applet`'s `getCodeBase().getHost()`. For standalone applications, the hostname should be specified explicitly.

continued

Example 15.1 continued

The `Naming.lookup()` method returns the remote object for the specified RMI URL. Once a remote object is found, it can be used just like a local object, although the stub and the skeleton are used behind the scenes to make the remote method invocation work.

If you run the client and the server on separate machines, you need to start RMIRegistry and run `StudentServer` on the server machine before running `StudentClient` on the client machine. To run `StudentClient` standalone, you need to deploy Student.class, StudentImpl_Stub.class, StudentClient.class on the client machine, and place Student.class, StudentImpl.class, StudentImpl_Skel.class, and StudentServer.class on the server machine. To run `StudentClient` from a Web browser, you need to place Student.class, StudentImpl.class, StudentImpl_Stub.class, StudentImpl_Skel.class, StudentClient.class, and StudentClient.html on the server machine.

CAUTION

If you modify the remote object implementation class, you must regenerate updated stub and skeleton classes. You need to restart the server class to reload the skeleton to the RMI registry. In some old versions of rmiregistry, you may have to restart rmiregistry.

RMI vs. Socket-Level Programming

Example 15.1 involves many files, but the stub and the skeleton were automatically generated by the rmic utility. These programs are easy to develop once you understand RMI. To demonstrate the power and elegance of the RMI concept, this section rewrites Example 15.1 using socket-level programming so that you can compare RMI programming with socket-level programming.

Example 15.2 Retrieving Student Scores from a Server Using Socket-Level Programming

This example rewrites Example 15.1 using socket-level programming. The purpose is to highlight the differences between RMI and socket-level programming and to demonstrate the superiority of RMI for client/sever applications. If you are not familiar with socket-level programming, please refer to Chapter 18, "Networking," in my *Introduction to Java Programming with JBuilder 4.*

Here are the steps to complete the example.

1. Create a new project named socketprogrammingdemo.jpr.
2. Create the server class named `SocketStudentServer`, as shown in Listing 15.5.

3. Create the client class named `SocketStudentClient`, as shown in Listing 15.6.
4. Start SocketStudentServer and then start SocketStudentClient. SocketStudentClient runs like StudentClient, as shown in Figure 15.7.

```
// SocketStudentServer.java
package socketprogrammingdemo;

import java.io.*;
import java.net.*;
import java.util.*;

public class SocketStudentServer {
  private HashMap scores = new HashMap();

  /** Constructor */
  public SocketStudentServer() {
    // Initialize scores hashtable
    initializeStudent();

    try {
      // Create a server socket
      ServerSocket serverSocket = new ServerSocket(8000);

      // Server the clients
      while (true) {
        // Listen for a new connection request
        Socket connectToClient = serverSocket.accept();
        System.out.println(
          "Starting a new server thread for a new client");

        // Create a new thread for the connection
        ThreadHandler thread = new ThreadHandler(connectToClient);

        // Start the new thread
        thread.start();
      }
    }
    catch(IOException ex) {
      System.err.println(ex);
    }
  }

  public static void main(String[] args) {
    // Initialize SocketStudentServer
    new SocketStudentServer();
  }

  /** Initialize student information */
  protected void initializeStudent() {
    scores.put("John", new Double(90.5));
    scores.put("Michael", new Double(100));
    scores.put("Michelle", new Double(98.5));
  }

  /** Get student score. Return -1 if score is not found */
  public double findScore(String name) {
    Double d = (Double)scores.get(name);

```

Listing 15.5 *SocketStudentServer.java*

continued

Example 15.2 continued

```
    if (d == null) {
      System.out.println("Student " + name + " is not found ");
      return -1;
    }
    else {
      System.out.println("Student " + name + "\'s score is "
        + d.doubleValue());
      return d.doubleValue();
    }
  }

  /** The server for handling a client, an inner class */
  class ThreadHandler extends Thread {
    private Socket connectToClient; // A connected socket

    public ThreadHandler(Socket socket) {
      connectToClient = socket;
    }

    public void run() {
      try {
        // Create data input and print streams
        BufferedReader isFromClient = new BufferedReader(
          new InputStreamReader(connectToClient.getInputStream()));
        PrintWriter osToClient =
          new PrintWriter(connectToClient.getOutputStream(), true);

        // Continuously serve the client
        while (true) {
          // Receive student name from the client in string
          String name = isFromClient.readLine();
          System.out.println(
            "Student name received from client is " + name);

          // Find score
          double score = findScore(name);

          // Send score back to the client
          osToClient.println(score);
        }
      }
      catch(IOException ex) {
        System.err.println(ex);
      }
    }
  } // End of the inner class
}
```

Listing 15.5 *Continued*

```
// SocketStudentClient.java: Student Client
package socketprogrammingdemo;

import javax.swing.*;
import java.awt.*;
import java.awt.event.*;
import javax.swing.border.*;
import java.io.*;
import java.net.*;
```

Listing 15.6 *SocketStudentClient.java*

```
import java.util.*;

public class SocketStudentClient extends JApplet {
  // Declare I/O streams
  protected BufferedReader isFromServer;
  protected PrintWriter osToServer;

  boolean isStandalone = false;
  JLabel jlblName = new JLabel();
  JTextField jtfName = new JTextField();
  JButton jbtGetScore = new JButton();
  JTextField jtfScore = new JTextField();
  JPanel jPanel1 = new JPanel();
  GridLayout gridLayout1 = new GridLayout();
  BorderLayout borderLayout1 = new BorderLayout();
  TitledBorder titledBorder1;
  JLabel jlblScore = new JLabel();

  /** Construct the applet */
  public SocketStudentClient() {
    try {
      // Create a socket to connect to the server
      Socket connectToServer = new Socket("localhost", 8000);

      // Create a buffered input stream to receive data
      // from the server
      isFromServer = new BufferedReader(
        new InputStreamReader(connectToServer.getInputStream()));

      // Create a buffered output stream to send data to the server
      osToServer =
        new PrintWriter(connectToServer.getOutputStream(), true);
    }
    catch (IOException ex) {
      System.err.println(ex);
    }
  }

  /** Initialize the applet */
  public void init() {
    try {
      jbInit();
    }
    catch (Exception e) {
      e.printStackTrace();
    }
  }

  /** Component initialization */
  private void jbInit() throws Exception {
    titledBorder1 = new TitledBorder("");
    this.getContentPane().setLayout(borderLayout1);
    jlblName.setText("Name");
    jbtGetScore.setText("Get Score");
    jbtGetScore.addActionListener(
      new java.awt.event.ActionListener() {
      public void actionPerformed(ActionEvent e) {
        jbtGetScore_actionPerformed(e);
      }
    });

```

Listing 15.6 *Continued*

continued

Example 15.2 continued

```
      jPanel1.setLayout(gridLayout1);
      gridLayout1.setRows(2);
      gridLayout1.setColumns(2);
      jPanel1.setBorder(titledBorder1);
      titledBorder1.setTitle("Enter Name and Get Score");
      jlblScore.setText("Score");
      this.getContentPane().add(jPanel1, BorderLayout.CENTER);
      jPanel1.add(jlblName, null);
      jPanel1.add(jtfName, null);
      jPanel1.add(jlblScore, null);
      jPanel1.add(jtfScore, null);
      this.getContentPane().add(jbtGetScore, BorderLayout.SOUTH);
    }

    /** Main method */
    public static void main(String[] args) {
      SocketStudentClient applet = new SocketStudentClient();
      applet.isStandalone = true;
      JFrame frame = new JFrame();
      frame.setTitle("SocketStudentClient");
      frame.getContentPane().add(applet, BorderLayout.CENTER);
      applet.init();
      applet.start();
      frame.setSize(250, 150);
      Dimension d = Toolkit.getDefaultToolkit().getScreenSize();
      frame.setLocation((d.width - frame.getSize().width) / 2,
        (d.height - frame.getSize().height) / 2);
      frame.setVisible(true);
      frame.setDefaultCloseOperation(3);
    }

    void jbtGetScore_actionPerformed(ActionEvent e) {
      try {
        // Send student name to the server
        osToServer.println(jtfName.getText().trim());

        // Get score from the server as a string
        StringTokenizer st = new StringTokenizer(
          isFromServer.readLine());

        // Convert string to double
        double score = new Double(
          st.nextToken()).doubleValue();

        // Display the result
        if (score < 0)
          jtfScore.setText("Not found");
        else
          jtfScore.setText(new Double(score).toString());
      }
      catch (IOException ex) {
        System.err.println(ex);
      }
    }
  }
```

Listing 15.6 *Continued*

Example Review

The server class `SocketStudentServer` does the following things:

1. It initializes the scores in the hash map, which is the same as in Example 15.1.
2. It creates an instance of `java.net.ServerSocket` named `serverSocket`, which is the base for listening to incoming connection requests from clients. The server socket is associated with a specific port. In this case, port 8000 is the server socket.
3. It creates an instance of `java.net.Socket` for connecting to a client, and starts a new server for handling the client on a separate thread. Since this server (`ThreadHandler`) is an inner class, `scores` and the `findScore` method defined in `SocketStudentServer` are directly accessible in this class. `ThreadHandler` continuously reads a name from the client, finds the score, and sends it to the client.

The client class `SocketStudentClient` is similar to `StudentClient` in Example 15.1 except that it communicates with the server through socket I/O, as follows:

1. Create an instance of `java.net.Socket` for connecting with the server at port 8000. Instantiate the I/O streams for sending and receiving data from the server.
2. In the handler for button Get Score, write the code to send the name to the server and receive the score from the server.

A comparison of Examples 15.1 and 15.2 clearly shows the advantages of using RMI against using socket-level programming.

- RMI enables you to program at a higher level of abstraction. It hides the details of socket server, socket, connection, and sending or receiving data. It even implements a multithreading server under the hood, while with socket-level programming you have to explicitly implement threads for handling multiple clients.
- RMI applications are scalable and easy to maintain. You can change the RMI server or move it to another machine without modifying the client program except for resetting the URL to locate the server. (To avoid resetting the URL, you can modify the client to pass the URL as a command-line parameter.) In socket-level programming, a client operation to send data requires a server operation to read it. The implementation of client and server at the socket-level is tightly synchronized.
- RMI clients can directly invoke the server method, whereas socket-level programming is limited to passing values.

As you can see, socket-level programming is very primitive. Avoid using it to develop client/server applications. As an analogy, socket-level programming is like programming in assembly language, while RMI programming is like programming in a high-level language.

Developing Three-Tier Applications Using RMI

Three-tier applications have gained considerable attention in recent years, largely because of the demand for more scalable and load-balanced systems to replace traditional two-tier client/server database systems. A centralized database system not only handles data access but also processes the business rules on data. Thus, a centralized database is usually heavily loaded because it requires extensive data manipulation and processing. In some situations, data processing is handled by the client and business rules are stored on the client side. It is preferable to use a middle tier as a buffer between a client and the database. The middle tier can be used to apply business logic and rules, and to process data to reduce the load on the database.

A three-tier architecture does more than just reduce the processing load on the server. It also provides access to multiple network sites. This is especially useful to Java applets that need to access multiple databases on different servers, since an applet can only connect with the server from which it is downloaded.

The following example demonstrates the use of RMI to create three-tier applications.

Example 15.3 Retrieving Student Scores on a Database Using RMI

This example rewrites Example 15.1 to find scores stored in a database rather than a hash map. In addition, the system is capable of blocking a client from accessing a student who has not given the university permission to publish his/her score. An RMI component is developed to serve as a middle tier between client and database; it sends a search request to the database, processes the result, and returns an appropriate value to the client.

For simplicity, this example reuses the `Student` interface and `StudentClient` class from Example 15.1 with no modifications. Here are the steps to complete the project.

1. Reopen project rmidemo.jpr, which was created in Example 15.1.
2. Create `Student3TierImpl` to implement the `Student` interface for accessing a JDBC data source, as shown in Listing 15.7. This implementation retrieves a record from the Scores table, processes the retrieved information, and sends the result back to the client.
3. At a DOS prompt, change to C:\radjb, and type the following command to generate the stub and skeleton for Student3TierImpl"

```
C:\radjb>rmic rmidemo.Student3TierImpl
```

4. Create `Student3TierServer` for creating an instance of `Student3TierImpl` and registering it with the RMI registry, as shown in Listing 15.8.

5. At a DOS prompt, change to C:\radjb, and type the following command to start the RMI registry and `Student3TierServer`:

```
start rmiregistry
java -Djava.security.policy=policy rmidemo.Student3TierServer
```

NOTE

The policy file is located at C:\radjb with the following contents to give global permission to anyone from anywhere:

```
grant {
  // Allow everything for now
  permission java.security.AllPermission;
};
```

This policy file is required to use JDBC drivers in RMI applications.

---

6. Run `StudentClient` to find student scores.

```
// Student3TierImpl.java: implementation for Student.java
// for accessing JDBC source
package rmidemo;

import java.rmi.*;
import java.rmi.server.*;
import java.sql.*;

public class Student3TierImpl extends UnicastRemoteObject
  implements Student {
  // Use prepared statement for querying DB
  private PreparedStatement pstmt;

  /** Constructor */
  public Student3TierImpl() throws RemoteException {
    initializeDB();
  }

  /** Load JDBC driver, establish connection and create statement */
  protected void initializeDB() {
    try {
      // Load the JDBC driver
      // Class.forName("oracle.jdbc.driver.OracleDriver");
      Class.forName("sun.jdbc.odbc.JdbcOdbcDriver");
      System.out.println("Driver registered");

      // Establish connection
      /*Connection conn = DriverManager.getConnection
        ("jdbc:oracle:thin:@drake.armstrong.edu:1521:test",
         "scott", "tiger");  */
      Connection conn = DriverManager.getConnection
        ("jdbc:odbc:LiangBookDB_MDB", "", "" );
      System.out.println("Database connected");

      // Create the Scores table and initialize it if necessary
      initializeTable(conn);

```

Listing 15.7 *Student3TierImpl.java*

continued

Example 15.3 continued

```
        // Create a prepared statement for querying DB
        pstmt = conn.prepareStatement(
          "select * from Scores where name = ?");
      }
      catch (Exception ex) {
        System.out.println(ex);
      }
    }

    /** Create the Scores table and initialize it if necessary */
    private void initializeTable(Connection conn) {
      try {
        // Create a statement
        Statement stmt = conn.createStatement();

        // stmt.executeUpdate("DROP TABLE Scores");

        // Create the table,
        // if already exists, an exception would be raised
        stmt.executeUpdate(
          "create table Scores" +
          "(name varchar(20), score number, permission number)");

        // Insert three records into the Scores TABLE
        stmt.executeUpdate(
          "insert into Scores values ('John', 90.5, 1)");
        stmt.executeUpdate(
          "insert into Scores values ('Michael', 100, 1)");
        stmt.executeUpdate(
          "insert into Scores values ('Michelle', 100, 0)");
      }
      catch (SQLException ex) {
        System.out.println(ex);
      }
    }

    /** Return the score for specified the name
     * Return -1 if score is not found.
     */
    public double findScore(String name) throws RemoteException {
      double score = -1;
      try {
        // Set the specified name in the prepared statement
        pstmt.setString(1, name);

        // Execute the prepared statement
        ResultSet rs = pstmt.executeQuery();

        // Retrieve the score
        if (rs.next()) {
          if (rs.getBoolean(3))
            score = rs.getDouble(2);
        }
      }
      catch (SQLException ex) {
        System.out.println(ex);
      }

```

Listing 15.7 *Continued*

```
    System.out.println(name + "\'s score is " + score);
    return score;
  }
}
```

Listing 15.7 *Continued*

```
// Student3TierServer.java: register Student3TierImpl
// with the RMI registry
package rmidemo;

import java.rmi.*;
import java.rmi.server.*;

public class Student3TierServer {
  public static void main(String args[]) {
    // Set RMI security manager
    if (System.getSecurityManager() == null) {
      System.setSecurityManager(new RMISecurityManager());
    }

    // Create and register the server implementation
    try {
      Student3TierImpl student3TierImpl = new Student3TierImpl();
      Naming.rebind("Student Server", student3TierImpl);
      System.out.println("Server " + student3TierImpl +
        " registered");
    }
    catch(Exception ex) {
      System.out.println(ex);
    }
  }
}
```

Listing 15.8 *Student3TierServer.java*

Example Review

This example is similar to Example 15.1 except that the `Student3TierImpl` class finds the score from a JDBC data source instead from a hash map.

The table named Scores consists of three columns, name, score, and permission, where permission indicates whether the student has given permission to show his/her score. Since SQL does not support a `boolean` type, permission is defined as a number whose value of 1 indicates true and 0 indicates false.

The `initializeDB()` method loads the appropriate JDBC driver, establishes connections with the database, initializes the table if necessary, and creates a prepared statement for processing the query. If the table does not exist, the `initializeTable()` method creates a table and initializes it with three records.

The `findScore` method sets the name in the prepared statement, executes the statement, processes the result, and returns the score for a student whose permission is true.

RMI Callbacks

In a traditional client/server system, a client sends a request to a server, and the server processes the request and returns the result to the client. The server cannot invoke the methods on a client. One of the important benefits of RMI is that it supports *callbacks*, which enable the server to invoke the methods on the client. With the RMI callback feature, you can develop interactive distributed applications.

The following example demonstrates the use of the RMI callback feature to develop an interactive TicTacToe game.

Example 15.4 Developing a TicTacToe Game with RMI

This example creates a distributed application for playing TicTacToe. In a TicTacToe game, two players alternate turns by marking an available cell in a 3 × 3 grid with their token (X or O). One player is X, and the other is O. When one player places three tokens in a row on the grid (whether horizontally, vertically, or diagonally), the game is over and that player has won. A draw (no winner) occurs when all spaces on the grid have been filled with tokens and a win has not been achieved by either player. Figures 15.8 and 15.9 are representative sample runs of the example.

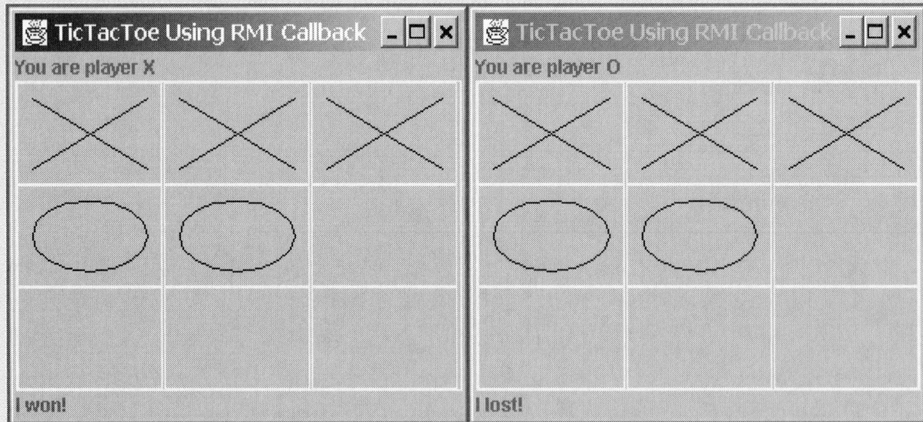

Figure 15.8 *This sample shows that player X has won.*

All the examples you have seen so far in this chapter have simple behaviors that are easy to model with classes. The behavior of the TicTacToe game is somewhat complex. To create the classes to model the game, you need to study and understand it and distribute the process appropriately between client and server.

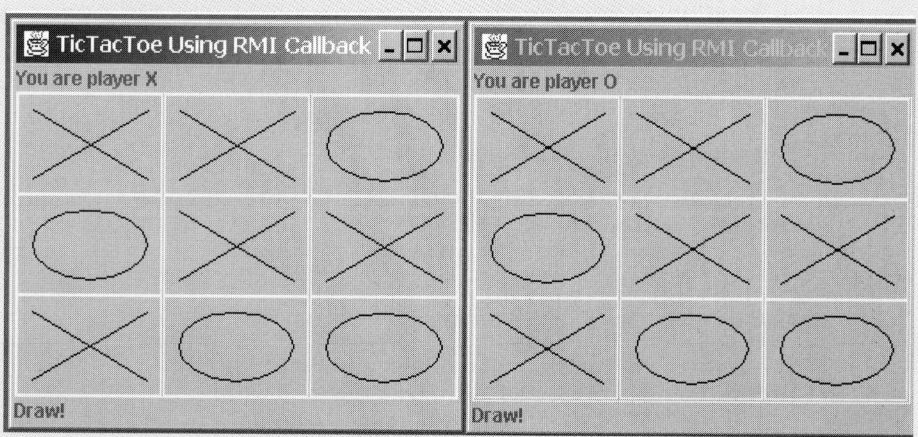

Figure 15.9 *This sample shows a draw with no winner.*

Clearly the client should be responsible for handling user interactions, and the server should coordinate with the client. Specifically, the client should register with the server, and the server can take two and only two players. Once a client makes a move, it should notify the server; the server then notifies the move to the other player. The server should determine the status of the game, that is, whether the game has been won or drawn, and should notify the players. The server should also coordinate the turns, that is, which client has the turn at a given time. The ideal approach for notifying a player is to invoke a method in the client to set appropriate properties in the client or to send messages to a player. Figure 15.10 illustrates the relationship between clients and server.

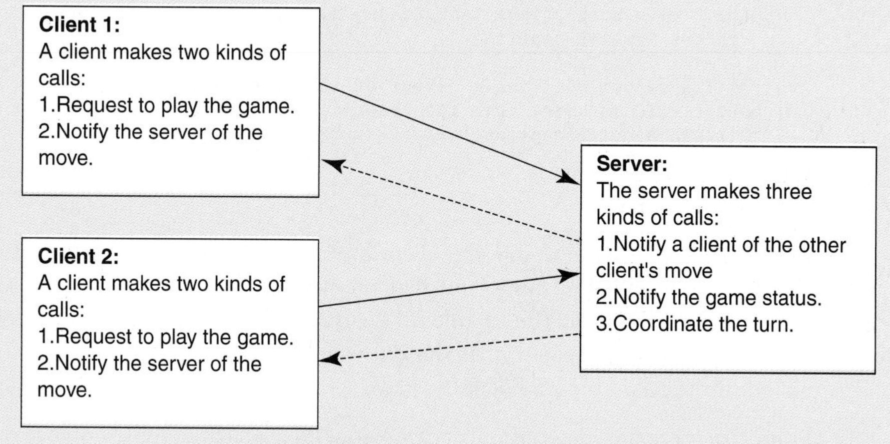

Figure 15.10 *The server coordinates the activities with the clients.*

continued

Example 15.4 continued

All the calls a client makes can be encapsulated in one remote interface named `TicTacToe` (Listing 15.9), and all the calls the server invokes can be defined in another interface named `CallBack` (Listing 15.10).

```
// TicTacToe.java: TicTacToe RMI interface, invoked by clients
package rmitictactoedemo;

import java.rmi.*;

public interface TicTacToe extends Remote {
  /**
   * Connect to the TicTacToe server and return the token.
   * If the returned token is ' ', the client is not connected to
   * the server
   */
  public char connect(CallBack client) throws RemoteException;

  /** A client invokes this method to notify the server of its move*/
  public void myMove(int row, int column, char token)
    throws RemoteException;
}
```

Listing 15.9 *TicTacToe.java*

```
// CallBack.java: CallBack RMI interface, invoked by the server
package rmitictactoedemo;

import java.rmi.*;

public interface CallBack extends Remote {
  /** The server notifies the client for taking a turn */
  public void takeTurn(boolean turn) throws RemoteException;

  /** The server sends a message to be displayed by the client */
  public void notify(java.lang.String message)
    throws RemoteException;

  /** The server notifies a client of the other player's move */
  public void mark(int row, int column, char token)
    throws RemoteException;
}
```

Listing 15.10 *CallBack.java*

What does a client need to do? The client interacts with the player. Assume that all the cells are initially empty, and that the first player takes the X token and the second player takes the O token. To mark a cell, the player points the mouse to the cell and clicks it. If the cell is empty, the token (X or O) is displayed. If the cell is already filled, the player's action is ignored.

From the preceding description, it is obvious that a cell is a GUI object that handles the mouse-click event and displays tokens. The candidate for such an object could be a button or a canvas. Canvases are more flexible than buttons. The token (X or O) can be drawn on a canvas in any size, but it only can be displayed as label on a button. `Canvas` is an AWT component, its Swing counterpart is `JPanel`. Therefore, a `JPanel` is used to model a cell in this example.

Let `Cell` be a subclass of `JPanel`. You can declare a 3 × 3 grid to be an array `Cell[][] cell = new Cell[3][3]` for modeling the game. How do you know the state of a cell (marked or not)? You can use a property named `marked` of the `boolean` type in the `Cell` class. How do you know whether the player has a turn? You can use a property named `myTurn` of `boolean`. This property (initially `false`) can be set by the server through a callback.

The `Cell` class is responsible for drawing the token when an empty cell is clicked, so you need to write the code for listening to the `MouseEvent` and for painting the shape for tokens X and O. To determine which shape to draw, introduce a variable named `marker` of the `char` type. Since this variable is shared by all the cells in a client, it is preferable to declare it in the client and to declare the `Cell` class as an inner class of the client so that this variable will be accessible to all the cells.

Now let us turn our attention to the server side. What does the server need to do? The server needs to implement the `TicTacToe` interface and notify the clients of the game status. The server has to record the moves in the cells and check the status every time a player makes a move. The status information can be kept in a 3 × 3 array of `char`. You can implement a method named `isFull()` to check whether the board is full and a method named `isWon(token)` to check whether a specific player has won.

Once a client is connected to the server, the server notifies the client which token to use; that is, X for the first client, and O for the second. Once a client notifies the server of its move, the server checks the game status and notifies the clients.

Now the most critical question is how the server notifies a client. You know that a client invokes a server method by creating a server stub on the client side. A server cannot directly invoke a client, because the client is not declared as a remote object. The `CallBack` interface was created to facilitate the server's callback to the client. In the implementation of `CallBack`, an instance of the client is passed as a parameter in the constructor of `CallBack`. The client creates an instance of `CallBack` and passes its stub to the server, using a remote method named `connect()` defined in the server. The server then invokes the client's method through a `CallBack` instance. The triangular relationship of client, `CallBack` implementation, and server is shown in Figure 15.11.

Here are the steps to complete the example.

1. Create a new project named rmitictactoe.jpr. Uncheck the option "Synchronize output directory" in the Build page of the Project Property dialog.

2. Create the `TicTacToe` interface and the `CallBack` interface, as shown in Listings 15.9 and 15.10.

continued

Example 15.4 continued

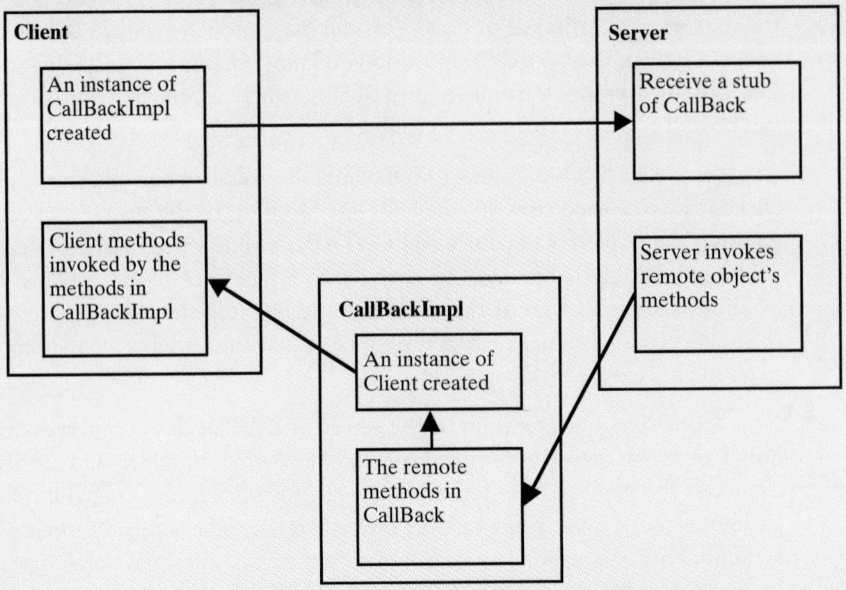

Figure 15.11 *The server receives a* `CallBack` *stub from the client and invokes the remote methods defined in the* `CallBack` *interface, which can invoke the methods defined in the client.*

3. Create `TicTacToeImpl` to implement the `TicTacToe` interface, as shown in Listing 15.11.
4. Create `CallBackImpl` to implement the `CallBack` interface, as shown in Listing 15.12.
5. Use the rmic utility to generate the stubs and the skeletons for `TicTacToeImpl` and `CallBackImpl`.
6. Create `TicTacToeServer` for creating and registering an instance of `TicTacToeImpl`, as shown in Listing 15.13.
7. Create `TicTacToeClient` for interacting with a player and communicating with the server, as shown in Listing 15.14.
8. Start an RMI registry and start `TicTacToeServer`. Start two instances of `TicTacToeClient` to play the game.

```
// TicTacToeImpl.java: The TicTacToe RMI Server Implementation
package rmitictactoedemo;

import java.rmi.*;
import java.rmi.server.*;

public class TicTacToeImpl extends UnicastRemoteObject
```

Listing 15.11 *TicTacToeImpl.java*

```
    implements TicTacToe {
    // Declare two players, used to call players back
    CallBack player1 = null;
    CallBack player2 = null;

    // board records players' moves
    char[][] board = new char[3][3];

    /**
     * Constructor, cannot be omitted since it requires to throw
     * an exception
     */
    public TicTacToeImpl() throws RemoteException {
    }

    /**
     * Connect to the TicTacToe server and return the token.
     * If the returned token is ' ', the client is not connected to
     * the server
     */
    public char connect(CallBack client) throws RemoteException {
      if (player1 == null) {
        // player1 (first player) registered
        player1 = client;
        player1.notify("Wait for a second player to join");
        return 'X';
      }
      else if (player2 == null) {
        // player2 (second player) registered
        player2 = client;
        player2.notify("Wait for the first player to move");
        player2.takeTurn(false);
        player1.notify("It is my turn (X token)");
        player1.takeTurn(true);
        return 'O';
      }
      else {
        // Already two players
        client.notify("Two players are already in the game");
        return ' ';
      }
    }

    /** A client invokes this method to notify the server of its move*/
    public void myMove(int row, int column, char token)
      throws RemoteException {
      // Set token to the specified cell
      board[row][column] = token;

      // Notify the other player of the move
      if (token == 'X')
        player2.mark(row, column, 'X');
      else
        player1.mark(row, column, 'O');

      // Check if the player with this token wins
      if (isWon(token)) {
        if (token == 'X') {
          player1.notify("I won!");
```

Listing 15.11 *Continued*

continued

Example 15.4 continued

```
        player2.notify("I lost!");
        player1.takeTurn(false);
      }
      else {
        player2.notify("I won!");
        player1.notify("I lost!");
        player2.takeTurn(false);
      }
    }
    else if (isFull()) {
      player1.notify("Draw!");
      player2.notify("Draw!");
    }
    else if (token == 'X') {
      player1.notify("Wait for the second player to move");
      player1.takeTurn(false);
      player2.notify("It is my turn, (O token)");
      player2.takeTurn(true);
    }
    else if (token == 'O') {
      player2.notify("Wait for the first player to move");
      player2.takeTurn(false);
      player1.notify("It is my turn, (X token)");
      player1.takeTurn(true);
    }
  }

  /** Check if a player with the specified token wins */
  public boolean isWon(char token) {
    for (int i=0; i<3; i++)
      if ((board[i][0] == token)
          && (board[i][1] == token)
          && (board[i][2] == token))
        return true;

    for (int j=0; j<3; j++)
      if ((board[0][j] == token)
          && (board[1][j] == token)
          && (board[2][j] == token))
        return true;

    if ((board[0][0] == token)
        && (board[1][1] == token)
        && (board[2][2] == token))
      return true;

    if ((board[0][2] == token)
        && (board[1][1] == token)
        && (board[2][0] == token))
      return true;

    return false;
  }

  /** Check if the board is full */
  public boolean isFull() {
    for (int i=0; i<3; i++)
```

Listing 15.11 *Continued*

```
        for (int j=0; j<3; j++)
          if (board[i][j] == '\u0000')
            return false;

      return true;
    }
  }
```

Listing 15.11 *Continued*

```
// CallBackImpl.java: The CallBack RMI interface implementation
package rmitictactoedemo;

import java.rmi.*;
import java.rmi.server.*;

public class CallBackImpl extends UnicastRemoteObject
  implements CallBack {
  // The client will be called by the server through callback
  TicTacToeClient thisClient;

  /** Constructor */
  CallBackImpl(Object client) throws RemoteException {
    thisClient = (TicTacToeClient)client;
  }

  /** The server notifies the client for taking a turn */
  public void takeTurn(boolean turn) throws RemoteException {
    thisClient.setMyTurn(turn);
  }

  /** The server sends a message to be displayed by the client */
  public void notify(java.lang.String message)
    throws RemoteException {
    thisClient.setMessage(message);
  }

  /** The server notifies a client of the other player's move */
  public void mark(int row, int column, char token)
    throws RemoteException {
    thisClient.mark(row, column, token);
  }
}
```

Listing 15.12 *CallBackImpl.java*

```
// TicTacToeServer.java: Launch TicTacTorImpl
package rmitictactoedemo;

import java.rmi.*;
import java.rmi.server.*;

public class TicTacToeServer {
  public static void main(String args[]) {
    System.setSecurityManager(new RMISecurityManager());
    try {
      TicTacToeImpl ticTacToeImpl = new TicTacToeImpl();
      Naming.rebind("TicTacToe Server", ticTacToeImpl);
      System.out.println("Server registered");
    }
```

Listing 15.13 *TicTacToeServer.java*

continued

Example 15.4 continued

```
      catch(Exception ex) {
        System.out.println(ex);
      }
    }
  }
```

Listing 15.13 *Continued*

```
// TicTacToeClient.java: TicTacToeClient applet
package rmitictactoedemo;

import java.rmi.*;
import java.awt.*;
import java.awt.event.*;
import java.applet.*;
import javax.swing.*;
import javax.swing.border.*;

public class TicTacToeClient extends JApplet {
  // marker is used to indicate the token type
  char marker;

  // myTurn indicates whether the player can move now
  private boolean myTurn = false;

  // Each cell can be empty or marked as 'O' or 'X'
  private Cell[][] cell;

  // ticTacToe is the game server for coordinating with the players
  TicTacToe ticTacToe;

  // Border for cells and panel
  Border lineBorder = BorderFactory.createLineBorder(Color.yellow, 1);

  boolean isStandalone = false;
  JLabel jlblStatus = new JLabel();
  JPanel jPanel1 = new JPanel();
  GridLayout gridLayout1 = new GridLayout();
  JLabel jlblIdentification = new JLabel();

  /** Initialize the applet */
  public void init() {
    try {
      jbInit();
    }
    catch (Exception e) {
      e.printStackTrace();
    }
  }

  /** Component and RMI initialization */
  private void jbInit() throws Exception {
    // Create user interface
    this.setSize(400,300);
    jPanel1.setLayout(gridLayout1);
    gridLayout1.setRows(3);
    gridLayout1.setHgap(1);
    gridLayout1.setColumns(3);
    jlblIdentification.setText("jLabel1");
    this.getContentPane().add(jlblStatus, BorderLayout.SOUTH);
```

Listing 15.14 *TicTacToeClient.java*

```
      this.getContentPane().add(jPanel1, BorderLayout.CENTER);
      this.getContentPane().add(jlblIdentification, BorderLayout.NORTH);

      jPanel1.setBorder(lineBorder);
      // Create cells and place cells in the panel
      cell = new Cell[3][3];
      for (int i=0; i<3; i++)
        for (int j=0; j<3; j++)
          jPanel1.add(cell[i][j] = new Cell(i, j));

      // Initialize the CORBA environment
      initializeRMI();
    }

    /** Initialize RMI */
    protected boolean initializeRMI() throws Exception {
      String url;

      if (isStandalone) {
        // Initialize RMI for a standalone application
        // System.setSecurityManager(new RMISecurityManager());
        url = "rmi:///";
        // Use rmi://hostname/ if the server is located on hostname,
        // i.e. rmi://liangy.liangy.edu/
      }
      else {
        // Initialize RMI for an applet
        url = getCodeBase().getHost();
        if (url.equals("default")) url = "";
        url = "rmi://" + url + "/";
      }

      ticTacToe = (TicTacToe)Naming.lookup(url + "TicTacToe Server");
      System.out.println("Server found");

      // Create callback for use by the server to control the client
      CallBackImpl callBackControl = new CallBackImpl(this);

      if (
        (marker = ticTacToe.connect((CallBack)callBackControl)) != ' ')
      {
        System.out.println("connected as " + marker + " player.");
        jlblIdentification.setText("You are player " + marker);
        return true;
      }
      else {
        System.out.println("already two players connected as ");
        return false;
      }
    }

    /** Set variable myTurn to true or false */
    void setMyTurn(boolean myTurn) {
      this.myTurn = myTurn;
    }

    /** Set message on the status label */
    public void setMessage(String message) {
      jlblStatus.setText(message);
    }

```

Listing 15.14 *Continued*

continued

Example 15.4 continued

```
  /** Mark the specified cell using the token */
  void mark(int row, int column, char token) {
    cell[row][column].setToken(token);
  }

  /** Inner class Cell for modeling a cell on the TicTacToe board */
  public class Cell extends JPanel implements MouseListener {
    // marked indicates whether the cell has been used
    private boolean marked = false;

    // row and column indicate where the cell appears on the board
    int row, column;

    // The token for the cell
    private char token;

    /** Construct a cell */
    public Cell(int row, int column) {
      this.row = row;
      this.column = column;
      addMouseListener(this);
      setBorder(lineBorder);
    }

    /** Set token on a cell (mark a cell) */
    public void setToken(char c) {
      token = c;
      marked = true;
      repaint();
    }

    /** Paint the cell to draw a shape for the token */
    public void paintComponent(Graphics g) {
      super.paintComponent(g);

      // Draw the border
      g.drawRect(0, 0, getSize().width, getSize().height);

      if (token == 'X') {
        g.drawLine(10, 10, getSize().width-10, getSize().height-10);
        g.drawLine(getSize().width-10, 10, 10, getSize().height-10);
      }
      else if (token == 'O') {
        g.drawOval(10, 10, getSize().width-20, getSize().height-20);
      }
    }

    public void mouseClicked(MouseEvent e) {
      // TODO: implement this java.awt.event.MouseListener method;
      if (myTurn && !marked) {
        // Mark the cell
        setToken(marker);

        // Notify the server of the move
        try {
          ticTacToe.myMove(row, column, marker);
        }
```

Listing 15.14 *Continued*

```
        catch (RemoteException ex) {
          System.out.println(ex);
        }
      }
    }

    public void mousePressed(MouseEvent e) {
      // TODO: implement this java.awt.event.MouseListener method;
    }

    public void mouseReleased(MouseEvent e) {
      // TODO: implement this java.awt.event.MouseListener method;
    }

    public void mouseEntered(MouseEvent e) {
      // TODO: implement this java.awt.event.MouseListener method;
    }

    public void mouseExited(MouseEvent e) {
      // TODO: implement this java.awt.event.MouseListener method;
    }
  }

  /** Main method */
  public static void main(String[] args) {
    // Omitted for brevity
  }
}
```

Listing 15.14 *Continued*

Example Review

The `TicTacToe` interface defines two remote methods, `connect(CallBack client)` and `myMove(int row, int column, char token)`. The `connect` method plays two roles: one is to pass a `CallBack` stub to the server, and the other is to let the server assign a token for the player. The `myMove` method notifies the server that the player has made a specific move.

The `CallBack` interface defines three remote methods, `takeTurn(boolean turn)`, `notify(String message)`, and `mark(int row, int column, char token)`. The `takeTurn` method sets the client's `myTurn` property to `true` or `false`. The `notify` method displays a message on the client's status label. The `mark` method marks the client's cell with the token at the specified location.

`TicTacToeImpl` is a server implementation for coordinating with the clients and managing the game. The variables `player1` and `player2` are instances of `CallBack`, each of which corresponds to a client, passed from a client when the client invokes the `connect` method. The variable `board` records the moves by the two players. This information is needed to determine the game status. When a client invokes the `connect` method, the server assigns a token X for the first player and O for the second player, and only two players are accepted by the server. You can modify the program to accept additional clients as observers. See Exercise 15.4 for more details.

continued

Example 15.4 continued

Once two players are in the game, the server coordinates the turns between them. When a client invokes the `myMove` method, the server records the move and notifies the other player by marking the other player's cell. It then checks to see whether the player wins or whether the board is full. If the game should continue, the server gives a turn to the other player.

The `CallBackImpl` implements the `CallBack` interface. It creates an instance of `TicTacToeClient` through its constructor. The `CallBackImpl` relays the server request to the client by invoking the client's methods. When the server invokes the `takeTurn` method, `CallBackImpl` invokes the client's `setMyTurn()` method to set the property `myTurn` in the client. When the server invokes the `notify()` method, `CallBackImpl` invokes the client's `setMessage()` method to set the message on the client's status label. When the server invokes the `mark` method, `CallBackImpl` invokes the client's `mark` method to mark the specified cell.

`TicTacToeClient` can run as a standalone application or as an applet. The `initializeRMI` method is responsible for creating the url for running as a standalone application or as an applet, for locating the `TicTacToe` server stub, for creating the `CallBack` server object, and for connecting the client with the server.

Interestingly, obtaining the `TicTacToe` stub for the client is different from obtaining the `CallBack` stub for the server. The `TicTacToe` stub is obtained by invoking the `lookup()` method through the RMI registry, and the `CallBack` stub is passed to the server through the `connect` method in the `TicTacToe` stub. It is a common practice to obtain the first stub with the `lookup` method, but to pass the subsequent stubs as parameters through remote method invocations.

Since the variables `myTurn` and `marker` are defined in `TicTacToeClient`, the `Cell` class is defined as an inner class within `TicTacToeClient` in order to enable all the cells in the client to access them. Exercise 15.4 suggests alternative approaches that implement the Cell as a non-inner class.

Chapter Summary

RMI is a high-level Java API for building distributed applications using distributed objects. The key idea of RMI is its use of stubs and skeletons to facilitate communications between objects. The stub and skeleton are automatically generated, which relieves programmers of tedious socket-level network programming. For an object to be used remotely, it must be defined in an interface that extends the `java.rmi.Remote` interface. In an RMI application, the initial remote object must be registered with the RMI registry on the server side and be obtained using the `lookup` method through the registry on the client side. Subsequent use of stubs of other remote objects may be passed as parameters through remote method invocations. RMI is especially useful for developing scalable and load-balanced multi-tier distributed applications. RMI is a pure Java solution, and it cannot be used to develop a distributed system involving different programming languages.

Review Questions

15.1 How do you define an interface for a remote object?

15.2 Describe the roles of the stub and the skeleton.

15.3 How do you generate the stub and the skeleton?

15.4 What is the RMI registry for? How do you create an RMI registry?

15.5 How do you register a remote object with the RMI registry?

15.6 How does a client locate a remote object stub through the RMI registry?

15.7 What can you do if you encounter a security violation?

15.8 Describe how parameters are passed in RMI.

15.9 What is the problem if the `connect()` method in the `TicTacToe` interface is defined as

```
public boolean connect(CallBack client, char token) throws Re-
moteException;
```

or as

```
public boolean connect(CallBack client, Character token) throws
RemoteException;
```

15.10 What is callback? How does callback work in RMI?

Programming Exercises

15.1 Modify Example 15.1 to limit the number of concurrent clients to 10.

15.2 Write an applet to show the number of visits made to a Web page. The count should be stored on the server side in a file. The applet should send a request to the server every time the page is visited or reloaded, and the server should increase the count and send it to the applet. The applet should then display the count in a message, such as *You are visitor number: 1000.* The server can read or write to the file using a random file access stream.

15.3 Use the three-tier approach to modify Example 13.2, "Using Statements to Execute Static SQL Statements," as follows:

- Create an applet client to manipulate student information, as shown in Figure 13.11.
- Create a remote object interface with methods for retrieving, inserting, and updating student information, and an object implementation for the interface.

15.4 Modify Example 15.4 as follows:

- Allow a client to connect to the server as an observer to watch the game.
- Rewrite the `Cell` class as a non-inner class.

CHAPTER 16

SERVLETS

Objectives

- Understand the concept of servlets.
- Become familiar with the HTML forms.
- Know the servlets API.
- Develop servlets to access databases.
- Use hidden fields, cookies, and `HttpSession` to track sessions.
- Send images from servlets.

Introduction

Servlet technology is primarily designed for use with the HTTP protocol of the Web. *Servlets* are Java programs that run on a Web server. Java servlets can be used to process client requests or produce dynamic Web pages. For example, you can write servlets to generate dynamic Web pages that display stock quotes or process client registration forms and store registration data in a database. This chapter introduces the concept of Java servlets. You will learn how to write Java servlets and run them from JBuilder.

HTML and Common Gateway Interface

Java servlets run in the Web environment. To understand Java servlets, let us review HTML and Common Gateway Interface (CGI).

Static Web Contents

You create Web pages using HTML. Your Web pages are stored as files on the Web server. The files are usually stored in the /htdocs on Unix, as shown in Figure 16.1. A user types a URL for the file from a Web browser. The browser contacts the Web server and requests the file. The server finds the file and returns it to the browser. The browser then displays the file to the user. This works fine for static information that does not change regardless of who requests it or when it is requested. Static information is stored in HTML files. The information in the files can be updated, but at any given time every request for the same document returns exactly the same result.

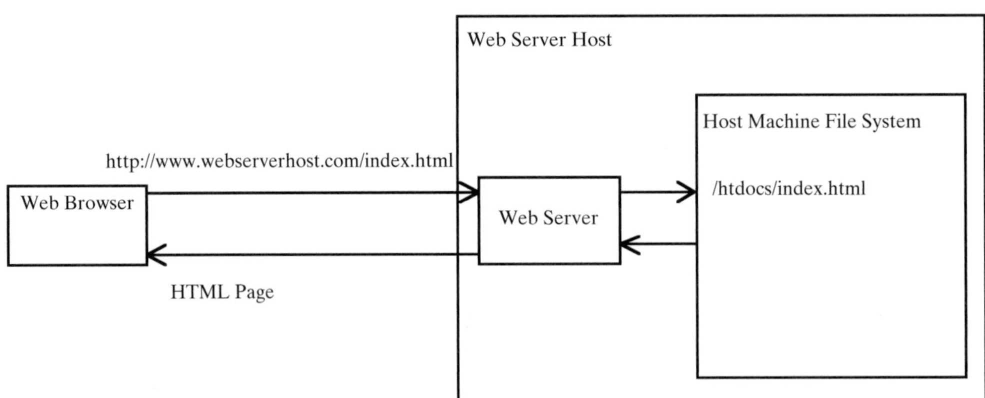

Figure 16.1 *A Web browser requests a static HTML page from a Web server.*

Dynamic Web Contents and Common Gateway Interface

Not all information, however, is static in nature. Stock quotes are updated every minute. Election vote counts are updated constantly on Election Day. Weather reports are frequently updated. The balance in a customer's bank account is updated whenever a transaction takes place. To view up-to-date information on the Web, the HTML pages for displaying this information must be generated dynamically. Dynamic Web pages are generated by Web servers. The Web server needs to run certain programs to process user requests from Web browsers in order to produce a customized response.

The *Common Gateway Interface*, or *CGI*, was proposed to generate dynamic Web content. The interface provides a standard framework for Web servers to interact with external programs, known as *CGI programs*. As shown in Figure 16.2, the Web server receives a request from a Web browser, and passes the request to the CGI program. The CGI program processes the request, and generates a response at runtime. CGI programs can be written in any language, but the *Perl* language is the most popular choice. CGI programs are typically stored in the /cgi-bin directory. Here is a pseudocode example of a CGI program for displaying a customer's bank account balance.

1. Obtain account ID and password.
2. Verify account ID and password. If it fails, generate an HTML page to report incorrect account ID and password, and exit.
3. Retrieve account balance from the database; generate an HTML page to display the account ID and balance.

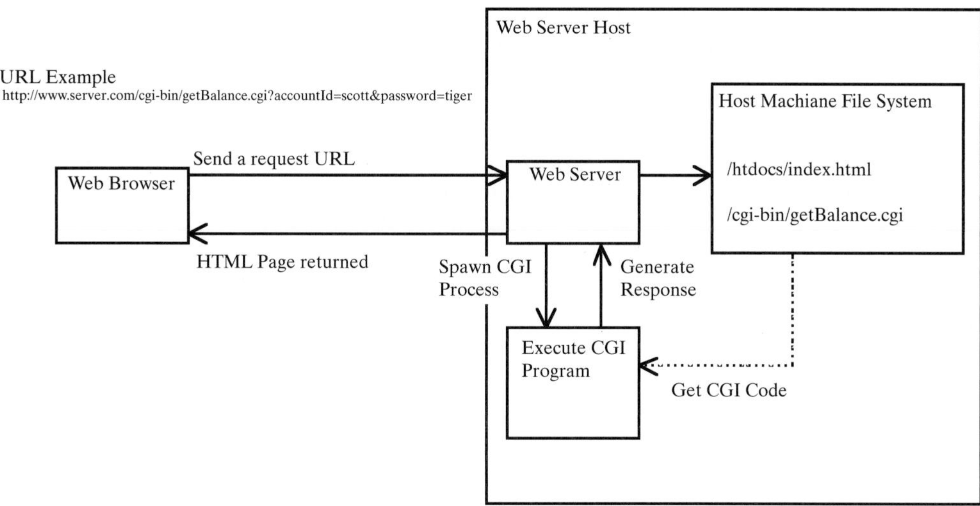

Figure 16.2 *A Web browser requests a dynamic HTML page from a Web server.*

The GET and POST Methods

The two most common HTTP requests, also known as *methods*, are GET and POST. The Web browser issues a request using a URL or an HTML form to trigger the Web server to execute a CGI program. When issuing a CGI request directly from a URL, the GET method is used. This URL is known as *a query string*. The URL query string consists of the location of the CGI program, parameters, and their values. For example, the following URL causes the CGI program `getBalance` to be invoked on the server side.

```
http://www.webserverhost.com/cgi-bin/
  getBalance.cgi?accountId=scott+smith&password=tiger
```

The **?** symbol separates the program from the parameters. The parameter name and value are associated using the **=** symbol. Parameter pairs are separated using the **&** symbol. The **+** symbol denotes a space character.

When issuing a request from an HTML form, either a GET method or a POST method can be used. The form explicitly specifies which of the two is used. If the GET method is used, the data in the form are appended to the request string as if it were submitted using a URL. If the POST method is used, the data in the form are packaged as part of the request file. The server program obtains the data by reading the file.

Note

The GET and POST methods both send requests to the Web server. The POST method always triggers the execution of the corresponding CGI program. The GET method may not cause the CGI program to be executed if the previous same request is cached in the Web browser. Web browsers often cache Web pages so that the same request can be quickly responded to without contacting the Web server. The browser checks the request sent through the GET method as a URL query string. If the results for the exact same URL are cached on disk, then the previous Web pages for the URL might be displayed. To ensure that a new Web page is always displayed, use the POST method. For example, use a POST method if the request will actually update the database. If your request is not time-sensitive, such as finding the address of a student in the database, use the GET method to speed up the performance.

HTML Forms

HTML forms enable you to submit data to the Web server in a convenient form. As shown in Figure 16.3, the form can contain text fields, text area, check boxes, combo boxes, lists, radio buttons, and buttons.

The HTML code for creating this form in Figure 16.3 is shown in Listing 16.1.

```
<html>
<head>
<title>Student Registration Form</title>
</head>
<body>
Student Registration Form

<form action="http://www.webserverhost.com/cgi-bin/register"
  method="POST">
  Last Name <input type="text" name="lastName" size="20">
  First Name <input type="text" name="firstName" size="20">
```

Listing 16.1 *An HTML Form Demo*

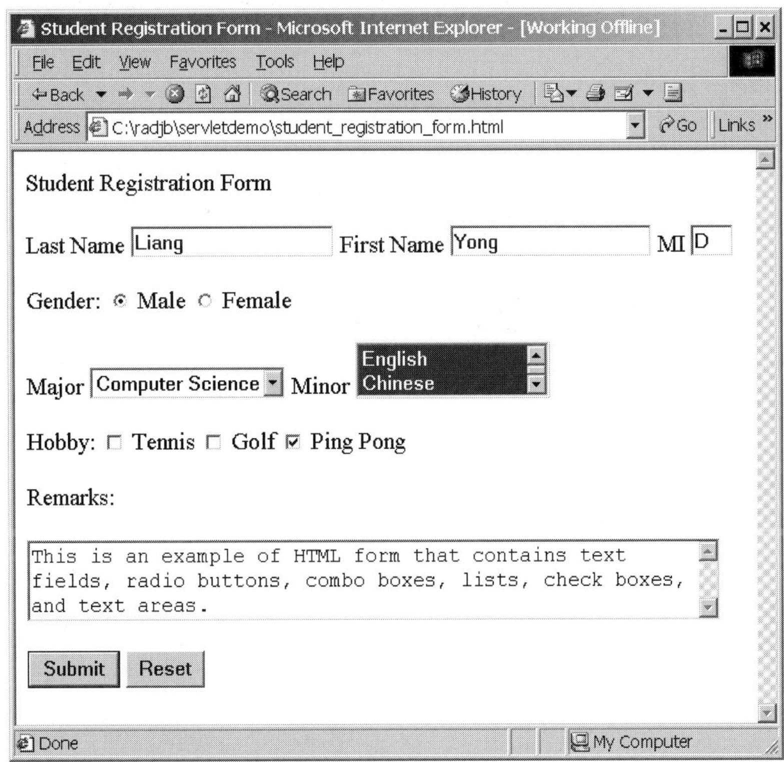

Figure 16.3 *This is an example of an HTML form that contains text fields, radio buttons, combo boxes, lists, check boxes, text areas, and buttons.*

```
    MI <input type="text" name="mi" size="1">
    <p>Gender: <input type="radio" name="gender"
                 value="male" checked> Male
              <input type="radio" name="gender"
                 value="Female"> Female</p>
    <p>Major <select name="major" size="1">
               <option>Computer Science
               <option>Mathematics
               <option>English
               <option>Chinese
            </select>
    Minor <select name="minor" size="2" multiple>
               <option>Computer Science
               <option>Mathematics
               <option>English
               <option>Chinese
          </select></p>
    <p>Hobby:
      <input type="checkbox" name="tennis"> Tennis
      <input type="checkbox" name="golf"> Golf
      <input type="checkbox" name="pingPong" checked> Ping Pong</p>
    <p>Remarks:</p>
    <p><textarea name="remarks" rows="3" cols="56"></textarea></p>
    <p><input type="submit" value="Submit">
       <input type="reset" value="Reset"></p>
  </form>
  </body>
```

Listing 16.1 *Continued*

The following HTML tags are used to construct HTML forms:

- **<form> . . . </form>**: Defines a form body. The attributes for the <form> tag are **action**, and **method**. The action attribute specifies the CGI program to be executed on the Web server when the form is submitted. The method attribute is either **GET** or **POST**.
- **<input>**: Defines an input field. The attributes for this tag are **type**, **name**, **value**, **checked**, **size**, and **maxlength**. The type attribute specifies the input type. Possible types are **text** for a one-line text field, **radio** for radio button, and **checkbox** for check box. The name attribute gives a formal name for the attribute. This name is used by the CGI program to retrieve its associated value. The names of radio buttons in a group must be identical. The value attribute specifies a default value for a text field and text area. The checked attribute indicates whether a radio button or a check box is initially checked. The size attribute specifies the size of a text field, and the maxlength attribute specifies the maximum length of a text field.
- **<select> . . . </select>**: Defines a combo box or a list. The attributes for this tag are **name**, **size**, and **multiple**. The size attribute specifies the number of rows visible in the list. The multiple attribute specifies that multiple values can be selected from a list. Set size to 1 and do not use a multiple for a combo box.
- **<option>**: Defines a selection list within a <select> ... </select> tags.
- **<textarea> . . . </textarea>**: Defines a text area. The attributes are **name**, **rows**, and **cols.** The rows and cols attributes specify the number of rows and columns in a text area.

From CGI to Java Servlets

CGI provides a relatively simple approach for creating dynamic Web applications that accept a user request, process it on the server side, and return responses to the Web browser. But CGI is very slow when handling a large number of requests simultaneously, because the Web server spawns a process for executing each CGI program. Each process has its own runtime environment that contains and runs the CGI program. It is not difficult to imagine what will happen when many CGI programs are executed simultaneously. System resource would be quickly exhausted, potentially causing the server to crash.

Several new approaches have been developed to remedy the performance problem of CGI programs. Java servlets are one successful technology for this purpose. Java servlets are Java programs that function like CGI programs. They are executed upon request from a Web browser. All the servlets run inside a *servlet container*, also referred to as a *servlet server* or a *servlet engine*. A servlet container is a single process that runs a Java Virtual Machine. The JVM creates a thread to handle each servlet. Java threads have much less overhead than full-brown processes. All the threads share the same memory allocated to the JVM. Since the JVM persists beyond the life cycle of a single servlet execution, servlets can share objects already created in the JVM. For example, if multiple servlets access the same database, they can share the connection object. Servlets are much more efficient than CGI.

Servlets have other benefits that are inherent in Java. Since servlets are Java programs, they are object-oriented, portable, and platform-independent. Since you know Java, you can develop servlets immediately with the support of Java API for accessing databases, and network resources.

Creating and Running Servlets from JBuilder

To run Java servlets, you need a servlet container. Many servlet containers are available. *Tomcat*, developed by Apache (`www.apache.org`), is a standard reference implementation for Java servlet 2.2 and Java Server Pages 1.1. It is free. It can be used standalone as a Web server or be plugged into a Web server like Apache, Netscape Enterprise Server, or Microsoft Internet Information Server. Tomcat has been integrated with JBuilder 4 and 5 Professional Edition. This section demonstrates how to create and run a Java servlet from JBuilder.

Creating a Servlet

1. Create a new project named servletdemo. In the Object Gallery, click the Servlet icon to display the Servlet wizard, as shown in Figure 16.4.

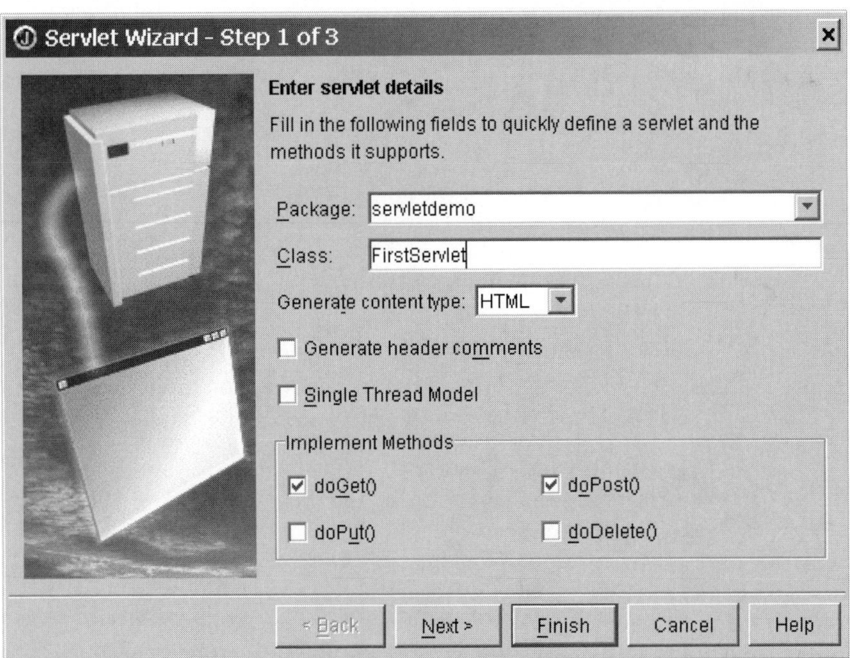

Figure 16.4 *Servlet wizard Step 1 of 3 enables you to specify a servlet class and method types.*

NOTE

If you check the Single Thread Model option, the generated servlet will implement the `SingleThreadModel` interface. This is a marker interface signifying that the servlet runs in a single-thread model. Normally, a servlet runs on multiple threads. Whenever a request arrives, the servlet engine spawns a new thread to handle the request. You have to be careful to ensure that data can be accessed simultaneously. If data might be corrupted because multiple threads access them simultaneously, you can implement the `SingleThreadModel` interface or synchronize the data in the `doGet` and `goPost` methods.

2. Type FirstServlet in the Class field. Choose HTML as the content type. Check the options to generate the `doGet()` and `doPost()` methods. Click Next to display Servlet wizard Step 2 of 3, as shown in Figure 16.5.

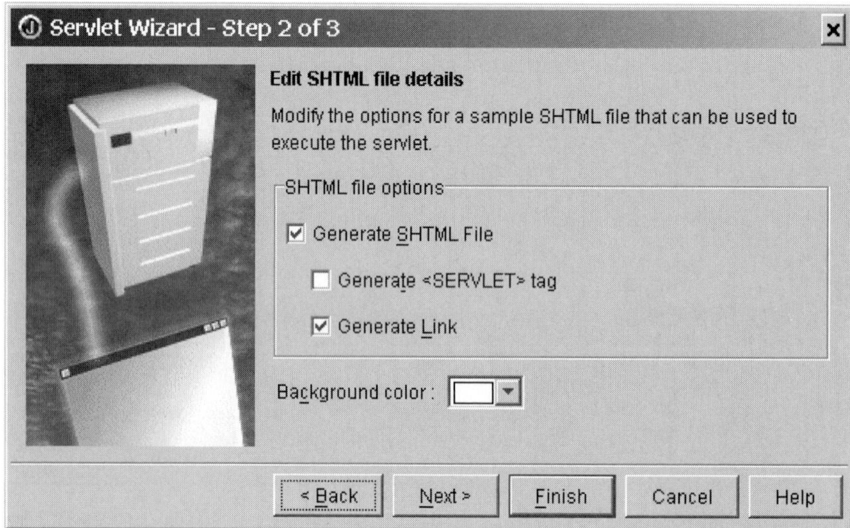

Figure 16.5 *Servlet wizard Step 2 of 3 enables you to specify the contents of the SHTML file.*

3. Check Generate SHTML File and Generate Link. Do not check Generate <SERVLET> tag, because at present it is not supported by most browsers Click Next to display Servlet wizard Step 3 of 3, as shown in Figure 16.6.

4. Type Your Name in the Desc field. Click Finish. JBuilder generates two files: FirstServlet.java (Listing 16.2) and FirstServlet.shtml (Listing 16.3). FirstServlet.shtml is displayed in Figure 16.7. JBuilder also automatically added a servlet in the Required Libraries for this project, as shown in Figure 16.8.

5. FirstServlet.java contains the source code for the Servlet class `FirstServlet`. In the `doPost` method of this class, add the following statement to send a text string to the browser

```
out.println("<p>Hi, " + var0 + "<p>");
```

before

```
out.println("</body></html>");
```

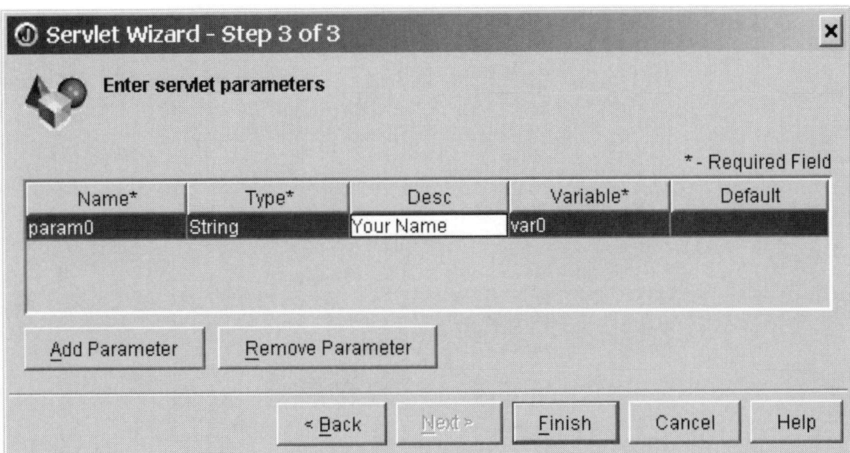

Figure 16.6 *Servlet wizard Step 3 of 3 enables you to specify servlet parameters.*

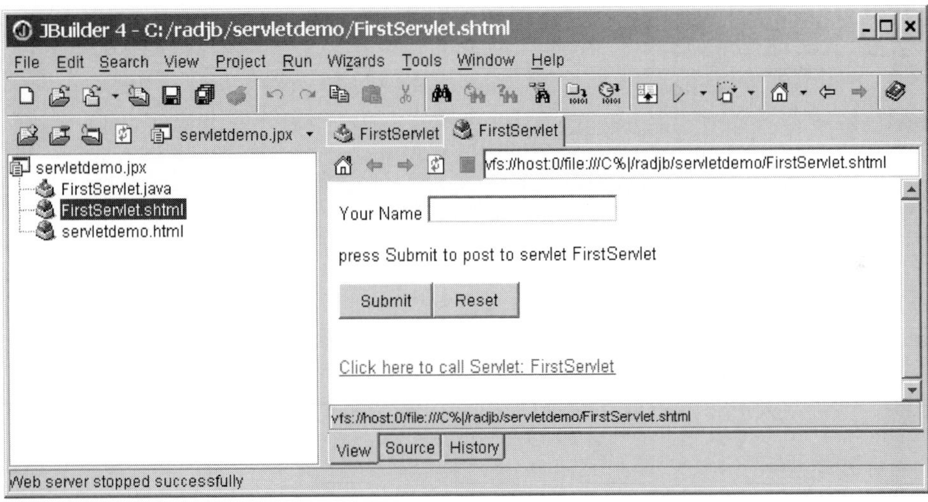

Figure 16.7 *Servlet wizard generated FirstServlet.java and FirstServlet.shtml.*

Note

The SHTML is the same as the HTML file except that the .shtml extension indicates the HTML file for the servlets.

JBuilder 5 Note

The Servlet icon in JBuilder 5 is in the Web page of the Object Gallery. The Servlet wizard has four steps. Specify a servlet class name in Step 1. Specify the methods used by the servlet and a sample SHTML file in Step 2. Skip Step 3. Specify parameters in Step 4.

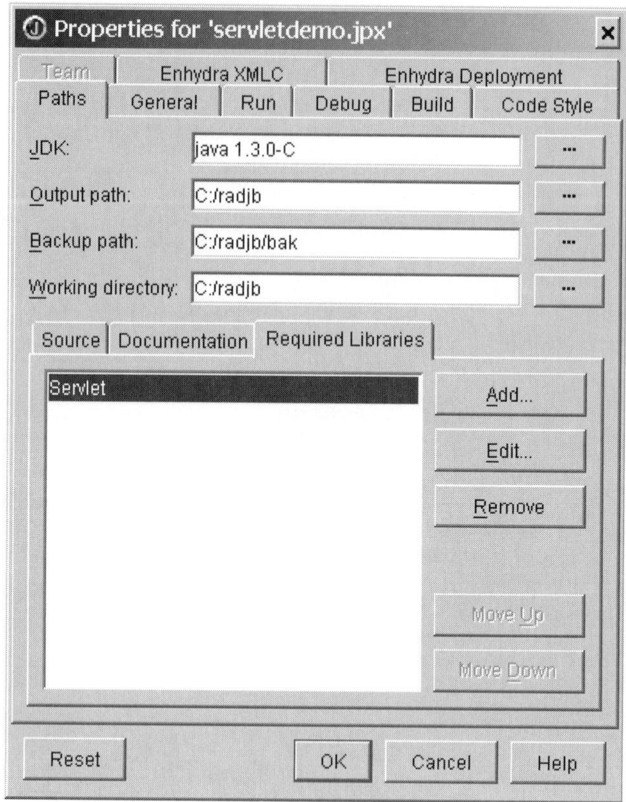

Figure 16.8 *The Servlet library was automatically placed in the project by the Servlet wizard.*

```
package servletdemo;

import javax.servlet.*;
import javax.servlet.http.*;
import java.io.*;
import java.util.*;

public class FirstServlet extends HttpServlet {
  private static final String CONTENT_TYPE = "text/html";

  /** Initialize global variables */
  public void init(ServletConfig config) throws ServletException {
    super.init(config);
  }

  /** Process the HTTP Get request */
  public void doGet(HttpServletRequest request, HttpServletResponse
    response) throws ServletException, IOException {
    String var0 = "";
    try {
      var0 = request.getParameter("param0");
    }
    catch(Exception e) {
      e.printStackTrace();
    }
    response.setContentType(CONTENT_TYPE);
    PrintWriter out = response.getWriter();
```

Listing 16.2 *FirstServlet.java*

```
      out.println("<html>");
      out.println("<head><title>FirstServlet</title></head>");
      out.println("<body>");
      out.println("<p>The servlet has received a GET. " +
        "This is the reply.</p>");
      out.println("</body></html>");
    }

    /** Process the HTTP Post request */
    public void doPost(HttpServletRequest request, HttpServletResponse
      response) throws ServletException, IOException {
      String var0 = "";
      try {
        var0 = request.getParameter("param0");
      }
      catch(Exception e) {
        e.printStackTrace();
      }
      response.setContentType(CONTENT_TYPE);
      PrintWriter out = response.getWriter();
      out.println("<html>");
      out.println("<head><title>FirstServlet</title></head>");
      out.println("<body>");
      out.println("<p>The servlet has received a POST. " +
        "This is the reply.</p>");
      out.println("<p>Hi, " + var0 + " <p>"); // Manually added
      out.println("</body></html>");
      out.close(); // Close stream
    }

    /** Clean up resources */
    public void destroy() {
    }
  }
```

Listing 16.2 *Continued*

```
<html>
<head>
<title>
FirstServlet
</title>
</head>
<body>

<form action="/servlet/servletdemo.FirstServlet" method="post">
<p>Your Name <input type="text" name="param0"></p>
<p>press Submit to post to servlet FirstServlet</p>
<p><input type="submit" name="Submit" value="Submit">
<input type="reset" value="Reset"></p>
</form>
<p><a href="/servlet/servletdemo.FirstServlet">
  Click here to call Servlet: FirstServlet</a></p>
</body>
</html>
```

Listing 16.3 *FirstServlet.shtml*

Running the Servlet

To run the servlet, choose FirstServlet.shtml in the project pane, right-click the mouse button to display the context menu. Click Web Run from the menu to start the Tomcat server and the servlet. The output from the server appears in the Message page, as shown in Figure 16.9.

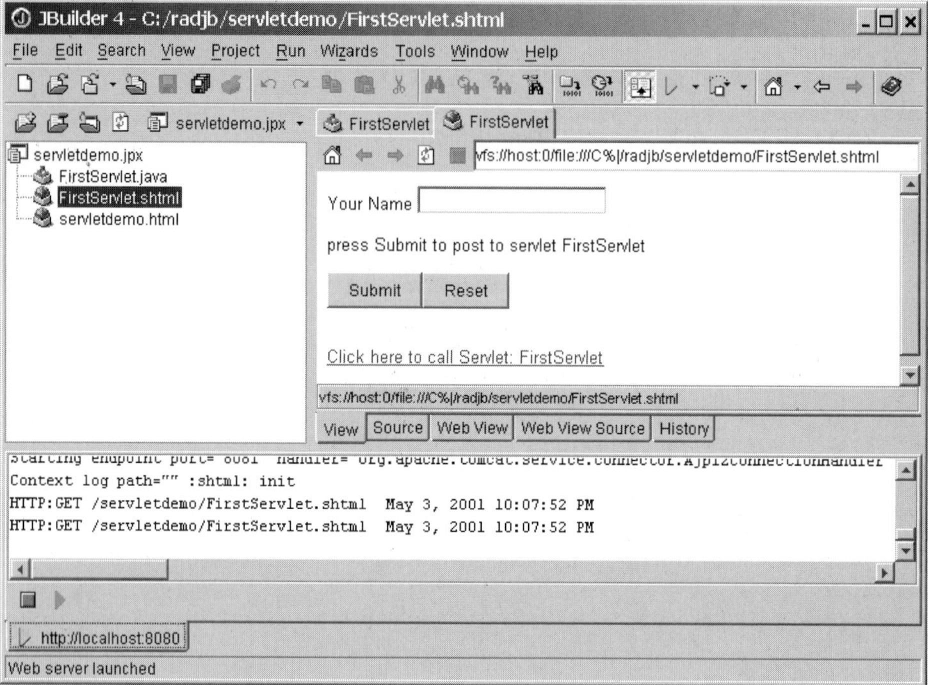

Figure 16.9 *Tomcat server and servlet are started from JBuilder.*

By default, Tomcat server starts at port 8080. If this port is in use, JBuilder automatically finds next available port.

JBUILDER 5 NOTE

When you click the Web Run menu from JBuilder 4, it always starts a new server at a new port. However, in JBuilder 5, it does not start a new server if the server has already been started by a previous Web Run.

JBUILDER 5 NOTE

If your servlet was created using JBuilder 4 and you wish to run it from JBuilder 5, you have to set the servlet to run from the Run page of the Project Properties dialog box.

Testing the Servlet

You can now test the servlet in JBuilder. Type Joe in the Your Name box, and click the Submit button, as shown in Figure 16.9. You will see a response from the servlet "Hi, Joe," displayed in the content pane, as shown in Figure 16.10. In Figure 16.10, the View tab renders FirstServlet.shtml, the Source tab displays the source code for FirstServlet.shtml, the Web View tab renders the generated Web

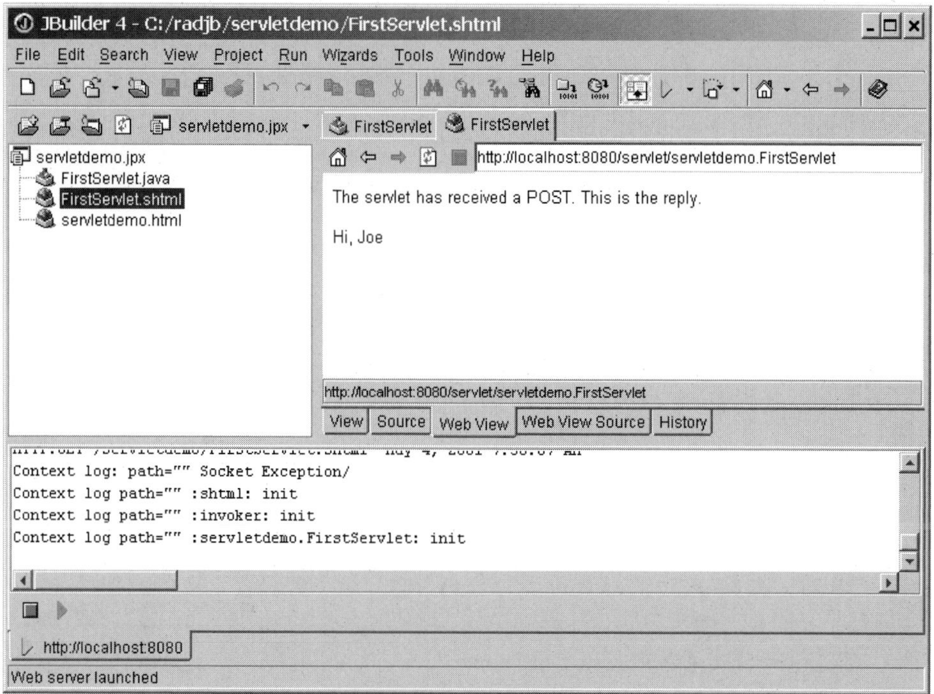

Figure 16.10 *You can test the servlet response from JBuilder.*

contents, and the Web View Source tab displays the source code of the generated Web text file.

You may also test it from the Web browser using the URL `http://localhost:8080/servletdemo/FirstServlet.shtml`, as shown in Figure 16.11. Type Joe in the Your Name box and click the Submit button. You will see a response from the Tomcat server displayed in Figure 16.12.

Note

You can use the servlet from anywhere on the Internet if your JBuilder is running on a host machine on the Internet. Suppose the host name is liang.armstrong.edu; use the URL http://liang.armstrong.edu:8080/servletdemo/FirstServlet.shtml to test the servlet.

The Servlet API

You have to know the servlet API in order to understand the source code in Listing 16.2. The servlet API provides the interfaces and classes that support servlets. These interfaces and classes are grouped into two packages, `javax.servlet` and `javax.servlet.http`, as shown in Figure 16.13. The `javax.servlet` package provides basic interfaces, and the `javax.servlet.http` package provides classes and in-

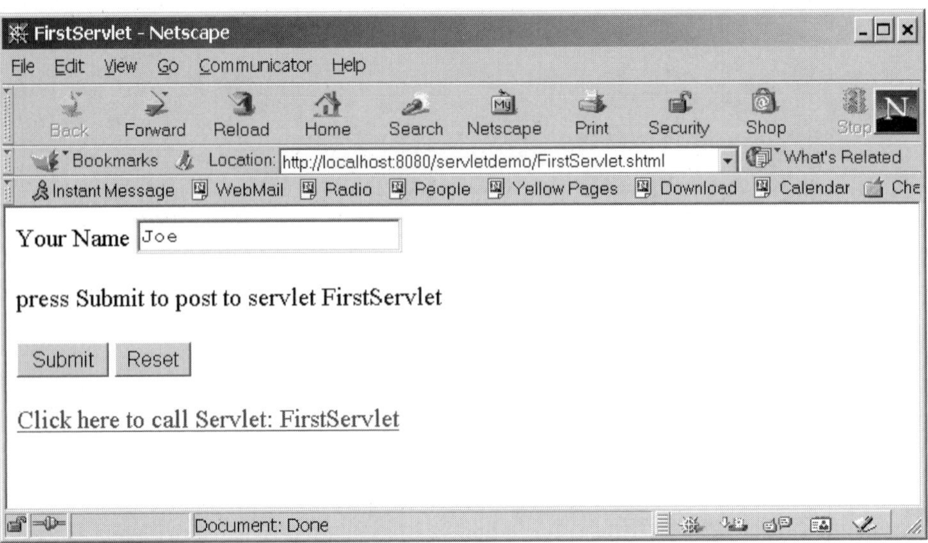

Figure 16.11 *You can test the servlet response from a Web browser.*

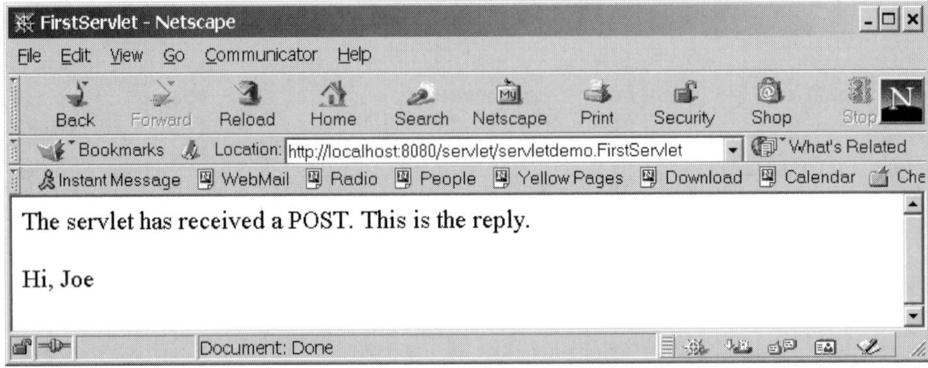

Figure 16.12 *The response from the servlet is shown in the Web browser.*

terfaces derived from them, which provide specific means for servicing HTTP requests.

The *Servlet* Interface

The `Servlet` interface defines the methods that all servlets must implement. The methods are listed below:

```
/** Invoked for every servlet constructed */
public void init(ServletConfig p0) throws ServletException;

/** Invoked to respond to incoming requests */
public void service(ServletRequest p0, ServletResponse p1)
  throws ServletException, IOException;

/** Invoked to release resource by the servlet */
public void destroy();
```

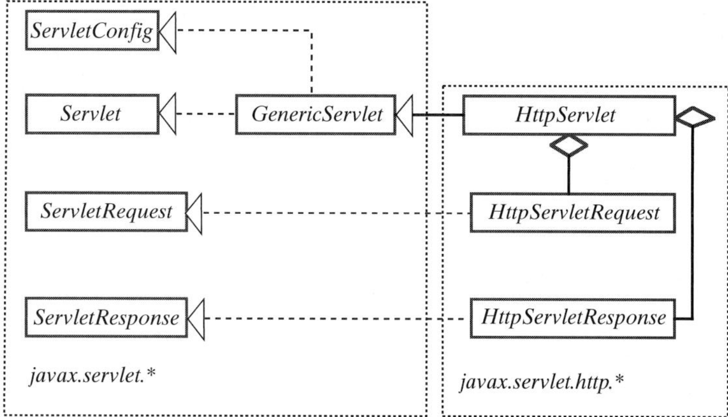

Figure 16.13 *The servlet API contains interfaces and classes that you use to develop and run servlets.*

```
/** Return information about the servlet */
public String getServletInfo();

/** Return configuration objects of the servlet */
public ServletConfig getServletConfig();
```

The `init`, `service`, and `destroy` methods are known as *life-cycle methods* and are called in the following sequence:

1. The `init` method is called when the servlet is first created, and is not called again as long as the servlet is not destroyed. This resembles the applet's `init` method, which is invoked when the applet is created, and is not invoked again as long as the applet is not destroyed.

2. The `service` method is invoked each time the server receives a request for the servlet. The server spawns a new thread and invokes `service`.

3. The `destroy` method is invoked once all the threads in the servlet's `service` method have exited or after a timeout period has passed. This method releases resources for the servlet.

The *GenericServlet* Class, *ServletConfig* Interface, and *HttpServlet* Class

The `GenericServlet` class defines a generic, protocol-independent servlet. It implements `Servlet` and `ServletConfig`. `ServletConfig` is an interface that defines four methods (`getInitParameter`, `getInitParameterNames`, `getServletContext`, and `getServletName`) for passing information to a servlet during initialization. All methods in `Servlet` and `ServletConfig` are implemented in `GenericServlet` except `service`. Therefore, `GenericServlet` is an abstract class.

The `HttpServlet` class defines a servlet for the HTTP protocol. It extends `GenericServlet` and implements the `service` method. The `service` method is implemented as a dispatcher of HTTP requests. The HTTP requests are processed in the following methods:

- `doGet` is invoked to respond to a GET request.
- `doPost` is invoked to respond to a POST request.
- `doDelete` is invoked to respond to a DELETE request. Such a request is normally used to delete a file on the server.
- `doPut` is invoked to respond to a PUT request. Such a request is normally used to send a file to the server.
- `doOptions` is invoked to respond to an OPTIONS request. This returns information about the server, such as which HTTP methods it supports.
- `doTrace` is invoked to respond to a TRACE request. Such a request is normally used for debugging. This method returns an HTML page that contains appropriate trace information.

All these methods have the same signature:

```
protected void doXxx(HttpServletRequest req, HttpServletResponse resp)
  throws ServletException, java.io.IOException
```

The `HttpServlet` class provides default implementation for these methods. You need to override `doGet`, `doPost`, `doDelete`, and `doPut` if you want the servlet to process a GET request, POST request, DELETE request, or PUT request. By default, nothing will be done. Normally, you should not override the `doOptions` method unless the servlet implements new HTTP methods beyond those implemented by HTTP 1.1. Nor is there any need to override the `doTrace` method.

NOTE

GET and POST requests are often used. DELETE, PUT, OPTIONS, and TRACE are not frequently used. For information about using these requests from a Web browser, please refer to HTTP 1.1 specification from www.cis.ohio-state.edu/htbin/rfc/rfc2068.html.

NOTE

Although the methods in `HttpServlet` are all nonabstract, `HttpServlet` is defined as an abstract class. Thus you cannot create a servlet directly from `HttpServlet`. Instead you have to define your servlet by extending `HttpServlet`.

The *ServletRequest* Interface and *HttpServletRequest* Interface

Every `doXxx` method in the `HttpServlet` class has an argument of the `HttpServletRequest` type, which is an object that contains HTTP request information, including parameter name and values, attributes, and an input stream. `HttpServletRequest` is a subinterface of `ServletRequest`. `ServletRequest` defines a more general interface to provide information for all kinds of clients.

Listed below are some frequently used methods in the `ServletRequest` interface.

- `public String getParameter(java.lang.String name)`

  Returns the value of a request parameter as a String, or null if the parameter does not exist. Request parameters are extra information sent with the request. For HTTP servlets, parameters are contained in the query string or posted from data. Only use this method when you are sure that the parameter has only one value. If it has more than one value, use `getParameterValues`.

- `public String[] getParameterValues(String name)`

  Returns an array of `String` objects containing all the values of the given request parameter, or null if the parameter does not exist.

- `public java.lang.String getRemoteAddr()`

  Returns the Internet Protocol (IP) address of the client that sent the request.

- `public String getRemoteHost()`

  Returns the fully qualified name of the client that sent the request, or the IP address of the client if the name cannot be determined.

In addition, the `HttpServletRequest` interface contains these commonly used methods:

- `public String getHeader(String name)`

  Returns the value of the specified request header as a String. If the request did not include a header of the specified name, this method returns null. Since the header name is case-insensitive, you can use this method with any request header.

- `public String getMethod()`

  Returns the name of the HTTP method with which this request was made; for example, GET, POST, DELETE, PUT, OPTIONS, or TRACE.

- `public String getQueryString()`

  Returns the query string that is contained in the request URL after the path. This method returns null if the URL does not have a query string.

- `public Cookie[] getCookies()`

  Returns an array containing all of the `Cookie` objects the client sent with the request. This method returns null if no cookies were sent. Using cookies is introduced in the section "Session Tracking Using Cookies."

- `public HttpSession getSession(boolean create)`

  `getSession(true)` returns the current session associated with this request. If the request does not have a session, it creates one. `getSession(false)` returns the current session associated with the request. If the request does not have a session, it returns `null`. The `getSession` method is used in session tracking, which is introduced in the section "Session Tracking Using Java Servlet API."

The *ServletResponse* Interface and *HttpServletResponse* Interface

Every `doXxx` method in the `HttpServlet` class has an argument of the `HttpServletResponse` type, which is an object that assists a servlet in sending a response to the client. `HttpServletResponse` is a subinterface of `ServletResponse`. `ServletRequest` defines a more general interface for sending output to the client.

Here are some frequently used methods in the `ServletResponse` interface:

- `public PrintWriter getWriter() throws IOException`

  Returns a `PrintWriter` object that can send character text to the client. The character encoding used is the one specified in the `charset` property of the `setContentType(String)` method, which must be called before calling this method for the `charset` to take effect.

- `public void setContentType(String type)`

  Sets the content type of the response being sent to the client. Before writing a response to the client, this method must be called to set the MIME type of HTTP response. The MIME type helps the browser determine how to display the data. When you are writing HTML to the client, the type should be set to "text/html." For plain text, use "text/plain." For sending a gif image to the browser, use "image/gif."

`HttpServletResponse` extends the `ServletResponse` interface to provide HTTP-specific functionality in sending a response. For example, it has the `addCookie` method to send an HTTP cookie to the browser. Cookies are introduced in the section "Session Tracking Using Cookies."

Creating Servlets

Servlets are the opposite of Java applets. Java applets run from a Web browser on the client side. To write Java programs, you define classes. To write a Java applet, you define a class that extends the `Applet` class. The Web browser runs and controls the execution of the applet through the methods defined in the `Applet` class. Similarly, to write a Java servlet, you define a class that extends the `HttpServlet` class. The servlet container runs and controls the execution of the servlet through the methods defined in the `HttpServlet` class. Like a Java applet, a servlet does not have a main method. A servlet depends on the servlet server to call the methods. Every servlet has a structure like the one shown in Listing 16.4.

```
import javax.servlet.*;
import javax.servlet.http.*;
import java.io.*;
import java.util.*;

public class MyServlet extends HttpServlet {
  /** Called by the servlet engine to initialize servlet */
  public void init(ServletConfig p0) throws ServletException {
    super.init(p0);
    ...
  }

  /** Process the HTTP Get request */
  public void doGet(HttpServletRequest request, HttpServletResponse
    response) throws ServletException, IOException {
    ...
  }

  /** Process the HTTP Post request */
  public void doPost(HttpServletRequest request, HttpServletResponse
    response) throws ServletException, IOException {
    ...
  }

  /** Called by the servlet engine to release resource */
  public void destroy() {
    ...
  }

  // Other methods if necessary
}
```

Listing 16.4 *Servlet Outline*

The servlet engine controls the servlets using `init`, `doGet`, `doPost`, `destroy`, and other methods. By default, the `doGet` and `doPost` methods do nothing. To handle a GET request, you need to override the `doGet` method; to handle a POST request, you need to override the `doPost` method.

Example 16.1 Obtaining Current Time from the Server

This example gives a simple Java servlet that generates a dynamic Web page for displaying current time to the browser. The servlet program is shown in Listing 16.5. A sample run is shown in Figure 16.14.

```
package servletdemo;

import javax.servlet.*;
import javax.servlet.http.*;
import java.io.*;
import java.util.*;

public class CurrentTime extends HttpServlet {
  /** Process the HTTP Get request */
  public void doGet(HttpServletRequest request, HttpServletResponse
```

Listing 16.5 *CurrentTime.java*

continued

Example 16.1 continued

```
        response) throws ServletException, IOException {
        response.setContentType("text/html");
        PrintWriter out = response.getWriter();
        out.println("<p>The current time is " + new Date());
        out.close(); // Close stream
    }
  }
```

Listing 16.5 *Continued*

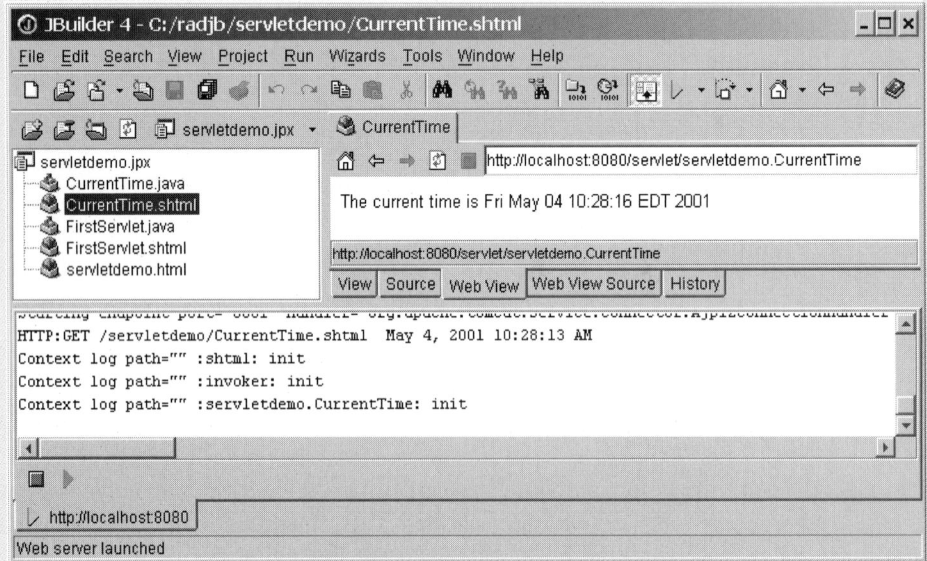

Figure 16.14 *Servlet CurrentTime displays the current time in JBuilder.*

Example Review

The `HttpServlet` class has a `doGet` method. The `doGet` method is invoked when the browser issues a request to the servlet using the GET method. So your servlet class should override the `doGet` method to respond to the GET request. In this case, you write the code to display the current time.

Servlets return responses to the browser through an `HttpServletResponse` object. Since the `setContentType("text/html")` method sets the MIME type to "text/html," the browser will display the response in HTML. The `getWriter` method returns a `PrintWriter` stream (`out`) for sending HTML back to the client.

After you have started a servlet from JBuilder, you can test it from a Web browser, as shown in Figure 16.15.

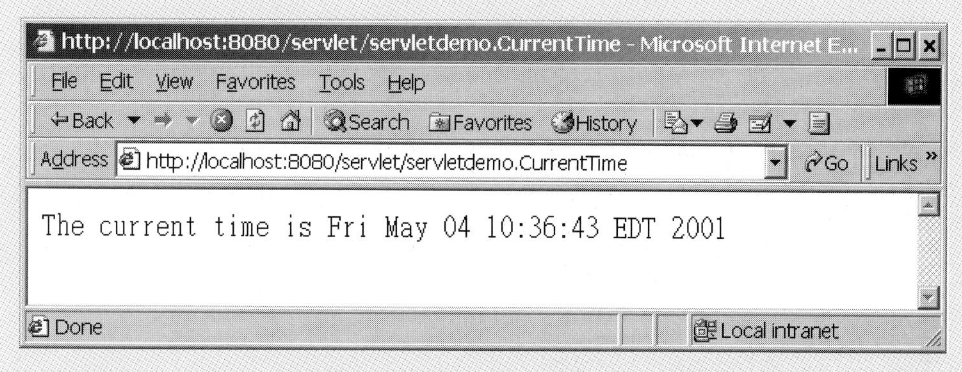

Figure 16.15 *Servlet CurrentTime displays the current time to the browser.*

NOTE

The URL query string uses the GET method to issue a request to the servlet. The current time may not be current if the Web page for displaying the current time is cached. To ensure that a new current time is displayed, refresh the page in the browser. In the next example, you will write a new servlet that uses the POST method to obtain the current time.

Example 16.2 Obtaining Current Time Based on Locale and Time Zone

This example creates a servlet that processes the GET and POST requests. The GET request generates a form that contains a combo box for locale and a combo box for time zone, as shown in Figure 16.16. The user can choose a locale and a time zone from this form to submit a POST request to obtain current time based on the locale and time zone, as shown in Figure 16.17. The servlet program is shown in Listing 16.6.

```
package servletdemo;

import javax.servlet.*;
import javax.servlet.http.*;
import java.io.*;
import java.util.*;
import java.text.*;

public class TimeForm extends HttpServlet {
  private static final String CONTENT_TYPE = "text/html";
  Locale[] allLocale = Locale.getAvailableLocales();
  String[] allTimeZone = TimeZone.getAvailableIDs();

  /** Process the HTTP Get request */
  public void doGet(HttpServletRequest request, HttpServletResponse
    response) throws ServletException, IOException {
```

Listing 16.6 *TimeForm.java*

continued

Example 16.2 continued

```
    response.setContentType(CONTENT_TYPE);
    PrintWriter out = response.getWriter();
    out.println("<h3>Choose locale and time zone</h3>");
    out.println("<form method=\"post\" action=" +
      "servletdemo.TimeForm>");
    out.println("Locale <select size=\"1\" name=\"locale\">");

    // Fill in all locales
    for (int i=0; i<allLocale.length; i++) {
      out.println("<option value=\"" + i +"\">" +
        allLocale[i].getDisplayName() + "</option>");
    }
    out.println("</select>");

    // Fill in all time zones
    out.println("<p>Time Zone<select size=\"1\" name=\"timezone\">");
    for (int i=0; i<allTimeZone.length; i++) {
      out.println("<option value=\"" + allTimeZone[i] +"\">" +
        allTimeZone[i] + "</option>");
    }
    out.println("</select>");

    out.println("<p><input type=\"submit\"" +
      " value=\"Submit\" name=\"B1\">");
    out.println("<input type=\"reset\" value=\"Reset\"></p>");
    out.println("</form>");
    out.close(); // Close stream
  }

  /** Process the HTTP Post request */
  public void doPost(HttpServletRequest request, HttpServletResponse
    response) throws ServletException, IOException {
    response.setContentType(CONTENT_TYPE);
    PrintWriter out = response.getWriter();
    out.println("<html>");
    int localeIndex = Integer.parseInt(
      request.getParameter("locale"));
    String timeZoneID = request.getParameter("timezone");
    out.println("<head><title>Current Time</title></head>");
    out.println("<body>");
    Calendar calendar =
      new GregorianCalendar(allLocale[localeIndex]);
    TimeZone timeZone = TimeZone.getTimeZone(timeZoneID);
    DateFormat dateFormat = DateFormat.getDateTimeInstance(
      DateFormat.FULL, DateFormat.FULL, allLocale[localeIndex]);
    dateFormat.setTimeZone(timeZone);
    out.println("Current time is " +
      dateFormat.format(calendar.getTime()) + "</p>");
    out.println("</body></html>");
    out.close(); // Close stream
  }
}
```

Listing 16.6 *Continued*

Example Review

When you use the URL `http://localhost:8080/servlet/servletdemo.TimeForm`, the servlet TimeForm's `doGet` method is invoked to generate the time form dynamically. The method of the form is POST, and the action invokes the

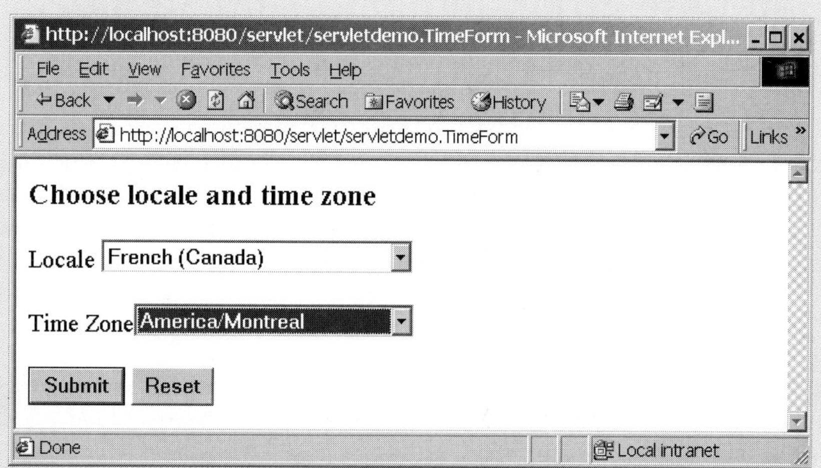

Figure 16.16 *The GET method in the* `TimeForm` *servlet displays a form.*

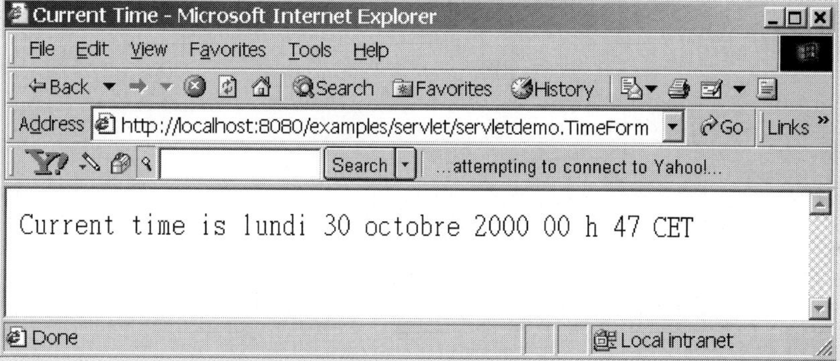

Figure 16.17 *The POST method in the* `TimeForm` *servlet displays the time based on locale and time zone.*

same servlet, `TimeForm`. When the form is submitted to the server, the `doPost` method is invoked to process the request.

The variables `allLocale` and `allTimeZone`, respectively, hold all available locales and time zone ids. The names of the locales are displayed in the locale list. The values for the locales are the indexes of the locales in the array `allLocale`. The time zone ids are strings. They are displayed in the time zone list. They are also the values for the list. The index of the locale and the time zone are passed to the servlet as parameters. The `doPost` method obtains the values of the parameters and finds the current time based on the locale and time zone.

Note

You can test this program from a Web browser, as long as Tomcat is started from JBuilder and your program has been compiled successfully.

Database Programming Using Servlets

Many dynamic Web applications use databases to store and manage data. Servlets can connect to any relational database via JDBC. In Part IV, "Java Database Programming," you learned how to create Java programs to access and manipulate relational databases via JDBC. Connecting a servlet to a database is no different from connecting a Java application or applet to a database. If you know Java servlets and JDBC, you can combine them to develop interesting and practical Web-based interactive projects. The following example demonstrates connecting to a database from a servlet.

Example 16.3 Registering a Student in a Database

This example creates a servlet that processes a registration form. The client enters data in an HTML form and submits it to the server, as shown in Figure 16.18. The result of the submission is shown in Figure 16.19. The server collects the data from the form and stores them in a database. The HTML file is shown in Listing 16.7, and the servlet is shown in Listing 16.8.

```
<html>
<head>
<title>Simple Registration without Confirmation</title>
</head>
<body>
Please register to your instructor's student address book.</font>

<form method="post" action=
  "http://localhost:8080/servlet/servletdemo.SimpleRegistration">
<p>Last Name <font color="#FF0000">*</font>
    <input type="text" name="lastName"> 
   First Name <font color="#FF0000">*</font>
    <input type="text" name="firstName"> 
   MI <input type="text" name="mi" size="3"></p>
<p>Telephone <input type="text" name="telephone" size="20"> 
   Email <input type="text" name="email" size="28"> </p>
<p>Street <input type="text" name="street" size="50"></p>
<p>City <input type="text" name="city" size="23"> 
   State <select size="1" name="state">
          <option value="GA">Georgia-GA</option>
          <option value="OK">Oklahoma-OK</option>
          <option value="IN">Indiana-IN</option>
         </select> 
   Zip <input type="text" name="zip" size="9"></p>
<p><input type="submit" name="Submit" value="Submit">
   <input type="reset" value="Reset"></p>
</form>
<p><font color="#FF0000">* required fields</font></p>
</body>
</html>
```

Listing 16.7 *SimpleRegistration.shtml*

Registration - Microsoft Internet Explorer

File Edit View Favorites Tools Help

Address http://localhost:8080/servletdemo/SimpleRegistration.shtml

Please register to your instructor's student address book.

Last Name * Smith First Name * John MI M

Telephone 322-223-1212 Email smith@yahoo.com

Street 100 Main Street

City Savannah State Georgia-GA Zip 31344

Submit Reset

* required fields

Done Local intranet

Figure 16.18 *The HTML form enables the user to enter student information.*

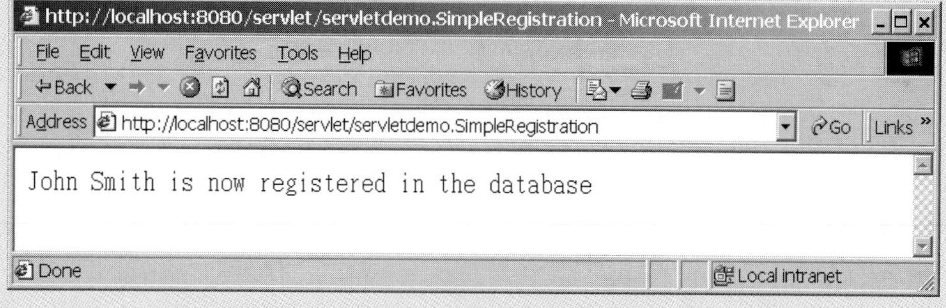

Figure 16.19 *The servlet processes the form and stores data in a database*

```
package servletdemo;

import javax.servlet.*;
import javax.servlet.http.*;
import java.io.*;
import java.sql.*;

public class SimpleRegistration extends HttpServlet {
  // Use a prepared statement to store a student into the database
  private PreparedStatement pstmt;

  /** Initialize global variables */
  public void init(ServletConfig config) throws ServletException {
    super.init(config);
```

Listing 16.8 *SimpleRegistration.java*

continued

Example 16.3 continued

```
      initializeJdbc();
    }

    /** Process the HTTP Post request */
    public void doPost(HttpServletRequest request, HttpServletResponse
      response) throws ServletException, IOException {
      response.setContentType("text/html");
      PrintWriter out = response.getWriter();

      // Obtain parameters from the client
      String lastName = request.getParameter("lastName");
      String firstName = request.getParameter("firstName");
      String mi = request.getParameter("mi");
      String phone = request.getParameter("telephone");
      String email = request.getParameter("email");
      String address = request.getParameter("street");
      String city = request.getParameter("city");
      String state = request.getParameter("state");
      String zip = request.getParameter("zip");

      if (lastName.length() == 0 || firstName.length() == 0) {
        out.println("Last Name and First Name are required");
        return; // End the method
      }

      try {
        storeStudent(lastName, firstName, mi, phone, email, address,
          city, state, zip);

        out.println(firstName + " " + lastName +
          " is now registered in the database");

        out.close(); // Close stream
      }
      catch(Exception ex) {
        out.println("Error: " + ex.getMessage());
        return; // End the method
      }
    }

    /** Initialize database connection */
    private void initializeJdbc() {
      try {
        // Declare driver and connection string
        String driver = "sun.jdbc.odbc.JdbcOdbcDriver";
        String connectionString = "jdbc:odbc:LiangBookDB_MDB";
        /* For Oracle
        String driver = "oracle.jdbc.driver.OracleDriver";
        String connectionString =
        "jdbc:oracle:thin:scott/tiger@liang.armstrong.edu:1521:oracle";
        */
        // Load the Oracle JDBC Thin driver
        Class.forName(driver);

        // Connect to the sample database
        Connection conn = DriverManager.getConnection
          (connectionString);

        // Create a Statement
        pstmt = conn.prepareStatement("insert into Address " +
          "(lastName, firstName, mi, telephone, email, street, city, "
```

Listing 16.8 *Continued*

```
          + "state, zip) values (?, ?, ?, ?, ?, ?, ?, ?, ?)");
      }
      catch (Exception ex) {
        System.out.println(ex);
      }
    }

    /** Store a student record to the database */
    private void storeStudent(String lastName, String firstName,
      String mi, String phone, String email, String address,
      String city, String state, String zip) throws SQLException {
      pstmt.setString(1, lastName);
      pstmt.setString(2, firstName);
      pstmt.setString(3, mi);
      pstmt.setString(4, phone);
      pstmt.setString(5, email);
      pstmt.setString(6, address);
      pstmt.setString(7, city);
      pstmt.setString(8, state);
      pstmt.setString(9, zip);
      pstmt.executeUpdate();
    }
  }
```

Listing 16.8 *Continued*

Example Review

The `init` method is executed once when the servlet starts. After the servlet has started, the servlet can be invoked many times as long as it is alive in the servlet container. Load the driver, and connect to the database from the servlet's `init` method. If a prepared statement or a callable statement is used, it should also be created in the `init` method. In this example, a prepared statement is desirable, because the servlet always uses the same insert statement with different values.

A servlet can connect to any relational database via JDBC. The `initializeJdbc` method in this example loads a JDBC-ODBC bridge driver. Use of the Oracle Thin driver is commented in the code. Once connected, it creates a prepared statement for inserting a student record into the database. The Access database and the Oracle database are the same as were used in Part IV, "Java Database Programming." To use the MS Access database, the ODBC data source LiangBookDB_MDB must be created. Please refer to Chapter 12, "Introduction to Java Database Programming," to create an ODBC data source. To use Oracle database, you must have the Oracle JDBC Thin driver in the library of the project.

Last name and first name are required fields. If either of them is empty, the servlet sends an error message to the client. Otherwise, the servlet stores the data in the database using the prepared statement.

NOTE

If a parameter `param` is not passed to the servlet, the `request.getParameter(param)` method returns `null`. If an empty value of the parameter is passed to the servlet, the `request.getParameter(param)` method returns a string with empty value. In this case, the length of the string is 0.

Session Tracking

Web servers use Hyper-Text Transport Protocol (HTTP). HTTP is a stateless protocol. An HTTP Web server cannot associate requests from a client, and therefore treats each request independently. This protocol works fine for simple Web browsing, where each request typically results in an HTML file or in a text file being sent back to the client. Such simple requests are isolated. However, the requests in interactive Web applications are often related. Consider the two requests in the following scenario:

- Request 1: A client sends registration data to the server; the server then returns the data to the user for confirmation.
- Request 2: The client confirms the data by resubmitting them.

In Request 2, the data submitted in Request 1 were sent back to the server. These two requests are related in a session. A *session* can be defined as a series of related interactions between a single client and the Web server over a period of time. Tracking data among requests in a session is known as *session tracking*.

This section introduces three techniques for session tracking: *using hidden values*, *using cookies*, and *using the session tracking tools from servlet API*.

Session Tracking Using Hidden Values

You can track a session by passing data from the servlet to the client as hidden value in a dynamically generated HTML form by including a field like the one shown below:

<input type="hidden" name="lastName" value="Smith">

The next request will submit the data back to the servlet. The servlet retrieves this hidden value just like any other parameter value using the `getParameter` method.

Example 16.4 Using Hidden Values in the Registration form

This example creates a servlet that processes a registration form. The client submits the form using the GET method, as shown in Figure 16.18. The server collects the data in the form, displays them to the client, and asks the client for confirmation, as shown in Figure 16.20. The client confirms the data by submitting the request with the hidden values using the POST method. Finally, the servlet writes the data to a database.

The HTML file is shown in Listing 16.9, which is the same as Listing 16.7, except that the method for the request is GET and the servlet program is named Registration. The servlet program is shown in Listing 16.10.

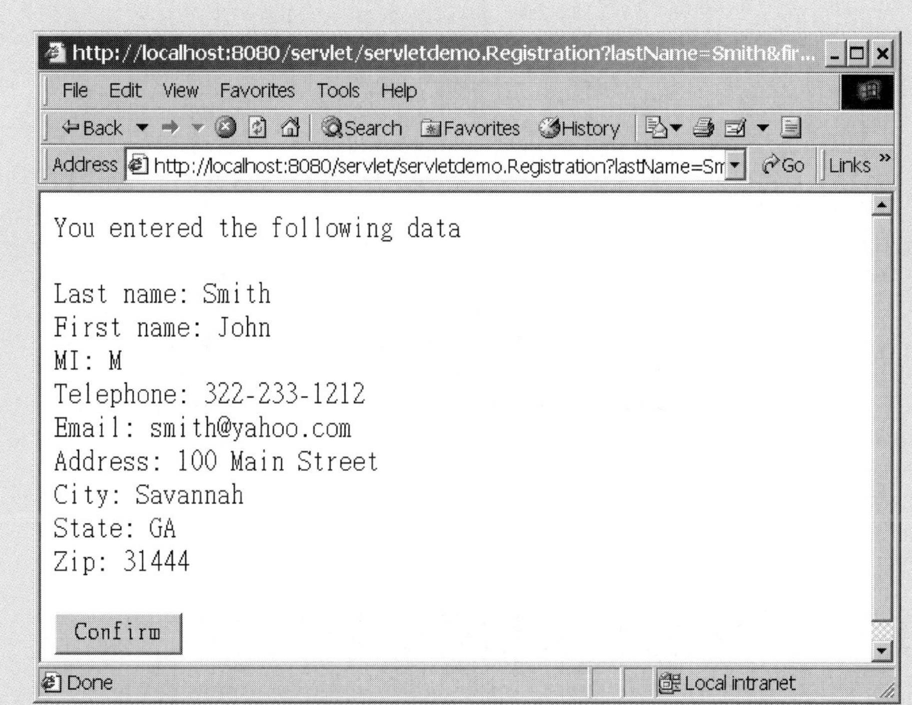

Figure 16.20 *The servlet asks the client for confirmation of the input.*

```
<html>
<head>
<title>Registration Using Hidden Data for Session Tracking</title>
</head>
<body>
Please register to your instructor's student address book.</font>

<form method="get"
  action="http://localhost:8080/servlet/servletdemo.Registration">
<p>Last Name <font color="#FF0000">*</font>
    <input type="text" name="lastName"> 
   First Name <font color="#FF0000">*</font>
    <input type="text" name="firstName"> 
   MI <input type="text" name="mi" size="3"></p>
<p>Telephone <input type="text" name="telephone" size="20"> 
   Email <input type="text" name="email" size="28"> </p>
<p>Street <input type="text" name="street" size="50"></p>
<p>City <input type="text" name="city" size="23"> 
   State <select size="1" name="state">
          <option value="GA">Georgia-GA</option>
          <option value="OK">Oklahoma-OK</option>
          <option value="IN">Indiana-IN</option>
         </select> 
   Zip <input type="text" name="zip" size="9"></p>
<p><input type="submit" name="Submit" value="Submit">
   <input type="reset" value="Reset"></p>
</form>
<p><font color="#FF0000">* required fields</font></p>
</body>
</html>
```

Listing 16.9 *Registration.shtml*

continued

Example 16.4 continued

```
package servletdemo;

import javax.servlet.*;
import javax.servlet.http.*;
import java.io.*;
import java.sql.*;

public class Registration extends HttpServlet {
  // Use a prepared statement to store a student into the database
  private PreparedStatement pstmt;

  /** Initialize global variables */
  public void init(ServletConfig config) throws ServletException {
    super.init(config);
    initializeJdbc();
  }

  /** Process the HTTP Get request */
  public void doGet(HttpServletRequest request, HttpServletResponse
    response) throws ServletException, IOException {
    response.setContentType("text/html");
    PrintWriter out = response.getWriter();

    // Obtain data from the form
    String lastName = request.getParameter("lastName");
    String firstName = request.getParameter("firstName");
    String mi = request.getParameter("mi");
    String telephone = request.getParameter("telephone");
    String email = request.getParameter("email");
    String street = request.getParameter("street");
    String city = request.getParameter("city");
    String state = request.getParameter("state");
    String zip = request.getParameter("zip");

    if (lastName.length() == 0 || firstName.length() == 0) {
      out.println("Last Name and First Name are required");
      return; // End the method
    }

    // Ask for confirmation
    out.println("You entered the following data");
    out.println("<p>Last name: " + lastName);
    out.println("<br>First name: " + firstName);
    out.println("<br>MI: " + mi);
    out.println("<br>Telephone: " + telephone);
    out.println("<br>Email: " + email);
    out.println("<br>Address: " + street);
    out.println("<br>City: " + city);
    out.println("<br>State: " + state);
    out.println("<br>Zip: " + zip);

    // Set the action for processing the answers
    out.println("<p><form method=\"post\" action=" +
      "servletdemo.Registration>");
    // Set hidden values
    out.println("<p><input type=\"hidden\" " +
      "value=" + lastName + " name=\"lastName\">");
    out.println("<p><input type=\"hidden\" " +
```

Listing 16.10 *Registration.java*

```
      "value=" + firstName + " name=\"firstName\">");
    out.println("<p><input type=\"hidden\" " +
      "value=" + mi + " name=\"mi\">");
    out.println("<p><input type=\"hidden\" " +
      "value=" + telephone + " name=\"telephone\">");
    out.println("<p><input type=\"hidden\" " +
      "value=" + email + " name=\"email\">");
    out.println("<p><input type=\"hidden\" " +
      "value=" + street + " name=\"street\">");
    out.println("<p><input type=\"hidden\" " +
      "value=" + city + " name=\"city\">");
    out.println("<p><input type=\"hidden\" " +
      "value=" + state + " name=\"state\">");
    out.println("<p><input type=\"hidden\" " +
      "value=" + zip + " name=\"zip\">");
    out.println("<p><input type=\"submit\"" +
      " value=\"Confirm\" name=\"B1\">");
    out.println("</form>");
  }

  /** Process the HTTP Post request */
  public void doPost(HttpServletRequest request, HttpServletResponse
    response) throws ServletException, IOException {
    response.setContentType("text/html");
    PrintWriter out = response.getWriter();

    try {
      String lastName = request.getParameter("lastName");
      String firstName = request.getParameter("firstName");
      String mi = request.getParameter("mi");
      String telephone = request.getParameter("telephone");
      String email = request.getParameter("email");
      String street = request.getParameter("street");
      String city = request.getParameter("city");
      String state = request.getParameter("state");
      String zip = request.getParameter("zip");

      storeStudent(lastName, firstName, mi, telephone, email,
        street, city, state, zip);

      out.println(firstName + " " + lastName +
        " is now registered in the database");
    }
    catch(Exception ex) {
      out.println("Error: " + ex.getMessage());
      return; // End the method
    }
  }

  /** Initialize database connection */
  private void initializeJdbc() {
    try {
      // Declare driver and connection string
      String driver = "sun.jdbc.odbc.JdbcOdbcDriver";
      String connectionString = "jdbc:odbc:LiangBookDB_MDB";
      /* For Oracle
      String driver = "oracle.jdbc.driver.OracleDriver";
      String connectionString =
      "jdbc:oracle:thin:scott/tiger@liang.armstrong.edu:1521:oracle";
```

Listing 16.10 *Continued*

continued

Example 16.4 continued

```
      */
      // Load the Oracle JDBC Thin driver
      Class.forName(driver);

      // Connect to the sample database
      Connection conn = DriverManager.getConnection
        (connectionString);

      // Create a Statement
      pstmt = conn.prepareStatement("insert into Address " +
        "(lastName, firstName, mi, telephone, email, street, city, "
        + "state, zip) values (?, ?, ?, ?, ?, ?, ?, ?, ?)");

      out.close(); // Close stream
    }
    catch (Exception ex) {
      System.out.println(ex);
    }
  }

  /** Store a student record to the database */
  private void storeStudent(String lastName, String firstName,
    String mi, String phone, String email, String address,
    String city, String state, String zip) throws SQLException {
    pstmt.setString(1, lastName);
    pstmt.setString(2, firstName);
    pstmt.setString(3, mi);
    pstmt.setString(4, phone);
    pstmt.setString(5, email);
    pstmt.setString(6, address);
    pstmt.setString(7, city);
    pstmt.setString(8, state);
    pstmt.setString(9, zip);
    pstmt.executeUpdate();
  }
}
```

Listing 16.10 *Continued*

Example Review

The servlet processes the GET request by generating an HTML page that displays the client's input and asks for the client's confirmation. The input data are hidden values in the newly generated forms. So the data will be sent back in the confirmation request. The confirmation request uses the POST method. The servlet retrieves the hidden values and stores them in the database.

Since the first request does not write anything to the database, it is appropriate to use the GET method. Since the second request results in an update to the database, the POST method must be used.

NOTE

The hidden values could also be sent from the URL query string if the next request uses the GET method.

Session Tracking Using Cookies

You can track sessions using cookies, which are small text files that store sets of name-value pairs on the disk in the client's computer. Cookies are sent from the server through the instructions in the header of the HTTP response. The instructions tell the browser to create a cookie with a given name and its associated value. If the browser already has a cookie with the key name, the value will be updated. The browser will then send the cookie with any request submitted to the same server. Cookies can have expiration dates set, after which they will not be sent to the server.

To create a cookie in the servlet, use the following constructor:

```
public Cookie(String name, String value)
```

The frequently used methods in the `Cookie` class are listed below:

- `public String getName()`

  Returns the name of the cookie.

- `public void setMaxAge(int expiry)`

  Specifies an integer that specifies how long (in seconds) the cookie will persist. Be default, this value is –1, which implies that the cookie persists until the browser exits. If you set this value to 0, the cookie is deleted. Use `getMaxAge` to obtain this value.

- `public void setValue(String newValue)`

  Assigns a new value in the cookie after the cookie is created. Use `getValue` to obtain this value.

- `public void setDomain(String pattern)`

  Sets the Internet domain, such as prenhall.com. By default, the cookie is sent to the server that originally created it. Use `getDomain` to obtain domain.

- `public void setSecure(boolean flag)`

  Sets `true` if a secure protocol should be used for the cookie. Use `getSecure` to obtain this value.

- `public void setPath(String uri)`

  Specifies a target directory under which the servlet can receive the cookie. Use `getPath` to obtain the path. Use `getPath` to obtain the path.

- `public void setComment(String purpose)`

  Sets a comment to describe the cookie. Use `getComment` to obtain the comment.

- `public void setVersion(int v)`

  Sets the version of the cookie protocol that this cookie complies with. Version 0 complies with the original Netscape cookie. Use `getVersion` to obtain the version.

To send a cookie to the browser, use the `addCookie` method in the `HTTPServletResponse` class, as shown below:

```
response.addCookie(cookie);
```

where `response` is an instance of `HTTPServletResponse`.

Example 16.5 Using Cookies in the Registration form

This example accomplishes the same task as Example 16.4. Instead of using hidden values for session tracking, it uses cookies. The new HTML file named RegistrationWithCookie.shtml can be found in the companion CD-ROM; it is the same as the one in Listing 16.9, except that the servlet is named RegistrationWithCookie. The servlet is shown in Listing 16.11.

```
package servletdemo;

import javax.servlet.*;
import javax.servlet.http.*;
import java.io.*;
import java.sql.*;

public class RegistrationWithCookie extends HttpServlet {
  private static final String CONTENT_TYPE = "text/html";
  // Use a prepared statement to store a student into the database
  private PreparedStatement pstmt;

  /** Initialize global variables */
  public void init(ServletConfig config) throws ServletException {
    super.init(config);
    initializeJdbc();
  }

  /** Process the HTTP Get request */
  public void doGet(HttpServletRequest request, HttpServletResponse
    response) throws ServletException, IOException {
    response.setContentType("text/html");
    PrintWriter out = response.getWriter();

    // Obtain data from the form
    String lastName = request.getParameter("lastName");
    String firstName = request.getParameter("firstName");
    String mi = request.getParameter("mi");
    String telephone = request.getParameter("telephone");
    String email = request.getParameter("email");
    String street = request.getParameter("street");
    String city = request.getParameter("city");
    String state = request.getParameter("state");
    String zip = request.getParameter("zip");

    // Create cookies and send cookies to browsers
    Cookie cookieLastName = new Cookie("lastName", lastName);
    // cookieLastName.setMaxAge(1000);
    response.addCookie(cookieLastName);
    Cookie cookieFirstName = new Cookie("firstName", firstName);
    response.addCookie(cookieFirstName);
    // cookieFirstName.setMaxAge(0);
```

Listing 16.11 *RegistrationWithCookie.java*

```
    Cookie cookieMi = new Cookie("mi", mi);
    response.addCookie(cookieMi);
    Cookie cookieTelephone = new Cookie("telephone", telephone);
    response.addCookie(cookieTelephone);
    Cookie cookieEmail = new Cookie("email", email);
    response.addCookie(cookieEmail);
    Cookie cookieStreet = new Cookie("street", street);
    response.addCookie(cookieStreet);
    Cookie cookieCity = new Cookie("city", city);
    response.addCookie(cookieCity);
    Cookie cookieState = new Cookie("state", state);
    response.addCookie(cookieState);
    Cookie cookieZip = new Cookie("zip", zip);
    response.addCookie(cookieZip);

    System.out.println("MaxAge? " + cookieLastName.getMaxAge());
    System.out.println("MaxAge fir? " + cookieFirstName.getMaxAge());

    if (lastName.length() == 0 || firstName.length() == 0) {
      out.println("Last Name and First Name are required");
      return; // End the method
    }

    // Ask for confirmation
    out.println("You entered the following data");
    out.println("<p>Last name: " + lastName);
    out.println("<br>First name: " + firstName);
    out.println("<br>MI: " + mi);
    out.println("<br>Telephone: " + telephone);
    out.println("<br>Email: " + email);
    out.println("<br>Street: " + street);
    out.println("<br>City: " + city);
    out.println("<br>State: " + state);
    out.println("<br>Zip: " + zip);

    // Set the action for processing the answers
    out.println("<p><form method=\"post\" action=" +
      "servletdemo.RegistrationWithCookie>");
    out.println("<p><input type=\"submit\"" +
      " value=\"Confirm\" name=\"B1\">");
    out.println("</form>");
    out.close(); // Close stream
  }

  /** Process the HTTP Post request */
  public void doPost(HttpServletRequest request, HttpServletResponse
    response) throws ServletException, IOException {
    response.setContentType(CONTENT_TYPE);
    PrintWriter out = response.getWriter();

    String lastName = "";
    String firstName = "";
    String mi = "";
    String telephone = "";
    String email = "";
    String street = "";
    String city = "";
    String state = "";
    String zip = "";

```

Listing 16.11 *Continued*

continued

Example 16.5 continued

```
      // Read the cookies
      Cookie[] cookies = request.getCookies();

      // Get cookie values
      for (int i=0; i<cookies.length; i++) {
        if (cookies[i].getName().equals("lastName"))
          lastName = cookies[i].getValue();
        else if (cookies[i].getName().equals("firstName"))
          firstName = cookies[i].getValue();
        else if (cookies[i].getName().equals("mi"))
          mi = cookies[i].getValue();
        else if (cookies[i].getName().equals("telephone"))
          telephone = cookies[i].getValue();
        else if (cookies[i].getName().equals("email"))
          email = cookies[i].getValue();
        else if (cookies[i].getName().equals("street"))
          street = cookies[i].getValue();
        else if (cookies[i].getName().equals("city"))
          city = cookies[i].getValue();
        else if (cookies[i].getName().equals("state"))
          state = cookies[i].getValue();
        else if (cookies[i].getName().equals("zip"))
          zip = cookies[i].getValue();
      }

      try {
        storeStudent(lastName, firstName, mi, telephone, email, street,
          city, state, zip);

        out.println(firstName + " " + lastName +
          " is now registered in the database");

        out.close(); // Close stream
      }
      catch(Exception ex) {
        out.println("Error: " + ex.getMessage());
        return; // End the method
      }
    }

    /** Initialize database connection */
    private void initializeJdbc() {
      try {
        // Declare driver and connection string
        String driver = "sun.jdbc.odbc.JdbcOdbcDriver";
        String connectionString = "jdbc:odbc:LiangBookDB_MDB";
        // For Oracle
        // String driver = "oracle.jdbc.driver.OracleDriver";
        // String connectionString = "jdbc:oracle:thin:scott/
        //   tiger@liang.armstrong.edu:1521:oracle";

        // Load the Oracle JDBC Thin driver
        Class.forName(driver);
        System.out.println("Driver " + driver + " loaded");

        // Connect to the sample database
        Connection conn = DriverManager.getConnection
          (connectionString);
```

Listing 16.11 *Continued*

```
        System.out.println("Database " + connectionString +
          " connected");

        // Create a Statement
        pstmt = conn.prepareStatement("insert into Address " +
          "(lastName, firstName, mi, telephone, email, street, city, "
          + "state, zip) values (?, ?, ?, ?, ?, ?, ?, ?, ?)");
      }
      catch (Exception ex) {
        System.out.println(ex);
      }
    }

    /** Store a student record to the database */
    private void storeStudent(String lastName, String firstName,
      String mi, String telephone, String email, String street,
      String city, String state, String zip) throws SQLException {
      pstmt.setString(1, lastName);
      pstmt.setString(2, firstName);
      pstmt.setString(3, mi);
      pstmt.setString(4, telephone);
      pstmt.setString(5, email);
      pstmt.setString(6, street);
      pstmt.setString(7, city);
      pstmt.setString(8, state);
      pstmt.setString(9, zip);
      pstmt.executeUpdate();
    }
  }
```

Listing 16.11 *Continued*

Example Review

You have to create a cookie for each value you want to track, using the `Cookie` class's only constructor, which defines a cookie's name and value as shown below:

```
Cookie cookieLastName = new Cookie("lastName", lastName);
```

To send the cookie to the browser, use a statement like this one:

```
response.addCookie(cookieLastName);
```

If a cookie with the same name already exists in the browser, its value is updated; otherwise, a new cookie is created.

Cookies are automatically sent to the Web server with each request from the client. The servlet retrieves all the cookies into an array using the `getCookies` method.

```
Cookie[] cookies = request.getCookies();
```

To obtain the name of the cookie, use the `getName` method:

```
String name = cookies[i].getName();
```

continued

Example 16.5 continued

The cookie's value can be obtained using the `getValue` method:

```
String value = cookies[i].getValue();
```

Cookies are stored as strings just like form parameters and hidden values. If a cookie represents a numeric value, you have to convert it into an integer or a double, using the `parseInt` method in the `Integer` class or the `parseDouble` method in the `Double` class.

By default, a newly created cookie persists until the browser exits. However, you can set the expiration date, using the `setMaxAge` method, to allow a cookie to stay in the browser for up to 2,147,483,647 seconds (approximately 24,855 days).

Session Tracking Using the Servlet API

You have now learned both session tracking using hidden values and session tracking using cookies. These two session-tracking methods have problems. They send data to the browser either as hidden values or as cookies. The data are not secure, and anybody with knowledge of computers can obtain them. The hidden data are in HTML form, which can be viewed from the browser. Cookies are stored in the Cache directory of the browser. Because of security concerns, some browsers do not accept cookies. The client can turn the cookies off and limit their number. Another problem is that hidden data and cookies pass data as strings. You cannot pass objects using these two methods. To address these problems, Java servlet API provides a session-tracking tool that enables tracking of a large set of data. The data can be stored as objects and are secure because they are kept on the server side.

To use the Java servlet API for session tracking, first create a session object using the `getSession` method in the `HttpServletRequest` interface:

```
HttpSession session = request.getSession(true);
```

This obtains the session or creates a new session if the client does not have a session on the server.

The `HttpSession` class provides the following methods for reading and storing data to the session, and for manipulating the session:

- `public Object getAttribute(String name)`

  Returns the object bound with the specified name in this session, or `null` if no object is bound under the name.

- `public void setAttribute(String name, Object value)`

  Binds an object to this session, using the specified name. If an object of the same name is already bound to the session, the object is replaced.

- `public String getId()`

  Returns a string containing the unique identifier assigned to this session. The identifier is assigned by the servlet container and is implementation-dependent.

- `public long getLastAccessedTime()`

  Returns the last time the client sent a request associated with this session as the number of milliseconds since midnight January 1, 1970 GMT.

- `public void invalidate()`

  Invalidates this session.

- `public boolean isNew()`

  Returns true if the session was just created in the current request.

- `public void removeAttribute(String name)`

  Removes the object bound with the specified name from this session. If the session does not have an object bound with the specified name, this method does nothing.

- `public void setMaxInactiveInterval(int interval)`

  Specifies the time, in seconds, between client requests before the servlet container will invalidate this session. A negative time indicates that the session will never time-out. Use `getMaxInactiveInterval` to retrieve this value.

NOTE

HTTP is stateless. So how does the server associate a session with multiple requests from the same client? This is handled behind the scenes by the servlet container and is transparent to the servlet programmer.

Example 16.6 Using HttpSession in the Registration Form

This example accomplishes the same task as Examples 16.4 and 16.5. Instead of using hidden values or cookies for session tracking, it uses servlet HttpSession. The new HTML file named RegistrationWithHttpSession.shtml can be found in the companion CD-ROM; it is the same as the one in Listing 16.9, except that the servlet is named RegistrationWithHttpSession. The servlet is shown in Listing 16.12.

```
package servletdemo;

import javax.servlet.*;
import javax.servlet.http.*;
import java.io.*;
```

Listing 16.12 *RegistrationWithHttpSession.java*

continued

Example 16.6 continued

```
import java.sql.*;
import java.util.*;

public class RegistrationWithHttpSession extends HttpServlet {
  // Use a prepared statement to store a student into the database
  private PreparedStatement pstmt;

  /** Initialize global variables */
  public void init(ServletConfig config) throws ServletException {
    super.init(config);
    initializeJdbc();
  }

  /** Process the HTTP Get request */
  public void doGet(HttpServletRequest request, HttpServletResponse
    response) throws ServletException, IOException {
    // Set response type and output stream to the browser
    response.setContentType("text/html");
    PrintWriter out = response.getWriter();

    // Obtain data from the form
    String lastName = request.getParameter("lastName");
    String firstName = request.getParameter("firstName");
    String mi = request.getParameter("mi");
    String telephone = request.getParameter("telephone");
    String email = request.getParameter("email");
    String street = request.getParameter("street");
    String city = request.getParameter("city");
    String state = request.getParameter("state");
    String zip = request.getParameter("zip");

    if (lastName.length() == 0 || firstName.length() == 0) {
      out.println("Last Name and First Name are required");
      return; // End the method
    }

    // Create a Student object
    Student student = new Student(lastName, firstName,
      mi, telephone, email, street, city, state, zip);

    // Get an HttpSession or create one if it does not exist
    HttpSession httpSession = request.getSession(true);

    // Store student object to the session
    httpSession.setAttribute("student", student);

    // Ask for confirmation
    out.println("You entered the following data");
    out.println("<p>Last name: " + lastName);
    out.println("<p>First name: " + firstName);
    out.println("<p>MI: " + mi);
    out.println("<p>Telephone: " + telephone);
    out.println("<p>Email: " + email);
    out.println("<p>Address: " + street);
    out.println("<p>City: " + city);
    out.println("<p>State: " + state);
    out.println("<p>Zip: " + zip);

```

Listing 16.12 *Continued*

```
      // Set the action for processing the answers
      out.println("<p><form method=\"post\" action=" +
        "servletdemo.RegistrationWithHttpSession>");
      out.println("<p><input type=\"submit\"" +
        " value=\"Confirm\" name=\"B1\">");
      out.println("</form>");

      out.close(); // Close stream
    }

    /** Process the HTTP Post request */
    public void doPost(HttpServletRequest request, HttpServletResponse
      response) throws ServletException, IOException {
      // Set response type and output stream to the browser
      response.setContentType("text/html");
      PrintWriter out = response.getWriter();

      // Obtain the HttpSession
      HttpSession httpSession = request.getSession(true);

      // Get the Student object in the HttpSession
      Student student = (Student)(httpSession.getAttribute("student"));

      try {
        storeStudent(student);

        out.println(student.firstName + " " + student.lastName +
          " is now registered in the database");
        out.close(); // Close stream
      }
      catch(Exception ex) {
        out.println("Error: " + ex.getMessage());
        return; // End the method
      }
    }

    /** Initialize database connection */
    private void initializeJdbc() {
      try {
        // Declare driver and connection string
        String driver = "sun.jdbc.odbc.JdbcOdbcDriver";
        String connectionString = "jdbc:odbc:LiangBookDB_MDB";

        // Load the Oracle JDBC Thin driver
        Class.forName(driver);
        System.out.println("Driver " + driver + " loaded");

        // Connect to the sample database
        Connection conn = DriverManager.getConnection
          (connectionString);
        System.out.println("Database " + connectionString +
          " connected");

        // Create a Statement
        pstmt = conn.prepareStatement("insert into Address " +
          "(lastName, firstName, mi, telephone, email, street, city, "
          + "state, zip) values (?, ?, ?, ?, ?, ?, ?, ?, ?)");
      }
```

Listing 16.12 *Continued*

continued

Example 16.6 continued

```
      catch (Exception ex) {
        System.out.println(ex);
      }
    }

    /** Store a student record to the database */
    private void storeStudent(Student student) throws SQLException {
      pstmt.setString(1, student.getLastName());
      pstmt.setString(2, student.getFirstName());
      pstmt.setString(3, student.getMi());
      pstmt.setString(4, student.getTelephone());
      pstmt.setString(5, student.getEmail());
      pstmt.setString(6, student.getAddress());
      pstmt.setString(7, student.getCity());
      pstmt.setString(8, student.getState());
      pstmt.setString(9, student.getZip());
      pstmt.executeUpdate();
    }

    class Student {
      private String lastName = "";
      private String firstName = "";
      private String mi = "";
      private String telephone = "";
      private String email = "";
      private String street = "";
      private String city = "";
      private String state = "";
      private String zip = "";

      Student(String lastName, String firstName,
        String mi, String telephone, String email, String street,
        String city, String state, String zip) {
        this.lastName = lastName;
        this.firstName = firstName;
        this.mi = mi;
        this.telephone = telephone;
        this.email = email;
        this.street = street;
        this.city = city;
        this.state = state;
        this.zip = zip;
      }

      public String getLastName() {
        return lastName;
      }

      public String getFirstName() {
        return firstName;
      }

      public String getMi() {
        return mi;
      }

      public String getTelephone() {
        return telephone;
      }

```

Listing 16.12 *Continued*

```
      public String getEmail() {
        return email;
      }

      public String getAddress() {
        return street;
      }

      public String getCity() {
        return city;
      }

      public String getState() {
        return state;
      }

      public String getZip() {
        return zip;
      }
    }
  }
```

Listing 16.12 *Continued*

Example Review

The statement

```
HttpSession httpSession = request.getSession(true);
```

obtains a session, or creates a new session if the session does not exist.

Since objects can be stored in `HttpSession`, this program defines a `Student` class. A `Student` object is created and is stored in the session using the `setAttribute` method, which binds the object with a name like the one shown below:

```
httpSession.setAttribute("student", student);
```

To retrieve the object, use the following statement:

```
Student student =  (Student)(httpSession.getAttribute("student"));
```

There is only one session between a client and a servlet. You can store any number of objects in a session. By default, a session stays alive as long as the servlet is not destroyed. You can explicitly set the session active time using the `setMaxInactiveInterval` method.

Sending Images from Servlets

So far you have learned how to write Java servlets that generate dynamic HTML text. Java servlets are not limited to sending text to a browser. They can return images in GIF, JPEG, or PNG format. This section demonstrates returning images in GIF format.

To send contents as a GIF image, the content type must be set to image/gif, as below:

```
response.setContentType("image/gif");
```

In the preceding examples, you used a `PrintWriter` object to return HTML text. Since images are binary data, you have to use a binary output stream:

```
OutputStream out = response.getOutputStream();
```

You can then create an instance of the `Image` class filled with content. Before the image is sent to a browser, it must be encoded into a format acceptable to the browser. Image encoders are not part of Java API, but several free encoders are available. One of them is the `GifEncoder` class from Acme (**http://www.acme.com/java/software/Acme.JPM.Encoders.GifEncoder.html**), which is included in the book's CD-ROM in \radjb\acme.zip.

Use the following statement to encode and send the image to the browser:

```
new GifEncoder(image, out, true).encode();
```

Example 16.7 Getting Images from Servlets

This example creates a servlet that dynamically generates the flag of a country, as shown in Figure 16.21. The servlet is given in Listing 16.13.

```
package servletdemo;

import javax.servlet.*;
import javax.servlet.http.*;
import java.io.*;
import java.util.*;
import java.awt.Image;
import javax.swing.ImageIcon;
import Acme.JPM.Encoders.GifEncoder;

public class ImageContent extends HttpServlet {
  /** Process the HTTP Get request */
  public void doGet(HttpServletRequest request, HttpServletResponse
    response) throws ServletException, IOException {
    response.setContentType("image/gif");
    OutputStream out = response.getOutputStream();

    // Obtain an image icon
    ImageIcon imageIcon = new ImageIcon("c:\\radjb\\image\\" +
      request.getParameter("country") + ".gif");

    // Obtain image from image icon
    Image image = imageIcon.getImage(); // Get the image

    // Encode the image and send to the output stream
    new GifEncoder(image, out, true).encode();

    out.close(); // Close stream
  }
}
```

Listing 16.13 *ImageContent.java*

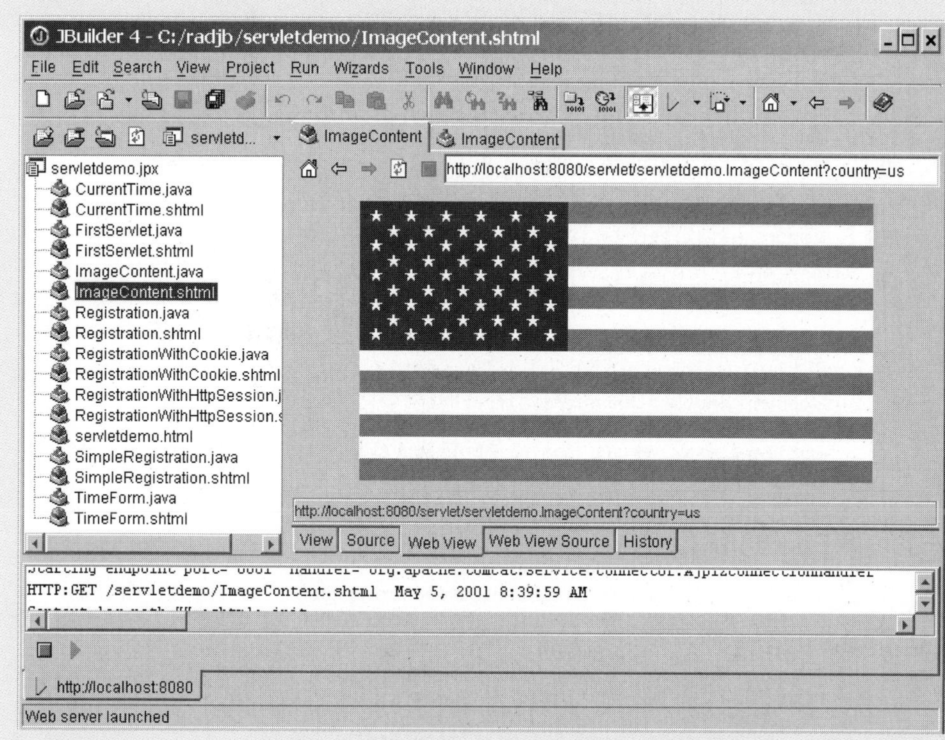

Figure 16.21 *The servlet returns an image of the country flag.*

Example Review

Before you start the Tomcat server from JBuilder, make sure that acme.zip is in the library of the project.

The content type of the response is image/gif, and the output stream is binary. The image is sent to the browser as binary data. The `GifEncoder` class is used to encode the image into content understood by the browser. The content is sent to the `OutputStream` object `out`.

Creating Images from Drawings

The preceding example creates an image from a GIF file. You can also create an image from a drawing and send it to the browser, as is demonstrated in the next example.

Example 16.8 Creating Images by Drawing

This example creates a servlet that displays a clock to show the current time, as shown in Figure 16.22. The servlet is given in Listing 16.14.

```
package servletdemo;

import javax.servlet.*;
import javax.servlet.http.*;
import java.io.*;
import java.util.*;
import java.text.*;
import java.awt.*;
import java.awt.image.BufferedImage;
import javax.swing.*;
import Acme.JPM.Encoders.GifEncoder;

public class ImageContentWithDrawing extends HttpServlet {
  /** Initialize global variables */
  private final static int width = 300;
  private final static int height = 300;

  /** Process the HTTP Get request */
  public void doGet(HttpServletRequest request, HttpServletResponse
    response) throws ServletException, IOException {
    response.setContentType("image/gif");
    OutputStream out = response.getOutputStream();

    // Create image
    Image image = new BufferedImage(width, height,
      BufferedImage.TYPE_INT_ARGB);

    // Get Graphics context of the image
    Graphics g = image.getGraphics();

    drawClock(g); // Draw a clock on graphics

    // Encode the image and send to the output stream
    new GifEncoder(image, out, true).encode();

    out.close(); // Close stream
  }

  private void drawClock(Graphics g) {
    // Initialize clock parameters
    int clockRadius =
      (int)(Math.min(width, height)*0.7*0.5);
    int xCenter = (width)/2;
    int yCenter = (height)/2;

    // Draw circle
    g.setColor(Color.black);
    g.drawOval(xCenter - clockRadius,yCenter - clockRadius,
      2*clockRadius, 2*clockRadius);
    g.drawString("12", xCenter-5, yCenter-clockRadius+12);
    g.drawString("9", xCenter-clockRadius+3, yCenter+5);
    g.drawString("3", xCenter+clockRadius-10, yCenter+3);
    g.drawString("6", xCenter-3, yCenter+clockRadius-3);

```

Listing 16.14 *ImageContentWithDrawing.java*

```
    // Get current time using GregorianCalendar
    TimeZone timeZone = TimeZone.getDefault();
    GregorianCalendar cal = new GregorianCalendar(timeZone);

    // Draw second hand
    int second = (int)cal.get(GregorianCalendar.SECOND);
    int sLength = (int)(clockRadius*0.9);
    int xSecond =
      (int)(xCenter + sLength*Math.sin(second*(2*Math.PI/60)));
    int ySecond =
      (int)(yCenter - sLength*Math.cos(second*(2*Math.PI/60)));
    g.setColor(Color.red);
    g.drawLine(xCenter, yCenter, xSecond, ySecond);

    // Draw minute hand
    int minute = (int)cal.get(GregorianCalendar.MINUTE);
    int mLength = (int)(clockRadius*0.75);
    int xMinute =
      (int)(xCenter + mLength*Math.sin(minute*(2*Math.PI/60)));
    int yMinute =
      (int)(yCenter - mLength*Math.cos(minute*(2*Math.PI/60)));
    g.setColor(Color.blue);
    g.drawLine(xCenter, yCenter, xMinute, yMinute);

    // Draw hour hand
    int hour = (int)cal.get(GregorianCalendar.HOUR_OF_DAY);
    int hLength = (int)(clockRadius*0.6);
    int xHour = (int)(xCenter +
      hLength*Math.sin((hour+minute/60.0)*(2*Math.PI/12)));
    int yHour = (int)(yCenter -
      hLength*Math.cos((hour+minute/60.0)*(2*Math.PI/12)));
    g.setColor(Color.green);
    g.drawLine(xCenter, yCenter, xHour, yHour);

    // Set display format in specified style, locale and timezone
    DateFormat formatter = DateFormat.getDateTimeInstance
      (DateFormat.MEDIUM, DateFormat.LONG);

    // Display current date
    g.setColor(Color.red);
    String today = formatter.format(cal.getTime());
    FontMetrics fm = g.getFontMetrics();
    g.drawString(today, (width -
      fm.stringWidth(today))/2, yCenter+clockRadius+30);
  }
}
```

Listing 16.14 *Continued*

Example Review

The program creates an image with the specified width, height, and image type, using the `BufferedImage` class:

```
Image image = new BufferedImage(width, height,
  BufferedImage.TYPE_INT_ARGB);
```

To draw things on the image, you need to get its graphics context using the `getGraphics` method:

```
Graphics g = image.getGraphics();
```

continued

Example 16.8 continued

You can use various drawing methods in the `Graphics` class to draw simple shapes, or you can use Java 2D to draw more sophisticated graphics. This example uses simple drawing methods to draw a clock that displays the current time.

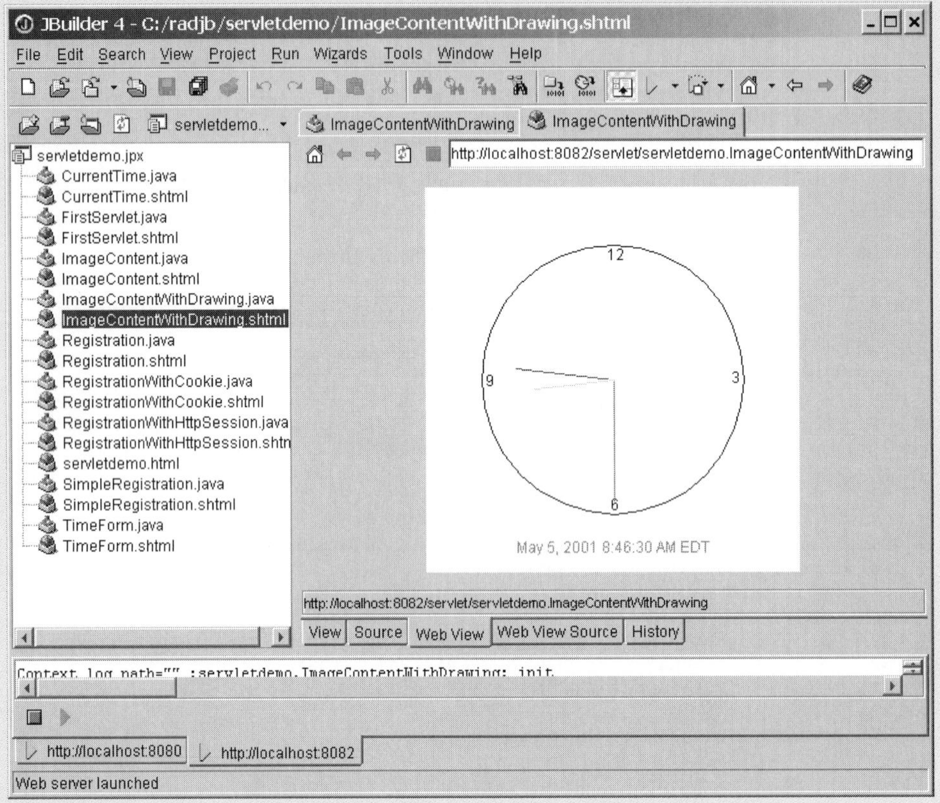

Figure 16.22 *The servlet returns a clock that displays the current time.*

Sending Images and Text Together

The servlets in the two preceding examples return images. Often images are mixed with text. In this case, you have to set the content type to "image/gif" before sending images, and set the content type to "text/html" before sending the text. However, the content type cannot be changed in one request. To circumvent this restriction, you may embed a get request for displaying the image in the HTML content. When the HTML content is displayed, a separate get request for retrieving the image is then sent to the server. Thus text and image are obtained through two separate get requests.

Example 16.9 Mixing Images and Texts

This example creates a servlet that dynamically generates the flag of a country and a text that describes the flag, as shown in Figure 16.23. The servlet is given in Listing 16.15.

```
package servletdemo;

import javax.servlet.*;
import javax.servlet.http.*;
import java.io.*;
import java.util.*;
import java.awt.*;
import javax.swing.*;
import Acme.JPM.Encoders.GifEncoder;

public class MixedContent extends HttpServlet {
  /** Process the HTTP Get request */
  public void doGet(HttpServletRequest request, HttpServletResponse
    response) throws ServletException, IOException {
    response.setContentType("text/html");
    PrintWriter out = response.getWriter();

    String country = request.getParameter("country");

    out.println("<img src = \"/servlet/servletdemo.ImageContent" +
      "?country=" + country + "\" align=left>");

    // Read description from a file and send it to the browser
    BufferedReader in = new BufferedReader(new FileReader(
      "c:\\radjb\\servletdemo\\" + country + ".txt"));

    // Text line from the text file for flag description
    String line;

    // Read a line from the text file and send it to the browser
    while ((line = in.readLine()) != null) {
      out.println(line);
    }

    out.close();
  }
}
```

Listing 16.15 *MixedContent.java*

Example Review

When you test the servlet using the URL `http://localhost:8080/servlet/servletdemo.MixedContent?country=ca`, it generates an HTML file with the image tag

```
<img src = "/servlet/servletdemo.ImageContent?country=ca" align=left>
```

followed by the text from the file ca.txt.

continued

Example 16.9 continued

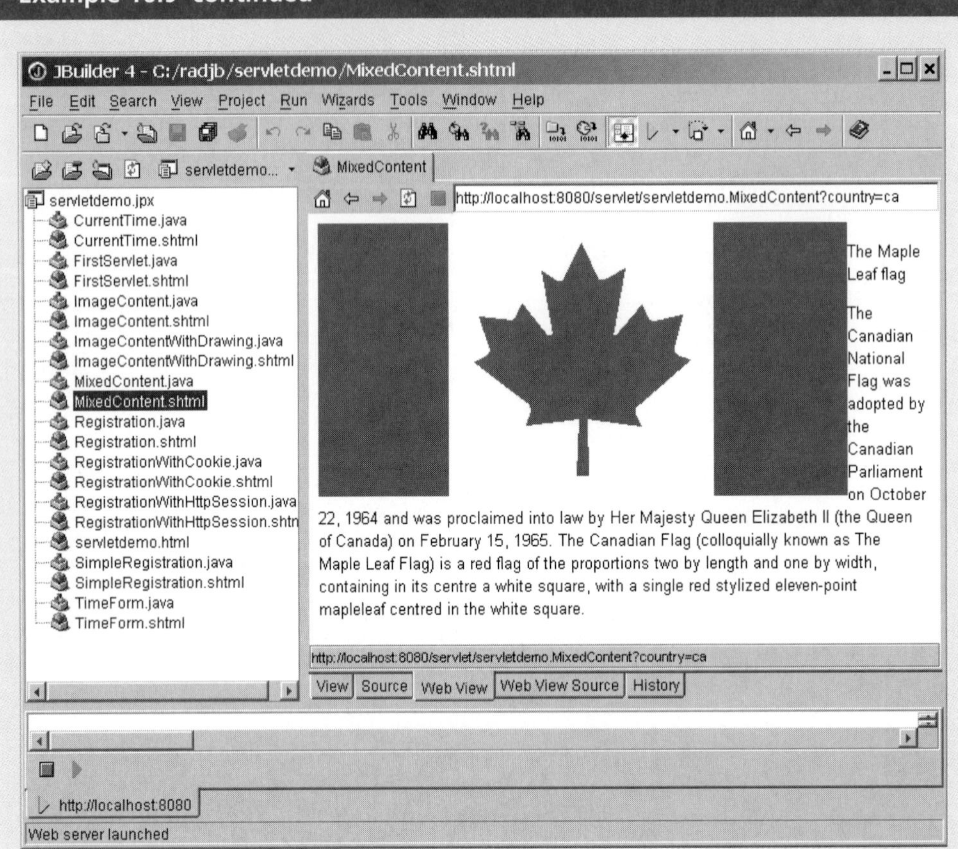

Figure 16.23 *The servlet returns an image along with the text.*

The HTML file is rendered by the browser. When the browser sees the image tag, it sends the request to the server. The servlet `ImageContent` created in Example 16.7 is invoked to retrieve the image file ca.gif. Thus the first get request dynamically prepared the second request. The content type for the first request is "text/html," and the second is "image/gif."

The first request invoked the servlet `MixedContent`, and the second request invoked the servlet `ImageContent`. Sometimes, it is convenient for both requests to invoke the same servlet. To do so, you can add a hidden value in the image tag to differentiate this request from the other. For example, use the following URL for the image tag:

```
<img src = "/servlet/servletdemo.MixedContentNew?country=ca&img=1">
```

Your servlet `doGet` method can check whether the hidden value is present in the request. If so, the request is for displaying image, otherwise, it is for rendering text. Here is the source code (Listing 16.16) that processes the two requests in one GET method.

```java
package servletdemo;

import javax.servlet.*;
import javax.servlet.http.*;
import java.io.*;
import java.util.*;
import java.awt.*;
import javax.swing.*;
import Acme.JPM.Encoders.GifEncoder;

public class MixedContentNew extends HttpServlet {
  /** Process the HTTP Get request */
  public void doGet(HttpServletRequest request, HttpServletResponse
    response) throws ServletException, IOException {
    if (request.getParameter("img") != null) {
      response.setContentType("image/gif");
      OutputStream out = response.getOutputStream();

      // Obtain an image icon
      ImageIcon imageIcon = new ImageIcon("c:\\radjb\\image\\" +
        request.getParameter("country") + ".gif");

      // Obtain image from image icon
      Image image = imageIcon.getImage(); // Get the image

      // Encode the image and send to the output stream
      new GifEncoder(image, out, true).encode();

      out.close(); // Close stream
    }
    else {
      response.setContentType("text/html");
      PrintWriter out = response.getWriter();

      String country = request.getParameter("country");

      out.println("<img src = \"" + request.getRequestURI() +
        "?country=" + country + "&img=1\" align=left>");

      // Read description from a file and send it to the browser
      BufferedReader in = new BufferedReader(new FileReader(
        "c:\\radjb\\servletdemo\\" + country + ".txt"));

      // Text line from the text file for flag description
      String line;

      // Read a line from the text file and send it to the browser
      while ((line = in.readLine()) != null) {
        out.println(line);
      }

      out.close();
    }
  }
}
```

Listing 16.16 *MixedContentNew.java*

Getting Images from Components

The preceding examples obtained images from drawings. Occasionally, the drawings already exist in a component. This section demonstrates how to obtain images from components.

Example 16.10 Getting Images from Components

In Example 16.8, you created an image of a clock by drawing the clock on a `Graphics` object. You wrote the code to draw clock. The code is the same as in the `Clock` component presented in Example 4.2, "The `Clock` Component." This example reuses the `Clock` component to create a clock image in a servlet, as shown in Listing 16.17.

```
package servletdemo;

import javax.servlet.*;
import javax.servlet.http.*;
import javax.swing.*;
import java.io.*;
import java.awt.*;
import java.awt.image.BufferedImage;
import Acme.JPM.Encoders.GifEncoder;
import clockdemo.Clock;

public class ImageContentFromComponent extends HttpServlet {
  /** Initialize global variables */
  private final static int width = 300;
  private final static int height = 300;

  // Create image
  private Image image = new BufferedImage(width, height,
    BufferedImage.TYPE_INT_ARGB);

  // Get Graphics context of the image
  private Graphics g = image.getGraphics();

  // Create clock
  private Clock clock = new Clock();

  // Create a frame to provide graphics environment for rendering
  // the clock
  private JFrame frame = new JFrame();

  /** Initialize global variables */
  public void init(ServletConfig config) throws ServletException {
    super.init(config);
    frame.setSize(width, height); // Set the frame size
    frame.getContentPane().add(clock); // Add clock to the frame
  }

  /** Process the HTTP Get request */
  public void doGet(HttpServletRequest request, HttpServletResponse
    response) throws ServletException, IOException {
    response.setContentType("image/gif");
    OutputStream out = response.getOutputStream();

```

Listing 16.17 *ImageContentFromComponent.java*

```
    frame.setVisible(true);
    g.setColor(Color.white);
    g.fillRect(0, 0, width, height);
    clock.paint(g);
    frame.setVisible(false);

    // Encode the image and send to the output stream
    new GifEncoder(image, out, true).encode();

    out.close(); // Close stream
  }
}
```

Listing 16.17 *Continued*

Example Review

This example displays the same clock as shown in Figure 16.22. Instead of writing the code to draw the clock, the example reuses the `Clock` component to draw the clock on a component. The image of the clock is then obtained through the `Graphics` object. The method `clock.paint(g)` invokes the `paint` method in the `Clock` component and draws the clock on `g`.

The `Clock` object is put into a frame. Why is a frame necessary in this example? There are two reasons. First, the `paint` method in the `Clock` component uses the `getWidth()` and `getHeight()` methods to obtain the component's width and height in order to draw a clock. Second, the `paint` method uses the `getLocale` method. In order to determine its locale, the clock must be placed in a frame or an applet.

Chapter Summary

This chapter introduced the creation of dynamic Web pages using Java servlets in JBuilder. You learned how to write HTML forms with the GET and POST methods. You wrote Java servlets that extended the `HttpServlet` class. Java servlets respond to GET requests with the `doGet` method and to POST requests with the `doPost` method.

The chapter introduced the Servlets API. You learned how to develop servlets with database applications. Three session-tracking techniques were introduced. You learned how to track sessions using HTML hidden values, HTML cookies, and `HttpSession` objects. Finally, you learned how to generate images from servlets.

Review Questions

16.1 What are the differences between CGI and servlets?

16.2 What is the difference between the GET and POST methods in an HTML form?

16.3 Can you submit a GET request directly from a URL? Can you submit a POST request directly from a URL?

16.4 What is wrong in the following URL for submitting a GET request to the servlet FindScore on host liang at port 8080 with parameters name?

```
http://liang:8080/servlet/servletdemo.FindScore?name="P Yates"
```

16.5 Does the Servlet wizard add the classpath for a servlet package in the project? If so, find out the servlet.jar file for the servlet package.

16.6 How do you ensure that the Servlet wizard generates the `doPost` method and the .shtml file?

16.7 When you run Tomcat from JBuilder, which port does it use? What happens if the port is already in use?

16.8 Describe the life-cycle of a servlet.

16.9 What would be displayed if you changed the content type to "html/plain" in Example 16.1?

16.10 What is session tracking? What are three techniques for session tracking?

16.11 What output stream should you use to send images to the browser?

16.12 How do you deal with dynamic contents with images and text?

Programming Exercises

16.1 Write a servlet that displays the number of visits on the servlet. Also display the client's host name, IP address, and request URL, as shown in Figure 16.24. This information can be obtained using the appropriate GET methods in the `HttpServletRequest` class.

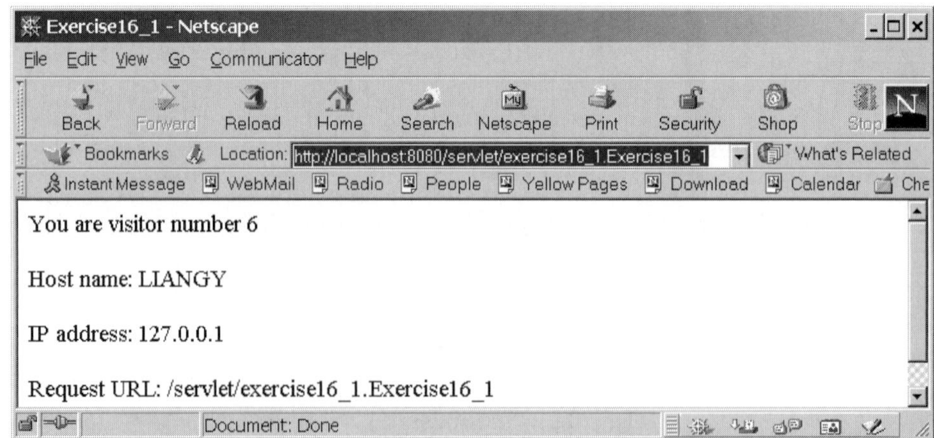

Figure 16.24 *The servlet displays the number of visits, client's host name, IP address, and request URL.*

(Can you modify the servlet to display the number of visits made by a client identified by the client's IP address? Hint: Use `Map` to store a pair of IP addresses and visit counts. For the first visit, an entry is created in the map. For subsequent visits, the visit count is updated.)

16.2 Write a servlet that displays the student name and the current score, given the ssn and class ID. For each class, a text file is used to store the student name, ssn, and current score. The file is named after the class id with .txt extension. For instance, if the class id were csci1301, the file name would be csci1301.txt. Suppose each line consists of student name, ssn, and score. These three items are separated by the # sign. Create an HTML form that enables the user to enter the ssn and class ID, as shown in Figure 16.25. Upon clicking the Submit button, the result is displayed, as shown in Figure 16.26. If the ssn or the class ID does not match, report an error.

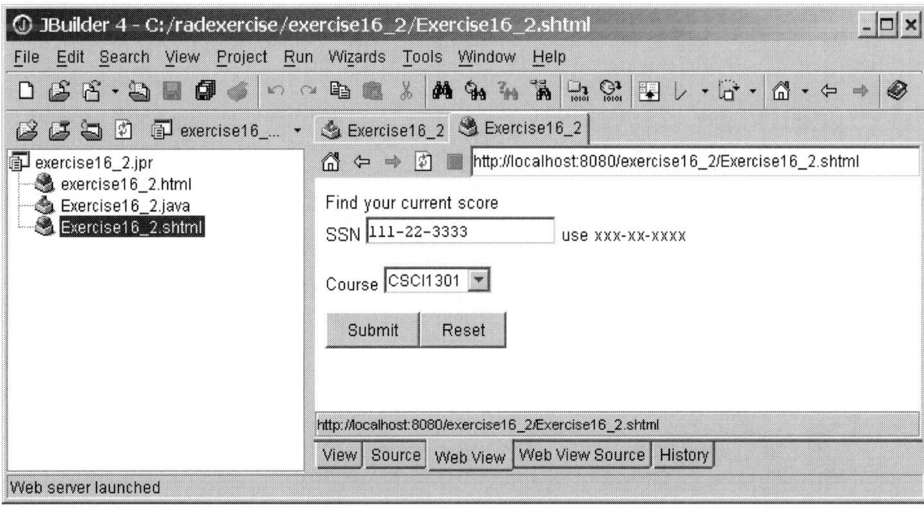

Figure 16.25 *The HTML form accepts the ssn and class ID from the user.*

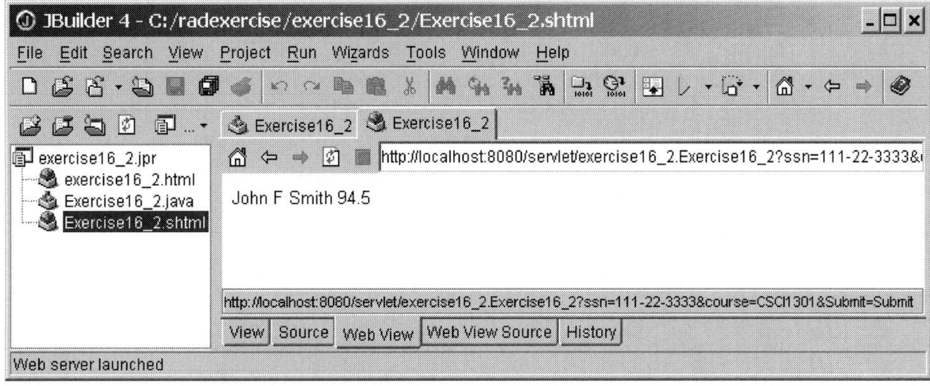

Figure 16.26 *Student name and score for the given ssn and class id are displayed.*

16.3 Rewrite the preceding servlet. Assume that for each class, a table is used to store the student name, ssn, and score. The table name is the same as the class ID. For instance, if the class id were csci1301, the table name would be csci1301.

16.4 Write a servlet that stores the following cookies in a browser, and set their max age for two days.

Cookie 1: name is "color" and value is red.

Cookie 2: name is "radius" and value is 5.5.

Cookie 3: name is "count" and value is 2.

16.5 Write a servlet that displays all cookies on the client. The client types the URL of the servlet from the browser to display all the cookies stored on the browser. See Figure 16.27.

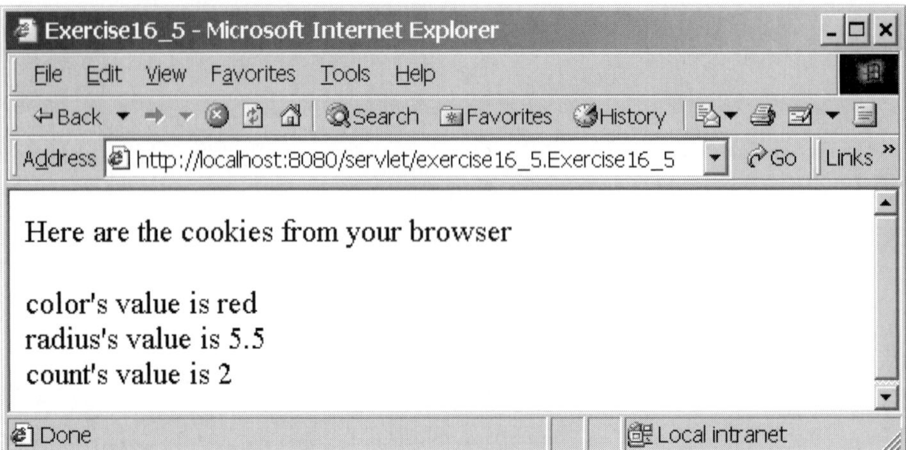

Figure 16.27 *All the cookies on the client are displayed in the browser.*

16.6 Write a servlet that enables the user to change the password from an HTML form, as shown in Figure 16.28. Suppose that the user information is stored in a database table named User with three columns: username, password, and name, where name is the real name of the user. The servlet performs the following tasks:

a. Verify that the username and old password are in the table. If not, report the error and redisplay the HTML form.

b. Verify that the new password and the confirmed password are the same. If not, report this error and redisplay the HTML form.

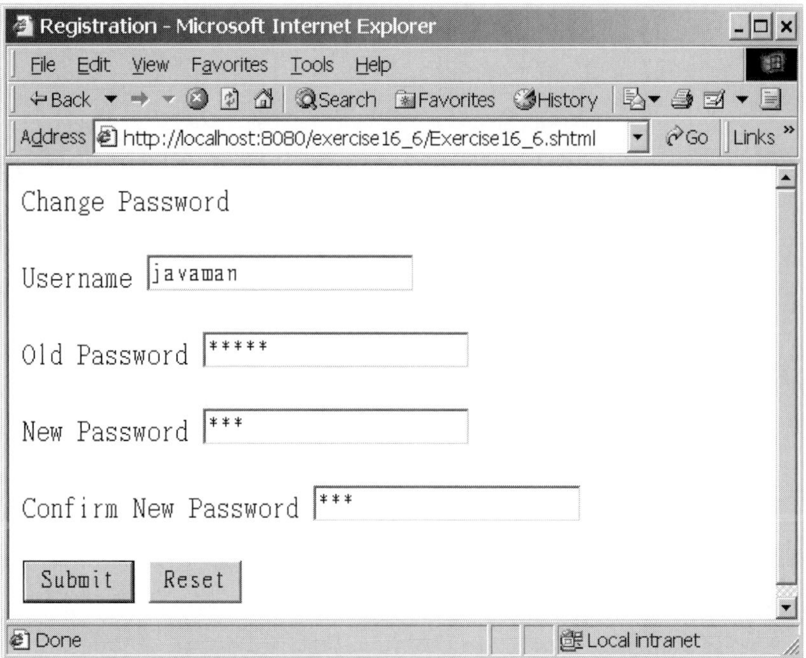

Figure 16.28 *The user enters the username and the old password and sets a new password.*

c. If the user information is entered correctly, update the password and report the status of the update to the user, as shown in Figure 16.29.

Figure 16.29 *The servlet reports the status of the update to the user.*

16.7 Write a servlet that displays a bar chart on the number of employees in each department from a database, as shown in Figure 16.30. The number of employees in each department can be obtained dynamically from the database tables Department and Employee. The Department table has three columns: deptno, deptname, and deptchair. The Employee table has four columns: empno, name, office, and deptno. The number of employees in each department can be obtained using the following SQL statement:

```
select deptname, count(*)
from Department, Employee
where department.deptno = employee.deptno
group by deptname;
```

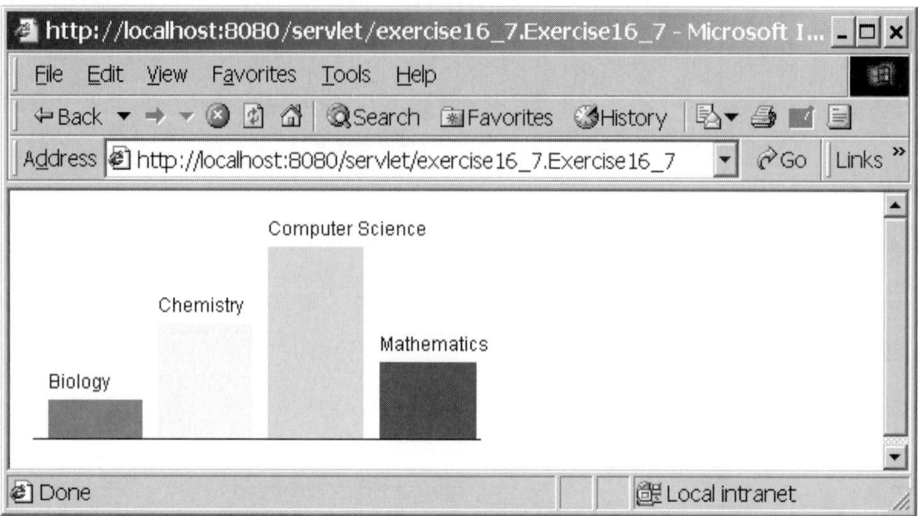

Figure 16.30 *The servlet sends a bar chart to display the number of employees for each department in the database.*

Write the code to draw the bar chart on a `Graphics` object.

16.8 Rewrite Exercise 16.7 using the `BarChart` component and the `ChartModel` from Exercise 4.8 so that you can reuse the code in the BarChart component to display the bar chart.

16.9 Write a servlet that displays the current calendar, as shown in Figure 16.31. The current calendar user interface can be obtained from the `CalendarPanel` component in Exercise 4.6.

16.10 Develop an interactive online test that meets the following requirements:

a. The test consists of multiple-choice questions. Each test is stored in a text file, as follows:

```
1. Question 1
a. Choice-a
b. Choice-b
c. Choice-c
d. Choice-d
e. Choice-e

# (Question separator)
2. Question 2
a. Choice-a
b. Choice-b
c. Choice-c
d. Choice-d
e. Choice-e

# (Question separator)
More questions

& End of the questions. Answers begins
1.d
2.c
More answers
```

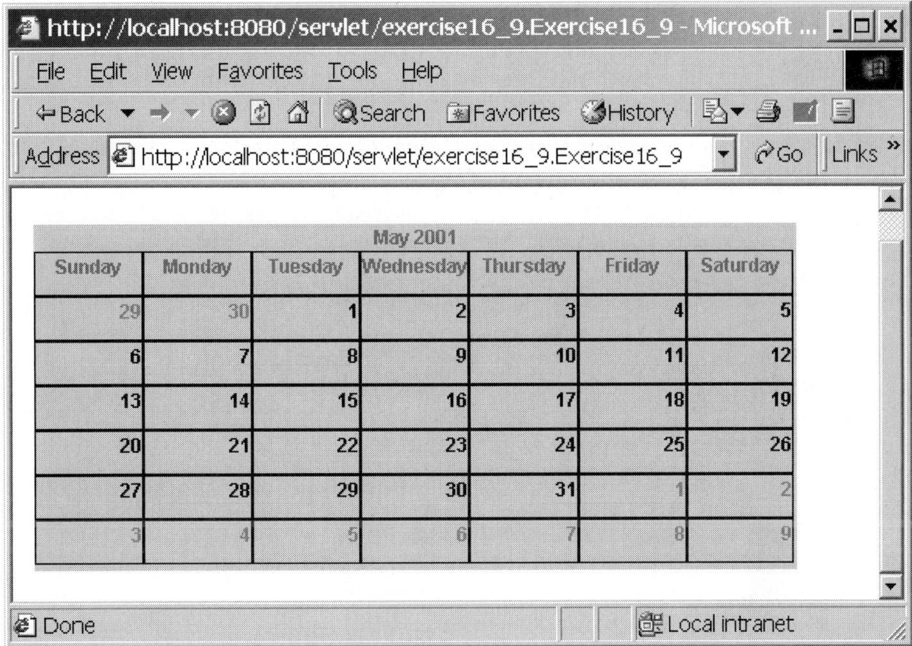

Figure 16.31 *The servlet uses the CalendarPanel component to create a user interface to display calendar and sends the image to the client.*

b. The user starts the test from a URL that consists of the servlet name and the parameter to specify a test, as shown in Figure 16.32.

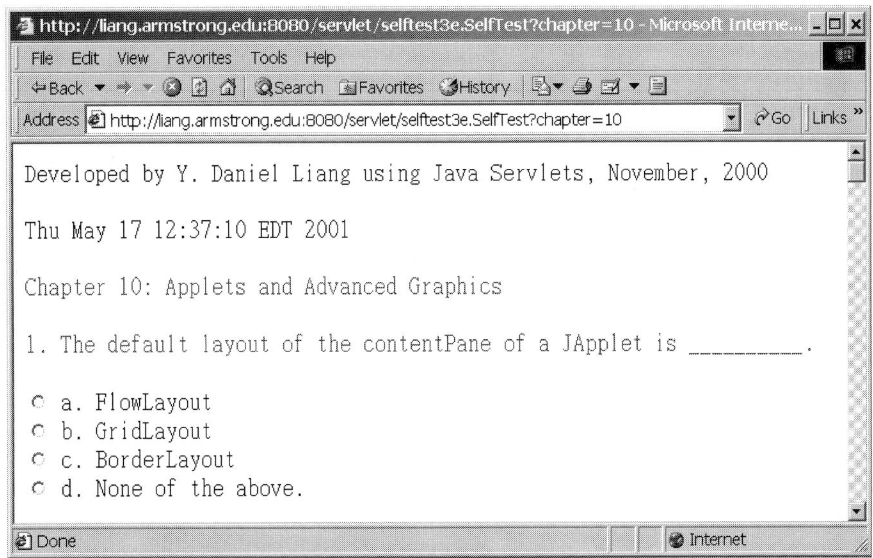

Figure 16.32 *The servlet dynamically generates the test.*

c. Upon submitting the test, the servlet grades it and sends the result back to the client. The servlet also generates a chart to show the number of correct answers, incorrect answers, and unanswered questions, as shown in Figure 16.33. (Please refer to **`www.cs.armstrong.edu/liang/introjb4.html`** and click Multiple Choice to see a live demo of this exercise. The source code for the servlet is at `http://liang.armstrong.edu:8080/selftestjb4/SelfTest.java`.

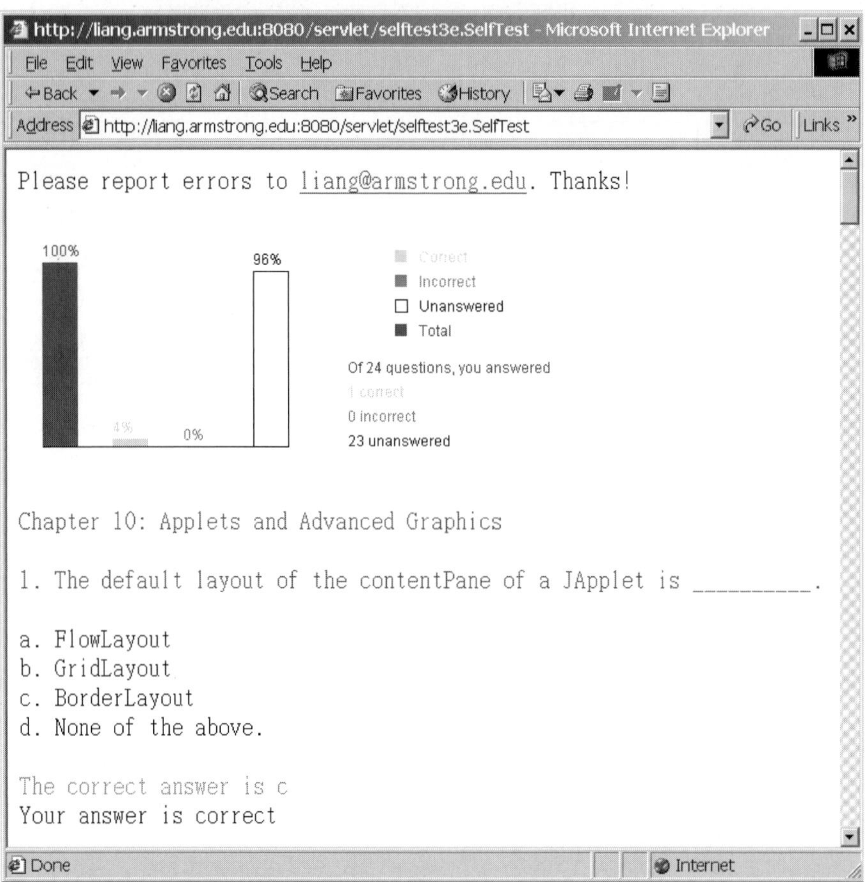

Figure 16.33 *The servlet grades the test and sends the result back to the client.*

INDEX

LICENSE AGREEMENT AND LIMITED WARRANTY

READ THE FOLLOWING TERMS AND CONDITIONS CAREFULLY BEFORE OPENING THIS DISK PACKAGE. THIS LEGAL DOCUMENT IS AN AGREEMENT BETWEEN YOU AND PRENTICE-HALL, INC. (THE "COMPANY"). BY OPENING THIS SEALED DISK PACKAGE, YOU ARE AGREEING TO BE BOUND BY THESE TERMS AND CONDITIONS. IF YOU DO NOT AGREE WITH THESE TERMS AND CONDITIONS, DO NOT OPEN THE DISK PACKAGE. PROMPTLY RETURN THE UNOPENED DISK PACKAGE AND ALL ACCOMPANYING ITEMS TO THE PLACE YOU OBTAINED THEM FOR A FULL REFUND OF ANY SUMS YOU HAVE PAID.

1. GRANT OF LICENSE: In consideration of your payment of the license fee, which is part of the price you paid for this product, and your agreement to abide by the terms and conditions of this Agreement, the Company grants to you a nonexclusive right to use and display the copy of the enclosed software program (hereinafter the "SOFTWARE") on a single computer (i.e., with a single CPU) at a single location so long as you comply with the terms of this Agreement. The Company reserves all rights not expressly granted to you under this Agreement.

2. OWNERSHIP OF SOFTWARE: You own only the magnetic or physical media (the enclosed disks) on which the SOFTWARE is recorded or fixed, but the Company retains all the rights, title, and ownership to the SOFTWARE recorded on the original disk copy(ies) and all subsequent copies of the SOFTWARE, regardless of the form or media on which the original or other copies may exist. This license is not a sale of the original SOFTWARE or any copy to you.

3. COPY RESTRICTIONS: This SOFTWARE and the accompanying printed materials and user manual (the "Documentation") are the subject of copyright. You may not copy the Documentation or the SOFTWARE, except that you may make a single copy of the SOFTWARE for backup or archival purposes only. You may be held legally responsible for any copying or copyright infringement which is caused or encouraged by your failure to abide by the terms of this restriction.

4. USE RESTRICTIONS: You may not network the SOFTWARE or otherwise use it on more than one computer or computer terminal at the same time. You may physically transfer the SOFTWARE from one computer to another provided that the SOFTWARE is used on only one computer at a time. You may not distribute copies of the SOFTWARE or Documentation to others. You may not reverse engineer, disassemble, decompile, modify, adapt, translate, or create derivative works based on the SOFTWARE or the Documentation without the prior written consent of the Company.

5. TRANSFER RESTRICTIONS: The enclosed SOFTWARE is licensed only to you and may not be transferred to any one else without the prior written consent of the Company. Any unauthorized transfer of the SOFTWARE shall result in the immediate termination of this Agreement.

6. TERMINATION: This license is effective until terminated. This license will terminate automatically without notice from the Company and become null and void if you fail to comply with any provisions or limitations of this license. Upon termination, you shall destroy the Documentation and all copies of the SOFTWARE. All provisions of this Agreement as to warranties, limitation of liability, remedies or damages, and our ownership rights shall survive termination.

7. MISCELLANEOUS: This Agreement shall be construed in accordance with the laws of the United States of America and the State of New York and shall benefit the Company, its affiliates, and assignees.

8. LIMITED WARRANTY AND DISCLAIMER OF WARRANTY: The Company warrants that the SOFTWARE, when properly used in accordance with the Documentation, will operate in substantial conformity with the description of the SOFTWARE set forth in the Documentation. The Company does not warrant that the SOFTWARE will meet your requirements or that the operation of the SOFTWARE will be uninterrupted or error-free. The Company warrants that the media on which the SOFTWARE is delivered shall be free from defects in materials and workmanship under normal use for a period of thirty (30) days from the date of your purchase. Your only remedy and the Company's only obligation under these limited warranties is, at the Company's option, return of the warranted item for a refund of any amounts paid by you or replacement of the item. Any replacement of SOFTWARE or media under the warranties shall not extend the original warranty period. The limited warranty set forth above shall not apply to any SOFTWARE which the Company determines in good faith has been subject to misuse, neglect, improper installation, repair, alteration, or damage by you. EXCEPT FOR THE EXPRESSED WARRANTIES SET FORTH ABOVE, THE COMPANY DISCLAIMS ALL WARRANTIES, EXPRESS OR IMPLIED, INCLUDING WITHOUT LIMITATION, THE IMPLIED WARRANTIES OF MERCHANTABILITY AND FITNESS FOR A PARTICULAR PURPOSE. EXCEPT FOR THE EXPRESS WARRANTY SET FORTH ABOVE, THE COMPANY DOES NOT WARRANT, GUARANTEE, OR MAKE ANY REPRESENTATION REGARDING THE USE OR THE RESULTS OF THE USE OF THE SOFTWARE IN TERMS OF ITS CORRECTNESS, ACCURACY, RELIABILITY, CURRENTNESS, OR OTHERWISE.

IN NO EVENT, SHALL THE COMPANY OR ITS EMPLOYEES, AGENTS, SUPPLIERS, OR CONTRACTORS BE LIABLE FOR ANY INCIDENTAL, INDIRECT, SPECIAL, OR CONSEQUENTIAL DAMAGES ARISING OUT OF OR IN CONNECTION WITH THE LICENSE GRANTED UNDER THIS AGREEMENT, OR FOR LOSS OF USE, LOSS OF DATA, LOSS OF INCOME OR PROFIT, OR OTHER LOSSES, SUSTAINED AS A RESULT OF INJURY TO ANY PERSON, OR LOSS OF OR DAMAGE TO PROPERTY, OR CLAIMS OF THIRD PARTIES, EVEN IF THE COMPANY OR AN AUTHORIZED REPRESENTATIVE OF THE COMPANY HAS BEEN ADVISED OF THE POSSIBILITY OF SUCH DAMAGES. IN NO EVENT SHALL LIABILITY OF THE COMPANY FOR DAMAGES WITH RESPECT TO THE SOFTWARE EXCEED THE AMOUNTS ACTUALLY PAID BY YOU, IF ANY, FOR THE SOFTWARE.

SOME JURISDICTIONS DO NOT ALLOW THE LIMITATION OF IMPLIED WARRANTIES OR LIABILITY FOR INCIDENTAL, INDIRECT, SPECIAL, OR CONSEQUENTIAL DAMAGES, SO THE ABOVE LIMITATIONS MAY NOT ALWAYS APPLY. THE WARRANTIES IN THIS AGREEMENT GIVE YOU SPECIFIC LEGAL RIGHTS AND YOU MAY ALSO HAVE OTHER RIGHTS WHICH VARY IN ACCORDANCE WITH LOCAL LAW.

ACKNOWLEDGMENT

YOU ACKNOWLEDGE THAT YOU HAVE READ THIS AGREEMENT, UNDERSTAND IT, AND AGREE TO BE BOUND BY ITS TERMS AND CONDITIONS. YOU ALSO AGREE THAT THIS AGREEMENT IS THE COMPLETE AND EXCLUSIVE STATEMENT OF THE AGREEMENT BETWEEN YOU AND THE COMPANY AND SUPERSEDES ALL PROPOSALS OR PRIOR AGREEMENTS, ORAL, OR WRITTEN, AND ANY OTHER COMMUNICATIONS BETWEEN YOU AND THE COMPANY OR ANY REPRESENTATIVE OF THE COMPANY RELATING TO THE SUBJECT MATTER OF THIS AGREEMENT.

Should you have any questions concerning this Agreement or if you wish to contact the Company for any reason, please contact in writing at the address below or call the at the telephone number provided.

PTR Customer Service
Prentice Hall PTR
One Lake Street
Upper Saddle River, New Jersey 07458

Telephone: 201-236-7105

INPRISE Corporation License Statement

JBuilder Foundation for Windows, Linux, and SolarisBorland C++ 5.5 Compiler

JECT TO ALL OF THE TERMS AND CONDITIONS OF THIS LICENSE STATEMENT. IF YOU DO NOT AGREE TO ALL OF THE TERMS AND CONDITIONS OF THIS STATEMENT, DO NOT USE THE SOFTWARE.

1. This Software is protected by copyright law and international copyright treaty. Therefore, you must treat this Software just like a book, except that you may copy it onto a computer to be used and you may make archive copies of the Software for the sole purpose of backing up our Software and protecting your investment from loss. You You may upload the JBuilder FoundationBorland C++ 5.5 Compiler in your labs across your entire campus for educational use.

2. INPRISE grants you a revocable, non-exclusive license to use the Software free of charge if you are a student, faculty member or staff member of an educational institution (K-12, junior college, college or library) ("Educational User"), or if your use of the Software is for the purpose of evaluating whether to purchase an ongoing license to the Software ("Evaluation User"). Government agencies (other than public schools and libraries) do not qualify as Educational Users under this License Statement. .

3. You may reproduce exact copies of the Software as provided by INPRISE and distribute such copies to Educational Users and Evaluation Users, so long as you do not charge or receive any compensation for such reproduction or distribution, and provided that the use of all such copies shall be subject to the terms of this License Statement.

4. If the Software is a INPRISE development tool, you can write and compile applications for your own personal use on the computer on which you have installed the Software, but you do not have a right to distribute or otherwise share those applications or any files of the Software which may be required to support those applications. APPLICATIONS THAT YOU CREATE MAY REQUIRE THE SOFTWARE IN ORDER TO RUN. UPON EXPIRATION OF THE EVALUATION PERIOD, THOSE APPLICATIONS MAY NO LONGER RUN. You should therefore take precautions to avoid any loss of data that might result.

5. INPRISE MAKES NO REPRESENTATIONS ABOUT THE SUITABILITY OF THIS SOFTWARE OR ABOUT ANY CONTENT OR INFORMATION MADE ACCESSIBLE BY THE SOFTWARE, FOR ANY PURPOSE. THE SOFTWARE IS PROVIDED 'AS IS' WITHOUT EXPRESS OR IMPLIED WARRANTIES, INCLUDING WARRANTIES OF MERCHANTABILITY AND FITNESS FOR A PARTICULAR PURPOSE OR NONINFRINGEMENT. THIS SOFTWARE IS PROVIDED GRATUITOUSLY AND, ACCORDINGLY, INPRISE SHALL NOT BE LIABLE UNDER ANY THEORY FOR ANY DAMAGES SUFFERED BY YOU OR ANY USER OF THE SOFTWARE. INPRISE WILL NOT SUPPORT THIS SOFTWARE AND IS UNDER NO OBLIGATION TO ISSUE UPDATES TO THIS SOFTWARE. INPRISE RESERVES THE RIGHT TO REVOKE THE LICENSE GRANTED HEREIN AT ANY TIME.

6. While INPRISE intends to distribute (or may have already distributed) a commercial release of the Software, INPRISE reserves the right at any time to not release a commercial release of the Software or, if released, to alter prices, features, specifications, capabilities, functions, licensing terms, release dates, general availability or other characteristics of the commercial release.

7. Title, ownership rights, and intellectual property rights in and to the Software shall remain in INPRISE and/or its suppliers. You agree to abide by the copyright law and all other applicable laws of the United States including, but not limited to, export control laws. You acknowledge that the Software in source code form remains a confidential trade secret of INPRISE and/or its suppliers and therefore you agree not to modify the Software or attempt to decipher, decompile, disassemble or reverse engineer the Software, except to the extent applicable laws specifically prohibit such restriction.

8. Use, duplication or disclosure by the Government is subject to restrictions set forth in subparagraphs (a) through (d) of the Commercial Computer-Restricted Rights clause at FAR 52.227-19 when applicable, or in subparagraph (c) (1) (ii) of the Rights in Technical Data and Computer Software clause at DFARS 252.227-7013, and in similar clauses in the NASA AR Supplement. Contractor/manufacturer is INPRISE Corporation, Inc., 100 INPRISE Way, Scotts Valley, CA 95066.

9. You may not download or otherwise export or reexport the Software or any underlying information or technology except in full compliance with all United States and other applicable laws and regulations. In particular, but without limitation, none of the Software or underlying information or technology may be downloaded or otherwise exported or reexported (i) into (or to a national or resident of) Cuba, Haiti, Iraq, Libya, Yugoslavia, North Korea, Iran, or

Syria or (ii) to anyone on the US Treasury Department's list of Specially Designated Nationals or the US Commerce Department's Table of Deny Orders. By downloading the Software, you are agreeing to the foregoing and you are representing and warranting that you are not located in, under control of, or a national or resident of any such country or on any such list.

10. INPRISE OR ITS SUPPLIERS SHALL NOT BE LIABLE FOR (a) INCIDENTAL, CONSEQUENTIAL, SPECIAL OR INDIRECT DAMAGES OF ANY SORT, WHETHER ARISING IN TORT, CONTRACT OR OTHERWISE, EVEN IF INPRISE HAS BEEN INFORMED OF THE POSSIBILITY OF SUCH DAMAGES, OR (b) FOR ANY CLAIM BY ANY OTHER PARTY. THIS LIMITATION OF LIABILITY SHALL NOT APPLY TO LIABILITY FOR DEATH OR PERSONAL INJURY TO THE EXTENT APPLICABLE LAW PROHIBITS SUCH LIMITATION. FURTHERMORE, SOME STATES DO NOT ALLOW THE EXCLUSION OR LIMITATION OF INCIDENTAL OR CONSEQUENTIAL DAMAGES, SO THIS LIMITATION AND EXCLUSION MAY NOT APPLY TO YOU.

11. HIGH RISK ACTIVITIES. The Software is not fault-tolerant and is not designed, manufactured or intended for use or resale as on-line control equipment in hazardous environments requiring fail-safe performance, such as in the operation of nuclear facilities, aircraft navigation or communication systems, air traffic control, direct life support machines, or weapons systems, in which the failure of the Software could lead directly to death, personal injury, or severe physical or environmental damage ("High Risk Activities"). INPRISE and its suppliers specifically disclaim any express or implied warranty of fitness for High Risk Activities.